THE COMPLETE

ELFQUEST®

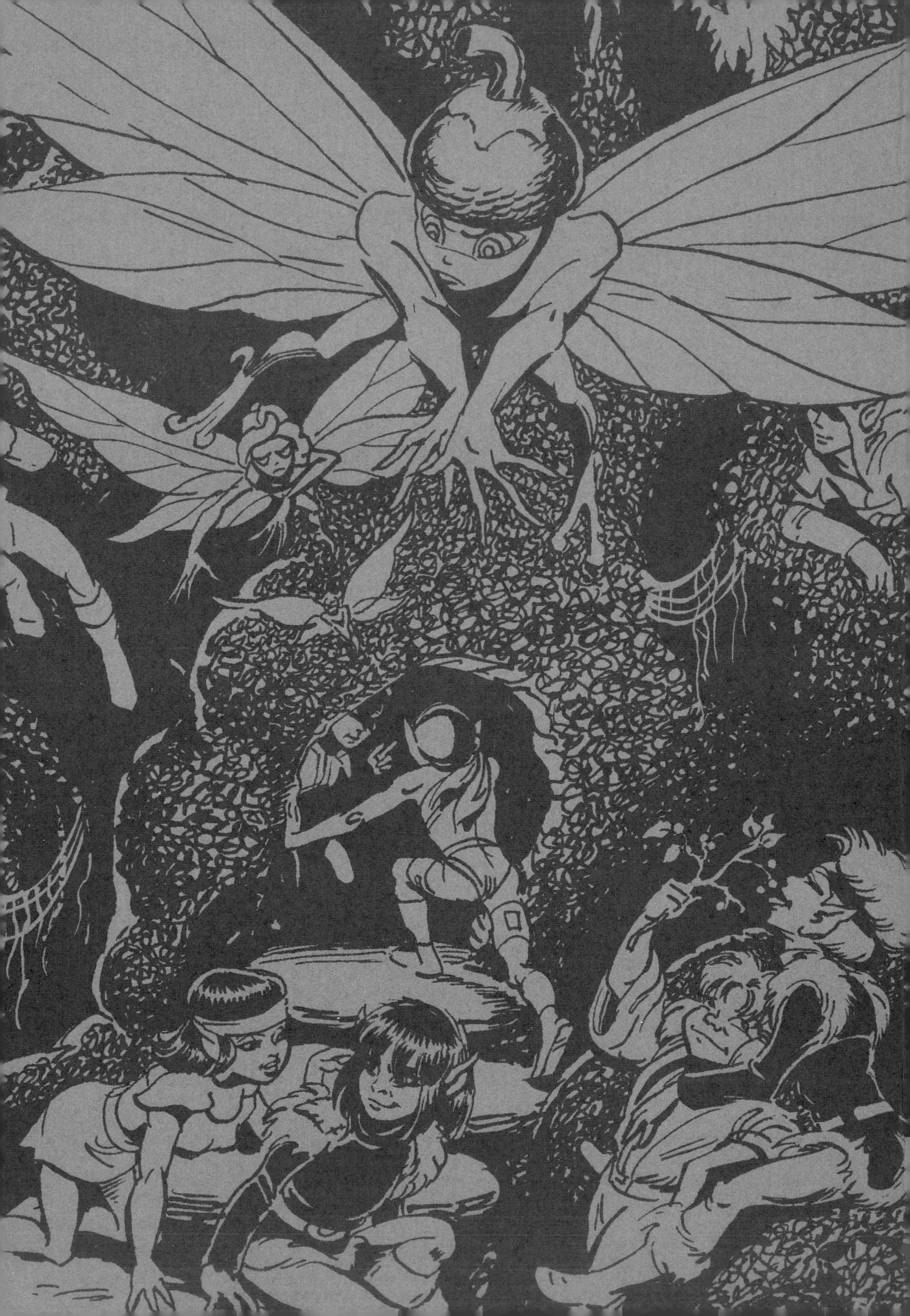

THE COMPLETE

ElfQuest®

VOLUME TWO

BY WENDY AND RICHARD PINI

INKS BY
JOE STATON
(SIEGE AT BLUE MOUNTAIN)

LETTERS BY
JANICE CHIANG
(SIEGE AT BLUE MOUNTAIN PARTS 1–4, 6–8)

CLEM ROBINS
(SIEGE AT BLUE MOUNTAIN PART 5)

NATE PIEKOS OF BLAMBOT®
(KINGS OF THE BROKEN WHEEL)

DARK HORSE BOOKS

President & Publisher MIKE RICHARDSON

Collection Editor SIERRA HAHN

Collection Assistant Editor SPENCER CUSHING

Digital Production ALLYSON HALLER

Collection Designer TINA ALESSI

Published by Dark Horse Books
A division of Dark Horse Comics, Inc.
10956 SE Main Street
Milwaukie, OR 97222

First edition: February 2015
ISBN 978-1-61655-408-8
5 7 9 10 8 6 4
Printed in China

International Licensing: (503) 905-2377
Comic Shop Locator Service: (888) 266-4226

LIBRARY OF CONGRESS CATALOGING-IN-PUBLICATION DATA

Pini, Wendy.
   The Complete ElfQuest Volume Two / by Wendy and Richard Pini. – First edition.
      pages cm
   Summary: "The Complete ElfQuest Volume 2 Collects ElfQuest: Siege at Blue Mountain
and ElfQuest: Kings of the Broken Wheel. This is the second volume in the Complete
ElfQuest Series"– Provided by publisher.
   ISBN 978-1-61655-408-8 (pbk.)
   1. Graphic novels. I. Pini, Richard. II. Title.

   PN6728.E45P54 2015
   741.5'973–dc23

                        2014039854

This volume collects and reprints the comic book series ElfQuest: Siege at Blue Mountain #1–#8 and ElfQuest: Kings of the Broken Wheel #1–#9.

TO EVERY STORYTELLER, YOUNG AND OLD,

WHO EVER UTTERED THE WORDS

"ONCE UPON A TIME."

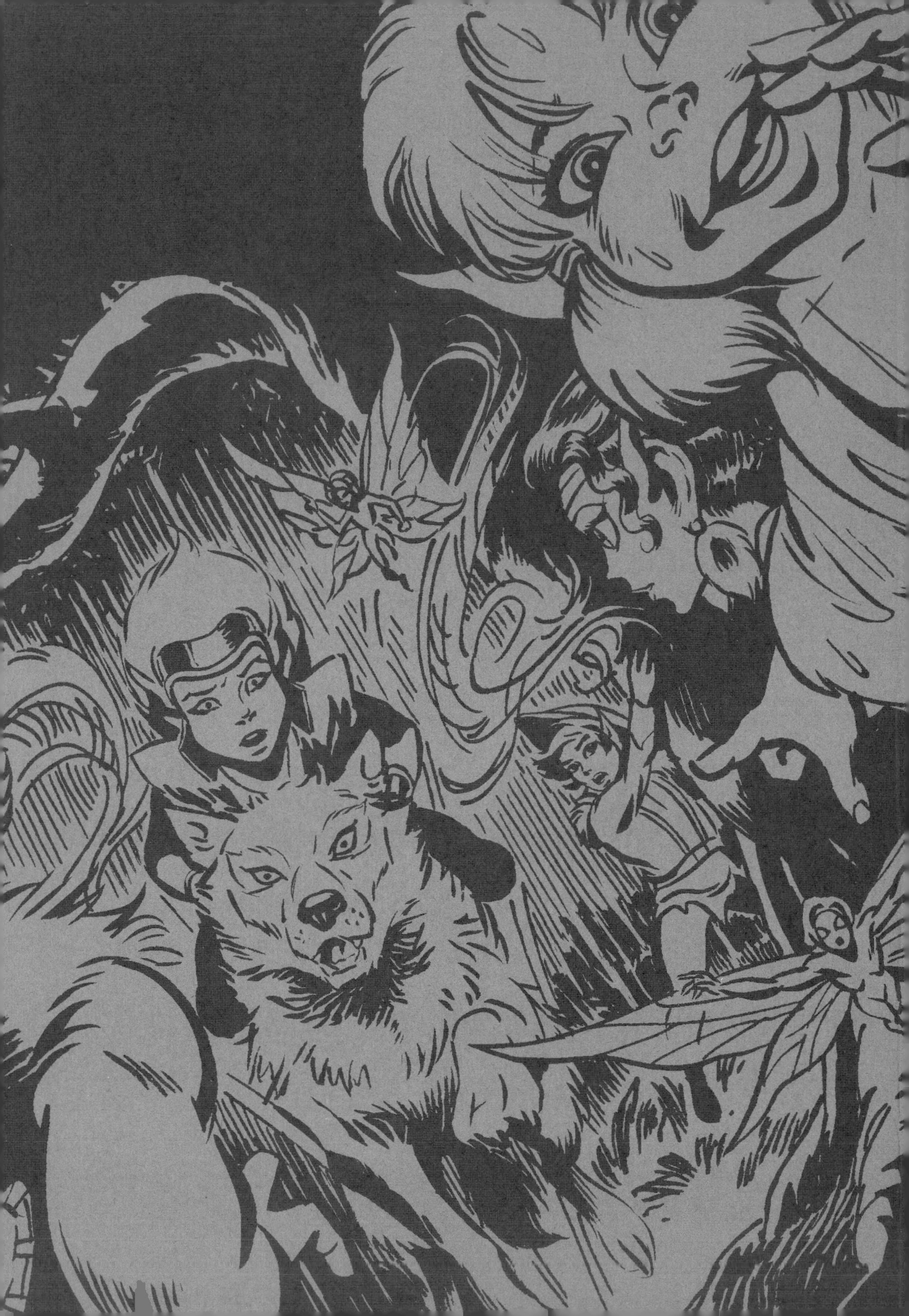

CONTENTS

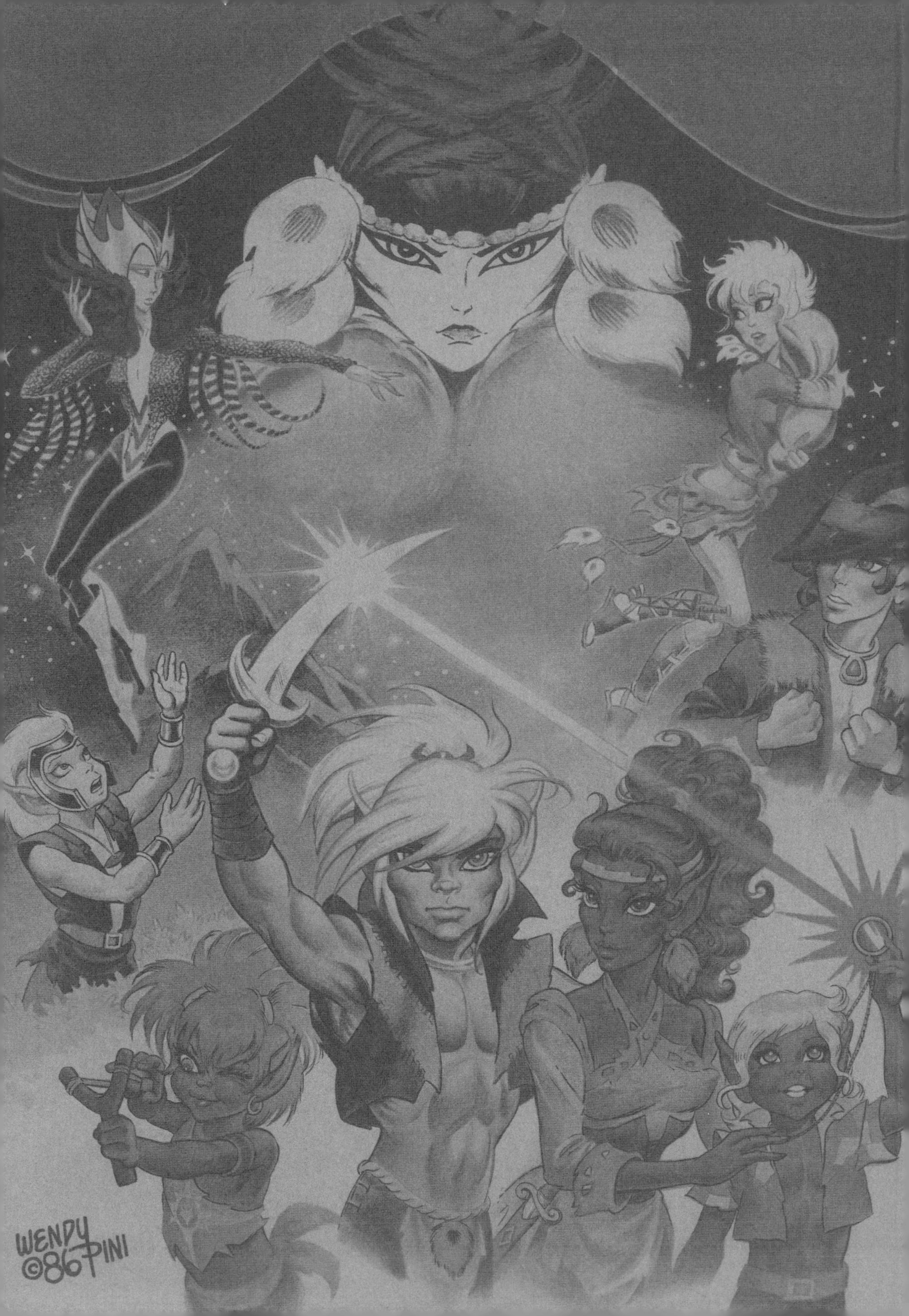
WENDY ©86 PINI

SIEGE AT BLUE MOUNTAIN

ARTIST / WRITER WENDY PINI   **CO-PLOT / EDITOR** RICHARD PINI   **PART 1**   **INKS** JOE STATON   **LETTERER** JANICE CHIANG

DUNG-HEADED, PUFFED UP, FROST BITTEN SUN-SUCKER! FROZEN STAG CHIP! BLACK-FACED, AIR WALKING--

UH... EH... K-KAHVI?

HE SHOULD FALL THROUGH THIN ICE!

HE SHOULD FRY IN BEAR FAT!

JUST WHO IN THE SHADOW OF THE GREAT ICE WALL DOES HE THINK HE IS?!

UH... AHEM!

WHAT HAS *HE* DONE NOW?

GO RECOGNIZE A TROLL, YOU MAGIC-SPURTING BAG OF WIND! ICE WATER FOR BLOOD--!

BLAP!

-- I BRING YOU MEAT AND YOU FLING IT IN MY FACE?!

STARVE, THEN! OR FEED ON MORE GIBBERISH FROM THE SCROLL!

YOU HEAR ME? GIBBERISH!

SAY THAT AGAIN AND--

--I'LL KILL YOU!

HAH!

AT LAST! YOU SPEAK WORDS I CAN UNDERSTAND!

NO...! NO, I–I SHOULDN'T HAVE...

I DID NOT MEAN...

¡TSK¡ COME OUT OF THERE, BLACK-HAIR! IT'S MAKING YOU *CRAZY*! YOU DON'T MEAN *HALF* WHAT YOU SAY LATELY––

––AND THE OTHER HALF MAKES NO SENSE!

GO AWAY, *KAHVI*. THIS IS BEYOND YOU. MAYBE... BEYOND ME.

UNTIL I AM SURE, LEAVE ME ALONE.

WHAT YOU NEED––

––IS A GOOD WRESTLE IN THE FURS, MY FRIEND. IT CLEARS THE HEAD.

IF ONLY IT WERE SO SIMPLE...

RAYEK HAS BEEN LOCK-SENDING WITH THE HIGH ONE FOR DAYS. HE IS TIRED OUT.

HMPH!

BEST LEAVE HIM TO ME.

OH! YOU UH--

--YOU MIGHT AS WELL LEAVE *THAT* TOO!

FINE!

TAKE A LOOK, ROCK-SHAPER!

THIS IS WHAT HE'LL BE IF HE STAYS IN THERE MUCH LONGER--

--COLD MEAT! THE SCROLL OF COLORS...SOME WAR PRIZE! WHAT GOOD IS IT--

--IF IT MELTS ELF BRAINS TO SLUSH?

. . . . . .

UP...DOWN... SIDE TO SIDE...

...BACK AND FORTH...THEN AND NOW...

SHE SAYS THEY MEAN NO MORE THAN *DEATH* DOES.

THAT *TIME* IS JUST THINGS AND ROOM TO PUT THEM IN.

UNCHOOSE *THINGS* AND YOU UNCHOOSE *TIME*.

BUT THE HIGH ONES CHOSE THEIR *BODIES*, BROWNSKIN!

EATING, SLEEPING, LOVING, HURTING--*LIFE!* THEY CHOSE IT. WHY? BECAUSE IT'S GOOD!

THEY *KNEW!*

AND *YOU* MUST NOT FORGET.

OH, *TIMMAIN!* YOU GAVE THE WOLFRIDERS A SPECK OF SAND PICKED FROM A MEASURELESS MOUNTAIN OF KNOWLEDGE.

YOU'VE GIVEN *ME* BUT FEW GRAINS MORE!

AS HE HAS DONE REPEATEDLY IN THE FEW DAYS SINCE THE ELVES WON THEIR BATTLE FOR THE PALACE OF THE HIGH ONES, *RAYEK* TURNS THE SCROLL OF COLORS, RELIVING THE HISTORY OF HIS ANCESTORS.

THE SWIRLING HUES TELL OF AN IMMORTAL RACE OF SHAPE-CHANGERS WHO, HAVING OUTLIVED THEIR OWN HOMEWORLD--

--VISITED IN DIFFERENT GUISES MANY OTHER WORLDS... EVEN TAKING THE SHAPE OF LEGEND.

WE WERE CREATURES OF FIRE, THEN, *TIMMAIN*, THE FIRE THAT CHANGES ALL.

HOW MAY I RECLAIM THAT POWER FOR OUR RACE? WE ARE WEAKENED, MADE SMALL BY THIS WORLD OF TWO MOONS! IT WAS A *MISTAKE*--!

--FOR THE HIGH ONES, SEEKING OTHERS OF THEIR KIND, TO ADOPT THE FORMS OF HUMAN FANCY. AND IT WAS A *FATAL* MISTAKE--

-- FOR THEM TO BRING THE BETRAYING *TROLLS* ALONG. THE HIGH ONES WOULD NEVER HAVE BEEN TRAPPED HERE IN THE WRONG PLACE AND TIME. BUT FOR--

--THOSE *CURSED, STINKING PETS!* WHY DIDN'T YOU LEAVE THEM BEHIND, *TIMMAIN*--

--WHEN WE ABANDONED OUR SPENT STAR, CHILD?

THE TROLLS WERE THE LAST BEINGS BESIDE OURSELVES TO SURVIVE-- THEY AND THE WINGED PRESERVERS.

WITHOUT US THEY'D HAVE PERISHED.

"BETTER THAT," *RAYEK INSOLENTLY RESPONDS,* "THAN TO HAVE FOUND MINDS OF THEIR OWN. THE TROLLS TOOK THEIR FREEDOM, BUT AT WHAT COST--TO *US!*"

WELL, FRIEND *TWO-EDGE*--

YOU PLAYED YOUR GAME, HERE IN THE FROZEN MOUNTAIN, BUT NOW IT'S DONE!

14

THE LITTLE WAR YOU SET US AND THE ELVES TO DIDN'T FINISH QUITE AS YOU EXPECTED, DID IT?

HOW DOES IT FEEL TO LOSE?

I WOULDN'T KNOW, MYSELF, AS YOU CAN SEE!

OOO, PICKY! HOW HE GLARES!

THAT'S ALL HE CAN DO, ODDBIT, MY QUEEN!

WHAT'S THE MATTER, HALF ELF? IS YOUR TONGUE PULPED LIKE YOUR FEET?

TOOK US ALL THIS TIME TO FIND 'IM IN ONE OF HIS HIDEY-HOLES.

DON'T KNOW HOW HE RAN SO FAST ON TWO FLESHBAGS OF BROKEN BONES, BUT A BLOOD TRAIL WILL TELL!

WHAT SHOULD WE DO WITH HIM, KING PICKNOSE?

"KING PICKNOSE"... AHH! I LIKE THE SOUND!

GOUGE THE HALF-BLOOD TRICKSTER!

SQUEEZE OUT HIS BRAINS THROUGH HIS POINTED EARS!

KILL 'IM!

TSK TSK... AND AFTER ALL YOU'VE DONE FOR THEM, MASTER SMITH! WHAT INGRATES!

NOW I...I STILL APPRECIATE YOUR LONG-FAMED SKILLS--

TWO-EDGE IS LED TO HIS OWN ONCE-SECRET ARMORY.

--IN FACT, I HAVE A PLACE FOR YOU IN MY COURT. AND ALL YOU NEED TO DO IS WHAT YOU LIKE--

--MAKE ARMOR FOR US--

--JUST AS YOU DID FOR THE LITTLE ELVES!

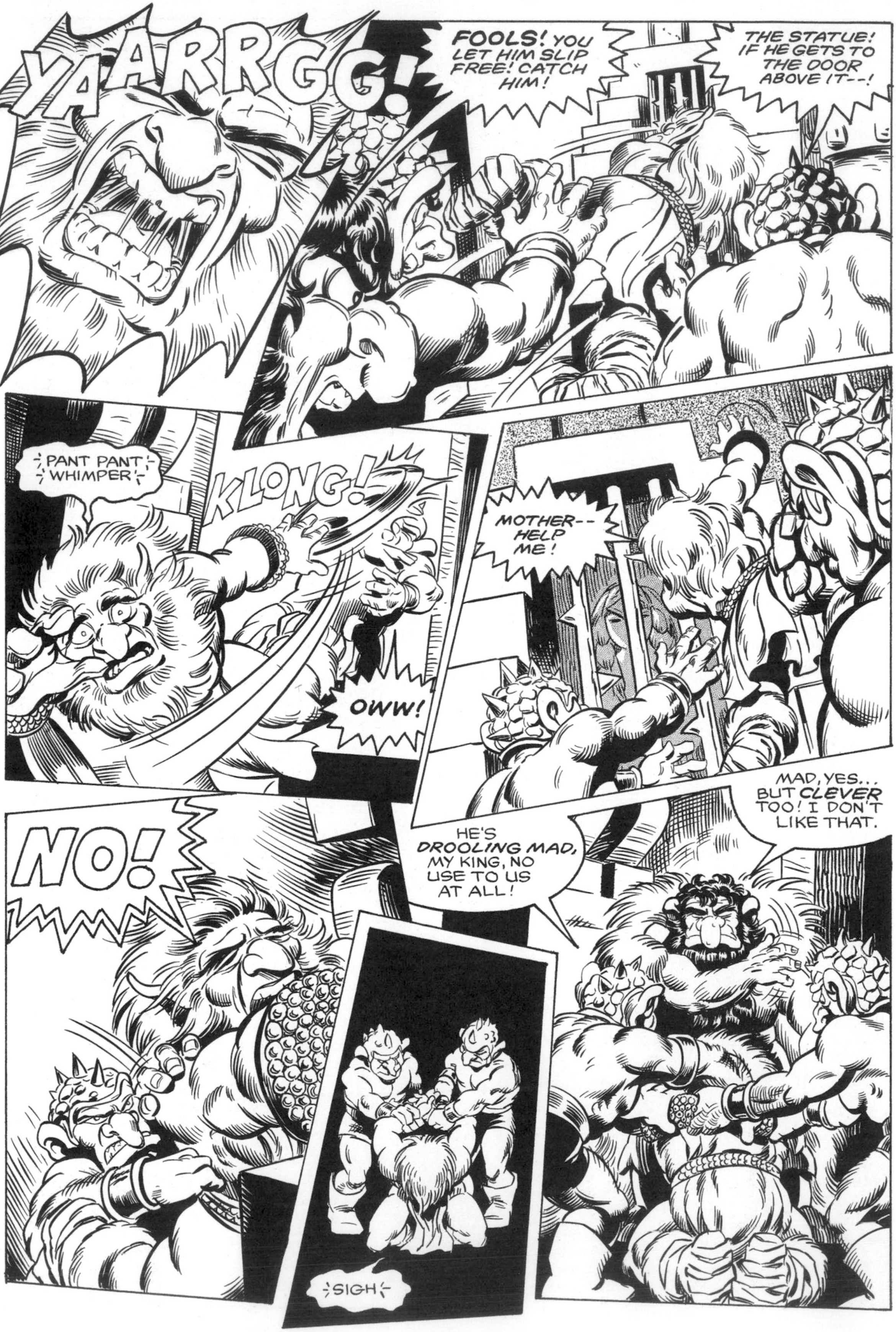
YA ARRGG!
FOOLS! YOU LET HIM SLIP FREE! CATCH HIM!
THE STATUE! IF HE GETS TO THE DOOR ABOVE IT--!
PANT PANT WHIMPER
KLONG!
OWW!
MOTHER-- HELP ME!
NO!
HE'S DROOLING MAD, MY KING, NO USE TO US AT ALL!
MAD, YES... BUT CLEVER TOO! I DON'T LIKE THAT.
SIGH

SOON... I THINK YOU'LL FIND YOUR TRICKS AND TALENTS LESS WARMING--

--THAN FURS AND A WELL-TENDED FIRE, MASTER SMITH. BUT I'LL GIVE YOU ONE LAST CHANCE.

BRING ME *EKUAR*, THE ROCK-SHAPER--

--AND I'LL TAKE YOU BACK UNDER MY CLOAK. I DOUBT THE GO BACKS WOULD DO AS MUCH, EXCEPT TO SMOKE YOU IN STRIPS--

--AND LIVE OFF YOU 'TIL THAW-TIME!

STILL SILENT, *TWO-EDGE* HOBBLES AWAY UP THE MOUNTAINSIDE.

THAT'S THAT. HE'LL BE STIFF AS AN ICICLE BY TOMORROW.

THE ONLY THING OF VALUE IN THE PALACE IS THAT ROCK SHAPER.

I WANT HIM.

ANYONE WHO'S LIVED AS LONG AS *TWO-EDGE*--

--DOESN'T JUST CURL UP AND DIE. WE'LL SEE IF HIS SENSIBLE TROLL HALF WINS HIM TO OUR USE. IF NOT...

WE'LL PAY THE PALACE A VISIT OUR-SELVES, EH? YOU KNOW, *KING PICKY*, IT WAS A LUCKY DAY--

--WHEN OLD *GUTTLEKRAW* CAUGHT YOU FOR A MINE PIT SLAVE!

MENTION THE PIT AGAIN--

KLOP!

AND YOU'LL SEE IT FOR YOURSELF-- *PERMANENTLY!*

17

THE RHYMES, THE COMFORTING RHYMES HAVE FLOWN.

THERE ARE NO MORE WORDS--

--TO CALM THE FURY OF THE STORM WITHIN HIS DIVIDED BRAIN.

A DAY PASSES...

THEN ANOTHER...

EACH CRACKING, THROBBING STEP--

--CARRIES HIM NEARER TO THE MOUNTAIN'S CREST!

AND ALL THE WHILE, MEMORIES SWIRL ABOUT HIM LIKE FLAKE-SPECKLED WIND.

AAAAAAHH!

GRRRRA

SUMETIME LATER...

THE CASTLE FLEW ONCE, *EKUAR*, ABOVE THE LAND--

--FROM ONE TIME TO ANOTHER, FROM ONE STAR TO ANOTHER!

MUNCH THERE IS A WAY TO MAKE IT FLY AGAIN...

...BUT I NEED *POWER*!

--THE SORT OF MAGIC THAT MOST ELVES NO LONGER EVEN DREAM OF USING!

WHY, BROWNSKIN?

¿ULP? WHAT?

WHY MAKE THE CASTLE FLY?

BECAUSE IT IS NOT IMPOSSIBLE!

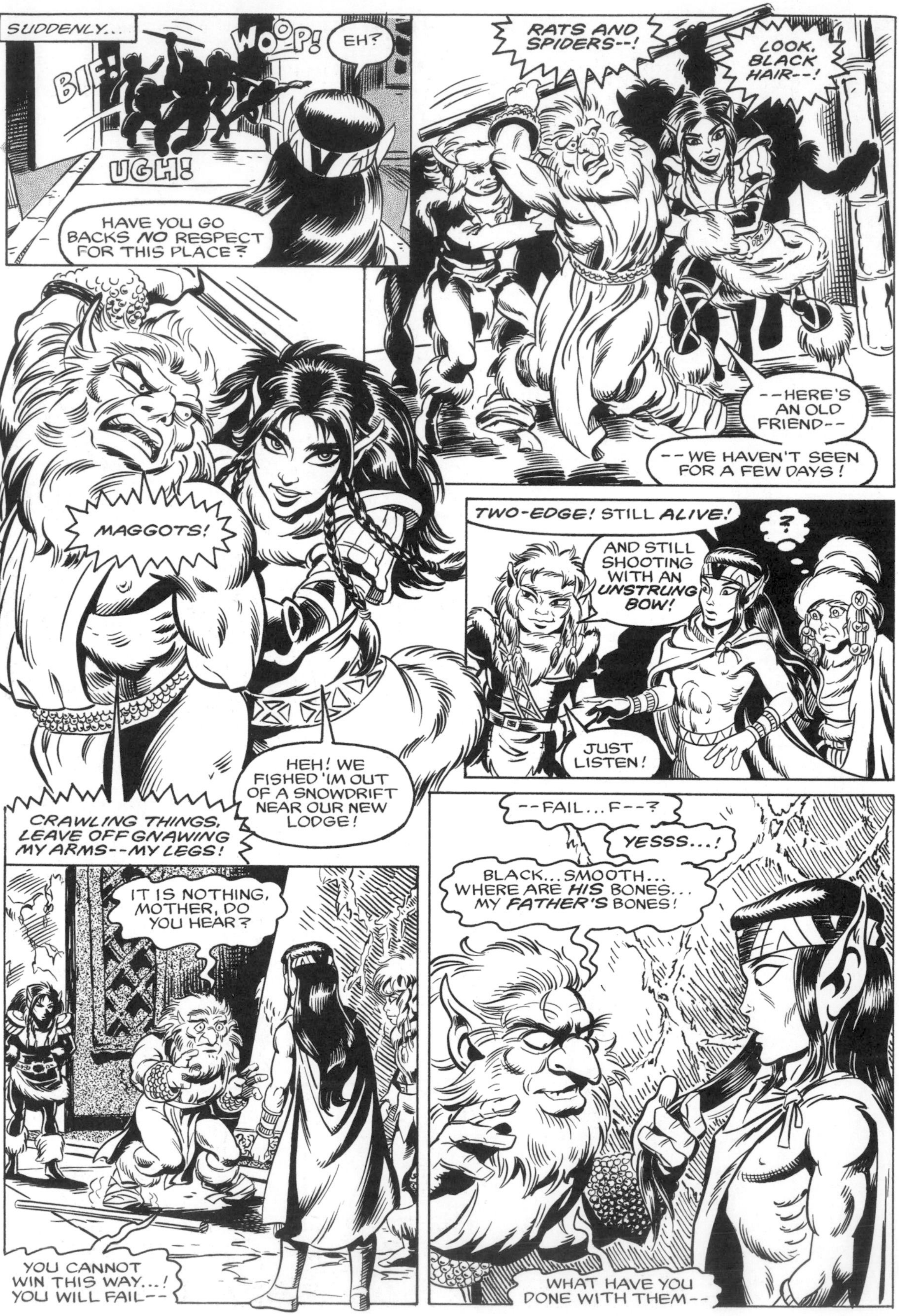
SUDDENLY...
BIF!
WOOP!
UGH!
EH?
HAVE YOU GO BACKS NO RESPECT FOR THIS PLACE?
RATS AND SPIDERS--!
LOOK, BLACK HAIR--!
--HERE'S AN OLD FRIEND--
--WE HAVEN'T SEEN FOR A FEW DAYS!
MAGGOTS!
TWO-EDGE! STILL ALIVE!
AND STILL SHOOTING WITH AN UNSTRUNG BOW!
?
JUST LISTEN!
HEH! WE FISHED 'IM OUT OF A SNOWDRIFT NEAR OUR NEW LODGE!
CRAWLING THINGS, LEAVE OFF GNAWING MY ARMS--MY LEGS!
IT IS NOTHING, MOTHER, DO YOU HEAR?
YOU CANNOT WIN THIS WAY...! YOU WILL FAIL--
--FAIL... F--?
YESSS...!
BLACK... SMOOTH... WHERE ARE HIS BONES... MY FATHER'S BONES!
WHAT HAVE YOU DONE WITH THEM--

--MOTHER...?

HO HO HO HA HA HA YA HA HA HOO HOO HOO

RAYEK *IGNORES THE JIBES, FOR A SUDDEN INSPIRATION STIRS HIM.*

POWER... WHAT AILS YOU, HALF-TROLL? ALL TROLL!

I AM NONE OF YOU--

--MATE-KILLER!

YOUNG-EATING CARRION BIRD! I AM ALL TROLL!!

NO...NO...I AM...YOUR SON! I AM A HIGH ONE! THE LOW BLOOD--

--DOES *NOT* CANCEL THE HIGH...!

THE GAME...

MY GAME--

--IS FINISHED!

LOOK...!

SEE WHAT WE BUILT FOR YOU, FATHER AND I...!

YOUR OWN SECRET KINGDOM IN THE DEPTHS OF BLUE MOUNTAIN!

NO ROCK-SHAPER CAN MATCH THE WORK OF A TROLL WHO SETS HIS HEART TO IT...

HEAR...? HIS *HEART!*

NO ONE WILL EVER SEE ALL THIS BUT YOU, MOTHER--

--AND *DOOR* THERE!

IT IS YOURS! YOURS!

21

I AM YOUR SON!!

NOW...GIVE IT BACK TO ME-- MY MIND! M-MY *SELF!* FOR PITY, *END* YOUR GAME!

¦SOB...SOB¦

IF EVER WE WISHED REVENGE ON *TWO EDGE*, THAT WISH WAS GRANTED LONG AGO. HE HAS BEEN A PRISONER SINCE CHILDHOOD--

--AS I WAS. I CAN TELL--

HE TAKES ME FOR *WINNOWILL*, THAT BLACK HAIRED PAIN-GIVER *LEETAH* FOUGHT--

¦SOB¦

--IN BLUE MOUNTAIN...WHERE THE *GLIDERS* DWELL. LEETAH SAID THEY THINK OF THEM SELVES AS HIGH ONES... AND THAT THEIR *POWERS* ALMOST BEAR THEM OUT!

UH HUM...

WHAT CAN HIS CRUEL MOTHER HAVE DONE TO HIM, BROWNSKIN? IF SHE WERE HERE, GENTLE *LEETAH* WOULD NOT HESITATE TO HEAL HIM!

WELL, SHE'S GONE, "*DOOR*", WITH THE WOLF- RIDERS TO THE *FORBIDDEN GROVE*--

"AND THAT LEAVES US TO SOLVE THIS UNWELCOMED RIDDLE OURSELVES... PERHAPS TO OUR ADVANTAGE!"

THE RIDDLE WAITS, GROWS MORE PROFOUND THROUGH THREE TURNS OF THE SEASONS.

THOSE WHO WILL HELP TO SOLVE IT KNOW NOTHING, YET, OF THE ROLES THEY WILL PLAY.

SWISH!

PAT PAT

-;GASP;-

LEETAH! A NEW JACKET!

AH!

AH... HAH!

RUSTLE!

GOT YOU, MOONSHADE!

SLY ONE!

-;CHUCKLE;-

HAPPY?

MMMHMMM! THE DYES ARE SO RICH, AND THE STITCHING-- SO PLAYFUL!

STRANGE...TO LIVE IN THE WOODS AND YET NOT FEEL ANXIOUS--

--TO HAVE EASE ENOUGH TO MAKE CLOTHES THAT ARE MORE THAN JUST USEFUL.

PEACE BRINGS GIFTS OF BEAUTY.

HERE WE HAVE TIME TO PLAY...TO DREAM.

HEH...ALL *CUTTER* HAD TO DO WAS LOSE HIS *HAIR*--

--TO MAKE *MOONSHADE* DREAM UP HIS NEW LEATHERS.

NIGHTFALL!

BAP!

AT LEAST *REDLANCE* WAS ABLE TO MEND THE BRANCH!

YOU AND *CUTTER* SHOULD HAVE PICKED A *STURDIER* ONE!

WE WEREN'T... PAYING ATTENTION.

LOOK!

SIGH A SHAME! BUT IF HE HADN'T CUT IT OFF--

--OUR CHIEF WOULD STILL BE TANGLED UP HERE, BARE AS A *BAGFROG!*

NO, STRONGBOW!

I CAN'T ALLOW IT!

THAT'S ALL!

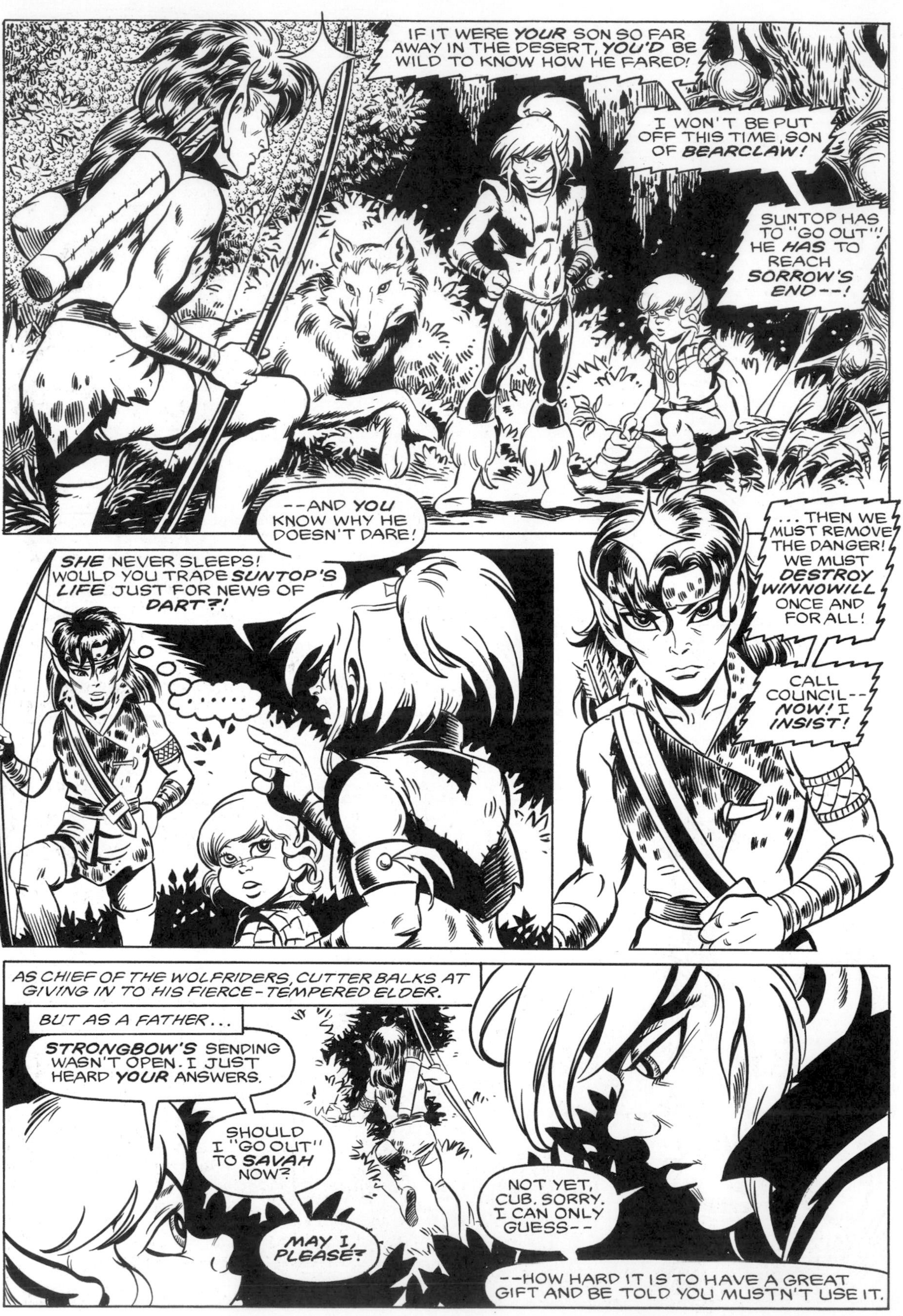
IF IT WERE YOUR SON SO FAR AWAY IN THE DESERT, YOU'D BE WILD TO KNOW HOW HE FARED!
I WON'T BE PUT OFF THIS TIME, SON OF BEARCLAW!
SUNTOP HAS TO "GO OUT"! HE HAS TO REACH SORROW'S END--!
--AND YOU KNOW WHY HE DOESN'T DARE!
SHE NEVER SLEEPS! WOULD YOU TRADE SUNTOP'S LIFE JUST FOR NEWS OF DART?!
......
...THEN WE MUST REMOVE THE DANGER! WE MUST DESTROY WINNOWILL ONCE AND FOR ALL!
CALL COUNCIL--NOW! I INSIST!
AS CHIEF OF THE WOLFRIDERS, CUTTER BALKS AT GIVING IN TO HIS FIERCE-TEMPERED ELDER.
BUT AS A FATHER...
STRONGBOW'S SENDING WASN'T OPEN. I JUST HEARD YOUR ANSWERS.
SHOULD I "GO OUT" TO SAVAH NOW?
MAY I, PLEASE?
NOT YET, CUB. SORRY. I CAN ONLY GUESS--
--HOW HARD IT IS TO HAVE A GREAT GIFT AND BE TOLD YOU MUSTN'T USE IT.

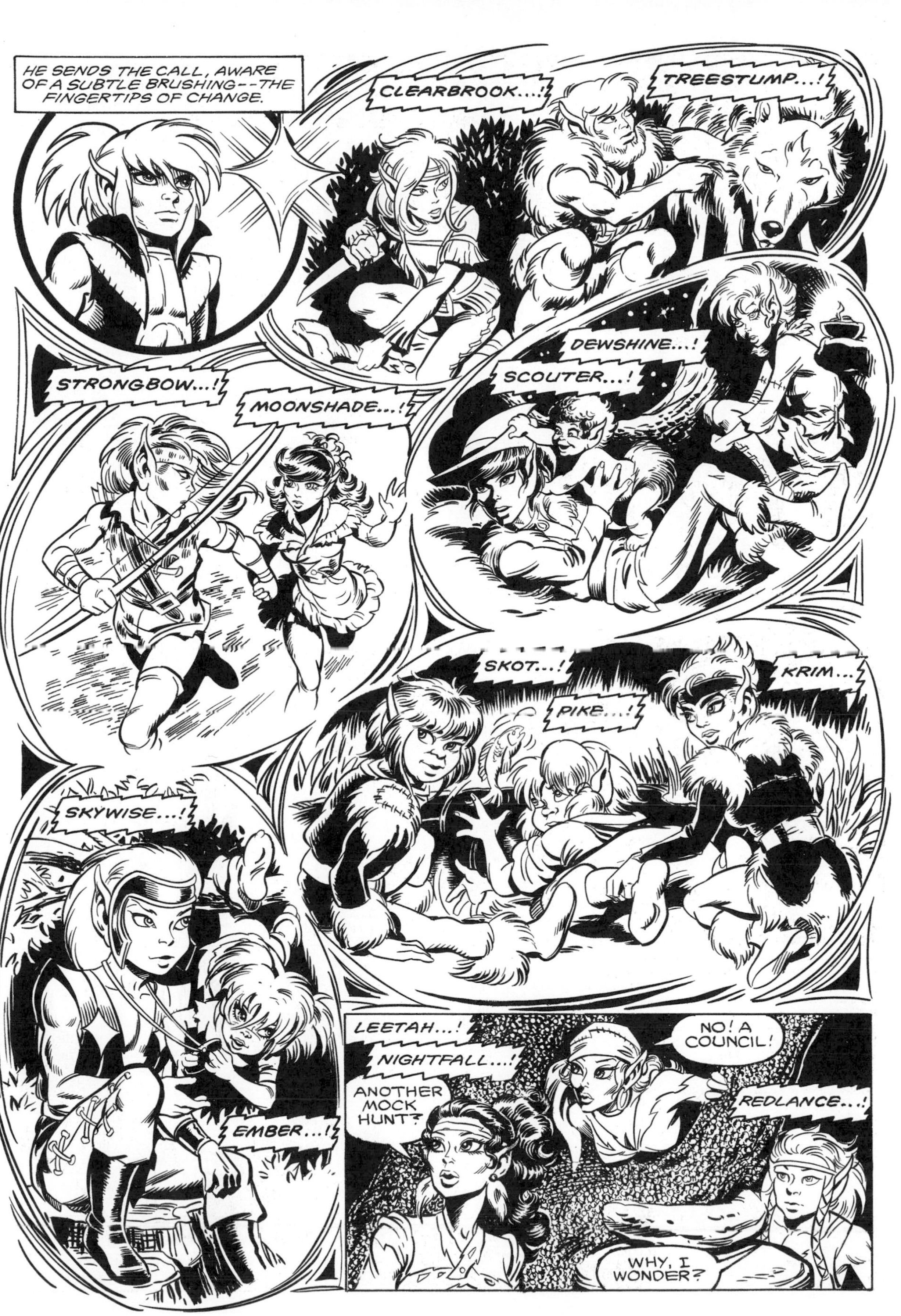

HE SENDS THE CALL, AWARE OF A SUBTLE BRUSHING--THE FINGERTIPS OF CHANGE.
CLEARBROOK...!
TREESTUMP...!
STRONGBOW...!
MOONSHADE...!
DEWSHINE...!
SCOUTER...!
SKOT...!
KRIM...
PIKE...!
SKYWISE...!
EMBER...!
LEETAH...!
NIGHTFALL...!
ANOTHER MOCK HUNT?
NO! A COUNCIL!
REDLANCE...!
WHY, I WONDER?

A RIOT OF SPRAWLING LIMBS WITH A BULGING, DEN-RIDDLED BOLE, ALL LOVINGLY SHAPED BY REDLANCE, THE NEW *FATHER TREE* IS THE GATHERING PLACE OF THE TRIBE.

YOUR EARS STILL AS SHARP AS YOUR EYES, *SCOUTER?*

-SIGH- I KNOW... "KEEP WATCH AND LISTEN IN".

WOA, *WINDKIN!* YOU'LL BUMP YOUR HEAD ON A BRANCH--LIKE LAST TIME! STAY DOWN!

KKHHGG!

SOON...

WELL... WE'RE ALL HERE, AND YET NOT ALL. WE HAVE BLOOD KIN IN THE SUN VILLAGE. *WOODLOCK* AND *RAINSONG*--

--HAD ANOTHER CUB ON THE WAY WHEN WE LEFT THEM.

AND THEY'VE PROBABLY HAD *FOUR MORE* SINCE!

NOW *THAT'S* RECOGNITION!

SO WHAT?

THAT'S JUST IT!

WE'VE KNOWN NOTHING OF THEM--

--OR OF OUR SON, *DART,* FOR THE THREE TURNS OF THE SEASONS!

SAID!

NOW LET SOME-ONE SAY WHY!

ME! *I'LL* SAY! BECAUSE OL' *"WINNOW-WICKED"* MIGHT, UM, TRY HER OLD, DIRTY TRICKS AGAIN IF, UM, *SAVAH--*

THE MOTHER OF MEMORY, WHO WOULD *ALSO* BE IN DANGER--

HEY!

--AND *SUNTOP* "WENT OUT" TO FIND EACH OTHER.

I WAS GOING TO SAY THAT!

NEXT TIME, *EMBER!*

WHAT'S ALL THIS "WENT OUT" SLUSH? I STILL CAN'T GET IT!

WE ELVES HAVE SPIRITS INSIDE US THAT WE CAN SEND OUT TO TALK TO OTHER SPIRITS FAR AWAY!

IF HE REMEMBERS *YESTERDAY,* HE'S DOING WELL!

A GO-BACK EVER CLEVER? *NEVER!*

LISTEN TO *SUNTOP!*

DON'T YOU REMEMBER THE SCROLL OF COLORS, *SKOT?*

ESPECIALLY *YOU, STRONGBOW!* YOU WANT TO BE RID OF *WINNOWILL--?*

29

"-- WELL, YOU CAN'T DO IT BY DESTROYING HER BODY -- SHE'S AN *ELF!* KILL HER, AND HER SPIRIT WILL LIVE ON--"

"--FREE TO DO WHATEVER HARM SHE LIKES--TO *ANY* OF US--"

"--FOREVER!"

IT IS SO! *WINNOWILL'S* WEB OF POWER MUST BE CUT WHILE SHE *LIVES*, ONE THREAD AT A TIME!

THEN, PERHAPS, WE MIGHT EVEN BECOME FRIENDS WITH THE GLIDERS--

--AND USE THEIR GIANT BIRDS TO VISIT THE SUN FOLK, OR THE GO-BACKS, OR OTHER TRIBES WE DON'T YET KNOW!

IT *IS* TIME TO STOP LIVING AFRAID...BUT WHICH THREAD TO CUT FIRST? HMMM...

AH!

THE *HOAN G'TAY SHO* WORSHIP *WINNOWILL!* IF WE CONVINCE THOSE HUMANS THAT THEY MUST *NOT* SERVE HER--

--I KNOW THAT LOOK...! *NONNA* AND *ADAR*, YES?

WELL, *NONNA'S* ONE OF THE *HOAN G'TAY SHO*, ISN'T SHE? SHE'LL HELP US TALK TO HER KIND.

IT WORKED ONCE BEFORE!

SORT OF...

AS DAWN APPROACHES AND THE COUNCIL ENDS, A TINY FEAR CLUTCHES AT LEETAH'S STOMACH.

30

HER LIFEMATE CHATS OF DOING A THING SHE STILL FINDS HARD TO IMAGINE--ASKING AID OF THE FIVE-FINGERED ONES!

I'LL LEAVE BEFORE DARK. THE SOONER I START, THE SOONER WE'LL KNOW IF THE PLAN IS GOOD.

YES, BUT...

...HE IS CUTTER, KINSEEKER, BLOOD OF TEN CHIEFS--

--AND FINDER OF THE PALACE OF THE HIGH ONES. THE QUICK DECISION QUICKLY ACTED UPON IS HIS WAY.

ALONE. NOT WISE.

DON'T WORRY. HE GETS ALONG WITH HUMANS JUST LIKE BEARCLAW DID WITH TROLLS!

AND SO...

IT'S A KNACK.

SCOUTER AND DEWSHINE SHARE SKY-WISE'S CONFIDENCE. HAVING SEEN CUTTER AWAY ON HIS MISSION, THE YOUNG PARENTS ENJOY THE EVENING.

OOF!

SO STRONG!

SOON HE'LL LIFT YOU IN THE AIR WITH HIM!

¡GIGGLE! WATCH!

WINDKIN! COME!

...! HE EVEN ANSWERS A SEND NOW! WHY WON'T HE EVER MIND ME THAT WELL?

HE LIKES ME--

"--BECAUSE I BROUGHT HIM CLOSE TO THE SKY EVERY DAY."

"EVEN ON THE DAY HE POPPED OUT!" ADDS SCOUTER.

NO WONDER.

JUST THEN... AYO-OAH-YOH!

SCOUTER! THERE'S A-A *SMUDGE* OF *LIGHT* IN THE SKY!

I JUST *SPOTTED* IT!

COME TELL ME WHAT *YOU* SEE!

RIGHT *BEHIND* YOU!

LOOKS LIKE IT'S STANDING STILL TO ME...

EH...?

HUNH! I'LL BE! IT HAS A *TAIL!*

A STAR WITH A TAIL... STRAIGHT OUT BEHIND, LIKE A RUNNING WOLF!

I BET IT'S GOING SOMEWHERE IN A HURRY!

UH OH!

OUT THERE! ONE OF THE *CHOSEN EIGHT!*

HEADED THIS WAY?

"--IT'S *AROREE!*

LOOKS LIKE. AND... I THINK I KNOW THE RIDER--!

LEADER IN CUTTER'S ABSENCE, **TREESTUMP** RECEIVES **SCOUTER'S** SILENT WARNING--

GLIDER! THIS WAY. SLOW. MAYBE HUNTING.

--AND SENDS AN ORDER WHICH GAINS AN INSTANT PRACTICED RESPONSE...

DEN-HIDE!

WHISPER-SWIFT, THE WOLFRIDERS SWARM THROUGH THE HOLLOWS OF THE FATHER TREE!

AND...

IT'S NOTHING, **DEWSHINE!** **AROREE** WON'T LAND-- HER HAWK'S TOO BIG. ALL SHE'LL SEE FROM THE SKY IS LEAVES!

IF **WINNOWILL** EVER LEARNS--

--THAT THIS IS OUR NEW HOLT--

--SHE'LL BE AFTER **SUNTOP** IN AN INSTANT! AND **WINDKIN** TOO! SHE COULDN'T RESIST!

WEBS! PERHAPS...?

COCOONS! AT LAST!

K·KRSSH!

DON'T MAKE A SOUND--

--OR MY TRIBE WILL ATTACK! YOU KNOW WHAT THAT MEANS...

I'VE BROKEN THE "DEN-HIDE". IT'S WRONG, BUT--

--AROREE, YOU *ABANDONED* US TO THE TROLLS!

WHY?

WHY HAVE YOU COME HERE NOW?

OH, SKYWISE, I DID NOT KNOW--

--THAT YOU WERE HERE IN THESE WOODS. BELIEVE ME! *SHE* SENT ME TO FIND THE LOST PRESERVERS!

I HAVE SEARCHED FOR DAYS!

BEHIND HER THOUGHTS HE SENSES IT...

...WINNOWILL! SHE'S DONE SOMETHING TO YOU!

COME ON! THEY'LL WANT TO KILL ME FOR THIS--

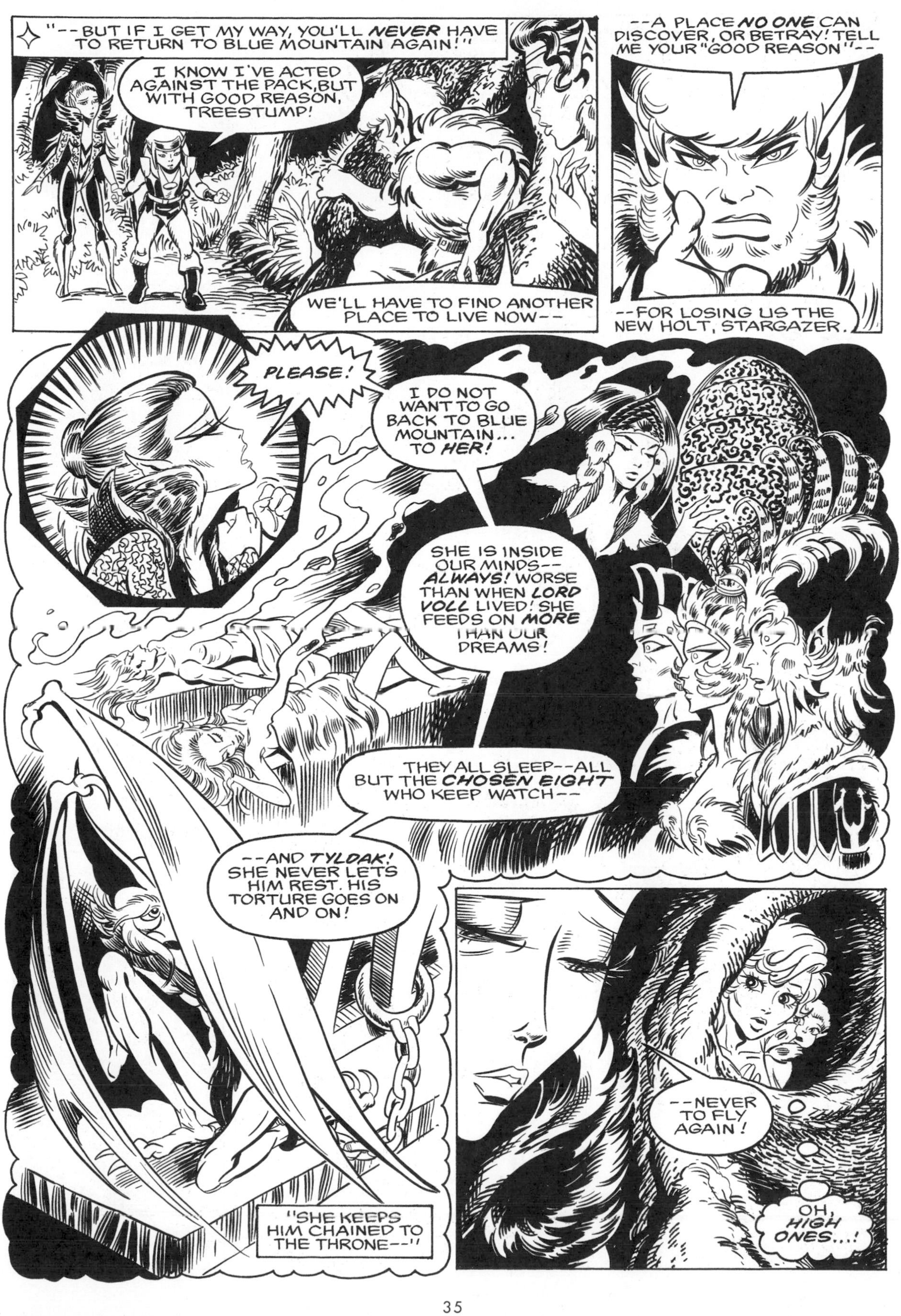
"--BUT IF I GET MY WAY, YOU'LL NEVER HAVE TO RETURN TO BLUE MOUNTAIN AGAIN!"
I KNOW I'VE ACTED AGAINST THE PACK, BUT WITH GOOD REASON, TREESTUMP!
WE'LL HAVE TO FIND ANOTHER PLACE TO LIVE NOW--
--A PLACE NO ONE CAN DISCOVER, OR BETRAY! TELL ME YOUR "GOOD REASON"--
--FOR LOSING US THE NEW HOLT, STARGAZER.
PLEASE!
I DO NOT WANT TO GO BACK TO BLUE MOUNTAIN... TO HER!
SHE IS INSIDE OUR MINDS-- ALWAYS! WORSE THAN WHEN LORD VOLL LIVED! SHE FEEDS ON MORE THAN OUR DREAMS!
THEY ALL SLEEP--ALL BUT THE CHOSEN EIGHT WHO KEEP WATCH--
--AND TYLDAK! SHE NEVER LETS HIM REST. HIS TORTURE GOES ON AND ON!
"SHE KEEPS HIM CHAINED TO THE THRONE--"
--NEVER TO FLY AGAIN!
OH, HIGH ONES...!

IF SOMETHING ISN'T DONE SOON, THAT BLACK *SHE-SNAKE* WILL MAKE *ALL* THE GLIDERS LIKE--

--DOOR!

DEAD, BUT LIVING TO SERVE *HER!*

NO!

THAT IS WHY *WINNOWILL* WANTS THE PRESERVERS--

TO BIND OUR BODIES IN ENDLESS SLEEP, SO THAT SHE MAY FEED ON OUR POWERS--LIKE A BLOOD-BAT!

SHE MUST BE STOPPED!

LET IT BEGIN HERE! I WILL CHASE HER FROM YOUR MIND, *AROREE.*

HEE HEE

WINDKIN!

GASP

A FLOATER! A CHANCE!

BLBLBL...!

DON'T! NO!!

SNAP!

MMM?

TO BE CONTINUED...

36

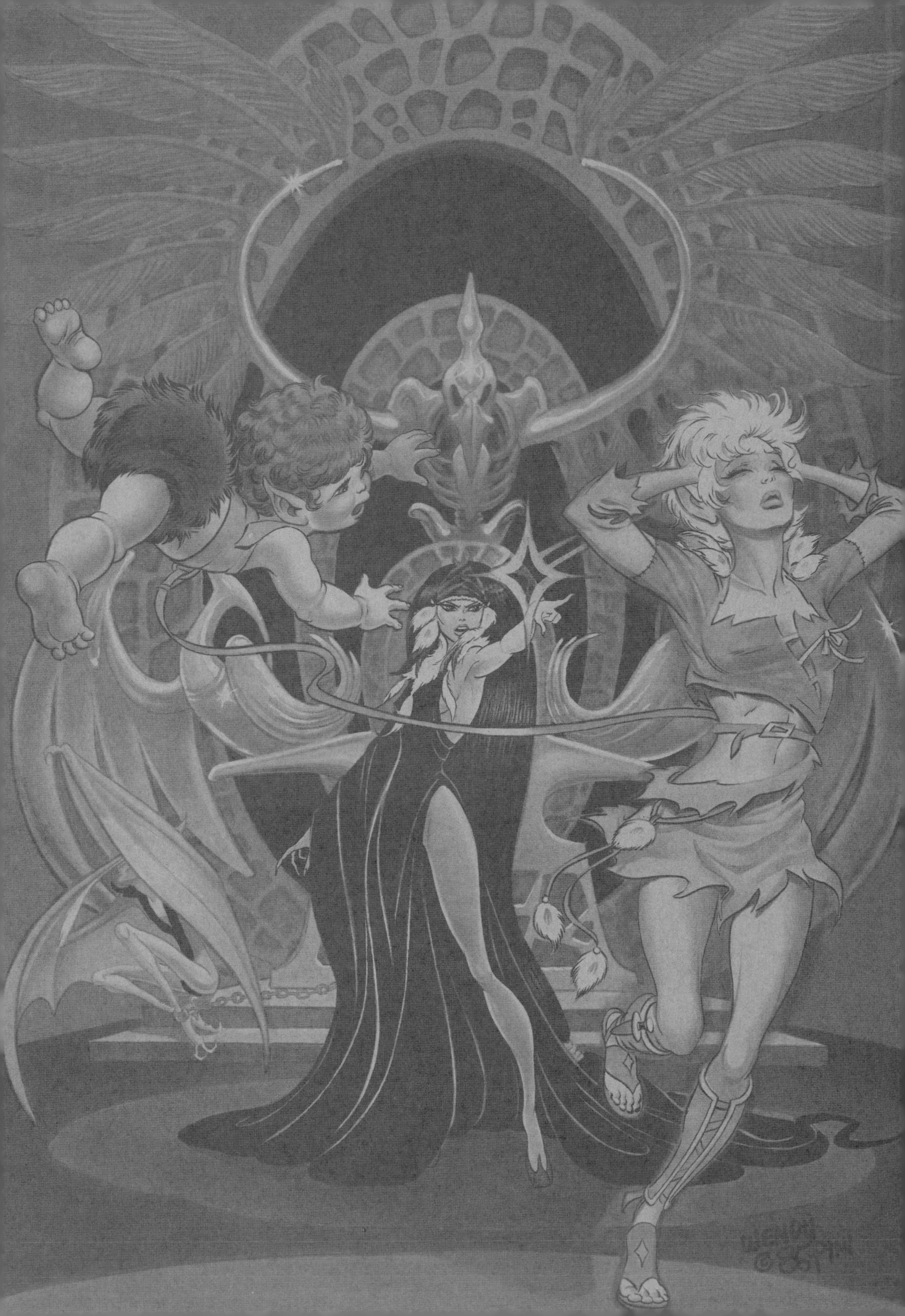

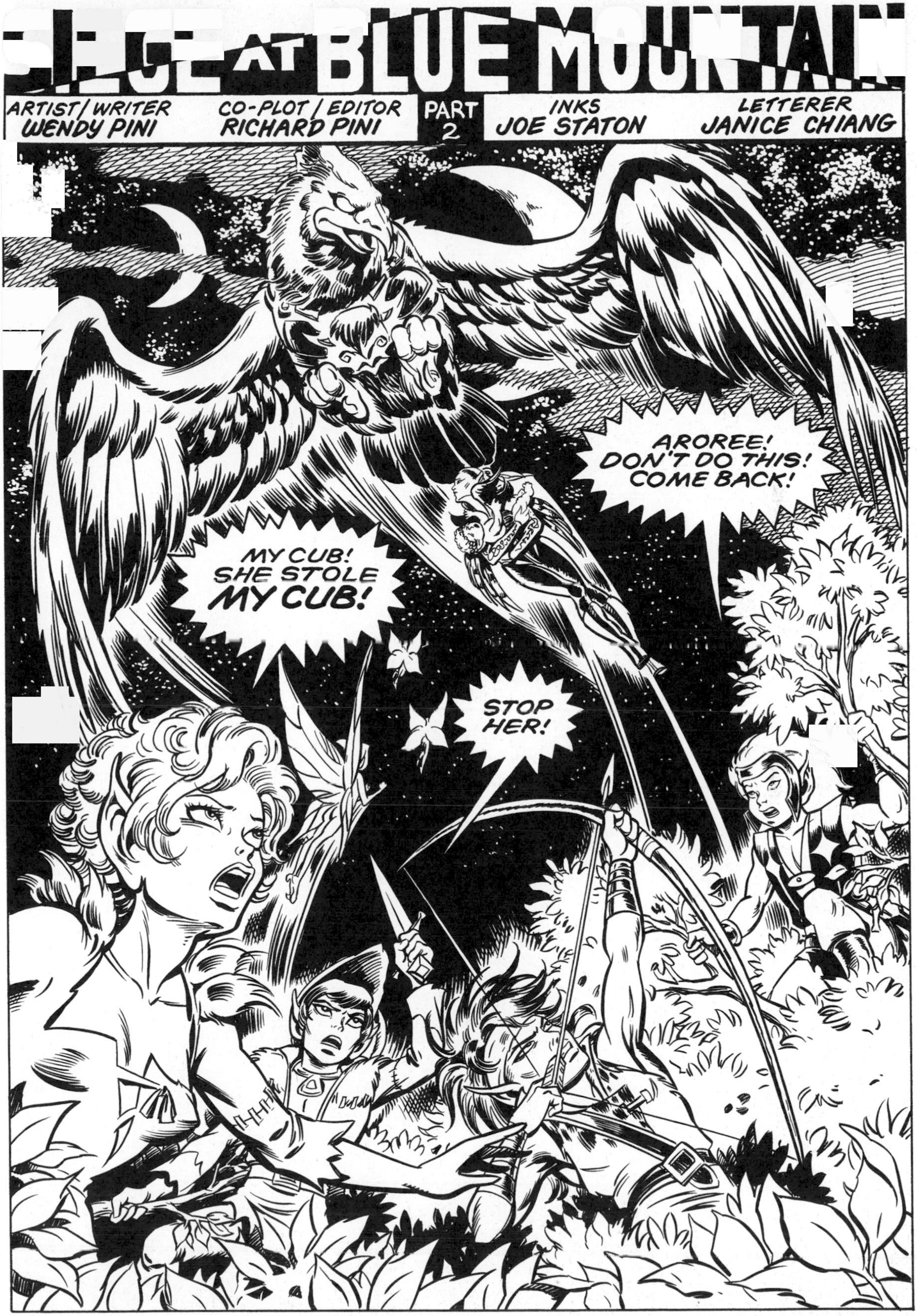
AT BLUE
ARTIST/WRITER WENDY PINI
CO-PLOT/EDITOR RICHARD PINI
PART 2
INKS JOE STATON
LETTERER JANICE CHIANG
AROREE! DON'T DO THIS! COME BACK!
MY CUB! SHE STOLE MY CUB!
STOP HER!

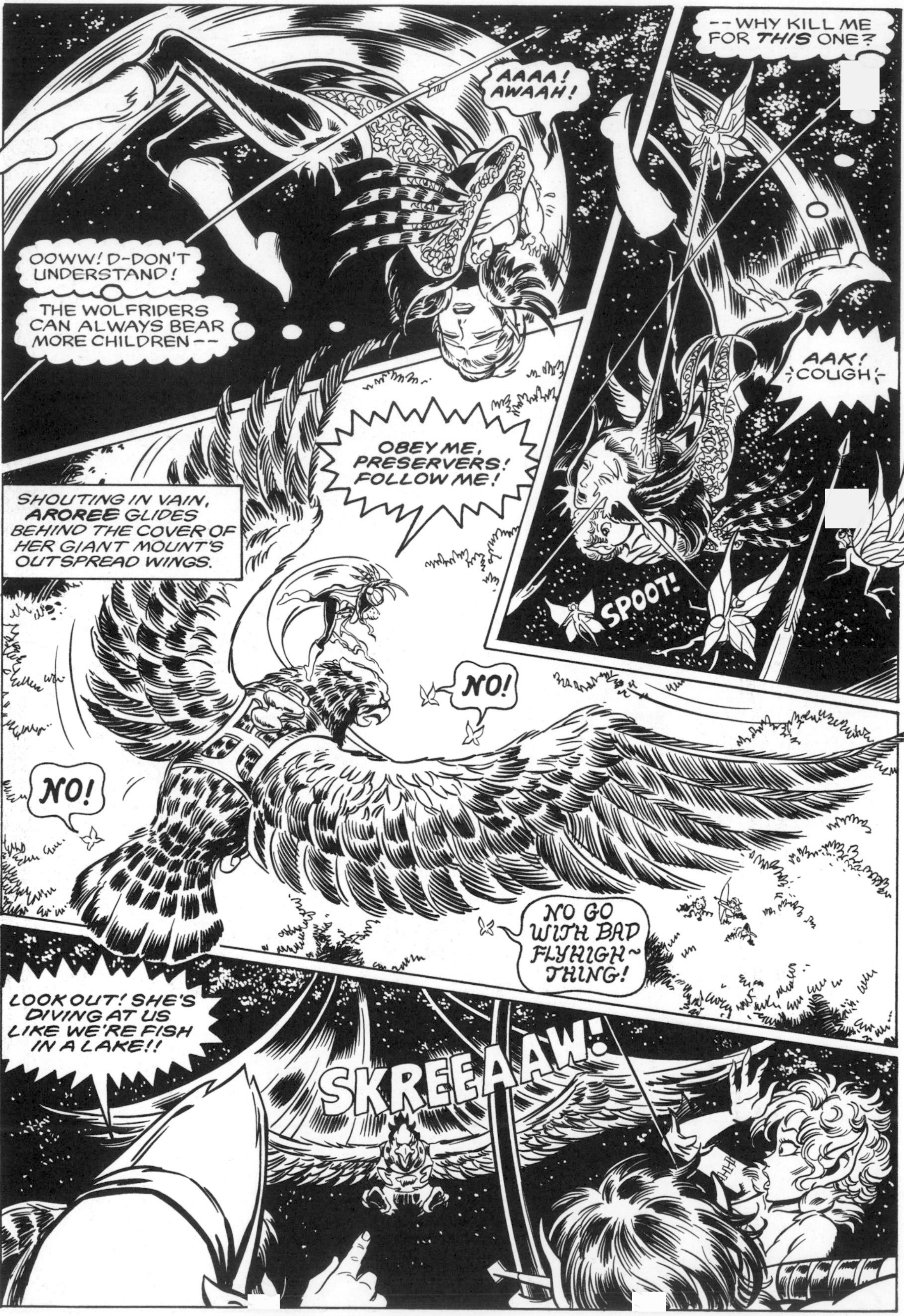
AAAA! AWAAH!
OOWW! D-DON'T UNDERSTAND!
THE WOLFRIDERS CAN ALWAYS BEAR MORE CHILDREN --
-- WHY KILL ME FOR THIS ONE?
AAK! COUGH
SPOOT!
OBEY ME, PRESERVERS! FOLLOW ME!
SHOUTING IN VAIN, AROREE GLIDES BEHIND THE COVER OF HER GIANT MOUNT'S OUTSPREAD WINGS.
NO!
NO!
NO GO WITH BAD FLYHIGH~THING!
LOOK OUT! SHE'S DIVING AT US LIKE WE'RE FISH IN A LAKE!!
SKREEAAAW!

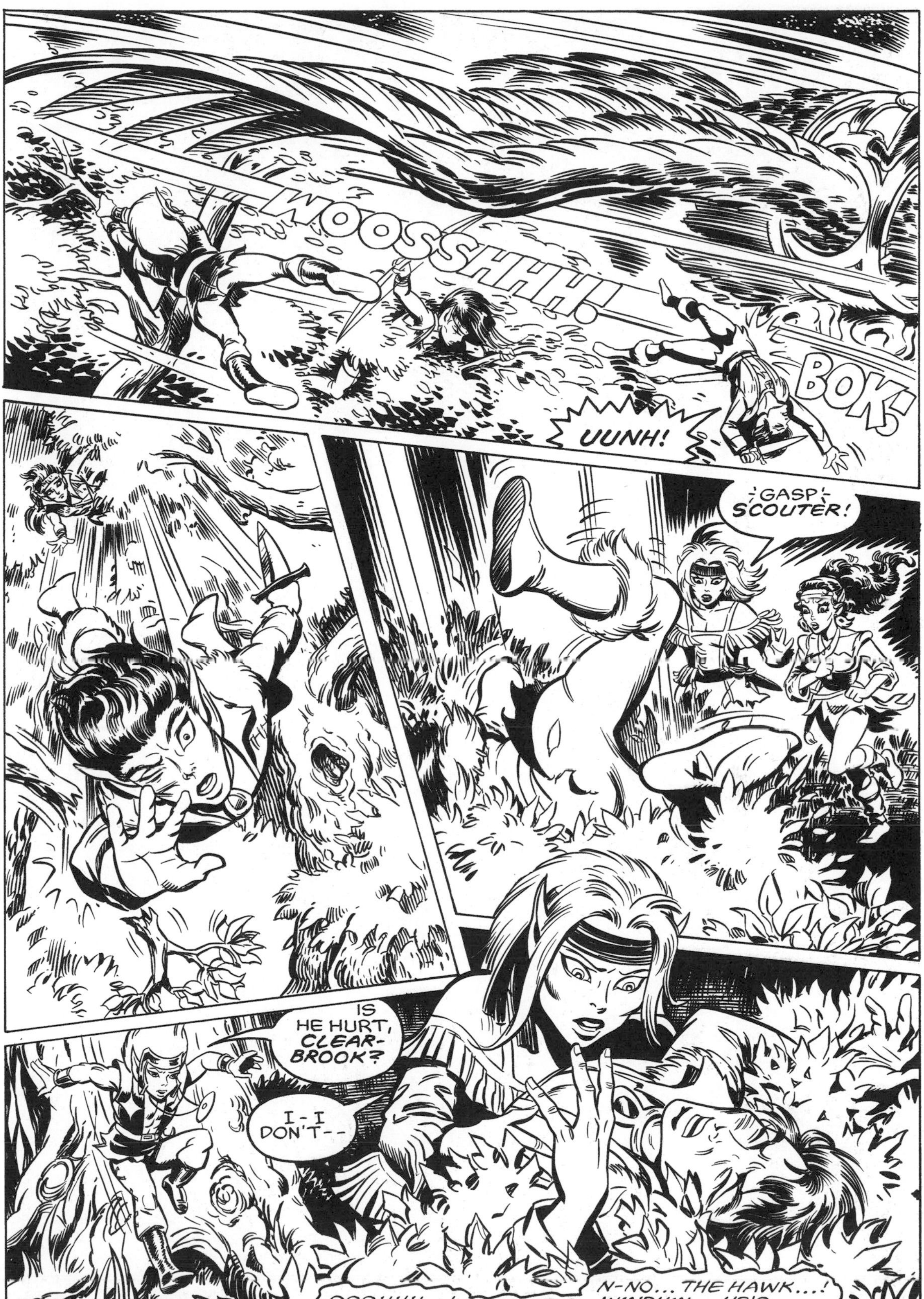
WOOSSHHH!
BOK!
UUNH!
GASP SCOUTER!
IS HE HURT, CLEARBROOK?
I-I DON'T--
OOOHHH...!
N-NO... THE HAWK...! WINDKIN... HE'S...

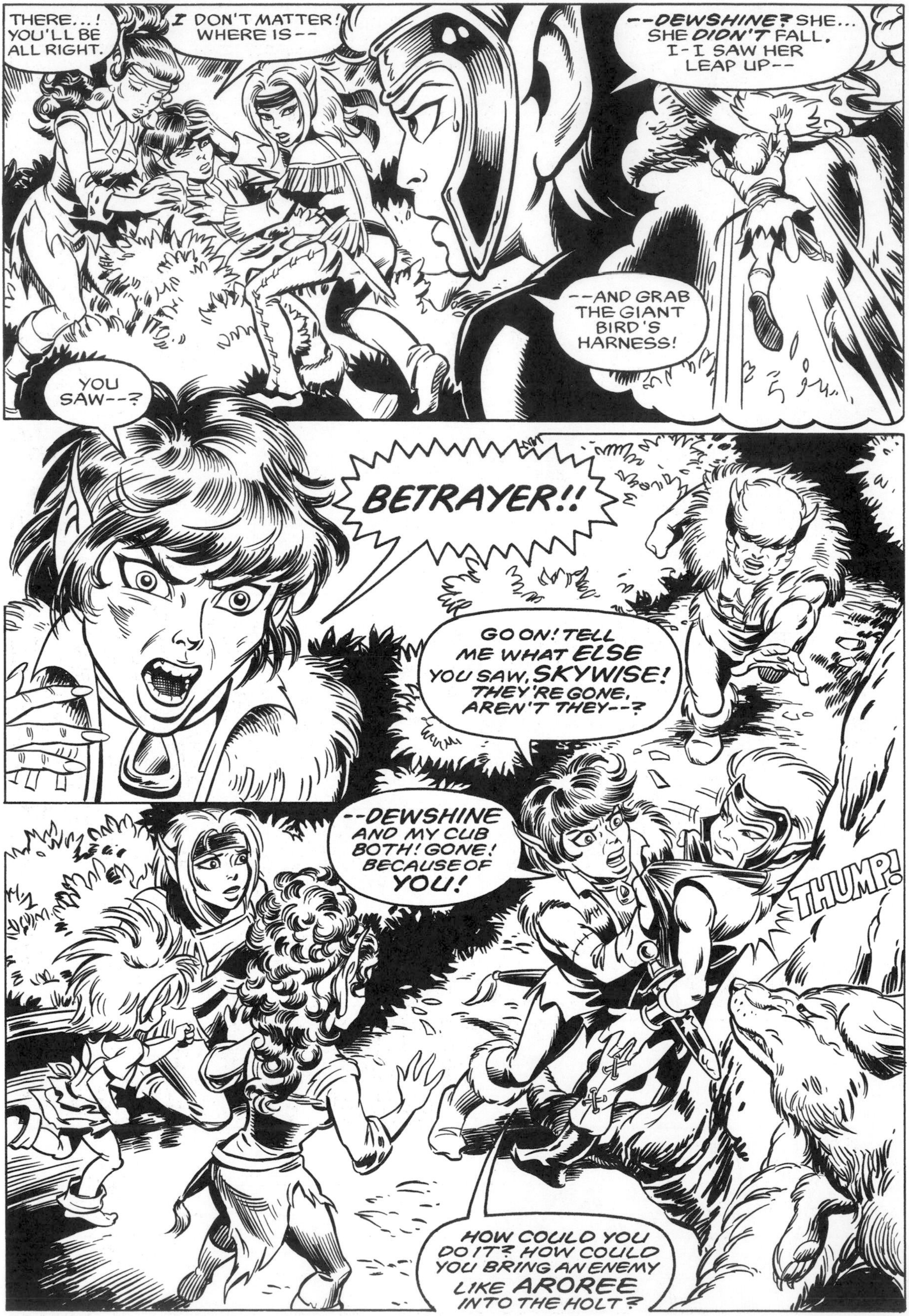

THERE...! YOU'LL BE ALL RIGHT.
I DON'T MATTER! WHERE IS--
--DEWSHINE? SHE... SHE DIDN'T FALL. I-I SAW HER LEAP UP--
--AND GRAB THE GIANT BIRD'S HARNESS!
YOU SAW--?
BETRAYER!!
GO ON! TELL ME WHAT ELSE YOU SAW, SKYWISE! THEY'RE GONE, AREN'T THEY--?
--DEWSHINE AND MY CUB BOTH! GONE! BECAUSE OF YOU!
THUMP!
HOW COULD YOU DO IT? HOW COULD YOU BRING AN ENEMY LIKE AROREE INTO THE HOLT?

EASE DOWN, NOW, LAD. LET GO OF HIM!

YOU LET GO, TREESTUMP!

WELL, SOMEBODY BETTER LET GO OF SOMEBODY OR SOMEBODY'S GOING TO LOSE A *FINGER!*

GRRRR....

NO, STAR-JUMPER! SEE? I'M ALL RIGHT...

ACTING CHIEF OF HIS TRIBE, AND ALL BUT A FATHER TO SCOUTER, TREESTUMP WINS WITH A FIRM SENDING. THE DISTRAUGHT YOUTH'S SHOULDERS SAG SUBMISSIVELY.

IT'S TRUE. THIS *IS* MY FAULT!

HALF THE NIGHT IS GONE SINCE *CUTTER* LEFT US TO SEEK HIS HUMAN FRIENDS' AID. HE THINKS THEY CAN HELP US UNDO BLUE MOUNTAIN'S POWER.

BUT *AROREE...* SHE'LL TAKE *DEWSHINE* AND *WINOKIN* TO THAT DARK PLACE-- TO *WINNOWILL!*

AYE, LEETAH.

AND WE DARE NOT GO RUSHING IN AFTER THEM!

WE NEED A PLAN--

--AND WE NEED *CUTTER* TO APPROVE IT QUICKLY!

THERE IS A SUBTLE LIST TO THE GIANT HAWK'S FLIGHT, ALMOST AS THOUGH HE BEARS THE EXTRA WEIGHT OF PREY IN HIS GREAT TALONS. BUT **AROREE** CHOOSES TO IGNORE IT.

THE TOPMOST CRAGS OF BLUE MOUNTAIN'S AERIE LOOM BEFORE HER--

--AND HER MIND IS OCCUPIED--

--LIKE HER ARMS, WITH A WRIGGLING, SQUEALING BUNDLE.

DON'T SCREAM DON'T SCREAM DON'T SCREAM!

THINK...! WHAT DO I HAVE WITH ME? ONLY *WINDKIN'S* TETHER--

--AND--

--MY *KNIFE!*

CAUTIOUSLY PULLING HERSELF UP TO PEER ACROSS THE LEDGE, **DEWSHINE** SEES THAT NOT ONLY SHE HAS NEED OF STEALTH.

AAA! AAH! AAA!

SHH! YOU TROUBLESOME LITTLE CREATURE! HUSH!

IF I ATTACK NOW, SHE MIGHT *HURT* HIM!

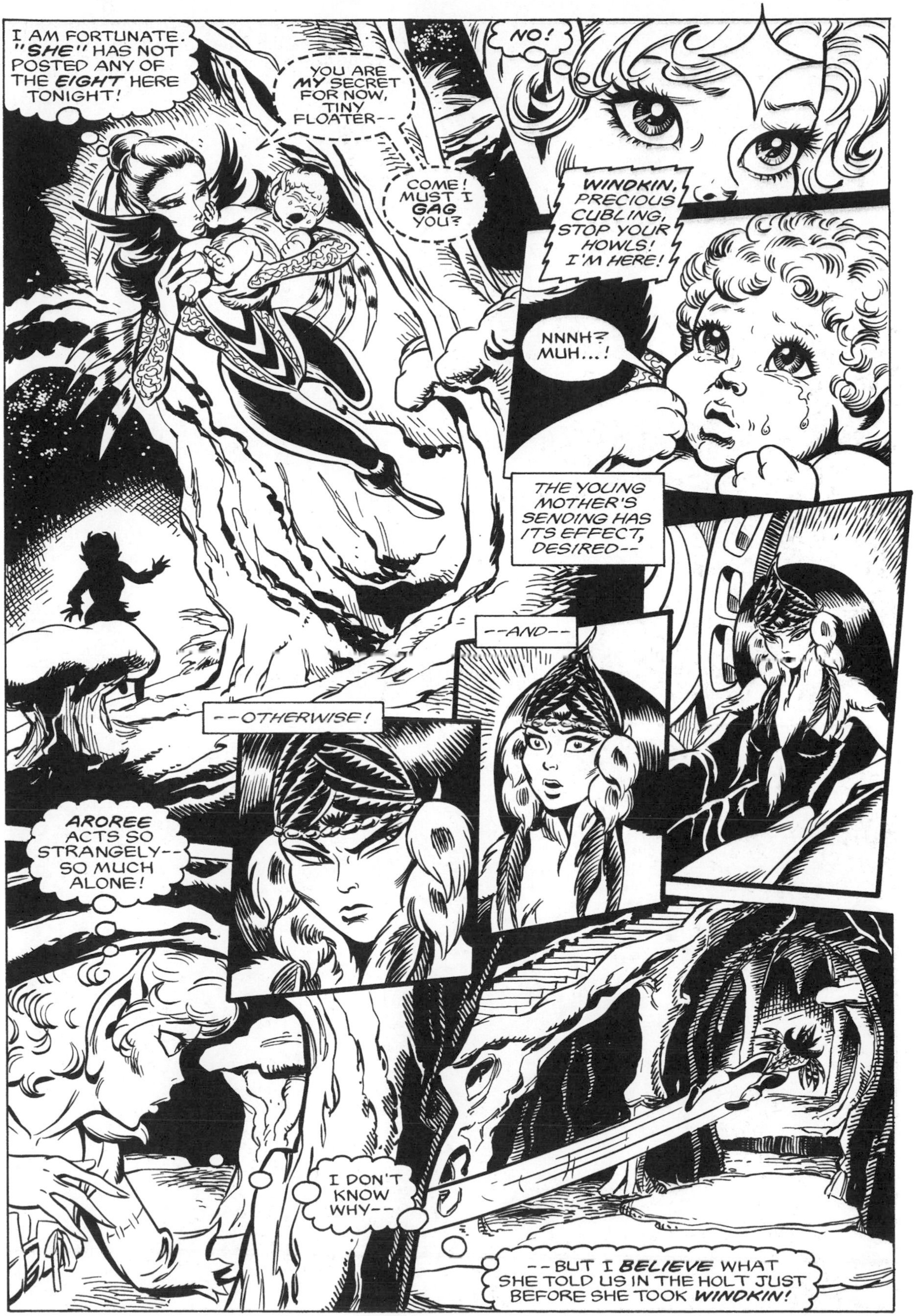

I AM FORTUNATE. "SHE" HAS NOT POSTED ANY OF THE EIGHT HERE TONIGHT!
YOU ARE MY SECRET FOR NOW, TINY FLOATER--
COME! MUST I GAG YOU?
NO!
WINDKIN, PRECIOUS CUBLING, STOP YOUR HOWLS! I'M HERE!
NNNH? MUH...!
THE YOUNG MOTHER'S SENDING HAS ITS EFFECT, DESIRED--
--AND--
--OTHERWISE!
AROREE ACTS SO STRANGELY-- SO MUCH ALONE!
I DON'T KNOW WHY--
--BUT I BELIEVE WHAT SHE TOLD US IN THE HOLT JUST BEFORE SHE TOOK WINDKIN!

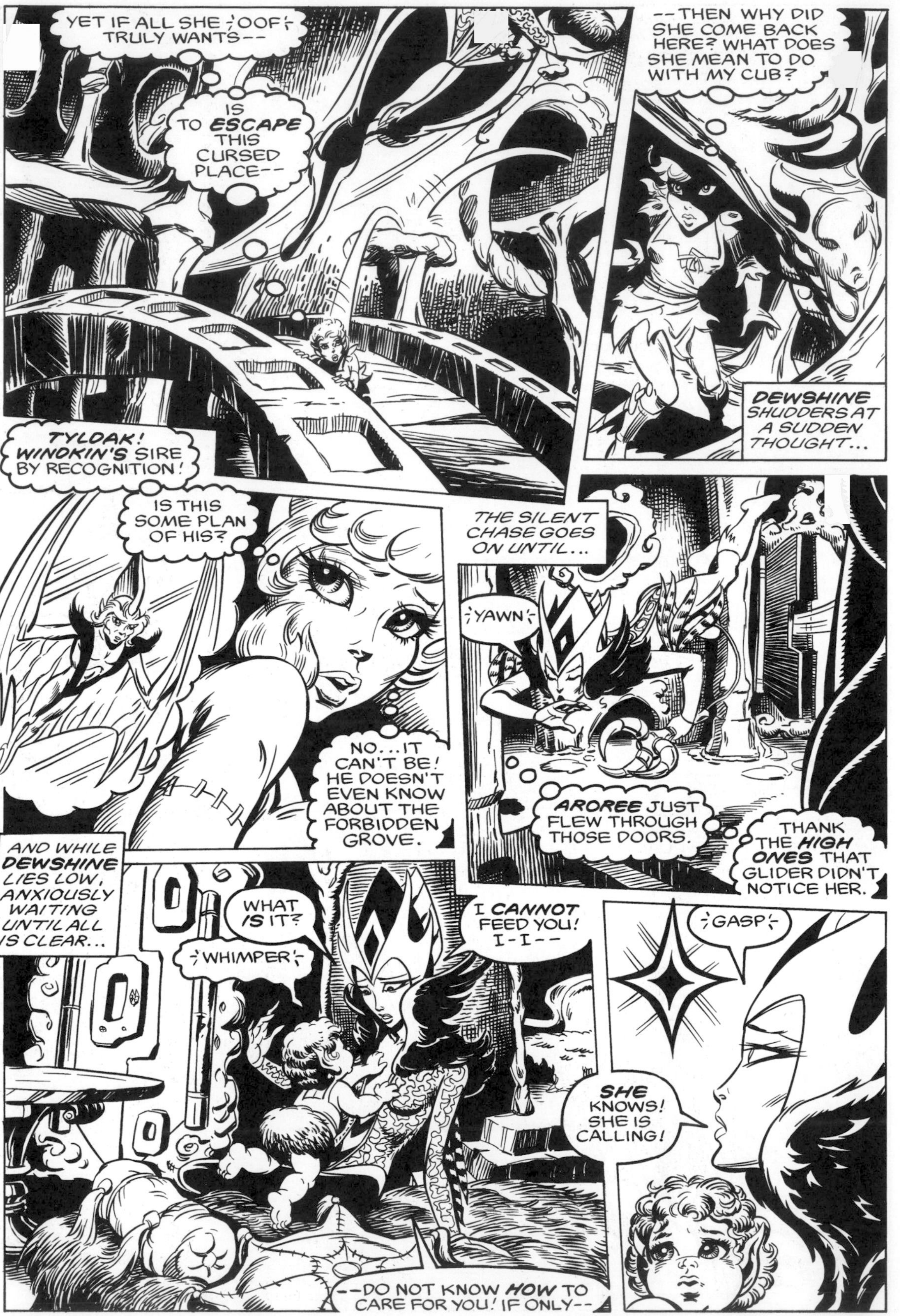
YET IF ALL SHE -OOF- TRULY WANTS--
IS TO ESCAPE THIS CURSED PLACE--
--THEN WHY DID SHE COME BACK HERE? WHAT DOES SHE MEAN TO DO WITH MY CUB?
DEWSHINE SHUDDERS AT A SUDDEN THOUGHT...
TYLDAK! WINOKIN'S SIRE BY RECOGNITION!
IS THIS SOME PLAN OF HIS?
NO...IT CAN'T BE! HE DOESN'T EVEN KNOW ABOUT THE FORBIDDEN GROVE.
THE SILENT CHASE GOES ON UNTIL...
-YAWN-
AROREE JUST FLEW THROUGH THOSE DOORS.
THANK THE HIGH ONES THAT GLIDER DIDN'T NOTICE HER.
AND WHILE DEWSHINE LIES LOW, ANXIOUSLY WAITING UNTIL ALL IS CLEAR...
WHAT IS IT?
-WHIMPER-
I CANNOT FEED YOU! I-I--
--DO NOT KNOW HOW TO CARE FOR YOU! IF ONLY--
-GASP-
SHE KNOWS! SHE IS CALLING!

ALMOST RELUCTANTLY, **ARORÉE** MUFFLES THE CHILD IN A BLANKET.

¡SIGH!

...SOONER THAN I EXPECTED.

IN MOMENTS...

AH! THERE THEY--

OH NO!

WINDKIN CAN'T COME TO MY SEND-CALL! I'VE GOT TO KEEP FOLLOWING--

--WAIT 'TIL SHE UNWRAPS HIM!

SOON...

I *KNOW* THIS PLACE!

IT'S THE ENTRANCE TO **LORD VOLL'S** THRONE ROOM!

"BUT THAT SAD, KINDLY ELDER IS DEAD," *THINKS DEWSHINE*--

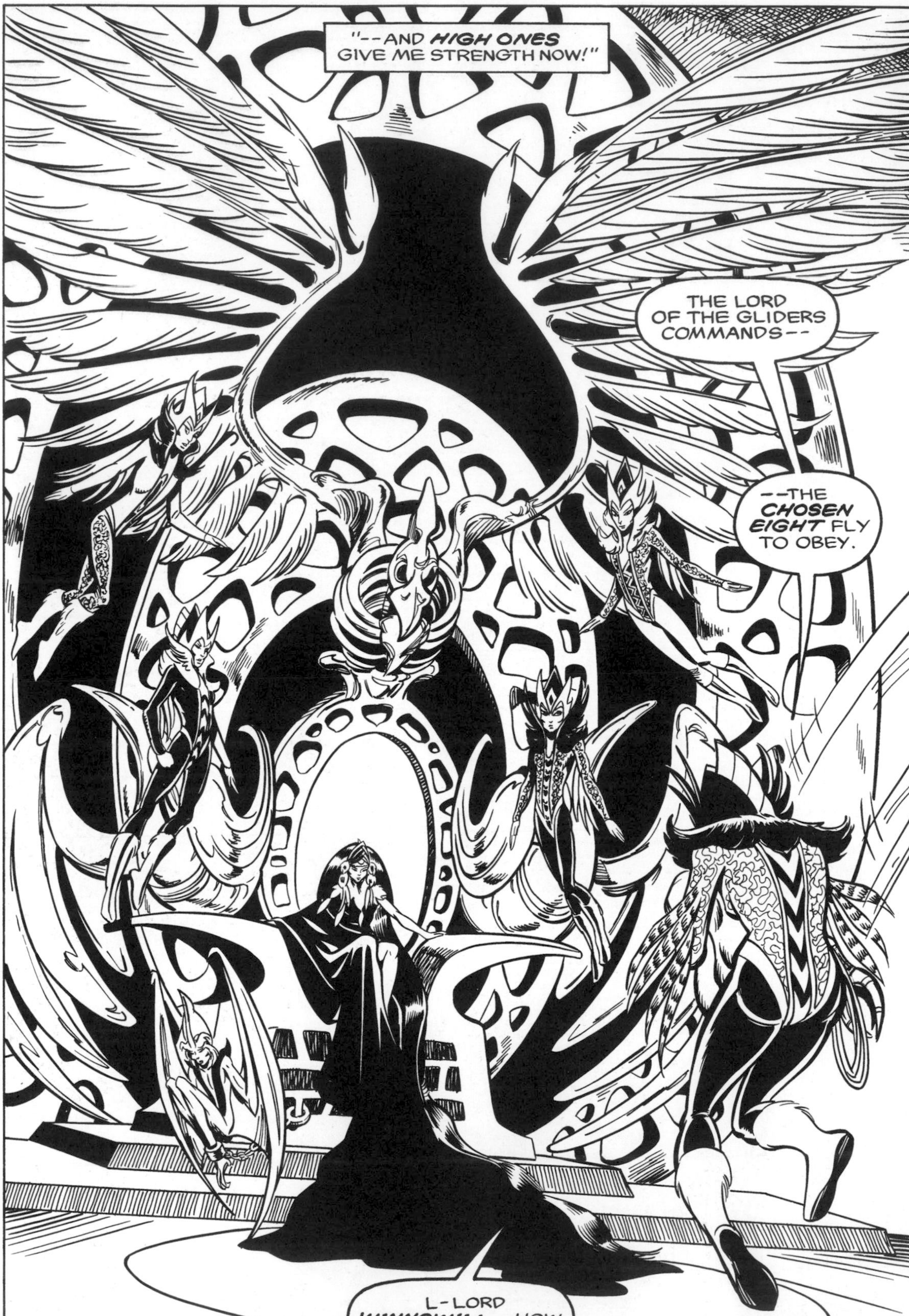
"--AND **HIGH ONES** GIVE ME STRENGTH NOW!"
THE LORD OF THE GLIDERS COMMANDS--
--THE **CHOSEN EIGHT** FLY TO OBEY.
L-LORD **WINNOWILL**... HOW MAY I SERVE?

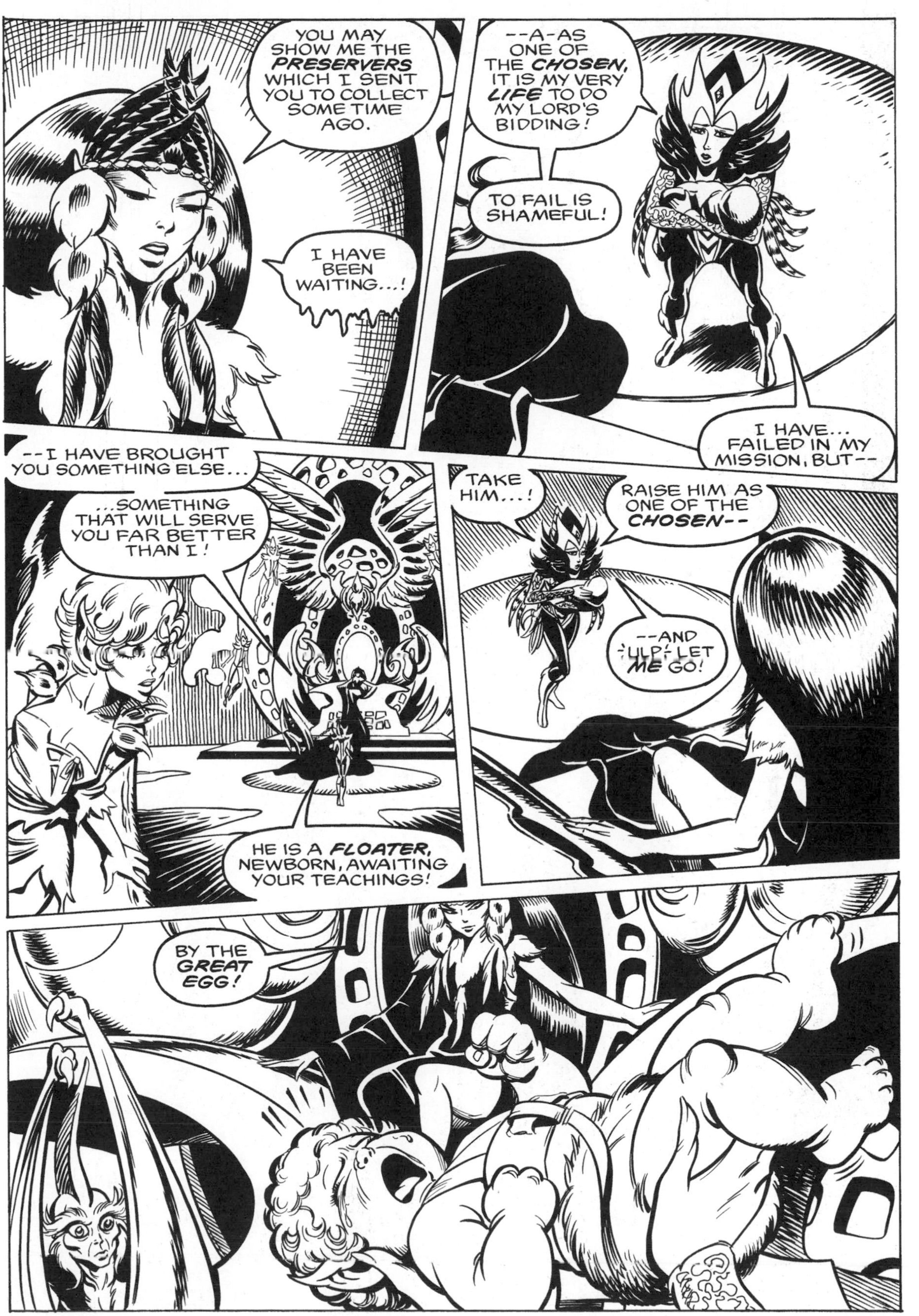
YOU MAY SHOW ME THE PRESERVERS WHICH I SENT YOU TO COLLECT SOME TIME AGO.
I HAVE BEEN WAITING...!
--A-AS ONE OF THE CHOSEN, IT IS MY VERY LIFE TO DO MY LORD'S BIDDING!
TO FAIL IS SHAMEFUL!
I HAVE... FAILED IN MY MISSION, BUT--
--I HAVE BROUGHT YOU SOMETHING ELSE...
...SOMETHING THAT WILL SERVE YOU FAR BETTER THAN I!
HE IS A FLOATER, NEWBORN, AWAITING YOUR TEACHINGS!
TAKE HIM...!
RAISE HIM AS ONE OF THE CHOSEN--
--AND -ULP- LET ME GO!
BY THE GREAT EGG!

SET ME *DOWN!*

SO...YOU WISH TO LEAVE THE *EIGHT*, AR_OREE?

Y-YES, LORD. BUT I COULD NOT ASK YOU TO GRANT ME FREEDOM IF IT MEANT LEAVING *YOU* WITH ONLY SEVEN!

SOMETHING IS... *WRONG* WITH ME! I-I CANNOT LIVE HERE IN BLUE MOUNTAIN ANY LONGER!

WA-AAH AAA-A!

YOU NEEDN'T EXPLAIN. AND YOU NEEDN'T SAY *WHOSE* LITTER OF ONE THIS IS.

IT IS OBVIOUS--

--IS IT NOT, *TYLDAK?*

JUST THEN...

WINDKIN! COME!

BD-D-D-T ÷GIGGLE÷

LREE!

WHA--?

NO!

AS THE CHILD FLIES ARROW STRAIGHT TO HIS MOTHER, *TYLDAK* STRAINS AGAINST HIS HEAVY CHAIN.

DEWSHINE'S SOUL NAME SINGS IN HIS MIND LIKE A BIRD REVIVED AFTER THE LONG WHITE-COLD.

HIGH ONES! I'D GIVE THE PALACE AND ALL TO BE ABLE TO FLY, BUT--

--EVEN THEN, *SHE* COULD STOP ME!

OH, PLEASE DON'T LET *HER* REMEMBER...!

THE DETERMINED YOUNG HUNTRESS WEAVES A PERPLEXING TRAIL FOR HER CASUAL, OVERCONFIDENT PURSUERS.

HOLD ON TIGHT TO ME, MY LITTLE TREE FROG! I'LL TELL *SCOUTER* AND ALL THE OTHER WOLFRIDERS HOW BRAVE YOU ARE!

AT LAST...A GLIMMER OF STARLIGHT...!

ANOTHER DOOR TO THE AERIE!

I'VE FOUND IT!

WE'RE ALMOST OUTSIDE!

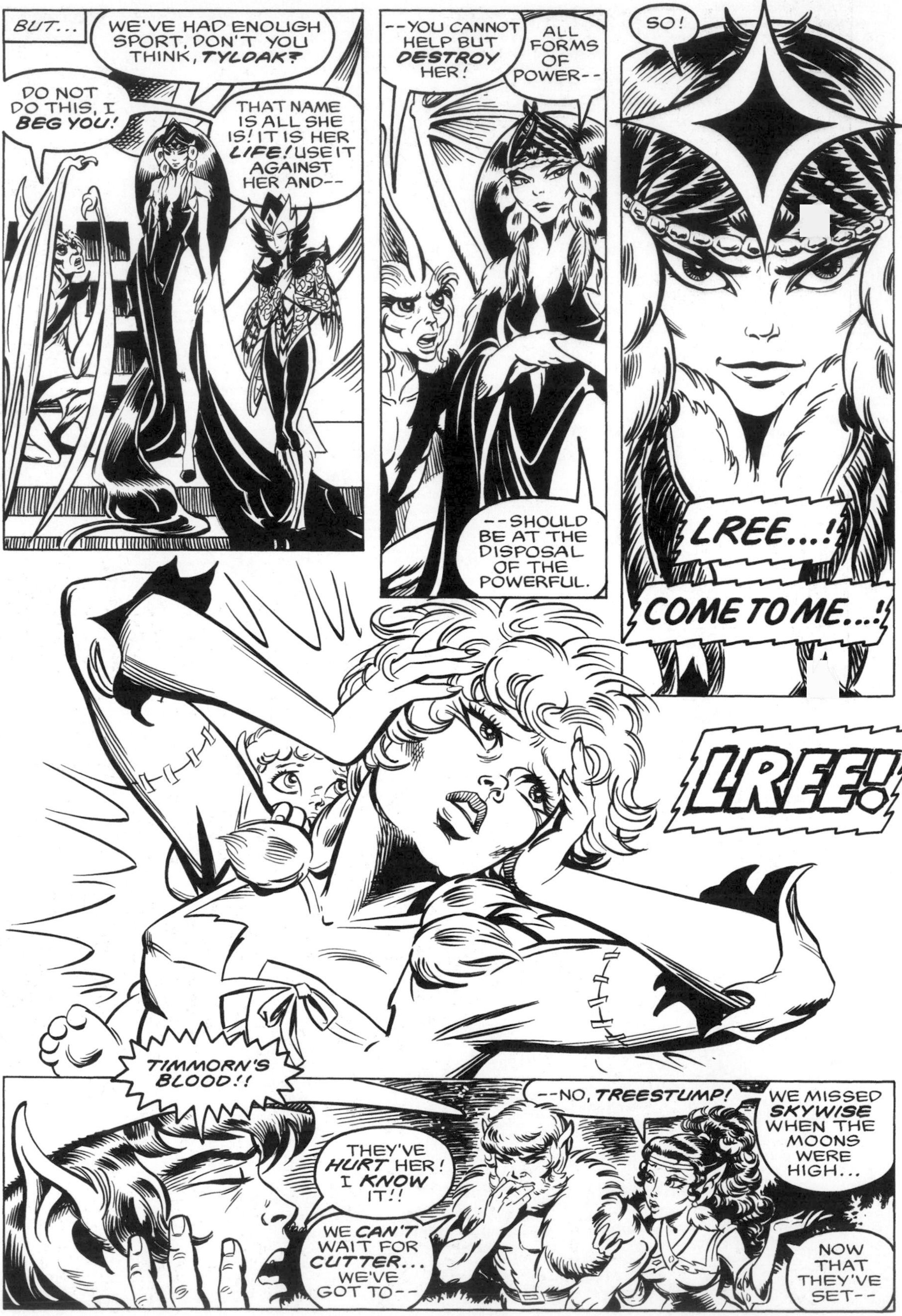

BUT...
WE'VE HAD ENOUGH SPORT, DON'T YOU THINK, TYLDAK?
DO NOT DO THIS, I BEG YOU!
THAT NAME IS ALL SHE IS! IT IS HER LIFE! USE IT AGAINST HER AND--
--YOU CANNOT HELP BUT DESTROY HER!
ALL FORMS OF POWER--
--SHOULD BE AT THE DISPOSAL OF THE POWERFUL.
SO!
LREE...!
COME TO ME...!
LREE!
TIMMORN'S BLOOD!!
THEY'VE HURT HER! I KNOW IT!!
WE CAN'T WAIT FOR CUTTER... WE'VE GOT TO--
--NO, TREESTUMP!
WE MISSED SKYWISE WHEN THE MOONS WERE HIGH...
NOW THAT THEY'VE SET--

"--SURELY HE IS CLOSE ON *CUTTER'S* TRAIL!"

HE'S FOLLOWING THE RIVER--

FOR ONCE I'M GLAD MY CHIEF-FRIEND DOESN'T GET SIDE-TRACKED BY CURIOSITY.

--OUGHT TO SPOT HIM ANY TIME NOW. ...*TROLL DUNG!* WHAT WILL HE SAY?

SKYWISE TURNS THE NIGHT'S EVENTS OVER AND OVER IN HIS MIND.

AROREE AND I LOCK-SENT!

I *KNOW* SHE DIDN'T HAVE IT ALL PLANNED! WHY--?

YI! YI! YI!

WHA--?

STARJUMPER!

MOMENTS LATER...

POOR OLD FRIEND! YOU WERE RUNNING YOUR PAWS OFF FOR ME, WEREN'T YOU?

CURSED THORN'S AS LONG AS MY FINGER! BUT IT'S OUT NOW!

RRF!

HMM?

OH... *HAIRBALLS!*

WELL--

--THEY WON'T KEEP US FROM FINDING *CUTTER!*

BUT... TWO DAYS LATER, THE WOLFRIDERS' YOUNG CHIEF *ARRIVES* AT DEATH-WATER FALLS, AS YET UNAWARE OF *DEWSHINE'S* PLIGHT.

» PANT PANT « *YOU* STILL WITH ME, *WARFROST?*

WE'RE ALMOST TO THE TOP.

HOWEVER NEAR THE HUMAN'S HUTS, HOWEVER VITAL THE MISSION--

--PRIORITIES--

--ARE PRIORITIES.

AND SO, SOMEWHAT LATER THAN PLANNED...

WELL... *OLBAR THE MOUNTAIN-TALL* IS *STILL* THEIR CHIEF. THAT'S HIS LAUGHTER COMING FROM THE BIGGEST HUT.

SOUNDS LIKE HE'S HAVING A FINE TIME WHILE EVERYBODY ELSE SLEEPS.

WHURF!

STAY THERE, *WARFROST.* I'LL KNOCK YOUR TEETH OUT IF YOU GIVE ME AWAY.

HAVING ESTABLISHED DOMINANCE IN HIS OWN MIND, IF NOT IN THE WOLF'S, *CUTTER* SNEAKS TOWARD A PARTICULAR DWELLING.

PUCKERNUTS! THEY'VE GOT A *NEAR-WOLF* GUARDING THEIR DOOR!

AS SILENTLY AS "CHILD MOON" SLIPS PAST "MOTHER MOON" IN THE SKY--

--CUTTER AVOIDS THE WATCHDOG--

--AND FINDS...

JUST BIG ENOUGH--

--FOR ME TO SQUEEZE THROUGH.

SNIFF *SNIFF*

THIS IS THEIR HUT--

--BUT THAT'S NOT THEM!

WHERE--?

THE FERAL FOREST-DWELLER'S KEEN NOSTRILS LEAD HIM STRAIGHT TO THE TWO HE SEEKS. BUT BEFORE WAKING NONNA AND ADAR, CUTTER TAKES IN HIS SURROUNDINGS.

HUNH! THEY'VE DONE WELL SINCE SKYWISE AND I LAST SAW THEM.

THEY HAVE SO MUCH STUFF-- ALMOST MORE THAN THEIR HUT CAN HOLD!

AND THREE CUBS, TOO. FAST WORK!

THE PLACE SMELLS OF NONNA'S PAINTS.

SHE'S PUT HER SYMBOLS ALL OVER THE WALLS.

WELL...

LET'S SEE IF THEY REMEMBER ME.

GASP!

GRRUMPH! MRRG!

SIGH

HEE HEE HEE HA HA HEH HEH HEH!

⟨N-NIMA...? TENCHI...! GERU!⟩

⟨QUIET! WE--?!⟩

OHH!

⟨OH, FINE!⟩

⟨DO I DREAM?! MY LITTLE *BIRD SPIRIT*!! ÷CHOKE÷⟩

⟨MY EYES SEE WITH JOY, *NONNA...ADAR.* THIS VILLAGE HAS TREATED YOU WELL.⟩

⟨AND *YOU* HAVE BEEN VERY BUSY!⟩

⟨÷CHUCKLE÷ YOU TEASE ME! THEY ARE TOO GROWN UP FOR *ME* TO HAVE BORNE THEM IN THREE SNOWS!!⟩

⟨WE TOOK THEM IN WHEN--EH?⟩

A SUDDEN RACKET AT THE DOOR--

--SENDS *CUTTER* LEAPING INTO THE SHADOWS.

HAAYEEAH!

⟨WAKE UP, SYMBOL MAKER!⟩

⟨GET YOUR POTS READY--!⟩

⟨MIX YOUR COLORS! CHANT, SWEAT OR WHATEVER YOU MUST DO!⟩

⟨I WANT YOU TO PAINT *GRAYSHA*, HERE, WITH--

⟨--BIG BELLY PICTURES!⟩ *HAR HAR HAR!*

⟨THE MOONS ARE RIGHT FOR THE MAKING OF ANOTHER *SON!*⟩

‹WELL? MUST I WAIT 'TIL SUNUP?›

‹UH...›

‹NO, MY CHIEF, BUT--›

HEH HEH HEH...

‹AIEEE! SPIRITS!›

‹SO *THIS* IS HOW OLBAR THE MOUNTAIN TALL--›

--MAKES USE OF HIS SYMBOL MAKER!›

‹WELL, BY MY GRANDMOTHER'S DROOPING DUGS!! *"BIRD-BONES"*!›

UFF!

‹OOHHH...! PLEASE, *OLBAR!* DO NOT TREAT THE HONORED ONE SO!›

‹WHY NOT?›

‹I DON'T MIND!›

‹Y-YOU ARE A *SACRED* BEING! MY FORMER TRIBEFOLK, THE *HOAN G'TAY SHO* HAVE ALWAYS WORSHIPPED BIRD SPIRITS!›

YOUR TRIBE HAS BEEN TRICKED BY AN EVIL ONE--

--WHO KEEPS THEM AS PLAYTHINGS! THAT'S WHY I'VE COME!›

‹NONNA AND ADAR, YOU MUST GO WITH ME TO SAVE THE HOAN G'TAY SHO!›

‹YES! THEY DON'T KNOW WHAT REALLY GOES ON INSIDE BLUE MOUNTAIN!›

WE...?

‹"PERHAPS YOU'VE SEEN HER FACE," INTONES THE ELF. "BEAUTIFUL... WHITE... LIKE A MASK MADE OF EGGSHELL, GLEAMING IN THE TUNNEL WHERE SHE STANDS TO RECEIVE HER HUMAN OFFERINGS!"›

‹"SHE'S CALLED--"›

‹"--WINNOWILL."›

‹"THOSE OF THE HOAN G'TAY SHO WHO ENTER THE MOUNTAIN TO SERVE HER THINK THEY'LL GAIN SOME SPECIAL BLESSING OF THE "BIRD SPIRITS."›

‹" BUT IN FACT, THEY BECOME WINNOWILL'S TOYS--PETS!"›

‹AND WHEN THEIR TIME FINALLY COMES, THEIR DEATHS, TOO, SERVE ONLY TO ENTERTAIN HER!›

‹I-I HAVE SEEN THE DARK-ROBED SPIRIT YOU SPEAK OF, BUT--›

‹BELIEVE ME, HUMANS!›

‹WINNOWILL HAS TURNED AGAINST EVEN HER OWN KIND!›

‹BELIEVE YOU? NOW WAIT JUST A MOMENT!›

‹YOU'RE NOT TALKING MY SYMBOL MAKER INTO SOME MAD-HEADED TREK TO BLUE MOUNTAIN!›

⟨I REMEMBER YOU WELL! YOU'RE NO SPIRIT! YOU'RE A *TRICKSTER!* IF I SAY *NO*, THERE'S NOTHING YOU CAN DO ABOUT IT!⟩

⟨I CAN CALL THE ANGER OF THE *FORBIDDEN GROVE* DOWN ON YOU!⟩

HAH!

⟨YOU WERE THERE ONCE. THE WINGED SPIRITS SCARED YOU, DIDN'T THEY?⟩

HAH!

⟨SO BRAVE?⟩

⟨LET'S JUST SEE...⟩

HELLO, HIGHTHING!

HELLO, BIG~ THING!

GAAH!

⟨TA-TAKE IT AWAY!!⟩

⟨EVIL SPIRIT! DON'T LET IT TRAP ME IN ITS *WEB!*⟩

YARK! YARK!

HEE HEE! BIGTHING RUN RUN RUN FROM BERRYBUZZ!

⟨THERE ARE MANY MORE WHERE *THIS* ONE COMES FROM, OLBAR! *BEWARE!*⟩

‹DON'T BE AFRAID CHIEF *OLBAR!* WE ARE STRONG WARRIORS!›

‹WE'LL KILL THE EVIL SPIRIT!›

‹*NO!* LET IT B-BE!›

BIGTHING BETTER BE NICE TO HIGHTHING OR : K-K-GH!

‹WH-WHAT IS IT SAYING?›

‹SOME THINGS ARE BEST NOT KNOWN, HUMAN!›

‹BUT YOU'D BE WISE TO LET ME BORROW *NONNA* AND *ADAR* FOR A WHILE!›

‹*OLBAR*, MY CHIEF. WITH YOUR CONSENT AND THAT OF MY MAN, I *DO* WISH TO HELP THE HOAN G'TAY SHO IN SOME WAY!›

‹PLEASE LET US GO TO THEM!›

‹I AGREE, *OLBAR*, THOUGH I'M NO GREAT BELIEVER IN SPIRITS, *THAT* ONE AND HIS FRIEND GUIDED *NONNA* AND ME SAFELY THROUGH THE WOODS ONCE.›

‹WE TRUST HIM.›

THANKS, *ADAR.*

YOU DON'T KNOW IT, BUT YOU'LL BE HELPING THE WOLF-RIDERS, TOO.

‹WELL...›

‹WE *WILL* RETURN. WE VOW TO! OUR HOME AND OUR CHILDREN ARE HERE!›

SETTLED! GOOD!

FIRST WE END THE HUMANS' SICK BONDAGE TO *WINNOWILL*--

--THEN WE GO TO WORK ON THE GLIDERS THEMSELVES!

MEANWHILE...

"--YET THE USE OF--APPROPRIATE--FORCE, NO MORE, NO LESS, RENDERS HER DOCILE. SUCH IS MY COMPASSION FOR THE MISBEGOTTEN OF OUR RACE."

WAA! AAA!

TWO ESCAPE ATTEMPTS IN AS MANY NIGHTS... ADMIRABLE! BUT I THINK SHE KNOWS NOW THAT SHE IS MINE.

THE WOLFRIDER IS SAVAGE, A BLOOD-SPILLER--

DON'T...

PLEASE DON'T TAKE MY CUB FROM ME...

OF COURSE NOT. IT WANTS FEEDING AND, OBVIOUSLY, CLEANING.

THE ONE WHO WHELPED IT CAN BEST DO THAT.

BY THE WAY--

--DISTASTEFUL AS IT IS TO TOUCH MINDS WITH YOU, I MUST THANK YOU FOR REVEALING THE PRESERVERS' WHEREABOUTS--

--AND YOUR TRIBE'S.

NO!

THIS IS NOT MY DOING--IS IT...? HOW CAN IT BE?

DEWSHINE IS TO BLAME! SHE SHOULD NOT HAVE CHASED ME HERE!

MUST LEAVE--NOW! I HAVE DONE MY DUTY BY *WINNOWILL.*

SHE HAS HER *EIGHTH.*

AND I HAVE A CLEANER WORLD WAITING-- --OUTSIDE.

SLOWLY, *ARØREE* GLIDES THROUGH BROODING, BAROQUE HALLWAYS WHOSE SINUOUS TWISTS AND TURNS SHE HAS KNOWN, IT SEEMS, FOR LONGER THAN SHE HAS LIVED.

AT LAST, SHE REACHES THE CHAMBER OF THE *GREAT EGG.*

FAREWELL, MY SLEEPING PEOPLE. MAY AT LEAST SOME OF YOUR DREAMS BE YOURS-- NOT *HERS!*

HER LAST LOOK TAKEN, THE HEAVY-HEARTED GLIDER RETURNS TO THE AERIE.

SHE WILL SUMMON *LITTLETRILL,* HER MAGNIFICENT MOUNT--

--AND, PLUNGING THROUGH THE OPEN SKY, SHE WILL FIND RELEASE FROM PRESSING, HONEST GUILT.

-¡GASP!- *KUREEL!*

YOU DO NOT TRULY INTEND TO SUNDER THE *EIGHT,* DO YOU, *ARØREE?*

YOUR RIGHT TO BE A *TALON WHIP*--

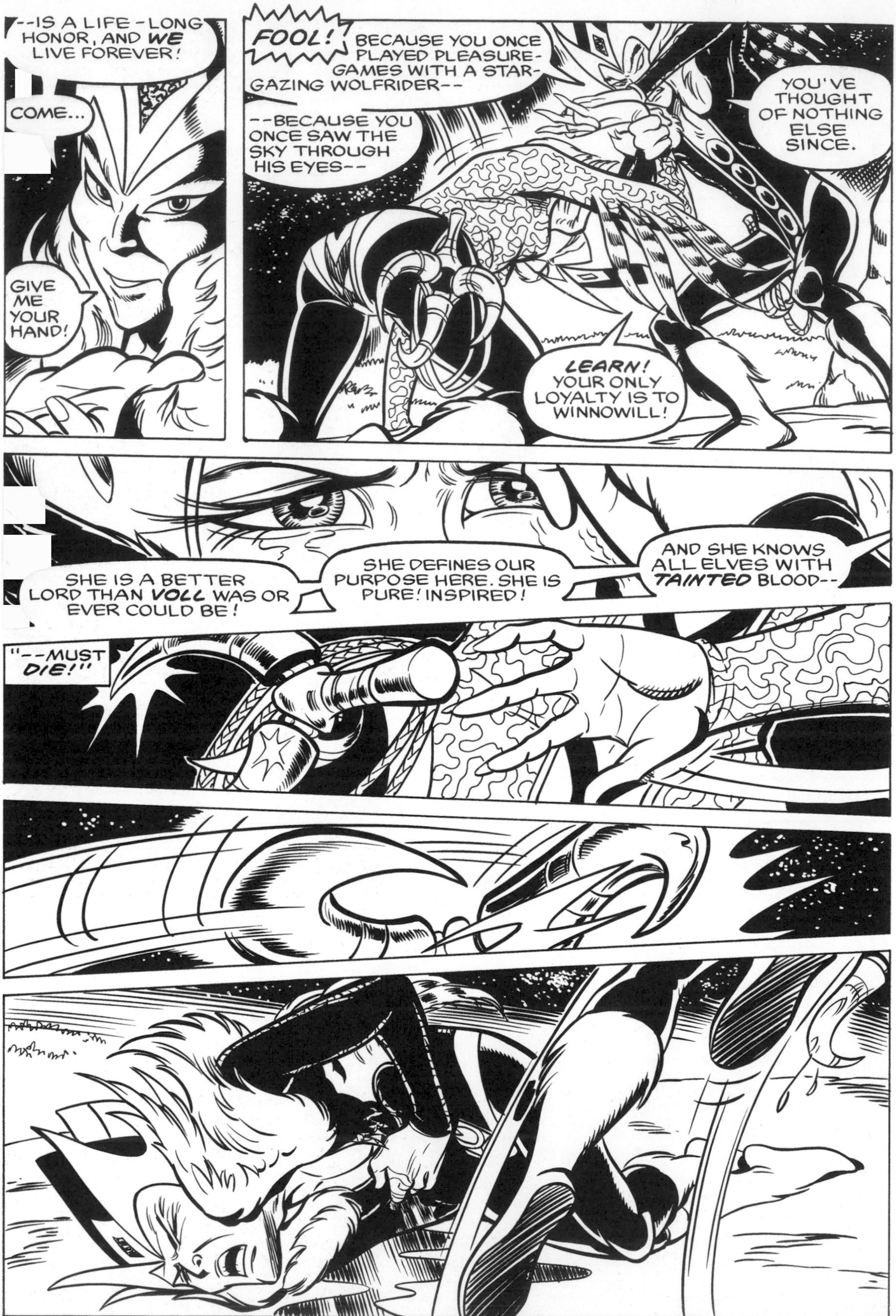
--IS A LIFE-LONG HONOR, AND WE LIVE FOREVER!
COME...
GIVE ME YOUR HAND!
FOOL!
BECAUSE YOU ONCE PLAYED PLEASURE-GAMES WITH A STAR-GAZING WOLFRIDER--
--BECAUSE YOU ONCE SAW THE SKY THROUGH HIS EYES--
YOU'VE THOUGHT OF NOTHING ELSE SINCE.
LEARN! YOUR ONLY LOYALTY IS TO WINNOWILL!
SHE IS A BETTER LORD THAN VOLL WAS OR EVER COULD BE!
SHE DEFINES OUR PURPOSE HERE. SHE IS PURE! INSPIRED!
AND SHE KNOWS ALL ELVES WITH TAINTED BLOOD--
"--MUST DIE!"

AS EASILY AS SLICING WARM FLESH, SHE HAS CUT ALL BONDS WITH THE ONLY LIFE SHE HAS KNOWN.

IF SHE SURVIVES, ALL POSSIBILITIES ARE OPEN TO HER.

BUT WHAT OF THOSE SHE HAS INADVERTENTLY BETRAYED?

SKY-WISE...

FORGIVE ME?

NEXT DAY... THE VALLEY OF ENDLESS SLEEP...

CUTTER IS QUIET, WATCHFUL. THOUGH HE HELPED ADAR BUILD THE RAFT, HE HAS NEVER TRAVELED BY WATER BEFORE.

I KNOW WE'LL MAKE BETTER TIME THAN ON FOOT, BUT...

⟨PARDON, HONORED ONE, DO YOU HAVE A NAME?⟩

⟨HUH?⟩

⟨YES.⟩

⟨I'M CALLED--⟩

?!

HE MUST HEAR SOMETHING WE CANNOT!

TAM!

WHUF!

ONLY ONE OTHER THAN LEETAH, FREELY USES CUTTER'S SOUL NAME--

--A BROTHER IN ALL BUT BLOOD!

TAM!!

65

‹HEY! WHERE DO YOU--?›

‹DON'T WAIT FOR ME! I'LL CATCH UP!›

SPOSH!

SHORTLY, NEAR THE RIVER BANK...

HOO! YOU LOOK LIKE YOU'VE BEEN GONE OVER BY A BEAR!

WORSE...

I FOUND NONNA AND ADAR. WE'RE LETTING THE RIVER TAKE US TO THE BLUE MOUNTAIN. COME ON--

NO!

I'VE HAD ENOUGH OF HUMANS!

THE MEMORIES ARE ALL TOO FRESH--TOO HUMILIATING FOR THE PROUD STARGAZER TO RECOUNT. INSTEAD, HE BREATHES A NAME...

"AROREE... SHE CAME INTO THE HOLT!"

IT'S MY DOING, TAM. I BROUGHT HER IN. I THOUGHT... SHE'D STAY. BUT SHE FLEW OFF... WITH WINDKIN! AND DEWSHINE'S GONE AFTER THEM!

WHAT?!

TO BE CONTINUED...

66

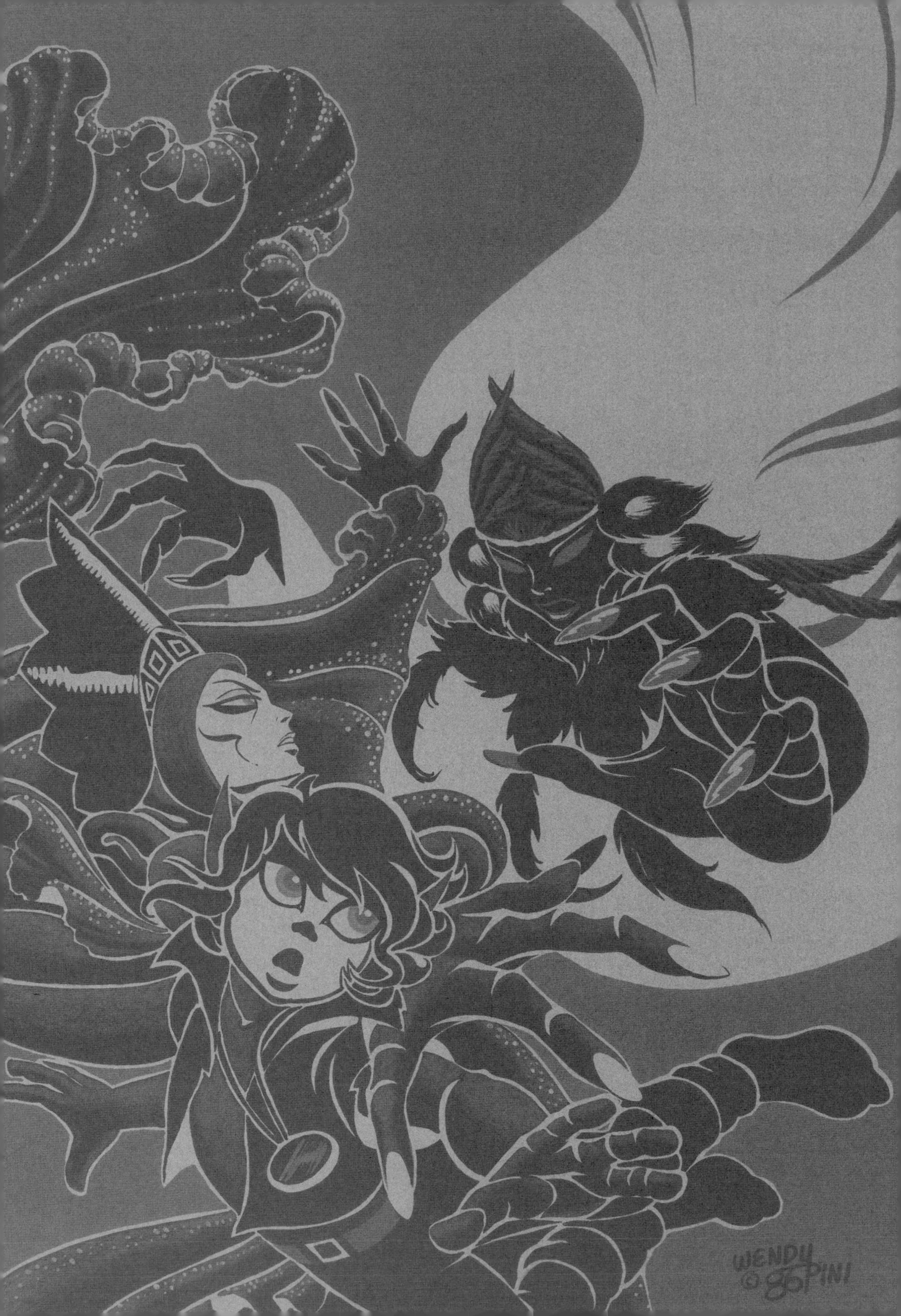
WENDY
© 80 PINI

SIEGE AT BLUE MOUNTAIN

ARTIST / WRITER
WENDY PINI

CO-PLOT / EDITOR
RICHARD PINI

PART 3

INKS
JOE STATON

LETTERER
JANICE CHIANG

SIMPLY, WITHOUT EXCUSES OR SHIFTING OF BLAME, **SKYWISE** TELLS **CUTTER** WHAT HAPPENED THREE NIGHTS AGO WITHIN THE FORBIDDEN GROVE.

AROREE SAID SHE WAS HUNTING **PRESERVERS**, NOT OUR TRIBE. SHE'D BEEN HURT-- INSIDE HER MIND-- BY **WINNOWILL**. I FELT IT, AND--

-- I WANTED TO HELP.

THE YOUNG WOLFRIDER CHIEF LISTENS... VERY QUIETLY.

AROREE SEEMED TO *WANT* THAT HELP MORE THAN ANYTHING--

--BUT ONE LOOK AT LITTLE *WINDKIN* AND... HER EYES JUST WENT *MAD!* SHE SNATCHED THE CUB AND FLEW OFF!

AND *DEWSHINE...?*

YOU KNOW YOUR COUSIN! SHE MADE ONE OF THOSE JUMPS THAT ALWAYS SCARE US TO DEATH--

--AND CAUGHT HOLD OF *AROREE'S* GIANT HAWK. YOU CAN GUESS WHERE THEY WERE HEADING.

BLUE MOUNTAIN.

÷SIGH÷

AN UNEXPECTED, GENTLE TOUCH AND THE SOUND OF HIS SOFTLY SPOKEN SOUL NAME TELL *SKYWISE* THAT HE IS ALREADY FORGIVEN.

FAHR... NO MATTER HOW MUCH YOU CARE, YOU CAN'T CHANGE *AROREE.* SHE'S A BACKSTAB--

NO!

MAYBE *I'M* MAD TOO, BUT I *KNOW* SHE MEANT NO HARM!

WELL... MEANT OR NOT, THE HARM'S BEEN DONE.

WE HAVE TO PLAN. MY HUMAN FRIENDS, *NONNA* AND *ADAR*, HAVE AGREED TO HELP US DETHRONE *WINNOWILL*.

IF *DEWSHINE* AND *WINDKIN* ARE PRISONERS INSIDE BLUE MOUNTAIN--

--THEN THE SOONER WE CAUSE *WINNOWILL* TROUBLE *OUTSIDE*, THE BETTER!

A DISTRACTION...? *GOOD!* MEANTIME, *I'LL* LEAD A WOLFRIDER RESCUE PARTY! WE'LL HACK OUR WAY--

--THROUGH STONE AND FLESH TO SAVE OUR KIN!

ON *CUTTER'S* JAW... A SILENT REMINDER...

WAR?

...NO.

YOU'RE RIGHT.

NEVER AGAIN!

BUT HOW--?

YATTA-YATTA-YAK! WE GO HOMETREES SOON, HIGHTHINGS?

SHUT UP, *BERRYBUZZ!*

WE'RE TRYING TO FIGURE OUT HOW TO FREE OUR FRIENDS! WE--

--WAIT! A *TRADE!* WE *DO* HAVE SOMETHING TO BARTER--

HEE HEE!

--SOMETHING *WINNOWILL* WANTS VERY MUCH!

THAT MORNING, IN THE FORBIDDEN GROVE...

POOR *SCOUTER*...!

THE LONGER WE HAVE TO WAIT FOR FATHER TO COME BACK, THE MORE *I* WORRY, TOO!

I KNOW. THERE ARE TEARS BEHIND HIS EYES ALL THE TIME NOW. HE WANTS SO MUCH TO GO RESCUE *DEWSHINE*--

--AND *WINDKIN*!

WE'RE *ALL* IN DANGER.

WINNOWILL CAN STEAL SECRETS FROM *ANYONE*! SHE'LL FIND OUT WHERE WE LIVE!

-*GASP*-

DEWSHINE WON'T BE ABLE TO FIGHT HER!

THEN *WE* BETTER DO SOMETHING BESIDES *SIT, SIT, SIT*!

SUNTOP, I'M TELLING YOU--

-- YOU *HAVE* TO "GO OUT" AND GET *SAVAH'S* ADVICE--

-- YOU JUST *HAVE* TO!

THE YOUNG MYSTIC DOES NOT ANSWER HIS TWIN SISTER. INSIDE HIM HIS FONDEST DESIRE WAGES EVEN BATTLE WITH THE OBEDIENCE HE OWES HIS ELDERS.

I KNOW... MOTHER AND FATHER SAID "NO"!

BUT EVEN THOUGH I HOPE I WON'T EVER *HAVE* TO TAKE FATHER'S PLACE, I CAN STILL *ACT* LIKE A CHIEF!

YOU DO WHAT I SAY AND *I'LL* TAKE THE BLAME!

B-BUT *EMBER*...!

GO ON! DO IT *NOW*!

TEMPTED PAST ENDURANCE, *SUNTOP* PREPARES TO ENTER A PROFOUND TRANCE--

--A FORBIDDEN STATE WHICH WILL LEAVE HIM UTTERLY VULNERABLE TO *WINNOWILL'S* PROWLING, PREYING SPIRIT!

BUT FIRST HE MUST EMPTY HIS MIND OF ALL MEMORIES...DREAMS...EVEN THE "NOW" OF WOLF-THOUGHT.

AN IMAGE COMES TO HIM—TIMMAIN, THE **HIGH ONE**...

TIMMAIN, WHO ENLIGHTENED THE WOLFRIDERS THROUGH **HIS** VOICE, AND CONFIRMED FOR HIM THE RIGHTNESS OF HIS CHOSEN SPIRITUAL PATH.

THE **HIGH ONE'S** FEATURES MELT, RESHAPE INTO THE DARK-SKINNED DIGNITY OF **SAVAH'S**.

WISE **SAVAH**, MOTHER OF MEMORY...BELOVED **SAVAH**, MENTOR AND TEACHER IN HIS DESERT BOUND BIRTH-HOME, THE SUN VILLAGE.

HER REGARD FOR HIM, HER EXPECTATIONS... SO HIGH!

BRIEFLY, A DISTRACTION—AMBITION—A DREAMED-OF MATURITY IN WHICH HIS GIFTS REACH FULL POTENTIAL. THE LAD DISCIPLINES HIS MIND AND...

AT LAST HIS SPIRIT FLOATS FREE! HE CALLS...

SAVAH?

SAVAH...!

IT'S ME!

SAAVAAAA

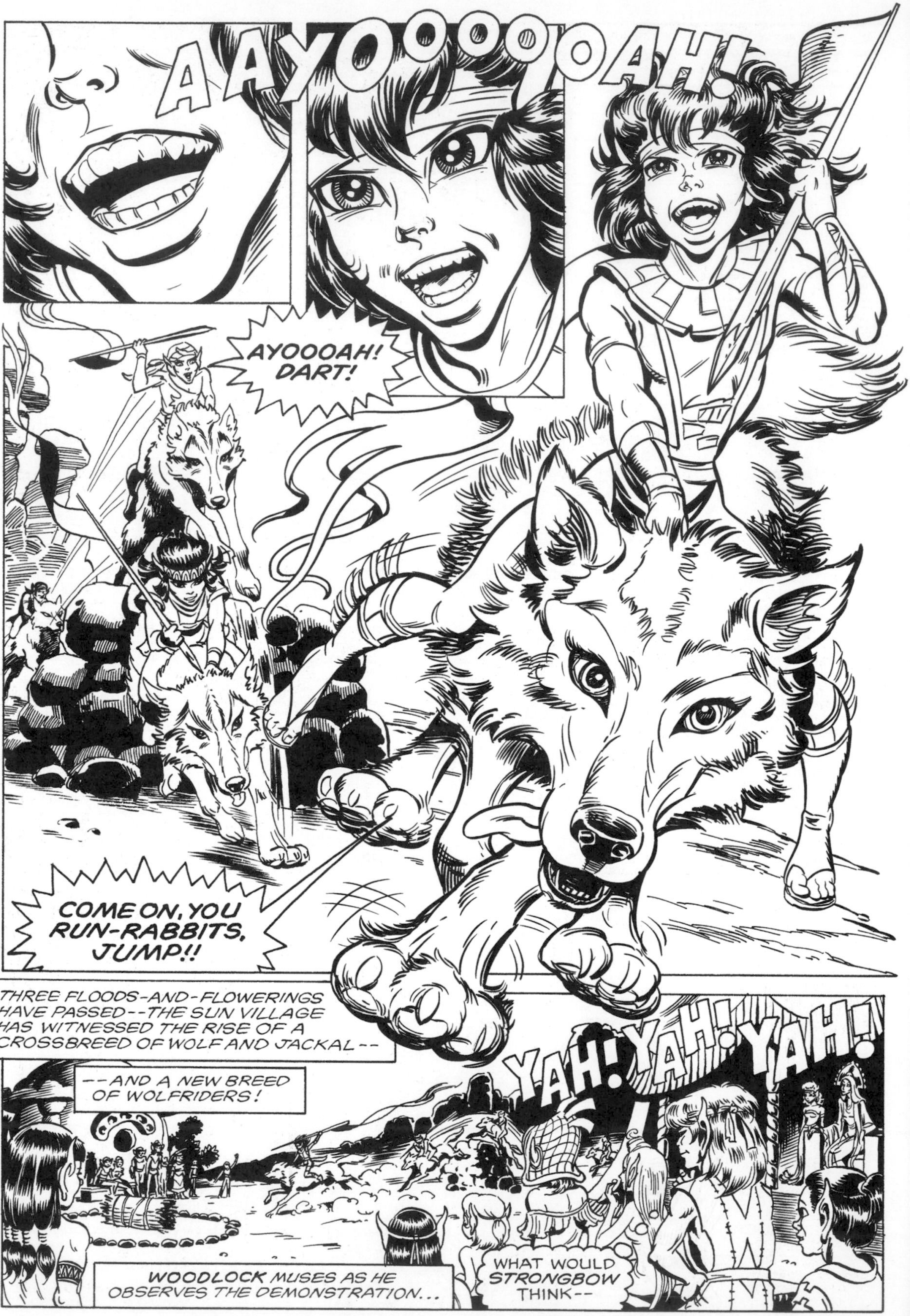
A AYOOOOOOAH!
AYOOOAH! DART!
COME ON, YOU RUN-RABBITS, JUMP!!
THREE FLOODS-AND-FLOWERINGS HAVE PASSED--THE SUN VILLAGE HAS WITNESSED THE RISE OF A CROSSBREED OF WOLF AND JACKAL--
--AND A NEW BREED OF WOLFRIDERS!
YAH! YAH! YAH!
WOODLOCK MUSES AS HE OBSERVES THE DEMONSTRATION...
WHAT WOULD STRONGBOW THINK--

"--OF HIS GROWN UP BOY-CUB NOW?"

THAK!

"LIKE SIRE, LIKE PUP--"

"--EXCEPT," *WOODLOCK* CHUCKLES TO HIMSELF--

HOO HAH

"--FOR THE *NOISE!*"

SEE HOW OUR SPEED HAS IMPROVED, *MOTHER OF MEMORY?* WE WERE DOWN FROM THE PLATEAU AND INTO THE RING--

--IN LESS TIME THAN EVER! YES!

THE SWIFTEST STRIPED DOE COULD NOT OUTRUN YOUR EIGHT-AND-FOUR HUNTERS!

SAVAH SMILES, REMINDED OF ANOTHER BOLD, PROUD YOUNGLING--HER WANDERER...

...RAYEK.

YOU'VE TURNED MEEK GARDENERS INTO WOLFRIDERS, *DART.* WE ARE ALL *MOST* IMPRESSED.

I, TOO! I'M *ALMOST* IMPRESSED! HE *COULD* STAND A BATH, THOUGH, RIGHT, *SHEN SHEN?*

--GIGGLE--*NEWSTAR!* YOU'RE TOO WICKED!

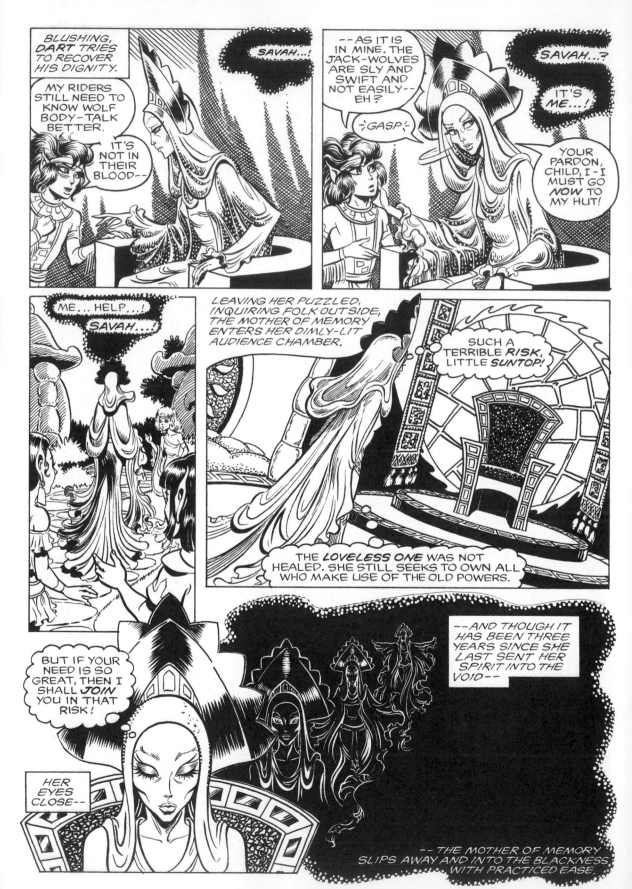

BLUSHING, *DART* TRIES TO RECOVER HIS DIGNITY.

MY RIDERS STILL NEED TO KNOW WOLF BODY-TALK BETTER.

IT'S NOT IN THEIR BLOOD--

SAVAH...!

--AS IT IS IN MINE. THE JACK-WOLVES ARE SLY AND SWIFT AND NOT EASILY-- EH?

¿GASP?

SAVAH...?

IT'S ME....!

YOUR PARDON, CHILD, I-I MUST GO *NOW* TO MY HUT!

ME... HELP...! SAVAH...!

LEAVING HER PUZZLED, INQUIRING FOLK OUTSIDE, THE MOTHER OF MEMORY ENTERS HER DIMLY-LIT AUDIENCE CHAMBER.

SUCH A TERRIBLE *RISK*, LITTLE *SUNTOP*!

THE *LOVELESS ONE* WAS NOT HEALED. SHE STILL SEEKS TO OWN ALL WHO MAKE USE OF THE OLD POWERS.

BUT IF YOUR NEED IS SO GREAT, THEN I SHALL *JOIN* YOU IN THAT RISK!

HER EYES--

--AND THOUGH IT HAS BEEN THREE YEARS SINCE SHE LAST SENT HER SPIRIT INTO THE VOID--

--THE MOTHER OF MEMORY SLIPS AWAY AND INTO THE BLACKNESS WITH PRACTICED EASE.

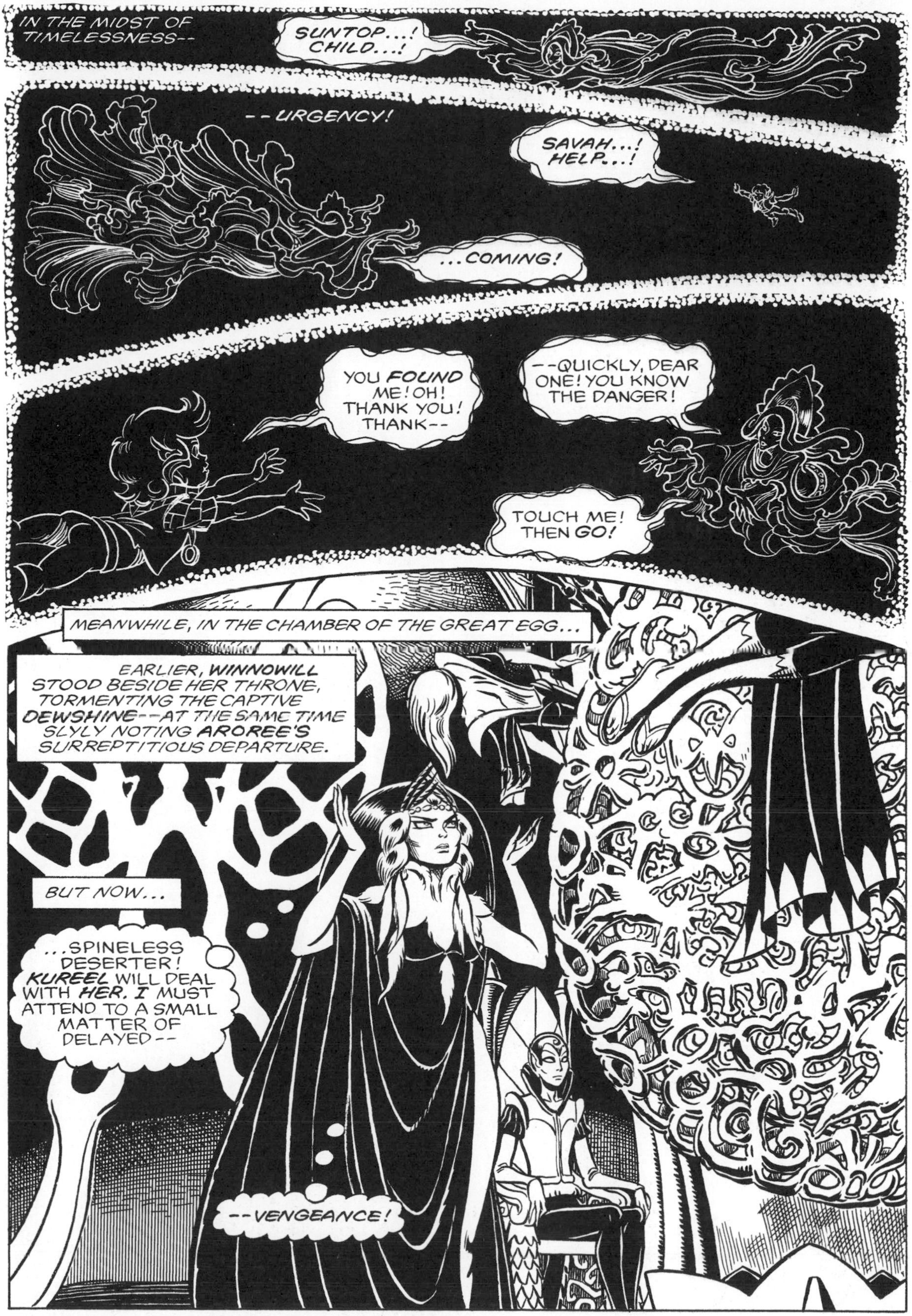

IN THE MIDST OF TIMELESSNESS--
SUNTOP...! CHILD...!
--URGENCY!
SAVAH...! HELP...!
...COMING!
YOU FOUND ME! OH! THANK YOU! THANK--
--QUICKLY, DEAR ONE! YOU KNOW THE DANGER!
TOUCH ME! THEN GO!
MEANWHILE, IN THE CHAMBER OF THE GREAT EGG...
EARLIER, WINNOWILL STOOD BESIDE HER THRONE, TORMENTING THE CAPTIVE DEWSHINE--AT THE SAME TIME SLYLY NOTING AROREE'S SURREPTITIOUS DEPARTURE.
BUT NOW...
...SPINELESS DESERTER! KUREEL WILL DEAL WITH HER. I MUST ATTEND TO A SMALL MATTER OF DELAYED--
--VENGEANCE!

CONTEMPLATING THE SHAPED STONE SYMBOLS ON THE MULTI-LAYERED SHELL OF THE FLOATING EGG, **WINNOWILL** SINKS TO HER KNEES. SHE LABORS TO CLEAR HER MIND OF FURIOUS, TRANCE-IMPEDING DREAMS.

VOLL, ONCE LORD, ONCE LOVEMATE-- FIRST-BORN OF THE **HIGH ONES...**

THEY SEDUCED HIM...KILLED HIM, THE WOLF- BLOODED ONES...

WHEN SHE LAY BROKEN BY HER OWN CHOICE, **VOLL** IGNORED HER FEEBLE SENDINGS AND FLEW TO HIS DEATH!

OH, HAD HE ONLY GIVEN HER TIME--TRUSTED HER TO DO HER WILL WITH THE GLIDERS--SHE'D HAVE GIVEN **HIM** FAR MORE THAN THE PALACE--HOME OF HIS DREAMS!

NOT MIND'S QUIET, BUT COLD PURPOSEFUL HATRED THRUSTS HER AT LAST THROUGH THE BLACK CURTAIN.

CURSED WOLFRIDERS! I **CAN** HURT THEM--

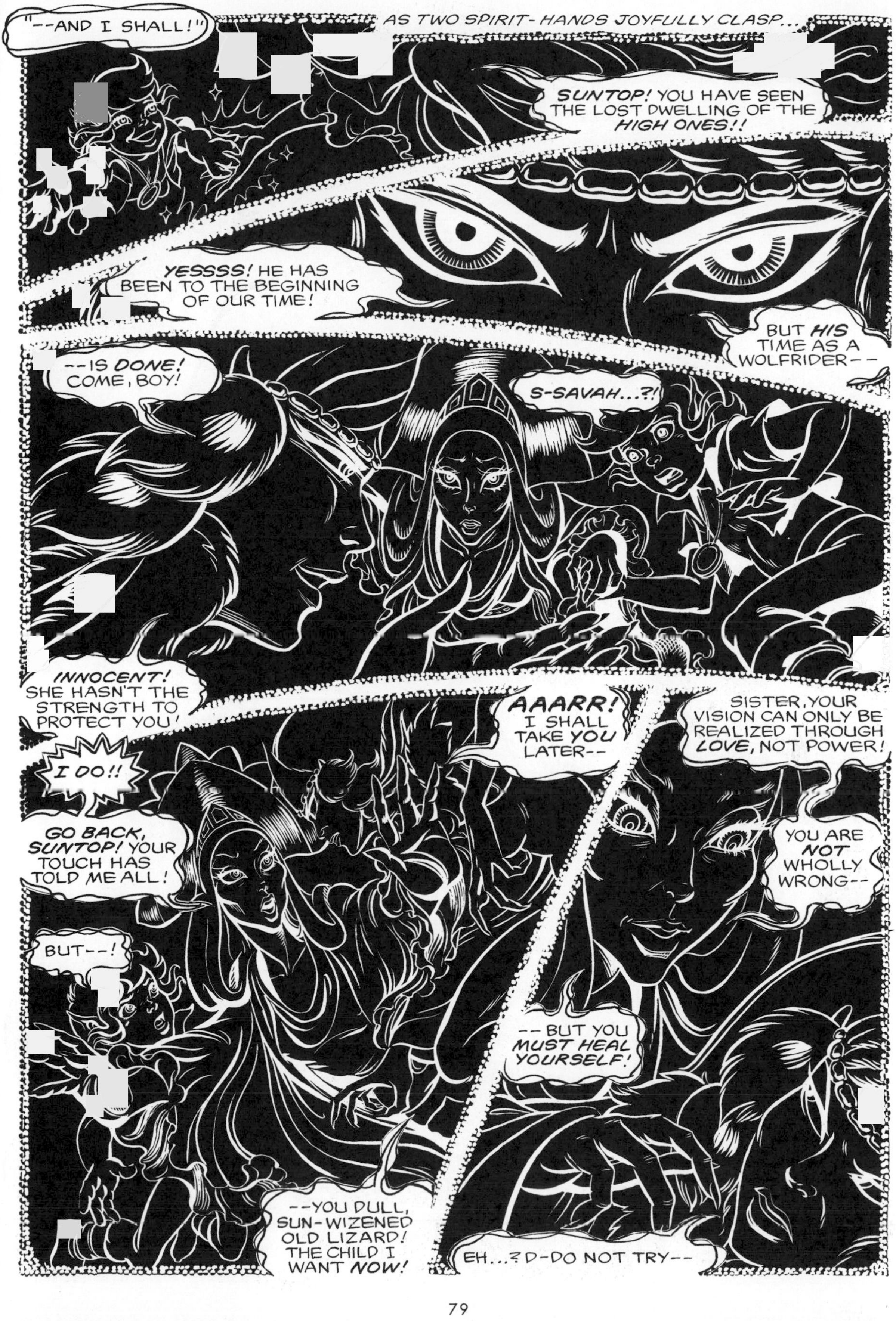
"--AND I SHALL!"
AS TWO SPIRIT-HANDS JOYFULLY CLASP...
SUNTOP! YOU HAVE SEEN THE LOST DWELLING OF THE HIGH ONES!!
YESSSS! HE HAS BEEN TO THE BEGINNING OF OUR TIME!
BUT HIS TIME AS A WOLFRIDER--
--IS DONE! COME, BOY!
S-SAVAH...?!
INNOCENT! SHE HASN'T THE STRENGTH TO PROTECT YOU!
I DO!!
GO BACK, SUNTOP! YOUR TOUCH HAS TOLD ME ALL!
BUT--!
--YOU DULL, SUN-WIZENED OLD LIZARD! THE CHILD I WANT NOW!
AAARR! I SHALL TAKE YOU LATER--
SISTER, YOUR VISION CAN ONLY BE REALIZED THROUGH LOVE, NOT POWER!
YOU ARE NOT WHOLLY WRONG--
--BUT YOU MUST HEAL YOURSELF!
EH...? D-DO NOT TRY--

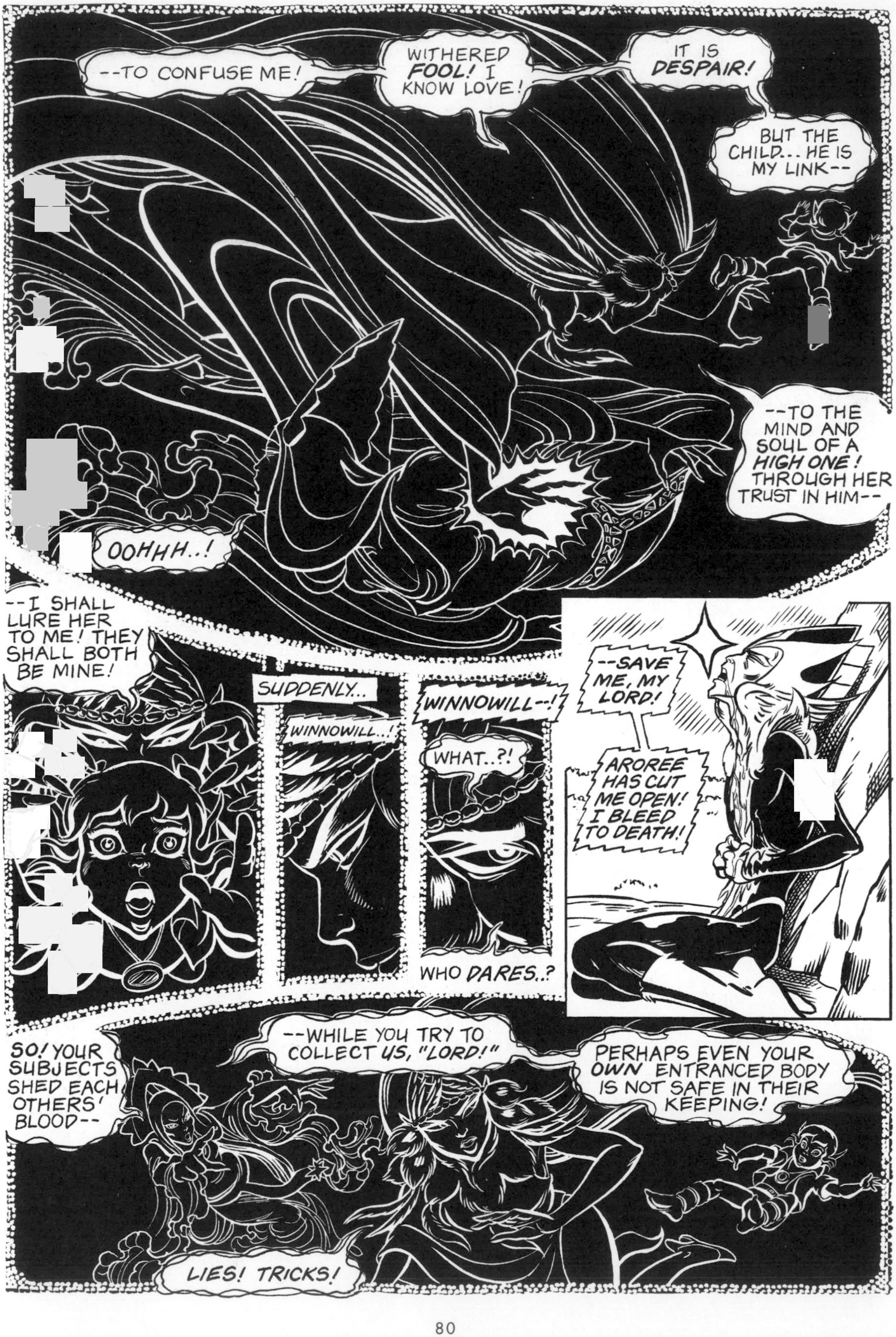
--TO CONFUSE ME!
WITHERED FOOL! I KNOW LOVE!
IT IS DESPAIR!
BUT THE CHILD... HE IS MY LINK--
--TO THE MIND AND SOUL OF A HIGH ONE! THROUGH HER TRUST IN HIM--
OOHHH..!
--I SHALL LURE HER TO ME! THEY SHALL BOTH BE MINE!
SUDDENLY...
WINNOWILL..!
WINNOWILL--!
WHAT..?!
WHO DARES..?
--SAVE ME, MY LORD!
AROREE HAS CUT ME OPEN! I BLEED TO DEATH!
SO! YOUR SUBJECTS SHED EACH OTHERS' BLOOD--
--WHILE YOU TRY TO COLLECT US, "LORD!"
PERHAPS EVEN YOUR OWN ENTRANCED BODY IS NOT SAFE IN THEIR KEEPING!
LIES! TRICKS!

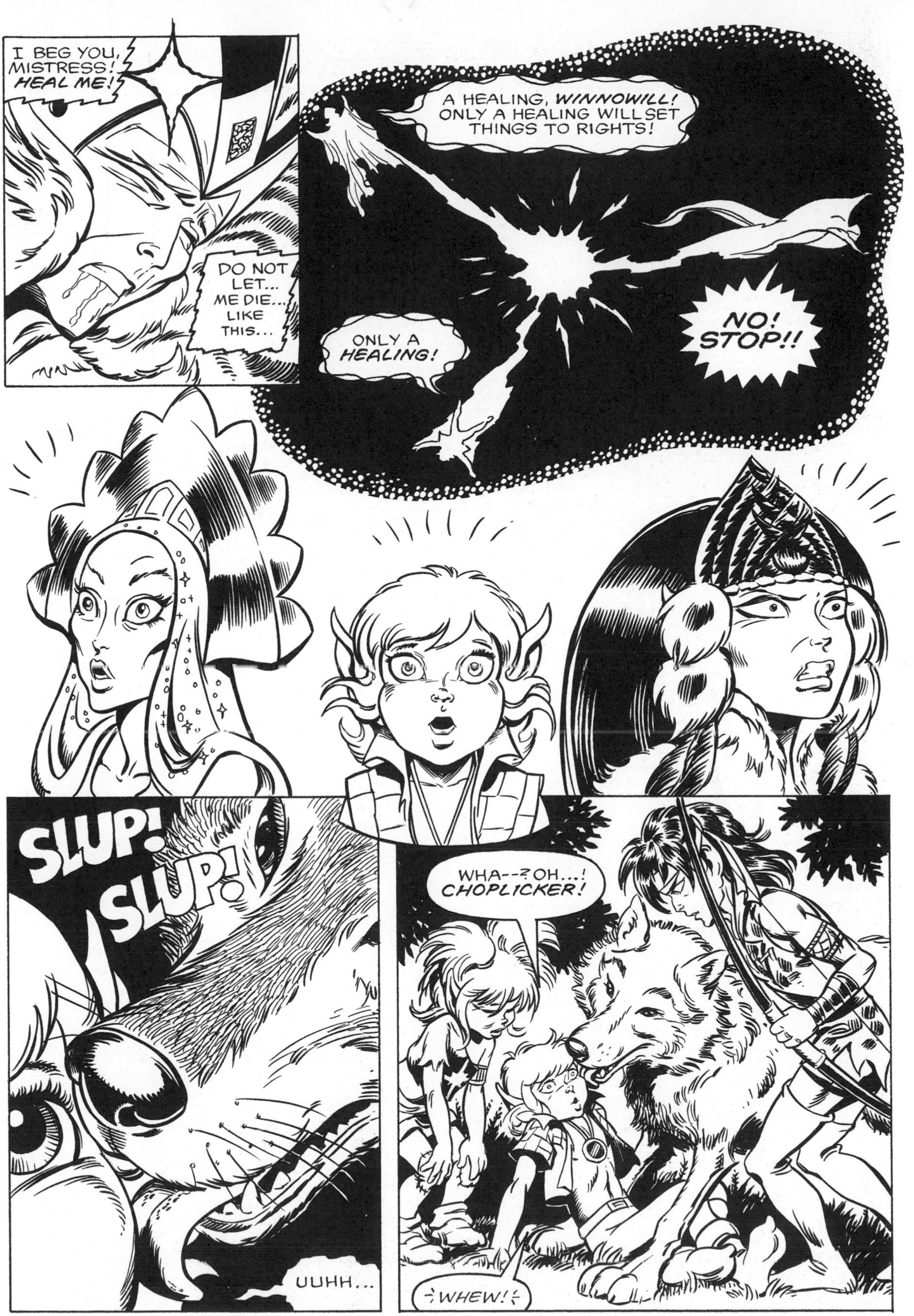
I BEG YOU, MISTRESS! HEAL ME!
DO NOT LET... ME DIE... LIKE THIS...
A HEALING, WINNOWILL! ONLY A HEALING WILL SET THINGS TO RIGHTS!
ONLY A HEALING!
NO! STOP!!
SLUP! SLUP!
UUHH...
WHA--? OH...! CHOPLICKER!
WHEW!

JUST WHAT WERE YOU UP TO, CUB?

YOU "WENT OUT", DIDN'T YOU, DESPITE *CUTTER'S* ORDERS!

PLEASE, *STRONGBOW!* SEND YOUR SCOLDING AT *ME!*

IT WAS MY IDEA. I TOLD *SUNTOP* TO "GO OUT"--

--AND ASK *SAVAH* WHAT TO DO ABOUT *WINNOWILL!*

PUNISHMENT THERE MUST BE, BUT *STRONGBOW* IS GLAD THAT IT WILL NOT BE HIS TO DECIDE. HAVING LISTENED TO ALL THAT BEFELL *SUNTOP* IN THE SPIRIT REALM, THE ARCHER CANNOT HELP BUT ASK ABOUT--

--DART? I-I'M NOT SURE...

BUT *SAVAH* GAVE ME THE FEELING THAT EVERYTHING'S *FINE* IN THE SUN VILLAGE.

SUNTOP? I-I FELT...

!? WHAT HAS HAPPENED?

TELL HER, CUBS. *I'M* HEADING FOR THE *TREES!*

COWARD!

THAT'S GOOD ENOUGH FOR *ME!* WE'RE IN IT UP TO OUR HACKLES NOW, CUBS, BUT I GUESS IT'S BEST WE KNOW THE BLACK SNAKE'S INTENTIONS.

SHE'D HAVE COME CALLING ON US SOONER OR LATER ANYWAY.

SHORTLY...

⸮ HARUMPH ⸮ ALL RIGHT...THIS MUCH *SUNTOP* COULD GATHER BEFORE *SAVAH* SAVED HIS *DISOBEDIENT* LITTLE TAIL FOR HIM...

AROREE STOLE *WINDKIN* FOR HER OWN REASONS-- THAT'S THE ONLY CRIME THE BLACK SNAKE *ISN'T* GUILTY OF.

WINNOWILL WANTS *SUNTOP, TIMMAIN*-- IN FACT *ANY* ELF GOOD AT MAGIC--UNDER HER CONTROL! THE REST OF US SHE WANTS BELLY UP!

SHE'S BOUND TO SEND THE GIANT BIRDS AGAINST US.

AND HER *HUMANS?*

WHO KNOWS?

WELL, DO WE FIGHT?

LET'S SAY WE DON'T *RUN!* DEFENDING OUR HOLT *ISN'T* MAKING WAR. SURELY *CUTTER* WOULD AGREE.

BUT *DEWSHINE*...IF WE FIGHT, WHAT OF *HER?*

AND IN SORROW'S END...

CHILDREN OF MY CHILDREN'S CHILDREN, I HAVE LEARNED THIS DAY WHAT BECAME OF *CUTTER,* HIS WOLFRIDERS AND HIS QUEST.

⸮ AAH! ⸮

AFTER RELEASING MY SPIRIT FROM *WINNOWILL'S* CLUTCHES, THEY FLEW FROM BLUE MOUNTAIN TO THE VERY PORTAL OF THE *HIGH ONES* LOST PALACE!

⸮ GASP ⸮

MORE!

IN TIME! FOR NOW, KNOW THAT ONCE AGAIN THE *LOVELESS ONE* THREATENS THE WOLFRIDERS--IN THEIR NEW FOREST HOLT.

HER SICKNESS WILL BRING GRIEF TO MANY!

MOTHER...FATHER...SO FAR AWAY! IS THERE SOME WAY I CAN HELP THEM?

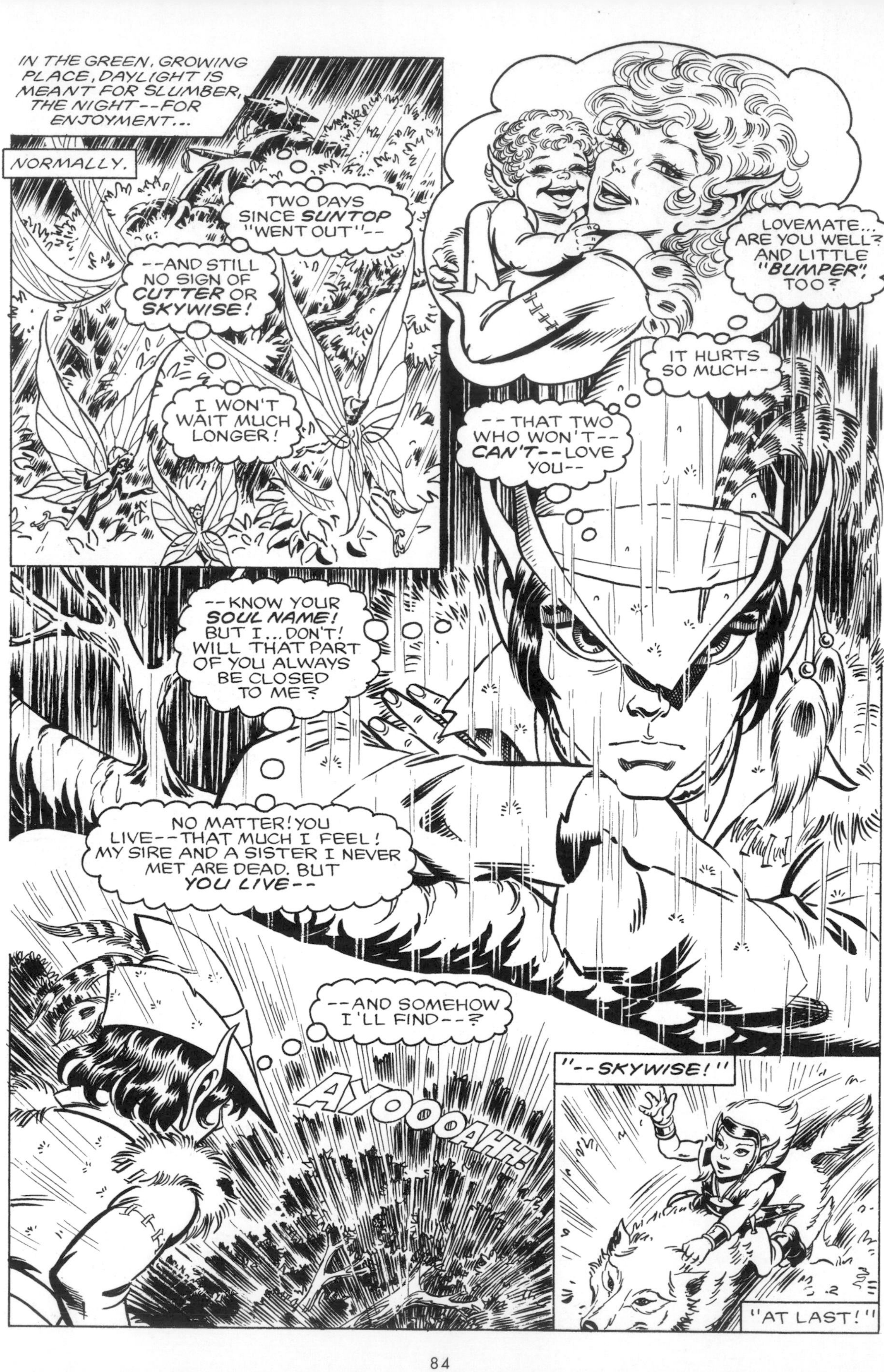

IN THE GREEN, GROWING PLACE, DAYLIGHT IS MEANT FOR SLUMBER, THE NIGHT--FOR ENJOYMENT...
NORMALLY.
TWO DAYS SINCE SUNTOP "WENT OUT"--
--AND STILL NO SIGN OF CUTTER OR SKYWISE!
I WON'T WAIT MUCH LONGER!
LOVEMATE... ARE YOU WELL? AND LITTLE "BUMPER", TOO?
IT HURTS SO MUCH--
--THAT TWO WHO WON'T--CAN'T--LOVE YOU--
--KNOW YOUR SOUL NAME! BUT I...DON'T! WILL THAT PART OF YOU ALWAYS BE CLOSED TO ME?
NO MATTER! YOU LIVE--THAT MUCH I FEEL! MY SIRE AND A SISTER I NEVER MET ARE DEAD. BUT YOU LIVE--
--AND SOMEHOW I'LL FIND--?
AYOOOAHH!
"--SKYWISE!"
"AT LAST!"

RAGGED, EXHAUSTED, THE *STARGAZER* AND HIS *WOLF* TEAR THROUGH DELICATE PRESERVER WEBBING AS THEY CHARGE TOWARD THE FATHER TREE.

IMMEDIATELY ROCKED BY A *BOMBARDMENT* OF ANXIOUS SENDINGS—

—*SKYWISE* DOES HIS LEVEL BEST TO ANSWER EVERYONE AT ONCE!

—YES, I FOUND *CUTTER*—

—I'M FINE—

—HE'S FINE—

—BLUE MOUNTAIN—

—RAFTING WITH THE HUMANS RIGHT NOW—

—YES! BY *RAFT*—!

—I DON'T KNOW HOW SOON—

—YES, THE PLAN TO TURN THE HUMANS AGAINST THE GLIDERS IS STILL ON—

—BUT LISTEN TO THIS—!

—*WINNOWILL* SURELY HAS MORE USE FOR *PRESERVERS* THAN FOR *DEWSHINE* AND HER CUB!

WE'LL OFFER A TRADE!

AYE, THERE'S AN IDEA!

BUT IS THAT *FAIR*? THE WINGED ONES THINK, AND IN A MANNER, *FEEL.* *SHE* HAS THE POWER TO HARM THEM!

TRUE...BUT I DOUBT SHE'LL GET THE CHANCE! THE PRESERVERS KNOW ALL ABOUT HER! BESIDES, REMEMBER HOW MUCH TROUBLE JUST *ONE* OF THEM GAVE HER?

"*JUST ONE!*"

⸮SIGH⸮ LITTLE *PETALWING*, WITH A WILL AS STRONG AS ITS SHELL—

85

"--AND PERSISTENCE TO MATCH! EVEN *RAYEK* COULD LEARN TO LIKE SUCH DEVOTION!"

GET AWAY FROM ME YOU, DOUBLE-CURSED SPY!

IF I WANT TO TRACK BEAR I'LL TRACK BEAR!

KAHVI! HAVE YOU NO SENSE AT ALL? THE CHILD--

SHARPDARK HIGHTHING SAY NO NO NO! IS COME GET YOU LIKE ALWAYS!

PETALWING AGREE!

--COULD GET DROPPED *TODAY*! WHY THE FLAP? IT'S HARDLY MY FIRST.

BUT IT MAY BE *MINE*!

YOU'VE DENIED YOUR TRUE ELF NATURE FOR SO LONG THAT NOT EVEN *TIMMAIN* CAN OPEN YOUR SOUL TO REVEAL THE FATHER'S NAME.

SO WHAT IF *YOU* TURN OUT TO BE THE BUCK, BLACK-HAIR?

THE YOUNG COME *THROUGH* US--THEY DON'T BELONG TO US!

I WAITED THROUGH MANY CYCLES OF THE GREATER MOON UNTIL *TWO-EDGE* WAS WELL ENOUGH TO TRAVEL.

HE WAS GOING TO SHOW ME *ALL* THE SECRETS OF BLUE MOUNTAIN--

--AND YOU'D HAVE BEEN THERE AND BACK LONG AGO BUT FOR ME, EH? *TSK*!

I CANNOT TRUST YOU. YOU ARE *RECKLESS*! ONLY WHEN THE BABE IS SAFELY IN THIS WORLD WILL I *GO*!

WHILE A POTENTIAL SIRE GRAPPLES WITH HIS CONFLICTING CONCERNS, A SIRE INDEED, WHO NEVER EXPECTED TO SEE OR KNOW HIS SON, STRIVES TO FEEL NOTHING AT ALL.

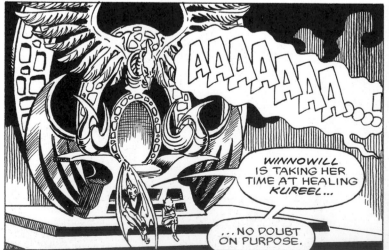

AAAAAAAAA!

WINNOWILL IS TAKING HER TIME AT HEALING *KUREEL*...

...NO DOUBT ON PURPOSE.

IT SEEMS HE INTERRUPTED SOME IMPORTANT BUSINESS--

--WITH HIS PETTY PLEAS FOR HIS LIFE.

HE'LL BE WONDROUS WHEN HE'S GROWN, DON'T YOU THINK...? *SCOUTER*... CALLS HIM "*BUMPER*"--

--BECAUSE HE HASN'T QUITE GOT THE KNACK OF DIRECTION YET...

YOU'RE STILL REPELLED BY WHAT YOU SEE INSIDE ME!

IT IS--

--DIFFICULT!

I GUESS I'M LUCKIER. YOU'RE ALMOST A *HIGH ONE*.

I GAVE *MUCH* TO BE ABLE TO FLY.

MY FOLK WILL FIND A WAY TO SAVE US BOTH, *TYLDAK*.

BEAR UP.

BUT... IF THEY FAIL... PROMISE ME *YOU* WILL FIND YOUR *KNIFE*... AND FREE ME FOREVER.

FLYING AND LIVING ARE THE *SAME*.

IF I CANNOT DO THE ONE...

HOWEVER... HOPELESSNESS ILL REFLECTS THE SPIRIT OF THE INTREPID THREESOME WHO ARRIVE SOMETIME LATER TO SCALE THE MOUNTAINSIDE.

I WISH CUTTER HAD ALREADY COME AND TALKED TO THE HOAN G'TAY SHO.

IF THEY SEE US, WHO KNOWS WHAT THEY'LL DO!

SO DON'T GET SEEN!

SOON...

THERE! THE TUNNEL WHERE THE HUMANS OFFER SACRIFICES!

CALL!

WINNOWILL...!

REMEMBER ME? I PUT AN ARROW IN YOU ONCE!

BUT NOW I'VE COME TO *TRADE* WITH YOU!

HEAR ME!

PRESERVERS! FOR THE RETURN OF MY *KIN*-- YOUR PRISONERS!

THE MOST POWERFUL SENDER OF ALL THE WOLFRIDERS, **STRONGBOW** FEARLESSLY COMMANDS THE "BLACK SNAKE'S" ATTENTION. NOT SHE, BUT ONE OF HER MINIONS FINALLY RESPONDS.

SKAAWW!

WITH MADDENING, LEISURELY GRACE THE GIGANTIC HAWK CIRCLES BLUE MOUNTAIN'S PEAK ONCE...TWICE... SLOWLY DRIFTING LOWER...

LOOK! PRAISE TIMMAIN--

--THAT GLIDER HAS *DEWSHINE* WITH HIM!

WOLF-BLOODED CURS, MY LORD MUST HAVE *PROOF* THAT YOU INDEED POSSESS THAT WHICH YOU OFFER.

SCOUTER...BELOVED... JUST TO *SEE* YOU ONCE MORE...!

AS HER SENDING PIERCES HIS HEART, *SCOUTER* SHARES ALL THAT SHE HAS SUFFERED--

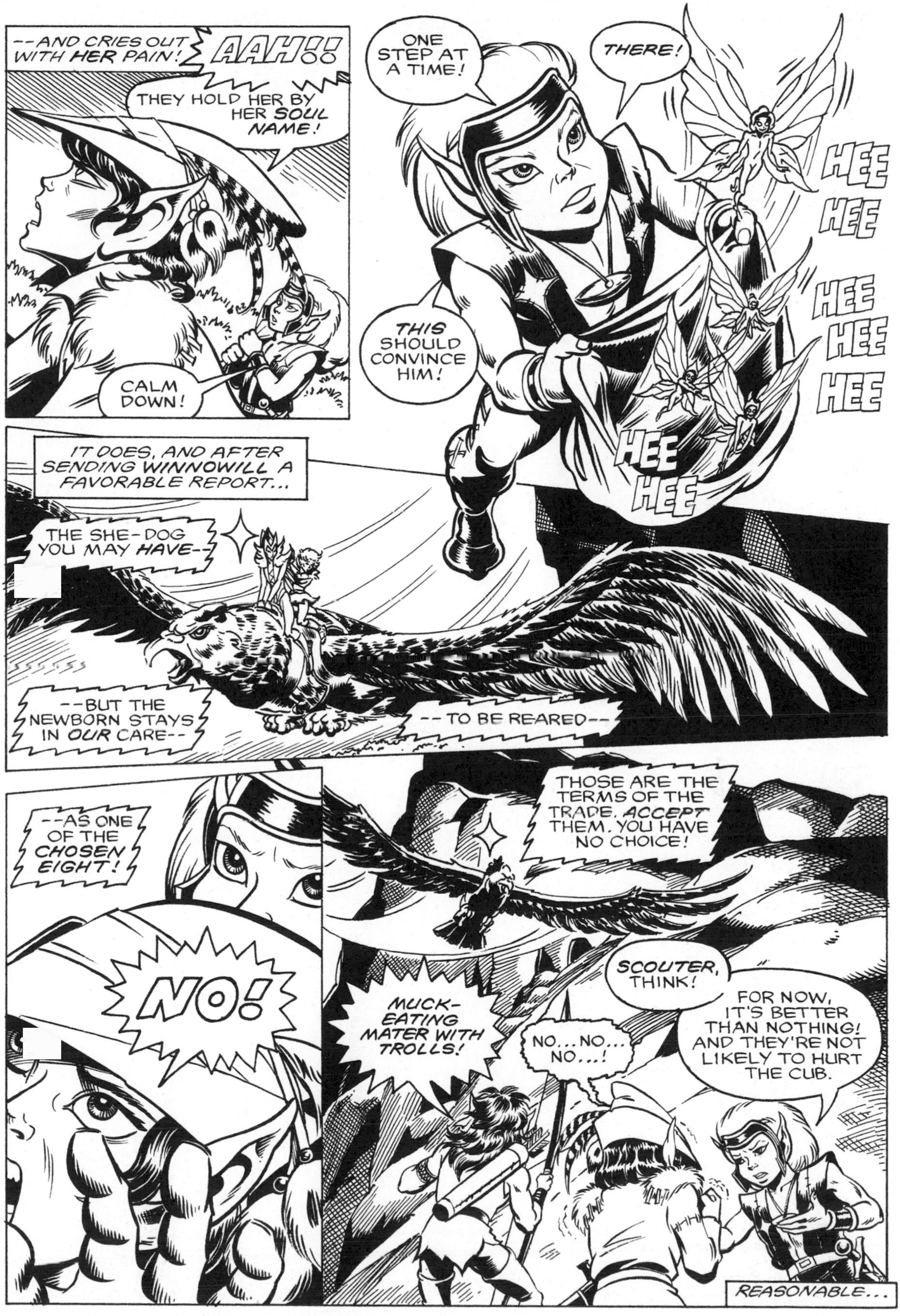
--AND CRIES OUT WITH HER PAIN!
AAH!!
THEY HOLD HER BY HER SOUL NAME!
CALM DOWN!
ONE STEP AT A TIME!
THERE!
HEE HEE
HEE HEE HEE
THIS SHOULD CONVINCE HIM!
HEE HEE
IT DOES, AND AFTER SENDING WINNOWILL A FAVORABLE REPORT...
THE SHE-DOG YOU MAY HAVE--
--BUT THE NEWBORN STAYS IN OUR CARE--
--TO BE REARED--
--AS ONE OF THE CHOSEN EIGHT!
NO!
THOSE ARE THE TERMS OF THE TRADE. ACCEPT THEM. YOU HAVE NO CHOICE!
MUCK-EATING MATER WITH TROLLS!
NO...NO... NO...!
SCOUTER, THINK!
FOR NOW, IT'S BETTER THAN NOTHING! AND THEY'RE NOT LIKELY TO HURT THE CUB.
REASONABLE...

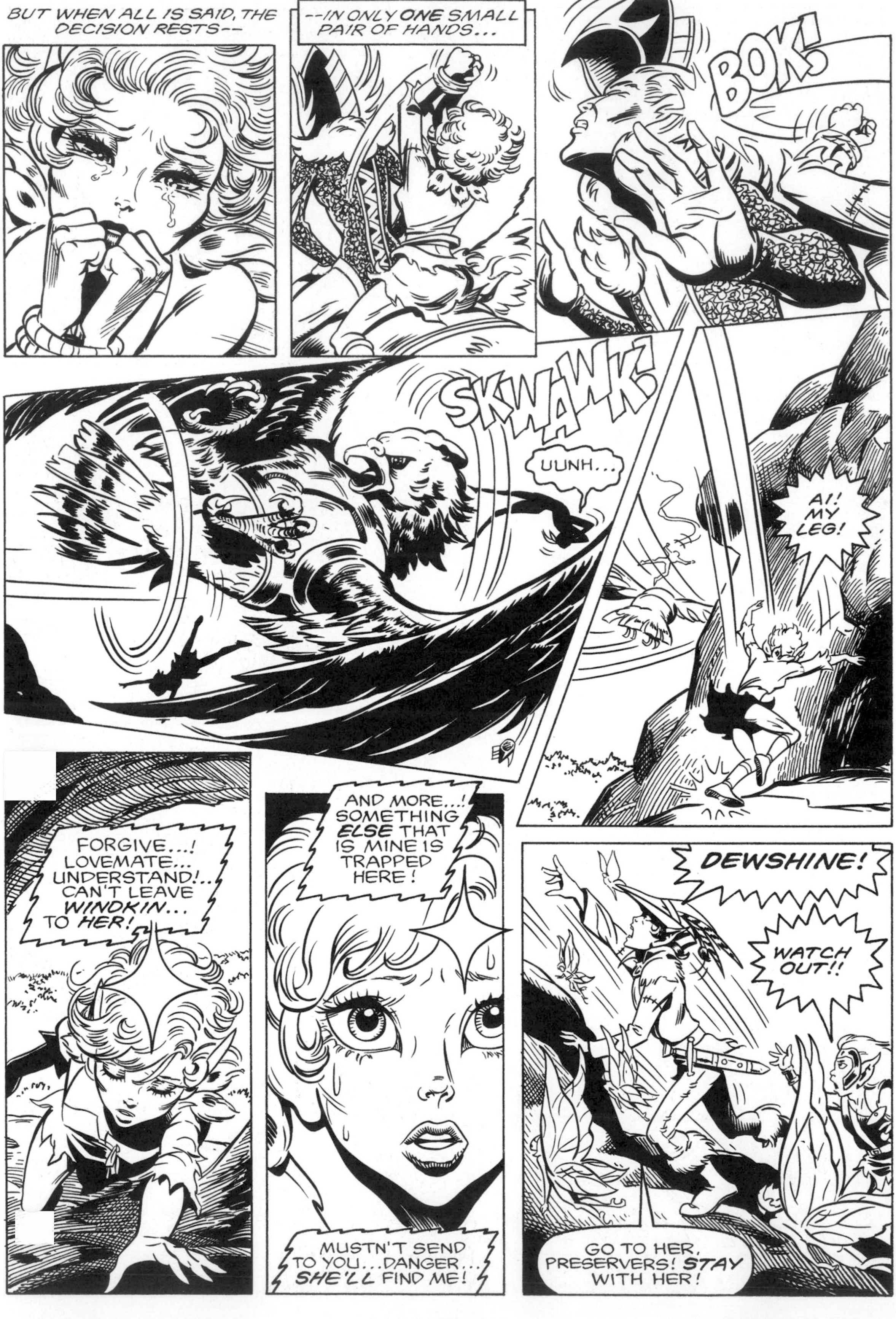
BUT WHEN ALL IS SAID, THE DECISION RESTS--
--IN ONLY ONE SMALL PAIR OF HANDS...
BOK!
SKWAWK!
UUNH...
AI! MY LEG!
FORGIVE...! LOVEMATE... UNDERSTAND!... CAN'T LEAVE WINDKIN... TO HER!
AND MORE...! SOMETHING ELSE THAT IS MINE IS TRAPPED HERE!
MUSTN'T SEND TO YOU... DANGER... SHE'LL FIND ME!
DEWSHINE!
WATCH OUT!!
GO TO HER, PRESERVERS! STAY WITH HER!

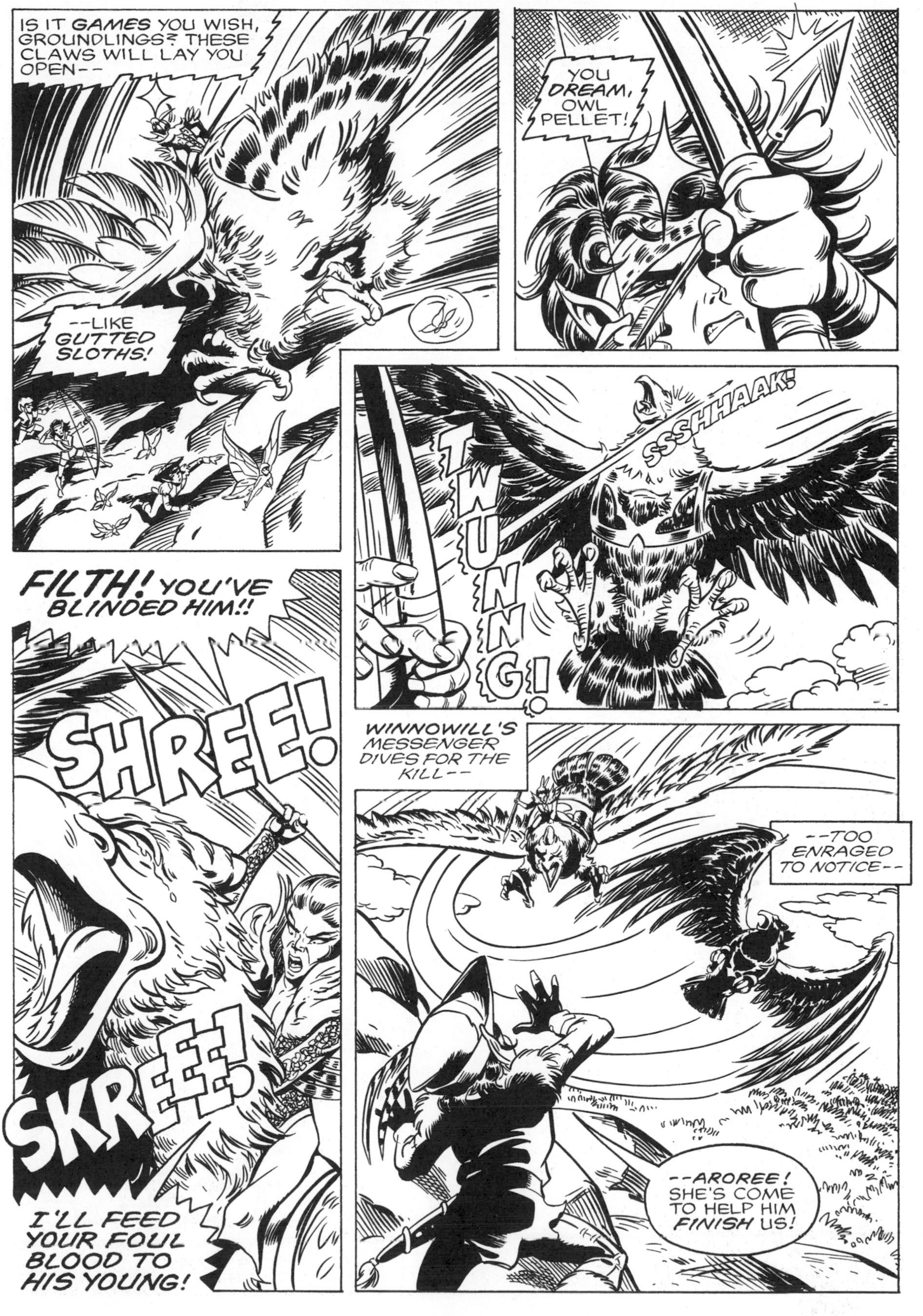

IS IT GAMES YOU WISH, GROUNDLINGS? THESE CLAWS WILL LAY YOU OPEN--
--LIKE GUTTED SLOTHS!
YOU DREAM, OWL PELLET!
SSSHHAAK!
TWUNNG!
FILTH! YOU'VE BLINDED HIM!!
SHREE!
SKREEE!
I'LL FEED YOUR FOUL BLOOD TO HIS YOUNG!
WINNOWILL'S MESSENGER DIVES FOR THE KILL--
--TOO ENRAGED TO NOTICE--
--AROREE! SHE'S COME TO HELP HIM FINISH US!

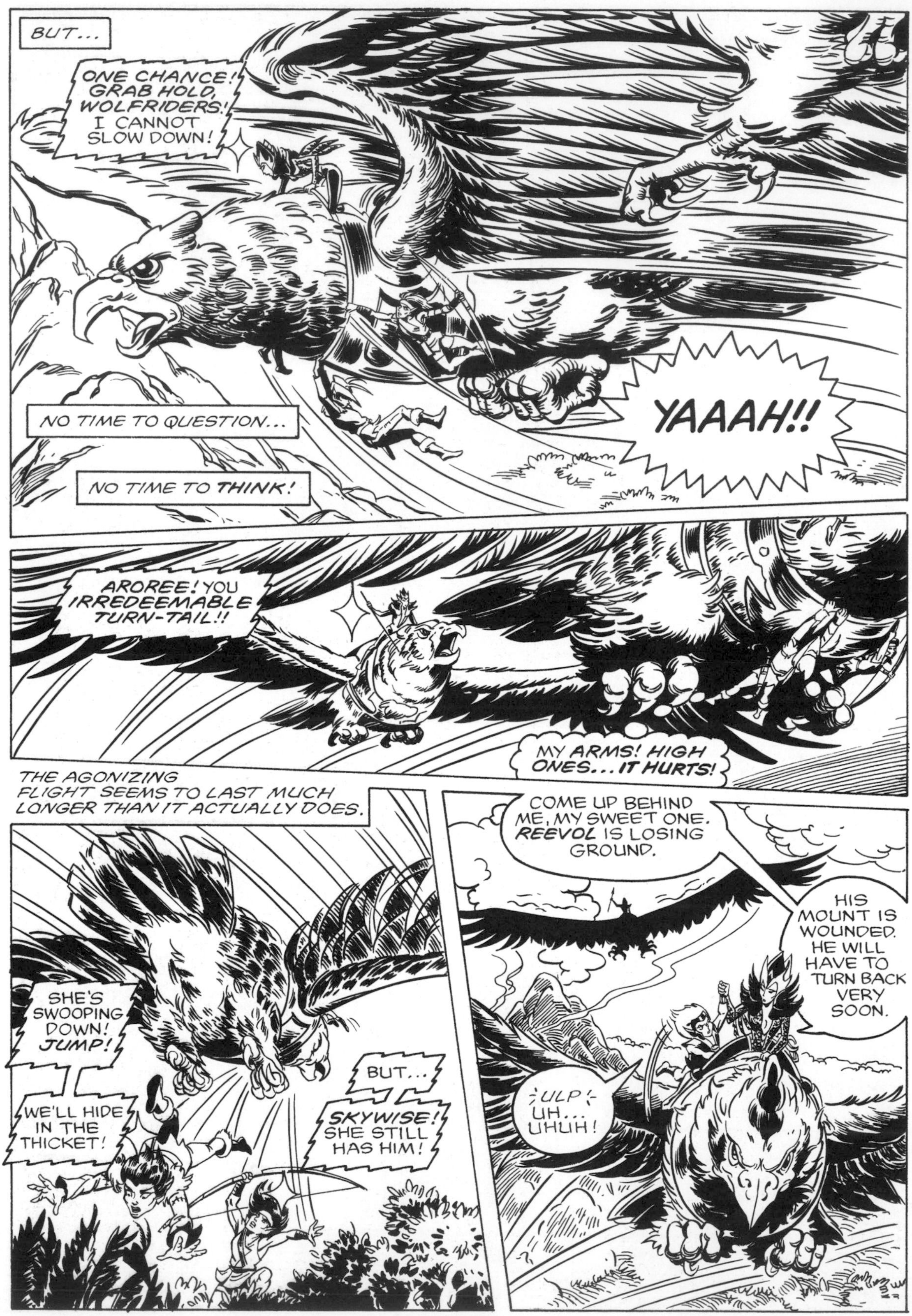
BUT...
ONE CHANCE! GRAB HOLD, WOLFRIDERS! I CANNOT SLOW DOWN!
NO TIME TO QUESTION...
NO TIME TO THINK!
YAAAH!!
AROREE! YOU IRREDEEMABLE TURN-TAIL!!
MY ARMS! HIGH ONES... IT HURTS!
THE AGONIZING FLIGHT SEEMS TO LAST MUCH LONGER THAN IT ACTUALLY DOES.
SHE'S SWOOPING DOWN! JUMP!
WE'LL HIDE IN THE THICKET!
BUT...
SKYWISE! SHE STILL HAS HIM!
COME UP BEHIND ME, MY SWEET ONE. REEVOL IS LOSING GROUND.
HIS MOUNT IS WOUNDED. HE WILL HAVE TO TURN BACK VERY SOON.
ULP UH... UHUH!

?!!© OOO

SKYWISE LOOKS BACK AND NOTES WITH RELIEF THAT *ARORE IS RIGHT.*

BUT WHETHER HE NOW EMBRACES SANITY--

--OR ANOTHER FORM OF BLUE MOUNTAIN'S MADNESS--

--HE DOES NOT KNOW!

MEANWHILE...

THE NOISY AERIAL ACTIVITY HAS HARDLY GONE UNNOTICED BY THE CAVE DWELLING *HOAN G'TAY SHO.*

⟨ MY PEOPLE, WE ARE THE FAVORED OF THOSE WHO DWELL ON HIGH. WHEN THE BIRD SPIRITS GIVE US SIGNS THAT WE OURSELVES CANNOT FATHOM, WE CALL UPON *THEM* TO MAKE THEIR WISHES CLEAR TO US! ⟩

THE HUMAN'S SHRILL PIPES CRY OUT--

--AND IN HER QUARTERS, DEEP IN THE BOWELS OF BLUE MOUNTAIN, *WINNOWILL* FEELS THE VIBRATION OF THOSE INSISTENT NOTES.

SHE SIGHS, HER SENSES RELIEVED. SHE HAS BEEN LISTENING TO THE INFANT CRY HIMSELF OUT LONG ENOUGH.

IT WILL BE INTERESTING TO DISCOVER WHETHER THE BEASTLY ELEMENTS--

--CAN BE REMOVED FROM HIS BLOOD.

AS HE IS, HE IS USELESS... *PERISHABLE.*

BUT I SHALL DEAL WITH THAT--

--LATER.

A SINGLE TOUCH... AND THE CRYING STOPS--

ZZZ...

--WITHOUT THE INCON-VENIENCE OF COMFORTING.

93

THESE, WHO ONCE LOVED HER, HAVE SEEN TOO MUCH -- DISAPPROVED ONCE TOO OFTEN...

THE HUMANS SHE GOES TO NOW HAVE NEVER LIVED WITH THE "BIRD SPIRITS". HENCE THEY BELIEVE ONLY IN THE PERFECTION THEY IMAGINE.

DOOR, OPEN!

A THREAD OF TWILIGHT...

L-LOOK..! A SPIRIT COMES!

SHE HAS NOT STEPPED SO FAR--

--OUTSIDE THE TUNNEL SINCE--

NO!

NO REMEMBERING!

⟨OOOHHH... SO BEAUTIFUL....!⟩

¡GASP!

⟨LIKE THE MOON...!⟩

⟨STARS!⟩

AHH...

⟨SHH!⟩

⟨SHE HOLDS A CHILD!!⟩

⟨FAITHFUL ONES...! GIFT GIVERS...!⟩

⟨YOU HAVE SEEN THEM, YOU KNOW THESE FALSE ONES!⟩

⟨BEWARE THE EVIL DEMONS WHO COME TO DESTROY YOUR LOVE OF THE BIRD SPIRITS--⟩

⟨THEY ARE SMALL... AND THEY DO NOT RIDE BIRDS!⟩

-- WHO COME TO DESTROY THE BIRD SPIRITS' CHILDREN AND MAKE BLUE MOUNTAIN AS A WOMAN BARREN!⟩

〈WOLVES! THEY RIDE FANGED WOLVES! WE REMEMBER! THREE SNOWS PAST WE SAW THEM GO INTO THE MOUNTAIN!〉

〈AND THREE SNOWS PAST, WE SAW THEM DRIVEN OUT! THEY SHALL NOT CLIMB UP AGAIN!〉

〈SO IT WAS.〉

〈SO IT WAS.〉

〈SO IT IS!〉

〈SO IT IS!〉

〈SO IT IS!〉

〈SEE, MY PEOPLE! WE HAVE WONDERED AT THE COMING OF THE LONG-TAILED STAR!〉

〈IT IS THE TORCH OF BATTLE AS THE SHAMAN FORTOLD!〉

〈SOON...BY WATER...〉

〈ONE WITH TWO FACES WILL COME AND SPEAK THE TRUTH FROM A THIRD MOUTH!〉

〈SOON...〉

〈LISTEN! ANOTHER VISION!〉

〈AND THE LIE WHICH IS THE TRUTH SHALL BRING MORE PAIN THAN THE TRUTH WHICH IS A LIE!〉

〈SO IT IS!〉

〈DEMONS LIE!〉

〈FALSE SPIRITS!〉

〈WE CANNOT BE TRICKED!〉

〈WE ARE FAVORED OF THOSE WHO DWELL ON HIGH!〉

〈THE FALSE SPIRITS WILL NOT PASS HERE!〉

〈WE WILL KILL THEM!〉

AND...

<BLUE MOUNTAIN... WE'RE ALMOST THERE. I EXPECT YOUR FOLK WILL BE GLAD TO SEE YOU AGAIN, NONNA.>

<NOT FOR ME, BUT FOR *YOU* WILL THEY SING PRAISES, HONORED ONE-->

<"--AFTER ALL, NEVER BEFORE HAS A *SPIRIT* GRACED THE CIRCLE OF OUR SACRED FIRE!">

TO BE CONTINUED...

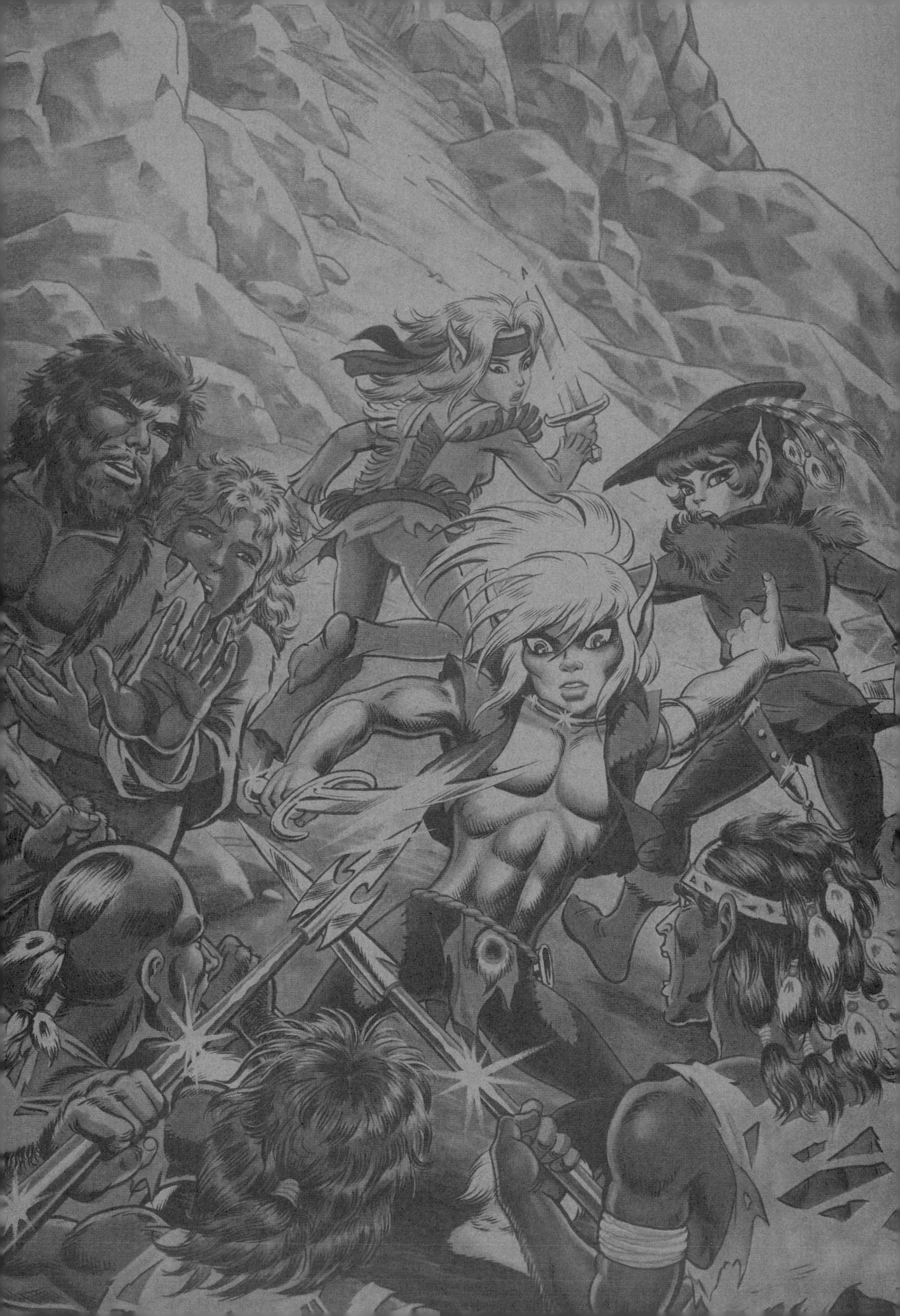

DAYBREAK...

KEEP...PLAYING...VOK!

WAAAAA! AA!

AH

WELL...

AAAA!

THAT ANSWERS THAT!

SIEGE AT BLUE MOUNTAIN

ARTIST / WRITER
WENDY PINI

CO-PLOT / EDITOR
RICHARD PINI

PART 4

INKS
JOE STATON

LETTERER
JANICE CHIANG

AS THE LOW-ANGLED SUN EASES ITS WAY TOWARD AFTERNOON, THE CASTLE'S METAL DOME, LEFT INCOMPLETE BY ITS TROLL BUILDERS, CASTS A SWELLING SHADOW OVER THE GO-BACKS' NEW LODGE.

HERE COMES *RAYEK.*

AGAIN.

UH HUH.

SAME AS YESTERDAY AND THE DAY BEFORE.

REMEMBER WHAT I TOLD YOU. *I'LL* HANDLE HIM. IF HE RAISES A STINK, JUST KEEP QUIET!

THIS ISSUE IS DEDICATED TO THE MEMORY OF OUR FRIEND *JOHN GAUG* WHO LOVED BEING AN ANIMATOR. THE MAGIC WAS IN HIM, HEAD, HAND AND HEART.

WELL, HELLO, BLACK-HAIR. ♪

KAHVI... *TELL ME!*

SHE CAME AT DAWN... DIDN'T LIVE TO SEE NOON.

PALE... *BLUE-* EYED.

SHE WASN'T *YOURS.*

HIGH ONES! FIRST YOUR OTHER CHILD, *VAYA,* AND NOW...

I–IS THERE ANYTHING I...?

YEP! STOP FUSSING LIKE A *FOOL,* AIR-WALKER. YOU'LL EMBARRASS US BOTH!

A *FOOL?!* YES! I AM *THAT,* FOR EXPECTING *SOME* MOTHERLY GRIEF--SOME SORROW FOR A LOST NEWBORN THAT MIGHT EASILY HAVE BEEN *OURS!*

WELL, SHE *WASN'T--*

--WHICH MEANS YOU CAN GO TO BLUE MOUNTAIN, NOW, AS YOU PLANNED.

NOT SOON ENOUGH! I AM *THROUGH* WITH YOU!

IT DISGUSTS ME THAT WE EVER TOUCHED!

¡SIGH¡- TOUCH AND GO, BLACK-HAIR. BUT I'VE GOT WHAT *I* WANT!

IT IS THE BITTERNESS OF THE MOUNTAIN WINDS-- ISN'T IT, "AIR-WALKER"?-- THAT BRINGS ON THE STINGING TEARS.

GO-BACKS... UNCARING!

IGNORANT! CONTEMPTUOUS OF MAGIC...!

SO PROUD--

--THAT THEY HAVE NO *NEED* OF HEALERS!

NO... NEED...

A LITTLE *GIRL* IT WAS...

HE FEELS ABOUT FOR HER SPIRIT.

IT IS NOT HERE YET.

THE CRUMBLING HALLS OF THE FIRSTCOMERS' ONCE-BURIED PALACE ARE AS TIDY AS A MAIMED ROCK SHAPER AND AN ADDLED HALF-TROLL HAVE BEEN ABLE TO MAKE THEM.

A FRIENDSHIP, SO UNLIKELY THAT IT *HAD* TO FORM--

HAH! CATCH ME *NOW*, MASTER SMITH!

--HAS QUIETED THE CLASHING OF *TWO-EDGE'S* FRACTURED THOUGHTS.

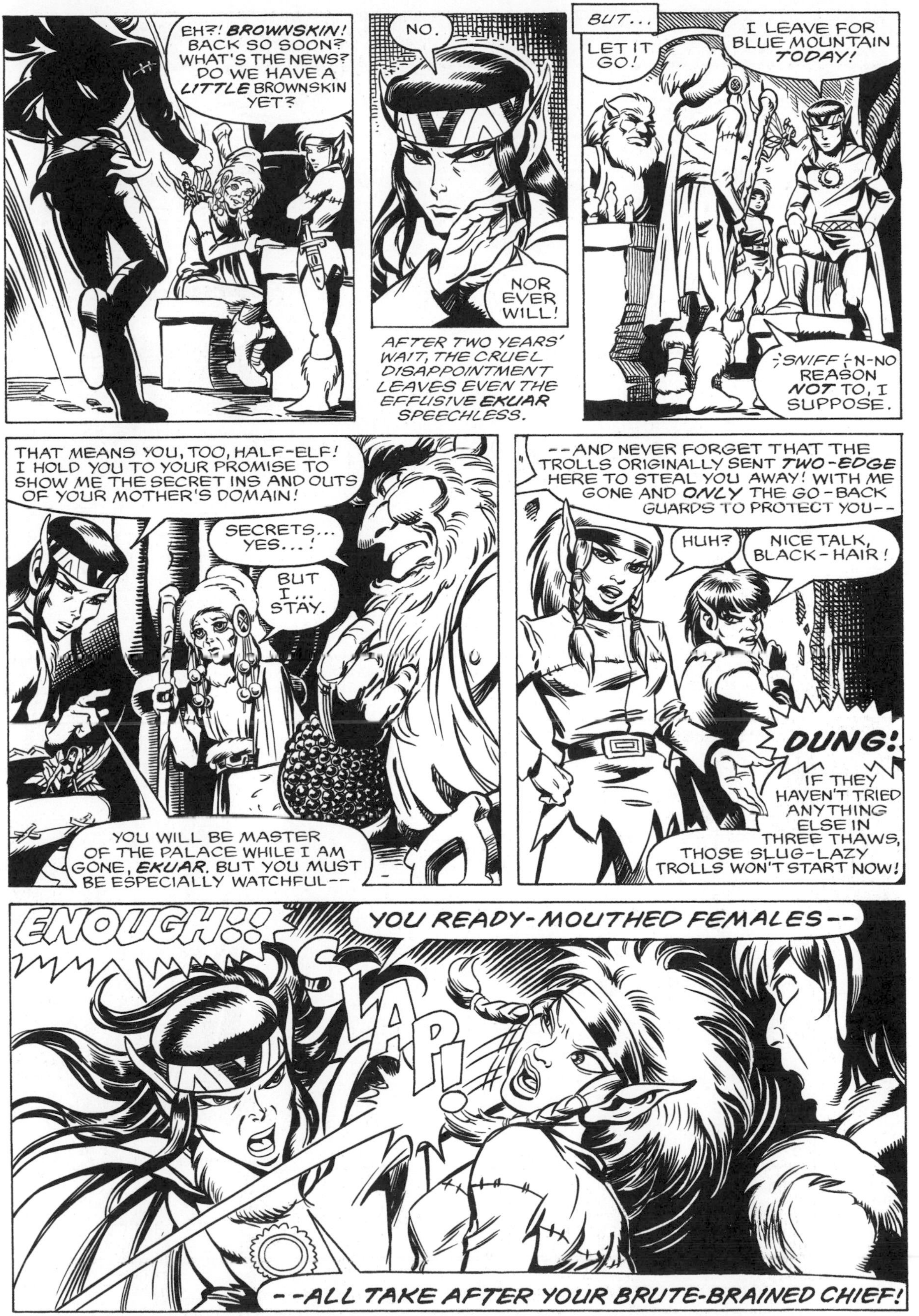

EH?! BROWNSKIN! BACK SO SOON? WHAT'S THE NEWS? DO WE HAVE A LITTLE BROWNSKIN YET?
NO.
NOR EVER WILL!
AFTER TWO YEARS' WAIT, THE CRUEL DISAPPOINTMENT LEAVES EVEN THE EFFUSIVE EKUAR SPEECHLESS.
BUT...
LET IT GO!
I LEAVE FOR BLUE MOUNTAIN TODAY!
SNIFF -N-NO REASON NOT TO, I SUPPOSE.
THAT MEANS YOU, TOO, HALF-ELF! I HOLD YOU TO YOUR PROMISE TO SHOW ME THE SECRET INS AND OUTS OF YOUR MOTHER'S DOMAIN!
SECRETS... YES...!
BUT I... STAY.
YOU WILL BE MASTER OF THE PALACE WHILE I AM GONE, EKUAR. BUT YOU MUST BE ESPECIALLY WATCHFUL--
--AND NEVER FORGET THAT THE TROLLS ORIGINALLY SENT TWO-EDGE HERE TO STEAL YOU AWAY! WITH ME GONE AND ONLY THE GO-BACK GUARDS TO PROTECT YOU--
HUH?
NICE TALK, BLACK-HAIR!
DUNG!
IF THEY HAVEN'T TRIED ANYTHING ELSE IN THREE THAWS, THOSE SLUG-LAZY TROLLS WON'T START NOW!
ENOUGH!!
YOU READY-MOUTHED FEMALES--
SLAP!
--ALL TAKE AFTER YOUR BRUTE-BRAINED CHIEF!

IF YOU FAIL TO PROTECT THE ROCK SHAPER, I *SWEAR* ON THE LIVING *HIGH ONE'S* SOUL-- --I WILL RETURN AND *WIPE* YOUR DEGENERATE TRIBE FROM THE FACE OF THIS WORLD!!

THERE ARE TIMES--

--WHEN THREATS *MUST BE* BELIEVED.

LATER, OUTFITTED FOR THE LONG JOURNEY, *RAYEK* STANDS BEFORE *TIMMAIN* IN THE ROOM OF THE SCROLL.

THE TIME HAS COME FOR ME TO BRING THE *GLIDERS*, MOST POWERFUL OF YOUR SURVIVING CHILDREN--

--HERE TO THE PALACE, *HIGH ONE*. I KNOW I CAN PERSUADE THEM--

--TO GIVE THEIR MAGIC TO MY CAUSE. THE PALACE *WILL FLY* AGAIN...!

AT OTHER TIMES HE HAS BEEN WARMLY RECEIVED.

BUT THE ROOM IS ICE COLD, AND *TIMMAIN*--STRANGELY SILENT. HER EXPECTED FAREWELL DOES NOT COME TO ENFOLD AND UPLIFT HIS HEART. HE SENSES--

--DISAPPROVAL...?

HOWEVER...

SMILE, MY FRIEND. REMEMBER, ALL THE SPIRITS OF OUR DEAD WITHIN THE PALACE WILL RALLY TO LEND YOU STRENGTH-- IF YOU NEED IT.

AND I AM SURE *TIMMAIN* WILL RECEIVE *YOUR* SENDINGS.

WELL! ER... ON YOUR WAY AT LAST! HEH. BUT...OH--

--LET ME BE A *LITTLE* SORRY FOR YOU...; SNIFF ;- THERE IS NO BABY BROWNSKIN! WHAT'S ALL THIS SCRAMBLING FOR--

--WITHOUT THE BABIES ?

FINALLY, NEAR THE DEER PENS...

THIS ONE'S OUR BEST, BUT THEN, *YOU* GAVE US THE BEST OF *WARS*, CRAZY-BRAIN! IT'S A FAIR EXCHANGE.

READY, HALF ELF?

READY *TOO!*

HMPH!

I HAVE AN EYE ON YOU. NO TRICKS!

SO THE TRAVELERS DEPART.

IS HE OFF, URDA?

BRRR! WITH-OUT SO MUCH AS A SALUTE.

ELF'S ICED OVER, THAT'S CERTAIN!

YOU COULD MAKE HIM LAUGH SOMETIMES. HE *WAS* BEGINNING TO LIKE YOU...

ARE YOU SORRY?

NOPE. WHEN *THAT* ONE LIKES YOU, HE LAYS CLAIM! I'VE NO USE FOR THAT!

SMART! BUT IT'S THE *LYING* THAT DOESN'T TASTE RIGHT, SOMEHOW.

HAD TO.

I WANTED HIS BLOOD RUNNING NEW IN OUR TRIBE--*HIS* FAWN, REARED *MY* WAY! THAT LEAVES *RAYEK* OUT!

HE'S THE SAME STUFF AS THE WOLF CHIEF, *CUTTER,* MEANT TO DO GREAT THINGS-- BUT LIKELY TO STUMBLE TRYING TO MANAGE TOO MUCH.

HE'D BE IN OUR WAY AND WE'D BE IN *HIS,* IF BLACK-HAIR KNEW.

GUESS SO. BUT IT'LL BE HARD--

--TO KEEP A BROWN SKINNED YELLOW-EYED GIRL A SECRET FOR VERY LONG.

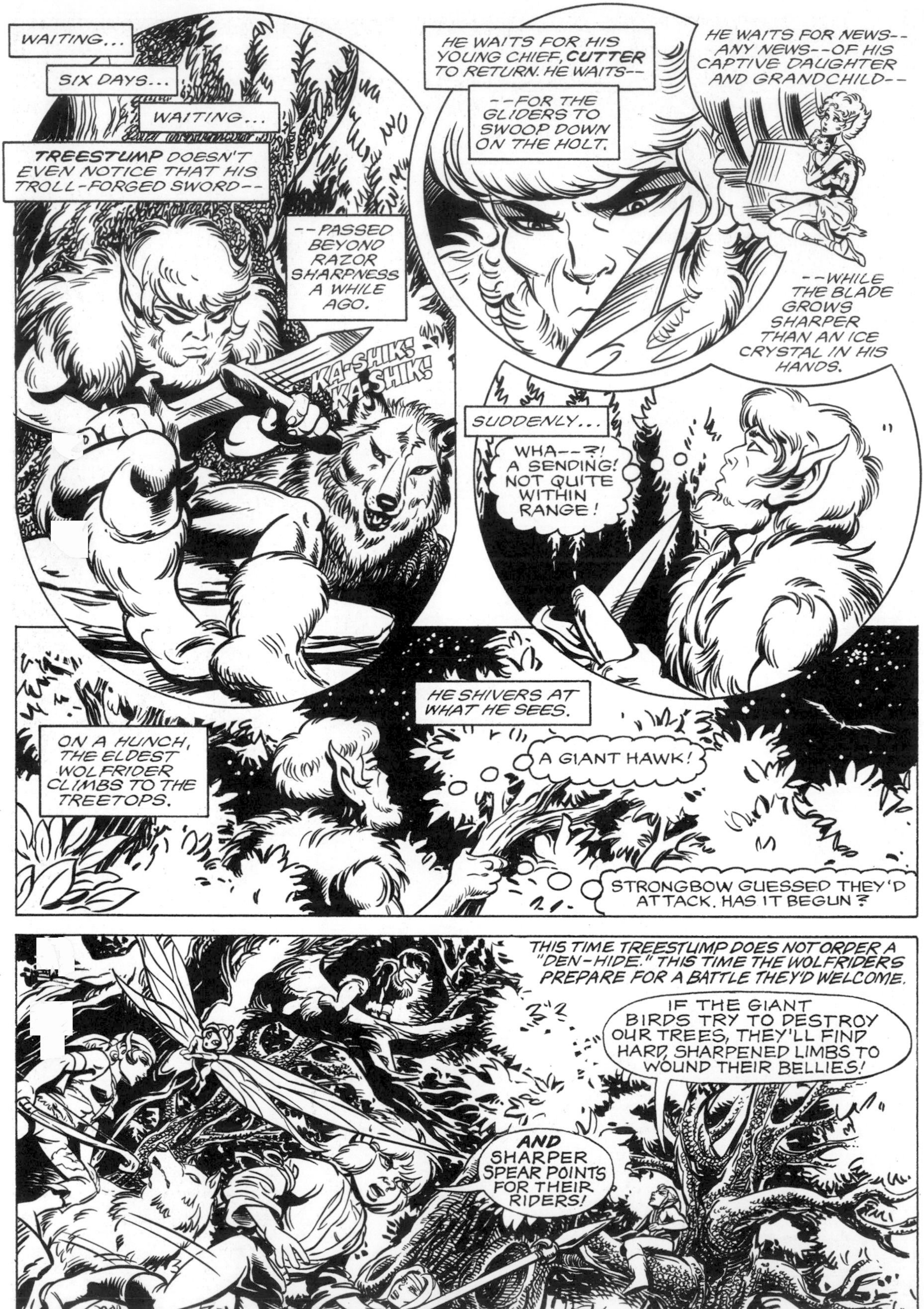
WAITING...
SIX DAYS...
WAITING...
TREESTUMP DOESN'T EVEN NOTICE THAT HIS TROLL-FORGED SWORD--
--PASSED BEYOND RAZOR SHARPNESS A WHILE AGO.
KA-SHIK! KA-SHIK!
HE WAITS FOR HIS YOUNG CHIEF, CUTTER TO RETURN. HE WAITS--
--FOR THE GLIDERS TO SWOOP DOWN ON THE HOLT.
HE WAITS FOR NEWS--ANY NEWS--OF HIS CAPTIVE DAUGHTER AND GRANDCHILD--
--WHILE THE BLADE GROWS SHARPER THAN AN ICE CRYSTAL IN HIS HANDS.
SUDDENLY...
WHA--?! A SENDING! NOT QUITE WITHIN RANGE!
ON A HUNCH, THE ELDEST WOLFRIDER CLIMBS TO THE TREETOPS.
HE SHIVERS AT WHAT HE SEES.
A GIANT HAWK!
STRONGBOW GUESSED THEY'D ATTACK. HAS IT BEGUN?
THIS TIME TREESTUMP DOES NOT ORDER A "DEN-HIDE." THIS TIME THE WOLFRIDERS PREPARE FOR A BATTLE THEY'D WELCOME.
IF THE GIANT BIRDS TRY TO DESTROY OUR TREES, THEY'LL FIND HARD, SHARPENED LIMBS TO WOUND THEIR BELLIES!
AND SHARPER SPEAR POINTS FOR THEIR RIDERS!

BUT...

--UMP! --STUMP...! TREESTUMP!

IT'S *SKYWISE*! *AROREE* RESCUED *SCOUTER*, *STRONGBOW* AND ME FROM HER OWN PEOPLE!

SHE'S *LEFT* THEM!

THE TRADE ALMOST WORKED--

--"PRESERVERS FOR *DEWSHINE* ONLY," THE GLIDERS SAID--

--BUT *DEWSHINE* WENT BACK INTO THE MOUNTAIN FOR *WINDKIN*!

WE COULDN'T REACH HER! SORRY!

AROREE DUMPED *STRONGBOW* AND *SCOUTER* SOMEWHERE BETWEEN HERE AND...

CURSE IT! OUT OF RANGE AGAIN!

AROREE, IF I'M *NOT* YOUR PRISONER, THEN YOU'VE *GOT* TO LET ME GO.

I SHOULD BE STANDING AT *CUTTER'S* SIDE WHEN HE TALKS TO THE HUMANS!

YOU LOVE HIM. *HE'LL NEVER* WANT FOR YOUR LOYALTY!

BUT I HAVE DEFIED MY LORD, *KILLED* ONE OF THE *EIGHT*! I HAVE NOTHING--

--NO FRIEND BUT *YOU*! I CANNOT BEAR THE FEAR! WITHOUT YOU, I AM *ALONE*!

HER HEART... BEATING LIKE A HUMMER'S WINGS...!

HIGH ONES! WHAT SHOULD I DO?

RELIEVED, AND YET MORE ANXIOUS THAN EVER, TREESTUMP GIVES THE STAR-GAZER'S MESSAGE TO THOSE IT AFFECTS MOST.

MOONSHADE!

CLEARBROOK!

YOUR MENFOLK ARE WELL. FAILED IN THEIR TASK... BUT THEY'RE WELL!

WE'RE BACK WHERE WE STARTED... NO WORSE AND... NO *BETTER!*

ALL WE HAVE GOING FOR US NOW IS *CUTTER'S* PLAN TO STIR UP THE HUMANS!

KA-SHIK! KA-SHIK!

KA-*

WHY?! ; *CHOKE!* - WHY WOULDN'T SHE ESCAPE WHEN SHE HAD THE CHANCE?! I DON'T UNDERSTAND!

YOU KNOW YOU DO! SHE COULDN'T DESERT WINNOKIN.

Y-YES! BUT *TIMMORN'S BLOOD!* YOU AND I'VE LOST LIFEMATES! ARE WE BOTH TO LOSE *DAUGHTERS* TOO?

WAITING...

WAITING...

SKYWISE'S NEWS, PASSED THROUGHOUT THE TRIBE, HAS GIVEN CUTTER'S FAMILY LITTLE REASSURANCE.

S-SAVAH! TIMMAIN...!

OHH... NO!

IT'S ANOTHER BAD DREAM, MOTHER.

NO...!

THE HEALER KNOWS WELL WHAT TO DO, BUT...

...SHE'LL CATCH YOU... SHE... SHE...

÷SIGH÷

UNFORTUNATELY, THE TRANQUILITY LEETAH CREATES CANNOT LAST.

THE CURSED VISIONS ALWAYS RETURN--

-- TO PLAGUE ALL WHO HAVE EVER LOCKED WILLS WITH THE "BLACK SNAKE"!

THESE VISIONS SHE, HERSELF, STILL SEES-- MIND-WOUNDS FROM THE ONE HEALING SHE REGRETS--

-- THAT SHE COULD NOT ACCOMPLISH!

HER OWN HANDS, **LEETAH** KNOWS, WOULD HAVE WON HAD THE BATTLE NOT BEEN WRENCHED FROM THEM.

BUT SHE HAS FEARED TO ERASE THE RESULTING DREAMS ENTIRELY--

--UNTIL SHE GRASPS THEIR FULL MEANING...

ARE THEY PUNISHMENTS, OR--

--PUZZLES? AND WOULD THE SOLUTIONS REVEAL THE WAY TO **WINNOWILL'S** UNDOING?

OR ARE THE NIGHT-MARES WARNINGS--

--FORESHADOWINGS OF THE PRICE THAT MUST BE PAID FOR FULL USE OF THE OLD POWERS?

HOW *SIMPLE*--IF WE WERE NOT WHAT WE ARE.

SINCE THE WAR FOR THE PALACE, *LEETAH* HAS WRESTLED WITH HERSELF...

WERE WE LIKE HUMANS, OUR MAGIC WOULD BE ASLEEP--WE'D HAVE NO POWERS ABLE TO *BE* ABUSED!

AND NO ABILITY TO REACH SHORE IN ONE PRODIGIOUS HOP!

THE FEAT, AS NATURAL TO *CUTTER* AS BREATHING, IS NOT CALCULATED TO IMPRESS.

BUT...

¡GASP!

¡WHEW!

IT'S LUCKY EVERY MOVE I MAKE SEEMS TO CONVINCE THEM MORE THAN EVER THAT I'M A "BIRD SPIRIT"!

THE HOAN G'TAY SHO *MUST* BELIEVE IN ME TOO-- MORE THAN IN THE GLIDERS!

BUT IF WE CONVINCE *NONNA'S* TRIBE THAT THE GLIDERS HAVE TRICKED THEM ALL ALONG, WHAT WILL KEEP THEM FROM DOUBTING *ME* TOO?

HMM...THAT COULD BE DANGEROUS!

IT'S *WINNOWILL* ALONE THAT WE MUST TURN THE HUMANS AGAINST.

IF THEY LOSE FAITH IN *ALL* "SPIRITS" THEN *I'M* AS GOOD AS COOKED--AND SO ARE *NONNA* AND *ADAR!*

SUDDENLY...AS IF TO UNDERSCORE *CUTTER'S* THOUGHTS...

RUMMA TUMMA TUM-TUM TUM TUM

〈DRUMS CALLING FOR-- GAMES?〉

〈NO! THEY PROMISE *BATTLE! REAL* FIGHTING! WHY? IN ALL MY SNOWS LIVING WITH THEM, I NEVER SAW MY PEOPLE SPILL ANOTHER TRIBE'S BLOOD!〉

〈IT IS BEST YOU WAIT HERE, HONORED ONE, UNTIL WE HAVE PREPARED THE *HOANG'TAY SHO* FOR YOUR COMING.〉

SHOULD I PRETEND I *KNOW* WHAT THE DRUMS MEAN?

NO. NO NEED. JUST STAY QUIET AND LOOK WISE. WISH I DIDN'T HAVE TO KEEP PLAYACTING FOR THESE GOOD TALL ONES.

BUT I WISH EVEN *MORE* THAT I KNEW WHAT THE HOANG'TAY SHO ARE SO WORKED UP ABOUT.

RUM TUM! RUM TUM!

DRUMMING LIKE THAT IS *NEVER* A GOOD SIGN--FROM *ANY* HUMAN CAMP!

SOON...

FOR FOURTEEN TURNS OF THE SEASONS, *NONNA* HAS DWELLED WITH HER MATE IN THE WOODS BEYOND "SUN-GOES-UP"--BEYOND THE VALLEY OF ENDLESS SLEEP.

BUT BEFORE *ADAR* CAME AND TOOK HER AWAY TO LIVE WITH HIS FAR-OFF TRIBE--

--*NONNA* WAS SYMBOL MAKER TO "THE FAVORED OF THOSE WHO DWELL ON HIGH"--

--AND THEY REMEMBER HER!

THE WAR DANCE CEASES...THE DRUMS FALL SILENT. AS HER BIRTH-TRIBE GATHERS AROUND HER IN GREETING, *NONNA* SEES YOUNG FACES THAT ARE NEW TO HER, WHILE SOME--

--BUT NOT ALL THE OLD ONES ARE GONE.

‹ MAY YOU SEE MANY MORE SNOWS, *KOHAHN*--CHIEF.›

‹ AS MANY AT LEAST AS *YOU* HAVE BEEN AWAY FROM US, *NONNA*.›

‹ WE HAD ALL BUT LOST HOPE OF SEEING YOU AGAIN.›

THE SIGHTS, SCENTS AND SOUNDS OF CHILDHOOD MEMORY MINGLE STRANGELY WITH IMPRESSIONS OF THE MOMENT AS *NONNA* PRESENTS THE GIFTS SHE HAS BROUGHT TO MEMBERS OF HER FAMILY.

‹ MY FATHER....›

‹ MAY WE ALWAYS BE CLOSE, THOUGH WE DWELL APART.›

‹ TROUBLE... ANGER IN THE AIR...WHY?›

SHORTLY, WHEN FORMAL GREETINGS ARE DONE...

‹ I-I BEG LEAVE TO SPEAK--AND TO HAVE THE HOAN G'TAY SHO HEAR ME AS THEY ONCE DID--›

‹ -- WHEN I WAS THEIR *SYMBOL MAKER*, PAINTER OF DREAMS.›

‹ ALTHOUGH I NOW LIVE FAR FROM BLUE MOUNTAIN, THE SPIRITS HAVE SOUGHT ME OUT AND THEY...›

‹ ...THEY HAVE... ASKED ME...TO...›

¡GASP!

‹ THAT BURNING SHAPE-- IT *FRIGHTENS* ME!›

‹ WHAT?! WHAT ARE YOU DOING?!›

‹WE PREPARE, SYMBOL MAKER, FOR BATTLE WITH *DEMONS!*›

‹THE BIRD SPIRITS HAVE SUMMONED US TO THEIR DEFENSE! WE ARE TO DESTROY THE *FALSE ONES!*›

‹IS THAT WHY *YOU* HAVE COME, *NONNA*-- TO USE YOUR PICTURE-MAGIC AGAINST THE DEMONS?›

‹DEMONS...?! FALSE ONES...?! WHAT DO YOU MEAN? THERE IS ONLY *ONE* EVIL SPIRIT AND I HAVE COME--›

‹--TO *WARN* YOU OF HER GREAT DECEPTION!›

‹THE HONORED ONES THEMSELVES WISH TO CAST HER FROM THEIR MIDST!›

‹IF YOU SPEAK OF THE DARK-ROBED MOTHER--THE BIRD SPIRIT WITH STARS FOR EYES AND A BABY AT HER BREAST, THEN THE *FALSE SPIRITS* HAVE MISLED YOU!›

‹--BUT A *DEMON* IN DISGUISE WOULD!›

‹MISLED...? HOW CAN THAT BE? MY GENTLE LITTLE MESSENGER WOULD NOT LIE TO ME--›

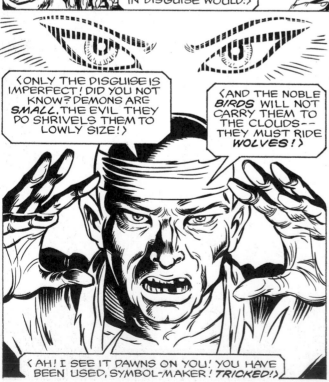

‹ONLY THE DISGUISE IS IMPERFECT! DID YOU NOT KNOW? DEMONS ARE *SMALL*. THE EVIL THEY DO SHRIVELS THEM TO LOWLY SIZE!›

‹AND THE NOBLE *BIRDS* WILL NOT CARRY THEM TO THE CLOUDS--THEY MUST RIDE *WOLVES!*›

‹AH! I SEE IT DAWNS ON YOU! YOU HAVE BEEN USED, SYMBOL-MAKER! *TRICKED!*›

‹THE DARK-ROBED ONE TOLD US TO BEWARE OF AN ATTACK BY WOLF-RIDING DEMONS--AND WE ARE SWORN TO *KILL THEM ON SIGHT!*›

AT THAT SAME MOMENT, WITHIN BLUE MOUNTAIN...

HERE! SHE WENT THROUGH *THIS* PASSAGE-WAY!

IT LEADS TO *TENSPAN'S HALL.* QUICKLY! WE MUST CATCH HER BEFORE SHE GOES FARTHER!

BUT...

AAAAGGH!

NOW WHAT?!

I'LL NOT FOLLOW TO FIND OUT!

IN THE NEXT INSTANT, *REEVOL'S* ANSWER BURSTS FROM THE TUNNEL, WRITHING IN "WRAPSTUFF".

⸳KAFF⸳ ⸳SPUTTER⸳

⸳GAG⸳ P-PRESERVERS!

THEY WILL ⸳COUGH⸳ OBEY *NONE* BUT THE WOLFRIDER CALLED *DEWSHINE!*

⸳COUGH COUGH⸳ SHE IS TOO WELL GUARDED! WE SHALL NEVER REACH HER!

WE *MUST* -- ELSE THE DISGRACE OF THE EIGHT IS COMPLETE!

AND IN A NOOK ABOVE THE POLISHED FLOOR OF *TENSPAN'S HALL...*

⸳PANT⸳ ⸳PANT⸳

THANK YOU, LITTLE FRIENDS!

MY SORE LEG MAKES IT HARD TO KEEP CLIMBING ⸳PANT⸳ -- NEED TO REST!

NASTY BAD FLYHIGH-THINGS GO 'WAY FOR AWHILE. SUNNYGOLD HIGHTHING MOSTLY SAFE.

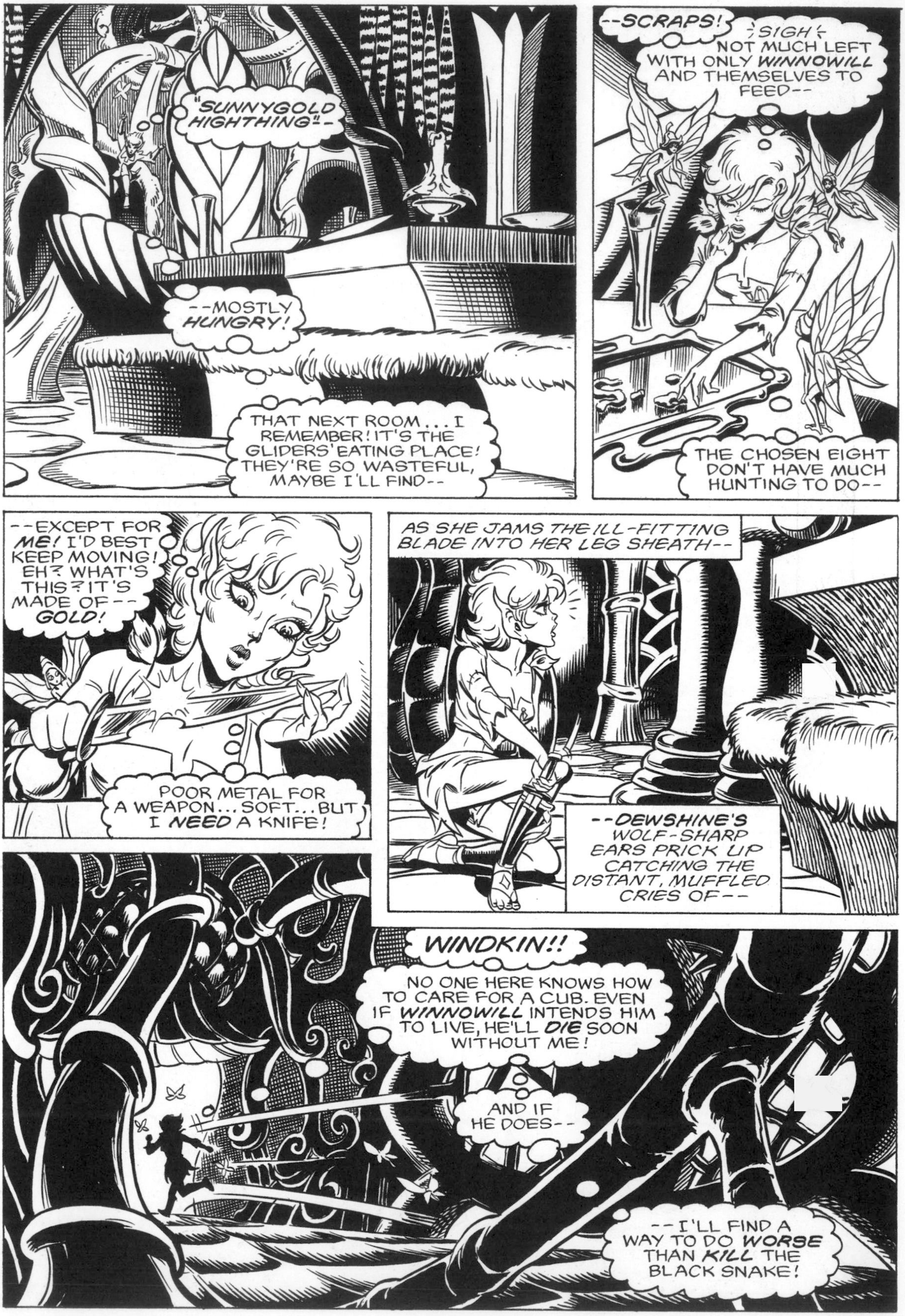
"SUNNYGOLD HIGHTHING"--
--MOSTLY HUNGRY!
THAT NEXT ROOM... I REMEMBER! IT'S THE GLIDERS' EATING PLACE! THEY'RE SO WASTEFUL, MAYBE I'LL FIND--
--SCRAPS!
SIGH
NOT MUCH LEFT WITH ONLY WINNOWILL AND THEMSELVES TO FEED--
THE CHOSEN EIGHT DON'T HAVE MUCH HUNTING TO DO--
--EXCEPT FOR ME! I'D BEST KEEP MOVING! EH? WHAT'S THIS? IT'S MADE OF--GOLD!
POOR METAL FOR A WEAPON... SOFT... BUT I NEED A KNIFE!
AS SHE JAMS THE ILL-FITTING BLADE INTO HER LEG SHEATH--
--DEWSHINE'S WOLF-SHARP EARS PRICK UP CATCHING THE DISTANT, MUFFLED CRIES OF--
WINDKIN!!
NO ONE HERE KNOWS HOW TO CARE FOR A CUB. EVEN IF WINNOWILL INTENDS HIM TO LIVE, HE'LL DIE SOON WITHOUT ME!
AND IF HE DOES--
--I'LL FIND A WAY TO DO WORSE THAN KILL THE BLACK SNAKE!

MEANWHILE...

SEVERAL TORTUOUSLY INTERCONNECTED HALLS AWAY, THE OBJECT OF *DEWSHINE'S* HATE REBUKES HER SEVEN FRUSTRATED GUARDS.

--SHAMEFUL! CLUMSY!

WAS *AROREE* SO VITAL TO YOUR NUMBER THAT YOU ARE *INEPT* WITHOUT HER?

NO OTHER EARS THAN THOSE OF *WINDKIN* AND THE EIGHT HEAR THE *"BLACK SNAKE'S"* CONTEMPTUOUS WORDS.

THE GREAT EGG, EVER SO SLOWLY, CONTINUES TO TURN. AROUND IT, THE SLEEPING GLIDERS CONTINUE TO DRIFT IN THEIR SILENT ORBITS.

LEAVE OFF YOUR SEARCH FOR THE SHE-DOG.

IF I SENSE HER NEAR, *I* SHALL STOP HER! GO *OUTSIDE!* TAKE *WEAPONS* TO THE HUMANS! *METAL* WEAPONS FOR KILLING WOLFRIDERS!

EAGER TO REGAIN THEIR LORD'S GOOD GRACES, THE GUARDS HASTEN AWAY, LEAVING--

--A VERY HUNGRY CHILD...!

SO HUNGRY... HE NO LONGER SHRINKS FROM MY TOUCH.

GOOD! IT IS TIME TO BEGIN!

AT ONCE, WARM, MAGICALLY-PRODUCED MILK FLOWS. *WINDKIN'S* WILL TO SURVIVE IS STRONGER THAN HIS NATURAL FEAR.

HE DOES NOT FEEL THE SUBTLE *INTRUSION*, THE SOFTLY SINISTER TOUCH THAT MEDDLES WITH THE VERY STUFF OF HIS BEING.

AND SO THE *CHANGE* BEGINS...

OUTSIDE, THE WORDS OF THE HOAN G'TAY SHO GROW MORE HEATED THAN THE CEREMONIAL FIRE...

‹NONNA LIES!›

‹FOOL! THE BIRD SPIRITS HAVE ALWAYS TALKED TO HER! SHE SPEAKS FOR THEM NOW! THE BLACK-ROBED ONE IS THE LIAR!›

‹SO IT IS!›

‹NO!›

‹STOP! PLEASE STOP SHOUTING AT EACH OTHER!›

BUT THE SYMBOL-MAKER'S PLEA ONLY ROUSES MORE VIOLENT CONFLICT.

‹WAIT! LISTEN! I KNOW NONNA'S MESSENGER! HE IS A GOOD SPIRIT!›

‹A DEMON, MASKED!›

NO! ADAR IS RIGHT!

‹BE QUIET, OLD MADMAN!›

‹WHY MUST THIS DIVIDE YOU? YOU KNOW THE SPIRITS! I KNOW THEM! I HAVE EVER TRIED, WITH MY POOR PAINTS, TO WORSHIP THEIR BEAUTY! WE KNOW THEM BY THEIR EYES, THEIR HANDS, THEIR GRACE!›

‹BUT ONLY THEY CAN KNOW WHICH ONE OF THEIR OWN KIND IS EVIL-- AND THIS THEY HAVE TOLD ME!›

AAIEEE!

SHUT YOUR MOUTH, WOMAN!

‹WE HEAR ONLY THE VOICE THAT COMES FROM BLUE MOUNTAIN!›

‹YOU LIE TO SET YOURSELVES ABOVE US! I DO NOT BELIEVE ANY SPIRIT EVER CAME TO YOU!›

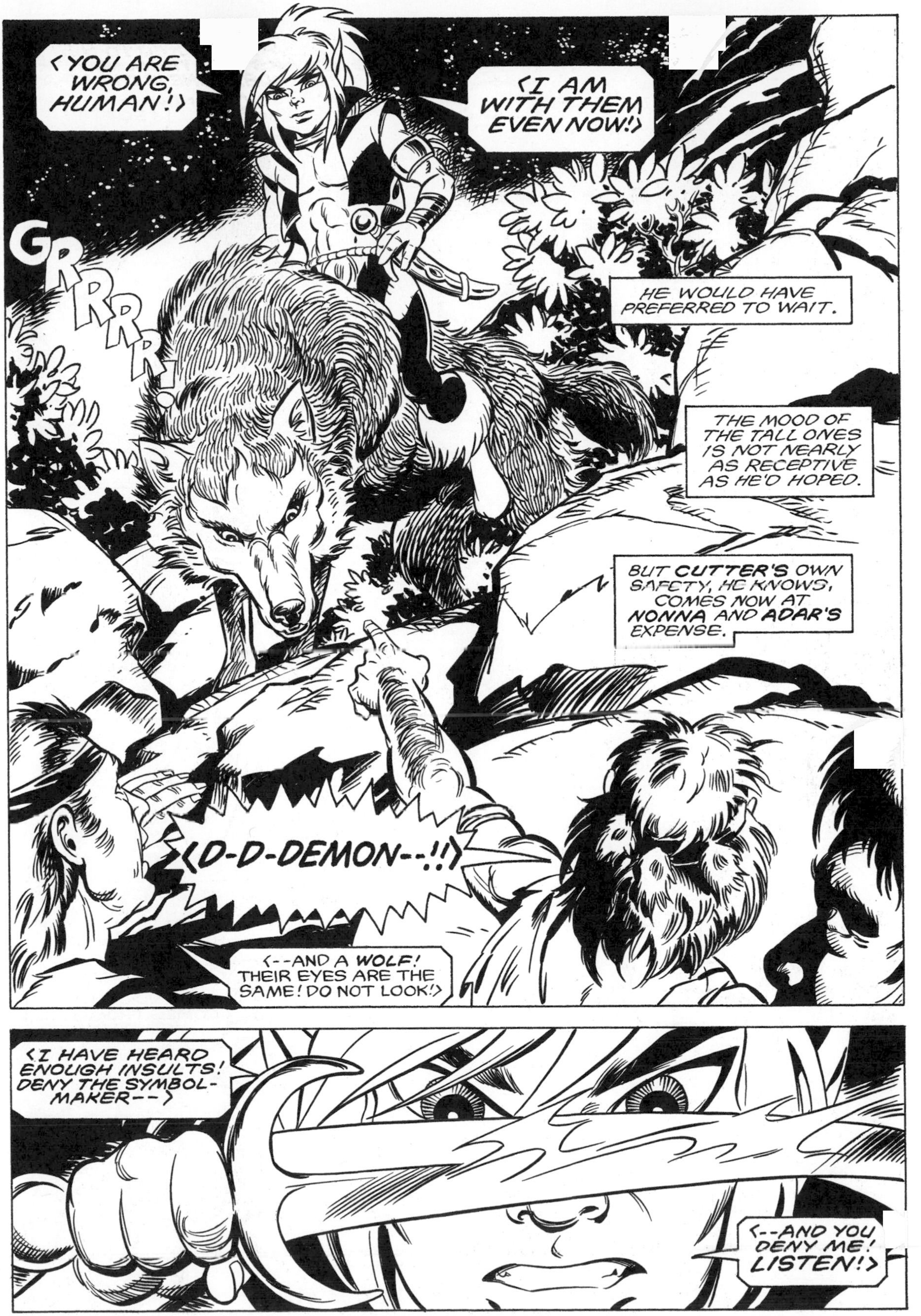
‹YOU ARE WRONG, HUMAN!›
‹I AM WITH THEM EVEN NOW!›
GRRRR!
HE WOULD HAVE PREFERRED TO WAIT.
THE MOOD OF THE TALL ONES IS NOT NEARLY AS RECEPTIVE AS HE'D HOPED.
BUT CUTTER'S OWN SAFETY, HE KNOWS, COMES NOW AT NONNA AND ADAR'S EXPENSE.
‹D-D-DEMON--!!›
‹--AND A WOLF! THEIR EYES ARE THE SAME! DO NOT LOOK!›
‹I HAVE HEARD ENOUGH INSULTS! DENY THE SYMBOL-MAKER--›
‹--AND YOU DENY ME! LISTEN!›

‹THE DARK-ROBED ONE IS AN ENEMY TO HER FELLOW SPIRITS! YOU MUST NOT FEED HER POWER WITH YOUR WORSHIP!›

‹SHE IS AN ENEMY TO *YOU*, MAKING SLAVES OF ALL WHO OFFER THEMSELVES UP TO HER!›

‹ALL THAT YOU HAVE BELIEVED OF HER 'TIL NOW--›

‹--IS UNTRUE!›

‹"AND THE LIE WHICH IS THE *TRUTH* SHALL BRING MORE PAIN THAN THE TRUTH WHICH IS A *LIE*...!"›

‹EXPLAIN, SHAMAN! WE ARE LOST!›

‹WHOSE WORDS ARE WE TO BELIEVE?›

‹I BELIEVE IN BLOOD!›

‹DEMON'S BLOOD!!›

LIE LIE LIE

KRAK!

WHHISSH!

KLUNK!

IMPRESSED, THE MAN HASTILY GATHERS UP HIS DEFTLY-DEFLECTED SPEAR.

THE HUMANS DO NOT KNOW WHAT TO THINK--

--AND NEITHER DOES *CUTTER* WHEN...

‹LOOK! MORE!›

‹WELL DONE, MY CHIEF!›

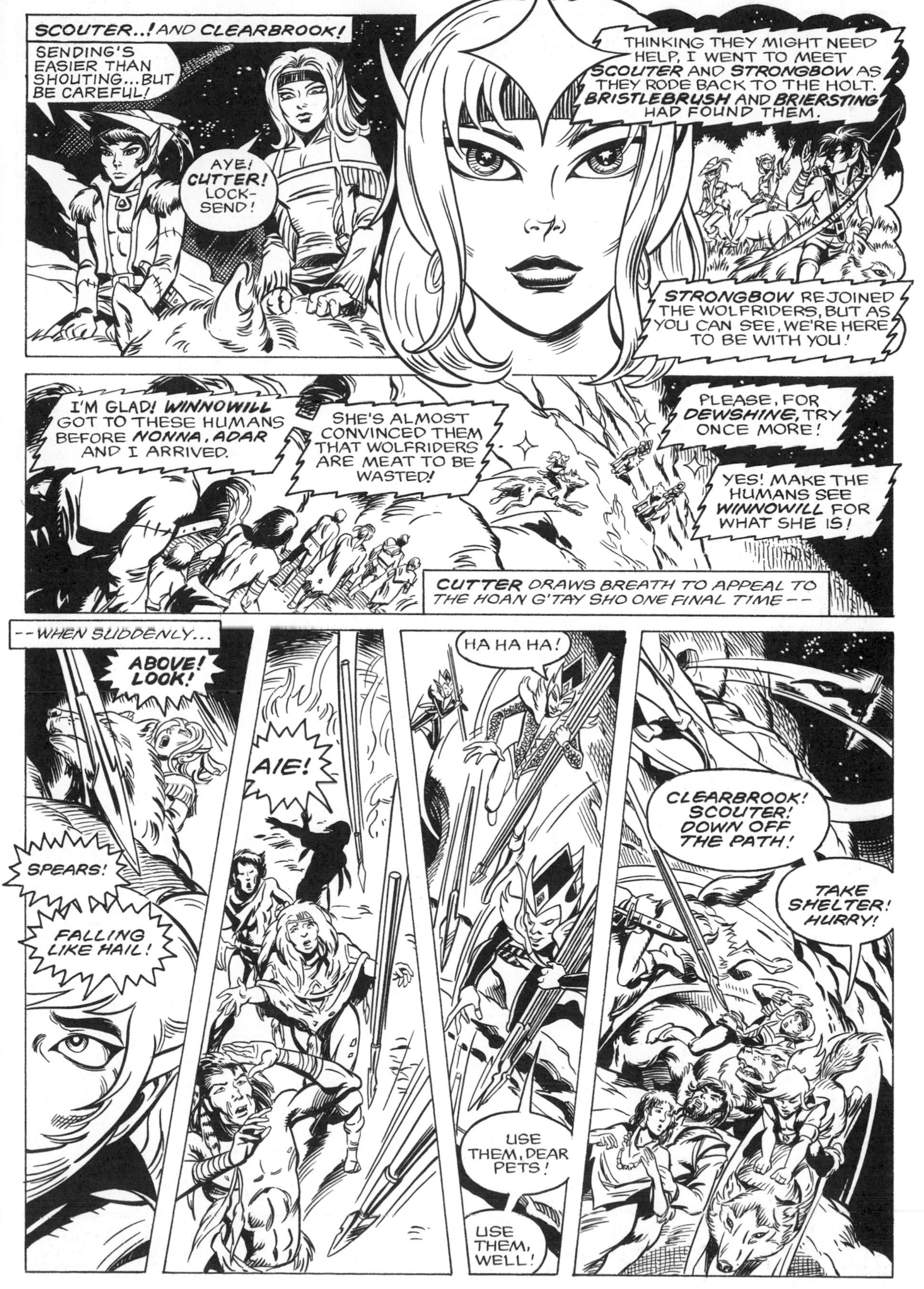

SCOUTER..! AND CLEARBROOK!
SENDING'S EASIER THAN SHOUTING... BUT BE CAREFUL!
AYE! CUTTER! LOCK-SEND!
THINKING THEY MIGHT NEED HELP, I WENT TO MEET SCOUTER AND STRONGBOW AS THEY RODE BACK TO THE HOLT. BRISTLEBRUSH AND BRIERSTING HAD FOUND THEM.
STRONGBOW REJOINED THE WOLFRIDERS, BUT AS YOU CAN SEE, WE'RE HERE TO BE WITH YOU!
I'M GLAD! WINNOWILL GOT TO THESE HUMANS BEFORE NONNA, ADAR AND I ARRIVED.
SHE'S ALMOST CONVINCED THEM THAT WOLFRIDERS ARE MEAT TO BE WASTED!
PLEASE, FOR DEWSHINE, TRY ONCE MORE!
YES! MAKE THE HUMANS SEE WINNOWILL FOR WHAT SHE IS!
CUTTER DRAWS BREATH TO APPEAL TO THE HOAN G'TAY SHO ONE FINAL TIME--
--WHEN SUDDENLY...
ABOVE! LOOK!
SPEARS!
FALLING LIKE HAIL!
AIE!
HA HA HA!
USE THEM, DEAR PETS!
USE THEM, WELL!
CLEARBROOK! SCOUTER! DOWN OFF THE PATH!
TAKE SHELTER! HURRY!

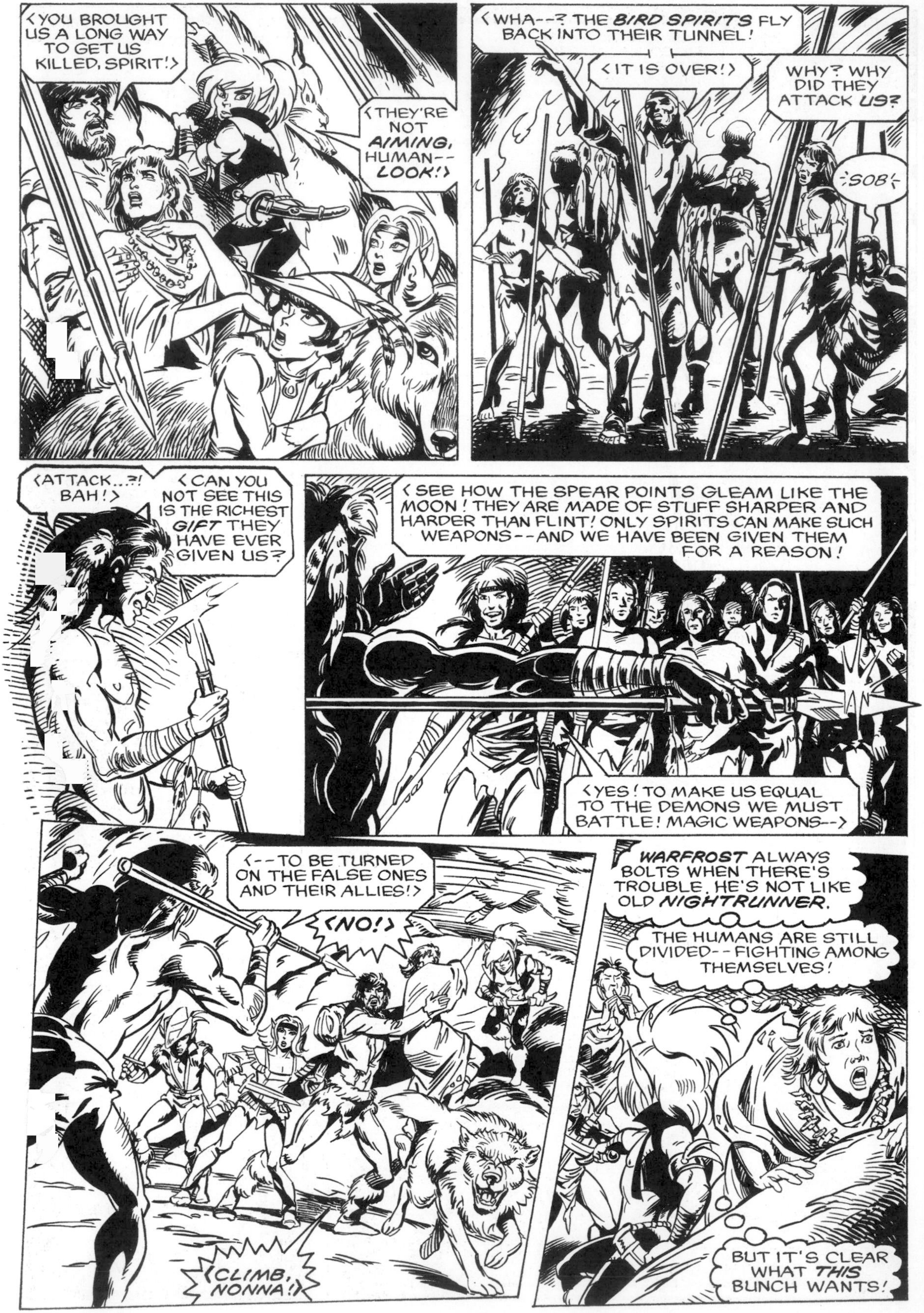
‹YOU BROUGHT US A LONG WAY TO GET US KILLED, SPIRIT!›
‹THEY'RE NOT AIMING, HUMAN-- LOOK!›
‹WHA--? THE BIRD SPIRITS FLY BACK INTO THEIR TUNNEL!
‹IT IS OVER!›
WHY? WHY DID THEY ATTACK US?
SOB
‹ATTACK...?! BAH!›
‹CAN YOU NOT SEE THIS IS THE RICHEST GIFT THEY HAVE EVER GIVEN US?
‹SEE HOW THE SPEAR POINTS GLEAM LIKE THE MOON! THEY ARE MADE OF STUFF SHARPER AND HARDER THAN FLINT! ONLY SPIRITS CAN MAKE SUCH WEAPONS--AND WE HAVE BEEN GIVEN THEM FOR A REASON!
‹YES! TO MAKE US EQUAL TO THE DEMONS WE MUST BATTLE! MAGIC WEAPONS--›
‹--TO BE TURNED ON THE FALSE ONES AND THEIR ALLIES!›
‹NO!›
‹CLIMB, NONNA!›
WARFROST ALWAYS BOLTS WHEN THERE'S TROUBLE. HE'S NOT LIKE OLD NIGHTRUNNER.
THE HUMANS ARE STILL DIVIDED--FIGHTING AMONG THEMSELVES!
BUT IT'S CLEAR WHAT THIS BUNCH WANTS!

AS THE HUMANS WHO HAVE SIDED WITH **WINNOWILL** TRY TO SURROUND THEM ON THE MOUNTAIN PATH, THE ELVES CREATE A FENCE OF FLASHING BRIGHT-METAL AROUND THEMSELVES, **NONNA** AND **ADAR**.

NO WAY TO JUMP ASIDE!

THEY'RE DRIVING US HIGHER!

SUDDENLY...

THE **TUNNEL!**

IT'S STILL OPEN!

HE MAKES A QUICK, MAD DECISION--

--THE ONLY ONE POSSIBLE!

RUN! RUN! FOR THE TUNNEL!

〈NONNA...! ADAR 'GO INSIDE THE MOUNTAIN!〉

WHEEEE

〈QUICKLY! BEFORE **DOOR** CLOSES THE ENTRANCE!〉

〈LOOK! TH-THE ROCK IS... **MOVING!**〉

'GASP'

〈DON'T STOP, HUMANS!〉

LAST TO SQUEEZE THROUGH THE SHRINKING APERTURE, **CUTTER** FEELS A SPEAR POINT JAB HIS BOOT.

'OW!' JUST IN TIME!

BLUE MOUNTAIN...

I NEVER THOUGHT WE'D SEE THIS SNAKE PIT AGAIN!

WHEN THIS IS ALL OVER, IF I STILL LIVE, I'M GOING TO HANG **SKYWISE** UP BY HIS **EARS** FOR GETTING US INTO THIS!

YOU ARE A PLEASURE-GIVER, MY LITTLE LOVE.

YOU KNOW ME BETTER THAN I KNOW MYSELF!

IF YOU DID KNOW YOUR-SELF YOU'D UNDERSTAND--

-- HOW WRONG IT WAS TO STEAL DEWSHINE'S CUB!

BUT--

--I HAVE KNOWN ONLY THE LAW--

--OF THE EIGHT. ANYTHING TO SERVE THEIR LORD.

HMPH! WINNOWILL!

DEAD OR ALIVE SHE'S A PAIN IN THE TAIL!

IF IT WERE SAFE TO KILL HER, I'D LIKE TO--

--TO....!

MORE....!

SOMETIME LATER...

; SIGH ; JOINING WITH YOU IS LIKE DREAM-BERRY WINE--

TOO MUCH DOESN'T FEEL LIKE ENOUGH. YOU'RE SO HUNGRY!

BUT EVEN THIS CAN'T FEED YOU LIKE THE SCROLL OF COLORS COULD!

SCROLL... OF COLORS?

THE SMALL QUESTION SETS **SKYWISE** TO RECOUNTING IN VIVID DETAIL THE STORY OF THE WOLFRIDERS' FIRST WAR-- THE BATTLE FOR THE PALACE OF THE HIGH ONES. LATER, AS THE TWO ELVES SOAR ABOVE THE CLOUDS, SKYWISE SPEAKS MOST REVERENTLY OF THE WONDERFUL SCROLL--THE THE MAGICAL CONTAINER OF ALL ELFIN HISTORY.

IT'S LIKE THE GLIDER'S GREAT STONE EGG--ONLY BETTER, **AROREE!** ONCE YOU SEE IT, YOU KNOW WHO YOU ARE-- WHO WE **ALL** ARE-- AND WHERE WE CAME FROM!

AFTER THAT, **NOTHING** CAN SCARE YOU!

YES...! I WANT TO SEE IT, **SKYWISE!** I WANT TO GO TO THE PALACE!

THE STARGAZER FEELS A SUDDEN TWINGE AS HE REALIZES--

--I-I'M SENDING HER AWAY! FOR **HER** SAKE! I DON'T HAVE TO. SHE'D DO ANYTHING I SAY. BUT...

HHHOOOWWW!

HEY!

DOWN THERE! **STARJUMPER!**

THE COUPLE PARTS AS NEAR TO BLUE MOUNTAIN AS **AROREE** DARES FLY.

FARE WELL, LITTLE LOVE!

REMEMBER--GO THE WAY YOU WENT ONCE BEFORE--

--BUT FLY **OVER** THE FROZEN MOUNTAINS THIS TIME! IT'S SAFE!

THE CASTLE WILL CALL YOU! GOOD LUCK!

THE WAY **AROREE** WENT ONCE BEFORE--

--IS THAT SAME PATH, REVERSED, ON WHICH **PETALWING** NOW GUIDES RAYEK TO BLUE MOUNTAIN.

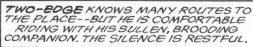

TWO-EDGE KNOWS MANY ROUTES TO THE PLACE--BUT HE IS COMFORTABLE RIDING WITH HIS SULLEN, BROODING COMPANION. THE SILENCE IS RESTFUL.

AND YET, THOUGH THE HALF-ELF UNDERSTANDS THE PLEASURE TO BE HAD IN NURSING OLD WOUNDS AND GRIEVANCES--

--RAYEK'S PARTICULAR CROW-TO-PLUCK BEWILDERS TWO-EDGE NO END.

KAHVI KEPT SOMETHING FROM ME!

THERE IS MORE TO THE CHILD'S DEATH THAN SHE TOLD.

NO ONE WANTS HIS OWN YOUNG!

WHY DOES HE GRIEVE OVER SUCH GOOD FORTUNE? HE MUST BE ...MAD...!

SORROWING FOR OTHERS IS A WASTE.

DEAD CHILDREN WISH TO BE FORGOTTEN--

--AS THE LIVE ONES ARE!

EH?!

SKREEAAAWWW!

NO!!

SHE HAS NOT FORGOTTEN!

I AM FOUND!

THE CELL!

THE GAMES! RATS! SPIDERS! PAIN! PAIN!!

TWO-EDGE!

EEYAAH!

TO BE CONTINUED...

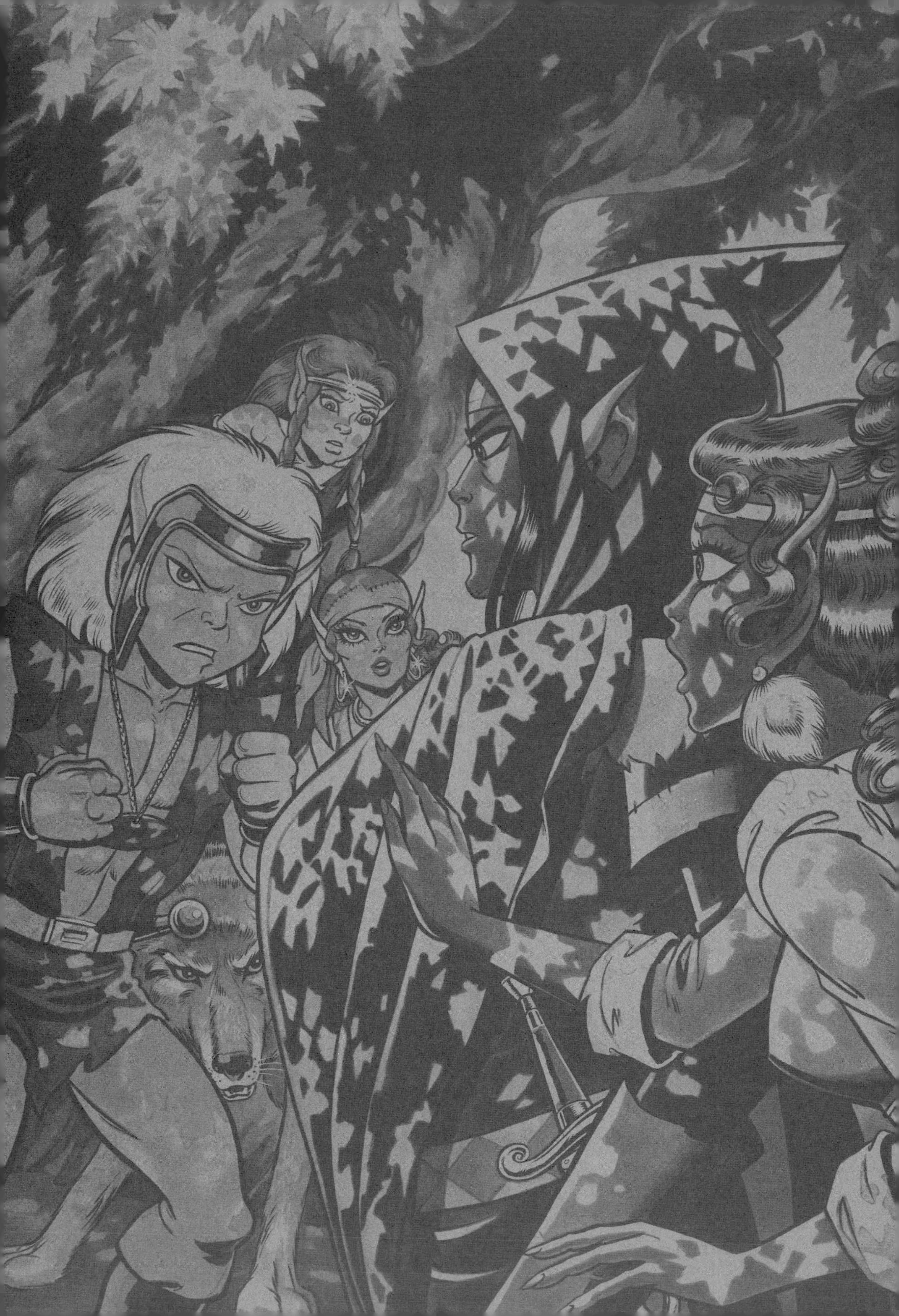

SIEGE AT BLUE MOUNTAIN

ARTIST / WRITER	CO-PLOT / EDITOR	PART	INKS	GUEST LETTERER
WENDY PINI	**RICHARD PINI**	**5**	**JOE STATON**	**CLEM ROBINS**

STRAINING AGAINST THE WIND AS HER WINGED MOUNT SUDDENLY DIVES TOWARD THE GROUND, **AROREE** DOES NOT ATTEMPT TO REGAIN HER NORTHWARD COURSE.

SHE KNOWS THE MOODS OF THE GIGANTIC BIRD OF PREY SHE RIDES.

THERE ARE LIMITS TO THE CONTROL HER BOND WITH HIM GIVES HER--PARTICULARLY WHEN HE IS VERY HUNGRY.

SHE HAS FLOWN HIM FAR AND FAST ON HER PILGRIMAGE TO THE PALACE OF THE HIGH ONES.

NOW IT IS TIME FOR HIM TO **FEED**.

LITTLETRILL...! WHAT HAVE YOU SPOTTED DOWN THERE?

AAWWK!

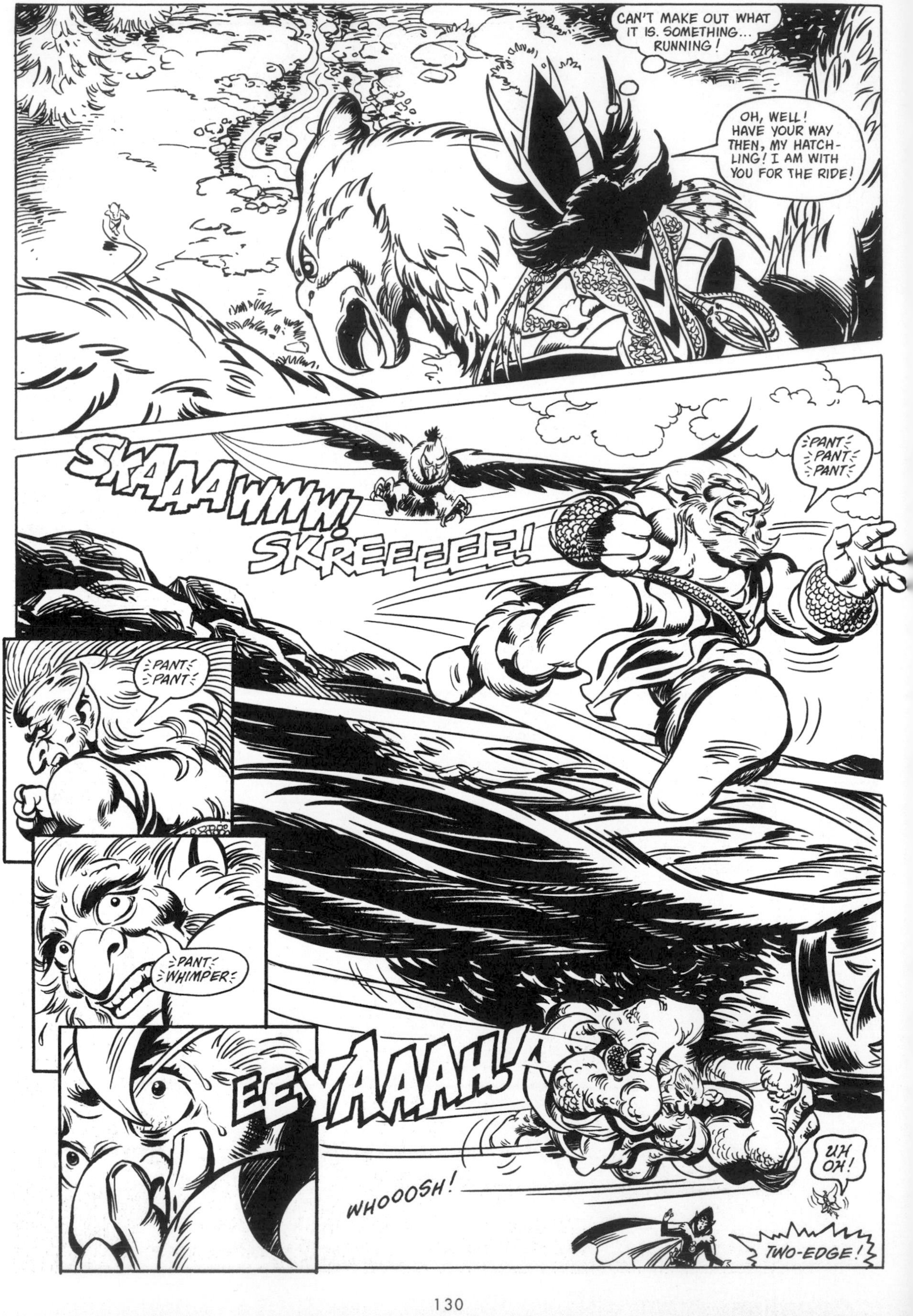
CAN'T MAKE OUT WHAT IT IS. SOMETHING... RUNNING!
OH, WELL! HAVE YOUR WAY THEN, MY HATCH-LING! I AM WITH YOU FOR THE RIDE!
SKAAAWWW!
SKREEEEEE!
PANT PANT PANT
PANT PANT
PANT WHIMPER
EEYAAAH!
WHOOOSH!
UH OH!
TWO-EDGE!

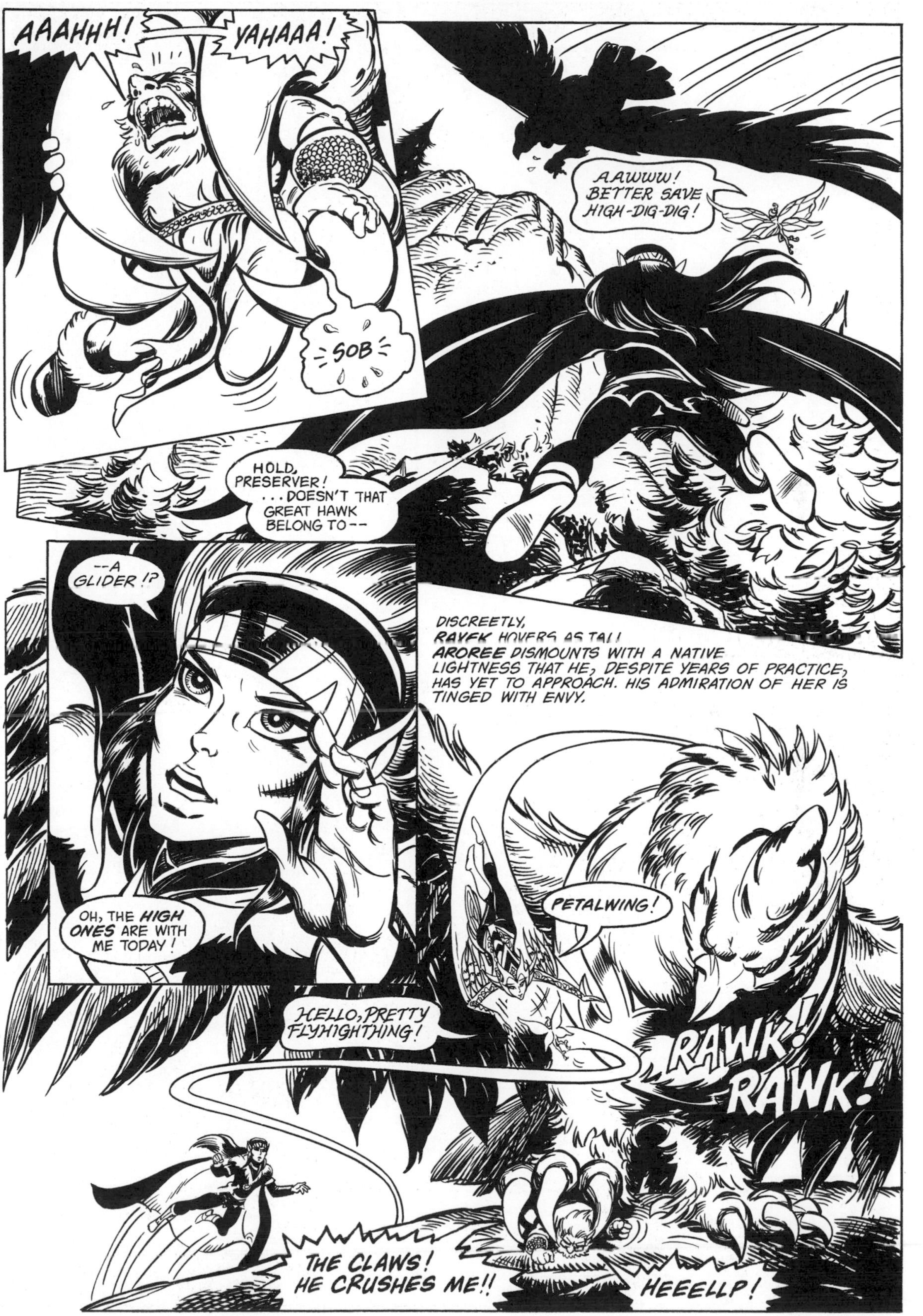

AAAHHH!
YAHAAA!
SOB
AAWWW! BETTER SAVE HIGH-DIG-DIG!
HOLD, PRESERVER! ...DOESN'T THAT GREAT HAWK BELONG TO--
--A GLIDER!?
OH, THE HIGH ONES ARE WITH ME TODAY!
DISCREETLY, RAYEK HOVERS AS TALL AROREE DISMOUNTS WITH A NATIVE LIGHTNESS THAT HE, DESPITE YEARS OF PRACTICE, HAS YET TO APPROACH. HIS ADMIRATION OF HER IS TINGED WITH ENVY.
PETALWING!
HELLO, PRETTY FLYHIGHTHING!
RAWK! RAWK!
THE CLAWS! HE CRUSHES ME!!
HEEELLP!

STARTLED, *AROREE* HESITATES...

THAT *VOICE*... THE VOICE FROM BEHIND THE WALLS...!

I HAVE HEARD IT OFTEN IN BLUE MOUNTAIN-- THOUGHT I DREAMED IT!

WHAT ARE YOU?

GNGH! NGUH!

HE CAN BETTER ANSWER YOU, MAIDEN, IF HE KNOWS HE WILL NOT BE DEVOURED!

:GASP!:

YOU...YOU *FLOATED* UP HERE?!

I AM PROUD TO SHARE THE GIFT, IF NOT THE GRACE, THAT YOU POSSESS.

MY NAME IS *RAYEK.*

AND IF ALL YOUR KIND ARE FORMED AS NOBLY AS YOURSELF--

--THEN THE *GLIDERS* ARE NEARER KIN TO THE *HIGH ONES* THAN I SUPPOSED!

I SHALL BE HONORED TO MEET THEM!

"*MEET THEM?!*"

OH, STRANGER...

YOU DO *NOT* WANT TO GO TO BLUE MOUNTAIN.

BABBLERS! TO THE ASH HEAP WITH YOUR *PLEASANTRIES!* NEXT YOU'LL BE *JOINING* ON TOP OF OLD TWO-EDGE'S PICKED BONES!

SILENTLY **RAYEK** STUDIES THE FEAR-HAUNTED GLIDER AS SHE COAXES THE GREAT BIRD'S CLAWS OPEN.

THEN...

BUT I AM *NOT* A STRANGER TO YOUR PEOPLE'S TROUBLES, MAIDEN.

I KNOW OF YOUR *LORD VOLL'S* DEATH--

--≋UHN≋ AND OF *WINNOWILL!*

THEN YOU KNOW WELL ENOUGH TO STAY FAR AWAY FROM HER!

AARK!

EVER SINCE *VOLL* DIED, *SHE* HAS BEEN OUR LORD. AND WE, EVEN TO THE LEAST GIFTED OF US, HAVE BEEN BOUND BY HER FOR A PURPOSE SOMEHOW CONNECTED TO THE GREAT *EGG.* OUR MAGIC IS HERS TO COMMAND--

"--AS *YOURS* WILL BE, DARK SKINNED ONE, IF YOU FALL INTO *WINNOWILL'S* HANDS!"

TSK! POOR CREATURE! SHE HAS THE RIGHT IDEA, FOCUSING THE COMBINED POWERS OF THE GLIDERS ON SOME TASK OR OTHER...BUT SHE GOES ABOUT IT IN THE WRONG WAY!

HER GOALS AND MINE, I SUSPECT, ARE SIMILAR. I'D SAY SHE HAS NEED OF ME.

NEED?! ALL WHO ANSWER HER NEEDS ARE CONSUMED! ALL WHO DENY HER NEEDS ARE CONDEMNED! GAMES! ONLY GAMES KEEP HER OFF BALANCE--AND ONLY WHEN THE RULES ARE YOURS, NOT HERS!

FOOL!

YOU DO NOT KNOW HOW TO PLAY!

I AM NOT HER TORMENTED SON. UNLIKE YOU, I HAVE NO CLINGING SHADOWS FROM THE PAST TO DARKEN MY VIEW OF WINNOWILL AS SHE IS.

THE MORE I HEAR, THE MORE I GATHER THAT SHE HAS LONG BEEN MISUNDERSTOOD--JUST AS I WAS IN THE SUN VILLAGE!

A BESTIAL SNARL, THEN FROTHING SPITTLE ERUPT FROM BETWEEN TWO-EDGE'S CLENCHED TEETH. WITH TEARS OF FRUSTRATION AND IMAGINED BETRAYAL, THE HALF-ELF TURNS AND STUMBLES DOWN THE ROCKY SLOPE.

WHAT DID YOU MEAN...HER SON?

LIES!! THE FUN WE WERE TO HAVE-- TRICKS WE WERE TO PLAY--

LIES!!

YOU MEANT TO COZY UP TO HER AT EVERY TURN! LYING ELF! ELF! ELF!! SHOULD'VE KNOWN, BUT YOU'LL SEE! HAHA! YOU'LL LEARN!

:SIGH: GONE RAVING AGAIN. BUT FORTUNATELY YOU ARE HERE!

I UNDERSTAND NONE OF THIS!

I MUST GO!

WAIT! YOUR GREAT HAWK FLIES FAST! TAKE ME TO BLUE MOUNTAIN--*NOW!*

NO!

THE EIGHT WOULD *KILL* ME!

BAH!

"ELVES DO NOT KILL...!" *CHOKE!*

ELVES DO NOT KILL *THEIR OWN!* YOU *MUST* DO AS I ASK--CAN YOU NOT SEE? THERE WILL *NEVER* BE A BETTER TIME!

WH-WHY SHOULD I RISK MY LIFE FOR *YOU?* I TRUST ONLY MY FRIEND, *SKYWISE.* HE PROMISED I'D SEE...I'D FIND... *SOMETHING*...IN THE PALACE OF THE *HIGH ONES!*

OH, YOU'LL FIND MUCH *MORE* THAN THAT PLAIN-SPOKEN WOLFRIDER COULD TELL YOU, MAIDEN!

IN SENDINGS THERE IS ONLY *TRUTH!*

HEED IT AND TRUST *ME!* I AM MASTER OF THE PALACE!

I INTEND TO SET THE GLIDERS FREE! WILL YOU HELP?

IT IS... SO HARD TO--

--RESIST ME...? DO NOT! TAKE MY USELESS DEER AND FEED IT TO YOUR HAWK! THEN FLY AT SWIFTEST SPEED!

THE SOONER I MEET *WINNOWILL* THE BETTER!

PERHAPS, *AROREE* THINKS, *THIS* ONE WHO LOOKS LIKE A BROTHER TO THE SOFT-HEARTED HEALER, *LEETAH,* WILL NOT SHRINK FROM DEALING PAIN FOR PAIN TO GAIN HIS ENDS.

PERHAPS HE IS, INDEED, A MATCH FOR THE BLACK SNAKE!

TWO DAYS LATER...

:MUNCH MUNCH:

WE'RE WASTING OUR TIME, *STARJUMPER.*

:SNIFF:

WHURF!

I HAVE A FEELING THE MOONS WILL RISE AND SET MANY TIMES--

--BEFORE *CUTTER* COMES DOWN FROM THE MOUNTAIN! IT'S A HARDER PLACE TO *LEAVE* THAN TO ENTER--AND GETTING IN IS HARD ENOUGH!

THOSE CURSED CARRION BIRDS WILL SHRED *ANYONE* WHO TRIES TO CLIMB UP TO THE AERIE.

GRRRR...

SCOUTER... CLEARBROOK... DEWSHINE... LITTLE WINDKIN... AND CUTTER, MY SOUL'S BROTHER--

--ALL INSIDE THAT *DUNG-HILL!* YOU WOLVES SAY THEY LIVE...

BUT ARE THEY HIDING...? FIGHTING...? CAPTURED...?

"IF ONLY I COULD KNOW!" SKYWISE GROWLS, REMEMBERING HOW HE FOUND HIS TRIBEMATES' MOUNTS PROWLING IN THE TALL SHRUBBERY AT THE FOOT OF THE MOUNTAIN.

IT WAS AGONY TO RESIST THE TEMPTATION TO SEND, BUT *SKYWISE* DARED NOT RISK HIS MENTAL CALL BEING DETECTED BY *WINNOWILL*--FOR THEN SHE WOULD KNOW--

--IF SHE DID NOT ALREADY, THAT *MORE* WOLFRIDERS HAD SECRETLY ENTERED HER STRONGHOLD.

SO *SKYWISE* WAITED, LISTENING TO THE QUARRELS OF THE DIVIDED HOAN G'TAY SHO. SOME OF THEM, IT *SEEMED,* HAD BELIEVED *CUTTER* AND *NONNA'S* WARNING ABOUT *WINNOWILL*--WHILE OTHERS--

--HAD DEFINITELY NOT BELIEVED!

RUM TUM! RUM TUM! RUMMA-TUMMA TUM!

THERE GO THE DRUMS AGAIN...*SIGH!* ANGRY HUMANS ARE ALL WE NEED NOW!

COME ON, *STARJUMPER.* BACK TO THE HOLT. WE'LL TELL THE OTHERS WHAT'S HAPPENED--

"--AND HOPE THAT, UNTIL WE CAN ALL COME AND HELP, *CUTTER* WILL SOMEHOW KEEP THINGS IN HAND."

THUD!

PSSST!

IT'S SAFE. COME ON.

⟨*NONNA*, THIS PLACE IS NOTHING LIKE YOUR TRIBE SAID IT WAS!⟩

⟨THE OLD SONGS AND STORIES YOU TAUGHT ME--⟩

⟨--DO NOT TELL OF THINGS AS THEY ARE! OH, *ADAR*, MY HEART HURTS!⟩

⟨WHERE IS THE *MUSIC?* WHERE ARE THE *CLOUDS* LINING SOFT NESTS MADE OF SUNLIGHT?⟩

⟨HUSH, HUMANS! THE *EIGHT* HAVE HUNTERS' EARS!⟩

IT HAS NOT BEEN DIFFICULT FOR *CUTTER* AND HIS ODDLY ASSORTED BAND TO SLIP UNDISCOVERED DOWN THE DARK, ECHOING PASSAGES WITHIN BLUE MOUNTAIN. ALTHOUGH CONSTANTLY ON THE ALERT FOR A SURPRISE ATTACK, THEY HAVE SEEN NO MOVEMENT, HEARD NO SOUND SAVE THE SETTLING OF ANCIENT ROCK AND THE MINDLESS DRIP OF SEEPING WATER.

NOW AND THEN A FAINT, FAMILIAR SCENT TEASES...

DEWSHINE CAME THIS WAY-- BUT WHEN? HER TRAIL CROSSES AND RECROSSES ITSELF!

POOR HUMANS. THEY'RE SCARED-- AND DISAPPOINTED.

AND WHY NOT? WONDERFUL AS IT IS, THE PALACE OF THE *HIGH ONES* WASN'T AS MY MIND PICTURED IT, EITHER. ARE ALL LEGENDS JUST WIND?

RUMBLING BELLIES ACHE FOR FOOD THAT HAS PROVED, SO FAR, UNOBTAINABLE. BUT AS FOR DRINK...

CUTTER, CLEARBROOK AND SCOUTER REMEMBER FROM THREE YEARS PAST A FATEFUL WOLFRIDER COUNCIL HELD IN A PLACE WHERE FRESH WATER FLOWED.

MEMORY AND NEED GUIDE THE SEARCH PARTY TO THAT RESTFUL GROTTO NOW.

⟨HUNH! *HERE* IS A WONDER!⟩

⟨A--A SACRED SPRING!⟩

HERE, TOO, *DEWSHINE'S* SCENT LINGERS. HERE, TOO, SHE SLAKED HER THIRST AND THEN RAN ON--IN PURSUIT? OR PURSUED?

SHORTLY...

THOUGH SHE HAS UNDERSTOOD PRECIOUS LITTLE OF *CUTTER'S* EXPLANATIONS, *NONNA* KNOWS THAT AN INFANT "SPIRIT" HAS BEEN ABDUCTED--

--AND THAT *SCOUTER* IS THE FATHER.

⟨I KNOW, LITTLE SPIRIT. I MISS *MY* CHILDREN, TOO!⟩

HUH?!

〈D-DON'T! PLEASE! PITY IS NO GOOD! HAVE TO--〉

SUDDENLY THE YOUNG WOLFRIDER STANDS AND TILTS BACK HIS HEAD...

NO!

BEFORE THE HIGH ONES' COMING THERE WERE WOLVES... AND BEFORE "SENDING" THERE WAS--

--HOWLING--COMMUNICATION PERFECT IN ITS SIMPLICITY!

BEAKS AND CLAWS! WHAT--?

AH, IT IS JUST THE SHE-DOG WAILING FOR HER WHELP.

RIGHT.

PAY IT NO MIND.

THE MERE CHANGE OF PITCH OR COLORATION OF TONE--

--SPEAKS VOLUMES TO THE RIGHT EARS!

SCOUTER! HERE!

TO THE STORM AND THE RAIN WITH THE CATERWAULING WOLFRIDER!

ONE HOWL! IT'S ALL I NEED. I KNOW WHERE HE IS. JUST HAVE TO GET PAST... THEM!

YES! I AM TIRED OF CHASING HER!

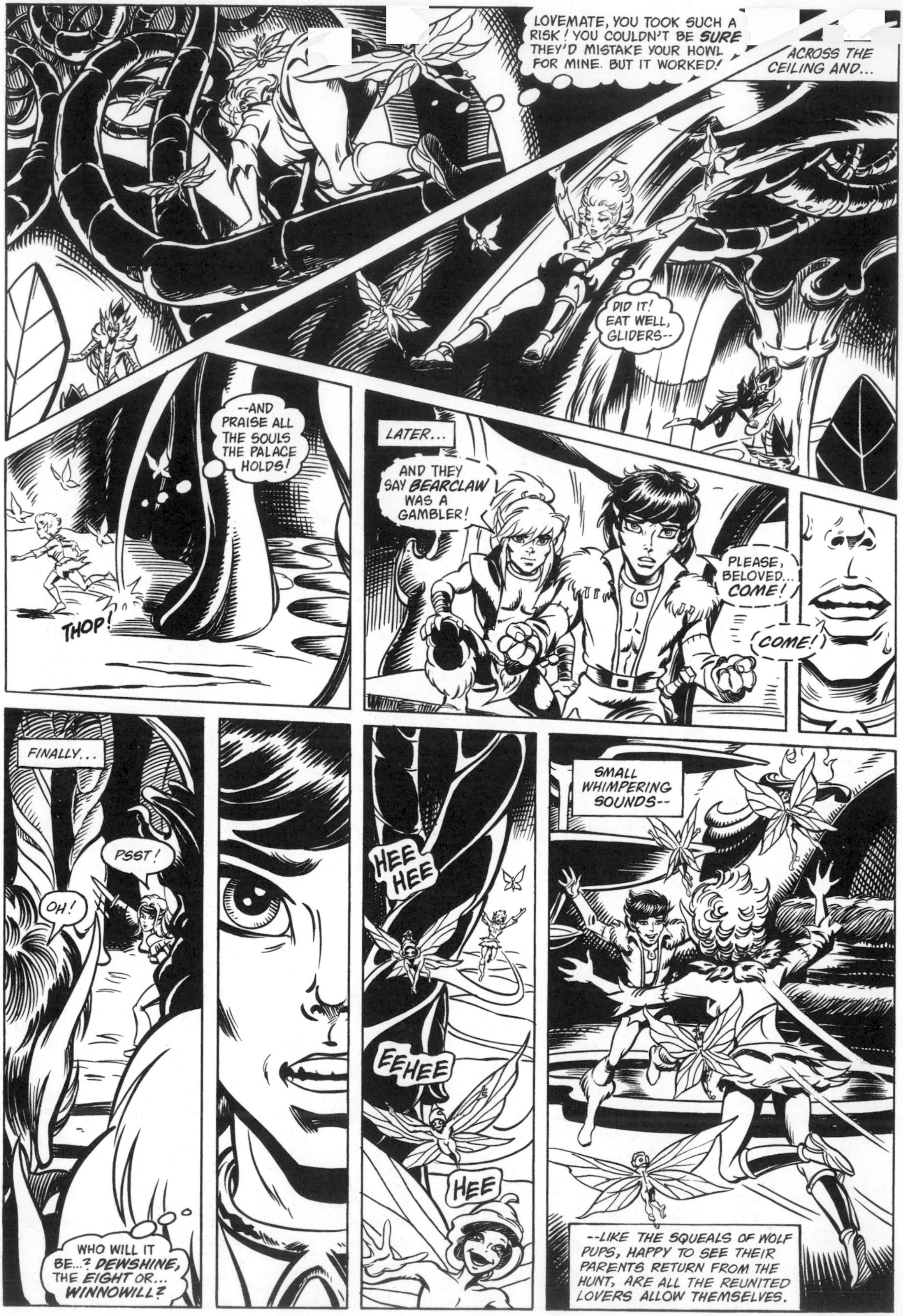

LOVEMATE, YOU TOOK SUCH A RISK! YOU COULDN'T BE SURE THEY'D MISTAKE YOUR HOWL FOR MINE. BUT IT WORKED!
ACROSS THE CEILING AND...
DID IT! EAT WELL, GLIDERS--
--AND PRAISE ALL THE SOULS THE PALACE HOLDS!
THOP!
LATER...
AND THEY SAY BEARCLAW WAS A GAMBLER!
PLEASE, BELOVED... COME!
COME!
FINALLY...
PSST!
OH!
WHO WILL IT BE...? DEWSHINE, THE EIGHT OR... WINNOWILL?
HEE HEE
EEHEE
HEE
SMALL WHIMPERING SOUNDS--
--LIKE THE SQUEALS OF WOLF PUPS, HAPPY TO SEE THEIR PARENTS RETURN FROM THE HUNT, ARE ALL THE REUNITED LOVERS ALLOW THEMSELVES.

OH, MY CUBS...!

YOUR LITTLE RIBS...! THEY *STARVED* YOU!

WE'LL MAKE THEM PAY!

THE SWEET, ELFIN LANGUAGE IS BEYOND *NONNA* AND *ADAR'S* KEN, BUT THE TEARS ARE ALL TOO EASILY UNDERSTOOD.

(ADAR--)

(--WHERE IS THEIR BABY?)

W-WINDKIN...?

SHE HAS HIM...ALWAYS! ...CARRIES HIM ABOUT LIKE A *DOLL!*

I THINK SHE'S DOWN BELOW IN HER DEN, NOW... I'M AFRAID ≷SOB≷ I-I'M AFRAID--

--SHE'LL *CHANGE* OUR CUB!

⟨WHY DO YOU LOOK AT *ME*, SPIRIT?⟩

⟨WHAT DO YOU THINK OF THIS PLACE, *ADAR?*⟩

⟨IT IS *FOUL!* AND SO ARE THE SPIRITS WHO MADE IT!⟩

⟨THERE ARE HUMAN SLAVES HERE, REMEMBER?⟩

⟨WANT TO DO SOMETHING ABOUT IT...?⟩

QUICKLY, WHEN THEY HAVE LEARNED THE *WHEREABOUTS* OF THE EIGHT FROM *DEWSHINE...*

⟨ALL THIS *DARK*--ALL THIS *SICKNESS* BECAUSE OF THIS--THIS BLACK-ROBED ONE?⟩

⟨WHY DO WE NOT *KILL* HER?⟩

UH...

⟨KILLING SPIRITS IS VERY BAD MAGIC FOR HUMANS-- *BELIEVE* ME!⟩

⟨IT IS AS I SAID: WE MUST BREAK HER *POWER!*⟩

"(AND TO DO THAT,)" CUTTER WHISPERS IN THE DIFFICULT HUMAN TONGUE, "(WE MUST FIRST GET RID OF HER WARRIORS!)"

(THERE THEY ARE...ALL TOGETHER... *FEEDING!*)

HEE HEE!

(GOOD! I'LL--)

(--PUT AWAY THAT SPEAR! WE MUST TRICK THEM --CATCH THEM OFF GUARD, THEN *SNARE* THEM IN OUR LITTLE WINGED FRIENDS' WEBS!)

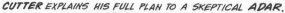

CUTTER EXPLAINS HIS FULL PLAN TO A SKEPTICAL *ADAR*.

(HMM...YOU KNOW, SPIRIT, YOUR FIRST IDEA, TO TALK TO *NONNA'S* TRIBE--

(--DID NOT GO SO WELL. ARE YOU *SURE* ABOUT THIS?)

(I AM SURE I CAN TRUST *YOU* TO DO YOUR BEST! NOT EVEN SPIRITS ARE PERFECT. ASK YOUR CHIEF, *OLBAR*, SOMETIME. HE'LL TELL YOU.)

(AND *ADAR*... MY NAME IS--) CUTTER. (CAN YOU SAY IT?)

:GRFL PLTZ:

SHORTLY...

WHAT IS *THIS?!*

ONE OF OUR LORD'S *PETS* HAS GOTTEN OUT OF ITS CAGE!

NONSENSE! *SHE* WOULD NEVER PERMIT IT! SHE HAS *SENT* HIM TO US.

OF COURSE! *WINNOWILL* HAS REALIZED THAT SHE HAS BEEN *NEGLECTING* US OF LATE.

:HEH-HEH: THOSE WHO SERVE MUST SOMETIMES *BE* SERVED!

THE LITTLE SPIRIT WITH THE TONGUE-TANGLING NAME SAID THIS SOUR JUICE WILL MAKE THESE BIRD-RIDERS DROWSY.

THEY SEEM TO LIKE IT WELL ENOUGH!

SO, HUMAN...HAS OUR LORD WHISPERED HER *SECRETS* TO YOU? WHAT OF THE *EGG?* WHEN WILL SHE AWAKEN THE SLEEPERS?

UUHH...

HMMM...A QUIET ONE! HE KNOWS NOT EVEN *ONE* OF OUR WORDS.

STRANGE...

DESPITE HIS VAGUE MISTRUST, *KUREEL* EATS AND DRINKS AS ZESTFULLY AS THE REST OF HIS COMPANIONS UNTIL...

GOOD FOR *ADAR!* THEY'RE STUFFED FULL AND MUZZY WITH WINE!

FLYHIGHTHINGS WOBBLE-WOBBLE?!

HEE HEE

HEE HEE

THE TINY *PRESERVERS* KNOW WHAT IS WANTED OF THEM--AND AT *CUTTER'S* SIGN--

HEE HEE HEE

HEE HEE

HEE

--THEY GLEEFULLY HURL THEM- SELVES INTO THEIR TASK!

AAAGK!!!

MY EYES!

OUT OF WAY, *BIGTHING!*

AAH!

PRESERVERS! BLINDING ME!

MY ARMS! THEY WILL WRAP US UP ≥UNH≤ MAKE US SLEEP!

MY LORD! MY LORD, HELP US!! IT IS THE *WOLFRIDER!*

SHE HAS SET HER *PRESERVERS* ON US! COME! DESTROY THEM!

NNG!

SPOOT!

HEE HEE HEE

HEE HEE

143

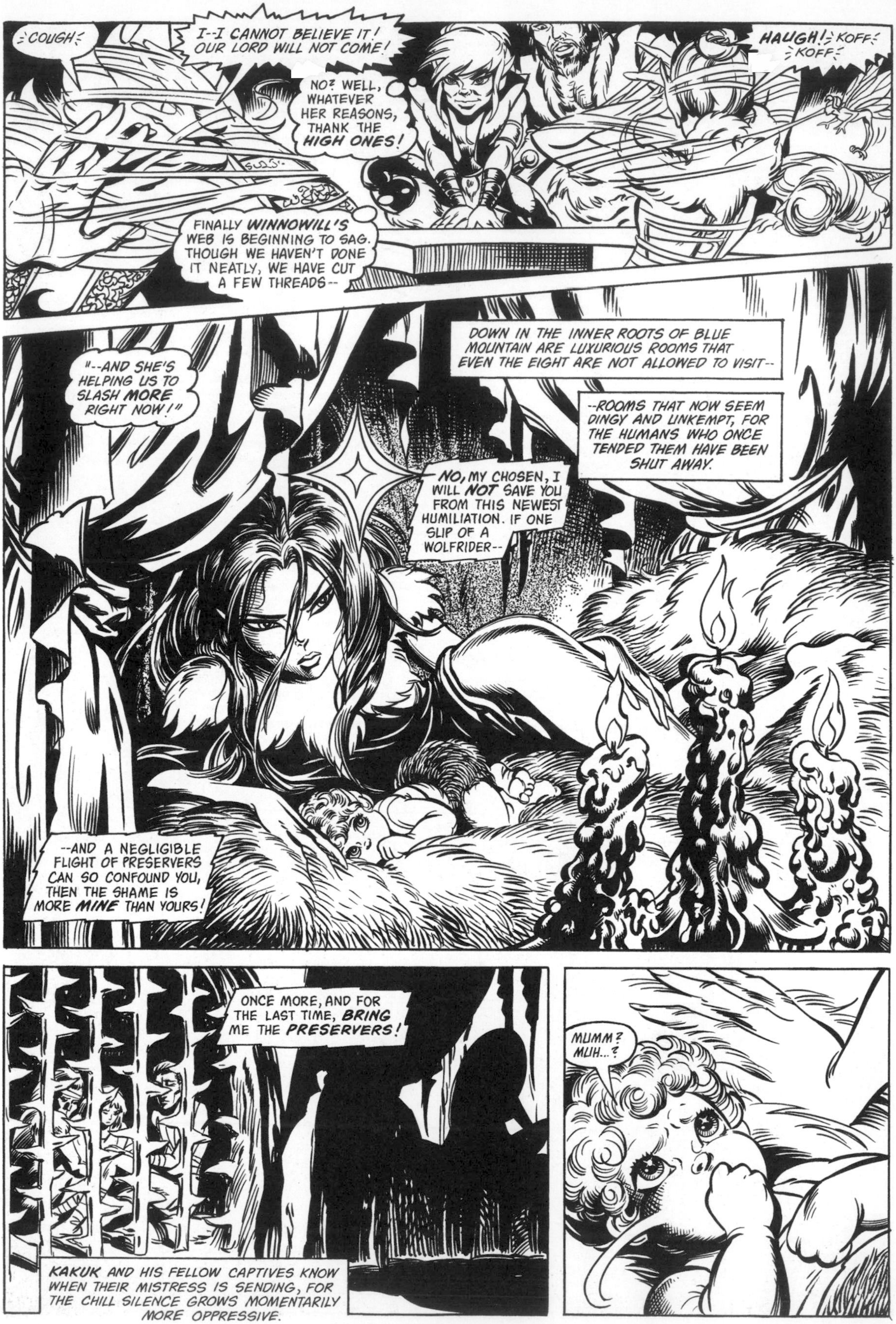
COUGH
I--I CANNOT BELIEVE IT! OUR LORD WILL NOT COME!
NO? WELL, WHATEVER HER REASONS, THANK THE HIGH ONES!
HAUGH! KOFF KOFF
FINALLY WINNOWILL'S WEB IS BEGINNING TO SAG. THOUGH WE HAVEN'T DONE IT NEATLY, WE HAVE CUT A FEW THREADS--
DOWN IN THE INNER ROOTS OF BLUE MOUNTAIN ARE LUXURIOUS ROOMS THAT EVEN THE EIGHT ARE NOT ALLOWED TO VISIT--
"--AND SHE'S HELPING US TO SLASH MORE RIGHT NOW!"
--ROOMS THAT NOW SEEM DINGY AND UNKEMPT, FOR THE HUMANS WHO ONCE TENDED THEM HAVE BEEN SHUT AWAY.
NO, MY CHOSEN, I WILL NOT SAVE YOU FROM THIS NEWEST HUMILIATION. IF ONE SLIP OF A WOLFRIDER--
--AND A NEGLIGIBLE FLIGHT OF PRESERVERS CAN SO CONFOUND YOU, THEN THE SHAME IS MORE MINE THAN YOURS!
ONCE MORE, AND FOR THE LAST TIME, BRING ME THE PRESERVERS!
KAKUK AND HIS FELLOW CAPTIVES KNOW WHEN THEIR MISTRESS IS SENDING, FOR THE CHILL SILENCE GROWS MOMENTARILY MORE OPPRESSIVE.
MUMM? MUH...?

MEANWHILE...

UNH!

WHOP!

‹LAST TWO!›

KLUD!

UUGH!

AAH!

WRAPSTUFF ALL FINISHED!

‹THESE BIRD RIDERS MUST BE MADE OF *FEATHERS!* THEY ARE LIGHTER THAN *YOU,* LITTLE SPIRIT!›

‹NO NEED TO WHISPER NOW. INSIDE THESE COCOONS THEY CANNOT SEE OR HEAR OR CRY OUT. THEY DO NOT KNOW YOU AND I ARE BEHIND THIS!›

‹BESIDES--›

--THERE IS MUCH ROCK BETWEEN US AND *WINNOWILL.* AS FAR AS SHE KNOWS, *WE* ARE NOT EVEN HERE!›

A SHORT WHILE LATER *ADAR* STUFFS THE LAST OF THE COCOONS INTO ONE OF SEVEN SEPARATE HIDING PLACES THAT HE AND *CUTTER* HAVE CHOSEN.

‹BUT THE BLACK-ROBED ONE STILL HAS THE BABY SPIRIT! SHE MAY HARM IT IF WE TRY TO DO *THIS* TO HER.›

‹MAYBE. BUT I HAVE FOUGHT HER BEFORE. I THINK SHE WOULD RATHER KILL *ME*--

‹--THAN HURT THE CHILD. IF I CAN KEEP HER BUSY--›

‹--THEN *MY* THREE WARRIORS MIGHT HAVE A CHANCE TO GRAB THE BABY AND RUN. IT WON'T BE EASY. BUT *WINNOWILL CAN* BE CAUGHT BY SURPRISE!›

THE SURPRISE WOULD, IN FACT, BE *CUTTER'S*, WERE HE PRIVY TO THE ONE-SIDED CONVERSATION TAKING PLACE IN HIS GREAT ENEMY'S CHAMBER.

SHE WHO BORE YOU IS MAKING AS MUCH TROUBLE AS SHE CAN.

INDEED, MUCH OF YOUR BRAVERY COMES FROM *DEWSHINE.*

BUT THIS... THE FLOATING ...IS YOUR TRUE SIRE'S GIFT TO YOU.

WERE YOU FULLY A WOLFRIDER AND NOT PARTLY THE PRODUCT OF *TYLDAK'S* WHOLESOME SEED--

--YOU WOULD NOT HAVE SURVIVED THE WORK I HAVE DONE ON YOU.

BUT MORE THAN THE TWO WHO JOINED TO GIVE YOU LIFE--

--*I* HAVE GIVEN YOU *TIME.* ALL TIME. YOU HAVE TAKEN MY MILK...AND I HAVE CLEANSED THE DEADLY WOLF BLOOD FROM YOUR VEINS.

YOU WILL LIVE *FOREVER* AND SEE THE FULFILLMENT OF A WISH I WAS FORCED TO SET ASIDE--

--BECAUSE MY POOR, CONSCIENCE-RIDDEN *VOLL* COULD NOT SHARE IT.

SO QUIET!

IF ONLY YOU WOULD LAUGH WITH JOY!

YOU ARE *PURE ELF* NOW--

--PURE...! N-NO!

WINNOWILL SHAKES HER SHINING MANE UNTIL WINDKIN'S FACE APPEARS AS HIS OWN AGAIN.

IT WAS AN ERROR!

A GRAVE ERROR! I CONFESS IT!

THAT IS WHAT COMES OF GOING OUTSIDE TO FIND WHAT HAS LAIN WITHIN ALL THE WHILE.

IT WAS THERE IN THE EGG--THERE FOR ALL TO SEE IF THEY HAD THE MINDS TO LOOK!

"BUT NO ONE GAZED AS LONG AS I DID--FROM THE CREATION OF THE VERY FIRST SHELL."

"THE GLIDERS HAD THEIR OWN CONCERNS BUILDING...SHAPING BLUE MOUNTAIN."

"THEY WERE ALL SO SAFE--JUST AS VOLL WANTED--THAT THEY NO LONGER NEEDED THEIR HEALER."

"A GIFT CAN FESTER, YOU KNOW, TURN IN UPON ITSELF, WHEN NO ONE ELSE HAS USE FOR IT."

"BUT I DID NOT LET THAT HAPPEN TO ME! I EXPLORED--

--MEDITATED UPON THE EGG--"

--BUT THEY REFUSED ME..! I SHOWED THEM HOW TERRIBLE IT COULD BE NOT TO GROW! AND THEY PREFERRED THAT!

MMBLE!

AH! HEAR...?

:GASP: FEEL?

RRRUUU

"--UNTIL I SAW THE MONUMENTAL JOKE WE HAD PLAYED ON OURSELVES--

I SHOWED THEM HOW TO GROW--"

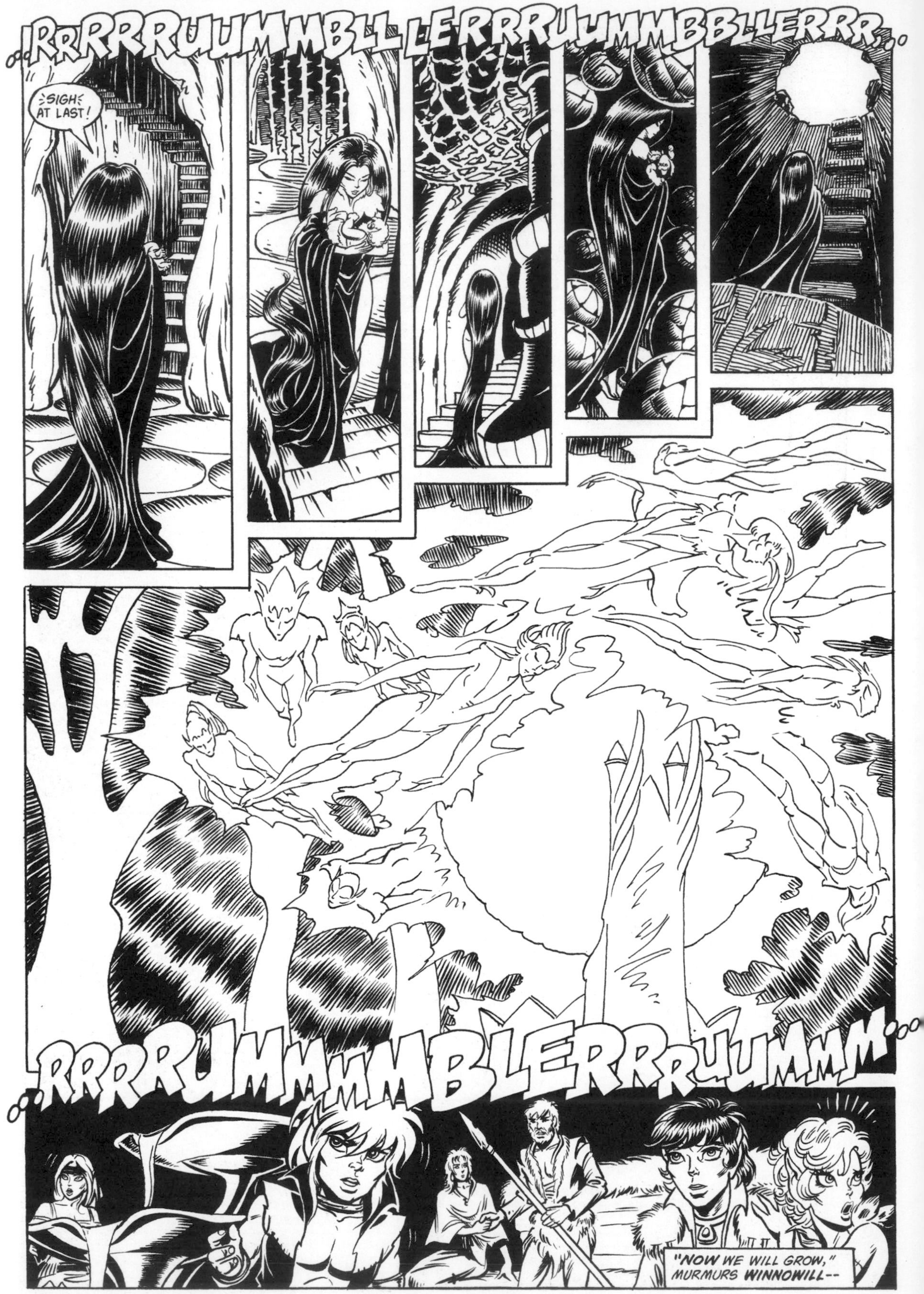
..RRRRRUUMMBLLLERRRRUUMMBBLLERRR..
SIGH AT LAST!
..RRRRUMMMMMBLERRRUUMMM..
"NOW WE WILL GROW," MURMURS WINNOWILL--

NOW WE WILL BE--

--WHAT WE WERE *MEANT* TO BE ALL ALONG!

YOU SEE, *AROREE?* ONLY THE POWERS OF THE GLIDERS--

--CAN BRING THE PALACE BACK TO LIFE! YOU WANT THAT, DON'T YOU?

I-I WANT...TO THINK FOR MYSELF! *YES!* THAT IS WHAT I WANT!

EVERYONE *USES* EVERYONE! *NO ONE* TELLS THE WHOLE TRUTH!

GO, *RAYEK!* THE WOLFRIDERS LIVE IN THOSE WOODS! GO TO THEM! I WILL *NOT* FLY YOU ANY CLOSER TO BLUE MOUNTAIN!

DULLARD! CHILD-THIEF! BUT PERHAPS THIS IS FOR THE BEST, AFTER ALL--

--LEETAH IS HERE!

AS *RAYEK* GLIDES TOWARD THE EDGE OF THE FORBIDDEN GROVE HIS AIR OF COCKSURENESS GIVES WAY TO UNEASE--

--AND WONDERMENT. NEARLY ALL HIS TRAVELING TO THE FROZEN MOUNTAINS WAS DONE UNDERGROUND.

UNTIL NOW HE HAS NOT TRULY SEEN OR SCENTED THE GREEN GROWING PLACE--OR HEARD ITS MANY VOICES CALLING, FACELESS, IN THE DARK.

THE WOLVES ANNOUNCE THE COMING OF BLOOD WHICH THEY HAVE SMELLED BEFORE. THE WOLFRIDERS, WITH SENSES ONLY SLIGHTLY MORE KEEN, ALLOW *RAYEK* TO APPROACH THE FATHER TREE IN THE HEART OF THE GROVE.

HEY, BROWNSKIN! HOW FARE THE *GO-BACKS*? THEY KILLED ANY TROLLS LATELY? HOW MANY LITTLE BEAR-STABBERS ARE ON THE WAY--OR FAWNED ALREADY?

RAYEK CASTS A WITHERING GLANCE AT *KRIM*, THE GO-BACK TURNED FOREST-DWELLER. BUT HIS FEATURES SOFTEN AT THE SIGHT OF THE ONLY FACE THAT INTERESTS HIM--THE ONLY EYES THAT MEET HIS WITH LOVE AND FELLOW-FEELING.

LEETAH...

MY FRIEND! MY EYES SEE WITH JOY!

SOFTPRETTY HIGH-THING! HELLO! HELLO!

:GIGGLE: PETALWING! YOU'RE HERE *TOO*!

SUCH A *SHORT* WHILE IT HAS BEEN SINCE WE LAST TOUCHED! IF ONLY THE TIME OF THIS MEETING WERE HAPPIER!

HAVING LEARNED ENOUGH FROM *SKYWISE*, THROUGH *ARORE*, TO HAVE FORMED HIS OWN ARCH OPINION OF RECENT EVENTS, *RAYEK* SMILES.

EEP!

I SEE SOFT LIVING HAS MADE YOU WOLFRIDERS LOSE YOUR NERVE, ELSE WHY HAVE YOU NOT CONFRONTED *WINNOWILL* OPENLY? YOU HAVE ALREADY PROVED THAT SHE CAN BE BEATEN!

SMART WORDS AT LAST--AND IT TOOK A MUCKING MAGIC-USER TO SPEAK 'EM OUT!

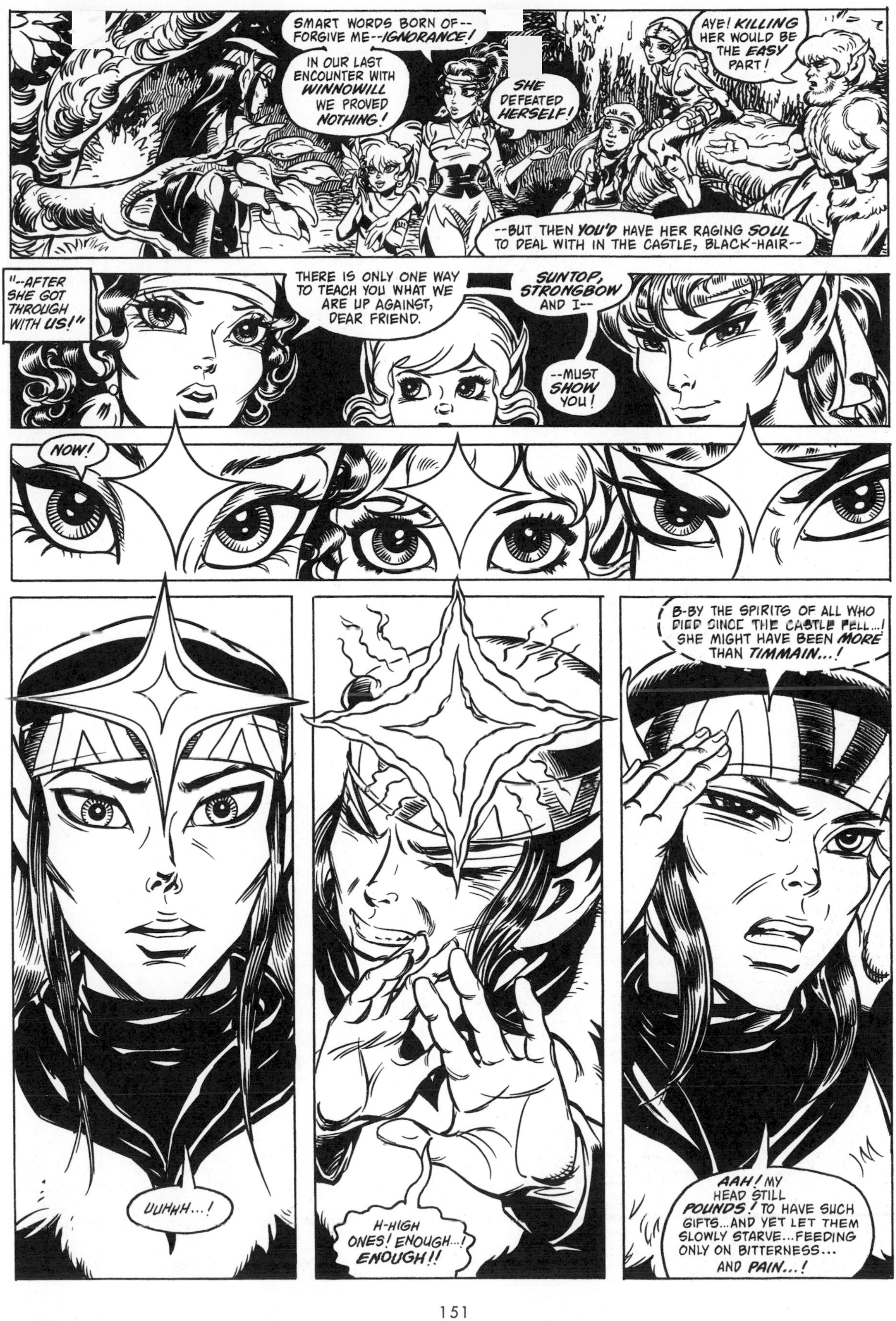

SMART WORDS BORN OF-- FORGIVE ME--IGNORANCE!
IN OUR LAST ENCOUNTER WITH WINNOWILL WE PROVED NOTHING!
SHE DEFEATED HERSELF!
AYE! KILLING HER WOULD BE THE EASY PART!
--BUT THEN YOU'D HAVE HER RAGING SOUL TO DEAL WITH IN THE CASTLE, BLACK-HAIR--
"--AFTER SHE GOT THROUGH WITH US!"
THERE IS ONLY ONE WAY TO TEACH YOU WHAT WE ARE UP AGAINST, DEAR FRIEND.
SUNTOP, STRONGBOW AND I--
--MUST SHOW YOU!
NOW!
UUHHH...!
H-HIGH ONES! ENOUGH...! ENOUGH!!
B-BY THE SPIRITS OF ALL WHO DIED SINCE THE CASTLE FELL...! SHE MIGHT HAVE BEEN MORE THAN TIMMAIN...!
AAH! MY HEAD STILL POUNDS! TO HAVE SUCH GIFTS...AND YET LET THEM SLOWLY STARVE...FEEDING ONLY ON BITTERNESS... AND PAIN...!

I--I AM SORRY--

--NO! THIS ONLY STRENGTHENED MY RESOLVE!

BUT YOU *DO* SEE, NOW?

SO LONG AS *WINNOWILL* HOLDS LITTLE *WINDKIN* BEFORE HER AS A SHIELD, NO ONE DARES STRIKE AT HER DIRECTLY!

THAT IS THE THINKING OF YOUR CHIEF, *CUTTER*-- ONE WHO *BELIEVES* THAT TO STRIKE, ONE MUST USE A *SWORD!*

ONE WHO, FOR ALL HIS EXPERIENCE, STILL UNDERVALUES THE *POWER* TO WHICH HE IS LIFEMATED! ONE WHOSE MIGHTIEST WEAPON HE STILL KEEPS SHEATHED!

LEETAH IS YOUR FIGHTING STRENGTH! YOUR WINNING IS IN *HER* HANDS!

NO, *RAYEK!* IT IS NOT SO SIMPLE AS THAT!

AYE! *CUTTER'S* WAY IS THE WISER!

YOU STILL DON'T GET IT, BLACK-HAIR! *WINNOWILL* MEANS US TO *DIE*--ALL OF US WHO AREN'T "CLEAN" IN HER SIGHT! SHE HAS MY DAUGHTER'S *SOUL NAME,* CURSE HER! IF WE STUPIDLY CHARGE INTO BLUE MOUNTAIN--

--*DEWSHINE'S* DEATH WILL BE BUT THE FIRST OF MANY! AND MOMENTS AGO *YOU* HAD A TASTE OF HOW IT CAN BE DONE!

WE HAVE TO GO SLOW, AS *CUTTER* SAID... CHIP AWAY AT THE BLACK SNAKE'S POWER BIT BY BIT--

WOLFRIDERS, YOU GIVE *WINNOWILL* TOO MUCH CREDIT! LET THOSE OF US WHO KNOW HOW TO BATTLE HER ON HER OWN GROUND DO THE WORK *FOR* YOU!

COME WITH ME--YOU AND *SUNTOP!* OUR POWERS COMBINED WILL *STUN* THE MIND OF BLUE MOUNTAIN'S SUFFERING LORD. THEN *YOU* MAY HEAL HER--AND WE WILL TAKE HER, WITH ALL THE OTHER GLIDERS, TO THE PALACE!

TH-THIS IS WHY YOU CAME TO US? TO FISH FOR MORE *POWER...?*

WHY NOT--?

--WE *ALL* STAND TO GAIN BY IT!

JUST THEN...

WHUF!

≋WHINE≋
≋WHINE≋

AAYOOOAH!!

SKYWISE'S CRY BRINGS THE WOLFPACK'S LEADER LOPING UP TO GREET HIM.

HULLO, BRIERSTING!

AFTER A FEW QUICK HUGS AND HEARTY LICKINGS--

GROWF!

--THE STARGAZER ONCE AGAIN ACTS AS TIDINGS-BEARER TO HIS APPREHENSIVE TRIBEFOLK.

...AND AS FAR AS I KNOW CUTTER AND THE OTHERS ARE WELL.

BUT, FOR WHATEVER REASON, THEY HAVEN'T YET ESCAPED FROM THE MOUNTAIN.

POOR PLANNING YIELDS POOR RESULTS. AS USUAL YOUR CHIEF RELIES TOO MUCH ON CHANCE. "MAYBE THE HUMANS WILL TURN AGAINST WINNOWILL." "MAYBE WE CAN TRADE PRESERVERS FOR THE GIRL AND HER BABY."

EVERY EFFORT HE HAS MADE, SO FAR, HAS HAD NO TRULY USEFUL EFFECT.

CUTTER DID MANAGE TO STIR UP THE HUMANS, THOUGH NOT ALL OF THEM DOUBT THE "BIRD SPIRITS." SOME HAVE BURRS UNDER THEIR TAILS NOW!

AND NOW HE HAS GOTTEN HIMSELF AND TWO MORE OF YOU TRAPPED! GOOD LEADERSHIP INDEED!

YOU...!

YOU ALWAYS TURN UP WITH A SNARL AND A GLARE AND A MOUTH FULL OF WRONG-TAILED SCRUB ABOUT YOUR OLD RIVAL! IT STILL STINGS, DOESN'T IT, *RAYEK*?

BEING MASTER OF THE PALACE HASN'T CHANGED YOU MUCH AT ALL!

AT LEAST I AM MASTER OF SOMETHING, *SKYWISE*. YOU HAVE NOT EVEN MASTERED *YOURSELF*!

WAS IT NOT YOUR CARELESS RUTTING AFTER THE DULL-WITTED *AROREE* THAT PLACED YOUR TRIBE IN ITS PRESENT DIFFICULTY?

ANTS TAKE YOUR EYES!

THE VERY OBJECTS OF *SKYWISE'S* OATH NOW BLAZE WITH AMBER FIRE—A FIRE WHICH *FREEZES*, RATHER THAN BURNS.

C-CAN'T MOVE...!

THE WOLVES WATCH WITH INTEREST, ABIDING BY THE AGE-OLD LAW OF THE "STARE-DOWN." THEY DO NOT INTERFERE.

SKYWISE'S FIST TREMBLES IN MID-SWING, BUT THE BLOW CANNOT BE DELIVERED!

IMPATIENTLY, *TREESTUMP* INTERVENES.

BACK OFF, BOTH OF YOU! ALL THAT MATTERS IS THE *TRUTH*!

AND THE TRUTH IS, IT'S NOT *WINNOWILL'S* STRENGTH GETTING EATEN UP LITTLE BY LITTLE—IT'S *OURS*!

THERE'S BEEN TOO MUCH RUNNING ALONE—OUTSIDE THE PACK—HERE!

Panel 1: CUTTER WENT OFF AND LEFT ME TO SPEAK FOR HIM *BEFORE* ANY OF THIS TROUBLE STARTED. I GUESS HE'S DONE HIS BEST TO ROLL WITH THE BLOWS SINCE.

BUT AS ACTING CHIEF, I SAY *RAYEK'S* MADE *ONE* POINT.

Panel 2: WE'RE *NOT* HELPLESS! THERE ARE FOUR AMONG US, NOW, WHO CAN STAND UP TO THE BLACK SNAKE'S MAGIC--AND THREE OF THEM HAVE ALREADY BEEN TESTED!

IT'S UP TO *ME* TO DECIDE HOW TO USE THEM!

Panel 3: I KNOW *CUTTER* WOULD GIVE UP HIS LIFE TO KEEP FRIEND--

Panel 4: --OR LIFEMATE--

Panel 5: --OR CUB--

--FROM SUFFERING *WINNOWILL'S* TORTURES. BUT THAT SHE-SPIDER CAN'T DO EVERYTHING AT ONCE.

Panel 6: IF SHE IS BUSY KEEPING THE GLIDERS ASLEEP, AND IF SHE *IS--HIGH ONES* HELP THEM--PLAYING HER PAIN-GAMES WITH THE FIVE OF US SHE'S GOT NOW, HER MIND'S ON *THEM*, NOT ON US!

Panel 7: THE TIME IS RIGHT AND WE HAVE THE RIGHT WEAPONS! WE'RE GOING TO BLUE MOUNTAIN!

TAM... LIFEMATE...

THIS JOINING OF LIVES, ALL FROM SEPARATE PATHS--

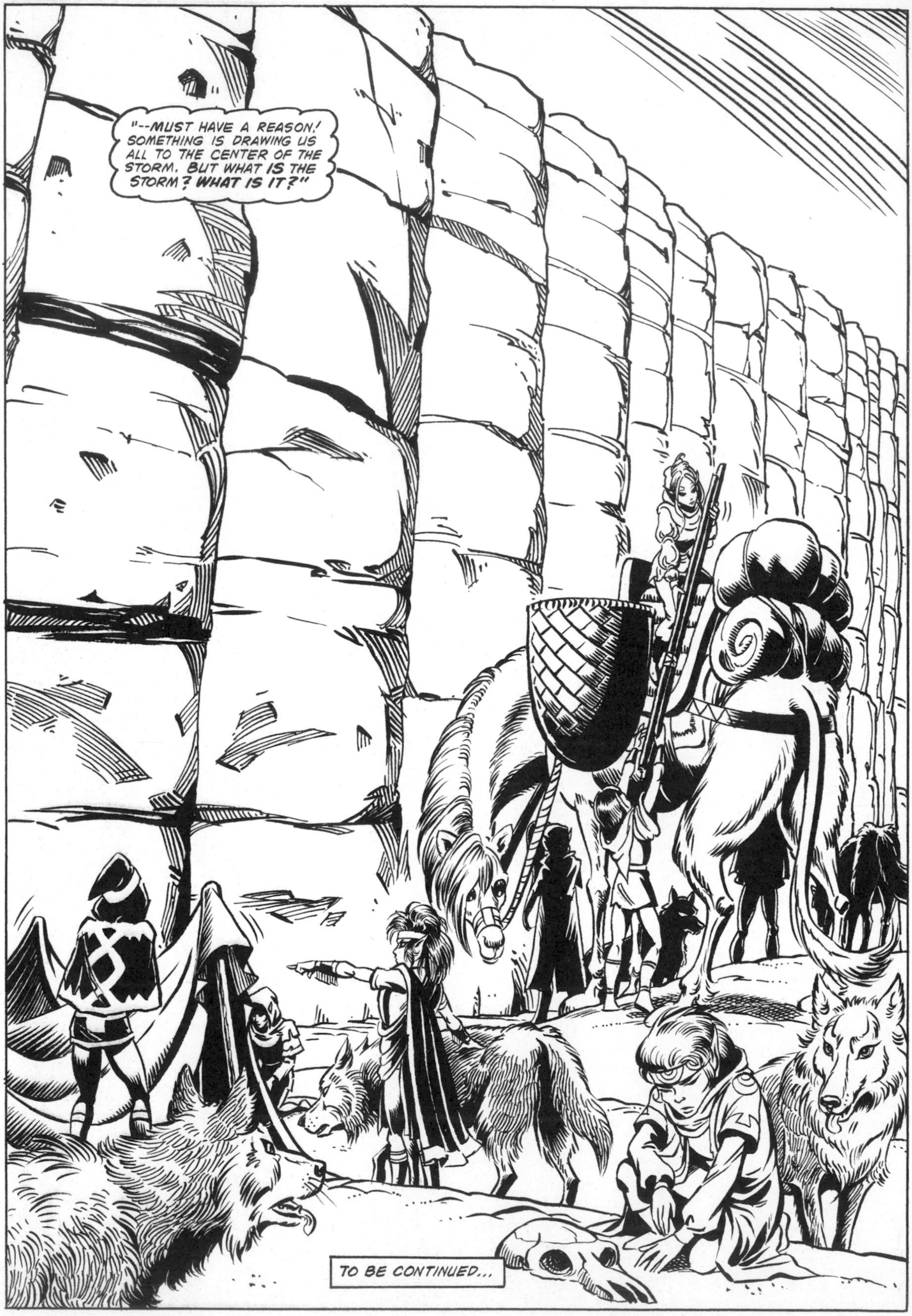
"--MUST HAVE A REASON! SOMETHING IS DRAWING US ALL TO THE CENTER OF THE STORM. BUT WHAT IS THE STORM? WHAT IS IT?"
TO BE CONTINUED...

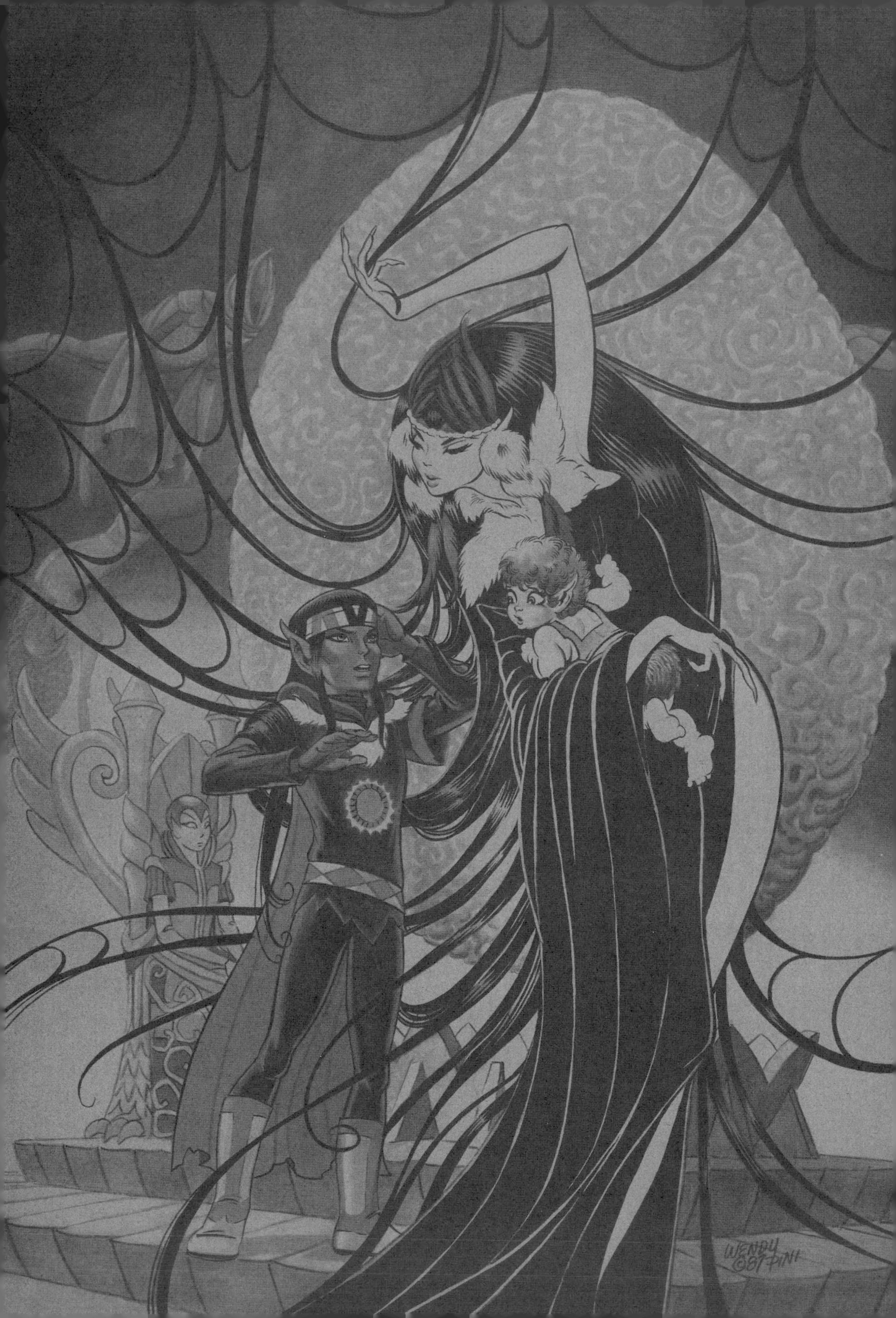
WENDY ©87 PINI

SIEGE AT BLUE MOUNTAIN

| ARTIST / WRITER **WENDY PINI** | CO-PLOT / EDITOR **RICHARD PINI** | PART **6** | INKS **JOE STATON** | LETTERER **JANICE CHIANG** |

WELCOME, *SAVAH.* TAKE CARE. THE WIND RISES WITH THE SUN.

MY FOOTING IS FIRM. BESIDES, THERE IS NO REST FOR ME BELOW.

I WILL STAND WITH YOU, *SUN TOUCHER*--

--AND FEEL THE WIND. DO *THEY* FEEL IT, TOO? IS IT HARSH OR GENTLE ON THEIR YOUNG FACES?

THEY MUST TAKE IT AS IT COMES, MOTHER OF MEMORY.

DART'S RIDERS MUST FACE THE STORM--GO THROUGH IT--ELSE THEY SHOULD NEVER HAVE LEFT THE SAFETY OF SORROW'S END.

THAT SAME MOMENT, FAR AWAY...

AS DAWNLIGHT PAINTS STRIPES OF GOLD ACROSS THE TOWERING CLIFFSIDE, HAGGARD ELFIN TRAVELERS THINK OF THE COOL UNDERGROUND CHAMBERS BENEATH THEIR HUTS--PLACES OF SHELTER FROM THE MIDDAY HEAT-- SHELTER WHICH NOW LIES DAYS BEHIND THEM.

SOON THE BLAZING DAYSTAR WILL SWEEP NIGHT'S LINGERING CHILL FROM THE SAND. THE JACK-WOLFRIDERS HASTEN TO PITCH THEIR TENTS.

WE WON'T CAMP HERE ALL DAY-- 'SOON AS THE HIGH WALL'S SHADOW IS LONG ENOUGH TO TRAVEL IN, WE'LL GO.

AYOOOAH! DART! LOOK AT THIS!

SOMEONE HAS SCRATCHED A SYMBOL INTO THE ROCK HERE...! LOOKS LIKE--

--THREE BEADS AND THREE CLAWS...

RAYEK! HE ALWAYS WORE THEM AROUND HIS NECK, REMEMBER?

I THINK I DO! HE LEFT THE SUN VILLAGE WHEN NEWSTAR AND I WERE JUST SMALL CUBS, DIDN'T HE?

HEY! WHAT'S THIS UNDER THE SAND...?

BITS OF BONE!

HOW DID THEY GET THERE?

AND WHO MARKED THE CAVE WITH A SYMBOL, AS IF IT WERE A-A BURIAL PLACE!?

160

DART SHUDDERS, STARING AT CHALKY FRAGMENTS RESTING IN HIS PALM.

IT **HAD** TO BE THE WOLFRIDERS, **NEWSTAR!**

SAVAH HAS GIVEN US THE SAME DIRECTIONS SHE GAVE **SUNTOP** THREE YEARS AGO. HE GUIDED MY PARENTS AND THE OTHERS THIS WAY LOOKING FOR **CUTTER**, BUT MAYBE THEY FOUND--

--_ULP!_ **RAYEK,** TOO!

TIRED...HUNGRY...SCARED... TOO HOT...TOO COLD...THAT'S ALL I REMEMBER OF THE FIRST TIME I CROSSED THE DESERT.

AND EVEN THOUGH **THIS** TIME WE HAVE SUPPLIES, IT'S ALMOST LIKE BEFORE...ESPECIALLY THE "SCARED" PART!

STILL...I KNOW **CUTTER** WASN'T MUCH OLDER THAN I WHEN HE LED THE WOLFRIDERS TO SORROW'S END.

I CAN BE LIKE HIM--AND LIKE MY PARENTS, TOO!

THE WOLF-RIDERS NEED HELP AND I WON'T STOP 'TIL I BRING IT TO THEM!

THAT EVENING...

COME, **LEETAH!** **BRIERSTING** WILL CARRY YOU AND **SUNTOP**! WE CAN GET THERE BEFORE SUNRISE! _HURRY!_

WE GOING BIG BLUE ROCKS! GET FLYIIIGHHBABY!

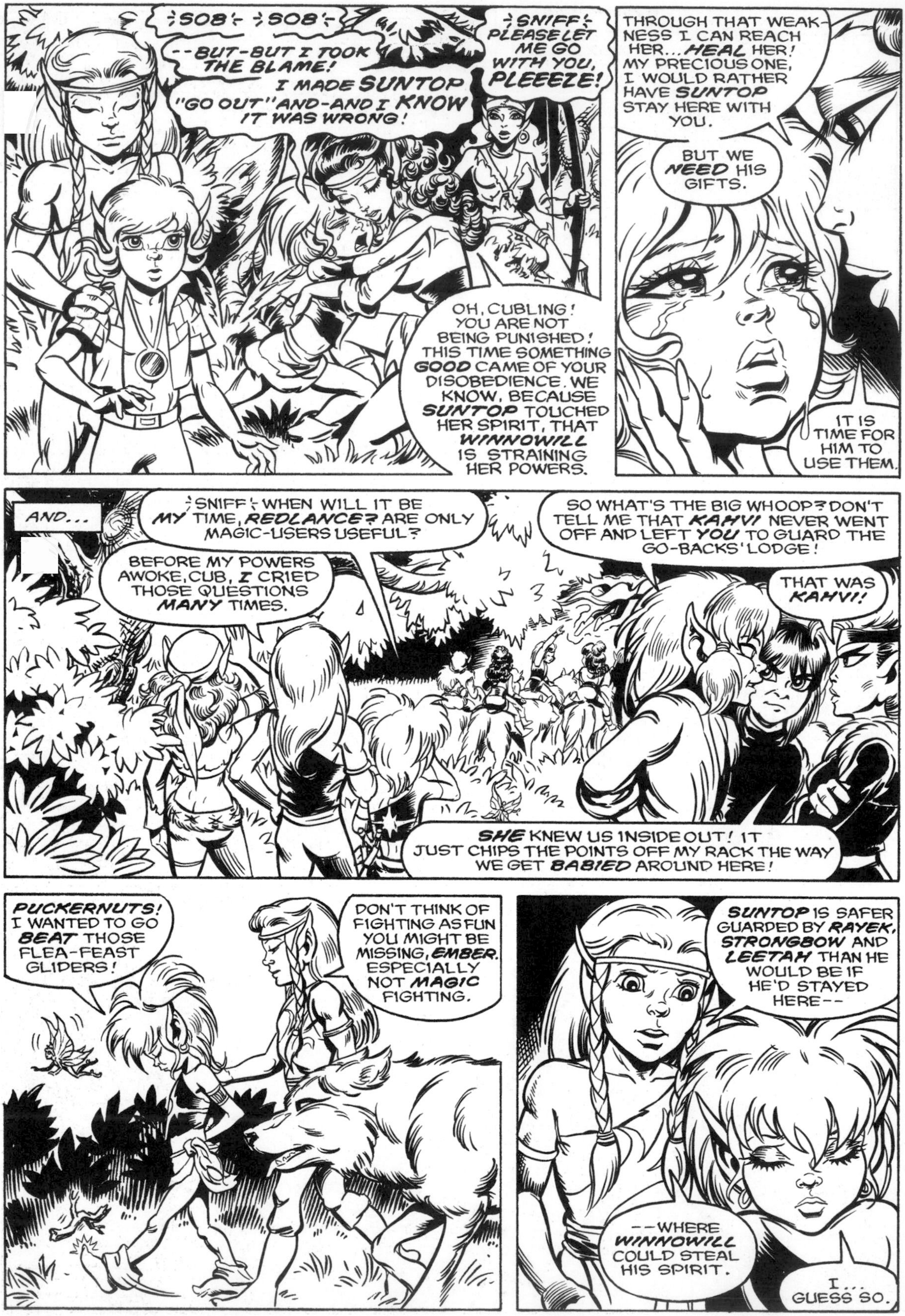

:SOB: :SOB:
--BUT-BUT I TOOK THE BLAME! I MADE SUNTOP "GO OUT" AND-AND I KNOW IT WAS WRONG!
:SNIFF: PLEASE LET ME GO WITH YOU, PLEEEZE!
OH, CUBLING! YOU ARE NOT BEING PUNISHED! THIS TIME SOMETHING GOOD CAME OF YOUR DISOBEDIENCE. WE KNOW, BECAUSE SUNTOP TOUCHED HER SPIRIT, THAT WINNOWILL IS STRAINING HER POWERS.
THROUGH THAT WEAKNESS I CAN REACH HER... HEAL HER! MY PRECIOUS ONE, I WOULD RATHER HAVE SUNTOP STAY HERE WITH YOU.
BUT WE NEED HIS GIFTS.
IT IS TIME FOR HIM TO USE THEM.
AND...
:SNIFF: WHEN WILL IT BE MY TIME, REDLANCE? ARE ONLY MAGIC-USERS USEFUL?
BEFORE MY POWERS AWOKE, CUB, I CRIED THOSE QUESTIONS MANY TIMES.
SO WHAT'S THE BIG WHOOP? DON'T TELL ME THAT KAHVI NEVER WENT OFF AND LEFT YOU TO GUARD THE GO-BACKS' LODGE!
THAT WAS KAHVI!
SHE KNEW US INSIDE OUT! IT JUST CHIPS THE POINTS OFF MY RACK THE WAY WE GET BABIED AROUND HERE!
PUCKERNUTS! I WANTED TO GO BEAT THOSE FLEA-FEAST GLIDERS!
DON'T THINK OF FIGHTING AS FUN YOU MIGHT BE MISSING, EMBER. ESPECIALLY NOT MAGIC FIGHTING.
SUNTOP IS SAFER GUARDED BY RAYEK, STRONGBOW AND LEETAH THAN HE WOULD BE IF HE'D STAYED HERE--
--WHERE WINNOWILL COULD STEAL HIS SPIRIT.
I... GUESS SO.

BESIDES, UNTIL *CUTTER* AND THE OTHERS COME HOME, *YOU* MUST BE, CHIEF! WHERE SHALL I GROW THE THORN FENCES AND STRANGLEWEED TRAPS TO KEEP ENEMIES OUT OF OUR HOLT?

⸴GIGGLE⸴ *HUM!* I'LL HAVE TO THINK ABOUT THAT!

THEN I'LL JUST STAND RIGHT HERE AND AWAIT YOUR ORDERS!

EMBER IS *CUTTER* REBORN. IT'S AS IF THE SEASONS HAD TURNED BACK SO WE MIGHT SEE HIM AS A CUB AGAIN.

THE ONLY THING *SHE* FEARS IS GETTING CAUGHT IN A MISTAKE.

I WOULD NOT BE A CHIEF...

I WOULD NOT *WISH* TO BE SO WATCHED--OR ALWAYS FEEL THAT I MUST WATCH MYSELF!

AS *NIGHTFALL* GAZES FONDLY AT HER LIFEMATE, HIS SOUL NAME RIPPLES THROUGH HER MIND...

ULM--

"--HE'S TURNED OUR TROUBLES INTO A *GAME!*

WOOPS!

SNAP!

AW, *CHOP-LICKER!* YOU *STONEHEAD!* YOU'VE WRECKED THE TRAP!

WE'LL MEND IT, LITTLE CHIEFTESS. STRANGLEWEED DOESN'T DIE WHEN YOU BREAK IT, IT JUST GROWS ITSELF RIGHT BACK.

MAY ONLY FOUR-LEGGED THINGS COME TO TEST YOUR TRAPS, BELOVED...

AND, PLEASE--

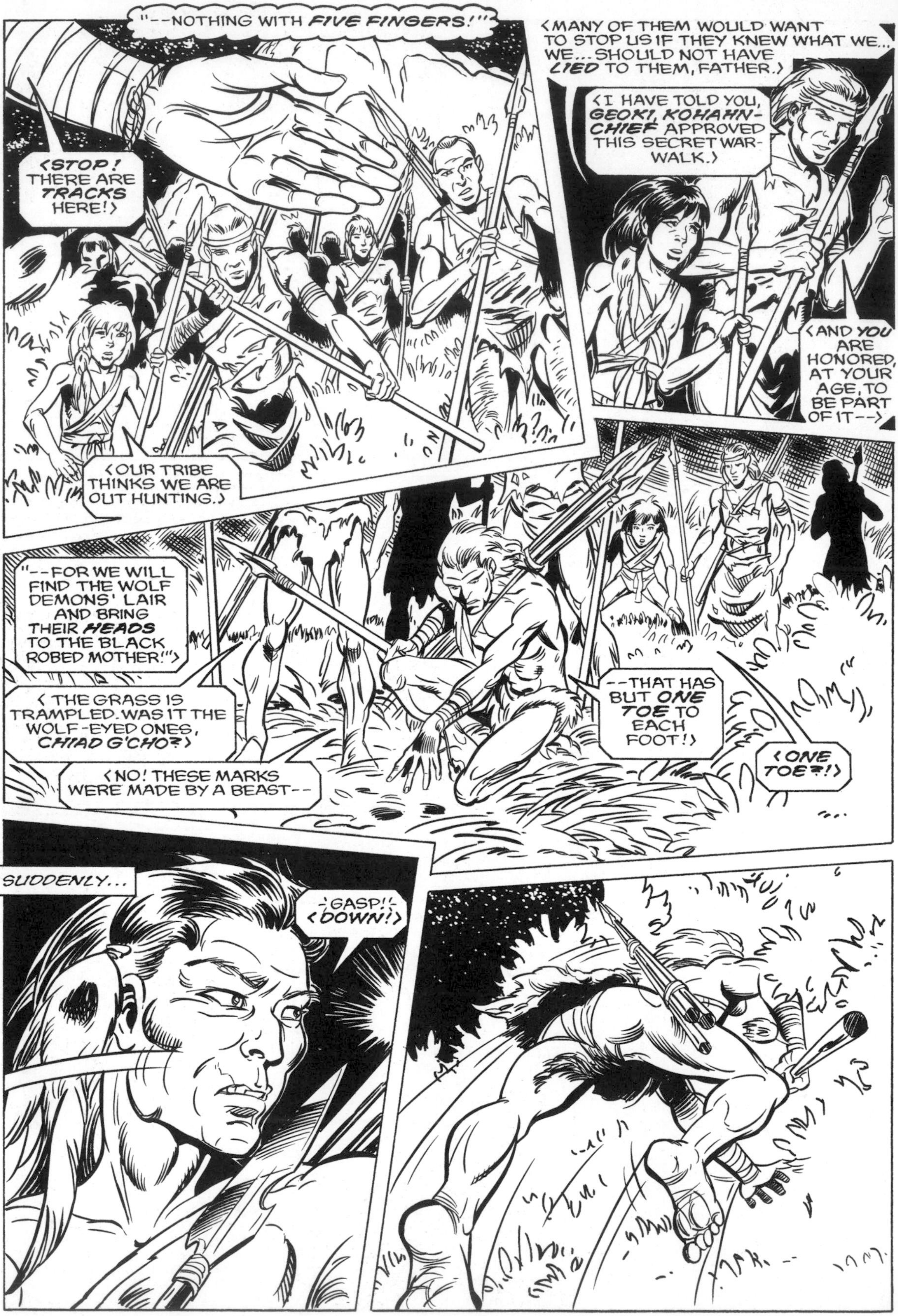
"--NOTHING WITH FIVE FINGERS!"
‹STOP! THERE ARE TRACKS HERE!›
‹OUR TRIBE THINKS WE ARE OUT HUNTING.›
‹MANY OF THEM WOULD WANT TO STOP US IF THEY KNEW WHAT WE... WE... SHOULD NOT HAVE LIED TO THEM, FATHER.›
‹I HAVE TOLD YOU, GEOKI, KOHAHN-CHIEF APPROVED THIS SECRET WAR-WALK.›
‹AND YOU ARE HONORED, AT YOUR AGE, TO BE PART OF IT--›
"--FOR WE WILL FIND THE WOLF DEMONS' LAIR AND BRING THEIR HEADS TO THE BLACK ROBED MOTHER!"›
‹THE GRASS IS TRAMPLED. WAS IT THE WOLF-EYED ONES, CHIAD G'CHO?›
‹NO! THESE MARKS WERE MADE BY A BEAST--
--THAT HAS BUT ONE TOE TO EACH FOOT!›
‹ONE TOE?!›
SUDDENLY...
-GASP!- ‹DOWN!›

‹ STOP, STRANGE ONES! COME NO CLOSER! WE HAVE STRONG MAGIC— *WEAPONS* GIVEN TO US BY THE *BIRD SPIRITS!* ›

‹ YOUR WAY OF SAYING OUR WORDS IS HARD TO UNDER-STAND. WE MEAN NO HARM. ›

TO MAKE HIMSELF CLEARER, THE SPEAKER BEGINS TO SIGN AS HE TALKS. THE OTHER MAN IS INCAPABLE OF SIGNING.

‹ WE ARE CHILDREN OF *GOTARA*, THE MASTER SPIRIT. WE COME FROM THE FLATLANDS BEYOND THE DARK WOODS TO THE EAST. WE HAVE BEEN WANDERERS, BUT NOW WE ARE *SEEKERS*. ›

‹ WE SEARCH FOR AN EVIL SPIRIT WITH HAIR LIKE FROST— AND WHEN WE FIND IT-- ›

‹ --WE WILL KILL IT! ›

‹ AH! THE FOUR-FINGERED ONES! THE WOLF-EYED ONES! WE HUNT THEM, TOO! ›

‹ WE WERE ABLE TO NET THE DEMON BECAUSE HIS WOLF WAS LAME AND COULD NOT OUTRUN OUR PONY. BUT HE ESCAPED AND CUT OFF *BRUGA'S* FINGERS. ›

‹ IF YOU WILL HAVE US, WE WILL JOIN YOU, FOR IT SEEMS WE ALL WANT THE SAME THING. ›

AND SO, WITH THE BARRIER OF ACCENT AND DIALECT BREACHED, THE MEN UNITE IN PURSUIT OF THEIR COMMON QUARRY.

ONLY THE BOY, GEOKI, SHOWS NO ENTHUSIASM AS THE HUNT RESUMES.

NOW ALL IS MOVEMENT AND PURPOSE IN THE NORMALLY PEACEFUL VALLEY OF ENDLESS SLEEP--

--AS THREE DETERMINED GROUPS, TWO ELFIN-- AND ONE HUMAN-- HURRY TOWARD THEIR GOALS.

LATER THAT NIGHT...

NOW THAT WE ARE SO NEAR BLUE MOUNTAIN, I FEEL--

--I FEAR-- I WAS TOO HASTY. LEETAH SHOULD NOT HAVE TO CROSS WILLS WITH THAT SICK PAIN-GIVER, AGAIN--

--AND NEITHER SHOULD HER LITTLE SON.

I KNOW WINNOWILL. SHE WILL LOSE ALL INTEREST IN HER CAPTIVES--

--IF I GIVE HER SOMETHING NEW TO FEED ON--

"--APPROVAL! THERE IS NOTHING WRONG WITH HER DESIRES--"

"--ONLY WITH HER METHODS. WHEN SHE KNOWS SHE IS LONGER ALONE--"

"--HER PAIN WILL END."

WHY THAT PUFFED-UP DESERT RAT! HE'S TAKEN OFF ON HIS OWN!

BUT I--I THOUGHT THE PLAN WAS SET.

OH, RAYEK! HE MISLED US!

SMALL LOSS!

WE STILL HAVE ALL THE STRENGTH WE NEED!

SOON...

THE GREAT HAWKS ARE LETTING ME PASS. THEY TAKE ME FOR A GLIDER.

PUH! WHAT A STENCH OF DROPPINGS.

A STAIRWAY!

NOW, WHY IN YUREK'S NAME WOULD THE GLIDERS HAVE NEED OF... STAIRS?

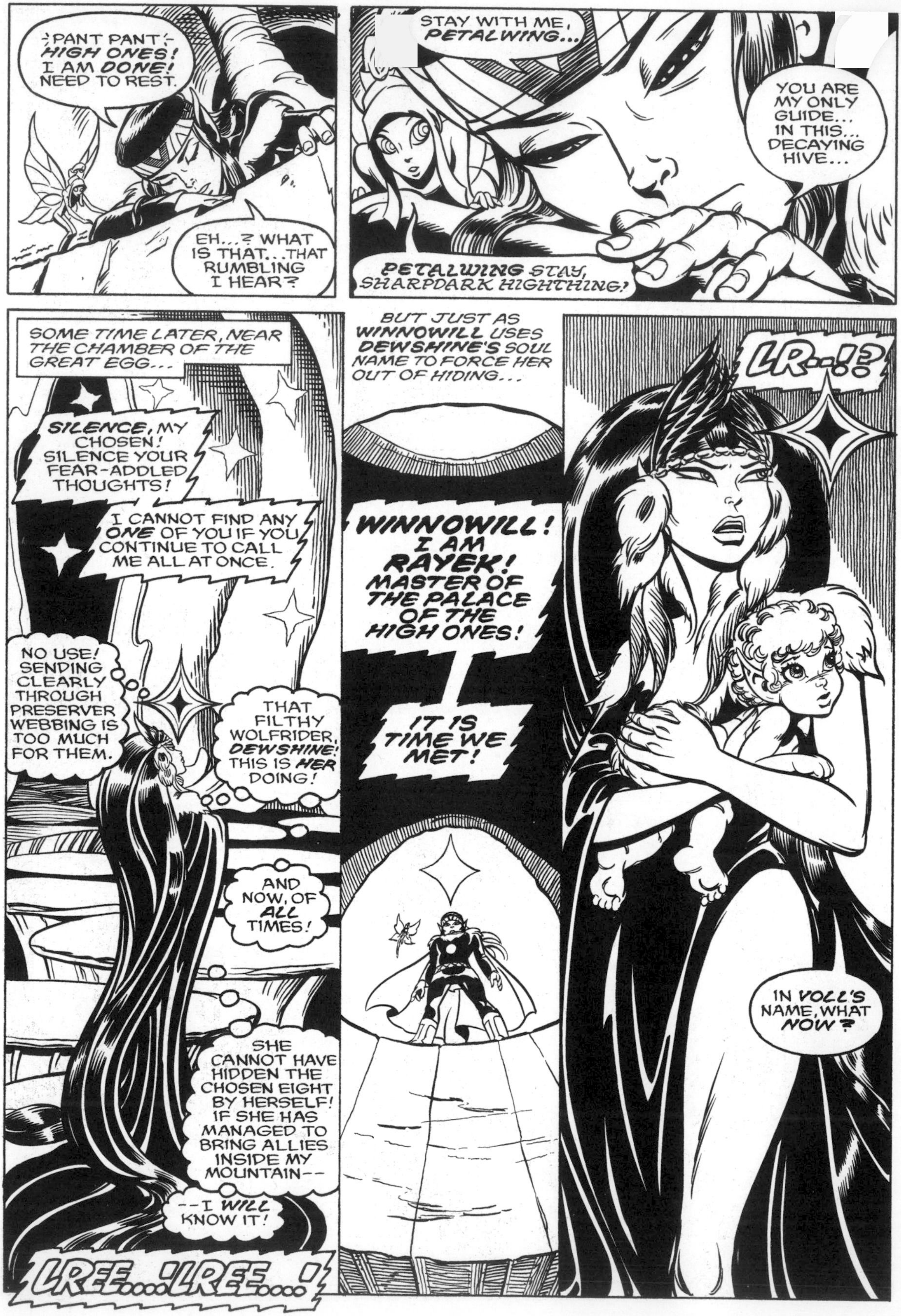

PANT PANT HIGH ONES! I AM DONE! NEED TO REST.
EH...? WHAT IS THAT...THAT RUMBLING I HEAR?
STAY WITH ME, PETALWING...
YOU ARE MY ONLY GUIDE... IN THIS... DECAYING HIVE...
PETALWING STAY, SHARPDARK HIGHTHING!
SOME TIME LATER, NEAR THE CHAMBER OF THE GREAT EGG...
SILENCE, MY CHOSEN! SILENCE YOUR FEAR-ADDLED THOUGHTS!
I CANNOT FIND ANY ONE OF YOU IF YOU CONTINUE TO CALL ME ALL AT ONCE.
NO USE! SENDING CLEARLY THROUGH PRESERVER WEBBING IS TOO MUCH FOR THEM.
THAT FILTHY WOLFRIDER, DEWSHINE! THIS IS HER DOING!
AND NOW, OF ALL TIMES!
SHE CANNOT HAVE HIDDEN THE CHOSEN EIGHT BY HERSELF! IF SHE HAS MANAGED TO BRING ALLIES INSIDE MY MOUNTAIN--
--I WILL KNOW IT!
LREE...LREE...!
BUT JUST AS WINNOWILL USES DEWSHINE'S SOUL NAME TO FORCE HER OUT OF HIDING...
WINNOWILL! I AM RAYEK! MASTER OF THE PALACE OF THE HIGH ONES!
IT IS TIME WE MET!
LR..!?
IN VOLL'S NAME, WHAT NOW?

OOOOHH...!

DEWSHINE!

IT-IT'S OVER...! SHE STOPPED!

AN OPEN SENDING! RAYEK IS HERE!

YES! DO YOU THINK HE'S COME TO HELP US?

WHO KNOWS? RAYEK AND WINNOWILL...HUH! NOW THERE'S A MEETING THAT WILL RATTLE THIS MOUNTAIN EVEN MORE THAN IT'S SHAKING NOW!

...RRRUMMRRRRRUUMMMMBLERRRUUM...

WHAT'S HAPPENING, BELOVED, DO YOU KNOW?

TYLDAK SAID...SOMETHING ABOUT...THE EGG! CUTTER, MY CUB! MY CUB!

YES, LITTLE COUSIN. WINNOWILL'S SCENT IS FRESH HERE. I THINK SHE CAME UP JUST A SHORT WHILE AGO.

‹SNIFF SNIFF›

I...CAN'T TELL IF SHE HAD WINDKIN WITH HER...

...SOMETHING'S STRANGE!

‹I DO NOT UNDERSTAND ALL THIS SPIRIT CHATTER!›

‹WHEN DO WE FREE THE SLAVES YOU SAY ARE DOWN THERE?›

‹RIGHT NOW, ADAR!›

WE'LL SEE IF WINNOWILL LEFT WINDKIN BELOW IN HER DEN. MEANTIME, YOU TRACK HER, CLEARBROOK.

AND FIND OUT WHAT RAYEK'S UP TO-- BUT DO NOTHING 'TIL WE JOIN YOU!

AYE, CUTTER!

CUTTER'S CURIOSITY IS NOTHING COMPARED TO THE LORD OF BLUE MOUNTAIN'S...

WHAT OF THIS NEW INTRUDER, *RAYEK?* AMBITION POWER AND *NEED* ARE ALL IN HIS SENDING.

HIS WILL ENJOYS LUSTY HEALTH. BUT THERE IS SOMETHING HE WANTS--

--FROM *ME!*

"SUCH A NATURE I HAVE DEALT WITH BEFORE."

"IN ELF, HUMAN OR TROLL, WHERE *NEED* IS PRESENT, *CONTROL* IS SIMPLE."

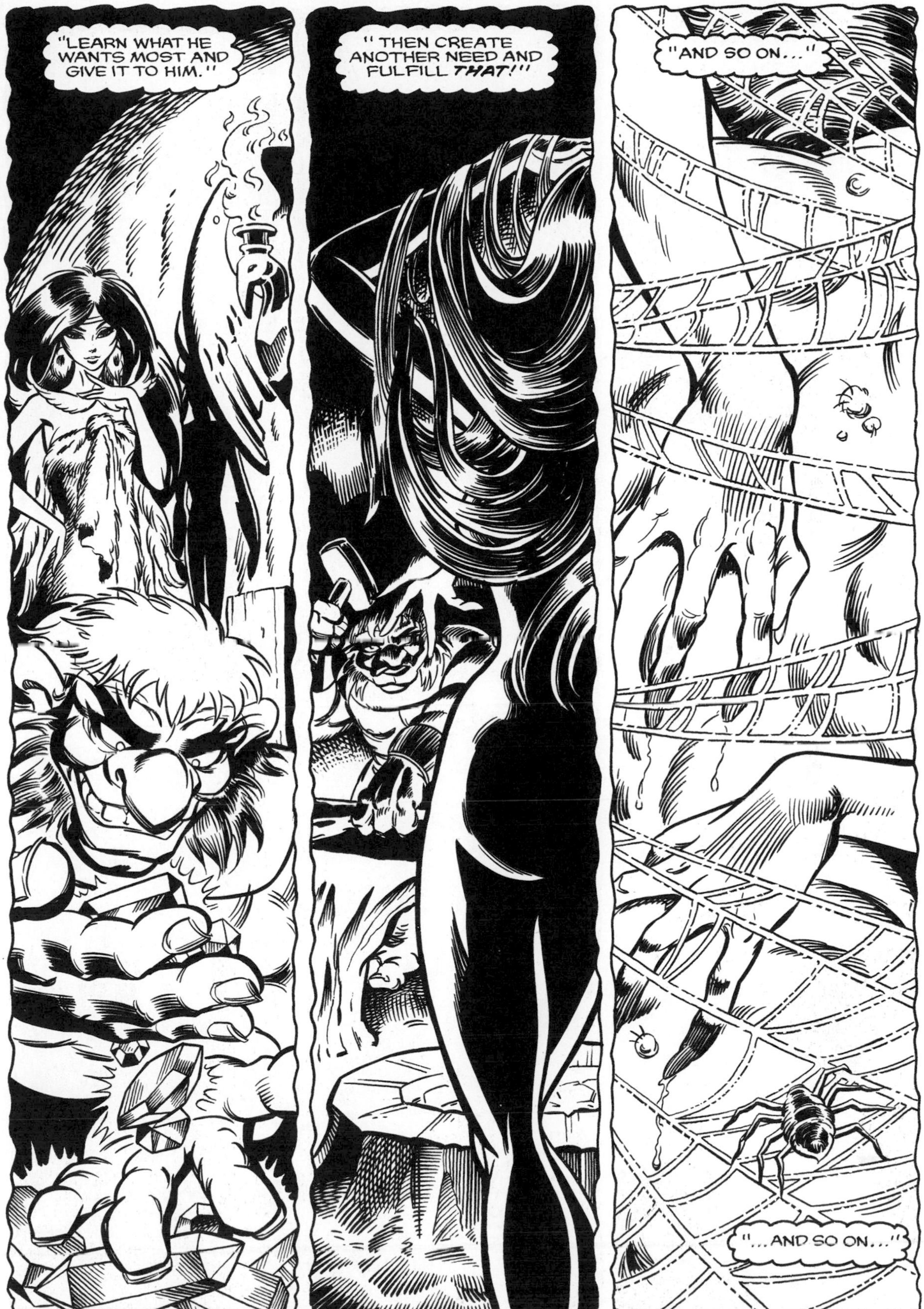
"LEARN WHAT HE WANTS MOST AND GIVE IT TO HIM."
" THEN CREATE ANOTHER NEED AND FULFILL THAT!"
"AND SO ON..."
"...AND SO ON..."

"THERE IS BEAUTY IN NEED, IT IS *LIFE* TO A HEALER."

"BUT IN GREED WAITS BETRAYAL AND MANY FORMS OF DEATH."

THIS *RAYEK* AND HIS ESTIMABLE POWERS--

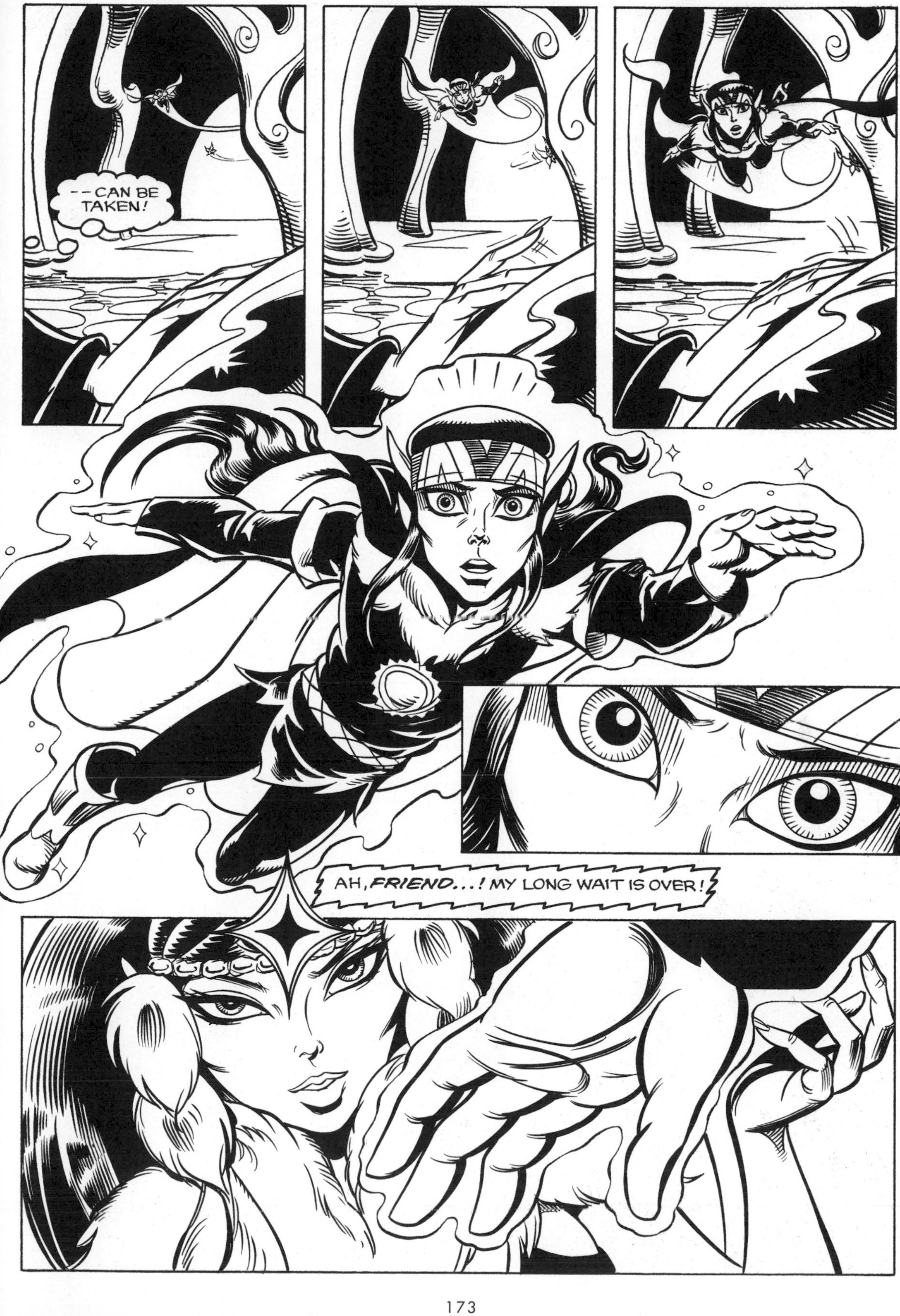
--CAN BE TAKEN!
AH, FRIEND...! MY LONG WAIT IS OVER!

RECOGNITION? NO, THIS IS NOT--

--THE UNION OF TWO SOULS TO GIVE LIFE AND BREATH TO A THIRD.

--THERE IS ONLY ONE SOUL HERE, *RAYEK*--

--SHARED BY TWO FORMS, YOURS AND MINE--

--YOU KNOW THIS--

--AS DO I .

MEANWHILE, *CUTTER* CAUTIONS *NONNA* AND *ADAR*...

< REMEMBER, HUMANS, NO MATTER WHAT, DO NOT TOUCH THESE ROUND THINGS!>

< IT COULD MEAN OUR LIVES!>

< HOW CAN SOMETHING MADE OF *STONE* BURST LIKE A NUT HEATED IN A FIRE?!>

BUBBLEBANGS!

< YOU QUESTION TOO MUCH, *ADAR!* TRUST!>

< WITHOUT THESE LITTLE ONES WE WOULD BE *LOST* IN THE GREAT CAVE OF SPIRITS!>

<*HMPH!* WITHOUT THESE LITTLE ONES WE WOULD BE *HOME* INSTEAD OF HERE!>

< SHHH! *WINNOWILL'S* CHAMBERS!>

WINDKIN ISN'T HERE... <CHOKE> HE ISN'T HERE!

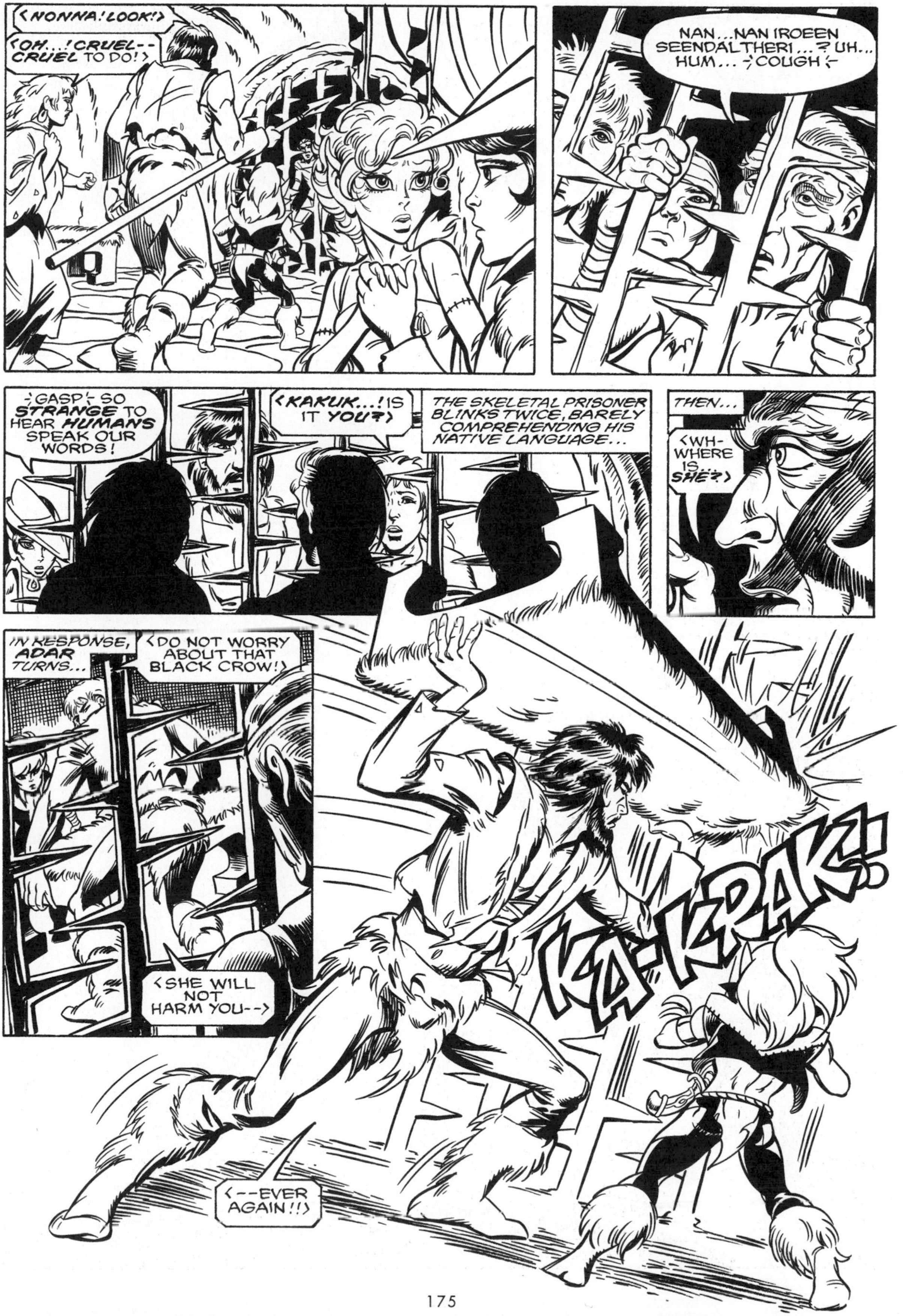
<NONNA! LOOK!>
<OH...! CRUEL--CRUEL TO DO!>
NAN...NAN IROEEN SEENDALTHERI...? UH... HUM... ;COUGH;
;GASP; SO STRANGE TO HEAR HUMANS SPEAK OUR WORDS!
<KAKUK...! IS IT YOU?>
THE SKELETAL PRISONER BLINKS TWICE, BARELY COMPREHENDING HIS NATIVE LANGUAGE...
THEN...
<WH-WHERE IS... SHE?>
IN RESPONSE, ADAR TURNS...
<DO NOT WORRY ABOUT THAT BLACK CROW!>
<SHE WILL NOT HARM YOU-->
KA-KRAK!
<--EVER AGAIN!!>

SLOWLY, DAZED AND INCREDULOUS, THE CAPTIVES EMERGE.

‹KAKUK, DO YOU REMEMBER ME? I AM NONNA! I WAS A CHILD--›

‹N-NONNA...›

--WHEN THE BIRD SPIRITS RECEIVED YOU, YOU WERE SO HAPPY...SO PROUD!›

‹AND THIS IS HOW THEY BLESSED YOU!›

‹OH, SUN AND MOONS! THE BIRD SPIRITS ARE EVIL!›

‹WE HAVE WORSHIPPED EVIL SPIRITS ALL THIS WHILE!!›

‹NONNA...THIS IS WINNOWILL'S DOING-- NO ONE ELSE'S. SHE IS NOT A "BIRD SPIRIT." NEITHER AM I, OR ANY OF MY KIND! BECAUSE OF OUR LOOKS AND WHAT WE CAN DO--›

‹--HUMANS HUNT US OR MAKE US GODS.›

÷SOB÷

‹BUT THERE IS NO PEACE FOR US EITHER WAY. WE CANNOT GO ON TRICKING YOU! IT IS WRONG AND I AM...SORRY.›

‹YOU! CH-CHILD SPIRITS! YOU CAME HERE ONCE BEFORE! TRIED... WARN US ABOUT THE MISTRESS!›

‹WE CANNOT HARM CHILDREN OF THE BIRD SPIRITS!›

‹WHY DID SHE COMMAND US TO? WHY?›

‹YOU'RE RIGHT! WINNOWILL'S CRAZY!›

‹SHE CARES NOTHING FOR YOU! YOU'RE JUST HER PETS! HER SLAVES!›

‹WE DID NOT BELIEVE...THEN.›

‹MANY OF THE HOAN G'TAY SHO DO NOT BELIEVE US EITHER. BUT NOW YOU CAN TELL THEM WHAT YOU HAVE LIVED THROUGH.›

‹YOU CAN TELL THEM THE TRUTH ABOUT BLUE MOUNTAIN.›

‹I... WILL! BUT--›

‹--I FEAR IT WILL DESTROY THEM!›

"AND THE LIE WHICH IS THE TRUTH SHALL BRING MORE PAIN--

"--THAN THE TRUTH WHICH IS A LIE!"

‹WHAT NOW? HOW DO WE GET OUT OF HERE?›

‹WE CAME IN THROUGH A DOOR MADE OF MOVING ROCK. CAN YOU MAKE THE ROCKS OPEN AGAIN, LITTLE SPIRIT?›

‹YOU *STILL* HAVE FAITH?›

‹I STILL *LOVE.*›

SCOUTER, DEWSHINE, TAKE THE HUMANS TO THE AERIE. THEY'LL HAVE TO CLIMB DOWN THE MOUNTAIN FROM THERE... SOMEHOW. HELP THEM.

BUT--

DON'T WORRY. WITH *CLEARBROOK'S* AID AND *RAYEK'S,* IF HE'S STILL A FRIEND, I'LL GET *WINDKIN!*

THEN... YOU STILL PLAN TO DO--

--WHAT I DID ONCE BEFORE: LOCK MINDS WITH THE BLACK SNAKE-- MAKE HER FORGET *EVERYTHING* BUT HER NEED TO KILL *ME!*

NO MATTER WHAT HAPPENS--

--YOUR *CUB* WILL BE BACK IN YOUR ARMS, *DEWSHINE,* SOON!

AT THAT MOMENT IN THE FORBIDDEN GROVE...

OOOOWWWWOOOOO

OOOOWWWWW

WWWOOO

WWWOOO

WWWOOO

HUMANS!

THEY'RE COMING THIS WAY, UP FROM THE WINDING RIVER!

ARE THEY THE HOAN G'TAY SHO?

DO THEY COME IN PEACE...?

THE INNOCENT HOPE IN REDLANCE'S SENDING SOON FADES, FOR--

177

--AS THE WAR PARTY APPROACHES THE HOLT, THE ELVES SENSE THE HUMANS' HOSTILE INTENT.

‹HEAR THE HOWLING OF THE WOLVES!›

‹HAH! THEY ARE WITH THEIR DEMON RIDERS IN THE WOOD OF DREAMS!›

‹REMEMBER, THE EVIL ONES' SIZE MEANS NOTHING. LIKE *ANTS*, THEY ARE MUCH STRONGER THAN THEY LOOK.›

‹BUT *WE* CAN CRUSH THEM, EVEN SO!›

DON'T LOOK SO WORRIED, *REDLANCE*. THIS'LL BE FUN! ALL OUR TRICKS AND TRAPS ARE READY AND THE PRESERVERS ARE *FULL* OF SPIT!

GRRUFF!

HOW MANY ARE THERE, BELOVED?

TWICE OUR NUMBER, PLUS TWO WHO RIDE A *NOHUMP*.

NOHUMP?

LATER!

WHY SEND? WHAT'S TO FEAR? IF *THOSE* ARE HUMANS, THEIR ARMS AND LEGS AREN'T *HALF* AS BIG AROUND AS A TROLL'S! *LET* THEM HEAR US LAUGH!

HUSH, SKOT!

LEGENDS OF THE MYSTERIOUS GROVE'S WINGED PROTECTORS, AND OTHER HAZARDS, REACHED THE HOAN G'TAY SHO GENERATIONS AGO. NOW, THE MEN CREEP STEALTHILY TOWARD THE PLACE, NOT KNOWING WHAT TO EXPECT.

THEY HAVE BEEN RAISED TO REVERE AND OBEY THE GLIDERS, WHOSE EXISTENCE IS A MATTER OF FACT, NOT FAITH. THE WARRIORS TAKE HEART IN THE BELIEF THAT THEY DO THE WILL OF THE BIRD SPIRITS.

BIGTHINGS BREAK UP IN BITTY BUNCHES!

IS GOOD! IS EASY PUT WRAPSTUFF 'ROUND TWOS AND THREES!

〈OW! THORNS!〉

〈THEY SURROUND THE WOOD! THERE IS NO WAY THROUGH!〉

〈DID YOU THINK THE DEMONS WOULD MAKE US WELCOME?〉

〈SHOW THEM! USE YOUR MAGIC *SPEARS!*〉

GRRAAH!

CHOKK!

EH?

YAAAH!

HAH HA HA HAH HA HA!

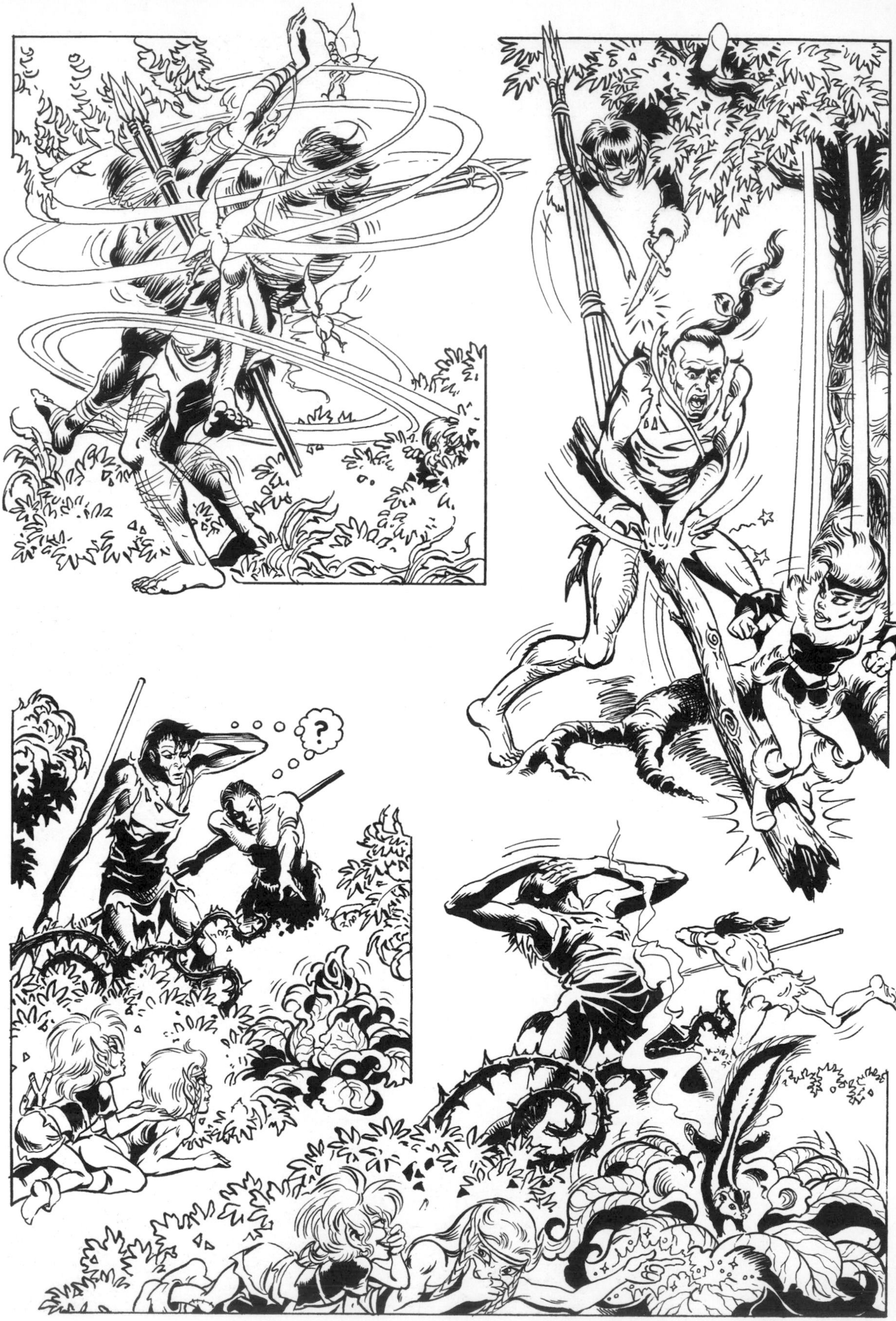
?

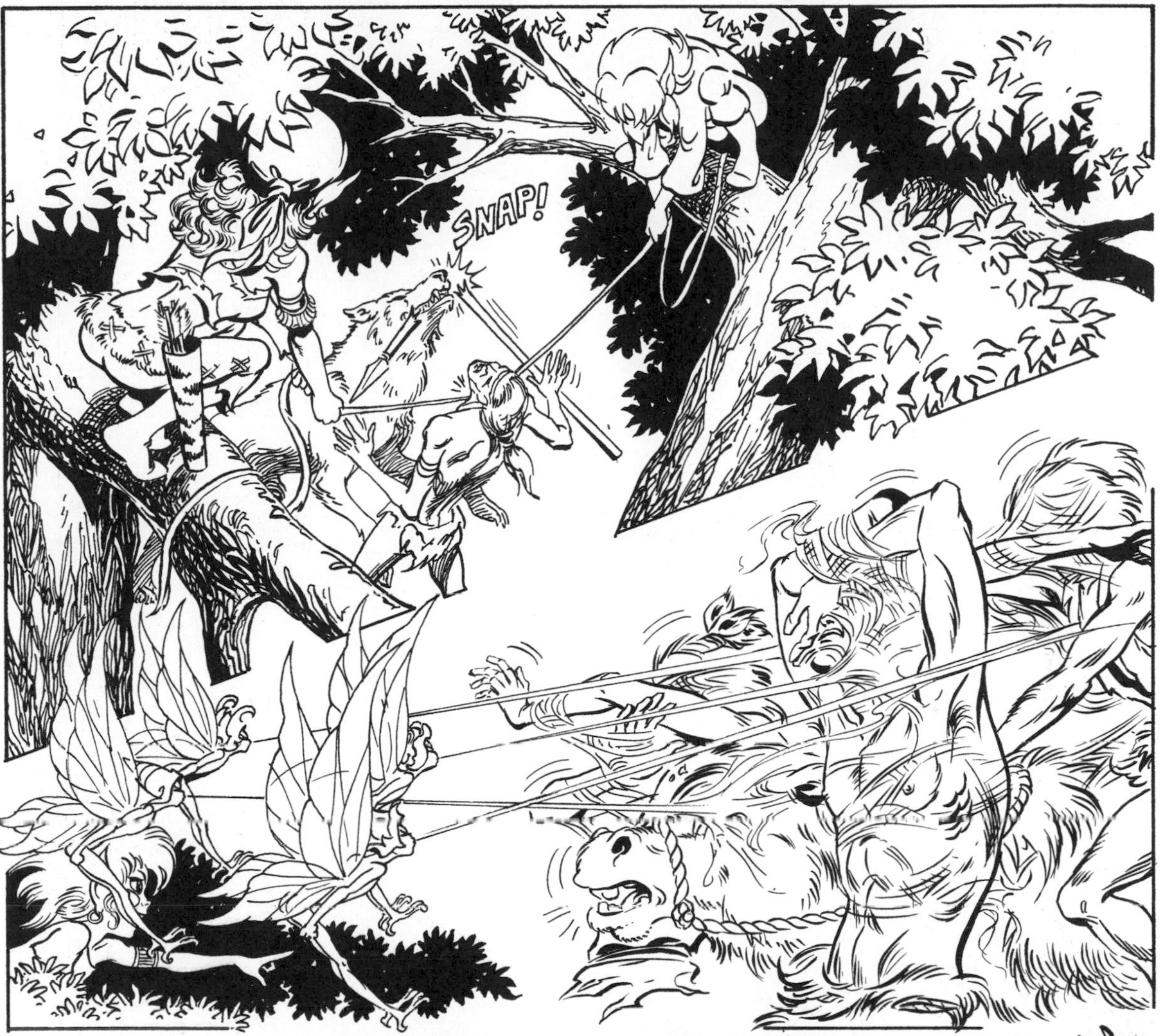
SNAP!

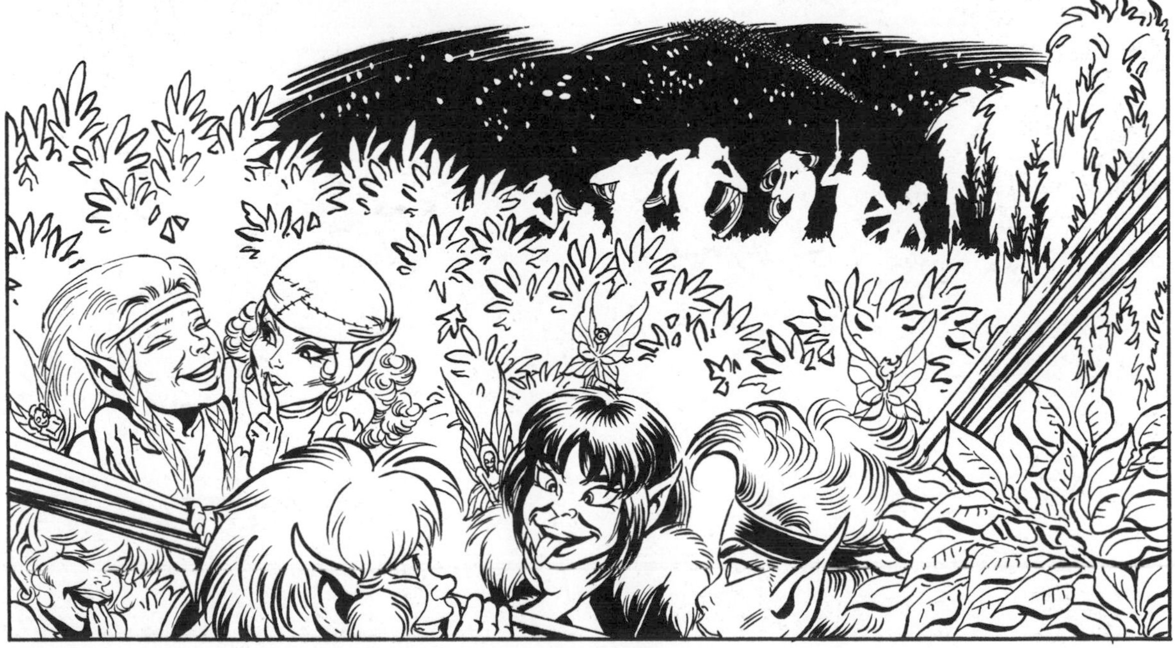

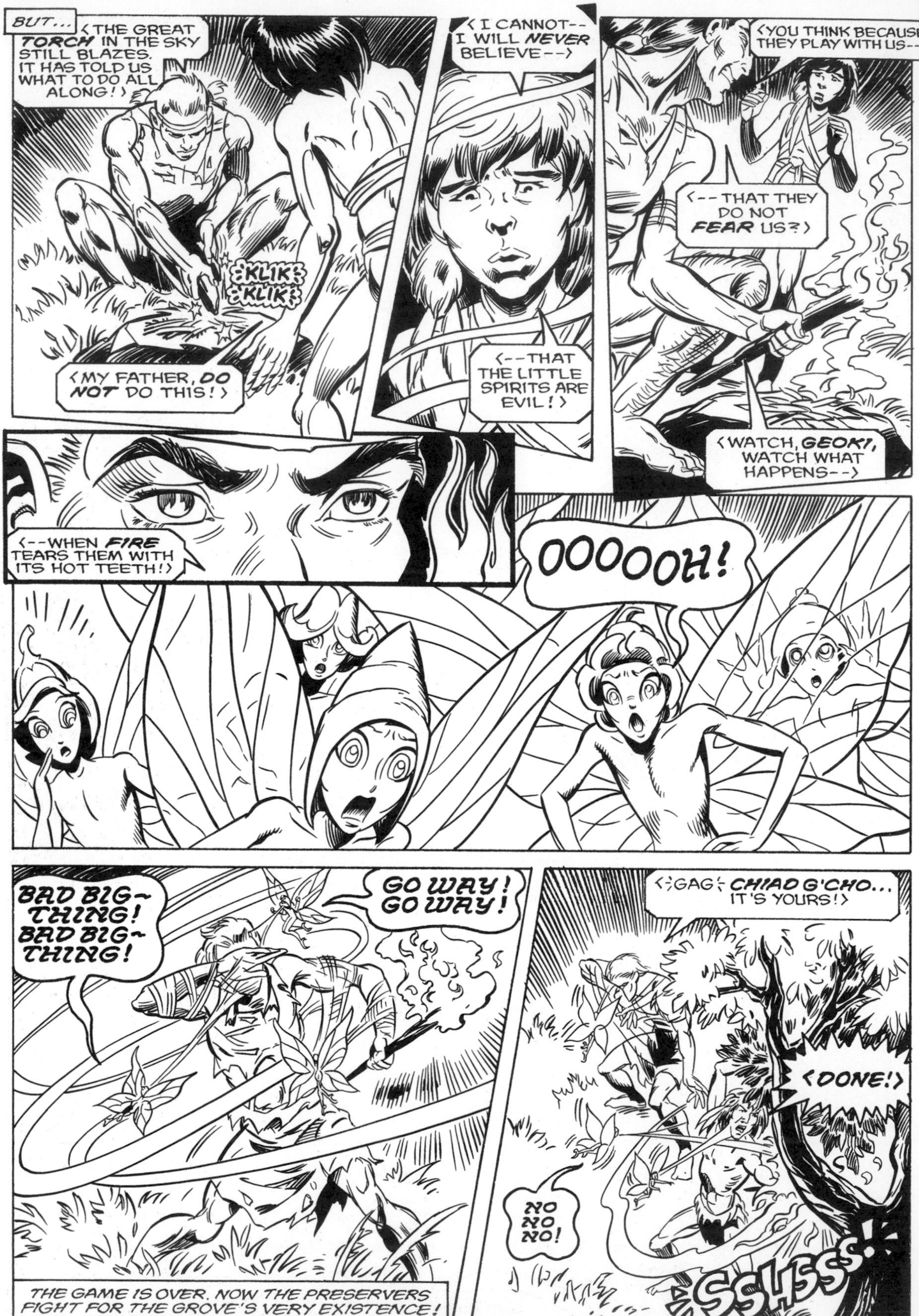
BUT...
<THE GREAT TORCH IN THE SKY STILL BLAZES. IT HAS TOLD US WHAT TO DO ALL ALONG!>
KLIK KLIK
<MY FATHER, DO NOT DO THIS!>
<I CANNOT-- I WILL NEVER BELIEVE-->
<--THAT THE LITTLE SPIRITS ARE EVIL!>
<YOU THINK BECAUSE THEY PLAY WITH US-->
<--THAT THEY DO NOT FEAR US?>
<WATCH, GEOKI, WATCH WHAT HAPPENS-->
<--WHEN FIRE TEARS THEM WITH ITS HOT TEETH!>
OOOOOH!
BAD BIG-THING! BAD BIG-THING!
GO WAY! GO WAY!
THE GAME IS OVER. NOW THE PRESERVERS FIGHT FOR THE GROVE'S VERY EXISTENCE!
<-GAG- CHIAD G'CHO... IT'S YOURS!>
<DONE!>
NO NO NO!
SSHSSS!

HIGH ONES!

CRACKLE

NO!

TEN YEARS AGO, **REDLANCE** WAS HELPLESS TO PREVENT THE BURNING OF ANOTHER HOLT--HIS BIRTHPLACE.

BUT TEN YEARS AGO HIS TREE SHAPING POWERS HAD NOT YET BLOSSOMED!

HE HUGS THE ROUGH TRUNK IN A LOVER'S EMBRACE--

--AND WITH THAT LOVE, MAGIC FLOWS!

FROM ROOTS TO LEAF TIPS MOISTURE OOZES, FORMING A THICK FILM OVER THE BARK!

AT SUCH A TABLE, HUNGRY FLAMES CANNOT DINE!

HSSST

TSSSSS

UNFORTUNATELY, THE FIRE, TOO, HAS ITS DEFENDERS--

--AND **REDLANCE** WILL NOT ABANDON THE TREE EVEN THOUGH HE MUST STAND WITHIN THE HUMAN'S SIGHT!

CURSED TORCHES! THEY'LL BURN US **OUT!** FIRE'S THE ONE THING STRONGER THAN WE ARE!

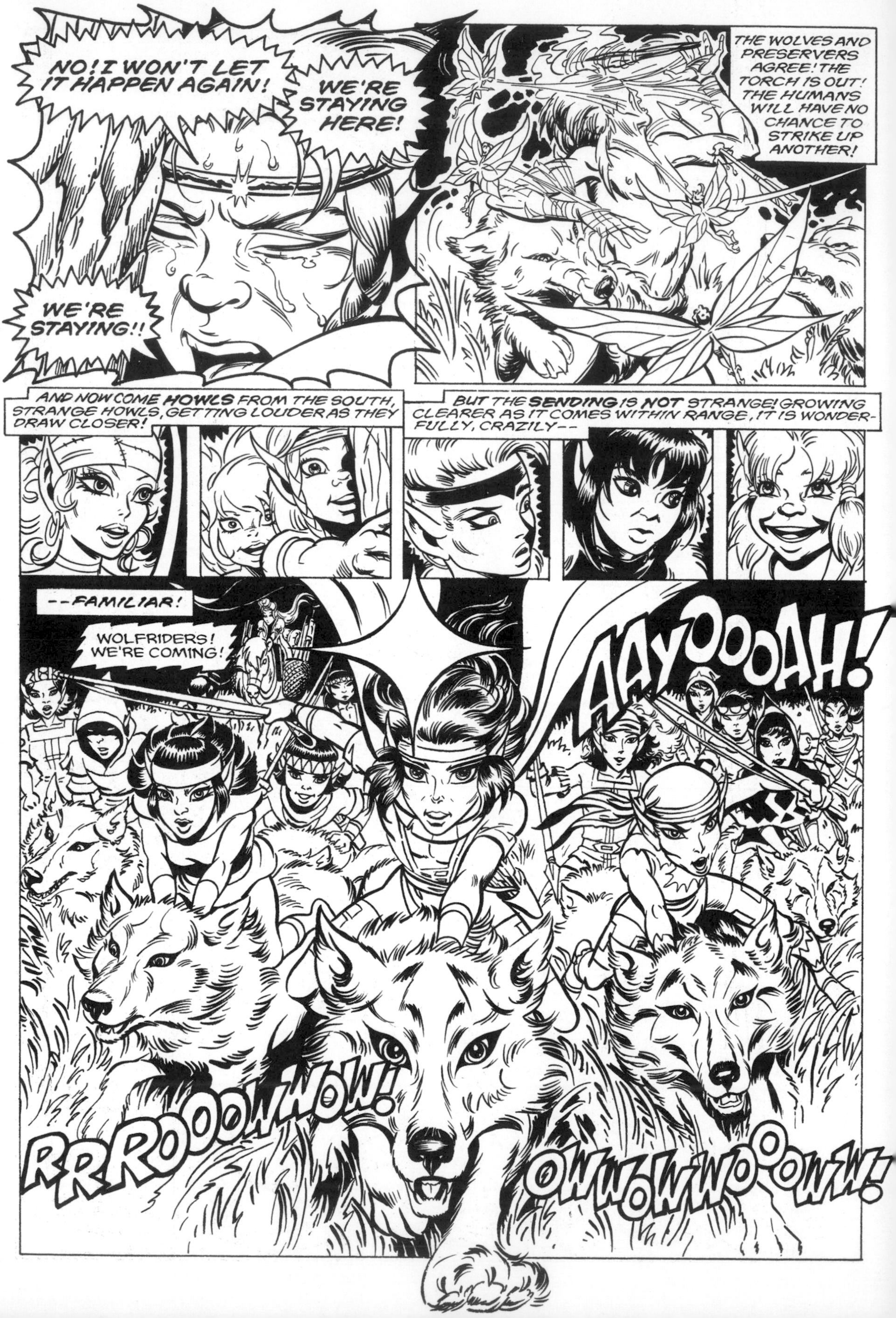
NO! I WON'T LET IT HAPPEN AGAIN!
WE'RE STAYING HERE!
WE'RE STAYING!!
THE WOLVES AND PRESERVERS AGREE! THE TORCH IS OUT! THE HUMANS WILL HAVE NO CHANCE TO STRIKE UP ANOTHER!
AND NOW COME HOWLS FROM THE SOUTH, STRANGE HOWLS, GETTING LOUDER AS THEY DRAW CLOSER!
BUT THE SENDING IS NOT STRANGE! GROWING CLEARER AS IT COMES WITHIN RANGE, IT IS WONDERFULLY, CRAZILY--
--FAMILIAR!
WOLFRIDERS! WE'RE COMING!
AAYOOOOAH!
RRROOOOWWOW!
OWWOWWOOOWW!

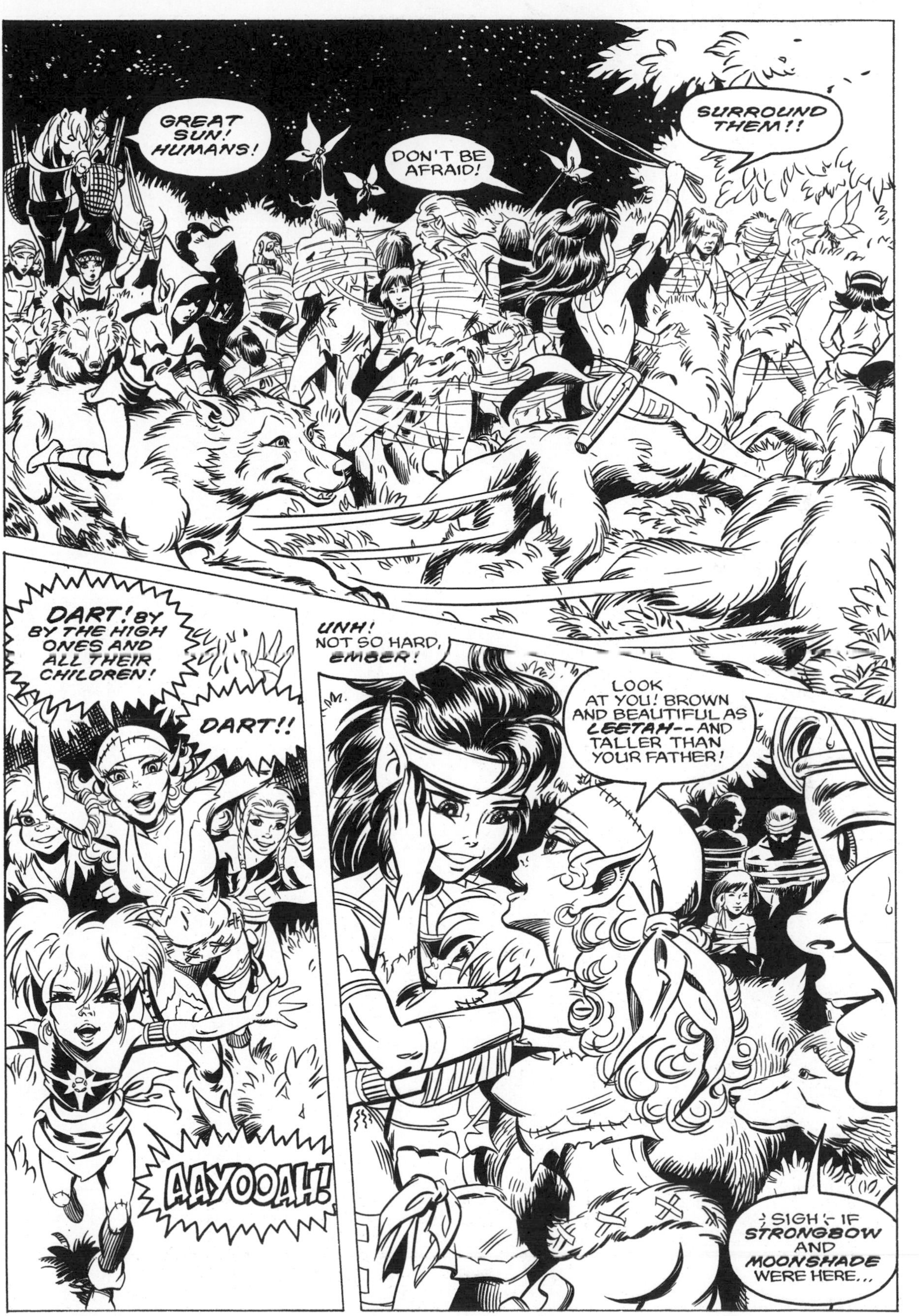
GREAT SUN! HUMANS!
DON'T BE AFRAID!
SURROUND THEM!!
DART! BY BY THE HIGH ONES AND ALL THEIR CHILDREN!
DART!!
AAYOOAH!
UNH! NOT SO HARD, EMBER!
LOOK AT YOU! BROWN AND BEAUTIFUL AS LEETAH--AND TALLER THAN YOUR FATHER!
SIGH IF STRONGBOW AND MOONSHADE WERE HERE...

REMEMBER ME? I REMEMBER A *LITTLE* CUB, SHY AND FRAGILE AS A NEWGREEN BUD--

NEWSTAR!

--NOT A *MAIDEN*, TALL AND GOLDEN AS A SUNFLOWER!

WE CAME BECAUSE OF *SUNTOP* AND WHAT *SAVAH* LEARNED FROM HIM.

WHILE THE HUMANS LOOK ON, SOME WITH LOATHING, MOST WITH FEAR, THE ELVES COMMUNICATE THROUGH SENDING ALL THAT HAS HAPPENED SINCE *WINOKIN* WAS STOLEN.

AND WHEN *DART* HAS LEARNED ALL ...

EVEN WHEN I WAS A CUB, I DIDN'T BELIEVE HUMANS WERE *ALL* BAD. I STILL DON'T. *THESE* ARE HERE BECAUSE OF THIS--THIS *WINNOWILL* CREATURE, SHE'S LIKE NO ELF I EVER HEARD OF!

AMONG THE GLUM FACES IN THE CAPTIVE WAR PARTY, *DART* SEES ONE WHOSE SMILE HE GENTLY RETURNS...

...FOR YOUTH KNOWS A BROTHER OF ITS OWN HEART AND HOPE—NO MATTER WHAT PHYSICAL DIFFERENCES EXIST.

DART HAS COME BACK TO THE GREEN GROWING *PLACE* WHERE HE SPENT HIS EARLIEST YEARS.

BUT HE HAS COME AT A TIME OF GREAT TROUBLE FOR THE WOLFRIDERS, AND HIS OWN PACK OF DESERT-BORN HUNTERS ARE FRIGHTENED BY HIS LAND'S STRANGENESS.

DART GAZES AT THE DISTANT MOONLIT PEAK OF BLUE MOUNTAIN AND WONDERS... WILL HE BE ANY HELP AT ALL?

TO BE CONTINUED...

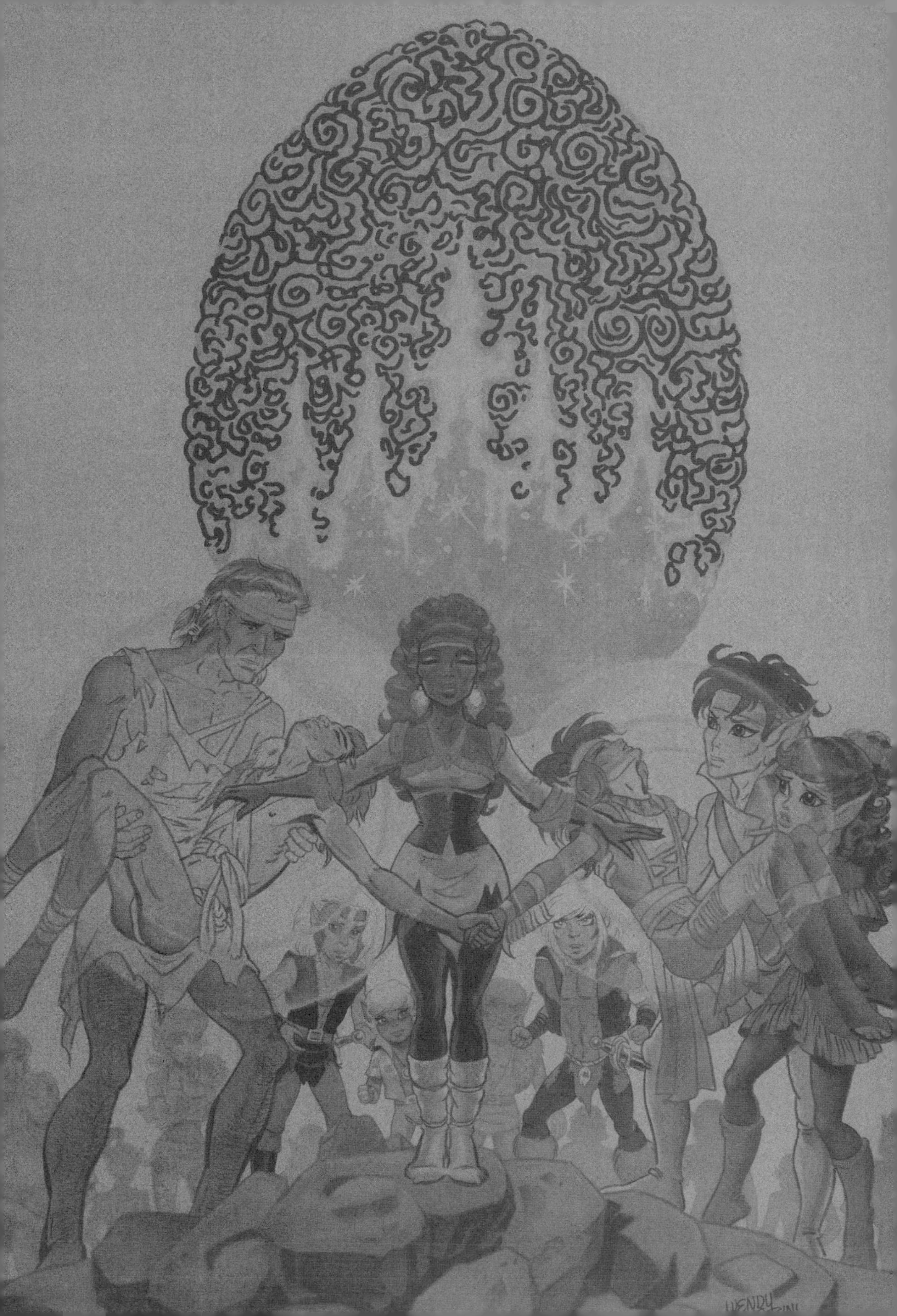

SIEGE AT BLUE MOUNTAIN

ARTIST / WRITER
WENDY PINI

CO-PLOT / EDITOR
RICHARD PINI

PART
7

INKS
JOE STATON

LETTERER
JANICE CHIANG

LORD VOLL'S HIGH-BACKED CHAIR STANDS EMPTY AT THE HEAD OF A BARREN TABLE. WHEN SHE LAST SAW IT, **CLEARBROOK** RECALLS, THE DINING CHAMBER GLOWED WARMLY WITH THE LIGHT OF MANY CANDLES, AND STRANGE, DELICIOUS MEATS WERE SERVED ON SHINING PLATTERS.

BUT THAT WAS THREE TURNS OF THE SEASONS AGO WHEN **VOLL** LIVED AND STILL HELD SOME SWAY WITHIN BLUE MOUNTAIN.

PRESERVER WEBS, CUPS AND TRAYS SCATTERED EVERY-WHERE! THE CHOSEN EIGHT PUT UP MORE OF A FIGHT THAN **CUTTER** AND **ADAR** BRAGGED!

NO MATTER! I'M GLAD THOSE GUARDS ARE OUT OF THE WAY. **WINNOWILL** IS ENOUGH TO DEAL WITH. ÷ MUNCH ÷ I'D BEST GET BACK ON HER TRAIL.

CLEARBROOK DELAYS BUT A MOMENT LONGER TO TUCK A FEW MORSELS INSIDE HER BELT POUCH. THEN SHE IS OFF DOWN ANOTHER DARK HALLWAY--

--FOLLOWING WINNOWILL'S DELICATE-BUT-RECENT SCENT TO THE THRONE ROOM, WHERE...

TYLDAK!

¿OOHHH...? Y-YOU HAVE A WEAPON...? GOOD!

USE IT!

I AM SICK... AND WEARY.

YOU'RE FAINT WITH HUNGER. HERE. EAT. BY TIMMORN'S BLOOD! THE BLACK SNAKE CAN MAKE ME PITY ANYONE--

--HUMANS... GLIDERS... EVEN YOU, WHO LEFT ME AND MINE TO THE TROLLS THAT KILLED MY LIFEMATE!

¿UUNNNH!? STUPID! WHAT MADE ME THINK I COULD BUDGE YOUR CHAIN!?

TELL ME WHERE IS WINNOWILL NOW?

IN THE CHAMBER OF THE GREAT EGG--

--WITH THE STRANGER, RAYEK!

I THINK HE MEANT TO TAKE MY...THE INFANT AWAY FROM HER--

--BUT SHE WORKED HER OLDEST AND BEST TRICKS ON HIM.

AND NOW, LIKE THE REST OF US, *RAYEK* IS HERS.

UNABLE TO DO ANYTHING MORE FOR *TYLDAK*, AND PRICKED BY HIS WORDS, *CLEARBROOK* DASHES OFF--

-- TO THE CHAMBER OF THE EGG...

AT LAST! *WINDKIN!* ASLEEP! AND I'D BET NOT NATURALLY!

THE SILVER-HAIRED HUNTRESS' BODY TENSES, READY TO SPRING FORWARD AND CATCH UP THE CHILD. BUT HE IS NOT ALONE!

YOU HAVE SEEN THIS BEFORE, HAVE YOU NOT?

THE ANCIENT MEMORIES, RETOLD NOT IN DANCING FIRE AND LIGHT--

BUT SHAPED AND SET IN LIVING ROCK!

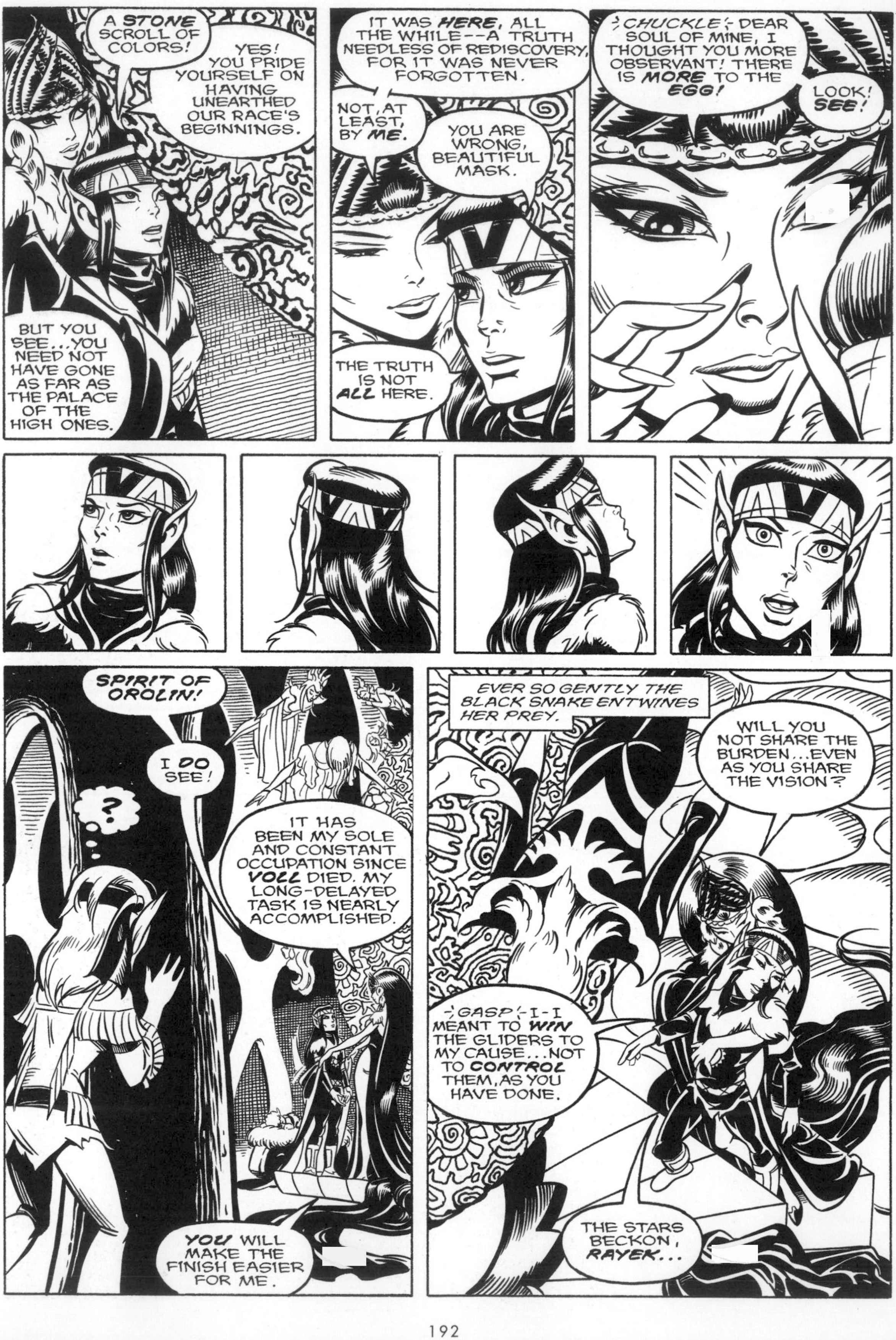
A STONE SCROLL OF COLORS!
YES! YOU PRIDE YOURSELF ON HAVING UNEARTHED OUR RACE'S BEGINNINGS.
BUT YOU SEE... YOU NEED NOT HAVE GONE AS FAR AS THE PALACE OF THE HIGH ONES.
IT WAS HERE, ALL THE WHILE--A TRUTH NEEDLESS OF REDISCOVERY, FOR IT WAS NEVER FORGOTTEN.
NOT, AT LEAST, BY ME.
YOU ARE WRONG, BEAUTIFUL MASK.
THE TRUTH IS NOT ALL HERE.
-CHUCKLE- DEAR SOUL OF MINE, I THOUGHT YOU MORE OBSERVANT! THERE IS MORE TO THE EGG!
LOOK! SEE!
SPIRIT OF OROLIN!
I DO SEE!
?
IT HAS BEEN MY SOLE AND CONSTANT OCCUPATION SINCE VOLL DIED. MY LONG-DELAYED TASK IS NEARLY ACCOMPLISHED.
YOU WILL MAKE THE FINISH EASIER FOR ME.
EVER SO GENTLY THE BLACK SNAKE ENTWINES HER PREY.
WILL YOU NOT SHARE THE BURDEN...EVEN AS YOU SHARE THE VISION?
-GASP- I-I MEANT TO WIN THE GLIDERS TO MY CAUSE...NOT TO CONTROL THEM, AS YOU HAVE DONE.
THE STARS BECKON, RAYEK...

NO! YOUR PEOPLE'S HEARTS ARE NOT IN IT!

AND NEITHER IS THEIR FULL POWER, YOU *KNOW* THAT!

THEY CANNOT RESIST THE TWO OF US.

RAYEK...

NOW THAT *YOU* ARE WITH ME--

--NO MORE WAITING--

--THERE WILL BE NO MORE WITHHOLDING--

--AND, ONCE WE ARE FREE OF THIS TWICE-CURSED WORLD, *NO MORE* MISTAKES!

UNDER M--*OUR* GUIDANCE THERE WILL NEVER BE ANOTHER "ACCIDENT" AS THAT WHICH EXILED THE FIRST COMERS HERE, WEAK AND ALL BUT DEFENSELESS.

BUT...THE PALACE--!

--IS NECESSARY! IT IS PART OF THE POWER WE NEED. WE WILL TAKE IT WITH US--

--BUT THE JOURNEY BEGINS WITH THE EGG!

CLEARBROOK STRUGGLES TO HOLD DOWN THE SLIGHT NOURISHMENT SHE TOOK A SHORT WHILE AGO.

SHE HAS NEVER DREAMED OF, MUCH LESS WITNESSED, SUCH A VIOLATION-- SUCH CALLOUS MANIPULATION OF ANOTHER'S NEEDS AND WEAKNESSES.

MEANWHILE, IN TENSPAN'S HALL...

⟨ADAR, C-COULD I NOT WAIT AND USE THE FOOT-HOLDS?⟩

⟨HEH...WOULD I HAVE COME THIS FAR TO DROP YOU *NOW*, WOMAN?⟩

LISTEN, LITTLE COUSIN. THESE HUMANS HAVE BEEN MISTREATED. THEY'RE WEAK. IF IT LOOKS LIKE THEY CAN'T MAKE IT DOWN THE MOUNTAIN FROM THE AERIE, JUST WAIT FOR ME.

WE'LL THINK OF SOMETHING.

I'M THINKING OF *STRONGBOW*. HE COULD GET "DOOR" TO OPEN.

OH, *CUTTER*, I KNOW YOU'VE STOOD UP TO *WINNOWILL* BEFORE-- BUT IF SHE GETS AT YOUR *SOUL*, SHE-SHE...FORGIVE ME! GOOD HUNT, MY CHIEF!

THAT'S WHAT I NEED TO HEAR, *DEWSHINE*.

AND *YOU*...!

LET'S SEE A *SMILE*!

GOOD HUNT, *CUTTER*!

SOON...

⟨FOLLOW, HUMANS! *THIS* WAY!⟩

⟨*PANT PANT*- THE CHILD SPIRITS RUN LIKE THE GREAT BIRDS FLY!⟩

⟨*TOO -GASP- SWIFTLY!*⟩

WE MAKE ROPES FOR CLIMBDOWN!

SPOOT!

HEE HEE!

GO, *BERRYBUZZ!* FLY OUTSIDE AND FIND US THE EASIEST WAY DOWN! AND *DON'T* GET EATEN BY GIANT HAWKS!

IN A SHORT WHILE...

⟨IT IS NOT MUCH FARTHER. DO NOT FEAR.⟩

SCOUTER IS SURPRISED BY HIS OWN CONCERN FOR "TALL ONES". THE LONGER HE IS WITH THEM, THE LESS THREATENING THEY SEEM.

⟨THERE NONNA!⟩

⟨THAT IS WHERE WE HID ONE OF THE BIRD RIDERS!⟩

AND...

RAAWK!

PRUMMMBLE!

HMMMM... ANYPLACE NOT SO GOOD FOR CLIMB DOWN!

TOO MUCH SHAKY~SHAKE!

OOPS!

NOSY OUTSIDE BIGTHINGS HEAR SHAKY~SHAKE, TOO!

WHY FOR EVERYBODY COME~GO COME~GO?

EEYIPE!

GROWLER HIGHTHINGS!

SHOULD JUST STAY HOME SAFE! SHOULD!!

195

HELLO! HELLO!

OH!

BERRYBUZZ! TELL US WHAT'S HAPPENED! WINDKIN..! CUTTER..! DEWSHINE...! TALK!

WHEN ONE ASKS A PRESERVER TO TALK, ONE DOES SO ADVISEDLY!

...THEN BIG BLUE ROCKS GO SHAKY-SHAKE AND WE LET LOOSE BIGTHINGS FROM CAGE...

...AND WE PUT WRAPSTUFF 'ROUND BAD FLYTHINGS, THEN PUT BAD FLYTHINGS IN HIDEY-HOLES...

...AND SHARPDARK HIGHTHING COME, THEN SHINYSWORD HIGHTHING SAY GO BY SELF, FIGHT BAD LONGSOFT-HAIR HIGHTHING GET FLYHIGHBABY BACK...

...AND LOOKSEE! LOOKSEE! MANY BIG-THINGS GUARD DOOR!

HUNH! I BET THEY'D SOONER FEED US TO THE GIANT BIRDS THAN BOW AND SCRAPE AS THEY ONCE DID FOR CUTTER, EH, STRONGBOW?

DEJECTEDLY, THE ARCHER NODS.

BUT WE HAVE TO GET IN--

--BEFORE CUTTER FACES WINNOWILL! I'D RATHER SLASH MY WAY THROUGH EIGHT EIGHTS OF HUMANS THAN LET HER EVEN BREATHE ON HIM!

SHH...SKYWISE, THERE IS ANOTHER DOOR, REMEMBER? IN WINNOWILL'S PRIVATE CHAMBERS.

SUNTOP CAN FIND IT FOR US.

LEETAH'S CALM ASSURANCE COOLS THE STARGAZER'S TEMPER.

IF ANYONE HAS A RIGHT TO WORRY ABOUT CUTTER, IT'S LEETAH. SHE DOESN'T BLAME ME FOR CAUSING THIS MESS--

--SO I'D BEST STOP BLAMING MYSELF, AND DO WHATEVER I CAN WITHOUT BARKING.

WITH PAINSTAKING SLOWNESS, THE ELFIN BAND PICKS IT'S WAY AROUND THE BASE OF BLUE MOUNTAIN. SUNTOP'S SPECIAL SENSE-- HIS "MAGIC FEELING"-- IS OPEN TO RECEIVE ANY TINGLING HINT OF DOOR THE ROCK-SHAPER'S PRESENCE.

OTHER SENSES, LUPINE ONES, ARE ALREADY DISTRACTED BY SOMETHING UNSEEN.

THE WOLVES... THEY KEEP LOOKING OFF TOWARD THE *HOLT!*

BUT BEFORE *STRONGBOW* CAN WHISPER HIS CONCERN TO HIS COMPANIONS...

GOLDEN DESERT CHILD, YOU SEEK A WAY *IN*, LIKE MICE YOU SQUEAK--

OH, NO...!

--BECAUSE YOU CANNOT FIND YOUR HOLE!

AND *THESE* ARE FINDERS OF THE *SCROLL!*

GRRRR...

HAHAHAHA!

WHAT?! THE WINNERS OF THE *PALACE*--

--LOST? MOTHER HAS YOU TURNED AND TOSSED!

WITHOUT EXPRESSION, WITHOUT SO MUCH AS THE BLINK OF AN EYE, *STRONGBOW* DRAWS AND AIMS.

WAIT.

THIS OLD ENEMY DESERVES A *SPECIAL* REVENGE--

--ONE THAT I HAVE IN MIND FOR HIS *MOTHER* AS WELL, IF I EVER GET MY HANDS ON HER...!

GLUH....

MOMENTS PASS QUIETLY. *LEETAH* WORKS SLOWLY, ADJUSTING TO THE ALIEN BLEND OF ELF AND TROLL BLOOD.

HEALER AND HEALED DESCEND TOGETHER TO THE BOTTOM OF THE PAIN--

--AND SUDDENLY, THE UNWEPT TEARS OF A FRIGHTENINGLY LONG AND LONELY LIFETIME GUSH FORTH.

THERE...MY GOOD CHILD... MY SWEET LITTLE SON... THERE...!

S-SON...?

WAIT! NO!

AFTER HIM!

A SON--

--BELONGS WITH THOSE WHO *WANT* HIM!

LEETAH...?

—SIGH!— CLOSE...! A MOMENT MORE——

——AND THE MADNESS WOULD HAVE LEFT HIM.

YOU CALLED THAT MONSTER "SON"! HOW COULD YOU?!

IT... WAS WHAT HE SEEMED TO NEED MOST!

TREESTUMP AND THE OTHERS CATCH UP WITH SKYWISE AND SUNTOP...

HURRY! COME LOOK! WE LOST TWO-EDGE——

BUT SEE WHAT WE FOUND!

A SECRET DOOR, HIDDEN BY THE BUSHES! WE'VE SEEN ITS LIKE BEFORE, EH?

TWO-EDGE'S SCENT IS STRONG THROUGH HERE!

AND THE OTHER "DOOR" ELF IS NEAR! HE JUST OPENED AT THE END OF THIS TUNNEL!

WELL, YOU WON'T BE NEEDING THAT BOW OF YOURS, STRONGBOW.

"BERRYBUZZ SAID THE ONLY ONE IN THE MOUNTAIN LEFT FOR US TO DEAL WITH IS WINNOWILL——"

"——AND, OF ALL CURSED THINGS, IT'S UP TO US KEEP HER ALIVE!"

RRRRRUUM...

RRRRUMMBLE...

RRRRUUM...

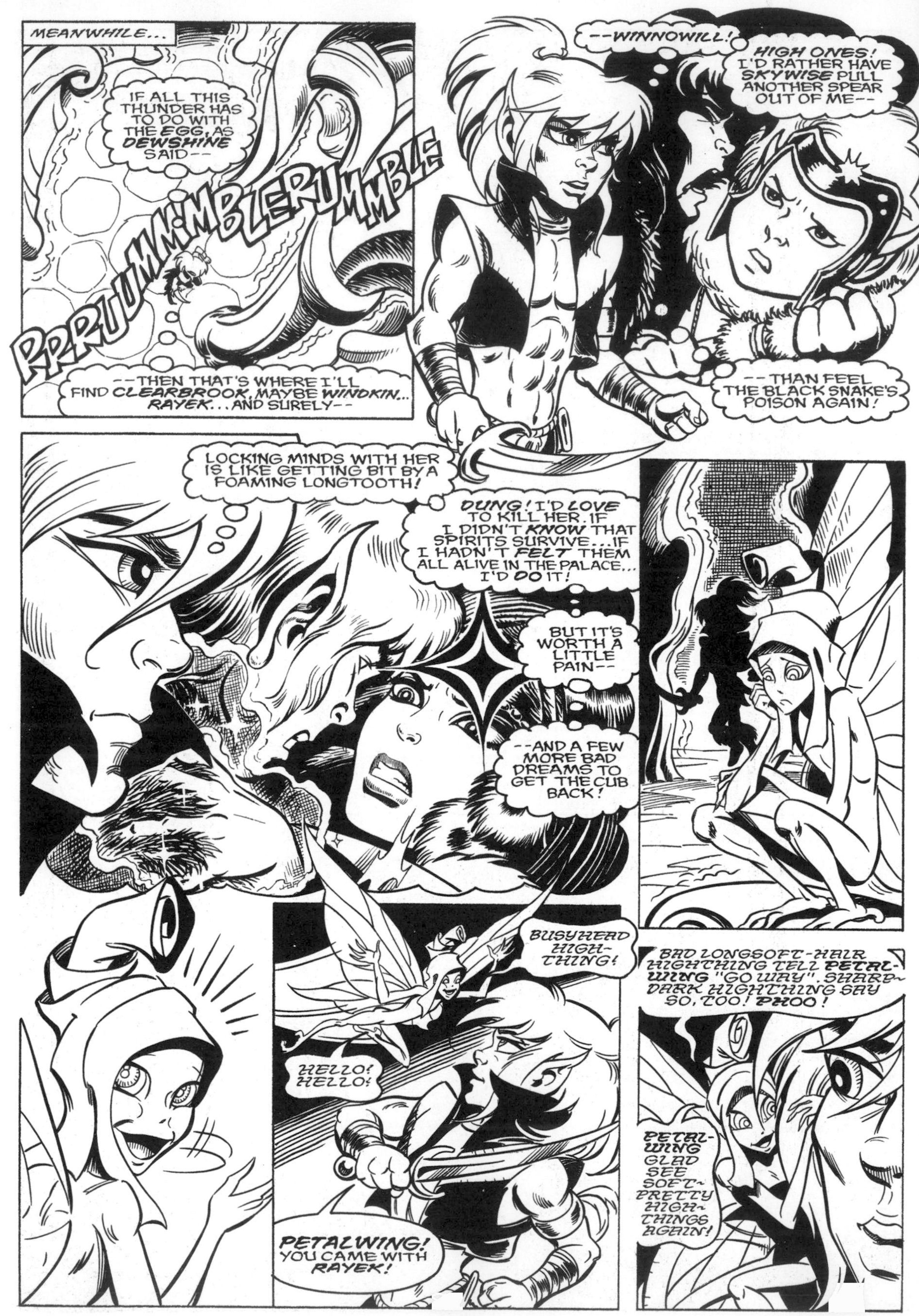
MEANWHILE...
IF ALL THIS THUNDER HAS TO DO WITH THE EGG, AS DEWSHINE SAID--
PPRUMMMBLERUMMBLE
--THEN THAT'S WHERE I'LL FIND CLEARBROOK, MAYBE WINDKIN... RAYEK... AND SURELY--
--WINNOWILL!
HIGH ONES! I'D RATHER HAVE SKYWISE PULL ANOTHER SPEAR OUT OF ME--
--THAN FEEL THE BLACK SNAKE'S POISON AGAIN!
LOCKING MINDS WITH HER IS LIKE GETTING BIT BY A FOAMING LONGTOOTH!
DUNG! I'D LOVE TO KILL HER. IF I DIDN'T KNOW THAT SPIRITS SURVIVE... IF I HADN'T FELT THEM ALL ALIVE IN THE PALACE... I'D DO IT!
BUT IT'S WORTH A LITTLE PAIN--
--AND A FEW MORE BAD DREAMS TO GET THE CUB BACK!
BUSYHEAD HIGH-THING!
HELLO! HELLO!
PETALWING! YOU CAME WITH RAYEK!
BAD LONGSOFT-HAIR HIGHTHING TELL PETALWING "GO WAY". SHARP-DARK HIGHTHING SAY SO, TOO! PHOO!
PETALWING GLAD SEE SOFT-PRETTY HIGH-THINGS AGAIN!

LEETAH? YOU'VE SEEN *LEETAH,* TOO?

CAME WITH IS HERE!

SO THAT'S WHAT'S BEEN GNAWING AT ME!

AND *SKYWISE...? TREESTUMP...?*

ALL OUTSIDE! WE GO GET FLYHIGHBABY NOW!

YES!

THE TIME YOU SPENT WITH *LEETAH...* YOU SEE NOW HOW MUCH *LESS* THAN FULFILLING IT WAS--

--HOW SHE WITHHELD HERSELF, PORTIONED OUT HER HEALER'S POWER TO COMPLETELY GRATIFY THE SENSES--

--PERHAPS, MISGUIDEDLY, TO PROTECT YOU. PERHAPS,... *HERSELF!*

I MAKE NO SUCH JUDGEMENTS UPON YOUR STRENGTH, FEAR NO LOSS OF SELF IN PLEASING YOU.

THE HUNGER YOU HAVE KNOWN ALL YOUR LIFE--

IS BUT THE LONELINESS OF THE *SUN* SHINING AMONG LESSER LIGHTS.

YOU HAVE ALWAYS YEARNED TO TAKE THE NEXT STEP, AND SCORNED ALL ELVES CONTENT WITH THEMSELVES AS THEY ARE.

WHAT IF YOU *COULD* TAKE THAT STEP?

WHAT IF THIS BODY, BURNED BROWN BY THE SUN--

-- THIS SLIGHT, SWEET FRAME THAT I HAVE COME TO KNOW — COULD, IN STATURE, BE WORTHY OF THE GREAT SPIRIT IT HOUSES?

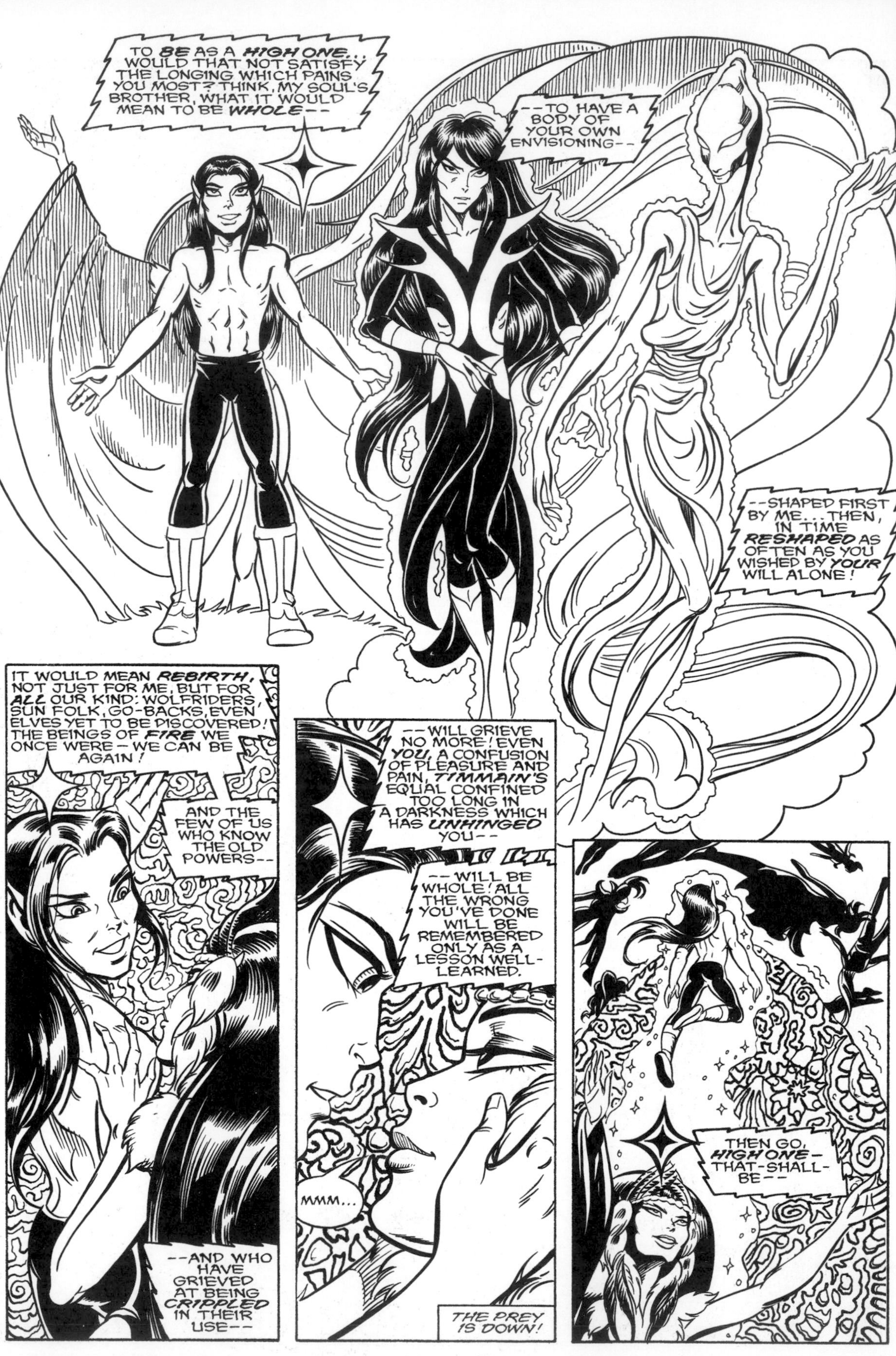
TO BE AS A HIGH ONE... WOULD THAT NOT SATISFY THE LONGING WHICH PAINS YOU MOST? THINK, MY SOUL'S BROTHER, WHAT IT WOULD MEAN TO BE WHOLE--
--TO HAVE A BODY OF YOUR OWN ENVISIONING--
--SHAPED FIRST BY ME... THEN, IN TIME RESHAPED AS OFTEN AS YOU WISHED BY YOUR WILL ALONE!
IT WOULD MEAN REBIRTH, NOT JUST FOR ME, BUT FOR ALL OUR KIND: WOLFRIDERS, SUN FOLK, GO-BACKS, EVEN ELVES YET TO BE DISCOVERED! THE BEINGS OF FIRE WE ONCE WERE--WE CAN BE AGAIN!
AND THE FEW OF US WHO KNOW THE OLD POWERS--
--AND WHO HAVE GRIEVED AT BEING CRIPPLED IN THEIR USE--
--WILL GRIEVE NO MORE! EVEN YOU, A CONFUSION OF PLEASURE AND PAIN, TIMMAIN'S EQUAL CONFINED TOO LONG IN A DARKNESS WHICH HAS UNHINGED YOU--
--WILL BE WHOLE! ALL THE WRONG YOU'VE DONE WILL BE REMEMBERED ONLY AS A LESSON WELL-LEARNED.
MMM...
THE PREY IS DOWN!
THEN GO, HIGH ONE-THAT-SHALL-BE--

"--AND MOVE THE GLIDERS WITH YOUR STRENGTH OF PURPOSE WHICH IS GREATER, EVEN, THAN MINE!"

WATCHING WITH HORRIFIED FASCINATION, CLEARBROOK STARTS AS *CUTTER* APPROACHES AT A WOLF-SOFT RUN.

THEY NOD A QUICK GREETING. THEIR EYES SPEAK.

THEY KNOW THEIR CHANCE TO SNATCH THE CUB IS NOW--

--OR NEVER!

BUT...

‡GASP!‡

WHA--?!

RRUM BE RRUMM.

CRRREEEEAKK!

EEP!

GRRREEAKKK!!

SQUEEALLL...

C—CAN'T STAND UU-U-UP!

...RRRUUMMBLLERRR...

OOF!

UNH!

TH—THE WHOLE PLACE IS MOVING— MELTING LIKE HOT MUD! TIMMORN'S BLOOD!

BUFFETED AND BRUISED, THE TWO TRIBEMATES STAGGER BACK TO THE CHAMBER OF THE EGG--

--WHERE THEY FIND A SMALL ISLAND OF STABILITY SURROUNDED BY MADLY UNDULATING STONE!

WHATEVER WINNOWILL IS DOING, RAYEK'S HELPING HER!

NOT ALL BY CHOICE, CUTTER! I SAW HER WORK ON HIM!

AND WITHIN TWO-EDGE'S SECRET TUNNEL...

SUNTOP! WHAT IS HAPPENING?

IT'S—IT'S LIKE A CROWD OF ROCK SHAPERS GONE CRAZY! SO MUCH POWER-- WHOA!!

IT'S A G-G- GROUND QUAKE THAT WON'T STOP!

THE SHAPING FORCE THAT SURGES THROUGH EVERY NOOK AND CRANNY OF BLUE MOUNTAIN IS LESS POTENT NEAR WINNOWILL'S PRIVATE QUARTERS.

DOOR, OPEN! DOOR, OPEN!

STRONGBOW "LOCK-SENDS", HOPING THAT WINNOWILL IS TOO BUSY ELSEWHERE TO PIERCE HIS MENTAL SHIELD.

DOOR, OPEN!!

SUNTOP IS ABLE TO SENSE THE SECOND "DOOR'S" LOCATION—ON THE OTHER SIDE OF THE WALL AT THE TUNNEL'S END.

DOOR, OPEN!!

HIS RECEPTIVITY MUDDLED BY THE GREAT UPHEAVAL, DOOR SHIFTS ON HIS SEAT.

HE HAS ALREADY PERFORMED FOR ONE HE KNOWS...

OPEN! OPEN! NOW!!

--TOO STRONG TO RESIST!

YES! OBEY ME! OPEN AND STAY OPEN!

BUT THIS NEW COMMAND IS SENT BY AN INTRUDER--A STRONG ONE--

HE DID IT! LEETAH! SUNTOP--

--GO!

BUT...

OH!

LOOK OUT!!

IT'S CLOSING AGAIN!

DOOR'S ERRATIC EFFORT TO DEFEND THE SANCTITY OF WINNOWILL'S QUARTERS FAILS AGAIN...

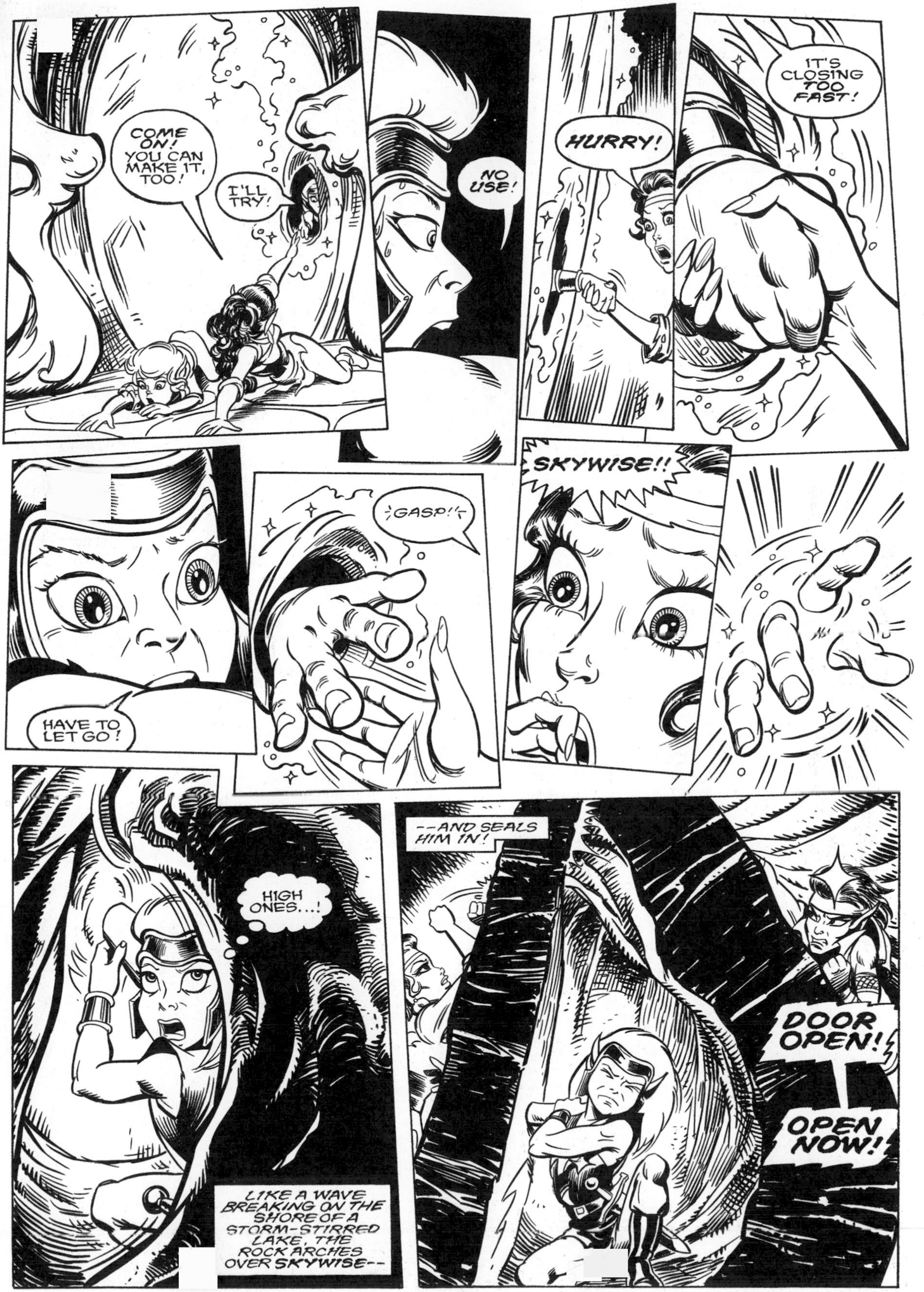
COME ON! YOU CAN MAKE IT, TOO!
I'LL TRY!
NO USE!
HURRY!
IT'S CLOSING TOO FAST!
HAVE TO LET GO!
GASP!
SKYWISE!!
HIGH ONES...!
LIKE A WAVE BREAKING ON THE SHORE OF A STORM-STIRRED LAKE, THE ROCK ARCHES OVER SKYWISE--
--AND SEALS HIM IN!
DOOR OPEN!!
OPEN NOW!

THIS TIME THERE IS NO APPEAL! THE KNOWLEDGE OF HIS FUNCTION NOT ENTIRELY SHAKEN FROM HIM--

--DOOR WILL NOT OPEN AGAIN!

OBEY CURSE YOU!

STRONGBOW, LOOK!

COME ON! WE CAN'T HELP SKYWISE--

--IF WE GET TRAPPED, TOO!

TREESTUMP AND THE ARCHER BARELY MANAGE TO SQUEEZE PAST ONE RISING LUMP OF TUNNEL FLOOR, ONLY TO FIND--

?!!!

--ANOTHER! AND IT'S STILL A WAYS TO THE OUTSIDE!

AFTER SEVERAL MORE NARROW SQUEAKS...

WATCH IT!

YOU'LL GET YOURSELF SQUASHED AND WE'LL NEVER GET DOOR OPEN AGAIN!

TREESTUMP WINCES GLADLY AT THE LIGHT WHICH STREAMS THROUGH THE TUNNEL ENTRANCE.

BUT FRAMED IN THAT DOORWAY STANDS A RIGID SILHOUETTE--

--MOONSHADE...? ARE YOU--?!

WELL, STRIKE ME WITH SKYFIRE!

208

MOTHER...!

M-MY EYES SEE WITH JOY! MY HANDS... TOUCH...

FATHER...?

YOU LOOK LIKE A THISTLE!

SUDDENLY... RRRUUUMMBLE-KRRK-KRAK!

KLOP!

...RRRRUUUU...MMMM!

BLERRR...

KLAT!

...RRRRUUUUT! BLERRRRUUMBLE...

GEGE!

AATIEE!

HURRY! CUT THE HUMANS FREE SO THEY CAN RUN!

YOU SURE DART?

DO IT!!

"G-GE-O-KI...!" RIGHT?

⟨GEOKI! MY NAME! I KNEW YOU WERE A FRIEND!⟩

SKREEEE!

RAAWK!

INSIDE THE AERIE *DEWSHINE, SCOUTER,* AND THE HUMANS CLING TO WHATEVER SHIFTING SUPPORT THEY CAN FIND!

THERE WILL BE NO CLIMBING DOWN UNDER *THESE* CONDITIONS!

AND IN THE CHAMBER OF THE EGG...

SOON...!

WINNOWILL!

OH...

IT IS *YOU,* LITTLE CHIEFTAIN.

GIVE ME THE CUB.

HE IS NO LONGER YOURS.

STRANGE... YOUR SENDING WAS A *SHOCK* THE FIRST TIME I FELT IT. NOW IT SEEMS QUITE TAME.

I CAN AFFORD A SLIGHT DISTRACTION NOW, WITH *RAYEK* HELPING TO KEEP THE GLIDERS' ATTENTION ON THEIR TASK.

YOU REMEMBER MY SENDING--

--DO YOU NOT WOLFLING?

THE CUB, CLEARBROOK ...QUICK!!

CUTTER SHIVERS, MAKING NO SOUND.

BUT, FAR BELOW, HIS PAIN IS FELT, AND HIS SILENT CRY IS HEARD BY ONE WHOSE SOUL IS LINKED WITH HIS!

OH, TAM!

SUNTOP, DO NOT SEND TO *SKYWISE!* THERE IS STILL A CHANCE WE CAN TAKE *WINNOWILL* BY SURPRISE!

LEETAH IS FORCED TO MAKE A HEARTBREAKING DECISION!

MOTHER, WE *CAN'T* LEAVE HIM LIKE THAT!

AND WE CANNOT STOP *WINNOWILL* UNLESS I *TOUCH* HER!

IN THE BLACKNESS OF THE STONE POCKET WHICH ENCLOSES HIM, THE STARGAZER CAN ONLY GUESS AT WHAT IS HAPPENING.

HE, TOO, SHARES CUTTER'S SOUL NAME. HE, TOO, FEELS HIS FRIEND'S PAIN-- MORE THAN HIS OWN FEAR.

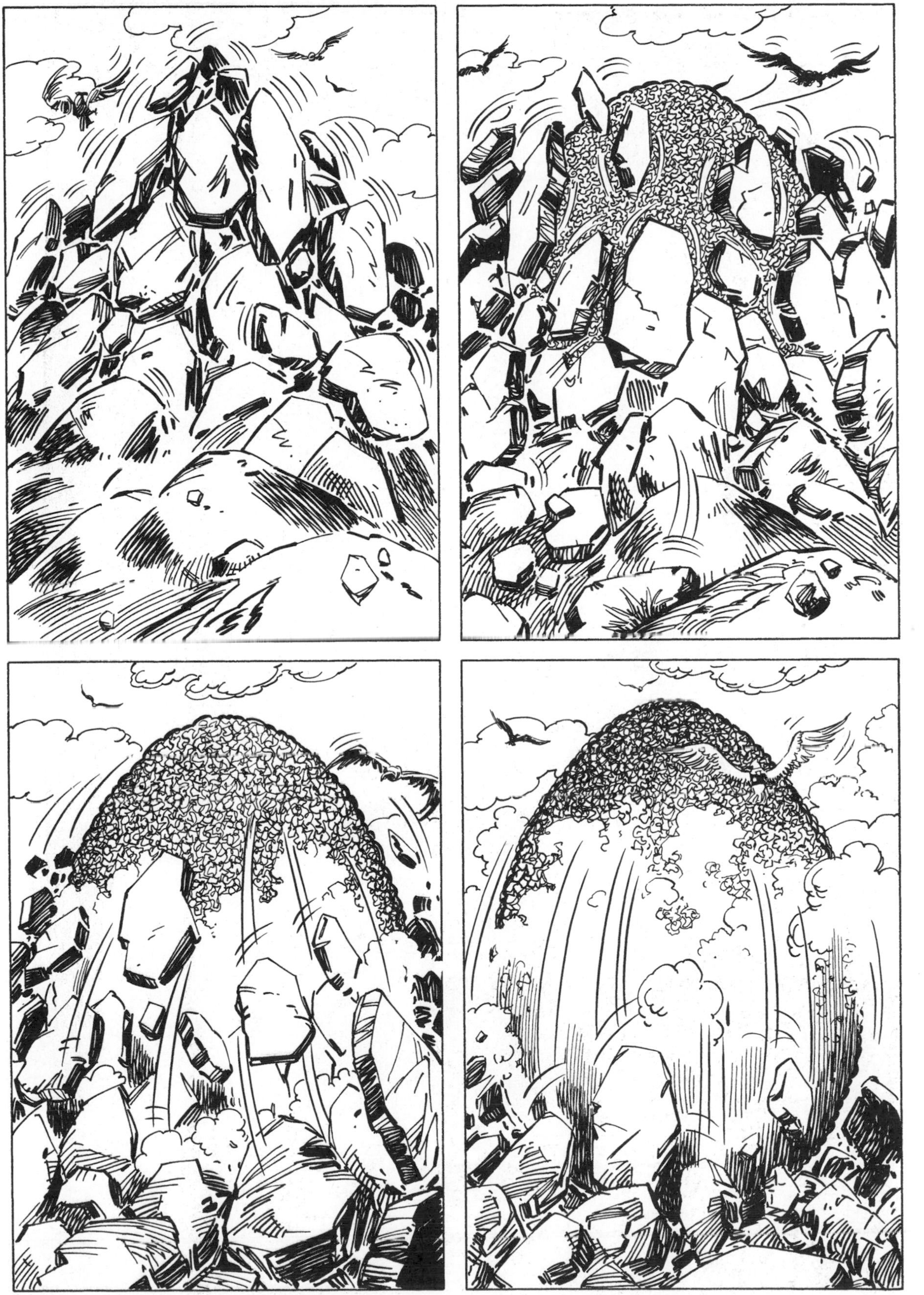

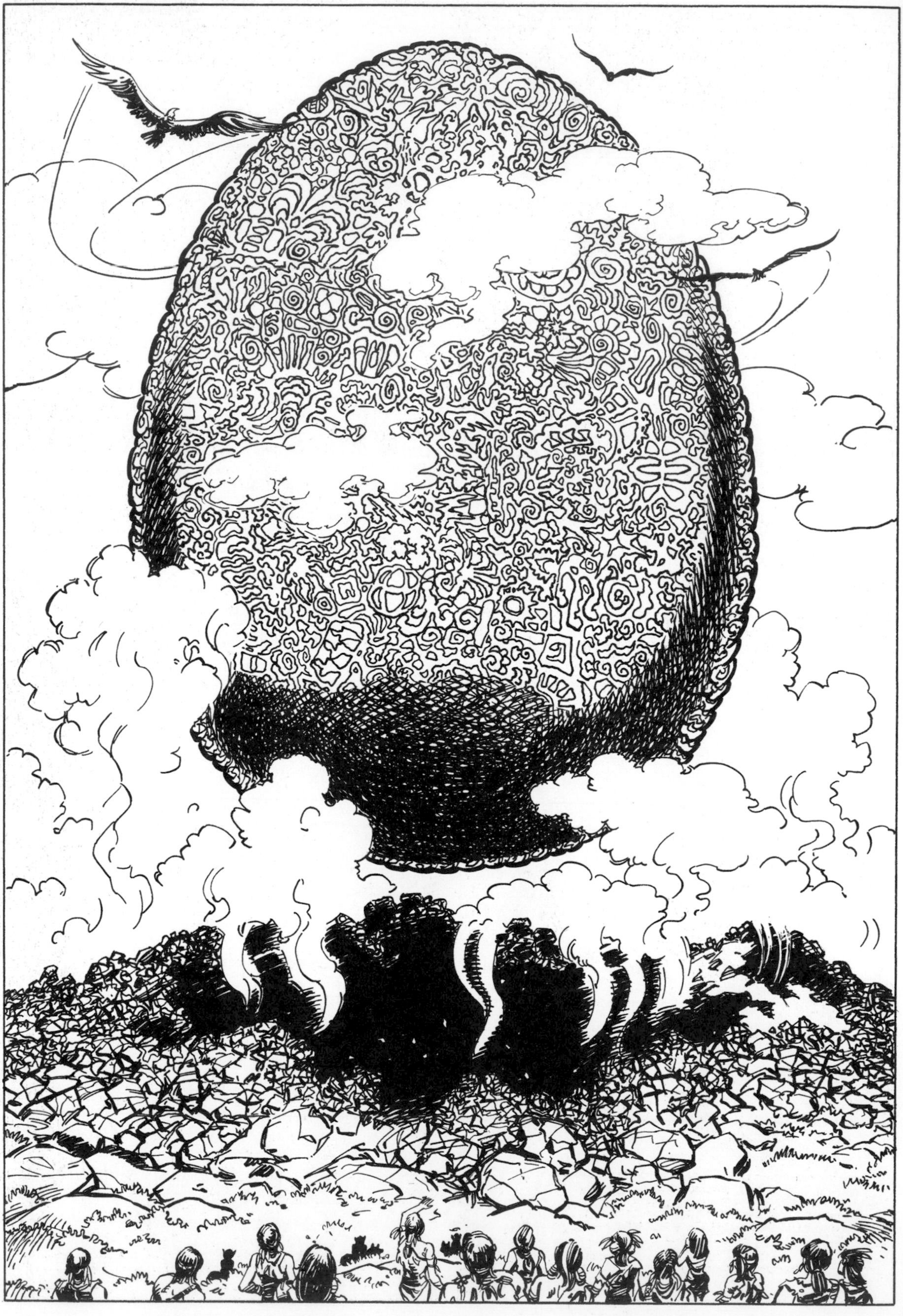

AS THE MOUNTAIN'S THROES SUBSIDE...

YOUR SWORD... IT REMAINS SHEATHED! YOU UNDERSTAND, THEN, THAT I MUST KEEP MY BODY. HOW FORTUNATE FOR YOU THAT I PREFER TO DO SO!

DO YOU KNOW WHAT HAS JUST BEGUN, LITTLE WOLF CHIEF? A *REBIRTH*, AS RAYEK CHARMINGLY PUT IT.

THE *EGG* IS NOW COMPLETE! TWO MORE LAYERS OF SHELL HAVE BEEN ADDED—EIGHT IN ALL. THE EGG WILL BE THE *NEW* CASTLE-SHIP. IT WILL TRAVEL TO THE FROZEN MOUNTAINS—

—AND ABSORB THE PALACE OF THE *HIGH ONES*—ALONG WITH ALL THE ATTENDANT SPIRITS BOUND TO THE TIME AND WORLD IN WHICH IT EXISTS!

ALL LIVING, *PURE-BLOODED* MAGIC USERS—ALL HEALERS AND FLOATERS, FIRE-MAKERS AND SHAPERS OF EVERY KIND—WILL THEN BE CALLED TO THE EGG!

WITH THAT MUCH POWER—

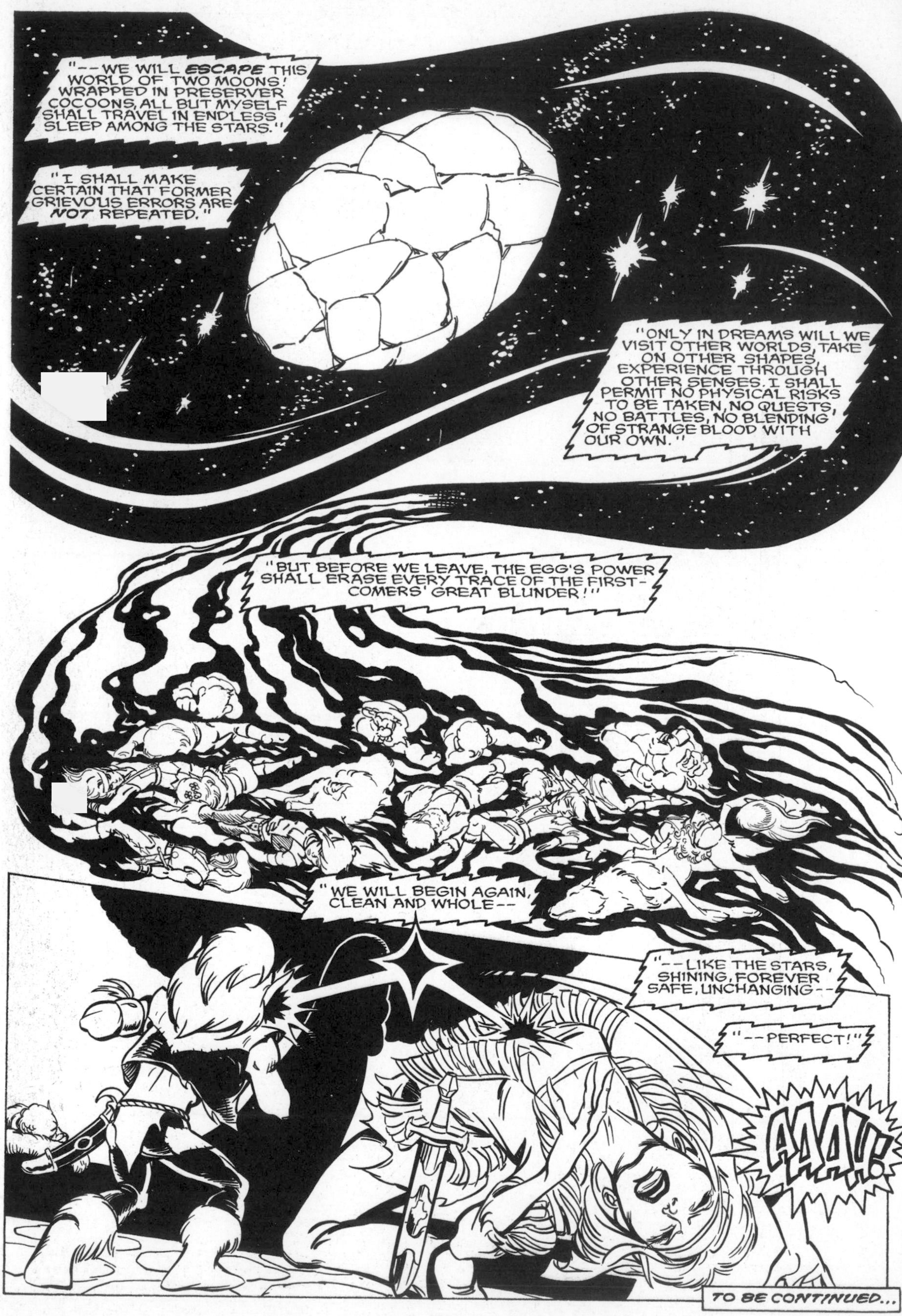
"--WE WILL ESCAPE THIS WORLD OF TWO MOONS! WRAPPED IN PRESERVER COCOONS, ALL BUT MYSELF SHALL TRAVEL IN ENDLESS SLEEP AMONG THE STARS."
"I SHALL MAKE CERTAIN THAT FORMER GRIEVOUS ERRORS ARE NOT REPEATED."
"ONLY IN DREAMS WILL WE VISIT OTHER WORLDS, TAKE ON OTHER SHAPES, EXPERIENCE THROUGH OTHER SENSES. I SHALL PERMIT NO PHYSICAL RISKS TO BE TAKEN, NO QUESTS, NO BATTLES, NO BLENDING OF STRANGE BLOOD WITH OUR OWN."
"BUT BEFORE WE LEAVE, THE EGG'S POWER SHALL ERASE EVERY TRACE OF THE FIRST-COMERS' GREAT BLUNDER!"
"WE WILL BEGIN AGAIN, CLEAN AND WHOLE--
"--LIKE THE STARS, SHINING, FOREVER SAFE, UNCHANGING--
"--PERFECT!"
AAAH!
TO BE CONTINUED...

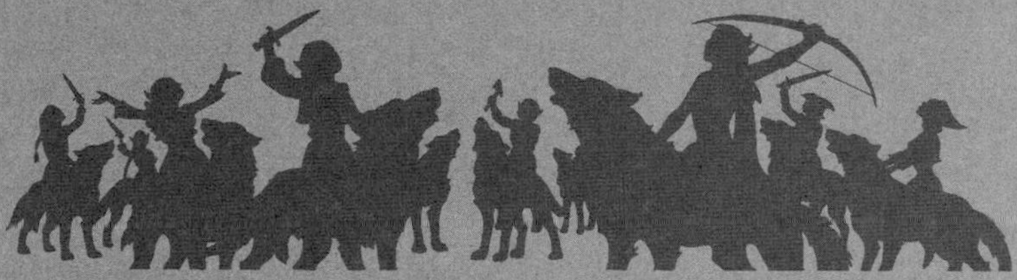

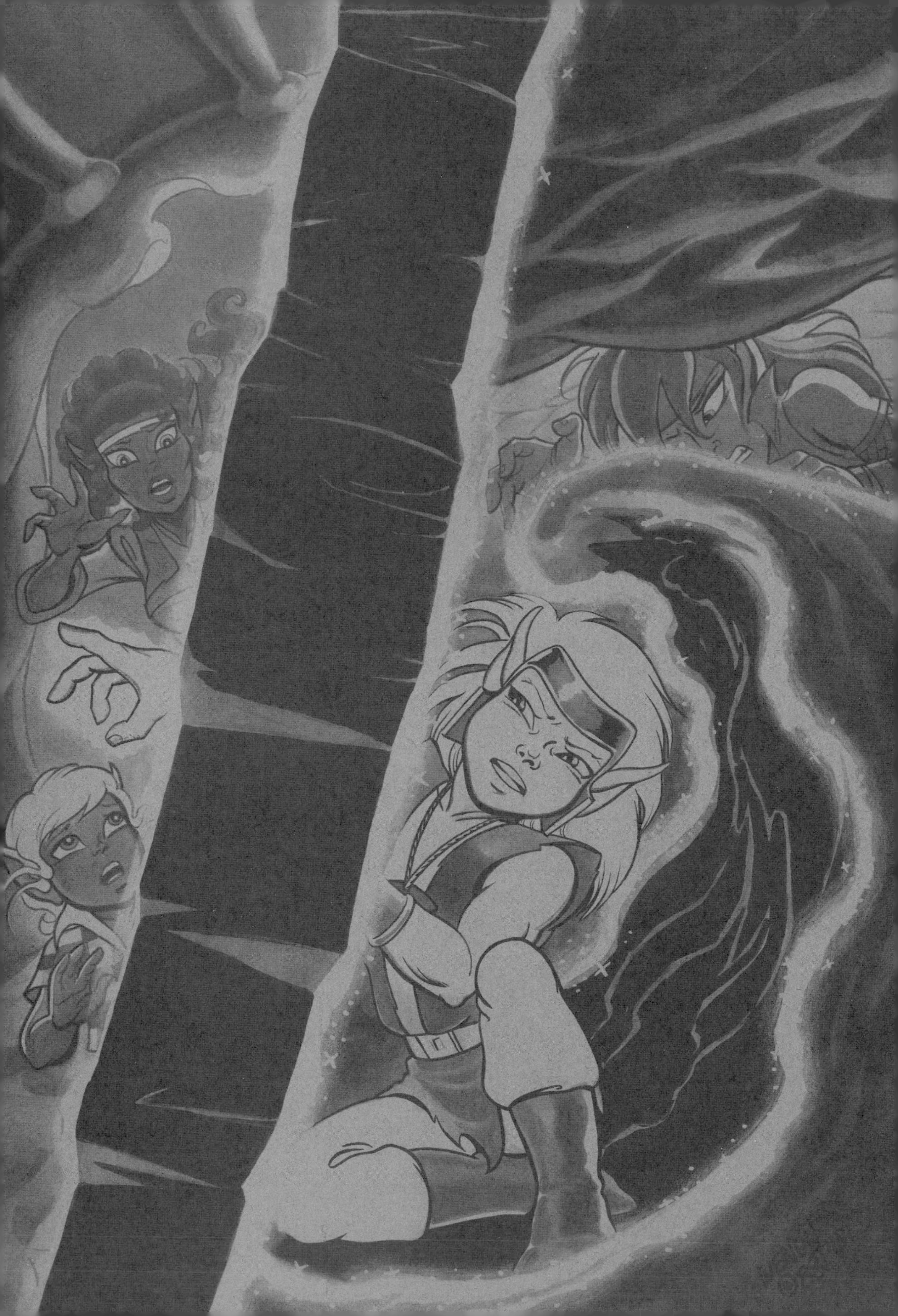

SIEGE AT BLUE MOUNTAIN

ARTIST / WRITER
WENDY PINI

CO-PLOT / EDITOR
RICHARD PINI

PART **8**

INKS
JOE STATON

LETTERER
JANICE CHIANG

EVERYONE KNOWS THE AIR IS **ALWAYS** THERE BETWEEN THE WORLD AND THE STAR-HOLDING SKY. AIR CANNOT BE DRAINED LIKE WATER... IT CANNOT BURN ITSELF OUT LIKE FIRE... NO, THE AIR IS **ALWAYS** THERE--

¡GASP!

--JUST AS A MOUNTAIN THAT HAS STOOD FOR TIME UNTOLD--

IS ALWAYS THERE. SACRED MOUNTAINS DO NOT CHANGE INTO STUPENDOUS **EGGS**--

--AND AIR DOES NOT ABANDON ITS BREATHER--

--EXCEPT, IT SEEMS, ON THE WORLD OF **TWO MOONS** WHERE BOTH EVENTS ARE PERCEIVED AS--

--MAGIC!

SPIRIT MAGIC!! WE WILL **DIE**!!

WHILE THE TERRIFIED HUMANS COWER IN THE VAST SHADOW OF BLUE MOUNTAIN – THAT – WAS, *SKYWISE* FIGHTS FOR CONSCIOUSNESS IN HIS SEALED TOMB WITHIN THE EGG.

PANT! PANT!

MY RIBS ACHE SO...!

WHY?

...IS IT SOME NEW PAIN-SENDING FROM *WINNOWILL?* NO! SHE'S FIGHTING *CUTTER* NOW... DOESN'T KNOW I'M HERE.

MY *ARM...!*

WANT TO BREAK SILENCE... SEND FOR HELP!

CAN'T! *LEETAH* MUST GET TO *CUTTER!*

IF IT'S HIM OR ME, SHE HAS TO HELP *HIM!*

HE *HAS* TO WIN, *HIGH ONES!* HE *HAS* TO!

AT THE SAME TIME...

THE INFANT LIES WITHIN REACH. THE INNOCENT ONE HAS BECOME THE PRIZE IN THIS DUEL BETWEEN CHIEF AND LORD.

THROUGH A RED HAZE OF PAIN, *CUTTER* SENSES HIS TRIBEMATE *CLEARBROOK,* HAS FALLEN.

BEAST-BLOODED *FOOL!* YOU ARE THE ONLY ONE OF YOUR KIND WITH STRENGTH ENOUGH TO SLAY ME. BUT KNOWLEDGE INHIBITS YOU.

BECAUSE YOU DARE NOT DESTROY *MY* BODY, I AM FREE TO DESTROY *YOURS*–– BY DEGREES!

AND YOUR SPIRIT, WOLFRIDER, THAT TOO WILL I KILL!

YOU AND YOUR TRIBE ARE *FINISHED!*

W-WINDKIN...! OOOHH...!

THE FLOORS NO LONGER HEAVE AS THEY DID MOMENTS AGO. WAVERING WALLS AND COLUMNS SETTLE INTO THE LACY PATTERNS THAT HELP TELL THE GREAT EGG'S EON-SPANNING TALE.

BUT *SUNTOP* AND *LEETAH,* ARRIVING AT ITS CORE, CARE NOTHING FOR THIS TWISTED STONE RECORD OF ELFIN LORE.

THEY SEE ONLY THE UNEQUAL BATTLE RAGING SILENTLY IN THE CHAMBER BEFORE THEM.

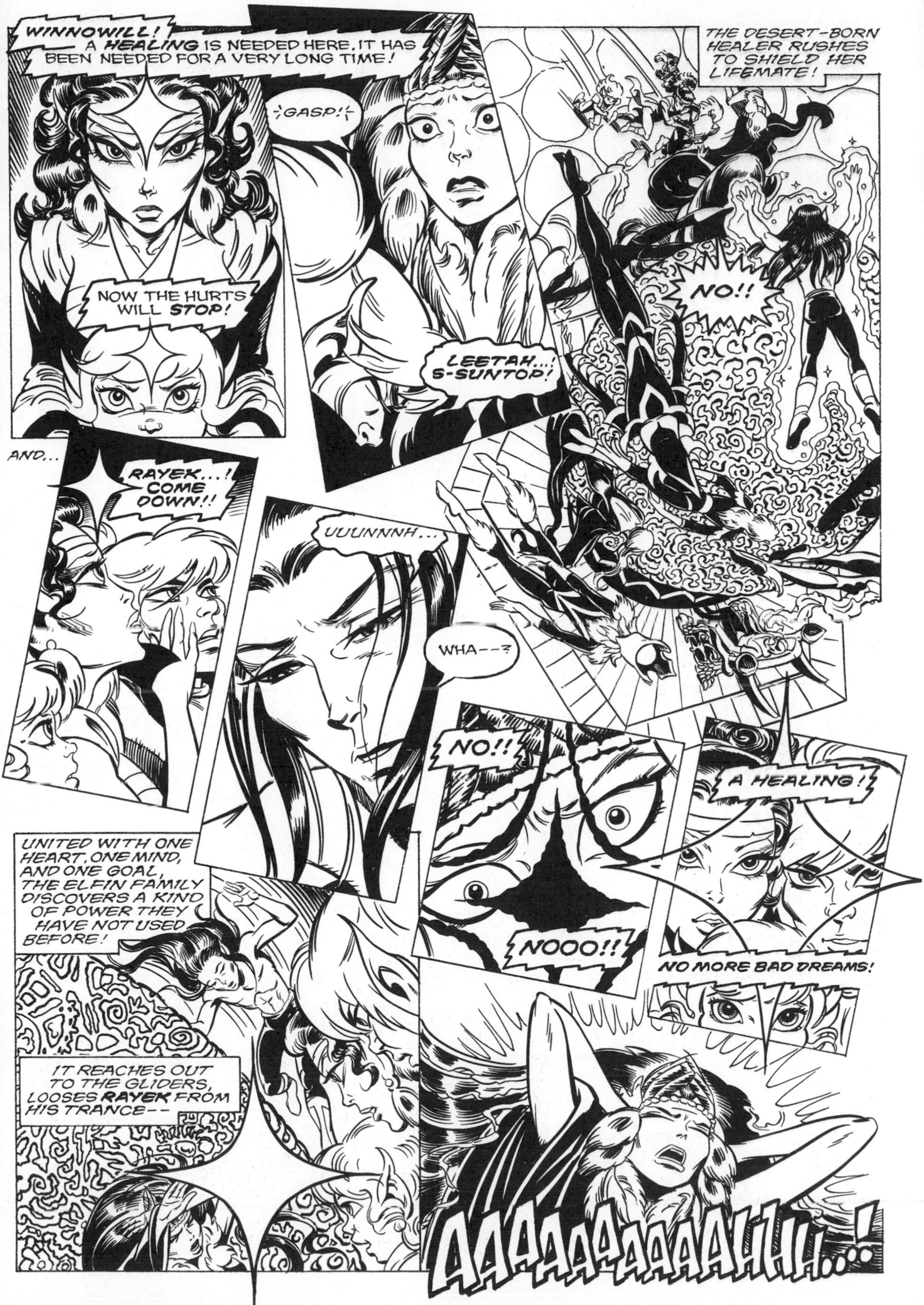
WINNOWILL!
A HEALING IS NEEDED HERE. IT HAS BEEN NEEDED FOR A VERY LONG TIME!
NOW THE HURTS WILL STOP!
GASP!
LEETAH...! S-SUNTOP!
THE DESERT-BORN HEALER RUSHES TO SHIELD HER LIFEMATE!
NO!!
AND...
RAYEK...! COME DOWN!!
UUUNNNH...
WHA--?
NO!!
NOOO!!
A HEALING!
NO MORE BAD DREAMS!
UNITED WITH ONE HEART, ONE MIND, AND ONE GOAL, THE ELFIN FAMILY DISCOVERS A KIND OF POWER THEY HAVE NOT USED BEFORE!
IT REACHES OUT TO THE GLIDERS, LOOSES RAYEK FROM HIS TRANCE--
AAAAAAAAAAAHHH...!

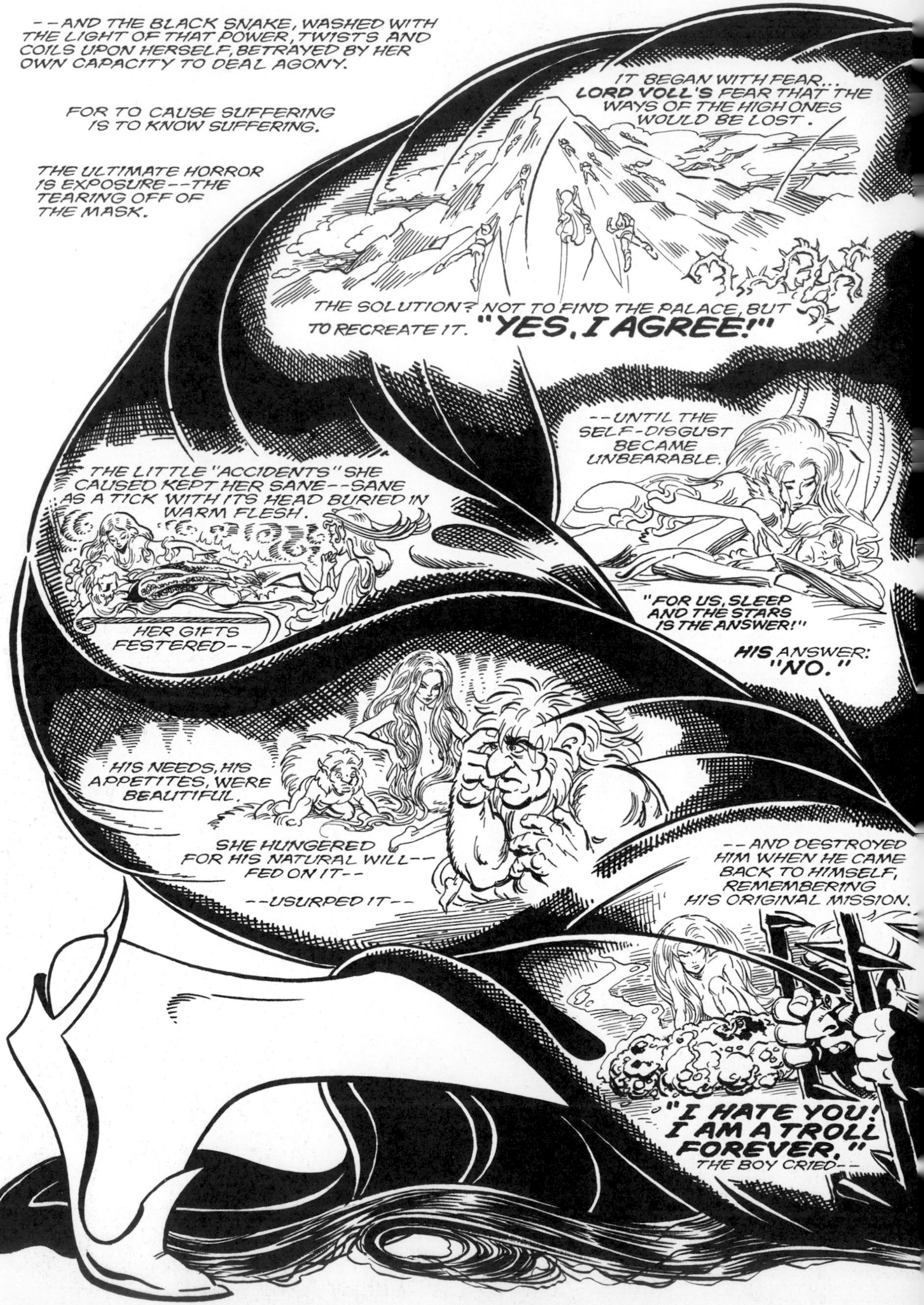
--AND THE BLACK SNAKE, WASHED WITH THE LIGHT OF THAT POWER, TWISTS AND COILS UPON HERSELF, BETRAYED BY HER OWN CAPACITY TO DEAL AGONY.
FOR TO CAUSE SUFFERING IS TO KNOW SUFFERING.
THE ULTIMATE HORROR IS EXPOSURE--THE TEARING OFF OF THE MASK.
IT BEGAN WITH FEAR... LORD VOLL'S FEAR THAT THE WAYS OF THE HIGH ONES WOULD BE LOST.
THE SOLUTION? NOT TO FIND THE PALACE, BUT TO RECREATE IT. "YES, I AGREE!"
--UNTIL THE SELF-DISGUST BECAME UNBEARABLE.
"FOR US, SLEEP AND THE STARS IS THE ANSWER!"
HIS ANSWER: "NO."
THE LITTLE "ACCIDENTS" SHE CAUSED KEPT HER SANE--SANE AS A TICK WITH ITS HEAD BURIED IN WARM FLESH.
HER GIFTS FESTERED--
HIS NEEDS, HIS APPETITES, WERE BEAUTIFUL.
SHE HUNGERED FOR HIS NATURAL WILL--FED ON IT--
--USURPED IT--
--AND DESTROYED HIM WHEN HE CAME BACK TO HIMSELF, REMEMBERING HIS ORIGINAL MISSION.
"I HATE YOU! I AM A TROLL FOREVER," THE BOY CRIED--

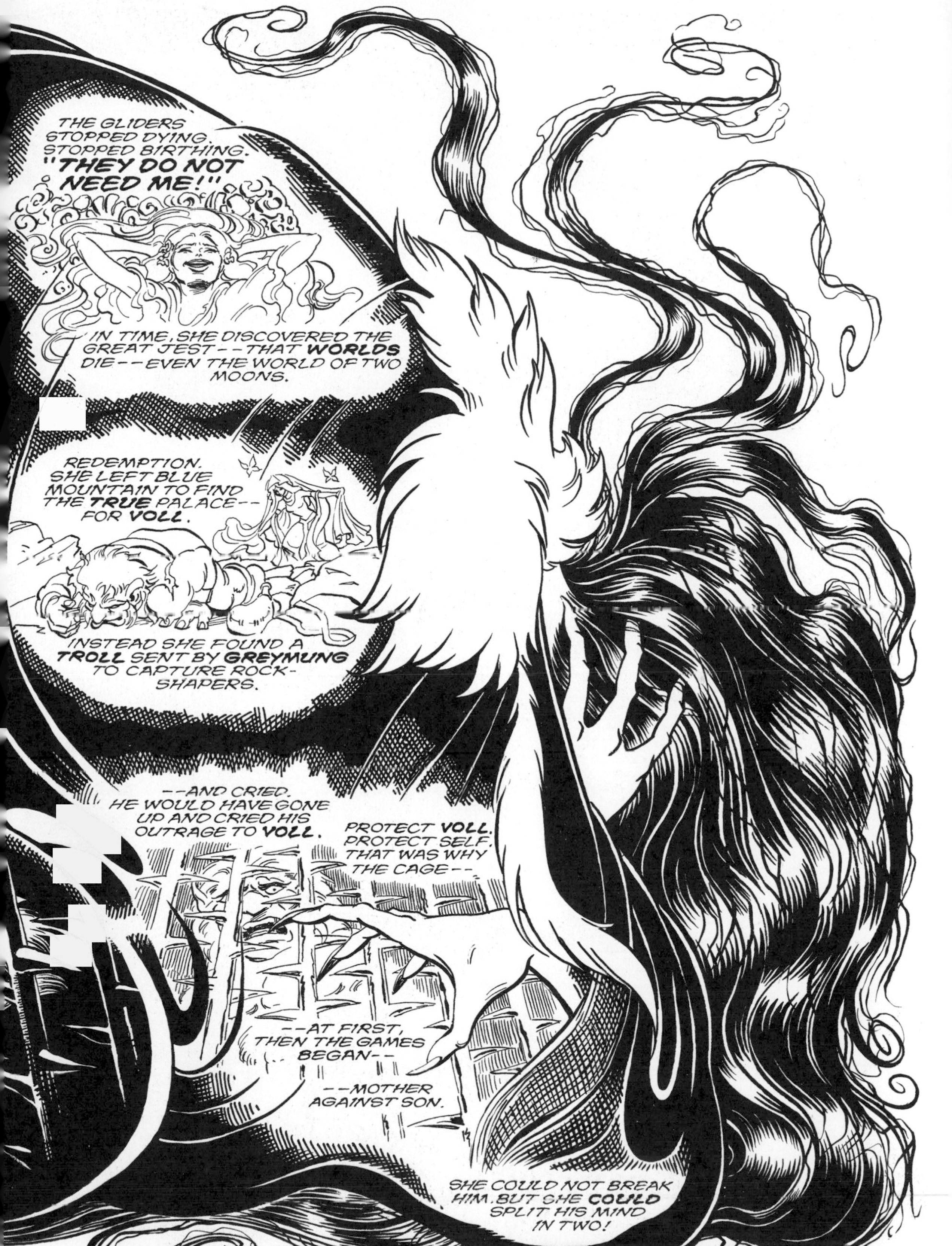
THE GLIDERS STOPPED DYING. STOPPED BIRTHING.
"THEY DO NOT NEED ME!"
IN TIME, SHE DISCOVERED THE GREAT JEST--THAT WORLDS DIE--EVEN THE WORLD OF TWO MOONS.
REDEMPTION. SHE LEFT BLUE MOUNTAIN TO FIND THE TRUE PALACE--FOR VOLL.
INSTEAD SHE FOUND A TROLL SENT BY GREYMUNG TO CAPTURE ROCK-SHAPERS.
--AND CRIED. HE WOULD HAVE GONE UP AND CRIED HIS OUTRAGE TO VOLL.
PROTECT VOLL. PROTECT SELF. THAT WAS WHY THE CAGE--
--AT FIRST, THEN THE GAMES BEGAN--
--MOTHER AGAINST SON.
SHE COULD NOT BREAK HIM. BUT SHE COULD SPLIT HIS MIND IN TWO!

THE FIRST TOUCH OF HEALING FORCES HER TO REMEMBER--

--HER CHILD'S FACE AT THE VERY MOMENT SHE MADE HIM MAD!

RAYEK...! AS YOU LOVE ME... SAVE ME!

AGAIN...

ALMOST...

HE ALMOST FALLS UNDER HER SPELL...

BUT THE PITEOUS SOUND-MEMORY OF YOUNG TWO-EDGE'S SOBS BLENDS IN RAYEK'S MIND WITH THE WAILS OF HIS OWN BABE--THE NEWBORN THAT SOMEHOW HE KNOWS IS ALIVE!

RAYEK DRAWS BACK, REPULSED BY THE CHILD-HARMER.

DO I STILL DREAM? THE CRIES...!

SHE TRICKED ME, MOCKED ME... EVEN IN JOINING!

AAAAA AWAAAAAA!

I UUINHH... CUB!

SCOUTER'S CUB!

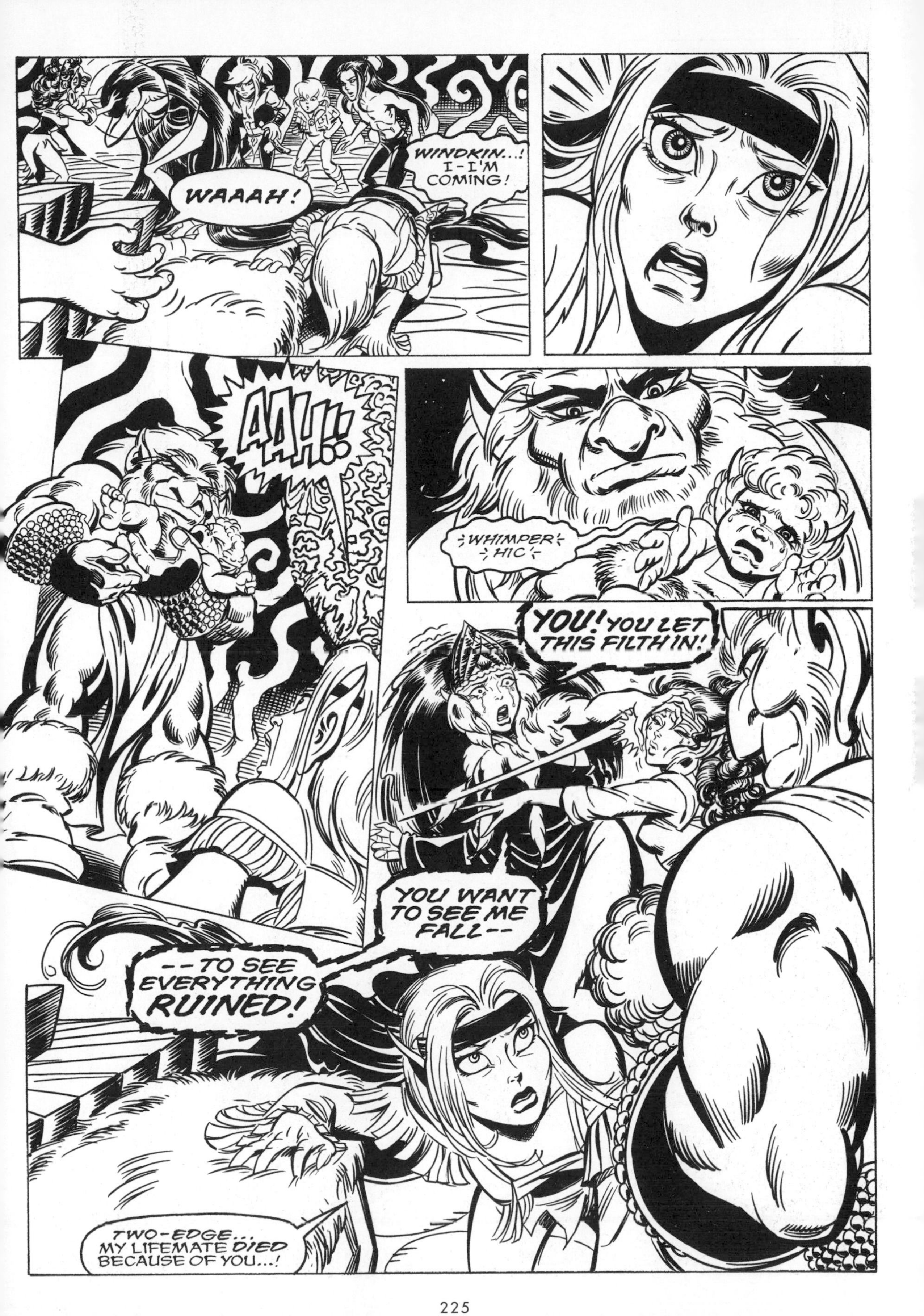
WINDKIN...! I-I'M COMING!
WAAAH!
AAH!!
WHIMPER HIC
YOU! YOU LET THIS FILTH IN!
YOU WANT TO SEE ME FALL--
--TO SEE EVERYTHING RUINED!
TWO-EDGE... MY LIFEMATE DIED BECAUSE OF YOU...!

LIKE HUNTED GAME BACKED TO THE EDGE OF A CLIFF--

--WINNOWILL LAUNCHES A LAST FRENZIED ATTACK!

BUT SHE IS EXHAUSTED, AND LEETAH'S MINISTRATIONS HAVE BEGUN TO TAKE EFFECT. THE BLACK SNAKE'S BITE IS VENOMLESS.

THEY KNOW HER.

SHE CANNOT FIGHT.

SHE CANNOT HIDE.

STILLQUIET...! IS GOOD! PETALWING MAKE WRAPSTUFF!

226

AND...

I'LL CHASE YOU TO THE END OF THE WORLD, HALF-TROLL! LET THE CUB GO!

--TO KNOW EMOTIONS OTHER THAN CONFUSION AND HATE. BUT CLEARBROOK WOULD NOT LIKELY LISTEN.

HE UNDER-STANDS HER FURY. HE WOULD LIKE TO TELL HER SO.

IT FEELS SO GOOD--

HER HEART IS SET ON REVENGE. HE KNOWS HOW THAT IS--

--SO HE RUNS--

--THROUGH A MISSHAPEN OPENING WHICH WAS ONCE THE ENTRANCE TO THE GLIDER LORD'S THRONE ROOM.

THERE TWO-EDGE FINDS ANOTHER OF HIS MOTHER'S TOYS PUNISHED FOR DEFIANCE--LIKE HIMSELF-- ABANDONED.

YOU ARE HIS FATHER. TAKE HIM!

EH?

TAKE HIM!

WHAM!

TAKE HIM WHERE HE'S WANTED MOST!

BAH...?! BABAH...?

TWO-EDGE...!

;HUULINNHH...;

...RRRPJJUUMMMMBLERRRRRRUUMMRRRUUMM... KRAK!

CRASH!!

EARLIER, BLUE MOUNTAIN'S CATACOMBED INTERIOR **WRITHED** AS IT SHAPED ITSELF INTO **WINNOWILL'S** ULTIMATE DREAM. BUT NOW THE COLOSSAL EGG BEGINS TO CRUMBLE FROM WITHIN! **SCOUTER, DEWSHINE** AND THEIR HUMAN CHARGES FEEL THE FLOOR OF THE AERIE GIVE WAY.

‹IT IS OUR **DEATH DAY**!›

THE HUMAN IS RIGHT, **BELOVED**!

WE'LL FALL WITH THE MOUNTAIN, AND SO WILL-- ≋GASP!≋

MUH!

MUH!

BABAH! MUUH!

OOOHH!

AM I DEAD **NOW**?! THIS IS **SPIRIT-JOY**!

NO...! THIS IS **LIVING-JOY**! THIS IS **WINDKIN**!

≋SOB≋-- **TIMMAIN** KEEP YOU, **TYLDAK**!

ALTHOUGH THE WORDS OF THE BLESSING MEAN LITTLE TO HIM, **DEWSHINE'S** ELATION IS STRANGELY PLEASING TO THE WINGED ELF. HE WILL DO MORE!

AAWK!

FRIGHTENED OUT OF THEIR AVIAN WITS BY THE CATASTROPHIC CHANGE IN THEIR NESTING PLACE, THE GIANT HAWKS RALLY AROUND **TYLDAK**.

RAWK! RAWK!

HE WHISTLES TO THEM, EASES THEIR CONFUSION--

--AND GIVES THEM SOME- THING FAMILIAR TO DO.

NONNA, THE SYMBOL MAKER, BREATHES A PRAYER, THEN FAINTS DEAD AWAY!

IT IS ONE THING TO HONOR THE GODS, BUT ANOTHER THING ALTOGETHER TO *FLY* WITH THEM!

THE FIVE HUMANS CANNOT "*SEND*" TO THEIR TRIBEFOLK BELOW, AS *SCOUTER* SENDS TO HIS--

--BUT HUMAN AND ELFIN ARMS BOTH ARE WAITING OUTSTRETCHED...

〈KAKUK!〉

GOT YOU, LAD!

AND SOON AFTERWARD, THE ASTOUNDED *HOAN G'TAY SHO* SEE *TYLDAK* UP CLOSE FOR THE FIRST TIME!

NOTHING--NEITHER FEAR FOR FRIENDS STILL TRAPPED WITHIN THE EGG, NOR THE WEIRD TANG OF LITTLE *WINDKIN'S* SCENT--MARS THE ECSTACY OF THIS REUNION. THE "NOW OF WOLF THOUGHT" ADMITS ONLY HAPPINESS--

--HOWEVER SHORT-LIVED IT MAY BE.

BE WELL, WOLFRIDERS!

DEW-SHINE! CUB!

I MUST RETURN TO *WINNOWILL,* THAT SHE MAY FEEL THE POWER--

--WAIT--!

--OF THE *TALONS* SHE GAVE ME!

HEEDLESS OF *DEWSHINE'S* PROTESTS THAT *WINNOWILL* MUST LIVE, *TYLDAK* SOARS BACK INTO THE EGG, WHERE...

SCOUTER... SENDING! *HAH!* THEY ESCAPED WITH THE CUB!

JUST IN TIME, TOO. THE WHOLE PLACE IS FALLING APART!

WHAT'S MAKING IT HAPPEN?

THE *GLIDERS!* IT IS WHAT THEY WANT. I HAVE BEEN PART OF THEM--THEIR SORROW. I *KNOW!*

LEETAH! COME OUT OF IT!

YOU CAN'T HEAL *WINNOWILL* HERE! IT'S NOT SAFE!

¬UH-- WHA--¬?!

WHERE ARE YOU, BROTHER? ANSWER ME!!

WE HAVE TO GET HER *OUTSIDE!*

OH...YES... YES! AND *SKYWISE,* TOO!

SKYWISE?!!

TAM...! YOUR SENDING'S OPEN! YOU...DID IT...!

YOU... WON!

NEED HELP...

TRAPPED...

CAN'T BREATHE! DON'T KNOW WHY... HURTS... HURRY...

RAYEK'S THE ONLY FLYING ELF I TRUST. GO WITH HIM, BOTH OF YOU.

YOU'RE ALL HE CAN CARRY AT ONE TIME!

PETALWING HELP!

COME BACK FOR *WINNOWILL* QUICK AS YOU CAN, BLACK-HAIR! SHE *HAS* TO BE HEALED, EVEN IF *SKYWISE* AND I DON'T GET OUT!

¬CHOKE¬

HIS BURDEN IS LIGHT DESPITE ITS SIZE, PELTED BY HAILSTONE-HARD DEBRIS--

THIS LOOKS LIKE THE PIT THAT LED TO *WINNOWILL'S* QUARTERS THIS MORNING!

HOPE I'M RIGHT.

WAIT FOR ME, *FAHR!* DON'T DIE!

SUDDENLY...

--CUTTER DASHES, DEER-LIKE, THROUGH MUCH-CHANGED HALLS.

STOP, WOLF-RIDER!

I WANT WHAT YOU CARRY!

TYLDAK! NO! NO TIME TO EXPLAIN!

NO *NEED* TO EXPLAIN! SHE IS *MINE!*

YOU FOOL! LET GO!!

DON'T IGNORE ME! YOU'VE GOT TO UNDERSTAND! SHE *MUSTN'T* BE KILLED!

SHE'S MORE TROUBLE DEAD THAN ALIVE!

GONE.

HE CAN PURSUE.

OR HE CAN SAVE HIS FRIEND.

TYLDAK!!

232

IT IS MADNESS! OF ALL THE WOLFRIDERS, ONLY **STRONGBOW** HAS THE STRENGTH OF WILL TO MAKE BLUE MOUNTAIN'S STONE-STILL "DOORS" RESPOND.

--OR I'LL OPEN YOU!! AND YOU'LL BE *AWAKE* FOR IT-- --BELIEVE ME!

IN SENDING, THERE IS ONLY TRUTH.

THE SHEER BRUTALITY OF *HIS* TRUTH SURPRISES EVEN *CUTTER.*

HOWEVER--

:GASP:

:GASP:

--ONLY RESULTS MATTER!

SKYWISE!

:COUGH: :COUGH:--*STARS!* I'VE MISSED YOU...!

WITH THE CHAMBER CRUMBLING AROUND THEIR EARS, THE TWO FRIENDS REMAIN LOCKED IN A GRATEFUL BEAR-HUG. THEN-- REALIZATION!

HAVE TO ESCAPE!

BUT SKYWISE IS WEAK!

AND DOOR'S LEGS ARE LIMP AS WATER WEEDS.

HE'S FORGOTTEN HOW TO WALK--

BUT HE'S *NOT* A MUSHROOM! HE WANTS TO LIVE-- LIKE ANYONE ELSE.

CUTTER GRABS DOOR BY THE SCRUFF OF THE NECK, HAULING HIM-- AND SKYWISE-- INTO THE DARK, SEALED TUNNEL.

PRODDED BY CUTTER'S SENDING, DOOR BEGINS TO REMOVE THE FROZEN WAVES OF ROCK WHICH OBSTRUCT THE PASSAGE.

CRRREEEAAK!

IT IS A RACE AGAINST DESTRUCTION AS THE TUNNEL CAVES IN BEHIND THEM!

AAH!

WORK FASTER, DOOR!

I SEE LIGHT!

AFTER DAYS OF CONFINEMENT IN THE OPPRESSIVE GLOOM OF BLUE MOUNTAIN, CUTTER BREATHES THE CLEAN, SUN-WARMED WIND THANKFULLY.

WE'RE OUT!

--ER...!

HELP...!

THERE YOU ARE, WOLFRIDER!

THERE WAS NO WAY BACK IN!

PRAISE THE HIGH ONES! IT'S ALMOST OV--

COME! I WILL LOWER YOU BOTH TO THE GROUND!

DOOR, TOO! WE CAN'T LEAVE HIM!

WHAT?!

NO! YOU OAF! I-I CANNOT! IT IS TOO--

WHOOOOOOAH!

UUPF!!

THERE'S MY LAD! DON'T EVER GO OFF ON YOUR OWN AGAIN!

WE NEED A CHIEF --AND I DON'T LIKE THE CHORE!

SMAT!

FLUMP!

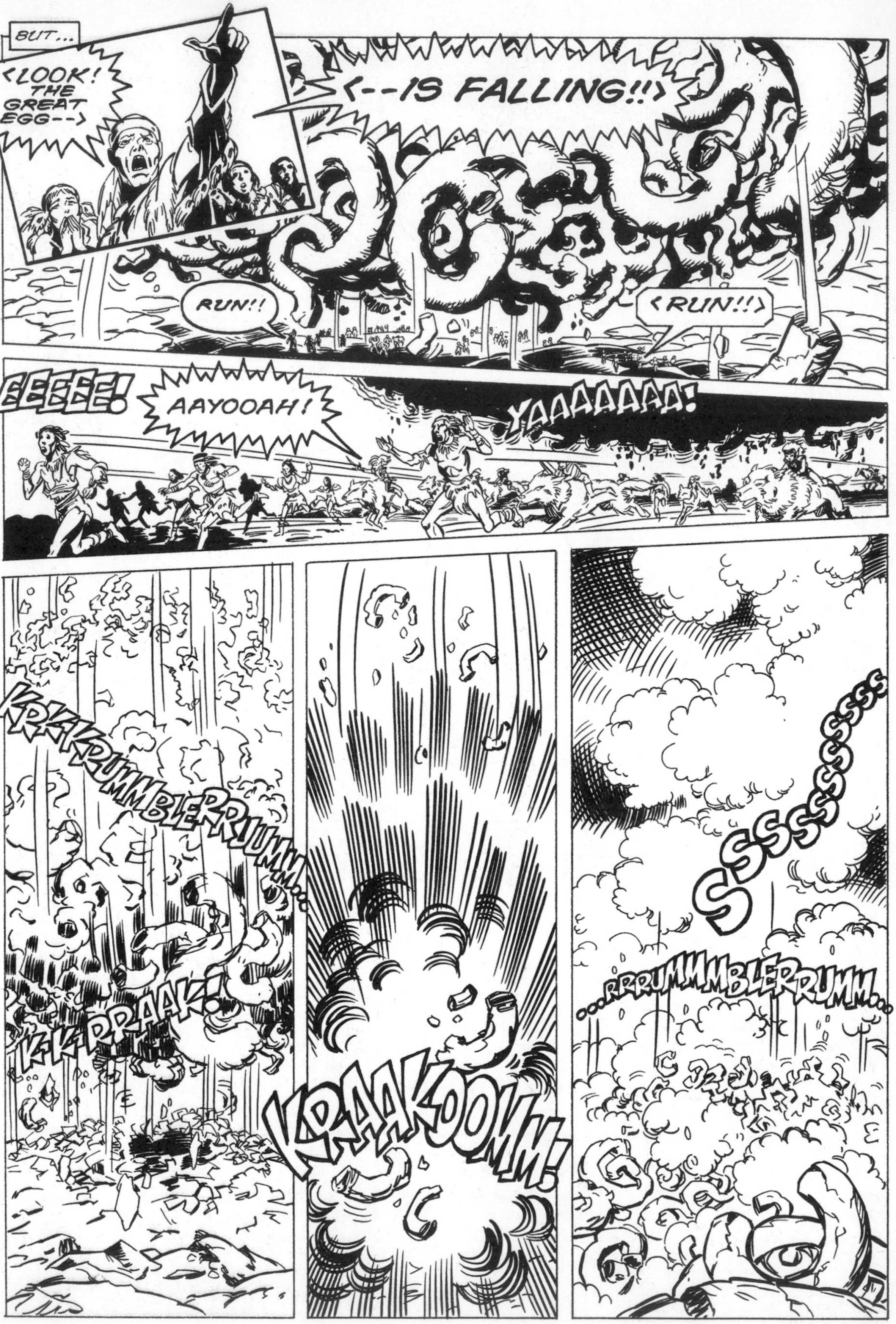
BUT...
<LOOK! THE GREAT EGG-->
<--IS FALLING!!>
RUN!!
<RUN!!>
EEEEE!
AAYOOAH!
YAAAAAAA!
KRKKRUMMBLERRUMM...
KKRRAAK!
KRAAKOOMM!
SSSSSSSSSS
...RRRUMMMBLERRUMM...

MOTHER!!

NO...!

SHE...DIDN'T GET OUT! SHE...

SHATTERED, LIKE THEIR SACRED MOUNTAIN, LIKE ALL THEIR ANCIENT BELIEFS, THE HOAN G'TAY SHO BEAR THEIR LOSS QUIETLY. IT IS A LOSS TOO GREAT TO PROTEST.

THE DUST OF CATACLYSM SWIRLS, A BROWN, SUN-VEILING CLOUD SO ENORMOUS THAT IT SEEMS TO MAKE A **SOUND**--

--A LOW THUNDEROUS GROAN.

SHE ISN'T DEAD... SHE ISN'T!

THAT MOTHERS AND FATHERS BOTH CAN PERISH UNTIMELY IS NO DELIBERATE INJUSTICE ON LIFE'S PART. **SCOUTER** KNOWS THAT LIFE IS JUST LIFE.

AND SO HE IS NOT QUITE ASTONISHED WHEN HIS SEND-CALL IS SWIFTLY ANSWERED.

MOTHER...? **PLEASE!**

I'M HERE CUB!

THIS, TOO, IS JUST LIFE.

H-HOW DID YOU--?

IT WAS **TWO-EDGE**...! HE CAN **SEND** NOW, DID YOU KNOW THAT...? **LEETAH** MUST HAVE WORKED ON HIM.

HE MADE THE FEMALE "**DOOR**" OPEN FOR ME...

SAVED ME...

AND HIM- SELF?

I DON'T KNOW. I STABBED HIM...ONLY THEN DID HE SEND. I FELT...SAW...FORGAVE. BUT HE STAYED BEHIND.

FOR SOME, FORGIVENESS IS AS HARD TO FIND AS IS THE SUN BEHIND ITS DARK CURTAIN OF DUST.

〈DEMONS! ‐SOB‐ THEY *MOCK* US IN THEIR VICTORY.〉

〈THEY HAVE DESTROYED THE BLACK-ROBED MOTHER! DESTROYED THE BIRD SPIRITS' HOME!〉

〈MY FATHER... ‐SNIFF‐ THEIR EYES ARE JUST VERY BIG!〉

〈AND *THERE THEY STAND*, GLARING WITH THEIR *EVIL EYES*!〉

〈I THINK...MAYBE... THEY ARE PEOPLE‐‐〉

〈‐‐SPIRIT *PEOPLE*!〉

I WISH I HAD WORKED HARDER AT LEARNING THE TALL ONES' WORDS.

DART HAS WON THAT YOUNG HUMAN'S HEART.

SEEMS SO.

RAYEK...?

YES... I SHALL!

〈*GEOKI* IS A FOOLISH *BOY*! IF THE DEMONS HAD NOT STOLEN OUR MAGIC SPEARS‐‐〉

CHUNK!

‐‐WEEEAAAGH!

YOU FAILED, HUMAN!

I WILL SHOW YOU HOW TO KILL HOWLING DOGS!

UUUUNNH...

KUREEL!

HA HA HA HAH HA!

238

THE INTENDED PREY IS SMALL AND FOUR-FINGERED.

BUT *KUREEL* IS A MINION OF THE BLACK SNAKE; HIS POISONOUS SOUL KNOWS DELIGHT AS RANDOM VICTIMS SCREAM AND DIE!

I'LL TURN THAT BIRD!

NO! THE ANGLE IS WRONG!

A TERRIBLE SHADOW FALLS OVER *GEOKI*. PETRIFIED, THE BOY CANNOT RUN.

WHIZZZ!

LITTLE STINGING WORM! WE'LL TEAR OFF YOUR *HEAD!*

GET DOWN!

GEOKI!!

WHOOOSH!

AAAA!

RAYEK! WHY DON'T YOU--?!

KUREEL IS PLEASED. CHILDREN OF BOTH TRIBES WILL DIE NOW, IN PARTIAL ATONEMENT FOR HIS LORD *WINNOWILL'S* FALL--

--AND EVEN FOR HIS PITIFUL FOLK, THE GLIDERS, WHO LIE CRUSHED BENEATH THE RUINS OF AN OLD, OLD DREAM.

THOUGH THEY WOULD HAVE TAKEN HIM DOWN WITH THEM, HE WILL AVENGE THEM, TOO.

MAN KILLS MAN. IT IS THE WAY OF HUMANS.

BUT WITHIN THE COLLECTIVE MEMORY OF THE FOUR KNOWN TRIBES, ELF HAS **NEVER** KILLED ELF.

THE WORLD HAS CHANGED--

--AGAIN.

‹GEOKI...! DO NOT BE DEAD!›

TH-THEIR HANDS! THEY WON'T COME APART!

GEOKI'S FATHER RECOILS, TRYING TO PULL HIS SON AWAY AS LEETAH HESITANTLY PLACES HER PALM ON THE SHATTERED BREAST.

MOMENTS LATER, SHE IS UNITED WITH HUMAN AND ELFIN YOUTH--

THE DESTRUCTION OF AN ENTIRE MOUNTAIN DOES NOT MEAN SO MUCH AS ONE HOPED-FOR SHUDDER OF BREATH.

BUT IF SPIRITS THEMSELVES CAN DIE, TO WHAT POWER CAN PRAYERS BE OFFERED?

--LOCKED, AS THE BOYS' HANDS ARE LOCKED, IN THE GRIP OF DEVOTION--

--TO LIFE!

SO MUCH TIME GOES BY THAT THE GREAT GRAY DUSTCLOUD DISPERSES.

THE SUN RETURNS.

UUNNNHHH...

AND...

TAM... I AM LOST! I—I THINK I WILL NEVER BE MYSELF AGAIN!

HUMANS... ARE SO—SO *SET* IN THEIR MOLD!

THEN LOOK AT WHAT YOU *KNOW*, BELOVED—

"—LOOK AT WHAT YOU'VE DONE!"

FOR THE FIRST TIME—IN HOW MANY DAYS, HE DOES NOT KNOW—CUTTER REALIZES THAT HIS BODY IS NOT TENSED TO FIGHT OR FLEE. HIS FAMILY IS SAFE. HIS TRIBE IS REUNITED WITH KIN AND FRIENDS FROM FAR AWAY. ONLY ONE THOUGHT TROUBLES HIS HARD-WON PEACE.

WINNOWILL...! IF TYLDAK KILLS HER, HER SPIRIT WILL BE ON US LIKE A *PLAGUE*!

AND ALL THIS WILL HAVE BEEN FOR NOTHING!

DON'T WORRY. TYLDAK WOULDN'T DO ANYTHING TO HURT US. I KNOW HIM. I *TRUST* HIM.

DEWSHINE WISHES SHE COULD BE AS CERTAIN OF HER OWN CUB'S NATURE. THE BRIGHT-EYED BABE SHE CHERISHES MORE THAN LIFE ITSELF HAS BEEN TAMPERED WITH.

THEY ARE ALL HERE... WITH *ME*! EVEN *KUREEL* REJOICES! *I* AM THEIR MOUNTAIN NOW...! *I* AM THEIR WAY TO THE *HIGH ONES'* HOME...!

THEIR POWER BELONGS TO THE PALACE!

A WOLF-LING NO MORE... WHAT *IS* HE?

¡GASP!¿

CLEARBROOK, LOOK AT HIS *EYES*, WILL YOU? HE'S MANY NUTS SHY OF A FULL POUCH!

HE TELLS THE TRUTH! THE AIR IS *FULL* OF SOULS! BUT HE'S NOT FIT, AS HE IS, TO TRAVEL ALONE TO THE FROZEN MOUNTAINS.

HMMHMM... POOR *GLIDERS*! BURIED ALIVE!

YES... ALIVE!

RAYEK! WHAT—?

THEN YOU AND I WILL TAKE HIM!

SOON...

‹NONNA...ADAR...WE WILL REMEMBER YOU ALWAYS IN OUR HOWLS-- THE FIRST HUMANS WE HAVE HONORED SO.›

‹NONE OF US WILL FORGET WHAT WE HAVE SEEN TODAY.›

‹I DO NOT KNOW WHY YOU HUMANS SET US SO HIGH ABOVE YOU. IT MAKES TOO MUCH FEELING,... TOO MUCH HATE...TOO MUCH LOVE. LEETAH HAS PROVED THAT WE ARE MORE LIKE YOU THAN NOT.›

‹BUT IT IS HARDER TO LOSE BELIEFS THAT MAKE YOU FEEL SAFE--›

‹--THAN IT IS TO LOSE A HOME! I KNOW!›

‹TODAY, YOUR MAGIC--›

‹BUT IF WORSHIP DISPLEASES YOU --›

‹--BROUGHT DOWN BLUE MOUNTAIN AND HEALED ONE OF OUR OWN! I BELIEVE WHAT I SEE.›

‹--THEN TAKE FRIEND- SHIP!›

"‹ I WILL MAKE THE HOAN G'TAY SHO A SYMBOL--›"

"‹-- THAT WILL SPEAK TO THEM OF THE HEALING MAGIC.›"

"‹THEY WILL WALK IN THE WORLD KNOWING WHAT THEY KNOW: THAT SPIRITS CAN BE POWERFUL HELPERS WHO SOMETIMES NEED HELP TOO.›"

TWO NIGHTS LATER...

THE PRESERVERS ARE NOT HAPPY. FOR TWO LIGHTS AND TWO DARKS, THEIR PRECIOUS COCOONS HAVE BEEN TRIPPED OVER, DANCED ON, TANGLED AND TORN. SPLASHED DREAMBERRY JUICE DRIPS LIKE STICKY DEW FROM THE WINGED SPRITES' WEBS.

THE WOLVES, TOO, ARE NOT HAPPY. HACKLES ARE UP AND TAILS ARE BRISTLING OVER THE INTRUDING PACK FROM THE DESERT.

BUT NONE OF THAT DISTURBS SUNTOP AS HE COMMUNES SERENELY WITH SAVAH--AND THEN SHYLY, REVERENTLY OFFERS HIS SPIRIT-HAND TO TIMMAIN, HERSELF.

EMBER, MEANWHILE, IS IN HER GLORY, ELABORATING YET AGAIN THE TERRORS AND TRIUMPHS OF HER GREAT BATTLE WITH THE HUMANS.

BUT THE SONG OF CELEBRATION, UNION, AND REUNION HOLDS A PENSIVE NOTE FOR SOME.

AND FOR THE ONE WHO FOUGHT HARDEST TO PRESERVE "THE WAY"--YET, WITH AN ARROW, CHANGED HIS WORLD FOREVER--THERE IS NO SONG BUT SILENCE.

MY CUB...! I'LL NEVER KNOW HIM BY SCENT AGAIN! WHAT DID SHE DO TO HIM?

WHAT DOES IT MATTER? HE'S STILL OUR "BUMPER". AND WE ARE HIS ONLY PARENTS.

÷GIGGLE÷

BA-BAH!

THERE!

HO!

THAT'S HOW MANY SNOWS I'VE BEEN CHIEF. YOU'D THINK I'D BE *SURE* OF MYSELF BY NOW!

THERE ARE *TWO* WAYS TO WIN AT "TOSS STONE"--

--BY PLAN OR BY LUCK!

YOU PLAYED MOSTLY BY LUCK IN BLUE MOUNTAIN, BUT WHO CARES? YOU WON!

WHAT ABOUT *WINNOWILL?*

TRUST LUCK AGAIN! IT SEEMS TO *WORK* FOR YOU!

"AND SOMETIMES..." *THINKS THE STARGAZER,* "BELIEVING THINGS WILL TURN OUT WELL IS THE ONLY THING WE CAN DO."

;CHIRR; ;CHIRR;

;KRIK; ;KRIK; ;KRIK;

HELLO ♪♫

OH...! *NEWSTAR!*

YOU SURELY GREW UP! THE SUN VILLAGE MUST *MISS* ITS PRETTIEST MAIDEN.

I LIKE IT HERE!

;SNORT;

AND I LIKE LOOKING AT THE STARS, TOO!

BUT DID YOU KNOW...YOU CAN SEE THEM *MUCH* BETTER--

--IF YOU LEAN BACK?

;SIGH...;

AND...

...STARS ARE SO BRIGHT. I CAN SEE THEM THROUGH THE LEAVES.

AND YOU KNOW...I LIKE 'EM RIGHT WHERE THEY ARE!

STRANGE HOW SOME OF US WOULD DO *ANYTHING* TO REACH THEM.

WHAT IS *FOR* US, DOES NOT PASS *BY* US, BELOVED.

THE GLIDERS NEVER WISHED TO BE PART OF THIS WORLD.

WHEN THEY WERE FREE, AT LAST, OF *WINNOWILL'S* CONTROL, THEY CHOSE TO EXIST ONLY IN SPIRIT.

I WOULDN'T! I *LIKE* HAVING SKIN.

THERE'S MY SKIN...AND THERE'S ME... AND WHEN I DIE ⸘YAWN⸘ THERE'LL STILL BE ME...!

BUT I'LL LET *THIS* WORLD DECIDE WHEN...! ZZZZ

NO!

HOW *EASY* IT WOULD BE TO BECOME LIKE *HER*--

--TO DENY OTHERS THEIR CHOICES EXCEPT AS THEY SUIT *MY* DESIRES!

THE ONLY DIFFERENCE IS *LOVE.* HIGH ONES... KEEP ME STRONG!

AND BE WITH MY SUFFERING SISTER--

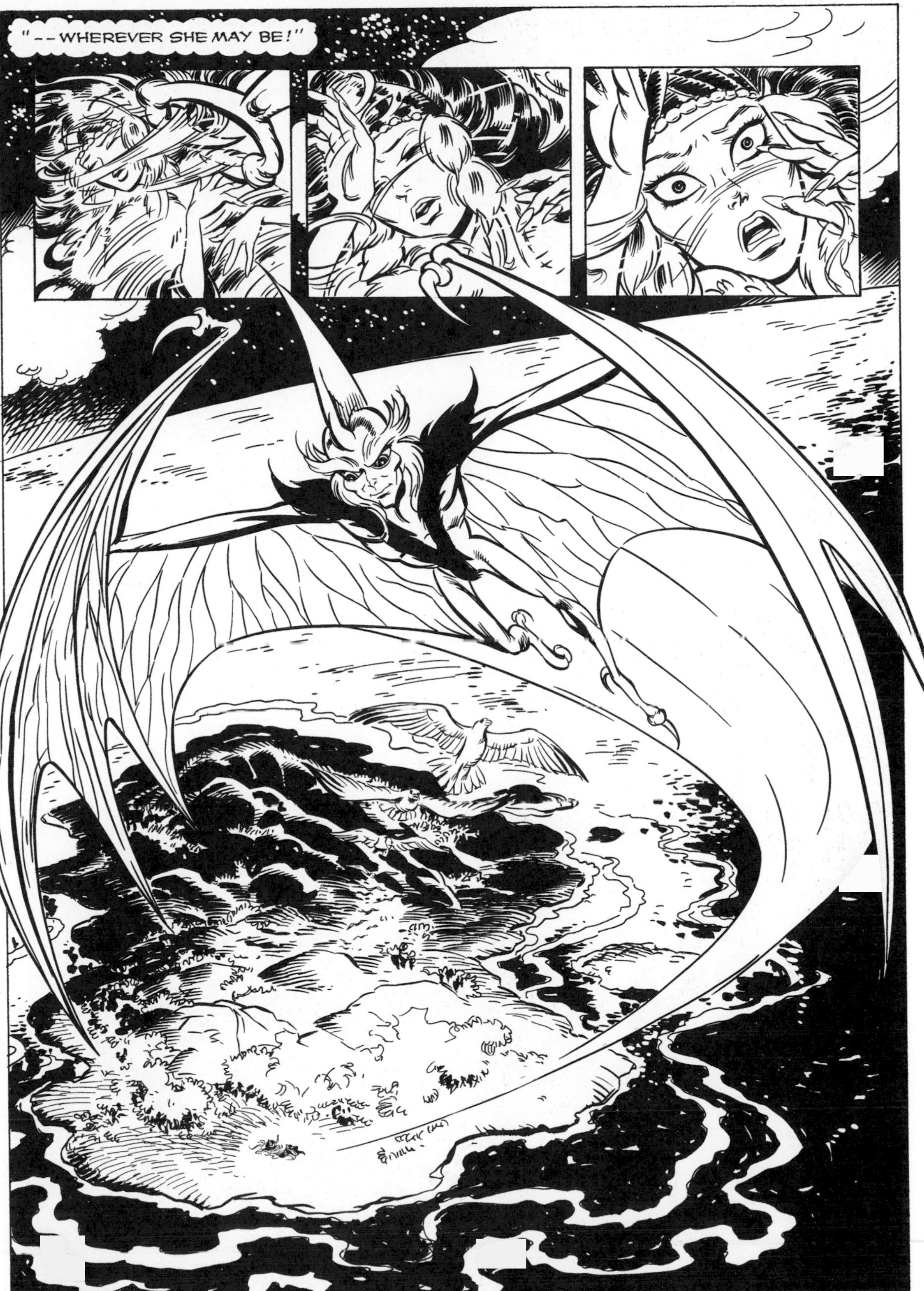
"--WHEREVER SHE MAY BE!"

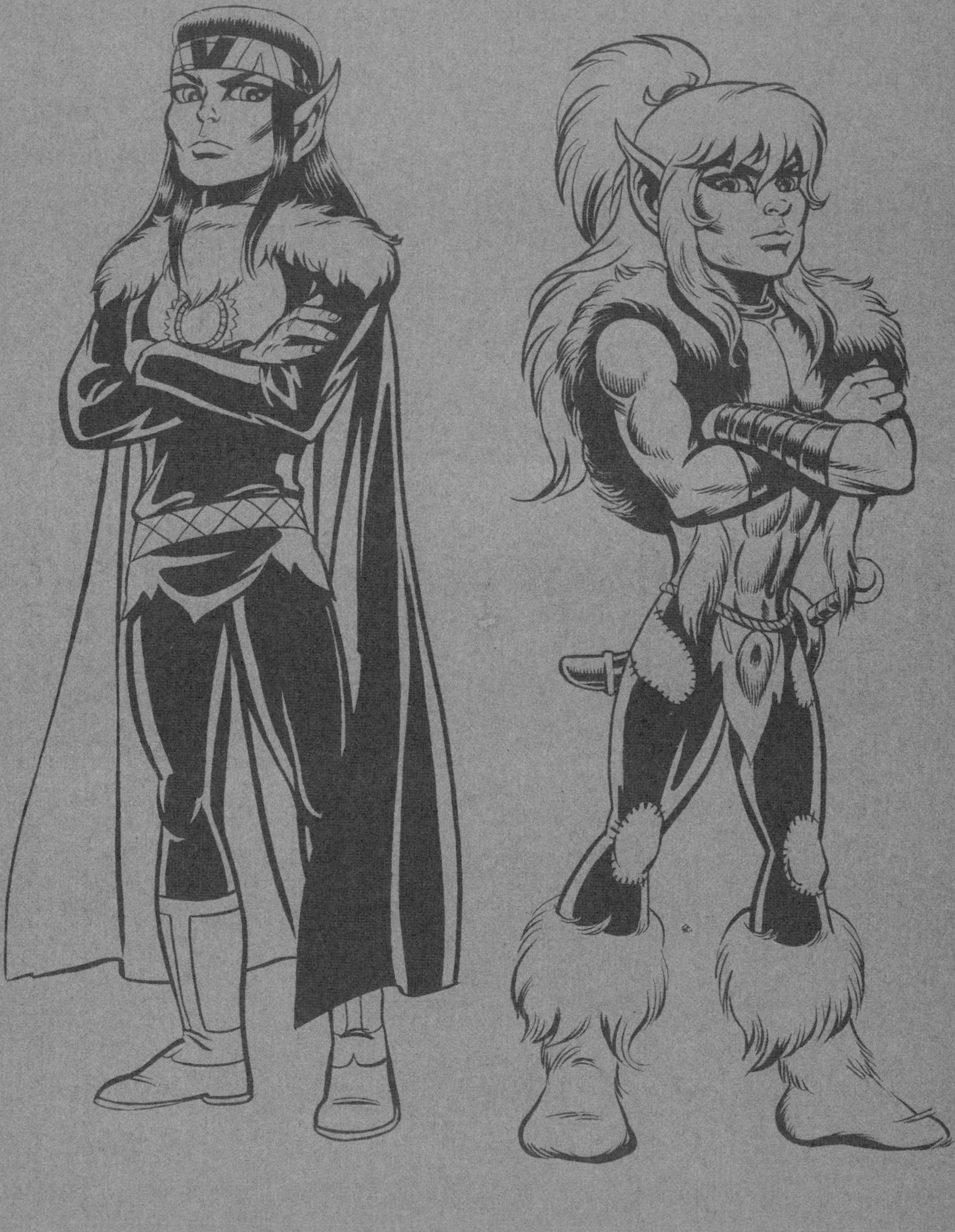

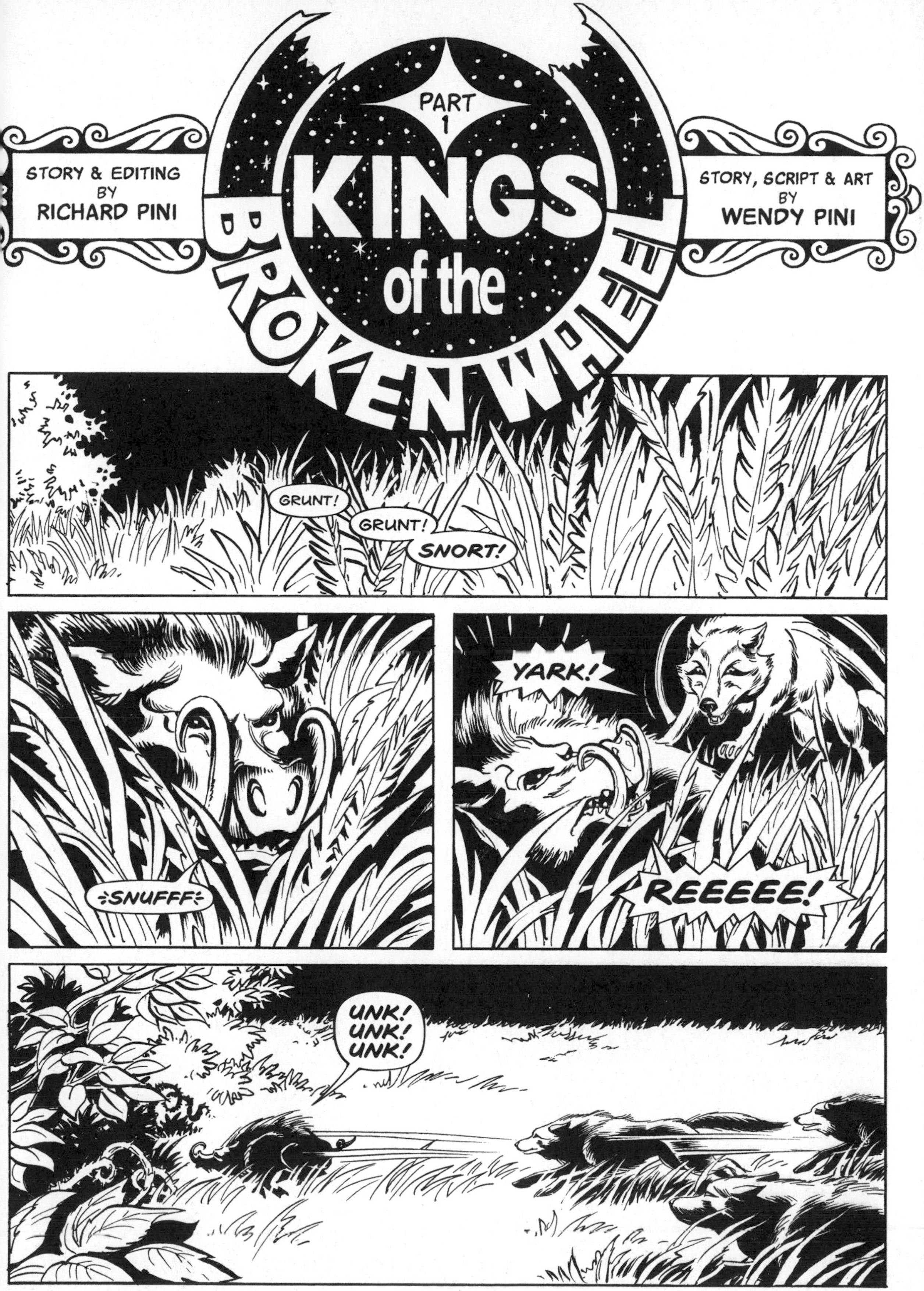
PART 1
KINGS of the BROKEN WHEEL
STORY & EDITING BY RICHARD PINI
STORY, SCRIPT & ART BY WENDY PINI
GRUNT!
GRUNT!
SNORT!
SNUFFF
YARK!
REEEEEE!
UNK! UNK! UNK!

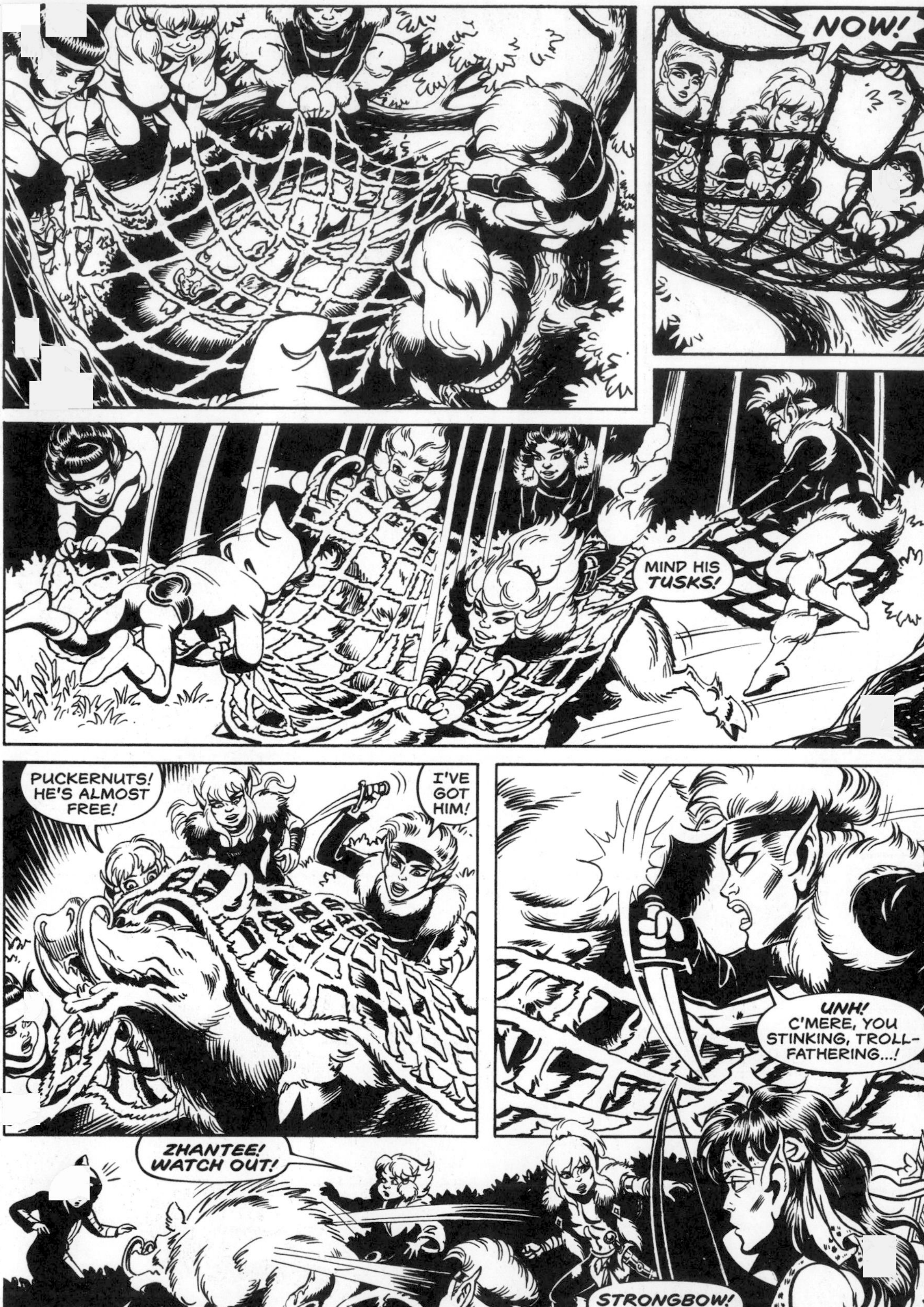

NOW!
MIND HIS TUSKS!
PUCKERNUTS! HE'S ALMOST FREE!
I'VE GOT HIM!
UNH! C'MERE, YOU STINKING, TROLL-FATHERING...!
ZHANTEE! WATCH OUT!
STRONGBOW! SHOOT!
RREEEE!

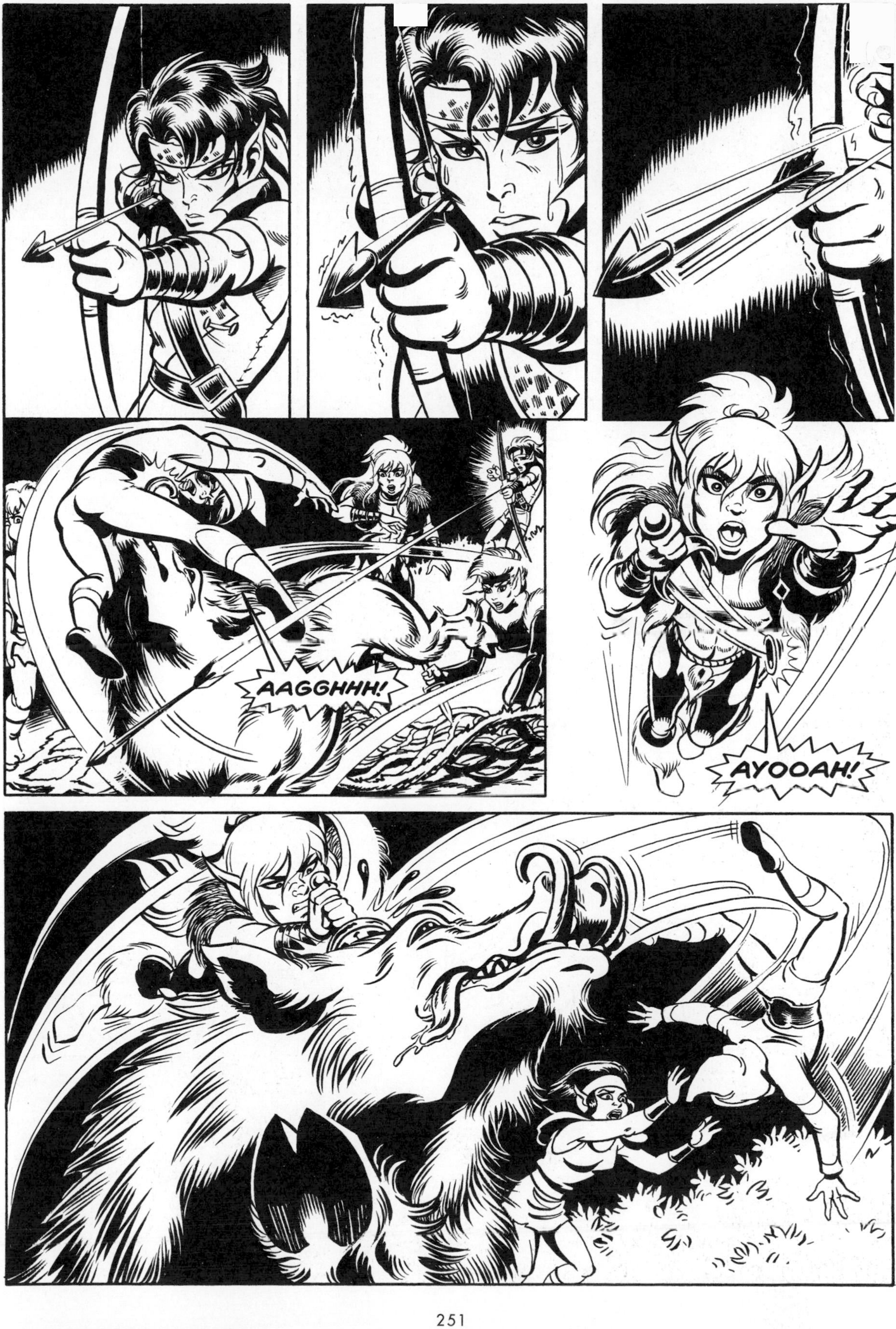
AAGGHHH!
AYOOAH!

B-BELT... ≡GASP≡ MY **BELT** SAVED ME.

HOW'S THE **GUT?**

WHAT WENT ≡COUGH≡ **WRONG?**

STRONGBOW NEVER MISSES... NEVER!

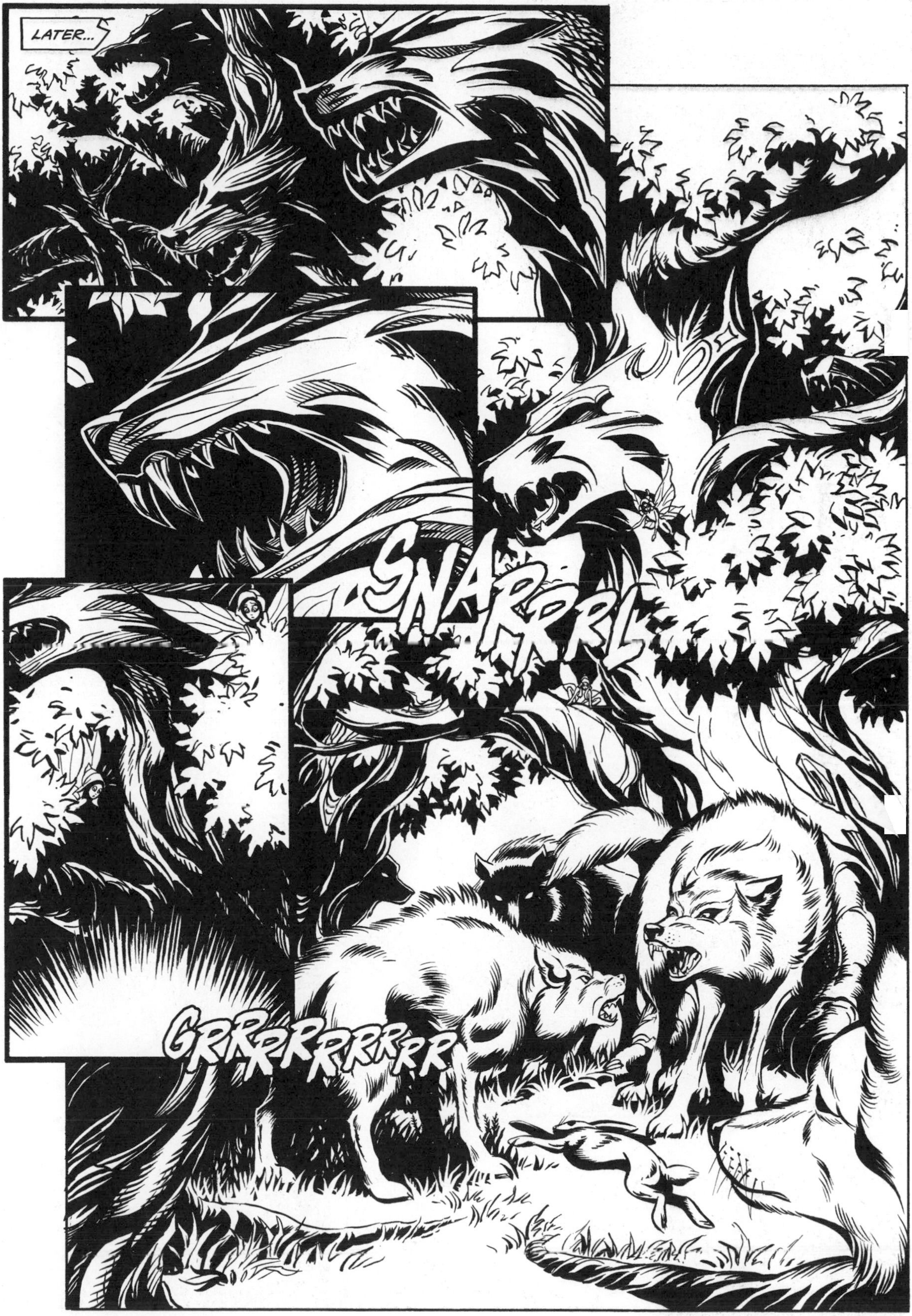
LATER...
SNARRRL
GRRRRRRRRR

STILL AT IT, EH? LOOKS LIKE *NOBODY* GETS AN EASY MEAL TONIGHT...

STRONGBOW NEARLY...

YOUR OLD WOLF FRIEND HAS MADE A REAL ENEMY, *SKYWISE.*

STARJUMPER? NOTHING TO IT! LOOK! HE'S PUT HIS TEETH OVER THAT BONY DESERT WOLF'S NOSE AGAIN!

BUT HE LOSES A BIT MORE GROUND EACH TIME THEY FIGHT. MAYBE...

NIGHTFALL! REDLANCE! YOU'RE FULL OF DREAMBERRIES! *STARJUMPER'S* LIVED SO LONG HE KNOWS ALL THE TRICKS!

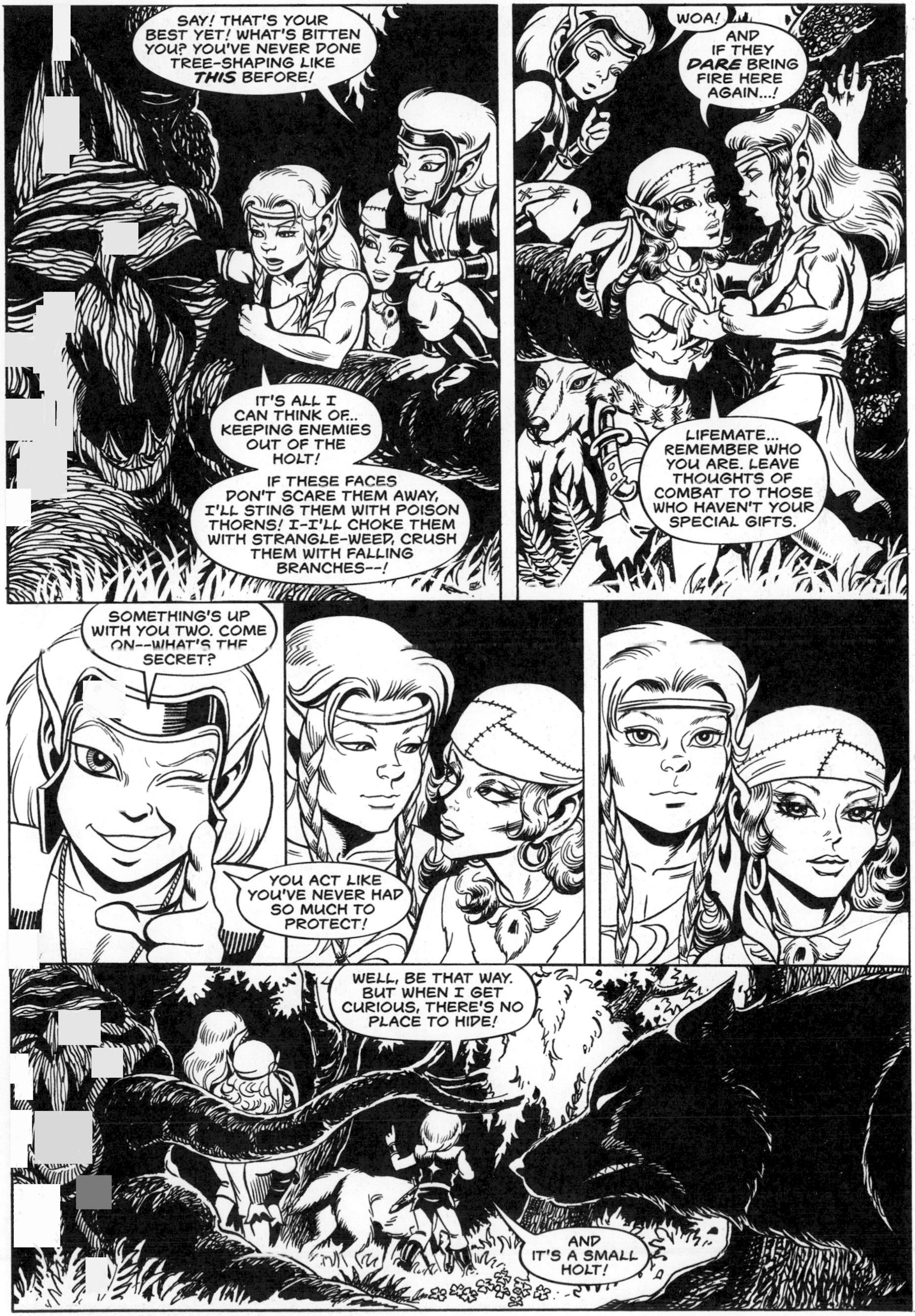
SAY! THAT'S YOUR BEST YET! WHAT'S BITTEN YOU? YOU'VE NEVER DONE TREE-SHAPING LIKE THIS BEFORE!
IT'S ALL I CAN THINK OF.. KEEPING ENEMIES OUT OF THE HOLT!
IF THESE FACES DON'T SCARE THEM AWAY, I'LL STING THEM WITH POISON THORNS! I-I'LL CHOKE THEM WITH STRANGLE-WEED, CRUSH THEM WITH FALLING BRANCHES--!
WOA!
AND IF THEY DARE BRING FIRE HERE AGAIN...!
LIFEMATE... REMEMBER WHO YOU ARE. LEAVE THOUGHTS OF COMBAT TO THOSE WHO HAVEN'T YOUR SPECIAL GIFTS.
SOMETHING'S UP WITH YOU TWO. COME ON--WHAT'S THE SECRET?
YOU ACT LIKE YOU'VE NEVER HAD SO MUCH TO PROTECT!
WELL, BE THAT WAY. BUT WHEN I GET CURIOUS, THERE'S NO PLACE TO HIDE!
AND IT'S A SMALL HOLT!

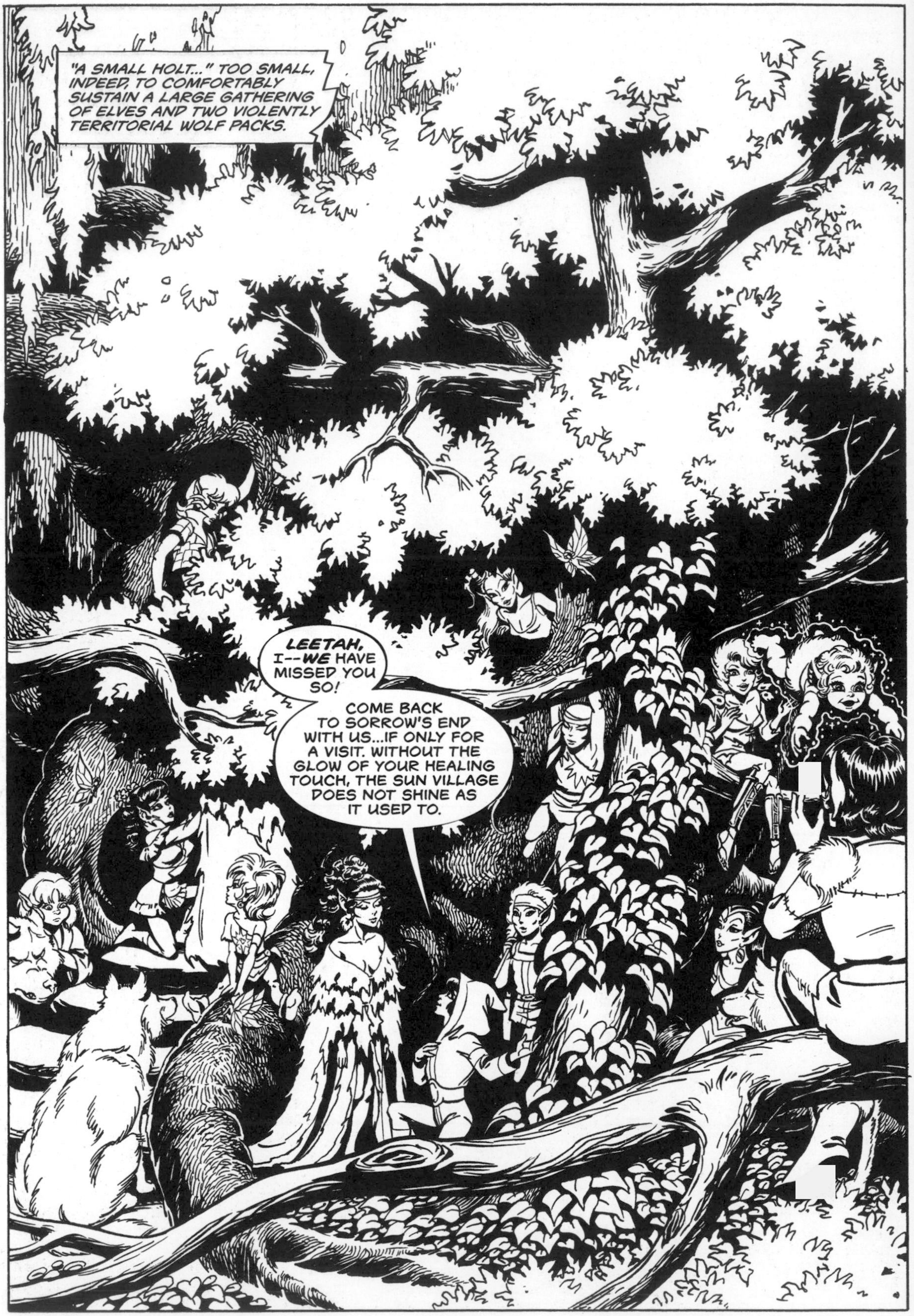
"A SMALL HOLT..." TOO SMALL, INDEED, TO COMFORTABLY SUSTAIN A LARGE GATHERING OF ELVES AND TWO VIOLENTLY TERRITORIAL WOLF PACKS.
LEETAH, I--WE HAVE MISSED YOU SO!
COME BACK TO SORROW'S END WITH US...IF ONLY FOR A VISIT. WITHOUT THE GLOW OF YOUR HEALING TOUCH, THE SUN VILLAGE DOES NOT SHINE AS IT USED TO.

LOOK AT YOU, *ZHANTEE.*

FROM OUR FARAWAY DESERT HOME YOU'VE COME, ACROSS BURNING WASTE AND THROUGH ECHOING GORGE TO THIS GREEN GROWING PLACE.

YOU, WHO WORKED THE CLAY OF SORROW'S END--AND THOUGHT NEVER TO LEAVE IT--ARE NOW A TRUE WOLF RIDER!

OUR FOREST BROTHERS CHANGED YOUR LIFE--AS THEY CHANGED MINE.

HE CHANGED YOU. HE CHANGED EVERYTHING.

THE TROLLS MAKE ROUND THINGS CALLED *WHEELS.* FOR STRENGTH THEY GIVE THEM UP TO *TEN* SPOKES--NO MORE. THEN THEY BEGIN ANOTHER WHEEL.

CUTTER IS BLOOD OF *TEN* CHIEFS.

AND THIS, THE UNION OF *FOUR* ELF TRIBES, IS THE BEGINNING OF A NEW CIRCLE. WE'VE ENTERED A TIME WHEN *NOTHING* IN THE WORLD CAN DIVIDE US--

NOT DISTANCE, NOT ROCK WALLS, NOT EVEN OLD BELIEFS.

FOUR TRIBES, CUTTER?

LOOK AROUND YOU, *NEWSTAR.* FROM "SUN-GOES-UP" WE *WOLFRIDERS* CAME...

...AND FROM THE WHITE-COLD LAND, WHERE THE PALACE OF THE HIGH ONES LIES, COME THE *GO-BACKS.*

FROM THE DESERT THE *SUN FOLK* RODE TO OUR AID--AND CAPTURED THE ENEMY HUMANS WHO TRIED TO TORCH OUR HOLT.

BUT THE CIRCLE IS *NOT* COMPLETE!

SHHHH!

BLUE MOUNTAIN NO LONGER STANDS WHERE "SUN-GOES-DOWN"! THE FLYING ELVES WHO LIVED THERE ALL *DIED* WHEN THE MOUNTAIN FELL!

WE HAVE OUR FULL CIRCLE. *WINDKIN* IS NOW A *GLIDER*--

--*NOT BY CHOICE!* HE WAS BORN HALF WOLFRIDER! HIS WOLF BLOOD WAS *STOLEN* FROM HIM IN BLUE MOUNTAIN!

WHEN THE TWINS WERE IN MY WOMB, *SCOUTER,* IT WAS *EMBER* WHO CALLED THE WOLF BLOOD TO HER. *SUNTOP* CALLED FOR SOMETHING ELSE.

IF *WINDKIN* IS HAPPY, AND HE SEEMS SO, LET HIM BE A GLIDER. REMEMBER, WE ARE *ELVES* FIRST.

ARE THEY *BOTH* WOLFRIDERS?

NO...*YES...!* I--I GUESS IT DOESN'T MATTER.

YES... THE CIRCLE *IS* WHOLE.

THEN THE HEALING CAN BEGIN. SPEAK NO MORE WORDS. SING. AND SEND.

WHO COMES TO RECEIVE THE POWER OF THE CIRCLE?

MY FATHER, *STRONGBOW,* COMES.

WHAT IS YOUR NEED?

I ASK RELEASE FROM THE *PAIN* THAT MAKES ME UNFIT TO HUNT OR GUARD.

I'VE KILLED AN ELF! KUREEL'S DEATH IS TURNING INTO MY OWN!

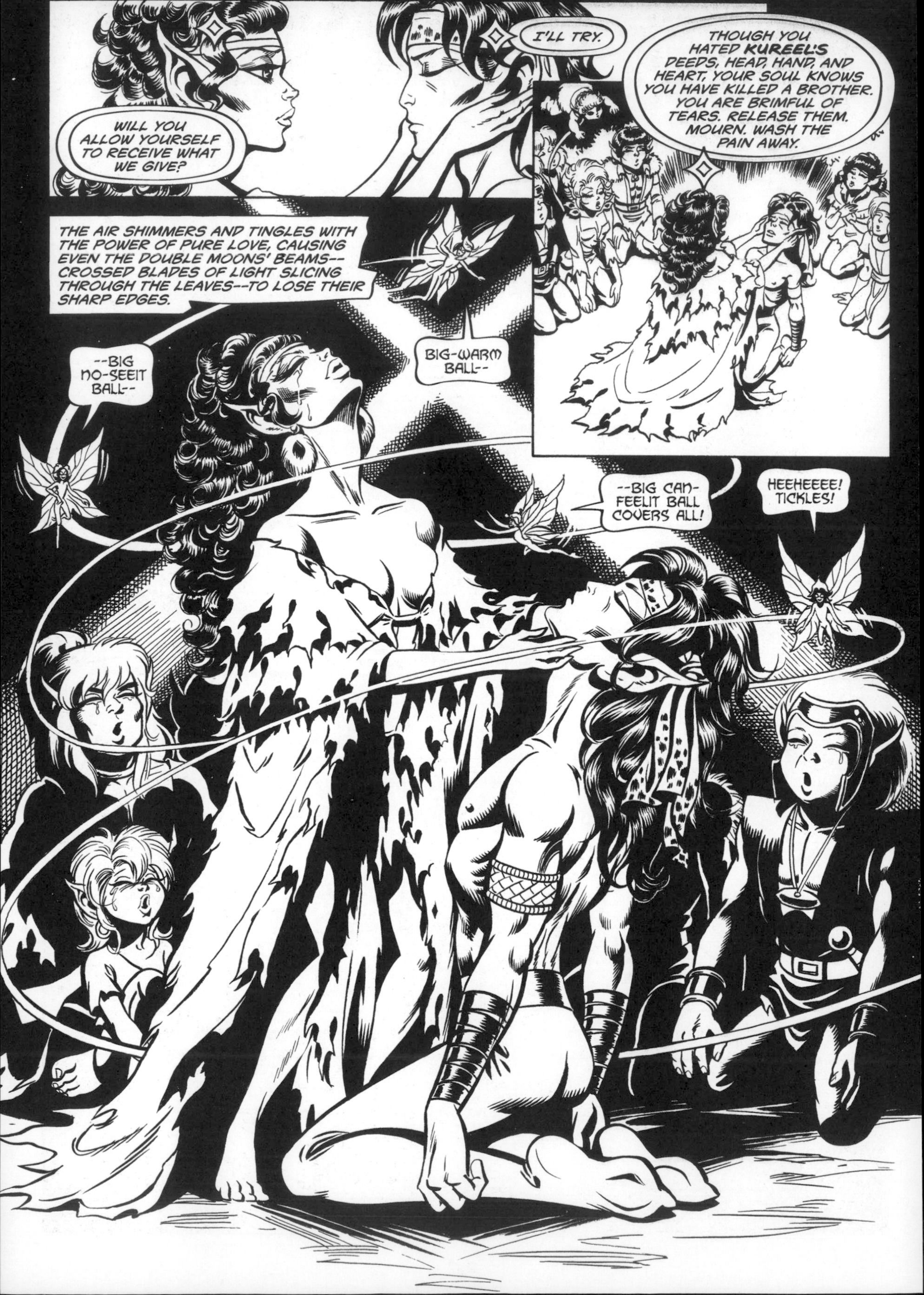
I'LL TRY.
WILL YOU ALLOW YOURSELF TO RECEIVE WHAT WE GIVE?
THOUGH YOU HATED KUREEL'S DEEDS, HEAD, HAND, AND HEART, YOUR SOUL KNOWS YOU HAVE KILLED A BROTHER. YOU ARE BRIMFUL OF TEARS. RELEASE THEM. MOURN. WASH THE PAIN AWAY.
THE AIR SHIMMERS AND TINGLES WITH THE POWER OF PURE LOVE, CAUSING EVEN THE DOUBLE MOONS' BEAMS--CROSSED BLADES OF LIGHT SLICING THROUGH THE LEAVES--TO LOSE THEIR SHARP EDGES.
--BIG NO-SEEIT BALL--
BIG-WARM BALL--
--BIG CAN-FEELIT BALL COVERS ALL!
HEEHEEEE! TICKLES!

GIVE AWAY YOUR SORROW, YOUR GUILT. LEAVE THEM TO FADE, HERE IN THE CIRCLE'S CENTER. LET THE TEARS COME.

I...CAN'T!

I HOPED THIS WOULD HELP, BUT IT DOESN'T.

THEN... WHAT WILL BELOVED?

WHY DON'T YOU TELL KUREEL YOU'RE SORRY, STRONGBOW?

THEN HE CAN FORGIVE YOU AND YOU CAN BE FRIENDS.

NOW THAT'S AN IDEA!

THINK WE CAN MAKE THE CARRION BIRDS COUGH UP ENOUGH TO APOLOGIZE TO?

AREN'T I RIGHT, FATHER? ELVES DON'T DIE--THEY JUST TURN INTO SPIRITS, DON'T THEY?

AND ELF SPIRITS GO TO THE PALACE OF THE HIGH ONES, DON'T THEY?

AND WE CAN *TALK* TO ELF SPIRITS IN THE PALACE, CAN'T WE?

WELL...?

THE PALACE OF THE HIGH ONES...

ONCE THERE WAS A QUEST--

--UNDERTAKEN PARTLY BY ACCIDENT, PARTLY BY DESIGN--WHICH LED THE WOLFRIDERS TO THE ANCIENT, ANCESTRAL DWELLING OF ALL ELVES.

THE PALACE OF THE HIGH ONES WAS FAR FROM WHAT THEY EXPECTED. WITHIN ITS TIMEWORN WALLS THE ELVES LEARNED MORE THAN THEY CARED TO--YET NOT NEARLY ENOUGH--OF THEIR RACE'S ORIGIN.

THE PALACE WAS NOT THE HOME, THE ETERNALLY SAFE HAVEN, THE WOLFRIDERS HAD HOPED FOR. YET THEY TOOK FROM IT--

--AND FROM TIMMAIN, THE LAST LIVING HIGH ONE--

--THE KNOWLEDGE THAT THEY, BEING PART WOLF, **BELONGED** TO THE WORLD OF TWO MOONS.

UNLIKE THOSE SLAIN IMMORTALS WHOSE SPIRITS MUST FOREVER INHABIT THE PALACE--

--THE MORTAL WOLFRIDERS WOULD FIND THEIR "SAFE PLACE" NOWHERE BUT WITHIN THEMSELVES.

SO THEY RETURNED TO THE FOREST. BUT **ONE** AMBITIOUS, PUREBLOODED ELF REMAINED IN THE PALACE--AND PROCLAIMED HIMSELF ITS MASTER.

RAYEK! GET YOUR TAIL BACK HERE!

HE'S TOO FAR UP. THE WIND...! HE CAN'T HEAR US!

SEND.

I HAVE! HE'S MISSING IT--

--OR IGNORING IT. :SIGH: WELL...WE STOP AGAIN.

SHORTLY...

YOU SURE? WE'RE CLOSE TO THE FROZEN MOUNTAINS.

:GRUMBLE: :GRUMPH:

BE PATIENT, TREESTUMP. HE'LL COME BACK.

MAYBE HE THINKS HE DOESN'T NEED US TO LOOK AFTER HIM ANYMORE.

HE NEEDS US--

--TO KEEP HIM SANE!

THEY ARE EAGER! THEY SENSE THE PALACE IS NEAR!

THE GLIDERS...?

THEIR SPIRITS URGE ME ONWARD. THEY MUST LEARN THAT *I* SET THE PACE.

CAREFUL. THEY'LL USE YOU UP LIKE THEY USED UP THEIR OWN MOUNTAIN.

USE ME...? *USE ME?!* I'LL SHOW YOU! ARE YOU COLD?

‡PANT‡ ‡PANT‡ ‡PANT‡

WHEW!

IN ALL THEIR UNSPEAKABLY LONG LIVES THE GLIDERS DID *NOTHING* OF THEIR OWN VOLITION!

IN DEATH, THEY STILL REQUIRE GUIDANCE. THEIR POWERS ARE MINE, TO USE AS I THINK BEST!

ARE YOU TAKING *WINNOWILL'S* PLACE, THEN? DO WE CALL *YOU* "BLACK SNAKE" NOW?

NO...! I DID NOT MEAN...I ONLY WANT TO *HELP* OUR KIND, NOT DOMINATE THEM!

WINNOWILL DIDN'T KNOW THE DIFFERENCE. DO YOU?

NONE BUT I UNDERSTAND HER. IN TIME...I COULD HAVE TAUGHT HER...IN TIME...SHE AND I...COULD HAVE...

BY MY AXE, HE'S ALL BUT *RECOGNIZED* HER! ALL THE MORE REASON NOT TO TRUST...

HI-I-I-M-M-M-M-M!

THE PALACE LIES JUST BEYOND THE FROZEN MOUNTAINS, MY FRIENDS.

NO NEED FOR YOU TO SCALE THOSE COLD, DEADLY PEAKS.

≥WHINE≥

YAAAAH! I *DON'T* LIKE THIS, BLACK-HAIR!

HA HA! YOU SHALL BE THE FIRST WOLFRIDERS TO SAY YOU HAVE RIDDEN YOUR MOUNTS THROUGH THE *CLOUDS!*

WE'RE UP HIGHER THAN THE TALLEST TREE EVER CLIMBED--HIGHER THAN THE TOPMOST AERIE OF BLUE MOUNTAIN, BEFORE IT FELL!

NOW I *KNOW* WHY *SKYWISE* ALWAYS DREAMS OF FLYING!

ALL I KNOW IS, BEFORE THOSE GLIDER SPIRITS GOT UNDER HIS SKIN--

RAYEK COULDN'T FLOAT MUCH MORE THAN HIS OWN WEIGHT!

WHAT IF HE GETS TIRED?

I DON'T THINK HE *CAN* GET TIRED...NOW!

EH?! WHAT NONSENSE IS HERE?

TOK TOK

TOK TOK

SPUNNNG

TIMMORN'S BLOOD! IT'S SLOWING DOWN--

--IT'S **STOPPED!**

SKRASSH

YOW!

GUTWORMS AND MUDWATER!

RAYEK... ARE YOU ALL RIGHT?

SPURRED BY A SUDDEN FOREBODING, **RAYEK** STREAKS OVER THE TROLLS' GLACIAL DOMAIN. BEHIND HIM HIS WOLFRIDER COMPANIONS GASP HURTLING HELPLESSLY THROUGH THE TOO-THIN AIR.

THREE YEARS WITHOUT A *PEEP* FROM THE TROLLS...!

THEN, WITHIN AN EIGHT-OF-DAYS, I JOURNEY TO BLUE MOUNTAIN AND RETURN...TO *THIS* GREETING!

BUT EVEN IN THEIR DISCOMFORT, **CLEARBROOK** AND **TREESTUMP** FEEL THE **PULL** OF THE PALACE OF THE HIGH ONES...

CLEARBROOK... SEE THE DOME?

I VOWED I'D RETURN TO THE PALACE ONE DAY--BUT, HIGH ONES, I MEANT ON FOOT!

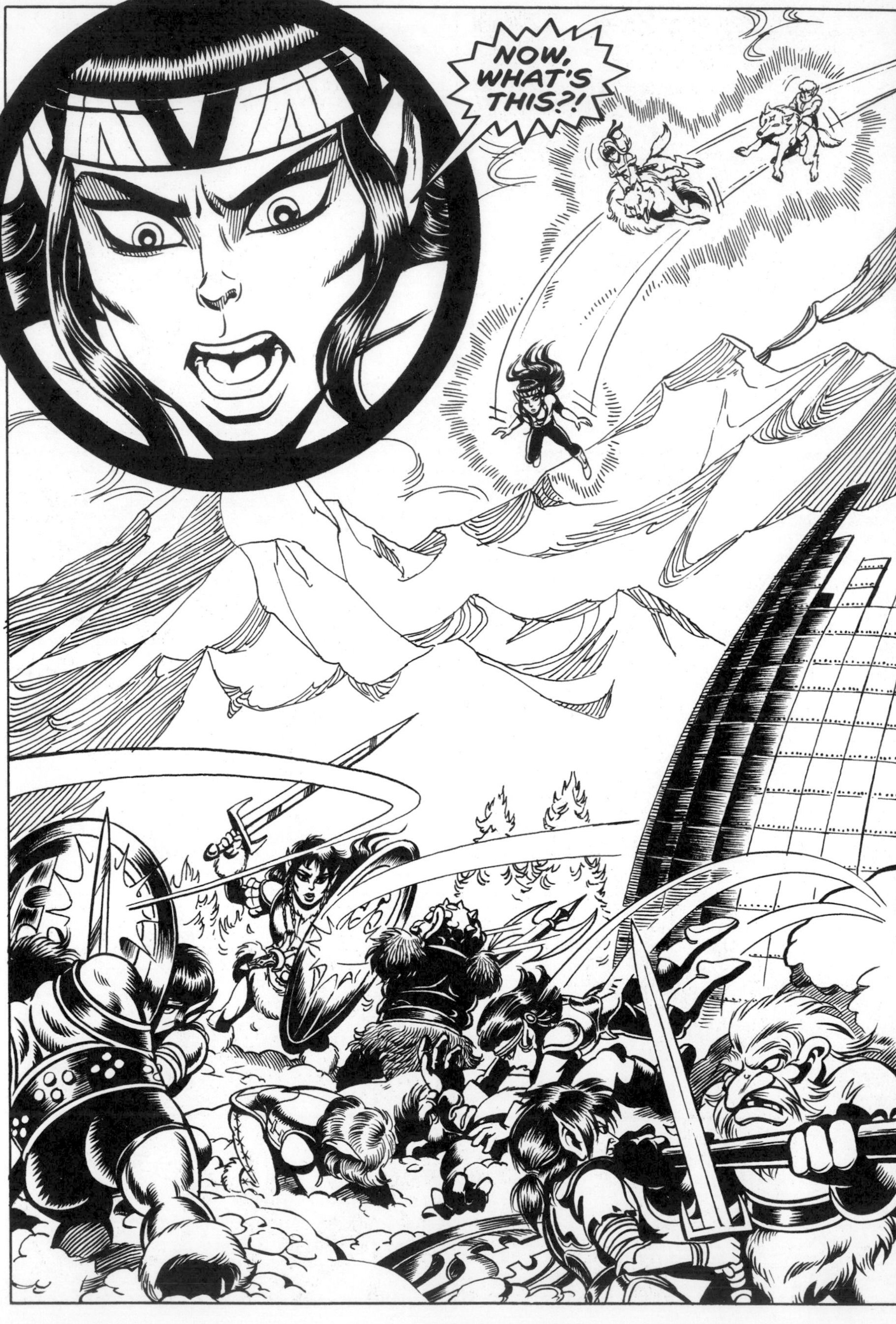
NOW, WHAT'S THIS?!

BACK, YOU GRAY-FACED FILTH! OR I'LL CUT OFF YOUR NETHER CHEEKS AND ROAST 'EM IN THE FIRE PIT!

ROTTEN FISH GUTS! WHAT--?!

AAHHH! PUT ME DOWN!

KAHVI!

C-CAN'T MOVE! HUNH! YOU LOOK TALLER, BLACK-HAIR. WHAT HAPPENED?

WHY DO YOU BATTLE? TELL ME--AT ONCE!

KNOWING RAYEK AS SHE DOES, THE GO-BACKS' CHIEF HAS GOOD REASON TO HESITATE. BUT, HAVING MORE COURAGE THAN REASON, SHE ANSWERS READILY.

THE TROLLS TOOK YOUR ONE-ARMED FRIEND, EKUAR, A FEW NIGHTS AGO.

WE'VE BEEN FIGHTING TO INVADE THEIR TUNNELS AND GET HIM BACK EVER SINCE.

SINCE YOU LEFT HIM ON OUR HANDS, THAT CRAZY ROCK SHAPER'S BEEN NOTHING BUT TROUBLE!

WE'D TAKE OUR EYES OFF HIM FOR A BLINK, AND HE'D LEAVE THE PALACE TO PUT DECORATIONS NOBODY WANTED ON THE ROCKS NEARBY!

HE JUST GOT HIMSELF CAUGHT...THAT'S ALL.

I... TOLD YOU... WHAT WOULD HAPPEN...

...IF YOU... FAILED...TO PROTECT EKUAR...!

RAYEK, NO!

MY CHIEF!

KRTCH

KRTCH

KRTCHH

OOWWFFF!

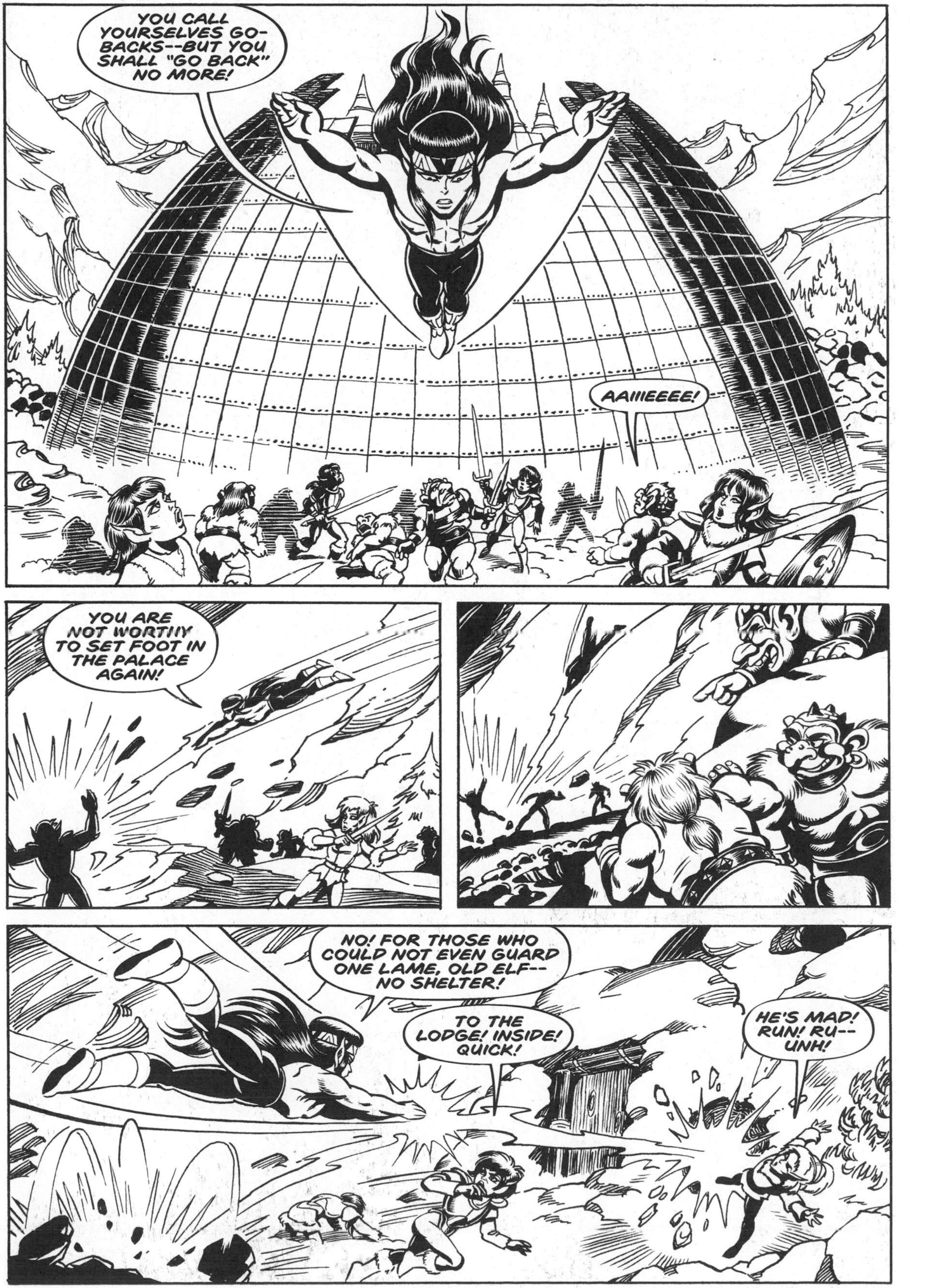
YOU CALL YOURSELVES GO-BACKS--BUT YOU SHALL "GO BACK" NO MORE!
AAIIEEEE!
YOU ARE NOT WORTHY TO SET FOOT IN THE PALACE AGAIN!
NO! FOR THOSE WHO COULD NOT EVEN GUARD ONE LAME, OLD ELF-- NO SHELTER!
TO THE LODGE! INSIDE! QUICK!
HE'S MAD! RUN! RU-- UNH!

AND INSIDE THE LODGE...

:GASP:

URDA! WHAT'S HAPPENING?!

A GROUND-QUAKE! RUN OUTSIDE! HURRY!

AAAAA! AAAWWWW-AAAAHHH!

UNGH!

WAAAAA-HAAAAAA... AAAA!

AANH! AANH! AANH!

STOP! CURSE YOU, STOP!

RAYEK! ENOUGH! ENOUGH!

THERE IS MORE TO HIS RAGE THAN EVEN EKUAR'S CAPTURE COULD INSPIRE.

THE POWER HE ALWAYS DREAMED OF IS NOW HIS TO COMMAND--

--YET, REFLECTED IN THE EYES OF THIS ONCE LOVEMATE HE SEES ALL HIS FRUSTRATIONS, ALL HIS WORST FAILURES.

DON'T KNOW HOW YOU'RE ABLE TO DO ALL THIS, BLACK-HAIR. BUT BY THE GREAT ICE WALL, YOU'D *BETTER* STOP...

...OR *I'LL STOP YOU!*

AAAAGHH!

YOU! CHIEF OF THE ONLY ELF TRIBE THAT *SPITS* ON MAGIC! YOU! WHO CAN BEAR A PRECIOUS CHILD AND WATCH, DRY-EYED, AS IT NEEDLESSLY DIES!

:COUGH:... TOLD YOU... SHE WASN'T... YOURS!

LIAR! YOU DIDN'T WANT HER! YOU KILLED HER!

THE PALACE IS DENIED TO ALL GO-BACKS! YOU SHALL NEVER DWELL NEAR IT AGAIN!

WAAAAA! AWAAAAAHH!

INSIDE, NO ONE IS LEFT WHO CAN HELP.

AAAAEEEE!

AND OUTSIDE, NO ONE CAN HEAR THE TINY WAILS OVER RAYEK'S BLASTS.

BUT EVEN SO...

NOOOO!

LISTEN! THE LODGE IS CAVING IN!

KAHVI WILL BE CRUSHED!

SAVE HER, RAYEK!

RAYEK...!

CURSE YOU FOREVER, BLACK-H--!

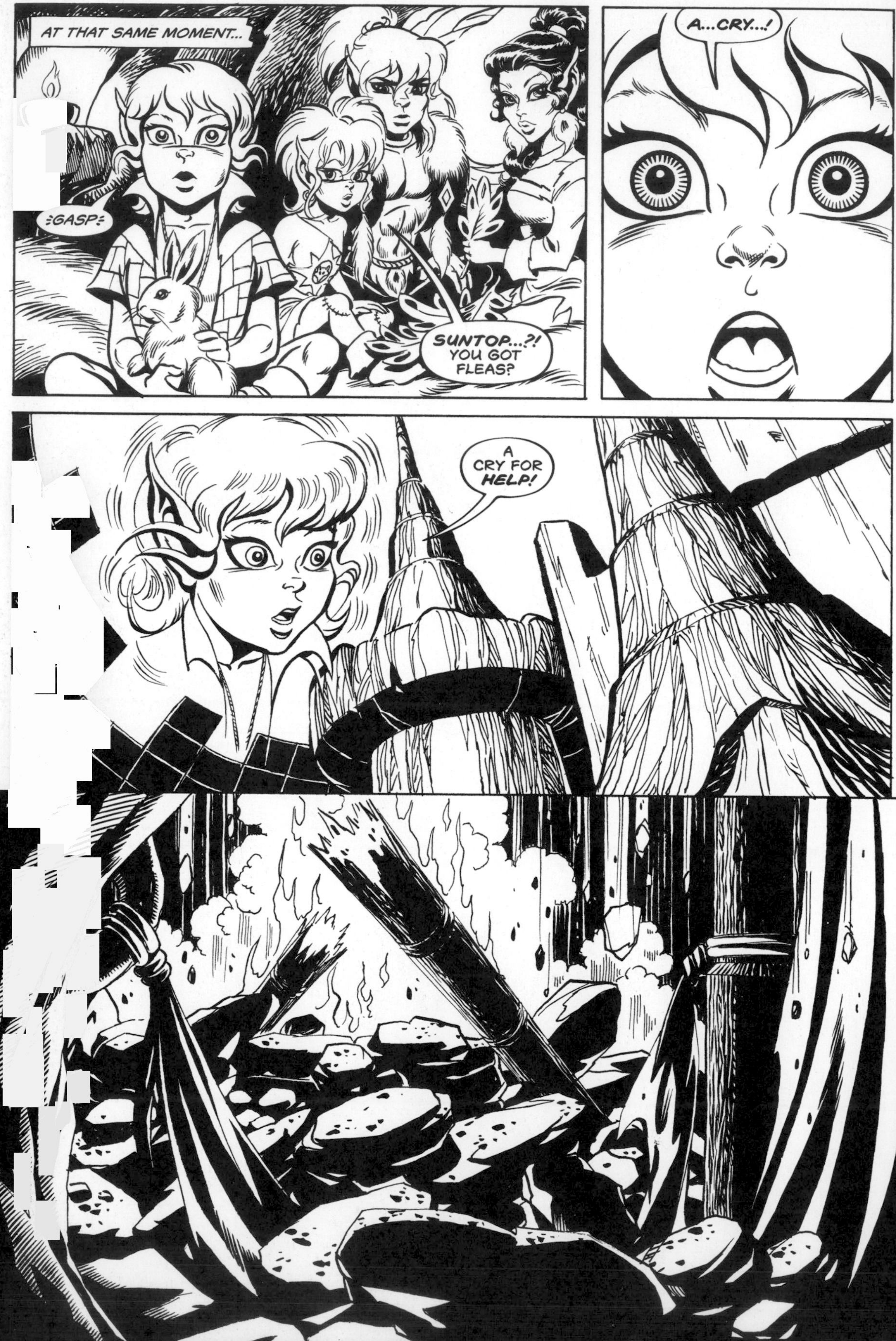
AT THAT SAME MOMENT...
:GASP:
SUNTOP...?! YOU GOT FLEAS?
A...CRY...!
A CRY FOR HELP!

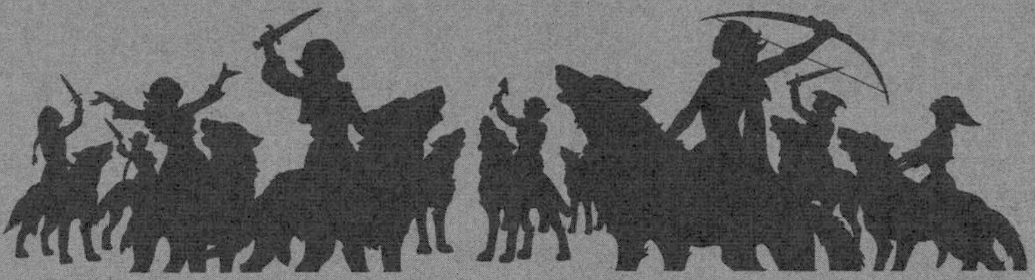

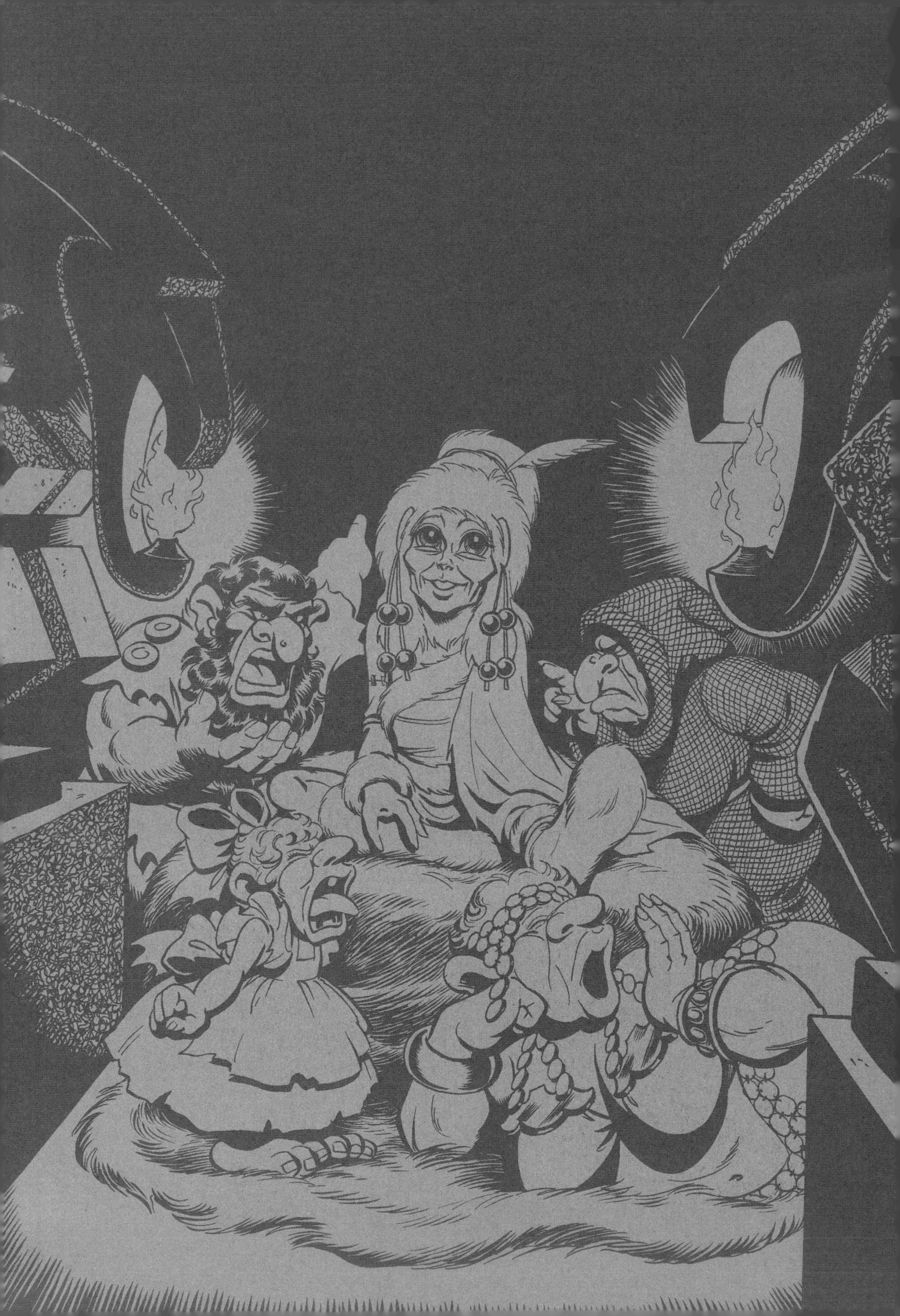

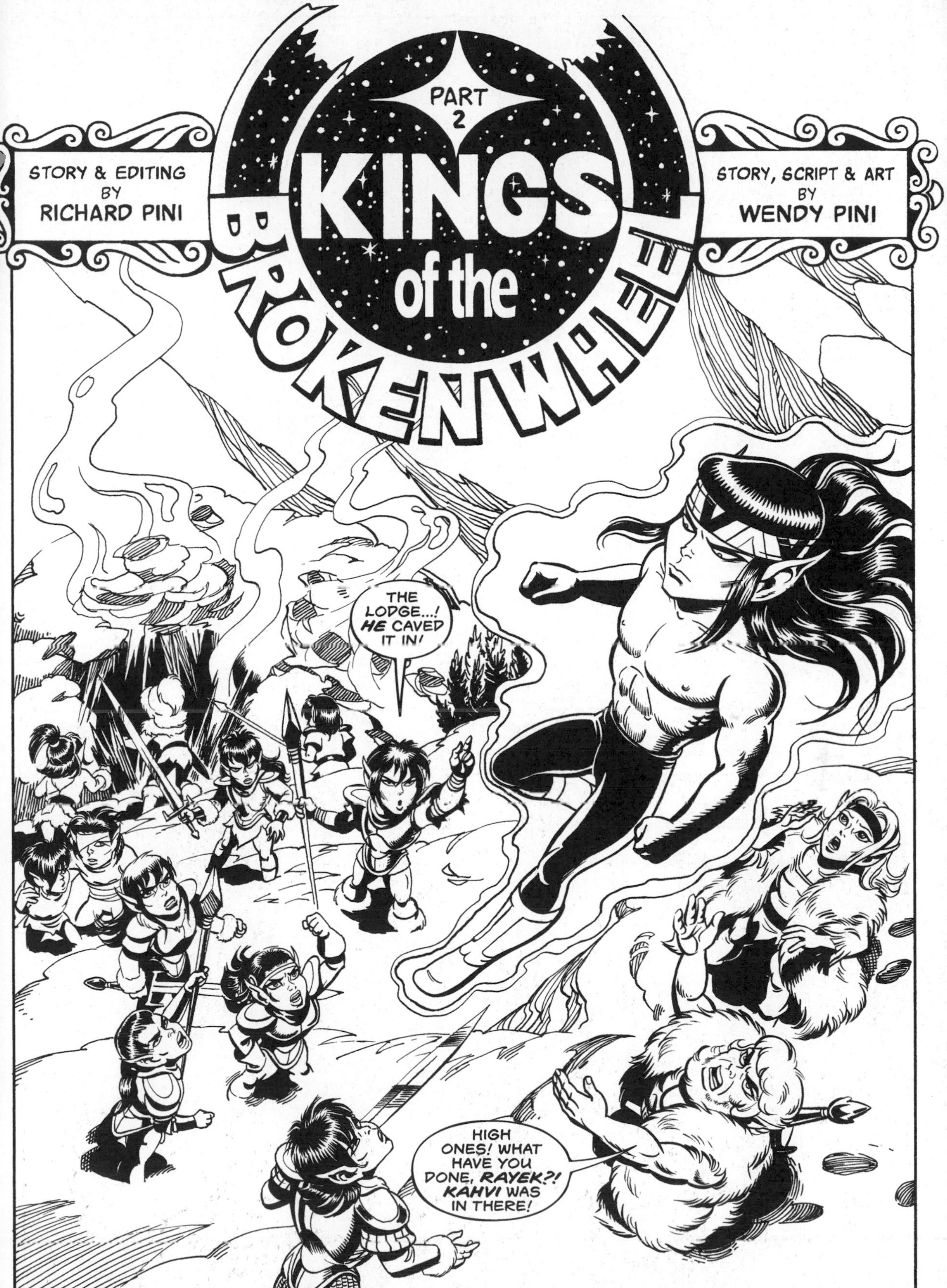
PART 2
KINGS of the BROKEN WHEEL
STORY & EDITING BY RICHARD PINI
STORY, SCRIPT & ART BY WENDY PINI
THE LODGE...! HE CAVED IT IN!
HIGH ONES! WHAT HAVE YOU DONE, RAYEK?! KAHVI WAS IN THERE!

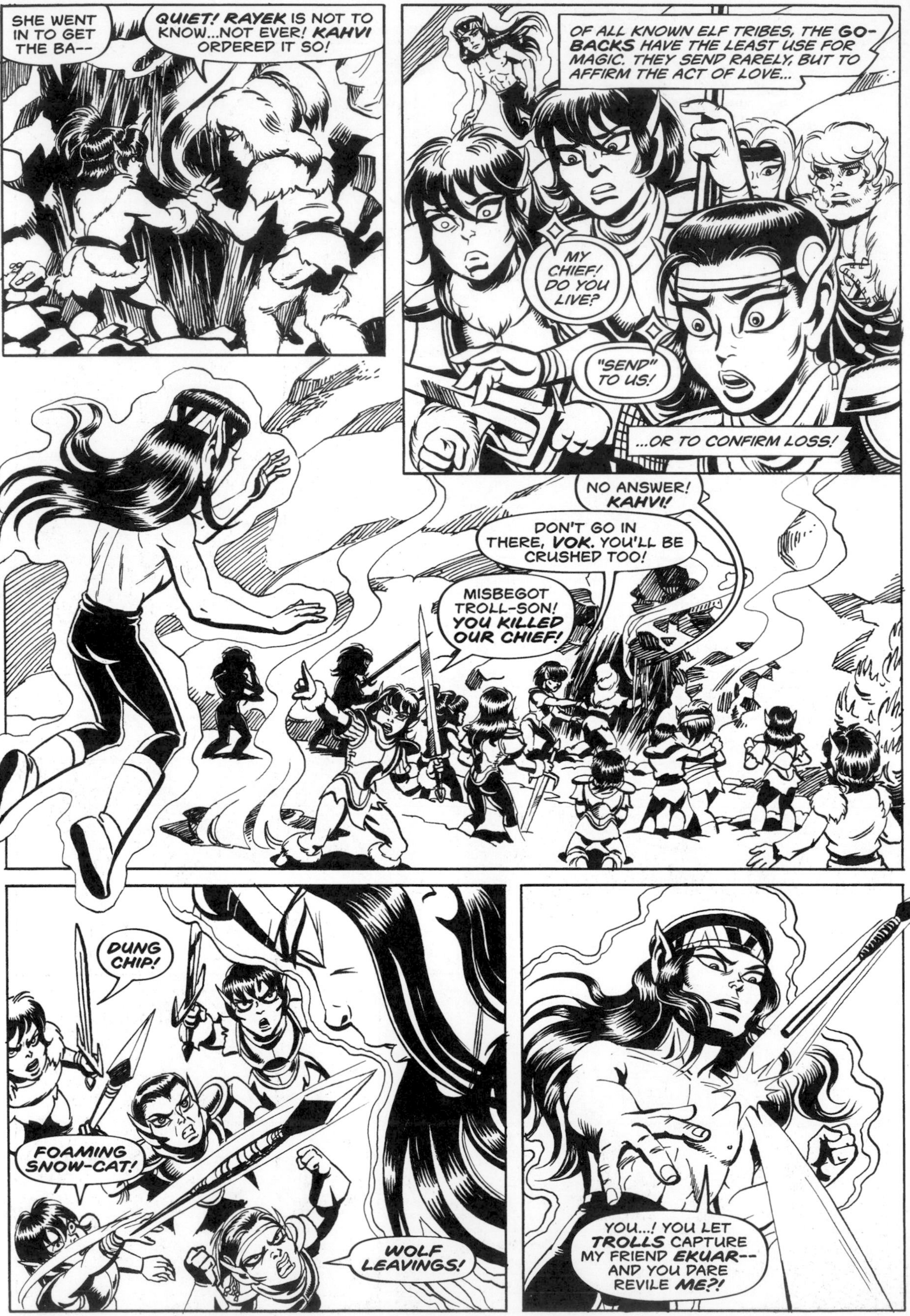
SHE WENT IN TO GET THE BA--
QUIET! RAYEK IS NOT TO KNOW...NOT EVER! KAHVI ORDERED IT SO!
OF ALL KNOWN ELF TRIBES, THE GO-BACKS HAVE THE LEAST USE FOR MAGIC. THEY SEND RARELY, BUT TO AFFIRM THE ACT OF LOVE...
MY CHIEF! DO YOU LIVE?
"SEND" TO US!
...OR TO CONFIRM LOSS!
NO ANSWER! KAHVI!
DON'T GO IN THERE, VOK. YOU'LL BE CRUSHED TOO!
MISBEGOT TROLL-SON! YOU KILLED OUR CHIEF!
DUNG CHIP!
FOAMING SNOW-CAT!
WOLF LEAVINGS!
YOU...! YOU LET TROLLS CAPTURE MY FRIEND EKUAR-- AND YOU DARE REVILE ME?!

OUCH! *PETALWING!* YOUR CLAWS!

HUMPH! SHARP-DARK HIGHTHING TOO BIG FOR BREECHES!

THAT'S THE CLEAR TRUTH, BUG! HIS BORROWED POWER'S MADE HIM BIGGER-- NOT BETTER!

PETALWING LIKE SHARP-DARK HIGHTHING...BUT NOT LIKE HURTFIRES AND NASTYBAD BANGBANGS!

BAD HIGHTHING! BAD! BAD! BAD!

SPOF

PWIFFF

OOOOOO!

NASTY! NASTY! PETALWING KNOW SOMEBODY TO STOP SHARPDARK HIGHTHING!

MOTHER-MOTHER HIGHTING HAS BIGGER HURTFIRES THAN SHARPDARK HIGHTING!

PETALWING GO GET MOTHER-MOTHER HIGHTING!

MOTHER-MOTHER HIGHTING SPANK SHARPDARK HIGHTING GOOD!

THE OPENING AT THE TOP OF THE TALL, PLAIN DOOR IS JUST PRESERVER-SIZED.

THE PORTAL TO THE ROOM OF THE **SCROLL OF COLORS** IS MADE OF THE SAME STAR-STUFF AS THE PALACE OF THE HIGH ONES--**VERY** OLD--

HUMDEDUM... PUSHPULL PUSHPULL!

--AND **PETALWING** IS ONLY SLIGHTLY YOUNGER! BUT A PRESERVER NEVER FORGETS ITS TASKS...OR HOW TO PERFORM THEM!

HEEHEEHEE! PETALWING OPEN DOOR! SHARPDARK HIGHTING IN BIG TROUBLE NOW!

SSSSHHHSSSHHHSS

284

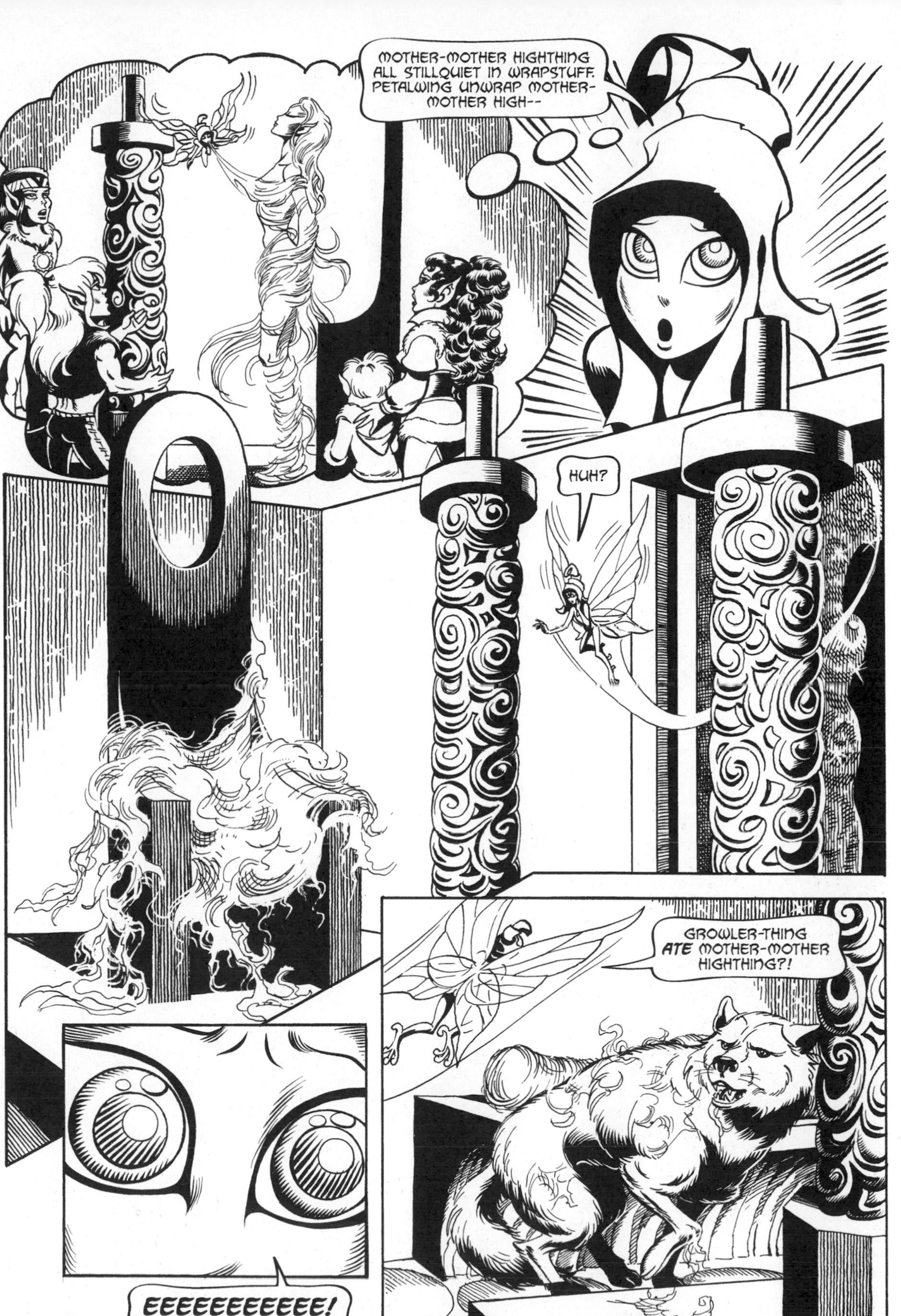
MOTHER-MOTHER HIGHTHING ALL STILLQUIET IN WRAPSTUFF. PETALWING UNWRAP MOTHER-MOTHER HIGH--
HUH?
GROWLER-THING ATE MOTHER-MOTHER HIGHTHING?!
EEEEEEEEEEEE!

UH OH! PETALWING REMEMBERS. MOTHER-MOTHER HIGHTHING *WAS* GROWLER-THING LONG LONG TIME!

:SNIFF:
:SNIFF:

MAYBE IS GROWLER-THING AGAIN?

CHOOF!

YEEEP!

MOTHER-MOTHER HIGHTHING CHANGE *INSIDE* WRAPSTUFF? WRAPSTUFF BREAK? CHEWCHEW OUT?

WAS GROWLER. WASN'T GROWLER. *IS* GROWLER--WHYFOR?!

WAIT! WAIT!

TIMMAIN, THE HIGH ONE, LAST OF THE FIRSTCOMERS, KNOWS MORE OF THE WORLD OF TWO MOONS AS WOLF THAN SHE EVER KNEW AS ELF...

THE WOLF MUST RUN FREE...ESCAPE... FOR THE ELFIN PART OF HER CANNOT BEAR THAT HER CHILDREN HAVE TURNED THEIR POWERS AGAINST EACH OTHER.

THE **GO-BACKS** CRY OUT IN RAGE AND GRIEF. THE FROZEN MOUNTAINS, BRISTLING WITH TROLLISH TRAPS, COULD NOT, IN THE END, BAR THE GO-BACKS FROM THE HIGH ONES' ANCIENT DWELLING.

BUT WHAT THE TROLLS FOUGHT TO DO FOR GENERATIONS, THE POWER OF ONE IMPLACABLE ELF WILL DO IN MOMENTS!

FOOLS! YOU KNOW THE PALACE'S TRUE NATURE NO BETTER THAN YOU KNOW YOUR OWN!

FILLED WITH THE SEEMINGLY LIMITLESS FORCE OF THE **GLIDERS'** SOULS, **RAYEK** DRIVES THE GO-BACKS ON AND ON...

YOU **LOST** YOUR CHANCE AT THE STARS EVEN AS YOU HELD IT IN YOUR HANDS!

CHOOSE **ANOTHER** NAME FOR YOURSELVES...

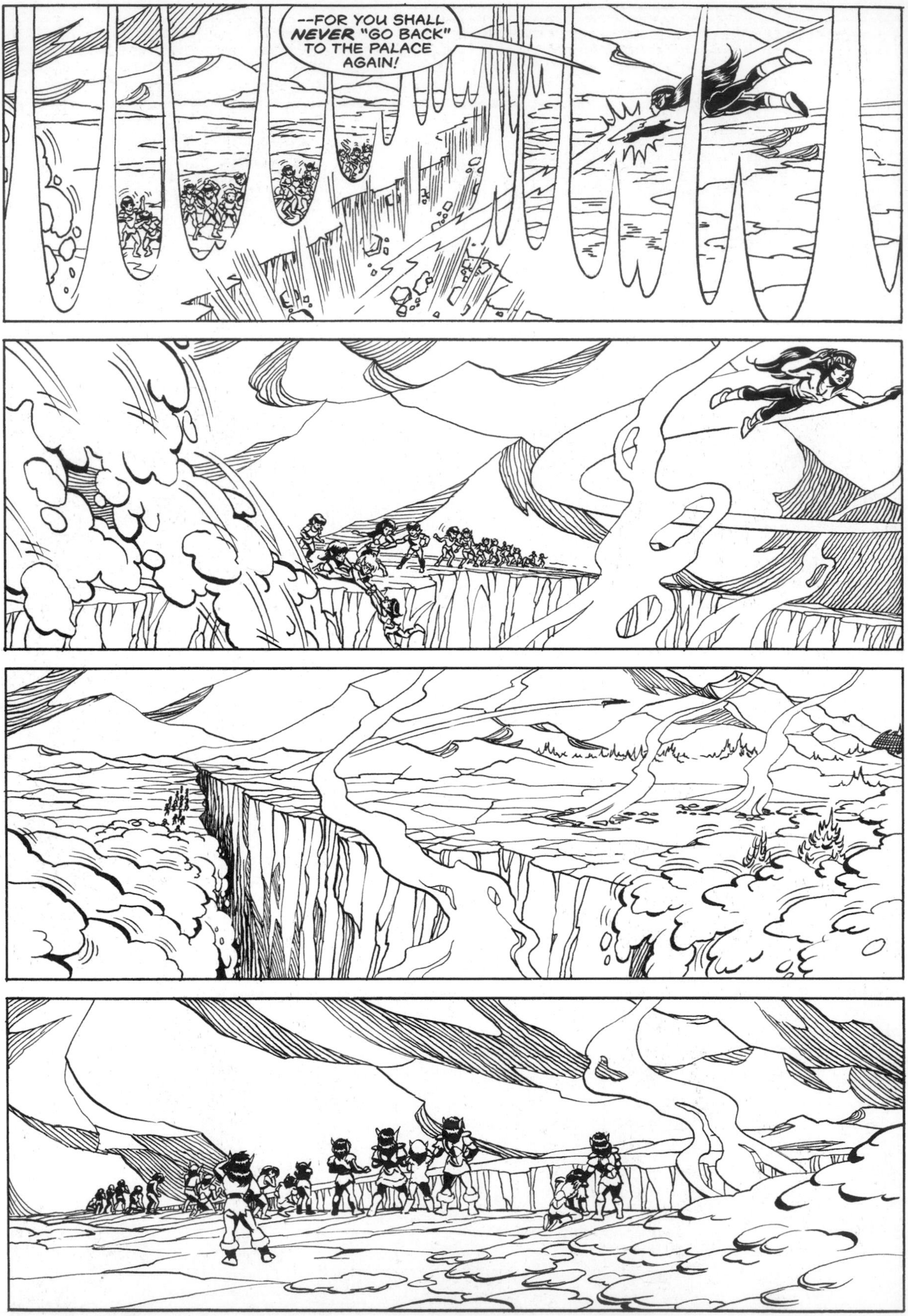
--FOR YOU SHALL NEVER "GO BACK" TO THE PALACE AGAIN!

MEANWHILE...

HIGH ONES! DO YOU THINK HE KILLED THEM ALL?

WE'D HAVE SENSED SO MANY DEATHS, I THINK... I HOPE...

WHAT'S HAPPENING, *CLEARBROOK*? FIRST *STRONGBOW* SHOOTS DOWN A GLIDER...AND NOW *RAYEK'S* FINISHED *KAHVI!*

ELVES ARE *KILLING* ELVES! HOW CAN IT BE?

AND HOW CAN *THEY* ALLOW IT-- THE SPIRITS OF ALL OUR DEAD KIN WHO HAUNT THE PALACE?

MAYBE THEY CAN'T SEE WHAT HAPPENS IN THE WORLD--OR IF THEY CAN, MAYBE THEY DON'T JUDGE!

WELL, I *DO!* I...

AAAGGHH!

LOOK OUT!

STAY CLEAR OF THE DOME! STAY CLEAR!

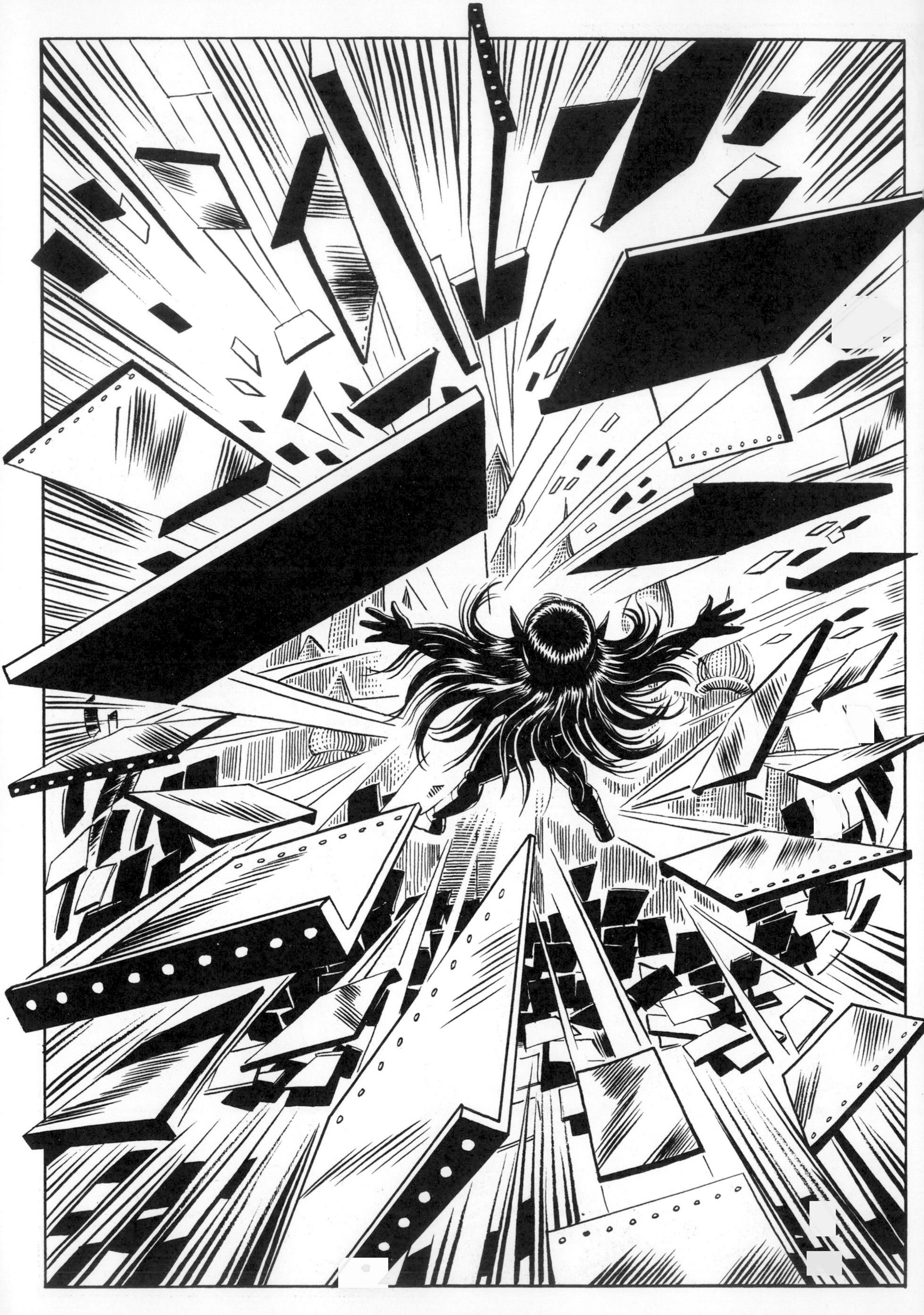

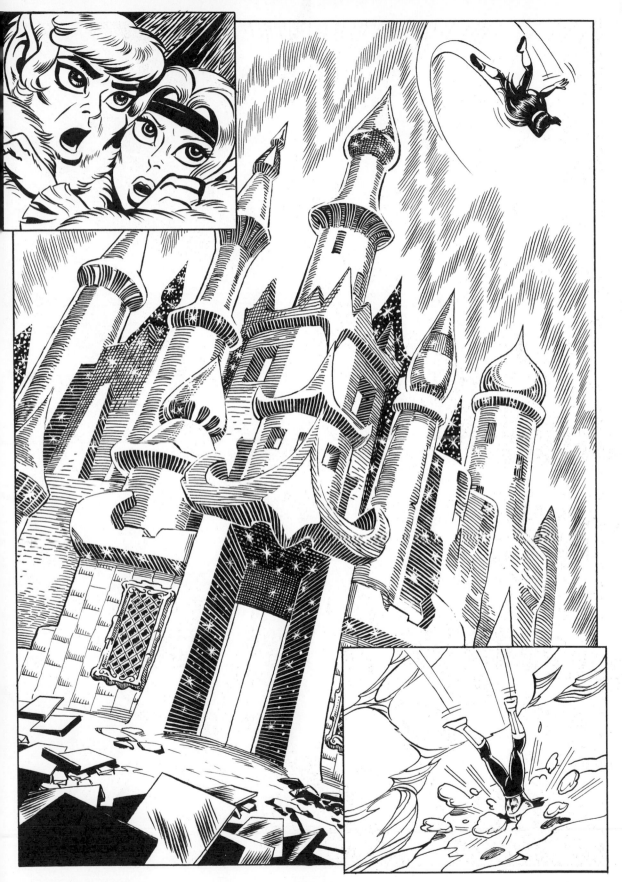

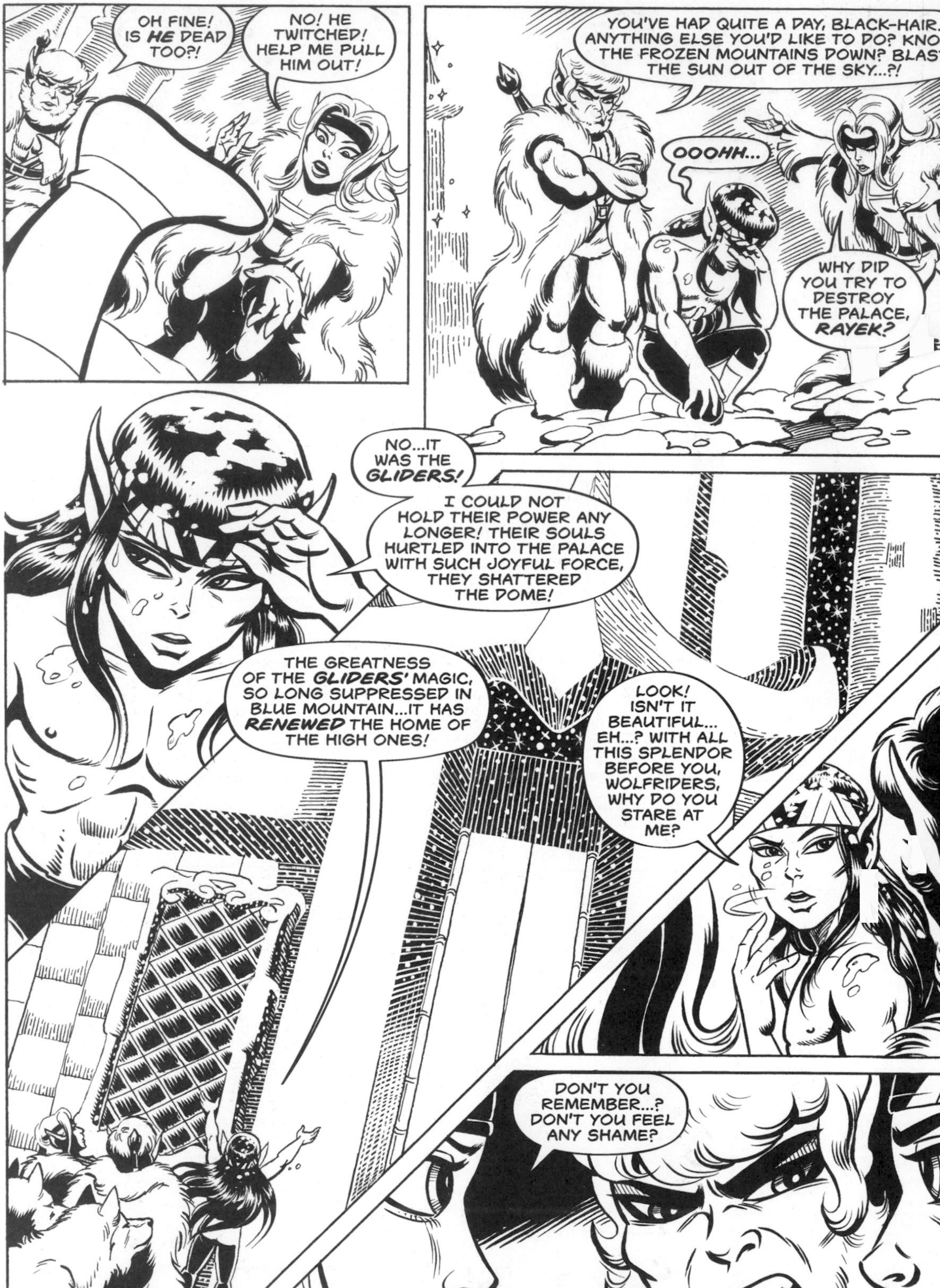

OH FINE! IS HE DEAD TOO?!
NO! HE TWITCHED! HELP ME PULL HIM OUT!
YOU'VE HAD QUITE A DAY, BLACK-HAIR. ANYTHING ELSE YOU'D LIKE TO DO? KNOCK THE FROZEN MOUNTAINS DOWN? BLAST THE SUN OUT OF THE SKY...?!
OOOHH...
WHY DID YOU TRY TO DESTROY THE PALACE, RAYEK?
NO...IT WAS THE GLIDERS!
I COULD NOT HOLD THEIR POWER ANY LONGER! THEIR SOULS HURTLED INTO THE PALACE WITH SUCH JOYFUL FORCE, THEY SHATTERED THE DOME!
THE GREATNESS OF THE GLIDERS' MAGIC, SO LONG SUPPRESSED IN BLUE MOUNTAIN...IT HAS RENEWED THE HOME OF THE HIGH ONES!
LOOK! ISN'T IT BEAUTIFUL... EH...? WITH ALL THIS SPLENDOR BEFORE YOU, WOLFRIDERS, WHY DO YOU STARE AT ME?
DON'T YOU REMEMBER...? DON'T YOU FEEL ANY SHAME?
TIMMORN'S BLOOD, BLACK-HAIR, YOU KILLED KAHVI! AND FOR ALL WE KNOW, THE GO-BACKS TOO!

I-I **WANTED** TO. PERHAPS I SHOULD HAVE. THE GO-BACKS ARE **BANISHED**, NOT DEAD. AS FOR THEIR WORTHLESS CHIEF... **BRRR!**

SHE'S A WHITE-STRIPE WITH MORE THAN **ONE** WAY OUT OF HER BURROW. IF YOU DID NOT FIND HER BODY...

--THEN SHE MIGHT YET **LIVE!** SEEMS, BY THAT REASONING, THERE'S A **CUB** SHE BORE WHOSE DEATH IS JUST AS DOUBTFUL. EVER THINK OF **THAT?**

ENOUGH! ALL THAT MATTERS NOW IS **EKUAR!** THE TROLLS HAVE HIM...AND I NO LONGER HAVE THE POWER TO **SAVE** HIM!

YOU FOOLISH ELF! ALWAYS CHOOSING THE THORNIEST PATH!

IT'S BEEN ALL OR NOTHING WITH YOU EVER SINCE WE'VE KNOWN YOU. WHEN WILL YOU LEARN?

THIS IS THE SECOND TIME **TREESTUMP** AND **CLEARBROOK** HAVE SET FOOT IN THE PALACE OF THE HIGH ONES. YET IT SEEMS THEY NEVER SAW IT...OR EVEN SENSED IT 'TIL NOW.

THE VOICES OF A HOST OF ELFIN SPIRITS ARE ALMOST AUDIBLE--THEIR WELCOME IS PALPABLE, AND THE PALACE'S **WARMTH,** BORN OF NO EARTHLY FIRE, PENETRATES THE WOLFRIDERS TO THEIR MARROW.

OOHHH! IF CUTTER AND THE REST COULD BE HERE...TO SEE IT--**FEEL** IT--LIKE THIS!

FIRST TIME, I DIDN'T KNOW WHAT TO MAKE OF IT. NOW, IT'S EVERYTHING I DREAMED!

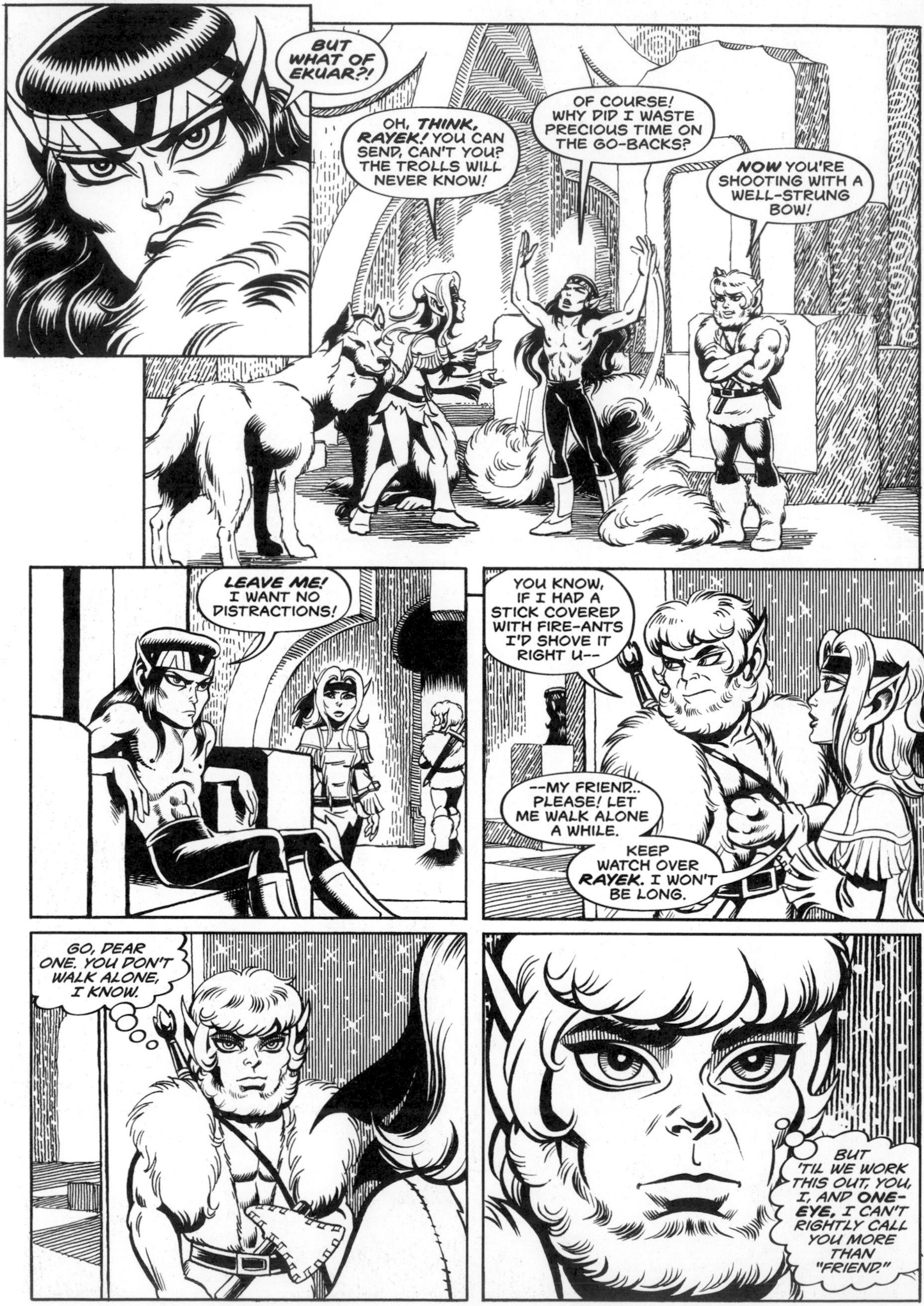
BUT WHAT OF EKUAR?!
OH, THINK, RAYEK! YOU CAN SEND, CAN'T YOU? THE TROLLS WILL NEVER KNOW!
OF COURSE! WHY DID I WASTE PRECIOUS TIME ON THE GO-BACKS?
NOW YOU'RE SHOOTING WITH A WELL-STRUNG BOW!
LEAVE ME! I WANT NO DISTRACTIONS!
YOU KNOW, IF I HAD A STICK COVERED WITH FIRE-ANTS I'D SHOVE IT RIGHT U--
--MY FRIEND.. PLEASE! LET ME WALK ALONE A WHILE.
KEEP WATCH OVER RAYEK. I WON'T BE LONG.
GO, DEAR ONE. YOU DON'T WALK ALONE, I KNOW.
BUT 'TIL WE WORK THIS OUT, YOU, I, AND ONE-EYE, I CAN'T RIGHTLY CALL YOU MORE THAN "FRIEND."

HE FELL THREE TURNS OF THE SEASONS AGO... IN THE SNOW...ON THE OTHER SIDE OF THE FROZEN MOUNTAINS. BUT THE DEATHLESS LOVE OF HER LIFEMATE **ONE-EYE** ENFOLDS HER, RELEASES HER UNWEPT TEARS.

SHE WHISPERS HIS SOUL NAME...

SUR...!

...AND HEARS HER OWN RETURNED.

AT THE SAME TIME, **RAYEK'S** MENTAL CALL GOES FAR FROM THE PALACE...DOWN...DOWN WHERE THE **TROLLS** DWELL IN THEIR SOOT-SMIRCHED KINGDOM BENEATH THE MOUNTAINS.

EKUAR...?

EKUAR... IT IS I, RAYEK!

SEND TO ME IF YOU CAN, MY MENTOR...WHERE ARE YOU? HOW DO YOU FARE...?

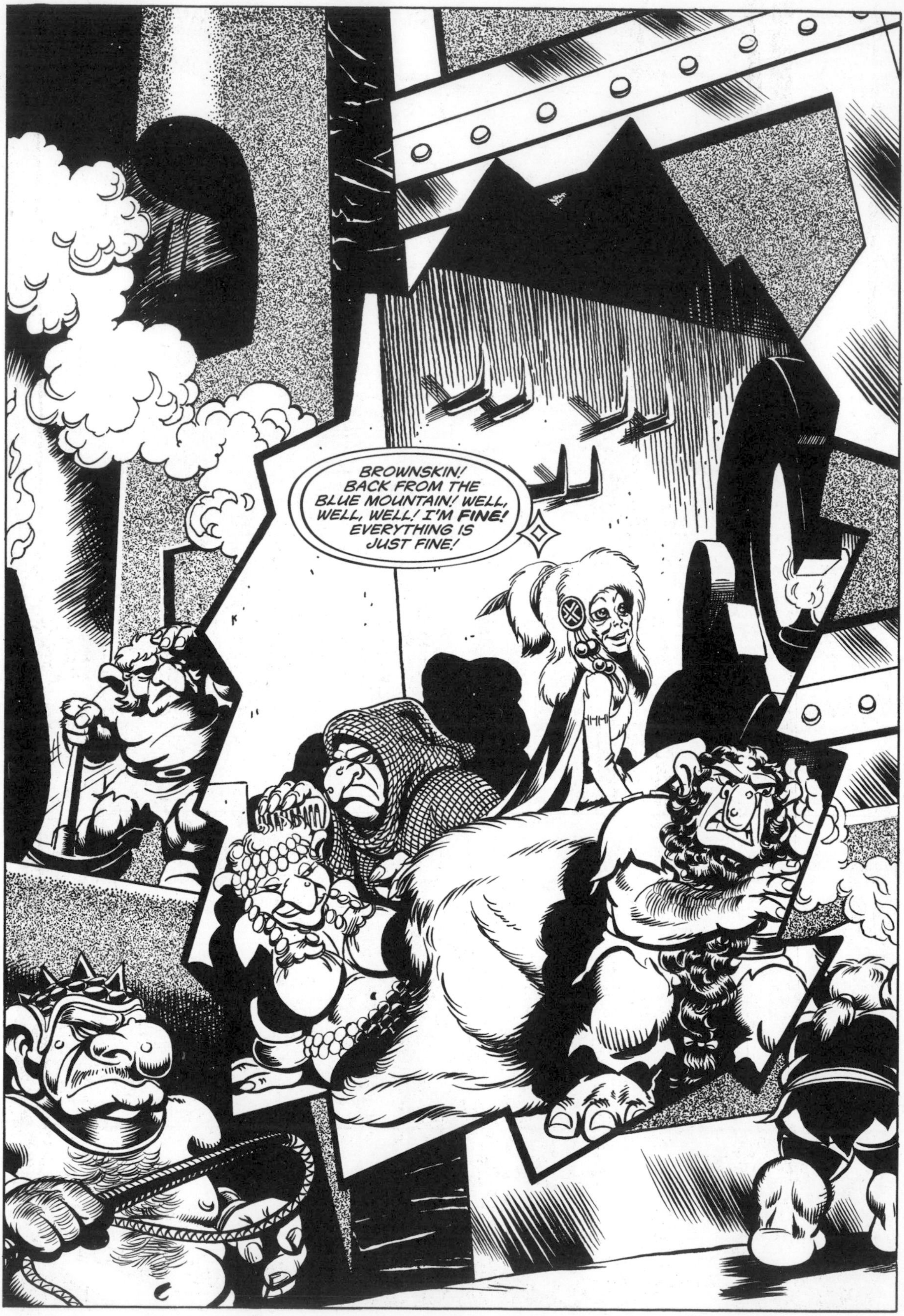
BROWNSKIN! BACK FROM THE BLUE MOUNTAIN! WELL, WELL, WELL! I'M **FINE!** EVERYTHING IS JUST FINE!

TH-THEY'RE ABOUT TO BREAK THROUGH THIS WALL AGAIN, ROCK SHAPER... *DO SOMETHING!*

"KING PICKNOSE..." *HAH!* STRUTLESS, GUTLESS, AND NUTL--

--NOT *THAT*, GRANDMAMA! ::*GIGGLE*:: AT *LEAST* NOT THAT!

POOR FELLOW, DON'T BOTHER YOURSELF! THERE'S PLENTY OF TIME TO SEAL UP THE WALL AGAIN!

NOK NOK

TOY BROKE! MAKE *TRINKET* A NEW TOY, PAPA *EKUAR!*

PAPA...? *PAPA?!* THAT DOES IT! THERE'S ONLY *ONE* PAPA HERE, ONE MASTER, AND ONE *KING!*

UNDERSTAND?!

AAWW-AAAHH! HE SCAAARED MEEEEEE! BAWWW!

BUT WE *MIGHT* THINK ABOUT COMING HOME NOW, BROWNSKIN....!

ELSEWHERE...FAR AWAY FROM THE FROZEN MOUNTAINS, IN THE WIDE, LUSH VALLEY OF ENDLESS SLEEP...

≠PANT PANT≠ THIS SONG... ALWAYS KEPT MY FEET DANCING...WHEN THE REST OF ME...WAS READY TO DROP!

NO OTHER DANCER FLASHES AND SPARKLES AS YOU DO, HEALER. WE'VE LONGED TO SEE YOUR SWIRLING, MANY-COLORED VEILS AGAIN.

YOU'VE LONGED ESPECIALLY, ZHANTEE! ≠HEH HEH≠

A VEIL WOULD CATCH AND TEAR HERE--AND I AM TORN BY YOUR PLEAS THAT I REVISIT SORROW'S END.

LEETAH...!

THERE MAY BE A REASON BEYOND MERE REUNIONS FOR ME TO RETURN WITH YOU NOW...

YES, THE CRY FOR HELP THAT SUNTOP HEARD.

SUNTOP'S POWERS ARE GROWING FASTER, IT SEEMS--

--THAN HIS ABILITY TO USE THEM.

HE DID SAY THE CRY CAME FROM FAR AWAY! BUT WHO...?

THE CRY PERSISTS, AND ITS SOURCE IS NOT WINNOWILL--THAT IS ALL SUNTOP KNOWS.

I HAVE TRIED TO SORT HIM OUT AS BEST I CAN... PERHAPS SAVAH COULD DO MORE.

SAVAH! YES!

SHE'D KNOW WHAT TO DO!

YES, HEALER! COME HOME WITH LITTLE SUNTOP!

NO! NOT NOW!

WE NEED HER HERE WITH **US**, MORE THAN EVER BEFORE!

:SIGH: THE DESERT IS DRY ALL YEAR-- THEN SUDDENLY THE FLOODS COME!

SO IT IS WITH PROBLEMS. I MUST KEEP MY PROMISE TO YOU, **NIGHTFALL**--

--AND A WAY MUST BE FOUND TO HELP **STRONGBOW**. UNTIL HE FORGIVES HIMSELF FOR KILLING **KUREEL**--

--HIS ARROWS WILL NEVER FLY TRUE.

WE'LL TALK OF YOUR PROMISE ANOTHER DAY, **LEETAH**. AND **STRONGBOW** HAS ALL THE WOLFRIDERS BEHIND HIM. YOUR CUB COMES FIRST.

HE IS WITH HIS FATHER. **CUTTER** HAS HEALING QUALITIES OF HIS OWN. MAYBE...

"...**SUNTOP** CAN TAKE STRENGTH FROM HIM."

CHIRRUP CHIRRUP

CHIRRR
*CHIRRR

CHIRRR

THE SUN FOLK ARE LEAVING TOMORROW. THEY BELONG IN THE DESERT WITH THEIR JACKAL-MIX WOLVES.

DO YOU WANT TO GO WITH THEM, CUB?

HMMM...?

YOUR MOTHER AND I TALKED. YOU NEED SPECIAL TEACHINGS WE CAN'T GIVE. I CAN PROTECT YOU FROM THE FOREST'S DANGERS...

BUT NOT FROM THE UNSEEN THINGS THAT GIVE YOU BAD DREAMS. I... I'M JUST A WOLFRIDER-- NOT A HIGH ONE.

YOU...YOU *WANT* ME TO GO AWAY?

HIGH ONES, *NO!*

I JUST WANT YOU TO BE HAPPY...

EVEN IF YOU MUST BE HAPPY FAR AWAY.

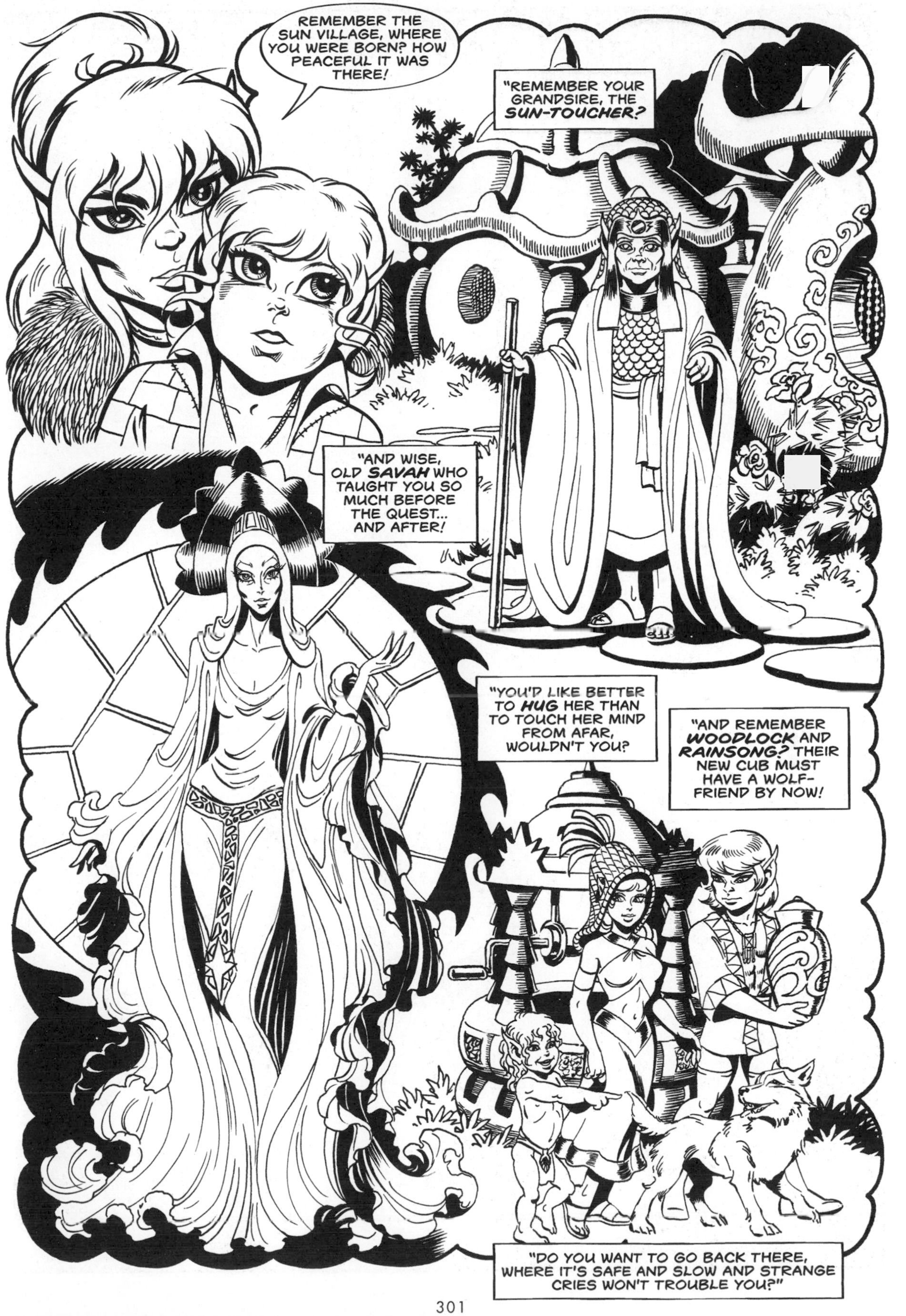

REMEMBER THE SUN VILLAGE, WHERE YOU WERE BORN? HOW PEACEFUL IT WAS THERE!
"REMEMBER YOUR GRANDSIRE, THE SUN-TOUCHER?
"AND WISE, OLD SAVAH WHO TAUGHT YOU SO MUCH BEFORE THE QUEST... AND AFTER!
"YOU'D LIKE BETTER TO HUG HER THAN TO TOUCH HER MIND FROM AFAR, WOULDN'T YOU?
"AND REMEMBER WOODLOCK AND RAINSONG? THEIR NEW CUB MUST HAVE A WOLF-FRIEND BY NOW!
"DO YOU WANT TO GO BACK THERE, WHERE IT'S SAFE AND SLOW AND STRANGE CRIES WON'T TROUBLE YOU?"

THERE'S NO PLACE TO RUN FROM THIS CRY, FATHER—IT'S IN MY HEAD! MANY VOICES...

...OR MAYBE JUST ONE...I DON'T KNOW...*ELF* VOICES! STRANGERS, SCREAMING FOR HELP!

WE *HAVE* TO GO TO THE PALACE AND FIND OUT! *STRONGBOW* TOO! NOTHING WILL BE RIGHT UNTIL WE DO!

:*SIGH*: PALACE OR SORROW'S END...NEITHER JOURNEY IS EASY. WE'LL SEE...

AYOOOAH!

HOW'S THE OLD NOISY SKULL, *SUNTOP?*

H'LO, *SKYWISE.*

WANT A GOOD SWING?

WELL...

SURE YOU DO! READY?

DON'T LET GO!

YIIIIIIII!

WOOO OOOOO OOOW!

LOOK OUT! *HIGHER! HIGHER!*

HOW'S *THIS?!*

WOOOP!

HAHA HAHA!

SEE? NOTHING LIKE A LITTLE WIND IN YOUR EARS TO CLEAR THE HEAD!

:GIGGLE:

UH-OH! THERE'S THAT SERIOUS FACE AGAIN...

YOU KNOW, WHEN *MY* HEAD BUZZES, *STARJUMPER* HELPS ME A LOT!

WOOO-OOOOOOO-AAHHHHH!

HA HA HA!

WOOP *WOOP* WOOPS!

HA HA!

HEH HEH!

...GRROOWWWLLL...

:SNIFF: :SNORT:

WHUFF!

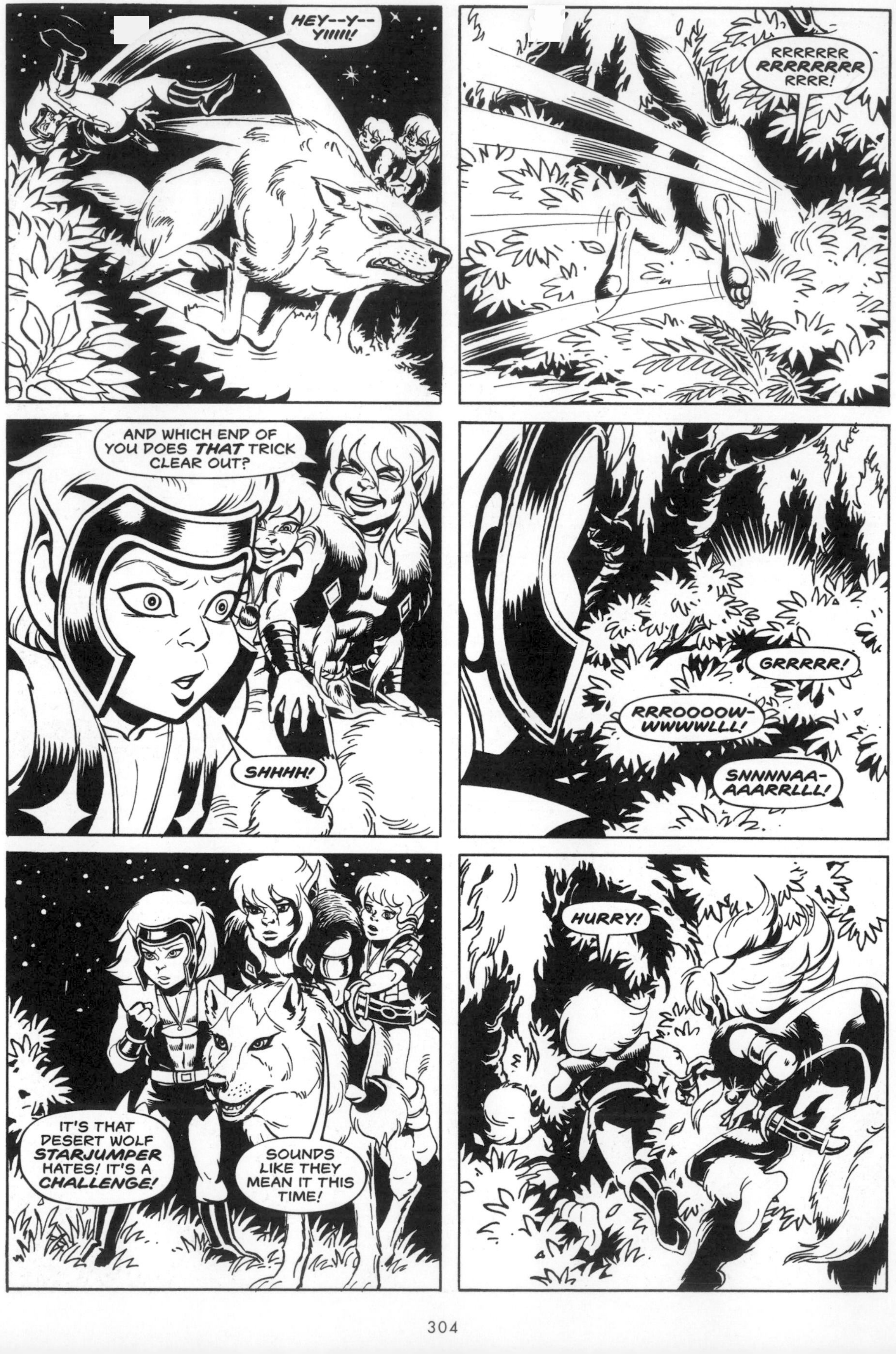
HEY--Y--YIIII!
RRRRRRR RRRRRRRR RRRR!
AND WHICH END OF YOU DOES THAT TRICK CLEAR OUT?
SHHHH!
GRRRRR!
RRROOOOW-WWWWLLL!
SNNNNAA-AAARRLLL!
IT'S THAT DESERT WOLF STARJUMPER HATES! IT'S A CHALLENGE!
SOUNDS LIKE THEY MEAN IT THIS TIME!
HURRY!

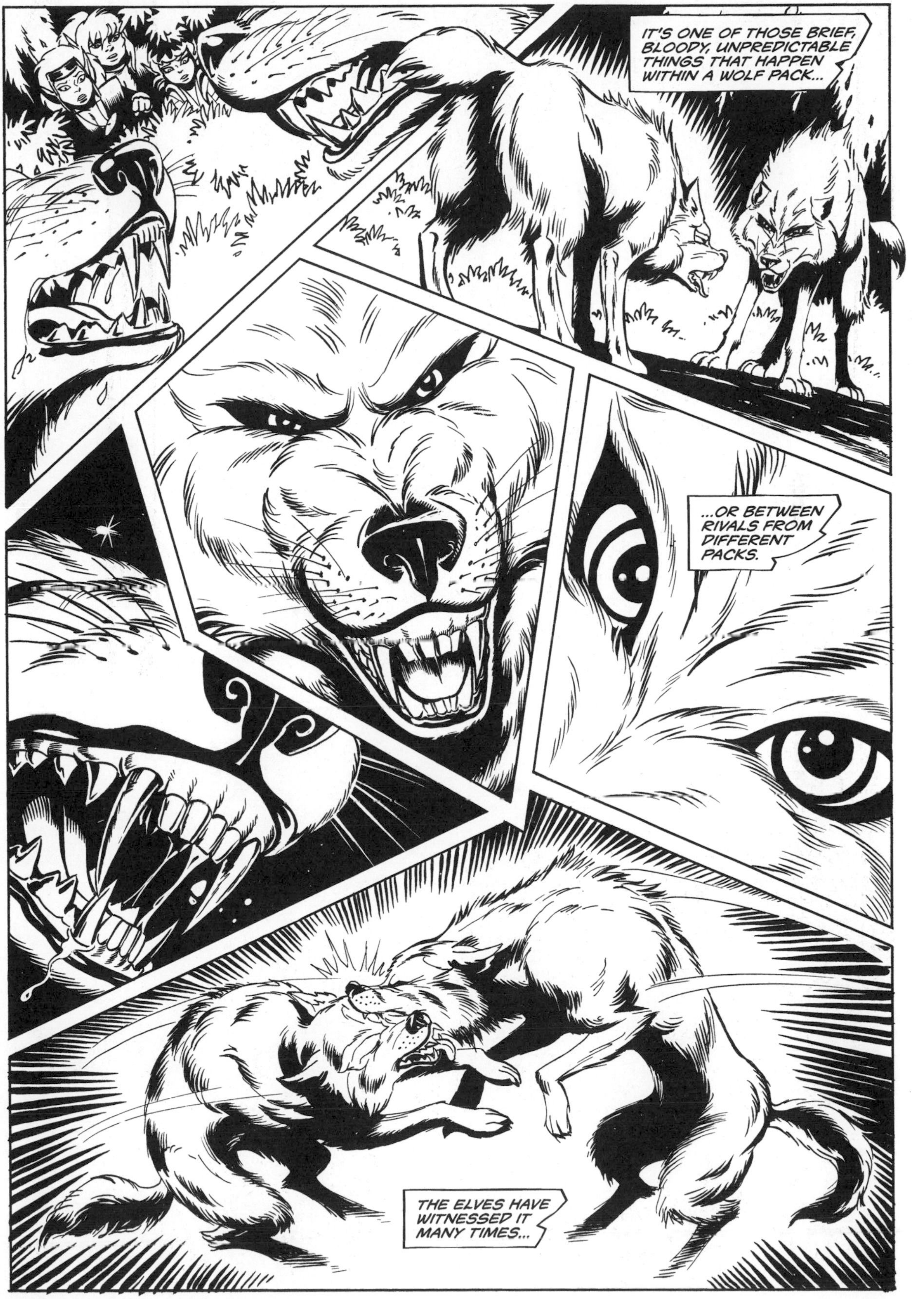

IT'S ONE OF THOSE BRIEF, BLOODY, UNPREDICTABLE THINGS THAT HAPPEN WITHIN A WOLF PACK...
...OR BETWEEN RIVALS FROM DIFFERENT PACKS.
THE ELVES HAVE WITNESSED IT MANY TIMES...

LIKE EVERY WOLFRIDER, *SKYWISE* FULLY KNOWS THE RULES...

STARJUMPER'S TOO OLD...TOO OLD FOR THIS!

...BUT UNLIKE MOST WOLFRIDERS, HE HAS KNOWN ONLY *ONE* WOLF-FRIEND SINCE BOYHOOD!

NO! DON'T DO IT!

GIVE UP, STARJUMPER! BACK OFF!

IT'S NO USE!

HAAH! YAAAH! BREAK IT UP! RUN!

GRRRR- RRRRARR!

AAAH!

SNNAAA- RRRRRLL!

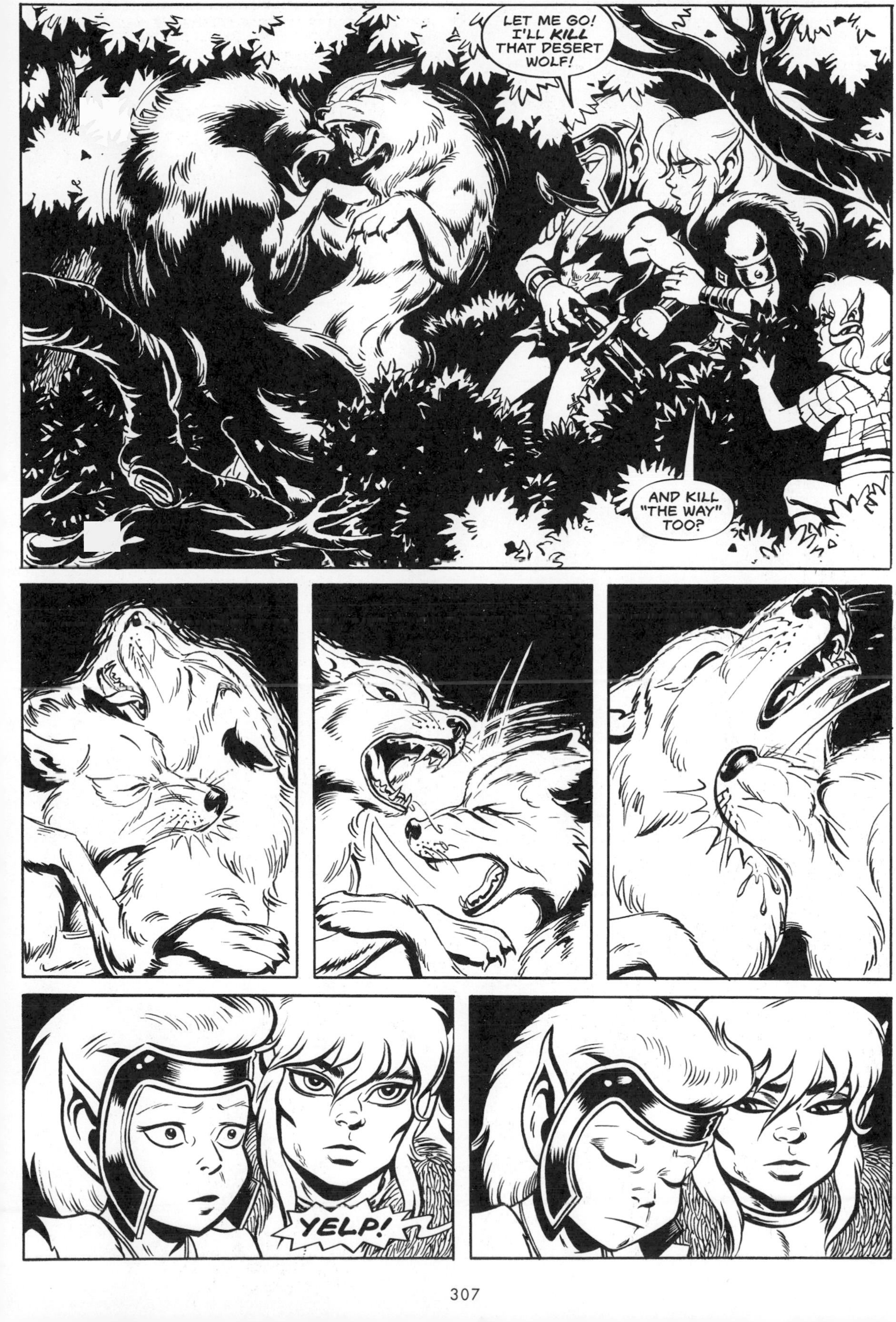
LET ME GO! I'LL KILL THAT DESERT WOLF!
AND KILL "THE WAY" TOO?
YELP!

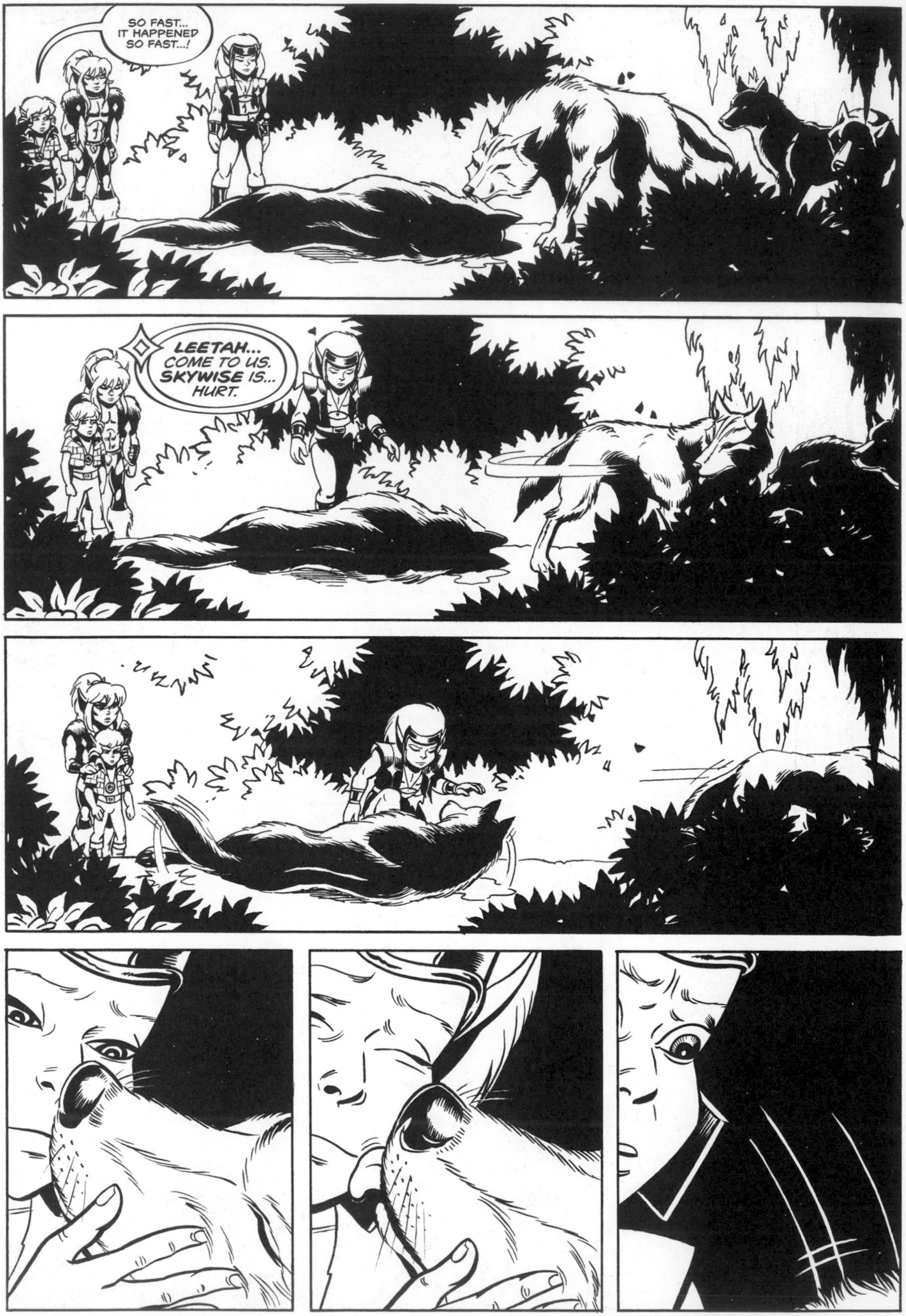
SO FAST... IT HAPPENED SO FAST...!
LEETAH... COME TO US. SKYWISE IS... HURT.

IT'S HIS THROAT...

LEETAH'S COMING. SHE KNOWS. SHE'LL BE HERE IN A HEARTBEAT.

YOU CAN SEE...AS WELL AS I...

...EVEN THAT'S TOO LONG TO WAIT!

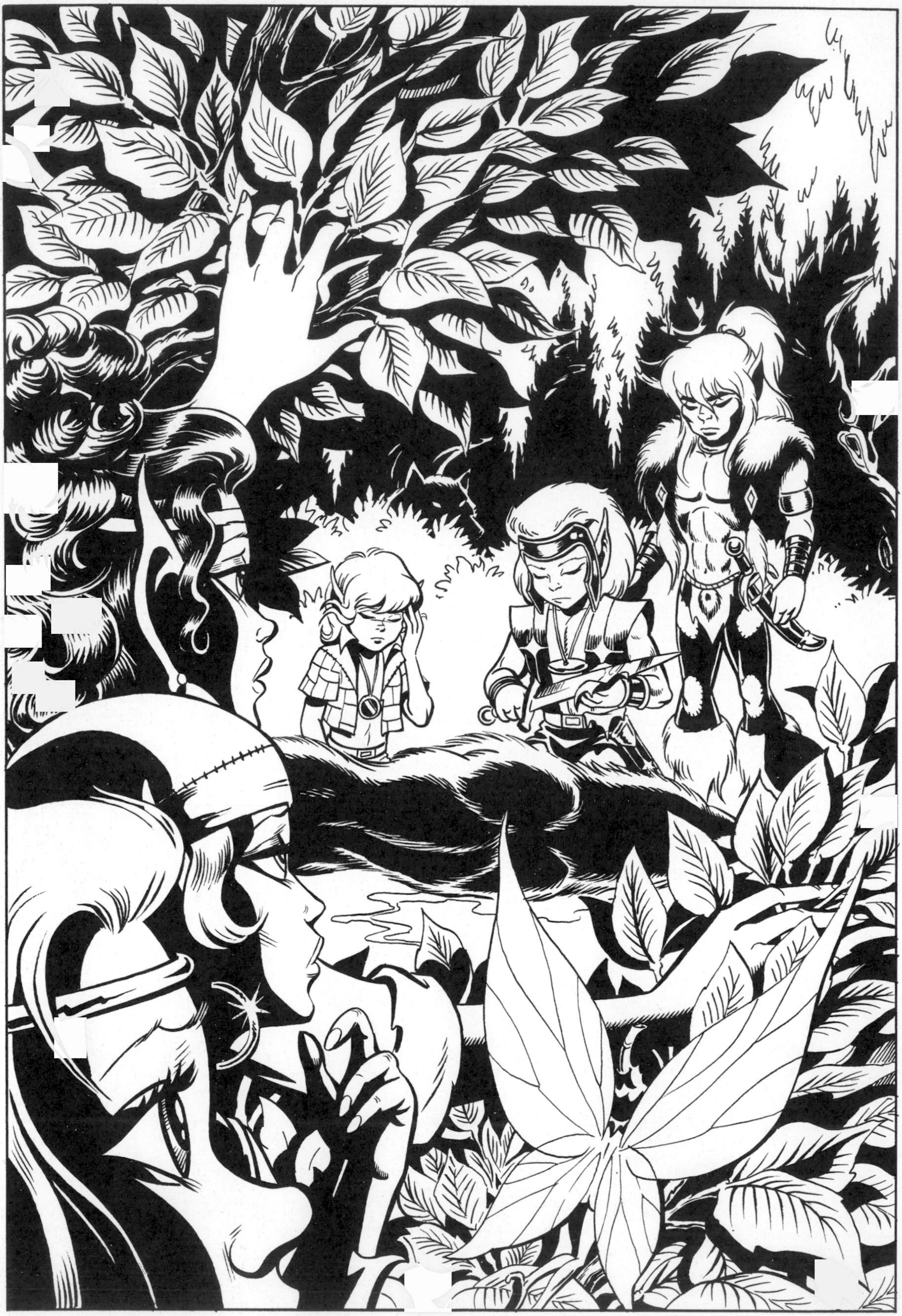

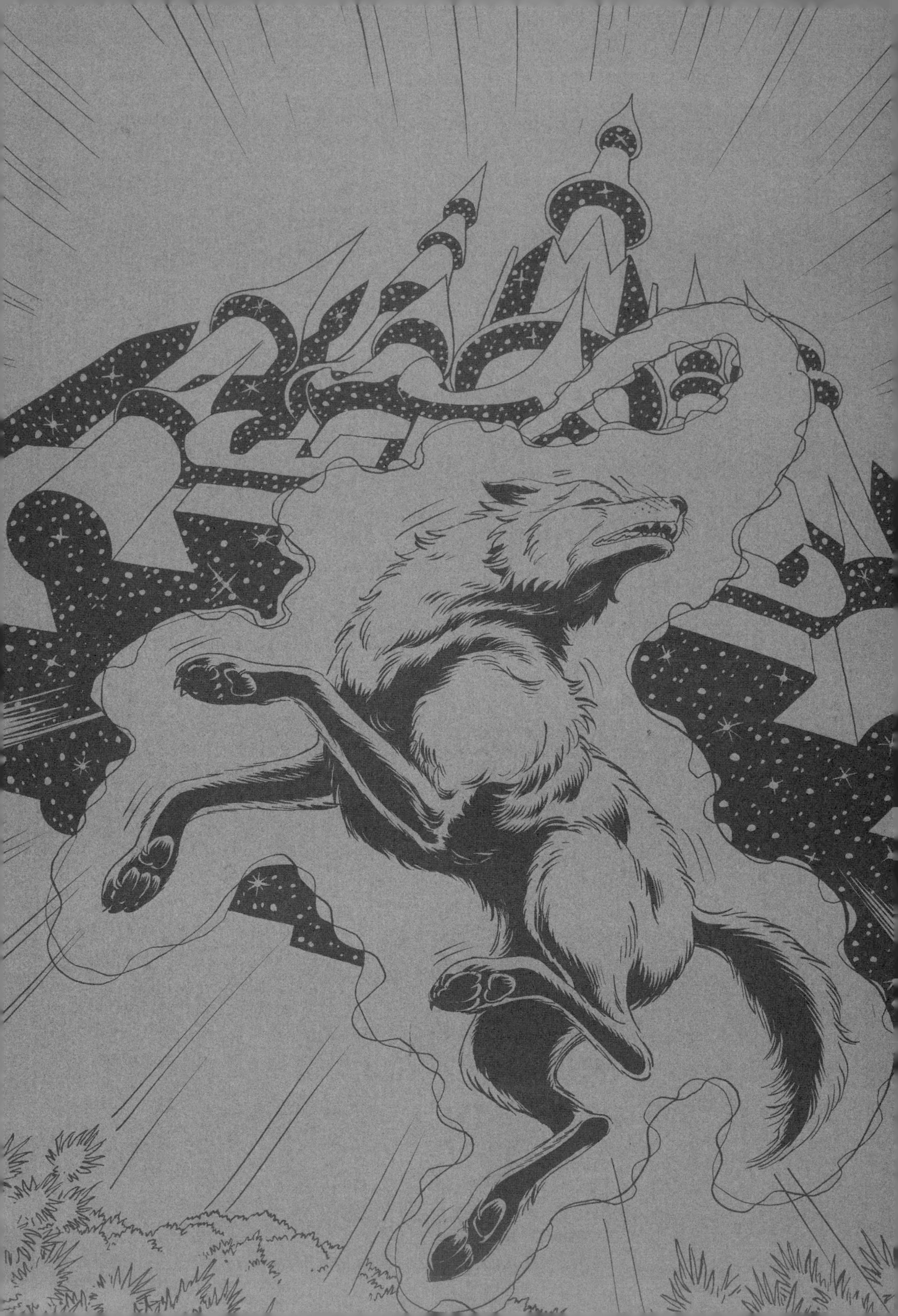

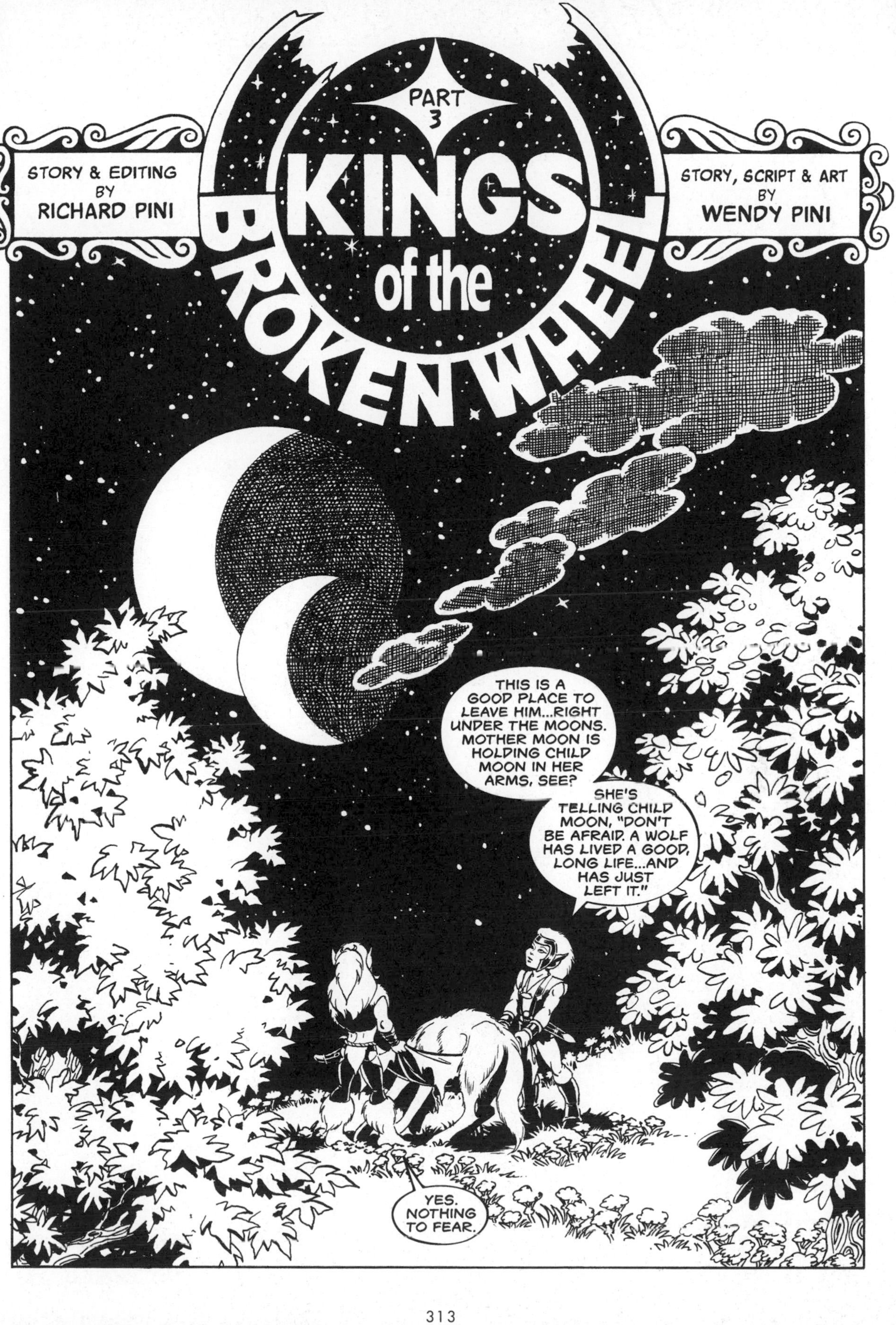
PART 3
KINGS of the BROKEN WHEEL
STORY & EDITING BY RICHARD PINI
STORY, SCRIPT & ART BY WENDY PINI
THIS IS A GOOD PLACE TO LEAVE HIM...RIGHT UNDER THE MOONS. MOTHER MOON IS HOLDING CHILD MOON IN HER ARMS, SEE?
SHE'S TELLING CHILD MOON, "DON'T BE AFRAID. A WOLF HAS LIVED A GOOD, LONG LIFE...AND HAS JUST LEFT IT."
YES. NOTHING TO FEAR.

THEN... WHY AM I SO COLD?

I WON'T FORGET HIS SCENT... EVER!

WANT HIS PELT?

NO. SOME PARTS OF DEATH I CAN LOOK AT. SOME PARTS I CAN'T. SOME...I CAN'T EVEN THINK ABOUT!

I KNOW. YOU DON'T LIKE IT WHEN THE LEAVES GO BROWN AND DROP OFF THE TREES--

--THOUGH YOU KNOW THE SEASON OF NEW-GREEN *ALWAYS* FOLLOWS THE DEATH-SLEEP.

I DON'T LIKE THINGS TO END.

WELL...EVEN THE *STARS* MAKE ROOM FOR NEW STARS.

NO!

NO? BUT... THE SCROLL OF COLORS SHOWED US...

ALL RIGHT! MAYBE STARS *DO* DIE, AND WOLVES AND WOLFRIDERS TOO!

BUT IF I *HAVE* TO GIVE MY BLOOD AND BONES BACK TO THE LAND THAT MADE ME...

WHY CAN'T *I* BE THE ONE TO SAY WHEN?

I'M GOING TO THE STARS, *TAM!*

ONE DAY I'LL WALK ON THE WORLD THE LODESTONE CAME FROM!

I'LL MISS YOU.

YOU'LL BE *WITH* ME! I CAN'T SEE IT ANY OTHER WAY!

A SHORT DISTANCE AWAY, IN THE FATHER TREE AT THE HEART OF THE FORBIDDEN GROVE...

WHO *ARE* YOU?! YOUR SCREAM'S COMING FROM SO FAR AWAY! WHAT'S HAPPENING TO YOU?! *TELL ME!*

TIMMAIN... TIMMAIN...!

PLEASE HELP ME, HIGH ONE! PLEASE!

HERE! THIS IS THE SPOT!

:HUFF HUFF: RIGHT ABOUT NOW :HUFF: I MISS THE POWER YOU HAD :UNH: TO *FLOAT* US UP, BLACK-HAIR!

MOVE YOUR BIG FEET, WILL YOU, *TREESTUMP?* I NEED THAT HANDHOLD!

EKUAR IS IN THE GREAT VAULT--WHERE *TWO-EDGE* STORED WEAPONS AND ARMOR--

--FOR OUR WAR WITH THE TROLLS. :PANT PANT: I REMEMBER THAT ROOM... AND *ONE-EYE* LYING THERE...

CLEARBROOK...!

THE VAULT LIES RIGHT BELOW OUR FEET...*FAR* BELOW.

EKUAR! COME UP! I WILL GUIDE YOU STRAIGHT TO THE SURFACE!

WHAT'S THAT? UP? OH MY!

ROCK SHAPER! GET YOUR SKINNY RUMP OVER HERE! THEY'RE BREAKING THROUGH!

NO! YOU ADDLE-HEADED ELF! CAN'T YOU SEE WE'RE DONE FOR IF YOU DON'T...!

WHA...?! WHY, YOU--! YOU--! HA HA HA!

ESCAPE! WE COULD'VE ESCAPED ALL ALONG! MADNESS!

COME, ODDBIT, MY ALL!

OH, YOU GO, PICKY, DEAR! I THINK I'LL STAY AND TAKE MY CHANCES HERE!

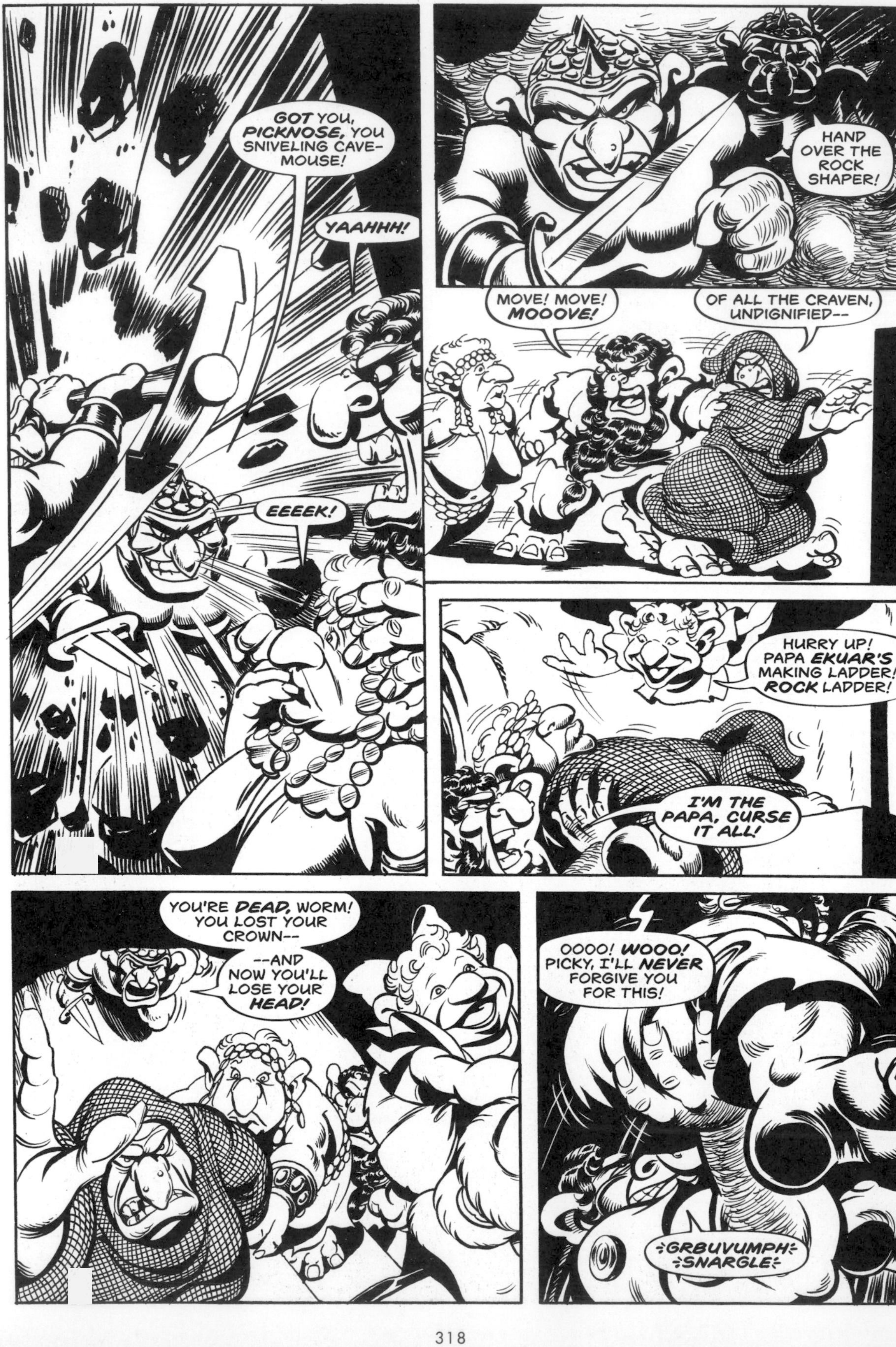
GOT YOU, PICKNOSE, YOU SNIVELING CAVE-MOUSE!
YAAHHH!
EEEEK!
HAND OVER THE ROCK SHAPER!
MOVE! MOVE! MOOOVE!
OF ALL THE CRAVEN, UNDIGNIFIED--
HURRY UP! PAPA EKUAR'S MAKING LADDER! ROCK LADDER!
I'M THE PAPA, CURSE IT ALL!
YOU'RE DEAD, WORM! YOU LOST YOUR CROWN--
--AND NOW YOU'LL LOSE YOUR HEAD!
OOOO! WOOO! PICKY, I'LL NEVER FORGIVE YOU FOR THIS!
GRBUVUMPH SNARGLE

DO SOMETHING, ELF! WE'RE ABOUT TO BE SPITTED!

:GASP: WHAT AN AWFUL THING TO SAY!

WAAAHH! AAAAWWW-AAAAHHH!

:SIGH:

HEH HEH HEH NOW...!

SLUG SCUM! HE'S PLUGGED IT! THE ROCK SHAPER'S HELPING THEM!

PICKY! I CAN'T SEE A THING!

TRAPPED INSIDE SOLID ROCK! :GASP: I'D RATHER GET STABBED THAN DIE LIKE THIS!

CALMLY, NOW--

--NOTHING AT ALL TO WORRY ABOUT!

319

AND SOON...

HELLO, BROWNSKIN! HOW WAS IT IN BLUE MOUNTAIN? DID YOU MEET THE GLIDERS?

AAH... YES!

WELL, WELL, *PICKNOSE!* LOOKS LIKE YOU SPROUTED A LITTLE *WART* SINCE WE LAST SAW YOU.

:THBTHBTHT:

YOURS. NO DOUBT ABOUT IT. YOURS!

WATCH YOUR TONGUE WHEN YOU ADDRESS A *KING'S* KINFOLK, WOLFRIDER!

KING? WHAT KING?

I DON'T SEE A KING HERE! JUST A FOOL WHO LOSES AT *TOSS-STONE*--AT *EVERYTHING!*

:GASP: SOMETHING'S CHANGED! YOU-YOU'VE *GROWN*, BROWN-SKIN!

YES, HEH HEH. I GUESS I NEED NEW CLOTHES!

I'LL EXPLAIN AS WE--

THAT CHILD...! *LEETAH'S* SON! GREAT, SHINING SUN! WHAT *POWER!*

SUNTOP? WHAT ABOUT HIM?

S-SENDING... WILD...CONFUSED...! *TIMMAIN!* HE CLAIMS... SOMETHING'S HAPPENED TO *TIMMAIN!*

TCH! *SUNTOP* DOESN'T "CLAIM," HE *KNOWS!* I WONDER WHAT...?

PICKY, I'M SOAKED WITH RIME! AND THE WIND IS MUSSING MY HAIR!

THAT'S A HERO'S FIRST CONCERN, ISN'T IT?

SHUT... UP!

OOOOOHHH...! MORE CHANGES! SO LOVELY! SO WARM! *MEKDA... OSEK...!*

THE ANCIENT ROCK SHAPER WEEPS QUIETLY, REMEMBERING FRIENDS FROM A TIME NEAR THE BEGINNING. THEY WERE ALL FIRSTBORN OF THE HIGH ONES. NOW, ONLY *EKUAR* IS LEFT.

BUT EVEN *HE* IS NOT THE OLDEST LIVING ELF. THERE REMAINS ONE WHO *IS* THE BEGINNING...

TIMMAIN!

TSK TSK TSK! WRAPSTUFF ALL RUINED! MOTHER-MOTHER HIGHTHING MAKE MESSYMUCH!

SHE'S GONE!

IS THIS YOUR DOING, PRESERVER? WHERE IS SHE? *TELL!*

EEEP!

MOTHER-MOTHER HIGHTHING IS *GROWLER* AGAIN! LOPPITY-LOP OFF TO TALLROCKS WHEN YOU MAKE NASTY HURTFIRES!

YOU *WOULD* LET THEM DRAG US HERE TO THIS FANCIED-UP RELIC! SERVING ELVES IS ALL YOU'RE GOOD FOR NOW!

OOOO, MUMKINS! *LOOK!* THERE'S *TRINKET!* PRETTY *TRINKET!*

TO SHAPE-CHANGE *INSIDE* A PRESERVER COCOON...OUTSIDE OF TIME! THAT IS MAGIC INDEED!

THE HIGH ONE...FLOWN... IN WOLF FORM! WHY? ALL THAT I PROMISED, I DID!

THE GLIDERS' MAGIC SERVES THE PALACE, AND *HER*, NOW!

WHY HAS SHE DESERTED ME?

WHOM DO *YOU* SERVE, BROWNSKIN?

ELVES, *EKUAR!* ALL ELVES WHO REMEMBER WHO THEY ARE...

:GASP:

OH! WHAT IS IT?!

AAGH! I HAVE IT, CHILD! ENOUGH!

:HEWH: HE IS GOOD, THAT LITTLE ONE! *VERY* GOOD! AND, BUT FOR *LEETAH*, HE IS *ALONE* AMONG THE WOLFRIDERS.

FAILING TO GAIN *TIMMAIN'S* AID, HE HAS WISELY SOUGHT MINE.

HE HAS HEARD SOMETHING--IN HIS MIND--A *CRY!* THE CRY OF *ELVES* IN A DISTANT PLACE! THEY CALL FOR HELP!

ELVES?! YOU MEAN... THOSE WE HAVE YET TO KNOW?

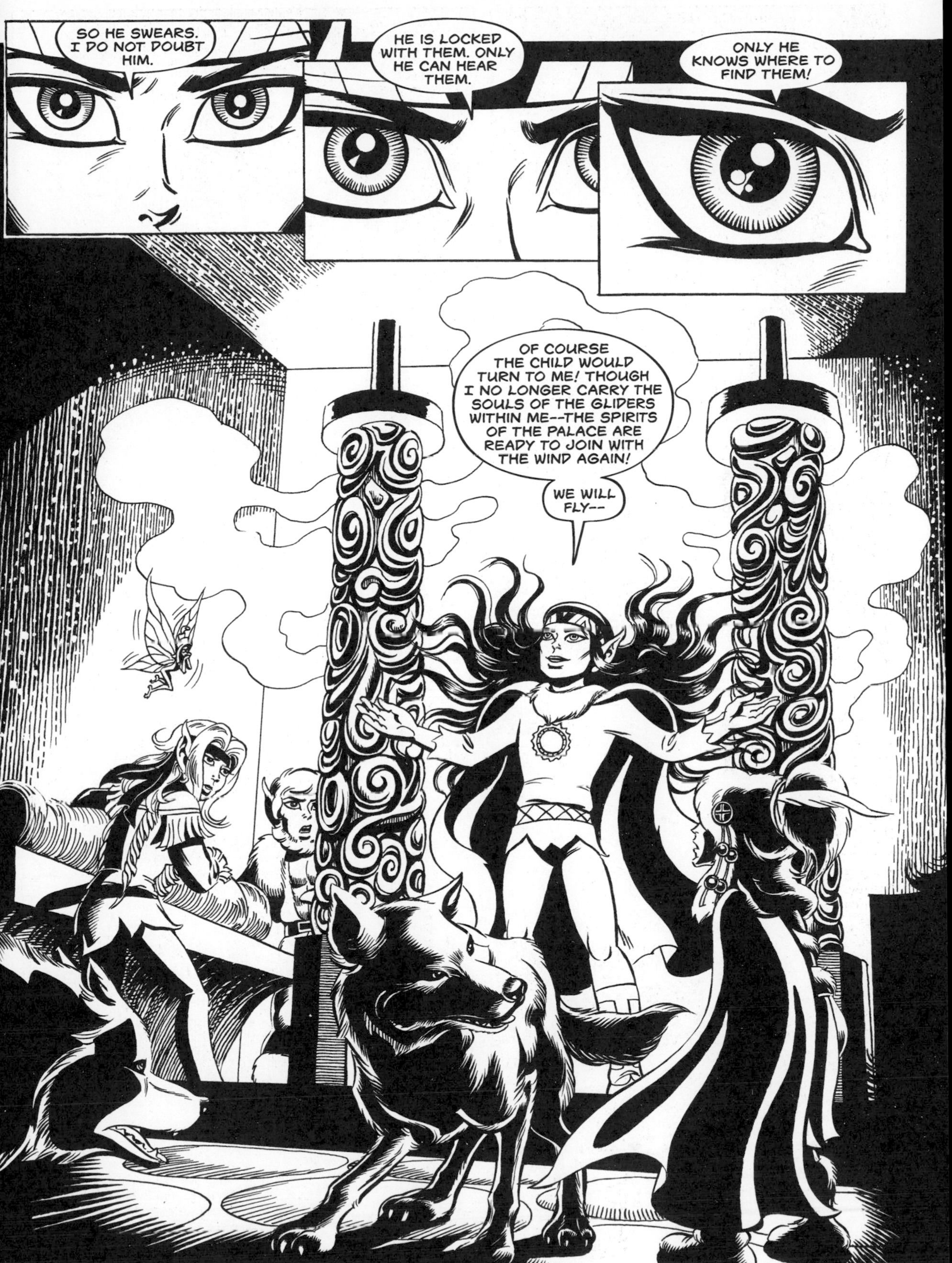
SO HE SWEARS. I DO NOT DOUBT HIM.
HE IS LOCKED WITH THEM. ONLY HE CAN HEAR THEM.
ONLY HE KNOWS WHERE TO FIND THEM!
OF COURSE THE CHILD WOULD TURN TO ME! THOUGH I NO LONGER CARRY THE SOULS OF THE GLIDERS WITHIN ME--THE SPIRITS OF THE PALACE ARE READY TO JOIN WITH THE WIND AGAIN!
WE WILL FLY--

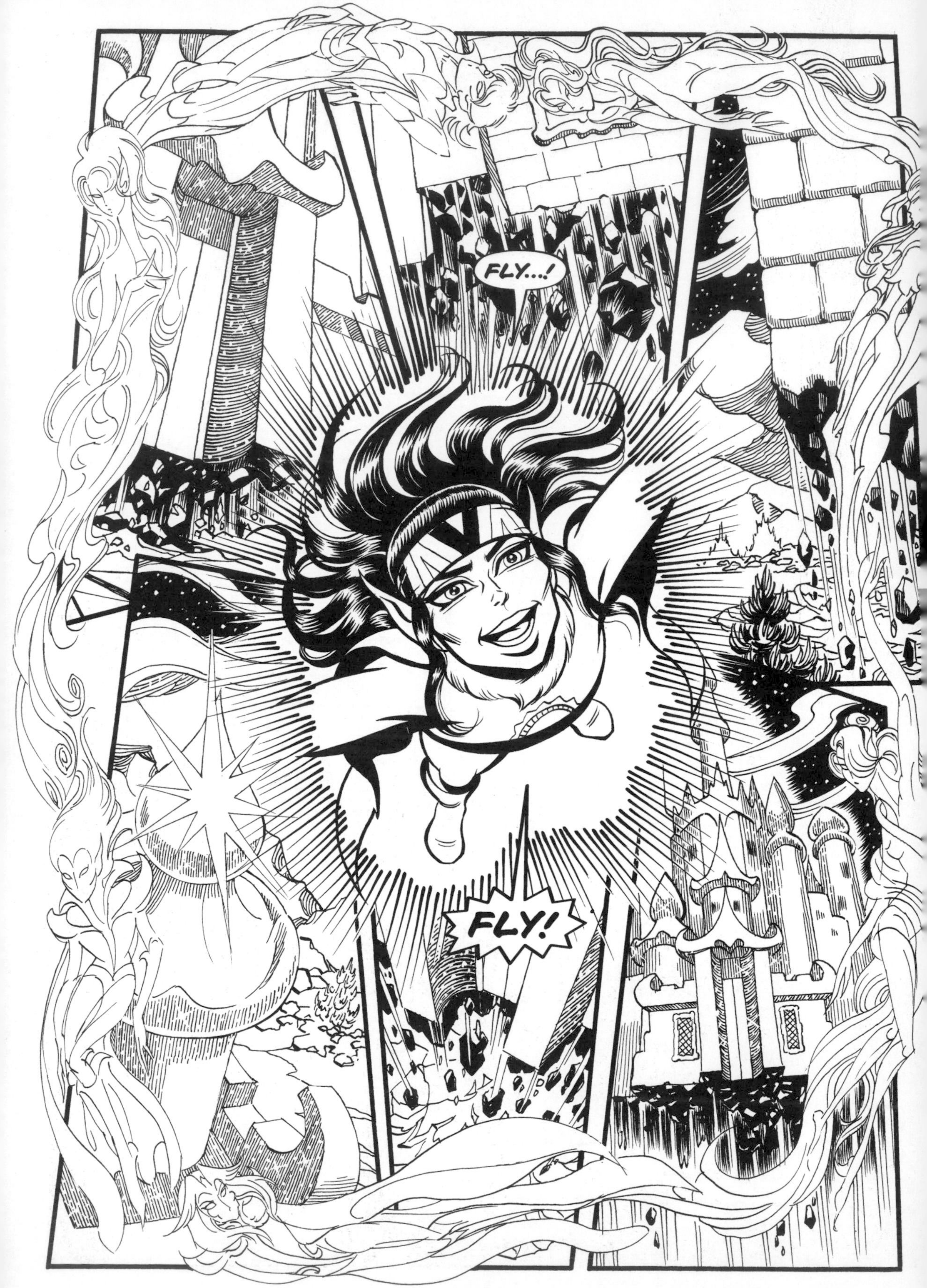
FLY...!
FLY!

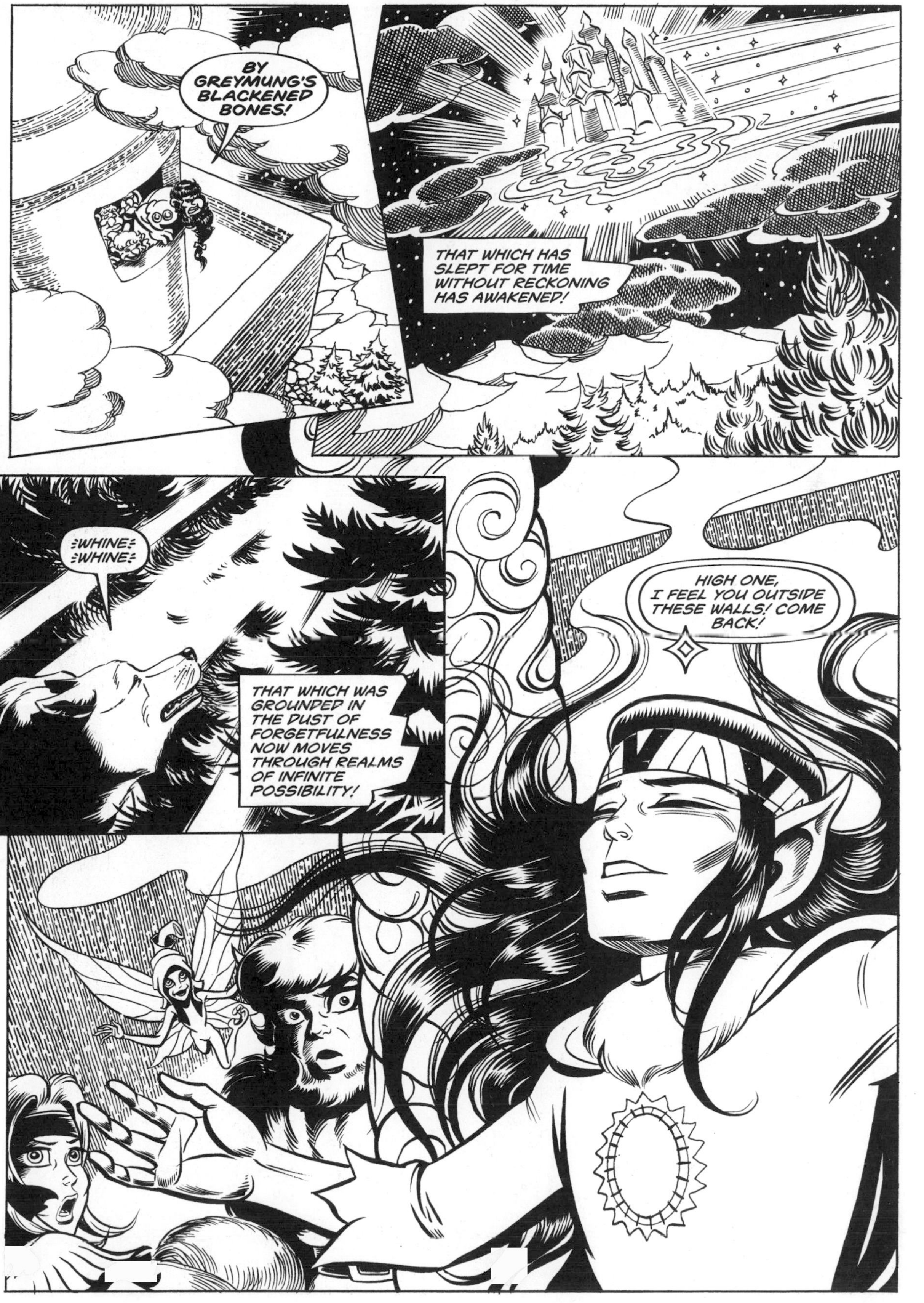
BY GREYMUNG'S BLACKENED BONES!
THAT WHICH HAS SLEPT FOR TIME WITHOUT RECKONING HAS AWAKENED!
WHINE WHINE
THAT WHICH WAS GROUNDED IN THE DUST OF FORGETFULNESS NOW MOVES THROUGH REALMS OF INFINITE POSSIBILITY!
HIGH ONE, I FEEL YOU OUTSIDE THESE WALLS! COME BACK!

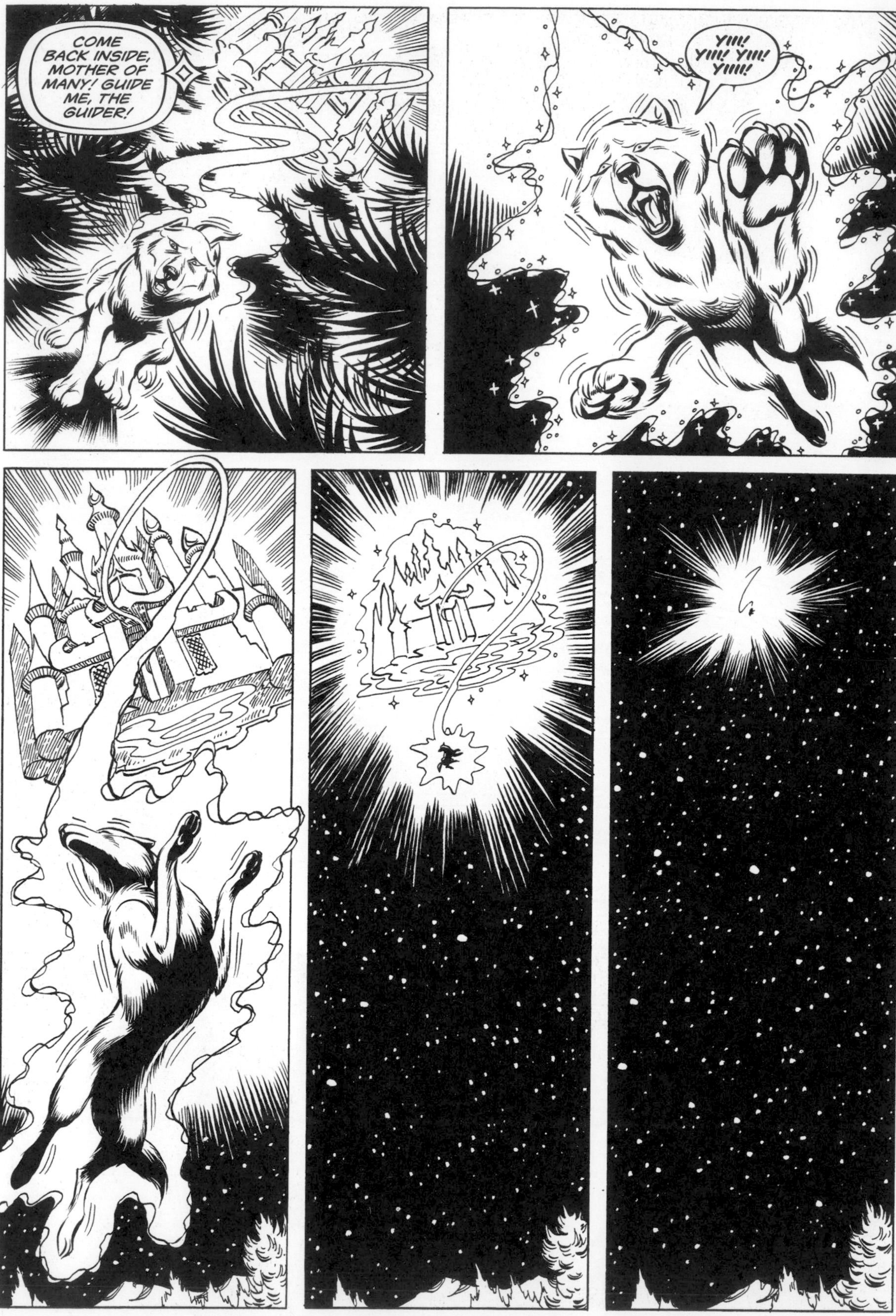
COME BACK INSIDE, MOTHER OF MANY! GUIDE ME, THE GUIDER!
YIII! YIII! YIII! YIIII!

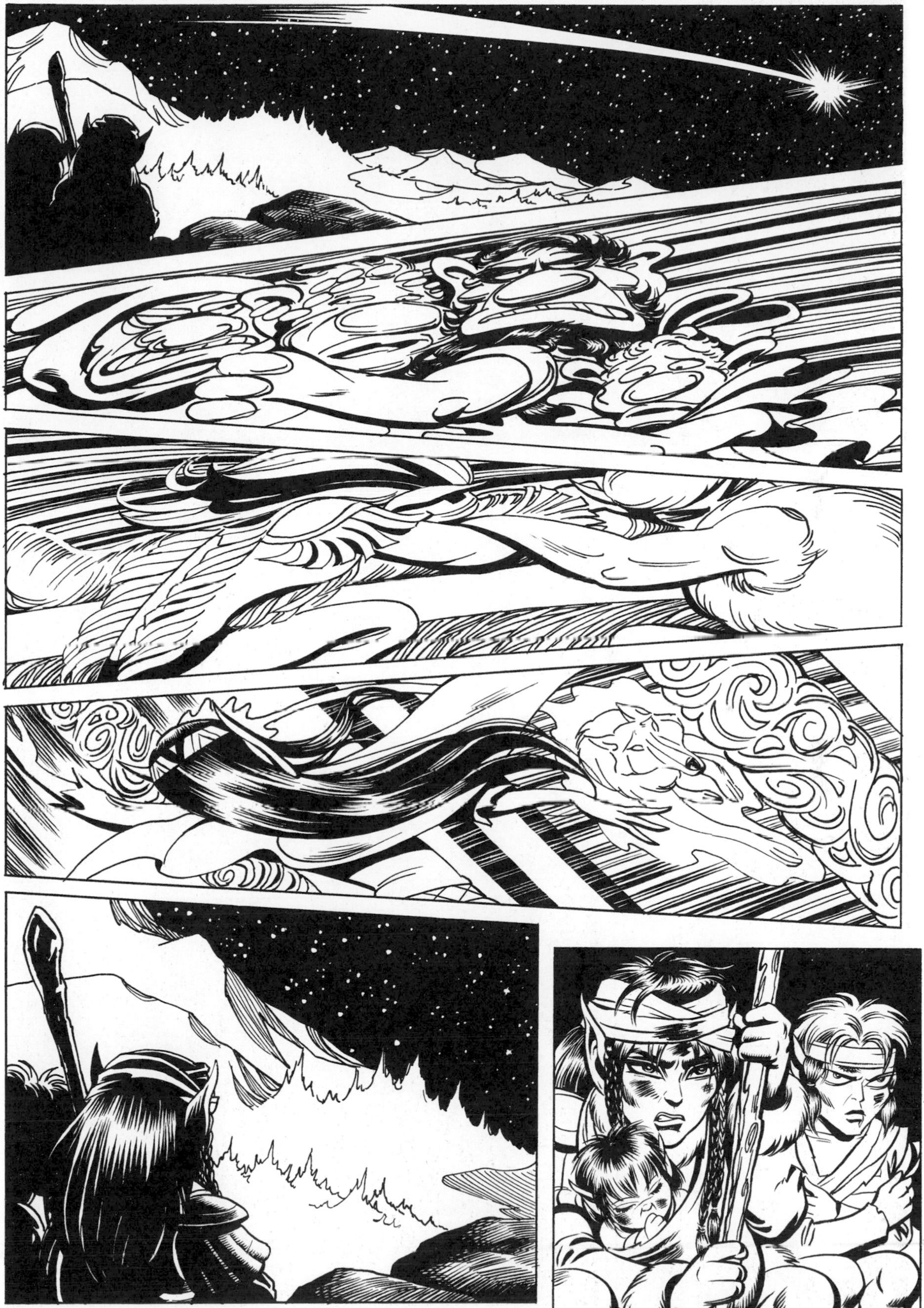

MEANWHILE, IN THE QUIET OF THE HOLT...

I AM SO SORRY, *SKYWISE*. MY *SKIMSAND* LOVES ROUGH PLAY... BUT I NEVER THOUGHT...

NO BLAME, *DODIA*. WOLVES CHOOSE THEIR BATTLES AS THEY WILL. WE HAVE NO SAY.

WE'LL MISS *STARJUMPER*.

SOMETIMES "THE WAY" SEEMS VERY HARD TO ME.

FATHER, THE HOLT CAN'T HOLD US ALL. MY RIDERS AND I MUST RETURN TO SORROW'S END. BUT YOU...

DO WHAT WILL SAVE LIVES IN BOTH WOLF PACKS, CUB. IT'S FOR ME TO WRESTLE ALONE WITH WHAT I'VE DONE.

BUT YOU KILLED *KUREEL* FOR ME! YOUR TROUBLE IS MINE! I CAN'T LEAVE!

YOU'RE A LEADER OF MANY, NOW, *DART*. ASK *CUTTER*. HE'LL TELL YOU THEY COME FIRST.

DART GETS TO ACT LIKE A CHIEF! NO FAIR! I WISH I HAD MAGIC TO MAKE ME GROW UP FAST!

THEN YOU'D BE A **BIG** LITTLE PEST!

GO ON! KNOCK ME OFF THE BRANCH! MAYBE IT'LL MAKE MY HEAD QUIET!

AAAAWWW! WHERE'S THE HIGH ONE, ANYWAY? WHY WASN'T SHE THERE TO HELP YOU?

THE ANSWERS ARE ALL IN THE PALACE...THAT'S ALL I KNOW--

--HUH?!

STAY HERE! SKYWISE AND I'LL GO SEE.

TWO-SPEAR'S SHAFT...!

SUNTOP...! DID YOU DO THAT?!

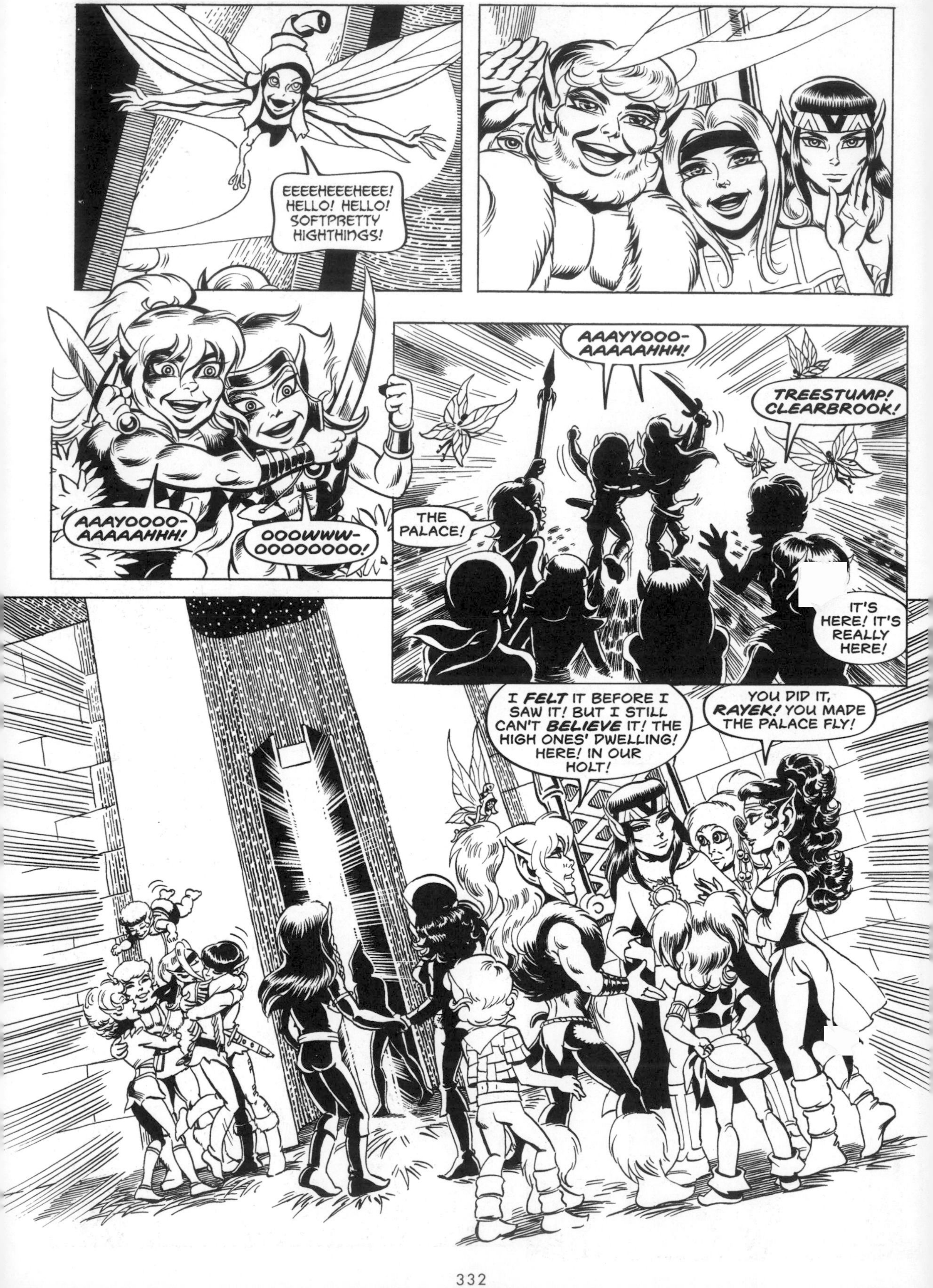
EEEEHEEEHEEE! HELLO! HELLO! SOFTPRETTY HIGHTHINGS!
AAAYOOOO-AAAAAAHHH!
OOOWWW-OOOOOOOO!
AAAYYOOO-AAAAAAHHH!
TREESTUMP! CLEARBROOK!
THE PALACE!
IT'S HERE! IT'S REALLY HERE!
I FELT IT BEFORE I SAW IT! BUT I STILL CAN'T BELIEVE IT! THE HIGH ONES' DWELLING! HERE! IN OUR HOLT!
YOU DID IT, RAYEK! YOU MADE THE PALACE FLY!

YOUR SON BROUGHT ME. I BELIEVE IN THE CRY HE HAS SENSED.

AND NOW WE HAVE THE MEANS TO ANSWER IT--TO GO WHEREVER IN THE WORLD THESE STRANGE ELVES ARE--AND AID THEM!

ANOTHER QUEST! SO MUCH TO GAIN IF WE FIND OTHER ELVES...SO MUCH TO LOSE IN THE TRYING!

SHU-SHEN! SHU-SHEN!

DON'T SHAKE HIM SO! HE'S JUST FAINTED!

I-I'M WEAK, TOO! THIS IS ALL TOO MUCH FOR ME!

THE PALACE OF THE HIGH ONES...!

AND LOOK AT RAYEK! HOW HE HAS CHANGED!

MMMMM! I'M LOOKING! =GASP= WHAT'S THAT IN THE DOORWAY?

...IS IT...?

IT IS.

TIMMAIN...! OH, HIGH ONE!

THE MOTHER OF TIMMORN YELLOW-EYES...OUR FIRST CHIEF! SHE'S COME BACK TO US AS A WOLF!

BACK TO SKYWISE ESPECIALLY! BUT WHERE IS STAR-JUMPER?

DEAD. KILLED IN A CHALLENGE. TIMMAIN MUST KNOW IT.

CAN'T LOOK AT HER...TOO ASHAMED! SHE KNOWS!

SHE KNOWS EVERY-THING--!

--ABOUT KUREEL?

COME WITH ME.

I'VE WISHED DEATH ON ENEMY ELVES BEFORE... BUT WISHING IS ONE THING. **KILLING** IS...LIKE KILLING MYSELF.

A GRIEF SO DEEP KEEPS YOU FROM LIVING IN THE **NOW** OF WOLF THOUGHT. I KNOW.

FOR **EMBER**, IT'S SO SIMPLE.

WHY DON'T YOU TELL **KUREEL** YOU'RE SORRY, **STRONGBOW?** THEN HE CAN FORGIVE YOU AND YOU CAN BE FRIENDS!

IF ONLY I COULD COME HERE AS A CUBLING, WITH OPEN, UNSTAINED HANDS.

IF ONLY I KNEW HOW! THE PALACE HAS BEEN DELIVERED INTO MY LAP...BUT IS **KUREEL** HERE? HOW CAN I BE CERTAIN?

I PROMISE YOU...YOU WILL KNOW!

ONE-EYE! HOW CAN YOU BEAR IT, KNOWING THAT HIS BODY LIVES BENEATH THOSE WRAPPINGS?

ONCE I THOUGHT I'D LIVE IN THE PALACE AND GUARD HIS BODY 'TIL HE RECLAIMED IT. BUT...

FIND HIM YOURSELF. HE'LL HELP YOU FIND KUREEL.

DO IT NOW!

HUNT BROTHER... PACK BROTHER...TRIBEMATE... FRIEND...! MY EYES SEE NOTHING BUT SORROW! MY HAND TOUCHES NOTHING BUT SORROW!

TAKE IT... AND PLACE IT IN KUREEL'S! I WANT HIM TO KNOW... I'M SORRY!

AT THAT SAME MOMENT...

THE BOY WILL BE *MY* LODESTONE! HE WILL GUIDE ME TO THE SOURCE OF THE CRY THAT TORMENTS HIM!

YOU DON'T HAVE A CUB. YOU'VE NEVER CARED FOR ONE.

NO, *RAYEK*. WE CAN'T LET YOU TAKE HIM.

BUT...I WOULD LOVE HIM AS MY OWN!

YOUR LOVE DEMANDS MORE STRENGTH THAN *SUNTOP* HAS.

HE WOULD WEAR HIMSELF OUT TRYING TO PLEASE YOU!

VERY WELL! I DO NOT CARE HOW MANY OF YOU ACCOMPANY THE BOY! THE PALACE CAN TRANSPORT US ALL-- ANYWHERE--SAFELY! I WILL PROVE IT!

...*IF* THAT'S WHAT EVERYONE HERE WANTS!

LOOK AT THEM! THEY KNOW A NEW TIME...A NEW *WAY* HAS COME TO THEM!

≋SIGH≋ WHATEVER ELSE THEY SAY WHEN THEY HOLD MY "HOWL," THEY'LL SAY, "*CUTTER* WAS CHIEF OF CHANGES. HIS DAYS WERE NEVER SIMPLE!"

THE PALACE IS RESTORED. *RAYEK* WANTS ALL ELVES TO BE LIKE THE HIGH ONES. MAYBE THE PUREBLOODED ONES CAN BE--

--BUT WHERE DOES THAT LEAVE THE WOLFRIDERS?

YOU WANT TO GO, DON'T YOU?

MORE THAN ANYTHING! *SHE* UNDERSTANDS.

SHE UNDERSTANDS YOU TOO. YOU ARE CHIEF. WE DON'T GO ANYWHERE UNLESS YOU SAY SO!

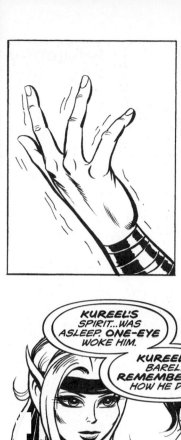

KUREEL'S SPIRIT...WAS ASLEEP. ONE-EYE WOKE HIM.

KUREEL... BARELY REMEMBERED... HOW HE DIED!

YOU'VE BOTH FORGIVEN...

AS I FORGAVE TWO-EDGE.

WHAT HAVE YOU DONE?!

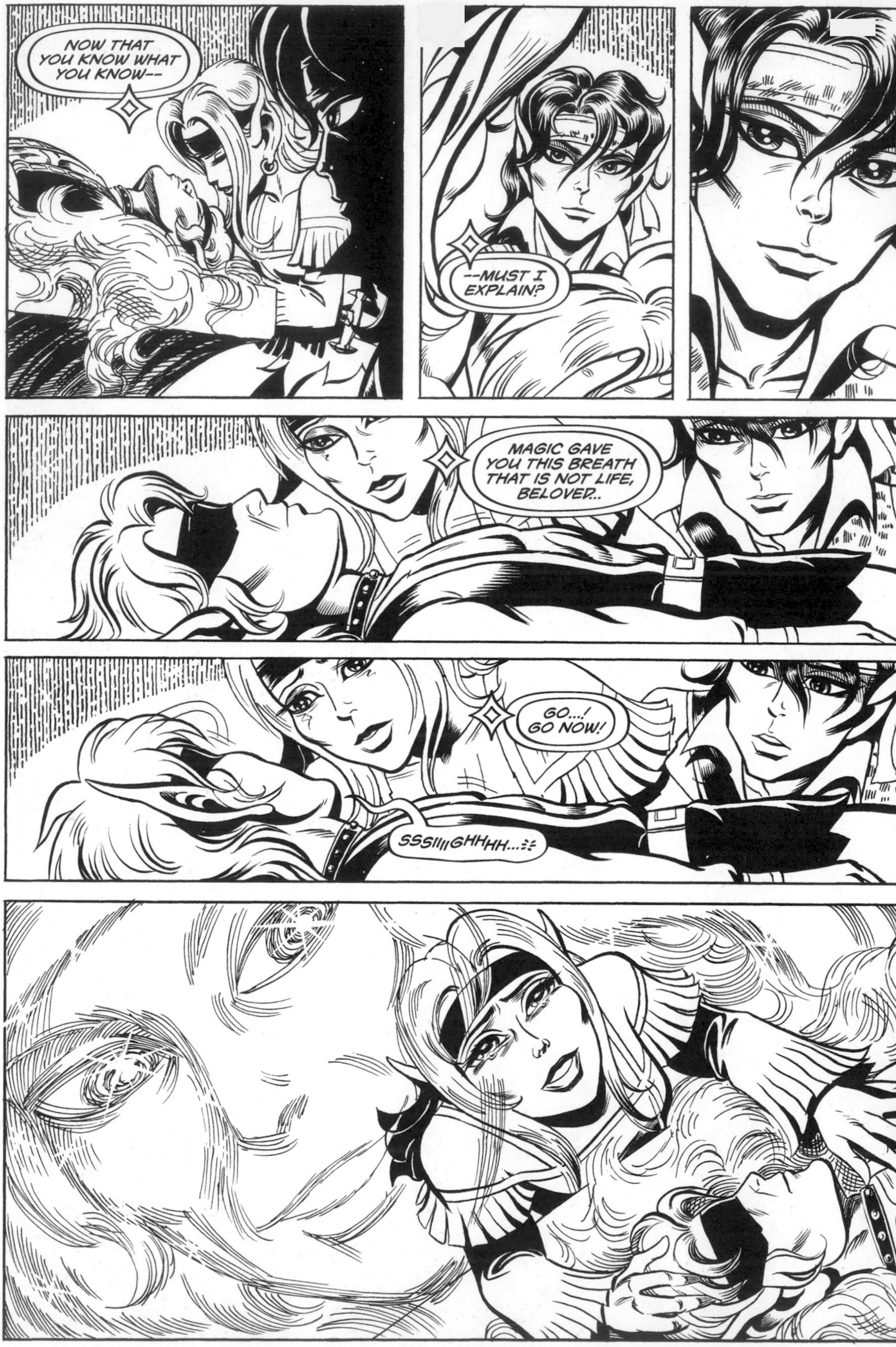
NOW THAT YOU KNOW WHAT YOU KNOW--
--MUST I EXPLAIN?
MAGIC GAVE YOU THIS BREATH THAT IS NOT LIFE, BELOVED..
GO...! GO NOW!
SSSIIIIGHHHH...

CLEARBROOK'S BEEN IN THERE WITH *STRONGBOW* A LONG TIME!

LET THEM BE.

GO ON... YOU SAY *RAYEK* BANISHED THE *GO-BACKS*...?!

AYE. AND I GUESS *TIMMAIN* DIDN'T LIKE IT, SO SHE--

HUH?! ONE-EYE...?! HERE AND GONE?!

LOOK!

FOLLOW ME.

LATER...LONG INTO THE NIGHT...

BARBARIC!

NO...PERFECT! WHEN YOU CAN SEE THAT, YOU'LL TRULY BE MASTER OF THE PALACE.

I HAVE OFFERED TO TAKE EVERYONE BACK TO THE SUN VILLAGE-- TO THAT FAMILIAR PLACE--AS PROOF OF THE PALACE'S SAFETY.

WILL CUTTER AGREE?

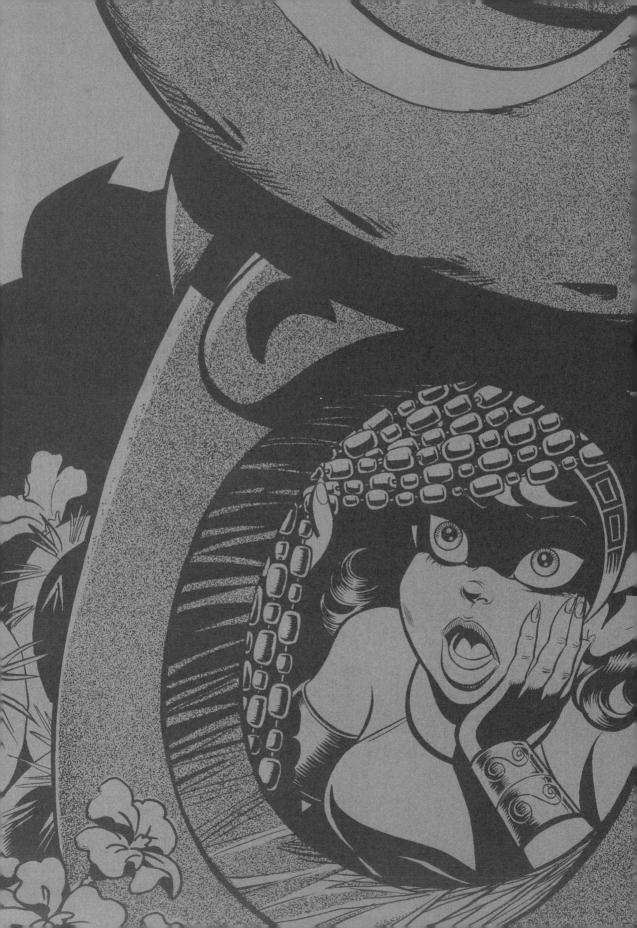

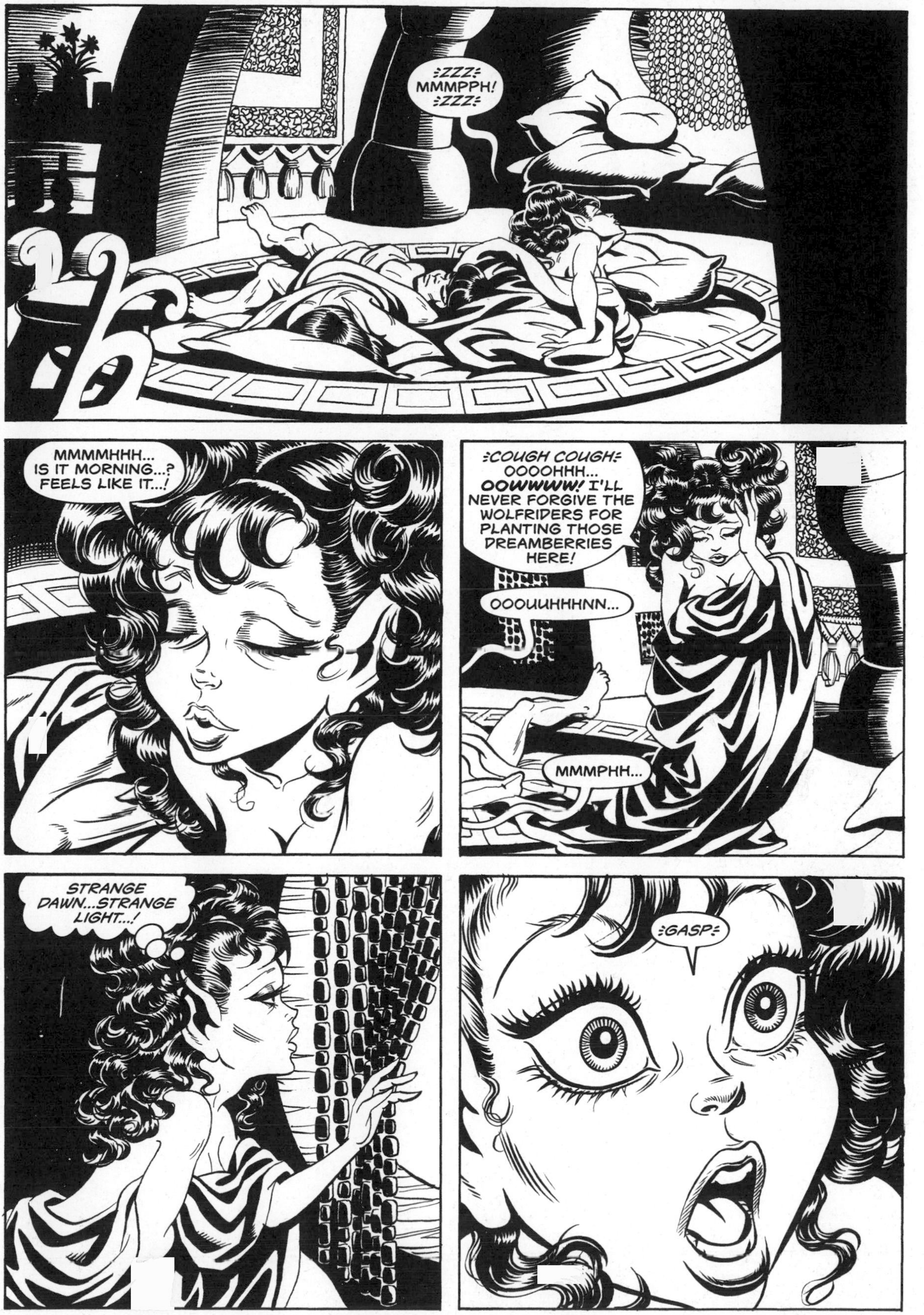

ZZZ MMMPPH! ZZZ
MMMMHHH... IS IT MORNING...? FEELS LIKE IT...!
COUGH COUGH OOOOHHH... **OOWWWW!** I'LL NEVER FORGIVE THE WOLFRIDERS FOR PLANTING THOSE DREAMBERRIES HERE!
OOOUUHHHNN...
MMMPHH...
STRANGE DAWN...STRANGE LIGHT...!
GASP

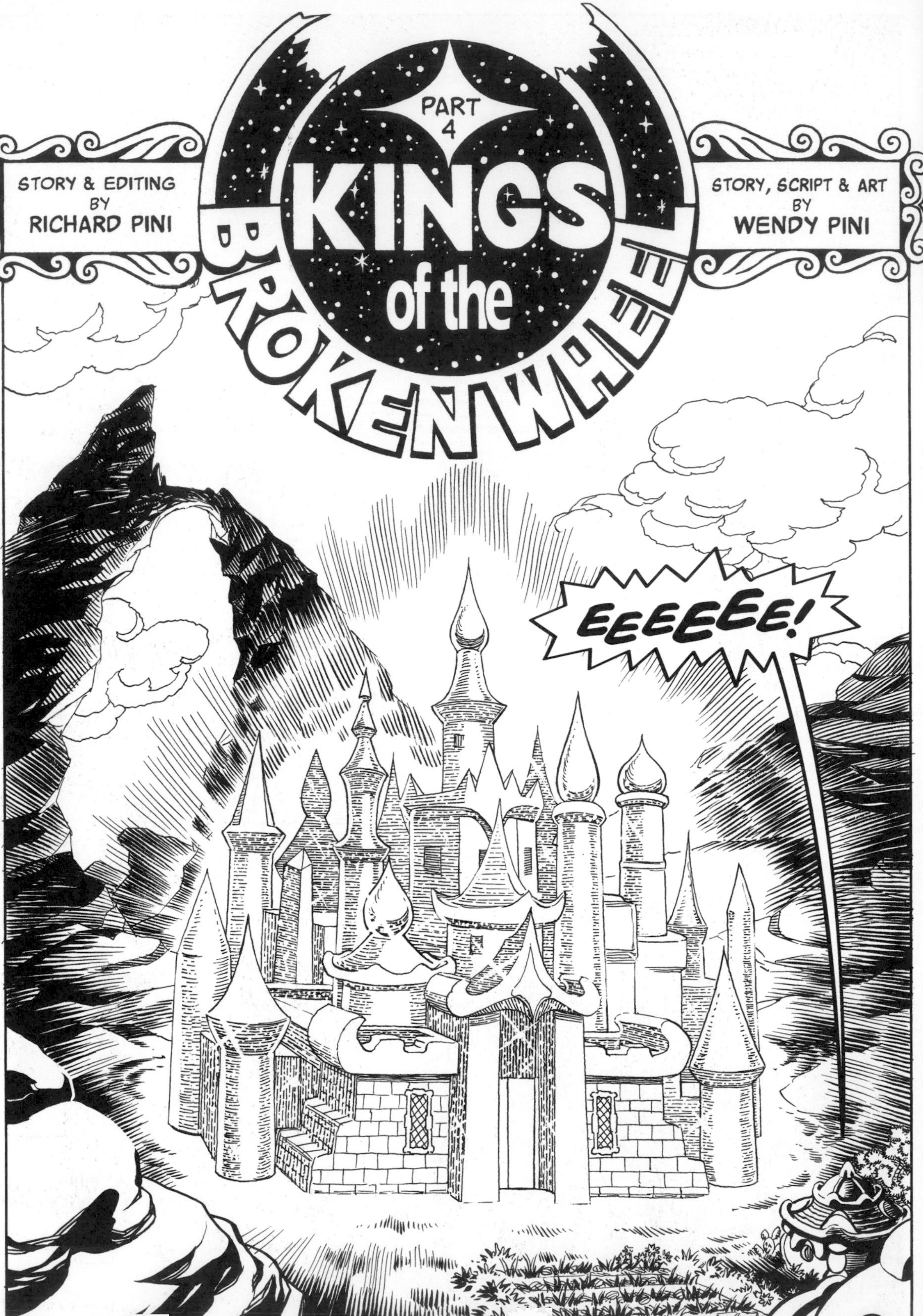
PART 4
KINGS of the BROKEN WHEEL
STORY & EDITING BY RICHARD PINI
STORY, SCRIPT & ART BY WENDY PINI
EEEEEEE!

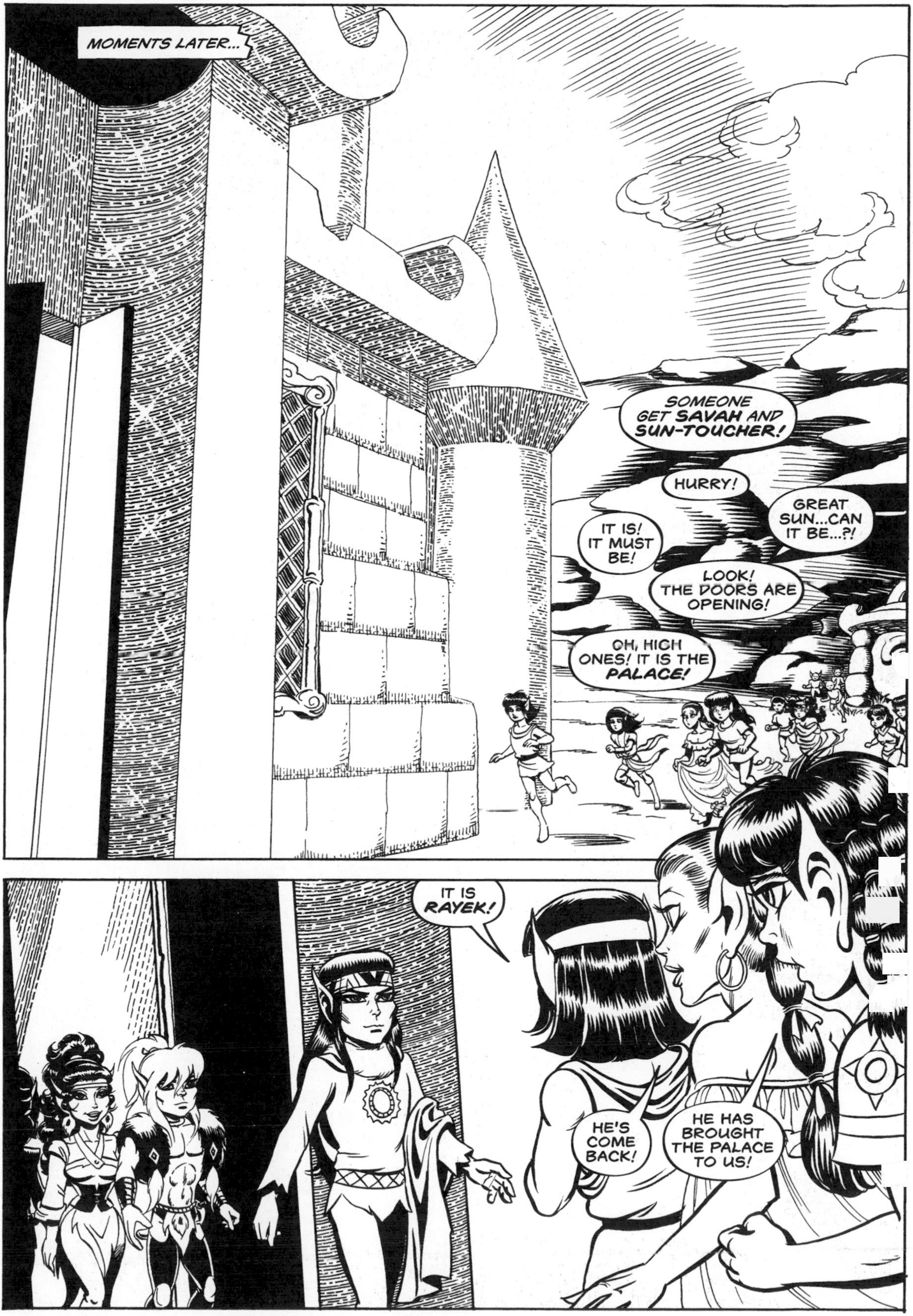
MOMENTS LATER...
SOMEONE GET SAVAH AND SUN-TOUCHER!
HURRY!
GREAT SUN...CAN IT BE...?!
IT IS! IT MUST BE!
LOOK! THE DOORS ARE OPENING!
OH, HIGH ONES! IT IS THE PALACE!
IT IS RAYEK!
HE'S COME BACK!
HE HAS BROUGHT THE PALACE TO US!

BEAUTIFUL! WONDROUS! SO BRAVE! NEVER SEEN ANYTHING LIKE...!

UNBELIEVABLE!

HOW DID YOU...?!

YOU LOOK...!

WHERE HAVE YOU...?

LONG AGO, WHEN THEIR LINE OF CHIEFS WAS MUCH SHORTER, THE WOLFRIDERS HUNTED THE WOODLANDS...

...UNAWARE THAT ANOTHER TRIBE OF ELVES HAD SETTLED IN THE OASIS OF SORROW'S END.

THE WOLFRIDERS WOULD NEVER HAVE DISCOVERED THEIR DESERT-DWELLING KIN, NOR WOULD THEY HAVE FOUND THE PALACE OF THE HIGH ONES...

...HAD IT NOT BEEN FOR CUTTER, BLOOD OF TEN CHIEFS' REPEATED WILLINGNESS TO TAKE THE FIRST STEP THROUGH FEAR--INTO KNOWLEDGE.

THEY SHOULD NOT BE CHEERING FOR RAYEK ALONE.

LOOK AT YOUR PEOPLE'S FACES, LEETAH.

THE PALACE FEEDS THE HUNGER THAT HAS NO VOICE...IN ALL OF US!

LEETAH! LEEEEETAH!

SHENSHEN! OH, MY LITTLE SISTER!

MOTHER... FATHER...!

...YES...I'VE MISSED YOU, TOO!

⁂GASP⁂ B-BUT YOU WEREN'T TALKING JUST NOW...WERE YOU?!

I WAS SENDING! I-I CANNOT HELP IT. THE PALACE...!

I DID IT! I RECEIVED YOUR SENDING! OH, IT IS MY FIRST TIME!

IT IS MAGIC!

I FEEL WARM AND SAFE AS A CHILD IN THE WOMB. IF ONLY YOU COULD SEE IT, BELOVED.

I CAN, TOORAH... EACH TIER, EACH RECESS...EVERY ROUNDED WALL AND SPARKLING SPIRE!

MY DEAR ONE, THIS IS THE GIFT OF GIFTS!

THIS COMPLETES US... MAKES THE SPAN OF TIME BETWEEN THE HIGH ONES' COMING AND NOW SEEM BUT AN INSTANT!

TIME MEANS NOTHING, MOTHER OF MEMORY. AND THE HIGH ONES ARE NOT ALL DEAD!

AS YOU ARE MOTHER OF THE SUN FOLK, *SAVAH,* SO THIS IS THE *WOLFRIDERS'* MOTHER.

SHE IS *TIMMAIN,* THE HIGH ONE... WITH US AGAIN AS IN THE YOUTH OF *TIMMORN YELLOW-EYES.*

I SEE... I *SEE* WHO SHE IS...!

FIRSTCOMER... YOU ARE *MY* MOTHER, TOO!

ALL YOUR CHILDREN THANK YOU, WITH LOVE, FOR THEIR BEGINNINGS.

LATER...

I FEEL AN URGENCY IN YOU, MY WANDERER. YOU HAVE NOT, AFTER ALL, BROUGHT THE PALACE HERE TO STAY. HOW SOON WILL YOU LEAVE US AGAIN?

THAT, UNFORTUNATELY, IS NOT FOR ME TO SAY.

RAYEK AND I MADE A PACT. HIS IS THE POWER TO SUMMON THE MAGIC OF THE PALACE-- TO MAKE IT FLY.

MINE IS THE POWER TO SAY WHEN.

MUST YOU FLING A PRIVATE MATTER TO THE CROWD?!

YOU'RE MASTER OF THE PALACE, BLACK-HAIR, BUT CUTTER'S MASTER OF YOU!

RAYEK HATES SHOWING THROAT TO CUTTER AGAIN! DON'T RUB IT IN, KRIM!

HE DESERVES IT FOR DRIVING THE GO-BACKS AWAY!

THE WOLFRIDERS WOULD TRAVEL WITH ME ONLY IF I AGREED TO THEIR CHIEF'S CONDITIONS.

WELL! SURELY THIS IS NO HOMECOMING! WHAT IS AT THE HEART OF THIS MISSION, RAYEK?

IT'S ME, SAVAH. I STARTED THE TROUBLE...!

SUNTOP...! YOUR EYES!

HE HAS NOT CLOSED THEM IN TWO DAYS.

NOR HAVE HIS PARENTS RESTED MUCH, I SEE!

IT--IT'S THE CRY, *SAVAH*. IT WON'T STOP!

THE CRY...?

EEEEYYYAAA-AAAGGGHHH!

OOF!

UGH!

CLOSETHEDOOR-CLOSETHEDOOR-CLOSETHE*DOOR*!

EEEEK!

RRROOOOOWWFFF!

GRRRR!

I GOT IT, DIDN'T I?

TAME WOLVES YOU SAID...USED TO SHARING...WALK RIGHT UP AND SNITCH A DEER JOINT FROM 'EM, EH?!

SO, PICKY! TREESTUMP AND CLEARBROOK SAID YOU WERE SQUIRRELED AWAY SOMEWHERE IN THE PALACE!

AH... AHEM!

WHY DID YOU LEAVE THOSE CURSED WOLVES OF YOURS INSIDE?! THEY MIGHT'VE TORN US TO BITS!

THEY'RE INSIDE AND DART'S DESERT WOLVES ARE OUTSIDE SO THERE WON'T BE ANY MORE CHALLENGES.

MAKES SENSE, DON'T YOU THINK?

☆⚡◎✳♨♩!

THOSE ARE TROLLS? OH! THEY LOOK DANGEROUS!

WE WOLFRIDERS DON'T FEAR TROLLS, DO WE, SKYWISE?

:CHUCKLE: NOT THESE PARTICULAR ONES!

FUNNY-LOOKING ELVES BETTER BE NICE TO TRINKET BECAUSE TRINKET ALWAYS DOES WHAT TRINKET WANTS...

AND BESIDES...GREAT-GRANDMAMA CAN THROW ANYBODY OVER HER SHOULDER!

HEEEHEEE HEEE!

POINK

AAAAIIIIIEEEEEE!

WAAAHHHH...! BAAAWWWW...! BAD BUG *BIT* TRINKET!

SILLY...! PRESERVERS DON'T HAVE TEETH!

:SNUFFLE: :SNUUCK:

BOO!

MMUUUUMM-MMKINNNS!

KEEP YOUR FLEA-BITTEN BRAT AWAY FROM US, ELF.

I DON'T WANT HER CONTAMINATING MY *TRINKET* WITH HER ROUGH WAYS!

OOOWWWW!

TRINKET WANTS TO PLAY WITH LITTLE RED-HAIRED ELF!

NOW, SWEETY BUMPS, THINK WHAT THAT DREADFUL SUN WILL DO TO YOUR LOVELY SKIN!

PALACE, TROLLS, AND PRESERVERS... THE SUN FOLK HAVE SEEN MUCH TODAY THAT IS NEW TO THEM. I AM GLAD THEY ARE NOT FRIGHTENED.

THE WOLFRIDERS LEFT US THEIR STRENGTH, THEIR READINESS TO DEAL WITH CHANGE. WE ARE NOT SO SOFT AS YOU REMEMBER, HEALER.

BUT I THINK YOUR LITTLE SON HAS TRIED TO BE TOO STRONG, TOO LONG. HE NEEDS REST.

SOMEONE'S IN TROUBLE, *SAVAH*... THEY KEEP SCREAMING AND SCREAMING...I HEAR THEM!

SHHHH... LATER, KITLING.

I WILL SEND YOU A SONG THAT WILL LIE LIKE A SOFT, MUFFLING BLANKET OVER THE CRY. YOU WILL SLEEP.

THANK YOU, MOTHER OF MEMORY.

:SIGHHHH:

THEIR CONCERN FOR *SUNTOP* ALLAYED FOR A WHILE, *CUTTER* AND *LEETAH* JOIN IN THE ONGOING MERRIMENT.

MORE SUBTLY COLORFUL THAN THE SUNSET, MORE LUMINOUS THAN MYRIAD GLOWING LANTERNS, THE PALACE IS THE FOCAL POINT OF GREAT JOY AND A NEW SENSE OF COMPLETENESS.

WILL YOU HAVE MORE DREAMBERRY JUICE...?

:GRUNT:

MY MY! WHAT... INTERESTING... JEWELRY! IT'S NOT TROLL-GOLD, IS IT?

WHY, NO! THE MOUNTAINS HERE ARE FULL OF DIFFERENT, SHINY METALS--

SOFT AND EASY TO WORK! WE DO IT OURSELVES!

DO TELL...!

THINGS ARE LOOKING UP FOR US, PETS. THOUGH I LOST MY CROWN IN A GAME OF TOSS-STONE, I MAY HAVE FOUND US A NEW KINGDOM OF OUR OWN--MANY TIMES RICHER THAN ANY WE'VE KNOWN!

TRINKET LOVES PAPA!

OOOOOO, PICKY! WHEN YOU TALK LIKE THAT, I JUST MELT!

EVEN AS THE PALACE IS HONORED, SO, TOO, DOES ITS MASTER RECEIVE HIS DUE.

RAYEK, YOUR DEEP HUNGER FOR GROWTH, AND YOUR COURAGE TO PURSUE IT AS FAR AND WIDE AS YOU MUST, HAS BROUGHT US ALL TO THIS HAPPY MOMENT.

WE ARE MORE THAN WE WERE, BECAUSE OF YOU.

HUNGER FOR GROWTH--OR FOR POWER?

WHEN THE TWO GO TOGETHER YOU FEEL FULL. BUT POWER ALONE NEVER FILLS YOU UP.

IF I KNOW RAYEK, HE'S STILL HUNGRY.

WERE YOU MY OWN FLESH AND BLOOD, I COULD NOT BE MORE PROUD!

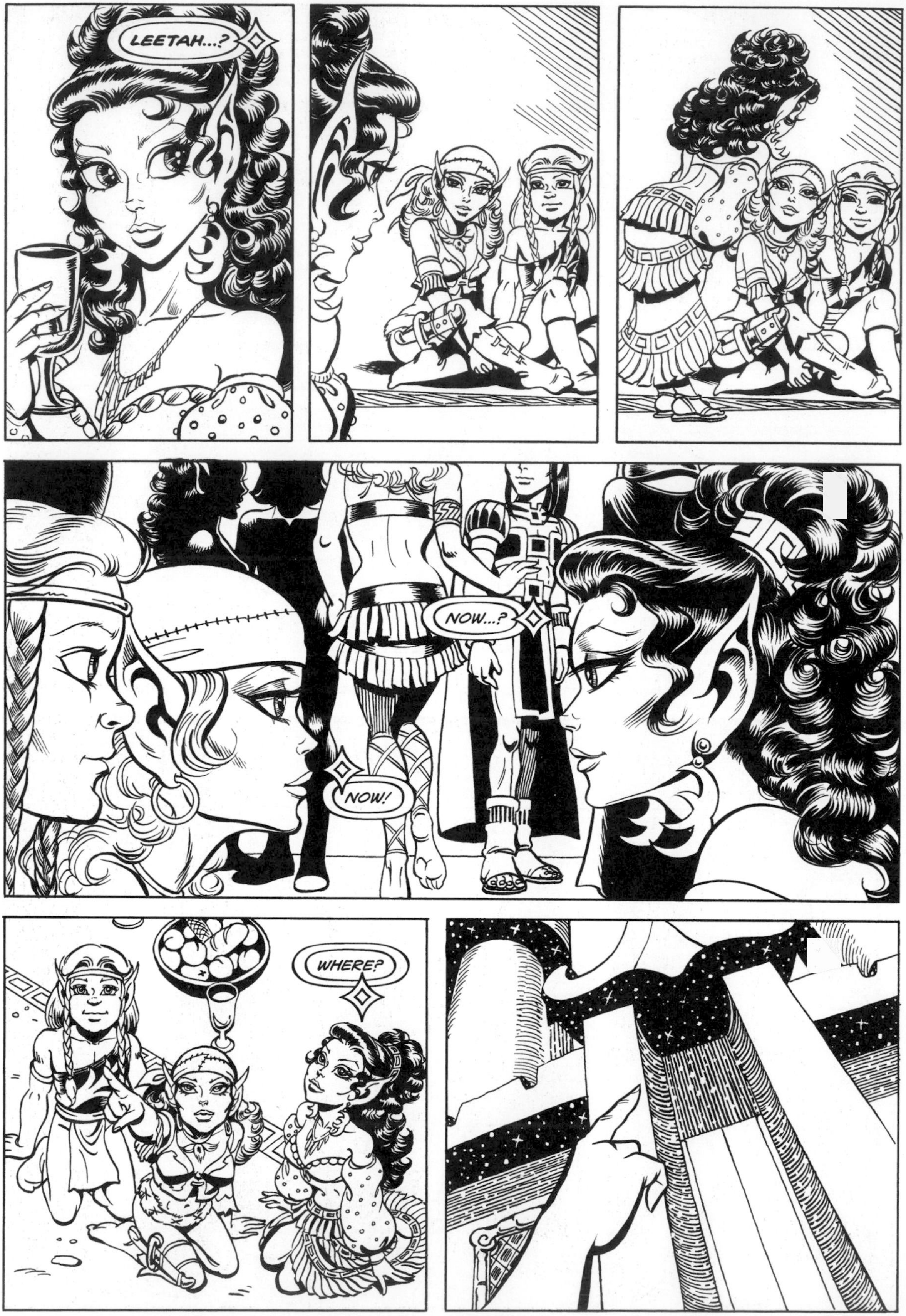
LEETAH...?
NOW...?
NOW!
WHERE?

WHAT'S UP?

DON'T KNOW. **NIGHTFALL** AND **REDLANCE** HAD HEADS TOGETHER WITH **LEETAH** BEFORE, BACK IN THE HOLT.

THEY'VE ALWAYS WANTED A CUB. I WONDER IF...?!

REMEMBER, WHEN YOU ARE READY, YOU WILL HAVE THIS **ONE** NIGHT. USE IT WELL.

ARE YOU SURE? CAN YOU REALLY...?

BELIEVE! IT IS WHAT I NEED FROM YOU MOST.

WHAT? **WHAT?** WHAT ARE THEY DOING?!

HAHAHA! SOMETHING **RAINSONG** AND I NEVER NEEDED A HEALER'S HELP TO DO!

YOU KNEW?

SOME. **LEETAH'S** NEVER TRIED IT BEFORE. IT'S COMPLICATED.

REDLANCE AND **NIGHTFALL** AREN'T REALLY RECOGNIZED, ARE THEY?

LIKE YOU AND ME...YES AND NO.

SNORT!

YES FOR THE SOUL...NO FOR HAVING CUBS.

FOR YOU AND ME I HOPE TO SAY SO! ⸘HIC⸘ SOOO... **LEETAH'S** HELPING THEM...?

THE MAIDENS HERE LIKE TO TELL TALES. THEY SAY **LEETAH** CAN... BZZZ...BZZ...

UH-HUH.

DOES SHE DO... **THAT**...EVERY TIME?!

UH-UH.

IF SHE DID, I'D BE NUT-MASH. COULDN'T EVEN WALK, LET ALONE BE CHIEF!

⸘SSIIIGHHH⸘

YIPE!

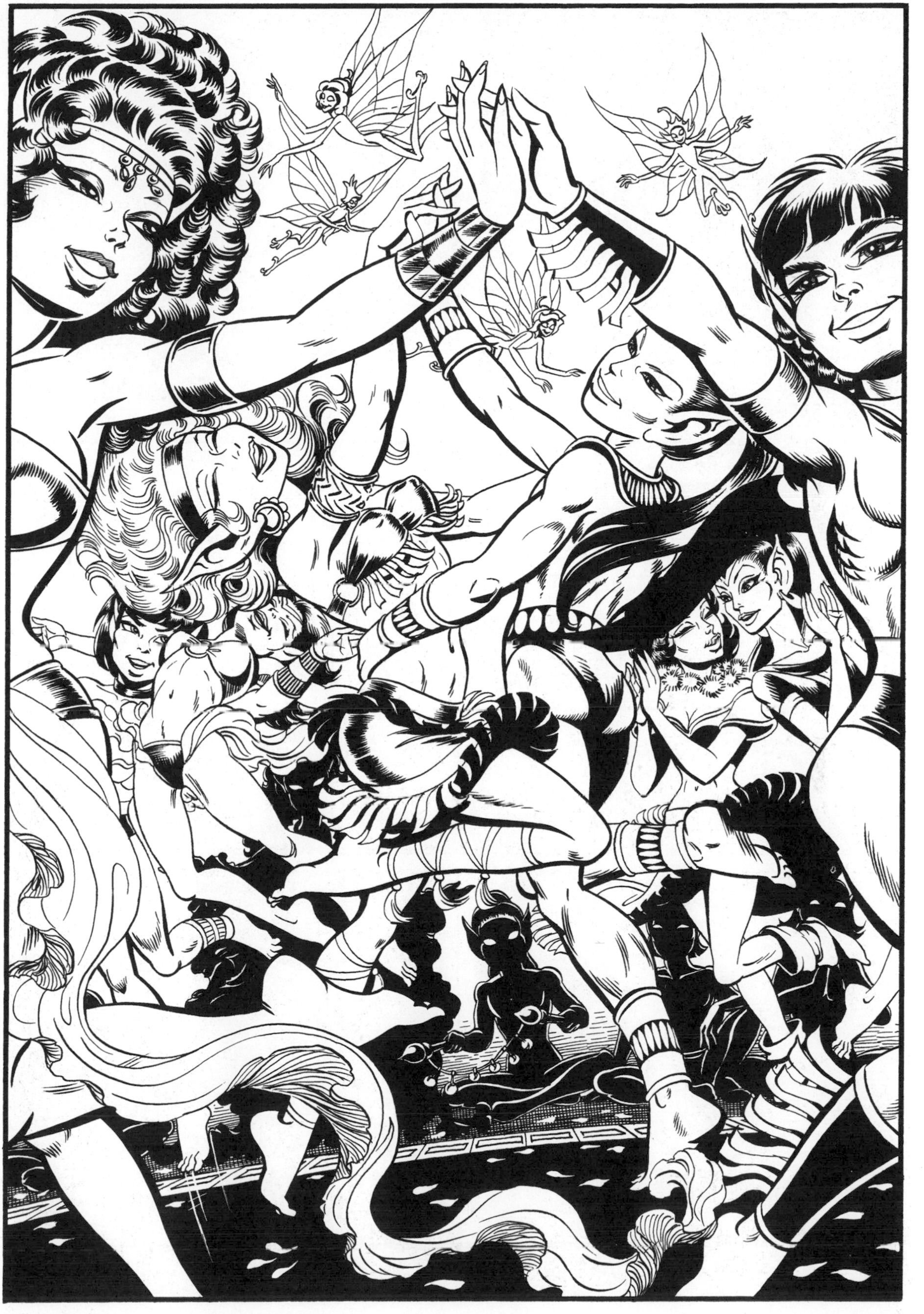

LATER...

LEETAH...? DID IT WORK?

OH...!

WHERE?

AAAYYYOO-OOOAAAAHHH! LIFEGIVER!

LUCKY LAD!

GOOD WORK, HEALER!

OOOWWWWW-OOOOOOOO!

SEE YOU TOMORROW-- MAYBE! HAHAHAHA!

COME TO OUR HUT, RAYEK...

NO! OURS! EKUAR, TOO!

THANK YOU...NO.

AWWWW!

AWWWWW!

WHAT, BROWNSKIN? IS IT LEETAH YOU THINK OF? OR PERHAPS WINNOWILL?

NO. THE BOY! HE MUST GUIDE US TO THOSE WHO CRY FOR OUR AID!

HOW LONG WILL CUTTER MAKE ME WAIT?

HOW LONG?!

ONLY SUNTOP SLEEPS. THE VILLAGE DOES NOT. AND THE TENDER CRIES THAT FILL THE NIGHT HAVE NOTHING TO DO WITH FEAR.

NEXT MORNING...

REMEMBERING...?

MMMHMM... THE TRIAL OF *HEAD, HAND, AND HEART.* YOU KNOW...

...MY FEAR OF HEIGHTS IS GONE.

HOW CAN I BE AFRAID TO LOOK UP OR DOWN OR ANY- WHERE...

...WHEN ALL THIS IS MINE?! THE WORLD BELONGS TO EACH ONE OF US.

AND WITH THE PALACE, THERE'S NO PART OF IT WE CAN'T EXPLORE!

BY NOW *SAVAH* HAS EXPLORED THE NATURE OF *SUNTOP'S* AILMENT. WE'LL SOON KNOW...

...IF KINFOLK OF OURS ARE TRULY IN DANGER SOMEWHERE!

AAYOOAAAAHH YOOOAAH--YOH!

≈MOAN≈ A WHOLE-TRIBE CALL...?! *CUTTER'S* JOKING! HE MUST BE!

...FATHER?! I HAVE TO GO, *SAVAH.* THE *WOLFRIDERS* ARE...

I KNOW, DEAR ONE. IT IS TIME TO GO INTO THE PALACE.

SOON...

SO THIS WAS THE HIGH ONES' HOME!

MORE THAN THAT, IT IS A VESSEL, MADE OF THE LIVING ROCK OF THEIR DISTANT BIRTH-STAR.

YOU WILL SEE ALL THAT HAS COME TO PASS IN THE *SCROLL OF COLORS,* SAVAH.

WELCOME, MOTHER OF MEMORY AND *SUN-TOUCHER!*

AAYOOOAAH! *TIMMAIN!*

LEETAH...

FOR WHAT YOU'VE GIVEN ME, MY LIFE IS YOURS!

AGGHKK!

WOLF FILTH! IN THIS SACRED PLACE!

GRRRRR...

EH...THE HIGH ONE REMINDS US ALL WHO EAT MUST GIVE SOMETHING BACK.

SO...!

DOWN AND INTO THE GROUND IT GOES!

WHILE YOU SLEPT, CHILD, I SHARED YOUR THOUGHTS...HEARD THE CRY.

SEND IT OUT, SO THAT ALL MAY HEAR!

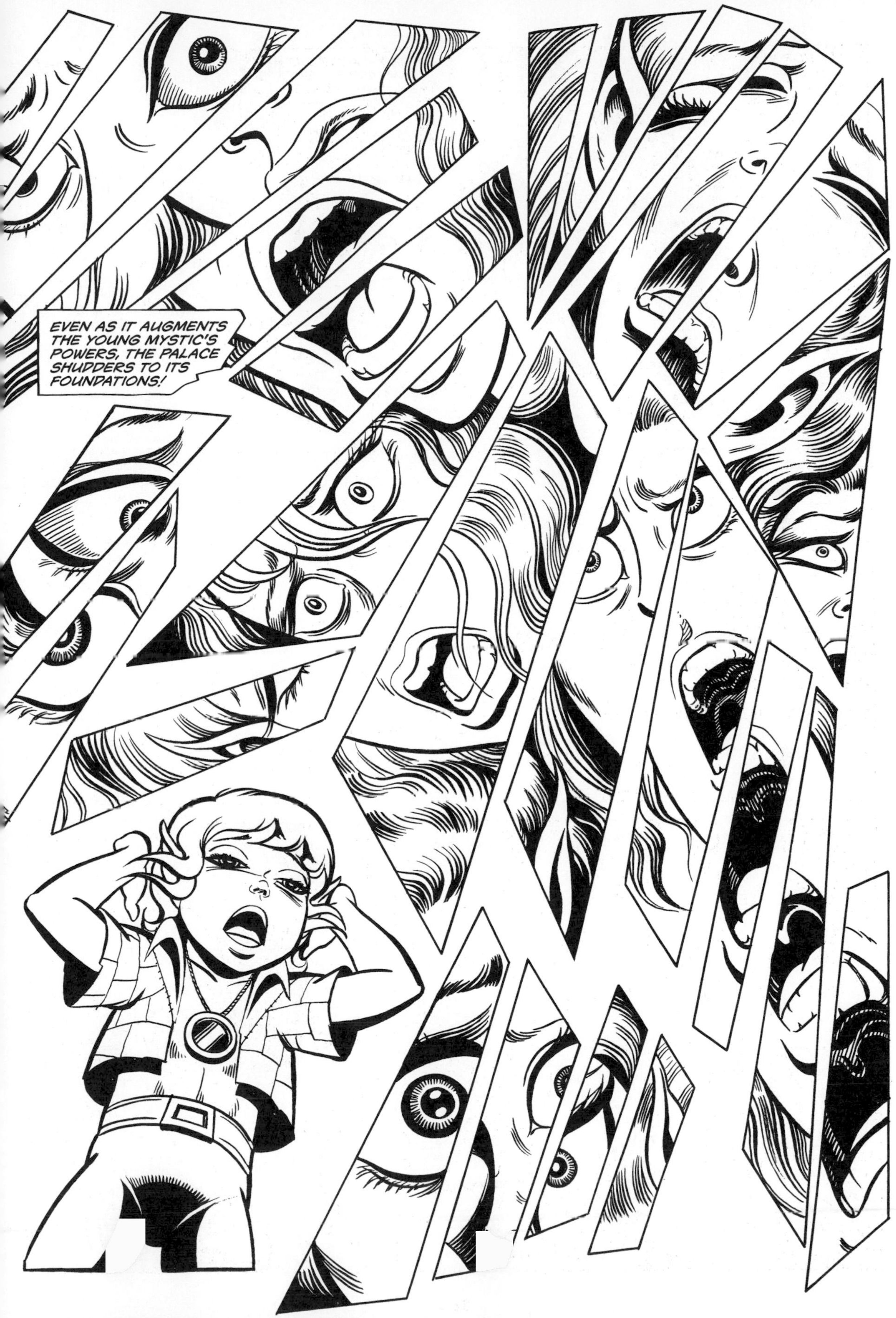
EVEN AS IT AUGMENTS THE YOUNG MYSTIC'S POWERS, THE PALACE SHUDDERS TO ITS FOUNDATIONS!

AND NO ONE HEARS THE CRY BUT TREMBLES WITH AWE--AND PITY!

GREAT SUN! WHAT *IS* IT?!

THE PALACE! THE PALACE IS... *SCREAMING!*

IS...IS *THAT* WHAT *SUNTOP'S* BEEN HEARING ALL THIS WHILE?!

TIMMORN'S BLOOD!

:PANT PANT: THAT'S ALL...! IT GOES ON LIKE THAT...OVER AND OVER!

IT'S COMING FROM...OH, WHAT DOES IT MEAN TO SAY WHERE?! IT'S A STRANGE PLACE! PLEASE! LET'S GO HELP NOW!

:WHINE: :WHIIINNNE: :YARK:

Y-YES, HIGH ONE! WE ALL HEARD! WE'RE GOING!

:GRRRRR: :WOOFWOOF:

WHAT...?! I-I DON'T...

WHAT MORE NEED YOU HEAR?! BUT FOR THE FOOLISH OATH I'M FORCED TO KEEP...

...THE BOY AND I WOULD BE GONE THIS INSTANT!

DO YOU KNOW...WHAT I COULD DO TO YOU... IF I WISHED...?

YOU BLIND, BOASTING BAT! OPEN YOUR EYES!

ONLY *YOU* SEE YOURSELF AS SEPARATE, ABOVE THE REST.

YOU'RE NOT! YOU'RE *LONELY!*

AND YOU THINK THE WAY TO FIX IT IS TO GET US ALL TO MATCH *YOUR* PACE!

BUT EVEN *TIMMAIN* WON'T RUN WITH YOU UNTIL YOU SEE WE'RE ALL ON THE SAME SIDE!

HIGH ONE...WE KNOW NOTHING OF WHAT LIES AHEAD. YOU CHOOSE WHO GOES. CHOOSE FOR STRENGTH, FOR WISDOM, AND FOR THE SKILLS MOST NEEDED ON THIS QUEST.

KNOWING THAT WHICH SHE CANNOT CONVEY, THE WHITE WOLF HESITATES. THEN, SLOWLY, SHE MAKES HER FIRST CIRCLE...

...ACCEPTING THAT HER CUB'S CUBS MUST FEND FOR THEMSELVES, COME WHAT MAY.

BUT...

DON'T WORRY. I WON'T BEGIN TO GET HEAVY FOR A FULL TURN OF THE SEASONS! WE'RE NEEDED!

AH! I'D'VE HAD TO *HIT* SOMEBODY IF WE WERE LEFT OUT!

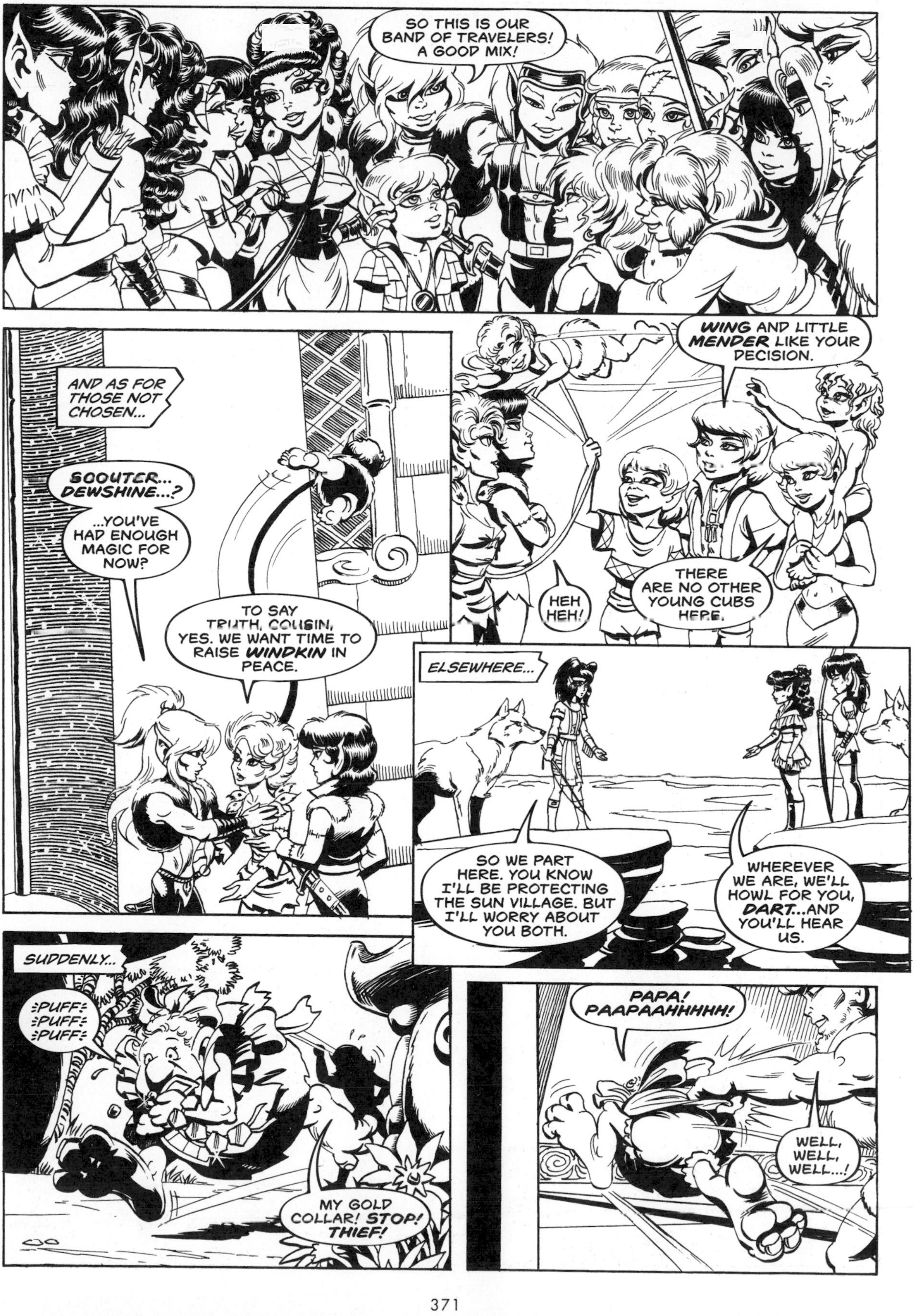
SO THIS IS OUR BAND OF TRAVELERS! A GOOD MIX!
AND AS FOR THOSE NOT CHOSEN...
SCOUTER... DEWSHINE...?
...YOU'VE HAD ENOUGH MAGIC FOR NOW?
TO SAY TRUTH, COUSIN, YES. WE WANT TIME TO RAISE WINDKIN IN PEACE.
WING AND LITTLE MENDER LIKE YOUR DECISION.
HEH HEH!
THERE ARE NO OTHER YOUNG CUBS HERE.
ELSEWHERE...
SO WE PART HERE. YOU KNOW I'LL BE PROTECTING THE SUN VILLAGE. BUT I'LL WORRY ABOUT YOU BOTH.
WHEREVER WE ARE, WE'LL HOWL FOR YOU, DART...AND YOU'LL HEAR US.
SUDDENLY...
PUFF PUFF PUFF
MY GOLD COLLAR! STOP! THIEF!
PAPA! PAAPAAHHHHH!
WELL, WELL, WELL...!

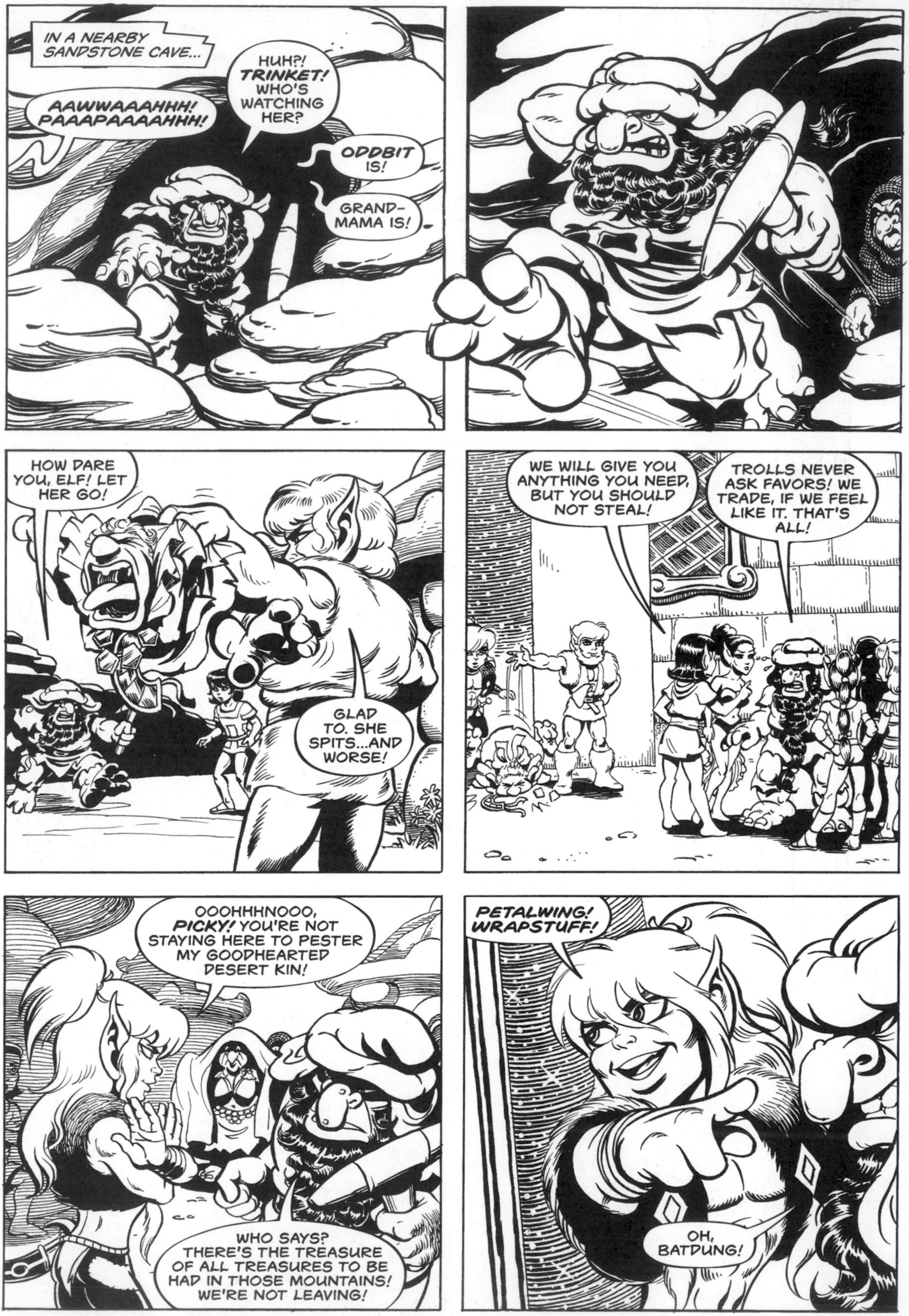
IN A NEARBY SANDSTONE CAVE...
AAWWAAAHHH! PAAAPAAAAHHH!
HUH?! TRINKET! WHO'S WATCHING HER?
ODDBIT IS!
GRAND-MAMA IS!
HOW DARE YOU, ELF! LET HER GO!
GLAD TO. SHE SPITS...AND WORSE!
WE WILL GIVE YOU ANYTHING YOU NEED, BUT YOU SHOULD NOT STEAL!
TROLLS NEVER ASK FAVORS! WE TRADE, IF WE FEEL LIKE IT. THAT'S ALL!
OOOHHHNOOO, PICKY! YOU'RE NOT STAYING HERE TO PESTER MY GOODHEARTED DESERT KIN!
WHO SAYS? THERE'S THE TREASURE OF ALL TREASURES TO BE HAD IN THOSE MOUNTAINS! WE'RE NOT LEAVING!
PETALWING! WRAPSTUFF!
OH, BATDUNG!

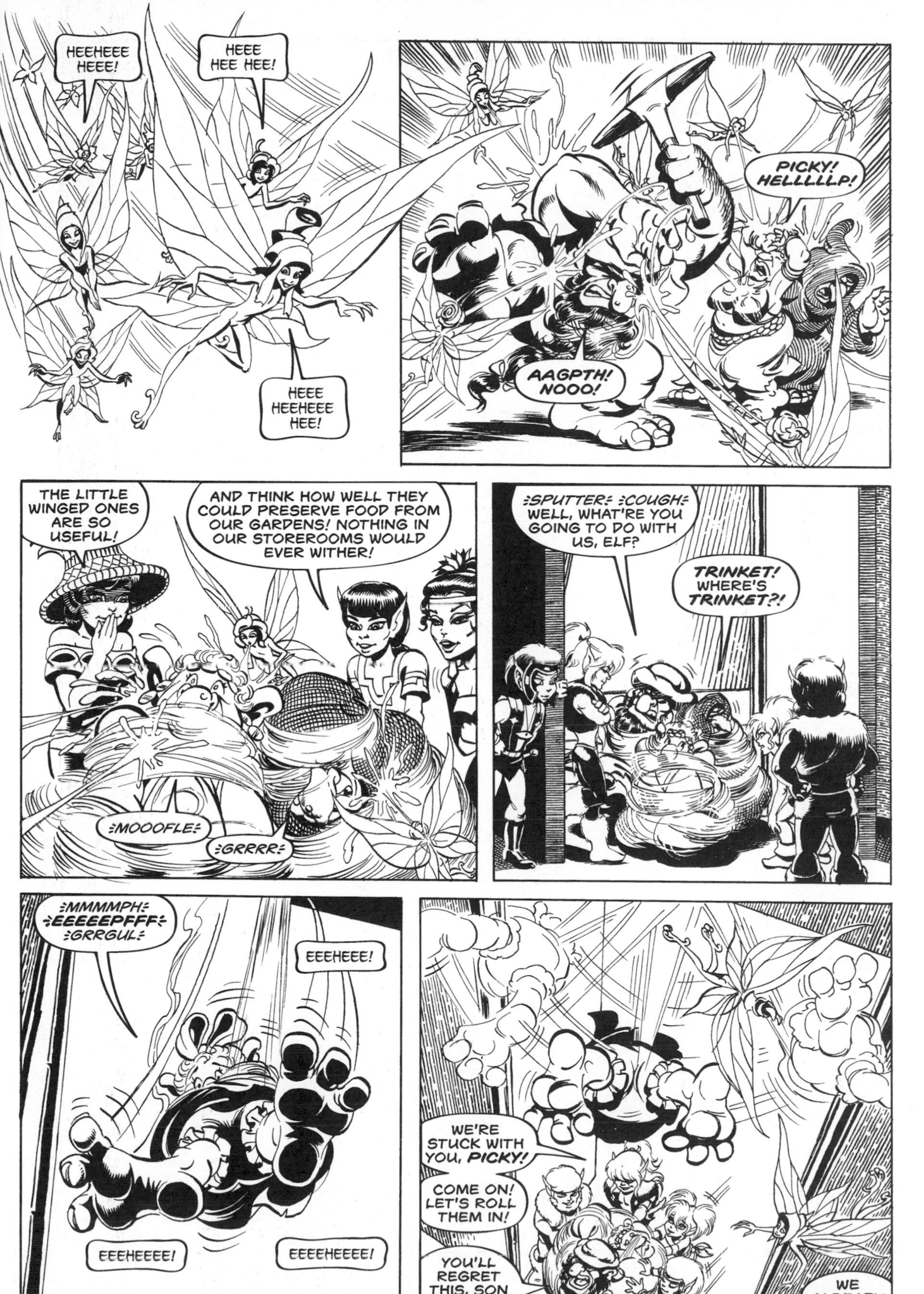
HEEHEEE HEEE!
HEEE HEE HEE!
HEEE HEEHEEE HEE!
PICKY! HELLLLLP!
AAGPTH! NOOO!
THE LITTLE WINGED ONES ARE SO USEFUL!
AND THINK HOW WELL THEY COULD PRESERVE FOOD FROM OUR GARDENS! NOTHING IN OUR STOREROOMS WOULD EVER WITHER!
MOOOFLE
GRRRR
SPUTTER COUGH WELL, WHAT'RE YOU GOING TO DO WITH US, ELF?
TRINKET! WHERE'S TRINKET?!
MMMMPH EEEEEPFFF GRRGUL
EEEHEEE!
EEEHEEEE!
EEEEHEEEE!
WE'RE STUCK WITH YOU, PICKY!
COME ON! LET'S ROLL THEM IN!
YOU'LL REGRET THIS, SON OF BEAR-CLAW!
WE ALREADY DO!

DESPITE THE COMMOTION IN THE ENTRANCE HALL, AN ATMOSPHERE OF QUIET REVERENCE PERVADES THE CHAMBER OF THE SCROLL OF COLORS.

YOU HAVE SEEN FOR YOURSELF WHAT THE HIGH ONES WERE, AND WHY WE ARE AS WE ARE NOW, MOTHER OF MEMORY.

I SHALL BE TRUE TO MY TITLE. WHOEVER WISHES TO SEE THE SCROLL MAY DO SO THROUGH ME.

IT HAS BECOME PART OF ME.

NOW I UNDERSTAND WHY THE PALACE SEEMS LESS A DWELLING PLACE THAN AN ORNAMENT FOR SHOW.

THEY WERE GUESSING, OUR DEAR FOREPARENTS, AT WHAT MIGHT BE INSIDE THE GREAT HUMAN-MADE HIVES THEY OBSERVED.

PERHAPS SOMEDAY WE DEATHLESS ONES WILL SEE THAT INSTANT IN TIME...BEFORE THE ACCIDENT...

...WHEN THE HIGH ONES FIRST APPEARED IN THE SKY. WHAT WILL HAPPEN THEN, I WONDER?

≡BUFF≡

AH, *SAVAH!* I HAVE SOMETHING FOR YOU!

FROM AN ANCIENT ELF TO A LOVELY, YOUNG ONE! A SMALL PIECE OF THE PALACE...

TO KEEP...SO YOU WON'T, ONE DAY, THINK IT WAS JUST A DREAM!

ALL FAREWELLS
HAVE BEEN SAID,
ALL HOPES
AND WISHES
EXPRESSED...

...ALL TREASURED
MEMENTOS EXCHANGED.

NOW, SUNTOP... YOU AND I WILL GUIDE THE PALACE TOGETHER!

FLY! FLY!

WE GO TO THE SOURCE OF THE CRY, TO THAT PLACE WHERE IT FIRST SOUNDED... AND STILL SOUNDS!

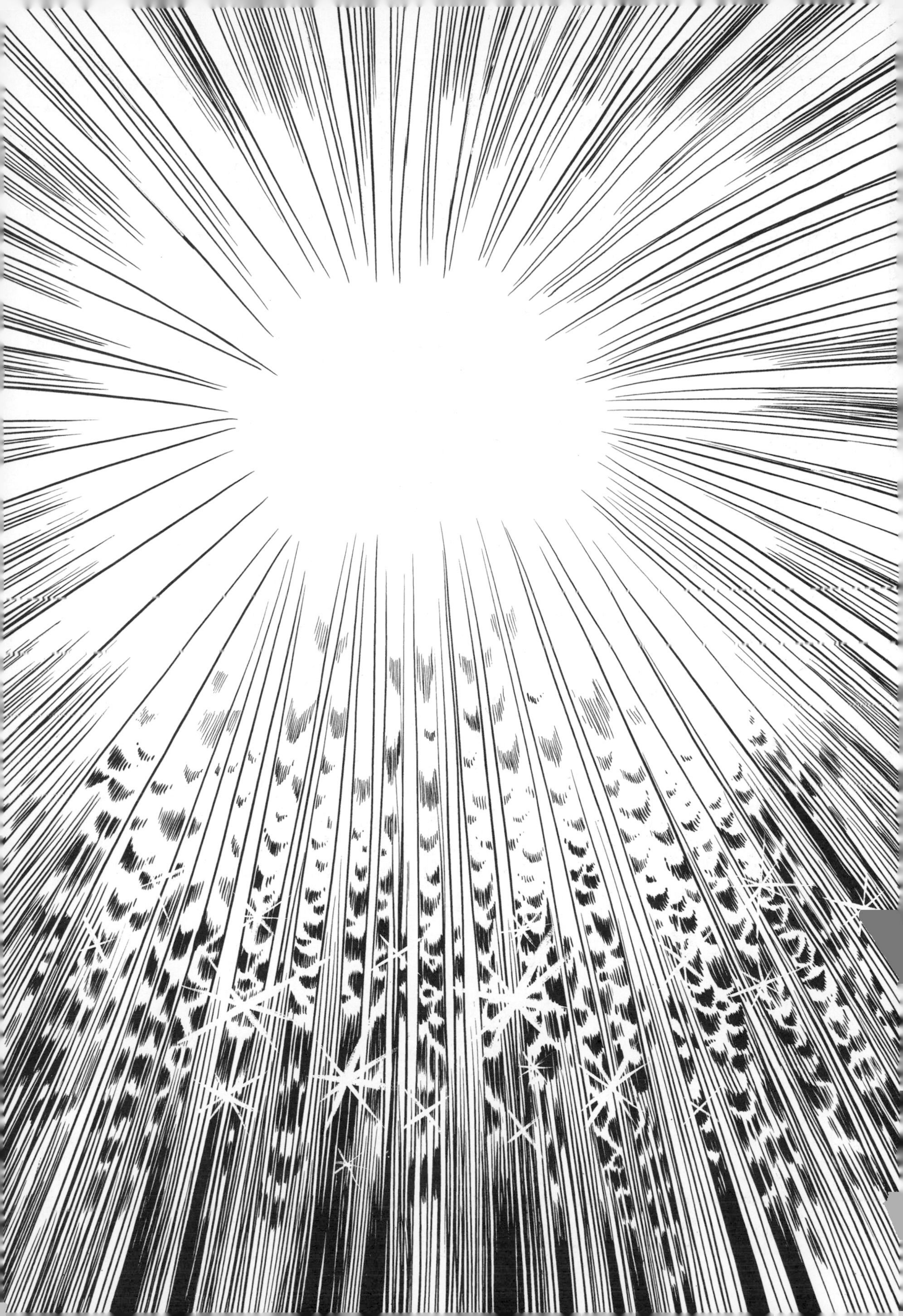

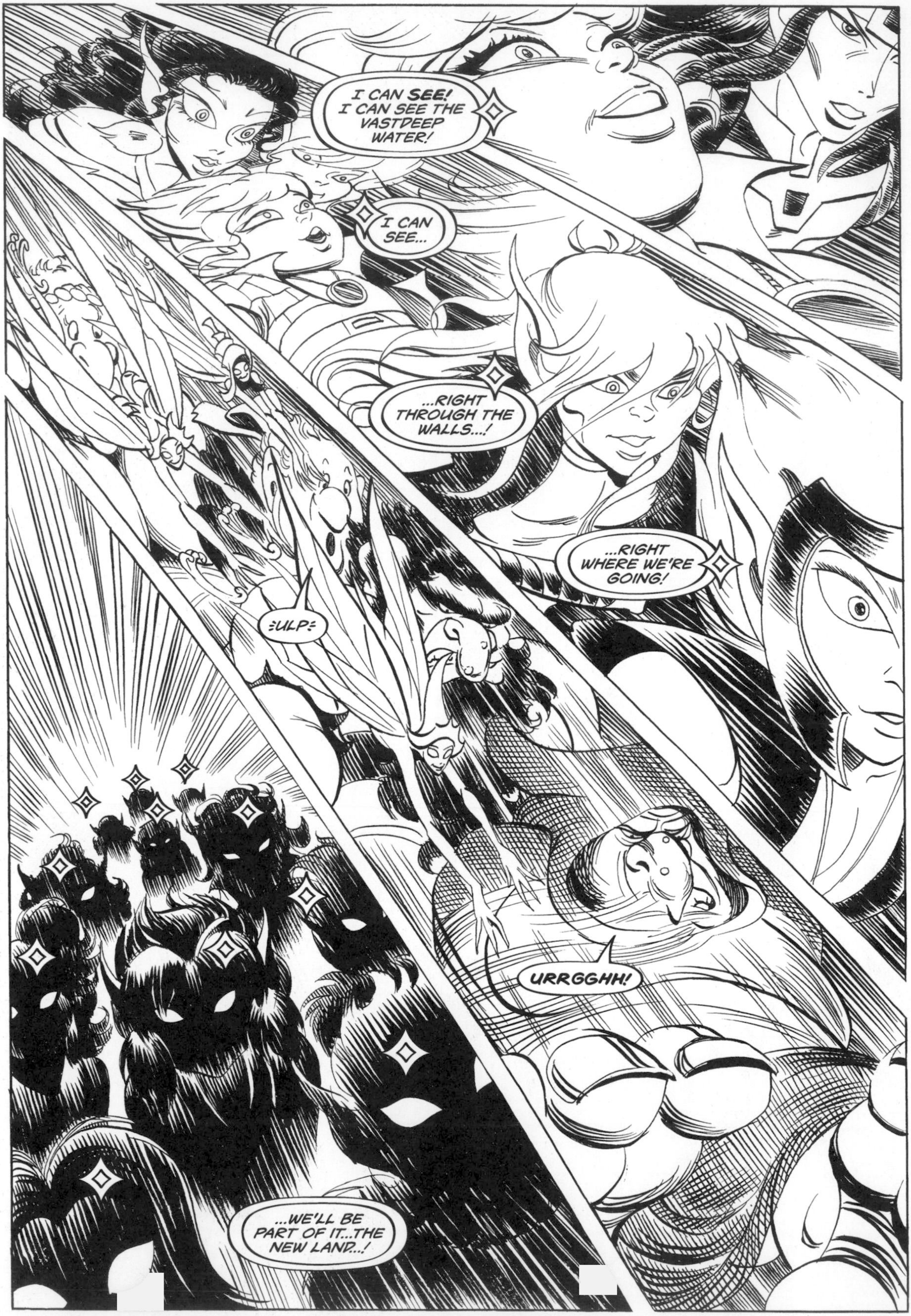
I CAN SEE! I CAN SEE THE VASTDEEP WATER!
I CAN SEE...
...RIGHT THROUGH THE WALLS...!
...RIGHT WHERE WE'RE GOING!
ULP
URRGGHH!
...WE'LL BE PART OF IT...THE NEW LAND...!

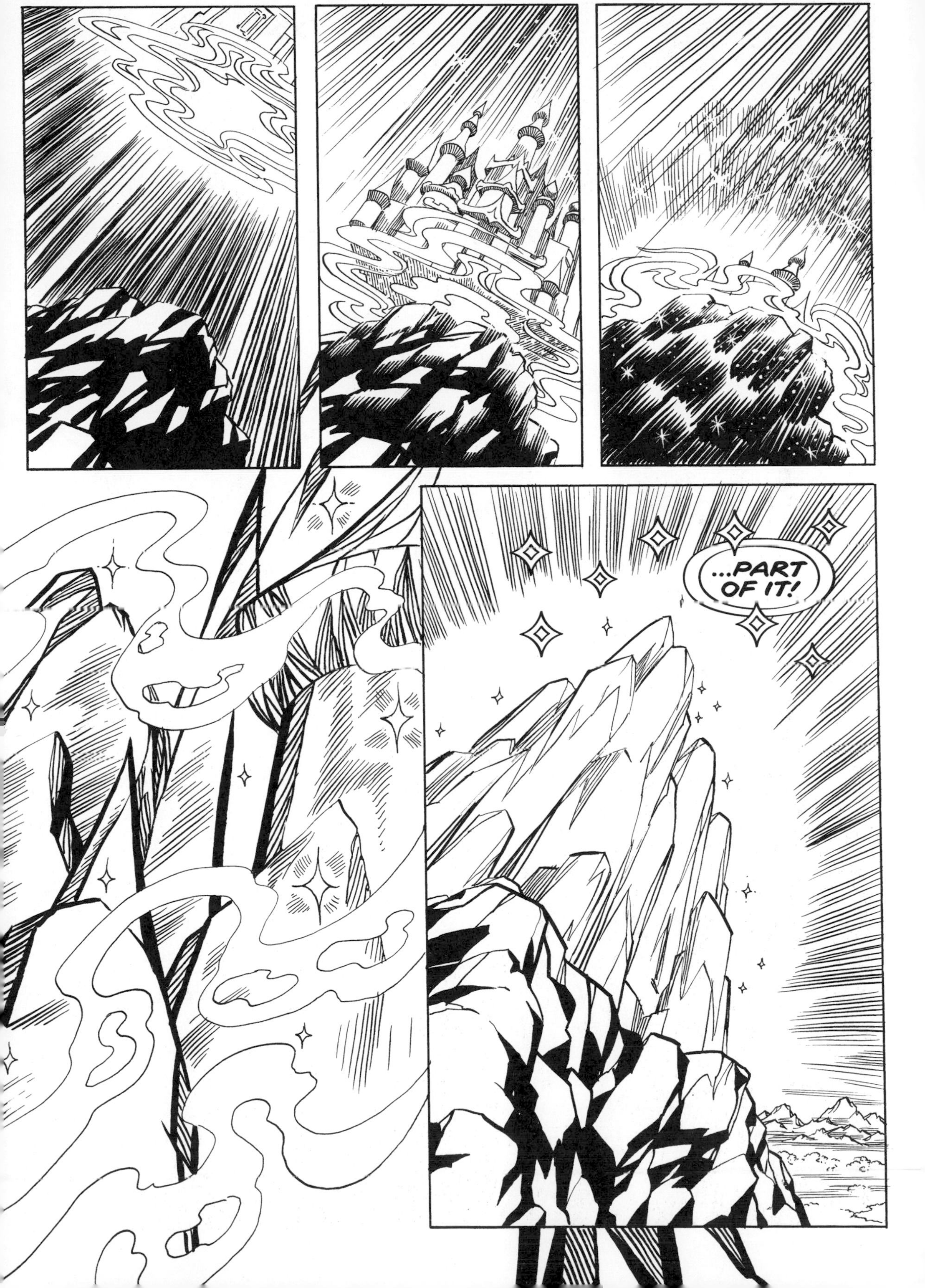
...PART OF IT!

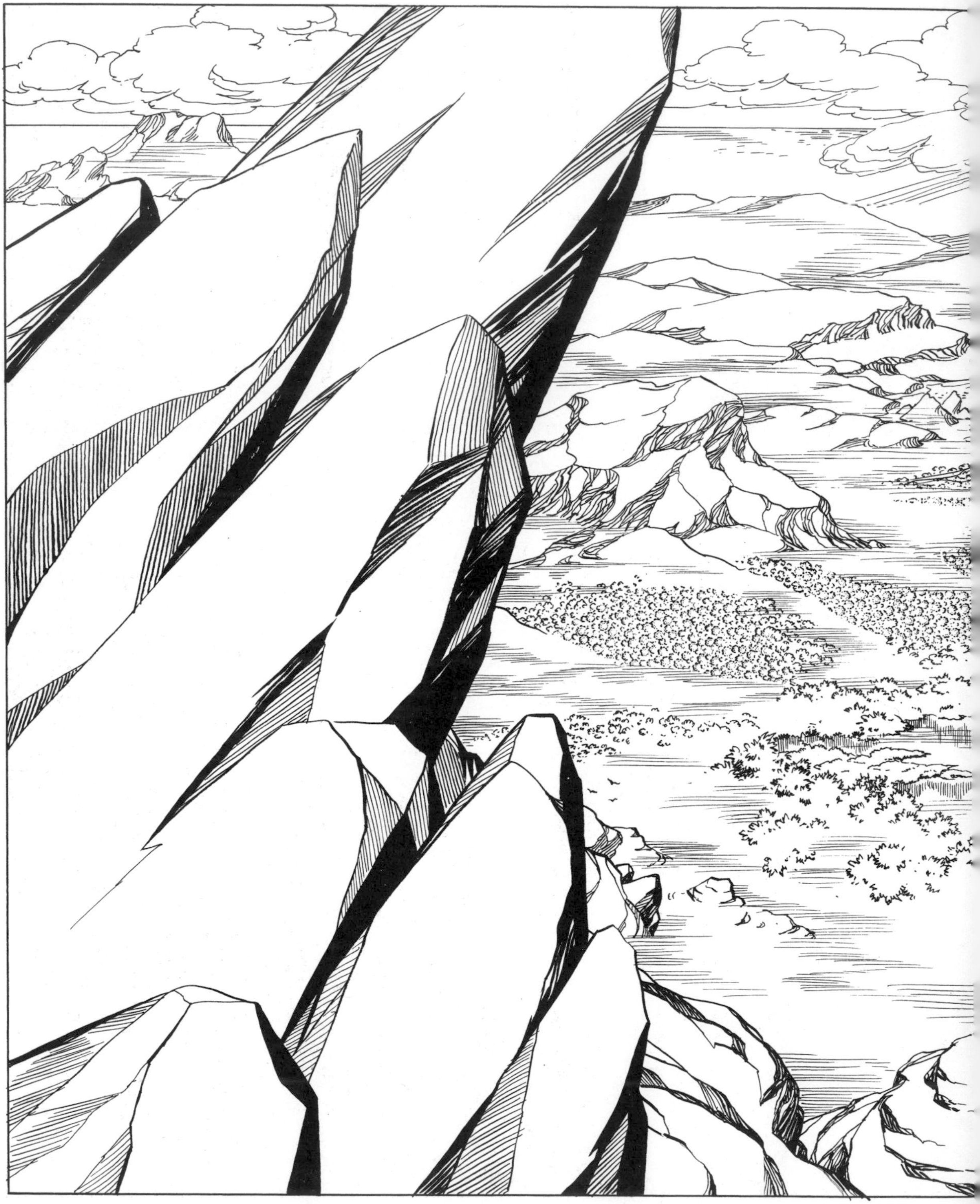

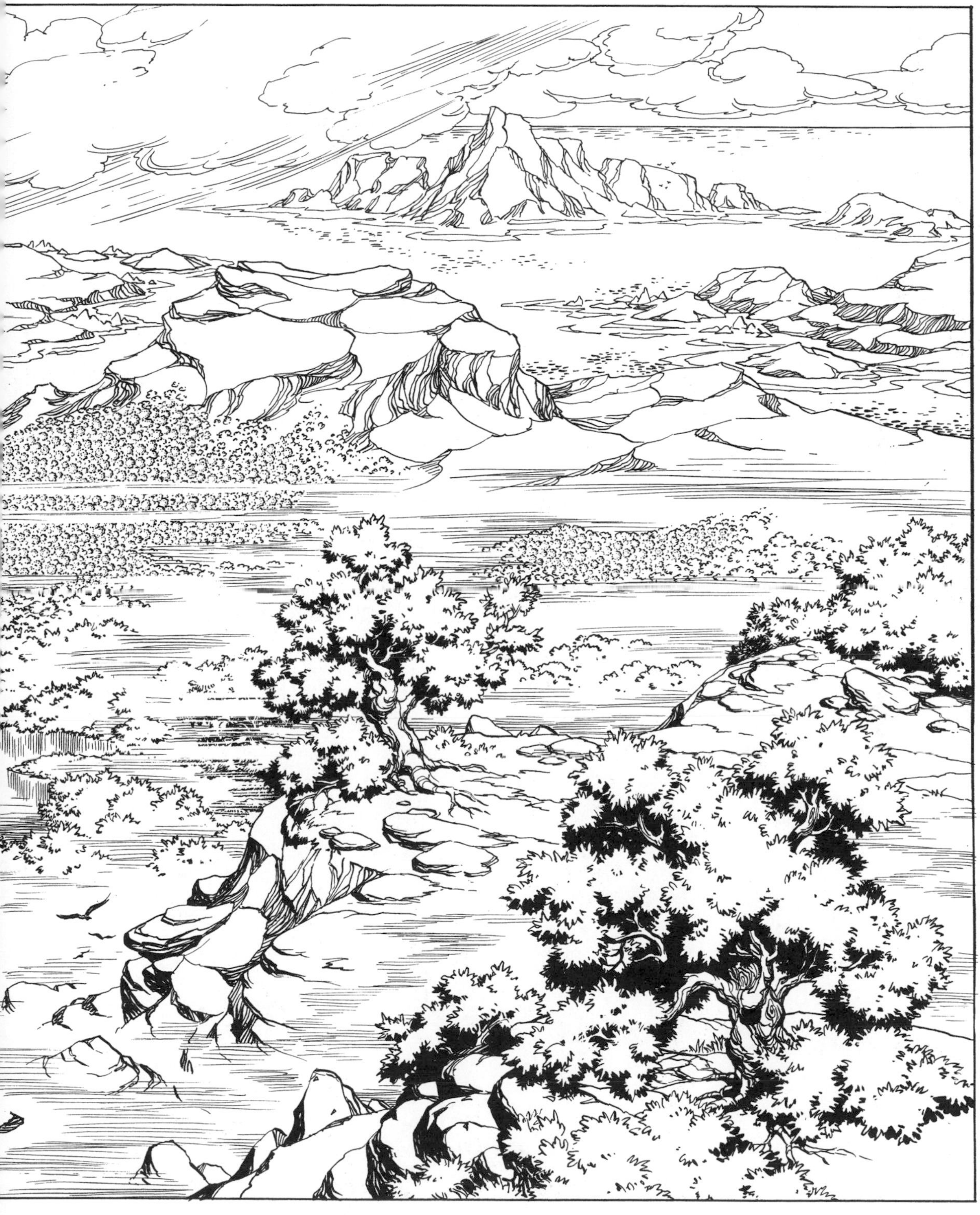

HIS SECRET SOUL NAME IS **TAM.** THE BLOOD OF TEN CHIEFS FLOWS IN HIS VEINS. HE WAS ONCE THE LEADER OF A SMALL ELFIN TRIBE KNOWN AS THE WOLFRIDERS. BUT NOW THEIR NUMBER HAS GROWN. THEIR WORLD HAS GROWN, TOO. AND NOTHING AWAITS THEM, **CUTTER** KNOWS, BUT MYSTERIES, RIDDLES, VERY FEW ANSWERS... AND THE WONDERFUL, TERRIBLE, ENDLESS GAME OF SURVIVAL.

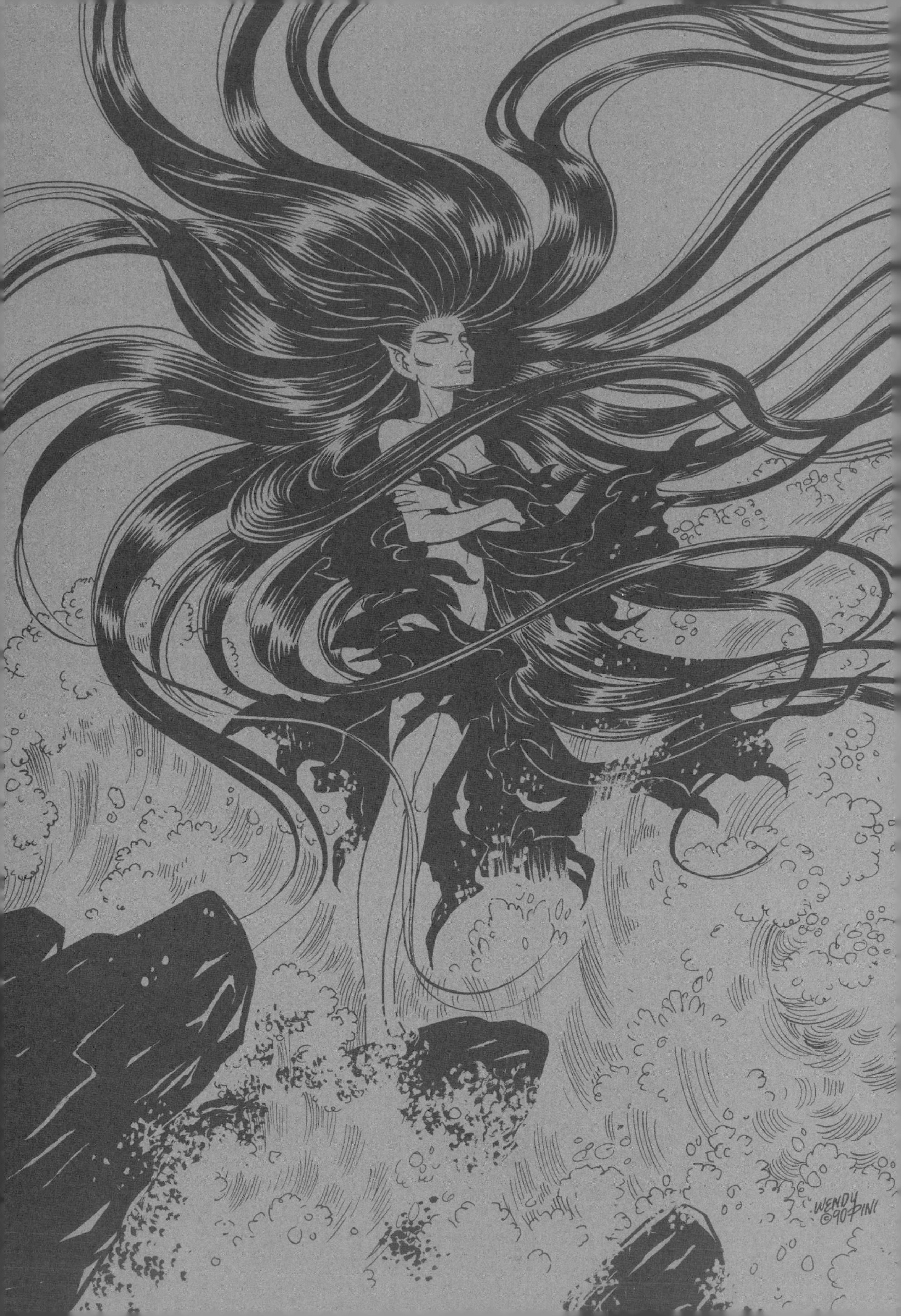
WENDY
©90 PINI

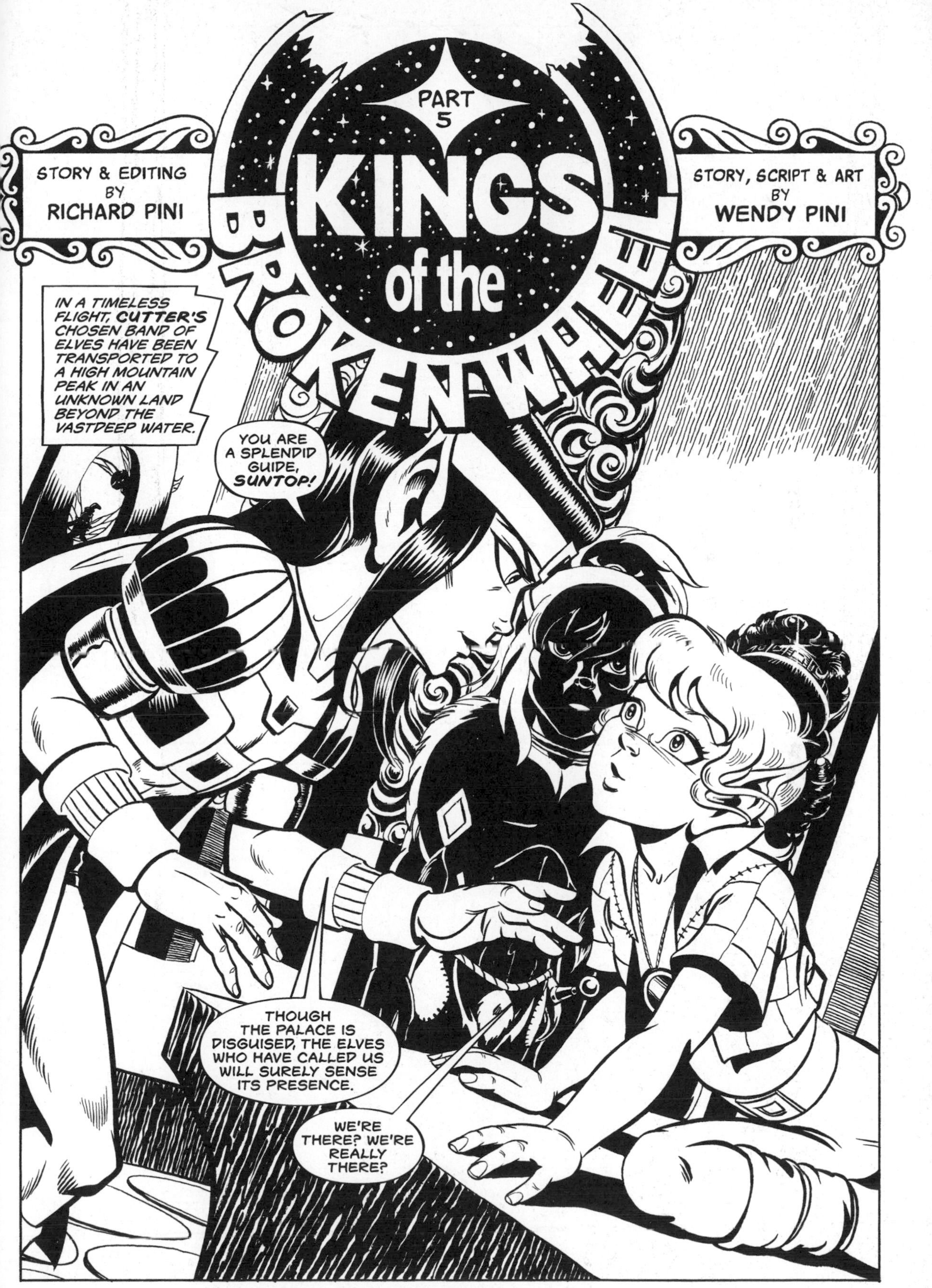
PART 5
KINGS of the BROKEN WHEEL
STORY & EDITING BY RICHARD PINI
STORY, SCRIPT & ART BY WENDY PINI
IN A TIMELESS FLIGHT, CUTTER'S CHOSEN BAND OF ELVES HAVE BEEN TRANSPORTED TO A HIGH MOUNTAIN PEAK IN AN UNKNOWN LAND BEYOND THE VASTDEEP WATER.
YOU ARE A SPLENDID GUIDE, SUNTOP!
THOUGH THE PALACE IS DISGUISED, THE ELVES WHO HAVE CALLED US WILL SURELY SENSE ITS PRESENCE.
WE'RE THERE? WE'RE REALLY THERE?

I-I STILL HEAR THE SCREAMING...!

THAT WILL END VERY SOON. WHEN THEY RECEIVE OUR SENDING, OUR KINDRED WILL HAVE NO MORE REASON TO CRY OUT!

QUICKLY! TOGETHER! OPEN SEND!

DO NOT STOP UNTIL YOU ARE ANSWERED!

FRIENDS, WE'VE COME!

A HIGH ONE IS HERE!

THE PALACE IS HERE!

WHATEVER YOUR NEED...

...WE'VE COME TO AID YOU!

WHERE ARE YOU?

ANSWER!

ANSWER!

THE SHIFTING OF MOUNTAIN WINDS, OCCASIONAL SHRIEKS OF SMALL BIRDS OF PREY...BUT FOR THESE SOUNDS, THE AFTERNOON CREEPS BY ON SILENT PAWS.

NOTHING YET! *IMPOSSIBLE!* TOGETHER OUR RANGE IS ALMOST UNLIMITED!

THERE IS NO CORNER OF THIS LAND OUR SENDING CANNOT REACH... NOT EVEN UNDER-GROUND!

IT–IT'S AWFUL! THE CRY KEEPS COMING, JUST THE SAME!

TH–THEY DON'T KNOW WE'RE HERE!

HOW CAN THAT BE?! ANYONE WITH THE POWER TO SEND SUCH A CRY...

...HAS TO BE ABLE TO RECEIVE! WHAT MORE CAN WE DO?!

SUNTOP!

≔CHOKE≕

WHERE ARE YOU?

WHERE ARE YOU?! WHERE ARE YOU?!

:SOB: :SOB:
...WHERE... ARE...YOU...!

OH, KITLING!

M— MOTHER! MY HEAD HURTS!

:SNIFF:...DIDN'T MEAN TO UPSET YOU! JUST...SO TIRED!

ENOUGH IS ENOUGH! I'M SICK OF SEEING THAT CUB IN PAIN!

SOMEONE'S PLAYED US A VERY DIRTY TRICK!

:RRRFFFF: :WHUFF:

TIMMAIN! WHY WON'T THE STRANGE ELVES ANSWER? DO YOU KNOW? IN YOUR WOLF FORM...CAN YOU KNOW?

:WHINE: :WHINE: :WHINE:

RAYEK...

HELP MY SON. PLEASE.

I WILL!

THE BURDEN SHOULD BE MINE.

WE WILL NEED YOUR POWER, LEETAH.

ONLY BECAUSE YOU ARE MUCH STRONGER THAN SUNTOP WILL I ALLOW THIS.

:GASP:

OOOOHHHHH...!

ENDLESS, YET IMMEDIATE, FILLED WITH THE FORCE OF SUDDEN TERROR, THE MULTIVOICED HOWL ENTERS RAYEK'S WAITING MIND. THOUGH LODGED FOR DAYS IN THE CHILD'S BRAIN, THE CRY SEEMS FRESH, A RESPONSE TO SUDDEN, UNEXPECTED DISASTER.

THE DOOR YOU HAVE KEPT OPEN...SHUT IT NOW.

RAYEK SHALL DEAL WITH THE STRANGERS.

AAAAAHHHHH...!

BROWNSKIN...?

THIS *IS* THE PLACE! THEY ARE RIGHT ON TOP OF US, YET OUR SENDING CANNOT GET THROUGH TO THEM!

A CRUEL RIDDLE, *EKUAR!* WHAT WILL BECOME OF THE STRANGERS IF WE FAIL TO SOLVE IT?

WOOPS! STEADY...!

YOUR EYES ARE BRIGHT AS FATHER'S SWORD! I'M GLAD YOUR SILLY OLD HEAD'S ALL YOURS AGAIN!

:GIGGLE:

NOW WHAT, CUTTER?

NOW... WE *EAT!*

SHORTLY, IN A CHAMBER WITHIN THE TRANSFORMED PALACE...

THESE OLD LEATHERS ARE DARK AND PLAIN...

A HUNT! GOOD!

I NEAR WENT CRAZY SITTING AROUND THAT SUN VILLAGE YESTERDAY!

...BUT 'TIL WE KNOW OUR WAY ABOUT, IT'S BEST WE BLEND WITH THE NIGHT.

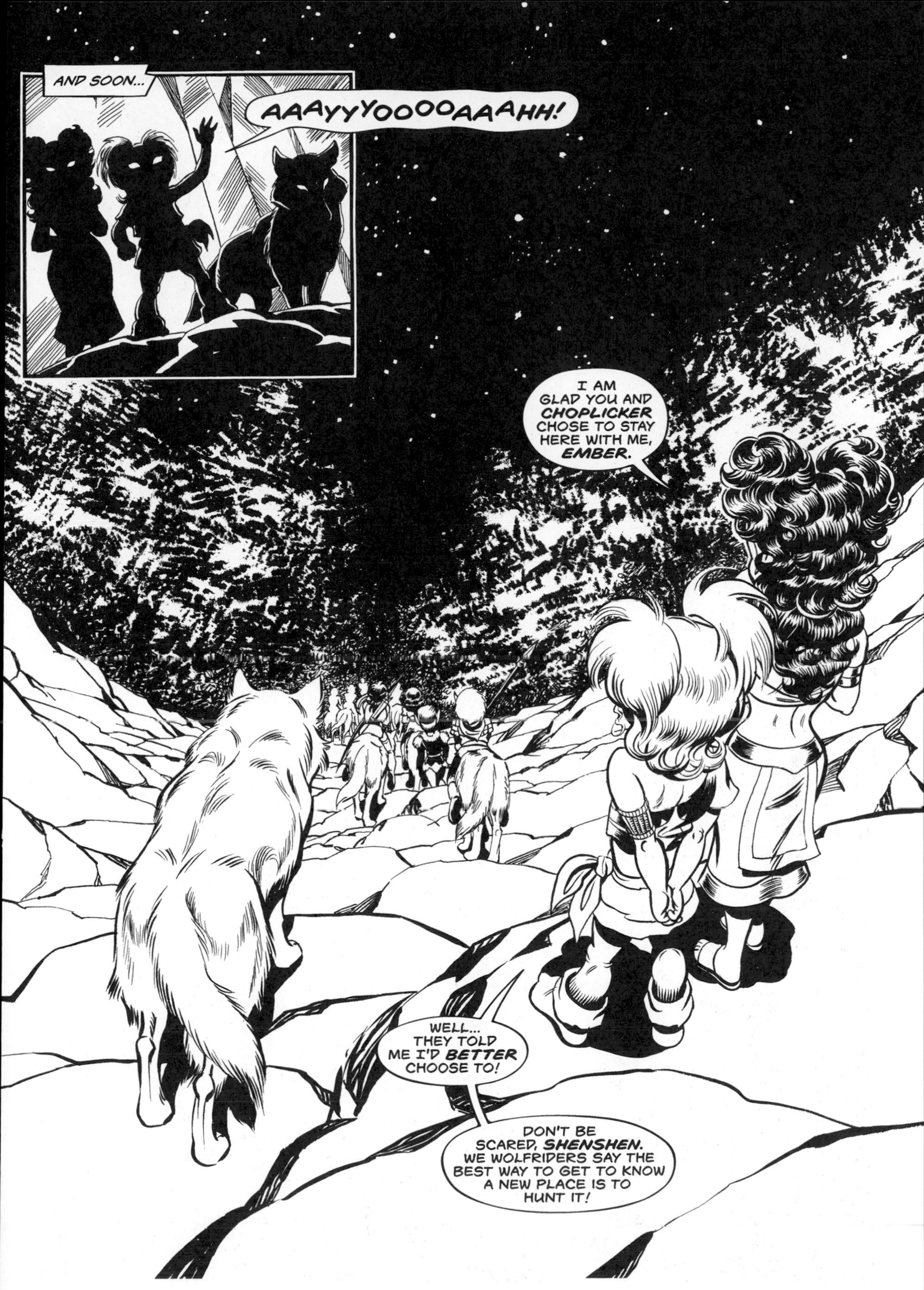
AND SOON...
AAAYYYOOOOAAAAHH!
I AM GLAD YOU AND CHOPLICKER CHOSE TO STAY HERE WITH ME, EMBER.
WELL... THEY TOLD ME I'D BETTER CHOOSE TO!
DON'T BE SCARED, SHENSHEN. WE WOLFRIDERS SAY THE BEST WAY TO GET TO KNOW A NEW PLACE IS TO HUNT IT!

THE DESCENT IS LENGTHY AND STEEP, BUT BARE ROCK FINALLY GIVES WAY TO FOREST.

THE TREES ARE BREATHTAKING... QUITE UNLIKE THEIR SMALLER, GNARLED BRETHREN IN THE VALLEY OF ENDLESS SLEEP.

SO MANY SOUNDS! SO MANY SMELLS! SLIDDERBACK IS SO EXCITED I CAN HARDLY CONTROL HER!

≠PANT≠
≠PANT≠
≠PANT≠

≠SNUFFLE≠
≠SNUFF≠

EVER MINDFUL OF THE REASON FOR THEIR ARRIVAL, THE WOLFRIDERS CONTINUE TO SEND...

...BUT THE HOPED-FOR RESPONSE STILL ELUDES THEM.

YOU KNOW...IT DOESN'T *FEEL* LIKE THERE ARE OTHER ELVES HERE--

OR THAT THEY EVER *WERE* HERE!

NO MATTER! SOMEONE MADE THAT CRY. WE'VE GOT TO KEEP TRYING!

FOR A WHILE LONGER THEY DO TRY. BUT, AT LAST, THEY GIVE IN TO THEIR SENSES...

...DRINKING IN THE NIGHT AIR MADE SWEET BY THE MASSIVE TREES' BREATH.

SUDDENLY...

I...I DON'T KNOW WHY I DID THAT...!

MAYBE NOT. BUT IT SOUNDS LIKE YOU SURE AS SPIT **HIT** SOMETHING!

LET'S GO SEE!

HOPE IT WASN'T A HUMAN!

HOPE IT WAS!

OH, BURY IT, **PIKE**!

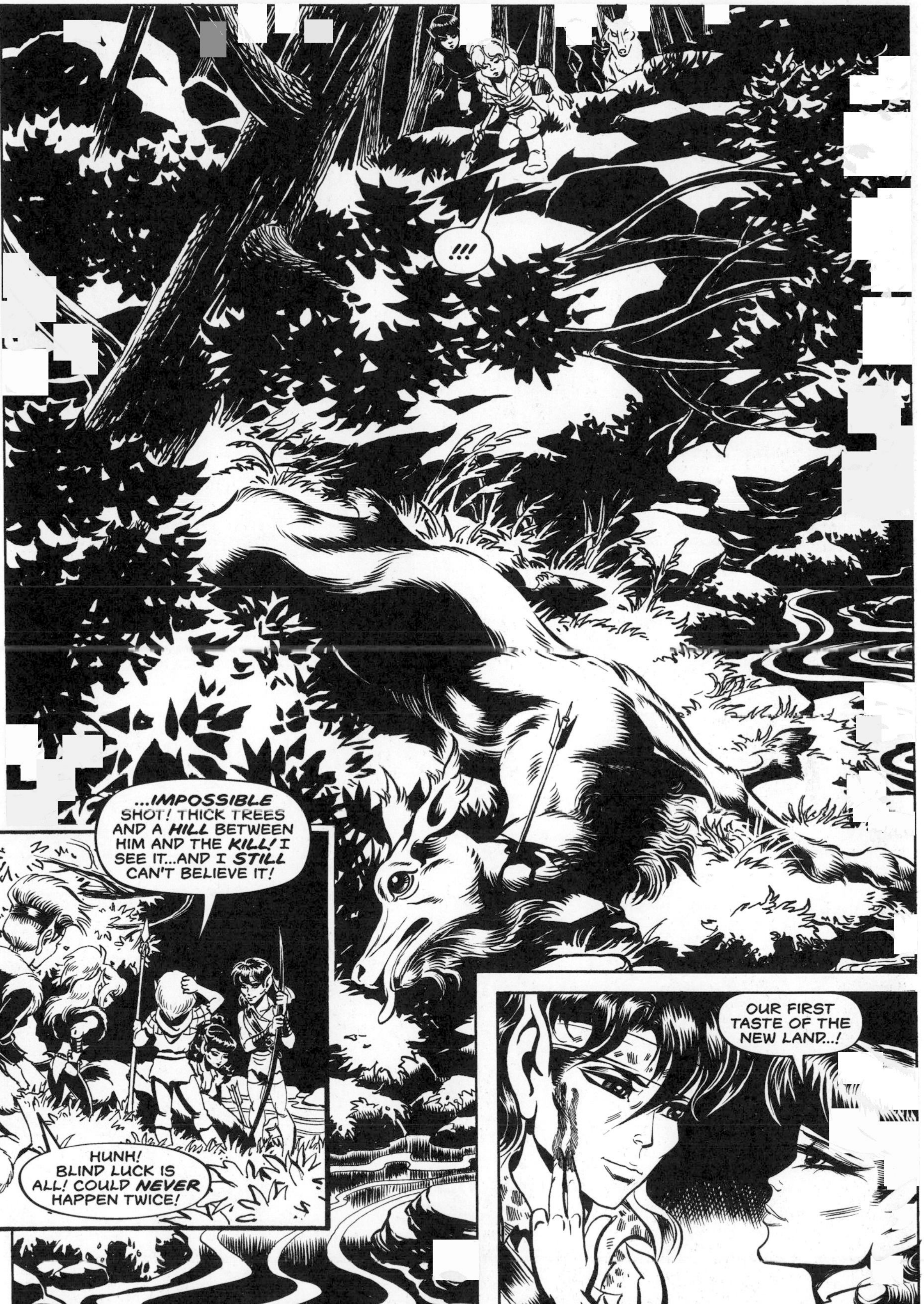
!!!
...IMPOSSIBLE SHOT! THICK TREES AND A HILL BETWEEN HIM AND THE KILL! I SEE IT...AND I STILL CAN'T BELIEVE IT!
HUNH! BLIND LUCK IS ALL! COULD NEVER HAPPEN TWICE!
OUR FIRST TASTE OF THE NEW LAND...!

MOMENTS LATER...

PIKE! YOU FAWN HEART! ALWAYS *THANKING* THE KILL FOR ITS MEAT! IT *CAN'T* HEAR YOU.

WHO KNOWS? IF A BEAR EATS YOU MAYBE HE'LL THANK YOU IN HIS OWN WAY!

OR MAYBE HE'LL JUST RETCH! WHAT'S BITING YOU? YOUR EARS ARE PRICKED UP LIKE A SCARED TREEWEE'S!

COME ON! EVEN I CAN FEEL IT...!

"...AND THE OTHERS MORE THAN ME! EVERYTHING'S *BIGGER* HERE THAN WE'RE USED TO...

"...THE NIGHT NOISES AND THE SCENTS...!

"...ONLY, IT'S NOT THE NEW LAND. IT'S US....!

"...SOMETHING INSIDE US IS GETTING...STRONGER!"

≡GASP≡

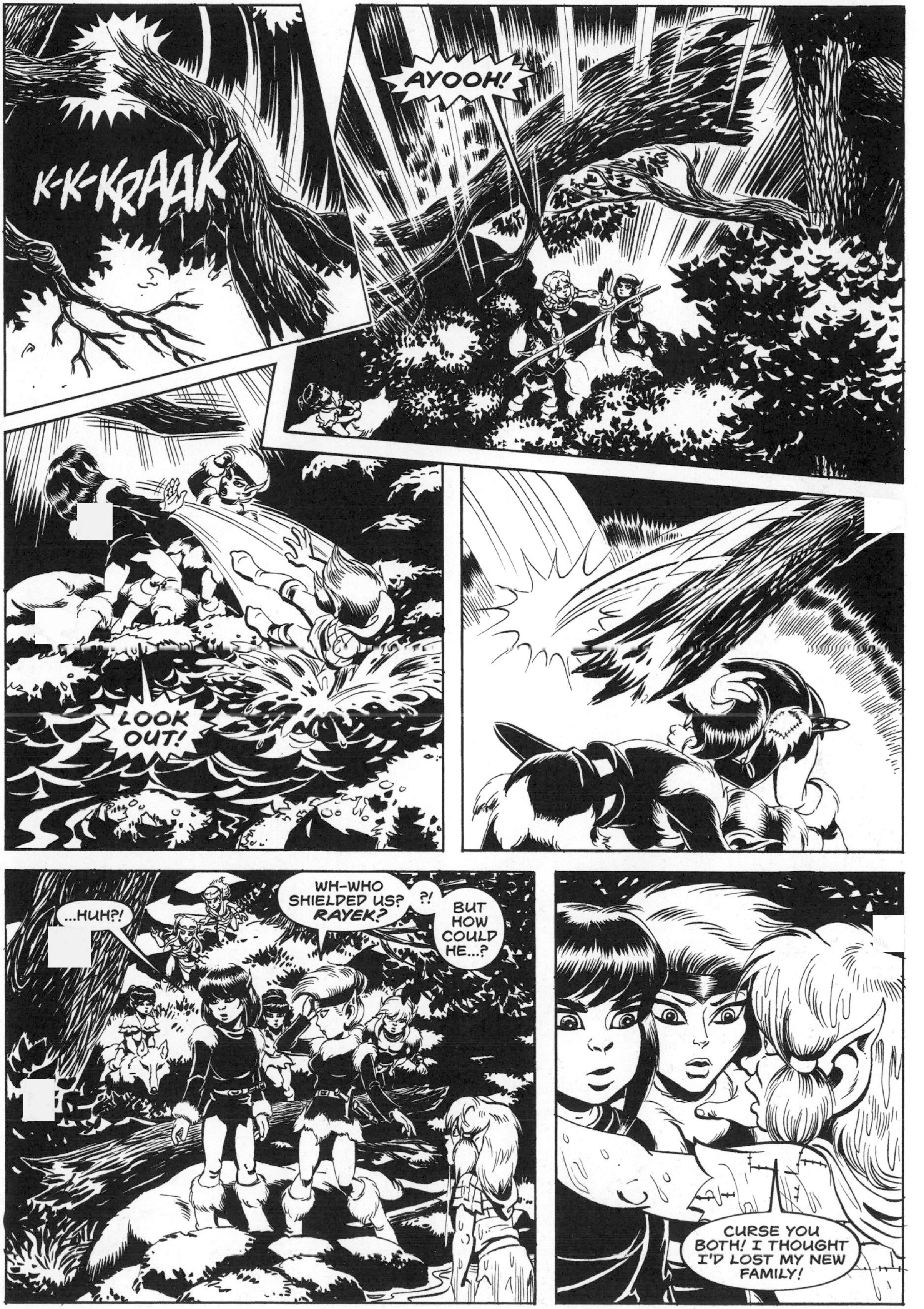

K-K-KRAAK
AYOOH!
LOOK OUT!
...HUH?!
WH-WHO SHIELDED US? RAYEK?
?!
BUT HOW COULD HE...?
CURSE YOU BOTH! I THOUGHT I'D LOST MY NEW FAMILY!

HIGH ONES...! THAT'S HOW *RILLFISHER*...!

RAIN THE HEALER HAD MAGIC ENOUGH TO BREAK HER FEVER...

"...BUT NOT TO CURE THE DEAFNESS IT CAUSED.

"SHE SAID SHE DIDN'T *NEED* EARS TO SNATCH FISH BARE HANDED FROM THE WATER.

"BUT IF ONCE... JUST ONCE... SHE COULD HAVE HEARD... HEARD THAT DEAD BRANCH GIVE WAY...!"

NEXT TIME DON'T WORRY ABOUT ME! JUST BE READY FOR ANYTHING!

SO SAYS THE CHIEF OF DREAM-BERRIES!

SKOT AND *KRIM*... I JUST *WISHED* THEM SAFE... AND THEY *WERE!*

QUIETLY, THOUGHTFULLY, THE WOLFRIDERS RETRACE THEIR PATH UP THE MOUNTAINSIDE... WITH **REDLANCE**, THE BEST OF TRACKERS, IN THE LEAD.

:SNIFF: :SNIFF: HMMM...

THE TRAIL IS SO HOT IT MIGHT AS WELL BE MADE OF FIRE! WITHOUT EYES, NOSE, OR EARS I COULD FOLLOW IT!

WHAT'S HAPPENING TO US?

WHERE ARE YOU GOING, **CUTTER**?

CAUGHT A WHIFF OF...SOME-THING.

JUST WANT TO MAKE SURE...!

ROCKS AND LOW-HANGING GROWTH MAKE RIDING DIFFICULT. THE THREE ELVES DISMOUNT AND CREEP CAUTIOUSLY FORWARD ON FOOT...

A CAVE!

SMELLS LIKE... HUMANS!

I THOUGHT SO.

LOOK! ASHES! DAYS OLD!

SO HUMANS DWELL IN THIS NEW LAND, TOO!

HUNH! AND WON'T THEY BE HAPPY TO SEE US! MAYBE THEY'RE THE CAUSE OF THE KIN-CRY THAT BROUGHT US HERE!

I EXPECTED TO DEAL WITH HUMANS AGAIN. BUT WE'D BETTER SEE THEM BEFORE WE JUDGE...

EH?!

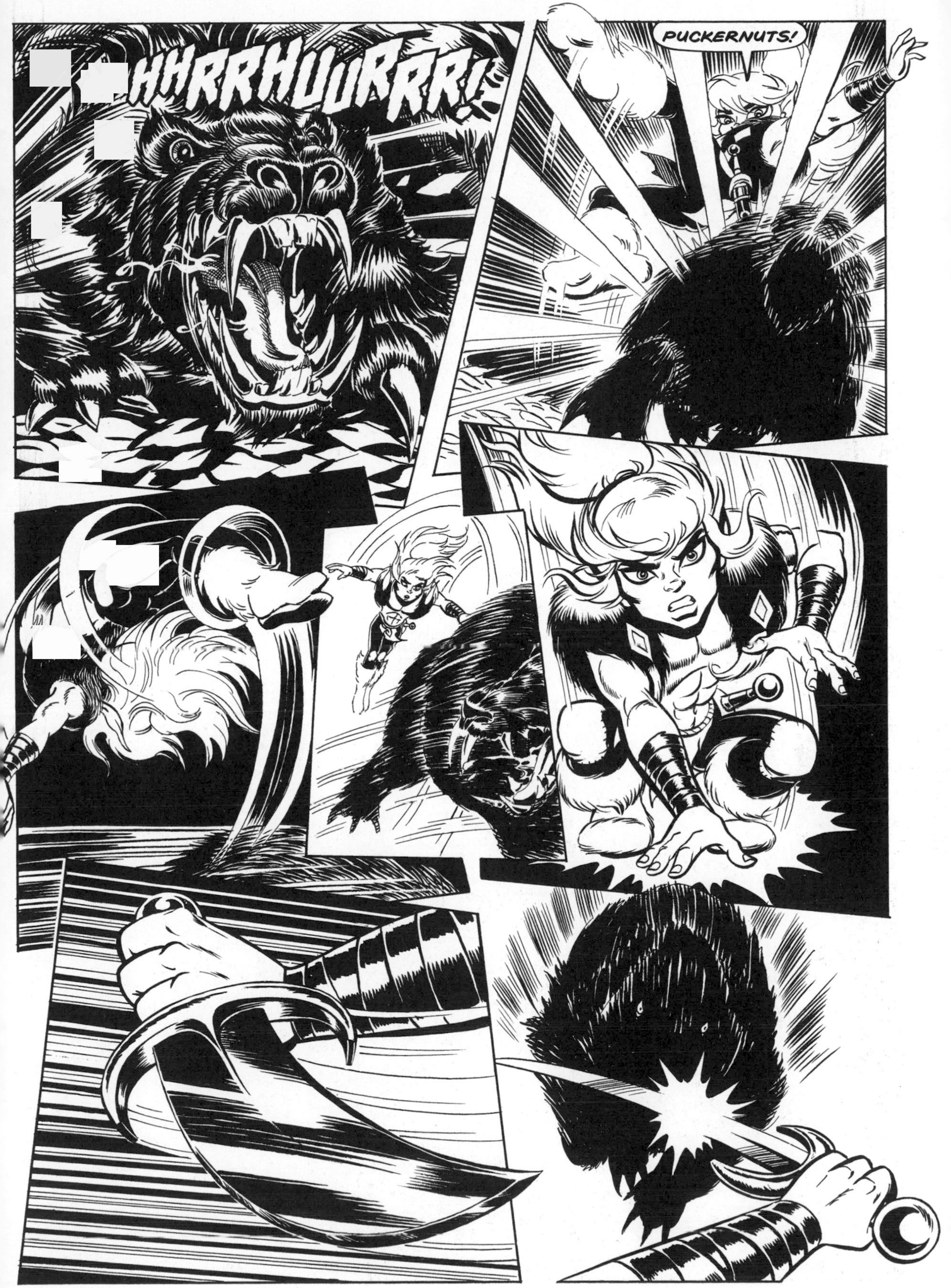
HHRRHUURRR!
PUCKERNUTS!

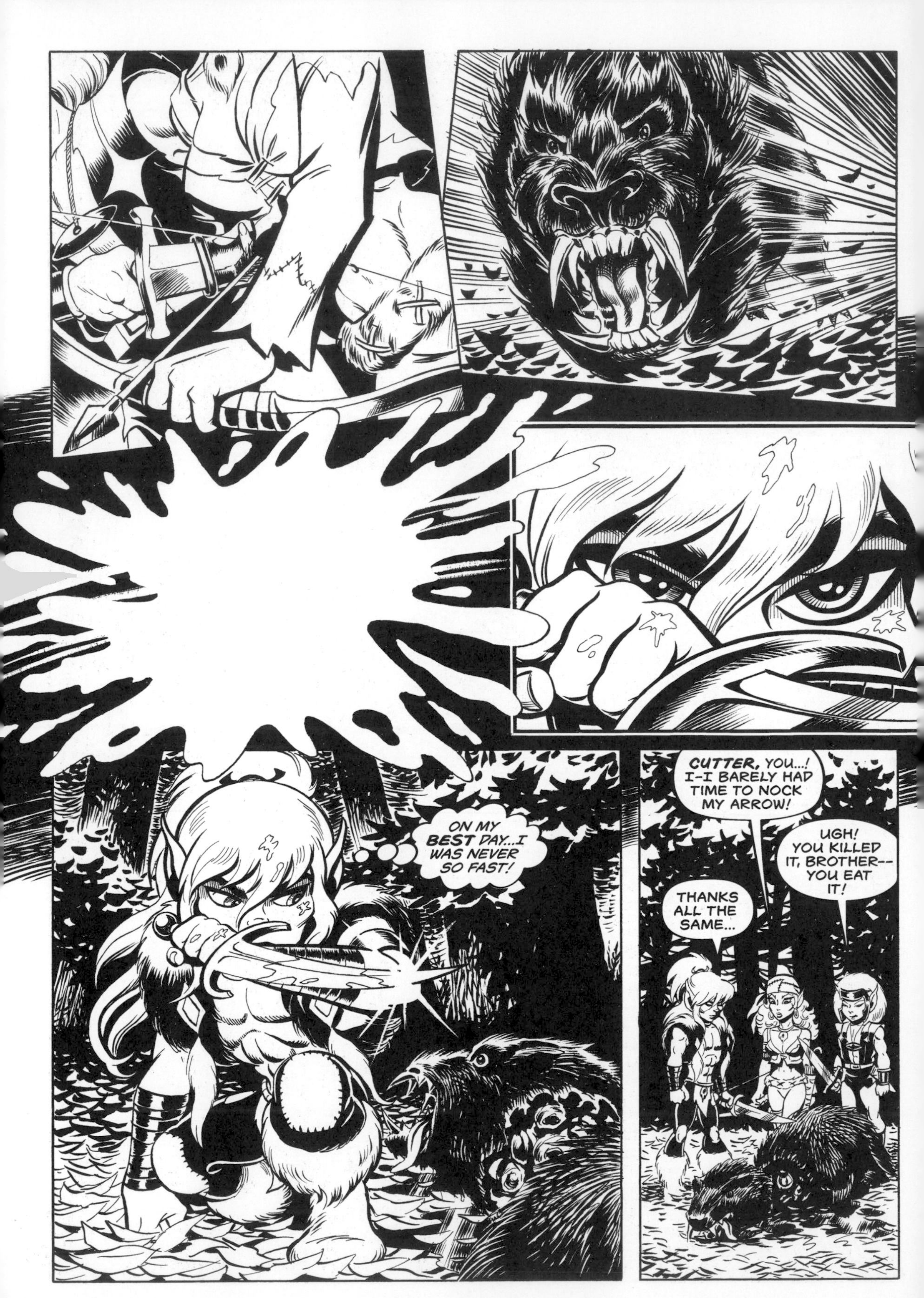
ON MY BEST DAY...I WAS NEVER SO FAST!
CUTTER, YOU...! I-I BARELY HAD TIME TO NOCK MY ARROW!
THANKS ALL THE SAME...
UGH! YOU KILLED IT, BROTHER-- YOU EAT IT!

NOT ONE OF THEM UNTOUCHED BY THE NIGHT'S WEIRD EVENTS, THE WOLFRIDERS GREET THEIR RETURNING CHIEF IN SILENCE.

WE FEED NEAR THE PALACE. AND AFTER...WE TALK! I CALL FOR A WHOLE-PACK COUNCIL.

ANTICIPATION OF THE FAMILIAR RITUAL CALMS THE SMALL HUNTERS.

THE SMOKY, CRYSTALLINE TOWERS OF THE PALACE RISE INTO VIEW, BECKONING THEM BACK TO THE ONLY HAVEN THEY NOW POSSESS.

AND WITHIN THE SCROLL ROOM...

MADDENING! THERE ARE MOMENTS... WHEN I THINK...I CAN ALMOST MAKE OUT WORDS!

WORDS... WITHIN THE CRY?

THOUGHTS, RATHER... FEELINGS.

SOMETHING... MORE THAN FEAR?

MUCH MORE!

A LOSS! A SHATTERING OF HOPE! LOVE BETRAYED!

LOVE...BETRAYED?! ONLY ONE IS CAPABLE OF THAT! IS IT SHE--?

NO. *WINNOWILL* HAS NO PART IN THIS. BUT...

...IT IS VERY PAINFUL!

MAYBE THE STRANGE ELVES AREN'T REALLY HERE! MAYBE THEIR CRY IS... IS LIKE AN ECHO BOUNCING OFF THIS MOUNTAIN!

'COURSE ECHOES COME AFTER YOU YELL... SO IT'S SURE SOMEONE YELLED SOMEWHERE, SOMETIME!

BUT WHO? AND WHERE ARE THEY NOW?

SHHHH! IN THE NEXT CHAMBER... HEAR THAT...?

WHY, THOSE SNEAKING, SNITCHING, STICKY-FINGERED...

"...*TROLLS!*"

THAT ONE TOO, *PICKY,* DEAR! I JUST LOOOVE WHITE FOX FUR!

:GRUMBLE: BETTER WE GO FOR WARMTH THAN FANCY LOOKS!

MMMMM! SNUGGY SNUGGY!

WHAT D'YOU THINK YOU'RE DOING?!

BAD DIGDIGS!

DROP THAT STUFF! IT'S NOT YOURS TO TAKE!

PETALWING! CHOPLICKER! GET 'EM!

GRROOOWFF!

405

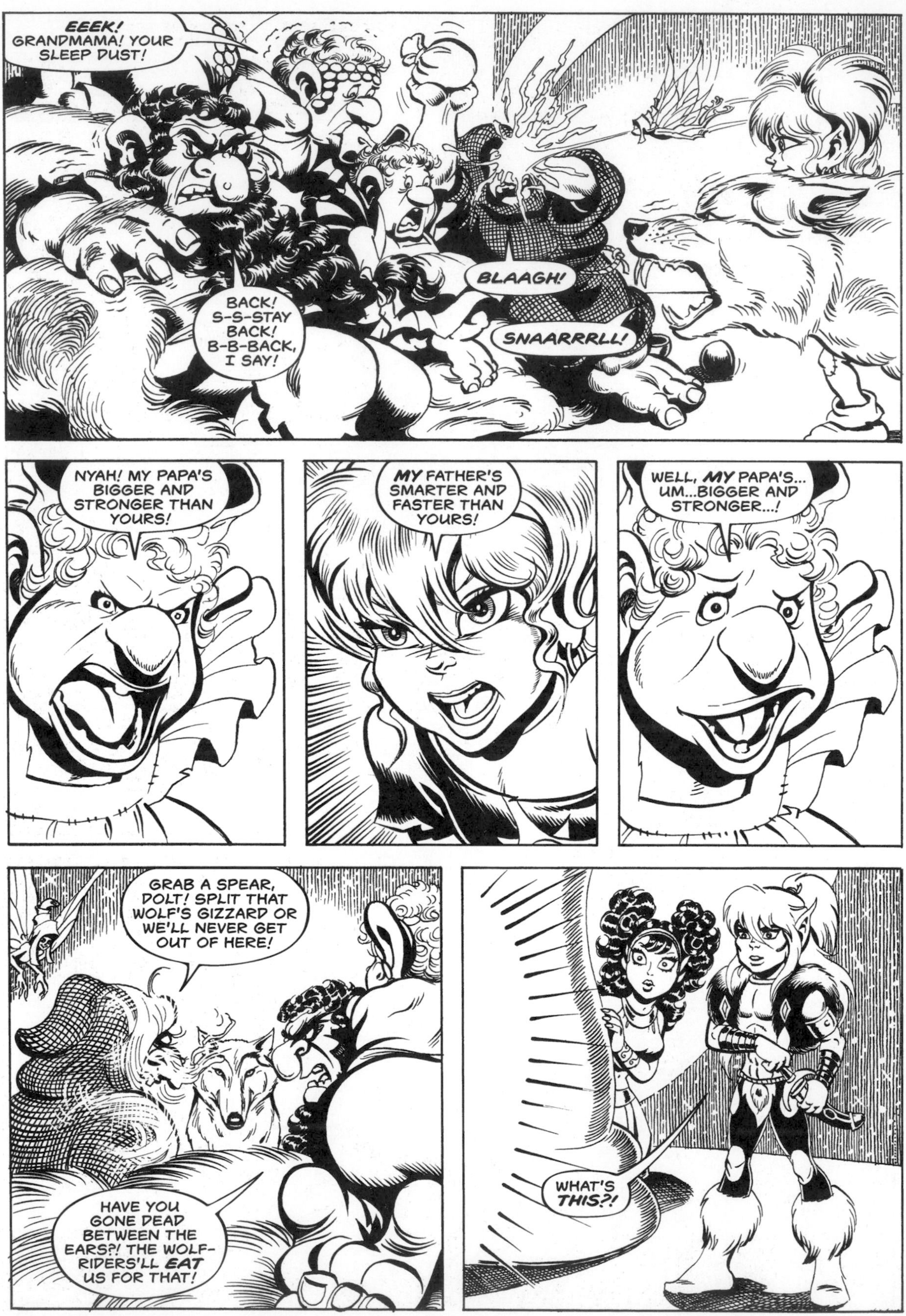
EEEK! GRANDMAMA! YOUR SLEEP DUST!
BLAAGH!
SNAARRRLL!
BACK! S-S-STAY BACK! B-B-BACK, I SAY!
NYAH! MY PAPA'S BIGGER AND STRONGER THAN YOURS!
MY FATHER'S SMARTER AND FASTER THAN YOURS!
WELL, MY PAPA'S... UM...BIGGER AND STRONGER...!
GRAB A SPEAR, DOLT! SPLIT THAT WOLF'S GIZZARD OR WE'LL NEVER GET OUT OF HERE!
HAVE YOU GONE DEAD BETWEEN THE EARS?! THE WOLF-RIDERS'LL EAT US FOR THAT!
WHAT'S THIS?!

PROBLEMS, *PICKY?*

YOU BIG-EYED, PINK-FACED TREE CLIMBERS! WE HAVE A *RIGHT* TO THESE SKINS!

YOU BROUGHT US HERE AGAINST OUR WILL!

'TIL WE'RE SETTLED UNDERGROUND, IT'S ONLY FAIR THAT YOU SHARE!

HMNH! FROM HERE "SHARING" LOOKS A LOT LIKE STEALING! STILL, FAIR'S FAIR! TAKE WHAT YOU WANT, BUT NO WEAPONS!

PUH! WHAT USE WOULD PUNY ELF BLADES BE IN MY MIGHTY HANDS?! I'LL SOON OWN THIS MOUNTAIN AND ALL THE REST!

TAKE A STEP ANYWHERE AND YOU'LL BE TREADING ON *KING PICKNOSE'S* ROOF! MARK ME!

SOMETHING TELLS ME OUR OLD DAYS OF TRADING AND BICKERING WITH THE TROLLS ARE ON THEIR WAY BACK.

BWAAAHHH! DON'T WANNA GO OUTSIDE! NNAAAHH!

SHORTLY...

ANY LUCK YET?

NONE. THE CRY IS...AS EVER. I-I AM FAILING EVERYONE!

SUNTOP IS FREE BECAUSE OF YOU! THE PALACE FLIES BECAUSE OF YOU!

RAYEK, WHATEVER YOU'RE ABLE TO DO...IS ENOUGH!

CAN YOU COME TO COUNCIL, LEETAH? WILL HE BE ALL RIGHT WITHOUT YOU?

I THINK SO.

A COUNCIL? WAS THERE TROUBLE IN THE HUNT?

NO...NO TROUBLE. BUT...

≡GASP≡ BELOVED! WHAT IS IT?!

WHAT HAS HAPPENED?

YOU'LL HAVE TO TELL US! WE'VE NEVER NEEDED YOUR WISDOM MORE!

WHEN THE WOLFRIDERS HAVE DIVIDED UP THE NIGHT'S CATCH...

HERE! TAKE THIS. IT'S BEST TO BUILD KINGDOMS ON A FULL BELLY!

!!! ≡MURBLE≡ O...≡HRUMPH≡ ...BLIGED! ≡GRUMBLE≡

AAWWAAAHHH! NOOOO! WON'T GO! WON'T GO!

:GIGGLE:

:WHIMPER: :WHIMPER:

BAAAWWWW!

BAAAWWW...
AAWW...
AWW...
AW...

UNOBTRUSIVELY, THE HEALER OBSERVES THE WOLFRIDERS AS THEY FEAST AND NOTES NO OUTWARD SIGN OF CHANGE.

BUT **LEETAH** KNOWS WHAT SHE HERSELF HAS SENSED SINCE HER FIRST FLIGHT IN THE PALACE.

LATELY I HAVE FELT AN INCREASE OF POWER AND CLARITY. HAVE ANY OF YOU...?

WASHING OVER THE INCOMPLETE QUERY COMES A FLOOD OF ANSWERS.

I COULD ALWAYS HIT WHAT I AIMED AT. BUT NOW I "SEE" MY TARGET IN MY HEAD...DON'T EVEN NEED TO AIM!

I CAN SEND NOW! IT IS AS SIMPLE AS BREATHING!

I CAN UNDERSTAND THE TREES' LANGUAGE... FAR BEYOND THE SOFT SIGHS AND CRIES I'VE KNOWN!

WHAT I WISH FOR COMES TRUE! THAT'S ALL I KNOW!

MY CHILD WAS MADE IN THE PALACE. SPIRITS SURROUND ME WITH LOVE!

I DON'T THINK HOW, I JUST DO! EVERYTHING'S EASY AND CLEAR NOW!

THIS IS THE PALACE'S INFLUENCE. REMEMBER TIMMAIN'S WORDS...

"THOSE BORN OF RECOGNITION ATTRACT INTERESTED SPIRITS WHO MAKE MAGIC MORE POTENT, VISIONS MORE CLEAR."

JUST THEN, FROM ANOTHER MOUNTAINTOP FAR AWAY...

OOOWWWOOO

OOOWWWWOOOo

OOOWOOOWWWWOOOWOOOo

SO, NOT JUST HUMANS BUT WOLVES LIVE HERE TOO. HEH HEH, OLD STARJUMPER WOULD'VE LED THE SONG TONIGHT...

OOWWWOOOo

?? EYES...!

TIMMAIN!

SEEK ONE VOICE AMONG THE MANY!

HUH?! YOU-YOU'RE SENDING!

SEEK ONE VOICE...? YOU MEAN AMONG THE WOLVES...? OR US? OR WHAT?!

EEEEEEEEEEEEEEEE

:GASP:

RAYEK! RAYEK'S SENT OUT THE CRY!

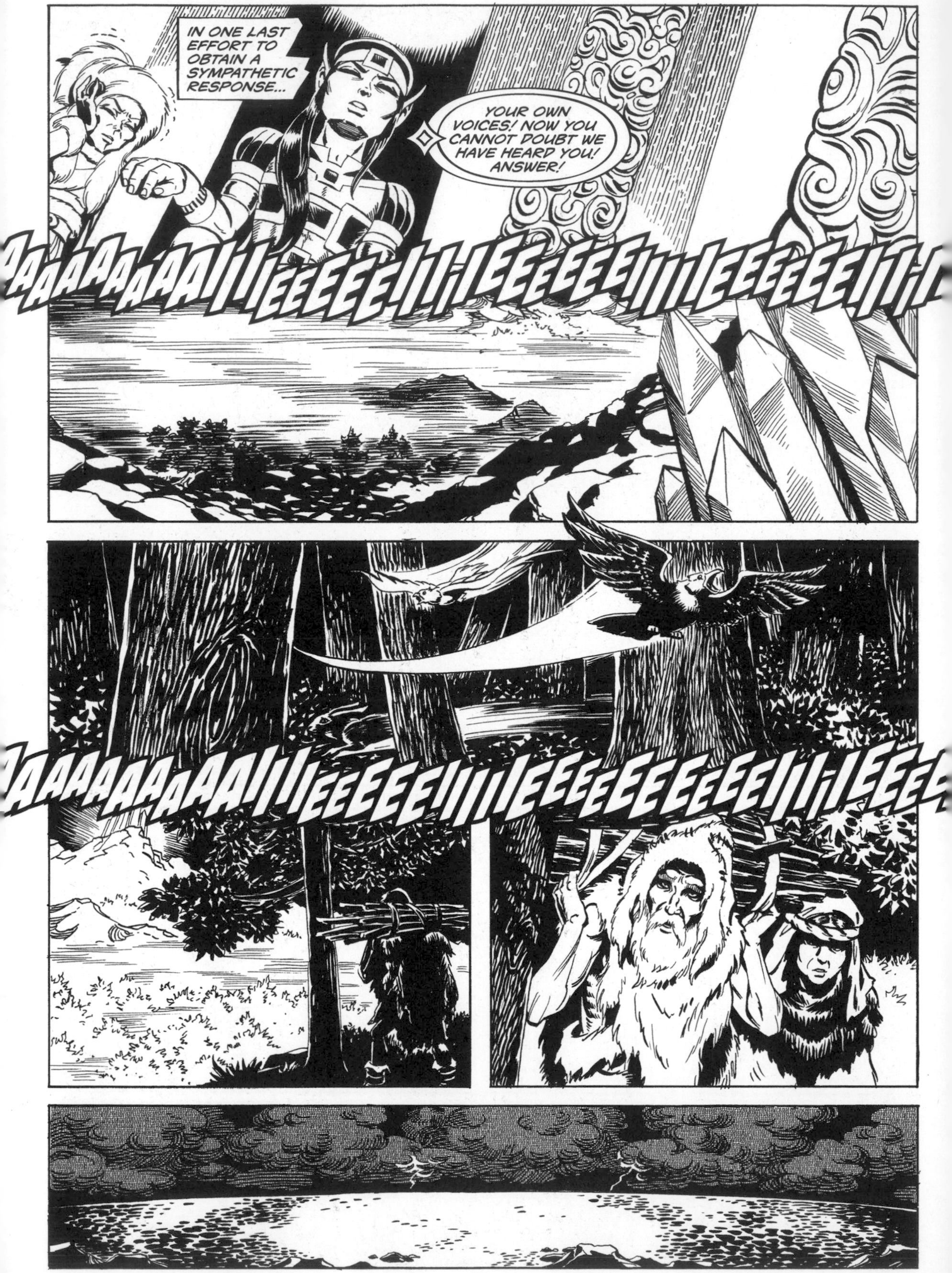
IN ONE LAST EFFORT TO OBTAIN A SYMPATHETIC RESPONSE...
YOUR OWN VOICES! NOW YOU CANNOT DOUBT WE HAVE HEARD YOU! ANSWER!
AAAAAAAAAIIIIEEEEEEIIIIEEEEEEIIIIEEEEEEEIIII
AAAAAAAAAIIIIEEEEEEIIIIEEEEEEEEEEEEIIIIEEEE

AAAAAAAIIIIIEEEEIIIIIAAAAAAEEEEEEIIIIIIE

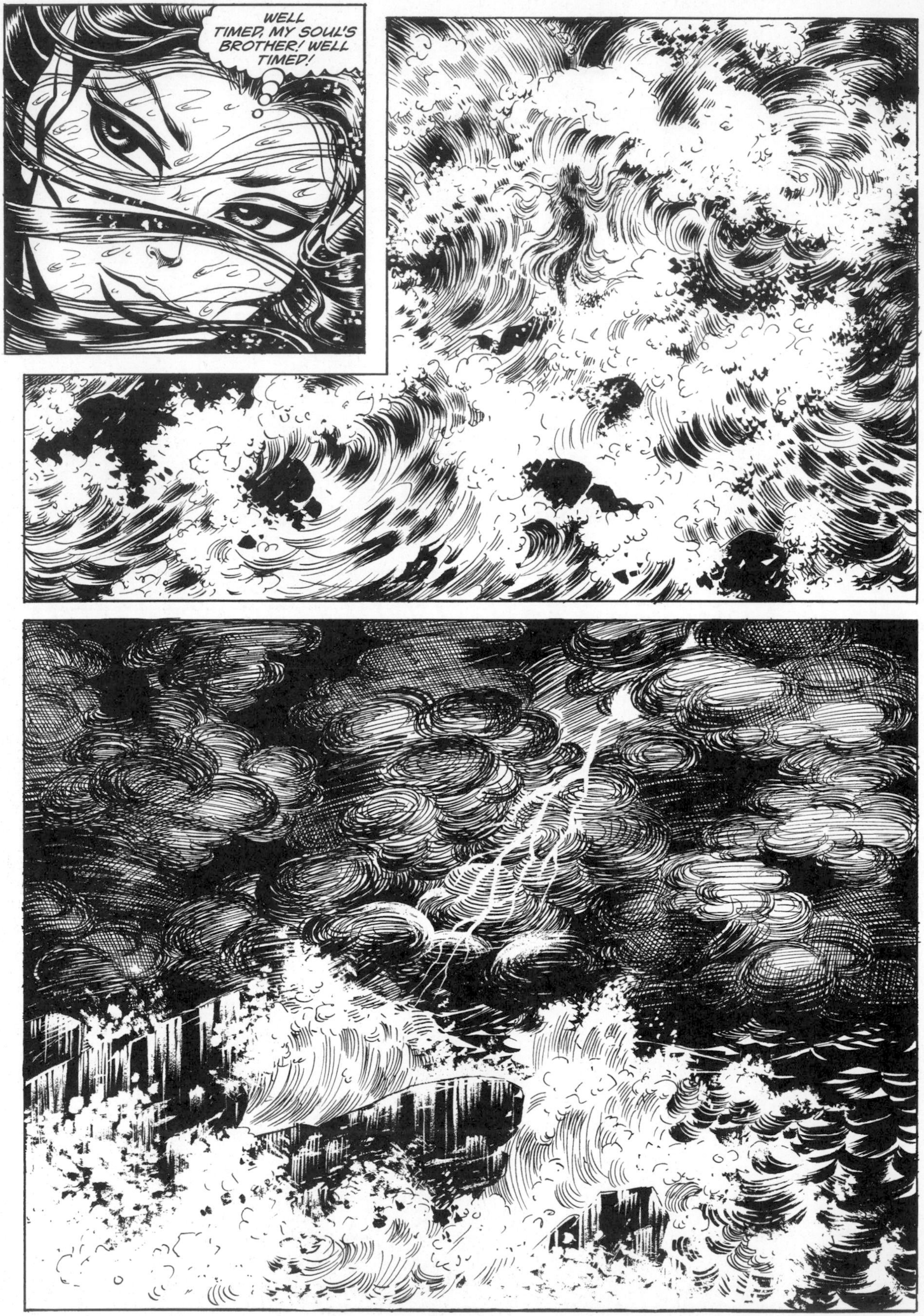
WELL TIMED, MY SOUL'S BROTHER! WELL TIMED!

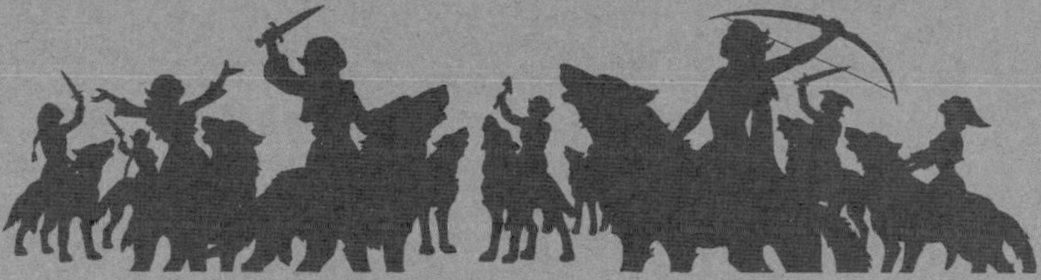

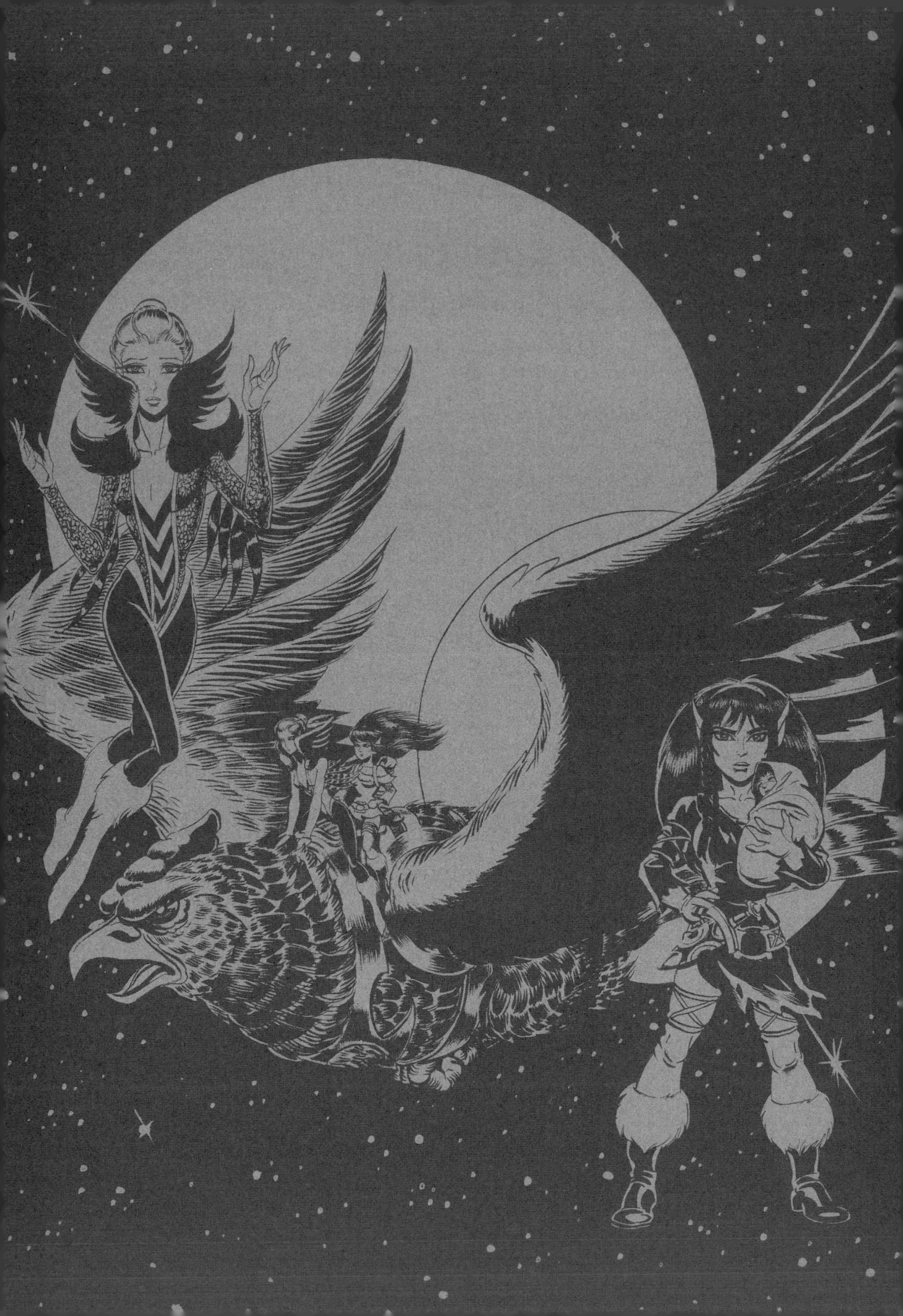

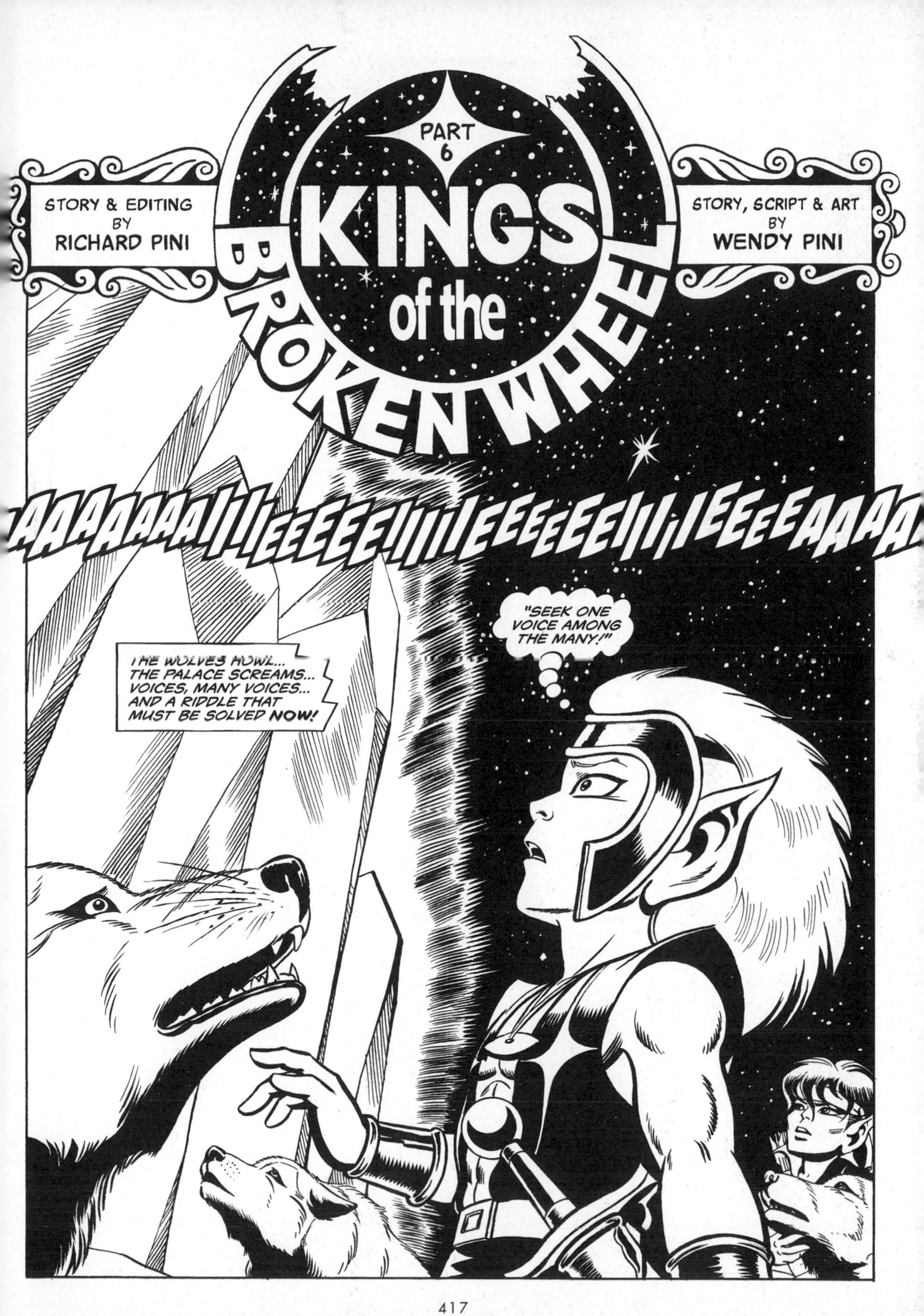
PART 6
KINGS of the BROKEN WHEEL
STORY & EDITING BY RICHARD PINI
STORY, SCRIPT & ART BY WENDY PINI
AAAAAAAIIIIEEEEEEIIIIIEEEEEEEIIIIEEEEAAAA
"SEEK ONE VOICE AMONG THE MANY!"
THE WOLVES HOWL... THE PALACE SCREAMS... VOICES, MANY VOICES... AND A RIDDLE THAT MUST BE SOLVED NOW!

AFTER DAYS AND NIGHTS SPENT WITHIN THE PALACE'S POWERFUL AURA, THE WOLFRIDERS--INCLUDING *SKYWISE* THE STARGAZER--FEEL A KEEN HEIGHTENING OF THEIR SENSES.

RAYEK!

TIMMAIN...HIGH ONE...THE ONE VOICE YOU WANT US TO FIND-- IT'S THE KEY, RIGHT? IT EXPLAINS THE CRY!

RRUUURRFFF!

RAAAAAAAAAAAAAAAAAIIIIEEEE!IIIIEEEEE!

RAYEK!

RAYEK, STOP...STOP! LISTEN TO ME!

SANDS OF THE BOUNDLESS WASTE! WHY DO YOU INTERRUPT?!

BECAUSE YOU'LL *NEVER* GET A RESPONSE FROM THE STRANGER ELVES THAT WAY!

THERE'S JUST *ONE* VOICE YOU SHOULD BE SEARCHING FOR, JUST *ONE* YOU MUST HEAR! *TIMMAIN* SAID...

TIMMAIN?! SHE HAS...SPOKEN TO YOU?

BY A WOLF SEND, YES!

"SEEK ONE VOICE AMONG THE MANY." SHE MEANT WITHIN THE *CRY*, I KNOW IT!

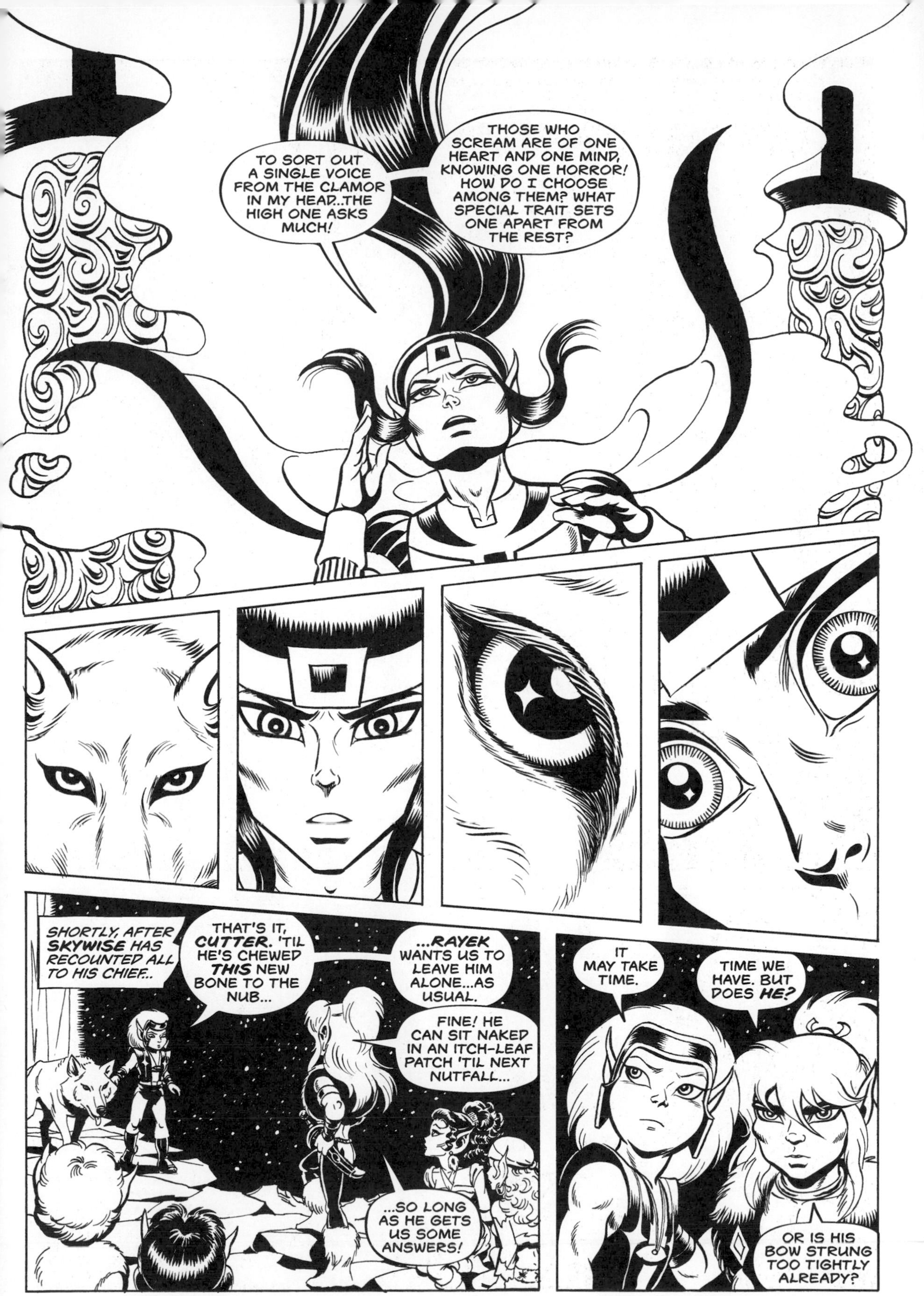
TO SORT OUT A SINGLE VOICE FROM THE CLAMOR IN MY HEAD..THE HIGH ONE ASKS MUCH!
THOSE WHO SCREAM ARE OF ONE HEART AND ONE MIND, KNOWING ONE HORROR! HOW DO I CHOOSE AMONG THEM? WHAT SPECIAL TRAIT SETS ONE APART FROM THE REST?
SHORTLY, AFTER SKYWISE HAS RECOUNTED ALL TO HIS CHIEF..
THAT'S IT, CUTTER. 'TIL HE'S CHEWED THIS NEW BONE TO THE NUB...
...RAYEK WANTS US TO LEAVE HIM ALONE...AS USUAL.
FINE! HE CAN SIT NAKED IN AN ITCH-LEAF PATCH 'TIL NEXT NUTFALL...
...SO LONG AS HE GETS US SOME ANSWERS!
IT MAY TAKE TIME.
TIME WE HAVE. BUT DOES HE?
OR IS HIS BOW STRUNG TOO TIGHTLY ALREADY?

THAT SAME NIGHT, HALF A WORLD AWAY...

SKYWISE...MY ONLY FRIEND... YOU HAVE ABANDONED ME!

KAWW KAWWW KAWWW

:GASP: LITTLETRILL! SOMEONE IS COMING?!

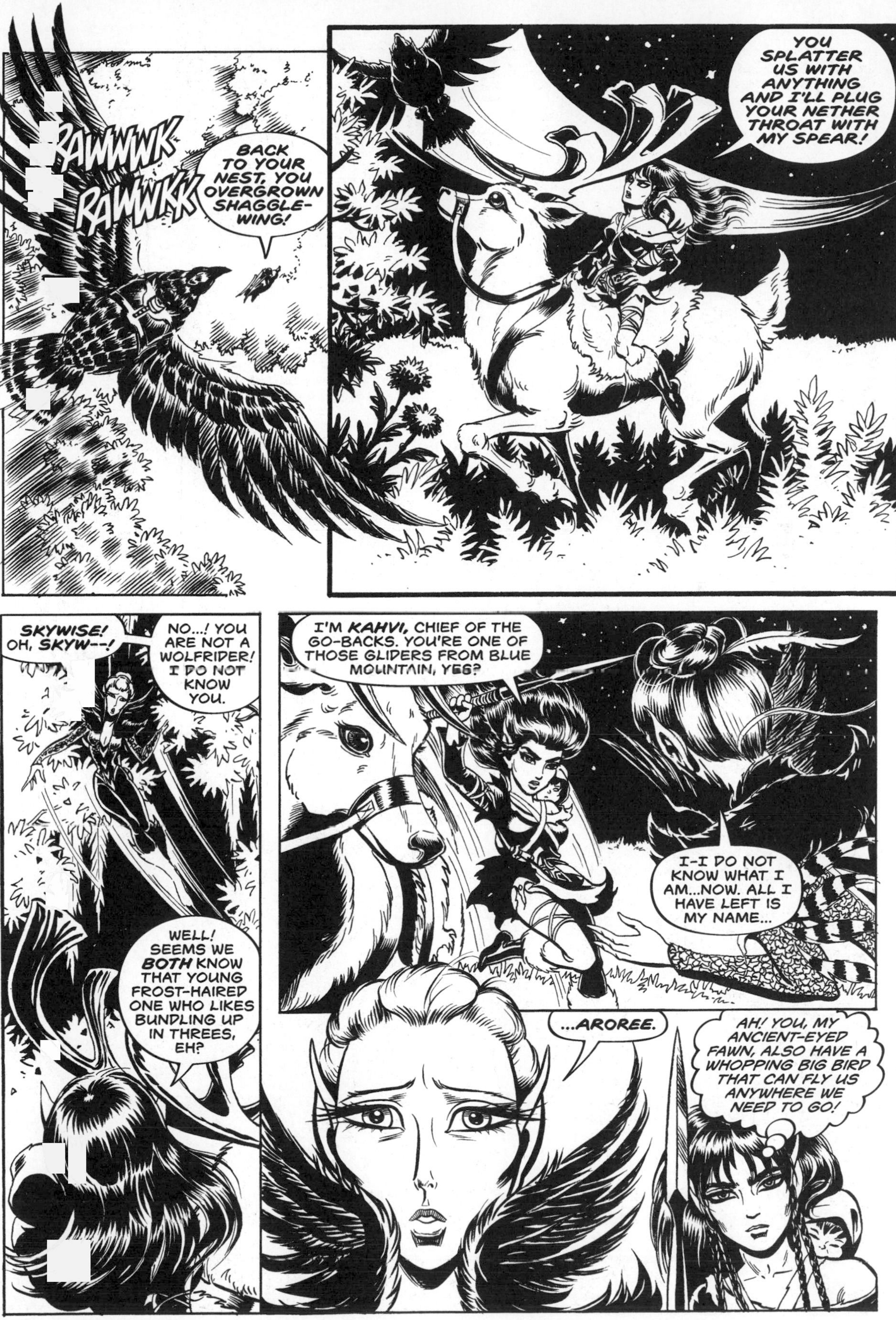
RAWWWK
RAWWKK
BACK TO YOUR NEST, YOU OVERGROWN SHAGGLE-WING!
YOU SPLATTER US WITH ANYTHING AND I'LL PLUG YOUR NETHER THROAT WITH MY SPEAR!
SKYWISE! OH, SKYW--!
NO...! YOU ARE NOT A WOLFRIDER! I DO NOT KNOW YOU.
I'M KAHVI, CHIEF OF THE GO-BACKS. YOU'RE ONE OF THOSE GLIDERS FROM BLUE MOUNTAIN, YES?
I-I DO NOT KNOW WHAT I AM...NOW. ALL I HAVE LEFT IS MY NAME...
WELL! SEEMS WE BOTH KNOW THAT YOUNG FROST-HAIRED ONE WHO LIKES BUNDLING UP IN THREES, EH?
...AROREE.
AH! YOU, MY ANCIENT-EYED FAWN, ALSO HAVE A WHOPPING BIG BIRD THAT CAN FLY US ANYWHERE WE NEED TO GO!

FEELING A TOUCH OF SYMPATHY BUT FEIGNING EVEN MORE, KAHVI HEARS **AROREE** OUT.

WHEN I FLED FROM BLUE MOUNTAIN AND MY LORD **WINNOWILL'S** GEM-HARD RULE, I COULD LOOK NOWHERE BUT TO MY FRIEND, **SKYWISE.**

"HE TOLD ME TO FLY TO THE PALACE OF THE HIGH ONES, TO VIEW THE SCROLL OF COLORS, AND...AND TO FILL MYSELF WITH KNOWLEDGE.

"ON MY WAY TO THE FROZEN MOUNTAINS, I WAS TURNED FROM MY PATH BY A DARK-SKINNED ONE NAMED **RAYEK...** WHO BEGGED ME TO TAKE HIM TO **WINNOWILL.**

"HE...HE WAS MOST PERSUASIVE! BUT IN THE END, HE HAD TO BE CONTENT WITH THE FORBIDDEN GROVE.

"AGAIN I FLEW NORTH! AGAIN I WAS TURNED FROM MY PATH...THIS TIME BY THE DREAD SIGHT OF BATTLE AND BLOODSHED SO CLOSE TO THE SACRED PALACE!

"AFTER THAT, MY MIND SEEMED FULL OF DARK CLOUDS. I LOST MY WAY... WANDERED. FINALLY MY HAWK BROUGHT ME BACK TO HIS REMEMBERED AERIE.

"BUT NOTHING... NOTHING REMAINED! SOMEHOW...BLUE MOUNTAIN HAD FALLEN! AND MY PEOPLE, **WINNOWILL,** EVEN THE CHOSEN EIGHT WERE GONE!

"MY LAST HOPE OF COMFORT LAY HERE IN THE FORBIDDEN GROVE, BUT, AS YOU SEE, EVEN THE WOLFRIDERS HAVE LEFT THEIR HOLT! PERHAPS THEY ARE ALL DEAD.

"I AM WITHOUT A LORD TO SERVE AND WITHOUT A SAFE PLACE TO DWELL... AMONG FRIENDS."

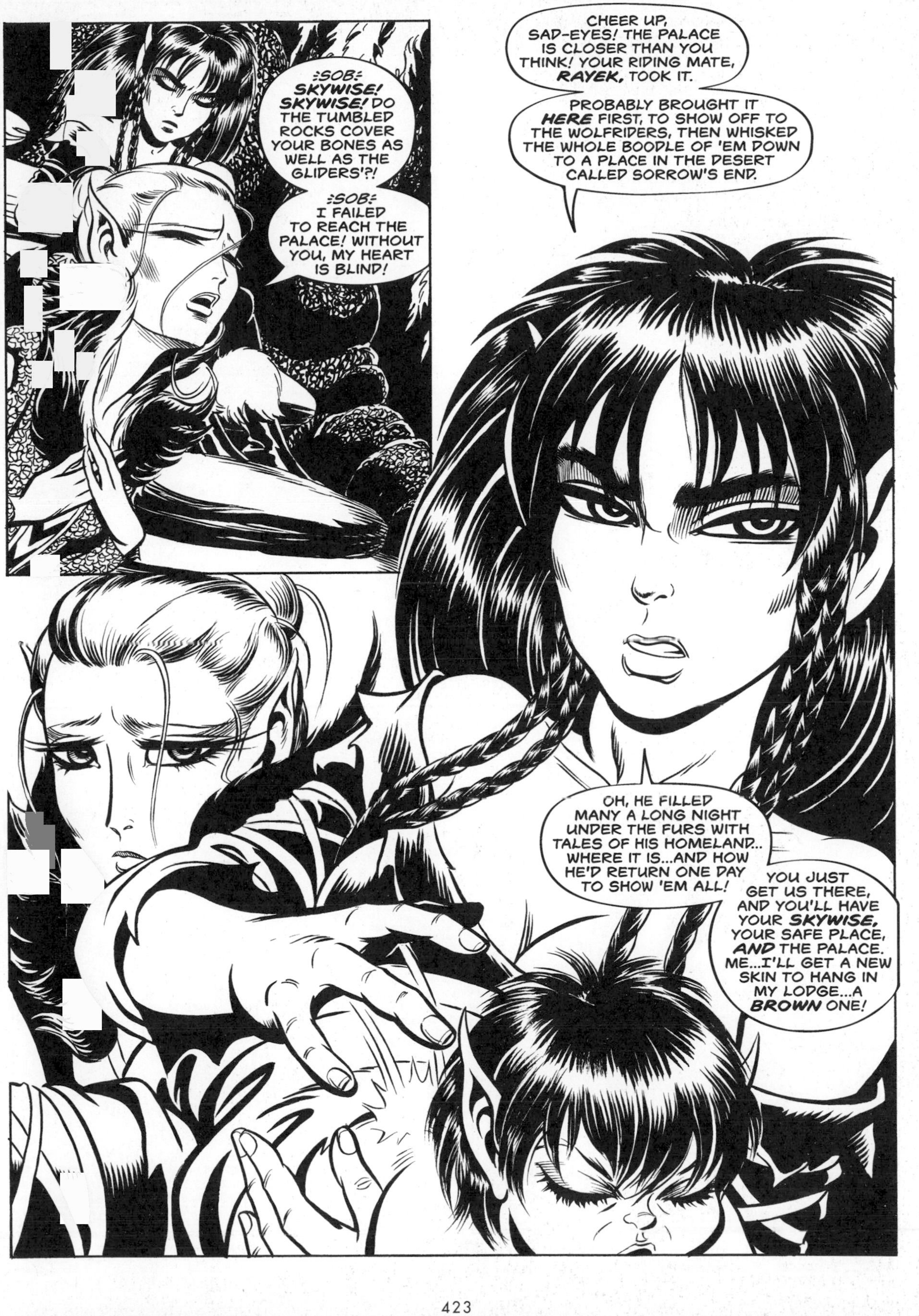

:SOB: SKYWISE! SKYWISE! DO THE TUMBLED ROCKS COVER YOUR BONES AS WELL AS THE GLIDERS'?!
:SOB: I FAILED TO REACH THE PALACE! WITHOUT YOU, MY HEART IS BLIND!
CHEER UP, SAD-EYES! THE PALACE IS CLOSER THAN YOU THINK! YOUR RIDING MATE, RAYEK, TOOK IT.
PROBABLY BROUGHT IT HERE FIRST, TO SHOW OFF TO THE WOLFRIDERS, THEN WHISKED THE WHOLE BOODLE OF 'EM DOWN TO A PLACE IN THE DESERT CALLED SORROW'S END.
OH, HE FILLED MANY A LONG NIGHT UNDER THE FURS WITH TALES OF HIS HOMELAND... WHERE IT IS...AND HOW HE'D RETURN ONE DAY TO SHOW 'EM ALL!
YOU JUST GET US THERE, AND YOU'LL HAVE YOUR SKYWISE, YOUR SAFE PLACE, AND THE PALACE. ME...I'LL GET A NEW SKIN TO HANG IN MY LODGE...A BROWN ONE!

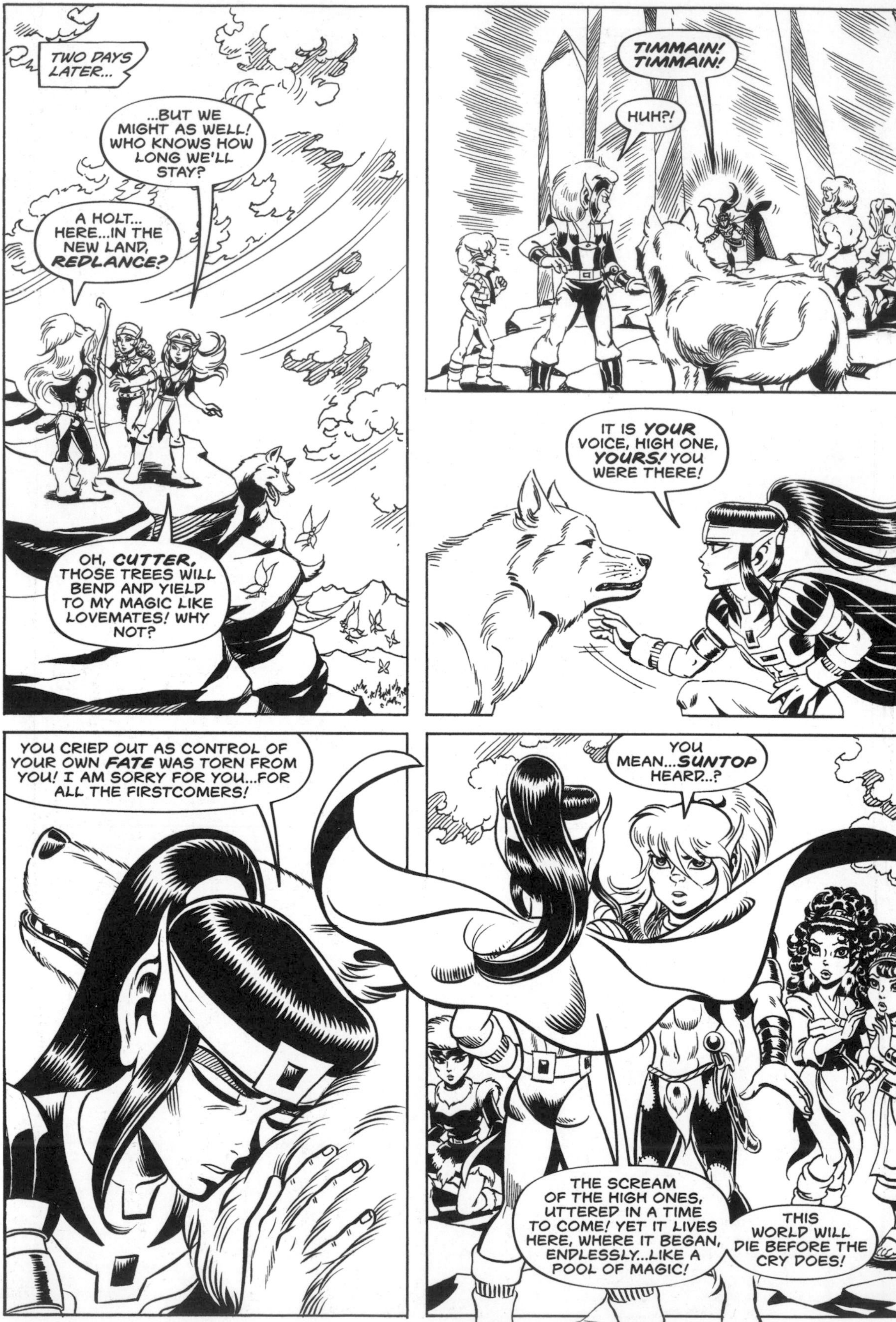
TWO DAYS LATER...
A HOLT... HERE...IN THE NEW LAND, REDLANCE?
...BUT WE MIGHT AS WELL! WHO KNOWS HOW LONG WE'LL STAY?
OH, CUTTER, THOSE TREES WILL BEND AND YIELD TO MY MAGIC LIKE LOVEMATES! WHY NOT?
TIMMAIN! TIMMAIN!
HUH?!
IT IS YOUR VOICE, HIGH ONE, YOURS! YOU WERE THERE!
YOU CRIED OUT AS CONTROL OF YOUR OWN FATE WAS TORN FROM YOU! I AM SORRY FOR YOU...FOR ALL THE FIRSTCOMERS!
YOU MEAN...SUNTOP HEARD...?
THE SCREAM OF THE HIGH ONES, UTTERED IN A TIME TO COME! YET IT LIVES HERE, WHERE IT BEGAN, ENDLESSLY...LIKE A POOL OF MAGIC!
THIS WORLD WILL DIE BEFORE THE CRY DOES!

...AND *SUNTOP* WAS THE FIRST OF US TO HEAR IT!

WHSSH! BY ALL THE WOLVES I'VE RIDDEN!

???

!!!

OHHH! I WISH THE HIGH ONES DIDN'T...THAT THEY WEREN'T SO SCARED...SO LOST! I WISH I COULD GO TO THEM AND SAY EVERYTHING WILL BE ALL RIGHT.

AND I WISH THEY COULD HAVE KNOWN ABOUT *YOU*, LITTLE ONE...THAT ONE DAY AN ELF CHILD WOULD BE BORN WHOSE POWERS THIS WORLD COULD NOT DRAIN!

TO TOUCH THE STARS WAS ALWAYS DREAM ENOUGH FOR ME. BUT *SUNTOP* AND *RAYEK*...! THEY'VE TOUCHED...*TIME!*

SUDDENLY...

"GO TO THEM," THE BOY SAID...

HUNH? WHAT'S GOT HOLD OF HIM *NOW?*

⸸SIGH⸸ *CLEARBROOK,* IF THIS MEANS WE'VE NO MORE REASON TO STAY HERE, I'LL BE SAD.

I TOO, DEAR ONE. EVERYTHING HAS A SOUL, EVEN A LAND. I COULD ALMOST SAY I'VE *RECOGNIZED* THIS ONE.

WHAT BEFALLS BY ACCIDENT CAN BE RE-CREATED... BY DESIGN!

MY AWARENESS AND CONTROL WILL MAKE ALL THE DIFFERENCE!

RAYEK, WAIT! WE CAME TO HELP STRANGERS IN NEED, AND THEY TURNED OUT TO BE THE HIGH ONES!

WE KNOW WHAT HAPPENED TO THEM...BUT YOU SAY IT HASN'T HAPPENED YET? EXPLAIN!

YES. OF ALL THE WOLFRIDERS, YOU MAY BEST BE ABLE TO GRASP IT.

CUTTER HEEDS YOU OVER ME. YOU MUST MAKE HIM UNDERSTAND!

∗GIGGLE∗

???

∗SHHH∗ TRINKET RAN AWAY! CAME TO PLAY WITH EMBER ELF!

HO! YOU LIGHT UP THE SCROLL OF COLORS WITH YOUR SMILE, BROWNSKIN!

I AM HAPPY, EKUAR! A DREAM OF SORROW AND LIMITATION IS ABOUT TO VANISH! WE AWAKE TO FREEDOM!

NEVER BEFORE HAS THE AIR IN THE SCROLL ROOM CRACKLED WITH THE FORCE OF A GATHERING STORM!

WHAT DO YOU KNOW OF TIME, WOLFRIDER?

THAT IT PASSES...THAT THE SEASONS TURN...

MUCH LIKE A *WHEEL*...

THE STARS TOO!

GOING ROUND AND ROUND FOREVER, EH?

TIME IS LIKE THAT--AT LEAST...OUR LITTLE PART IN IT. WHEN THE HIGH ONES FIRST APPEARED, THEY WERE EXILED INTO THE "LONG AGO."

BUT WE, THEIR UNDYING CHILDREN, ARE SLOWLY CATCHING UP...

T-TO WHAT?

TO THAT "FAR-AHEAD" TIME...TO THE MOMENT OF THE HIGH ONES' ARRIVAL.

YOU MEAN... IT'S LIKE A CIRCLE?

A *FULL* CIRCLE, TO BE COMPLETED COUNTLESS YEARS FROM NOW...

...OR...

...IN THE BLINK OF AN EYE!

HUH?!

WISE *SAVAH!* SHE SAW THE POSSIBILITY. NOW I AM SURE IT CAN BE DONE!

WHAT? WHAT?!

WE CAN BE THERE TO GREET THE FIRSTCOMERS!

WE CAN PREVENT THE TROLL REBELLION WHICH HURLED THEM BACK INTO THE WRONG PLACE AND TIME!

SLOW DOWN, BROWNSKIN! YOU'RE SAYING...WE CAN FLY THROUGH *TIME?*

INDEED! THE CRY STILL RESOUNDS IN MY MIND. IT IS THE TORCH WE SHALL FOLLOW IN THE DARK!

WITH THE POWER OF THE PALACE, WE WILL GO FROM *NOW* TO *THEN* AND RESCUE THE HIGH ONES!

THEIR CRY OF TERROR WILL NEVER EXIST...

...AND NEITHER, I DARESAY, WILL THE OFFSPRING OF THOSE BETRAYING TROLLS!

HOLD IT!

THAT ONE CHANGE WILL WIPE OUT ALL THE TROLLS? WH-WHAT ABOUT THE SUN FOLK, THE GO-BACKS, AND US?

WE'RE HERE BECAUSE OF THAT ACCIDENT, JUST LIKE THE TROLLS! WILL *WE* BE WIPED OUT TOO?

NOT IF YOU ARE WITH ME IN THE PALACE.

THE WOLFRIDERS AND THE SUN FOLK WILL LEAVE THIS TIME BEHIND!

THIS PALACE...AND THAT OF THE FIRSTCOMERS... ARE ONE AND THE SAME!

WE WILL MERGE THEM AND FIND OUR TRUE FORTUNES AMONG THE STARS!

NO!

WHAT?!

I SAID NO.

THE TROLLS AND GO-BACKS WEREN'T INVITED, I NOTICE. WHY STOP THERE?

WHY NOT DITCH THE WOLFRIDERS TOO? WE'RE "TAINTED" AFTER ALL. AND WHY BOTHER WITH THE SUN FOLK? THEY FAILED TO APPRECIATE YOU.

WHO'S LEFT? *TYLDAK?* OR...

AH, YES, *WINNOWILL!* NOW, *SHE'S* FIT COMPANY FOR YOU. HER VISION IS LIKE YOURS, AND SHE'S VERY CLEAR ABOUT WHO SHOULD AND SHOULDN'T LIVE!

FOOL! YOU'VE TWISTED ALL I--

CURSE YOU! I'VE NEVER UNDERSTOOD *WINNOWILL* OR YOU! *TIMMORN'S BLOOD!* WHAT DO YOU WANT? WHAT'S MISSING?

NOTHING STICKS WITH YOU! KINDNESS, RESPECT, LOVE... NONE OF IT'S ENOUGH!

YOU'VE NEVER KNOWN PEACE HERE! WHAT MAKES YOU THINK YOU'LL FIND IT IN ANY OTHER PLACE OR TIME?!

I PITY YOU, WOLF CHIEF, THAT THIS IS YOUR BE-ALL AND END-ALL! I PITY YOU, THAT YOUR BODY MUST AGE AND DECAY.

ALL THIS WORLD'S CREATURES WALK THAT PATH, BLACK-HAIR.

MUST WE?

AND WE IMMORTALS, WHO ARE NOT PART OF THIS WORLD, WHAT ARE WE TO DO?

GO CRAZY, IT SEEMS.

LOOK, EITHER YOU TAKE EVERY LAST LIVING ELF, TROLL, AND PRESERVER WITH YOU ON THIS MAD ZWOOT CHASE...

IMPOSSIBLE!

...OR YOU DON'T GO!

IF I HEARD RIGHT...YOU RESCUE THE HIGH ONES, AND EVERYTHING THEIR CHILDREN HAVE FOUGHT FOR THROUGH THE MANY SEASONS--HOME, KIN, LIFE ITSELF-- WILL DISAPPEAR!

I CAN'T ALLOW YOUR CHOICE TO WIPE OUT SO MANY OTHERS' CHOICES.

YOUR MIND IS TOO SMALL TO FORESEE THE GREATER GOOD—

ENOUGH! WE'RE *HERE* AND *NOW* AND I SAY NO!

KEEP TO YOUR OATH, OR YOU'RE NO LONGER MASTER OF THE PALACE!

YOU... DARE...?!

SHALL I MAKE YOU A SPIRIT? MAYBE *THEN* YOU'LL SEE THINGS DIFF—

UNH!

YOU...!

:GASP: N-NO, *SKYWISE!* IT'S ALL RIGHT.

I JUST FORGOT...

MOST OF *RAYEK'S* POWER IS BORROWED FROM THE PALACE. BUT *MINE* IS IN MY FAMILY!

THE TWINS ARE TIED TOGETHER. *EMBER* WAS WITH US WHEN WE BROKE *WINNOWILL'S* SPELL OVER THE EGG SLAVES!

DON'T TRY US, *RAYEK!* YOU'LL FALL LIKE THE BLACK SNAKE DID!

RRRRRUUUFFFF!

THEN LET THE HIGH ONE CHOOSE...BETWEEN THE BEAST LIFE SHE LIVES NOW...

AND A TIMELY RESCUE WHICH WOULD PREVENT ANY NEED FOR SUCH A SHAPE CHANGE.

TIMMAIN, YOU CRIED OUT WITH THE OTHERS. THIS BANISHMENT... THIS-THIS GROUNDING CANNOT BE WHAT YOU WANTED!

IT CAN UN-HAPPEN! AND YET YOUR CHILDREN, THE WOLFRIDERS, CAN STILL BE WITH YOU. IS THAT NOT BEST?

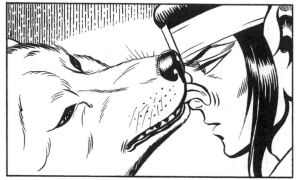

SHE WON'T TAKE SIDES. FOR GOOD OR ILL, WHAT HAPPENED TO THE HIGH ONES HAPPENED.

I SAY IT WAS FOR THE GOOD.

YOU FOUR REASON WITH HIM. YOU'RE THE ONLY ONES, HERE, THAT HE RESPECTS. I NEED TO COOL OFF.

I SAY WE DON'T TRY TO CHANGE IT.

TAM...!

"NO ELF MUST DIE."

BUT RAYEK'S MEDDLING WITH ALL THAT HAS BEEN OR WILL BE! THE WAY DOESN'T TAKE THAT IN!

WE CAN'T JUST BIND HIM IN WRAPSTUFF AND DUMP HIM SOMEWHERE!

WE DON'T KNOW THE HALF OF WHAT HE CAN DO. STRONGBOW SAYS DEATH CAN GENTLE AN ELF'S SPIRIT...

BELOVED! YOU... YOU REALLY WOULD KILL RAYEK IF...?

UNLESS YOU CAN WEAN HIM AWAY FROM HIS SCHEME...

...IT MAY COME TO THAT.

ELSEWHERE...

THERE, *AROREE!* THAT MUST BE THE MOUNTAIN RANGE *RAYEK* CALLED WORLD'S SPINE.

ALMOST DAWN...THIS BIG DUCK IS TIRED AND HUNGRY. HE'LL FRY IN THE HEAT OF DAY...AND SO WILL WE!

YOUR LAND FREEZES, HIS LAND BURNS. YOU ARE ICE AND HE IS FIRE. NO WONDER YOU HATE HIM!

WRONG, GIRL! DIFFERENCES MAKE GOOD SPARKS! IT'S HIS HAUGHTY AIRS I HATE. HE'S CROSSED A DEADLY LINE AND HE'LL PAY FOR IT!

"YOU KNOW, FOR ONCE I WAS THANKFUL FOR OLD *EKUAR'S* PUTTERING. THE COLD, UNDERGROUND STOREROOM HE SHAPED BENEATH THE LODGE FLOOR WAS SHELTER ENOUGH FOR *URDA*, THE BABE, AND ME.

"AFTER *RAYEK* STOLE THE PALACE AWAY, I FOUND MY TRIBE...AND SAW HIS FURTHER INSULT TO US!"

WE'VE NEVER LIVED WITHOUT THE STEADY TUG OF THE PALACE NEARBY. BUT WE'RE SURVIVORS! DIG IN YOUR CLAWS, GO-BACKS! DEPEND ON YOUR CHIEF'S VOW! I'LL GET EVEN WITH BLACK-HAIR...

AND IF NOT ME, MY DAUGHTER!

SO...YOUR TASK IS CLEAR. I SHALL NOT INTERFERE.

MY ONLY DESIRE IS TO FIND *SKYWISE.* HE IS MORE TO ME THAN THE PALACE OF THE HIGH ONES!

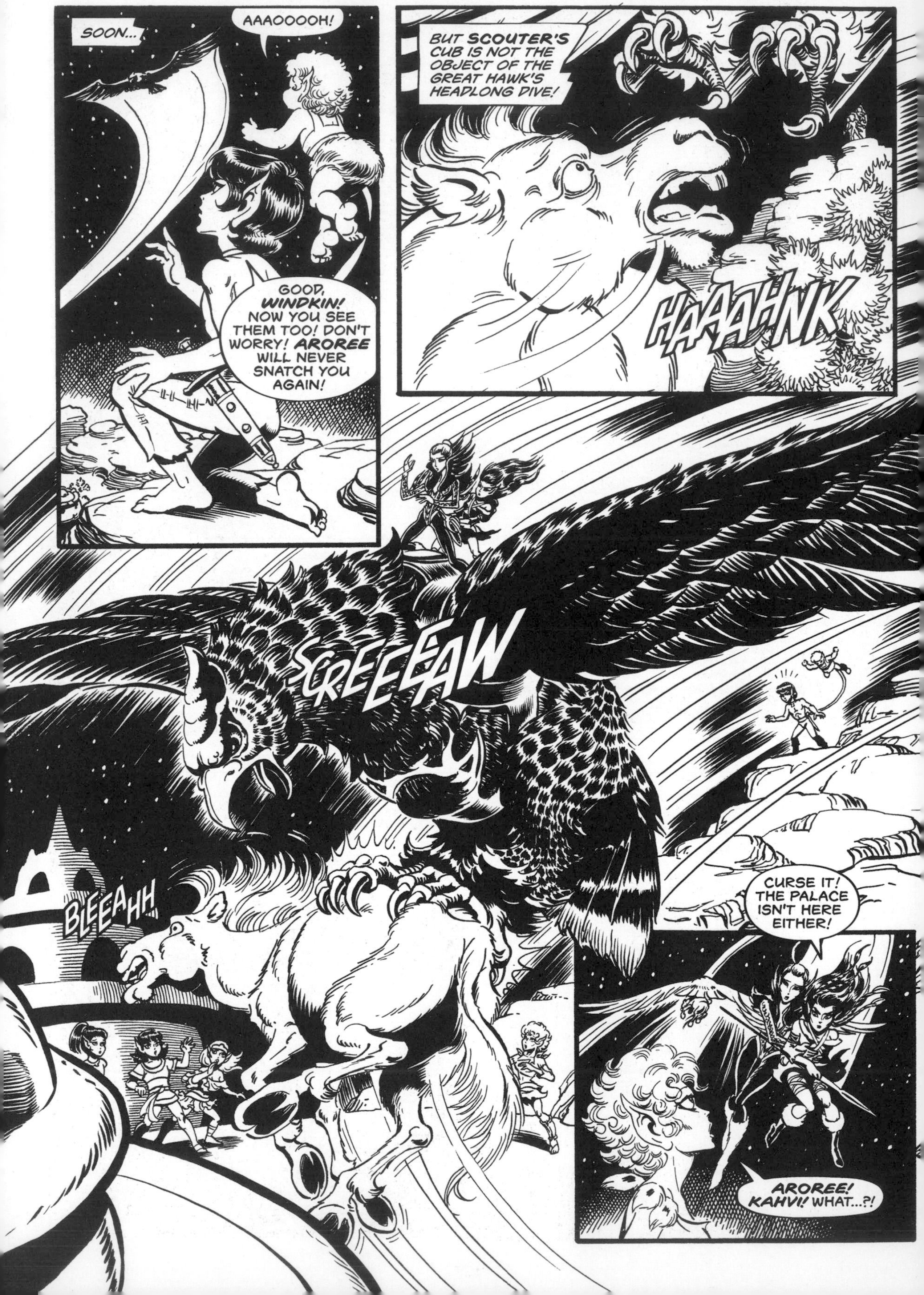
SOON...
AAAOOOOH!
GOOD, WINDKIN! NOW YOU SEE THEM TOO! DON'T WORRY! AROREE WILL NEVER SNATCH YOU AGAIN!
BUT SCOUTER'S CUB IS NOT THE OBJECT OF THE GREAT HAWK'S HEADLONG DIVE!
HAAAHNK
SCREEEEAW
BLEEAHH
CURSE IT! THE PALACE ISN'T HERE EITHER!
AROREE! KAHVI! WHAT...?!

SOME *DAINTY DIGGINGS!* THAT CROWNED ONE MUST BE *RAYEK'S* MUCH PRAISED MOTHER OF MEMORY!

MORE SUDDEN VISITORS TO THE SUN VILLAGE! AND WITH *NEW* FACES THIS TIME! *DEWSHINE,* YOU KNOW THEM?

NOT ALTOGETHER AS FRIENDS, *SAVAH...*BUT I THINK THEY MEAN NO HARM.

IT HAS BEEN LONG SINCE I LOOKED ONE OF *EQUAL* HEIGHT IN THE EYES.

AND SUCH *HAUNTED EYES!* WHO ARE YOU, PALE SISTER?

AH-AH-*AROREE...* ONCE OF BLUE MOUNTAIN!

CAREFUL... PLAY IT GENTLY!

YOU MAY HAVE HEARD THE *WOLFRIDERS'* TALES OF ME. I'M *KAHVI,* AND I'VE COME SEEKING MY LOVEMATE, *RAYEK...*

...TO SHOW HIM HIS *FIRSTBORN!*

OOOHHH...! PRECIOUS BEYOND WORDS! HER NAME?

VENKA!

HAD YOU COME BUT A FEW DAYS EARLIER, YOU COULD HAVE PLACED THE BABE IN *RAYEK'S* OWN ARMS!

FOR JUST ONE NIGHT HE BROUGHT THE PALACE OF THE HIGH ONES TO US. THEN HE AND THE WOLFRIDERS DEPARTED ON AN URGENT QUEST!

SKYWISE?! SKYWISE TOO?

YES, AS EVER, AT *CUTTER'S* SIDE! YOU SEE, HERE IN MY HUT, A FRAGMENT OF THE HIGH ONES' DWELLING.

SO IT IS! THE ROCK SHAPER'S WORK, I BET!

WHERE IS THE PALACE NOW, *SAVAH?* WHERE HAVE *SKYWISE* AND THE OTHERS GONE?

IT MEANS MUCH TO US TO KNOW...

...SO WE CAN BE WITH OUR LOVEMATES AND SHARE WHATEVER TRIALS AWAIT THEM.

THE PALACE CANNOT BE SEPARATED FROM ITSELF. THIS SMALL REPLICA KNOWS ALL THAT THE ORIGINAL KNOWS.

BEING NEAR IT ENHANCES MY VISIONS.

THE TRAVELERS ARE FAR AWAY IN ANOTHER LAND. THE MISTS DO NOT PART COMPLETELY.

BUT, AS IF FROM A HIGH VANTAGE, I CAN GLIMPSE GREAT EXPANSES OF GREEN AND BLUE, THE FLESH OF THAT LAND, BARELY COVERING THE MIGHTY MOUNTAINS THAT ARE ITS BONES!

TO GET THERE THE PALACE FLEW TOWARD THE SUN'S SETTING PLACE, ACROSS A VAST BODY OF WATER. OUR DEAR ONES ARE SAFE AND WELL.

AH, THAT'S GOOD NEWS! VERY GOOD NEWS INDEED!

SOON...

QUESTIONS! FOOD! GIFTS! UNASKED-FOR ADVICE! THE SUN FOLK GIVE YOU EVERYTHING BUT A MOMENT'S PEACE!

IF SKYWISE WERE HERE, I THINK I COULD BE HAPPY. BUT IT HARDLY MATTERS WHERE I DWELL NOW.

I TRULY DOUBT THAT LITTLETRILL COULD MAKE THE FLIGHT ACROSS THE VASTDEEP SEA. YOU AND THE CHILD WOULD DROWN WITH HIM.

AND I WOULD LAST BUT LITTLE LONGER!

EVEN IF WE WERE TO REACH THE NEW LAND, RAYEK IS MASTER OF THE PALACE AND ALL POWERFUL!

SUCH A ONE SEES ALL OTHERS AS MINIONS!

FROM SUCH A ONE, BELIEVE ME, IT IS BEST TO FLEE!

LOOK THERE!

ANTS CAN LIVE ANYWHERE! THEY'RE TINY, BUT THEY'RE SURVIVORS, LIKE MY TRIBE! IF YOU STEP ON THEM...

THEY SWARM BACK TO BITE YOU, THEY AND THEIR YOUNG!

AND SOMETIMES THE CHILDREN HAVE SHARPER STINGS THAN THEIR MOTHERS!

MEANWHILE...

YOU WASTE YOUR BREATH, *LEETAH!* THAT ROCK-SKULLED BARBARIAN DARED CHALLENGE MY MASTERY OF THE PALACE!

DEAR FRIEND, UNDERSTAND THAT THIS IS FAR MORE THAN THE SNARLING AND TESTING THAT HAVE ALWAYS GONE ON BETWEEN YOU AND *CUTTER.*

HIS DECISION IS FINAL.

IF YOU DO NOT BACK DOWN, HE WILL SIMPLY PUT AN END TO YOU!

OR I TO HIM!

YOU WILL STILL LOSE EVERYTHING. NO ONE WILL STAND WITH YOU!

YET, IF HE KILLS ME...NO ONE WILL BLAME HIM. IS IT SO, *LEETAH?* DO YOU NOT SEE, AS I DO, THAT OUR RACE'S ENTIRE EXISTENCE ON THIS WORLD IS A SHAM?

DOES NO ONE ELSE HUNGER TO BE WITH THE HIGH ONES...TO SAVE THEM AND OURSELVES FROM THIS WHEEL OF EMPTY STRUGGLE?

THE HIGH ONES ARE WITH *US,* SILLY! *TIMMAIN* IS A WOLF, AND ALL HER FRIENDS' SPIRITS LIVE RIGHT HERE!

YOU CAN'T FLY *THIS* PALACE TO A PLACE WHERE THE HIGH ONES' SPIRITS STILL LIVE IN THEIR *BODIES!* THEY'LL *POP* OR SOMETHING!

BLEND ONE CANDLE FLAME WITH ANOTHER...AND YOU REALIZE THEY NEVER WERE, NEVER COULD BE ANYTHING BUT *ONE.*

ANY FIRE IS *ALL* FIRE. AND ANY SPIRIT IS *ALL* SPIRIT. FOREVER! THE BLENDING TAKES UP NO SPACE INSIDE A BODY.

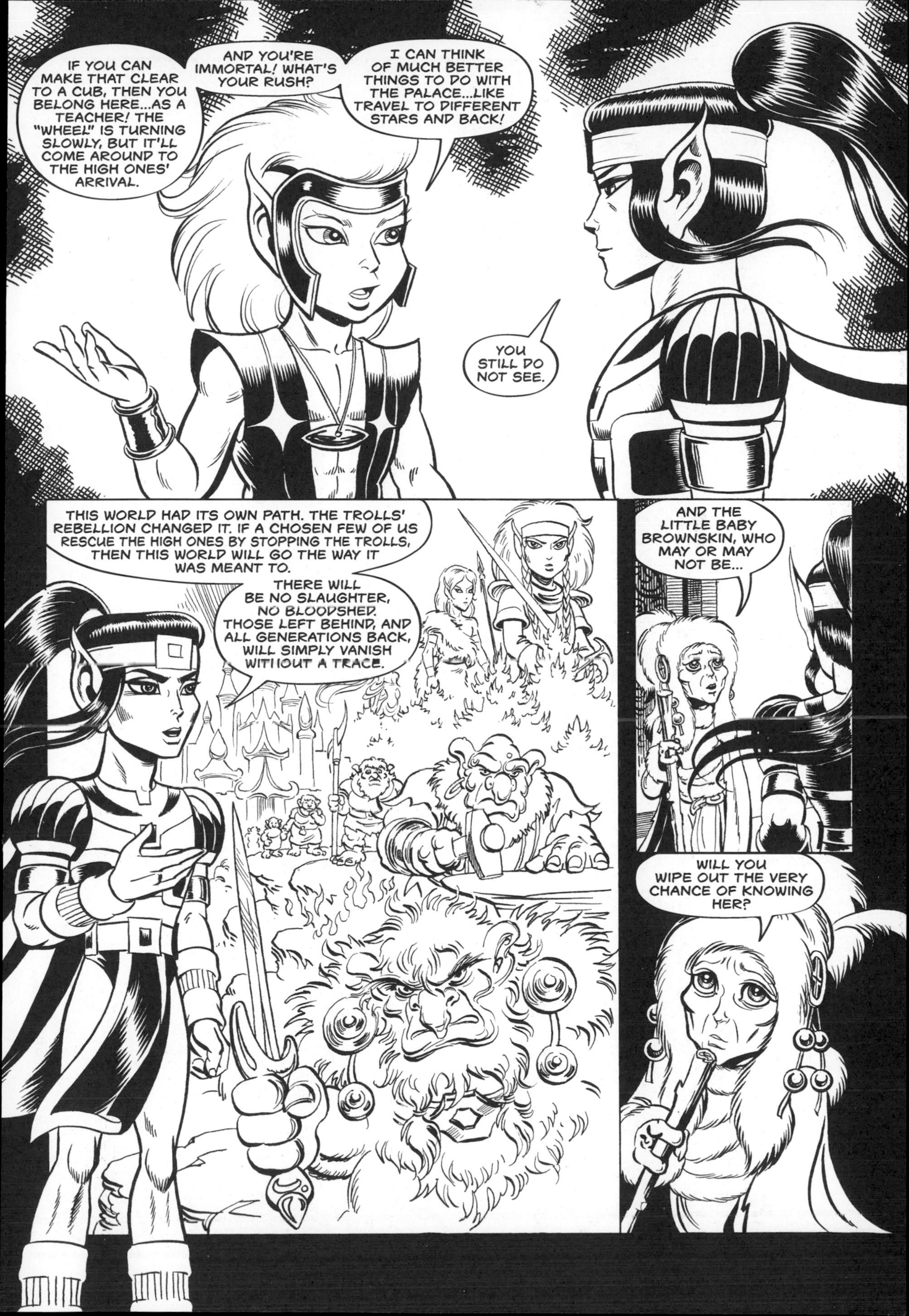
IF YOU CAN MAKE THAT CLEAR TO A CUB, THEN YOU BELONG HERE...AS A TEACHER! THE "WHEEL" IS TURNING SLOWLY, BUT IT'LL COME AROUND TO THE HIGH ONES' ARRIVAL.
AND YOU'RE IMMORTAL! WHAT'S YOUR RUSH?
I CAN THINK OF MUCH BETTER THINGS TO DO WITH THE PALACE...LIKE TRAVEL TO DIFFERENT STARS AND BACK!
YOU STILL DO NOT SEE.
THIS WORLD HAD ITS OWN PATH. THE TROLLS' REBELLION CHANGED IT. IF A CHOSEN FEW OF US RESCUE THE HIGH ONES BY STOPPING THE TROLLS, THEN THIS WORLD WILL GO THE WAY IT WAS MEANT TO.
THERE WILL BE NO SLAUGHTER, NO BLOODSHED. THOSE LEFT BEHIND, AND ALL GENERATIONS BACK, WILL SIMPLY VANISH WITHOUT A TRACE.
AND THE LITTLE BABY BROWNSKIN, WHO MAY OR MAY NOT BE...
WILL YOU WIPE OUT THE VERY CHANCE OF KNOWING HER?

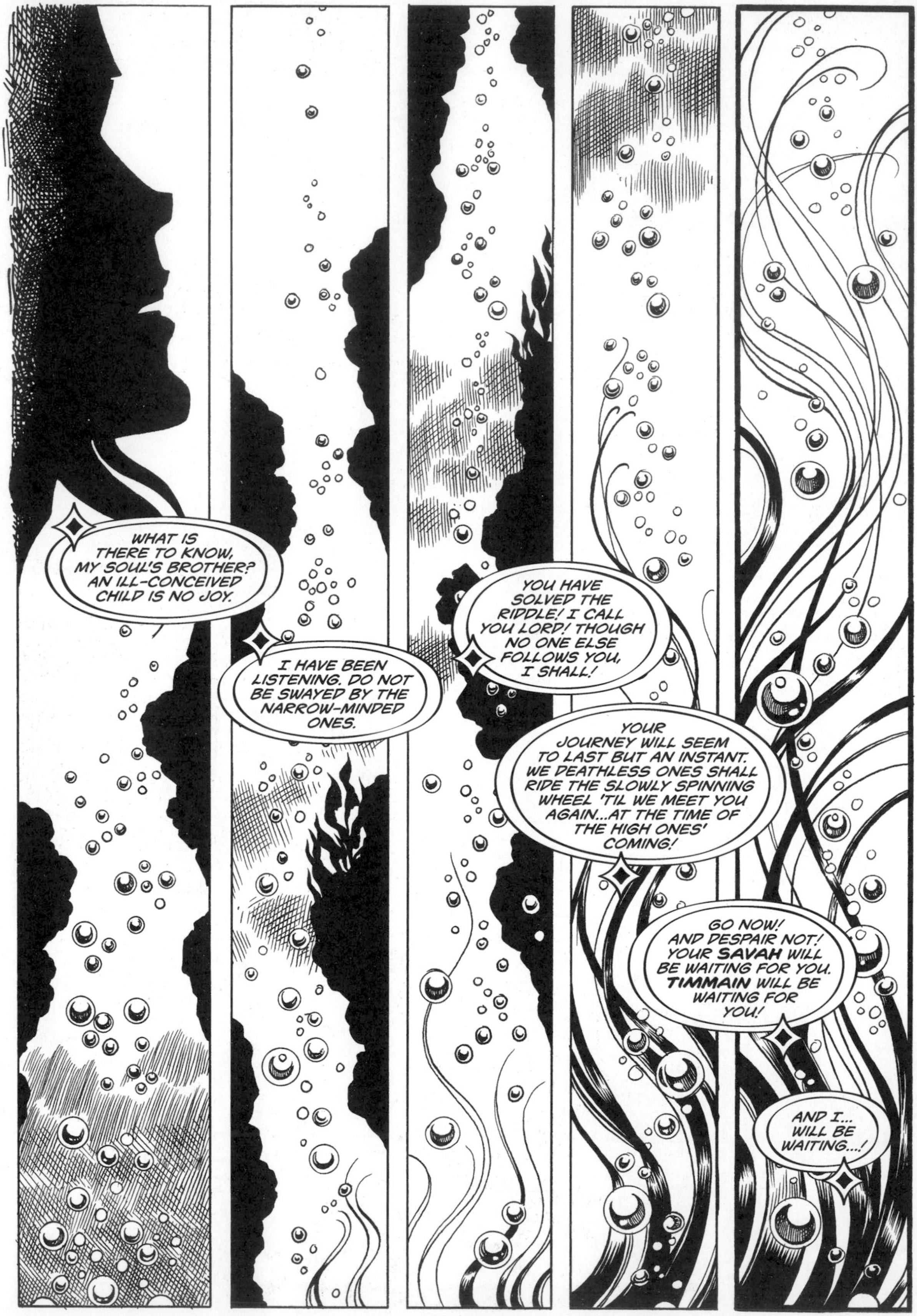
WHAT IS THERE TO KNOW, MY SOUL'S BROTHER? AN ILL-CONCEIVED CHILD IS NO JOY.
I HAVE BEEN LISTENING. DO NOT BE SWAYED BY THE NARROW-MINDED ONES.
YOU HAVE SOLVED THE RIDDLE! I CALL YOU LORD! THOUGH NO ONE ELSE FOLLOWS YOU, I SHALL!
YOUR JOURNEY WILL SEEM TO LAST BUT AN INSTANT. WE DEATHLESS ONES SHALL RIDE THE SLOWLY SPINNING WHEEL 'TIL WE MEET YOU AGAIN...AT THE TIME OF THE HIGH ONES' COMING!
GO NOW! AND DESPAIR NOT! YOUR SAVAH WILL BE WAITING FOR YOU. TIMMAIN WILL BE WAITING FOR YOU!
AND I... WILL BE WAITING...!

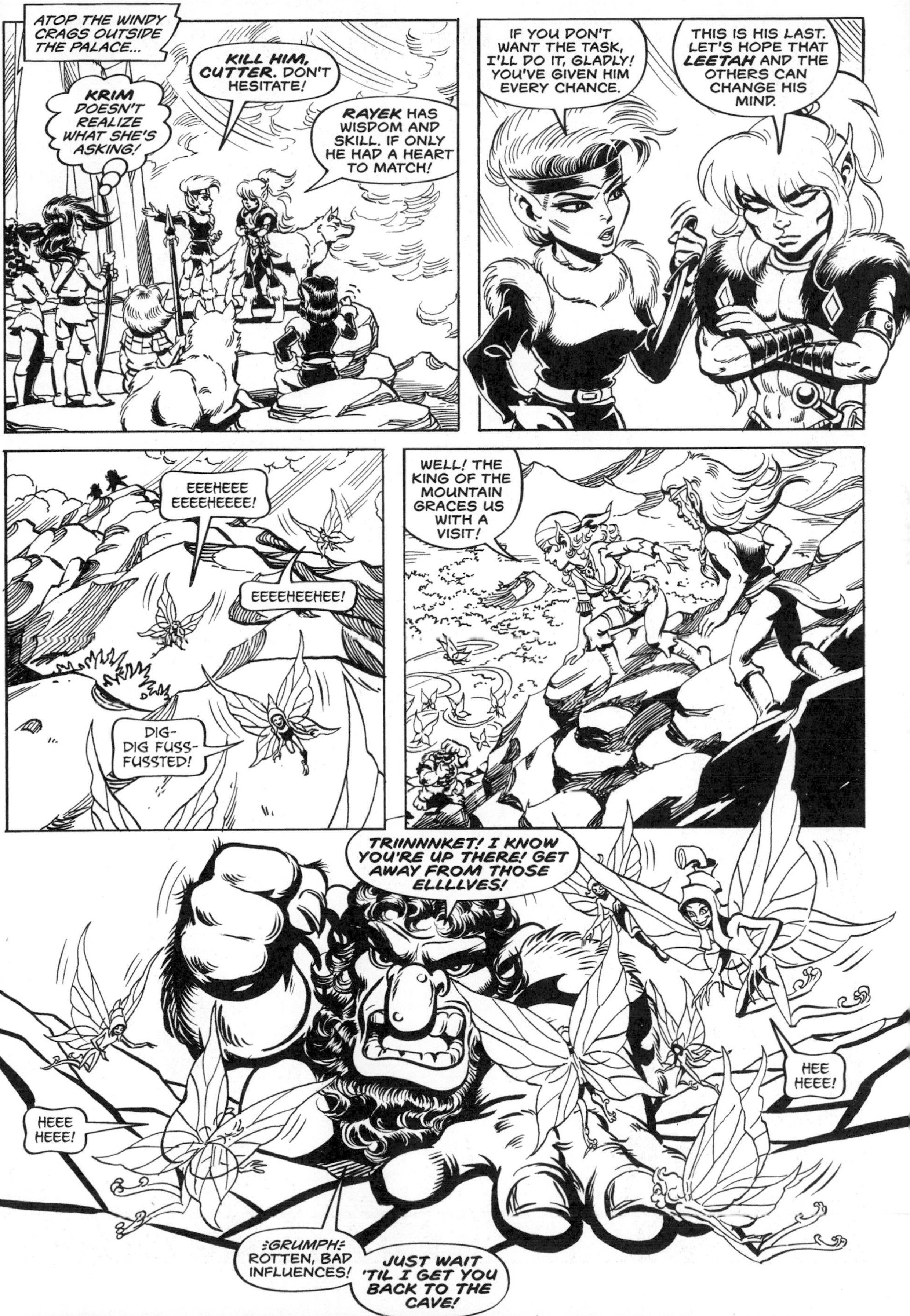

ATOP THE WINDY CRAGS OUTSIDE THE PALACE...
KRIM DOESN'T REALIZE WHAT SHE'S ASKING!
KILL HIM, CUTTER. DON'T HESITATE!
RAYEK HAS WISDOM AND SKILL. IF ONLY HE HAD A HEART TO MATCH!
IF YOU DON'T WANT THE TASK, I'LL DO IT, GLADLY! YOU'VE GIVEN HIM EVERY CHANCE.
THIS IS HIS LAST. LET'S HOPE THAT LEETAH AND THE OTHERS CAN CHANGE HIS MIND.
EEEHEEE EEEEHEEEE!
EEEEHEEHEE!
DIG-DIG FUSS-FUSSTED!
WELL! THE KING OF THE MOUNTAIN GRACES US WITH A VISIT!
TRIINNNKET! I KNOW YOU'RE UP THERE! GET AWAY FROM THOSE ELLLLVES!
HEE HEEE!
HEEE HEEE!
:GRUMPH: ROTTEN, BAD INFLUENCES!
JUST WAIT 'TIL I GET YOU BACK TO THE CAVE!

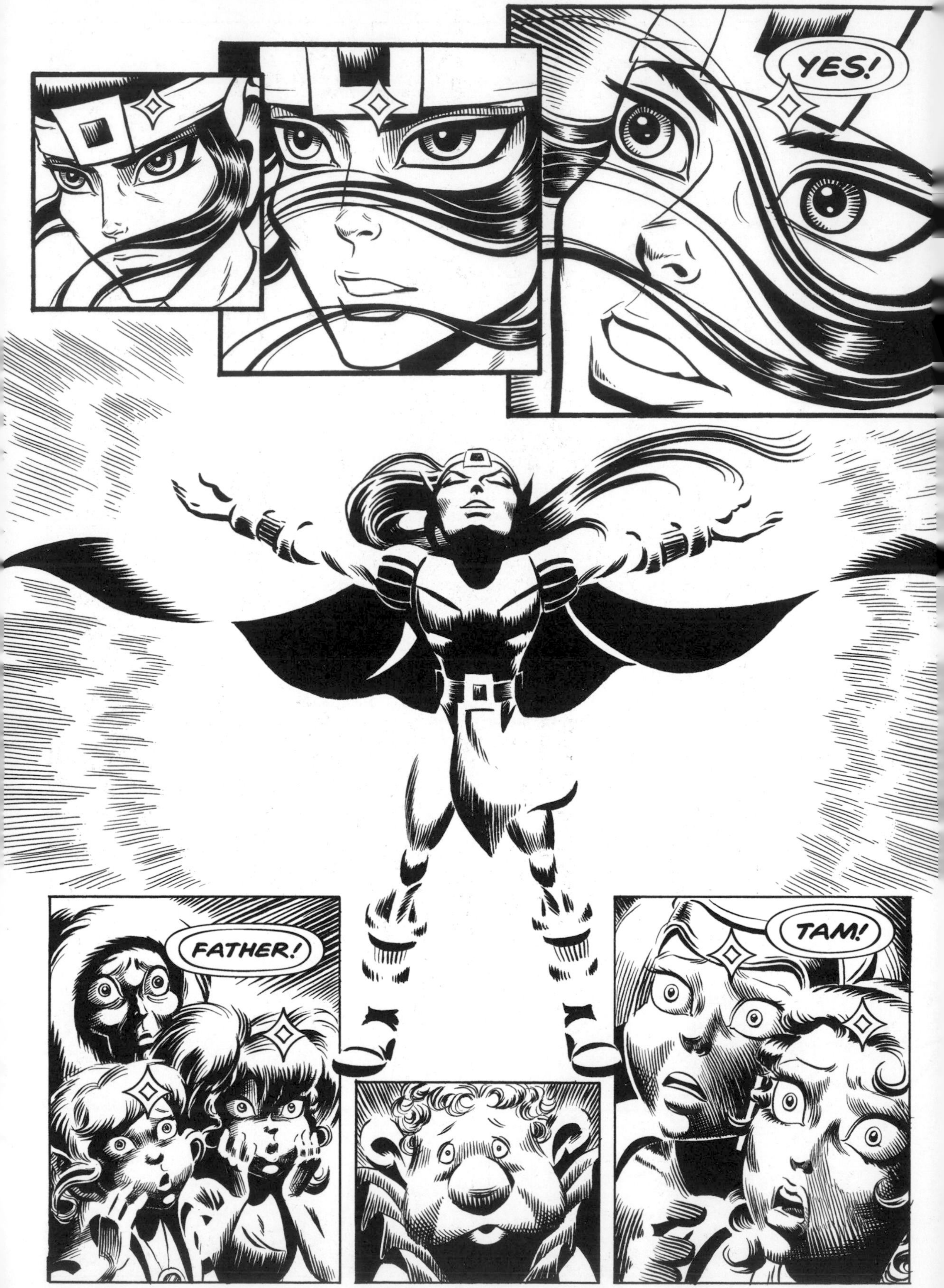
YES!
FATHER!
TAM!

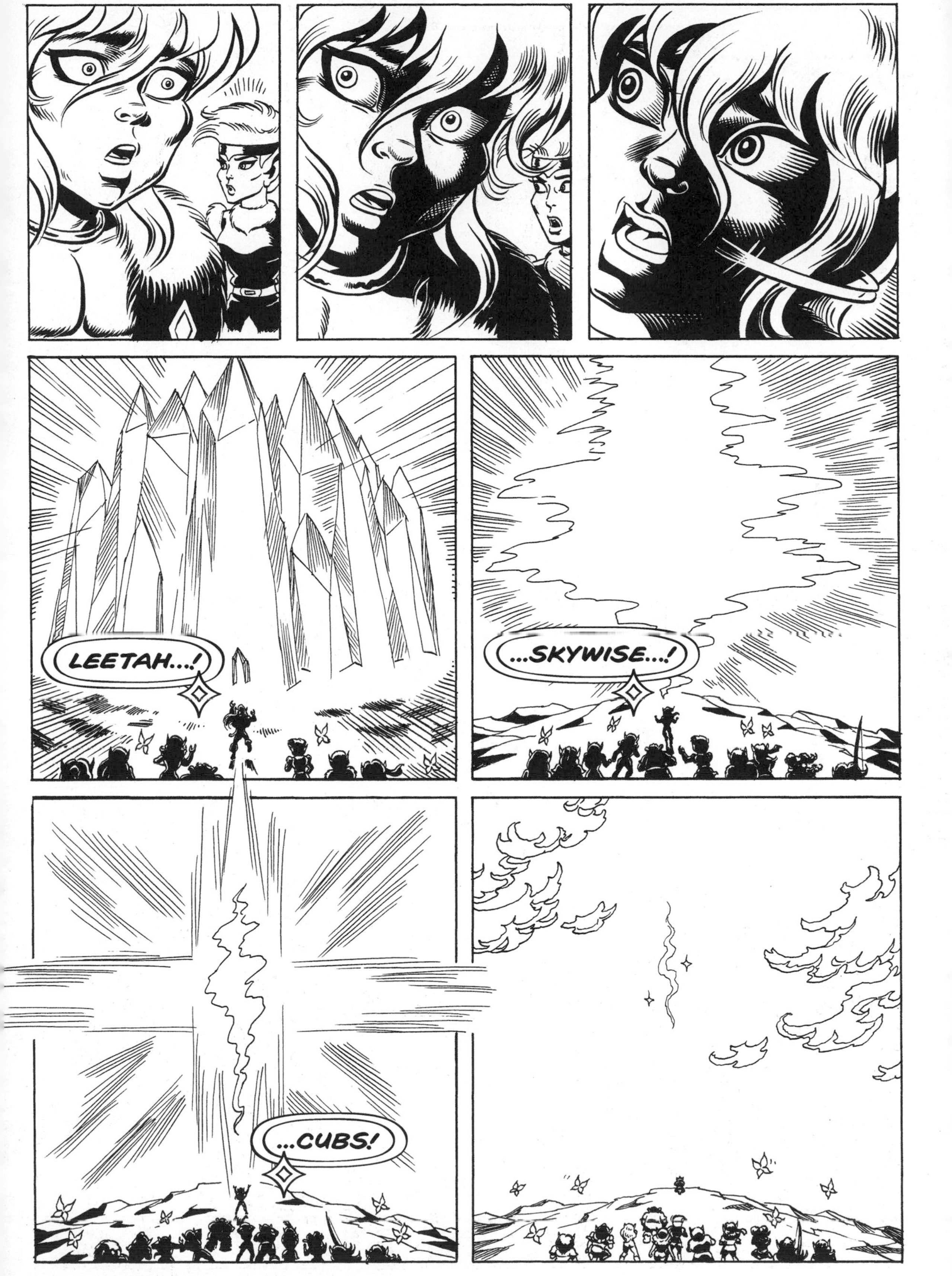
LEETAH...!
...SKYWISE...!
...CUBS!

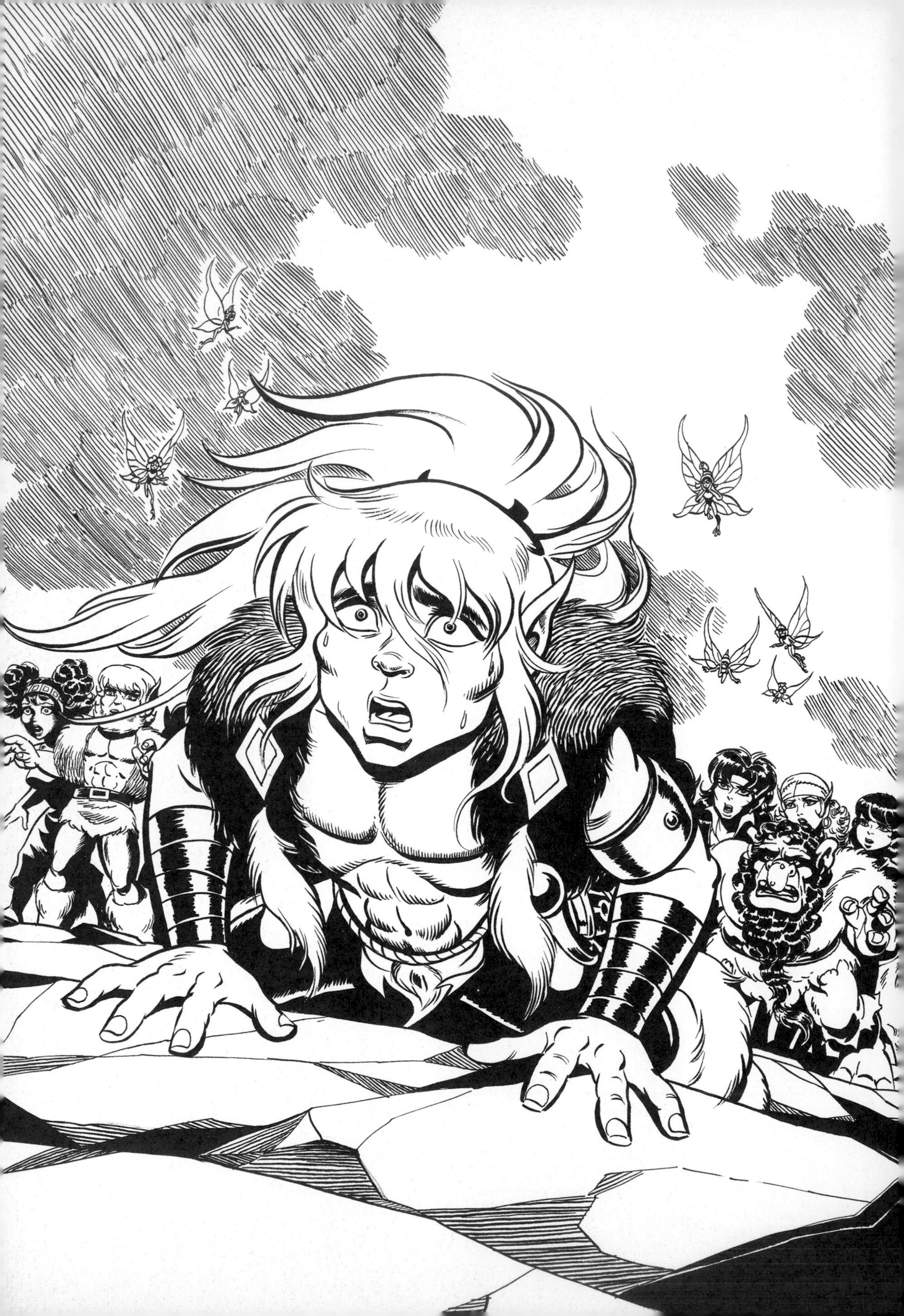

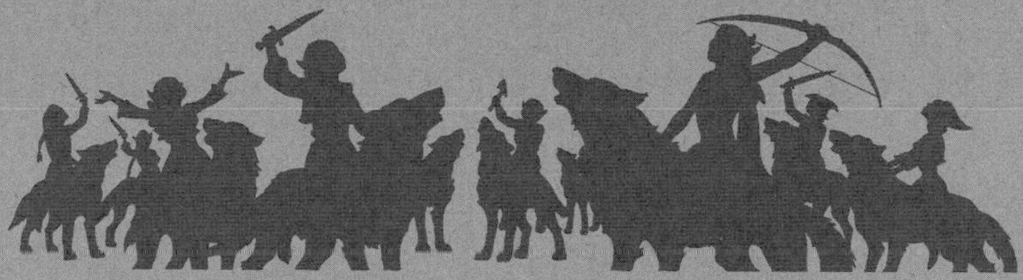

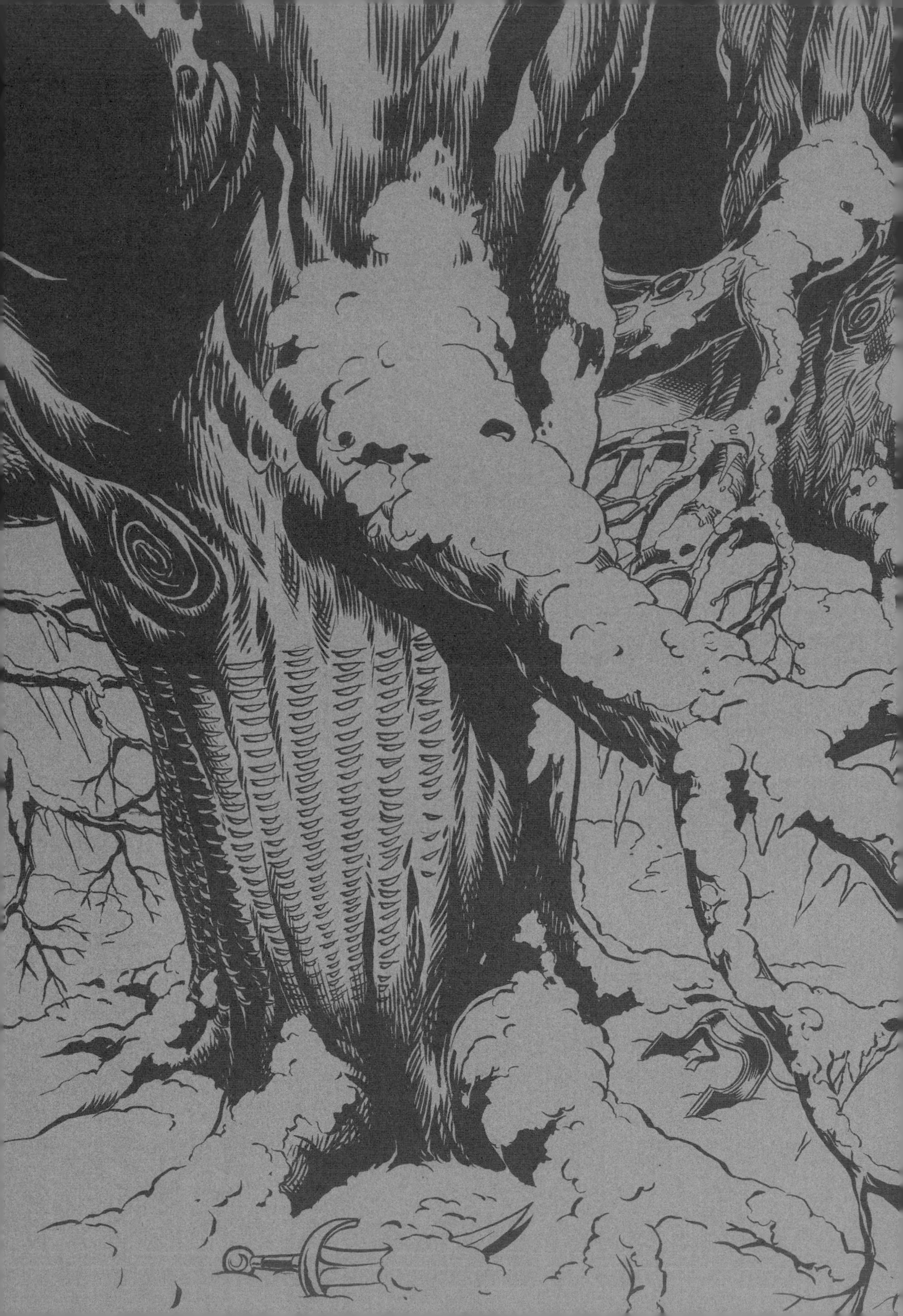

PART 7

KINGS of the BROKEN WHEEL

STORY & EDITING BY RICHARD PINI

STORY, SCRIPT & ART BY WENDY PINI

LIFEMATE FROM LIFEMATE...FRIEND FROM FRIEND... PARENTS FROM CHILD...SEVERED-- IN ONE SWIFT, UNFORESEEABLE STROKE!

RAYEK HAS SWEPT THE PALACE OF THE HIGH ONES, AND HIS UNWILLING COMPANIONS, INTO A FAR-AHEAD TIME--THERE TO MERGE THE PALACE WITH ITS FUTURE SELF AND OBLITERATE ALL THAT HAS GONE BEFORE!

I WONDER... WHAT IT WILL FEEL LIKE WHEN...

DEATH IS ANOTHER BEGINNING, MOONSHADE.

WHAT'S COMING IS MORE THAN DEATH! WE'LL NEVER HAVE BEEN... AND NEVER BE!

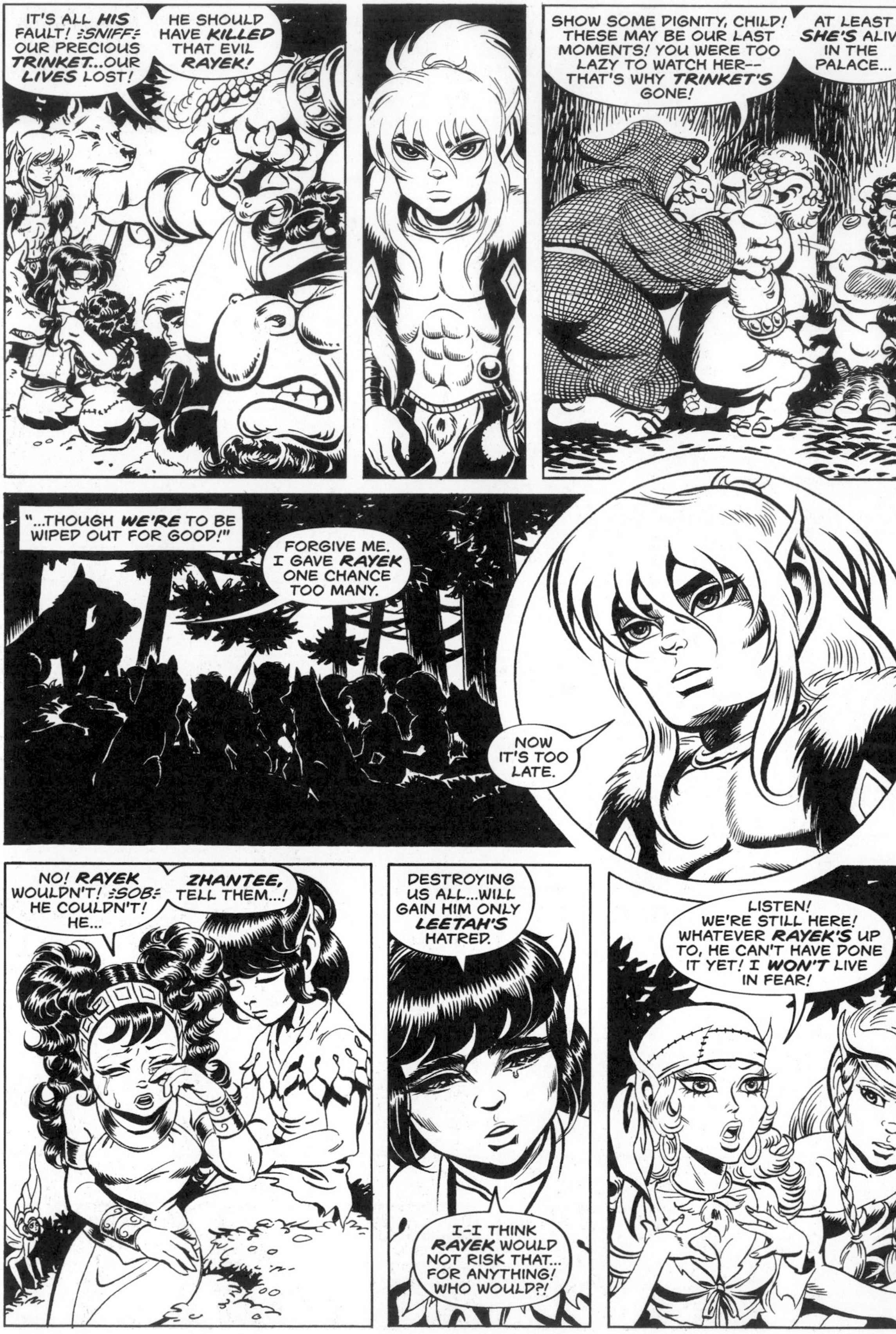
IT'S ALL HIS FAULT! =SNIFF= OUR PRECIOUS TRINKET...OUR LIVES LOST!
HE SHOULD HAVE KILLED THAT EVIL RAYEK!
SHOW SOME DIGNITY, CHILD! THESE MAY BE OUR LAST MOMENTS! YOU WERE TOO LAZY TO WATCH HER-- THAT'S WHY TRINKET'S GONE!
AT LEAST SHE'S ALIVE IN THE PALACE...
"...THOUGH WE'RE TO BE WIPED OUT FOR GOOD!"
FORGIVE ME. I GAVE RAYEK ONE CHANCE TOO MANY.
NOW IT'S TOO LATE.
NO! RAYEK WOULDN'T! =SOB= HE COULDN'T! HE...
ZHANTEE, TELL THEM...!
DESTROYING US ALL...WILL GAIN HIM ONLY LEETAH'S HATRED.
I-I THINK RAYEK WOULD NOT RISK THAT... FOR ANYTHING! WHO WOULD?!
LISTEN! WE'RE STILL HERE! WHATEVER RAYEK'S UP TO, HE CAN'T HAVE DONE IT YET! I WON'T LIVE IN FEAR!

NIGHTFALL'S RIGHT. WE'RE ALIVE...AND TIMMAIN IS WITH US. WE'LL DO WHAT WE'VE ALWAYS DONE...

...HUNT, HOWL, AND SURVIVE!

YOU CAN START ON THE NEW HOLT RIGHT NOW, REDLANCE.

MY CHIEF... COUNT ON ME!

COUNT ON US ALL!

SOON...

IT HAS TO BE DIFFERENT FROM OTHER HOLTS. WE'LL LIVE HIGH UP, LIKE BIRDS IN THEIR NESTS...

"...HIGH UP, WHERE NO ONE CAN SEE US FROM BELOW.

"AND WE'LL HAVE A NEW RULE: TO THE HUMANS IN THIS STRANGE LAND, WE'LL BE NEITHER FRIENDS NOR FOES.

"TO THEM WE WON'T EXIST."

THE FOLLOWING NIGHT...

YOU HAVEN'T CHOSEN A DEN FOR YOURSELF YET, CUTTER.

NO HURRY. BY AND BY.

REDLANCE'S TREE-SHAPING EXCEEDS HIS TRIBE'S WILDEST FANCIES. WHETHER SOMETHING OF THE VANISHED PALACE'S INFLUENCE REMAINS WITH HIM, OR WHETHER HE HAS SIMPLY RISEN TO MEET A GREAT CHALLENGE, EVEN HE CANNOT SAY.

AH, TREESTUMP! THERE'S ROOM ENOUGH FOR YOUR BIG FEET...AND FOR MY HAIR TO GROW AS LONG AS IT WILL!

ZHANTEE, IT IS SO CLEVER! SO MUCH LIKE THE HUTS IN THE SUN VILLAGE!

NOT WHEN YOU LOOK DOWN!

IT'S TIME CUTTER CHOSE. WHERE IS HE, TREESTUMP?

UP THERE. DOESN'T SEEM TO CARE WHERE HE LIVES...OR IF, CURSE IT...

"...IT'S BEARCLAW ALL OVER AGAIN!"

452

CUTTER?

DON'T BE ALONE.

TREE WITH US...FOR AS LONG AS YOU WANT!

THE NEW LIFE GROWING IN ME--LET IT GIVE YOU HOPE!

PLEASE...

DAYS LATER...

EAT! LEETAH, SKYWISE, THE TWINS... THEY'RE ALIVE!

LIVE FOR THEM! AND FOR US!

AND SO...

THE GO-BACKS KEEP TRACK OF THE TURNING SEASONS LIKE SO. IF I KILL THIS TREE WITH TOO MANY NOTCHES, I'LL START ON ANOTHER, AND ANOTHER...

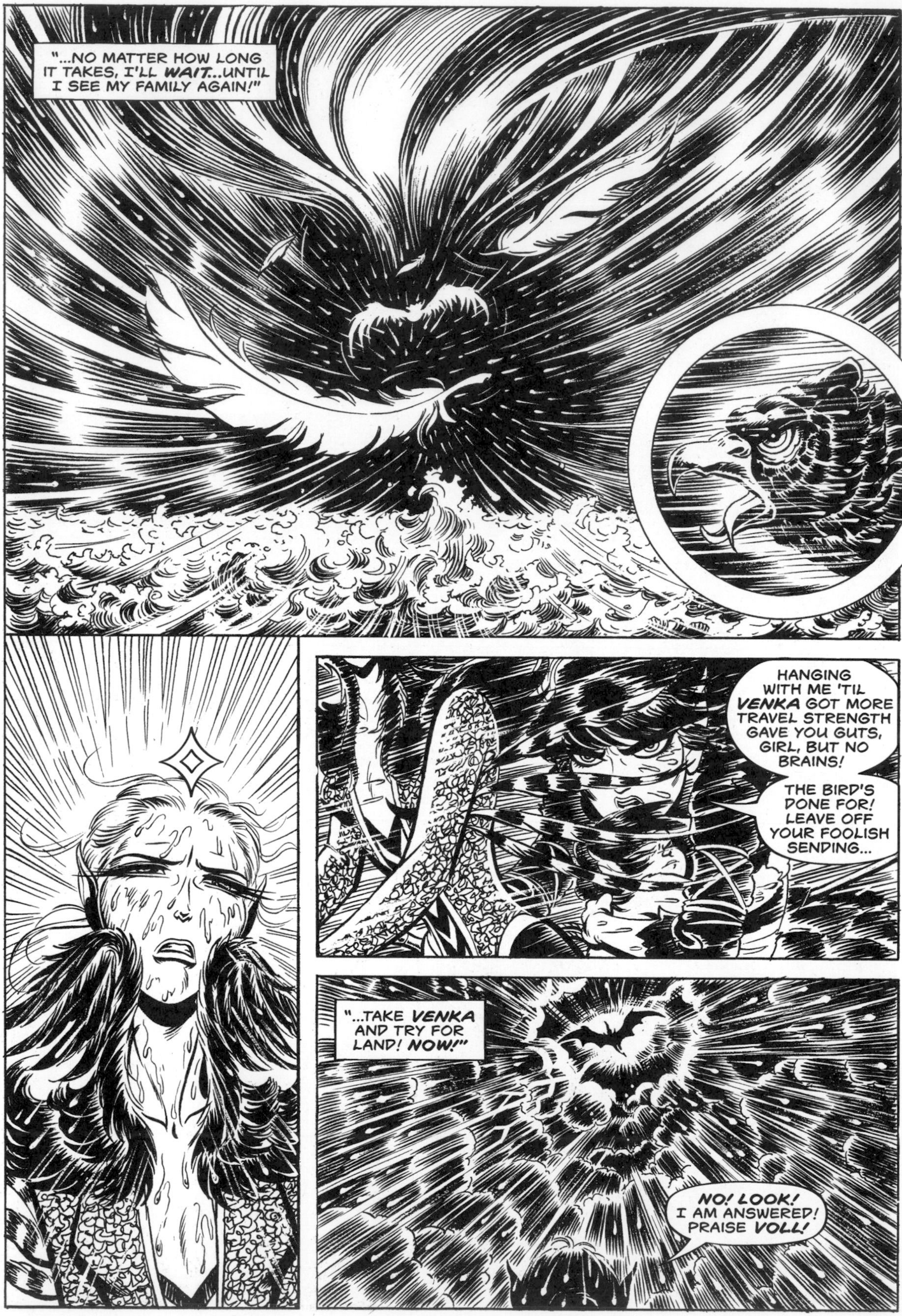
"...NO MATTER HOW LONG IT TAKES, I'LL WAIT...UNTIL I SEE MY FAMILY AGAIN!"
HANGING WITH ME 'TIL VENKA GOT MORE TRAVEL STRENGTH GAVE YOU GUTS, GIRL, BUT NO BRAINS!
THE BIRD'S DONE FOR! LEAVE OFF YOUR FOOLISH SENDING...
"...TAKE VENKA AND TRY FOR LAND! NOW!"
NO! LOOK! I AM ANSWERED! PRAISE VOLL!

I-I'VE SEEN *YOU* BEFORE... JUST DIDN'T *BELIEVE* IT! A WINGED ELF!

YOU ARE A BLESSED SIGHT, *TYLDAK!* COME, *VENKA!*

RIDE ON MY WAKE, *AROREE!* THERE IS AN ISLAND NOT FAR FROM HERE!

LITTLETRILL... MY BOND-BIRD...!

:GASP:

WHAT'S WRONG?!

COME BACK! COME BACK TO ME!

LORD *WINNOWILL!*

A-ALIVE!

HEY!

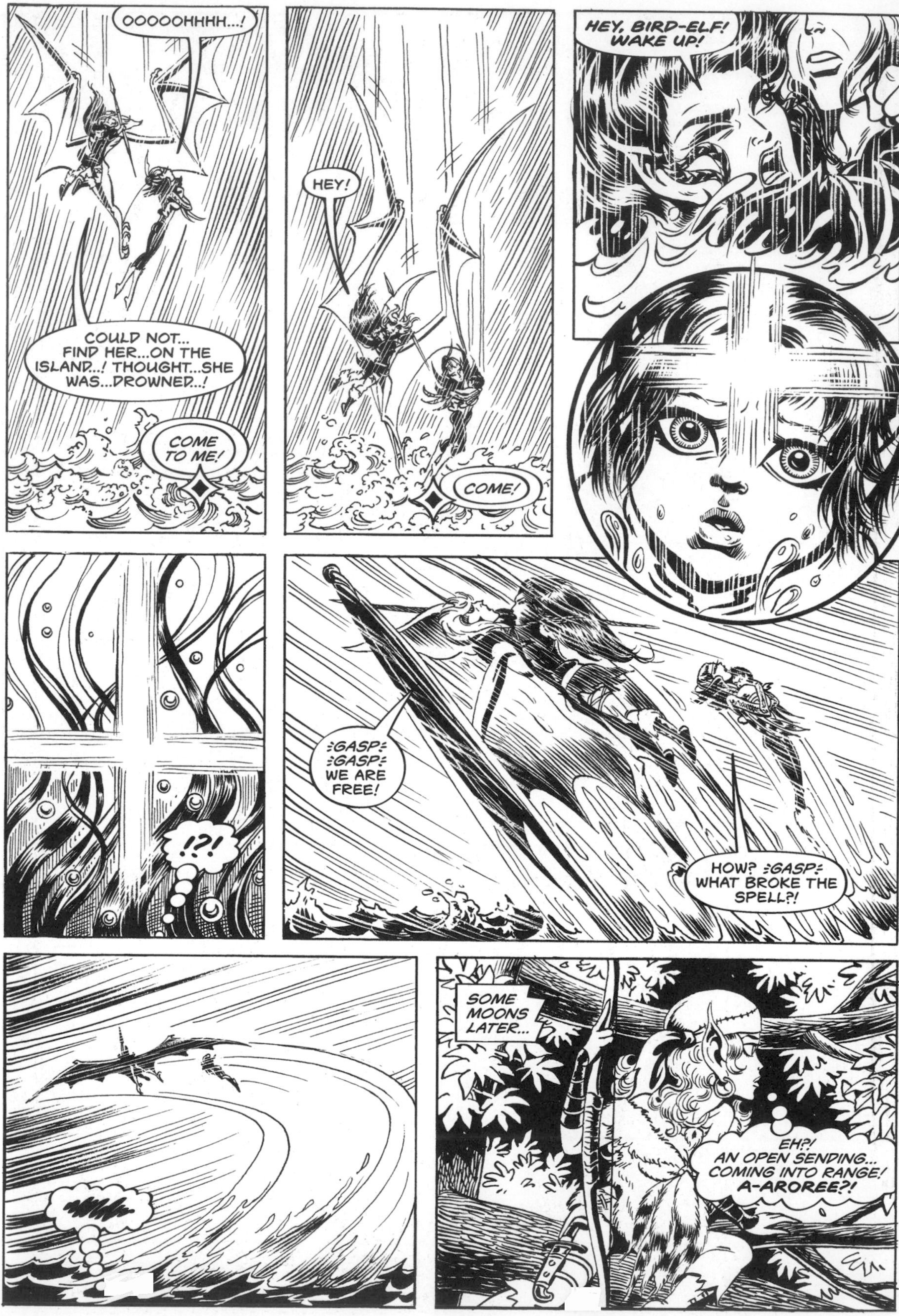
OOOOOHHHH...!
COULD NOT... FIND HER...ON THE ISLAND...! THOUGHT...SHE WAS...DROWNED...!
COME TO ME!
HEY!
COME!
HEY, BIRD-ELF! WAKE UP!
!?!
GASP GASP WE ARE FREE!
HOW? GASP WHAT BROKE THE SPELL?!
SOME MOONS LATER...
EH?! AN OPEN SENDING... COMING INTO RANGE! A-AROREE?!

EVER WARY, THE WOLFRIDERS GATHER TO AWAIT THE MOTLEY GROUP'S ARRIVAL. FINALLY...

SO...KAHVI'S CUB *DID* MAKE IT! AND RAYEK'S THE SIRE, OR I'M A ZWOOT!

LEARNING THAT **RAYEK** HAS ONCE MORE SLIPPED THROUGH HER FINGERS, **KAHVI** CAN BARELY CONTAIN HER RAGE. BUT AS **CUTTER'S** TALE OF LOSS QUIETLY UNFOLDS...

I'M SORRY FOR YOU, WOLF-CHIEF...TRULY. YOUR KIN-CLOSENESS...

...I'VE NEVER SEEN THE LIKE...!

SHHH!

HUMANS! BELOW IN THE MIST! THEY SELDOM COME THIS FAR UP THE MOUNTAIN!

IF YOU KEEP TO OUR RULES, YOU FOUR ARE WELCOME TO STAY.

WHAT CHOICE HAVE WE? BUT RAISING **VENKA** IN A TREE...THAT'S OUT!

MOTHER, FATHER, AND CHILD...LOCKED IN SENDING. THREE SHARE THE WORK AS ONE!

UHM! PERFECTLY DONE! YOU'VE GIVEN ME FAR TOO LITTLE TO DO TODAY!

≤GASP≥

AHH...!

HERS IS A WOLFRIDER'S SOUL NAME. BUT THE TRIBE CAN CALL HER *TYLEET.*

"HEALER'S GIFT"! SHE'S AS WELCOME AS WATER IN THE DESERT!

A SHAPE-CHANGED HIGH ONE...!

NO BETTER NURSE FOR OUR TWO PRIZE FAWNS!

STRANDS OF WHITE BLENDING WITH THE RED-GOLD...

...MEANS AN EARLY WHITE-COLD! OUR CUB'S CHANGING PELT NEVER LIES!

I SAW YOU AND *STRONGBOW* DOWN BY THE WATERFALL LAST NIGHT.

NEXT HOWL I'M GOING TO SING A SONG ABOUT IT!

WILL I GET FACE FUR WHEN I'M OLD AS YOU, *TREESTUMP*?

YOU'LL BE AS BEAUTIFUL, AS WISE...AND MAYBE EVEN AS *QUIET* AS CLEARBROOK!

HEE HEE HEE! ALL RIGHT, *ALL RIGHT, BUNDLES!* YOU'RE MY WOLF FRIEND FOREVER!

...SO WE WON THE PALACE IN A BLOODY WAR, BUT LOST IT AGAIN WHEN *RAYEK* STOLE IT AWAY.

MAYBE... HE DIDN'T MEAN TO.

SO *THAT'S* WHY *VENKA'S* BROWN LIKE YOU! ARE YOU TWO LOVEMATES?

WELL... *SHENSHEN* AND I ARE *VERY* OLD FRIENDS!

WAS *EMBER* LIKE ME?

SOME. TOUGHER, MAYBE.

MOTHER AND FATHER SAY, BECAUSE OF ME, THEY KNOW JUST HOW YOU FEEL.

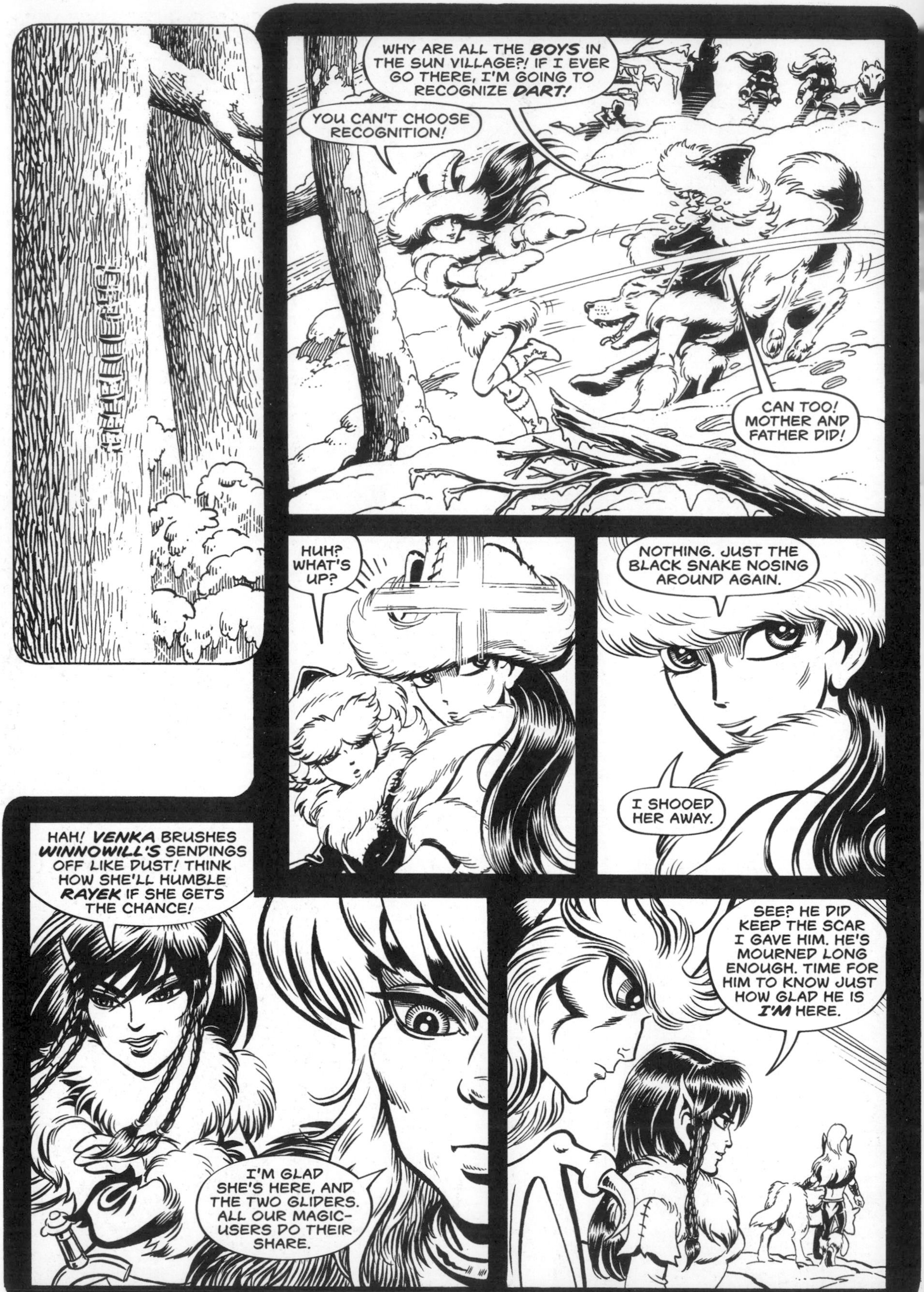
WHY ARE ALL THE BOYS IN THE SUN VILLAGE?! IF I EVER GO THERE, I'M GOING TO RECOGNIZE DART!
YOU CAN'T CHOOSE RECOGNITION!
CAN TOO! MOTHER AND FATHER DID!
HUH? WHAT'S UP?
NOTHING. JUST THE BLACK SNAKE NOSING AROUND AGAIN.
I SHOOED HER AWAY.
HAH! VENKA BRUSHES WINNOWILL'S SENDINGS OFF LIKE DUST! THINK HOW SHE'LL HUMBLE RAYEK IF SHE GETS THE CHANCE!
I'M GLAD SHE'S HERE, AND THE TWO GLIDERS. ALL OUR MAGIC-USERS DO THEIR SHARE.
SEE? HE DID KEEP THE SCAR I GAVE HIM. HE'S MOURNED LONG ENOUGH. TIME FOR HIM TO KNOW JUST HOW GLAD HE IS I'M HERE.

YOUR BODY IS WITH ME, TO BE SURE, WOLF CHIEF. BUT *YOU* NEVER ARE!

I'M SORRY... I CAN'T GIVE YOU MORE.

IT BOTHERS ME THAT I NEED MORE. I NEVER HAVE BEFORE.

YOU MISS THE GO-BACKS. YOU MISS BEING CHIEF.

WHEN YOU'RE KEPT APART FROM ALL YOU KNOW AND LOVE MOST...

WHAT YOU NEED...

...DON'T LOOK FOR IT IN ME.

SOME LIFE, EH, SAD-EYES? YOU BIRD-FOLK AND I LIVE IN THESE CAVES LIKE *TROLLS!*

ALL THE WOLFRIDERS WANT IS A FULL BELLY AND A HOLLOW TREE. I WANT BATTLE AND SPOILS!

I WANT THE PALACE BACK! I WANT...

POOR OLD *WARFROST!* THERE WASN'T MUCH LOVE LOST BETWEEN US. STILL... I'LL MISS HIM.

:BUFF:

RUN WITH ME ALWAYS, *TIMMAIN.* I'M TIRED OF LOSING FRIENDS!

BEING NEAR THE PALACE MADE OUR SMALL MAGIC BURN BRIGHTER. MOTHER OF WOLFRIDERS...

...WITH YOU WATCHING OVER US, OUR FLAME BURNS STEADY AND WARM.

"AND BECAUSE A BIT OF THE PALACE REMAINS IN THE SUN VILLAGE...

"...WE CAN KNOW HOW OUR KINFOLK FARE...AT LEAST...THOSE WHO LIVE NOW, IN *THIS* TIME.

"I LEAD A PACK MADE OF MANY SHAPES AND COLORS...ALL TOUCHING, ALL DOING *THEIR* PART.

"BUT FOR ME, EACH DAY IS A *FIGHT* TO RIDE ABOVE THE SORROW AND DO *MINE.*"

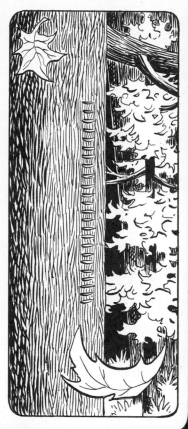

WATCH, GIRL! FIRE AND SONG IS THE GO-BACKS' WAY!

THE DANCE IS PART OF YOU, *VENKA*, AS MUCH AS THAT SHOWY MAGIC OF YOURS!

"IN THE TREES, AS YOU PLEASE. ON THE GROUND, NOT A SOUND!" YOU KNOW THE RULES, YET YOU BREAK THEM AGAIN AND AGAIN!

THOUGHT *YOU* KNEW BETTER, PIKE!

SORRY...!

EVEN THOSE WHO WERE ONCE MINE CHOOSE THE WOLFRIDERS' WAY.

SO MUCH FOR MY REVENGE! *RAYEK'S* FAR BEYOND SPEAR-POINT'S REACH. AND WHAT'S A SPEAR TO *HIM* ANYWAY?

IT'S TOO LONG A WAIT TO FIND OUT, EVEN FOR ME. WE EACH DO WHAT WE'RE SUITED FOR, EH?

AND WHAT SHOULD I DO, MOTHER, THAT WOULD PLEASE YOU MOST?

ALL THAT WAS BEST IN *RAYEK*, AND NONE OF THE WORST, I SEE IN YOU.

TEACH HIM A LESSON, THAT'S ALL I ASK.

TEACH HIM SO HE *LEARNS!*

WHAT DO YOU SEE?

A KINDRED SPIRIT...

...ONE WHO NEEDS NEITHER EXPLAIN NOR ASK LEAVE. ONE WHO IS NOT AFRAID TO FLY!

VENKA! THE HUNT'S ON. WHERE'S **KAHVI?**

SHE'S FLOWN OFF...WITH **TYLDAK.** THEY HOPE TO FIND A WAY BACK TO THE FROZEN MOUNTAINS OVER LAND!

::SPLUTTER:: **THOSE** TWO?!

"**DIFFERENCES** MAKE GOOD SPARKS," SHE SAID.

ZHANTEE... SHARE A MEMORY WITH ME.

IN THE SUN VILLAGE, BEFORE... BEFORE ALL THIS, WHAT WAS MY FATHER LIKE?

I WAS ONE OF THOSE WHO ADMIRED HIM...EVEN **LIKED** HIM. WHEN HE REACHED A GOAL, HE WOULD NOT REST, BUT ALWAYS AIMED HIGHER.

I THINK PERHAPS I AM A WOLFRIDER NOW, BECAUSE OF **RAYEK'S** EXAMPLE THEN.

MANY TWILIGHTS AND MANY HUNTS FOLLOW. AND SOMETIMES MEMORY SEEMS STRONG ENOUGH TO BRING A MUCH-MISSED BROTHER, IN SPIRIT, TO THE CHASE.

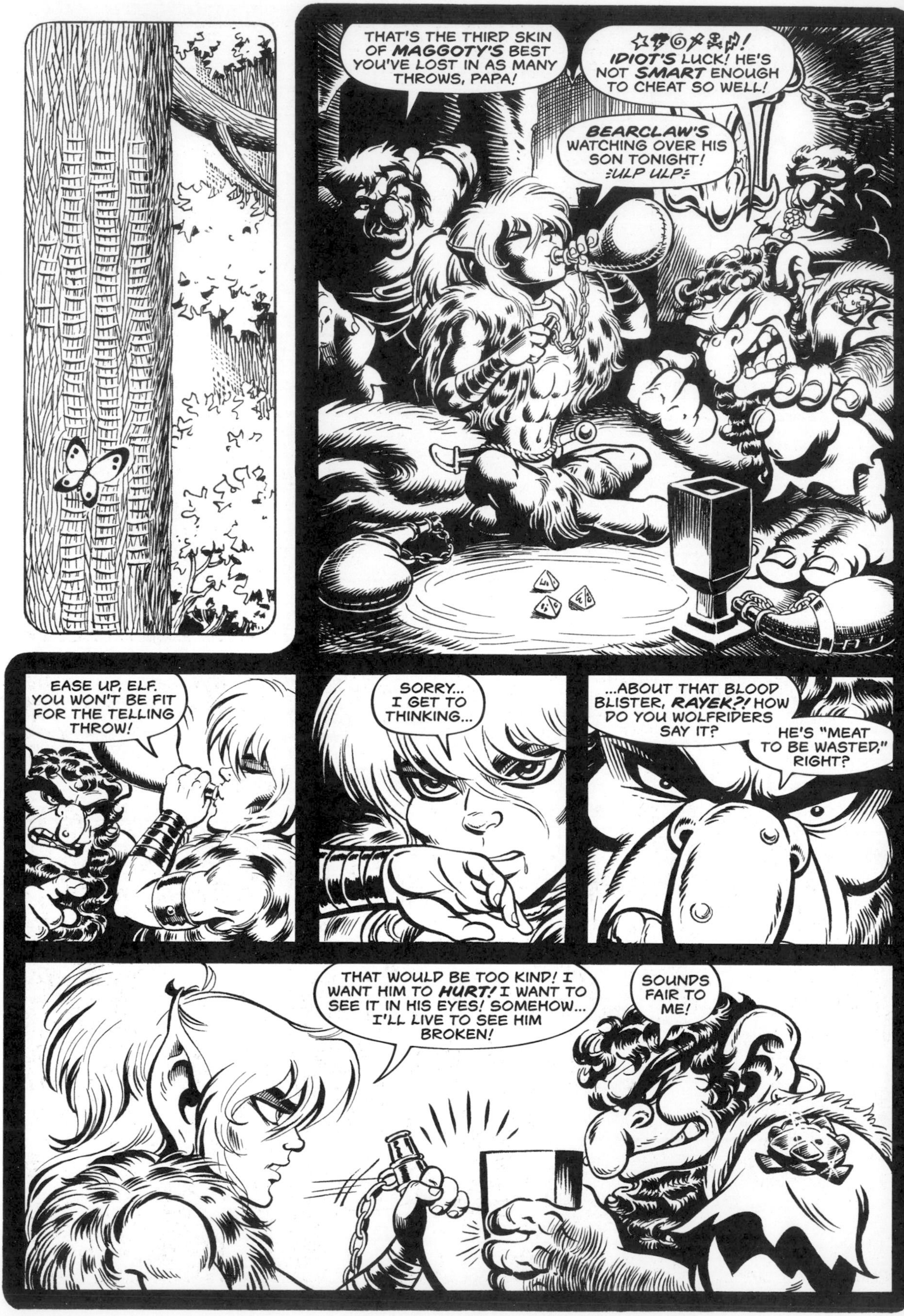

THAT'S THE THIRD SKIN OF MAGGOTY'S BEST YOU'VE LOST IN AS MANY THROWS, PAPA!
IDIOT'S LUCK! HE'S NOT SMART ENOUGH TO CHEAT SO WELL!
BEARCLAW'S WATCHING OVER HIS SON TONIGHT! ULP ULP
EASE UP, ELF. YOU WON'T BE FIT FOR THE TELLING THROW!
SORRY... I GET TO THINKING...
...ABOUT THAT BLOOD BLISTER, RAYEK?! HOW DO YOU WOLFRIDERS SAY IT?
HE'S "MEAT TO BE WASTED," RIGHT?
THAT WOULD BE TOO KIND! I WANT HIM TO HURT! I WANT TO SEE IT IN HIS EYES! SOMEHOW... I'LL LIVE TO SEE HIM BROKEN!
SOUNDS FAIR TO ME!

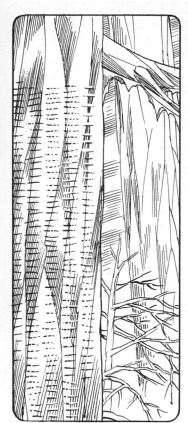

STARVED...! FROZEN! AT LEAST SHE'S NOT ONE OF OURS.

DEATH'S IN THE AIR, **CLEARBROOK.** THIS IS THE CRUELEST WHITE COLD EVER!

KRIM... YOUR LITTLE **CHEIPAR** IS...

IT WAS THE WRONG TIME TO BREED. MAYBE THERE **IS** SOMETHING TO THIS RECOGNITION BUSINESS.

HE WAS FRAIL FROM THE START.

WE'LL TRY AGAIN...THE FOUR OF US.

HIGHTHINGS GO IN WRAPSTUFF NOW?

"A LIVING DEATH," **LEETAH** CALLED IT. "MONSTROUS!"

TO SLEEP THROUGH THE WHITE-COLD LIKE MUD RATS... NO! IT'S NOT **THE WAY!**

467

THE WAY, AN UNSPOKEN LAW BORN OF BLOOD BLENDING BETWEEN WOLF AND ELF IN THE TIME OF THE FIRSTCOMERS. TO FOLLOW IT IS TO BE AWARE OF NOTHING...READY FOR NOTHING...BUT WHAT HAPPENS IN THE MOMENT. IT IS THE COMFORT OF FORGETFULNESS, THE WISDOM OF BEING FULLY AWAKE. IT IS THE NOW OF WOLF-THOUGHT.

TO CHOOSE ANY OTHER PATH IS TO BE OTHER THAN A WOLFRIDER.

TO BE CHIEF, KEEPER OF THE WAY, AND YET UNABLE TO FORGET...

...IS TO BE... ALMOST...OTHER THAN AN ELF.

AGAIN SHE'S CHEWED HERSELF FREE!

IT'S SHE...THE *DEATHLESS* ONE MY FATHER SOUGHT, AND HIS FATHER BEFORE HIM, AND *HIS!*

I'LL *HAVE* HER SACRED HIDE, THOUGH IT TAKES THE WHOLE OF MY LIFE!

PUT THAT GRIN AWAY! LISTEN! IT'S YOUR SNOWY *PELT* THEY WANT, HIGH ONE!

HUMANS *CRAVE* RARE PRIZES!

BE GRAY AGAIN! CAN'T YOU UNDERSTAND? OH, *TIMMAIN!*

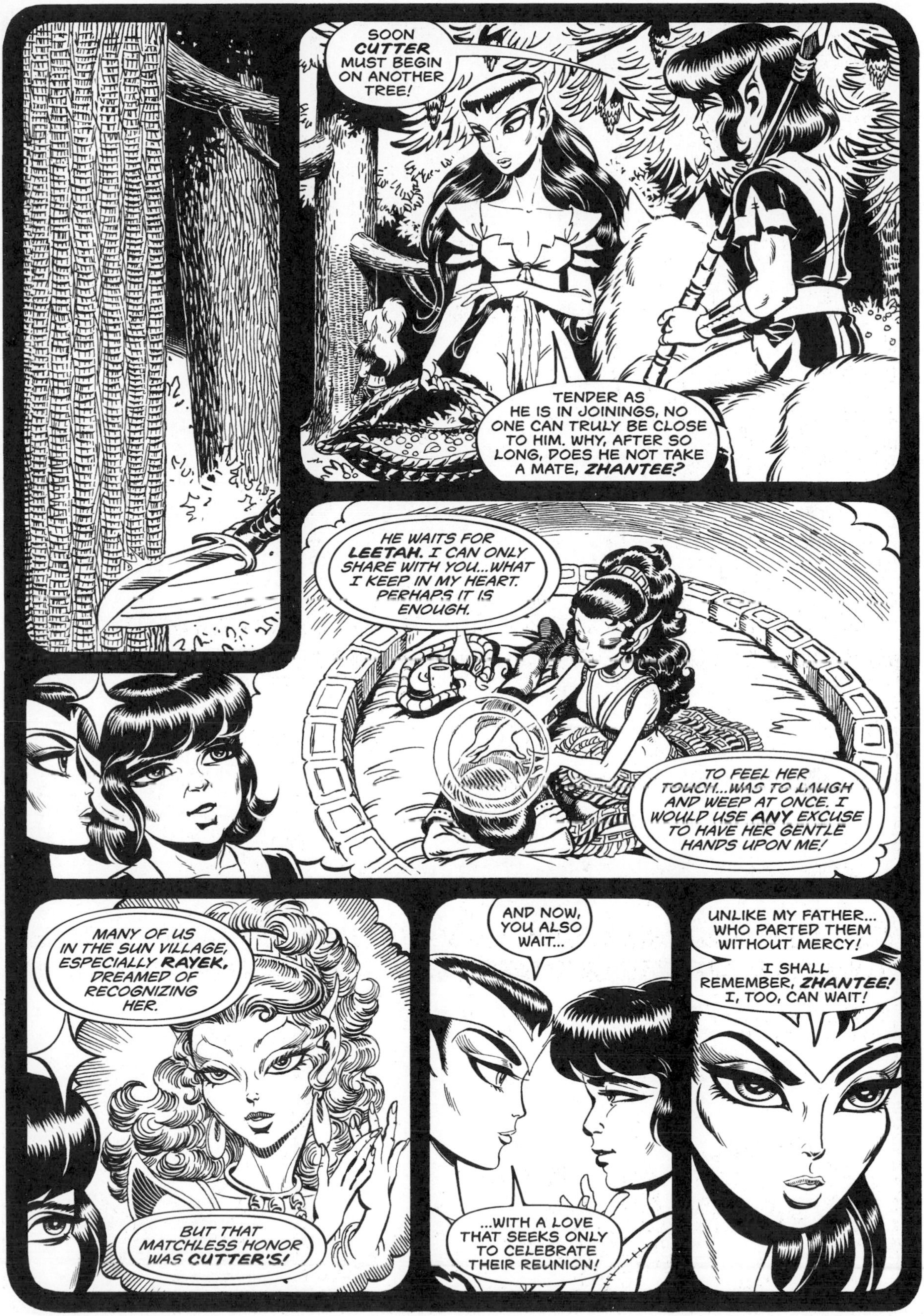
SOON CUTTER MUST BEGIN ON ANOTHER TREE!
TENDER AS HE IS IN JOININGS, NO ONE CAN TRULY BE CLOSE TO HIM. WHY, AFTER SO LONG, DOES HE NOT TAKE A MATE, ZHANTEE?
HE WAITS FOR LEETAH. I CAN ONLY SHARE WITH YOU...WHAT I KEEP IN MY HEART. PERHAPS IT IS ENOUGH.
TO FEEL HER TOUCH...WAS TO LAUGH AND WEEP AT ONCE. I WOULD USE ANY EXCUSE TO HAVE HER GENTLE HANDS UPON ME!
MANY OF US IN THE SUN VILLAGE, ESPECIALLY RAYEK, DREAMED OF RECOGNIZING HER.
BUT THAT MATCHLESS HONOR WAS CUTTER'S!
AND NOW, YOU ALSO WAIT...
...WITH A LOVE THAT SEEKS ONLY TO CELEBRATE THEIR REUNION!
UNLIKE MY FATHER... WHO PARTED THEM WITHOUT MERCY!
I SHALL REMEMBER, ZHANTEE! I, TOO, CAN WAIT!

ONE DAY...

OH! ONE OF **CURLNECK'S** CUBS IS MISSING!

:SNIFF: :SNIFF: :WHINE:

DIRE THINGS OFTEN BEFALL THE HELPLESS IN THE WIDE WOODS.

A NORMAL WOLF GRIEVES A MOMENT, THEN GOES ON.

BUT A HIGH ONE IN LUPINE FORM, WHO REGARDS WOLVES AND ELVES, BOTH, AS HER CHILDREN...

:SNIFF: :SNUFFLE: :SNUFF:

AAAWWWWW! POOR BABY GROWLER!

SOMEBODY CATCH-KILL, BUT NO EAT!

GENTLY **TIMMAIN** MOVES TO CARRY THE DEAD CUB BACK TO ITS DEN...

A TRAP! SET BY ONE WHO KNOWS HER WAYS WELL!

YIIPE!

THE SNARE IS COATED WITH A STINGING VENOM!

THIS TIME SHE CANNOT BITE THROUGH!

PETALWING STREAKS TO THE NEAREST HELP!

MOTHER-MOTHER HIGHTHING ALL STICKY-STUCK! COME QUICK!

CUTTER! YOU'RE TOO FAST FOR ME! WAIT!

HE *HAS* WAITED, STRIVING TO BE TRUE TO *THE WAY*, FINDING ANY REASON TO KEEP ON UNTIL THOSE HE LOVES MOST CAN BE WITH HIM.

NOW HE MUST PUT ASIDE THAT FRAGILE HOPE...

...TO PROTECT THE SOURCE, THE VERY SOUL, OF HIS TRIBE!

AT LAST!

≶WHINE≶ ≶WHINE≶

WHITE GODDESS WOLF! SO BEAUTIFUL! ...MINE!

?!!

MAKE THE KILL QUICK AND CLEAN. SHE MUST NOT SUFFER!

473

NO!

NAUGHTY NAUGHTY BIGTHINGS! PTOO!

BY ALL THE... GNSH!

EEEEP!

PETALWING'S OUT! NO TIME...

OOWWW!

IT BURNS! STICKY! WON'T CUT!

WOA!

LET THE STRANGE BOY BE! GET THE WOLF!

TIMMAIN!

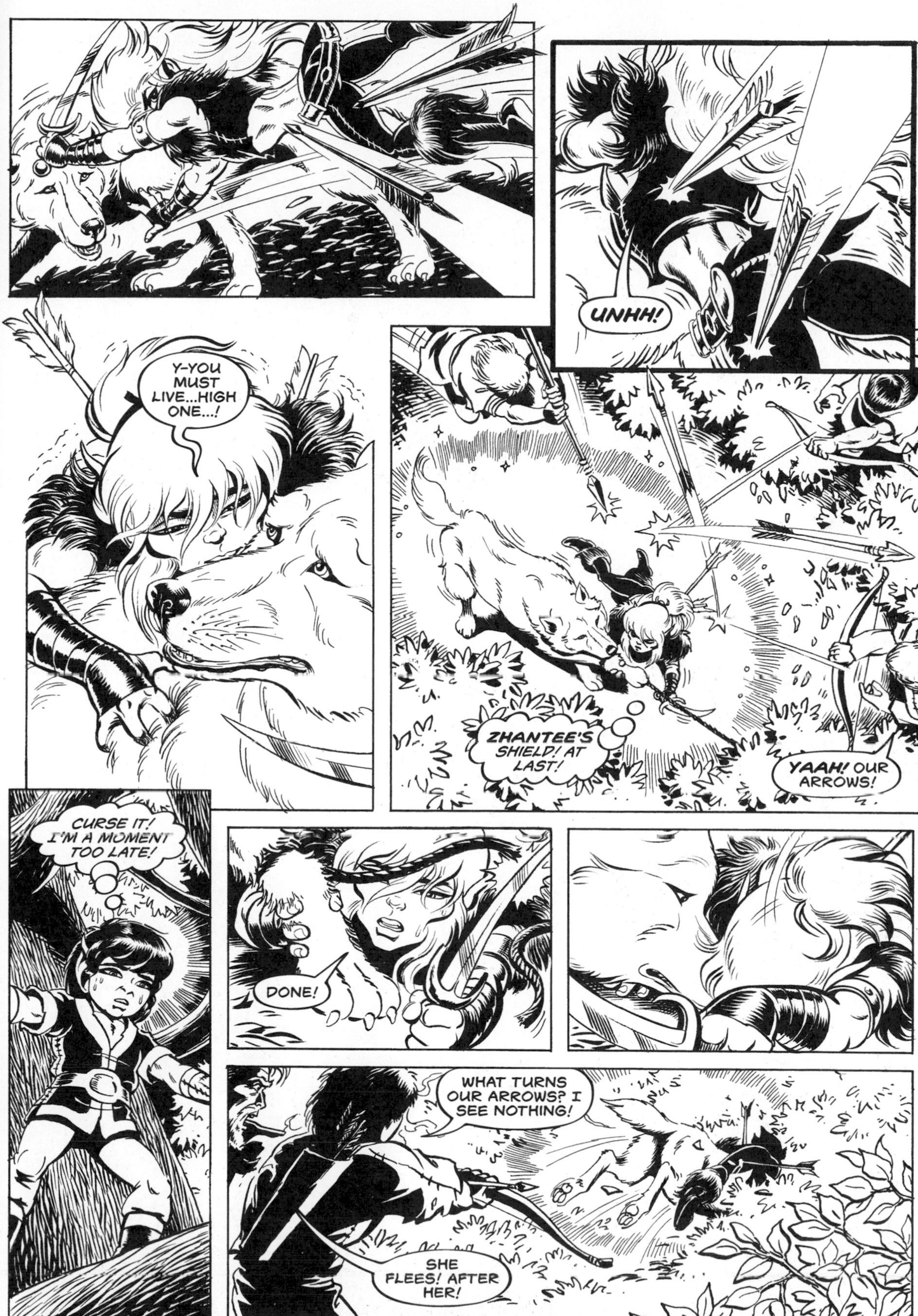

UNHH!
Y-YOU MUST LIVE...HIGH ONE...!
ZHANTEE'S SHIELD! AT LAST!
YAAH! OUR ARROWS!
CURSE IT! I'M A MOMENT TOO LATE!
DONE!
WHAT TURNS OUR ARROWS? I SEE NOTHING!
SHE FLEES! AFTER HER!

PLEASE... BE ALIVE!

WHERE ARE YOU, LAD?

...WITH...THE TROLLS! DON'T... WORRY...!

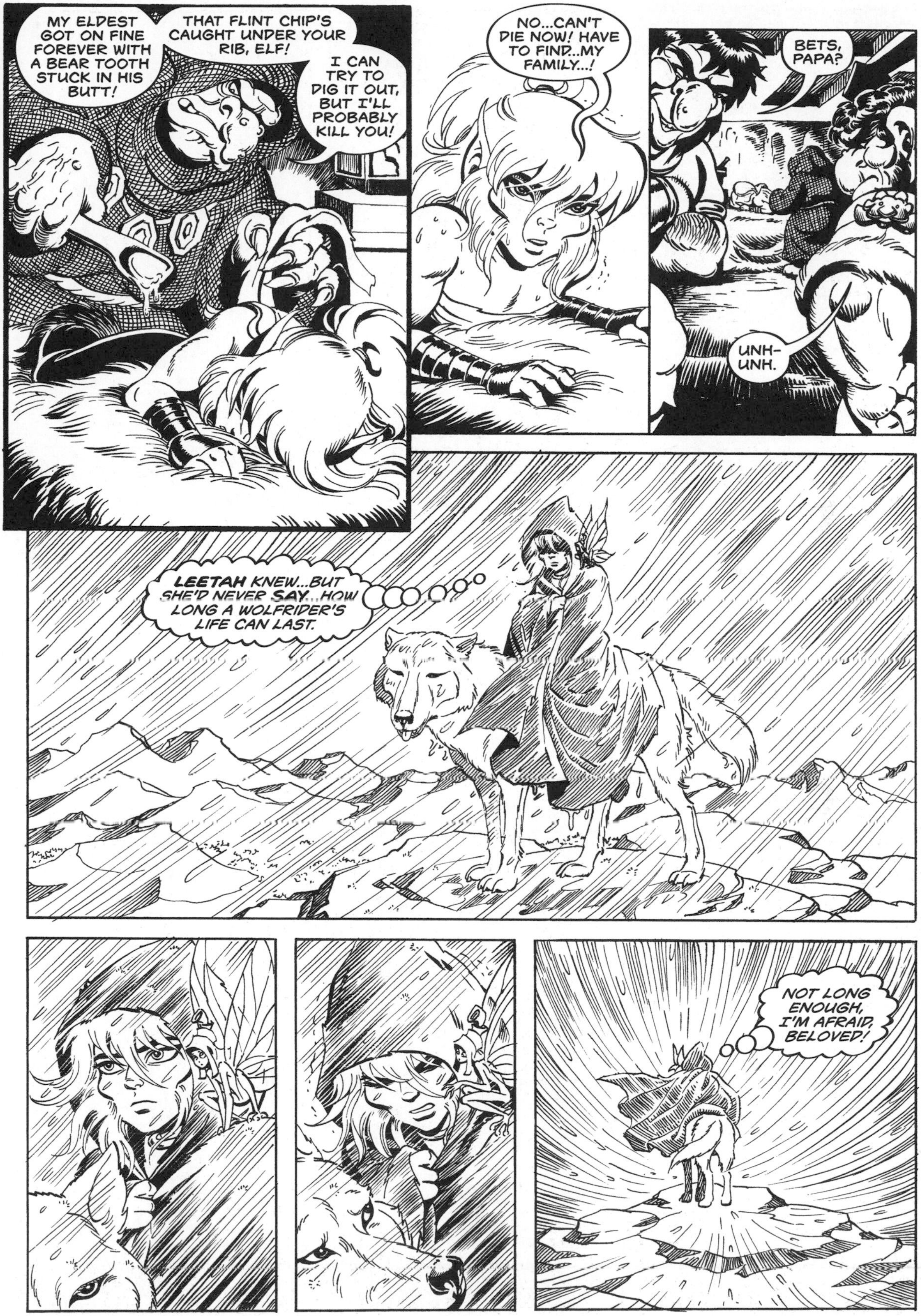
MY ELDEST GOT ON FINE FOREVER WITH A BEAR TOOTH STUCK IN HIS BUTT!
THAT FLINT CHIP'S CAUGHT UNDER YOUR RIB, ELF!
I CAN TRY TO DIG IT OUT, BUT I'LL PROBABLY KILL YOU!
NO...CAN'T DIE NOW! HAVE TO FIND...MY FAMILY...!
BETS, PAPA?
UNH-UNH.
LEETAH KNEW...BUT SHE'D NEVER SAY...HOW LONG A WOLFRIDER'S LIFE CAN LAST.
NOT LONG ENOUGH, I'M AFRAID, BELOVED!

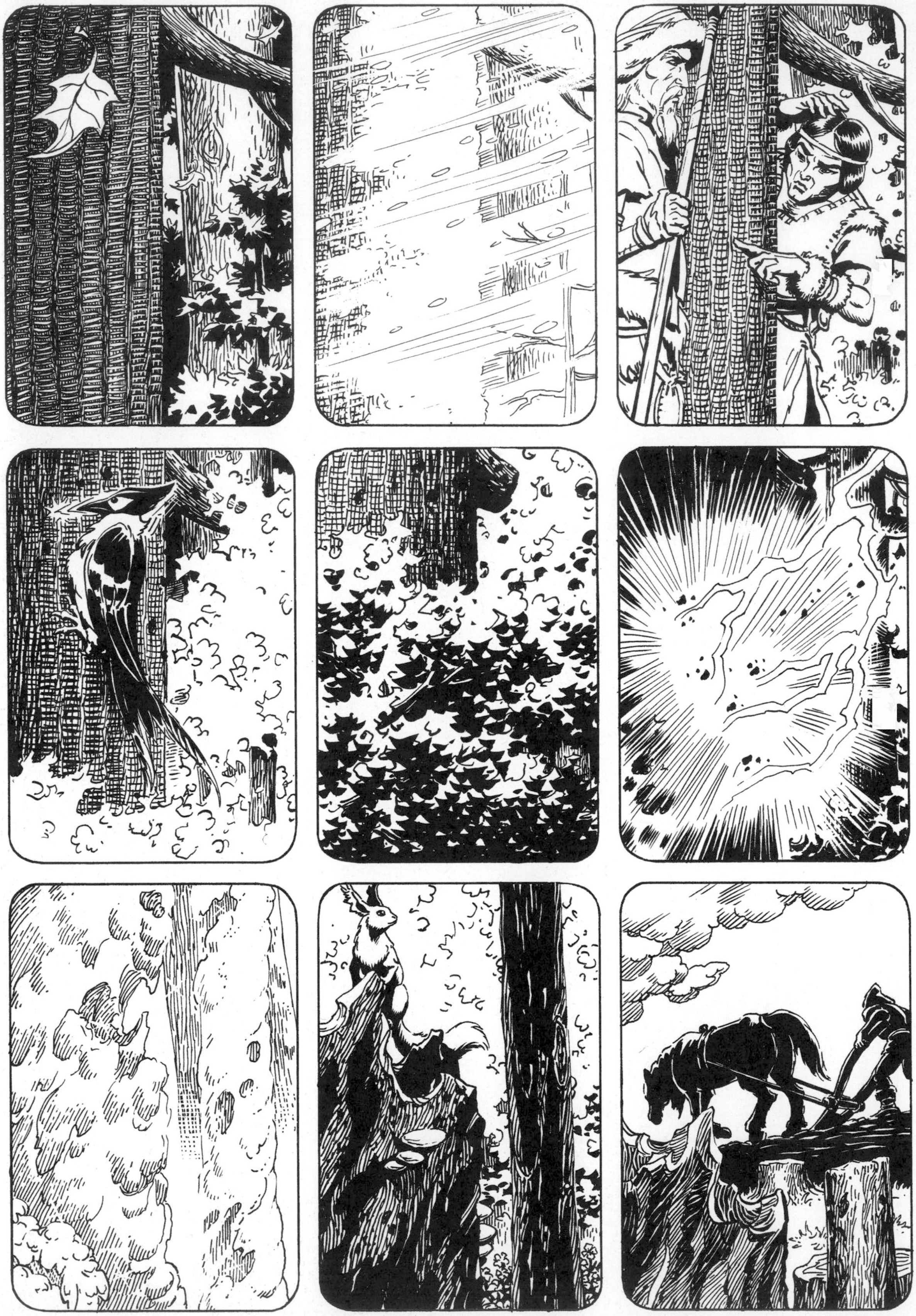

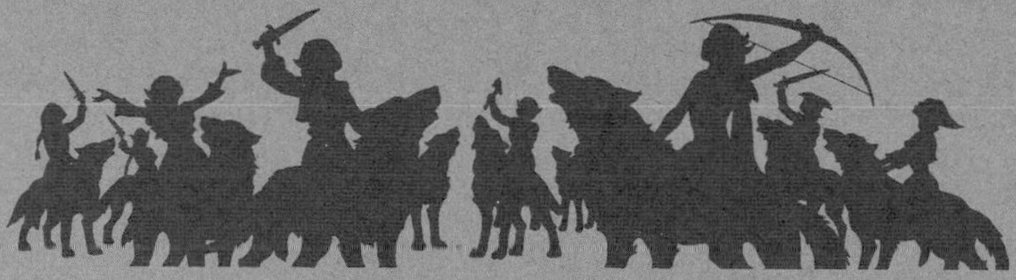

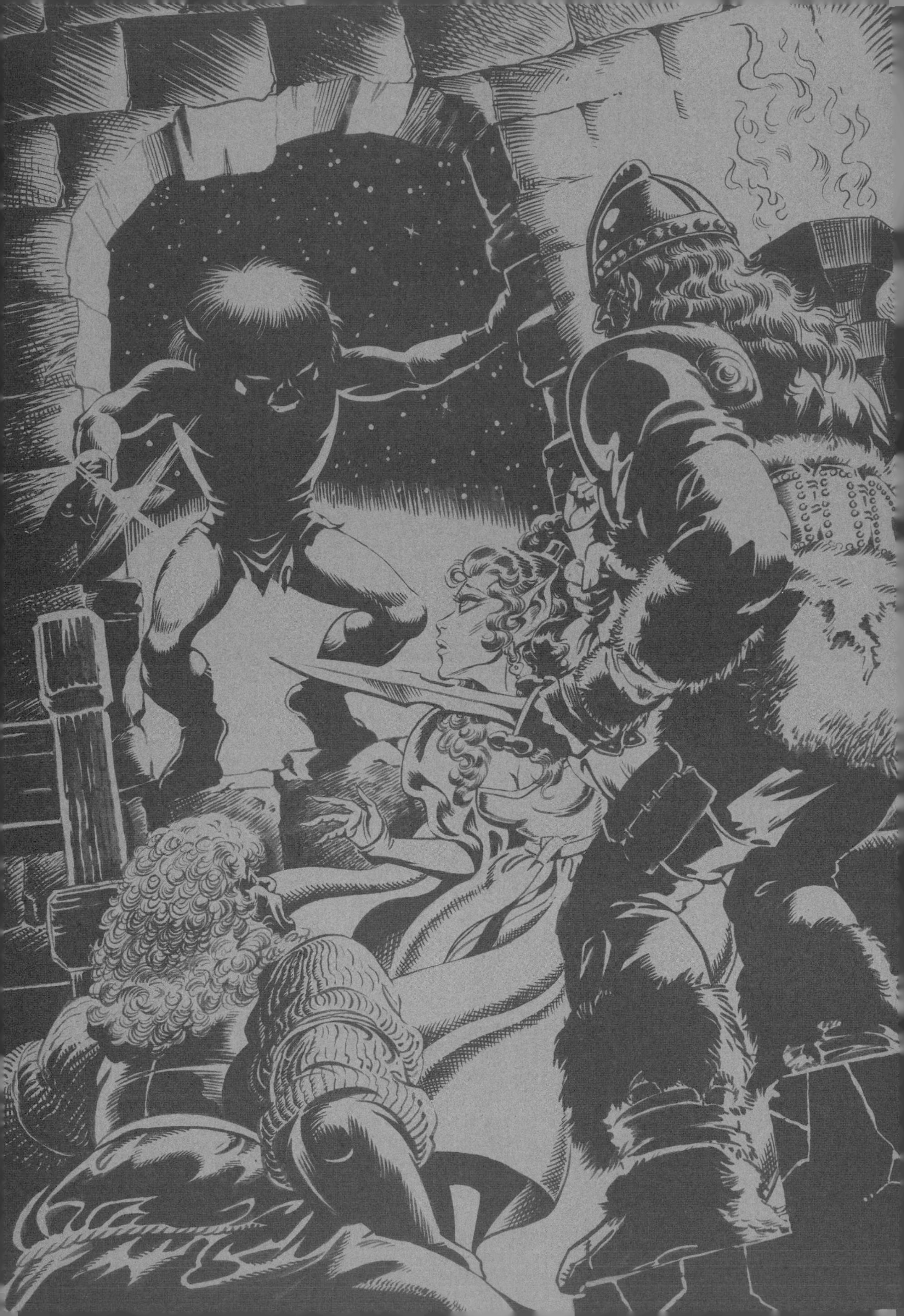

STORY & EDITING BY RICHARD PINI

PART 8

KINGS of the BROKENWHEEL

STORY, SCRIPT & ART BY WENDY PINI

WH–WHAT HAPPENED...?!

MUMKINS...? PAPA...?!

AS THE ABDUCTED TRAVELERS SLOWLY REGAIN THEIR SENSES...

BROWNSKIN?! BROWNSKIN!

IS-IS RAYEK ALIVE, EKUAR?

BLESS THE HIGH ONES!

HE IS SPENT...BUT BREATHING!

BAAAWWWW! WHERE'S PAPA?!

TRINKET WANTS PAPAAAAAHHHH!

DON'T LIKE IT HERE! WANT HOME! WANT HOOOOME! WAAAAAHHH!

TRINKET! DON'T GO OUT THERE!

MOMENTS LATER...

≈WHEW≈ YOU ALMOST FELL OVER THE EDGE!

≈SNIFFLE≈ ≈WHIMPER≈

BE CAREFUL!

?!?

WE ARE ON THE SAME MOUNTAIN PEAK...BUT...THOSE LIGHTS! THOSE STRANGE HUTS! HOW DID THEY...?

EKUAR, J-JUST HOW...MUCH... TIME HAS PASSED SINCE *RAYEK* SNATCHED US? CAN YOU TELL?

TREMBLING, THE ANCIENT ROCK SHAPER KNEELS...

...AND BECOMES ONE WITH THE WEATHERED STONE.

≡GASP≡

MERCIFUL MOONS ABOVE...!

MY POOR HEAD THINKS *CUTTER* LEFT THE SCROLL ROOM JUST A WHILE AGO, BUT...

...FROM MY DAYS AS A FIRSTCOMER TOT... TO THE DAY BROWNSKIN FREED ME FROM THE TROLLS' PRISON HOLE... THAT IS HOW MUCH THIS MOUNTAIN HAS AGED!

NOOOOOOOO!

LEETAH!

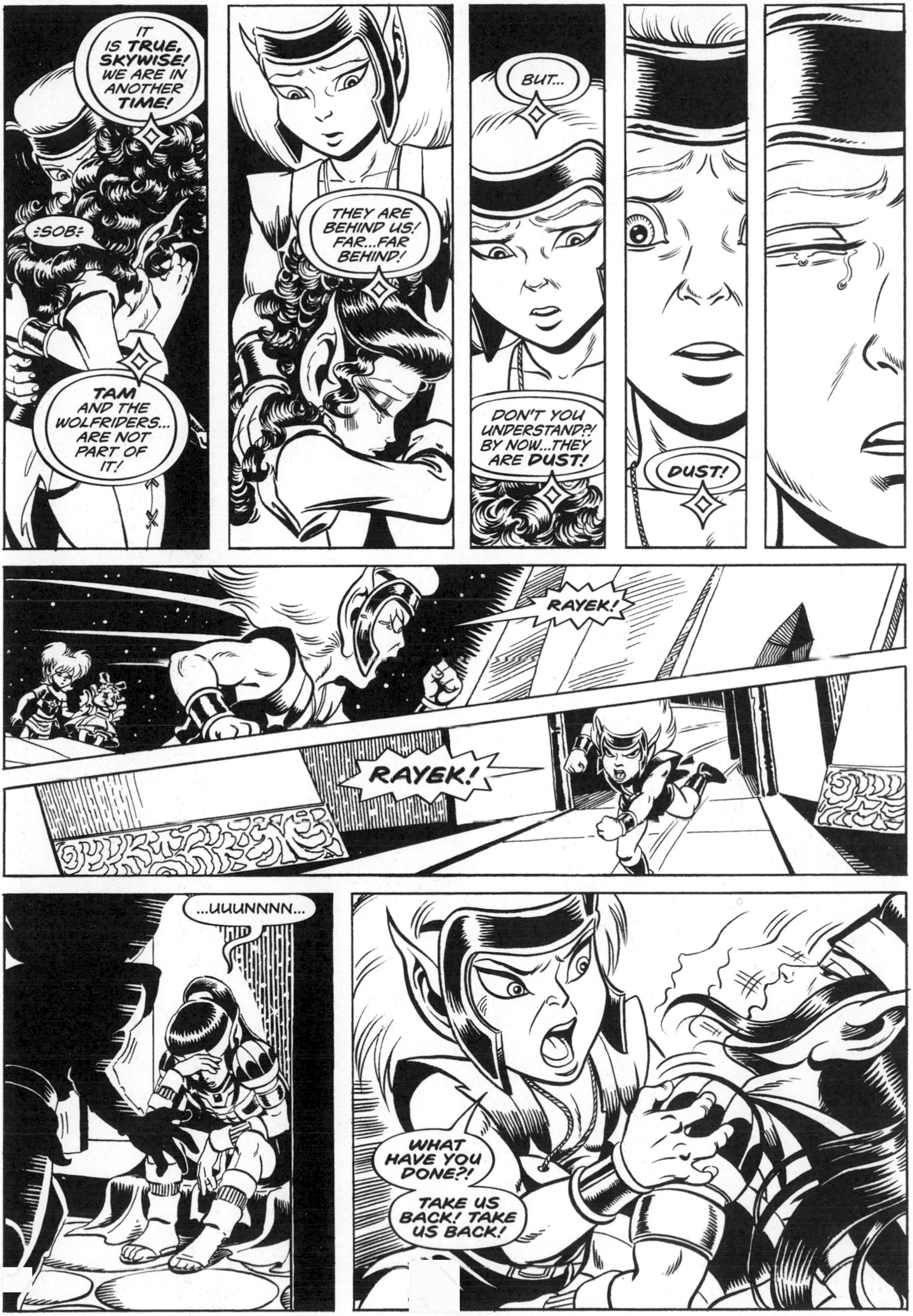

IT IS TRUE, SKYWISE! WE ARE IN ANOTHER TIME!
:SOB:
TAM AND THE WOLFRIDERS... ARE NOT PART OF IT!
THEY ARE BEHIND US! FAR...FAR BEHIND!
BUT...
DON'T YOU UNDERSTAND?! BY NOW...THEY ARE DUST!
DUST!
RAYEK!
RAYEK!
...UUUNNNN...
WHAT HAVE YOU DONE?!
TAKE US BACK! TAKE US BACK!

"BACK"...? THEN THE THING IS DONE?!

HUNH!

YOU SEE?! NO IDLE BOASTS, MINE! I WAS *RIGHT! I AM RIGHT!*

BROWNSKIN, PLEASE! WHERE DO YOU GO?!

HER CALL IS ONLY FOR THE MASTER OF THE PALACE. A MANY-THOUSAND-YEAR-OLD RENDEZVOUS HAS BEEN FAITHFULLY KEPT.

ENTICED BY HIS RECENT MEMORIES OF SENSUAL BLISS, YET WARY THAT THE BLACK SNAKE'S TEMPER HAS HAD MYRIAD TIDES IN WHICH TO SOUR...

...RAYEK HASTENS TO MOVE HIS MOST VALUABLE GAME PIECE...

...SO THAT WINNER *MUST* TAKE ALL!

MOTHERRRRR!

LEAVE ME WITH MY CHILDREN! DO *THAT* AT LEAST!

HUSH! ALL WILL BE WELL, *LEETAH...BETTER* THAN WELL!

486

YOU BEGAN YOUR TASK, STRANGE TO SAY, JUST *DAYS* AGO. *WINNOWILL*, HALF HEALED BY YOU, WAITS IN THE SEA BELOW.

SOON YOU WILL MAKE HER WHOLE...AS FIT AS *YOU* ARE, NOW, TO STAND WITH ME AND GREET THE HIGH ONES!

FOR HER OWN GOOD, SHE MUST BE TAKEN BY SURPRISE! DO AS I DO AND CONCEAL THE PLAN IN YOUR MIND!

SHE...EVEN SHE...WILL HAVE HER CHOICES MADE... BY *YOU?*

I-I ALWAYS BELIEVED THAT ONE DAY YOUR HEART WOULD OPEN FULLY.

I WAS PATIENT...BECAUSE I THOUGHT THERE WAS *TIME...*

...TIME ENOUGH FOR YOU TO LEARN HOW TO LOVE. I NEVER DREAMED YOU WOULD HARM ME SO!

HARM YOU?!

MY LIFEMATE...

BUT-BUT I *SPARED* YOU SEEING HIM AGE AND DIE LIKE AN ANIMAL! YOU *KNEW* HE WOULD!

YOU WERE WITH HIM ALL OF EIGHT AND THREE YEARS! HE WAS JUST A BREEZE THROUGH YOUR HAIR!

HE... WAS...MY... *SOUL!*

AAAGH!

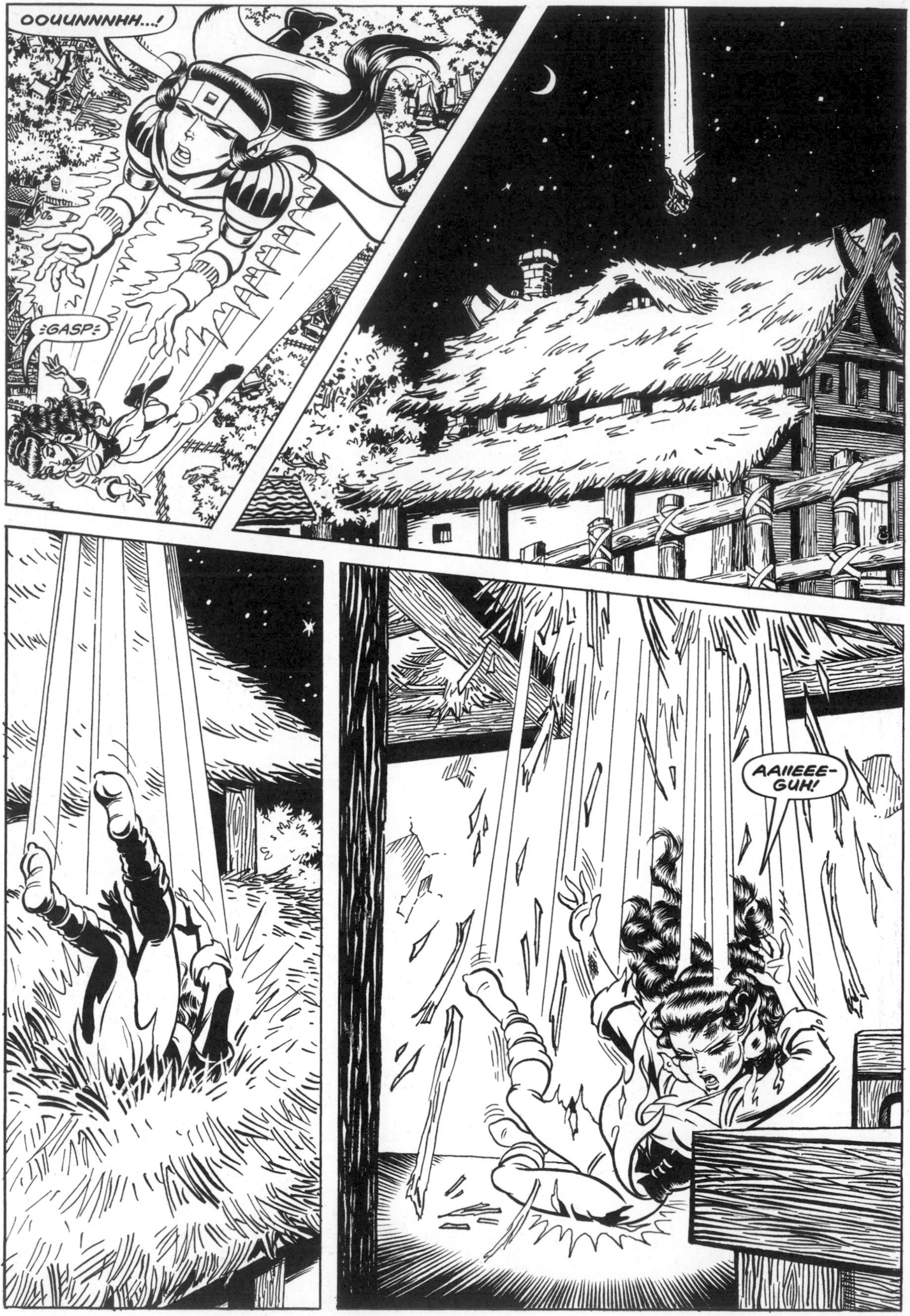
OOUUNNNHH...!
GASP
AAIIEEE-GUH!

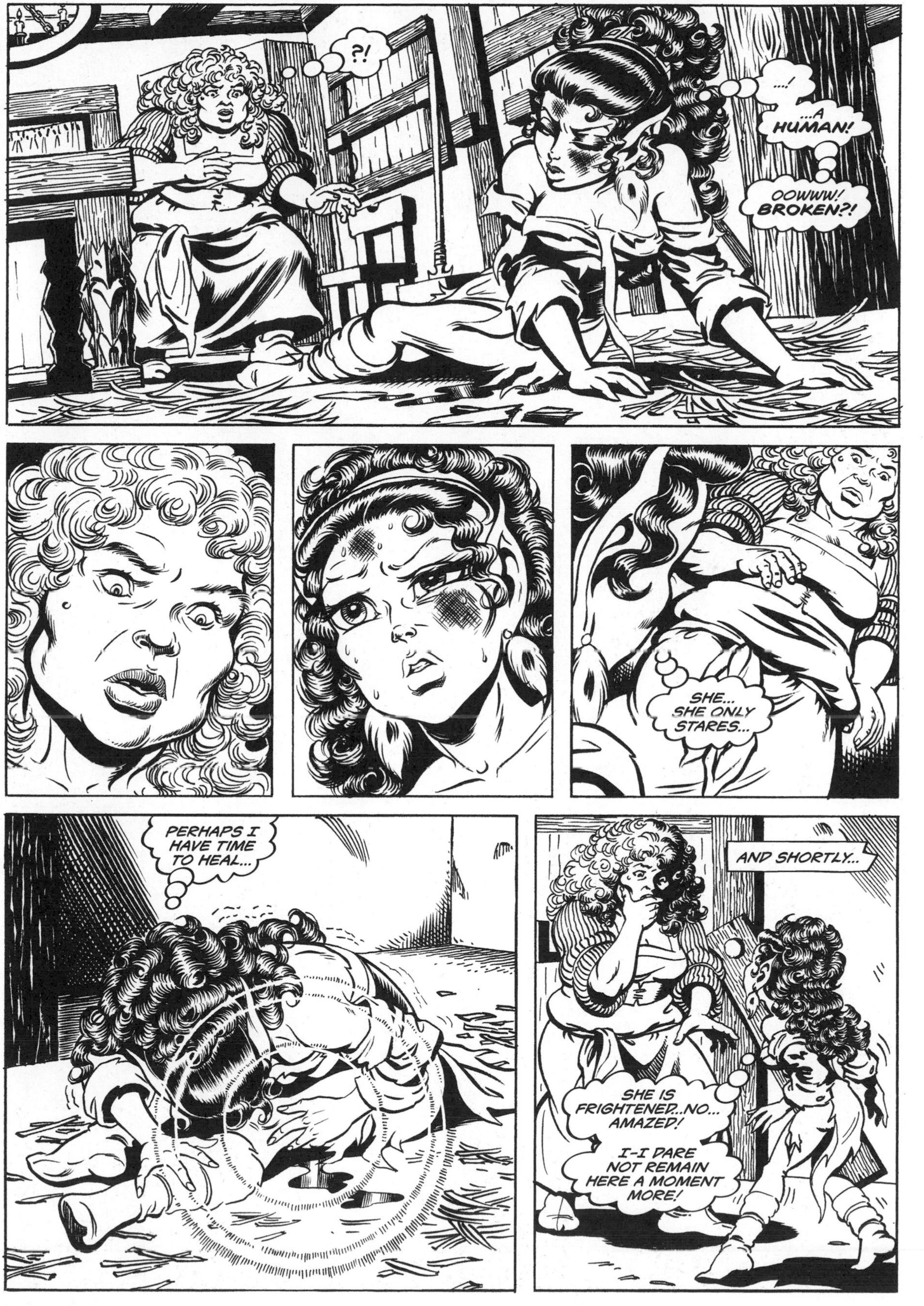
?!
...!
...A HUMAN!
OOWWW! BROKEN?!
SHE... SHE ONLY STARES...
PERHAPS I HAVE TIME TO HEAL...
AND SHORTLY...
SHE IS FRIGHTENED...NO... AMAZED!
I-I DARE NOT REMAIN HERE A MOMENT MORE!

SUNTOP AND EMBER NEED M--!

OH!

THE WOMAN'S HAND IS CALLUSED, HER GRIP STRONG.

BUT HER HEART IS NOT SO EASILY ASSESSED.

SHE DRAWS ME TOWARD THAT CURTAIN. WHY?

THIS YOUNG HUMAN IS DYING! SHE MUST BE TELLING ME SO!

SHE KNOWS I MENDED MYSELF. I...UNDERSTAND WHAT YOU WANT... POOR MOTHER.

BUT MY OWN CUBS... WHAT OF THEM?

IN THE END, LEETAH CANNOT TURN HER BACK ON SO MUCH SUFFERING.

AND SO, IMMERSED IN THE DEEPEST OF HEALING TRANCES, SHE MISSES AN ANXIOUS FRIEND'S REPEATED SENDINGS.

...NOT IN RANGE YET? NO! FROM THE MOUNTAINTOP, I *SAW* HER FALL AMONG THESE WEIRD HUTS!

SHE'S ALIVE! SHE **MUST** BE! I'LL FIND HER, **TAM!** WE'LL COME BACK TO YOU, I SWEAR IT!

WATCH IT! HUMANS KEEP NEAR-WOLVES TO GUARD THEM IN **THIS** TIME TOO!

≤PANT≥
≤PANT≥
≤PANT≥

BUT EVERYTHING ELSE IS SO...SO DIFFERENT! SO CROWDED TOGETHER! SO SMELLY! *PHEW!*

"AND THE SYMBOLS... ALL OVER!

"THEY LOOK SOMETHING LIKE US! I WONDER...?"

LEETAH! LEETAH! WHERE ARE YOU?

FOR TAM'S SAKE, HEALER, ANSWER ME!

NOTHING...!

LATER...

THERE!

...FEEL...TATTERED...AS MY LEATHERS! MUST GO...!

≡SSSIIIIGHHHH≡

HMMM? WHAT NOW?!

?!

...A GARMENT! HER EYES SEEM TO SAY, "THANK YOU!"

SOFT AS A BABY MOUSE'S FUR!

HUMANS... MAKING SUCH FINE THINGS! WONDROUS!

DO YOU FEEL THIS, MY *TAM?* I THINK YOU DO.

I THINK YOUR SPIRIT IS WITH ME.

IT MUST BELONG TO THE YOUNG ONE.

INDEED WE ARE OF A HEIGHT...

...THOUGH NOT OF A SIZE!

HER MATE...? ≡GASP≡ HUGE!

CAREFULLY... QUIETLY...!

ZZZZZ...

???

STAY BUSY WITH THE YOUNG ONE...PLEASE... PLEASE...PL--

OH!

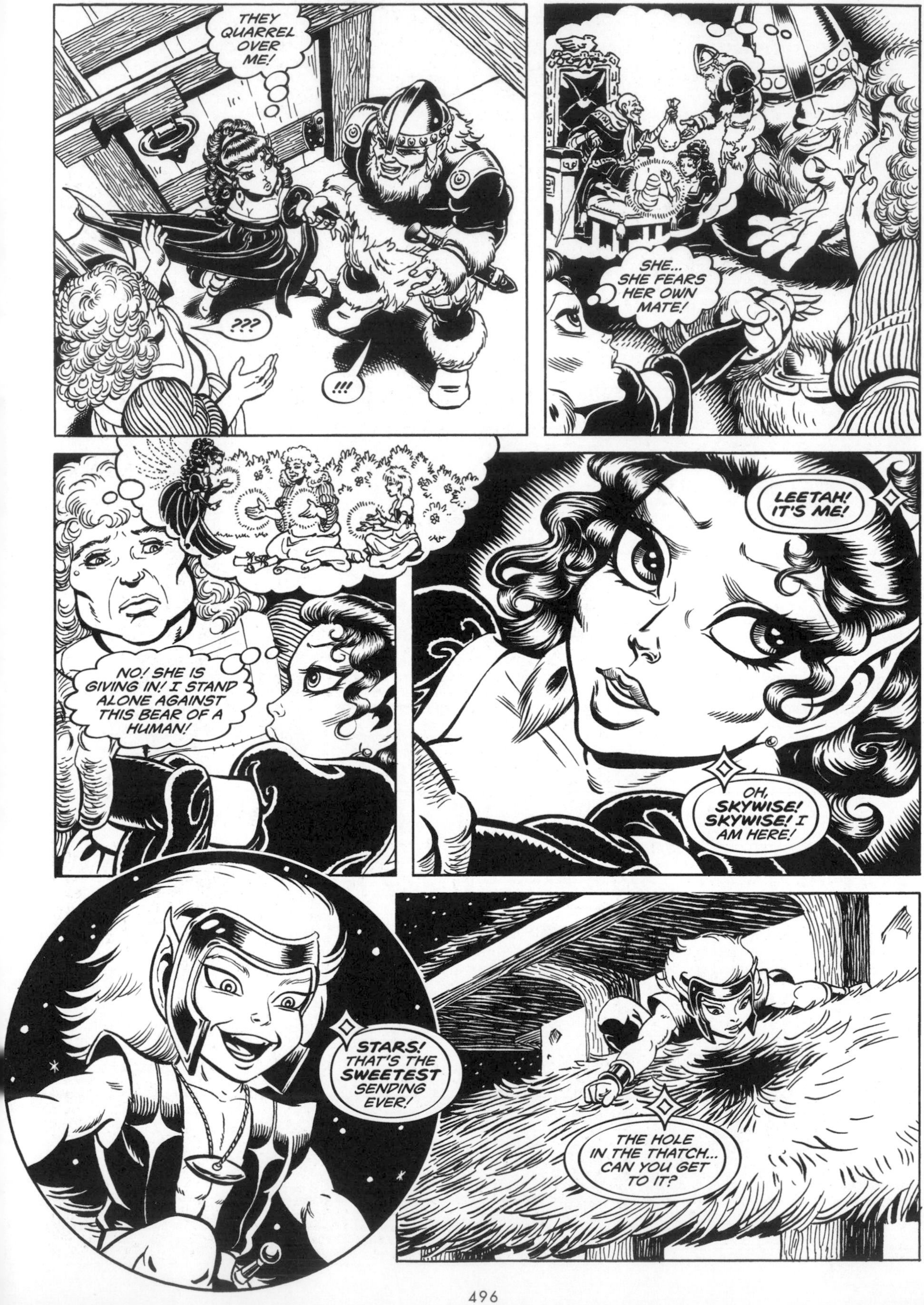
THEY QUARREL OVER ME!
???
!!!
SHE... SHE FEARS HER OWN MATE!
NO! SHE IS GIVING IN! I STAND ALONE AGAINST THIS BEAR OF A HUMAN!
LEETAH! IT'S ME!
OH, SKYWISE! SKYWISE! I AM HERE!
STARS! THAT'S THE SWEETEST SENDING EVER!
THE HOLE IN THE THATCH... CAN YOU GET TO IT?

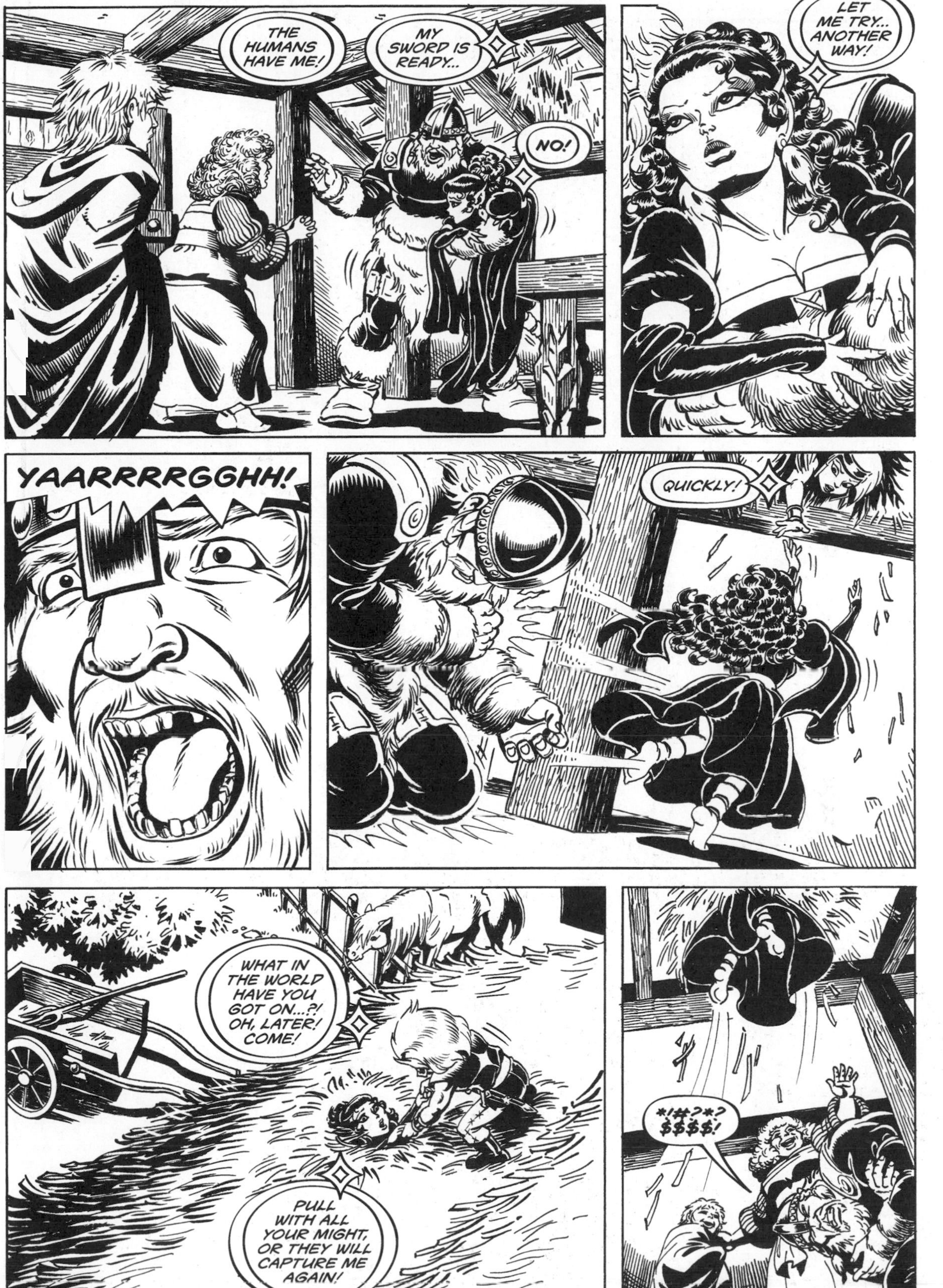
THE HUMANS HAVE ME!
MY SWORD IS READY...
NO!
LET ME TRY... ANOTHER WAY!
YAARRRRGGHH!
QUICKLY!
WHAT IN THE WORLD HAVE YOU GOT ON...?! OH, LATER! COME!
PULL WITH ALL YOUR MIGHT, OR THEY WILL CAPTURE ME AGAIN!
!#?? $$$$!

FLEEING THE SNARLS OF WAKENED HOUNDS AND AN OUTWITTED MERCENARY'S OATHS, THE TWO ELVES VANISH AMID PATCHES OF MOON SHADOW.

THE MINGLED SCENTS OF GROWTH AND DECAY ARE SOOTHING. TIME'S LENGTHY PASSAGE, UNNOTICED BY THE ELVES DURING THE PALACE'S FLIGHT, HAS NOT ALTERED THE NATURAL RHYTHMS OF THE FOREST.

DID RAYEK RETURN? ARE SUNTOP AND EMBER...?

EKUAR'S WATCHING THEM. EVEN TRINKET BEHAVES AROUND HIM! AS FOR RAYEK, LET HIM...JUST LET HIM SHOW UP!

TIRED? WE CAN AFFORD A REST.

SHORTLY...

PRETTY SOON IT'LL BE MORNING. IF THEY SPOT THE PALACE, THE HUMANS ARE BOUND TO COME SNOOPING UP THE MOUNTAIN.

ONLY RAYEK IS ABLE TO MAKE IT FLY. UNTIL HE RETURNS, WE MUST DEFEND IT AS BEST WE CAN.

:CHOKE: I–I STARTED TO SEND FOR TAM AND THE OTHERS...CAN'T BELIEVE THEY'RE...

I, TOO, HAVE SENT IN HOPE, BUT... SILENCE...ONLY SILENCE!

PERHAPS THEY CONTINUED WANDERING TO OTHER LANDS. PERHAPS SOMEWHERE, FAR OUT OF SENDING RANGE, THEIR CUBS' CUBS DWELL IN PEACE.

BUT THE WOLFRIDERS WE KNEW...DIED OUT...LONG AGO! =SIGH= TAM... BELOVED...!

"WHEN HE LEARNED OF HIS TRIBE'S MORTALITY, I HOPED HE WOULD CHOOSE, BY MY AID, TO DEFY FATE.

FOR WHAT?

I KNOW WHY YOU HID THE TRUTH. I UNDERSTAND.

WE'LL KEEP IT *OUR* SECRET --FOR NOW.

CAN YOU FORGIVE ME... MY LIFEMATE?

"INSTEAD, HE *EMBRACED* IT!"

AND SO DID ALL OF YOU! TO THE END, YOU CHOSE TO BE LIKE *WOLVES!*

NOT ALL OF US...NOT *NOW!* MY SOUL BROTHER, MY FRIENDS, MY *TIME*... THEY'VE BEEN *STOLEN* FROM ME!

YOU HAVE ENDLESS TURNS OF THE SEASONS AHEAD OF YOU, *LEETAH!* I DON'T! BUT *YOU* CAN GIVE THEM TO ME!

IF THERE'S A WAY BACK...EVEN IF IT TAKES A STAR'S LIFETIME... I WANT THAT CHANCE!

BUT... WITHOUT YOUR WOLF BLOOD, YOU WILL NO LONGER BE A...

I'LL BE WHAT I'LL BE! GIVE ME *TIME*, HEALER!

PLEASE!

PAIN GIVEN... BLOOD CHANGED. THOUGH THE DIFFERENCE LIES IN THE *WHY* OF IT...

...THERE IS NOTHING I DO, IT SEEMS, THAT *WINNOWILL* HAS NOT ALREADY DONE...

"...NOTHING!"

500

OOOHHHH... FINALLY... THE ACHE CEASES!

NO INJURY, BUT...GREAT SUN! WHAT DID SHE *DO?!*

SHE-SHE HURT ME! **LEETAH ATTACKED ME!** DID HER STAY WITH THE WOLFRIDERS CHANGE THE GENTLE ONE SO MUCH?

ONCE SHE WAS DRIVEN TO KILL...BUT ONLY TO SAVE HER CHILD. WHAT CAN HAVE PROVOKED HER, NOW, TO...?

≈GASP≈ CAN SHE POSSIBLY HAVE WANTED **CUTTER** MORE... **MORE** THAN DWELLING FOREVER WITH THE HIGH ONES?

STRIVE NOT TO UNRAVEL THE TWISTED INTENT OF ONE WHO WILLINGLY EMBRACES LIMITATION.

WINNOWILL! YOU SPY ON MY THOUGHTS!

RISE AND SEE, **RAYEK!** LAUGH AT HOW LITTLE THE WORLD HAS CHANGED! YOU LEAVE NOTHING BEHIND BUT A TIRED SONG, REPETITIOUS OF THEME, ENDLESS OF VERSE.

THE HIGH ONES APPEAR AT DAWN! I WILL HAVE BUT AN INSTANT TO UNITE MY PALACE WITH ITS ORIGINAL SELF. **SAVAH**...THE SUN FOLK... **TIMMAIN**...DID THEY SURVIVE?

YOU KNEW THEY WOULD, ELSE YOU'D NOT SO READILY HAVE COME FORWARD IN TIME.

DO YOU FEEL IT? EVEN NOW THE FIRST TROLLS PLOT REBELLION...AS THEIR GUARDIANS PART THE STARDUST FOR A HAZY GLIMPSE OF THIS WORLD.

GO, CHANGER OF WHAT WAS! GATHER THE SUN FOLK AS A GIFT TO CELEBRATE THE HIGH ONES' SALVATION.

AND MAKE OF **TIMMAIN** AN OFFERING TO HER **SELF!**

THAT I WILL DO! BUT FIRST I WISH TO SEE **YOU.** HOW HAVE YOU SURVIVED YOUR EXILE BENEATH THE WAVES?

AND WHY DO YOU SEEM AT EASE, WHERE I ENVISIONED YOU **WRITHING** FOR LACK OF ELFIN HEARTS AND MINDS TO RULE?!

RAGE CANNOT STAY ABOIL FOREVER IN THE VASTDEEP'S CALM! I HAVE **CHANGED!** AND I HAVE BEEN ENTERTAINED THIS LONG WHILE!

THE DEAR, FOOLISH HUMANS... THEIR DREAMS HAVE FED ME! I HAVE EVEN SENT THEM...PLAY-THINGS...TO KEEP THEIR FEARFUL FANCIES RICH AND AMUSING.

BY MY OWN KIND I WAS SPURNED...SHUT OUT! I HAVE FORGOTTEN THEM ALL! ALL SAVE YOU, MY LORD!

YOU WAITED FOR ME. I AM HONORED.

THE GLIDERS PERISHED THAT YOU MIGHT RESTORE THE PALACE.

YOU SHALL RESTORE **ME** TOO. AMONG THE HIGH ONES I SHALL BE REBORN, CLEANSED IN EVERY WAY OF THIS WORLD!

HOW I WANT YOU, LOVELY SNAKE!

BUT YOU ARE BY NO MEANS HEALED OF YOUR OVERPOWERING WAYS!

"AND UNTIL YOU ARE, PART OF ME MUST REMAIN CLOSED TO YOU...THE PART THAT NEEDS, AND **WILL** HAVE, **LEETAH'S** AID!"

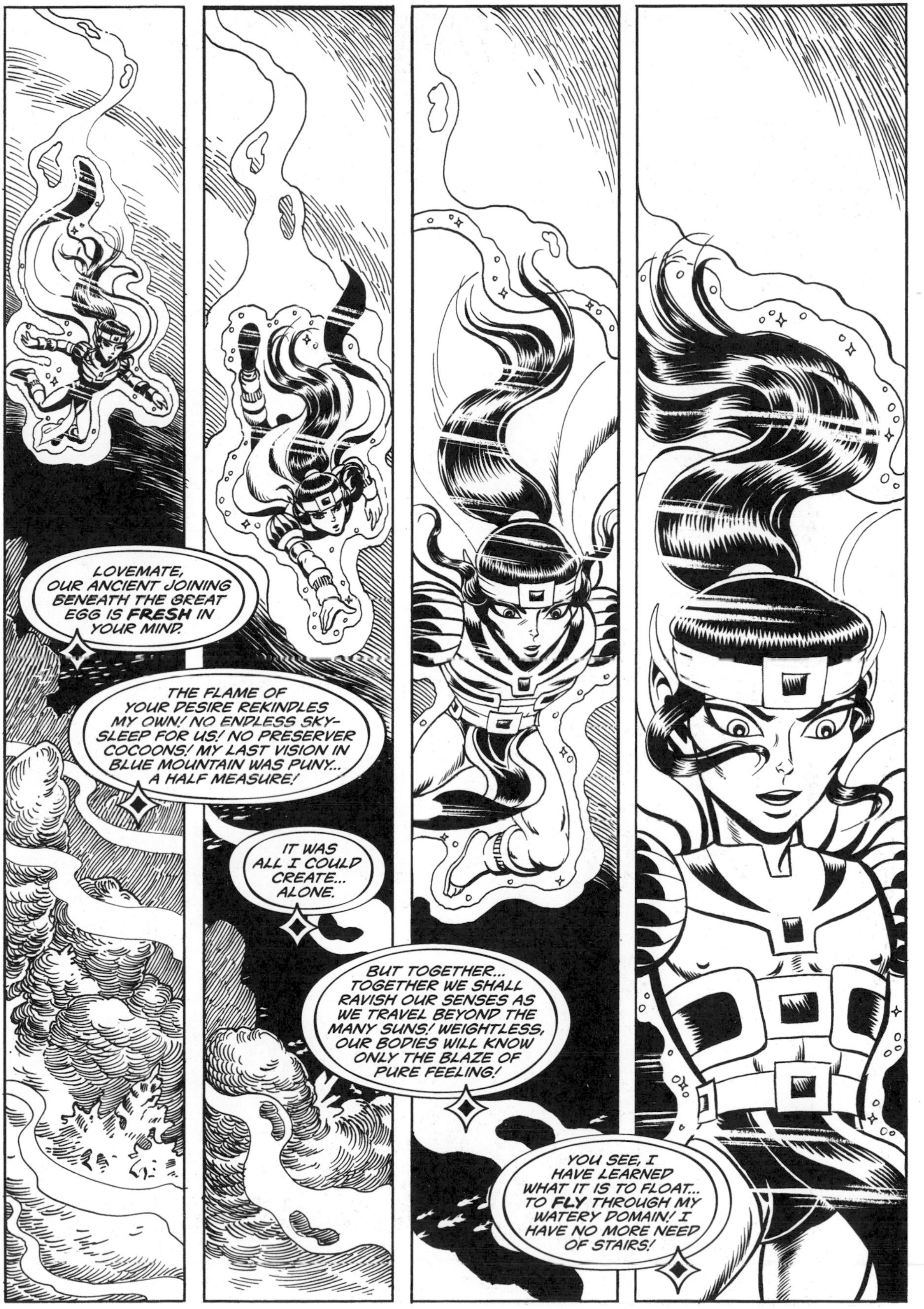
LOVEMATE, OUR ANCIENT JOINING BENEATH THE GREAT EGG IS FRESH IN YOUR MIND.
THE FLAME OF YOUR DESIRE REKINDLES MY OWN! NO ENDLESS SKY-SLEEP FOR US! NO PRESERVER COCOONS! MY LAST VISION IN BLUE MOUNTAIN WAS PUNY... A HALF MEASURE!
IT WAS ALL I COULD CREATE... ALONE.
BUT TOGETHER... TOGETHER WE SHALL RAVISH OUR SENSES AS WE TRAVEL BEYOND THE MANY SUNS! WEIGHTLESS, OUR BODIES WILL KNOW ONLY THE BLAZE OF PURE FEELING!
YOU SEE, I HAVE LEARNED WHAT IT IS TO FLOAT... TO FLY THROUGH MY WATERY DOMAIN! I HAVE NO MORE NEED OF STAIRS!

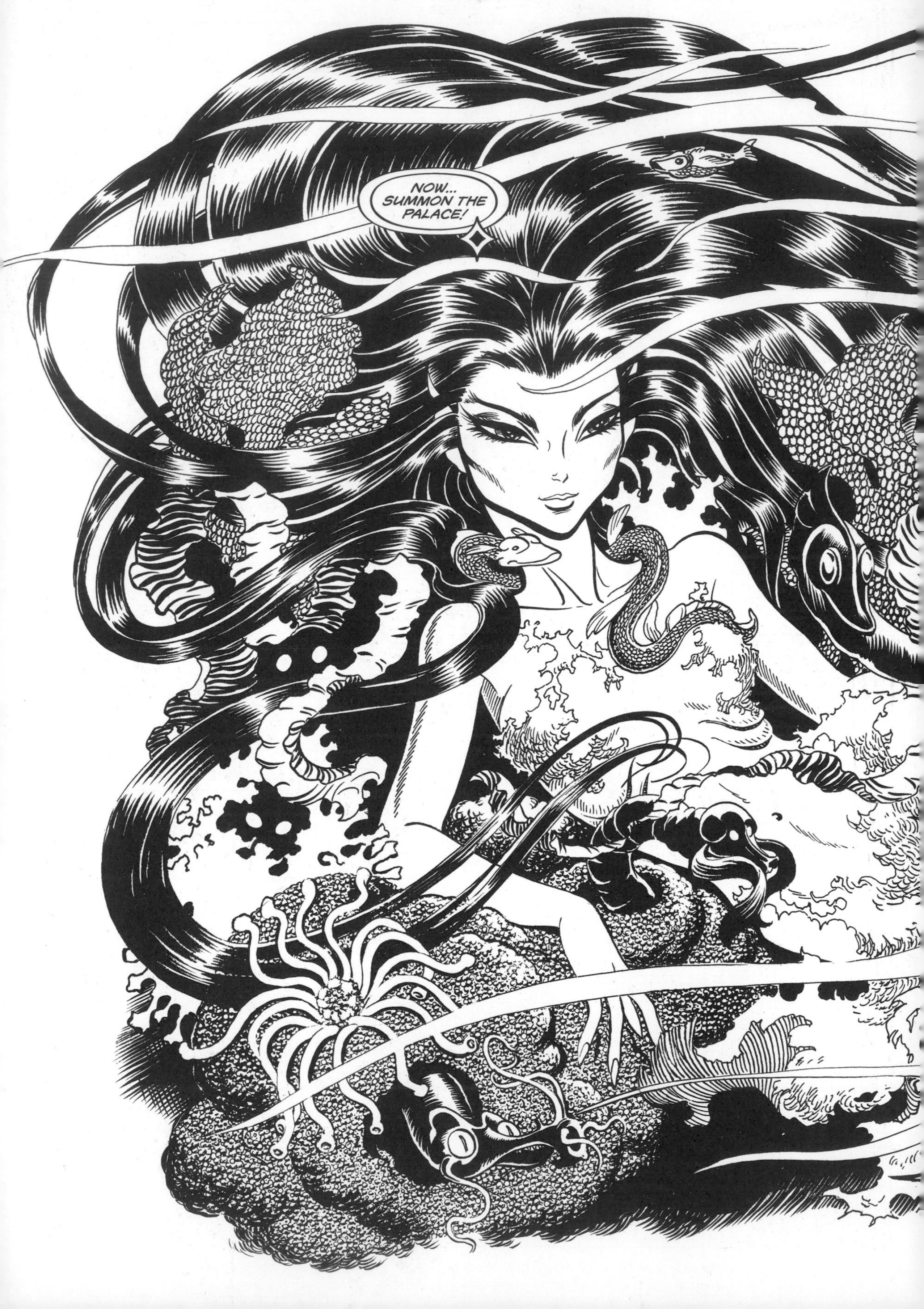
NOW... SUMMON THE PALACE!

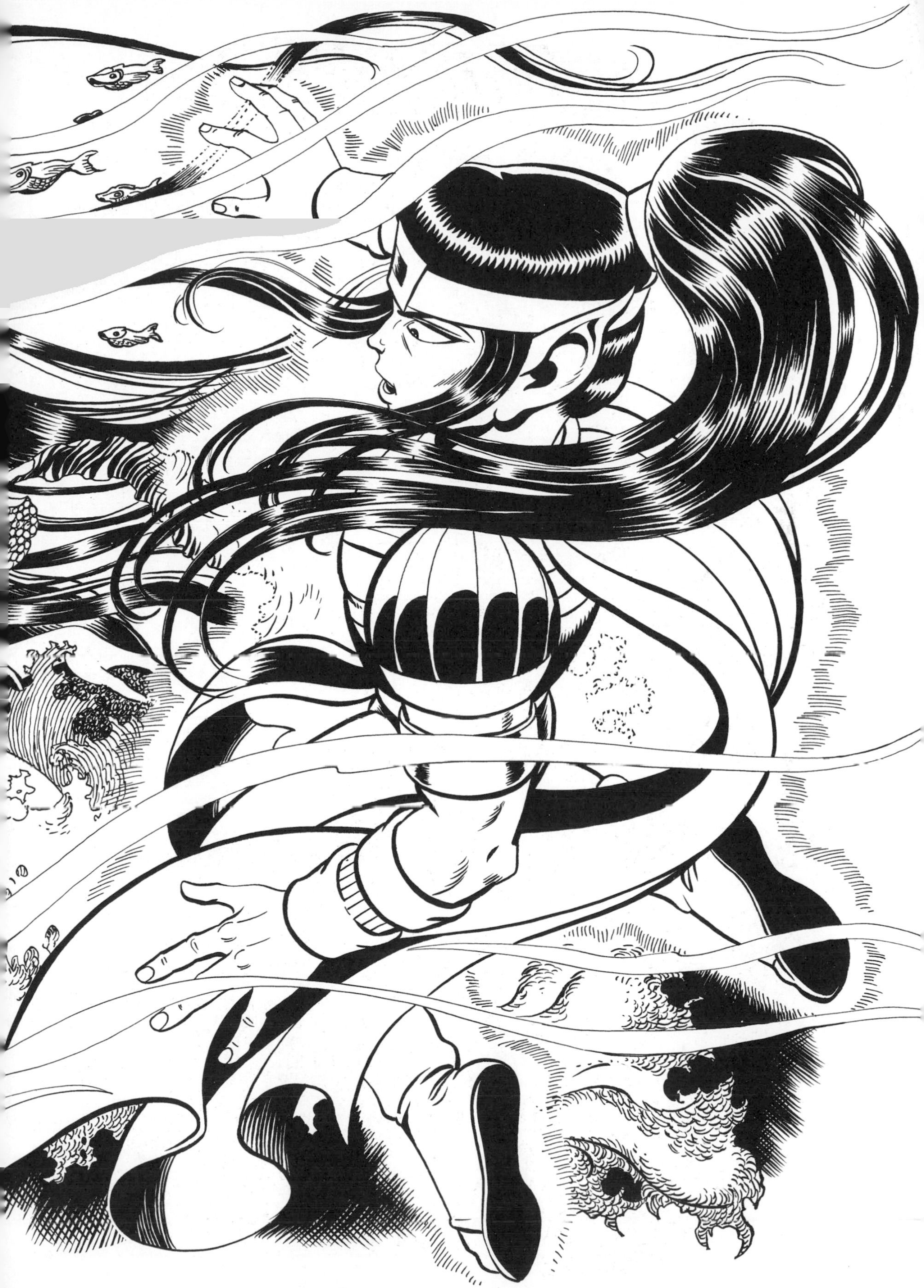

MEANWHILE, SEQUESTERED IN THE SCROLL ROOM...

THINK NOW. IF WE COULD COME TO THIS TIME, AND WE DID, THEN SURELY WE CAN GO BACK! THINGS WILL TURN OUT FOR THE BEST--

--NOT WHILE *RAYEK* TRIES TO BE CHIEF!

THERE IS KINDNESS IN HIM, YOUNG AND IMPATIENT AS HE IS.

:SIGH: BUT IT DOES SEEM HIS DESIRE TO RESCUE THE HIGH ONES HAS BLINDED HIM TO ALL ELSE.

AND I'M THE ONE WHO GOT HIM STARTED!

I HEARD THE CRY...DIDN'T THINK IT OVER...JUST BOTHERED EVERYBODY 'TIL THEY DID SOMETHING ABOUT IT!

NOW FATHER IS... IS...WHAT IF WE NEVER SEE HIM AGAIN?!

SOMETIMES... I THINK I GET A "MAGIC FEELING"...LIKE SOMEBODY'S... REACHING. BUT WHAT DO I KNOW?

"I WAS WRONG ABOUT THE CRY."

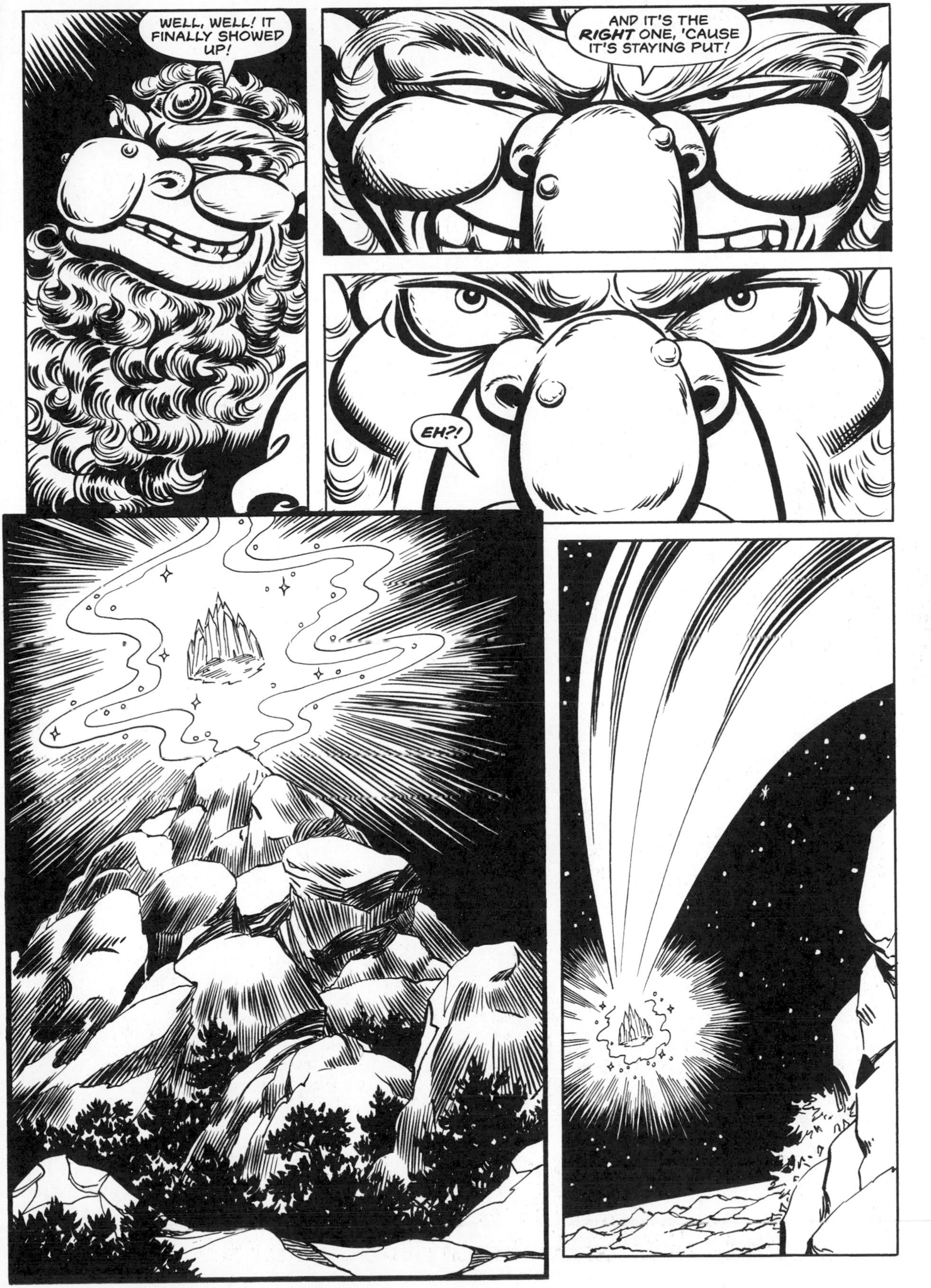
WELL, WELL! IT FINALLY SHOWED UP!
AND IT'S THE RIGHT ONE, 'CAUSE IT'S STAYING PUT!
EH?!

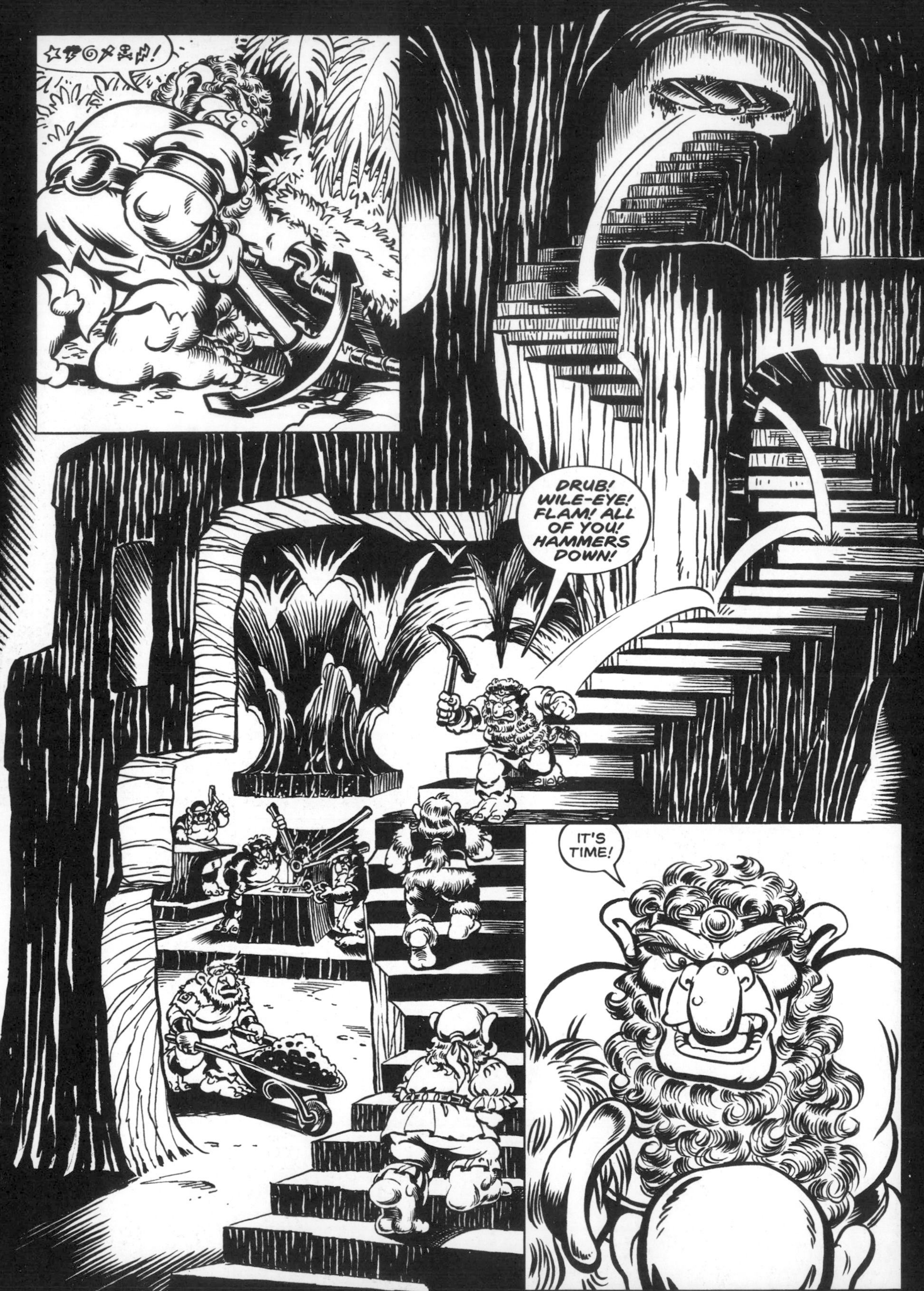
DRUB! WILE-EYE! FLAM! ALL OF YOU! HAMMERS DOWN!
IT'S TIME!

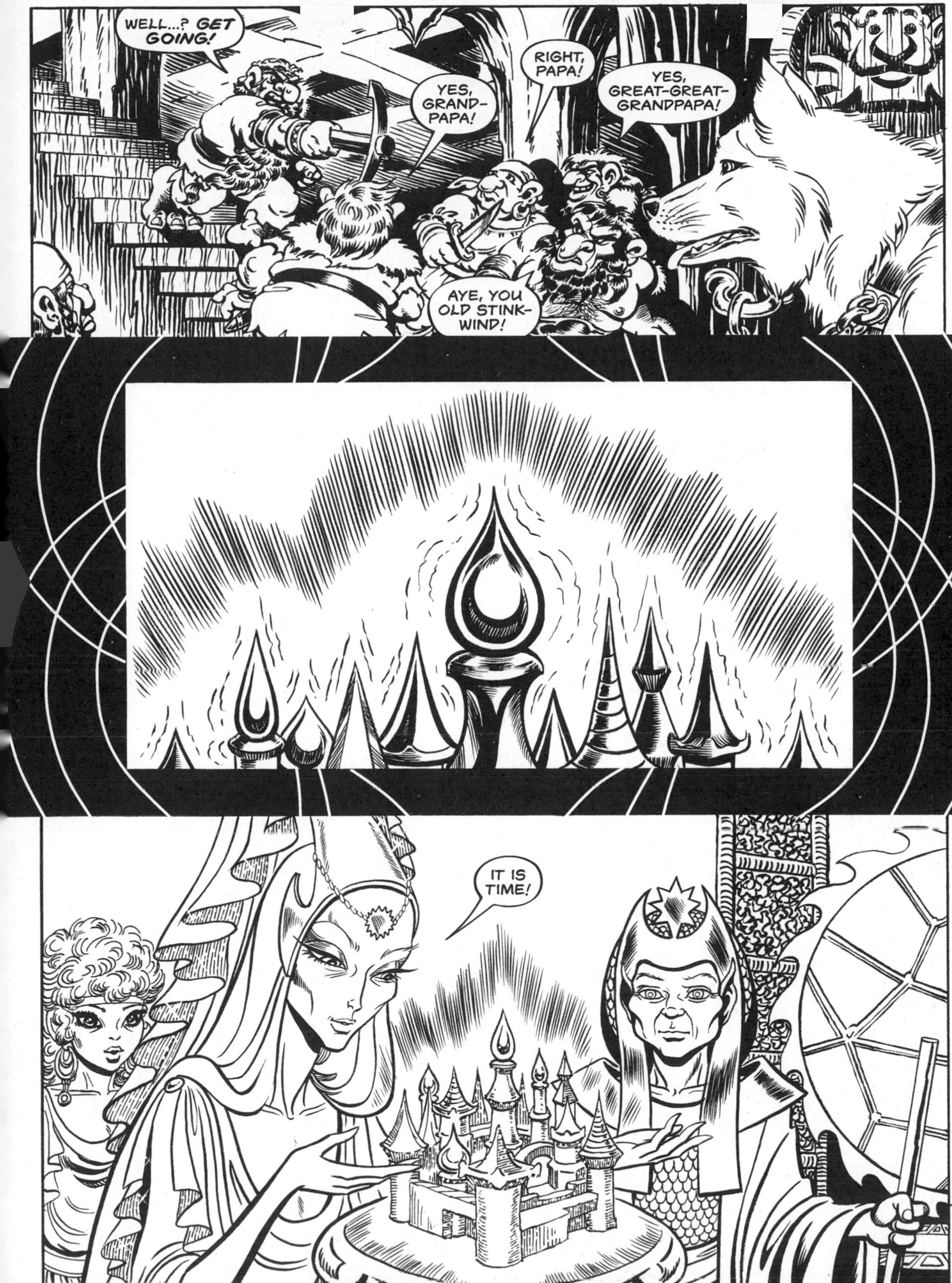
WELL...? GET GOING!
YES, GRAND-PAPA!
RIGHT, PAPA!
YES, GREAT-GREAT-GRANDPAPA!
AYE, YOU OLD STINK-WIND!
IT IS TIME!

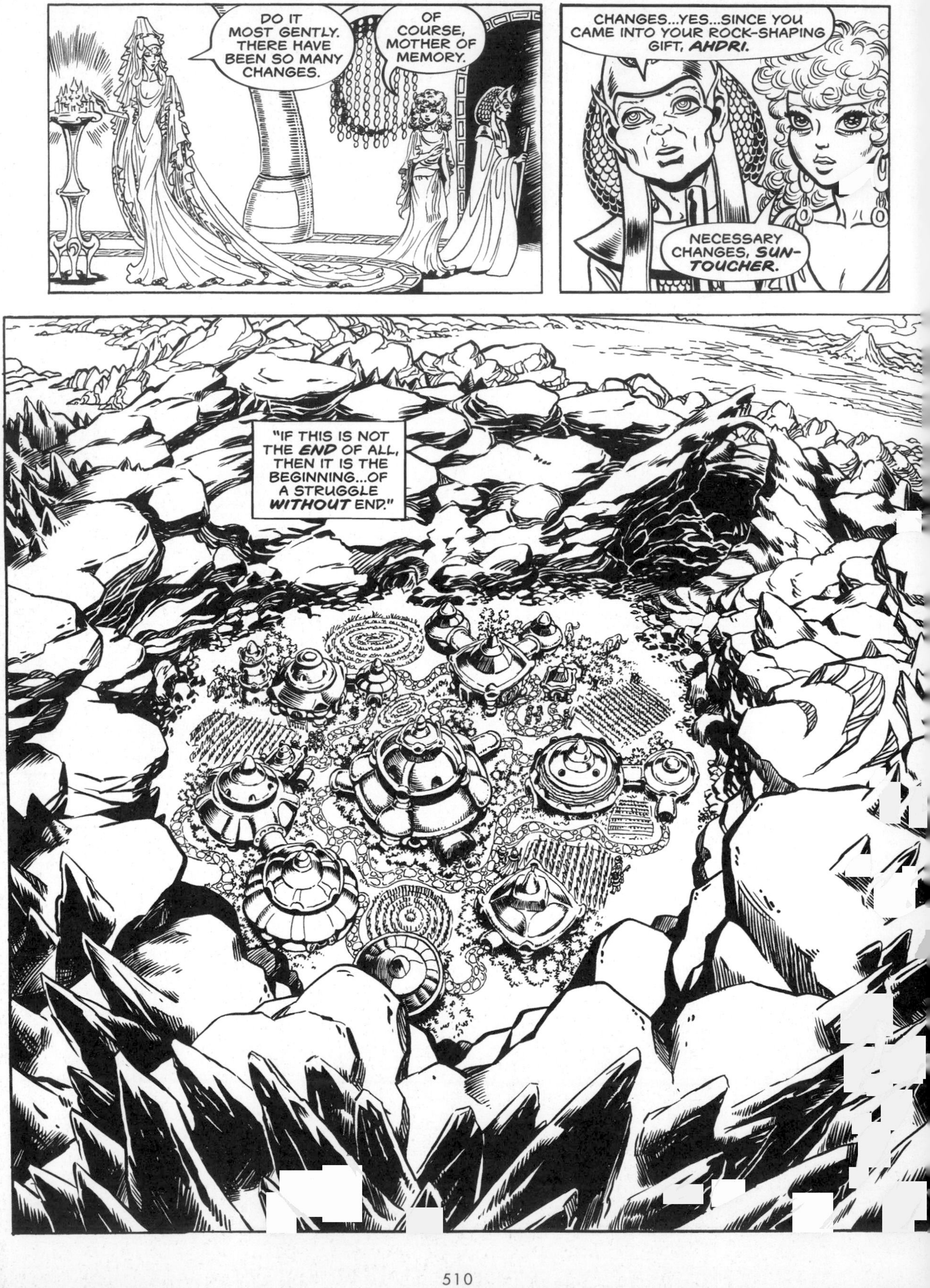
DO IT MOST GENTLY. THERE HAVE BEEN SO MANY CHANGES.
OF COURSE, MOTHER OF MEMORY.
CHANGES...YES...SINCE YOU CAME INTO YOUR ROCK-SHAPING GIFT, AHDRI.
NECESSARY CHANGES, SUN-TOUCHER.
"IF THIS IS NOT THE END OF ALL, THEN IT IS THE BEGINNING...OF A STRUGGLE WITHOUT END."

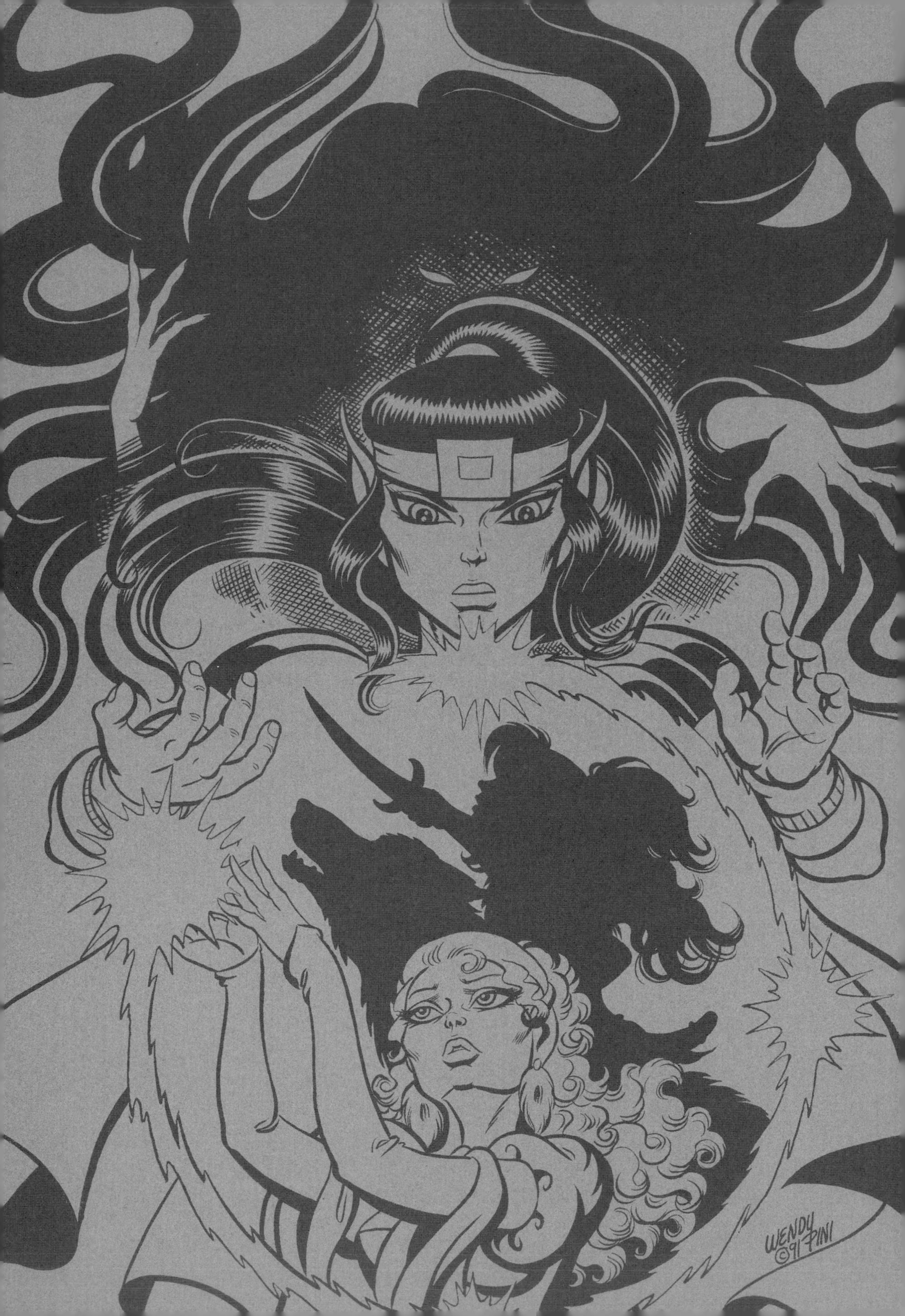
WENDY
©91 PINI

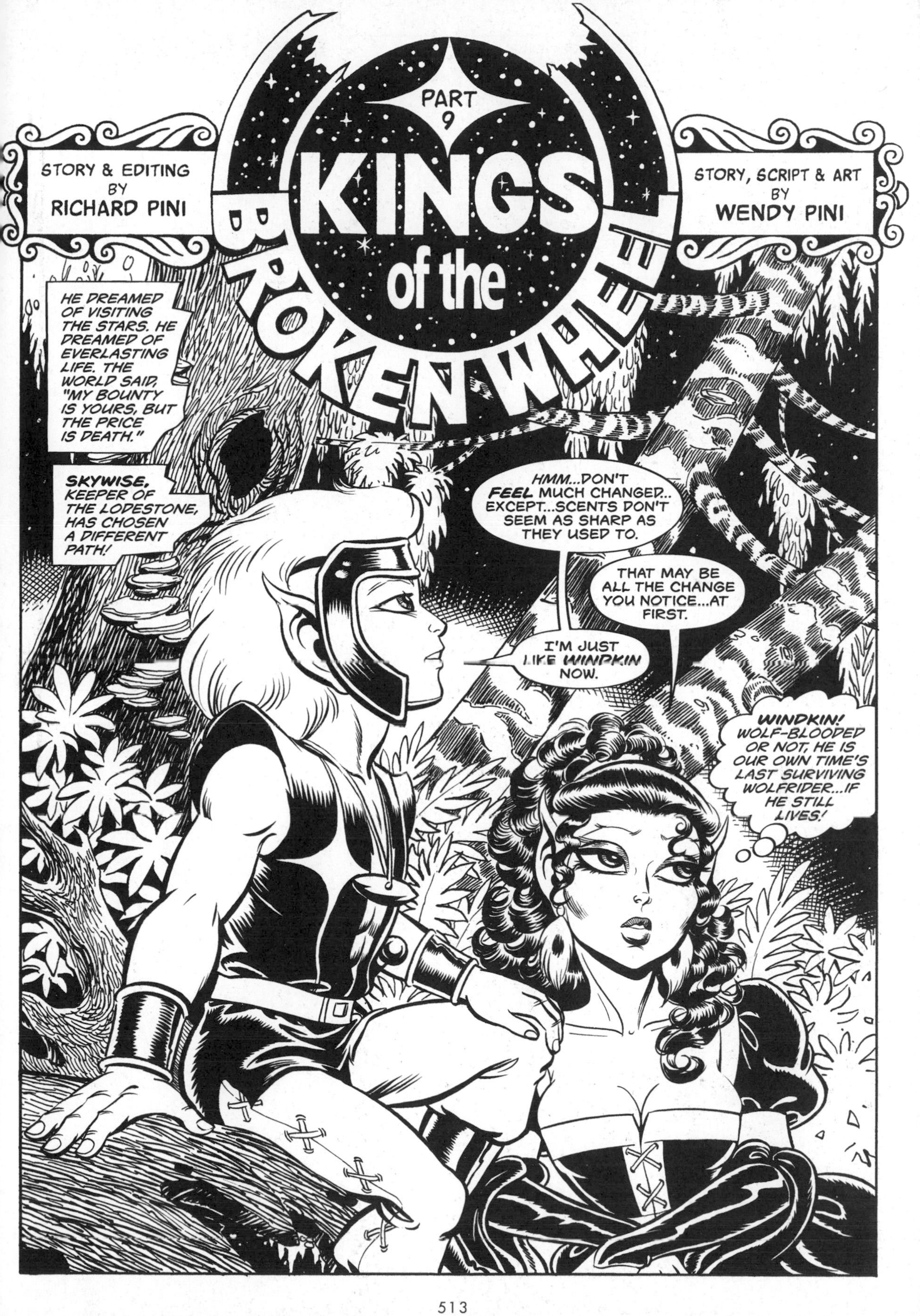
PART 9
KINGS of the BROKEN WHEEL
STORY & EDITING BY RICHARD PINI
STORY, SCRIPT & ART BY WENDY PINI
HE DREAMED OF VISITING THE STARS. HE DREAMED OF EVERLASTING LIFE. THE WORLD SAID, "MY BOUNTY IS YOURS, BUT THE PRICE IS DEATH."
SKYWISE, KEEPER OF THE LODESTONE, HAS CHOSEN A DIFFERENT PATH!
HMM...DON'T FEEL MUCH CHANGED... EXCEPT...SCENTS DON'T SEEM AS SHARP AS THEY USED TO.
THAT MAY BE ALL THE CHANGE YOU NOTICE...AT FIRST.
I'M JUST LIKE WINDKIN NOW.
WINDKIN! WOLF-BLOODED OR NOT, HE IS OUR OWN TIME'S LAST SURVIVING WOLFRIDER...IF HE STILL LIVES!

LET'S GET BACK TO *SUNTOP!* HE CAN "GO OUT," SEARCH FOR *SAVAH!* SHE'LL TELL US WHAT HAPPENED...

...MAYBE EVEN HOW TO STOP *RAYEK!*

YOUR FAITH MUST CARRY US BOTH. MINE IS GONE.

DON'T GIVE U-UU-UUUUUUPPP?!

≈GASP≈ *RAYEK!*

HA! POINT-EARED BABY-SNATCHER! AFTER ALL THIS TIME, HE COULDN'T FOOL OLD *PICKNOSE!* HOLD HER DOWN!

WHINE! WHINE!

AYE! ELSE WE'LL BE *DAYS* SCRAPING WOLF GUTS OFF THE CEILING!

WOOOAAAAA!

AAAYOOOOAAHHH!

MOTHER! SKYWISE! YOU'RE BACK! YOU'RE BACK!

WHAT'RE YOU WEARING, MOTHER...? YOU SMELL ALL OVER LIKE *HUMANS!* *CHOPLICKER,* HE'S...HE WENT OUTSIDE...JUST FOR A BIT! THE PALACE FLEW AWAY SO FAST, WE LEFT HIM BEHIND ON THE MOUNTAINTOP!

HE IS A STRONG AND CRAFTY WOLF, KITLING. HE CAN PROTECT HIMSELF.

FEELS LIKE THE PALACE HAS SETTLED!

"OOOHH! MY *EARS*...ALL PLUGGED UP!"

"MINE TOO, *EMBER!* WHERE IN *FREEFOOT'S* NAME ARE WE NOW?!"

BWAAAAAAHH! DON'T LIKE IT!

I KNOW LITTLE OF THE SEA...AND EVEN LESS OF GETTING ABOUT IN IT!

A SURGE OF WATER CARRIES US FORWARD! SHE IS CREATING IT SOMEHOW! SO THAT IS HOW *WINNOWILL* "FLIES"!

THE PALACE...AT LAST!

I HAVE DISGUISED IT.

NO MATTER! I KNOW I BEHOLD MY FREEDOM! YOU CANNOT SEE MY TEARS, *RAYEK*, BUT...

....I-I FEEL *JOY*!

SEEING **YOU**...FILLED WITH A CHILD'S WONDER... IS A JOY GREATER STILL!

I LOVE YOU...AS I LOVE NO OTHER!

ONLY IN **WINNOWILL'S** INFINITELY YOUNGER DAYS DID **VOLL**, FIRST LORD OF THE GLIDERS, GLIMPSE HER THUS-- OPEN, ALIVE, AND UNWARY.

THE AURA WHICH KEEPS YOU DRY AND BREATHING SURROUNDS THE PALACE TOO. IF I AM TO ENTER, I MUST RESHAPE MYSELF FOR AIR-LIVING.

A PITY! NOT ONE OF OUR KIND IS UNPLEASANT TO LOOK ON. BUT **YOU**! THE HIGH ONES MUST **SEE**, MUST **KNOW** THEIR MOST GLORIOUS CHILD!

HA HA! NONE BUT YOU ARE SO OUTRAGEOUS IN YOUR USE OF THE OLD POWERS!

MY LORD...!

WHEN THE TWO PALACES BECOME ONE...SO SHALL YOU AND I!

...!?

THAT IS... ONCE **LEETAH** HAS SWEPT OUT THE LAST OF YOUR DARK CORNERS!

TIME GROWS SHORT. MUST COLLECT *SAVAH* AND THE SUN FOLK. AND WHERE IS *TIMMAIN?*

HOPE *LEETAH* CAN WORK THE HEALING QUICKLY!

TRINKET WANTS TO GO HOME NOW...:SNIFF: PLEEEEZE?!

...ONLY...ONLY SO MUCH OF THE PALACE'S POWER I CAN CONTAIN AT ONE TIME! CAREFUL! MUST BE FIT...FOR THE MERGING!

RAYEK... TAKE US BACK TO *CUTTER.* **NOW!**

NOT EVEN IF I COULD AND STILL KEEP TO MY PLAN!

ACCEPT IT! YOU ARE ONE OF THE *FEW* CHOSEN TO HELP SAVE THE HIGH ONES!

WHAT MAKES YOU THINK THAT WILL MATTER TO THEM? YOU DO NOT KNOW WHAT MATTERS AT ALL!

WINNOWILL'S CURE MATTERS!

IF ONLY I COULD CURE *YOU!* BUT YOU ARE NOT MAD, YOU ARE JUST WRONG...AS WRONG AS ANYONE HAS EVER BEEN!

ENOUGH! SHE WILL SHAKE OFF MY SPELL AT ANY MOMENT! *COME!*

HOW *DARE* YOU GIVE ORDERS?!

YOU'RE NO *CHIEF!* I CHALLENGE YOU FOR THE PALACE!

BETTER FOR YOU, HAD YOU BEEN LEFT BEHIND WITH YOUR MORTAL TRIBE, WOLFRIDER!

OOOWWW!

BETTER?! YOU FOOL! *SKYWISE* HAS BECOME...

BROWNSKIN... YOU—YOU SHOULDN'T...

DO NOT WASTE THE POWER OF YOUR TOUCH ON ME, *LEETAH!* HE WILL SUFFER TOO!

PUCKERNUTS! I HATE YOU, YOU BIG COWARD!

WHAT'RE YOU AFRAID OF?!

WHY ARE YOU RUNNING AWAY?

YOU HAVE BEEN FILLED BY THE SCROLL OF COLORS, *SUNTOP!* YOU KNOW WHAT WE IMMORTALS *COULD* BE!

BUT HERE, WE ARE HOBBLED, DISGRACED...EVEN *YOU!* YOU DESERVE BETTER!

I MEAN TO ESCAPE THIS CURSED WORLD WITH AS MANY OTHERS LIKE ME AS I CAN!

WHEN WE PREVENT THEIR FALL, WHEN THEY REALIZE THE HARDSHIP WE'VE SPARED THEM, THE HIGH ONES WILL HONOR US!

BUT IT MUST BE *NOW!* I MAY *NEVER* BE ABLE TO CREATE SUCH A CHANCE FOR US AGAIN!

RAYEK! LET SKYWISE GO!

IF IT TAKES *THIS* TO MAKE YOU COME WITH ME, SO BE IT!

DO NOT BE AFRAID. YOU SHALL NOT DROWN.

I AM SORRY... ABOUT *CUTTER.* IN THE HIGH ONES' ARMS, I PRAY YOUR GRIEF ENDS!

YOU THINK I DO NOT KNOW HOW TO LOVE. BUT IF NOT FOR LOVE OF YOU... OF ALL *TRUE* ELVES... WHY WOULD I HAVE RISKED SO MUCH?

FINISH HEALING *WINNOWILL!* THEN YOU WILL UNDER-STAND!

YOU!

YOU *TRICKED* ME, *LOVEMATE. FAIR ENOUGH!*

BUT NOW... YOU BRING THIS *TORTURER* TO ME?!

ONLY TO MAKE YOU COMPLETELY *WELL!*

YOU HAVE SHED SO MUCH SICKNESS ALREADY THAT--

SICKNESS! YOU, MY SOUL'S *BROTHER,* JUDGE ME SO?!

WE *USE* EACH OTHER'S *FLAWS* TO OUR ADVANTAGE! WHY ELSE WOULD I CALL YOU "LORD"? WE ARE *ALIKE!*

ONLY...*SHE* HAS NOT RAKED YOU RAW WITH HER TOUCH AND LEFT *YOU* TO BLEED... *ALONE!*

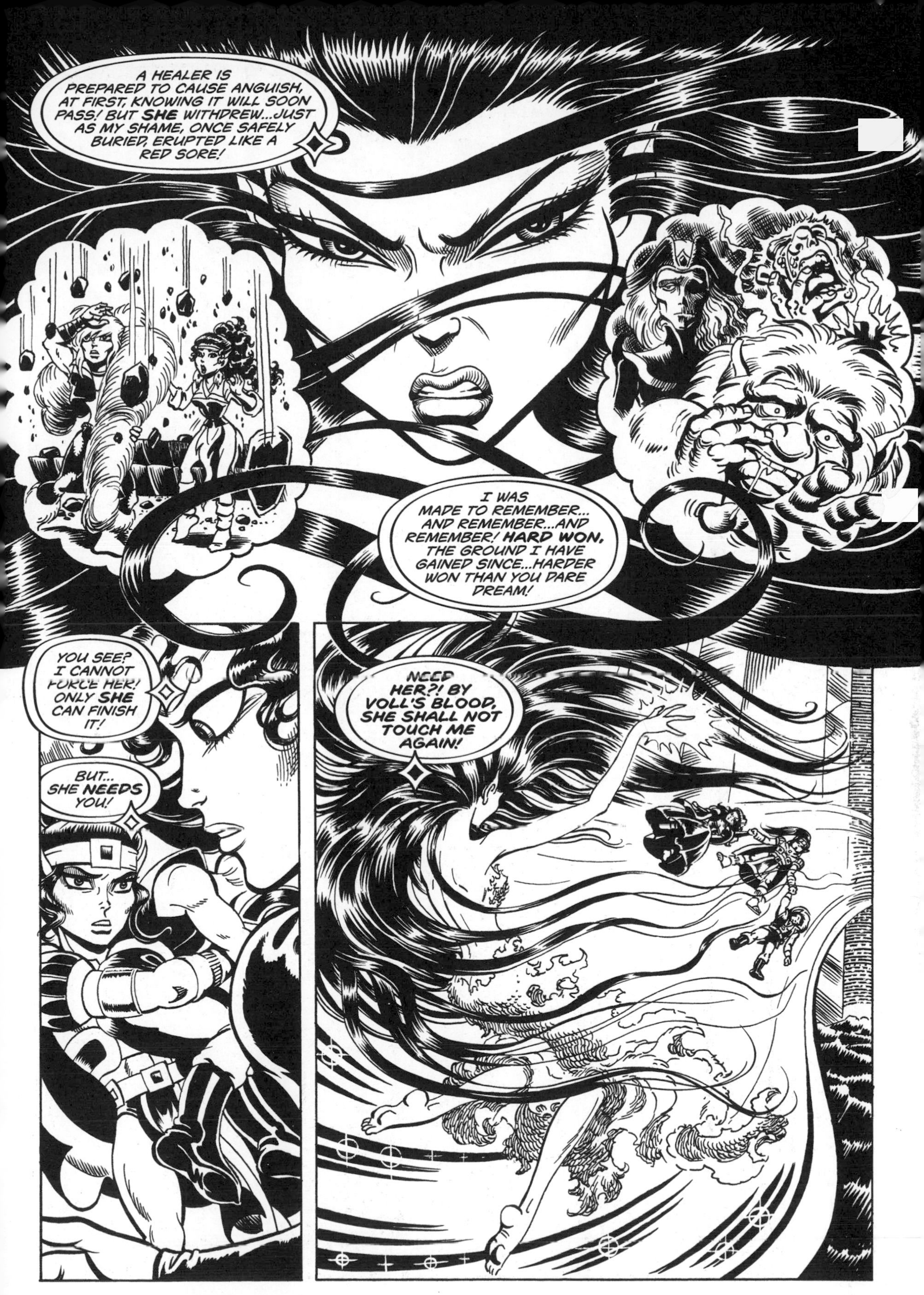
A HEALER IS PREPARED TO CAUSE ANGUISH, AT FIRST, KNOWING IT WILL SOON PASS! BUT SHE WITHDREW...JUST AS MY SHAME, ONCE SAFELY BURIED, ERUPTED LIKE A RED SORE!
I WAS MADE TO REMEMBER... AND REMEMBER...AND REMEMBER! HARD WON, THE GROUND I HAVE GAINED SINCE...HARDER WON THAN YOU DARE DREAM!
YOU SEE? I CANNOT FORCE HER! ONLY SHE CAN FINISH IT!
BUT... SHE NEEDS YOU!
NEED HER?! BY VOLL'S BLOOD, SHE SHALL NOT TOUCH ME AGAIN!

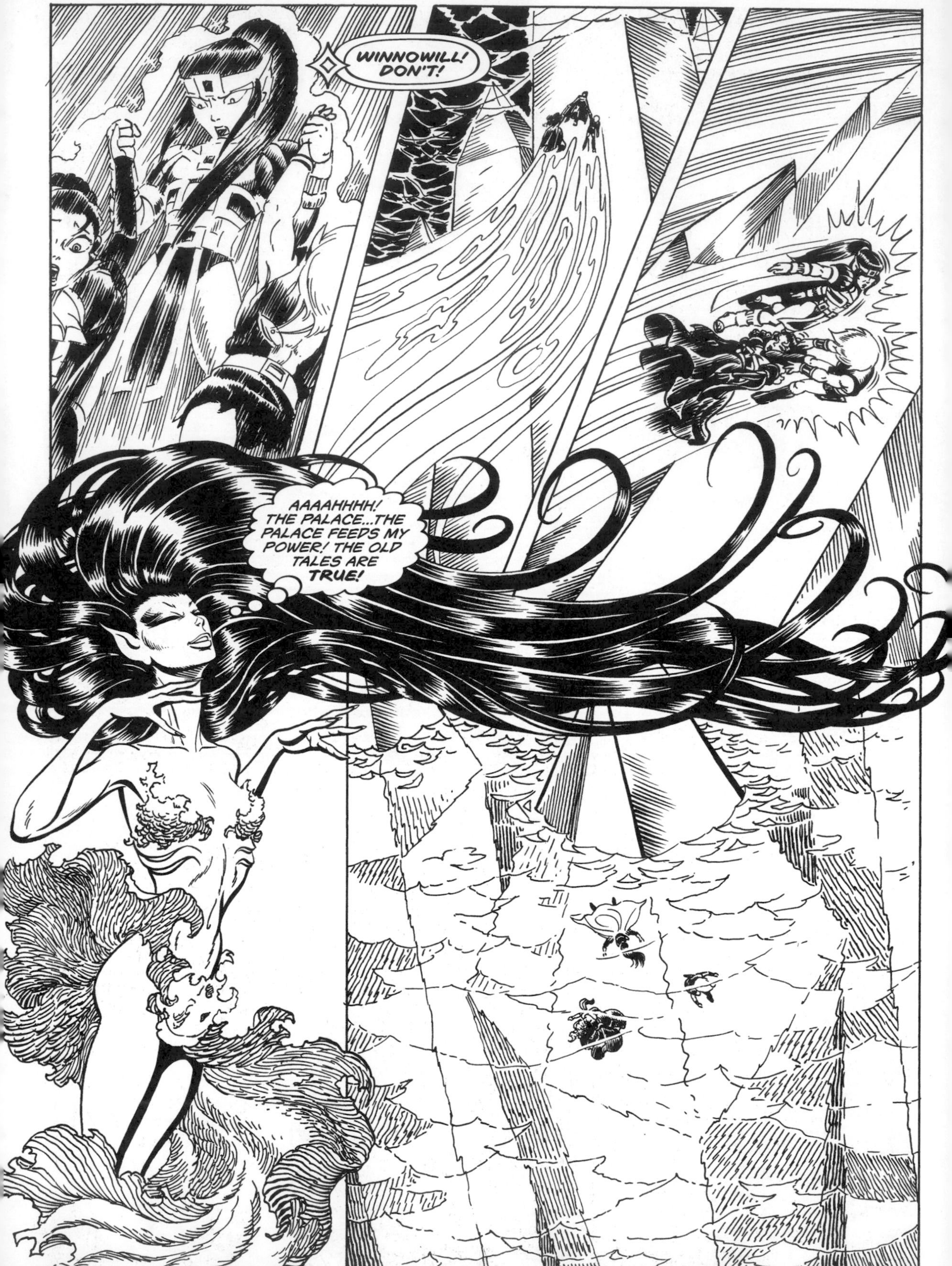
WINNOWILL! DON'T!
AAAAHHHH! THE PALACE...THE PALACE FEEDS MY POWER! THE OLD TALES ARE TRUE!

NEARBY, ABOVE THE JAGGED SHORELINE...

:PANT:
:PANT:
:PANT:

:COUGH:
:COUGH:

:GASP:

LEETAH!
SHE'S
DROWNING!

HUUUUPH!

LITTLE FRIEND OF MY BODY AND SPIRIT...I REMEMBER!

STILL WEAK....! NEED TO CATCH MY BREATH!

:PANT:
:PANT:

UNF!

MMMNN...

...WHITE.

MEANWHILE...

SOMEONE SEEKS TO SAVE YOU, DARK SISTER? I THINK NOT!

THERE IS **NO** PLACE FOR YOU AND ME TOGETHER... HERE, IN THE PALACE, OR ANYWHERE BEYOND!

WH-WHAT'S HAPPENING?!

HIGH ONES HELP US...!

AAAIIIEEE...✳

AAAAAHHHHH HA HA HAAAHH!

LEETAH! NO!

AA-AAGH!

...CAN BARELY... MOVE...

MOVE!

UUUHHHHNNN...

THE DEADLY WAVES, THRASHED TO MAGICAL HEIGHTS, QUICKLY SETTLE...

=HACK=
=COUGH=
=COUGH=

?!?

YOU...YOU'RE...

TAKE ME TO THE BLACK SNAKE!

SOOOO... EVEN THE SACRED DWELLING OF THE HIGH ONES CAN BE INFESTED WITH FLEAS!

A WATER-RAM, SUCH AS I HAVE USED ON HUMAN VESSELS...A POWERFUL CURRENT TO PIERCE THE AURA...

...AND FLOOD EVERY CHAMBER, WILL RID ME OF THEM!

WINNOWILL!

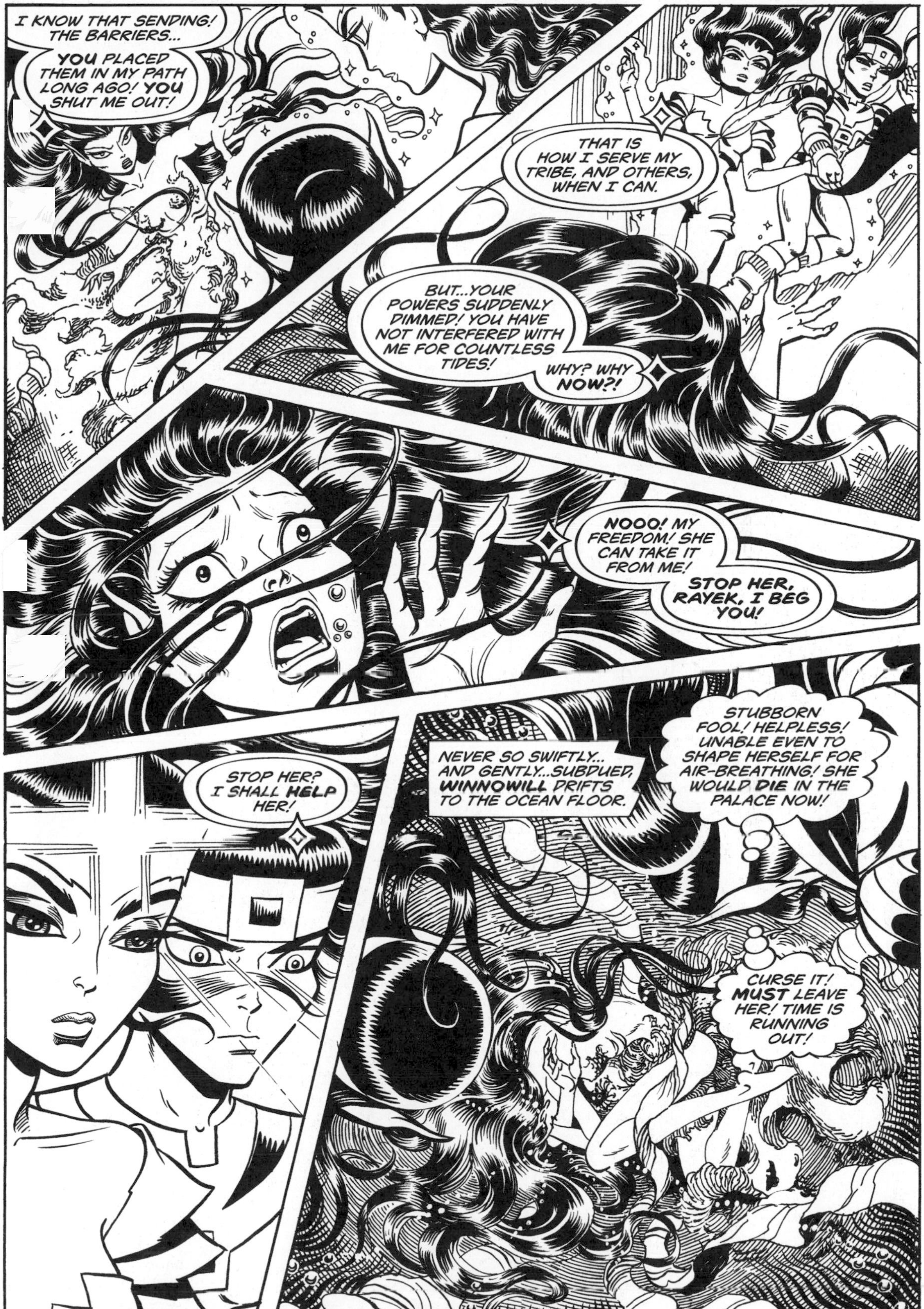
I KNOW THAT SENDING! THE BARRIERS...
YOU PLACED THEM IN MY PATH LONG AGO! YOU SHUT ME OUT!
THAT IS HOW I SERVE MY TRIBE, AND OTHERS, WHEN I CAN.
BUT...YOUR POWERS SUDDENLY DIMMED! YOU HAVE NOT INTERFERED WITH ME FOR COUNTLESS TIDES!
WHY? WHY NOW?!
NOOO! MY FREEDOM! SHE CAN TAKE IT FROM ME!
STOP HER, RAYEK, I BEG YOU!
STOP HER? I SHALL HELP HER!
NEVER SO SWIFTLY... AND GENTLY...SUBDUED, WINNOWILL DRIFTS TO THE OCEAN FLOOR.
STUBBORN FOOL! HELPLESS! UNABLE EVEN TO SHAPE HERSELF FOR AIR-BREATHING! SHE WOULD DIE IN THE PALACE NOW!
CURSE IT! MUST LEAVE HER! TIME IS RUNNING OUT!

SHORTLY...

ALMOST *DAWN!* THE HIGH ONES WILL *APPEAR,* THEN *VANISH* IN *THREE HEARTBEATS!*

I SHOULD BE IN THE SCROLL ROOM, *PREPARING!*

HOLD IT! DON'T MOVE! WHERE'S MOTHER AND *SKYWISE?* AND JUST WHO ARE *YOU?!*

KAHVI, CHIEF OF THE *GO-BACKS,* NAMED ME *VENKA.*

VENKA...!

COME BACK HERE, RAYEK! WHAT DID YOU DO WITH MOTHER?!

WHY ARE HER SENDINGS SO *WEAK?* WHY DON'T THEY MAKE *SENSE?!*

WHO KNOWS, CHILD?! *NOTHING* MAKES SENSE, NOW! I-I HAVE LOST *WINNOWILL!* AND *SAVAH* TOO! IT IS *PAST* TIME TO GATHER THE SUN FOLK!

VENKA! HOW....?

NO MATTER! FIND *LEETAH...* AND *TIMMAIN.* BUT FIRST...

THE SCROLL OF COLORS IS A RECORD OF THE HIGH ONES' TRAVELS... STAR-JOURNEYS PAST AND, I THINK, THOSE YET TO COME!

I HAVE YET TO RECOGNIZE *MYSELF* IN THE COLORS, BUT PERHAPS... AFTER THE MERGING...

THE HIGH ONES ARE *NEAR!* I MUST LINK THE SCROLL TO *THEM...*

"...AND FORGET ALL ELSE!"

HOW CAN THIS BE?! ZHANTEE...! ZHANTEE!

...TRIED TO... SHIELD HER... UUNH!

SH-SHE'LL LIVE! TELL ME SHE'LL LIVE...!

HUSH! YOU'RE...

...AFTER ALL THIS TIME...SHE MUST!

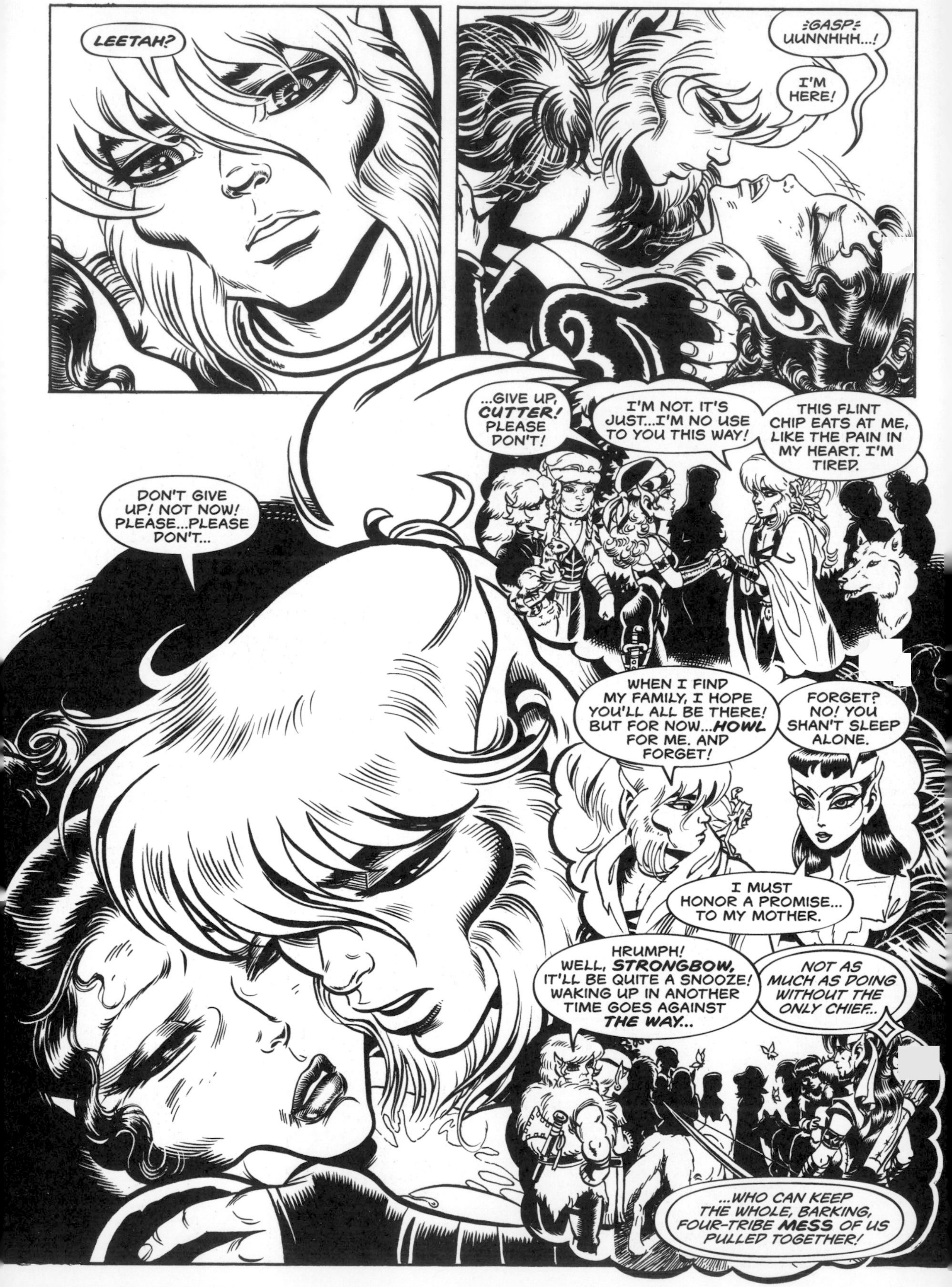

LEETAH?
:GASP: UUNNHHH...!
I'M HERE!
...GIVE UP, CUTTER! PLEASE DON'T!
I'M NOT. IT'S JUST...I'M NO USE TO YOU THIS WAY!
THIS FLINT CHIP EATS AT ME, LIKE THE PAIN IN MY HEART. I'M TIRED.
DON'T GIVE UP! NOT NOW! PLEASE...PLEASE DON'T...
WHEN I FIND MY FAMILY, I HOPE YOU'LL ALL BE THERE! BUT FOR NOW...HOWL FOR ME. AND FORGET!
FORGET? NO! YOU SHAN'T SLEEP ALONE.
I MUST HONOR A PROMISE... TO MY MOTHER.
HRUMPH! WELL, STRONGBOW, IT'LL BE QUITE A SNOOZE! WAKING UP IN ANOTHER TIME GOES AGAINST THE WAY...
NOT AS MUCH AS DOING WITHOUT THE ONLY CHIEF...
...WHO CAN KEEP THE WHOLE, BARKING, FOUR-TRIBE MESS OF US PULLED TOGETHER!

TAM... TAM...!

I TURNED MY BACK ON THE WAY, BELOVED! BETTER TO SLEEP AND KNOW NOTHING...

...THAN WAKE TO ONE MORE NIGHT WITHOUT YOU!

I...I WILL RETURN SWIFTLY, SKYWISE.

AND IN THE ENTRANCE HALL OF THE PALACE...

IT'S TRUE, CUBS! AROREE WILL TAKE YOU TO THEM!

SUNTOP, EMBER, AND YOU, LITTLE TROLL...YOU WILL BRING SUCH JOY WHEN YOU ARE SEEN!

QUICKLY, NOW!

AS AROREE FLIES OFF WITH HER PRECIOUS BURDEN...

I KNOW YOU. WHAT WILL YOU DO TO HIM?

THE WOLFRIDERS FINISHED MY UPBRINGING.

THEY DID NOT TEACH ME TO HATE.

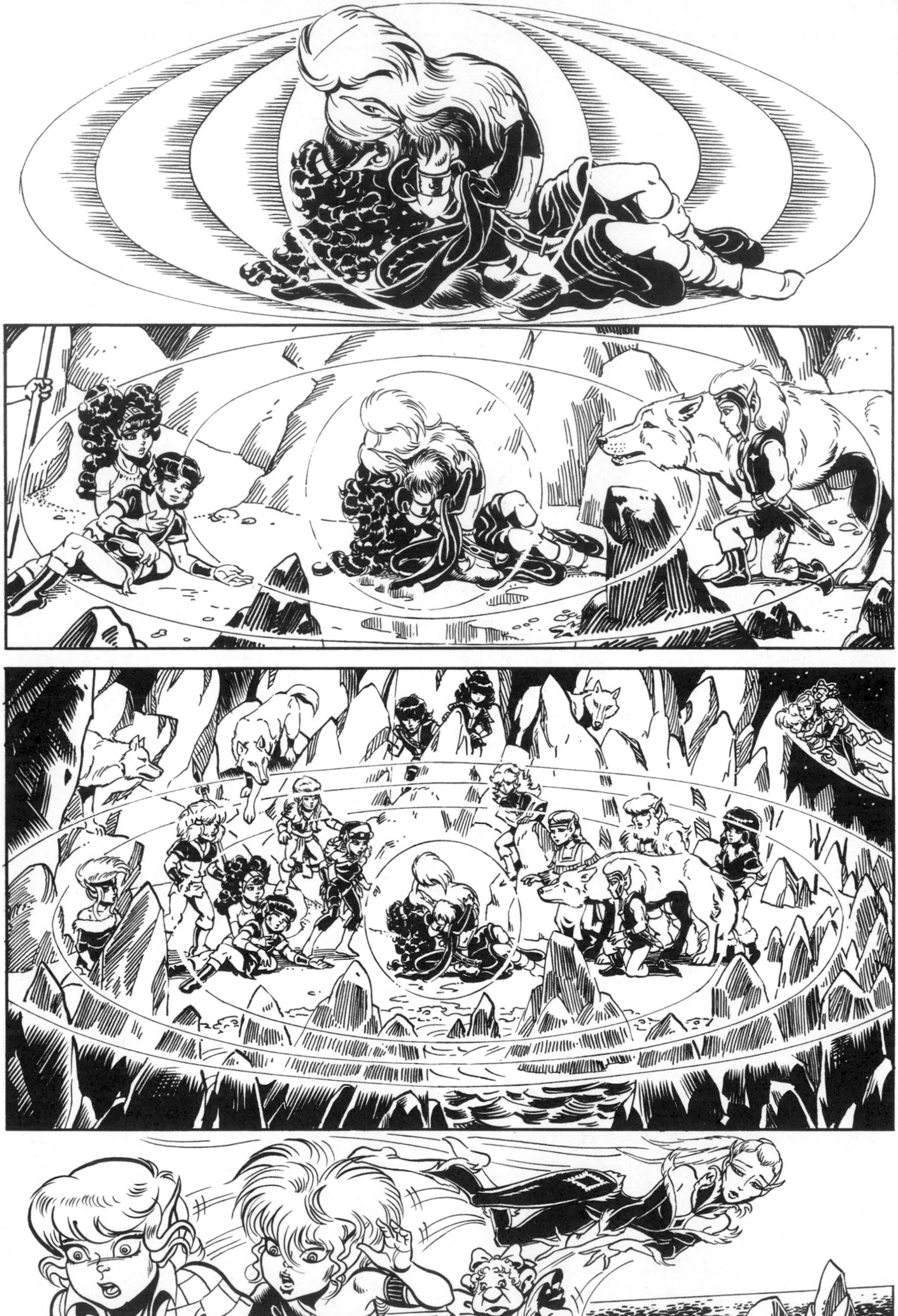

WHO IS THERE...? OH! COME CLOSER.

YOU SEE? THE SCROLL MIRRORS WHAT GOES ON ABOVE. IT WILL TELL ME THE EXACT MOMENT TO UNITE THE PALACE WITH ITS TWIN SELF.

THE HIGH ONES ARE BETWEEN FLESH AND SPIRIT NOW, RESHAPING THEMSELVES AND THEIR SHELL. SHOULD I TRY, BEFORE WE MERGE, TO WARN THEM OF THEIR TROLLS' TREACHERY?

HMM...UNWISE TO MUCK WITH EVENTS TOO MUCH. MIGHT WIPE MYSELF OUT! BESIDES...

...THIS WORLD SO CLOUDS THE HIGH ONES' PERCEPTIONS, IT IS THE HUMANS THEY NOTICE...THEIR SONGS, THEIR SYMBOLS. NO WONDER! THEY'VE SWARMED OVER THE LAND LIKE FIRE ANTS!

RIGHT NOW ONE CALLED OROLIN TURNS HIS SCROLL AND PUZZLES AS HIS PALACE SINGS TO ITSELF DOWN HERE.

HE WILL LIVE... BECAUSE VERY SOON WE WILL SAVE HIM!

THEN YOU'D BEST SAY YOUR FAREWELLS TO EKUAR NOW.

WHAT?!

EKUAR, WHY ARE YOU NOT WITH ME? IT IS NEARLY TIME! I DARE NOT TAKE MY EYES FROM THE SCROLL!

MUST I CARRY YOU BACK?!

DAWN IS IN THE WIND, DEAR ONE. THE SKY IS GROWING LIGHTER. LOOK! LOOK OUT...OVER THE WATER!

I TOLD YOU MY POWER WAS IN MY FAMILY.

NOTHING YOU CAN DO WILL PART US!

THEN... THEN COME WITH ME! ALL OF YOU!

HURRY! ANYONE WHO IS IN THE PALACE WILL SURVIVE THE MERGING--

SURVIVE?! KNOWING THOSE WE LEAVE BEHIND ARE WORSE THAN DEAD?! NO! WE COULDN'T!

NOR COULD I.

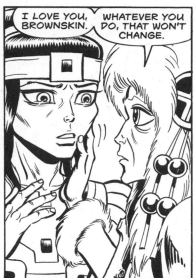

I LOVE YOU, BROWNSKIN. WHATEVER YOU DO, THAT WON'T CHANGE.

EKUAR...!

HE-HE NEVER SAID A WORD! I DID NOT KNOW...

IT WAS EASY WHEN YOU THOUGHT WE WERE ALL LONG DEAD.

CAN YOU DO IT NOW... WIPE THEM OUT...

...WITH ALL OF THEM THERE, WATCHING?

I HAVE THE POWER TO STOP YOU. IT'S WHAT I WAS RAISED TO DO.

BUT I WON'T. IT MUST BE YOUR CHOICE.

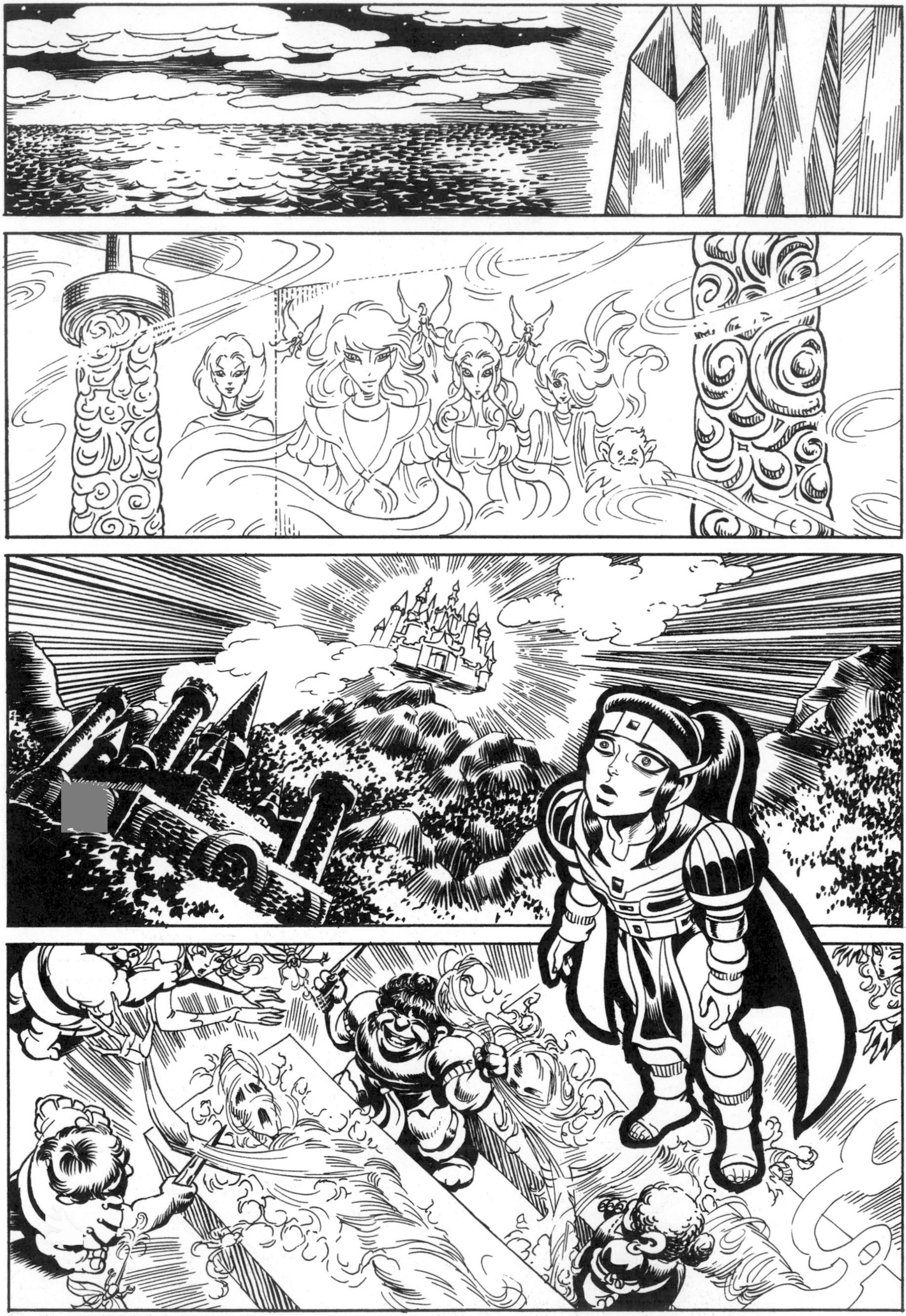

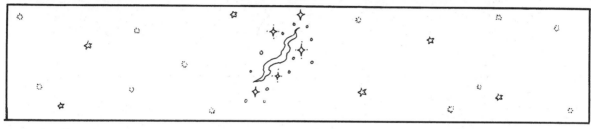

ZHANTEE! YOU ARE WELL!

...I AM! AND SHE DIDN'T EVEN *TOUCH* ME!

FATHER...?

MUCH NEEDS PUTTING RIGHT.

MUCH.

I'LL HELP YOU...

...BEGINNING WITH WINNOWILL.

SOON, IN **PICKNOSE'S** CAVERNOUS STRONGHOLD...

OOO, MUMKINS! SO *WRINKLY!*

YOU SHELTERED OUR COCOONS WELL, KING TROLL.

I DID. I SAW *RAYEK'S* EYES.

YOU SENT?! GUESS THAT WRAPSTUFF WAS TOO MUCH FOR US!

HOW... SWEET!

BAH! IT WAS WORTH THE BOTHER! AND DID YOU GET *YOURS,* WOLF CHIEF?

HUNH! WAY DOWN HERE, WE WERE OUT OF RANGE ANYWAY!

TIMMAIN GUARDED US AND HUNTED MEAT FOR THE TROLLS ALL ALONG! SHE'S MORE WOLF THAN EVER!

AND NOW I GET TO DO WHAT I COULDN'T BEFORE. *SPOIL* THIS LITTLE *DREAMBERRY ROTTEN!* GITCHY GITCHY GITCH!

HOO HOO HOO HEE HEEEE!

SAVAH... SAVAH...I'M *SUNTOP.* REMEMBER ME? FOR YOU IT'S BEEN MANY, MANY NIGHTS...FOR ME, JUST ONE.

THE CRY SCARED ME, BUT NOW I KNOW WE CAN NEVER LOSE EACH OTHER.

I'M COMING BACK TO SORROW'S END JUST AS SOON AS I CAN. I WANT YOU FOR MY TEACHER, SAVAH...MORE THAN EVER!

I HATE THIS!

I *LIKE* THIS! YOU ARE NO LONGER MY CHILD-MATE. WE ARE OF AN AGE!

LEETAH...

WHAT YOU DID FOR *SKYWISE*...GO ON! DO IT FOR ME!

OH, BELOVED! I HAVE WAITED SO LONG TO HEAR YOU...

GREAT SUN! I KNOW NOTHING AT ALL OF WAITING!

"WHEN *SKYWISE* ASKED FOR TIME, IT WAS FROM HIS HEART. ONLY THE TRIAL YOU'VE ENDURED MAKES YOU SPEAK NOW. WHEN YOUR HEART IS CLEAR, ASK ME AGAIN."

<STICKY NIGHT...MIGHT AS WELL LET THE FIRE DIE, *BOLL!* HALF A MOMENT AND I'LL BE IN!>

<SHY AND SECRET FOREST FOLK, TEACH ME AS I SLEEP...>

<WHICH TREES, NEXT DAY, ARE MINE TO CUT, AND WHICH ARE YOURS TO KEEP.>

<THERE YOU ARE... WARM, SWEET MILK!>

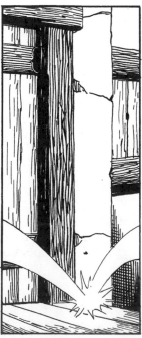

542

WE STAY HIDDEN FROM THEM, BUT STILL THEY BELIEVE IN US!

MAYBE THEY WOULD WHETHER THEY EVER SAW US OR NOT. ⸫SSSUUUPP⸫

MAYBE THAT'S HOW HUMANS ARE!

⸫ULP ULP⸫ SO NOW YOU *WOULDN'T* RATHER HATE THEM?

WELL, I HAVE THE STARS' OWN TIME TO MAKE UP MY MIND!

YOUR FACE FUR WON'T EVER COME IN, YOU KNOW.

THAT TROUBLES YOU?

NO...

THE WIND'S BOTH YOUNG AND OLD. IT CHANGES, BUT STAYS THE SAME, I GUESS, NO MATTER HOW MANY SEASONS TURN.

YOU AND THE WIND, *FAHR.*

TO THE HOLT...?

KLUNK

...NOT THE END

MAKING OF ElfQuest

COMMENTARY BY WENDY AND RICHARD PINI

August 25, 1986

Some thoughts on the layout of the ELFQUEST book

The story will be 28 pages in each issue, and we will be responsible for 2 more pages (i.e., we will supply you with a 30 page package). This does not include the inside front cover, which I supply for all the books, EQ included.

Whichever two pages we get (in addition to the 28), I want them to be contiguous. It doesn't matter if they are facing pages or if one has to turn the page to get from one to the other, but I do want them to follow. The reason for this is that I intend to use those two pages for whatever Wendy and I think will go best on them; that may be two full pages of letters one issue, a page and a half of letters and a half page of EQ-editorial, a page and a page, or whatever. Maybe a page of sketches one issue. Who knows? But the two pages will be laid out by us to be a continuous "entity."

You will ask "Where will I put the subscription coupon I said I wanted?" and the answer will be: on whatever page you put the "coming next issue" ad for the next EQ issue, just as has been done for all the books from time to time. (I'm assuming that there will be a "coming next issue" thing for EQ.) Point being, if I'm going to be responsible for supplying a 30-page package, then I want 30 full pages.

Which leaves you with three pages for ads (two of newsprint and the inside back cover) -- plus the back cover if we all so choose. I will be responsible for plugging things like the Fan Club and other EQ related things out of our two pages, so you don't have to further shave from your pages.

One thing, however, that I will insist on, which I don't as much for the other books, and that is that I will want to approve every page of EQ before it goes to press. This does not need to become a company-wide thing (as you pointed out, giving us a "personal" editorial on the inside front cover could lead to everyone wanting one) but given the relationship between the two companies, I think I can ask this.

Two years after The Original Quest *ended, Warp Graphics launched the next chapter,* Siege at Blue Mountain. *Warp partnered with Apple Comics as copublishers, so Wendy and Richard could concentrate on writing and drawing* ElfQuest, *while Apple also managed its other fantasy and science-fiction titles.*

Dart and his Dirty Dozen (Jack-wolf Riders) have been following Savah's directions (the same she gave Suntop three years ago when the child led the Wolfriders to find Cutter on the original quest). The jack-wolves have made good time; less than ten days and already they've arrived at Osek's tomb. Dart wonders about Osek's crumbling bones -- he's never seen an elf die before. Newstar and Dart's other companions, all Sun Villagers, are nervous and humbled at being out in the wide world for the first time. But Dart remembers the story of how Cutter led the Wolfriders across the desert and he tries to be the same kind of confident, purposeful leader to his own band. He has brought them this far to be whatever help to the Wolfriders they can be. But what they're getting into -- they have no idea.

Treestump leads Rayek, Petalwing, Leetah, Suntop, Skywise, Strongbow and Moonshade to Blue Mountain while Redlance, Nightfall, Ember, Pike, Skot, Krim and the remaining preservers stay in the Forbidden Grove. Ember cries at being left behind, thinking it's her punishment for making Suntop "go out" against Cutter's orders. But Redlance explains that if Suntop didn't have his special sending gift -- one that makes him both highly vulnerable and a potent weapon at once -- he would be staying behind in the Grove as well. Redlance adds that Ember should never look at fighting as fun she might be missing out on.

1

As independent comics publishing matured from its early, scrappy roots, so did the process of putting together an issue of ElfQuest. Once, issue treatments would have been jotted down on whatever lined paper was handy; here, we'd advanced to word processing with the ability to edit. No more scribbled-out corrections!

she to deal with this new intruder, Rayek, whose sending suggests
such power and purpose?

Winnowill's memory flashes back to her first encounter with
Two-Edge's father -- a troll sent by Greymung to find the escaped
rock shaper, Osek (pg.77, EQ Book 4). Since she was able to
seduce a troll, she thinks, surely it will be simple enough to use
the same witchery on Rayek; all she need do is find out what he
wants most and give it to him as she did to the troll, and to
Tyldak.

Seated in all her dark splendor, with Windkin cradled in her arms,
Winnowill receives Rayek in the throne room. He is absolutely
dazzled by her, and though recognition does not occur, Rayek is
knocked off balance by the powerful attraction he feels toward
her.

Elsewhere, Cutter and his band find their way to Winnowill's
quarters, only to learn that she is not there. Adar shatters the
cage of Winnowill's human pets and sets them free. Kakuk, their
spokesman, promises they will tell the Hoan G'Tay Sho the
disillusioning truth about the Gliders -- if they can all escape
the mountain. But Dewshine and Scouter refuse to escape without
Windkin.

His party now enlarged with more human allies, Cutter determines
to confront Winnowill and do psychic battle with her once again.
Even if he is hurt or killed, he hopes he may buy the preservers

3

On this page you can read (in the third full paragraph) the broad action that will eventually end up on page 18 of the comic. The words may be simple and bare bones, but—while waiting for Wendy to interpret them on a blank sheet of drawing paper—they hold the promise of drama.

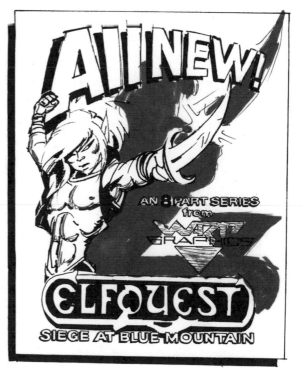

Before Siege launched in 1986, we needed posters so comic shops could advertise the new ElfQuest series. Wendy's initial concept is at upper left. Artist and animator Joe Barruso took that design and played with it, adding and changing elements and ultimately infusing typographic sizzle into the final concept (at lower right).

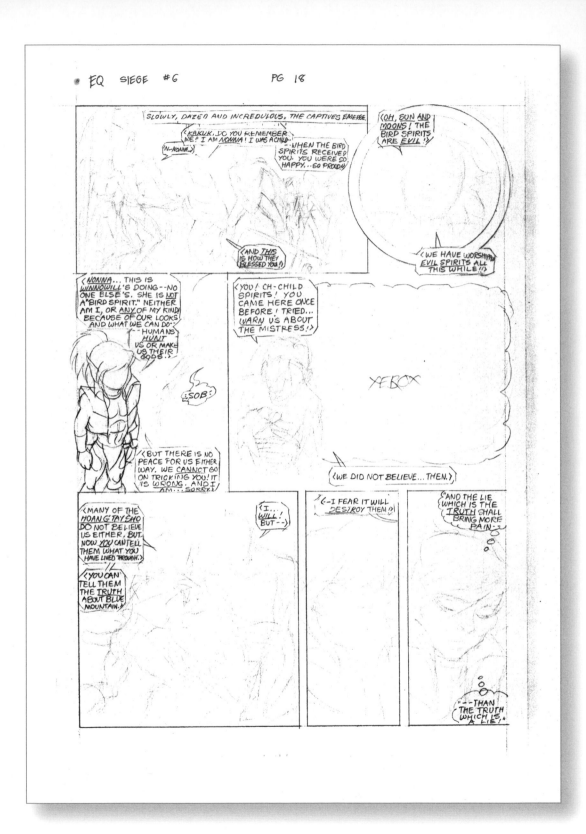

When ElfQuest was lettered by outside talent (in this case, Janice Chiang), Wendy first provided a very light layout with suggestions of word balloon placement. Drawing a comic book isn't only about the artwork; there must also be a balance between art and words, so the entire page appears pleasing and reads well.

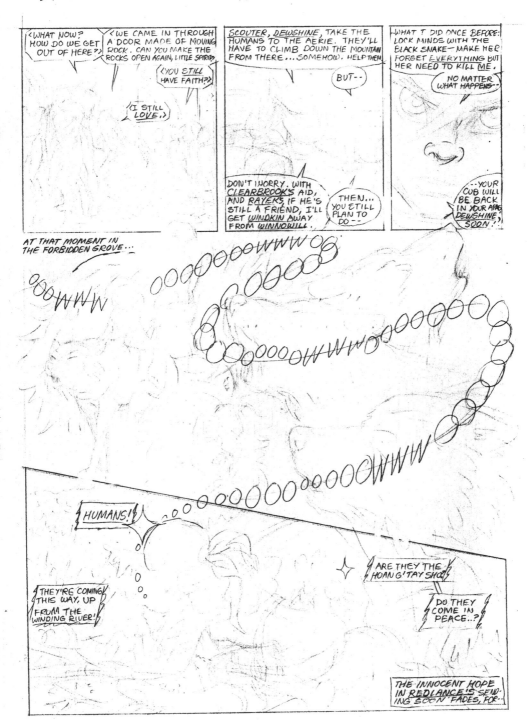

<WHAT NOW? HOW DO WE GET OUT OF HERE?>

<WE CAME IN THROUGH A DOOR MADE OF MOVING ROCK. CAN YOU MAKE THE ROCKS OPEN AGAIN, LITTLE SPIRIT?>

<YOU *STILL* HAVE FAITH?>

<I STILL *LOVE*.>

SCOUTER, DEWSHINE, TAKE THE HUMANS TO THE AERIE. THEY'LL HAVE TO CLIMB DOWN THE MOUNTAIN FROM THERE...SOMEHOW. HELP THEM.

BUT--

DON'T WORRY. WITH CLEARBROOK'S AID, AND RAYEK, IF HE'S STILL A FRIEND, I'LL GET WINDKIN AWAY FROM WINNOWILL.

THEN... YOU STILL PLAN TO DO--

-WHAT I DID ONCE BEFORE: LOCK MINDS WITH THE BLACK SNAKE—MAKE HER FORGET *EVERYTHING* BUT HER NEED TO KILL ME.

NO MATTER WHAT HAPPENS--

--YOUR CUB WILL BE BACK IN YOUR ARMS, DEWSHINE, SOON.

AT THAT MOMENT IN THE FORBIDDEN GROVE...

HUMANS!!

THEY'RE COMING THIS WAY, UP FROM THE WINDING RIVER!

ARE THEY THE HOAN G'TAY SHO?

DO THEY COME IN PEACE...?

THE INNOCENT HOPE IN REDLANCE'S SENDING SOON FADES, FOR-

The letterer has taken the rough suggestions of placement and rendered all the words strongly and nicely formatted. At this stage, Wendy has also begun to tighten up the pencils for the inker (Joe Staton), indicating areas of solid black (marked with x's) for dramatic lighting and contrast.

ELFQUEST®

DISCOVER THE LEGEND OF *ELFQUEST*! ALLIANCES ARE FORGED, ENEMIES DISCOVERED, AND SAVAGE BATTLES FOUGHT IN THIS EPIC FANTASY ADVENTURE, HANDSOMELY PRESENTED BY DARK HORSE BOOKS!

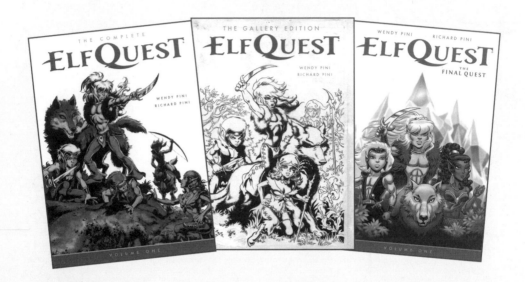

THE COMPLETE ELFQUEST
Volume 1: The Original Quest
978-1-61655-407-1 | $24.99

Volume 2
978-1-61655-408-8 | $24.99
Coming in 2015!

ELFQUEST: THE ORIGINAL QUEST GALLERY EDITION
978-1-61655-411-8 | $125.00
Coming Fall 2014!

ELFQUEST: THE FINAL QUEST
Volume 1
978-1-61655-409-5 | $17.99
Coming in 2015!

Volume 2
978-1-61655-410-1 | $17.99
Coming in 2016!

"I'll be here," Pie told him. "Your body needs rest. Let it do what it needs to do."

The mystif had been warming Gentle's shirt in front of the fire, and now helped him put it on, a delicate business. Gentle's joints were already stiffening. He pulled on his trousers without Pie's help, however, up over limbs that were a mass of bruises and abrasions.

"Whatever I did out there I certainly made a mess of myself," he remarked.

"You heal quickly," Pie said. This was true, though Gentle couldn't remember sharing that information with the mystif. "Lie down. I'll wake you when it's light."

Gentle put his head on the small heap of hides Pie had made as a pillow and let the mystif pull his coat up over him.

"Dream of sleeping," Pie said, laying a hand on Gentle's face. "And wake whole."

2

When Pie shook him awake, what seemed mere minutes later, the sky visible between the rock faces was still dark, but it was the gloom of snow-bearing cloud rather than the purple black of a Jokalaylaurian night. He sat up feeling wretched, aching in every bone.

"I'd kill for coffee," he said, resisting the urge to torture his joints by stretching. "And warm *pain au chocolat.*"

"If they don't have it in Yzordderrex, we'll invent it," Pie said.

"Did you brew up?"

"There's nothing left to burn."

"And what's the weather like?"

"Don't ask."

"That bad?"

"We should get a move on. The thicker the snow gets, the more difficult it'll be to find the pass."

They roused the doeki, which made plain its disgruntlement at having to breakfast on words of encouragement rather than hay, and, with the meat Pie had prepared the day before loaded, left the shelter of the rock and headed out into the snow. There had been a short debate before they left as to whether they should ride or not, Pie insisting that Gentle should do so, given his present delicacy, but he'd argued that they might need the doeki's strength to carry them both if they got into worse difficulties, and they should preserve such energies as it still possessed for such an emergency. But he soon began to stumble in snow that was waist high in places,

of it, but the tears crystallized on the ledge of his eye and would not fall.

Twice he stopped, because he sensed that there was something more than snow on the storm's back. He remembered Pie's talk of agents left in this wilderness to guard the murder site and, though he was only dreaming and knew it, he was still afraid. If these entities were charged to keep witnesses from the glacier, they would not simply drive the wakeful off but the sleeping too; and those who came as he came, in reverence, would earn their special ire. He studied the spattered air, looking for some sign of them, and once thought he glimpsed a form overhead that would have been invisible but that it displaced the snow: an eel's body with a tiny ball of a head. But it was come and gone too quickly for him to be certain he'd even seen it.

The glacier was in sight, however, and his will drove his limbs to motion, until he was standing at its edge. He raised his hands to his face and wiped the snow from his cheeks and forehead, then stepped onto the ice. The women gazed up at him as they had when he'd stood here with Pie 'oh' pah, but now, through the dust of snow blowing across the ice, they saw him naked, his manhood shrunk, his body trembling; on his face and lips a question he had half an answer to. Why, if this was indeed the work of Hapexamendios, had the Unbeheld, with all His powers of destruction, not obliterated every last sign of His victims? Was it because they were women or, more particularly, women of power? Had He brought them to ruin as best He could—overturning their altars and unseating their temples—but at the last been unable to wipe them away? And if so, was this ice a grave or merely a prison?

He dropped to his knees and laid his palms on the glacier. This time he definitely heard a sound in the wind, a raw howl somewhere overhead. The invisibles had entertained his dreaming presence long enough. They saw his purpose and were circling in preparation for descent. He blew against his palm and made a fist before the breath could slip, then raised his arm and slammed his hand against the ice, opening it as he did so.

The pneuma went off like a thunderclap. Before the tremors had died he snatched a second breath and broke it against the ice; then a third and fourth in quick succession, striking the steely surface so hard that had the pneuma not cushioned the blow he'd have broken every bone from wrist to fingertip. But his efforts had effect. There were hairline cracks spreading from the point of impact.

Encouraged, he began a second round of blows, but he'd delivered only three when he felt something take hold of his hair, wrenching his head back. A second grip instantly seized his raised arm. He had time to feel the ice splintering beneath his legs; then he was hauled up off the glacier by wrist and hair. He struggled against the claim, knowing that if his assaulters carried him too high death was assured; they'd either tear him apart in the clouds or simply drop him. The hold on his head was the less secure of the two, and his gyrations were sufficient to slip it, though blood ran down his brow.

Freed, he looked up at the entities. There were two, six feet long, their bodies scantily fleshed spines sprouting innumerable ribs, their limbs twelvefold and bereft of bone, their heads vestigial. Only their motion had beauty: a sinuous knotting and unknotting. He reached up and snatched at the closer of the two heads. Though it had no discernible features, it looked tender, and his hand had sufficient echo of the pneumas it had discharged to do harm. He dug his fingers into the flesh of the thing, and it instantly began to writhe, coiling its length around its companion for support, its limbs flailing wildly. He twisted his body to the left and right, the motion violent enough to wrench him free. Then he fell, a mere six feet but hard, onto slivered ice. The breath went from him as the pain came. He had time to see the agents descending upon him, but none in which to escape. Waking or sleeping, this was the end of him, he knew; death by these limbs had jurisdiction in both states.

But before they could find his flesh, and blind him, and unman him, he felt the shattered glacier beneath him shudder, and with a roar it rose, throwing him off its back into the snow. Shards pelted down upon him, but he peered up through their hail to see that the women were emerging from their graves, clothed in ice. He hauled himself to his feet as the tremors increased, the din of this unshackling echoing off the mountains. Then he turned and ran.

The storm was discreet and quickly drew its veil over the resurrection, so that he fled not knowing how the events he'd begun had finished. Certainly the agents of Hapexamendios made no pursuit; or, if they did, they failed to find him. Their absence comforted him only a little. His adventures had done him harm, and the distance he had to cover to get back to the camp was substantial. His run soon deteriorated into stumbling and staggering, blood marking his route. It was time to be done with this dream of endurance, he thought, and open his eyes; to roll over and put his arms around Pie 'oh' pah; to kiss the mystif's cheek and share this vision with it. But his thoughts were too confounded to take hold of wakefulness long enough for him to rouse himself, and he dared not lie down in the snow in case a dreamed death came to him before morning woke him. All he could do was push himself on, weaker by the step, putting out of his head the possibility that he'd

lost his way and that the camp didn't lie ahead but off in another direction entirely.

He was looking down at his feet when he heard the shout, and his first instinct was to peer up into the snow above him, expecting one of the Unbeheld's creatures. But before his eyes reached his zenith they found the shape approaching him from his left. He stopped and studied the figure. It was shaggy and hooded, but its arms were outspread in invitation. He didn't waste what little energy he had calling Pie's name. He simply changed his direction and headed towards the mystif as it came to meet him. It was the faster of the two, and as it came it shrugged off its coat and held it open, so that he fell into its luxury. He couldn't feel it; indeed he could feel little, except relief. Borne up by the mystif he let all conscious thought go, the rest of the journey becoming a blur of snow and snow, and Pie's voice sometimes, at his side, telling him that it would be over soon.

"Am I awake?" He opened his eyes and sat up, grasping hold of Pie's coat to do so. "Am I awake?"

"Yes."

"Thank God! Thank God! I thought I was going to freeze to death."

He let his head sink back. The fire was burning, fed with fur, and he could feel its warmth on his face and body. It took a few seconds to realize the significance of this. Then he sat up again and realized he was naked: naked and covered with cuts.

"I'm not awake," he said. "Shit! I'm not awake!"

Pie took the pot of herders' brew from the fire, and poured a cup.

"You didn't dream it," the mystif said. It handed the cup over to Gentle. "You went to the glacier, and you almost didn't make it back."

Gentle took the cup in raw fingers. "I must have been out of my mind," he said. "I remember thinking: I'm dreaming this, then taking off my coat and my clothes . . . why the hell did I do that?"

He could still recall struggling through the snow and reaching the glacier. He remembered pain, and splintering ice, but the rest had receded so far he couldn't grasp it. Pie read his perplexed look.

"Don't try and remember now," the mystif said. "It'll come back when the moment's right. Push too hard and you'll break your heart. You should sleep for a while."

"I don't fancy sleeping," he said. "It's a little too much like dying."

his body, though somewhat healed by sleep, not equal to the demands upon it.

"We'll go more quickly if you ride," Pie told him.

He needed little persuasion and mounted the doeki, his fatigue such that he could barely sit upright with the wind so strong, and instead slumped against the beast's neck. He only occasionally raised himself from that posture, and when he did the scene had scarcely changed.

"Shouldn't we be in the pass by now?" he murmured to Pie at one point, and the look on the mystif's face was answer enough. They were lost. Gentle pushed himself into an upright position and, squinting against the gale, looked for some sign of shelter, however small. The world was white in every direction but for them, and even they were being steadily erased as ice clogged the fur of their coats and the snow they were trudging through deepened. Until now, however arduous the journey had become, he hadn't countenanced the possibility of failure. He'd been his own best convert to the gospel of their indestructibility. But now such confidence seemed self-deception. The white world would strip all color from them, to get to the purity of their bones.

He reached to take hold of Pie's shoulder, but misjudged the distance and slid from the doeki's back. Relieved of its burden the beast slumped, its front legs buckling. Had Pie not been swift and pulled Gentle out of harm's way, he might have been crushed beneath the creature's bulk. Hauling back his hood and swiping the snow from the back of his neck, he got to his feet and found Pie's exhausted gaze there to meet him.

"I thought I was leading us right," the mystif said.

"Of course you did."

"But we've missed the pass somehow. The slope's getting steeper. I don't know where the fuck we are, Gentle."

"In trouble is where we are, and too tired to think our way out of it. We have to rest."

"Where?"

"Here," Gentle said. "This blizzard can't go on forever. There's only so much snow in the sky, and most of it's already fallen, right? *Right?* So if we can just hold on till the storm's over, and we can see where we are—"

"Suppose by that time it's night again? We'll freeze, my friend."

"Do we have any other choice?" Gentle said. "If we go on we'll kill the beast and probably ourselves. We could march right over a gorge and never know it. But if we stay here ... *together* ... maybe we're in with a chance."

"I thought I knew our direction."

"Maybe you did. Maybe the storm'll blow over, and we'll find

ourselves on the other side of the mountain." Gentle put his hands
on Pie's shoulders, sliding them around the back of the mystif's
neck. "We have no choice," he said slowly.

Pie nodded, and together they settled as best they could in the
dubious shelter of the doeki's body. The beast was still breathing,
but not, Gentle thought, for long. He tried to put from his mind
what would happen if it died and the storm failed to abate, but what
was the use of leaving such plans to the last? If death seemed
inevitable, would it not be better for him and Pie to meet it
together—to slit their wrists and bleed to death side by side—
rather than slowly freeze, pretending to the end that survival was
plausible? He was ready to voice that suggestion now, while he still
had the energy and focus to do so, but as he turned to the mystif
some tremor reached him that was not the wind's tirade but a
voice beneath its harangue, calling him to stand up. He did so.

The gusts would have blown him over had Pie not stood up with
him, and his eyes would have missed the figures in the drifts but
that the mystif caught his arm and, putting its head close to Gentle's, said, "How the hell did they get out?"

The women stood a hundred yards from them. Their feet were
touching the snow but not impressing themselves upon it. Their
bodies were wound with cloth brought from the ice, which billowed
around them as the wind filled it. Some held treasures, claimed
from the glacier: pieces of their temple, and ark, and altar. One, the
young girl whose corpse had moved Gentle so much, held in her
arms the head of a Goddess carved in blue stone. It had been badly
vandalized. There were cracks in its cheeks, and parts of its nose,
and an eye, were missing. But it found light from somewhere and
gave off a serene radiance.

"What do they want?" Gentle said.

"You, maybe?" Pie ventured.

The woman standing closest to them, her hair rising half her
height again above her head, courtesy of the wind, beckoned.

"I think they want us both to go," Gentle said.

"That's the way it looks," Pie said, not moving a muscle.

"What are we waiting for?"

"I thought they were dead," the mystif said.

"Maybe they were."

"So we take the lead from phantoms? I'm not sure that's wise."

"They came to find us, Pie," Gentle said.

Having beckoned, the woman was turning slowly on her toe tips,
like a mechanical Madonna that Clem had once given Gentle,
which had played "Ave Maria" as it turned.

"We're going to lose them if we don't hurry. What's your problem, Pie? You've talked with spirits before."

"Not like these," Pie said. "The Goddesses weren't all forgiving mothers, you know. And their rites weren't all milk and honey. Some of them were cruel. They sacrificed men."

"You think that's why they want us?"

"It's possible."

"So we weigh that possibility against the absolute certainty of freezing to death where we stand," Gentle said.

"It's your decision."

"No, this one we make together. You've got fifty percent of the vote and fifty percent of the responsibility."

"What do you want to do?"

"There you go again. Make up your own mind for once."

Pie looked at the departing women, their forms already disappearing behind a veil of snow. Then at Gentle. Then at the doeki. Then back at Gentle. "I heard they eat men's balls."

"So what are you worried about?"

"All right!" the mystif growled, "I vote we go."

"Then it's unanimous."

Pie started to haul the doeki to its feet. It didn't want to move, but the mystif had a fine turn of threat when pressed, and began to berate it ripely.

"Quick, or we'll lose them!" Gentle said.

The beast was up now, and tugging on its bridle Pie led it in pursuit of Gentle, who was forging ahead to keep their guides in sight. The snow obliterated the women completely at times, but he saw the beckoner glance back several times, and knew that she'd not let her foundlings get lost again. After a time, their destination came in sight. A rock face, slate-gray and sheer, loomed from the murk, its summit lost in mist.

"If they want us to climb, they can think again," Pie yelled through the wind.

"No, there's a door," Gentle shouted over his shoulder. "See it?"

The word rather flattered what was no more than a jagged crack, like a bolt of black lightning burned into the face of the cliff. But it represented some hope of shelter, if nothing else.

Gentle turned back to Pie. "Do you see it, Pie?"

"I see it," came the response. "But I don't see the women."

One sweeping glance along the rock face confirmed the mystif's observation. They'd either entered the cliff or floated up its face into the clouds. Whichever, they'd removed themselves quickly.

"Phantoms," Pie said, fretfully.

"What if they are?" Gentle replied. "They brought us to shelter."

He took the doeki's rein from Pie's hands and coaxed the animal on, saying, "See that hole in the wall? It's going to be warm inside. Remember warm?"

The snow thickened as they covered the last hundred yards, until it was almost waist deep again. But all three—man, animal, and mystif—made the crack alive. There was more than shelter inside; there was light. A narrow passageway presented itself, its black walls encased in ice, with a fire flickering somewhere out of sight in the cavern's depths.

Gentle had let slip the doeki's reins, and the wise animal was already heading away down the passage, the sound of its hooves echoing against the glittering walls. By the time Gentle and Pie caught up with it, a slight bend in the passage had revealed the source of the light and warmth it was heading towards. A broad but shallow bowl of beaten brass was set in a place where the passage widened, and the fire was burning vigorously in its center. There were two curiosities, however: one, that the flame was not gold but blue; two, that it burned without fuel, the flames hovering six inches above the bottom of the bowl. But oh, it was warm. The cobs of ice in Gentle's beard melted and dropped off; the snowflakes became beads on Pie's smooth brow and cheek. The warmth brought a whoop of pure pleasure to Gentle's lips, and he opened his aching arms to Pie 'oh' pah.

"We're not going to die!" he said. "Didn't I tell you? We're not going to die!"

The mystif hugged him in return, its lips first pressed to Gentle's neck, then to his face.

"All right, I was wrong," it said. "There! I admit it!"

"So we go on and find the women, yes?"

"Yes!" it said.

A sound was waiting for them when the echoes of their enthusiasm died. A tinkling, as of ice bells.

"They're calling us," Gentle said.

The doeki had found a little paradise by the fire and was not about to move, for all Pie's attempts to tug it to its feet.

"Leave it awhile," Gentle said, before the mystif began a fresh round of profanities. "It's given good service. Let it rest. We can come back and fetch it later."

The passage they now followed not only curved but divided many times, the routes all lit by fire bowls. They chose between them by listening for the sound of the bells, which didn't seem to be getting any closer. Each choice, of course, made the likelihood of finding their way back to the doeki more uncertain.

"This place is a maze," Pie said, with a touch of the old unease creeping back into its voice. "I think we should stop and assess exactly what we're doing."

"Finding the Goddesses."

"And losing our transport while we do it. We're neither of us in any state to go much farther on foot."

"I don't feel so bad. Except for my hands." He raised them in front of his face, palm up. They were puffy and bruised, the lacerations livid. "I suppose I look like that all over. Did you hear the bells? They're just around the corner, I swear!"

"They've been just around the corner for the last three quarters of an hour. They're not getting any closer, Gentle. It's some kind of trick. We should go back for the animal before it's slaughtered."

"I don't think they'd shed blood in here," Gentle replied. The bells came again. "Listen to that. They *are* closer." He went to the next corner, sliding on the ice. "Pie. Come look."

Pie joined him at the corner. Ahead of them the passageway narrowed to a doorway.

"What did I tell you?" Gentle said, and headed on to the door and through it.

The sanctum on the other side wasn't vast—the size of a modest church, no more—but it had been hewn with such cunning it gave the impression of magnificence. It had sustained great damage, however. Despite its myriad pillars, chased by the finest craft, and its vaults of ice-sleek stone, its walls were pitted, its floor gouged. Nor did it take great wit to see that the objects that had been buried in the glacier had once been part of its furniture. The altar lay in hammered ruins at its center, and among the wreckage were fragments of blue stone, matching that of the statue the girl had carried. Now, more certainly than ever, they were standing in a place that carried the marks of Hapexamendios' passing.

"In His footsteps," Gentle murmured.

"Oh, yes," Pie murmured. "He was here."

"And so were the women," Gentle said. "But I don't think they ate men's balls. I think their ceremonies were more loving than that." He went down on his haunches, running his fingers over the carved fragments. "I wonder what they did? I'd like to have seen the rites."

"They'd have ripped you limb from limb."

"Why?"

"Because their devotions weren't for men's eyes."

"You could have got in, though, couldn't you?" Gentle said. "You would have been a perfect spy. You could have seen it."

"It's not the seeing," Pie said softly, "it's the feeling."

Gentle stood up, gazing at the mystif with new comprehension. "I think I envy you, Pie," he said. "You know what it feels like to be both, don't you? I never thought of that before. Will you tell me how it feels, one of these days?"

"You'd be better off finding out for yourself," Pie said.

"And how do I do that?"

"This isn't the time—"

"Tell me."

"Well, mystifs have their rites, just like men and women. Don't worry, I won't make you spy on me. You'll be *invited,* if that's what you want."

The remotest twinge of fear touched Gentle as he listened to this. He'd become almost blasé about the many wonders they'd witnessed as they traveled, but the creature that had been at his side these many days remained, he realized, undiscovered. He had never seen it naked since that first encounter in New York; nor kissed it the way a lover might kiss; nor allowed himself to feel sexual towards it. Perhaps it was because he'd been thinking of the women here, and their secret rites, but now, like it or not, he was looking at Pie 'oh' pah and was aroused.

Pain diverted him from these thoughts, and he looked down at his hands to see that in his unease he'd made fists of them and reopened the cuts in his palms. Blood dropped onto the ice underfoot, shockingly red. With the sight of it came a memory he'd consigned to the back of his head.

"What's wrong?" Pie said.

But Gentle didn't have the breath to reply. He could hear the frozen river cracking beneath him, and the howl of the Unbeheld's agents wheeling overhead. He could feel his hand slamming, slamming, slamming against the glacier and the thorns of ice flying up into his face.

The mystif had come to his side. "Gentle," it said, anxious now. "Speak to me, will you? What's wrong?"

It put its arms around Gentle's shoulders, and at its touch Gentle drew breath.

"The women . . ." he said.

"What about them?"

"It was me who freed them."

"How?"

"Pneuma. How else?"

"You *undid* the Unbeheld's handiwork?" the mystif said, its voice barely audible. "For our sake I hope the women were the only witnesses."

"There were agents, just as you said there'd be. They almost killed me. But I hurt them back."

"This is bad news."

"Why? If I'm going to bleed, let *Him* bleed a little too."

"Hapexamendios doesn't bleed."

"Everything bleeds, Pie. Even God. Maybe especially God. Or else why did He hide Himself away?"

As he spoke the tinkling bells sounded again, closer than ever, and glancing over Gentle's shoulder Pie said, "She must have been waiting for that little heresy."

Gentle turned to see the beckoning woman standing halfway in shadow at the end of the sanctum. The ice that still clung to her body hadn't melted, suggesting that, like the walls, the flesh it was encrusted upon was still below zero. There were cobs of ice in her hair, and when she moved her head a little, as she did now, they struck each other and tinkled like tiny bells.

"I brought you out of the ice," Gentle said, stepping past Pie to approach her.

The woman said nothing.

"Do you understand me?" Gentle went on. "Will you lead us out of here? We want to find a way through the mountain."

The woman took a step backwards, retreating into the shadows.

"Don't be afraid of me," Gentle said. "Pie! Help me out here."

"How?"

"Maybe she doesn't understand English."

"She understands you well enough."

"Just talk to her, will you?" Gentle said.

Ever obedient, Pie began to speak in a tongue Gentle hadn't heard before, its musicality reassuring even if the words were unintelligible. But neither music nor sense seemed to impress the woman. She continued to retreat into the darkness, Gentle pursuing cautiously, fearful of startling her but more fearful still of losing her entirely. His additions to Pie's persuasions had dwindled to the basest bargaining.

"One favor deserves another," he said.

Pie was right, she did indeed understand. Even though she stood in shadow, he could see that a little smile was playing on her sealed lips. Damn her, he thought, why wouldn't she answer him? The bells still rang in her hair, however, and he kept following them even when the shadows became so heavy she was virtually lost among them. He glanced back towards the mystif, who had by now given up any attempt to communicate with the woman and instead addressed Gentle.

"Don't go any further," it said.

Though he was no more than fifty yards from where the mystif stood, its voice sounded unnaturally remote, as though another law besides that of distance and light held sway in the space between them.

"I'm still here. Can you see me?" he called back, and, gratified to hear the mystif reply that it could, he returned his gaze to the shadows.

The woman had disappeared however. Cursing, he plunged on

towards the place where she'd last stood, his sense that this was
equivocal terrain intensifying. The darkness had a nervous quality, like a bad liar attempting to shoo him off with shrugs. He
wouldn't go. The more it trembled, the more eager he became to
see what it was hiding. Sightless though he was, he wasn't blind to
the risk he was taking. Minutes before he'd told Pie that everything
was vulnerable. But nobody, not even the Unbeheld, could make
darkness bleed. If it closed on him he could claw at it forever and
not make a mark on its hideless back.

He heard Pie calling behind him now: "Where the hell are you?"
The mystif was following him into the shadows, he saw.

"Don't come any further," he told it.

"Why not?"

"I may need a marker to find my way back."

"Just turn around."

"Not till I find her," Gentle said, forging on with his arms
outstretched.

The floor was slick beneath him, and he had to proceed with extreme caution. But without the woman to guide them through the
mountain, this maze might prove as fatal as the snows they'd escaped. He had to find her.

"Can you still hear me?" he called back to Pie.

The voice that told him *yes* was as faint as a long-distance call
on a failing line.

"Keep talking," he yelled.

"What do you want me to say?"

"Anything. Sing a song."

"I'm tone deaf."

"Talk about food, then."

"All right," said Pie, "I already told you about the ugichee and
the bellyful of eggs—"

"It's the foulest thing I ever heard," Gentle replied.

"You'll like it once you taste it."

"As the actress said to the bishop."

He heard Pie's muted laughter come his way. Then the mystif
said, "You hated me almost as much as you hated fish, remember?
And I converted you."

"I never hated you."

"In New York you did."

"Not even then. I was just confused. I'd never slept with a mystif before."

"How did you like it?"

"It's better than fish but not as good as chocolate."

"What did you say?"

"I said—"

"Gentle? I can hardly hear you."

"I'm still here!" he replied, shouting now. "I'd like to do it again sometime, Pie."

"Do what?"

"Sleep with you."

"I'll have to think about it."

"What do you want, a proposal of marriage?"

"That might do it."

"All right!" Gentle called back. "So marry me!"

There was silence behind him. He stopped and turned. Pie's form was a blurred shadow against the distant light of the sanctum.

"Did you hear me?" he yelled.

"I'm thinking it over."

Gentle laughed, despite the darkness and the unease it had wrung from him. "You can't take forever, Pie," he hollered. "I need an answer in—" He stopped as his outstretched fingers made contact with something frozen and solid. "Oh, *shit*."

"What's wrong?"

"It's a fucking dead end!" he said, stepping right up to the surface he'd encountered and running his palms over the ice. "Just a blank wall."

But that wasn't the whole story. The suspicion he'd had that this was nebulous territory was stronger than ever. There was something on the other side of this wall, if he could only reach it.

"Make your way back," he heard Pie entreating.

"Not yet," he said to himself, knowing the words wouldn't reach the mystif. He raised his hand to his mouth and snatched an expelled breath.

"Did you hear me, Gentle?" Pie called.

Without replying he slammed the pneuma against the wall, a technique his palm was now expert in. The sound of the blow was swallowed by the murk, but the force he unleashed shook a freezing hail down from the roof. He didn't wait for the reverberations to settle but delivered a second blow, and a third, each impact opening further the wounds in his hand, adding blood to the violence of his blows. Perhaps it fueled them. If his breath and spittle did such service, what power might his blood contain, or his semen?

As he stopped to draw a fresh lungful, he heard the mystif yelling, and turned to see it moving towards him across a gulf of frantic shadow. It wasn't just the wall and the roof above that was shaken by his assault: the very air was in a furor, shaking Pie's silhouette into fragments. As his eyes fought to fix the image, a vast spear of ice divided the space between them, hitting the ground and shattering. He had time to raise his arms over his face before the shards struck him, but their impact threw him back against the wall.

"You'll bring the whole place down!" he heard Pie yell as new spears fell.

"It's too late to change our minds!" Gentle replied. *"Move, Pie!"*

Light-footed, even on this lethal ground, the mystif dodged through the ice towards Gentle's voice. Before it was even at his side, he turned to attack the wall afresh, knowing that if it didn't capitulate very soon they'd be buried where they stood. Snatching another breath from his lips he delivered it against the wall, and this time the shadows failed to swallow the sound. It rang out like a thunderous bell. The shock wave would have pitched him to the floor had the mystif's arms not been there to catch him.

"This is a passing place!" it yelled.

"What does that mean?"

"Two breaths this time," was its reply. "Mine as well as yours, in one hand. Do you understand me?"

"Yes."

He couldn't see the mystif, but he felt it raise his hand to its mouth.

"On a count of three," Pie said. *"One."*

Gentle drew a breathful of furious air.

"Two."

He drew again, deeper still.

"Three!"

And he expelled it, mingled with Pie's, into his hand. Human flesh wasn't designed to govern such force. Had Pie not been beside him to brace his shoulder and wrist, the power would have erupted from his palm and taken his hand with it. But they flung themselves forward in unison, and he opened his hand the instant before it struck the wall.

The roar from above redoubled, but it was drowned out moments later by the havoc they'd wrought ahead of them. Had there been room to retreat they'd have done so, but the roof was pitching down a fusillade of stalactites, and all they could do was shield their bare heads and stand their ground as the wall stoned them for their crime, knocking them to their knees as it split and fell. The commotion went on for what seemed like minutes, the ground shuddering so violently they were thrown down yet again, this time to their faces. Then, by degrees, the convulsions slowed. The hail of stone and ice became a drizzle, and stopped, and a miraculous gust brought warm wind to their faces.

They looked up. The air was murky, but light was catching glints off the daggers they lay on, and its source was somewhere up ahead. The mystif was first to its feet, hauling Gentle up beside it.

"A passing place," it said again.

It put its arm around Gentle's shoulders, and together they

stumbled towards the warmth that had roused them. Though the
gloom was still deep, they could make out the vague presence of
the wall. For all the scale of the upheaval, the fissure they'd made
was scarcely more than a man's height. On the other side it was
foggy, but each step took them closer to the light. As they went,
their feet sinking into a soft sand that was the color of the fog, they
heard the ice bells again and looked back, expecting to see the
women following. But the fog already obscured the fissure and the
sanctum beyond, and when the bells stopped, as they did moments
later, they lost all sense of its direction.

"We've come out into the Third Dominion," Pie said.

"No more mountains? No more snow?"

"Not unless you want to find your way back to thank them."

Gentle peered ahead into the fog. "Is this the only way out of
the Fourth?"

"Lord, no," said Pie. "If we'd gone the scenic route we'd have
had the choice of a hundred places to cross. But this must have
been their secret way, before the ice sealed it up."

The light showed Gentle the mystif's face now, and it bore a wide
smile.

"You did fine work," Pie said. "I thought you'd gone crazy."

"I think I did, a little," Gentle replied. "I must have a destructive streak. Hapexamendios would be proud of me." He halted to
give his body a moment's rest. "I hope there's more than fog in the
Third."

"Oh, believe me, there is. It's the Dominion I've longed to see
more than any other, while I've been in the Fifth. It's full of light
and fertility. We'll rest, and we'll feed, and we'll get strong again.
Maybe go to L'Himby and see my friend Scopique. We deserve to
indulge ourselves for a few days before we head for the Second and
join the Lenten Way."

"Will that take us to Yzordderrex?"

"Indeed it will," Pie said, coaxing Gentle into motion again.
"The Lenten Way's the longest road in the Imajica. It must be the
length of the Americas, and more."

"A map!" said Gentle. "I *must* start making that map."

The fog was beginning to thin, and with the growing light came
plants: the first greenery they'd seen since the foothills of the
Jokalaylau. They picked up their pace as the vegetation became
lusher and scented, calling them on to the sun.

"Remember, Gentle," Pie said, when they'd gone a little way, "I
accepted."

"Accepted what?" Gentle asked.

The fog was wispy now; they could see a warm new world awaiting them.

"You proposed, my friend, don't you remember?"

"I didn't hear you accept."

"But I did," the mystif replied, as the verdant landscape was unveiled before them. "If we do nothing else in this Dominion, we should at the very least get married!"

24

I

England saw an early spring that year, with the days becoming balmy at the end of February and, by the middle of March, warm enough to have coaxed April and May flowers forth. The pundits were opining that if no further frosts came along to kill the blooms and chill the chicks in their nests, there would be a surge of new life by May, as parents let their fledglings fly and set about a second brood for June. More pessimistic souls were already predicting drought, their divining dampened when, at the beginning of March, the heavens opened over the island.

When—on that first day of rain—Jude looked back over the weeks since she'd left the Godolphin estate with Oscar and Dowd, they seemed well occupied; but the details of what had filled that time were at best sketchy. She had been made welcome in the house from the beginning and was allowed to come and go whenever it pleased her to do so, which was not often. The sense of belonging she'd discovered when she'd set eyes on Oscar had not faded, though she had yet to uncover its true source. He was a generous host, to be sure, but she'd been treated well by many men and not felt the devotion she felt now. That devotion was not returned, at least not overtly, which was something of a fresh experience for her. There was a certain reserve in Oscar's manner—and a consequent formality in their exchanges—which merely intensified her feelings for him. When they were alone together she felt like a long-lost mistress miraculously returned to his side, each with sufficient knowledge of the other that overt expressions of affection were superfluous; when she was with him in company—at the theater or at dinner with his friends—she was mostly silent, and happily so. This too was odd for her. She was accustomed to volubility, to handing out opinions on whatever subject was at issue, whether said opinions were requested or even seriously held. But now it didn't trouble her not to speak. She listened to the tittle-tattle and the chat (politics, finance, social gossip) as to the dialogue of a play. It wasn't her drama. She *had* no drama, just the ease of being where she wanted to be. And with such contentment to be had from simply witnessing, there seemed little reason to demand more.

Godolphin was a busy man, and though they spent some portion of every day together, she was more often than not alone. When she was, a pleasant languor overcame her, which contrasted forcibly with the confusion that had preceded her coming to stay with him. In fact she tried hard to put thoughts of that time out of her mind, and it was only when she went back to her flat to pick up belongings or bills (which, on Oscar's instruction, Dowd paid) that she was reminded of friends whose company she was at present not disposed to keep. There were telephone messages left for her, of course, from Klein, Clem, and half a dozen others. Later, there were even letters—some of them concerned for her health— and notes pushed through her door asking her to make contact. In the case of Clem she did so, guilty that she'd not spoken to him since the funeral. They lunched near his office in Marylebone, and she told him that she'd met a man and had gone to live with him on a temporary basis. Inevitably, Clem was curious. Who was this lucky individual? Anyone he knew? How was the sex: sublime or merely wonderful? And was it love? Most of all, was it love? She answered as best she could: named the man and described him; explained that there was nothing sexual between them as yet, though the thought had passed through her mind on several occasions; and as to love, it was too soon to tell. She knew Clem well and could be certain that this account would be public knowledge in twenty-four hours, which suited her fine. At least with this telling she'd allayed her friends' fears for her health.

"So when do we get to meet this paragon?" Clem asked her as they parted.

"In a while," she said.

"He's certainly had quite an effect on you, hasn't he?"

"Has he?"

"You're so—I don't know the word exactly—tranquil, maybe? I've never seen you this way before."

"I'm not sure I've ever felt this way before."

"Well, just make sure we don't lose the Judy we all know and love, huh?" Clem said. "Too much serenity's bad for the circulation. Everybody needs a good rage once in a while."

The significance of this exchange didn't really strike her until the evening after, when—sitting downstairs in the quiet of the house, waiting for Oscar to come home—she realized how passive she'd become. It was almost as if the woman she'd been, the Jude of furies and opinions, had been shed like a dead skin, and now, tender and new, she had entered a time of waiting. Instruction would come, she assumed; she couldn't live the rest of her life so becalmed. And she knew to whom she had to look for that instruction: the man whose voice in the hall made her heart rise and her head light, Oscar Godolphin.

If Oscar was the good news that those weeks brought, Kuttner Dowd was the bad. He was astute enough to realize after a very short time that she knew far less about the Dominions and their mysteries than their conversation at the Retreat had suggested, and far from being the source of information she'd hoped he'd prove, he was taciturn, suspicious, and on occasion rude, though never the last in Oscar's company. Indeed, when all three of them were together he lavished her with respect, its irony lost on Oscar, who was so used to Dowd's obsequious presence he barely seemed to notice the man.

Jude soon learned to match suspicion with suspicion, and several times verged on discussing Dowd with Oscar. That she didn't was a consequence of what she'd seen at the Retreat. Dowd had dealt almost casually with the problem of the corpses, dispatching them with the efficiency of one who had covered for his employer in similar circumstances before. Nor had he sought commendation for his labor, at least not within earshot of her. When the relationship between master and servant was so ingrained that a criminal act—the disposal of murdered flesh—was passed over as an unremarkable duty, it was best, she thought, not to come between them. It was *she* who was the interloper here, the new girl who dreamed she'd belonged to the master forever. She couldn't hope to have Oscar's ear the way Dowd did, and any attempt to sow mistrust might easily rebound upon her. She kept her silence, and things went on their smooth way. Until the day of rain.

2

A trip to the opera had been planned for March second, and she had spent the latter half of the afternoon in leisurely preparation for the evening, idling over her choice of dress and shoes, luxuriating in indecision. Dowd had gone out at lunchtime, on urgent business for Oscar which she knew better than to inquire about. She'd been told upon her arrival at the house that any questions as to Oscar's business would not be welcomed, and she'd never challenged that edict: it was not the place of mistresses to do so. But today, with Dowd uncharacteristically flustered as he left, she found herself wondering, as she bathed and dressed, what work Godolphin was about. Was he off in Yzordderrex, the city whose streets she assumed Gentle now walked with his soul mate the assassin? A mere two months before, with the bells of London

pealing in the New Year, she'd sworn to go to Yzordderrex after
him. But she'd been distracted from that ambition by the very man
whose company she'd sought to take her there. Though her
thoughts returned to that mysterious city now, it was without her
former appetite. She'd have liked to know if Gentle was safe in
those summer streets—and might have enjoyed a description of its
seamier quarter—but the fact that she'd once sworn an oath to get
there now seemed almost absurd. She had all that she needed
here.

It wasn't only her curiosity about the other Dominions that had
been dulled by contentment; her curiosity about events in her own
planet was similarly cool. Though the television burbled constantly
in the corner of her bedroom, its presence soporific, she attended
to its details scarcely at all and would not have noticed the
midafternoon news bulletin, but that an item she caught in passing put her in mind of Charlie.

Three bodies had been found in a shallow grave on Hampstead
Heath, the condition of the mutilated corpses implying, the report
said, some kind of ritualistic murder. Preliminary investigations
further suggested that the deceased had been known to the community of cultists and black magic practitioners in the city, some
of whom, in the light of other deaths or disappearances among
their number, believed that a vendetta against them was under way.
To round the piece off, there was footage of the police searching
the bushes and undergrowth of Hampstead Heath, while the rain
fell and compounded their misery. The report distressed her for two
reasons, each related to one of the brothers. The first, that it
brought back memories of Charlie, sitting in that stuffy little room
in the clinic, watching the heath and contemplating suicide. The second, that perhaps this vendetta might endanger Oscar, who was as
involved in occult practices as any man alive.

She fretted about this for the rest of the afternoon, her concern
deepening still further when Oscar failed to return home by six.
She put off dressing for the opera and waited for him downstairs,
the front door open, the rain beating the bushes around the step.
He returned at six-forty with Dowd, who had barely stepped
through the door before he pronounced that there would be no
opera visit tonight. Godolphin contradicted him immediately,
much to his chagrin, telling Jude to go and get ready; they'd be leaving in twenty minutes.

As she dutifully headed upstairs, she heard Dowd say, "You
know McGann wants to see you?".

"We can do both," Oscar replied. "Did you put out the black
suit? No? What have you been doing all day? No, don't tell me. Not
on an empty stomach."

Oscar looked handsome in black, and she told him so when, twenty-five minutes later, he came downstairs. In response to the compliment, he smiled and made a small bow.

"And you were never lovelier," he replied. "You know, I don't have a photograph of you? I'd like one, for my wallet. We'll have Dowd organize it."

By now, Dowd was conspicuous by his absence. Most evenings he would play chauffeur, but tonight he apparently had other business.

"We're going to have to miss the first act," Oscar said as they drove. "I've got a little errand to run in Highgate, if you'll bear with me."

"I don't mind," she said.

He patted her hand. "It won't take long," he said.

Perhaps because he didn't often take the wheel himself he concentrated hard as he drove, and though the news item she'd seen was still very much in her mind she was loath to distract him with talk. They made good time, threading their way through the back streets to avoid thoroughfares clogged by rain-slowed traffic, and arriving in a veritable cloudburst.

"Here we are," he said, though the windshield was so awash she could barely see ten yards ahead. "You stay in the warm. I won't be long."

He left her in the car and sprinted across a courtyard towards an anonymous building. Nobody came to the front door. It opened automatically and closed after him. Only when he'd disappeared, and the thunderous drumming of the rain on the roof had diminished somewhat, did she lean forward to peer out through the watery windshield at the building itself. Despite the rain, she recognized instantly the tower from the dream of blue eye. Without conscious instruction her hand went to the door and opened it, as her breath quickened with denials.

"Oh, no. Oh, no. . . ."

She got out of the car and turned her face up to the cold rain and to an even colder memory. She'd let this place—and indeed the journey that had brought her here, her mind moving through the streets touching this woman's grief and that woman's rage— slip into the dubious territory that lay between recollections of the real and those of the dreamed. In essence, she'd allowed herself to believe it had never happened. But here was the very place, to the window, to the brick. And if the exterior was so exactly as she'd seen it, why should she doubt that the interior would be any different?

There'd been a labyrinthine cellar, she remembered, lined with shelves piled high with books and manuscripts. There'd been a wall (lovers coupling against it) and, behind it, hidden from every sight but hers, a cell in which a bound woman had lain in darkness for a suffering age. She heard the prisoner's scream now, in her mind's ear: that howl of madness that had driven her up out of the ground and back through the dark streets to the safety of her own house and head. Was the woman still screaming, she wondered, or had she sunk back into the comatose state from which she'd been so unkindly woken? The thought of her pain brought tears to Jude's eyes, mingling with the rain.

"What are you doing?"

Oscar had reappeared from the tower and was hurrying across the gravel towards her, his jacket raised and tented over his head.

"My dear, you'll freeze to death. Get in the car. Please, *please*. Get in the car."

She did as he suggested, the rain running down her neck.

"I'm sorry," she said. "I . . . I wondered where you'd gone, that was all. Then . . . I don't know . . . the place seemed familiar."

"It's a place of no importance," he said. "You're shivering. Would you prefer we didn't go to the opera?"

"Would you mind?"

"Not in the least. Pleasure shouldn't be a trial. You're wet and cold, and we can't have you getting a chill. One sickly individual's enough."

She didn't question this last remark; there was too much else on her mind. She wanted to sob, though whether out of joy or sorrow she wasn't sure. The dream she'd come to dismiss as fancy was founded in solid fact, and this solid fact beside her—Godolphin— was in turn touched by something momentous. She'd been per- suaded by his practiced understatement: the way he talked of traveling to the Dominions as he would of boarding a train, and his expeditions in Yzordderrex as a form of tourism as yet un- available to the great unwashed. But his reductionism was a screen—whether he was aware of the fact or not—a ploy to con- ceal the greater significance of his business. His ignorance, or ar- rogance, might well kill him, she began to suspect: which thought was the sorrow in her. And the joy? That she might save him, and he learn to love her out of gratitude.

Back at the house they both changed out of their formal attire. When she emerged from her room on the top floor she found him on the stairs, waiting for her.

"I wonder . . . perhaps we should talk?"

They went downstairs into the tasteful clutter of the lounge. The rain beat against the window. He drew the curtains and poured them brandies to fortify them against the cold. Then he sat down opposite her.

"We have a problem, you and I."

"We do?"

"There's so much we have to say to each other. At least . . . here am I presuming it's reciprocal, but for myself, certainly . . . certainly I've got a good deal I want to say, and I'm damned if I know where to begin. I'm aware that I owe you explanations, about what you saw at the estate, about Dowd and the voiders, about what I did to Charlie. The list goes on. And I've tried, really I have, to find some way to make it all clear to you. But the truth is, I'm not sure of the truth myself. Memory plays such tricks"—she made a murmur of agreement—"especially when you're dealing with places and people who seem to belong half in your dreams. Or in your nightmares." He drained his glass and reached for the bottle he'd set on the table beside him.

"I don't like Dowd," she said suddenly. "And I don't trust him."

He looked up from refilling his glass. "That's perceptive," he said. "You want some more brandy?" She proffered her glass, and he poured her an ample measure. "I agree with you," he said. "He's a dangerous creature, for a number of reasons."

"Can't you get rid of him?"

"He knows too much, I'm afraid. He'd be more dangerous out of my employ than in it."

"Has he got something to do with these murders? Just today, I saw the news—"

He waved her inquiry away. "You don't need to know about any of that, my dear," he said.

"But if you're at risk—"

"I'm not. I'm not. At least be reassured about that."

"So you know all about it?"

"Yes," he said heavily. "I know a little something. And so does Dowd. In fact, he knows more about this whole situation than you and I put together."

She wondered about this. Did Dowd know about the prisoner behind the wall, for instance, or was that a secret she had entirely to herself? If so, perhaps she'd be wise to keep it that way. When so many players in this game had information she lacked, sharing anything—even with Oscar—might weaken her position; perhaps threaten her life. Some part of her nature not susceptible to the blandishments of luxury or the need for love was lodged behind that wall with the woman she'd woken. She would leave it there, safe in the darkness. The rest—anything else she knew—she'd share.

"You're not the only one who crosses over," she said. "A friend of mine went."

"Really?" he said. "Who?"

"His name's Gentle. Actually, his real name's Zacharias. John Furie Zacharias. Charlie knew him a little."

"Charlie...." Oscar shook his head. "Poor Charlie." Then he said, "Tell me about Gentle."

"It's complicated," she said. "When I left Charlie he got very vengeful. He hired somebody to kill me...."

She went on to tell Oscar about the murder attempt in New York and Gentle's later intervention; then about the events of New Year's Eve. As she related this she had the distinct impression that at least some of what she was telling him he already knew, a suspicion confirmed when she'd finished her description of Gentle's removal from this Dominion.

"The mystif took him?" he said. "My God, that's a risk!"

"What's a mystif?" she asked.

"A very rare creature indeed. One would be born into the Eurhetemec tribe once in a generation. They're reputedly extraordinary lovers. As I understand it, they have no sexual identity, except as a function of their partner's desire."

"That sounds like Gentle's idea of paradise."

"As long as you know what you want," Oscar said. "If you don't I daresay it could get very confusing."

She laughed. "He knows what he wants, believe me."

"You speak from experience?"

"Bitter experience."

"He may have bitten off more than he can chew, so to speak, keeping the company of a mystif. My friend in Yzordderrex—Peccable—had a mistress for a while who'd been a madam. She'd had a very plush establishment in Patashoqua, and she and I got on famously. She kept telling me I should become a white slaver and bring her girls from the Fifth, so she could start a new business in Yzordderrex. She reckoned we'd have made a fortune. We never did it, of course. But we both enjoyed talking about things venereal. It's a pity that word's so tainted, isn't it? You say *venereal,* and people immediately think of disease, instead of Venus...." He paused, seeming to have lost his way, then said, "Anyway, she told me once that she'd employed a mystif for a while in her bordello, and it caused her no end of problems. She'd almost had to close her place, because of the reputation she got. You'd think a creature like that would make the ultimate whore, wouldn't you? But apparently a lot of customers just didn't want to see their desires made flesh." He watched her as he spoke, a smile playing around his lips. "I can't imagine why."

"Maybe they were afraid of what they were."

"You'd consider that foolish, I assume."

"Yes, of course. What you are, you are."

"That's a hard philosophy to live up to."

"No harder than running away."

"Oh, I don't know. I've thought about running away quite a lot of late. Disappearing forever."

"Really?" she said, trying to stifle any show of agitation. "Why?"

"Too many birds coming home to roost."

"But you're staying?"

"I vacillate. England's so pleasant in the spring. And I'd miss the cricket in the summer months."

"They play cricket everywhere, don't they?"

"Not in Yzordderrex they don't."

"You'd go there forever?"

"Why not? Nobody would find me, because nobody would ever guess where I'd gone."

"I'd know."

"Then maybe I'd have to take you with me," he said tentatively, almost as though he were making the proposal in all seriousness and was afraid of being refused. "Could you bear that thought?" he said. "Of leaving the Fifth, I mean."

"I could bear it."

He paused. Then: "I think it's about time I showed you some of my treasures," he said, rising from his chair. "Come on."

She'd known from oblique remarks of Dowd's that the locked room on the second floor contained some kind of collection, but its nature, when he finally unlocked the door and ushered her in, astonished her.

"All this was collected in the Dominions," Oscar explained, "and brought back by hand."

He escorted her around the room, giving her a capsule summary of what some of the stranger objects were and bringing from hiding tiny items she might otherwise have overlooked. Into the former category, among others, went the Boston Bowl and Gaud Maybellome's *Encyclopedia of Heavenly Signs;* into the latter a bracelet of beetles caught by the killing jar in their daisy chain coupling—fourteen generations, he explained, male entering female, and female in turn devouring the male in front, the circle joined by the youngest female and the oldest male, who, by dint of the latter's suicidal acrobatics, were face to face.

She had many questions, of course, and he was pleased to play the teacher. But there were several inquiries he had no answers to. Like the empire looters from whom he was descended, he'd assembled the collection with commitment, taste, and ignorance in equal measure. Yet when he spoke of the artifacts, even those whose function he had no clue to, there was a touching fervor in his tone, familiar as he was with the tiniest detail of the tiniest piece.

"You gave some objects to Charlie, didn't you?" she said.

"Once in a while. Did you see them?"

"Yes, indeed," she said, the brandy tempting her tongue to confess the dream of the blue eye, her brain resisting it.

"If things had been different," Oscar said, "Charlie might have been the one wandering the Dominions. I owe him a glimpse."

" 'A piece of the miracle,' " she quoted.

"That's right. But I'm sure he felt ambivalent about them."

"That was Charlie."

"True, true. He was too English for his own good. He never had the courage of his feelings, except where you were concerned. And who could blame him?"

She looked up from the trinket she was studying to find that she too was a subject of study, the look on his face unequivocal.

"It's a family problem," he said. "When it comes to . . . matters of the heart."

This confession made, a look of discomfort crossed his face, and his hand went to his ribs. "I'll leave you to look around if you like," he said. "There's nothing in here that's really volatile."

"Thank you."

"Will you lock up after yourself?"

"Of course."

She watched him go, unable to think of anything to detain him, but feeling forsaken once he'd gone. She heard him go to his bedroom, which was down the hall on the same floor, and close the door behind him. Then she turned her attention back to the treasures on the shelves. It wouldn't stay there, however. She wanted to touch, and be touched by, something warmer than these relics. After a few moments of hesitation she left them in the dark, locking the door behind her. She would take the key back to him, she'd decided. If his words of admiration were not simply flattery—if he had bed on his mind—she'd know it soon enough. And if he rejected her, at least there'd be an end to this trial by doubt.

She knocked on the bedroom door. There was no reply. There was light seeping from under the door, however, so she knocked again and then turned the handle and, saying his name softly, entered. The lamp beside the bed was burning, illuminating an ancestral portrait that hung over it. Through its gilded window a severe and sallow individual gazed down on the empty sheets. Hearing the sound of running water from the adjacent bathroom, Jude crossed the bedroom, taking in a dozen details of this, his most private chamber, as she did so: the plushness of the pillows and the linen; the spirit decanter and glass beside the bed; the cigarettes and ashtray on a small heap of well-thumbed paperbacks. Without declaring herself, she pushed the door open. Oscar was sitting on the edge of the bath in his undershorts, dabbing a washcloth to a partially healed wound in his side. Reddened water ran over the furry swell of his belly. Hearing her, he looked up. There was pain on his face.

She didn't attempt to offer an excuse for being there, nor did he request one. He simply said, "Charlie did it."

"You should see a doctor."

"I don't trust doctors. Besides, it's getting better." He tossed the washcloth into the sink. "Do you make a habit of walking into bathrooms unannounced?" he said. "You could have walked in on something even less—"

"Venereal?" she said.

"Don't mock me," he replied. "I'm a crude seducer, I know. It comes from years of buying company."

"Would you be more comfortable buying me?" she said.

"My God," he replied, his look appalled. "What do you take me for?"

"A lover," she said plainly. *"My* lover?"

"I wonder if you know what you're saying?"

"What I don't know I'll learn," she said. "I've been hiding from myself, Oscar. Putting everything out of my head so I wouldn't feel anything. But I feel a lot. And I want you to know that."

"I know," he said. "More than you can understand, I know. And it makes me afraid, Judith."

"There's nothing to be afraid of," she said, astonished that it was she who was mouthing these words of reassurance when he was the elder and presumably the stronger, the wiser. She reached out and put her palm flat against his massive chest. He bent forward to kiss her, his mouth closed until he met hers and found it open. One hand went around her back, the other to her breast, her murmur of pleasure smeared between their mouths. His touch moved down, over her stomach, past her groin, to hoist up her skirt and retrace its steps. His fingers found her sopping—she'd been wet since first stepping into the treasure room—and he slid his whole hand down into the hot pouch of her underwear, pressing the heel of his palm against the top of her sex while his long middle digit sought out her fundament, gently catching its flukes with his nail.

"Bed," she said.

He didn't let her go. They made an ungainly exit from the bathroom, with him guiding her backwards until she felt the edge of the bed behind her thighs. There she sat down, taking hold of the waistband of his blood-stained shorts and easing them down while she kissed his belly. Suddenly bashful, he reached to stop her, but she pulled them down until his penis appeared. It was a curiosity. Only a little engorged, it had been deprived of its foreskin, which made its outlandishly bulbous, carmine head look even more inflamed than the wound in its wielder's side. The stem was very considerably thinner and paler, its length knotted with veins bearing blood to its crown. If it was this disproportion that embarrassed him he had no need, and to prove her pleasure she put her lips against the head. His objecting hand was no longer in evidence. She heard him make a little moan above, and looked up to see him staring down at her with something very like awe on his face. Sliding her fingers beneath testicles and stem, she raised the curiosity to her mouth and took it inside; then she dropped both hands to her blouse and began to unbutton. But he'd no sooner started to harden in her mouth than he murmured a denial, withdrew his member, and stepped back from her, pulling up his underwear.

"Why are you doing this?" he said.

"I'm enjoying it."

He was genuinely agitated, she saw, shaking his head, covering the bulge in his underwear in a new fit of bashfulness.

"For whose sake?" he said. "You don't have to, you know."

"I know."

"I wonder?" he said, genuine puzzlement in his voice.

"I don't want to use you."

"I wouldn't let you."

"Maybe you wouldn't know."

This remark inflamed her. A rage rose such as she'd not felt in a long while. She stood up.

"I know what I want," she said, "but I'm not about to beg for it."

"That's not what I'm saying."

"What *are* you saying?"

"That I want you, too."

"So do something about it," she said.

He seemed to find her fury freshly arousing and stepped towards her again, saying her name in a voice almost pained with feeling. "I'd like to undress you," he said. "Would you mind?"

"No."

"I don't want you to do anything—"

"Then I won't."

"—except lie down."

She did so. He turned off the bathroom light, then came to the edge of the bed and looked down at her. His bulk was emphasized by the light from the lamp, which threw his shadow up to the ceiling. Quantity had never seemed an arousing quality hitherto, but in him she found it intensely attractive, evidence as it was of his excesses and his appetites. Here was a man who would not be contained by one world, one set of experiences, but who was kneeling now like a slave in front of her, his expression that of one obsessed.

With consummate tenderness, he began to undress her. She'd known fetishists before—men to whom she was not an individual but a hook upon which some particular item was hung for worship. If there was any such particular in this man's head, it was the body he now began to uncover, proceeding to do so in an order and manner that made some fevered sense to him. First he slipped off her underpants; then he finished unbuttoning her blouse, without removing it. Next he teased her breasts from her bra, so that they were available to his toying, but then didn't play there but went to her shoes, removing them and setting them beside the bed before hoisting up her skirt so as to have a view of her sex. Here his eyes lingered, his fingers advancing up her thigh to the crease of her groin, then retreating. Not once did he look at her face. She looked at his, however, enjoying the zeal and veneration there. Finally he rewarded his own diligence with kisses. First on her lower legs, moving up towards her knees; then her stomach and her breasts, and finally returning to her thighs and up into the place he'd forbidden them both till now. She was ready for pleasure, and he supplied it, his huge hand caressing her breasts as he tongued her. She closed her eyes as he unfolded her, alive to every drop of moisture on her labia and legs. When he rose from this to finish undressing her—skirt first, then blouse and bra—her face was hot and her breath fast. He tossed the clothes onto the floor and stood up again, taking her knees and pushing them up and back, spreading her for his delectation, and holding her there, prettily exposed.

"Finger yourself," he said, not letting her go.

She put her hands between her legs and made a show for him. He'd slickened her well, but her fingers went deeper than his tongue, readying herself for the curiosity. He gorged on the sight, meanwhile, glancing up to her face several times, then returning to the spectacle below. All trace of his previous hesitation had gone. He encouraged her with his admiration, calling her a host of sweet names, his tented underwear proof—as if she needed it—of his arousal. She started to push her hips up from the bed to meet her fingers, and he took firmer grip of her knees as she moved, opening her wider still. Lifting his right hand to his mouth he licked his middle finger and put it down against her pucker of her other hole, rubbing it gently.

"Will you suck me now?" he asked her. "Just a little?"

"Show me it," she said.

He stepped away from her and took off his underwear. The

curiosity was now fully risen and florid. She sat up and put it back between her lips, one hand holding it by its pulsing root while the other continued its dalliance with her own sex. She'd never been good at guessing the point at which the milk boiled over, so she took it from the heat of her mouth to cool him a little, glancing up at him as she did so. Either the extraction or her glance set him off, however.

"Damn!" he said. "Damn!", and started to step back from her, his hand going down to his groin to take the curiosity in a stranglehold.

It seemed he might have succeeded, as two desultory dribbles ran from its head. Then his testicles unleashed their flood, and it came forth in uncommon abundance. He moaned as it came, as much in self-admonishment as pleasure, she thought, that assumption confirmed when he'd emptied his sac upon the floor.

"I'm sorry . . ." he said, ". . . I'm sorry. . . ."

"There's no need," she said, standing up and putting her lips to his. He continued to murmur his apologies, however.

"I haven't done that in a long time," he said. "So adolescent."

She kept her silence, knowing anything she said would only begin a further round of self-reproach. He slipped away into the bathroom to find a towel. When he returned she was picking up her clothes.

"Are you going?" he said.

"Only to my room."

"Do you have to?" he said. "I know that wasn't much of a performance, but . . . the bed's big enough for us both. And I don't snore."

"The bed's enormous."

"So . . . would you stay?" he said.

"I'd like to."

He made a charming smile. "I'm honored," he said. "Will you excuse me a moment?"

He switched the bathroom light back on and disappeared inside, closing the door, leaving her to lie back on the bed and wonder at this whole turn of events. Its very oddness seemed appropriate. After all, this whole journey had begun with an act of misplaced love: love become murder. Now a new dislocation. Here she was, lying in the bed of a man with a body far from beautiful, whose bulk she longed to have upon her; whose hands were capable of fratricide but aroused her like none she'd ever known; who'd walked more worlds than an opium poet, but couldn't speak love without stumbling; who was a titan, and yet afraid. She made a nest among his duck-down pillows and waited there for him to come back and tell her a story of love.

He reappeared after a long while and slipped beneath the sheets beside her. True to her imaginings, he said he loved her at last, but only once he'd turned the light out, and his eyes were not available for study.

When she slept, it was deeply, and when she woke again, it was like sleeping, dark and pleasurable, the former because the drapes were still drawn, and between their cracks she could see that the sky was still benighted, the latter because Oscar was behind her, and inside. One of his hands was upon her breast, the other lifting her leg so that he could ease his upward stroke. He'd entered her with skill and discretion, she realized. Not only had he not stirred her until he was embedded, but he'd chosen the virgin passage, which—had he suggested it while she was awake—she'd have attempted to coax him from, fearing the discomfort. In truth, there was none, though the sensation was quite unlike anything she'd felt before. He kissed her neck and shoulder blade, light kisses, as though he was unaware of her wakefulness. She made it known with a sigh. His stroke slowed and stopped, but she pressed her buttocks back to meet his thrust, satisfying his curiosity as to the limit of its access, which was to say none. She was happy to accept him entirely, trapping his hand against her breast to press it to rougher service, while putting her own at the connecting place. He'd dutifully slipped on a condom before entering her, which, together with the fact that he'd already poured forth once tonight, made him a near perfect lover: slow and certain.

She didn't use the dark to reconfigure him. The man pressing his face into her hair, and biting at her shoulder, wasn't—like the mystif he'd described—a reflection of imagined ideals. It was Oscar Godolphin, paunch, curiosity, and all. What she *did* reconfigure was herself, so that she became in her mind's eye a glyph of sensation: a line dividing from the coil of her pierced core, up through her belly to the points of her breasts, then intersecting again at her nape, crossing and becoming woven spirals beneath the hood of her skull. Her imagination added a further refinement, inscribing a circle around this figure, which burned in the darkness behind her lips like a vision. Her rapture was perfected then: being an abstraction in his arms, yet pleasured like flesh. There was no greater luxury.

He asked if they might move, saying only, "The wound . . . ," by way of explanation.

She went onto her hands and knees, he slipping from her for a tormenting moment while she did so, then putting the curiosity back to work. His rhythm instantly became more urgent, his fingers in her sex, his voice in her head, both expressing ecstasy. The glyph brightened in her mind's eye, fiery from end to end. She yelled out to him, first only *yes* and *yes,* then plainer demands, inflaming him to new invention. The glyph became blinding, burning away all thought of where she was, or what; all memory of conjunctions past subsumed in this perpetuity.

She was not even aware that he'd spent himself until she felt him withdrawing, and then she reached behind her to keep him inside a while longer. He obliged. She enjoyed the sensation of his softening inside her, and even, finally, his exiting, the tender muscle yielding its prisoner reluctantly. Then he rolled over onto the bed beside her and reached for the light. It was dim enough not to sting, but still too bright, and she was about to protest when she saw that he was putting his fingers to his injured side. Their congress had unknitted the wound. Blood was running from it in two directions: down towards the curiosity, still nestled in the condom, and down his side to the sheet.

"It's all right," he said as she made to get up. "It looks worse than it is."

"It still needs something to staunch it," she said.

"That's good Godolphin blood," he said, wincing and grinning at the same moment. His gaze went from her face to the portrait above the bed. "It's always flowed freely," he said.

"He doesn't look as though he approved of us," she said.

"On the contrary," Oscar replied. "I know for a fact he'd adore you. Joshua understood devotion."

She looked at the wound again. Blood was seeping between his fingers.

"Won't you let me cover that up?" she said. "It makes me queasy."

"For you . . . anything."

"Have you got any dressing?"

"Dowd's probably got some, but I don't want him knowing about us. At least, not yet. Let's keep it our secret."

"You, me, and Joshua," she said.

"Even Joshua doesn't know what we got up to," Oscar said, without a trace of irony audible in his voice. "Why do you think I turned the light out?"

In lieu of fresh dressing she went through to the bathroom to find a towel. While she was doing so he spoke to her through the open door.

"I meant what I said, by the way," he told her.

"About what?"

"That I'll do anything for you. At least, anything that's in my power to do or give. I want you to stay with me, Judith. I'm no Adonis, I know that. But I learned a lot from Joshua . . . about devotion, I mean." She emerged with the towel to be greeted by the same offer. "Anything you want."

"That's very generous."

"The pleasure's in the giving," he said.

"I think you know what I'd like most."

He shook his head. "I'm no good at guessing games. Only cricket. Just tell me."

She sat down on the edge of the bed and gently tugged his hand from the wound in his side, wiping the blood from between his fingers.

"Say it," he told her.

"Very well," she said. "I want you to take me out of this Dominion. I want you to show me Yzordderrex."

25

I

Twenty-two days after emerging from the icy wastes of the Jokalaylau into the balmier climes of the Third Dominion—days which had seen Pie and Gentle's fortunes rise dramatically as they journeyed through the Third's diverse territories—the wanderers were standing on a station platform outside the tiny town of Mai-ké, waiting for the train that once a week came through on its way from the city of Iahmandhas, in the northeast, to L'Himby, half a day's journey to the south.

They were eager to be departing. Of all the towns and villages they'd visited in the past three weeks, Mai-ké had been the least welcoming. It had its reasons. It was a community under siege from the Dominion's two suns, the rains which brought the region its crops having failed to materialize for six consecutive years. Terraces and fields that should have been bright with shoots were virtually dust bowls, stocks hoarded against this eventuality critically depleted. Famine was imminent, and the village was in no mood to entertain strangers. The previous night the entire populace had been out in the drab streets praying aloud, these imprecations led by their spiritual leaders, who had about them the air of men whose invention was nearing its end. The noise, so unmusical Gentle had observed that it would irritate the most sympathetic of deities, had gone on until first light, making sleep impossible. As a consequence, exchanges between Pie and Gentle were somewhat tense this morning.

They were not the only travelers waiting for the train. A farmer from Mai-ké had brought a herd of sheep onto the platform, some of them so emaciated it was a wonder they could stand, and the flock had brought with them clouds of the local pest: an insect called a zarzi, that had the wingspan of a dragonfly and a body as fat and furred as a bee. It fed on sheep ticks, unless it could find something more tempting. Gentle's blood fell into this latter category, and the lazy whine of the zarzi was never far from his ears as he waited in the midday heat. Their one informant in Mai-ké, a woman called Hairstone Banty, had predicted that the train would be on time, but it was already well overdue, which didn't augur well for the hundred other pieces of advice she'd offered them the night before.

Swatting zarzi to left and right, Gentle emerged from the shade of the platform building to peer down the track. It ran without crook or bend to its vanishing point, empty every mile of the way. On the rails a few yards from where he stood, rats, a gangrenous variety called graveolents, to-ed and fro-ed, gathering dead grasses for the nests they were constructing between the rails and the gravel the rails were set upon. Their industry only served to irritate Gentle further.

"We're stuck here forever," he said to Pie, who was squatting on the platform making marks on the stone with a sharp pebble. "This is Hairstone's revenge on a couple of hoopreo."

He'd heard this term whispered in their presence countless times. It meant anything from exotic stranger to repugnant leper, depending on the facial expression of the speaker. The people of Mai-ké were keen face-pullers, and when they'd used the word in Gentle's company there was little doubt which end of the scale of affections they had in mind.

"It'll come," said Pie. "We're not the only ones waiting."

Two more groups of travelers had appeared on the platform in the last few minutes: a family of Mai'kéacs, three generations represented, who had lugged everything they owned down to the station; and three women in voluminous robes, their heads shaved and plastered with white mud, nuns of the Goetic Kicaranki, an order as despised in Mai-ké as any well-fed hoopreo. Gentle took some comfort from the appearance of these fellow travelers, but the track was still empty, the graveolents, who would surely be the first to sense any disturbance in the rails, going about their nest building unperturbed. He wearied of watching them very quickly and turned his attention to Pie's scrawlings.

"What are you doing?"

"I'm trying to work out how long we've been here."

"Two days in Mai-ké, a day and a half on the road from Attaboy—"

"No, no," said the mystif, "I'm trying to work it out in Earth days. Right from first arriving in the Dominions."

"We tried that in the mountains, and we didn't get anywhere."

"That's because our brains were frozen stiff."

"So have you done it?"

"Give me a little time."

"Time, we've got," Gentle said, returning his gaze to the antics of graveolents. "These little buggers'll have grandchildren by the time the damn train arrives."

The mystif went on with its calculations, leaving Gentle to wander back into the comparative comfort of the waiting room, which, to judge by the sheep droppings on the floor, had been used to pen entire flocks in the recent past. The zarzi followed him, buzzing around his brow. He pulled from his ill-fitting jacket (bought with money he and Pie had won gambling in Attaboy) a dog-eared copy of *Fanny Hill*—the only volume in English, besides *Pilgrim's Progress,* which he'd been able to purchase—and used it to flail at the insects, then gave up. They'd tire of him eventually, or else he'd become immune to their attacks. Whichever; he didn't care.

He leaned against the graffiti-covered wall and yawned. He was bored. Of all things, bored! If, when they'd first arrived in Vanaeph, Pie had suggested that a few weeks later the wonders of the Reconciled Dominions would have become tedious, Gentle would have laughed the thought off as nonsense. With a gold-green sky above and the spires of Patashoqua gleaming in the distance, the scope for adventure had seemed endless. But by the time he'd reached Beatrix—the fond memories of which had not been entirely erased by images of its ruin—he was traveling like any man in a foreign land, prepared for occasional revelations but persuaded that the nature of conscious, curious bipeds was a constant under any heaven. They'd seen a great deal in the last few days, to be sure, but nothing he might not have imagined had he not stayed at home and got seriously drunk.

Yes, there had been glorious sights. But there had also been hours of discomfort, boredom, and banality. On their way to Mai-ké, for instance, they'd been exhorted to stay in some nameless hamlet to witness the community's festival: the annual donkey drowning. The origins of this ritual were, they were told, shrouded in fabulous mystery. They declined, Gentle remarking that this surely marked the nadir of their journey, and traveled on in the back of a wagon whose driver informed them that the vehicle had served his family for six generations as a dung carrier. He then proceeded to explain at great length the life cycle of his family's ancient foe, the pensanu, or shite rooster, a beast that with one turd could render an entire wagonload of dung inedible. They didn't press the man as to who in the region dined thusly, but they peered closely at their plates for many days following.

As he sat rolling the hard pellets of sheep dung under his heel, Gentle turned his thoughts to the one high point in their journey across the Third. That was the town of Effatoi, which Gentle had rechristened Attaboy. It wasn't that large—the size of Amsterdam, perhaps, and with that city's charm—but it was a gambler's paradise, drawing souls addicted to chance from across the Dominion. Here every game in the Imajica could be played. If your credit wasn't good in the casinos or the cock pits, you could always find a desperate man somewhere who'd bet on the color of your next piss if it was the only game on offer. Working together with what was surely telepathic efficiency, Gentle and the mystif had made a small fortune in the city—in eight currencies, no less— enough to keep them in clothes, food, and train tickets until they reached Yzordderrex. It wasn't profit that had almost seduced Gentle into setting up house there, however. It was a local delicacy: a cake of strudel pastry and the honey-softened seeds of a marriage between peach and pomegranate, which he ate before they gambled to give him vim, then while they gambled to calm his nerves, and then again in celebration when they'd won. It was only when Pie assured him that the confection would be available elsewhere (and if it wasn't they now had sufficient funds to hire their own pastry chef to make it) that Gentle was persuaded to depart. L'Himby called.

"We have to move on," the mystif had said. "Scopique will be waiting."

"You make it sound like he's expecting us."

"I'm always expected," Pie said.

"How long since you were in L'Himby?"

"At least . . . two hundred and thirty years."

"Then he'll be dead."

"Not Scopique," Pie said. "It's important you see him, Gentle. Especially now, with so many changes in the air."

"If that's what you want to do, then we'll do it," Gentle had replied. "How far is L'Himby?"

"A day's journey, if we take the train."

That had been the first mention Gentle had heard of the iron road that joined the city of Iahmandhas and L'Himby: the city of furnaces and the city of temples.

"You'll like L'Himby," Pie had said. "It's a place of meditation."

Rested and funded, they'd left Attaboy the following morning, traveling along the River Fefer for a day, then, via Happi and

Omootajive, into the province called the Ched Lo Ched, the Flowering Place (now bloomless), and finally to Mai-ké, caught in the twin pincers of poverty and puritanism.

On the platform outside, Gentle heard Pie say, "Good."

He raised himself from the comfort of the wall and stepped out into the sunshine again. "The train?" he said.

"No. The calculations. I've finished them." The mystif stared down at the marks on the platform at its feet. "This is only an approximation, of course, but I think it's sound within a day or two. Three at the most."

"So what day is it?"

"Take a guess."

"March . . . the tenth."

"Way off," said Pie. "By these calculations, and remember this is only an approximation, it's the seventeenth of May."

"Impossible."

"It's true."

"Spring's almost over."

"Are you wishing you were back there?" Pie asked.

Gentle chewed on this for a while, then said, "Not particularly. I just wish the fucking trains ran on time."

He wandered to the edge of the platform and stared down the line.

"There's no sign," Pie said. "We'd be quicker going by doeki."

"You keep doing that—"

"Doing what?"

"Saying what's on the tip of my tongue. Are you reading my mind?"

"No," said the mystif, rubbing out its calculation with its sole.

"So how did we win all that in Attaboy?"

"You don't need teaching," Pie replied.

"Don't tell me it comes naturally," Gentle said. "I've got through my entire life without winning a thing, and suddenly, when you're with me, I can do no wrong. That's no coincidence. Tell me the truth."

"That *is* the truth. You don't need teaching. *Reminding*, maybe. . . ." Pie gave a little smile.

"And that's another thing," Gentle said, snatching at one of the zarzi as he spoke.

Much to his surprise, he actually caught it. He opened his palm. He'd cracked its casing, and the blue mush of its innards was oozing out, but it was still alive. Disgusted, he flicked his wrist, depositing the body on the platform at his feet. He didn't scrutinize the remains, but pulled up a fistful of the sickly grass that sprouted between the slabs of the platform and set about scrubbing his palm with it.

"What were we talking about?" he said. Pie didn't reply. "Oh, yes . . . things I'd forgotten." He looked down at his clean hand. "Pneuma," he said. "Why would I ever forget having a power like the pneuma?"

"Either because it wasn't important to you any longer—"

"Which is doubtful."

"—or you forgot because you wanted to forget."

There was an oddness in the way the mystif pronounced its reply which grated on Gentle's ear, but he pursued the argument anyway.

"Why would I want to forget?" he said.

Pie looked back along the line. The distance was obscured by dust, but there were glimpses through it of a clear sky.

"Well?" said Gentle.

"Maybe because remembering hurts too much," it said, without looking around.

The words were even uglier to Gentle's ear than the reply that had preceded it. He caught the sense, but only with difficulty.

"Stop this," he said.

"Stop what?"

"Talking in that damn-fool way. It turns my gut."

"I'm not doing anything," the mystif said, its voice still distorted, but now more subtly. "Trust me. I'm doing nothing."

"So tell me about the pneuma," Gentle said. "I want to know how I came by a power like that."

Pie started to reply, but this time the words were so badly disfigured, and the sound itself so ugly, it was like a fist in Gentle's stomach, stirring the stew there.

"Jesus!" he said, rubbing his belly in a vain attempt to soothe the churning. "Whatever you're playing at—"

"It's not me," Pie protested. "It's you. You don't want to hear what I'm saying."

"*Yes, I do,*" Gentle said, wiping beads of chilly sweat from around his mouth. "I want answers. I want straight answers!"

Grimly, Pie started to speak again, but immediately the waves of nausea climbed Gentle's gut with fresh zeal. The pain in his belly was sufficient to bend him double, but he was damned if the mystif was going to keep anything from him. It was a matter of principle now. He studied Pie's lips through narrowed eyes, but after a few words the mystif stopped speaking.

"Tell me!" Gentle said, determined to have Pie obey him even if he could make no sense of the words. "What have I done that I want to forget so badly? *Tell me!*"

Its face all reluctance, the mystif once again opened its mouth. The words, when they came, were so hopelessly corrupted Gentle could barely grasp a fraction of their sense. Something about power. Something about death.

Point proved, he waved the source of this excremental din away and turned his eyes in search of a sight to calm his belly. But the scene around him was a convention of little horrors: a graveolent making its wretched nest beneath the rails; the perspective of the track, snatching his eye into the dust; the dead zarzi at his feet, its egg sac split, spattering its unborn onto the stone. This last image, vile as it was, brought food to mind. The harbor meal in Yzord-derrex: fish within fish within fish, the littlest filled with eggs. The thought defeated him. He tottered to the edge of the platform and vomited onto the rails, his gut convulsing. He didn't have that much in his belly, but the heaves went on and on until his abdomen ached and tears of pain ran from his eyes. At last he stepped back from the platform edge, shuddering. The smell of his stomach was still in his nostrils, but the spasms were steadily diminishing. From the corner of his eye he saw Pie approach.

"Don't come near me!" he said. "I don't want you touching me!"

He turned his back on the vomit and its cause and retired to the shade of the waiting room, sitting down on the hard wood bench, putting his head against the wall, and closing his eyes. As the pain eased and finally disappeared, his thoughts turned to the purpose behind Pie's assault. He'd quizzed the mystif several times over the past four and a half months about the problem of power: how it was come by and—more particularly—how he, Gentle, had come to possess it. Pie's replies had been oblique in the extreme, but Gentle hadn't felt any great urge to get to the bottom of the question. Perhaps subconsciously he hadn't really wanted to know. Classically, such gifts had consequences, and he was enjoying his role as getter and wielder of power too much to want it spoiled with talk of hubris. He'd been content to be fobbed off with hints and equivocation, and he might have continued to be content, if he hadn't been irritated by the zarzi and the lateness of the L'Himby train, bored and ready for an argument. But that was only half the issue. He'd pressed the mystif, certainly, but he'd scarcely goaded it. The attack seemed out of all proportion to the offense. He'd asked an innocent question and been turned inside out for doing so. So much for all that loving talk in the mountains.

"Gentle . . ."

"Fuck you."

"The train, Gentle . . ."

"What about it?"

"It's coming."

He opened his eyes. The mystif was standing in the doorway, looking forlorn.

"I'm sorry that had to happen," it said.

"It didn't have to," Gentle said. "You made it happen."

"Truly I didn't."

"What was it then? Something I ate?"

"No. But there are some questions—"

"That make me sick."

"—that have answers you don't want to hear."

"What do you take me for?" Gentle said, his tone all quiet contempt. "I ask a question, you fill my head with so much shit for an answer that I throw up, and then it's my fault for asking in the first place? What kind of fucked-up logic is that?"

The mystif raised its hands in mock surrender. "I'm not going to argue," it said.

"Damn right," Gentle replied.

Any further exchange would have been impractical anyway, with the sound of the train's approach steadily getting louder, and its arrival being greeted by cheers and clapping from an audience that had gathered on the platform. Still feeling delicate when he stood, Gentle followed Pie out into the crowd.

It seemed half the inhabitants of Mai-ké had come down to the station. Most, he assumed, were sightseers rather than potential travelers; the train a distraction from hunger and unanswered prayers. There were some families here who planned to board, however, pressing through the crowd with their luggage. What privations they'd endured to purchase their escape from Mai-ké could only be imagined. There was much sobbing as they embraced those they were leaving behind, most of whom were old folk, who to judge by their grief did not expect to see their children and grandchildren again. The journey to L'Himby, which for Gentle and Pie was little more than a jaunt, was for them a departure into memory.

That said, there could be few more spectacular means of departure in the Imajica than the massive locomotive which was only now emerging from a cloud of evaporating steam. Whoever had made blueprints for this roaring, glistening machine knew its earth counterpart—the kind of locomotives outdated in the West but still serving in China and India—very well. Their imitation was not so slavish as to suppress a certain decorative joie de vivre—it had been painted so gaudily it looked like the male of the species in search of a mate—but beneath the daubings was a machine that might have steamed into King's Cross or Marylebone in the years following the Great War. It drew six carriages and as many freight vehicles again, two of the latter being loaded with the flock of sheep.

Pie had already been down the line of carriages and was now coming back towards Gentle.

"The second. It's fuller down the other end."

They got in. The interiors had once been lush, but usage had taken its toll. Most of the seats had been stripped of both padding and headrests, and some were missing backs entirely. The floor was dusty, and the walls—which had once been decorated in the same riot as the engine—were in dire need of a fresh coat of paint. There were only two other occupants, both male, both grotesquely fat, and both wearing frock coats from which elaborately bound limbs emerged, lending them the look of clerics who'd escaped from an accident ward. Their features were minuscule, crowded in the center of each face as if clinging together for fear of drowning in fat. Both were eating nuts, cracking them in their pudgy fists and dropping little rains of pulverized shell on the floor between them.

"Brothers of the Boulevard," Pie remarked as Gentle took a seat, as far from the nut-crackers as possible.

Pie sat across the aisle from him, the bag containing what few belongings they'd accrued to date alongside. There was then a long delay, while recalcitrant animals were beaten and cajoled into boarding for what they perhaps knew was a ride to the slaughterhouse and those on the platform made their final farewells. It wasn't just the vows and tears that came in through the windows. So did the stench of the animals, and the inevitable zarzi, though with the Brothers and their meal to attract them the insects were uninterested in Gentle's flesh.

Wearied by the hours of waiting and wrung out by his nausea, Gentle dozed and finally fell into so deep a sleep that the train's long-delayed departure didn't stir him, and when he woke two hours of their journey had already passed. Very little had changed outside the window. Here were the same expanses of gray-brown earth that had stretched around Mai-ké, clusters of dwellings, built from mud in times of water and barely distinguishable from the ground they stood upon, dotted here and there. Occasionally they would pass a plot of land—either blessed with a spring or better irrigated than the ground around it—from which life was rising; even more occasionally saw workers bending to reap a healthy crop. But generally the scene was just as Hairstone Banty had predicted. There would be many hours of dead land, she'd said; then they would travel through the Steppes, and over the Three Rivers, to the province of Bem, of which L'Himby was the capital city. Gentle had doubted her competence at the time (she'd been smoking

a weed too pungent to be simply pleasurable, and wearing something unseen elsewhere in the town: a smile) but dope fiend or no,
she knew her geography.

As they traveled, Gentle's thoughts turned once again to the origins of the power Pie had somehow awakened in him. If, as he suspected, the mystif had touched a hitherto passive portion of his
mind and given him access to capabilities dormant in all human
beings, why was it so damned reluctant to admit the fact? Hadn't
Gentle proved in the mountains that he was more than willing to
accept the notion of mind embracing mind? Or was that co-
mingling now an embarrassment to the mystif, and its assault on
the platform a way to reestablish a distance between them? If so,
it had succeeded. They traveled half a day without exchanging a
single word.

In the heat of the afternoon, the train stopped at a small town
and lingered there while the flock from Mai-ké disembarked. No
less than four suppliers of refreshments came through the train
while it waited, one exclusively carrying pastries and candies,
among which Gentle found a variation on the honey and seed
cake that had almost kept him in Attaboy. He bought three slices,
and then two cups of well-sweetened coffee from another merchant, the combination of which soon enlivened his torpid system.
For its part, the mystif bought and ate dried fish, the smell of which
drove Gentle even farther from its side.

As the shout came announcing their imminent departure, Pie
suddenly sprang up and darted to the door. The thought went
through Gentle's head that the mystif intended to desert him, but
it had spotted newspapers for sale on the platform and, having
made a hurried purchase, clambered aboard again as the train
began to move off. Then it sat down beside the remains of its fish
dinner and had no sooner unfolded the paper than it let out a low
whistle.

"Gentle. You'd better look at this."

It passed the newspaper across the aisle. The banner headline
was in a language Gentle neither understood nor even recognized,
but that scarcely mattered. The photographs below were plain
enough. Here was a gallows, with six bodies hanging from it, and,
inset, the death portraits of the executed individuals: among them,
Hammeryock and Pontiff Farrow, the lawgivers of Vanaeph. Below
this rogues' gallery a finely rendered etching of Tick Raw, the crazy
evocator.

"So," Gentle said, "they got their comeuppance. It's the best
news I've had in days."

"No, it's not," Pie replied.

"They tried to kill us, remember?" Gentle said reasonably,

determined not to be infuriated by Pie's contentiousness. "If they
got hanged I'm not going to mourn 'em! What did they do, try and
steal the Merrow Ti' Ti'?"

"The Merrow Ti' Ti' doesn't exist."

"That was a joke, Pie," Gentle said, dead pan.

"I missed the humor of it, I'm sorry," the mystif said, unsmiling.
"Their crime—" It stopped and crossed the aisle to sit opposite
Gentle, claiming the paper from his hands before continuing.
"Their crime is far more significant," it went on, its voice lowered.
It began to read in the same whisper, précising the text of the
paper. "They were executed a week ago for making an attempt on
the Autarch's life while he and his entourage were on their peace
mission in Vanaeph—"

"Are you kidding?"

"No joke. That's what it says."

"Did they succeed?"

"Of course not." The mystif fell silent while it scanned the
columns. "It says they killed three of his advisers with a bomb and
injured eleven soldiers. The device was . . . wait, my Omootajivac
is rusty . . . the device was smuggled into his presence by Pontiff
Farrow. They were all caught alive, it says, but hanged dead, which
means they died under torture but the Autarch made a show of the
execution anyway."

"That's fucking barbaric."

"It's very common, particularly in political trials."

"What about Tick Raw? Why's his picture in there?"

"He was named as a co-conspirator, but apparently he escaped.
The damn fool!"

"Why'd you call him that?"

"Getting involved in politics when there's so much more at
stake. It's not the first time, of course, and won't be the last—"

"I'm not following."

"People get frustrated with waiting and they end up stooping to
politics. But it's so shortsighted. Stupid sod."

"How well do you know him?"

"Who? Tick Raw?" The placid features were momentarily confounded. Then Pie said, "He has . . . a certain reputation, shall we
say? They'll find him for certain. There isn't a sewer in the Dominions he'll be able to hide his head in."

"Why should you care?"

"Keep your voice down."

"Answer the question," Gentle replied, dropping his volume as
he spoke.

"He was a Maestro, Gentle. He called himself an evocator, but
it amounts to the same thing: he had power."

"Then why was he living in the middle of a shithole like Vanaeph?"

"Not everybody cares about wealth and women, Gentle. Some souls have higher ambition."

"Such as?"

"Wisdom. Remember why we came on this journey? To understand. That's a fine ambition." Pie looked at Gentle, making eye-to-eye contact for the first time since the episode on the platform. "*Your* ambition, my friend. You and Tick Raw had a lot in common."

"And he knew it?"

"Oh, yes. . . ."

"Is that why he was so riled when I wouldn't sit down and talk with him?"

"I'd say so."

"Shit!"

"Hammeryock and Farrow must have taken us for spies, come to wheedle out plots laid against the Autarch."

"But Tick Raw saw the truth."

"He did. He was once a great man, Gentle. At least . . . that was the rumor. Now I suppose he's dead or being tortured. Which is grim news for us."

"You think he'll name us?"

"Who knows? Maestros have ways of protecting themselves from torture, but even the strongest man can break under the right kind of pressure."

"Are you saying we've got the Autarch on our tails?"

"I think we'd know it if we had. We've come a long way from Vanaeph. The trail's probably cold by now."

"And maybe they didn't arrest Tick, eh? Maybe he escaped."

"They still caught Hammeryock and the Pontiff. I think we can assume they've got a hair-by-hair description of us."

Gentle laid his head back against the seat. "Shit," he said. "We're not making many friends, are we?"

"All the more reason that we don't lose each other," the mystif replied. The shadows of passing bamboo flickered on its face, but it looked at him unblinking. "Whatever harm you believe I may have done you, now or in the past, I apologize for it. I'd never wish you any hurt, Gentle. Please believe that. Not the slightest."

"I know," Gentle murmured, "and I'm sorry too, truly."

"Shall we agree to postpone our argument until the only opponents we've got left in the Imajica are each other?"

"That may be a very long time."

"All the better."

Gentle laughed. "Agreed," he said, leaning forward and taking the mystif's hand. "We've seen some amazing sights together, haven't we?"

"Indeed we have."

"Back there in Mai-ké I was losing my sense of how marvelous all this is."

"We've got a lot more wonders to see."

"Just promise me one thing?"

"Ask it."

"Don't eat raw fish in eyeshot of me again. It's more than a man can take."

2

From the yearning way that Hairstone Banty had described L'Himby, Gentle had been expecting some kind of Khatmandu— a city of temples, pilgrims, and free dope. Perhaps it had been that way once, in Banty's long-lost youth. But when, a few minutes after night had fallen, Gentle and Pie stepped off the train, it was not into an atmosphere of spiritual calm. There were soldiers at the station gates, most of them standing idle, smoking and talking, but a few casting their eyes over the disembarking passengers. As luck had it, however, another train had arrived at an adjacent platform minutes before, and the gateway was choked with passengers, many hugging their life's belongings. It wasn't difficult for Pie and Gentle to dig their way through to the densest part of the crowd and pass unnoticed through the turnstiles and out of the station.

There were many more troops in the wide lamplit streets, their presence no less disturbing for the air of lassitude that hung about them. The uncommissioned ranks wore a drab gray, but the officers wore white, which suited the subtropical night. All were conspicuously armed. Gentle made certain not to study either men or weaponry too closely for fear of attracting unwelcome attention, but it was clear from even a furtive glance that both the armaments and the vehicles parked in every other alleyway were of the same elaborately intimidating design as he'd seen in Beatrix. The warlords of Yzordderrex were clearly past masters in the crafts of death, their technology several generations beyond that of the locomotive that had brought the travelers here.

To Gentle's eye the most fascinating sight was not the tanks or the machine guns, however, it was the presence among these troops of a subspecies he'd not encountered hitherto. Oethacs, Pie called them. They stood no taller than their fellows, but their heads made up a third or more of that height, their squat bodies grotesquely broad to bear the weight of such a massive load of bone. Easy targets, Gentle remarked, but Pie whispered that their brains were small, their skulls thick, and their tolerance for pain heroic, the latter evidenced by the extraordinary array of livid scars and disfigurements they all bore on skin that was as white as the bone it concealed.

It seemed this substantial military presence had been in place for some time, because the populace went about their evening business as if these men and their killing machines were completely commonplace. There was little sign of fraternization, but there was no harassment either.

"Where do we go from here?" Gentle asked Pie once they were clear of the crowds around the station.

"Scopique lives in the northeast part of the city, close to the temples. He's a doctor. Very well respected."

"You think he may be still practicing?"

"He doesn't mend bones, Gentle. He's a doctor of theology. He used to like the city because it was so sleepy."

"It's changed, then."

"It certainly has. It looks as though it's got rich."

There was evidence of L'Himby's newfound wealth everywhere: in the gleaming buildings, many of them looking as though the paint on their doors was barely dry; in the proliferation of styles among the pedestrians and in the number of elegant automobiles on the street. There were a few signs still remaining of the culture that had existed here before the city's fortunes had boomed: beasts of burden still wove among the traffic, honked at and cursed; a smattering of façades had been preserved from older buildings and incorporated—usually crudely—into the designs of the newer. And then there were the living façades, the faces of the people Gentle and Pie were mingling with. The natives had a physical peculiarity unique to the region: clusters of small crystalline growths, yellow and purple, on their heads, sometimes arranged like crowns or coxcombs but just as often erupting from the middle of the forehead or irregularly placed around the mouth. To Pie's knowledge, they had no particular function, but they were clearly viewed as a disfigurement by the sophisticates, many of whom went to extraordinary lengths to disguise their commonality of stock with the undecorated peasants. Some of these stylists wore hats, veils, and makeup to conceal the evidence; others had tried surgery to remove the growths and went proudly about unhatted, wearing their scars as proof of their wealth.

"It's grotesque," Pie said when Gentle remarked upon this. "But that's the pernicious influence of fashion for you. These people want to look like the models they see in the magazines from

Patashoqua, and the stylists in Patashoqua have always looked to the Fifth for their inspiration. Damn fools! Look at them! I swear if we were to spread the rumor that everyone in Paris is cutting off their right arms these days, we'd be tripping over hacked-off limbs all the way to Scopique's house."

"It wasn't like this when you were here?"

"Not in L'Himby. As I said, it was a place of meditation. But in Patashoqua, yes, always, because it's so close to the Fifth, so the influence is very strong. And there's always been a few minor Maestros, you know, traveling back and forth, bringing styles, bringing ideas. A few of them made a kind of business of it, crossing the In Ovo every few months to get news of the Fifth and selling it to the fashion houses, the architects, and so on. So damn decadent. It revolts me."

"But you did the same thing, didn't you? You became part of the Fifth Dominion."

"Never here," the mystif said, its fist to its chest. "Never in my heart. My mistake was getting lost in the In Ovo and letting myself be summoned to earth. When I was there I played the human game, but only as much as I had to."

Despite their baggy and by now well-crumpled clothes, both Pie and Gentle were bare-headed and smooth-skulled, so they attracted a good deal of attention from envious poseurs parading on the pavement. It was far from welcome, of course. If Pie's theory was correct and Hammeryock or Pontiff Farrow had described them to the Autarch's torturers, their likenesses might very well have appeared in the broadsheets of L'Himby. If so, an envious dandy might have them removed from the competition with a few words in a soldier's ear. Would it not be wiser, Gentle suggested, if they hailed a taxi, and traveled a little more discreetly? The mystif was reluctant to do so, explaining that it could not remember Scopique's address, and their only hope of finding it was to go on foot, while Pie followed its nose. They made a point of avoiding the busier parts of the street, however, where café customers were outside enjoying the evening air or, less frequently, where soldiers gathered. Though they continued to attract interest and admiration, nobody challenged them, and after twenty minutes they turned off the main thoroughfare, the well-tended buildings giving way within a couple of blocks to grimier structures, the fops to grimmer souls.

"This feels safer," Gentle said, a paradoxical remark given that the streets they were wandering through now were the kind they would have instinctively avoided in any city of the Fifth: ill-lit backwaters, where many of the houses had fallen into severe disrepair. Lamps burned in even the most dilapidated, however, and

children played in the gloomy streets despite the lateness of the
hour. Their games were those of earth, give or take a detail—not
filched, but invented by young minds from the same basic materials: a ball and a bat, some chalk and a pavement, a rope and a
rhyme. Gentle found it reassuring to walk among them and hear
their laughter, which was indistinguishable from that of human
children.

Eventually the tenanted houses gave way to total dereliction,
and it was clear from the mystif's disgruntlement that it was no
longer sure of its whereabouts. Then, a little noise of pleasure, as
it caught sight of a distant structure.

"That's the temple." Pie pointed to a monolith some miles from
where they stood. It was unlit and seemed forsaken, the ground in
its vicinity leveled. "Scopique had that view from his toilet window,
I remember. On fine days he said he used to throw open the window and contemplate and defecate simultaneously."

Smiling at the memory, the mystif turned its back on the sight.

"The bathroom faced the temple, and there were no more
streets between the house and the temple. It was common land, for
the pilgrims to pitch their tents."

"So we're walking in the right direction," Gentle said. "We just
need the last street on our right."

"That seems logical," Pie said. "I was beginning to doubt my
memory."

They didn't have much farther to look. Two more blocks, and the
rubble-strewn streets came to an abrupt end.

"This is it."

There was no triumph in Pie's voice, which was not surprising,
given the scene of devastation before them. While it was time that
had undone the splendor of the streets they'd passed through, this
last had been prey to more systematic assault. Fires had been set
in several of the houses. Others looked as though they'd been used
for target practice by a Panzer division.

"Somebody got here before us," Gentle said.

"So it seems," Pie replied. "I must say I'm not altogether surprised."

"So why the hell did you bring us here?"

"I had to see for myself," Pie said. "Don't worry, the trail doesn't
end here. He'll have left a message."

Gentle didn't remark on how unlikely he thought this, but followed the mystif along the street until it stopped in front of a
building that, while not reduced to a heap of blackened stones,
looked ready to succumb. Fire had eaten out its eyes, and the
once-fine door had been replaced with partially rotted timbers; all

this illuminated not by lamplight (the street had none) but by a
scattering of stars.

"Better you stay out here," Pie 'oh' pah said. "Scopique may
have left defenses."

"Like what?"

"The Unbeheld isn't the only one who can conjure guardians,"
Pie replied. "Please, Gentle . . . I'd prefer to do this alone."

Gentle shrugged. "Do as you wish," he said. Then, as an afterthought, "You usually do."

He watched Pie climb the debris-covered steps, pull several of
the timbers off the door, and slip out of sight. Rather than wait at
the threshold, Gentle wandered farther along the row to get another view of the temple, musing as he went that this Dominion,
like the Fourth, had confounded not only his expectations but
those of Pie as well. The safe haven of Vanaeph had almost seen
their execution, while the murderous wastes of the mountains had
offered resurrections. And now L'Himby, a sometime city of meditation, reduced to gaud and rubble. What next? He wondered.
Would they arrive in Yzordderrex only to find it had spurned its
reputation as the Babylon of the Dominions and become a New
Jerusalem?

He stared across at the shadowy temple, his mind straying back
to a subject that had occupied him several times on their journey
through the Third: how best to address the challenge of making a
map of the Dominions, so that when they finally returned to the Fifth
Dominion he could give his friends some sense of how the lands lay.
They'd traveled on all kinds of roads, from the Patashoquan Highway to the dirt tracks between Happi and Mai-ké; they'd wound
through verdant valleys and scaled heights where even the hardiest moss would perish; they'd had the luxury of chariots and the loyalty of doeki; they'd sweated and frozen and gone dreamily, like
poets into some place of fancy, doubting their senses and themselves.
All this needed setting down: the routes, the cities, the ranges, and
the plains all needed laying in two dimensions, to be pored over at
leisure. In time, he thought, putting the challenge off yet again;
in time.

He looked back towards Scopique's house. There was no sign
of Pie emerging, and he began to wonder if some harm had befallen
the mystif inside. He walked back to the steps, climbed them, and—
feeling a little guilty—slid through the gap between the timbers.
The starlight had more difficulty getting in than he did, and his
blindness put a chill in him, bringing to mind the measureless darkness of the ice cathedral. On that occasion the mystif had been behind him; this time, in front. He waited a few seconds at the door,
until his eyes began to make out the interior. It was a narrow

house, full of narrow places, but there was a voice in its depths, barely above a whisper, which he pursued, stumbling through the murk. After only a few paces he realized it was not Pie speaking but someone hoarse and panicked. Scopique, perhaps, still taking refuge in the ruins?

A glimmer of light, no brighter than the dimmest star, led him to a door through which he had sight of the speaker. Pie was standing in the middle of the blackened room, turned from Gentle. Over the mystif's shoulder Gentle saw the light's fading source: a shape hanging in the air, like a web woven by a spider that aspired to portraiture, and held aloft by the merest breeze. Its motion was not arbitrary, however. The gossamer face opened its mouth and whispered its wisdom.

"—no better proof than in these cataclysms. We must hold to that, my friend, hold to it and pray ... no, better not pray ... I doubt every God now, especially the Aboriginal. If the children are any measure of the Father, then He's no lover of justice or goodness."

"Children?" said Gentle.

The breath the word came upon seemed to flutter in the threads. The face grew long, the mouth tearing.

The mystif glanced behind and shook its head to silence the trespasser. Scopique—for this was surely his message—was talking again.

"Believe me when I say we know only the tenth part of a tenth part of the plots laid in this. Long before the Reconciliation, forces were at work to undo it; that's my firm belief. And it's reasonable to assume that those forces have not perished. They're working in this Dominion, and the Dominion from which you've come. They strategize not in terms of decades, but centuries, just as we've had to. And they've buried their agents deeply. Trust nobody, Pie 'oh' pah, not even yourself. Their plots go back before we were born. We could either one of us have been conceived to serve them in some oblique fashion and not know it. They're coming for me very soon, probably with voiders. If I'm dead you'll know it. If I can convince them I'm just a harmless lunatic, they'll take me off to the Cradle, put me in the *maison de santé*. Find me there, Pie 'oh' pah. Or if you have more pressing business, then forget me; I won't blame you. But, friend, whether you come for me or not, know that when I think of you I still smile, and in these days that is the rarest comfort."

Even before he'd finished speaking the gossamer was losing its power to capture his likeness, the features softening, the form sinking in upon itself, until, by the time the last of his message had been uttered, there was little left for it to do but flutter to the ground.

The mystif went down on its haunches and ran its fingers through the inert threads. "Scopique," it murmured.

"What's the cradle he talked about?"

"The Cradle of Chzercemit. It's an inland sea, two or three days' journey from here."

"You've been there?"

"No. It's a place of exile. There's an island in the Cradle which was used as a prison. Mostly for criminals who'd committed atrocities but were too dangerous to execute."

"I don't follow that."

"Ask me another time. The point is, it sounds like it's been turned into an asylum." Pie stood up. "Poor Scopique. He always had a terror of insanity—"

"I know the feeling," Gentle remarked.

"—and now they've put him in a madhouse."

"So we must get him out," Gentle said very simply.

He couldn't see Pie's expression, but he saw the mystif's hands go up to its face and heard a sob from behind its palms.

"Hey," Gentle said softly, embracing Pie. "We'll find him. I know I shouldn't have come spying like that, but I thought maybe something had happened to you."

"At least you've heard him for yourself. You know it's not a lie."

"Why would I think that?"

"Because you don't trust me," Pie said.

"I thought we'd agreed," Gentle said. "We've got each other and that's our best hope of staying alive and sane. Didn't we agree to that?"

"Yes."

"So let's hold to it."

"It may not be so easy. If Scopique's suspicions are correct, either one of us could be working for the enemy and not know it."

"By enemy you mean the Autarch?"

"He's one, certainly. But I think he's just a sign of some greater corruption. The Imajica's sick, Gentle, from end to end. Coming here and seeing the way L'Himby's changed makes me want to despair."

"You know, you should have forced me to sit down and talk with Tick Raw. He might have given us a few clues."

"It's not my place to force you to do anything. Besides, I'm not sure he'd have been any wiser than Scopique."

"Maybe he'll know more by the time we speak with him."

"Let's hope so."

"And this time I won't take umbrage and waltz off like an idiot."

"If we get to the island, there'll be nowhere to waltz to."

"True enough. So now we need a means of transport."

"Something anonymous."

"Something fast."

"Something easy to steal."

"Do you know how to get to the Cradle?" Gentle asked.

"No, but I can inquire around while you steal the car."

"Good enough. Oh, and Pie? Buy some booze and cigarettes while you're at it, will you?"

"You'll make a decadent of me yet."

"My mistake. I thought it was the other way round."

3

They left L'Himby well before dawn, in a car that Gentle chose for its color (gray) and its total lack of distinction. It served them well. For two days they traveled without incident, on roads that were less trafficked the farther from the temple city and its spreading suburbs they went. There was some military presence beyond the city perimeters, but it was discreet, and no attempt was made to stop them. Only once did they glimpse a contingent at work in a distant field, vehicles maneuvering heavy artillery into position behind barricades, pointing back towards L'Himby, the work just public enough to let the citizens know whose clemency their lives were conditional upon.

By the middle of the third day, however, the road they were traveling was almost entirely deserted, and the flatlands in which L'Himby was set had given way to rolling hills. Along with this change of landscape came a change of weather. The skies clouded; and with no wind to press them on, the clouds thickened. A landscape that might have been enlivened by sun and shadow became drear, almost dank. Signs of habitation dwindled. Once in a while they'd pass a homestead, long since fallen into ruin; more infrequently still they'd catch sight of a living soul, usually unkempt, always alone, as though the territory had been given over to the lost.

And then, the Cradle. It appeared suddenly, the road taking them up over a headland which presented them with a sudden panorama of gray shore and silver sea. Gentle had not realized how oppressed he'd been by the hills until this vista opened in front of them. He felt his spirits rise at the sight.

There were peculiarities, however, most particularly the thousands of silent birds on the stony beach below, all sitting like an audience awaiting some spectacle to appear from the arena of the sea, not one in the air or on the water. It wasn't until Pie and Gentle reached the perimeter of this roosting multitude and got out of the car that the reason for their inactivity became apparent. Not only were they and the sky above them immobile, so was the Cradle itself. Gentle made his way through the mingled nations of birds—a close relation of the gull predominated, but there were also geese, oyster catchers, and a smattering of parrots—to the edge, testing it first with his foot, then with his fingers. It wasn't frozen—he knew what ice felt like from bitter experience—it was simply solidified, the last wave still plainly visible, every curl and eddy fixed as it broke against the shore.

"At least we won't have to swim," the mystif said.

It was already scanning the horizon, looking for Scopique's prison. The far shore wasn't visible, but the island was, a sharp gray rock rising from the sea several miles from where they stood, the *maison de santé,* as Scopique had called it, a cluster of buildings teetering on its heights.

"Do we go now or wait until dark?" Gentle asked.

"We'll never find it after dark," Pie said. "We have to go now."

They returned to the car and drove down through the birds, who were no more inclined to move for wheels than they'd been for feet. A few took to the air briefly, only to flutter down again; many more stood their ground and died for their stoicism.

The sea made the best road they'd traveled since the Patashoquan Highway; it had apparently been as calm as a millpond when it had solidified. They passed the corpses of several birds who'd been caught in the process, and there was still meat and feathers on their bones, suggesting that the solidification had occurred recently.

"I've heard of walking on water," Gentle said as they drove. "But *driving* . . . that's a whole other miracle."

"Have you any idea of what we're going to do when we get to the island?" Pie said.

"We ask to see Scopique, and when we've found him we leave with him. If they refuse to let us see him, we use force. It's simple as that."

"They may have armed guards."

"See these hands?" Gentle said, taking them off the wheel and thrusting them at Pie. "These hands are lethal." He laughed at the expression on the mystif's face. "Don't worry, I won't be indiscriminate." He seized the wheel again. "I like having the power, though. I really like it. The idea of using it sort of arouses me. Hey, will you look at that? The suns are coming out."

The parting clouds allowed a few beams through, and they lit the island, which was within half a mile of them now. The visitors' approach had been noticed. Guards had appeared on the cliff top and along the prison's parapet. Figures could be seen hurrying down the steps that wound down the cliff face, heading for the boats moored at its base. From the shore behind them rose the clamor of birds.

"They finally woke up," Gentle said.

Pie looked around. Sunlight was lighting the beach, and the wings of the birds as they rose in a squalling cloud.

"Oh, Jesu," Pie said.

"What's wrong?"

"The sea—"

Pie didn't need to explain, for the same phenomenon that was crossing the Cradle's surface behind them was now coming to meet them from the island: a slow shock wave, changing the nature of the matter it passed through. Gentle picked up speed, closing the gap between the vehicle and solid ground, but the road had already liquified completely at the island's shore, and the message of transformation was spreading at speed.

"Stop the car!" Pie yelled. "If we don't get out we'll go down in it."

Gentle brought the car to a skidding halt, and they flung themselves out. The ground beneath them was still solid enough to run on, but they could feel tremors in it as they went, prophesying dissolution.

"Can you swim?" Gentle called to Pie.

"If I have to," the mystif replied, its eyes on the approaching tide. The water looked mercurial, and seemed to be full of thrashing fish. "But I don't think this is something we want to bathe in, Gentle."

"I don't think we're going to have any choice."

There was at least some hope of rescue. Boats were being launched off the island's shore, the sound of the oars and the rhythmical shouts of the oarsmen rising above the churning of the silver water. The mystif wasn't looking for hope from that source, however. Its eyes had found a narrow causeway, like a path of softening ice, between where they stood and the land. Grabbing Gentle's arm, it pointed the way.

"I see it!" Gentle replied, and they headed off along this zigzag route, checking on the position of the two boats as they went. The oarsmen had comprehended their strategy and changed direction to intercept them. Though the flood was eating at their causeway from either side, the possibility of escape had just seemed plausible when the sound of the car upending and slipping into the waters distracted Gentle from his dash. He turned and collided with Pie as he did so. The mystif went down, falling on its face. Gentle hauled it back onto its feet, but it was momentarily too dazed to know their jeopardy.

There were shouts of alarm coming from the boats now, and the frenzy of water yards from their heels. Gentle half hoisted Pie onto his shoulders and picked up the race again. Precious seconds had been lost, however. The lead boat was within twenty yards of them, but the tide was half that distance behind, and half again between his feet and the bow. If he stood still, the floe beneath him would go before the boat reached them. If he tried to run, burdened with the semiconscious mystif, he'd miss his rendezvous with his rescuers.

As it was, the choice was taken from him. The ground beneath the combined weight of man and mystif fractured, and the silver waters of the Chzercemit bubbled up between his feet. He heard a shout of alarm from the creature in the nearest boat—an Oethac, huge-headed and scarred—then felt his right leg lose six inches as his foot plunged through the brittle floe. It was Pie's turn to haul him up now, but it was a lost cause: the ground would support neither of them.

In desperation he looked down at the waters that he was going to have to swim in. The creatures he'd seen thrashing were not *in* the sea but *of* the sea. The wavelets had backs and necks; the glitter of the spume was the glitter of countless tiny eyes. The boat was still speeding in their direction, and for an instant it seemed they might bridge the gap with a lunge.

"*Go!*" he yelled to Pie, pushing as he did so.

Though the mystif flailed, there was sufficient power in its legs to turn the fall into a jump. Its fingers caught the edge of the boat, but the violence of its leap threw Gentle from his precarious perch. He had time to see the mystif being hauled onto the rocking boat, and time too to think he might reach the hands outstretched in his direction. But the sea was not about to be denied both its morsels. As he dropped into the silver spume, which pressed around him like a living thing, he threw his hands up above his head in the hope that the Oethac would catch hold of him. All in vain. Consciousness went from him, and, uncaptained, he sank.

26

I

Gentle woke to the sound of a prayer. He knew before sight came to join the sound that the words were a beseechment, though the language was foreign to him. The voices rose and fell in the same unmelodious fashion as did earth congregations, one or two of the half dozen speakers lagging a syllable behind, leaving the verses ragged. But it was nevertheless a welcome sound. He'd gone down thinking he'd never rise again.

Light touched his eyes, but whatever lay in front of him was murky. There was a vague texture to the gloom, however, and he tried to focus upon it. It wasn't until his brow, cheeks, and chin reported their irritation to his brain that he realized why his eyes couldn't make sense of the scene. He was lying on his back, and there was a cloth over his face. He told his arm to rise and pluck it away, but the limb just lay stupid at his side. He concentrated, demanding it obey, his irritation growing as the timber of the supplications changed and a distressing urgency came into them. He felt the bed he was lying on jostled, and tried to call out in alarm, but there was something in his throat that prevented him from making a sound. Irritation became unease. What was wrong with him? Be calm, he told himself. It'll come clear; just be calm. But damn it, the bed was being lifted up! Where was he being taken? To hell with calm. He couldn't just lie still while he was paraded around. He wasn't dead, for God's sake!

Or was he? The thought shredded every hope of equilibrium. He was being lifted up, and carried, lying inert on a hard board with his face beneath a shroud. What was *that,* if it wasn't dead? They were saying prayers for his soul, hoping to waft it heavenward, meanwhile carrying his remains to what dispatch? A hole in the ground? A pyre? He had to stop them: raise a hand, a moan, anything to signal that this leave-taking was premature. As he was concentrating on making a sign, however primitive, a voice cut through the prayers. Both prayers and bier bearers stumbled to a halt and the same voice—it was Pie!—came again.

"Not yet!" it said.

Somebody off to Gentle's right murmured something in a language Gentle didn't recognize: words of consolation, perhaps. The mystif responded in the same tongue, its voice fractured with grief.

A third speaker now entered the exchange, his purpose undoubtedly the same as his compatriot's: coaxing Pie to leave the body alone. What were they saying? That the corpse was just a husk; an empty shadow of a man whose spirit was gone into a better place? Gentle willed Pie not to listen. The spirit was here! *Here!*

Then—joy of joys!—the shroud was pulled back from his face, and Pie appeared in his field of vision, staring down at him. The mystif looked half dead itself, its eyes raw, its beauty bruised with sorrow.

I'm saved, Gentle thought. Pie sees that my eyes are open, and there's more than putrefaction going on in my skull. But no such comprehension came into Pie's face. The sight simply brought a new burst of tears. A man came to Pie's side, his head a cluster of crystalline growths, and laid his hands on the mystif's shoulders, whispering something in its ear and gently tugging it away. Pie's fingers went to Gentle's face and lay for a few seconds close to his lips. But his breath—which he'd used to shatter the wall between Dominions—was so piffling now it went unfelt, and the fingers were withdrawn by the hand of Pie's consoler, who then reached down and drew the shroud back over Gentle's face.

The prayer sayers picked up their dirge, and the bearers their burden. Blinded again, Gentle felt the spark of hope extinguished, replaced with panic and anger. Pie had always claimed such sensitivity. How was it possible that *now,* when empathy was essential, the mystif could be immune to the jeopardy of the man it claimed as a friend? More than that: a soul mate; someone it had reconfigured its flesh for.

Gentle's panic slowed for an instant. Was there some half hope buried amid these rebukes? He scoured them for a clue. Soul mate? Reconfigured flesh? Yes, of course: as long as he had *thought* he had *desire,* and desire could touch the mystif; *change* the mystif. If he could put death from his mind and turn his thoughts to sex he might still touch Pie's protean core: bring about some metamorphosis, however small, that would signal his sentience.

As if to confound him, a remark of Klein's drifted into his head, recalled from another world. "All that time wasted," Klein had said, "meditating on death to keep yourself from coming too soon...."

The memory seemed mere distraction, until he realized that it was precisely the mirror of his present plight. Desire was now his only defense against premature extinction. He turned his thoughts to the little details that were always a stimulus to his erotic imagination: a nape bared by lifted curls, lips rewetted by a slow tongue, looks, touches, dares. But thanatos had eros by the neck. His terror drove arousal away. How could he hold a sexual thought in his head long enough to influence Pie when either the flame or the grave was waiting at his feet? He was ready for neither. One was too hot, the other too cold; one bright, the other so very dark. What he wanted was a few more weeks, days—hours, even; he'd be grateful for hours—in the space between such poles. Where flesh was; where love was.

Knowing the death thoughts couldn't be mastered, he attempted one final gambit: to embrace them, to fold them into the texture of his sexual imaginings. Flame? Let that be the heat of the mystif's body as it was pressed against him, and cold the sweat on his back as they coupled. Let the darkness be a night that concealed their excesses, and the pyre blaze like their mutual consumption.

He could feel the trick working as he thought this through. Why should death be so unerotic? If they blistered or rotted together, mightn't their dissolution show them new ways to love, uncovering them layer by layer and joining their moistures and their marrows until they were utterly mingled?

He'd proposed marriage to Pie and been accepted. The creature was his to have and hold, to make over and over, in the image of his fondness and most forbidden desires. He did so now. He saw the creature naked and astride him, changing even as he touched it, throwing off skins like clothes. Jude was one of those skins, and Vanessa another, and Martine another still. They were all riding him high: the beauty of the world impaled on his prick.

Lost in this fantasy, he wasn't even aware that the prayers had stopped until the bier was halted once again. There were whispers all around him, and in the middle of the whispers soft and astonished laughter. The shroud was snatched away, and his beloved was looking down at him, grinning through features blurred by tears and Gentle's influence.

"He's alive! Jesu, he's *alive!*"

There were doubting voices raised, but the mystif laughed them down.

"I feel him in me!" it said. "I swear it! He's still with us. Put him down! *Put him down!*"

The pallbearers did as they were instructed, and Gentle had his first glimpse of the strangers who'd almost bade him farewell. Not a happy bunch, even now. They stared down at the body, still disbelieving. But the danger was over, at least for the time being. The mystif leaned over Gentle and kissed his lips. Its face was fixed once more, its features exquisite in their joy.

"I love you," it murmured to Gentle. "I'll love you until the death of love."

2

Alive he was; but not healed. He was moved to a small room of gray brick and laid on a bed only marginally more comfortable than the boards they'd laid him on as a corpse. There was a window, but being unable to move he had to rely upon Pie 'oh' pah to lift him up and show him the view through it, which was scarcely more interesting than the walls, being simply an expanse of sea— solid once again—under a cloudy sky.

"The sea only changes when the suns come out," Pie explained. "Which isn't very often. We were unlucky. But everyone is amazed that you survived. Nobody who fell into the Cradle ever came out alive before."

That he was something of a curiosity was evidenced by the number of visitors he had, both guards and prisoners. The regime seemed to be fairly relaxed, from what little he could judge. There were bars on the windows, and the door was unbolted and bolted up again when anybody came or went, but the officers, particularly the Oethac who ran the asylum, named Vigor N'ashap, and his number two—a military peacock named Aping, whose buttons and boots shone a good deal more brightly than his eyes, and whose features drooped on his head as though sodden—were polite enough.

"They get no news out here," Pie explained. "They just get sent prisoners to look after. N'ashap knows there was a plot against the Autarch, but I don't believe he knows whether it's been successful or not. They've quizzed me for hours, but they haven't really asked about us. I just told them we were friends of Scopique's, and we'd heard he'd lost his sanity, so we came to visit him. All innocence, in other words. And they seemed to swallow it. But they get supplies of food, magazines, and newspapers every eight or nine days—always out of date, Aping says—so our luck may not hold out too long. Meanwhile I'm doing what I can to keep them both happy. They get very lonely."

The significance of this last remark wasn't lost on Gentle, but all he could do was listen and hope his healing wouldn't take too long. There was some easing in his muscles, allowing him to open and close his eyes, swallow, and even move his hands a little, but his torso was still completely rigid.

His other regular visitor, and by far the most entertaining of those who came to gawk, was Scopique, who had an opinion on everything, including the patient's rigidity. He was a tiny man, with the perpetual squint of a watchmaker and a nose so upturned and so tiny his nostrils were virtually two holes in the middle of his face, which was already gouged with laugh lines deep enough to plant in. Every day he would come and sit on the edge of Gentle's bed, his gray asylum clothes as crumpled as his features, his glossy black wig never in the same place on his pate from hour to hour. Sitting, sipping coffee, he'd pontificate: on politics, on the various psychoses of his fellow inmates; on the subjugation of L'Himby by commerce; on the deaths of his friends, mostly by what he called despair's slow sword; and, of course, on Gentle's condition. He had seen people made rigid in such a fashion before, he claimed. The reason was not physiological but psychological, a theory which seemed to carry weight with Pie. Once, when Scopique had left after a session of theorizing, leaving Pie and Gentle alone, the mystif poured out its guilt. None of this would have come about, it said, if it had been sensitive to Gentle's situation from the beginning. Instead, it had been crude and un-kind. The incident on the platform at Mai-ké was a case in point. Would Gentle ever forgive it? Ever believe that its actions were the product of ineptitude, not cruelty? Over the years it had won-dered what would happen if they ever took the journey they were taking, and had tried to rehearse its responses, but it had been alone in the Fifth Dominion, unable to confess its fears or share its hopes, and the circumstances of their meeting and departure had been so haphazard that those few rules it had set itself had been thrown to the wind.

"Forgive me," it said over and over. "I love you and I've hurt you, but please, forgive me."

Gentle expressed what little he could with his eyes, wishing his fingers had the strength to hold a pen, so that he could simply write *I do*, but the small advances he'd made since his resurrection seemed to be the limit of his healing, and though he was fed and bathed by Pie, and his muscles massaged, there was no sign of fur-ther improvement. Despite the mystif's constant words of en-couragement, there was no doubt that death still had its finger in him. In them both, in fact, for Pie's devotion seemed to be taking its own toll, and more than once Gentle wondered if the mystif's dwindling was simply fatigue, or whether they were symbiotically linked after their time together. If so, his demise would surely take them both to oblivion.

He was alone in his cell the day the suns came out again, but Pie had left him sitting up, with a view through the bars, and he was able to watch the slow unfurling of the clouds and the appearance of the subtlest beams, falling on the solid sea. This was the first time since their arrival that the suns had broken over the Chzercemit, and he heard a chorus of welcome from other cells, then the sound of running feet as guards went to the parapet to watch the trans-formation. He could see the surface of the Cradle from where he was sitting, and felt a kind of exhilaration at the imminent specta-cle, but as the beams brightened he felt a tremor climbing through his body from his toes, gathering force as it went until by the time it reached his head it had force enough to throw his senses from his skull. At first he thought he'd stood up and run to the window— he was peering out through the bars at the sea below—but a noise at the door drew his gaze around to meet the sight of Scopique, with Aping at his side, crossing the cell to the sallow, bearded derelict sitting with a glazed expression against the far wall. He was that man.

"You have to come and see, Zacharias!" Scopique was enthus-ing, putting his arm beneath the derelict and hoisting him up.

Aping lent a hand, and together they began to carry Gentle to the window, from which his mind was already departing. He left them to their kindness, the exhilaration he'd felt like an engine in him. Out and along the dreary corridor he went, passing cells in which prisoners were clamoring to be released to see the suns. He had no sense of the building's geography, and for a few moments his speeding soul lost its way in the maze of gray brick, until he encountered two guards hurrying up a flight of stone stairs and went with them, an invisible mind, into a brighter suite of rooms. There were more guards here, forsaking games of cards to head out into the open air.

"Where's Captain N'ashap?" one of them said.

"I'll go and tell him," another said, and broke from his comrades towards a closed door, only to be called back by another, who told him, "He's in conference—with the mystif," the reply winning a ribald laugh from his fellows.

Turning his spirit's back on the open air, Gentle flew towards the door, passing through it without harm or hesitation. The room beyond was not, as he'd expected, N'ashap's office but an antechamber, occupied by two empty chairs and a bare table. On the wall behind the table hung a painting of a small child, so wretchedly rendered the subject's sex was indeterminate. To the left of the picture, which was signed *Aping,* lay another door, as securely closed as the one he'd just passed through. But there was a voice audible from the far side: Vigor N'ashap, in a little ecstasy.

"Again! Again!" he was saying, then an outpouring in a foreign tongue, followed by cries of "Yes!" and "There! There!"

Gentle went to the door too quickly to prepare himself for what lay on the other side. Even if he had—even if he'd conjured the sight of N'ashap with his breeches down and his Oethac prick purple—he could not have imagined Pie 'oh' pah's condition, given that in all their months together he had never once seen the mystif naked. Now he did, and the shock of its beauty was second only to that of its humiliation. It had a body as serene as its face, and as ambiguous, even in plain sight. There was no hair on any part of it; nor nipples; nor navel. Between its legs, however, which were presently spread as it knelt in front of N'ashap, was the source of its transforming self, the core its couplers touched with thought. It was neither phallic nor vaginal, but a third genital form entirely, fluttering at its groin like an agitated dove and with every flutter reconfiguring its glistening heart, so that Gentle, mesmerized, found a fresh echo in each motion. His own flesh was mirrored there, unfolding as it passed between Dominions. So was the sky above Patashoqua and the sea beyond the shuttered window, turning its solid back to living water. And breath, blown into a closed fist; and the power breaking from it: all there, all there.

N'ashap was disdainful of the sight. Perhaps, in his heat, he didn't even see it. He had the mystif's head clamped between his scarred hands and was pushing the sharp tip of his member into its mouth. The mystif made no objection. Its hands hung by its sides, until N'ashap demanded their attention upon his shaft. Gentle could bear the sight no longer. He pitched his mind across the room towards the Oethac's back. Hadn't he heard Scopique say that thought was power? If so, Gentle thought, I'm a mote, diamond hard. Gentle heard N'ashap gasp with pleasure as he pierced the mystif's throat; then he struck the Oethac's skull. The room disappeared, and hot meat pressed on him from all sides, but his momentum carried him out the other side, and he turned to see N'ashap's hands go from the mystif's head to his own, a shriek of pain coming from his lipless mouth.

Pie's face, slack until now, filled with alarm as blood poured from N'ashap's nostrils. Gentle felt a thrill of satisfaction at the sight, but the mystif rose and went to the officer's assistance, picking up a piece of its own discarded clothing to help staunch the flow. N'ashap twice waved its help away at first, but Pie's pliant voice softened him, and after a time the captain sank back in his cushioned chair and allowed himself to be tended. The mystif's cooings and caresses were almost as distressing to Gentle as the scene he'd just interrupted, and he retreated, confounded and repulsed, first to the door, then through it into the antechamber.

There he lingered, his sight fixed upon Aping's picture. In the room behind him, N'ashap had begun to moan again. The sound drove Gentle out, through the labyrinth and back to his room. Scopique and Aping had laid his body back on the bed. His face was devoid of expression, and one of his arms had slid from his chest and hung off the edge of the boards. He looked dead already. Was it any wonder Pie's devotion had become so mechanical, when all it had before it to inspire hope of recovery was this gaunt mannequin, day in, day out? He drew closer to the body, half tempted never to enter it again, to let it wither and die. But there was too much risk in that. Suppose his present state was conditional upon the continuance of his physical self? Thought without flesh was certainly possible—he'd heard Scopique pronounce on the subject in this very cell—but not, he guessed, for spirits so unevolved as his. Skin, blood, and bone were the school in which the soul learned flight, and he was still too much a fledgling to dare truancy. He had to go, vile as that notion was, back behind the eyes.

He went one more time to the window and looked out at the

glittering sea. The sight of its waves beating at the rocks below brought back the terror of his drowning. He felt the living waters squirming around him, pressing at his lips like N'ashap's prick, demanding he open up and swallow. In horror, he turned from the sight and crossed the room at speed, striking his brow like a bullet. Returning into his substance with the images of N'ashap and sea on his mind, he comprehended instantly the nature of his sickness. Scopique had been wrong, all wrong! There was a solid—oh, *so* solid—physiological reason for his inertia. He felt it in his belly now, wretchedly real. He'd swallowed some of the waters and they were still inside him, living, prospering at his expense.

Before intellect could caution him he let his revulsion loose upon his body; threw his demands into each extremity. Move! he told them, move! He fueled his rage with the thought of N'ashap using him as he'd used Pie, imagining the Oethac's semen in his belly. His left hand found power enough to take hold of the bed board, its purchase sufficient to pull him over. He toppled onto his side, then off the bed entirely, hitting the floor hard. The impact dislodged something in the base of his belly. He felt it scrabble to catch hold of his innards again, its motion violent enough to throw him around like a sack full of thrashing fish, each twist unseating the parasite a little more and in turn releasing his body from its tyranny. His joints cracked like walnut shells; his sinews stretched and shortened. It was agony, and he longed to shriek his complaint, but all he could manage was a retching sound. It was still music: the first sound he'd made since the yell he'd given as the Cradle swallowed him up. It was short-lived, however. His wracked system was pushing the parasite up from his stomach. He felt it in his chest, like a meal of hooks he longed to vomit up but could not, for fear he'd turn himself inside out in the attempt. It seemed to know they'd reached an impasse, because its flailing slowed, and he had time to draw a desperate breath through pipes half clogged by its presence. With his lungs as full as he had hope of getting them, he hauled himself up off the ground by clinging to the bed, and before the parasite had time to incapacitate him with a fresh assault he stood to his full height, then threw himself face down. As he hit the ground the thing came up into his throat and mouth in a surge, and he reached between his teeth to snatch it out of him. It came with two pulls, fighting to the end to crawl back down his gullet. It was followed immediately by his last meal.

Gasping for air he dragged himself upright and leaned against the bed, strings of puke hanging from his chin. The thing on the floor flapped and flailed, and he let it suffer. Though it had felt huge when inside him, it was no bigger than his hand: a formless scrap

of milky flesh and silver vein with limbs no thicker than string but
fully twenty in number. It made no sound, except for the slap its
spasms made in the bilious mess on the cell floor.

Too weak to move, Gentle was still slumped against the bed
when, some minutes later, Scopique came back to look for Pie.
Scopique's astonishment knew no bounds. He called for help, then
hoisted Gentle back onto the bed, question following question so
fast Gentle barely had breath or energy to answer. But sufficient
was communicated for Scopique to berate himself for not grasping the problem earlier.

"I thought it was in your *head,* Zacharias, and all the time—all
the time it was in your *belly.* This bastard thing!"

Aping arrived, and there was a new round of questions, answered this time by Scopique, who then went off in search of Pie,
leaving the guard to arrange for the filth on the floor to be cleaned
up and the patient brought fresh water and clean clothes.

"Is there anything else you need?" Aping wanted to know.

"Food," Gentle said. His belly had never felt emptier.

"It'll be arranged. It's strange to hear your voice and see you
move. I got used to you the other way." He smiled. "When you're
feeling stronger," he said, "we must find some time to talk. I hear
from the mystif you're a painter."

"I was, yes," said Gentle, adding an innocent inquiry. "Why?
Are you?"

Aping beamed. "I am," he said.

"Then we must talk," Gentle said. "What do you paint?"

"Landscapes. Some figures."

"Nudes? Portraits?"

"Children."

"Ah, children . . . do you have any yourself?"

A trace of anxiety crossed Aping's face. "Later," he said, glancing out towards the corridor, then back at Gentle. "In private."

"I'm at your disposal," Gentle replied.

There were voices outside the room. Scopique returning with
N'ashap, who glanced down into the bucket containing the parasite as he entered. There were more questions, or rather the same
rephrased, and answered on this third occasion by both Scopique
and Aping. N'ashap listened with only half an ear, studying Gentle as the drama was recounted, then congratulating him with a curious formality. Gentle noted with satisfaction the plugs of dried
blood in his nose.

"We must make a full account of this incident to Yzordderrex,"
N'ashap said. "I'm sure it will intrigue them as much as it does me."

So saying, he left, with an order to Aping that he follow immediately.

"Our commander looked less than well," Scopique observed. "I wonder why."

Gentle allowed himself a smile, but it went from his face at the sight of his final visitor. Pie 'oh' pah had appeared in the door.

"Ah, well!" said Scopique. "Here you are. I'll leave you two alone."

He withdrew, closing the door behind him. The mystif didn't move to embrace Gentle, or even take his hand. Instead it went to the window and gazed out over the sea, upon which the suns were still shining.

"Now we know why they call this the Cradle," it said.

"What do you mean?"

"Where else could a man give birth?"

"That wasn't birth," Gentle said. "Don't flatter it."

"Maybe not to us," Pie said. "But who knows how children were made here in ancient times? Maybe the men immersed themselves, drank the water, let it grow—"

"I saw you," Gentle said.

"I know," Pie replied, not turning from the window. "And you almost lost us both an ally."

"N'ashap? An ally?"

"He's the power here."

"He's an Oethac. And he's scum. And I'm going to have the satisfaction of killing him."

"Are you my champion now?" Pie said, finally looking back at Gentle.

"I saw what he was doing to you."

"That was nothing," Pie replied. "I knew what I was doing. Why do you think we've had the treatment we've had? I've been allowed to see Scopique whenever I want. You've been fed and watered. And N'ashap was asking no questions, about either of us. Now he will. Now he'll be suspicious. We'll have to move quickly before he gets his questions answered."

"Better that than you having to service him."

"I told you, it was nothing."

"It was to me," Gentle said, the words scraping in his bruised throat.

It took some effort, but he got to his feet so as to meet the mystif, eye to eye.

"At the beginning, you talked to me about how you thought you'd hurt me, remember? You kept talking about the station at Mai-ké, and saying you wanted me to forgive you, and I kept thinking there would never be anything between us that couldn't be forgiven or forgotten, and that when I had the words again I'd say so. But now I don't know. He saw you naked, Pie. Why him and not me? I think that's maybe unforgivable, that you granted him the mystery but not me."

"He saw no mystery," Pie replied. "He looked at me, and he saw a woman he'd loved and lost in Yzordderrex. A woman who looked like his mother, in fact. That's what he was obsessing on. An echo of his mother's echo. And as long as I kept supplying the illusion, discreetly, he was compliant. That seemed more important than my dignity."

"Not any more," Gentle said. "If we're to go from here—together—then I want whatever you are to be mine. I won't share you, Pie. Not for compliance. Not for life itself."

"I didn't know you felt like this. If you'd told me—"

"I couldn't. Even before we came here, I felt it, but I couldn't bring myself to say anything."

"For what it's worth, I apologize."

"I don't want an apology."

"What then?"

"A promise. An oath." He paused. "A marriage."

The mystif smiled. "Really?"

"More than anything. I asked you once, and you accepted. Do I need to ask again? I will if you want me to."

"No need," Pie said. "Nothing would honor me more. But here? Here, of all places?" The mystif's frown became a grin. "Scopique told me about a Dearther who's locked up in the basement. He could do the honors."

"What's his religion?"

"He's here because he thinks he's Jesus Christ."

"Then he can prove it with a miracle."

"What miracle's that?"

"He can make an honest man of John Furie Zacharias."

3

The marriage of the Eurhetemec mystif and the fugitive John Furie Zacharias, called Gentle, took place that night in the depths of the asylum. Happily, their priest was passing through a period of lucidity and was willing to be addressed by his real name, Father Athanasius. He bore the evidence of his dementia, however: scars on his forehead, where the crowns of thorns he repeatedly fashioned and wore had dug deep, and scabs on his hands where he'd driven nails into his flesh. He was as fond of the frown as Scopique of the grin, though the look of a philosopher sat badly on a face better suited to a comedian: with its blob nose that perpetually ran, its teeth too widely spread, and eyebrows, like hairy caterpillars, that concertinaed when he furrowed his forehead. He

was kept, along with twenty or so other prisoners judged excep-
tionally seditious, in the deepest part of the asylum, his windowless cell guarded more vigorously than those of the prisoners on
higher floors. It had thus taken some fancy maneuvering on
Scopique's part to get access to him, and the bribed guard, an
Oethac, was only willing to turn a hooded eye for a few minutes.
The ceremony was therefore short, conducted in an ad hoc mixture of Latin and English, with a few phrases pronounced in the
language of Athanasius' Second Dominion order, the Dearthers,
the music of which more than compensated for its unintelligibil-
ity. The oaths themselves were necessarily spare, given the con-
straints of time and the redundance of most of the conventional
vocabulary.

"This isn't done in the sight of Hapexamendios," Athanasius
said, "nor in the sight of any God, or the agent of any God. We pray
that the presence of our Lady may however touch this union with
Her infinite compassion, and that you go together into the great
union at some higher time. Until then, I can only be as a glass held
up to your sacrament, which is performed in your sight for your
sake."

The full significance of these words didn't strike Gentle until
later, when, with the oaths made and the ceremony done, he lay
down in his cell beside his partner.

"I always said I'd never marry," he whispered to the mystif.

"Regretting it already?"

"Not at all. But it's strange to be married and not have a wife."

"You can call me wife. You can call me whatever you want.
Reinvent me. That's what I'm for."

"I didn't marry you to use you, Pie."

"That's part of it, though. We must be functions of each other.
Mirrors, maybe." It touched Gentle's face. "I'll use *you,* believe me."

"For what?"

"For everything. Comfort, argument, pleasure."

"I do want to learn from you."

"About what?"

"How to fly out of my head again, the way I did this afternoon.
How to travel by mind."

"By mote," Pie said, echoing the way Gentle had felt as he'd driven his thoughts through N'ashap's skull. "Meaning: a particle of
thought, as seen in sunlight."

"It can only be done in sunlight?"

"No. It's just easier that way. Almost everything's easier in
sunlight."

"Except this," Gentle said, kissing the mystif. "I've always preferred the night for this. . . ."

He had come to their marriage bed determined that he would make love with the mystif as it truly was, allowing no fantasy to intrude between his senses and the vision he'd glimpsed in N'ashap's office. That oath made him as nervous as a virgin groom, demanding as it did a double unveiling. Just as he unbuttoned and discarded the clothes that concealed the mystif's essential sex, so he had to tear from his eyes the comfort of the illusions that lay between his sight and its object. What would he feel then? It was easy to be aroused by a creature so totally reconfigured by desire that it was indistinguishable from the thing desired. But what of the configurer itself, seen naked by naked eyes?

In the shadows its body was almost feminine, its planes serene, its surface smooth, but there was an austerity in its sinew he couldn't pretend was womanly; nor were its buttocks lush, or its chest ripe. It was not his wife, and though it was happy to be imagined that way, and his mind teetered over and over on the edge of giving in to such invention, he resisted, demanding his eyes hold to their focus and his fingers to the facts. He began to wish it were lighter in the cell, so as not to give ease to ambiguity. When he put his hand into the shadow between its legs and felt the heat and motion there, he said, "I want to see," and Pie dutifully stood up in the light from the window so that Gentle could have a plainer view. His heart was pumping furiously, but none of the blood was reaching his groin. It was filling his head, making his face burn. He was glad he sat in shadow, where his discomfort was less visible, though he knew that shadow concealed only the outward show, and the mystif was perfectly aware of the fear he felt. He took a deep breath and got up from the bed, crossing to within touching distance of this enigma.

"Why are you doing this to yourself?" Pie asked softly. "Why not let the dreams come?"

"Because I don't want to dream you," he said. "I came on this journey to understand. How can I understand anything if all I look at is illusions?"

"Maybe that's all there is."

"That isn't true," he said simply.

"Tomorrow, then," Pie said, temptingly. "Look plainly tomorrow. Just enjoy yourself tonight. I'm not the reason we're in the Imajica. I'm not the puzzle you came to solve."

"On the contrary," Gentle said, a smile creeping into his voice. "I think maybe you *are* the reason. And the puzzle. I think if we stayed here, locked up together, we could heal the Imajica from what's between us." The smile appeared on his face now. "I never realized that till now. That's why I want to see you clearly, Pie, so there're no lies between us." He put his hand against the mystif's sex. "You could fuck or be fucked with this, right?"

"Yes."

"And you could give birth?"

"I haven't. But it's been known."

"And fertilize?"

"Yes."

"That's wonderful. And is there something else you can do?"

"Like what?"

"It isn't all doer or done to, is it? I know it isn't. There's something else."

"Yes, there is."

"A third way."

"Yes."

"Do it with me, then."

"I can't. You're male, Gentle. You're a fixed sex. It's a physical fact." The mystif put its hand on Gentle's prick, still soft in his trousers. "I can't take this away. You wouldn't want me to." It frowned. "Would you?"

"I don't know. Maybe."

"You don't mean that."

"If it meant finding a way, maybe I do. I've used my dick every way I know how. Maybe it's redundant."

Now it was Pie's turn to smile, but such a fragile smile, as though the unease Gentle had felt now burdened the mystif instead. It narrowed its shining eyes.

"What are you thinking?" Gentle said.

"How you make me a little afraid."

"Of what?"

"Of the pain ahead. Of losing you."

"You're not going to lose me," Gentle said, putting his hand around the back of Pie's neck and stroking the nape with his thumb. "I told you, we could heal the Imajica from here. We're strong, Pie."

The anxiety didn't go from the mystif's face, so Gentle coaxed its face towards his and kissed it, first discreetly, then with an ardor it seemed reluctant to match. Only moments before, sitting on the bed, he'd been the tentative one. Now it was the other way around. He put his hand down to its groin, hoping to distract it from its sadness with caresses. The flesh came to meet his fingers, warm and fluted, trickling into the shallow cup of his palm a moisture his skin drank like liquor. He pressed deeper, feeling the elaboration grow at his touch. There was no hesitation here; no shame or sorrow in this flesh, to keep it from displaying its need, and need had never failed to arouse him. Seeing it on a woman's face was a sure aphrodisiac, and it was no less so now.

He reached up from this play to his belt, unbuckling it with one hand. But before he could take hold of his prick, which was becoming painfully hard, the mystif did so, guiding him inside it with an urgency its face still failed to betray. The bath of its sex soothed his ache, immersing him balls and all. He let out a long sigh of pleasure, his nerve endings—starved of this sensation for months—rioting. The mystif had closed its eyes, its mouth open. He put his tongue hard between its lips, and it responded with a passion he had never seen it manifest before. Its hands wrapped around his shoulders, and in possession of them both it fell back against the wall, so hard the breath went from it into Gentle's throat. He drew it down into his lungs, inciting a hunger for more, which the mystif understood without need of words, inhaling from the heated air between them and filling Gentle's chest as though he were a just-drowned man being pumped back to life. He answered its gift with thrusts, its fluids running freely down the inside of his thighs. It gave him another breath, and another. He drank them all, eating the pleasure off its face in the moments between, the breath received as his prick was given. In this exchange they were both entered and enterer: a hint, perhaps, of the third way Pie had spoken of, the coupling between unfixed forces that could not occur until his manhood had been taken from him. Now, as he worked his prick against the warmth of the mystif's sex, the thought of relinquishing it in pursuit of another sensation seemed ludicrous. There could be nothing better than this; only different.

He closed his eyes, no longer afraid that his imagination would put a memory, or some invented perfection, in Pie's place, only that if he looked at the mystif's bliss too much longer he'd lose all control. What his mind's eye pictured, however, was more potent still: the image of them locked together as they were, inside each other, breath and prick swelling inside each other's skins until they could swell no further. He wanted to warn the mystif that he could hold on no longer, but it seemed to have that news already. It grasped his hair, pulling him off its face, the sting of it just another spur now, and the sobs too, coming out of them both. He let his eyes open, wanting to see its face as he came, and in the time it took for his lashes to unknit, the beauty in front of him became a mirror. It was *his* face he was seeing, *his* body he was holding. The illusion didn't cool him. Quite the reverse. Before the mirror softened into flesh, its glass becoming the sweat on Pie's sweet face, he passed the point of no return, and it was with that image in his eye—his face mingled with the mystif's—that his body unleashed its little torrent. It was, as ever, exquisite and racking, a short delirium followed by a sense of loss he'd never made peace with.

The mystif began to laugh almost before he was finished, and when Gentle drew his first clear breath it was to ask, "What's so funny?"

"The silence," Pie said, suppressing the music so that Gentle could share the joke.

He'd lain here in this cell hour after hour, unable to make a moan, but he'd never heard a silence such as this. The whole asylum was listening, from the depths where Father Athanasius wove his piercing crowns to N'ashap's office, its carpet indelibly marked with the blood his nose had shed. There was not a waking soul who'd not heard their coupling.

"Such a silence," the mystif said.

As it spoke, the hush was broken by the sound of someone yelling in his cell, a rage of loss and loneliness that went on unchecked for the rest of the night, as if to cleanse the gray stone of the joy that had momentarily tainted it.

27

I

If pressed, Jude could have named a dozen men—lovers, suitors, slaves—who'd offered her any prize she set her heart on in return for her affections. She'd taken several up on their largesse. But her requests, extravagant as some of them had been, were as nothing beside the gift she'd asked of Oscar Godolphin. *Show me Yzord-derrex,* she'd said, and watched his face fill with trepidation. He'd not refused her out of hand. To have done so would have crushed in a moment the affection growing between them, and he would never have forgiven himself that loss. He listened to her request, then made no further mention of it, hoping, no doubt, she'd let the subject lie.

She didn't, however. The blossoming of a physical relationship between them had cured her of the strange passivity that had afflicted her when they'd first met. She had knowledge of his vulnerability now. She'd seen him wounded. She'd seen him ashamed of his lack of self-control. She'd seen him in the act of love, tender and sweetly perverse. Though her feelings for him remained strong, this new perspective removed the veil of unthinking acceptance from her eyes. Now, when she saw the desire he felt for her—and he several times displayed that desire in the days following their consummation—it was the old Judith, self-reliant and fearless, who watched from behind her smiles; watched and waited, knowing that his devotion empowered her more by the day. The tension between these two selves—the remnants of the compliant mistress his presence had first conjured and the willful, focused woman she'd been (and now was again)—scourged the last dregs of dreaminess from her system, and her appetite for Dominion-hopping returned with fresh intensity. She didn't shrink from reminding him of his promise to her as the days went by, but on the first two occasions he made some polite but spurious excuse so as to avoid talking further about it.

On the third occasion her insistence won her a sigh, and eyes cast to heaven.

"Why is this so important to you?" he asked. "Yzordderrex is an overpopulated cesspit. I don't know a decent man or woman there who wouldn't prefer to be here in England."

"A week ago you were talking about disappearing there forever. But you couldn't you said, because you'd miss the cricket."

"You've got a good memory."

"I hang on your every word," she said, not without a certain sourness.

"Well, the situation's changed. There's most likely going to be revolution. If we went now, we'd probably be executed on sight."

"You've come and gone often enough in the past," she pointed out. "So have hundreds of others, haven't they? You're not the only one. That's what magic is for: passing between Dominions."

He didn't reply.

"I want to see Yzordderrex, Oscar," she said, "and if you won't take me I'll find a magician who will."

"Don't even joke about it."

"I mean it," she said fiercely. "You can't be the only one who knows the way."

"Near enough."

"There are others. I'll find them if I have to."

"They're all crazy," he told her. "Or dead."

"Murdered?" she said, the word out of her mouth before she'd fully grasped its implication.

The look on his face, however (or rather its absence: the willed blankness), was enough to confirm her suspicion. The bodies she'd seen on the news being carted away from their games were not those of burned-out hippies and sex-crazed satanists. They were possessors of true power, men and women who'd maybe walked where she longed to walk: in the Imajica.

"Who's doing it, Oscar? It's somebody you know, isn't it?"

He got up and crossed to where she sat, his motion so swift she thought for an instant he meant to strike her. But instead he dropped to his knees in front of her, holding her hands tight and staring up at her with almost hypnotic intensity.

"Listen to me carefully," he said. "I have certain familial duties, which I wish to God I didn't have. They make demands upon me I'd willingly shrug off if I could—"

"This is all to do with the tower, isn't it?"

"I'd prefer not to discuss that."

"We *are* discussing it, Oscar."

"It's a very private and a very delicate business. I'm dealing with individuals quite without any sense of morality. If they were to know that I've said even this much to you, both our lives would be in the direst jeopardy. I beg you, never utter another word about this to anyone. I should never have taken you up to the tower."

If its occupants were half as murderous as he was suggesting, she thought, how much more lethal would they be if they knew how many of the tower's secrets she'd seen?

"Promise me you'll let this subject alone," he went on.

"I want to see Yzordderrex, Oscar."

"Promise me. No more talk about the tower, in this house or out of it. *Say it,* Judith."

"All right. I won't talk about the tower."

"In this house—"

"—or out of it. But Oscar—"

"What, sweet?"

"I still want to see Yzordderrex."

2

The morning after this exchange she went up to Highgate. It was another rainy day, and failing to find an unoccupied cab she braved the Underground. It was a mistake. She'd never liked traveling by tube at the best of times—it brought out her latent claustrophobia—but she recalled as she rode that two of those murdered in the spate of killings had died in these tunnels: one pushed in front of a crowded train as it drew into Piccadilly station, the other stabbed to death at midnight, somewhere on the Jubilee Line. This was not a safe way to travel for someone who had even the slightest inkling of the prodigies half hidden in the world; and she was one of those few. So it was with no little relief she stepped out into the open air at Archway station (the clouds had cleared) and started up Highgate Hill on foot. She had no difficulty finding the tower itself, though the banality of its design, together with the shield of trees in full leaf in front of it, meant few eyes were likely to look its way.

Despite the dire warnings issued by Oscar it was difficult to find much intimidating about the place, with the spring sunshine warm enough to make her slip off her jacket, and the grass busy with sparrows quarreling over worms raised by the rain. She scanned the windows, looking for some sign of occupation, but saw none. Avoiding the front door, with its camera trained on the step, she headed down the side of the building, her progress unimpeded by walls or barbed wire. The owners had clearly decided the tower's best defense lay in its utter lack of character, and the less they did to keep trespassers out the fewer would be attracted in the first place. There was even less to see from the back than the front. There were blinds down over most of the windows, and those few that were not covered let onto empty rooms. She made a complete circuit of the tower, looking for some other way into it, but there was none.

As she returned to the front of the building she tried to imagine the passageways buried beneath her feet—the books piled in the darkness, and the imprisoned soul lying in a deeper darkness still—hoping her mind might be able to go where her body could not. But that exercise proved as fruitless as her window-watching. The real world was implacable; it wouldn't shift a particle of soil to let her through. Discouraged, she made one final circuit of the tower, then decided to give up. Maybe she'd come back here at night, she thought, when solid reality didn't insist on her senses so brutally. Or maybe seek another journey under the influence of the blue eye, though this option made her nervous. She had no real grasp of the mechanism by which the eye induced such flights, and she feared giving it power over her. Oscar already had enough of that.

She put her jacket back on and headed away from the tower. To judge by the absence of traffic on Hornsey Lane, the hill—which had been clogged with traffic—was still blocked, preventing drivers from making their way in this direction. The gulf usually filled with the din of vehicles was not empty, however. There were footsteps close behind her; and a voice.

"Who are you?"

She glanced around, not assuming the question was directed at her, but finding that she and the questioner—a woman in her sixties, shabbily dressed and sickly—were the only people in sight. Moreover, the woman's stare was fixed upon her with a near manic intensity. Again, the question, coming from a mouth that had about it a spittle-flecked asymmetry that suggested the speaker had suffered a stroke in the past.

"Who are you?"

Already irritated by her failure at the tower, Judith was in no mood to humor what was plainly the local schizophrenic and was turning on her heel to walk away when the woman spoke again.

"Don't you know they'll hurt you?"

"Who will?" she said.

"The people in the tower. The Tabula Rasa. What were you looking for?"

"Nothing."

"You were looking very hard for nothing."

"Are you spying for them?"

The woman made an ugly sound that Judith took to be a laugh. "They don't even know I'm alive," she said. Then, for the third time, "Who are you?"

"My name's Judith."

"I'm Clara Leash," the woman said. She cast a glance back in the direction of the tower. "Walk on," she said. "There's a church halfway up the hill. I'll meet you there."

"What is all this about?"

"At the church, not here."

So saying, she turned her back on Judith and walked off, her agitation enough to dissuade Judith from following. Two words in their short exchange convinced her she should wait at the church and find out what Clara Leash had to say, however. Those words were *Tabula Rasa*. She hadn't heard them spoken since her conversation with Charlie at the estate, when he'd told her how he'd been passed over for membership in favor of Oscar. He'd made light of it at the time, and much of what he'd said had been blotted from her mind by the violence and the revelations that followed. Now she found herself digging for recollections of what he'd said about the organization. Something about the tainted soil of England, and her saying tainted by what?, and Charlie making some comical reply. Now she knew what that taint was: magic. In that bland tower the lives of the men and women whose bodies had been found in shallow graves or scraped from the rails of the Piccadilly Line had been judged and found corrupt. No wonder Oscar was losing weight and sobbing in his sleep. He was a member of a Society formed for the express purpose of eradicating a second, and diminishing, society, to which he also belonged. For all his self-possession he was the servant of two masters: magic and its despoiler. It fell to her to help him by whatever means she could. She was his lover, and without her aid he would eventually be crushed between contrary imperatives. And he in his turn was her ticket to Yzordderrex, without whom she would never see the glories of the Imajica. They needed each other, alive and sane.

She waited at the church for half an hour before Clara Leash appeared, looking fretful.

"Out here's no good," she said. "Inside."

They stepped into the gloomy building and sat close to the altar so as not to be overheard by the three noontime supplicants who were at their prayers towards the back. It was not an ideal place in which to have a whispered conversation; their sibilance carried even if the sense did not, its echoes coming back to meet them off the bare walls. Nor was there much trust between them to begin with. To defend herself from Clara's glare, Judith spent the early part of their exchange with her back half turned to the woman, only facing her fully when they'd disposed of the circumlocutions and she felt confident enough to ask the question most on her mind.

"What do you know about the Tabula Rasa?"

"Everything there is to know," Clara replied. "I was a member of the Society for many years."

"But they think you're dead?"

"They're not far wrong. I haven't got more than a few months left, which is why it's important I pass along what I know."

"To me?"

"That depends," she said. "First I want to know what you were doing at the tower."

"I was looking for a way in."

"Have you ever been inside?"

"Yes and no."

"Meaning what?"

"My mind's been inside even though my body hasn't," Judith said, fully expecting a repeat of Clara's weird little laugh in response.

Instead, the woman said, "On the night of December the thirty-first."

"How the hell did you know that?"

Clara put her hand up to Judith's face. Her fingers were icy cold. "First, you should know how I departed the Tabula Rasa."

Though she told her story without embellishments, it took some time, given that so much of what she was explaining required footnotes for Judith to fully comprehend its significance. Clara, like Oscar, was the descendant of one of the Society's founding members and had been brought up to believe in its basic principles: England, tainted by magic—indeed, almost destroyed by it—had to be protected from any cult or individual who sought to educate new generations in its corrupt practices. When Judith asked how this near destruction had come about, Clara's answer was a story in itself. Two hundred years ago this coming midsummer, she explained, a ritual had been attempted that had gone tragically awry.

Its purpose had been to reconcile the reality of earth with those of four other dimensions.

"The Dominions," Judith said, dropping her voice, which was already low, lower still.

"Say it out loud," Clara replied. "Dominions! Dominions!" She only raised her voice to speaking volume, but after such a time whispering it was shockingly loud. "It's been a secret for too long," she said. "And that gives the enemy power."

"Who is the enemy?"

"There are so many," she said. "In this Dominion, the Tabula Rasa and its servants. And it's got plenty of those, believe me, in the very highest places."

"How?"

"It's not difficult, when your members are the descendants of kingmakers. And if influence fails, you can always buy your way past democracy. It's going on all the time."

"And in the other Dominions?"

"Getting information's more difficult, especially now. I knew two women who regularly passed between here and the Reconciled Dominions. One of them was found dead a week ago, the other's disappeared. She may also have been murdered—"

"By the Tabula Rasa."

"You know a good deal, don't you? What's your source?"

Judith had known Clara would ask that question eventually and had been trying to decide how she would answer it. Her belief in Clara Leash's integrity grew apace, but wouldn't it be precipitous to share with a woman she'd taken for a bag lady only two hours before a secret that could be Oscar's death warrant if known to the Tabula Rasa?

"I can't tell you my source," she said. "This person's in great danger as it is."

"And you don't trust me." She raised her hand to ward off any protest. "Don't sweet-talk me!" she said. "You don't trust me, and why should I blame you? But let me ask this: Is this source of yours a man?"

"Yes. Why?"

"You asked me before who the enemy was, and I said the Tabula Rasa. But we've got a more obvious enemy: the opposite sex."

"What?"

"*Men,* Judith. The destroyers."

"Oh, now wait—"

"There used to be Goddesses throughout the Dominions. Powers that took our sex's part in the cosmic drama. They're all dead, Judith. They didn't just die of old age. They were systematically eradicated by the enemy."

"Ordinary men don't kill Goddesses."

"Ordinary men serve extraordinary men. Extraordinary men get their visions from the Gods. And Gods kill Goddesses."

"That's too simple. It sounds like a school lesson."

"Learn it, then. And if you can, disprove it. I'd like that, truly I would. I'd like to discover that the Goddesses are all in hiding somewhere—"

"Like the woman under the tower?"

For the first time in this dialogue, Clara was lost for words. She simply stared, leaving Jude to fill the silence of her astonishment.

"When I said I've been into the tower in my mind, that isn't strictly true," Jude said. "I've only been *under* the tower. There's a cellar there, like a maze. It's full of books. And behind one of the walls there's a woman. I thought she was dead at first, but she isn't. She's maybe close to it, but she's holding on."

Clara was visibly shaken by this account. "I thought I was the only one who knew she was there," she said.

"More to the point, do you know who she is?"

"I've got a pretty good idea," Clara said, and picked up the story she'd been diverted from earlier: the tale of how she'd come to leave the Tabula Rasa.

The library beneath the tower, she explained, was the most comprehensive collection of manuscripts dealing with the occult sciences—but more particularly the legends and lore of the Imajica—in the world. It had been gathered by the men who'd founded the Society, led by Roxborough and Godolphin, to keep from the hands and minds of innocent Englishmen the stain of things Imajical; but rather than cataloguing the collection—making an index of these forbidden books—generations of the Tabula Rasa had simply left them to fester.

"I took it upon myself to sort through the collection. Believe it or not, I was once a very ordered woman. I got it from my father. He was in the military. At first I was watched by two other members of the Society. That's the law. No member of the Society is allowed into the library alone, and if any one judges either of the other two to be in any way unduly interested or influenced by the volumes, they can be tried by the Society and executed. I don't think it's ever been done. Half the books are in Latin, and who reads Latin? The other half—you've seen for yourself—they're rotting on their spines, like all of us. But I wanted order, the way Daddy would have liked it. Everything neat and tidy.

"My companions soon got tired of my obsession and left me to it. And in the middle of the night I felt something . . . or somebody . . . pulling at my thoughts, plucking them out of my scalp one by one, like hairs. Of course I thought it was the books, at first.

I thought the words had got some power over me. I tried to leave, but you know I really didn't want to. I'd been Daddy's repressed little daughter for fifty years, and I was about ready to crack. Celestine knew it too—"

"Celestine is the woman in the wall?"

"I believe it's her, yes."

"But you don't know who she is?"

"I'm coming to that," Clara said. "Roxborough's house stood on the land where the tower now stands. The cellar is the cellar of that house. Celestine was—indeed, still is—Roxborough's prisoner. He walled her up because he didn't dare kill her. She'd seen the face of Hapexamendios, the God of Gods. She was insane, but she'd been touched by divinity, and even Roxborough didn't dare lay a finger on her."

"How do you know all this?"

"Roxborough wrote a confession, a few days before he died. He knew the woman he'd walled up would outlive him by centuries, and I suppose he also knew that sooner or later somebody would find her. So the confession was also a warning to whatever poor, victimized man came along, telling him that she was not to be touched. *Bury her again,* he said, I remember that very clearly. *Bury her again, in the deepest abyss your wits may devise*—"

"Where did you find this confession?"

"In the wall, that night when I was alone. I believe Celestine led me to it, by plucking thoughts out of my head and putting new ones in. But she plucked too hard. My mind gave up. I had a stroke down there. I wasn't found for three days."

"That's horrible—"

"My suffering's nothing compared to hers. Roxborough had found this woman in London, or his spies had, and he knew she was a creature of immense power. He probably realized it more clearly than she did, in fact, because he says in the confession she was a stranger to herself. But she'd seen sights no other human being had ever witnessed. She'd been snatched from the Fifth Dominion, escorted across the Imajica, and taken into the presence of Hapexamendios."

"Why?"

"It gets stranger. When he interrogated her, she told him she'd been brought back into the Fifth Dominion pregnant."

"She was having God's child?"

"That's what she told Roxborough."

"She could have been inventing it all, just to keep him from hurting her."

"I don't think he'd have done that. In fact I think he was half in love with her. He said in the confession he felt like his friend Godolphin. *I'm broken by a woman's eye,* he wrote."

"That's an odd phrase," Jude thought, thinking of the stone as she did so: its stare, its authority.

"Well, Godolphin died obsessing on some mistress he'd loved and lost, claiming he'd been destroyed by her. The men were always the innocents, you see. Victims of female connivings. I daresay Roxborough'd persuaded himself that walling Celestine up was an act of love. Keeping her under his thumb forever."

"What happened to the child?" Judith said.

"Maybe she can tell us herself," Clara replied.

"Then we have to get her out."

"Indeed."

"Do you have any idea how?"

"Not yet," Clara said. "Until you appeared I was ready to despair. But between the two of us we'll find some way to save her."

It was getting late, and Jude was anxious that her absence not be noted, so the plans they laid were sketchy in the extreme. A further examination of the tower was clearly in order, this time—Clara proposed—under cover of darkness.

"Tonight," she suggested.

"No, that's too soon. Give me a day to make up some excuse for being out for the night."

"Who's the watchdog?" Clara said.

"Just a man."

"Suspicious?"

"Sometimes."

"Well, Celestine's waited a long time to be set free. She can wait another twenty-four hours. But please, no longer. I'm not a well woman."

Jude put her hand over Clara's hand, the first contact between them since the woman had touched her icy fingers to Jude's cheek. "You're not going to die," she said.

"Oh, yes, I am. It's no great hardship. But I want to see Celestine's face before I leave."

"We will," Judith said. "If not tomorrow night, soon after."

3

She didn't believe what Clara had said about men pertained to Oscar. He was no destroyer of Goddesses, either by hand or proxy. But Dowd was another matter entirely. Though his façade was civilized—almost prissy at times—she would never forget the casual way he'd disposed of the voiders' bodies, warming his hands at the pyre as though they were branches, not bones, that were cracking in the flames. And, as bad luck would have it, Dowd was back at the house when she returned, and Oscar was not, so it was his questions she was obliged to answer if she wasn't to arouse his suspicions with silence. When he asked her what she'd done with the day, she told him she'd gone out for a long walk along the Embankment. He then inquired as to whether the tube had been crowded, though she'd not told him she'd traveled that way. She said it was. You should take a cab next time, he said. Or, better still, allow me to drive you. I'm certain Mr. Godolphin would prefer you to travel in comfort, he said. She thanked him for his kindness. Will you be planning other trips soon? he asked. She had her story for the following evening already prepared, but Dowd's manner never failed to throw her off balance, and she was certain any lie she told now would be instantly spotted, so she said she didn't know, and he let the subject drop.

Oscar didn't come home until the middle of the night, slipping into bed beside her as gently as his bulk allowed. She pretended to wake. He murmured a few words of apology for stirring her, and then some of love. Feigning a sleepy tone, she told him she was going to see her friend Clem tomorrow night, and did he mind? He told her she should do whatever she wanted, but keep her beautiful body for him. Then he kissed her shoulder and neck and fell asleep.

She had arranged to meet Clara at eight in the evening, outside the church, but she left for that rendezvous two hours before in order to go via her old flat. She didn't know what place in the scheme of things the carved blue eye had, but she'd decided the night before that it should be with her when they made their attempt to liberate Celestine.

The flat felt cold and neglected, and she spent only a few minutes there, first retrieving the eye from her wardrobe, then quickly leafing through the mail—most of it junk—that had arrived since she'd last visited. These tasks completed, she set out for Highgate, taking Dowd's advice and hailing a taxi to do so. It delivered her to the church twenty-five minutes early, only to find that Clara was already there.

"Have you eaten, my girl?" Clara wanted to know.

Jude told her she had.

"Good," Clara said. "We'll need all our strength tonight."

"Before we go any further," Jude said, "I want to show you something. I don't know what use it can be to us, but I think you ought to see it." She brought the parcel of cloth out of her bag. "Remember what you said about Celestine plucking the thoughts out of your head?"

"Of course."

"This is what did the same to me."

She began to unwrap the eye, a subtle tremor in her fingers as she did so. Four months and more had passed since she'd hidden it away with such superstitious care but her memory of its effect was undimmed, and she half expected it to exercise some power now. It did nothing, though; it lay in the folds of its covering, looking so unremarkable she was almost embarrassed to have made such a show of unveiling it. Clara, however, stared at it with a smile on her lips.

"Where did you get this?" she said.

"I'd rather not say."

"This is no time for secrets," Clara snapped. "How did you come by it?"

"It was given to my husband. My ex-husband."

"Who by?"

"His brother."

"And who's his brother?"

She took a deep breath, undecided even as she drew it whether she'd expel it again as truth or fabrication.

"His name's Oscar Godolphin," she said.

At this reply Clara physically retreated from Judith, almost as though this name was proof of the plague.

"Do you *know* Oscar Godolphin?" she said, her tone appalled.

"Yes, I do."

"Is he the watchdog?" she said.

"Yes, he is."

"Cover it up," she said, shunning the eye now. "Cover it up and put it away." She turned her back on Judith, running her crabbed hands through her hair. "You and Godolphin?" she said, half to herself. "What does that mean? What does that mean?"

"It doesn't mean anything," Jude said. "What I feel for him and what we're doing now are completely different issues."

"Don't be naïve," Clara replied, glancing back at Jude. "Godolphin's a member of the Tabula Rasa, and a man. You and Celestine are both women, and his prisoners—"

"I'm not his prisoner," Jude said, infuriated by Clara's condescension. "I do what I want when I want."

"Until you defy history," Clara said. "Then you'll see how much he thinks he owns you." She approached Jude again, taking her voice down to a pained whisper. "Understand this," she said. "You can't save Celestine and keep his affections. You're going to be digging at the very foundations—literally, the foundations—of his family and his faith, and when he finds out—and he will, when the Tabula Rasa starts to crumble—whatever's between you will mean nothing. We're not another sex, Judith, we're another species. What's going on in our bodies and our heads isn't remotely like what's going on in theirs. Our hells are different. So are our heavens. We're *enemies,* and you can't be on both sides in a war."

"It isn't war," Jude said. "If it was war I'd be angry, and I've never been calmer."

"We'll see how calm you are, when you see how things really stand."

Jude took another deep breath. "Maybe we should stop arguing and do what we came to do," she said. Clara looked at her balefully. "I think stubborn bitch is the phrase you're looking for," Jude remarked.

"I never trust the passive ones," Clara said, betraying a trace of admiration.

"I'll remember that."

The tower was in darkness, and the trees clogged the lamplight from the street, leaving the forecourt shadowy and the route down the flank of the building virtually lightless. Clara had obviously wandered here by night many times, however, because she went with confidence, leaving Jude to trail, snared by the brambles and stung by the nettles it had been easy to avoid in the sunshine. By the time she reached the back of the tower, her eyes were better accustomed to the murk and found Clara standing twenty yards from the building, staring at the ground.

"What are you doing back here?" Jude said. "We know there's only one way in."

"Barred and bolted," she said. "I'm thinking there may be some other entrance to the cellar under the turf, even if it's only a ventilation pipe. The first thing we should do is locate Celestine's cell."

"How do we do that?"

"We use the eye that took you traveling," Clara said. "Come on, come on, give it over."

"I thought it was too tainted to be touched."

"Not at all."

"The way you looked at it . . ."

"It's loot, my girl. That's what repulsed me. It's a piece of women's history traded between two men."

"I'm sure Oscar didn't know what it was," she said, thinking even as she defended him that this was probably untrue.

"It belongs to a great temple—"

"He certainly doesn't loot temples," Jude said, taking the contentious item from her pocket.

"I'm not saying he does," Clara replied. "The temples were

brought down long before the line of the Godolphins was even founded. Well, are you going to hand it over or not?"

Jude unwrapped the eye, discovering in herself a reluctance to share it she hadn't anticipated. It was no longer as unremarkable as it had been. It gave off a subtle luminescence, blue and steady, by which she and Clara could see each other, albeit faintly.

Their gazes met, the eye's light gleaming between them like the glance of a third conspirator, a woman wiser than them both, whose presence—despite the dull murmur of traffic, and jets droning through the clouds above—exalted the moment. Jude found herself wondering how many women had gathered in the glow of this light or its like down the ages: gathered to pray, or make sacrifice, or shelter from the destroyer. Countless numbers, no doubt, dead and forgotten but, in this brief time out of time, reclaimed from anonymity; not named, but at least acknowledged by these new acolytes. She looked away from Clara, towards the eye. The solid world around her suddenly seemed irrelevant—at best a game of veils, at worst a trap in which the spirit struggled and, struggling, gave credence to the lie. There was no need to be bound by its rules. She could fly beyond it with a thought. She looked up again to confirm that Clara was also ready to move, but her companion was glancing out of the circle, towards the corner of the tower.

"What is it?" Jude said, following the direction of Clara's gaze. Somebody was approaching them through the darkness, in the walk a nonchalance she could name in a syllable: "Dowd."

"You know him?" Clara said.

"A little," Dowd said, his voice as casual as his gait. "But really, there's so much she doesn't know."

Clara's hands dropped from Jude's, breaking the charm of three.

"Don't come any closer," Clara said.

Surprisingly, Dowd stopped dead in his tracks, a few yards from the women. There was sufficient light from the eye for Jude to pick out his face. Something, or things, seemed to be crawling around his mouth, as though he'd just eaten a handful of ants and a few had escaped from between his lips.

"I would so love to kill you both," he said, and with the words further mites escaped and ran over his cheeks and chin. "But your time will come, Judith. Very soon. For now, it's just Clara. . . . It *is* Clara, isn't it?"

"Go to hell, Dowd," Jude said.

"Step away from the old woman," Dowd replied.

Jude's response was to take hold of Clara's arm. "You're not going to hurt anybody, you little shit," she said.

There was a fury rising in her the like of which she'd not felt in months. The eye was heavy in her hand; she was ready to brain the bastard with it if he took a step towards them.

"Did you not understand me, whore?" he said, moving towards her as he did so. "I told you: Step *away!*"

In her rage she went to meet his approach, raising her weighted hand as she did so, but in the instant that she let go of Clara he side-stepped her, and she lost sight of him. Realizing that she'd done exactly as he'd planned, she reeled around, intending to take hold of Clara again. But he was there before her. She heard a shout of horror and saw Clara staggering away from her attacker. The mites were at her face already, blinding her. Jude ran to catch hold of her before she fell, but this time Dowd moved towards her, not away, and with a single blow struck the stone from Jude's hand. She didn't turn to reclaim it but went to Clara's aid. The woman's moans were terrible; so were the tremors in her body.

"What have you done to her?" she yelled at Dowd.

"Undone, lovely, undone. Let her be. You can't help her now."

Clara's body was light, but when her legs buckled she carried Jude down with her. Her moans had become howls now, as she reached up to her face as if to scratch out her eyes, for there the mites were at some agonizing work. In desperation Jude tried to feel for the creatures in the darkness, but either they were too fast for her fingers or they'd gone where fingers couldn't follow. All she could do was beg for a reprieve.

"Make them stop," she said to Dowd. "Whatever you want, I'll do, but *please* make them stop."

"They're voracious little sods, aren't they?" he said.

He was crouching in front of the eye, the blue light illuminating his face, which wore a mask of chilling serenity. As she watched he picked mites from around his mouth and let them drop to the ground.

"I'm afraid they've got no ears, so I can't call them back," he said. "They only know how to *unmake.* And they'll unmake anything but their maker. In this case, that's me. So I'd leave her alone, if I were you. They're indiscriminate."

She turned her attention back to the woman in her arms. Clara had given up scratching at her eyes, and the tremors in her body were rapidly diminishing.

"Speak to me," Jude said. She reached for Clara's face, a little ashamed of how tentative Dowd's warning had made her.

There was no answer from the body, unless there were words in Clara's dying moans. Jude listened, hoping to find some vestigial sense there, but there was none. She felt a single spasm pass down Clara's spine, as though something in her head had snapped, and then the whole system stopped dead. From the moment when

Dowd had first appeared, perhaps ninety seconds had passed. In that time every hope that had gathered here had been undone. She wondered if Celestine had heard this tragedy unfold, another's suffering adding to her own sum.

"Dead, then, lovey," Dowd said.

Jude let Clara's body slip from her arms into the grass.

"We should be going," he went on, his tone so bland they might have been forsaking a picnic instead of a corpse. "Don't worry about Clara. I'll fetch what's left of her later."

She heard the sound of his feet behind her and stood up, rather than be touched by him. Overhead, another jet was roaring in the clouds. She looked towards the eye, but it too had been unmade.

"Destroyer," she said.

28

I

Gentle had forgotten his short exchange with Aping about their shared enthusiasm for painting, but Aping had not. The morning after the wedding in Athanasius' cell, the sergeant came to fetch Gentle and escorted him to a room at the other end of the building, which he had turned into a studio. It had plenty of windows, so the light was as good as this region was ever likely to supply, and he had gathered over the months of his posting here an enviable selection of materials. The products of this workplace were, however, those of the most uninspired dilettante. Designed without compositional skill and painted without sense of color, their only real point of interest lay in their obsessiveness. There were, Aping proudly told Gentle, one hundred and fifty-three pictures, and their subject was unchanging: his child, Huzzah, the merest mention of whom had caused the loving portraitist such unease. Now, in the privacy of his place of inspiration, he explained why. His daughter was young, he said, and her mother dead; he'd been obliged to bring her with him when orders from Iahmandhas moved him to the Cradle.

"I could have left her in L'Himby," he told Gentle. "But who knows what kind of harm she'd have come to if I'd done that? She's a child."

"So she's here on the island?"

"Yes, she is. But she won't step out of her room in the daytime. She's afraid of catching the madness, she says. I love her very much. And as you can see"—he indicated the paintings—"she's very beautiful."

Gentle was obliged to take the man's word for it. "Where is she now?" he asked.

"Where she always is," Aping said. "In her room. She has very strange dreams."

"I know how she feels," Gentle said.

"Do you?" Aping replied, with a fervor in his voice that suggested that art was not, after all, the subject Gentle had been brought here to debate. "You dream too, then?"

"Everybody does."

"That's what my wife used to tell me." He lowered his voice. "She had prophetic dreams. She knew when she was going to die, to the very hour. But I don't dream at all. So I can't share what Huzzah feels."

"Are you suggesting that maybe I could?"

"This is a very delicate matter," Aping said. "Yzordderrexian law prohibits all prophetics."

"I didn't know that."

"Especially women, of course," Aping went on. "That's the real reason I keep her out of sight. It's true, she fears the madness, but I'm afraid for what's inside her even more."

"Why?"

"I'm afraid if she keeps company with anyone but me she'll say something out of turn, and N'ashap will realize she has visions like her mother."

"And that would be—"

"Disastrous! My career would be in tatters. I should never have brought her." He looked up at Gentle. "I'm only telling you this because we're both artists, and artists have to trust each other, like brothers, isn't that right?"

"That's right," said Gentle. Aping's large hands were trembling, he saw. The man looked to be on the verge of collapse. "Do you want me to speak to your daughter?" he asked.

"More than that . . ."

"Tell me."

"I want you to take her with you, when you and the mystif leave. Take her to Yzordderrex."

"What makes you think we're going there—or anywhere, come to that?"

"I have my spies, and so does N'ashap. Your plans are better known than you'd like. Take her with you, Mr. Zacharias. Her mother's parents are still alive. They'll look after her."

"It's a big responsibility to take a child all that way."

Aping pursed his lips. "I would of course be able to ease your departure from the island, if you were to take her."

"Suppose she won't go?" Gentle said.

"You must persuade her," he said simply, as though he knew Gentle had long experience of persuading little girls to do what he wanted.

Nature had played Huzzah Aping three cruel tricks. One, it had lent her powers that were expressly forbidden under the Autarch's regime; two, it had given her a father who, despite his sentimental dotings, cared more for his military career than for her; and, three, it had given her a face that only a father could ever have described as beautiful. She was a thin, troubled creature of nine or ten, her black hair cut comically, her mouth tiny and tight. When, after much cajoling, those lips deigned to speak, her voice was wan and despairing. It was only when Aping told her that her visitor was the man who'd fallen into the sea and almost died that her interest was sparked.

"You went down into the Cradle?" she said.

"Yes, I did," Gentle replied, coming to the bed on which she sat, her arms wrapped around her knees.

"Did you see the Cradle Lady?" the girl said.

"See who?" Aping started to hush her, but Gentle waved him into silence. "See who?" he said again.

"She lives in the sea," Huzzah said. "I dream about her—and I hear her sometimes—but I haven't seen her yet. I want to see her."

"Does she have a name?" Gentle asked.

"Tishalullé," Huzzah replied, pronouncing the run of the syllables without hesitation. "That's the sound the waves made when she was born," she explained. "Tishalullé."

"That's a lovely name."

"I think so," the girl said gravely. "Better than Huzzah."

"Huzzah's pretty too," Gentle replied. "Where I come from, Huzzah's the noise people make when they're happy."

She looked at him as though the idea of happiness was utterly alien to her, which Gentle could believe. Now he saw Aping in his daughter's presence, he better understood the paradox of the man's response to her. He was frightened of the girl. Her illegal powers upset him for his reputation's sake, certainly, but they also reminded him of a power he had no real mastery over. The man painted Huzzah's fragile face over and over as an act of perverse devotion, perhaps, but also of exorcism. Nor was the child much better served by her gift. Her dreams condemned her to this cell and filled her with obscure longings. She was more their victim than their celebrant.

Gentle did his best to draw from her a little more information on this woman Tishalullé, but she either knew very little or was unprepared to vouchsafe further insights in her father's presence.

Gentle suspected the latter. As he left, however, she asked him quietly if he would come and visit her again, and he said he would.

He found Pie in their cell, with a guard on the door. The mystif looked grim.

"N'ashap's revenge," it said, nodding towards the guard. "I think we've outstayed our welcome."

Gentle recounted his conversation with Aping and the meeting with Huzzah.

"So the law prohibits prophetics, does it? That's a piece of legislation I hadn't heard about."

"The way she talked about the Cradle Lady—"

"Her mother, presumably."

"Why do you say that?"

"She's frightened and she wants her mother. Who can blame her? And what's a Cradle Lady if not a mother?"

"I hadn't thought of it that way," Gentle said. "I'd supposed there might be some literal truth to what she was saying."

"I doubt it."

"Are we going to take her with us or not?"

"It's your choice, of course, but I say absolutely not."

"Aping said he'd help us if we took her."

"What's his help worth, if we're burdened with a child? Remember, we're not going alone. We've got to get Scopique out too, and he's confined to his cell the way we are. N'ashap has ordered a general clamp-down."

"He must be pining for you."

Pie made a sour face. "I'm certain our descriptions are on their way to his headquarters even now. And when he gets an answer he's going to be a very happy Oethac, knowing he's got a couple of desperadoes under lock and key. We'll *never* get out once he knows who we are."

"So we have to escape before he realizes. I just thank God the telephone never made it to this Dominion."

"Maybe the Autarch banned it. The less people talk, the less they can plot. You know, I think maybe I should try and get access to N'ashap. I'm sure I could persuade him to give us a freer rein, if I could just talk with him for a few minutes."

"He's not interested in conversation, Pie," Gentle said. "He'd prefer to keep your mouth busy some other way."

"So you simply want to fight your way out?" Pie replied. "Use pneuma against N'ashap's men?"

Gentle paused to think this option through. "I don't think that'd be too clever," he said. "Not with me still weak. In a couple of days, maybe we could take them on. But not yet."

"We don't have that long."

"I realize that."

"And even if we did, we'd be better avoiding a face-to-face conflict. N'ashap's troops may be lethargic, but there's a good number of them."

"Perhaps you *should* see him, then, and try to mellow him a little. I'll talk to Aping and praise his pictures some more."

"Is he any good?"

"Put it this way: As a painter he makes a damn fine father. But he trusts me, with us being fellow artists and all."

The mystif got up and called to the guard, requesting a private interview with Captain N'ashap. The man mumbled something smutty and left his post, having first beaten the bolts on the door with his rifle butt to be certain they were firmly in place. The sound drove Gentle to the window, to stare out at the open air. There was a brightness in the cloud layer that suggested the suns might be on their way through. The mystif joined him, slipping its arms around his neck.

"What are you thinking?" it said.

"Remember Efreet's mother, in Beatrix?"

"Of course."

"She told me she'd dreamt about me coming to sit at her table, though she wasn't certain whether I'd be a man or a woman."

"Naturally you were deeply offended."

"I would have been once," Gentle said. "But it didn't mean that much when she said it. After a few weeks with you, I didn't give a shit what sex I was. See how you've corrupted me?"

"My pleasure. Is there any more to this story, or is that it?"

"No, there's more. She started talking about Goddesses, I remember. About how they were hidden away. . . ."

"And you think Huzzah's found one?"

"We saw acolytes in the mountains, didn't we? Why not a Deity? Maybe Huzzah did go dreaming for her mother . . ."

". . . but instead she found a Goddess."

"Yes. Tishalullé, out there in the Cradle, waiting to rise."

"You like the idea, don't you?"

"Of hidden Goddesses? Oh, yes. Maybe it's just the woman chaser in me. Or maybe I'm like Huzzah, waiting for someone I can't remember, wanting to see some face or other, come to fetch me away."

"I'm already here," Pie said, kissing the back of Gentle's neck. "Every face you ever wanted."

"Even a Goddess?"

"Ah—"

The sound of the bolts being drawn aside silenced them. The

guard had returned with the news that Captain N'ashap had con-
sented to see the mystif.

"If you see Aping," Gentle said as it left, "will you tell him I'd
love to sit and talk painting with him?"

"I'll do that."

They parted, and Gentle returned to the window. The clouds had
thickened their defenses against the suns, and the Cradle lay still
and empty again beneath their blanket. Gentle said again the name
Huzzah had shared with him, the word that was shaped like a
breaking wave.

"Tishalullé."

The sea remained motionless. Goddesses didn't come at a call.
At least, not his.

He was just estimating the time that Pie had been away—and deciding it was an hour or more—when Aping appeared at the cell
door, dismissing the guard from his post while he talked.

"Since when have you been under lock and key?" he asked
Gentle.

"Since this morning."

"But why? I understood from the captain that you and the mystif were guests, after a fashion."

"We were."

A twitch of anxiety passed over Aping's features. "If you're a
prisoner here," he said stiffly, "then of course the situation's
changed."

"You mean we won't be able to debate painting?"

"I mean you won't be leaving."

"What about your daughter?"

"That's academic now."

"You'll let her languish, will you? You'll let her die?"

"She won't die."

"I think she will."

Aping turned his back on his tempter. "The law is the law," he
said.

"I understand," Gentle replied softly. "Even artists have to bow
to that master, I suppose."

"I understand what you're doing," Aping said. "Don't think I
don't."

"She's a child, Aping."

"Yes. I know. But I'll have to tend to her as best I can."

"Why don't you ask her whether she's seen her own death?"

"Oh, Jesu," Aping said, stricken. He began to shake his head.
"Why must this happen to me?"

"It needn't. You can save her."

"It isn't so clear-cut," Aping said, giving Gentle a harried look. "I have my duty."

He took a handkerchief from his trouser pocket and wiped hard at his mouth, back and forth, as though a residue of guilt clung there and he was afraid it would give him away.

"I have to think," he said, going back to the door. "It seemed so easy. But now . . . I have to think."

The guard was at his post again when the door opened, and Gentle was obliged to let the sergeant go without having the chance to broach the subject of Scopique.

There was further frustration when Pie returned. N'ashap had kept the mystif waiting two hours and had finally decided not to grant the promised interview.

"I heard him even if I didn't see him," Pie said. "He sounded to be roaring drunk."

"So both of us were out of luck. I don't think Aping's going to help us. If the choice is between his daughter and his duty he'll choose his duty."

"So we're stuck here."

"Until we plot another plot."

"Shit."

2

Night fell without the suns appearing again, the only sound throughout the building that of the guards proceeding up and down the corridors, bringing food to the cells, then slamming and locking the doors until dawn. Not a single voice was raised to protest the fact that the privileges of the evening—games of Horsebone, recitations of scenes from Quexos, and Malbaker's *Numbubo,* works many here knew by heart—had been withdrawn. There was a universal reluctance to make a peep, as if each man, alone in his cell, was prepared to forgo every comfort, even that of praying aloud, to keep themselves from being noticed.

"N'ashap must be dangerous when drunk," Pie said, by way of explanation for this breathless hush.

"Maybe he's fond of midnight executions."

"I'd take a bet on who's top of his list."

"I wish I felt stronger. If they come for us, we'll fight, right?"

"Of course," Pie said. "But until they do, why don't you sleep for a while?"

"You must be kidding."

"At least stop pacing about."

"I've never been locked up by anybody before. It makes me claustrophobic."

"One pneuma and you could be out of here," Pie reminded him.

"Maybe that's what we should be doing."

"If we're pressed. But we're not yet. For Christ's sake, lie down."

Reluctantly, Gentle did so, and despite the anxieties that lay down beside him to whisper in his ear, his body was more interested in rest than their company, and he quickly fell asleep.

He was woken by Pie, who murmured, "You've got a visitor."

He sat up. The cell's light had been turned off, and had it not been for the smell of oil paint he'd not have known the identity of the man at the door.

"Zacharias. I need your help."

"What's wrong?"

"Huzzah is . . . I think she's going crazy. You've got to come." His whispering voice trembled. So did the hand he laid on Gentle's arm. "I think she's dying," he said.

"If I go, Pie comes too."

"No, I can't take that risk."

"And I can't take the risk of leaving my friend here," Gentle said.

"And I can't take the risk of being found out. If there isn't somebody in the cell when the guard passes—"

"He's right," said Pie. "Go on. Help the child."

"Is that wise?"

"Compassion's always wise."

"All right. But stay awake. We haven't said our prayers yet. We need both our breaths for that."

"I understand."

Gentle slipped out into the passage with Aping, who winced at every click the key made as he locked the door. So did Gentle. The thought of leaving Pie alone in the cell sickened him. But there seemed to be no other choice.

"We may need a doctor's help," Gentle said as they crept down the darkened corridors. "I suggest you fetch Scopique from his cell."

"Is he a doctor?"

"He certainly is."

"It's you she's asking for," Aping said. "I don't know why. She just woke up, sobbing and begging me to fetch you. She's so cold!"

With Aping's knowledge of how regularly each floor and passageway was patrolled to aid them, they reached Huzzah's cell without encountering a single guard. The girl wasn't lying on her bed, as Gentle had expected, but was crouched on the floor, with her head and hands pressed against one of the walls. A single wick burned in a bowl in the middle of the cell, her face unwarmed by its light. Though she registered their appearance with a glance, she didn't move from the wall, so Gentle went to where she was crouching and did the same. Shudders passed through her body, though her bangs were plastered to her brow with sweat.

"What can you hear?" Gentle asked her.

"She's not in my dreams any more, Mr. Zacharias," she said, pronouncing his name with precision, as though the proper naming of the forces around her would offer her some little control over them.

"Where is she?" Gentle inquired.

"She's outside. I can hear her. Listen."

He put his head to the wall. There was indeed a murmur in the stone, though he guessed its source was either the asylum's generator or its furnace rather than the Cradle Lady.

"Do you hear?"

"Yes, I hear."

"She wants to come in," Huzzah said. "She tried to come in through my dreams, but she couldn't, so now she's coming through the wall."

"Maybe . . . we should move away then," Gentle said, reaching to put his hand on the girl's shoulder. She was icy. "Come on, let me take you back to bed. You're cold."

"I was in the sea," she said, allowing Gentle to put his arms around her and draw her to her feet.

He looked towards Aping and mouthed the word *Scopique*. Seeing his daughter's frailty, the sergeant went from the door as obediently as a dog, leaving his Huzzah clinging to Gentle. He set her down on the bed and wrapped a blanket around her.

"The Cradle Lady knows you're here," Huzzah said.

"Does she?"

"She told me she almost drowned you, but you wouldn't let her."

"Why would she want to do that?"

"I don't know. You'll have to ask her, when she comes in."

"You're not afraid of her?"

"Oh, no. Are you?"

"Well, if she tried to drown me—"

"She won't do that again, if you stay with me. She likes me, and if she knows I like you she won't hurt you."

"That's good to know," Gentle said. "What would she think if we were to leave here tonight?"

"We can't do that."

"Why not?"

"I don't want to go up there," she said. "I don't like it."

"Everybody's asleep," he said. "We could just tiptoe away. You and me and my friends. That wouldn't be so bad, would it?" She looked unpersuaded. "I think your papa would like us to go to Yzordderrex. Have you ever been there?"

"When I was very little."

"We could go again."

Huzzah shook her head. "The Cradle Lady won't let us," she said.

"She might, if she knew that was what you wanted. Why don't we go up and have a look?"

Huzzah glanced back towards the wall, as if she was expecting Tishalullé's tide to crack the stone there and then. When nothing happened, she said, "Yzordderrex is a very long way, isn't it?"

"It's quite a journey, yes."

"I've read about it in my books."

"Why don't you put on some warm clothes?" Gentle said.

Her doubts banished by the tacit approval of the Goddess, Huzzah got up and went to select some clothes from her meager wardrobe, which hung from hooks on the opposite wall. Gentle took the opportunity to glance through the small stack of books at the end of the bed. Several were entertainments for children, keepsakes, perhaps, of happier times; one was a hefty encyclopedia by someone called Maybellome, which might have made informative reading under other circumstances but was too densely printed to be skimmed and too heavy to be taken along. There was a volume of poems that read like nonsense rhymes, and what appeared to be a novel, Huzzah's place in it marked with a slip of paper. He pocketed it when her back was turned, as much for himself as her, then went to the door in the hope that Aping and Scopique were within sighting distance. There was no sign. Huzzah had meanwhile finished dressing.

"I'm ready," she said. "Shall we go? Papa will find us."

"I hope so," Gentle replied.

Certainly remaining in the cell was a waste of valuable time. Huzzah asked if she could take Gentle's hand, to which he said of course, and together they began to thread their way through the passageways, all of which looked bewilderingly alike in the semi-darkness. Their progress was halted several times when the sound of boots on stone announced the proximity of guards, but Huzzah was as alive to their danger as Gentle and twice saved them from discovery.

And then, as they climbed the final flight of stairs that would bring them out into the open air, a din erupted not far from them. They both froze, drawing back into the shadows, but they weren't the cause of the commotion. It was N'ashap's voice that came echoing along the corridor, accompanied by a dreadful hammering. Gentle's first thought was of Pie, and before common sense could intervene he'd broken cover and was heading towards the source of the sound, glancing back once to signal that Huzzah should stay where she was, only to find that she was already on his heels. He recognized the passageway ahead. The open door twenty yards from where he stood was the door of the cell he'd left Pie in. And it was from there that the sound of N'ashap's voice emerged, a garbled stream of insults and accusations that was already bringing guards running. Gentle drew a deep breath, preparing for the violence that was surely inevitable now.

"No further," he told Huzzah, then raced towards the open door.

Three guards, two of them Oethacs, were approaching from the opposite direction, but only one of the two had his eyes on Gentle. The man shouted an order which Gentle didn't catch over N'ashap's cacophony, but Gentle raised his arms, open-palmed, fearful that the man would be trigger-happy, and at the same time slowed his run to a walk. He was within ten paces of the door, but the guards were there ahead of him. There was a brief exchange with N'ashap, during which Gentle had time to halve the distance between himself and the door, but a second order—this time plainly a demand that he stand still, backed up by the guard's training his weapon at Gentle's heart—brought him to a halt.

He'd no sooner done so than N'ashap emerged from the cell, with one hand in Pie's ringlets and the other holding his sword, a gleaming sweep of steel, to the mystif's belly. The scars on N'ashap's swollen head were inflamed by the drink in his system; the rest of his skin was dead white, almost waxen. He reeled as he stood in the doorway, all the more dangerous for his lack of equilibrium. The mystif had proved in New York it could survive traumas that would have laid any human dead in the gutter. But N'ashap's blade was ready to gut it like a fish, and there'd be no surviving that. The commander's tiny eyes fixed as best they could on Gentle.

"Your mystif's very faithful all of a sudden," he said, panting. "Why's that? First it comes looking for me, then it won't let me near it. Maybe it needs your permission, is that it? So give it." He pushed the blade against Pie's belly. "*Go on.* Tell it to be friendly, or it's dead."

Gentle lowered his hands a little, very slowly, as if in an attempt to appeal to Pie. "I don't think we have much choice," he said, his eyes going between the mystif's impassive face and the sword poised at its belly, putting the time it would take for a pneuma to blow N'ashap's head off against the speed of the captain's blade.

N'ashap was not the only player in the scene, of course. There were three guards already here, all armed, and doubtless more on their way.

"You'd better do what he wants," Gentle said, drawing a deep breath as he finished speaking.

N'ashap saw him do so, and saw too his hand going to his mouth. Even drunk, he sensed his danger and loosed a shout to the men in the passageway behind him, stepping out of their line of fire, and Gentle's, as he did so.

Denied one target, Gentle unleashed his breath against the other. The pneuma flew at the guards as their trigger fingers tightened, striking the nearest with such violence his chest erupted. The force of the blow threw the body back against the other two. One went down immediately, his weapon flying from his hand. The other was momentarily blinded by blood and a shrapnel of innards but was quick to regain his balance, and would have blown Gentle's head off had his target not been on the move, flinging himself towards the corpse. The guard fired once wildly, but before he could fire again Gentle had snatched up the dropped weapon and answered the fire with his own. The guard had enough Oethac blood to be indifferent to the bullets that came his way, till one found his spattered eye and blew it out. He shrieked and fell back, dropping his gun to clamp both hands to the wound.

Ignoring the third man, still moaning on the floor, Gentle went to the cell door. Inside, Captain N'ashap stood face to face with Pie 'oh' pah. The mystif's hand was on the blade. Blood ran from the sliced palm, but the commander was making no attempt to do further damage. He was staring at Pie's face, his own expression perplexed.

Gentle halted, knowing any intervention on his part would snap N'ashap out of his distracted state. Whoever he was seeing in Pie's place—the whore who resembled his mother, perhaps; another echo of Tishalullé, in this place of lost mamas?—it was sufficient to keep the blade from removing the mystif's fingers.

Tears began to well in N'ashap's eyes. The mystif didn't move, nor did its gaze flicker from the captain's face for an instant. It seemed to be winning the battle between N'ashap's desire and his murderous intention. His hand unknotted from around the sword. The mystif opened its own fingers, and the weight of the sword carried it out of the captain's grip to the ground. The noise it made striking the stone was too loud to go unheard by N'ashap, however entranced he was, and he shook his head violently, his gaze going instantly from Pie's face to the weapon that had fallen between them.

The mystif was quick: at the door in two strides. Gentle drew breath, but as his hand went to his mouth he heard a shriek from Huzzah. He glanced down the corridor towards the child, who was retreating before two more guards, both Oethacs, one snatching at her as she fled, the other with his sights on Gentle. Pie seized his arm and dragged him back from the door as N'ashap, still rising as he came, ran at them with his sword. The time to dispatch him with a pneuma had passed. All Gentle had space to do was seize the door handle and slam the cell closed. The key was in the lock, and he turned it as N'ashap's bulk slammed against the other side.

Huzzah was running now, her pursuer between the second guard and his target. Tossing the gun to Pie, Gentle went to snatch Huzzah up before the Oethac took her. She was in his arms with a stride to spare, and he flung them both aside to give Pie a clear line of fire. The pursuing Oethac realized his jeopardy and went for his own weapon. Gentle looked around at Pie.

"Kill the fuckers!" he yelled, but the mystif was staring at the gun in its hand as though it had found shite there.

"Pie! For Christ's sake! Kill them!"

Now the mystif raised the gun, but still it seemed incapable of pulling the trigger.

"*Do it!*" Gentle yelled.

The mystif shook its head, however, and would have lost them all their lives had two clean shots not struck the back of the guards' necks, dropping them both to the ground.

"*Papa!*" Huzzah said.

It was indeed the sergeant, with Scopique in tow, who emerged through the smoke. His eyes weren't on his daughter, whom he'd just saved from death. They were on the soldiers he'd dispatched to do so. He looked traumatized by the deed. Even when Huzzah went to him, sobbing with relief and fear, he barely noticed her. It wasn't until Gentle shook him from his daze of guilt, saying they should get going while they had half a chance, that he spoke.

"They were my men," he said.

"And this is your daughter," Gentle replied. "You made the right choice."

N'ashap was still battering at the cell door, yelling for help. It could only be moments before he got it.

"What's the quickest way out?" Gentle asked Scopique.

"I want to let the others out first," Scopique replied. "Father Athanasius, Izaak, Squalling—"

"There's no time," Gentle said. "Tell him, Pie! We have to go now or not at all. Pie? Are you with us?"

"Yes. . . ."

"Then stop dreaming and let's get going."

Still protesting that they couldn't leave the rest under lock and key, Scopique led the quintet up by a back way into the night air. They came out not onto the parapet but onto bare rock.

"Which way now?" Gentle asked.

There was already a proliferation of shouts from below. N'ashap had doubtless been liberated and would be ordering a full alert.

"We have to head for the nearest landfall."

"That's the peninsula," Scopique said, redirecting Gentle's gaze across the Cradle towards an arm of low-lying land that was barely discernible in the murk of the night.

That murk was their best ally now. If they moved fast enough it would cloak them before their pursuers even knew which direction they'd headed in. There was a beetling pathway down the island's face to the shore, and Gentle led the way, aware that every one of the four who were following was a liability: Huzzah a child, her father still racked by guilt, Scopique casting backwards glances, and Pie still dazed by the bloodshed. This last was odd in a creature he'd first encountered in the guise of assassin, but then this journey had changed them both.

As they reached the shore, Scopique said, "I'm sorry. I can't go. You all head on. I'm going to try and get back in and let the others out."

Gentle didn't attempt to persuade him otherwise. "If that's what you want to do, good luck," he said. "We have to go."

"Of course you do! Pie, I'm sorry, my friend, but I couldn't live with myself if I turned my back on the others. We've suffered too long together." He took the mystif's hand. "Before you say it, I'll stay alive. I know my duty, and I'll be ready when the time comes."

"I know you will," the mystif replied, drawing the handshake into an embrace.

"It will be soon," Scopique said.

"Sooner than I'd wish," Pie replied; then, leaving Scopique to head back up the cliff face, the mystif joined Gentle, Huzzah, and Aping, who were already ten yards from the shore.

The exchange between Pie and Scopique—with its intimation of a shared agenda hitherto kept secret—had not gone unnoted by Gentle; nor would it go unquestioned. But this was not the time. They had at least half a dozen miles to travel before they reached the peninsula, and there was already a swell of noise from behind them, signaling pursuit. Torch beams raked the shore as the first of N'ashap's troops emerged to give chase, and from within the walls of the asylum rose the din of the prisoners, finally giving voice to their rage. That, like the murk, might confound the hounds, but not for long.

The torches had found Scopique, and the beams now scanned the shore he'd been ascending from, each sweep wider than the one that preceded it. Aping was carrying Huzzah, which speeded their progress somewhat, and Gentle was just beginning to think that they might stand a chance of survival when one of the torches caught them. It was weak at such a distance, but strong enough that its light picked them out. Gunfire followed immediately. They were difficult targets, however, and the bullets went well wide.

"They'll catch us now," Aping gasped. "We should surrender." He set his daughter down and threw his gun to the ground, turning to spit his accusations in Gentle's face. "Why did I ever listen to you? I was *crazy.*"

"If we stay here they'll shoot us on the spot," Gentle replied. "Huzzah as well. Do you want that?"

"They won't shoot us," he said, taking hold of Huzzah with one hand and raising the other to catch the beams. "Don't shoot!" he yelled. "Don't shoot! Captain? Captain! Sir! We surrender!"

"Fuck this," Gentle said, and reached to haul Huzzah from her father's grip.

She went into Gentle's arms readily, but Aping wasn't about to relinquish her so easily. He turned to snatch her back, and as he did so a bullet struck the ice at their feet. He let Huzzah go and turned to attempt a second appeal. Two shots cut him short, the first striking his leg, the second his chest. Huzzah let out a shriek and wrenched herself from Gentle's hold, dropping to the ground at her father's head.

The seconds they'd lost in Aping's surrender and death were the difference between the slimmest hope of escape and none. Any one of the twenty or so troops advancing upon them now could pick them off at this distance. Even N'ashap, who was leading the group, his walk still unsteady, could scarcely have failed to bring them down.

"What now?" said Pie.

"We have to stand our ground," Gentle replied. "We've got no choice."

That very ground, however, was no steadier than N'ashap's walk. Though this Dominion's suns were in another hemisphere and there was only midnight from horizon to horizon, a tremor was moving through the frozen sea that both Pie and Gentle recognized from almost fatal experience. Huzzah felt it too. She raised her head, her sobs quieting.

"The Lady," she murmured.

"What about her?" said Gentle.

"She's near us."

Gentle put out his hand, and Huzzah took it. As she got up she scanned the ground. So did he. His heart had started to pound furiously, as the memories of the Cradle's liquification flooded back.

"Can you stop her?" he murmured to Huzzah.

"She's not come for us," the girl said, and her gaze went from the still solid ground beneath their feet to the group that N'ashap was still leading in their direction.

"Oh, Goddess . . ." Gentle said.

A cry of alarm was rising from the middle of the approaching pack. One of the torch beams went wild, then another, and another, as one by one the soldiers realized their jeopardy. N'ashap let out a shout himself: a demand for order among his troops that went unobeyed. It was difficult to see precisely what was going on, but Gentle could imagine it well enough. The ground was softening, and the Cradle's silver waters were bubbling up around their feet. One of the men fired into the air as the sea's shell broke beneath him; another two or three started back towards the island, only to find their panic excited a quicker dissolution. They went down as if snatched by sharks, silver spume fountaining where they'd stood. N'ashap was still attempting to preserve some measure of command, but it was a lost cause. Realizing this, he began to fire towards the trio, but with the ground rocking beneath him, and the beams no longer trained on his targets, he was virtually shooting blind.

"We should get out of here," Gentle said, but Huzzah had better advice.

"She won't hurt us if we're not afraid," she said.

Gentle was half tempted to reply that he was indeed afraid, but he kept his silence and his place, despite the fact that the evidence of his eyes suggested the Goddess had no patience with dividing the bad from the misguided or the unrepentant from the prayerful. All but four of their pursuers—N'ashap numbered among them—had already been claimed by the sea, some gone beneath the tide entirely, others still struggling to reach some solid place. Gentle saw one man scrambling up out of the water, only to have the ground he was crawling upon liquify beneath him with such speed the Cradle had closed over him before he had time to scream. Another went down shouting at the water that was bubbling up around him, the last sight of him his gun, held high and still firing.

All the torch carriers had succumbed now, and the only illumination was from the cliff top, where soldiers who'd had the luck to be left behind were training their beams on the massacre, throwing into silhouette the figures of N'ashap and the other three survivors, one of whom was making an attempt to race towards the solid ground where Gentle, Pie, and Huzzah stood. His panic undid him. He'd only run five strides when silvery foam bubbled up in front of him. He turned to retrace his steps, but the route had already gone to seething silver. In desperation he flung away his weapons and attempted to leap to safety, but fell short and went from sight in an instant.

One of the remaining trio, an Oethac, had fallen to his knees to pray, which merely brought him closer to his executioner, who drew him down in the throes of his imprecation, giving him time only to snatch at his comrade's leg and pull him down at the same time. The place where they'd vanished did not cease to seethe but redoubled its fury now. N'ashap, the last alive, turned to face it, and as he did so the sea rose up like a fountain, until it was half his height again.

"Lady," Huzzah said.

It was. Carved in water, a breasted body, and a face dancing with glints and glimmers: the Goddess, or her image, made of her native stuff, then gone the same instant as it broke and dropped upon N'ashap. He was borne down so quickly, and the Cradle left rocking so placidly the instant after, it was as though his mother had never made him.

Slowly, Huzzah turned to Gentle. Though her father was dead at her feet, she was smiling in the gloom, the first open smile Gentle had seen on her face.

"The Cradle Lady came," she said.

They waited awhile, but there were no further visitations. What the Goddess had done—whether it was to save the child, as Huzzah would always believe, or because circumstance had put within her reach the forces that had tainted Her Cradle with their cruelty—She had done with an economy She wasn't about to spoil with gloating or sentiment. She closed the sea with the same efficiency She'd employed to open it, leaving the place unmarked.

There was no further attempt at pursuit from the guards left on the cliff, though they kept their places, torches piercing the murk.

"We've got a lot of sea to cross before dawn," Pie said. "We don't want the suns coming up before we reach the peninsula."

Huzzah took Gentle's hand. "Did Papa ever tell you where we're going in Yzordderrex?"

"No," he said. "But we'll find the house."

She didn't look back at her father's body, but fixed her eyes on the gray bulk of the distant headland and went without complaint, sometimes smiling to herself, as she remembered that the night had brought her a glimpse of a parent that would never again desert her.

29

I

The territory that lay between the shores of the Cradle and the limits of the Third Dominion had been, until the Autarch's intervention, the site of a natural wonder universally held to mark the center of the Imajica: a column of perfectly hewn and polished rock to which as many names and powers had been ascribed as there were shamans, poets, and storytellers to be moved by it. There was no community within the Reconciled Dominions that had not enshrined it in their mythology and found an epithet to mark it as their own. But its truest name was also perhaps its plainest: the Pivot. Controversy had raged for centuries about whether the Unbeheld had set it down in the smoky wastes of the Kwem to mark the midpoint between the perimeters of the Imajica, or whether a forest of such columns had once stood in the area, and some later hand (moved, perhaps, by Hapexamendios' wisdom) had leveled all but this one.

Whatever the arguments about its origins, however, nobody had ever contested the power that it had accrued standing at the center of the Dominions. Lines of thought had passed across the Kwem for centuries, carrying a freight of force which the Pivot had drawn to itself with a magnetism that was virtually irresistible. By the time the Autarch came into the Third Dominion, having already established his particular brand of dictatorship in Yzordderrex, the Pivot was the single most powerful object in the Imajica. He laid his plans for it brilliantly, returning to the palace he was still building in Yzordderrex and adding several features, though their purpose did not become apparent until almost two years later, when, acting with the kind of speed that usually attends a coup, he had the Pivot toppled, transported, and set in a tower in his palace before the blood of those who might have raised objections to this sacrilege was dry.

Overnight, the geography of the Imajica was transformed. Yzordderrex became the heart of the Dominions. Thereafter, there would be no power, either secular or sacred, that did not originate in that city; there would be no crossroads sign in any of the Reconciled Dominions that did not carry its name, nor any highway that did not have upon it somewhere a petitioner or penitent who'd turned his eyes towards Yzordderrex in hope of salvation. Prayers were still uttered in the name of the Unbeheld, and blessings murmured in the forbidden names of the Goddesses, but Yzordderrex was the true Lord now, the Autarch its mind and the Pivot its phallus.

One hundred and seventy-nine years had passed since the day the Kwem had lost its great wonder, but the Autarch still made pilgrimages into the wastes when he felt the need for solitude. Some years after the removal of the Pivot he'd had a small palace built close to the place where it had stood, spartan by comparison with the architectural excesses of the folly that crowned Yzordderrex. This was his retreat in confounding times, where he could meditate upon the sorrows of absolute power, leaving his Military High Command, the generals who ruled the Dominions on his behalf, to do so under the eye of his once-beloved Queen, Quaisoir. Lately she had developed a taste for repression that was waning in him, and he'd several times thought of retiring to the palace in the Kwem permanently and leaving her to rule in his stead, given that she took so much more pleasure from it than he. But such dreams were an indulgence, and he knew it. Though he ruled the Imajica invisibly—not one soul, outside the circle of twenty or so who dealt with him daily, would have known him from any other white man with good taste in clothes—his vision had shaped the rise of Yzordderrex, and no other would ever competently replace it.

On days like this, however, with the cold air off the Lenten Way whining in the spires of the Kwem Palace, he wished he could send the mirror he met in the morning back to Yzordderrex in his place and let his reflection rule. Then he could stay here and think about the distant past: England in midsummer. The streets of London bright with rain when he woke, the fields outside the city peaceful and buzzing with bees. Scenes he pictured longingly when he was in elegiac mood. Such moods seldom lasted long, however. He was too much of a realist, and he demanded truth from his memory. Yes, there had been rain, but it had come with such venom it had bruised every fruit it hadn't beaten from the bough. And the hush of those fields had been a battlefield's hush, the murmur not trees but flies, come to find laying places.

His life had begun that summer, and his early days had been filled with signs not of love and fruitfulness but of Apocalypse. There wasn't a preacher in the park who didn't have Revelation by heart that year, nor a whore in Drury Lane who wouldn't have told you she'd seen the Devil dancing on the midnight roofs. How could those days not have influenced him: filled him with a horror of imminent destruction, given him an appetite for order, for law, for Empire? He was a child of his times, and if they'd made him cruel in his pursuit of system, was that *his* fault or that of the *age*?

The tragedy lay not in the suffering that was an inevitable consequence of any social movement, but in the fact that his achievements were now in jeopardy from forces that—if they won the
day—would return the Imajica to the chaos from which he had
brought it, undoing his work in a fraction of the time it had taken
for it to be achieved. If he was to suppress these subversive elements he had a limited number of options, and after the events in
Patashoqua, and the uncovering of plots against him, he had retreated to the quiet of the Kwem Palace to decide between them.
He could continue to treat the rebellions, strikes, and uprisings as
minor irritations, limiting his reprisals to small but eloquent acts
of suppression, such as the burning of the village of Beatrix and
the trials and executions at Vanaeph. This route had two significant disadvantages. The most recent attempt upon his life, though
still inept, was too close for comfort, and until every last radical and
revolutionary had been silenced or dissuaded, he would be in danger. Furthermore, when his whole reign had been dotted with
episodes that had required some measured brutalities, would this
new spate of purges and suppressions make any significant mark?
Perhaps it was time for a more ambitious vision: cities put under
martial law, tetrarchs imprisoned so that their corruptions could
be exposed in the name of a just Yzordderrex, governments toppled, and resistance met with the full might of the Second Dominion's armies. Maybe Patashoqua would have to burn the way
Beatrix had. Or L'Himby and its wretched temples.

If such a route were followed successfully, the slate would be
wiped clean. If not—if his advisers had underestimated the scale
of unrest or the quality of leaders among the rabble—he might find
the circle closing and the Apocalypse into which he'd been born
that faraway summer coming around again, here in the heart of his
promised land.

What then, if Yzordderrex burned instead of Patashoqua?
Where would he go for comfort? Back to England, perhaps? Did
the house in Clerkenwell still stand, he wondered, and if so were
its rooms still sacred to the workings of desire, or had the Maestro's
undoing scoured them to the last board and nail? The questions
tantalized him. As he sat and pondered them he found a curiosity
in his core—no, more than curiosity, an appetite—to discover what
the Unreconciled Dominion was like almost two centuries after his
creation.

His musings were interrupted by Rosengarten, a name he'd be-
queathed to the man in the spirit of irony, for a more infertile
thing never walked. Piebald from a disease caught in the swamps
of Loquiot in the throes of which he had unmanned himself,
Rosengarten lived for duty. Among the generals, he was the only

one who didn't sin with some excess against the austerity of these rooms. He spoke and moved quietly; he didn't stink of perfumes; he never drank; he never ate kreauchee. He was a perfect emptiness, and the only man the Autarch completely trusted.

He had come with news and told it plainly. The asylum on the Cradle of Chzercemit had been the scene of a rebellion. Almost all the garrison had been killed, under circumstances which were still under investigation, and the bulk of the prisoners had escaped, led by an individual called Scopique.

"How many were there?" the Autarch asked.

"I have a list, sir," Rosengarten replied, opening the file he'd brought with him. "There are fifty-one individuals unaccounted for, most of them religious dissidents."

"Women?"

"None."

"We should have had them executed, not locked them away."

"Several of them would have welcomed martyrdom, sir. The decision to incarcerate them was taken with that in mind."

"So now they'll return to their flocks and preach revolution all over again. This we must stop. How many of them were active in Yzordderrex?"

"Nine. Including Father Athanasius."

"Athanasius? Who was he?"

"The Dearther who claimed he was the Christos. He had a congregation near the harbor."

"Then that's where he'll return, presumably."

"It seems likely."

"All of them'll go back to their flocks, sooner or later. We must be ready for them. No arrests. No trials. Just have them quietly dispatched."

"Yes, sir."

"I don't want Quaisoir informed of this."

"I think she already knows, sir."

"Then she must be prevented from anything showy."

"I understand."

"Let's do this discreetly."

"There *is* something else, sir."

"What's that?"

"There were two other individuals on the island before the rebellion—"

"What about them?"

"It's difficult to know exactly what to make of the report. One of them appears to have been a mystif. The description of the other may be of interest."

He passed the report to the Autarch, who scanned it quickly at first, then more intently.

"How reliable is this?" he asked Rosengarten.

"At this juncture I don't know. The descriptions were corroborated, but I haven't interrogated the men personally."

"Do so."

"Yes, sir."

He handed the report back to Rosengarten. "How many people have seen this?"

"I had all other copies destroyed as soon as I read it. I believe only the interrogating officers, their commander, and myself have been party to this information."

"I want every one of the survivors from the garrison silenced. Court-martial them all and throw away the key. The officers and the commander must be instructed that they will be held accountable for any leakage of this information, from any source. Such leakage to be punishable by death."

"Yes, sir."

"As for the mystif and the stranger, we must assume they're making way to the Second Dominion. First Beatrix, now the Cradle. Their destination must be Yzordderrex. How many days since this uprising?"

"Eleven, sir."

"Then they'll be in Yzordderrex in a matter of days, even if they're traveling on foot. Track them. I'd like to know as much about them as I can."

He looked out the window at the wastes of the Kwem.

"They probably took the Lenten Way. Probably passed within a few miles of here." There was a subtle agitation in his voice. "That's twice now our paths have come close to crossing. And now the witnesses, describing him so well. What does it mean, Rosengarten? What does it mean?"

When the commander had no answers, as now, he kept his silence: an admirable trait.

"I don't know either," the Autarch said. "Perhaps I should go out and take the air. I feel old today."

The hole from which the Pivot had been uprooted was still visible, though the driving winds of the region had almost healed the scar. Standing on the lips of the hole was a fine place to meditate on absence, the Autarch had discovered. He tried to do so now, his face swathed in silk to keep the stinging gust from his mouth and nostrils, his long fur coat closely buttoned, and his gloved hands driven into his pockets. But the calm he'd always derived from such meditations escaped him now. Absence was a fine discipline for the spirit when the world's bounty was a step away, and boundless. Not so now. Now it reminded him of an emptiness that he both feared and feared to be filled, like the haunted place at the shoulder of a twin who'd lost its other in the womb. However high he built his fortress walls, however tightly he sealed his soul, there was one who would always have access, and that thought brought palpitations. This other knew him as well as he knew himself: his frailties, his desires, his highest ambition. Their business together—most of it bloody—had remained unrevealed and unrevenged for two centuries, but he had never persuaded himself that it would remain so forever. It would be finished at last, and soon.

Though the cold could not reach his flesh through his coat, the Autarch shuddered at the prospect. He had lived for so long like a man who walks perpetually in the noonday sun, his shadow falling neither in front of him nor behind. Prophets could not predict him, nor accusers catch his crimes. He was inviolate. But that would change now. When he and his shadow met—as they inevitably would—the weight of a thousand prophecies and accusations would fall upon them both.

He pulled the silk from his face and let the eroding wind assault him. There was no purpose in staying here any longer. By the time the wind had remade his features he would have lost Yzordderrex, and even though that seemed like a small forfeit now, in the space of hours it might be the only prize he'd be able to preserve from destruction.

2

If the divine engineers who had raised the Jokalaylau had one night set their most ambitious peak between a desert and an ocean, and returned the next night and for a century of nights thereafter to carve its steeps and sheers from foothills to clouded heights with lowly habitations and magnificent plazas, with streets, bastions, and pavilions—and if, having carved, they had set in the core of that mountain a fire that smoldered but never burned—then their handiwork, when filled to overflowing with every manner of life, might have deserved comparison with Yzordderrex. But given that no such masterwork had ever been devised, the city stood without parallel throughout the Imajica.

The travelers' first sight of it came as they crossed the causeway that skipped like a well-aimed stone across the delta of the River Noy, rushing in twelve white torrents to meet the sea. It was early morning when they arrived, the fog off the river conspiring with the uneasy light of dawn to keep the city from sight until they were so close to it that when the fog was snatched the sky was barely visible, the desert and the sea no more than marginal, and all the world was suddenly Yzordderrex.

As they'd walked the Lenten Way, passing from the Third Dominion into the Second, Huzzah had recited all she'd read about the city from her father's books. One of the writers had described Yzordderrex as a god, she reported, a notion Gentle had thought ludicrous until he set eyes upon it. Then he understood what the urban theologian had been about, deifying this termite hill. Yzordderrex was worthy of worship; and millions were daily performing the ultimate act of veneration, living on or within the body of their Lord. Their dwellings clung like a million panicked climbers to the cliffs above the harbor and teetered on the plateaus that rose, tier on tier, towards the summit, many so crammed with houses that those closest to the edge had to be buttressed from below, the buttresses in turn encrusted with nests of life, winged, perhaps, or else suicidal. Everywhere, the mountain teemed, its streets of steps, lethally precipitous, leading the eye from one brimming shelf to another: from leafless boulevards lined with fine mansions to gates that let onto shadowy arcades, then up to the city's six summits, on the highest of which stood the palace of the Autarch of the Imajica. There was an abundance of a different order here, for the palace had more domes and towers than Rome, their obsessive elaboration visible even at this distance. Rising above them all was the Pivot Tower, as plain as its fellows were baroque. And high above that again, hanging in the white sky above the city, the comet that brought the Dominion's long days and languid dusks: Yzordderrex's star, called Giess, the Witherer.

They stood for only a minute or so to admire the sight. The daily traffic of workers who, having found no place of residence on the back or in the bowels of the city, commuted in and out daily, had begun, and by the time the newcomers reached the other end of the causeway they were lost in a dusty throng of vehicles, bicycles, rickshaws, and pedestrians all making their way into Yzordderrex. Three among tens of thousands: a scrawny young girl wearing a wide smile; a white man, perhaps once handsome but sickly now, his pale face half lost behind a ragged brown beard; and a Eurhetemec mystif, its eyes, like so many of its breed, barely concealing a private grief. The crowd bore them forward, and they went unresisting where countless multitudes had gone before: into the belly of the city-god Yzordderrex.

30

I

When Dowd brought Judith back to Godolphin's house after the murder of Clara Leash, it was not as a free agent but as a prisoner. She was confined to the bedroom she'd first occupied, and there she waited for Oscar's return. When he came in to see her it was after a half-hour conversation with Dowd (she heard the murmur of their exchange, but not its substance), and he told her as soon as he appeared that he had no wish to debate what had happened. She'd acted against his best interests, which were finally—did she not realize this yet?—against her own too, and he would need time to think about the consequences for them both.

"I trusted you," he said, "more than I've ever trusted any woman in my life. You betrayed me, exactly the way Dowd predicted you would. I feel foolish, and I feel hurt."

"Let me explain," she said.

He raised his hands to hush her. "I don't want to hear," he said. "Maybe in a few days we'll talk, but not now."

Her sense of loss at his retreat was almost overwhelmed by the anger she felt at his dismissal of her. Did he believe her feelings for him were so trivial she'd not concerned herself with the consequences of her actions on them both? Or worse: had Dowd convinced him that she'd been planning to betray him from the outset, and she'd calculated everything—the seduction, the confessions of devotion—in order to weaken him? This latter scenario was the likelier of the two, but it didn't clear Oscar of guilt. He had still failed to give her a chance to justify herself.

She didn't see him for three days. Her food was served in her room by Dowd, and there she waited, hearing Oscar come and go, and on occasion hints of conversation on the stairs, enough to gather the impression that the Tabula Rasa's purge was reaching a critical point. More than once she contemplated the possibility that what she'd been up to with Clara Leash made her a potential victim, and that day by day Dowd was eroding Oscar's reluctance to dispatch her. Paranoia, perhaps; but if he had any scrap of feeling for her why didn't he come and see her? Didn't he pine, the way she did? Didn't he want her in his bed, for the animal comfort of it if nothing else? Several times she asked Dowd to tell Oscar she needed to speak with him, and Dowd—who affected the detachment of a jailer with a thousand other such prisoners to deal with daily—had said he'd do his best, but he doubted that Mr. Godolphin would want to have any dealings with her. Whether the message was communicated or not, Oscar left her solitary in her confinement, and she realized that unless she took more forcible action she might never see daylight again.

Her escape plan was simple. She forced the lock on her bedroom door with a knife unreturned after one of her meals—it wasn't the lock that kept her from straying, it was Dowd's warning that the mites which had murdered Clara were ready to claim her if she attempted to leave—and slipped out onto the landing. She'd deliberately waited until Oscar was home before she made the attempt, believing, perhaps naïvely, that despite his withdrawal of affection he'd protect her from Dowd if her life was threatened. She was sorely tempted to seek him out there and then. But perhaps it would be easier to treat with him when she was away from the house and felt more like a mistress of her own destiny. If, once she was safely away from the house, he chose to have no further contact with her, then her fear that Dowd had soured his feelings towards her permanently would be confirmed, and she would have to look for another way to get to Yzordderrex.

She made her way down the stairs with the utmost caution and, hearing voices at the front of the house, decided to make her exit through the kitchen. The lights were burning everywhere, as usual. The kitchen was deserted. She crossed quickly to the door, which was bolted top and bottom, crouching to slide the lower bolt aside.

As she stood up Dowd said, "You won't get out that way."

She turned to see him standing at the kitchen table, bearing a tray of supper dishes. His laden condition gave her hope that she might yet outmaneuver him, and she made a dash for the hallway. But he was faster than she'd anticipated, setting down his burden and moving to stop her so quickly she had to retreat again, her hand catching one of the glasses on the table. It fell, smashing musically.

"Now look what you've done," he said, with what seemed to be genuine distress. He crossed to the shards and bent down to gather them up. "That glass had been in the family for generations. I'd have thought you'd have had some fellow feeling for it."

Though she was in no temper to talk about broken glasses, she replied nevertheless, knowing her only hope lay in alerting Godolphin to her presence.

"Why should I give a damn about a glass?" she said.

Dowd picked up a piece of the bowl, holding it to the light.

"You've got so much in common, lovey," he said. "Both made in ignorance of yourselves. Beautiful, but fragile." He stood up.

"You've *always* been beautiful. Fashions come and go, but Judith is always beautiful."

"You don't know a damn thing about me," she said.

He put the shards on the table beside the rest of the dirty plates and cutlery. "Oh, but I do," he said. "We're more alike than you realize."

He'd kept a glittering fragment back, and as he spoke he put it to his wrist. She only just had time to register what he was about to do before he cut into his own flesh. She looked away, but then—hearing the piece of glass dropped among the litter—glanced back. The wound gaped, but there was no blood forthcoming, just an ooze of brackish sap. Nor was the expression on Dowd's face pained. It was simply intent.

"You have a piffling recall of the past," he said; "I have too much. You have heat; I have none. You're in love; I've never understood the word. But Judith: *we are the same.* Both slaves."

She looked from his face to the cut to his face to the cut to his face, and with every move of her pupils her panic increased. She didn't want to hear any more from him. She despised him. She closed her eyes and conjured him at the voider's pyre, and in the shadow of the tower, crawling with mites, but however many horrors she put between them his words won through. She'd given up attempting to solve the puzzle of herself a long time ago, but here he was, spilling pieces she couldn't help but pick up.

"Who are you?" she said to him.

"More to the point, who are you?"

"We're not the same," she said. "Not even a little. I bleed. You don't. I'm human. You're not."

"But is it *your* blood you bleed?" he said. "Ask yourself that."

"It comes out of my veins. Of course it's mine."

"Then who are you?" he said.

The inquiry was made without overt malice, but she didn't doubt its subversive purpose. Somehow Dowd knew she was forgetful of her past and was pricking her to a confession.

"I know what I'm *not,"* she said, earning herself the time to invent an answer. "I'm not a glass. I'm not fragile or ignorant. And I'm not—"

What was the other quality he'd mentioned besides beauty and fragility? He'd been stopping to pick up the pieces of broken glass, and he described her some way or other.

"You're not what?" he said, watching her wrestle with her own reluctance to seize the memory.

She pictured him crossing the kitchen. Now look what you've done, he'd said. Then he'd stooped (she saw him do so, in her mind's eye) and as he'd begun to pick up the pieces, the words had come to his lips. And now to her memory too.

"That glass had been in the family for generations," he'd said. "I'd have thought you'd have had some fellow feeling for it."

"No," she said aloud, shaking her head to keep the sense of this from congealing there. But the motion only shook up other memories: of her trip to the estate with Charlie, when that pleasurable sense of belonging had suffused her and voices had called her sweet names from the past; of meeting Oscar on the threshold of the Retreat and knowing instantly she belonged at his side, without question, or care to question; of the portrait above Oscar's bed, gazing down on the bed with such a possessive stare he had turned off the light before they made love.

As these thoughts came, the shaking of her head grew wilder, the motion possessing her like a fit. Tears spat from her eyes. Her hands went out for help even as the power to request it went from her throat. Through a blur of motion she was just able to see Dowd standing beside the table, his hand covering his wounded wrist, watching her impassively. She turned from him, terrified that she'd choke on her tongue or break her head open if she fell, and knowing he'd do nothing to help her. She wanted to cry out for Oscar, but all that came was a wretched gargling sound. She stumbled forward, her head still thrashing, and as she did so saw Oscar in the hallway, coming towards her. She pitched her arms in his direction and felt his hands upon her, to pull her up out of her collapse. He failed.

2

He was beside her when she woke. She wasn't lying in the narrow bed she'd been consigned to for the last few nights but in the wide four-poster in Oscar's room, the bed she'd come to think of as theirs. It wasn't, of course. Its true owner was the man whose image in oils had come back to her in the throes of her fit: the Mad Lord Godolphin, hanging above the pillows on which she lay and sitting beside her in a later variation, caressing her hand and telling her how much he loved her. As soon as she came to consciousness and felt his touch, she withdrew from it.

"I'm . . . not a pet," she struggled to say. "You can't just . . . stroke me when . . . it suits you."

He looked appalled. "I apologize unconditionally," he said in his gravest manner. "I have no excuse. I let the Society's business take precedence over understanding you and caring for you. That was unforgivable. Then Dowd, of course, whispering in my ear . . . Was he very cruel?"

"You're the one who's been cruel."

"I've done nothing intentionally. Please believe that, at least."

"You've lied to me over and over again," she said, struggling to sit up in bed. "You know things about me that I don't. Why didn't you share them with me? I'm not a child."

"You've just had a fit," Oscar said. "Have you ever had a fit before?"

"No."

"Some things are better left alone, you see."

"Too late," she said. "I've had my fit, and I survived it. I'm ready to hear the secret, whatever it is." She glanced up at Joshua. "It's something to do with him, isn't it? He's got a hold on you."

"Not on me—"

"You liar! You liar!" she said, throwing the sheets aside and getting onto her knees, so that she was face to face with the deceiver. "Why do you tell me you love me one moment and lie to me the next? Why don't you trust me?"

"I've told you more than I've ever told anybody. But then I find you've plotted against the Society."

"I've done more than plot," she said, thinking of her journey into the cellars of the tower.

Once again, she teetered on the edge of telling him what she'd seen, but Clara's advice was there to keep her from falling. *You can't save Celestine and keep his affections,* she'd said, *you're digging at the foundations of his family and his faith.* It was true. She understood that more clearly than ever. And if she told him all she knew, pleasurable as that unburdening would be, could she be absolutely certain that he wouldn't cleave to his history, at the last, and use what he knew against her? What would Clara's death and Celestine's suffering have been worth then? She was now their only agent in the living world, and she had no right to gamble with their sacrifices.

"What have you done," Oscar said, "besides plot? What have you done?"

"You haven't been honest with me," she replied. "Why should I tell you anything?"

"Because I can still take you to Yzordderrex," he said.

"Bribes now?"

"Don't you want to go any longer?"

"I want to know the truth about myself more."

He looked faintly saddened by this. "Ah." He sighed. "I've been lying for so long I'm not sure I'd know the truth if I tripped over it. Except . . ."

"Yes?"

"What we felt for each other," he murmured, "at least, what I feel for you . . . that was *true,* wasn't it?"

"It can't be much," Jude said. "You locked me away. You left me to Dowd—"

"I've already explained—"

"Yes, you were distracted. You had other business. So you forgot me."

"No," he protested, "I never forgot. Never, I swear."

"What then?"

"I was afraid."

"Of me?"

"Of everything. You, Dowd, the Society. I started to see plots everywhere. Suddenly the idea of your being in my bed seemed too much of a risk. I was afraid you'd smother me, or—"

"That's ridiculous."

"Is it? How can I be sure who you belong to?"

"I belong to myself."

He shook his head, his gaze going from her face up to the painting of Joshua Godolphin that hung above the bed.

"How can you know that?" he said. "How can you be certain that what you feel for me comes from your heart?"

"What does it matter where it comes from? It's there. Look at me."

He refused her demand, his eyes still fixed on the Mad Lord.

"He's dead," she said.

"But his legacy—"

"Fuck his legacy!" she said, and suddenly got to her feet, taking hold of the portrait by its heavy, gilded frame and wrenching it from the wall.

Oscar rose to protest, but her vehemence carried the day. The picture came from its hooks with a single pull, and she summarily pitched it across the room. Then she dropped back onto the bed in front of Oscar.

"He's dead and gone," she said. "He can't judge us. He can't control us. Whatever it is we feel for each other—and I don't pretend to know what it is—it's *ours.*" She put her hands to his face, her fingers woven with his beard. "Let go of the fears," she said. "Take hold of me instead."

He put his arms around her.

"You're going to take me to Yzordderrex, Oscar. Not in a week's time, not in a few days: tomorrow. I want to go tomorrow. Or else"—her hands dropped from his face— "let me go now. Out of here. Out of your life. I won't be your prisoner, Oscar. Maybe *his* mistresses put up with that, but I won't. I'll kill myself before I'll let you lock me up again."

She said all of this dry-eyed. Simple sentiments, simply put. He took hold of her hands and raised them to his cheeks again, as if inviting her to possess him. His face was full of tiny creases she'd not seen before, and they were wet with tears.

"We'll go," he said.

3

There was a balmy rain falling as they left London the next day, but by the time they'd reached the estate the sun was breaking through, and the parkland gleamed around them as they entered. They didn't make any detours to the house but headed straight to the copse that concealed the Retreat. There was a breeze in the branches, and they flickered with light leaves. The smell of life was everywhere, stirring her blood for the journey ahead.

Oscar had advised her to dress with an eye to practicality and warmth. The city, he said, was subject to rapid and radical shifts in temperature, depending on the direction of the wind. If it came off the desert, the heat in the streets could bake the flesh like unleavened bread. And if it swung and came off the ocean, it brought marrow-chilling fogs and sudden frosts. None of this daunted her, of course. She was ready for this adventure as for no other in her life.

"I know I've gone on endlessly about how dangerous the city's become," Oscar said as they ducked beneath the low-slung branches, "and you're tired of hearing about it, but this isn't a civilized city, Judith. About the only man I trust there is Peccable. If for any reason we were to be separated—or if anything were to happen to me—you can rely upon him for help."

"I understand."

Oscar stopped to admire the pretty scene ahead, dappled sunlight falling on the pale walls and dome of the Retreat. "You know, I used only to come here at night," he said. "I thought that was the sacred time, when magic had the strongest hold. But it's not true. Midnight Mass and moonlight is fine, but miracles are here at noon as well; just as strong, just as strange."

He looked up at the canopy of trees.

"Sometimes you have to go away from the world to see the world," he said. "I went to Yzordderrex a few years back and stayed—oh, I don't know, two months, maybe two and a half, and when I came back to the Fifth I saw it like a child. I swear, like a child. This trip won't just show you other Dominions. If we get back safe and sound—"

"We will."

"Such faith. If we do, this world will be different, too. Everything changes after this, because you'll be changed."

"So be it," she said.

She took hold of his hand, and they started towards the Retreat. Something made her uneasy, however. Not his words—his talk of change had only excited her—but the hush between them, perhaps, which was suddenly deep.

"Is there something wrong?" he said, feeling her grip tighten.

"The silence. . . ."

"There's always an odd atmosphere here. I've felt it before. A lot of fine souls died here, of course."

"At the Reconciliation?"

"You know about that, do you?"

"From Clara. It was two hundred years ago this midsummer, she said. Perhaps the spirits are coming back to see if someone's going to try again."

He stopped, tugging on her arm. "Don't talk about it, even in jest. Please. There'll be no Reconciliation, this summer or any other. The Maestros are dead. The whole thing's—"

"All right," she said. "Calm down. I won't mention it again."

"After this summer it'll be academic anyway," he said, with a feigned lightness, "at least for another couple of centuries. I'll be dead and buried long before this hoopla starts again. I've got my plot, you know? I chose it with Peccable. It's on the edge of the desert, with a fine view of Yzordderrex."

His nervous babble concealed the quiet until they reached the door; then he let it drop. She was glad he was silent. The place deserved reverence. Standing at the step, it wasn't difficult to believe phantoms gathered here, the dead of centuries past mingling with those she'd last seen living on this very spot: Charlie for one, of course, coaxing her inside, telling her with a smile that the place was nothing special, just stone; and the voiders too, one burned, one skinned, both haunting the threshold.

"Unless you see any just impediment," Oscar said, "I think we should do this."

He led her inside, to the middle of the mosaic.

"When the time comes," he said. "We have to hold on to each other. Even if you think there's nothing to hold on to, there is; it's just changed for a time. I don't want to lose you between here and there. The In Ovo's no place to go wandering."

"You won't lose me," she said.

He went down on his haunches and dug into the mosaic, pulling from the pattern a dozen or so pieces of pyramidal stone the size of two fists, which had been so designed as to be virtually invisible when set in their places.

"I don't fully understand the mechanisms that carry us over," he said as he worked. "I'm not sure anybody does completely. But according to Peccable there's a sort of common language into which anybody can be translated. And all the processes of magic involve this translation."

He was laying the stones around the edge of the circle as he spoke, the arrangement seemingly arbitrary.

"Once matter and spirit are in the same language, one can influence the other in any number of ways. Flesh and bone can be transformed, transcended—"

"Or transported?"

"Exactly."

Jude remembered how the removal of a traveler from this world into another looked from the outside: the flesh folding upon itself, the body distorted out of all recognition.

"Does it hurt?" she said.

"At the beginning, but not badly."

"When will it begin?" she said.

He stood up. "It already has," he said.

She felt it, as he spoke: a pressure in her bowels and bladder, a tightness in her chest that made her catch her breath.

"Breathe slowly," he said, putting his palm against her breastbone. "Don't fight it. Just let it happen. There's no harm going to come to you."

She looked down at his hand, then beyond it to the circle that enclosed them, and out through the door of the Retreat to the sunlit grass that lay just a few paces from where she stood. Close as it was, she couldn't return there. The train she'd boarded was gathering speed around her. It was too late for doubts or second thoughts. She was trapped.

"It's all right," she heard Oscar say, but it didn't feel that way at all.

There was a pain in her belly so sharp it felt as though she'd been poisoned, and an ache in her head, and an itch too deep in her skin to be scratched. She looked at Oscar. Was he enduring the same discomforts? If so he was bearing them with remarkable fortitude, smiling at her like an anesthetist.

"It'll be over soon," he was saying. "Just hold on . . . it'll be over soon."

He drew her closer to him, and as he did so she felt a tingling pass through her cells, as though a rainstorm was breaking inside her, sluicing the pain away.

"Better?" he said, the word more shape than sound.

"Yes," she told him and, smiling, put her lips to his, closing her eyes with pleasure as their tongues touched.

The darkness behind her lids was suddenly brightened by gleaming lines, falling like meteors across her mind's eye. She lifted her lids again, but the spectacle came out of her skull, daubing Oscar's face with streaks of brightness. A dozen vivid hues picked out the furrows and creases of his skin; another dozen, the geology of bone beneath; and another, the lineaments of nerves and veins and vessels, to the tiniest detail. Then, as though the mind interpreting them had done with its literal translation and could now rise to poetry, the layered maps of his flesh simplified. Redundancies and repetitions were discarded, the forms that emerged so simple and so absolute that the matter they represented seemed wan by comparison, and receded before them. Seeing this show, she remembered the glyph she'd imagined when she and Oscar had first made love: the spiral and curve of her pleasure laid on the velvet behind her eyes. Here was the same process again, only the mind imagining them was the circle's mind, empowered by the stones and by the travelers' demand for passage.

A motion at the door distracted her gaze momentarily. The air around them was close to dropping its sham of sights altogether, and the scene beyond the circle was blurred. But there was enough color in the suit of the man at the threshold for her to know him even though she couldn't make out his face. Who else but Dowd wore that absurd shade of apricot? She said his name, and though she heard no sound from her throat, Oscar understood her alarm and turned towards the door.

Dowd was approaching the circle at speed, his intention perfectly clear: to hitch a ride to the Second Dominion. She'd seen the gruesome consequences of such interference before, on this very spot, and she braced herself against Oscar for the coming shock. Instead of trusting to the circle to dispatch the hanger-on, however, Oscar turned from her and went to strike Dowd. The circle's flux multiplied his violence tenfold, and the glyph of his body became an illegible scrawl, the colors dirtied in an instant. The pain she'd thought washed away swept back over her. Blood ran from her nose and into her open mouth. Her skin itched so violently she'd have brought blood to that too had the pain in her joints not kept her from moving.

She could make no sense of the scribble in front of her until her glance caught sight of Oscar's face, smeared and raw, screaming back at her as he toppled from the circle. She reached to haul him back, despite the searing pain her motion brought, and took hold of an arm, determined that wherever they were delivered, to Yzordderrex or death, they'd go there together. He returned her grasp, seizing her outstretched arms and dragging himself back onto the Express. As his face emerged from the blur beyond the smile she realized her error. It was Dowd she'd hauled aboard.

She let go of her hold, in revulsion more than rage. His face was horribly contorted, blood streaming from eyes, ears, and nose. But the mind of passage was already working on this fresh text, preparing to translate and transport it. She had no way of braking the process, and to leave the circle now would be certain suicide. Beyond it, the scene was blurred and darkening, but she caught sight of Oscar, rising from the ground, and thanked whatever deities protected these circles that he was at least alive. He was moving towards the circle again, she saw, as though to dare its flux a second time, but it seemed he judged the train to be moving too swiftly now, because he retreated, arms up over his face. Seconds later the whole scene disappeared, the sunlight at the threshold burning on for a heartbeat longer than the rest, then that too folding away into obscurity.

The only sight left to her now was the matrix of lines which were the translator's rendering of her fellow traveler, and though she despised him beyond words she kept her eyes fixed upon them, having no other point of reference. All bodily sensation had disappeared. She didn't know if she was floating, falling, or even breathing, though she suspected she was doing none of these things. She had become a sign, transmitted between Dominions, encoded in the mind of passage. The sight before her—Dowd's shimmering glyph—was not secured by sight but by thought, which was the only currency valid on this trip. And now, as if her powers to purchase were increasing with familiarity, the absence around her began to gain detail. The In Ovo, Oscar had called this place. Its darkness swelled in a million places, their skins stretching until they gleamed and split, glutinous forms breaking out and in their turn swelling and splitting, like fruit whose seeds were sown inside each other and nourished to corruption by their predecessors' decay. Repulsive as this was, there was worse to come, as new entities appeared, these no more than scraps from a cannibal's table, sucked bloodless and gnawed: idiot doodles of life that didn't bear translation into any material form. Primitive though they were, they sensed the presence of finished life forms in their midst and rose towards the travelers like the damned to passing angels. But they swarmed too late. The visitors moved on and away, the darknesses sealing up their tenants and receding.

Jude could see Dowd's body in the midst of his glyph, still insubstantial but brightening by the moment. With the sight, the agonies of ferriage returned, though not as sharply as those that had pained her at the outset of the journey. She was glad to have them if they proved her nerves were hers again; surely it meant the journey was almost over. The horrors of the In Ovo had almost disappeared entirely when she felt the faint heat on her face. But the scent this heat raised to her nostrils brought more certain proof that the city was near: a mingling of the sweets and sours she'd first smelled on the wind that had issued from the Retreat months before.

She saw a smile come over Dowd's face, cracking the blood already dried on it: a smile which became a laugh in a beat or two, ringing off the walls of the merchant Peccable's cellar as it grew solid around them. She didn't want to share his pleasure, after all the harms he'd devised, but she couldn't help herself. Relief that the journey hadn't killed her, and sheer exhilaration that after all this time she was here, brought laughter onto her face and, with every breath between, the air of the Second Dominion into her lungs.

I

Five miles up the mountainside from the house in which Jude and Dowd were taking their first gasps of Yzordderrexian air, the Autarch of the Reconciled Dominions sat in one of his watchtowers and surveyed the city he had inspired to such notorious excess. It was three days since his return from the Kwem Palace, and almost every hour somebody—it was usually Rosengarten—had brought news of further acts of civil defiance, some in regions of the Imajica so remote that word of the mutinies had been weeks in coming, some—these more disturbing—barely beyond the palace walls. As he mused he chewed on kreauchee, a drug to which he'd been addicted for some seventy years. Its side effects were severe and unpredictable for those unused to it. Periods of lethargy alternated with bouts of priapism and psychotic hallucination. Sometimes the fingers and toes swelled to grotesque proportions. But the Autarch's system had been steeped in kreauchee for so many years the drug no longer assaulted either his physique or his faculties, and he could enjoy its capacity to lift him from dolor without having to endure its discomforts.

Or at least such had been the case until recently. Now, as if in league with the forces that were destroying his dream below, the drug refused to give him relief. He'd demanded a fresh supply while meditating at the place of the Pivot, only to get back to Yzordderrex to find that his procurers in the Scoriae Kesparate had been murdered. Their killers were reputedly members of the

Dearth, an order of renegade shammists—worshipers of the
Madonna, he'd heard it rumored—who'd been fulmigating revolution for years and had until now presented so little threat to the
status quo that he'd let them be for entertainment's sake. Their
pamphlets—a mingling of castration fantasies and bad theology—
had made farcical reading, and with their leader Athanasius in
prison many of them had retreated to the desert to worship at the
margins of the First Dominion, the so-called Erasure, where the
solid reality of the Second paled and faded. But Athanasius had
escaped his custody and returned to Yzordderrex with fresh calls
to arms. His first act of defiance, it seemed, had been the slaughter of the kreauchee pushers. A small deed, but the man was wily
enough to know what an inconvenience he'd caused with it. No
doubt he was touting it as an act of civil healing, performed in the
name of the Madonna.

The Autarch spat out the wad of kreauchee he was chewing and
vacated the watchtower, heading off through the monumental
labyrinth of the palace towards Quaisoir's quarters in the hope that
she had some small supply he could filch. To left and right of him
were corridors so immense no human voice would carry along
them, each lined with dozens of chambers—all exquisitely finished, all exquisitely empty—the ceilings of many so high that thin
clouds formed there. Though his architectural endeavors had once
been the wonder of the Dominions, the enormity of his ambition,
and indeed of his achievement, mocked him now. He'd wasted his
energies with these follies, when he should have been concerning
himself with the shock waves his empire building had sent through
the Imajica.

It wasn't the pogroms he'd instigated that were causing these
troubles, his analysts informed him. The present unrest was a consequence of less violent changes in the fabric of the Dominions,
the rise of Yzordderrex and its companion cities being one of those
changes, and perhaps its most significant. All eyes had been turned
towards the tinsel glories of those cities, and a new pantheon had
been created for tribes and communities that had long since lost
faith in the deities of rock and tree. Peasants had left their dust
bowls in their hundreds of thousands to claim their slice of this
miracle, only to end up fermenting their envy and despair in hell-
holes like Vanaeph.

That was one way revolutionaries were made, the analysts said:
not out of ideologies but out of frustration and rage. Then there
were those who saw a chance to profit by anarchy, like the new
species of nomads that were making portions of the Lenten Way
impassable—crazed and merciless bandits who took pleasure in
their own notoriety. And finally, there were the new rich, the

dynasties created by the boom in consumption that had come with
Yzordderrex's rise. In the early days they'd repeatedly turned to
the regime for protection against the acquisitive poor. But the
Autarch had been too busy building his palace, and the help had
not been forthcoming, so the dynasties had formed private armies
to police their lands, swearing their continued allegiance to the Empire even as they plotted against it. Now those plots were no longer
theory. With their armies primed to defend their estates, the boom
barons were announcing themselves independent of Yzordderrex
and its taxes.

There was, the analysts said, no evidence of collusion among
these elements. How could there be? They didn't have a single
philosophical notion in common. They were neo-feudalists, neo-
communists, neo-anarchists, all enemies of the others. It was purely
coincidence that had roused them to rebellion at the same moment. Either that, or unfortuitous stars.

The Autarch barely listened to such assessments. What little
pleasure he'd taken in politics at the beginning of his regime had
quickly staled. It wasn't the craft he'd been born to, and he found
it tiresome and dull. He'd appointed his Tetrarchs to rule over the
four Reconciled Dominions—the Tetrarch of the First doing so *in
absentia,* of course—leaving him to obsess upon making Yzordderrex the city to end all cities, and the palace its glorious crown.
What he'd in fact created was a monument to purposelessness,
which, when he was under the influence of kreauchee, he would
rail against as at some enemy.

One day, for instance, in visionary mood, he'd had all the windows in the chambers facing the desert smashed, and great ton-
nages of rancid meat laid on the mosaics. Within a day, flocks of
carrion birds had forsaken the hot high winds above the sands and
were feasting and breeding on tables and beds prepared for the
royalty of the Dominions. In another such mood he'd had fishes
brought up from the delta and housed in the baths. The water was
warm, the food plentiful, and they proved so fecund he could have
walked on their backs within weeks. Then they became over-
crowded, and he spent many hours watching the consequences:
patricide, fratricide, infanticide. But the cruelest revenge he
wreaked against his folly was the most private. One by one he was
using the high halls with their drizzling clouds as stages for dramas
in which nothing was feigned, not even death; and when the final
act had been performed he had each theater sealed as elaborately
as a king's tomb and moved on to another chamber. Little by little, the glorious palace of Yzordderrex was becoming a mausoleum.

The suite of chambers he was entering now was exempt from

this process, however. Quaisoir's bathrooms, bedrooms, lounges, and chapel were a state unto themselves, and he'd long ago sworn to her he would never violate them. She'd decorated the rooms with any lush or luxurious item that pleased her eclectic eye. It was an aesthetic he himself had favored, before his present melancholia. He'd filled the bedrooms now nested by carrion birds with immaculate copies of baroque and rococo furniture, had commissioned the walls to be mirrored like Versailles, and had the toilets gilded. But he'd long since lost his taste for such extravagances, and now the very sight of Quaisoir's rooms nauseated him so much that if he hadn't been driven by need he'd have retreated, appalled by their opulence.

He called his wife's name as he went. First through the lounges, strewn with the leavings of a dozen meals; all were empty. Then into the state room, which was appointed even more grandly than the lounges, but also empty. Finally, to the bedroom. At its threshold, he heard the slap of feet on the marble floor, and Quaisoir's servant Concupiscentia paddled into view. She was naked, as always, her back a field of multicolored extremities each as agile as an ape's tail, her forelimbs withered and boneless things, bred to such vestigial condition over generations. Her large green eyes seeped constantly, the feathery fans to either side of her face dipping to brush the moisture from her rouged cheeks.

"Where's Quaisoir?" he demanded.

She drew a coquettish fan of her tails over her lower face and giggled behind them like a geisha. The Autarch had slept with her once, in a kreauchee fugue, and the creature never let him by without a show of flirtation.

"Not now, for Christ's sake," he said, disgusted at the display. "I want my wife! Where is she?"

Concupiscentia shook her head, retreating from his raised voice and fist. He pushed past her into the bedroom. If there was any tiny wad of kreauchee to be had, it would be here, in her boudoir, where she lazed away so many days, listening to Concupiscentia sing hymns and lullabies. The chamber smelled like a harbor bordello, a dozen sickly perfumes draping the air like the veils that hung around the bed.

"I want kreauchee!" he said. "Where is it?"

Again, a great shaking of the head from Concupiscentia, this time accompanied by whimpering.

"Where?" he shouted. *"Where?"*

The perfume and the veils sickened him, and he began to rip at the silks and gossamers in his rage. The creature didn't intervene until he picked up the Bible lying open on the pillows and threatened to rip out its onion-leaf pages.

"Pleas ep!" she squealed. "Please ep! Shellem beat I if ye tau-rat the Book. Quaisoir lovat the Book."

It wasn't often he heard the gloss, the pidgin English of the is-lands, and the sound of it—as misshapen as its source—infuriated him even more. He tore half a dozen pages from the Bible, just to make her squeal again. She obliged.

I want kreauchee! he said.

"I havat! I havat!" the creature said, and led him from the bed-room into the enormous dressing room that lay next door, where she began to search through the gilded boxes on Quaisoir's dress-ing table.

Catching sight of the Autarch's reflection in the mirror, she made a tiny smile, like a guilty child, before bringing a package out of the smallest of the boxes. He snatched it from her fingers be-fore she had a chance to proffer it. He knew from the smell that stung his nostrils that this was good quality, and without hesitat-ing he unwrapped it and put the whole wad into his mouth.

"Good girl," he told Concupiscentia. "Good girl. Now, do you know where your mistress got it?"

Concupiscentia shook her head. "She goallat alon unto the Kesparates, many nights. Sometimes shellem a goat beggar, some-times shellem goat—"

"A whore."

"No, no. Quaisoir isem a whore."

"Is that where she is now?" the Autarch said. "Is she out whor-ing? It's a little early for that, isn't it, or is she cheaper in the af-ternoon?"

The kreauchee was better than he'd hoped; he felt it striking him as he spoke, lifting his melancholy and replacing it with a vehement buzz. Even though he'd not penetrated Quaisoir in four decades (nor had any desire to), in some moods news of her infidelities could still depress him. But the drug took all that pain away. She could sleep with fifty men a day, and it wouldn't take her an inch from his side. Whether they felt contempt or passion for each other was irrelevant. History had made them indivisible and would hold them together till the Apocalypse did them part.

"Shellem not whoring," Concupiscentia piped up, determined to defend her mistress's honor. "Shellem downer ta Scoriae."

"The Scoriae? Why?"

"Executions," Concupiscentia replied, pronouncing this word—learned from her mistress's lips—perfectly.

"Executions?" the Autarch said, a vague unease surfacing through the kreauchee's soothings. "What executions?"

Concupiscentia shook her head. "I dinnet knie," she said. "Jest executions. Allovat executions. She prayat to tem—"

"I'm sure she does."

"We all prayat far the sols, so ta go intat the presence of the Unbeheld washed—"

Here were more phrases repeated parrot fashion, the kind of Christian cant he found as sickening as the decor. And, like the decor, these were Quaisoir's work. She'd embraced the Man of Sorrows only a few months ago, but it hadn't taken her long to claim she was His bride. Another infidelity, less syphilitic than the hundreds that had gone before, but just as pathetic.

The Autarch left Concupiscentia to babble on and dispatched his bodyguard to locate Rosengarten. There were questions to be answered here, and quickly, or else it wouldn't only be the Scoriae where heads would roll.

2

Traveling the Lenten Way, Gentle had come to believe that, far from being the burden he'd expected her to be, Huzzah was a blessing. If she hadn't been with them in the Cradle he was certain the Goddess Tishalullé would not have intervened on their behalf; nor would hitchhiking along the highway have been so easy if they hadn't had a winsome child to thumb rides for them. Despite the months she'd spent hidden away in the depths of the asylum (or perhaps because of them), Huzzah was eager to engage everyone in conversation, and from the replies to her innocent inquiries he and Pie gleaned a good deal of information he doubted they'd have come by otherwise. Even as they'd crossed the causeway to the city, she'd struck up a dialogue with a woman who'd happily supplied a list of the Kesparates and even pointed out those that were visible from where they'd walked. There were too many names and directions for Gentle to hold in his head, but a glance towards Pie confirmed that the mystif was attending closely and would have all of them by heart by the time they reached the other side.

"Wonderful," Pie said to Huzzah when the woman had departed. "I wasn't sure I'd be able to find my way back to my people's Kesparate. Now I know the way."

"Up through the Oke T'Noon, to the Caramess, where they make the Autarch's sweetmeats," Huzzah said, repeating the directions as if she was reading them off a blackboard. "Follow the wall of the Caramess till we get to Smooke Street, then up to the Viaticum, and we'll be able to see the gates from there."

"How did you remember all that?" Gentle said, to which Huzzah somewhat disdainfully asked how he could have allowed himself to forget.

"We mustn't get lost," she said.

"We won't," Pie replied. "There'll be people in my Kesparate who'll help us find your grandparents."

"If they don't it doesn't matter," Huzzah said, looking gravely from Pie to Gentle. "I'll come with you to the First Dominion. I don't mind. I'd like to see the Unbeheld."

"How do you know that's where we're going?" Gentle said.

"I've heard you talking about it," she replied. "That's what you're going to do, isn't it? Don't worry, I'm not scared. We've seen a Goddess, haven't we? He'll be the same, only not as beautiful."

This unflattering notion amused Gentle mightily.

"You're an angel, you know that?" he said, going down on his haunches and sliding his arms around her.

She'd put on a few pounds in weight since they'd begun their journey together, and her hug, when she returned it, was strong.

"I'm hungry," she murmured in his ear.

"Then we'll find somewhere to eat," he replied. "We can't have our angel going hungry."

They walked up through the steep streets of the Oke T'Noon until they were clear of the throng of itinerants coming off the causeway. Here there were any number of establishments offering breakfast, from stalls selling barbecued fish to cafés that might have been transported from the streets of Paris, but that the customers sipping coffee were more extraordinary than even that city of exotics could boast. Many were species whose peculiarities he now took for granted: Oethacs and Heratea; distant relatives of Mother Splendid and Hammeryock; even a few who resembled the one-eyed croupier from Attaboy. But for every member of a tribe whose features he recognized, there were two or three he did not. As in Vanaeph, Pie had warned him that staring too hard would not be in their best interests, and he did his best not to enjoy too plainly the array of courtesies, humors, lunacies, gaits, skins, and cries that filled the streets. But it was difficult. After a time they found a small café from which the smell of food was particularly tempting, and Gentle sat down beside one of the windows, from which he could watch the parade without drawing too much attention.

"I had a friend called Klein," he said as they ate, "back in the Fifth Dominion. He liked to ask people what they'd do if they knew they only had three days to live."

"Why three?" Huzzah asked.

"I don't know. Why three anything? It's one of those numbers."

" 'In any fiction there's only ever room for three players,' " the mystif remarked. " 'The rest must be . . .' "—its flow faltered in mid-quotation—" 'agents,' something, and something else. That's a line from Pluthero Quexos."

"Who's he?"

"Never mind."

"Where was I?"

"Klein," said Huzzah.

"When he got around to asking me this question, I told him, If I had three days left I'd go to New York, because you've got more chance of living out your wildest dreams there than anywhere. But now I've seen Yzordderrex—"

"Not much of it," Huzzah pointed out.

"It's enough, angel. If he asks me again I'm going to tell him I'd like to die in Yzordderrex."

"Eating breakfast with Pie and Huzzah," she said.

"Perfect."

"Perfect," she replied, echoing his intonation precisely.

"Is there anything I couldn't find here if I looked hard enough?"

"Some peace and quiet," Pie remarked.

The hubbub from outside was certainly loud, even in the café.

"I'm sure we'll find some little courtyards up in the palace," Gentle said.

"Is that where we're going?" Huzzah asked.

"Now listen," said Pie. "For one thing, Mr. Zacharias doesn't know what the hell he's talking about—"

"Language, Pie," Gentle put in.

"And for another, we brought you here to find your grandparents, and that's our first priority. Right, Mr. Zacharias?"

"What if you can't find them?" Huzzah said.

"We will," Pie replied. "My people know this city from top to bottom."

"Is that possible?" Gentle said. "I somehow doubt it."

"When you've finished your coffee," Pie said, "I'll allow them to prove you wrong."

With their bellies filled, they headed on through the streets, following the route they'd had laid out for them: from the Oke T'Noon to the Caramess, following the wall until they reached Smooke Street. In fact the directions were not entirely reliable. Smooke Street, which was a narrow thoroughfare, and far emptier than those they'd left, did not lead them onto the Viaticum as they'd been told it would, but rather into a maze of buildings as plain as barracks. There were children playing in the dirt, and among them wild ragemy, an unfortunate cross between porcine and canine strains that Gentle had seen spitted and served in Mai-ké but which here seemed to be treated as pets. Either the mud, the children, or the ragemy stank, and their smell had attracted zarzi in large numbers.

"We must have missed a turning," the mystif said. "We'd be best to—"

It stopped in mid-sentence as the sound of shouting rose from nearby, bringing the children up out of the mud and sending them off in pursuit of its source. There was a high unmusical holler in the midst of the din, rising and falling like a warrior cry. Before either Pie or Gentle could remark on this, Huzzah was following the rest of the children, darting between the puddles and the rooting ragemy to do so. Gentle looked at Pie, who shrugged; then they both headed after Huzzah, the trail leading them down an alleyway into a broad and busy street, which was emptying at an astonishing rate as pedestrians and drivers alike sought cover from whatever was racing down the hill in their direction.

The hollerer came first: an armored man of fully twice Gentle's height, carrying in each fist scarlet flags that snaked behind him as he ran, the pitch and volume of his cry undimmed by the speed at which he moved. On his heels came a battalion of similarly armored soldiers—none, even in the troop, under eight feet tall—and behind them again a vehicle which had clearly been designed to mount and descent the ferocious slopes of the city with minimum discomfort to its passengers. The wheels were the height of the hollerer, the carriage itself low-slung between them, its bodywork sleek and dark, its windows darker still. A gull had become caught between the spokes of the wheels on the way down the hill, and it flapped and bled there as the wheels turned, its screeches a wretched but perfect complement to the cacophony of wheels, engine, and hollerer.

Gentle took hold of Huzzah as the vehicle raced past, though she was in no danger of being struck. She looked around at him, wearing a wide grin.

"Who was that?" she said.

"I don't know."

A woman sheltering in the doorway beside them furnished the answer. "Quaisoir," she said. "The Autarch's woman. There's arrests being made down in the Scoriae. More Dearthers."

She made a small gesture with her fingers, moving them across her face from eye to eye, then down to her mouth, pressing the knuckles of first and third fingers against her nostrils while the middle digit tugged at her lower lip, all this with the speed of one who made the sign countless times in a day. Then she turned off down the street, keeping close to the wall as she went.

"Athanasius was a Dearther, wasn't he?" Gentle said. "We should go down and see what's happening."

"It's a little too public," Pie said.

"We'll stay to the back of the crowd," Gentle said. "I want to see how the enemy works."

Without giving Pie time to object, Gentle took Huzzah's hand and headed after Quaisoir's troop. It wasn't a difficult trail to follow. Everywhere along the route faces were once more appearing at windows and doors, like anemones showing themselves again after being brushed by the underbelly of a shark: tentative, ready to hide their tender heads again at the merest sign of a shadow. Only a couple of tots, not yet educated in terror, did as the three strangers were doing and took to the middle of the street, where the comet's light was brightest. They were quickly reclaimed for the relative safety of the doorways in which their guardians hovered.

The ocean came into view as the trio descended the hill, and the harbor was now visible between the houses, which were considerably older in this neighborhood than in the Oke T'Noon or up by the Caramess. The air was clean and quick here; it enlivened their step. After a short while the domestic dwellings gave way to docklands: warehouses, cranes, and silos reared around them. But the area was by no means deserted. The workers here were not so easily cowed as the occupants of the Kesparate above, and many were leaving off their labors to see what this rumpus was all about. They were a far more homogenized group than Gentle had seen elsewhere, most a cross between Oethac and *Homo sapiens,* massive, even brutish men who in sufficient numbers could certainly trounce Quaisoir's battalion. Gentle hoisted Huzzah up to ride on his back as they joined this congregation, fearful she'd be trampled if he didn't. A few of the dockers gave her a smile, and several stood aside to let her mount secure a better place in the crowd. By the time they came within sight of the troops again they were thoroughly concealed.

A small contingent of the soldiers had been charged to keep onlookers from straying too close to the field of action, and this they were attempting to do, but they were vastly outnumbered, and as the crowd swelled it steadily pushed the cordon towards the site of the hostilities, a warehouse some thirty yards down the street, which had apparently been laid siege to. Its walls were pitted with bullet strikes, and its lower windows smoked. The besieging troops—who were not dressed showily like Quaisoir's battalion, but in the monochrome Gentle had seen paraded in L'Himby— were presently hauling bodies out of the building. Some were on the second story, pitching dead men—and a couple who still had life in them—out of the windows onto the bleeding heap below. Gentle remembered Beatrix. Was this cairn building one of the marks of the Autarch's hand?

"You shouldn't be seeing this, angel," Gentle told Huzzah, and tried to lift her off his shoulders. But she held fast, taking fistfuls of his hair as security.

"I want to see," she said. "I've seen it with Daddy, lots of times."

"Just don't get sick on my head," Gentle warned.

"I won't," she said, outraged at the suggestion.

There were fresh brutalities unfolding below. A survivor had been dragged from the building and was kicked to the ground a few yards from Quaisoir's vehicle, the doors and windows of which were still closed. Another was defending himself as best he could from bayonet jabs, yelling in defiance as his tormentors encircled him. But everything came to a sudden halt with the appearance on the warehouse roof of a man wearing little more than ragged underwear, who opened his arms like a soul in search of martyrdom and proceeded to harangue the assembly below.

"That's Athanasius!" Pie murmured in astonishment.

The mystif was far sharper sighted than Gentle, who had to squint hard to confirm the identification. It was indeed Father Athanasius, his beard and hair longer than ever, his hands, brow, and flank running with blood.

"What the hell's he doing up there," Gentle said, "giving a sermon?"

Athanasius' address wasn't simply directed at the troops and their victims on the cobblestones below. He repeatedly turned his head towards the crowd, shouting in their direction too. Whether he was issuing accusations, prayers, or a call to arms, the words were lost to the wind, however. Soundless, his display looked faintly absurd and undoubtedly suicidal. Rifles were already being raised below, to put him in their sights.

But before a shot could be fired the first prisoner, who'd been kicked to his knees close to Quaisoir's vehicle, slipped custody. His captors, distracted by Athanasius' performance, were slow to respond, and by the time they did so their victim was already dashing towards the crowd, ignoring quicker escape routes to do so. The crowd began to part, anticipating the man's arrival in its midst, but the troops behind him were already turning their muzzles his way. Realizing they intended to fire in the direction of the crowd, Gentle dropped to his haunches, yelling for Huzzah to clamber down. This time she didn't protest. As she slipped from his shoulders several shots were fired. He glanced up and through the mesh of bodies caught sight of Athanasius falling back, as if struck, and disappearing behind the parapet around the roof.

"Damn fool," he said to himself, and was about to scoop Huzzah up and carry her away when a second round of shots froze him in his tracks.

A bullet caught one of the dockers a yard from where he crouched, and the man went down like felled timber. Gentle looked around for Pie, rising as he did so. The escaping Dearther had also been hit, but he was still staggering forward, heading towards a crowd that was now in confusion. Some were fleeing, some standing their ground in defiance, some going to the aid of the fallen docker.

It was doubtful the Dearther saw any of this. Though the momentum of his flight still carried him forward, his face—too young to boast a beard—was slack and expressionless, his pale eyes glazed. His lips worked as though to impart some final word, but a sharpshooter below denied him the comfort. Another bullet struck the back of his neck and appeared on the other side, where three fine blue lines were tattooed across his throat, the middle one bisecting his Adam's apple. He was thrown forward by the bullet's impact, the few men between him and Gentle parting as he fell. His body hit the ground a yard from Gentle, with only a few twitches of life left in it. Though his face was to the ground, his hands still moved, making their way through the dirt towards Gentle's feet as if they knew where they were going. His left arm ran out of power before it could reach its destination, but the right had sufficient will behind it to find the scuffed toe of Gentle's shoe.

He heard Pie murmuring to him from close by, coaxing him to come away, but he couldn't forsake the man, not in these last seconds. He started to stoop, intending to clasp the dying fingers in his palm, but he was too late by seconds. The arm lost its power, and the hand dropped back to the ground lifeless.

"Now will you come?" Pie said.

Gentle tore his eyes from the corpse and looked up. The scene had gained him an audience, and there was a disturbing anticipation in their faces, puzzlement and respect mingled with the clear expectation of some pronouncement. Gentle had none to offer and opened his arms to show himself empty-handed. The assembly stared on, unblinking, and he half thought they might assault him if he didn't speak, but a further burst of gunfire from the siege site broke the moment, and the starers gave up their scrutiny, some shaking their heads as though waking from a trance. The second of the captives had been executed against the warehouse wall, and shots were now being fired into the pile of bodies to silence some survivor there. Troops had also appeared on the roof, presumably intending to pitch Athanasius' body down to crown the cairn. But they were denied that satisfaction. Either he'd faked being struck, or else he'd survived the wounding and crawled off to safety while the drama unfolded below. Whichever, he'd left his pursuers empty-handed.

Three of the cordon keepers, all of whom had fled for cover as their comrades fired on the crowd, now reappeared to claim the body of the escapee. They encountered a good deal of passive resistance, however, the crowd coming between them and the dead youth, jostling them. They forced their way through with well-aimed jabs from bayonets and rifle butts, but Gentle had time to retreat from in front of the corpse as they did so.

He had also had time to look back at the corpse-strewn stage visible beyond the heads of the crowd. The door of Quaisoir's vehicle had opened, and with her elite guard forming a shield around her she finally stepped out into the light of day. This was the consort of the Imajica's vilest tyrant, and Gentle lingered a dangerous moment to see what mark such intimacy with evil had made upon her.

When she came into view the sight of her, even with eyes that were far from perfect, was enough to snatch the breath from him. She was human, and a beauty. Nor was she simply *any* beauty. She was Judith.

Pie had hold of his arm, drawing him away, but he wouldn't go. "Look at her. Jesus. Look at her, Pie. *Look!*"

The mystif glanced towards the woman.

"It's Judith," Gentle said.

"That's impossible."

"It is! It is! Use your fucking eyes! It's Judith!"

As if his raised voice was a spark to the bone-dry rage of the crowd all around, violence suddenly erupted, its focus the trio of soldiers who were still attempting to claim the dead youth. One was bludgeoned to the ground while another retreated, firing as he did so. Escalation was instantaneous. Knives were slid from their sheaths, machetes unhooked from belts. In the space of five seconds the crowd became an army and five seconds later claimed its first three lives. Judith was eclipsed by the battle, and Gentle had little choice but to go with Pie, more for the sake of Huzzah than for his own safety. He felt strangely inviolate here, as though that circle of expectant stares had lent him a charmed life.

"It was Judith, Pie," he said again, once they were far enough from the shouts and shots to hear each other speak.

Huzzah had taken firm hold of his hand and swung on his arm excitedly. "Who's Judith?" she said.

"A woman we know," Gentle said.

"How could that be her?" The mystif's tone was as fretful as it was exasperated. "Ask yourself: How could that be her? If you've got an answer, I'm happy to hear it. Truly I am. Tell me."

"I don't know how," Gentle said. "But I trust my eyes."

"We left her in the Fifth, Gentle."

"If *I* got through, why shouldn't she?"

"And in the space of two months she takes over as the Autarch's wife? That's a meteoric rise, wouldn't you say?"

A fresh fusillade of shots rose from the siege site, followed by a roar of voices so profound it reverberated in the stone beneath their feet. Gentle stopped, walked, and looked back down the slope towards the harbor.

"There's going to be a revolution," he said simply.

"I think it's already begun," Pie replied.

"They'll kill her," he said, starting back down the hill.

"Where the hell are you going?" Pie said.

"I'm coming with you," Huzzah piped up, but the mystif took hold of her before she could follow.

"You're not going anywhere," Pie said, "except home to your grandparents. Gentle, will you listen to me? It's not Judith."

Gentle turned to face the mystif, attempting a reasoning tone. "If it's not her then it's her double; it's her echo. Some part *of* her, here in Yzordderrex."

The mystif didn't reply. It merely studied Gentle, as if coaxing him with its silence to articulate his theory more fully.

"Maybe people can be in two places at one time," Gentle said. Frustration made him grimace. "I *know* it was her, and nothing you can say's going to change my mind. You two go in to the Kesparate. Wait for me. I'll—"

Before he could finish his instructions, the holler that had first announced Quaisoir's descent from the heights of the city was raised again, this time at a higher pitch, to be drowned out almost instantly by a surge of celebratory cheering.

"That sounds like a retreat to me," Pie said, and was proved right twenty seconds later with the reappearance of Quaisoir's vehicle, surrounded by the tattered remnants of her retinue.

The trio had plenty of time to step out of the path of wheels and boots as they thundered up the slope, for the pace of the retreat was not as swift as that of the advance. Not only was the ascent steep but many of the elite had sustained wounds in defending the vehicle from assault and trailed blood as they ran.

"There's going to be such reprisals now," Pie said.

Gentle murmured his agreement as he stared up the slope where the vehicle had gone. "I have to see her again," he said.

"That's going to be difficult," Pie replied.

"She'll see me," Gentle said. "If I know who she is, then she's going to know who I am. I'll lay money on it."

The mystif didn't take up the bet. It simply said, "What now?"

"We go to your Kesparate, and we send out a search party to look for Huzzah's folks. Then we go up"—he nodded towards the palace—"and get a closer look at Quaisoir. I've got some questions to ask her. Whoever she is."

3

The wind veered as the trio retraced their steps, the relatively clear ocean breeze giving sudden way to a blisteringly hot assault off the desert. The citizens were well prepared for such climatic changes, and at the first hint of a shift in the wind, scenes of almost mechanical, and therefore comical, efficiency were to be seen high and low. Washing and potted plants were gathered from windowsills; ragemy and cats gave up their sun traps and headed inside; awnings were rolled up and windows shuttered. In a matter of minutes the street was emptied.

"I've been in these damn storms," the mystif said. "I don't think we want to be walking about in one."

Gentle told it not to fret, and hoisting Huzzah onto his shoulders, he set the pace as the storm scourged the streets. They'd asked for fresh directions a few minutes before the wind veered, and the shopkeeper who'd supplied them had known his geography. The directions were good even if walking conditions were not. The wind smelt like flatulence and carried a blinding freight of sand, along with ferocious heat. But they at least had the freedom of the streets. The only individuals they glimpsed were either felonious, crazy, or homeless, into all three of which categories they themselves fell.

They reached the Viaticum without error or incident, and from there the mystif knew its way. Two hours or more after they'd left the siege at the harbor they reached the Eurhetemec Kesparate. The storm was showing signs of fatigue, as were they, but Pie's voice fairly sang when it announced, "This is it. This is the place where I was born."

The Kesparate in front of them was walled, but the gates were open, swinging in the wind.

"Lead on," Gentle said, setting Huzzah down.

The mystif pushed the gate wide and led the way into streets the wind was unveiling before them as it fell, dropping sand underfoot. The streets rose towards the palace, as did almost every street in Yzordderrex, but the dwellings built upon it were very different from those elsewhere in the city. They stood discreet from one another, tall and burnished, each possessed of a single window that ran from above the door to the eaves, where the structure branched into four overhanging roofs, lending the buildings, when side by side, the look of a stand of petrified trees. In the street in front of the houses were the real thing: trees whose branches still swayed in the dying gusts like kelp in a tidal pool, their boughs so supple and their tight white blossoms so hardy the storm had done them no harm.

It wasn't until he caught the tremulous look on Pie's face that Gentle realized what a burden of feeling the mystif bore, stepping back into its birthplace after the passage of so many years. Having such a short memory, he'd never carried such luggage himself. There were no cherished recollections of childhood rites, no Christmas scenes or lullabies. His grasp of what Pie might be feeling had to be an intellectual construct and fell—he was sure—well shy of the real thing.

"My parents' home," the mystif said, "used to be between the chianculi"—it pointed off to its right, where the last remnants of sand-laden gusts still shrouded the distance—"and the hospice." It pointed to its left, a white-walled building.

"So somewhere near," Gentle said.

"I think so," Pie said, clearly pained by the tricks memory was playing.

"Why don't we ask somebody?" Huzzah suggested.

Pie acted upon the suggestion instantly, walking over to the nearest house and rapping on the door. There was no reply. It moved next door and tried again. This house was also vacated. Sensing Pie's unease, Gentle took Huzzah to join the mystif on the third step. The response was the same here, a silence made more palpable by the drop in the wind.

"There's nobody here," Pie said, remarking, Gentle knew, not simply on the empty houses but on the whole hushed vista.

The storm was completely exhausted now. People should have been appearing in their doorsteps to brush off the sand and peer at their roofs to see they were still secure. But there was nobody. The elegant streets, laid with such precision, were deserted from end to end.

"Maybe they've all gathered in one place," Gentle suggested. "Is there some kind of assembly place? A church or a senate?"

"The chianculi's the nearest thing," Pie said, pointing towards a quartet of pale yellow domes set amid trees shaped like cypresses but bearing Prussian blue foliage. Birds were rising from them into the clearing sky, their shadows the only motion on the streets below.

"What happens at the chianculi?" Gentle said as they started towards the domes.

"Ah! In my youth," the mystif said, attempting a lightness of tone it clearly didn't feel, "in my youth it was where we had the circuses."

"I didn't know you came from circus stock."

"They weren't like any Fifth Dominion circus," Pie replied. "They were ways we remembered the Dominion we'd been exiled from."

"No clowns and ponies?" Gentle said.

"No clowns and ponies," Pie replied, and would not be drawn on the subject any further.

Now that they were close to the chianculi, its scale—and that of the trees surrounding it—became apparent. It was fully five stories high from the ground to the apex of its largest dome. The birds, having made one celebratory circuit of the Kesparate, were now settling in the trees again, chattering like myna birds that had been taught Japanese.

Gentle's attention was briefly claimed by the spectacle, only to be grounded again when he heard Pie say, "They're not all dead."

Emerging from between the Prussian blue trees were four of the mystif's tribe, negroes wrapped in undyed robes like desert nomads, some folds of which they held between their teeth, covering their lower faces. Nothing about their gait or garments offered any clue to their sex, but they were evidently prepared to oust trespassers, for they came armed with fine silver rods, three feet or so in length and held across their hips.

"On no account move or even speak," the mystif said to Gentle as the quartet came within ten yards of where they stood.

"Why not?"

"This isn't a welcoming party."

"What is it then?"

"An execution squad."

So saying, the mystif raised its hands in front of its chest, palms out, then—breaking its own edict—it stepped forward, addressing the squad as it did so. The language it spoke was not English but had about it the same oriental lilt Gentle had heard from the beaks of the settling birds. Perhaps they'd indeed been speaking in their owners' tongue.

One of the quartet now let the bitten veil drop, revealing a woman in early middle age, her expression more puzzled than aggressive. Having listened to Pie for a time, she murmured something to the individual at her right, winning only a shaken head by way of response. The squad had continued to approach Pie as it talked, their stride steady; but now, as Gentle heard the syllables *Pie 'oh' pah* appear in the mystif's monologue, the woman called a halt. Two more of the veils were dropped, revealing men as finely boned as their leader. One was lightly mustached, but the seeds of sexual ambiguity that blossomed so exquisitely in Pie were visible here. Without further word from the woman, her companion went on to reveal a second ambiguity, altogether less attractive. He let one hand drop from the silver rod he carried and the wind caught it, a ripple passing through its length as though it were made not of steel but of silk. He lifted it to his mouth and draped it over his tongue. It fell in soft loops from his lips and fingers, still glinting like a blade even though it folded and fluttered.

Whether this gesture was a threat or not Gentle couldn't know, but in response to it the mystif dropped to its knees and indicated with a wave of its hand that Gentle and Huzzah should do the same. The child cast a rueful glance in Gentle's direction, looking to him for endorsement. He shrugged and nodded, and they both knelt, though to Gentle's way of thinking this was the last position to adopt in front of an execution squad.

"Get ready to run," he whispered across to Huzzah, and she returned a nervous little nod.

The mustachioed man had now begun to address Pie, speaking in the same tongue the mystif had used. There was nothing in either his tone or attitude that was particularly threatening, though neither, Gentle knew, were foolproof indications. There was some comfort in the fact of dialogue, however, and at a certain point in the exchange the fourth veil was dropped. Another woman, younger than the leader and altogether less amiable, was taking over the conversation with a more strident tone, waving her ribbon blade in the air inches from Pie's inclined head. Its lethal capacity could not be in doubt. It whistled as it sliced and hummed as it rose again, its motion, for all its ripples, chillingly controlled. When she'd finished talking, the leader apparently ordered them to their feet. Pie obliged, glancing around at Gentle and Huzzah to indicate they should do the same.

"Are they going to kill us?" Huzzah murmured.

Gentle took her hand. "No, they're not," he said. "And if they try, I've got a trick or two in my lungs."

"Please, Gentle," Pie said. "Don't even—"

A word from the squad leader silenced the appeal, and the mystif answered the next question directed at it by naming its companions: Huzzah Aping and John Furie Zacharias. There then followed another short exchange between the members of the squad, during which time Pie snatched a moment to explain.

"This is a very delicate situation," Pie said.

"I think we've grasped that much."

"Most of my people have gone from the Kesparate."

"Where?"

"Some of them tortured and killed. Some taken as slave labor."

"But now the prodigal returns. Why aren't they happy to see you?"

"They think I'm probably a spy, or else I'm crazy. Either way, I'm a danger to them. They're going to keep me here to question me. It was either that or a summary execution."

"Some homecoming."

"At least there's a few of them left alive. When we first got here, I thought—"

"I know what you thought. So did I. Do they speak any English?"

"Of course. But it's a matter of pride that they don't."

"But they'll understand me?"

"Don't, Gentle."

"I want them to know we're not their enemies," Gentle said, and turned his address to the squad. "You already know my name," he said. "I'm here with Pie 'oh' pah because we thought we'd find friends here. We're not spies. We're not assassins."

"Let it alone, Gentle," Pie said.

"We came a long way to be here, Pie and me. All the way from the Fifth. And right from the beginning Pie's dreamed about seeing you people again. Do you understand? You're the dream Pie's come all this way to find."

"They don't care, Gentle," Pie said.

"They have to care."

"It's their Kesparate," Pie replied. "Let them do it their way."

Gentle mused on this a moment. "Pie's right," he said. "It's your Kesparate, and we're just visitors here. But I want you to understand something." He turned his gaze on the woman whose ribbon blade had danced so threateningly close to the mystif's pate. "Pie's my friend," he said. "I will protect my friend to the very last."

"You're doing more harm than good," the mystif said. "Please stop."

"I thought they'd welcome you with open arms," Gentle said, surveying the quartet's unmoved faces. "What's wrong with them?"

"They're protecting what little they've got left," Pie said. "The Autarch's sent in spies before. There've been purges and abductions. Children taken. Heads returned."

"Oh, Jesus." Gentle made a small, apologetic shrug. "I'm sorry," he said, not just to Pie but to them all. "I just wanted to say my piece."

"Well, it's said. Will you leave it to me now? Give me a few hours, and I can convince them we're sincere."

"Of course, if that's what it'll take. Huzzah and I can wait around until you've worked it all out."

"Not here," Pie said. "I don't think that would be wise."

"Why not?"

"I just don't," Pie said, softly insisting.

"You're afraid they're going to kill us all, aren't you?"

"There is . . . some doubt . . . yes."

"Then we'll all leave now."

"That's not an option. I stay and you leave. That's what they're offering. It's not up for negotiation."

"I see."

"I'll be all right, Gentle," Pie said. "Why don't you go back to the café where we had breakfast? Can you find it again?"

"I can," Huzzah said. She'd spent the time of this exchange with downcast eyes. Now that they were raised, they were full of tears.

"Wait for me there, angel," Pie said, conferring Gentle's epithet upon her for the first time. "Both of you angels."

"If you're not with us by twilight we'll come back and find you," Gentle said. He threw his gaze wide as he said this, a smile on his lips and threat in his eyes.

Pie put out a hand to be shaken. Gentle took it, drawing the mystif closer.

"This is very proper," he said.

"Any more would be unwise," Pie replied. "Trust me."

"I always have. I always will."

"We're lucky, Gentle," Pie said.

"How so?"

"To have had this time together."

Gentle met the mystif's gaze, as it spoke, and realized there was a deeper farewell beneath this formality, which he didn't want to hear. For all its bright talk, the mystif was by no means certain they would be meeting again.

"I'm going to see you in a few hours, Pie," Gentle said. "I'm depending on that. Do you understand? We have vows."

The mystif nodded and let its hand slip from Gentle's grasp. Huzzah's smaller, warmer fingers were there, ready to take its place.

"We'd better go, angel," he said, and led Huzzah back towards the gate, leaving Pie in the custody of the squad.

She glanced back at the mystif twice as they walked, but Gentle resisted the temptation. It would do Pie no good to be sentimental at this juncture. Better just to proceed on the understanding that they'd be reunited in a matter of hours, drinking coffee in the Oke T'Noon. At the gate, however, he couldn't keep himself from glancing down the street of blossom-laden trees for one last glimpse of the creature he loved. But the execution squad had already disappeared into the chianculi, taking the prodigal with them.

32

I

With the long Yzordderrexian twilight still many hours from falling, the Autarch had found himself a chamber close to the Pivot Tower where the day could not come. Here the consolations brought by the kreauchee were not spoiled by light. It was easy to believe that everything was a dream and, being a dream, not worth mourning if—or rather when—it passed. In his unerring fashion Rosengarten had discovered the niche, however, and to it he brought news as disruptive as any light. A quiet attempt to eradicate the cell of Dearthers led by Father Athanasius had been turned into a public spectacle by Quaisoir's arrival. Violence had flared and was already spreading. The troops who had mounted the original siege were thought to have been massacred to a man, though this could not now be verified because the docklands had been sealed off by makeshift barricades.

"This is the signal the factions have been waiting for," Rosengarten opined. "If we don't stamp this out immediately, every little cult in the Dominion's going to tell its disciples that the Day's come."

"Time for judgment, eh?"

"That's what they'll say."

"Perhaps they're right," the Autarch replied. "Why don't we let them run riot for a while? None of them like each other. The Scintillants hate the Dearthers, the Dearthers hate the Zenetics. They can all slit each other's throats."

"But the city, sir."

"The city! The city! What about the frigging city? It's *forfeit*, Rosengarten. Don't you see that? I've been sitting here thinking, If I could call the comet down on top of it I would. Let it die the way it's lived: beautifully. Why so tragic, Rosengarten? There'll be other cities. I can build another Yzordderrex."

"Then maybe we should get you out now, before the riots spread."

"We're safe here, aren't we?" the Autarch said. A silence followed. "You're not so sure."

"There's such a swell of violence out there."

"And you say she started it?"

"It was in the air."

"But she was the inspiring spark?" He sighed. "Oh, damn her, damn her. You'd better fetch the generals."

"All of them?"

"Mattalaus and Racidio. They can turn this place into a fortress."
He got to his feet. "I'm going to speak with my loving wife."

"Shall we come and find you there?"

"Not unless you want to witness murder, no."

As before, he found Quaisoir's chambers empty, but this time
Concupiscentia—no longer flirtatious but trembling and dry-eyed,
which was like tears to her seeping clan—knew where her mistress
was: in her private chapel. He stormed in, to find Quaisoir lighting candles at the altar.

"I was calling for you," he said.

"Yes, I heard," she replied. Her voice, which had once made
every word an incantation, was drab; as was she.

"Why didn't you answer?"

"I was praying," she said. She blew out the taper she'd lit the candles with and turned from him to face the altar. It was, like her
chamber, a study in excess. A carved and painted Christ hung on
a gilded cross, surrounded by cherubim and seraphim.

"Who were you praying for?" he asked her.

"For myself," she said simply.

He took hold of her shoulder, spinning her around. "What about
the men who were torn apart by the mob? No prayers for them?"

"They've got people to pray for them. People who loved them.
I've got nobody."

"My heart bleeds," he said.

"No, it doesn't," she replied. "But the Man of Sorrows bleeds
for me."

"I doubt that, lady," he said, more amused by her piety than irritated.

"I saw Him today," she said.

This was a new conceit. He pandered to it. "Where was this?"
he asked her, all sincerity.

"At the harbor. He appeared on a roof, right above me. They
tried to shoot Him down, and He was struck. I saw Him struck. But
when they looked for the body it had gone."

"You know you should go down to the Bastion with the rest of
the madwomen," he told her. "You can wait for the Second Coming there. I'll have all this transported down there if you'd like."

"He'll come for me here," she said. "He's not afraid. *You're* the
one who's afraid."

The Autarch looked at his palm. "Am I sweating? No. Am I on
my knees begging Him to be kind? No. Accuse me of most crimes,
and I'm probably guilty. But not fear. You know me better than
that."

"He's here, in Yzordderrex."

"Then let Him come. I won't be leaving. He'll find me if He wants me so badly. He won't find me praying, you understand. Pissing maybe, if He could bear the sight." The Autarch took Quaisoir's hand and tugged it down between his legs. "He might find He's the one who's humbled." He laughed. "You used to pray to this fellow, lady. Remember? Say you remember."

"I confess it."

"It's not a crime. It's the way we were made. What are we to do but suffer it?" He suddenly drew close. "Don't think you can desert me for Him. We belong to each other. Whatever harm you do me, you do yourself. Think about that. If our dreams burn, we cook in them together."

His message was getting through. She didn't struggle in his embrace, but shook with terror.

"I don't want to take your comforts from you. Have your Man of Sorrows if He helps you sleep. But remember how our flesh is joined. Whatever little sways you learned down in the Bastion, it doesn't change what you are."

"Prayers aren't enough," she said, half to herself.

"Prayers are useless."

"Then I have to find Him. Go to Him. Show Him my adoration."

"You're going nowhere."

"I have to. It's the only way. He's in the city, waiting for me."

She pressed him away from her.

"I'll go to Him in rags," she said, starting to tear at her robes. "Or naked! Better naked!"

The Autarch didn't attempt to catch hold of her again but withdrew from her, as though her lunacy were contagious, letting her tear at her clothes and draw blood with the violence of her revulsion. As she did so she started to pray aloud, her prayer full of promises to come to Him, on her knees, and beg His forgiveness. As she turned, delivering this exhortation to the altar, the Autarch lost patience with her hysteria and took her by the hair—twin fistfuls of it—drawing her back against him.

"You're not listening!" he said, both compassion and disgust overwhelmed by a rage even the kreauchee couldn't quell. "There's only one Lord in Yzordderrex!"

He threw her aside and mounted the steps of the altar in three strides, clearing the candles from it with one backward sweep of his arm. Then he clambered up onto the altar itself to drag down the crucifix. Quaisoir was on her feet to stop him, but neither her appeals nor her fists slowed him. The gilded seraphim came first, wrenched from their carved clouds and pitched behind him to the ground. Then he put his hands behind the Savior's head and pulled.

The crown He wore was meticulously carved, and the thorns punctured his fingers and palms, but the sting only gave fire to his sinews, and a snarl of splintered wood announced his victory. The crucifix came away from the wall, and all he had to do was step aside to let gravity take it. For an instant he thought Quaisoir intended to fling herself beneath its weight, but a heartbeat before it toppled she stumbled back from the steps, and it fell amid the litter of dismembered seraphim, cracking as it struck the stone floor.

The commotion had of course brought witnesses. From his place on the altar the Autarch saw Rosengarten racing down the aisle, his weapon drawn.

"It's all right, Rosengarten!" he panted. "The worst is over."

"You're bleeding, sir."

The Autarch sucked at his hand. "Will you have my wife escorted to her chambers?" he said, spitting out the gold-flecked blood. "She's to be allowed no sharp instruments, nor any object with which she could do herself any harm. I'm afraid she's very sick. We'll have to watch over her night and day from now on."

Quaisoir was kneeling among the pieces of the crucifix, sobbing there.

"Please, lady," the Autarch said, jumping down from the altar to coax her up. "Why waste your tears on a dead man? Worship nothing, lady, except in adoration . . ." He stopped, puzzled by the words; then he took them up again. "In adoration of your True Self."

She raised her head, heeling away the tears with her hands to stare at him.

"I'll have some kreauchee found for you," he said. "To calm you a little."

"I don't want kreauchee," she murmured, her voice washed of all color. "I want forgiveness."

"Then I forgive you," he replied, with flawless sincerity.

"Not from you," she said.

He studied her grief for a time. "We were going to love and live forever," he said softly. "When did you become so *old?*"

She made no reply, so he left her there, kneeling in the debris. Rosengarten's underling, Seidux, had already arrived to take charge of her.

"Be considerate," he told Seidux as they crossed at the door. "She was once a great lady."

He didn't wait to watch her removal but went with Rosengarten to meet Generals Mattalaus and Racidio. He felt better for his exertion. Though like any great Maestro he was untouched by age, his system still became sluggish and needed an occasional stirring up. What better way to do it than by demolishing idols?

As they passed by a window which gave onto the city the spring went from his step, however, seeing the signs of destruction visible below. For all his defiant talk of building another Yzordderrex, it would be painful to watch this one torn apart, Kesparate by Kesparate. Half a dozen columns of smoke were already rising from conflagrations across the city. Ships were burning in the harbor, and there were bordellos aflame around Lickerish Street. As Rosengarten had predicted, all the apocalyptics in the city would fulfill their prophecies today. Those who'd said corruption came by sea were burning boats; those who railed against sex had lit their torches for the brothels. He glanced back towards Quaisoir's chapel as his consort's sobs were raised afresh.

"It's best we don't stop her weeping," he said. "She has good reason."

2

The full extent of the harm Dowd had done himself in his late boarding of the Yzordderrexian Express did not become apparent until their arrival in the icon-filled cellar beneath the merchant's house. Though he'd escaped being turned inside out, his trespass had wounded him considerably. He looked as though he'd been dragged face down over a freshly graveled road, the skin on his face and hands shredded and the sinew beneath oozing the meager filth he had in his veins. The last time Jude had seen him bleed, the wound had been self-inflicted and he'd seemed to suffer scarcely at all; but not so now. Though he held on to her wrist with an implacable grip and threatened her with a death that would make Clara's seem merciful if she attempted to escape him, he was a vulnerable captor, wincing as he hauled her up the stairs into the house above.

This was not the way she had imagined herself entering Yzordderrex. But then the scene she met at the top of the stairs was not as she'd imagined either. Or rather, it was all too imaginable. The house—which was deserted—was large and bright, its design and decoration almost depressingly recognizable. She reminded herself that this was the house of Oscar's business partner Peccable, and the influence of Fifth Dominion aesthetics was likely to be strong in a dwelling that had a doorway to Earth in its cellar. But the vision of domestic bliss this interior conjured was depressingly bland. The only touch of exoticism was the parrot sulking on its perch by the window; otherwise this nest was irredeemably suburban, from the row of family photographs beside the clock on the mantelpiece to the drooping tulips in the vase on the well-polished dining room table.

She was sure there were more remarkable sights in the street outside, but Dowd was in no mood, or indeed condition, to go exploring. He told her they would wait here until he was feeling fitter, and if any of the family returned in the meanwhile she was to keep her silence. He'd do the talking, he said, or else she'd put not only her own life in jeopardy but that of the whole Peccable clan.

She believed him perfectly capable of such violence, especially in his present pain, which he demanded she help him ameliorate. She dutifully bathed his face, using water and towels from the kitchen. The damage was regrettably more superficial than she'd initially believed, and once the wounds were cleaned he rapidly began to show signs of recovery. She was now presented with a dilemma. Given that he was healing with superhuman speed, if she was going to exploit his vulnerability and escape it had to be soon. But if she did—if she fled the house there and then—she'd have turned her back on the only guide to the city she had. And, more importantly, she would be gone from the spot to which she still hoped Oscar would come, following her across the In Ovo. She couldn't afford to take the risk of his arriving and finding her gone into a city that from all reports was so vast they might search for each other ten lifetimes and never cross paths.

A wind began to get up after a while, and it carried a member of the Peccable family to the door. A gangling girl in her late teens or early twenties, dressed in a long coat and flower-print dress, who greeted the presence of two strangers in the house, one clearly recovering from injury, in a studiedly sanguine fashion.

"Are you friends of Papa's?" she asked, removing her spectacles to reveal eyes that were severely crossed.

Dowd said they were and began to explain how they'd come to be here, but she politely asked him if he'd hold off his story until the house had been shuttered against the coming storm. She turned to Jude for help in this, and Dowd made no objection, correctly assuming that his captive was not going to venture out into an unknown city as a storm came upon it. So, with the first gusts already rattling the door, Jude followed Hoi-Polloi around the house, locking any windows that were open even an inch, then closing the shutters in case the glass was blown in.

Even though the sandy wind was already obscuring the distance, Jude got a glimpse of the city outside. It was frustratingly brief, but sufficient to reassure her that when she finally got to walk the streets of Yzordderrex her months of waiting would be rewarded with wonders. There were myriad tiers of streets set on the slopes above the house, leading up to the monumental walls and towers of what Hoi-Polloi identified as the Autarch's palace, and just visible from the attic room window was the ocean, glittering through the thickening storm. But these were sights—ocean, rooftops, and towers—she might have seen in the Fifth. What marked this place as another Dominion was the people in the streets outside, some human, many not, all retreating from the wind or the commotions it carried. A creature, its head vast, stumbled up the street with what looked to be two sharp-snouted pigs, barking furiously, under each arm. A group of youths, bald and robed, ran in the other direction, swinging smoking censers above their heads like bolas. A man with a canary-yellow beard and china-doll skin was carried, wounded but yelling furiously, into a house opposite.

"There's riots everywhere," Hoi-Polloi said. "I wish Papa would come home."

"Where is he?" Jude asked.

"Down at the harbor. He had a shipment coming in from the islands."

"Can't you telephone him?"

"Telephone?" Hoi-Polloi said.

"Yes, you know, it's a—"

"I know what it is," Hoi-Polloi said testily. "Uncle Oscar showed me one. But they're against the law."

"Why?"

Hoi-Polloi shrugged. "The law's the law," she said. She peered out into the storm before shuttering the final window. "Papa will be sensible," she went on. "I'm always telling him, Be sensible, and he always is."

She led the way downstairs to find Dowd standing on the front step, with the door flung wide. Hot, gritty air blew in, smelling of spice and distance. Hoi-Polloi ordered Dowd back inside with a sharpness that made Jude fear for her, but Dowd seemed happy to play the erring guest and did as he was asked. She slammed the door and bolted it, then asked if anybody wanted tea. With the lights swinging in every room, and the wind rattling every loose shutter, it was hard to pretend nothing was amiss, but Hoi-Polloi did her best to keep the chat trivial while she brewed a pot of Darjeeling and passed around slices of Madeira cake. The sheer absurdity of the situation began to amuse Jude. Here they were having a tea party while a city of untold strangeness was racked by storm and revolution all around. If Oscar appears now, she thought, he'll be most entertained. He'll sit down, dunk his cake in his tea, and talk about cricket like a perfect Englishman.

"Where's the rest of your family?" Dowd asked Hoi-Polloi, when the conversation once more returned to her absentee father.

"Mama and my brothers have gone to the country," she said, "to be away from the troubles."

"Didn't you want to go with them?"

"Not with Papa here. Somebody has to look after him. He's sensible most of the time, but I have to remind him." A particularly vehement gust brought slates rattling off the roof like gunshots. Hoi-Polloi jumped. "If Papa was here," she said, "I think he'd suggest we had something to calm our nerves."

"What do you have, lovey?" Dowd said. "A little brandy, maybe? That's what Oscar brings, isn't it?"

She said it was and fetched a bottle, dispensing it to all three of them in tiny glasses.

"He brought us Dotterel too," she said.

"Who's Dotterel?" Jude inquired.

"The parrot. He was a present to me when I was little. He had a mate but she was eaten by the ragemy next door. The brute! Now Dotterel's on his own, and he's not happy. But Oscar's going to bring me another parrot soon. He said he would. He brought pearls for Mama once. And for Papa he always brings newspapers. Papa loves newspapers."

She babbled on in a similar vein with barely a break in the flow. Meanwhile, the three glasses were filled and emptied and filled again several times, the liquor steadily taking its toll on Jude's concentration. In fact she found the monologue, and the subtle motion of the light overhead, positively soporific and finally asked if she might lie down for a while. Again, Dowd made no objection and let Hoi-Polloi escort Jude up to the guest bedroom, offering only a slurred "sweet dreams, lovey" as she retired.

She laid her buzzing head down gratefully, thinking as she dozed that it made sense to sleep now, while the storm prevented her from taking to the streets. When it was over her expedition would begin, with or without Dowd. Oscar was not coming for her, that much seemed certain. Either he'd sustained too much injury to follow or else the Express had been somehow damaged by Dowd's late boarding. Whichever, she could not delay her adventures here any longer. When she woke, she'd emulate the forces rattling the shutters and take Yzordderrex by storm.

She dreamt she was in a place of great grief: a dark chamber, its shutters closed against the same storm that raged outside the room in which she slept and dreamt—and knew she slept and dreamt even as she did so—and in this chamber was the sound of a woman sobbing. The grief was so palpable it stung her, and she wanted to soothe it, as much for her own sake as that of the griever. She moved through the murk towards the sound, encountering curtain after curtain as she went, all gossamer thin, as though the trousseaus of a hundred brides had been hung in this chamber. Before she could reach the weeping woman, however, a figure moved through the darkness ahead of her, coming to the bed where the woman lay and whispering to her.

"Kreauchee . . ." the other said, and through the veils Jude glimpsed the lisping speaker.

No figure as bizarre as this had ever flitted through her dreams before. The creature was pale, even in the gloom, and naked, with a back from which sprawled a garden of tails. Jude advanced a little to see her better, and the creature in her turn saw her, or at least her effect upon the veils, for she looked around the chamber as if she knew there was a haunter here. Her voice carried alarm when it came again.

"There's som'ady here, ledy," it said.

"I'll see nobody. Especially Seidux."

"It's notat Seidux. I seeat no'ady, but I feelat som'ady here stell."

The weeping diminished. The woman looked up. There were still veils between Jude and the sleeper's face, and the chamber was indeed dark, but she knew her own features when she saw them, though her hair was plastered to her sweating scalp, and her eyes puffed up with tears. She didn't recoil at the sight, but stood as still as spirits were able amid gossamer, and watched the woman with her face rise up from the bed. There was bliss in her expression.

"He's sent an angel," she said to the creature at her side. "Concupiscentia . . . He's sent an angel to summon me."

"Yes?"

"Yes. For certain. This is a sign. I'm going to be forgiven."

A sound at the door drew the woman's attention. A man in uniform, his face lit only by the cigarette he drew upon, stood watching.

"Get out," the woman said.

"I came only to see that you were comfortable, Ma'am Quaisoir."

"I said get out, Seidux."

"If you should require anything—"

Quaisoir got up suddenly and pitched herself through the veils in Seidux's direction. The suddenness of this assault took Jude by surprise, as it did its target. Though Quaisoir was a head shorter than her captor, she had no fear of him. She slapped the cigarette from his lips.

"I don't want you watching me," she said. "Get out. Hear me? Or shall I scream rape?"

She began to tear at her already ragged clothes, exposing her breasts. Seidux retreated in confusion, averting his eyes.

"As you wish!" he said, heading out of the chamber. "As you wish!"

Quaisoir slammed the door on him and turned her attention back to the haunted room.

"Where are you, spirit?" she said, moving back through the veils. "Gone? No, not gone." She turned to Concupiscentia. "Do you feel its presence?" The creature seemed too frightened to speak. "I feel nothing," Quaisoir said, now standing still amid the shifting veils. "Damn Seidux! The spirit's been driven out!"

Without the means to contradict this, all Jude could do was wait beside the bed and hope that the effect of Seidux's interruption—which had seemingly blinded them to her presence—would wear off now that he'd been exiled from the chamber. She remembered as she waited how Clara had talked about men's power to destroy. Had she just witnessed an example of that, Seidux's mere presence enough to poison the contact between a dreaming spirit and a waking one? If so, he'd done it all unknowing: innocent of his power, but no more forgivable for that. How many times in any day did he and the rest of his kind—hadn't Clara said they were another species?—spoil and mutilate in their unwitting way, Jude wondered, preventing the union of subtler natures?

Quaisoir sank back down on the bed, giving Jude time to ponder the mystery her face represented. She hadn't doubted from the moment she'd entered this chamber that she was traveling here much as she'd first traveled to the tower, using the freedom of a dream state to move invisibly through the real world. That she no longer needed the blue eye to facilitate such movement was a puzzle for another time. What concerned her now was to find out how this woman came to have her face. Was this Dominion somehow a mirror of the world she'd left? And if not—if she was the only woman in the Fifth to have a perfect twin—what did that echo signify?

The wind was beginning to abate, and Quaisoir dispatched her servant to the window to remove the shutters. There was still a red dust hanging in the atmosphere, but, moving to the sill beside the creature, Jude was presented with a vista that, had she possessed breath in this state, would have taken it away. They were perched high above the city, in one of the towers she'd briefly glimpsed as she'd gone around the Peccable house with Hoi-Polloi, bolting and shuttering. It was not simply Yzordderrex that lay before her, but signs of the city's undoing. Fires were raging in a dozen places beyond the palace walls, and within those walls the Autarch's troops were mustering in the courtyards. Turning her dream gaze back towards Quaisoir, Jude saw for the first time the sumptuousness of the chamber in which she'd found the woman. The walls were tapestries, and there was no stick of furniture that did not compete in its gilding. If this was a prison, then it was fit for royalty.

Quaisoir now came to the window and looked out at the panorama of fires.

"I have to find Him," she said. "He sent an angel to bring me to Him, and Seidux drove the angel out. So I'll have to go to Him myself. Tonight . . ."

Jude listened, but distractedly, her mind more occupied by the opulence of the chamber and what it revealed about her twin. It seemed she shared a face with a woman of some significance, a possessor of power, now dispossessed, and planning to break the bonds set upon her. Romance seemed to be her reason. There was a man in the city below with whom she desperately wanted to be reunited, a lover who sent angels to whisper sweet nothings in her ear. What kind of man? she wondered. A Maestro, perhaps, a wielder of magic?

Having studied the city for a time, Quaisoir left the window and went through to her dressing room.

"I mustn't go to Him like this," she said, starting to undress. "That would be shameful."

The woman caught sight of herself in one of the mirrors and sat down in front of it, peering at her reflection with distaste. Her tears had made mud of the kohl around her eyes, and her cheeks and neck were blotchy. She took a piece of linen from the dressing table, sprinkled some fragrant oil upon it, and began to roughly clean her face.

"I'll go to Him naked," she said, smiling in anticipation of that pleasure. "He'll prefer me that way."

This mystery lover intrigued Jude more and more. Hearing her own voice musky with talk of nakedness, she was tantalized. Would it not be a fine thing to see the consummation? The idea of watching herself couple with some Yzordderrexian Maestro had not been among the wonderments she'd anticipated discovering in this city, but the notion carried an erotic *frisson* she could not deny herself. She studied the reflection of her reflection. Though there were a few cosmetic differences, the essentials were hers, to the last nick and mole. This was no approximation of her face, but the thing exactly, which fact strangely excited her. She had to find a way to speak with this woman tonight. Even if their twinning was simply a freak of nature, they would surely be able to illuminate each other's lives with an exchange of histories. All she needed was a clue from her doppelgänger as to where in the city she intended to go looking for her Maestro lover.

With her face cleansed, Quaisoir got up from in front of the mirror and went back into the bedroom. Concupiscentia was sitting by the window. Quaisoir waited until she was within inches of her servant before she spoke, and even then her words were barely audible.

"We'll need a knife," she said.

The creature shook her head. "They tookat em all," she said. "You seem how ey lookat and lookat."

"Then we must make one," Quaisoir replied. "Seidux will try to oppose our leaving."

"You wishat to kill em?"

"Yes, I do."

This talk chilled Jude. Though Seidux had retreated before Quaisoir when she'd threatened to cry rape, Jude doubted that he'd be so passive if challenged physically. Indeed, what more perfect excuse would he need to regain his dominance than her coming at him with a knife? If she'd had the means, she would have been Clara's mouthpiece now and echoed her sentiments on man the desolator, in the hope of keeping Quaisoir from harm. It would be an unbearable irony to lose this woman now, having found her way (surely not by accident, though at present it seemed so) across half the Imajica into her very chamber.

"I cet shapas te knife," Concupiscentia was saying.

"Then do it," Quaisoir replied, leaning still closer to her fellow conspirator.

Jude missed the next exchange, because somebody called her name. Startled, she looked around the room, but before she'd half scanned it she recognized the voice. It was Hoi-Polloi, and she was rousing the sleeper after the storm.

"Papa's here!" Jude heard her say. "Wake up, Papa's here!"

There was no time to bid farewell to the scene. It was there in front of her one moment, and replaced the next with the face of Peccable's daughter, leaning to shake her awake.

"Papa—" she said again.

"Yes, all right," Jude said brusquely, hoping the girl would leave without further exchanges coming between her and the sights sleep had brought. She knew she had scant moments to drag the dream into wakefulness with her, or it would subside and the details become hazy the deeper it sank.

She was in luck. Hoi-Polloi hurried back down to her father's side, leaving Jude to recite aloud all she'd seen and heard. Quaisoir and her servant Concupiscentia; Seidux and the plot against him. And the lover, of course. She shouldn't forget the lover, who was presumably somewhere in the city even now, pining for his mistress who was locked up in her gilded prison. With these facts fixed in her head, she ventured first to the bathroom, then down to meet Peccable.

Well dressed and better fed, Peccable had a face upon which his present ire sat badly. He looked slightly absurd in his fury, his features too round and his mouth too small for the rhetoric they were producing. Introductions were made, but there was no time for pleasantries. Peccable's fury needed venting, and he seemed not to care much who his audience was, as long as they sympathized. He had reason for fury. His warehouse near the harbor had been burned to the ground, and he himself had only narrowly escaped death at the hands of a mob that had already taken over three of the Kesparates and declared them independent city-states, thereby issuing a challenge to the Autarch. So far, he said, the palace had done little. Small contingents of troops had been dispatched to the Caramess, to the Oke T'Noon, and the seven Kesparates on the other side of the hill, to suppress any sign of uprisings there. But no offensive had been launched against the insurgents who had taken the harbor.

"They're nothing more than rabble," the merchant said. "They've no care for property or person. Indiscriminate destruction, that's all they're good for! I'm no great lover of the Autarch, but he's got to be the voice of decent people like me in times like this! I should have sold my business a year ago. I talked with Oscar about it. We planned to move away from this wretched city. But I hung on and hung on, because I believe in people. That's my mistake," he said, throwing his eyes up to the ceiling like a man martyred by his own decency. "I have too much faith." He looked at Hoi-Polloi. "Don't I?"

"You do, Papa, you do."

"Well, not any more. You go and pack our belongings, sweet. We're getting out tonight."

"What about the house?" Dowd said. "And all the collectibles downstairs?"

Peccable cast a glance at Hoi-Polloi. "Why don't you start packing now?" he said, clearly uncomfortable with the idea of debating his black market activities in front of his daughter.

He cast a similar glance at Jude, but she pretended not to comprehend its significance and remained seated. He began to talk anyway.

"When we leave this house we leave it forever," he said. "There'll be nothing left to come back to, I'm convinced of that." The outraged bourgeois of minutes before, appealing for civil stability, was now replaced by an apocalyptic. "It was bound to happen sooner or later. They couldn't control the cults in perpetuity."

"They?" said Jude.

"The Autarch. And Quaisoir."

The sound of the name was like a blow to her heart. "Quaisoir?" she said.

"His wife. The consort. Our lady of Yzordderrex: Ma'am Quaisoir. She's been his undoing, if you ask me. He always kept himself hidden away, which was wise; nobody thought about him much as long as trade was good and the streets were lit. The taxes, of course: the taxes have been a burden upon us all, especially family men like myself, but let me tell you we're better off here than they are in Patashoqua or Iahmandhas. No, I don't think he's done badly by us. The stories you hear about the state of things when he first took over: Chaos! Half the Kesparates at war with the other half. He brought stability. People prospered. No, it's not his policies, it's *her:* she's his undoing. Things were fine until she started to interfere. I suppose she thinks she's doing us a favor, deigning to appear in public."

"Have you . . . seen her then?" Jude asked.

"Not personally, no. She stays out of sight, even when she attends executions. Though I heard that she showed herself today, out in the open. Somebody said they'd actually seen her face. Ugly, they said. Brutish. I'm not surprised. All these executions were her idea. She enjoys them, apparently. Well, people don't like that. Taxes, yes. An occasional purge, some political trials—well, yes, those too; we can accept those. But you can't make the law into a public spectacle. That's a mockery, and we've never mocked the law in Yzordderrex."

He went on in much the same vein, but Jude wasn't listening. She was attempting to conceal the heady mixture of feelings that was coursing through her. Quaisoir, the woman with her face, was not some minor player in the life of Yzordderrex but one of its two potentates; by extension, therefore, one of the great rulers of the Imajica. Could she now doubt that there was purpose in her coming to this city? She had a face which owned power. A face that went in secret from the world, but that behind its veils had made the Autarch of Yzordderrex pliant. The question was: What did that mean? After so unremarkable a life on earth, had she been called into this Dominion to taste a little of the power that her other took for granted? Or was she here as a diversion, called to suffer in place of Quaisoir for the crimes she'd supposedly committed? And if so, who was the summoner? Clearly it had to be a Maestro with ready access to the Fifth Dominion and agents there to conspire with. Was Godolphin some part of this plot? Or Dowd, perhaps? That seemed more likely. And what about Quaisoir? Was she in ignorance of the plans being laid on her behalf or a fellow plotter?

Tonight would tell, Jude promised herself. Tonight she'd find some way to intercept Quaisoir as she went to meet her angel-dispatching lover, and before another day had gone by Jude would know whether she'd been brought from the Fifth to be a sister or a scapegoat.

33

GENTLE DID AS HE'D PROMISED PIE, and stayed with Huzzah at the café where they'd breakfasted until the comet's arc took it behind the mountain and the light of day gave way to twilight. Doing so tried not only his patience but his nerve, because as the afternoon wore on the unrest from the lower Kesparates spread up through the streets, and it became increasingly apparent that the establishment would stand in the middle of a battlefield by evening. Party by party, the customers vacated their tables as the sound of rioting and gunfire crept closer. A slow rain of smuts began to fall, spiraling from a sky which was intermittently darkened now by smoke rising from the burning Kesparates.

As the first wounded began to be carried up the street, indicating that the field of action was now very near, the owners of several nearby shops gathered in the café for a short council, debating, presumably, the best way to defend their property. It ended in accusation, the insults an education to both Gentle and Huzzah. Two of the owners returned with weapons a few minutes later, at which point the manager, who introduced himself as Bunyan Blew, asked Gentle if he and his daughter didn't have a home to go to. Gentle replied that they had promised to meet somebody here earlier in the day, and they would be most obliged if they could remain until their friend arrived.

"I remember you," Blew replied. "You came in this morning, didn't you, with a woman?"

"That's who we're waiting for."

"She put me in mind of somebody I used to know," Blew said. "I hope she's safe out there."

"So do we," Gentle replied.

"You'd better stay then. But you'll have to lend me a hand barricading the place."

Bunyan explained that he'd known this was going to happen sooner or later and was prepared for the eventuality. There were timbers to nail over the windows, and a supply of small arms should the mob try to loot his shelves. In fact, his precautions proved unnecessary. The street became a conduit for ferrying the wounded army from the combat zone, which was moving up the hill one street east of the café. There were two nerve-racking hours, however, when the din of shouting and gunfire was coming from all compass points, and the bottles on Blew's shelves tinkled every time the ground shook, which was often. One of the shopkeepers who'd left in high dudgeon earlier came beating at the door during this siege, and stumbled over the threshold with blood streaming from his head and tales of destruction from his mouth. The army had called up heavy artillery in the last hour, he reported, and it had practically leveled the harbor and rendered the causeway impassable, thereby effectively sealing the city. This was all part of the Autarch's plan, he said. Why else were whole neighborhoods being allowed to burn unchecked? The Autarch was leaving the city to consume its own citizens, knowing the conflagration would not be able to break the palace walls.

"He's going to let the mob destroy the city," the man went on, "and he doesn't care what happens to us in the meantime. Selfish bastard! We're all going to burn, and he's not going to lift a finger to help us!"

This scenario certainly fitted the facts. When, at Gentle's suggestion, they went up onto the roof to get a better view of the situation, it seemed to be exactly as described. The ocean was obliterated by a wall of smoke climbing from the embers of the harbor; further flame-shot columns rose from two dozen neighborhoods, near and far; and through the dirty heat coming off the Oke T'Noon's pyre the causeway was just visible, its rubble damming the delta. Clogged by smoke, the comet shed a diminished light on the city, and even that was fading as the long twilight deepened.

"It's time to leave," Gentle told Huzzah.

"Where are we going to go?"

"Back to find Pie 'oh' pah," he replied. "While we still can."

It had been apparent from the roof that there was no safe route back to the mystif's Kesparate. The various factions warring in the streets were moving unpredictably. A street that was empty one moment might be thronged the next, and rubble the moment after that. They would have to go on instinct and a prayer, taking as direct a path back to where they'd left Pie 'oh' pah as circumstance allowed. Dusk in this Dominion usually lasted the length of an English midwinter day—five or six hours—the tail of the comet keeping traces of light in the sky long after its fiery head had dropped beneath the horizon. But the smoke thickened as Gentle and Huzzah traveled, eclipsing the languid light and plunging the city into a filthy gloom. There were still the fires to compensate, of course, but between the conflagration, in streets where the lamps hadn't been lit and the citizens had shuttered their windows and blocked their keyholes to keep any sign of occupation from showing, the darkness was almost impenetrable. In such thoroughfares Gentle hoisted Huzzah onto his shoulders, from which vantage point she was able to snatch sights to steer him by.

It was slow going, however, halting at each intersection to calculate the least dangerous route to follow, and taking refuge at the approach of both governmental and revolutionary troops. But for every soldier in this war there were half a dozen bystanders, people daring the tide of battle like beachcombers, retreating before each wave, only to return to their watching places when it receded: a sometimes lethal game. A similar dance was demanded of Gentle and Huzzah. Driven off course again and again, they were obliged to trust to instinct as to their direction, and inevitably instinct finally deserted them.

In an uncommon hush between clamors and bombardments, Gentle said, "Angel? I don't know where we are any more."

A comprehensive fusillade had brought down most of the Kesparate around them, and there were precious few places of refuge amid the rubble, but Huzzah insisted they find one: a call of nature that could be delayed no longer. Gentle set her down, and she headed off for the dubious cover of a semidemolished house some yards up the street. He stood guard at the door, calling inside to her and telling her not to venture too far. He'd no sooner offered this warning than the appearance of a small band of armed men drove him back into the shadows of the doorway. But for their weapons, which had presumably been plucked from dead men, they looked ill suited to the role of revolutionaries. The eldest, a barrel of a man in late middle age, still wore the hat and tie he'd most likely gone to work in that morning, while two of his accomplices were barely older than Huzzah. Of the two remaining members, one was an Oethac woman, the other of the tribe to which the executioner in Vanaeph had belonged: a Nullianac, its head like hands joined in prayer.

Gentle glanced back into the darkness, hoping to hush Huzzah before she emerged, but there was no sign of her. He left the step and headed into the ruins. The floor was sticky underfoot, though he couldn't see with what. He did see Huzzah, however, or her silhouette, as she rose from relieving herself. She saw him too and made a little noise of protest, which he hushed as loudly as he dared. A fresh bombardment close by brought shock waves and bursts of light, by which he glimpsed their refuge: a domestic interior, with a table set for the evening meal, and its cook dead beneath it, her blood the stickiness under his heel.

Beckoning Huzzah to him and holding her tight, he ventured back towards the door as a second bombardment began. It drove the looters to the step for cover, and the Oethac caught sight of

Gentle before he could retreat into shadow. She let out a shout, and one of the youths fired into the darkness where Gentle and Huzzah had stood, the bullets spattering plaster and wood splinters in all directions. Backing away from the door through which their attackers were bound to come, Gentle ushered Huzzah into the darkest corner and drew a breath. He barely had time to do so before the trigger-happy youth was at the doorway, firing indiscriminately. Gentle unleashed a pneuma from the darkness, and it flew towards the door. He'd underestimated his strength. The gunman was obliterated in an instant, but the pneuma took the door frame and much of the wall to either side of it at the same time.

Before the dust could clear and the survivors come after them, he went to find Huzzah, but the wall against which she'd been crouching was cracked and curling like a stone wave. He yelled her name as it broke. Her shriek answered him, off to his left. The Nullianac had snatched her up, and for a terrifying instant Gentle thought it intended to annihilate her, but instead it drew her to it like a doll and disappeared into the dust clouds.

He started in pursuit without a backward glance, an error that brought him to his knees before he'd covered two yards of ground, as the Oethac woman delivered a stabbing blow to the small of his back. The wound wasn't deep, but the shock drove his breath from him as he fell, and her second blow would have taken out the back of his skull had he not rolled out of its way. The small pick she was wielding, wet with his blood, buried itself in the ground, and before she could pull it free he hauled himself to his feet and started after Huzzah and her abductor. The second youth was moving after the Nullianac, squealing with drugged or drunken glee, and Gentle followed the sound when he lost the sight, the chase taking him out of the wasteland and into a Kesparate that had been left relatively untouched by the conflict.

There was good reason. The trade here was in sexual favors, and business was booming. Though the streets were narrower than in any other district Gentle had passed through, there was plenty of light spilling from the doorways and windows, the lamps and candles arranged to best illuminate the wares lolling on step and sill. Even a passing glance confirmed that there were anatomies and gratifications on offer here that beggared the most dissolute backwaters of Bangkok or Tangiers. Nor was there any paucity of customers. The imminence of death seemed to have whipped up the consensual libido. Even if the flesh pushers and pill pimps who offered their highs as Gentle passed never made it to morning, they'd die rich. Needless to say, the sight of a Nullianac carrying a protesting child barely warranted a look in a street sacred to depravity, and Gentle's calls for the abductor to be stopped went ignored.

The crowd thickened the farther down the street he ventured, and he finally lost both sight and sound of those he was pursuing. There were alleyways off the main thoroughfare (its name—Lickerish Street—daubed on one of the bordello walls), and the darkness of any of them might be concealing the Nullianac. He started to yell Huzzah's name, but in the come-ons and hagglings two shouted syllables were drowned out. He was about to run on when he glimpsed a man backing out of one of the alleyways with distress on his face. He pushed his way through to the man and took hold of his arm, but he shrugged it off and fled before Gentle could ask what he'd seen. Rather than call Huzzah's name again, Gentle saved his breath and headed down the alley.

There was a fire of mattresses burning twenty yards down it, tended by a masked woman. Insects had nested in the ticking and were being driven out by the flames, some attempting to fly on burning wings, only to be swatted by the fire maker. Ducking her wild swings, Gentle asked after the Nullianac, and the woman directed him on down the alley with a nod. The ground was seething with refugees from the mattresses, and he broke a hundred shells with every step until he was well clear of the fumigator's fire. Lickerish Street was now too far behind him to shed any light on the scene, but the bombardment which the crowd behind him had been so indifferent to still continued all around, and explosions farther up the city's slopes briefly but garishly lit the alleyway. It was narrow and filthy, the buildings blinded by brick or boarded up, the road between scarcely more than a gutter, choked with trash and decaying vegetable matter. Its stench was sickening, but he breathed it deeply, hoping the pneuma born of and on that fetid air would be all the more potent for its foulness. The theft of Huzzah had already earned her abductors their deaths, but if they had done the least hurt to her he swore to himself he'd return that hurt a hundredfold before he executed them.

The alleyway twisted and turned, narrowing to a man's width in some places, but the sense that he was closing on them was confirmed when he heard the youth whooping a little way ahead. He slowed his pace a little, advancing through shin-deep refuse, until he came in sight of a light. The alleyway ended a few yards from where he stood, and there, squatting with its back to the wall, was the Nullianac. The light source was neither lamp nor fire but the creature's head, between the sides of which arcs of energy passed back and forth.

By their flickers, Gentle saw his angel, lying on the ground in front of her captor. She was quite still, her body limp, her eyes closed, for which fact Gentle was grateful, given the Nullianac's present labors. It had stripped the lower half of her body, and its long, pale hands were busy upon her. The whooper was standing a little way off from the scene. He was unzipped, his gun in one hand, his half-hard member in the other. Every now and then he aimed the gun at the child's head, and another whoop came from his lips.

Nothing would have given Gentle more satisfaction at that moment than unleashing a pneuma against them both from where he stood, but he still wielded the power ineptly and feared that he'd do Huzzah some accidental harm, so he crept a little closer, another explosion on the hill throwing its brutal light down on the scene. By it he caught a glimpse of the Nullianac's work, and then, more stomach-turning still, heard Huzzah gasp. The light withered as she did so, leaving the Nullianac's head to shed its flickering gleam on her pain. The whooper was silent now, his eyes fixed on the violation. Looking up, the Nullianac uttered a few syllables shaped out of the chamber between its skulls, and reluctantly the youth obeyed its order, retreating from the scene a little way. Some crisis was near. The arcs in the Nullianac's head were flaring with fresh urgency, its fingers working as if to expose Huzzah to their discharge. Gentle drew breath, realizing he would have to risk hurting Huzzah if he was to prevent the certainty of worse harm. The whooper heard his intake and turned to peer into the darkness. As he did so another lethal brightness dropped around them from on high. By it, Gentle stood revealed.

The youth fired on the instant, but either his ineptitude or his arousal spoiled his aim. The shots went wide. Gentle didn't give him a second chance. Reserving his pneuma for the Nullianac, he threw himself at the youth, striking the weapon from his hand and kicking the legs from under him. The whooper went down within inches of his gun, but before he could reclaim it Gentle drove his foot down on the outstretched fingers, bringing a very different kind of whoop from the kid's throat.

Now he turned back on the Nullianac, in time to see it raising its fireful head, the arcs cracking like slapsticks. Gentle's fist went to his mouth, and he was discharging the pneuma when the whooper seized hold of his leg. The death warrant went from Gentle's hand, but it struck the Nullianac's flank rather than its head, wounding but not dispatching it. The kid hauled on Gentle's leg again, and this time he toppled, falling into the muck where he'd put the whooper seconds before, his punctured back striking the ground hard. The pain blinded him, and when sight returned the youth was up, and rummaging among the arsenal at his belt. Gentle glanced towards the Nullianac. It had dropped against the wall, its head thrown back and spitting darts of fire. Their light was little, but enough for Gentle to catch the gleam of the dropped gun at his side. He reached for it as the delinquent's hand fumbled with another weapon, and he had it leveled before the youth could get his cracked finger on the trigger. He pointed not at the youth's head or heart, but at his groin. A littler target, but one which made the kid drop his gun instantly.

"Don't do that, sirrah!" he said.

"The belt," Gentle said, getting to his feet as the youth unbuckled and unburdened himself of his filched arsenal.

By another blaze from above he saw the boy now full of tics and jitters, pitiful and powerless. There would be no honor in shooting him down, whatever crimes he'd been responsible for.

"Go home," he said. "If I see your face ever again—"

"You won't, sirrah!" the boy said. "I swear! I swear you won't!"

He didn't give Gentle time to change his mind, but fled as the light that had revealed his frailty faded. Gentle turned the gun and his gaze upon the Nullianac. It had raised itself from the ground and slid up the wall into a standing position, its fingers, their tips red with its deed, pressed to the place where the pneuma had struck it. Gentle hoped it was suffering, but he had no way of knowing until it spoke. When it did, when the words came from its wretched head, they were faltering and barely comprehensible.

"Which is it to be," it said, "you or her? I will kill one of you before I pass. Which is it to be?"

"I'll kill you first," Gentle said, the gun pointed at the Nullianac's head.

"You could," it said. "I know. You murdered a brother of mine outside Patashoqua."

"Your brother, huh?"

"We're rare, and know each other's lives," it said.

"So don't get any rarer," Gentle advised, taking a step towards Huzzah as he spoke, but keeping his eyes fixed on her violator.

"She's alive," it said. "I wouldn't kill a thing so young. Not quickly. Young deserves slow."

Gentle risked a glance away from the creature. Huzzah's eyes were indeed wide open and fixed upon him in her terror.

"It's all right, angel," he said, "nothing's going to happen to you. Can you move?"

He glanced back at the Nullianac as he spoke, wishing he had some way of interpreting the motions of its little fires. Was it more grievously wounded than he'd thought, and preserving its energies for healing? Or was it biding its time, waiting for its moment to strike?

Huzzah was pulling herself up into a sitting position, the motion bringing little whimpers of pain from her. Gentle longed to cradle and soothe her, but all he'd dared do was drop to his haunches, his eyes fixed on her violator, and reach for the clothes she'd had torn from her.

"Can you walk, angel?"

"I don't know," she sobbed.

"Please try. I'll help you."

He put his hand out to do so but she avoided him, saying no through her tears and pulling herself to her feet.

"That's good, sweetheart," he said. There was a reawakening in the Nullianac's head, the arcs dancing again. "I want you to start walking, angel," Gentle said. "Don't worry about me, I'm coming with you."

She did as he instructed, slowly, the sobs still coming. The Nullianac started to speak again as she went.

"Ah, to see her like that. It makes me ache." The arcs had begun their din again, like distant firecrackers. "What would you do to save her little soul?" it said.

"Just about anything," Gentle replied.

"You deceive yourself," it said. "When you killed my brother, we inquired after you, my kin and I. We know how foul a savior you are. What's my crime beside yours? A small thing, done because my appetite demands it. But you—*you*—you've laid waste the hopes of generations. You've destroyed the fruit of great men's trees. And *still* you claim you would give yourself to save her little soul?"

This eloquence startled Gentle, but its essence startled him more. Where had the creature plucked these conceits from, that it could so easily spill them now? They were inventions, of course, but they confounded him nevertheless, and his thoughts strayed from his present jeopardy for a vital moment. The creature saw him drop his guard and acted on the instant. Though it was no more than two yards from him, he heard the sliver of silence between the light and its report, a void confirming how foul a savior he was. Death was on its way towards the child before his warning cry was even in his throat.

He turned to see his angel standing in the alleyway some distance from him. She had either turned in anticipation, or had been listening to the Nullianac's speech, because she stood full face to the blow coming at her. Still, time ran slow, and Gentle had several aching moments in which to see how her eyes were fixed upon him, her tears all dried, her gaze unblinking. Time too for that warning shout, in acknowledgment of which she closed her eyes, her face becoming a blank upon which he could inscribe any accusation his guilt wished to contrive.

Then the Nullianac's blow was upon her. The force struck her body at speed, but it didn't break her flesh, and for an instant he dared hope she had found some defense against it. But its hurt was more insidious than a bullet or a blow, its light spreading from the point of impact up to her face, where it entered by every means it could, and down to where its dispatcher's fingers had already pried.

He let out another shout, this time of revulsion, and turned back on the Nullianac, raising the gun its words had made him so forgetful of and firing at its heart. It fell back against the wall, its arms slack at its side, the space between its skulls still issuing its lethal light. Then he looked back at Huzzah, to see that it had eaten her away from the inside, and that she was flowing back along the line of her destroyer's gaze, into the chamber from which the stroke had been delivered. Even as he watched, her face collapsed, and her limbs, never substantial, decayed and went the same way. Before she was entirely consumed, however, the harm Gentle's bullet had done the Nullianac took its toll. The stream of power fractured and failed. When it did, darkness descended, and for a time Gentle couldn't even see the creature's body. Then the bombardment on the hill began afresh, its blaze brief but bright enough to show him the Nullianac's corpse, lying in the dirt where it had squatted.

He watched it, expecting some final act of retaliation, but none came. The light died, and left Gentle to retreat along the alleyway, weighed down not only by his failure to save Huzzah's life, but by his lack of comprehension of what had just happened. In plain terms, a child in his care had been slaughtered by her molester, and he'd failed to prevent that slaughter. But he'd been wandering in the Dominions too long to be content with simple assessments. There was more here than stymied lust and sudden death. Words had been uttered more appropriate to pulpit than gutter. Hadn't he himself called Huzzah his angel? Hadn't he seen her grow seraphic at the end, knowing she was about to die and accepting that fate? And hadn't he in his turn been dubbed a deficient savior—and proved that accusation true by failing to deliver her? These were high-flown words, but he badly needed to believe them apt, not so that he could indulge messianic fantasies, but so that the grief welling in him might be softened by the hope that there was a higher purpose here, which in the fullness of time he'd come to know and understand.

A burst of fire threw light down the alleyway, and Gentle's shadow fell across something twitching in the filth. It took him a moment to comprehend what he was seeing, but when he did he loosed a shout. Huzzah had not quite gone. Small scraps of her skin and sinew, dropped when the Nullianac's claim upon her was cut short, moved here in the rot. None were recognizable; indeed, had they not been moving in the folds of her bloodied clothes he'd not even have known them as her flesh. He reached down to touch them, tears stinging his eyes, but before his fingers could make contact, what little life the scraps had owned went out.

He rose raging; rose in horror at the filth beneath his feet, and the dead, empty houses that channeled it, and in disgust at himself, for surviving when his angel had not. Turning his gaze on the nearest wall, he drew breath and put not one hand but two against his lips, intending to do what little he could to bury these remains.

But rage and revulsion were fueling his pneuma, and when it went from him it brought down not one wall but several, passing through the teetering houses like a bullet through a pack of cards. Shards of pulverized stone flew as the houses toppled, the collapse of one initiating the fall of the next, the dust cloud growing in scale as each house added to its sum.

He started up the alleyway in pursuit of the pneuma, fearing that his disgust had given it more purpose than he'd intended. It was heading towards Lickerish Street, where the crowds were still milling, oblivious to its approach. They were not wandering that street innocent of its corruption, of course, but neither did their presence there deserve death. He wished he could draw the breath as he exhaled it, call the pneuma back into himself. But it had its head, and all he could do was run after it as it brought down house after house, hoping it would spend its power before it reached the crowd.

He could see the lights of Lickerish Street through the hail of demolition. He picked up his pace, to try and outrun the pneuma, and was a little ahead of it when he set eyes on the throng itself, thicker than ever. Some had interrupted their window-shopping to watch the spectacle of destruction. He saw their gawking faces, their little smiles, their shaking heads: saw they didn't comprehend for an instant what was coming their way. Knowing any attempt to warn them verbally would be lost in the furor, he raced to the end of the alleyway and flung himself into their midst, intending to scatter them, but his antics only drew a larger audience, who were in turn intrigued by the alleyway's capitulation. One or two had grasped their jeopardy now, their expressions of curiosity become looks of fear; finally, too late, their unease spread to the rest, and a general retreat began.

The pneuma was too quick, however. It broke through the last of the walls in a devastating shower of rock shards and splinters, striking the crowd at its densest place. Had Hapexamendios, in a fit of cleansing ire, delivered a judgment on Lickerish Street He could scarcely have scoured it better. What had seconds before been a crowd of puzzled sightseers was blood and bone in a heartbeat.

Though he stood in the midst of this devastation, Gentle

remained unharmed. He was able to watch his terrible weapon at work, its power apparently undecayed despite the fact that it had demolished a string of houses. Nor, having cut a swath through the crowd, was it following the trajectory set at his lips. It had found flesh and clearly intended to busy itself in the midst of living stuff until there was none left to undo.

He was appalled at the prospect. This hadn't been his intention, or anything like it. There seemed to be only one option available to him, and that he instantly took: he stood in the pneuma's path. He'd used the power in his lungs many times now—first against the Nullianac's brother in Vanaeph, then twice in the mountains, and finally on the island, when they were making their escape from Vigor N'ashap's asylum—but in all that time he'd only had the vaguest impression of its appearance. Was it like a fire-breather's belch, or like a bullet made of will and air, nearly invisible until it did its deed?

Perhaps it had been the latter once, but now, as he set himself in its path, he saw that it had gathered dust and blood along its route, and from those essential elements it had made itself a likeness of its maker. It was *his* face that was coming at him, albeit roughly sculpted: his brow, his eyes, his open mouth, expelling the very breath it had begun with. It didn't slow as it approached its maker, but struck Gentle's chest the way it had struck so many before him. He felt the blow but was not felled by it. Instead the power, knowing its source, discharged itself through his system, running to his fingertips and coursing across his scalp. Its shock was come and gone in a moment, and he was left standing in the middle of the devastation with his arms spread wide and the dust falling around him.

Silence followed. Distantly, he could hear the wounded sobbing, and half-demolished walls going to rubble, but he was encircled by a hush that was almost reverential. Somebody dropped to his knees nearby, to tend, he thought, to one of the wounded. Then he heard the hallelujahs the man was uttering and saw his hands reaching up towards him. Another of the crowd followed suit, and then another, as though this scene of their deliverance was a sign they'd been waiting for and a long-suppressed flood of devotion was breaking from each of their hearts.

Sickened, Gentle turned his gaze away from their grateful faces, up the dusty length of Lickerish Street. He had only one ambition now: to find Pie and take comfort from this insanity in the mystif's arms. He broke from his ring of devotees and started up the street, ignoring their clinging hands and cries of adoration. He wanted to berate them for their naïveté, but what good would that do? Any pronouncement he made now, however self-deprecatory, would

probably be taken as the jotting for some gospel. Instead he kept
his silence and picked his way over the stones and corpses, his
head down. The hosannas followed him, but he didn't once acknowledge them, knowing even as he went that his reluctance
might seem like divine humility, but unable to escape the trap circumstance had set.

The wasteland at the head of the street was as daunting as ever,
but he started across it not caring what fires might come. Its terrors were nothing beside the memory of Huzzah's scrap, twitching
in the muck, or the hallelujahs he could still hear behind him,
raised in ignorance of the fact that he—the savior of Lickerish
Street—was also its destroyer, but no less tempting for that.

I

Every trace of the joy that the vast halls of the chianculi had once
seen—no clowns or ponies, but circuses such as any showman in
the Fifth would have wept to own—had gone. The echoing halls
had become places of mourning and of judgment. Today, the accused was the mystif Pie 'oh' pah; its accuser one of the few lawyers
in Yzordderrex the Autarch's purges had left alive, an asthmatic
and pinched individual called Thes 'reh' ot. He had an audience of
two for his prosecution—Pie 'oh' pah, and the judge—but he delivered his litany of crimes as if the hall were full to the rafters. The
mystif was guilty enough to warrant a dozen executions, he said.
It was at very least a traitor and coward, but probably also an informant and a spy. Worse, perhaps, it had abandoned this Dominion for another without the consent of its family or its teachers,
denying its people the benefit of its rarity. Had it forgotten in its
arrogance that its condition was sacred, and that to prostitute itself in another world (the Fifth, of all places, a mire of unmiracu-
lous souls!) was not only a sin upon itself but upon its species? It
had gone from this place clean and dared to return debauched and
corrupted, bringing a creature of the Fifth with it and then freely
confessing that said creature was its husband.

Pie had expected to be met with some recriminations upon
return—the memories of Eurhetemec were long, and they clung
strongly to tradition as the only contact they had with the First Dominion—but the vehemence of this catalogue was still astonishing.
The judge, Culus 'su' erai, was a woman of great age but diminished physique, who sat bundled in robes as colorless as her skin,

listening to the litany of accusations without once looking at either accuser or accused. When Thes 'reh' ot had finished, she offered the mystif the chance to defend itself, and it did what it could.

"I admit I've made many errors," Pie said. "Not least leaving my family—and my people were my family—without telling them where I was going or why. But the simple fact is: I didn't know. I fully intended to return, after maybe a year or so. I thought it'd be fine to have traveler's tales to tell. Now, when I finally return, I find there's nobody to tell them to."

"What possessed you to go into the Fifth?" Culus asked.

"Another error," Pie said. "I went to Patashoqua and I met a theurgist there who said he could take me over to the Fifth. Just for a jaunt. We'd be back in a day, he said. A day! I thought this was a fine idea. I'd come home having walked in the Fifth Dominion. So I paid him—"

"In what currency?" said Thes 'reh' ot.

"Cash. And some little favors. I didn't prostitute myself, if that's what you're suggesting. If I had, maybe he'd have kept his promises. Instead, his ritual delivered me into the In Ovo."

"And how long were you there?" Culus 'su' erai inquired.

"I don't know," the mystif replied. "The suffering there seemed endless and unendurable, but it was perhaps only days."

Thes 'reh' ot snorted at this. "Its *sufferings* were of its own making, ma'am. Are they strictly relevant?"

"Probably not," Culus 'su' erai, conceded. "But you were claimed out of the In Ovo by a Maestro of the Fifth, am I right?"

"Yes, ma'am. His name was Sartori. He was the Fifth's representative in the Synod preparing for the Reconciliation."

"And you served him?"

"I did."

"In what capacity?"

"In any way he chose to request. I was his familiar."

Thes 'reh' ot made a sound of disgust. His response was not feigned, Pie thought. He was genuinely appalled at the thought of one of his people—especially a creature so blessed as a mystif—serving the will of a *Homo sapiens*.

"Was Sartori, in your estimation, a good man?" Culus asked Pie.

"He was the usual paradox. Compassion when it was least expected. Cruelty the same. He had an extraordinary ego, but then I don't believe he could have carried the responsibility of the Reconciliation without one."

"Was he cruel to you?" Culus inquired.

"Ma'am?"

"Do you not understand the question?"

"Yes. But not its relevance."

Culus growled with displeasure. "This court may be much reduced in pomp and ceremony," she said, "and its officers a little withered, but the authority of both remains undiminished. Do you understand me, mystif? When I ask a question I expect it answered, promptly and truthfully."

Pie murmured apologies.

"So," said Culus. "I will repeat the question. Was Sartori cruel to you?"

"Sometimes," Pie replied.

"And yet when the Reconciliation failed you didn't forsake his company and return to this Dominion?"

"He'd summoned me out of the In Ovo. He'd bound me to him. I had no jurisdiction."

"Unlikely," Thes 'reh' ot remarked. "Are you asking us to believe—"

"Did I hear you ask permission to question the accused again?" Culus snapped.

"No, ma'am."

"Do you request such permission?"

"Yes, ma'am."

"Denied," Culus replied and turned her eye back upon Pie. "I think you learned a great deal in the Fifth Dominion, mystif," she said. "And you're the worse for it. You're arrogant. You're sly. And you're probably just as cruel as your Maestro. But I don't believe you're a spy. You're something worse than that. You're a fool. You turned your back on people who loved you and let yourself be enslaved by a man responsible for the deaths of a great many fine souls across the Imajica. I can tell you've got something to say, Thes 'reh' ot. Spit it out, before I give judgment."

"Only that the mystif isn't here simply charged with spying, ma'am. In denying its people the benefits of its birthright, it committed a grievous crime against us."

"I don't doubt that," Culus said. "And it frankly sickens me to look on something so tainted that once had perfectibility within its grasp. But, may I remind you, Thes 'reh' ot, how few we are? The tribe is diminished to almost nothing. And this mystif, whose breed was always rare, is the last of its line."

"The last?" said Pie.

"Yes, the last!" Culus replied, her voice trembling as it rose. "While you were at play in the Fifth Dominion our people have been systematically decimated. There are now fewer than fifty souls here in the city. The rest are either dead or scattered. Your own line is destroyed, Pie 'oh' pah. Every last one of your clan is murdered or dead of grief."

The mystif covered its face with its hands, but Culus didn't spare it the rest of her report.

"Two other mystifs survived the purges," she went on, "until just a year ago. One was murdered here in the chiancula, while it was healing a child. The other went into the desert—the Dearth are there, at the edge of the First, and the Autarch's troops don't like to go so near to the Erasure—but they caught up with it before it reached the tents. They brought its body back and hung it on the gates."

She stepped down from her chair and approached Pie, who was sobbing now.

"So you see, it may be that you did the right thing for the wrong reasons. If you'd stayed you'd be dead by now."

"Ma'am, I protest," Thes 'reh' ot said.

"What would you prefer I did?" Culus said. "Add this foolish creature's blood to the sea already spilt? No. Better we try and turn its taint to our advantage."

Pie looked up, puzzled.

"Perhaps we've been too pure. Too predictable. Our stratagems foreseen, our plots easily uncovered. But you're from another world, mystif, and maybe that makes you potent." She paused for breath. Then she said, "This is my judgment. Take whomsoever you can find among our number and use your tainted ways to murder our enemy. If none will go with you, go alone. But don't return here, mystif, while the Autarch is still breathing."

Thes 'reh' ot let out a laugh that rang around the chamber. "Perfect!" he said. "Perfect!"

"I'm glad my judgment amuses you," Culus replied. "Remove yourself, Thes 'reh' ot." He made to protest but she brought forth such a shout he flinched as if struck. "I said, *remove yourself!*"

The laughter fell from his face. He made a small formal bow, murmuring some chilly words of parting as he did so, and left the chamber. She watched him go.

"We have all become cruel," she said. "You in your way. Us in ours." She looked back at Pie 'oh' pah. "Do you know why he laughed, mystif?"

"Because he thinks your judgment is execution by another name?"

"Yes, that's precisely what he thinks. And, who knows, perhaps that's what it is. But this may be the last night of the Dominion, and last things have power tonight they never had before."

"And I'm a last thing."

"Yes, you are."

The mystif nodded. "I understand," it said. "And it seems just."

"Good," she said. Though the trial was over, neither moved. "You have a question?" Culus asked.

"Yes, I do."

"Better ask it now."

"Do you know if a shaman called Arae 'ke' gei is still alive?"

Culus made a little smile. "I wondered when you'd get to him," she said. "He was one of the survivors of the Reconciliation, wasn't he?"

"Yes."

"I didn't know him that well, but I heard him speak of you. He held on to life long after most people would have given up, because he said you'd come back eventually. He didn't realize you were bound to your Maestro, of course."

She said all this disingenuously, but there was a penetrating look in her rheumy eyes throughout.

"Why didn't you come back, mystif?" she said. "And don't spin me some story about jurisdiction. You could have slipped your bondage if you'd put your mind to it, especially in the confusion after the failure of the Reconciliation. But you didn't. You chose to stay with your wretched Sartori, even though members of your own tribe had been victims of his ineptitude."

"He was a broken man. And I was more than his familiar, I was his friend. How could I leave him?"

"That's not all," Culus said. She'd been a judge too long to let such simplifications pass unchallenged. "What else, mystif? This is the night of last things, remember. Tell it now or run the risk of not telling it at all."

"Very well," said Pie. "I always nurtured the hope that there would be another attempt at Reconciliation. And I wasn't the only one who nurtured such a hope."

"Arae 'ke' gei indulged it too, huh?"

"Yes, he did."

"So that's why he kept your name alive. And himself too, waiting for you to come back." She shook her head. "Why do you wallow in these fantasies? There'll be no Reconciliation. If anything, it'll be the other way about. The Imajica'll come apart at the seams, and every Dominion will be sealed up in its own little misery."

"That's a grim vision."

"It's an honest one. And a rational one."

"There are still people in every Dominion willing to try again. They've waited two hundred years, and they're not going to let go of their hope now."

"Arae 'ke' gei let go," Culus said. "He died two years ago."

"I was . . . prepared for that eventuality," Pie said. "He was old when I knew him last."

"If it's any comfort, your name was on his lips at the very end. He never gave up believing."

"There are others who can perform the ceremonies in his place."

"I was right," Culus said. "You are a fool, mystif." She started towards the door. "Do you do this in memory of your Maestro?"

Pie went with her, opening the door and stepping out into a twilight sharp with smoke. "Why would I do that?" Pie said.

"Because you loved him," Culus said, her gaze accusatory. "And that's the real reason why you never came back here. You loved him more than your own people."

"Perhaps that's true," Pie said. "But why would I do anything in memory of the living?"

"The living?"

The mystif smiled, bowing to its judge as it retreated from the light at the door, fading into the gloom like a phantom. "I told you Sartori was a broken man, not a dead one," it said as it went. "The dream is still alive, Culus 'su' erai. And so is my Maestro."

2

Quaisoir was waiting behind the veils when Seidux came in. The windows were open, and within the warm dusk came a din aphrodisiacal to a soldier like Seidux. He peered at the veils, trying to make out the figure behind them. Was she naked? It seemed so.

"I have an apology to make," she said to him.

"There's no need."

"There's every need. You were doing your duty, watching me." She paused. When she spoke again, her voice was sinuous. "I like to be watched, Seidux. . . ."

He murmured, "You do?"

"Certainly. As long as my audience is appreciative."

"I'm appreciative," he said, surreptitiously dropping his cigarette and grinding it out beneath the heel of his boot.

"Then why don't you close the door?" she said to him. "In case we get noisy. Maybe you should tell the guards to go and get drunk?"

He did so. When he returned to the veils he saw that she was kneeling up on the bed, her hand between her legs. And, yes, she was naked. When she moved the veils moved with her, some of them sticking momentarily to the oiled gloss of her skin. He could see how her breasts rode up as she raised her arms, inviting his kisses there. He put his hand out to part the veils, but they were too abundant, and he could find no break in them, so he simply pressed on towards her, half blinded by their luxury.

Her hand went down once more between her legs, and he couldn't conceal a moan of anticipation at the thought of replacing it with his own. There was swelling in her fingers, he thought: some device she'd been pleasuring herself with, most likely, anticipating his arrival, easing herself open to accommodate his every inch. Thoughtful, pliant thing that she was, she was even handing it to him now, as though in confession of her little sin; thinking perhaps that he'd want to feel its warmth and wetness. She pushed it through the veils towards him, as he in turn pressed towards her, murmuring as he went a few promises that ladies liked to hear.

Between those promises he caught the sound of tearing fabric, and assuming that she was clawing her way through the veils in her hunger to reach him, began to do the same himself, until he felt a sharp pain in his belly. He looked down through the layers that clung about his face and saw a stain spreading through the weave. He let out a cry and started to disentangle himself, catching sight of her pleasuring device buried deep in him as he wrestled to be out of her way. She withdrew the blade, only to plunge it into him a second time, and a third, leaving it in his heart as he fell backwards, his fingers dragging the veils down with him.

Standing at one of the upper windows of Peccable's house, watching the fires that raged in every direction, Jude shuddered, and looking down at her hands saw them glistening, wet with blood. The vision lasted only the briefest time, but she had no doubt of what she'd seen, nor what it signified. Quaisoir had committed the crime she'd been plotting.

"It's quite a sight, isn't it?" she heard Dowd say, and turned to look at him, momentarily disoriented. Had he seen the blood, too? No, no. He was talking about the fires.

"Yes, it is," she said.

IIe came to join her at the glass, which rattled with each fusillade. "The Peccables are almost ready to leave. I suggest we do the same. I'm feeling much renewed." He had indeed healed with astonishing speed. The wounds on his face were barely visible now.

"Where will we go?" she said.

"Around the other side of the city," he said. "To where I first trod the boards. According to Peccable the theater is still standing. The Ipse, it's called. Built by Pluthero Quexos himself. I'd like to see it again."

"You want to be a tourist on a night like this?"

"The theater may not be standing tomorrow. In fact, the whole of Yzordderrex could be in ruins by daybreak. I thought you were the one who was so hungry to see it."

"If it's a sentimental visit," she said, "maybe you should go alone."

"Why, have you got some other agenda?" he asked her. "You have, haven't you?"

"How could I have?" she protested lightly. "I've never set foot here before."

He studied her, his face all suspicion. "But you always wanted to come here, didn't you? Right from the start. Godolphin used to wonder where you got the obsession from. Now I'm wondering the same." He followed her gaze through the window. "What's out there, Judith?"

"You can see for yourself," she replied. "We'll probably get killed before we reach the top of the street."

"No," he said. "Not us. We're blessed."

"Are we?"

"We're the same, remember? Perfect partners."

"I remember," she replied.

"Ten minutes, then we'll go."

"I'll be ready."

She heard the door close behind her, then looked down at her hands again. All trace of the vision had faded. She glanced back towards the door, to be certain that Dowd had gone, then put her hands to the glass and closed her eyes. She had ten minutes to find the woman who shared her face, ten minutes before she and Dowd were out in the tumult of the streets and all hope of contact would be dashed.

"Quaisoir," she murmured.

She felt the glass vibrate against her palms and heard the din of the dying across the roofs. She said her double's name a second time, turning her thoughts to the towers that would have been visible from this very window if the air between hadn't been so thick with smoke. The image of that smoke filled her head, though she hadn't consciously conjured it, and she felt her thoughts rise in its clouds, wafted on the heat of destruction.

It was difficult for Quaisoir to find something discreet to wear among garments she had acquired for their immodesty, but by tearing all the decoration from one of her simpler robes she had achieved something like seemliness. Now she left her chambers and prepared for her final journey through the palace. She had already plotted her route once she was out of the gates: back down to the harbor, where she'd first seen the Man of Sorrows, standing on the roof. If He wasn't there, she would find somebody who knew His whereabouts. He hadn't come into Yzorderrex simply to disappear again. He would leave trails for His acolytes to follow, and trials, no doubt, for them to endure, proving in their endurance how much they desired to come into His presence. But first, she had to get out of the palace, and to do so she took corridors and stairways that had not been used in decades, familiar only to her, the Autarch, and the masons who'd laid these cold stones, cold themselves now. Only Maestros and their mistresses preserved their youth, and doing so was no longer the bliss it had been. She would have liked the years to show on her face when she knelt before the Nazarene, so that He would know that she'd suffered, and that she deserved His forgiveness. But she would have to trust that He would see through the veil of her perfection to the pain beneath.

Her feet were bare, and the chill rose through her soles, so that by the time she reached the humid air outside, her teeth were chattering. She halted for a moment, to orient herself in the maze of courtyards that surrounded the palace, and as she turned her thoughts from the practical to the abstract she met another thought, waiting at the back of her skull for just such a turn. She didn't doubt its source for a moment. The angel that Seidux had driven from her chamber that afternoon had waited at the threshold all this time, knowing she would come at last, seeking guidance. Tears started to her eyes when she realized she'd not been forsaken. The Son of David knew her agony and sent this messenger to whisper in her head.

Ipse, it said. *Ipse.*

She knew what the word meant. She'd patronized the Ipse many times, masked, as were all the women of the *haut monde* when visiting places of moral dubiety. She'd seen all the works of Quexos performed there; and translations of Flotter; even, on occasion, Koppocovi's farces, crude as they were. That the Man of Sorrows should have chosen such a place was certainly strange, but who was she to question His purposes?

"I hear," she said aloud.

Even before the voice in her had faded, she was making her way through the courtyards to the gate by which she would be delivered most readily into the Deliquium Kesparate, where Pluthero Quexos had built his shrine to artifice, soon to be reconsecrated in the name of Truth.

Jude took her hands from the window and opened her eyes. There had been none of the clarity she'd experienced when asleep in this contact—in truth she was not even certain she'd made it—but there was no time left to try again. Dowd was calling her, and so were the streets of Yzordderrex, blazing though they were. She'd seen blood spilt from her place by the window; numerous assaults and beatings; troop charges and retreats; civilians warring in rabid packs, and others marching in brigades, armed and ordered. In such a chaos of factions she had no way of judging the legitimacy of any cause; nor, in truth, did she much care. Her mission was seek out her sister in this maelstrom, and hope that she in her turn was seeking out Jude.

Quaisoir would be disappointed, of course, if and when they finally met. Jude was not the messenger of the Lord she was hurrying to find. But then lords divine or secular were not the redeemers and salvers of the world legend made them out to be. They were spoilers; they were destroyers. The evidence of that was out there, in the very streets Jude was about to tread, and if she could only make Quaisoir share and understand that vision, perhaps the promise of sisterhood would not be so unwelcome a gift to bring to this meeting, which she could not help but think of as a reunion.

35

I

Demanding directions as he went, usually from wounded men, Gentle took several hours to get from the hosannas of Lickerish Street to the mystif's Kesparate, during which period the city's decline into chaos quickened, so that he went half expecting that the streets of straight houses and blossom-clad trees would be ashes and rubble by the time he arrived. But when he finally came to the city-within-a-city he found it untouched by looters or demolishers, either because they knew there was little of worth to them here or—more likely—because the lingering superstition about a people who'd once occupied the Unbeheld's Dominion kept them from doing their worst.

Entering, he went first to the chiancula, prepared to do whatever was necessary—threaten, beg, cajole—in order to be returned into the mystif's company. The chiancula and all the adjacent buildings were deserted, however, so he began a systematic search of the streets. They, like the chiancula, were empty, and as his desperation grew his discretion fled, until he was shouting Pie's name to the empty streets like a midnight drunkard.

Eventually, these tactics earned him a response. One of the quartet who'd appeared to offer such chilly welcome when he'd first come here appeared: the mustached young man. His robes were not held between his teeth this time, and when he spoke he deigned to do so in English. But the lethal ribbon still fluttered in his hands, its threat undisguised.

"You came back," he said.

"Where's Pie?"

"Where's the girl child?"

"Dead. Where's Pie?"

"You seem different."

"I am. Where's Pie?"

"Not here."

"Where then?"

"The mystif's gone up to the palace," the man replied.

"Why?"

"That was the judgment upon it."

"Just to go?" Gentle said, taking a step towards the man. "There must have been more to it than that."

Though the silk sword protected the man, Gentle came with a burden of power that beggared his own, and sensing this he answered less obliquely.

"The judgment was that it kill the Autarch," he said.

"So it's been sent up there alone?"

"No. It took some of our tribe with it and left a few of us to guard the Kesparate."

"How long ago since they went?"

"Not very long. But you won't get into the palace. Neither will they. It's suicide."

Gentle didn't linger to argue but headed back towards the entrance, leaving the man to guard the blossoms and the empty streets. As he approached the gate, however, he saw that two individuals, a man and a woman, had just entered and were looking his way. Both were naked from the waist up, their throats painted with the blue triple stripe he remembered from the siege at the harbor, marking them as members of the Dearth. At his approach, both acknowledged him by putting palm to palm and inclining their heads. The woman was half as big again as her companion, her body a glorious machine, her head—shaved but for a ponytail—set on a neck wider than her cranium and, like her arms and belly, so elaborately muscled the merest twitch was a spectacle.

"I said he'd be here!" she told the world.

"I don't know what you want," he said, "but I can't supply it."

"You *are* John Furie Zacharias?"

"Yes."

"Called Gentle?"

"Yes. But—"

"Then you have to come. Please. Father Athanasius sent us to find you. We heard what happened on Lickerish Street, and we knew it had to be you. I'm Nikaetomaas," the woman said. "This is Floccus Dado. We've been waiting for you since Estabrook arrived."

"Estabrook?" said Gentle. There was a man he hadn't given a thought to in many a month. "How do you know him?"

"We found him in the street. We thought he was the one. But he wasn't. He knew nothing."

"And you think I do?" Gentle said, exasperated. "Let me tell you, I know fuck-all! I don't know who you think I am, but I'm not your man."

"That's what Father Athanasius said. He said you were in ignorance—"

"Well, he was right."

"But you married the mystif."

"So what?" said Gentle. "I love it, and I don't care who knows it."

"We realize that," Nikaetomaas said, as though nothing could have been plainer. "That's how we tracked you."

"We knew it would come here," Floccus said. "And wherever it had gone, you would be."

"It isn't here," Gentle said. "It's up in the palace."

"In the palace?" said Nikaetomaas, turning her gaze up towards the lowering walls. "And you intend to follow it?"

"Yes."

"Then I'll come with you," she said. "Mr. Dado, go back to Athanasius. Tell him who we've found and where we've gone."

"I don't want company," Gentle said. "I don't even trust myself."

"How will you get into the palace without someone at your side?" Nikaetomaas said. "I know the gates. I know the courtyards."

Gentle turned the options over in his head. Part of him wanted to go as a rogue, carrying the chaos he'd brought to Lickerish Street as his emblem. But his ignorance of palace geography could indeed slow him, and minutes might make the difference between finding the mystif alive or dead. He nodded his consent, and the parties divided at the gate: Floccus Dado back to Father Athanasius, Gentle and Nikaetomaas up towards the Autarch's fortress.

The only subject he broached as they traveled was that of Estabrook. How was he, Gentle asked: still crazy?

"He was almost dead when we found him," Nikaetomaas said. "His brother left him here for dead. But we took him to our tents on the Erasure, and we healed him there. Or, more properly, his being there healed him."

"You did all this, thinking he was me?"

"We knew that somebody was going to come from the Fifth to begin the Reconciliation again. And of course we knew it had to be soon. We just didn't know what he looked like."

"Well, I'm sorry to disappoint you, but that's twice you've got it wrong. I'm no more your man than Estabrook."

"Why did you come here, then?" she said.

That was an inquiry that deserved a serious reply, if not for her sake, then for his own.

"There were questions I wanted answered, that I couldn't answer on earth," he said. "A friend of mine died, very young. A woman I knew was almost murdered—"

"Judith."

"Yes, Judith."

"We've talked about her a great deal," Nikaetomaas said. "Estabrook was obsessed with her."

"Is he still?"

"I haven't spoken to him for a long time. But you know he was trying to bring her to Yzordderrex when his brother intervened."

"Did she come?"

"Apparently not," Nikaetomaas said. "But Athanasius believes she will eventually. He says she's part of the story of the Reconciliation."

"How does he work that out?"

"From Estabrook's obsession with her, I suppose. The way he talked about her, it was though she was something holy, and Athanasius loves holy women."

"Let me tell you, I know Judith very well, and she's no Virgin."

"There are other kinds of sanctity among our sex," Nikaetomaas replied, a little testily.

"I'm sorry. I didn't mean any offense. But if there's one thing Jude's always hated it's being put on a pedestal."

"Then maybe it's not the idol we should be studying, but the worshiper. Athanasius says obsession is fire to our fortress."

"What does that mean?"

"That we have to burn down the walls around us, but it takes a very bright flame to do so."

"An obsession, in other words."

"That's one such flame, yes."

"Why would we want to burn down these walls in the first place? Don't they protect us?"

"Because if we don't, we die inside, kissing our own reflections," Nikaetomaas said, the reply too well turned to be improvised.

"Athanasius again?" Gentle said.

"No," said Nikaetomaas. "An aunt of mine. She's been locked up in the Bastion for years, but in here"—Nikaetomaas pointed to her temple—"she's free."

"And what about the Autarch?" Gentle said, turning his gaze up towards the fortress.

"What about him?"

"Is he up there, kissing his reflection?"

"Who knows? Maybe he's been dead for years, and the state's running itself."

"Do you seriously believe that?"

Nikaetomaas shook her head. "No. He's alive, behind his walls."

"What's he keeping out, I wonder?"

"Who knows? Whatever he's afraid of, I don't think it breathes the same air that we do."

Before they left the rubble-strewn thoroughfares of the Kesparate called Hittahitte, which lay between the gates of the Eurhetemec Kesparate and the wide Roman streets of Yzordderrex's bureaucratic district, Nikaetomaas dug around in the ruins of a garret for some means of disguise. She found a collection of filthy garments which she insisted Gentle don, then found some equally disgusting for herself. Their faces and physiques had to be concealed, she explained, so that they could mingle freely with the wretched they'd find gathered at the gates. Then they headed on, their climb bringing them into streets lined with buildings of classical severity and scale, as yet unscorched by the torches that were being passed from hand to hand, roof to roof, in the Kesparates below. They would not remain pristine much longer, Nikaetomaas predicted. When the rebels' fire reached these edifices—the Taxation Courts and the Bureaus of Justice—it would leave no pillar unblackened. But for now the travelers moved between monoliths as quiet as mausoleums.

On the other side, the reason for their donning of stinking and louse-ridden clothes became apparent. Nikaetomaas had brought them not to one of the great gates of the palace but to a minor opening, around which a group dressed in motley indistinguishable from their own was gathered. Some of them carried candles. By their fitful light Gentle could see that there was not a single body that was whole among them.

"Are they waiting to get in?" he asked his guide.

"No. This is the gate of Saint Creaze and Saint Evendown. Have you not heard of them in the Fifth? I thought that's where they were martyred."

"Very possibly."

"They appear everywhere in Yzordderrex. Nursery rhymes, puppet plays—"

"So what happens here? Do the saints make personal appearances?"

"After a fashion."

"And what are these people hoping for?" Gentle asked, casting a glance among the wretched assembly. "Healing?"

They were certainly in dire need of such miracles. Crippled and diseased, suppurating and broken, some of them looked so weak they'd not make it till morning.

"No," Nikaetomaas replied. "They're here for sustenance. I only hope the saints aren't too distracted by the revolution to put in an appearance."

She'd no sooner spoken than the sound of an engine chugging into life on the far side of the gates pitched the crowd into frenzy. Crutches became weapons, and diseased spittle flew, as the invalids fought for a place close to the bounty they knew was imminent. Nikaetomaas pushed Gentle forward into the brawl, where he was obliged to fight, though he felt ashamed to do so, or else have his limbs torn from their sockets by those who had fewer than he. Head down, arms flailing, he dug his way forward as the gates began to open.

What appeared on the other side drew gasps of devotion from all sides and one of incredulity from Gentle. Trundling forward to fill the breadth of the gates was a fifteen-foot study in kitsch: a sculpted representation of Saints Creaze and Evendown, standing shoulder to shoulder, their arms stretched out towards the yearning crowd, while their eyes rolled in their carved sockets like those of carnival dummies, looking down on their flock as if affrighted by them one moment and up to heaven the next. But it was their apparel that drew Gentle's appalled gaze. They were clothed in their largesse: dressed in food from throat to foot. Coats of meat, still smoking from the ovens, covered their torsos; sausages hung in steaming loops around their necks and wrists; at their groins hung sacks heavy with bread, while the layers of their skirts were of fruit and fish. The crowd instantly surged forward to denude them, the brawlers merciless in their hunger, beating each other as they climbed for their share.

The saints were not without defense, however; there were penalties for the gluttonous. Hooks and spikes, expressly designed to wound, were set among the bountiful folds of skirts and coats. The devotees seemed not to care, but climbed up over the statues, disdainful of fruit and fish, in order to reach the steaks and sausages above. Some fell, doing themselves bloody mischief on the way down; others—scrambling over the victims—reached their goals with shrieks of glee and set about loading the bags on their backs. Even then, in their triumph, they were not secure. Those behind either dragged them from their perches or pulled the bags from their backs and pitched them to accomplices in the crowd, where they in turn were set upon and robbed.

Nikaetomaas held on to Gentle's belt so that they wouldn't be separated in this mêlée, and after much maneuvering they reached the base of the statues. The machine had been designed to block the gates, but Nikaetomaas now squatted down in front of the plinth, and—her activities concealed from the guards watching from above the gate—tore at the casing that housed the vehicle's wheels. It was beaten metal, but it came away like cardboard beneath her assault, its rivets flying. Then she ducked into the gap she'd created. Gentle followed. Once below the saints, the din of the crowd became remoter, the thump of bodies punctuating the general hubbub. It was almost completely dark, but they shimmied forward on their stomachs, the engine—huge and hot—dripping its fluids on them as they went. As they reached the other side, and Nikaetomaas began to prize away the casing there, the sound of shouting became louder. Gentle looked around. Others had discovered Nikaetomaas' handiwork and, perhaps thinking there were new treasures to be discovered beneath the idols, were following: not two or three, now, but many. Gentle began to lend Nikaetomaas a hand, as the space filled up with bodies, new brawls erupting as the pursuers fought for access. The whole structure, enormous as it was, began to shudder, the combination of brawlers below and above conspiring to tip it. With the violence of the rocking increasing by the moment, Gentle had sight of escape. A sizable courtyard lay on the other side of the saints, scored by the tracks of the engine and littered with discarded food.

The instability of the machine had not gone unnoticed, and two guards were presently forsaking their meal of prime steak and raising the alarm with panicked shouts. Their retreat allowed Nikaetomaas to wriggle free unnoticed, then turn to haul Gentle after her. The juggernaut was now close to toppling, and shots were being fired on the other side as the guards above the gate sought to dissuade the crowd from further burrowings. Gentle felt hands grasping at his legs, but he kicked back at them, as Nikaetomaas dragged him forward, and slid out into the open air as several cracks, like sudden thunder, announced that the saints were tired of teetering and ready to fall. Backs bent, Gentle and Nikaetomaas darted across the rind- and crust-littered ground to the safety of the shadows as, with a great din the saints fell backwards like comic drunkards, a mass of their adherents still clinging to arms and coats and skirts. The structure came apart as it hit the ground, pitching pieces of carved, cooked, and crippled flesh in all directions.

The guards were descending from the ramparts now, to stem with bullets the flow of the crowd. Gentle and Nikaetomaas didn't linger to watch this fresh horror but took to their heels, up and away from the gates, the pleas and howls of those maimed by the fall following them through the darkness.

2

"What's the din, Rosengarten?"

"There's a minor problem at the Gate of Saints, sir."

"Are we under siege?"

"No. It was merely an unfortunate accident."

"Fatalities?"

"Nothing significant. The gate's now been sealed."

"And Quaisoir? How's she?"

"I haven't spoken with Seidux since early evening."

"Then find out."

"Of course."

Rosengarten withdrew, and the Autarch returned his attention to the man transfixed in the chair close by.

"These Yzordderrexian nights," he said to the fellow, "they're so very long. In the Fifth, you know, they're half this length, and I used to complain they were over too soon. But now"—he sighed—"now I wonder if I wouldn't be better off going back there and founding a New Yzordderrex. What do you think?"

The man in the chair didn't reply. His cries had long since ceased, though the reverberations, more precious than the sound itself, and more tantalizing, continued to shake the air, even to the ceiling of this chamber, where clouds sometimes formed and shed delicate, cleansing rains.

The Autarch drew his own chair up closer to the man. A sac of living fluid the size of his head was clamped to the victim's chest, its limbs, fine as thread, puncturing him, and reaching into his body to touch his heart, lungs, liver, and lights. He'd summoned the entity, which was the shreds of a once much more fabulous beast, the renunciance, from the In Ovo, selecting it as a surgeon might choose some instrument from a tray, to perform a delicate and very particular task. Whatever the nature of such summoned beasts, he had no fear of them. Decades of such rituals had familiarized him with every species that haunted the In Ovo, and while there were certainly some he would never have dared bring into the living world, most had enough base instinct to know their master's voice and would obey him within the confines of their wit. This creature he'd called Abelove, after a lawyer he'd known briefly in the Fifth, who'd been as leechlike as this scrap of malice, and almost as foul smelling.

"How does it feel?" the Autarch asked, straining to catch the merest murmur of a reply. "The pain's passed, hasn't it? Didn't I say it would?"

The man's eyes flickered open, and he licked his lips. They made something very close to a smile.

"You feel a kind of union with Abelove, am I right? It's worked its way into every little part. Please speak, or I'll take it from you. You'll bleed from every hole it's made, but that pain won't be anything beside the loss you'll feel."

"Don't . . ." the man said.

"Then talk to me," the Autarch replied, all reason. "Do you know how difficult it is to find a leech like this? They're almost extinct. But I gave this one to you, didn't I? And all I'm asking is that you tell me how it feels."

"It feels . . . good."

"Is that Abelove talking, or you?"

"We're the same," came the reply.

"Like sex, is it?"

"No."

"Like love, then?"

"No. Like I'm unborn again."

"In the womb?"

"In the womb."

"Oh, God, how I envy you. I don't have that memory. I never floated in a mother."

The Autarch rose from his chair, his hand covering his mouth. It was always like this when the dregs of kreauchee moved in his veins. He became unbearably tender at such times, moved to expressions of grief and rage at the obscurest cue.

"To be joined with another soul," he said, "indivisibly. Consumed and made whole in the same moment. What a precious joy."

He turned back to his prisoner, whose eyes were closing again. The Autarch didn't notice.

"It's times like this," he said, "I wish I were a poet. I wish I had the words to express my yearning. I think that if I knew that one day—I don't care how many years from now, centuries even, I don't care—if I *knew* that one day I was going to be united, indivisibly, with another soul, I could begin to be a good man."

He sat down again beside the captive, whose eyes were completely closed.

"But it won't happen," he said, tears beginning to come. "We're too much ourselves. Afraid of letting go of what we are in case we're nothing, and holding on so tight we lose everything else." Agitation was shaking the tears out of his eyes now. "Are you listening to me?" he said.

He shook the man, whose mouth fell open, a trickle of saliva dribbling from one corner.

"Listen!" he raged. "I'm giving you my pain here!"

Receiving no response, he stood up and struck his captive across the face so hard the man toppled over, the chair to which he was bound falling with him. The creature clamped to his chest convulsed in sympathy with its host.

"I didn't bring you here to sleep!" the Autarch said. "I want you to share your pain with me."

He put his hands on the leech and began to tear it from the man's chest. The creature's panic flooded its host, and instantly the man began to writhe, the cords drawing blood as he fought to keep the leech from being stolen. Less than an hour before, when Abelove had been brought out of the shadows and displayed to the prisoner, he'd begged to be spared its touch. Now, finding his tongue again, he pleaded twice as hard not to be separated from it, his pleas swooping into screams when the parasite's filaments, barbed so as to prevent their removal, were wrenched from the organs they'd pierced. As soon as they broke surface they began to flail wildly, seeking to return to their host or find a new one. But the Autarch was unmoved by the panic of either lover and divided them like death itself, pitching Abelove across the chamber and taking the man's face in fingers sticky with his infatuate's blood.

"Now," he said. "How does it feel?"

"Give it back . . . *please* . . . give it back."

"Is this like being born?" the Autarch said.

"Whatever you say! Yes! Yes! Just give it back!"

The Autarch left the man's side and crossed the chamber to the spot where he'd made the summoning. He picked his way through the spirals of human gut he'd arranged on the floor as bait and snatched up the knife still lying in the blood beside the blindfolded head, returning at no more than an amble to where the victim was lying. There he cut the prisoner's bonds and stood back to watch the rest of the show. Though he was grievously wounded, his punctured lungs barely able to draw breath, the man fixed his eyes on the object of his desire and began to crawl towards it. Ashen, the Autarch let him crawl, knowing as he went that the distance was too great, and the scene must end in tragedy.

The lover had advanced no more than a couple of yards when there was a rapping on the door.

"Go away!" the Autarch said, but the rapping came again, this time accompanied by Rosengarten's voice.

"Quaisoir's gone, sir," he said.

The Autarch watched the crawling man's despair and despaired himself. Despite all his indulgences, the woman had deserted him for the Man of Sorrows.

"Come in!" he called.

Rosengarten entered and made his report. Seidux was dead, stabbed and thrown from a window. Quaisoir's quarters were empty, her servant vanished, her dressing room overturned. A search for her abductors was already under way.

"Abductors?" the Autarch said. "No, Rosengarten. There are no abductors. She's gone of her own accord."

Not once as he spoke did he take his eyes off the lover, who had covered a third of the distance between his chair and his darling but was weakening fast.

"It's over," the Autarch said. "She's gone to find her Redeemer, the poor bitch."

"Then shouldn't I dispatch troops to find her?" Rosengarten said. "The city's dangerous."

"So's she when she wants to be. The women in the Bastion taught her some unholy stuff."

"I hope that cesspit's been burned to the ground," Rosengarten said, with a rare passion.

"I doubt it is," the Autarch replied. "They've got ways of protecting themselves."

"Not from me, they haven't," Rosengarten boasted.

"Yes, even from you," the Autarch told him. "Even from me. The power of women can't be scoured away, however hard we try. The Unbeheld attempted it, but he didn't succeed. There's always some corner—"

"Just say the word," the commander broke in, "and I'll go down there now. Hang the bitches in the streets."

"No, you don't understand," the Autarch said, his voice almost monotonous, but all the more sorrowful for that. "The corner isn't out there, it's in here." He pointed to his skull. "It's in our minds. Their mysteries obsess us, even though we put them out of sight. Even me. God knows, I should be free of it. I wasn't cast out like the rest of you were. How can I yearn for something I never had? But I do." He sighed. "Oh, I do."

He looked around at Rosengarten, whose expression was uncomprehending.

"Look at him." The Autarch glanced back at the captive as he spoke. "He's got seconds left to live. But the leech gave him a taste and he wants it back again."

"A taste of what?"

"Of the womb, Rosengarten. He said it was like being in the womb. We're all *cast out*. Whatever we build, wherever we hide, we're cast out."

As he spoke the prisoner gave a last exhausted moan and lay still. The Autarch watched the body awhile, the only sound in the vastness of the chamber the weakening motions of the leech on the cold floor.

"Lock the doors and seal them up," the Autarch said, turning to leave without looking back at Rosengarten. "I'm going to the Pivot Tower."

"Yes, sir."

"Come and find me when it's light. These nights, they're too long. Too long. I wonder, sometimes . . ."

But what he wondered had gone from his head before it could reach his lips, and when he left the lovers' tomb it was in silence.

36

I

Gentle's thoughts had not often turned to Taylor as he and Pie journeyed, but when, in the streets outside the palace, Nikaetomaas had asked him why he'd come to the Imajica, it had been Taylor's death he'd spoken of first, and only then of Judith and the attempt upon her life. Now, as he and Nikaetomaas passed through the balmy, benighted courtyards and up into the palace itself, he thought of the man again, lying on his final pillow, talking about floating and charging Gentle to solve mysteries that he'd not had time to solve himself.

"I had a friend in the Fifth who would have loved this place," Gentle said. "He loved desolation."

It was here, in every courtyard. Gardens had been planted in many of them and left to riot. But riot took energy, and nature was weary here, the plants throttling themselves after a few spurts and withering back into earth the color of ash. The scene was not so different once they got inside, wandering mapless down galleries where the dust was as thick as the soil in the dead gardens, into forsaken annexes and chambers laid out for guests who had breathed their last decades before. Most of the walls, whether of chambers or galleries, were decorated: some with tapestries, many others with immense frescoes, and while there were scenes Gentle recognized from his travels—Patashoqua under a green-gold sky, with a flight of air balloons rising from the plain outside its walls; a festival at the L'Himby temples—the suspicion grew on him that the finest of these images were of earth; or, more particularly, of England. Doubtless the pastoral was a universal mode, and shepherds wooed nymphs in the Reconciled Dominions just as sonnets described them doing in the Fifth, but there were details of these scenes that were indisputably English: swallows swooping in mild summer skies; cattle drinking in water meadows while their herders slept; the Salisbury spire rising from a bank of oaks; the distant towers and domes of London, glimpsed from a slope on which maids and swains made dalliance; even Stonehenge, relocated for drama's sake to a hill and set against thunderheads.

"England," Gentle said as they went. "Somebody here remembers England."

Though they passed by these works too fast for him to scrutinize them carefully, he saw no signature on any. The artists who'd sketched England, and returned to depict it so lovingly, were apparently content to remain anonymous.

"I think we should start climbing," Nikaetomaas suggested when by chance their wanderings brought them to the foot of a monumental staircase. "The higher we are the more chance we'll have of grasping the geography."

The ascent was five flights long—more deserted galleries presenting themselves on every floor—but it finally delivered them onto a roof from which they were able to glimpse the scale of the labyrinth they were lost in. Towers twice and three times the height of the one they'd climbed loomed above them while, below, the courtyards were laid out in all directions, some crossed by battalions but most as deserted as every other corridor and chamber. Beyond them lay the palace walls, and beyond the walls themselves the smoke-shrouded city, the sound of its convulsions dim at such a distance.

Lulled by the remoteness of this aerie, both Gentle and Nikaetomaas were startled by a commotion that erupted much closer by. Almost grateful for signs of life in this mausoleum, even if it was the enemy, they headed in pursuit of the din makers, back down a flight of stairs and across an enclosed bridge between towers.

"Hoods!" Nikaetomaas said, tucking her ponytail back into her shirt and pulling the crude cowl over her head. Gentle did the same, though he doubted such a disguise would offer them much protection if they were discovered.

Orders were being given in the gallery ahead, and Gentle drew Nikaetomaas into hiding to listen. The officer had words of inspiration for his squad, promising every man who brought a Eurhetemec down a month's paid leave. Somebody asked him how many there were, and he replied that he'd heard six, but he didn't believe it because they'd slaughtered ten times that number. However many there are, he said—six, sixty, six hundred—they're outnumbered and trapped. They won't get out alive. So saying, he divided his contingent and told them to shoot on sight.

Three soldiers were dispatched in the direction of Nikaetomaas and Gentle's hiding place. They had no sooner passed than she stepped out of the shadows and brought two of the three down with single blows. The third turned to defend himself, but Gentle—

lacking the mass or muscle power that made Nikaetomaas so effective—used momentum instead, flinging himself against the man with such force he threw both of them to the ground. The soldier raised his gun towards Gentle's skull, but Nikaetomaas took hold of both weapon and hand, hauling the man up by his arm until he was head to head with her, the gun pointing at the roof, the fingers around it too crushed to fire. Then she pulled his helmet off with her free hand and peered at him.

"Where's the Autarch?"

The man was too pained and too terrified to claim ignorance. "The Pivot Tower," he said.

"Which is where?"

"It's the tallest tower," he sobbed, scrabbling at the arm he was dangling by, down which blood was running.

"Take us there," Nikaetomaas said. "Please."

Teeth gritted, the man nodded his head, and she let him go. The gun went from his pulverized fingers as he struck the ground. She invited him to stand with a hooked finger.

"What's your name?" she asked him.

"Yark Lazarevich," he told her, nursing his hand in the crook of his arm.

"Well, Yark Lazarevich, if you make any attempt—or I choose to interpret any act of yours as an attempt—to alert help, I will swat the brains from your pan so fast they'll be in Patashoqua before your pants fill. Is that plain?"

"That's plain."

"Do you have children?"

"Yes. I've got two."

"Think of them fatherless and take care. You have a question?"

"No, I just wanted to explain that the tower's quite a way from here. I don't want you thinking I'm leading you astray."

"Be fast, then," she said, and Lazarevich took her at her word, leading them back across the bridge towards the stairs, explaining as he went that the quickest route to the tower was through the Cesscordium, and that was two floors down.

They had descended perhaps a dozen steps when shots were fired behind them, and one of Lazarevich's two comrades staggered into view, adding shouts to his gunfire to raise the alarm. Had he not been groggy he might have put a bullet in Nikaetomaas or Gentle, but they were away down the stairs before he'd even reached the top, Lazarevich protesting as he went that none of this was his doing, and he loved his children and all he wanted to do was see them again.

There was the sound of running in the lower gallery, and shouts answering those of the alarm raiser above. Nikaetomaas unleashed a series of expletives which could not have been fouler had Gentle understood them, and reached for Lazarevich, who hared off down the stairs before she could snatch hold of him, meeting a squad of his comrades at the bottom. Nikaetomaas' pursuit had taken her past Gentle, directly into their line of fire. They didn't hesitate. Four muzzles flared; four bullets found their mark. Her physique availed her nothing. She dropped where she stood, her body tumbling down the stairs and coming to a halt a few steps from the bottom. Watching her fall, three thoughts went through Gentle's head. One, that he'd have these bastards for this. Two, that stealth was irrelevant now. And three, that if he brought the roof down on their murderous heads, and word spread that there was another power in the palace besides the Autarch, that would be no bad thing. He'd regretted the deaths he'd caused in Lickerish Street, but he would not regret these. All he had to do was get his hand to his face to tear away the cloth before the bullets flew. There were more soldiers converging on the spot from several directions. Come on, he thought, raising his hands in feigned surrender as the others approached: come on, join the jubilee.

One of the gathering number was clearly a man of authority. Heels clicked together as he appeared, salutes were exchanged. He looked up the staircase towards his hooded prisoner.

"General Racidio," one of the captains said. "We have two of the rebels here."

"These aren't Eurhetemecs." His gaze went from Gentle to the body of Nikaetomaas, then back up to Gentle again. "I think we have two Dearthers here."

He started up the stairs towards Gentle, who was surreptitiously drawing breath through the open weave of the cloth around his face in preparation for his unveiling. He would have two or three seconds at best. Time perhaps to seize Racidio and use him as a hostage if the pneuma failed to kill every one of the gunmen.

"Let's see what you look like," the commander said, and tore the cloth from Gentle's face.

The instant that should have seen the pneuma loosed instead saw Racidio drop back in stupefaction from the features he'd uncovered. Whatever he saw was missed by the soldiers below, who kept their guns trained on Gentle until Racidio spat an order that they be lowered. Gentle was as confounded as they, but he wasn't about to question the reprieve. He dropped his hands and, stepping over the body of Nikaetomaas, came to the bottom of the stairs. Racidio retreated further, shaking his head as he did so, and wetting his lips, but apparently unable to find the words to express himself. He looked as though he was expecting the ground to open up beneath him; indeed, was silently willing it to do so. Rather than

risk disabusing the man of his error by speaking, Gentle summoned his guide Lazarevich forward with the hooked finger
Nikaetomaas had used minutes before. The man had taken refuge
behind a shield of soldiers and only came out of hiding reluctantly,
glancing at his captain and Racidio in the hope that Gentle's summons would be countermanded. It was not, however. Gentle went
to meet him, and Racidio uttered the first words he'd been able to
find since setting eyes on the trespasser's face.

"Forgive me," he said. "I'm mortified."

Gentle didn't give him the solace of a response but, with Lazarevich at his side, took a step towards the knot of soldiers at the top
of the next flight of stairs. They parted without a word and he
headed between their ranks, fighting the urge to pick up his pace,
tempting though it was. And he regretted too not being able to say
his farewells to Nikaetomaas. But neither impatience nor sentiment would profit him now. He'd been blessed, and maybe in the
fullness of time he'd understand why. In the short term, he had to
get to the Autarch and hope that the mystif was there also.

"You still want to go to the Pivot Tower?" Lazarevich said.

"Yes."

"When I get you there, will you let me go?"

Again he said, "Yes."

There was a pause, while Lazarevich oriented himself at the
bottom of the stairs. Then he said, "Who are you?"

"Wouldn't you like to know," Gentle replied, his answer as much
for his own benefit as that of his guide.

2

There had been six of them at the start. Now there were two. One
of the casualties had been Thes 'reh' ot, shot down as he etched
with a cross a corner they'd turned in the maze of courtyards. It
had been his inspiration to mark their route and so facilitate a
speedy exit when they'd finished their work.

"It's only the Autarch's will that holds these walls up," he'd said
as they'd entered the palace. "Once he's down, they'll come too.
We need to beat a quick retreat if we're not to get buried."

That Thes 'reh' ot had volunteered for a mission his laughter had
dubbed fatal was surprising enough, but this further show of optimism teetered on the schizophrenic. His sudden death not only
robbed Pie of an unlooked-for ally, but also of the chance to ask
him why he'd joined the assault. But then several such conundrums had accrued around this endeavor, not least the sense of inevitability that had attended every phase, as though this judgment
had been laid down long before Pie and Gentle had ever appeared

in Yzordderrex, and any attempt to flout it would defy the wisdom of greater magistrates than Culus. Such inevitability bred fatalism, of course, and though the mystif had encouraged Thes 'reh' ot to plot their route of return, it entertained few delusions about making that journey. It willfully kept from its mind the losses that extinction would bring until its remaining comrade, Lu 'chur' chem—a purebred Eurhetemec, his skin blue-black, his eyes double-irised—raised the subject. They were in a gallery lined with frescoes that evoked the city Pie had once called home: the painted streets of London, depicted as they'd been in the age into which the mystif had been born, replete with pigeon hawkers, mummers, and dandies.

Seeing the way Pie gazed at these sights, Lu 'chur' chem said, "Never again, eh?"

"Never again what?"

"Out in a street, seeing the way the world is some morning."

"No?"

"No," Lu 'chur' chem said. "We're not coming back this way, and we both know it."

"I don't mind," Pie replied. "I've seen a lot of things. I've felt even more. I've got no regrets."

"You've had a long life?"

"Yes, I have."

"And your Maestro? He had a long life too?"

"Yes, he did," Pie said, looking again at the scenes on the walls.

Though the renderings were relatively unsophisticated, they touched the mystif's memories awake, evoking the bustle and din of the crowded thoroughfares it and its Maestro had walked in the bright, hopeful days before the Reconciliation. Here were the fashionable streets of Mayfair, lined with fine shops and paraded by finer women, abroad to buy lavender water and mantua silk and snow-white muslin. Here was the throng of Oxford Street, where half a hundred vendors clamored for custom: purveyors of slippers, wildfowl, cherries, and gingerbread, all vying for a niche on the pavement and a space in the air to raise their cries. Here too was a fair, St. Bartholomew's most likely, where there was more sin to be had by daylight than Babylon ever boasted by dark.

"Who made these?" Pie wondered aloud as they proceeded.

"Diverse hands, by the look of 'em," Lu 'chur' chem replied. "You can see where one style stops and another starts."

"But somebody directed these painters, gave them the details, the colors. Unless the Autarch just stole artists from the Fifth Dominion."

"Perfectly possible," Lu 'chur' chem said. "He stole architects. He put tribes in chains to build the place."

"And nobody ever challenged him?"

"People tried to stir up revolutions over and over again, but he suppressed them. Burnt down the universities, hanged the theologians and the radicals. He had a stranglehold. *And* he had the Pivot, and most people believe that's the Unbeheld's seal of approval. If Hapexamendios didn't want the Autarch to rule Yzordderrex, why did He allow the Pivot to be moved here? That's what they said. And I don't—"

Lu 'chur' chem stopped in his tracks, seeing that Pie had already done so.

"What is it?" he asked.

The mystif stared up at the picture they had come abreast of, its breath quickened by shock.

"Is something wrong?" Lu 'chur' chem said.

It took a few moments to find the words. "I don't think we should go any further," it said.

"Why not?"

"Not together, at least. The judgment fell on me, and I should finish this alone."

"What's wrong with you? I've come this far. I want to have the satisfaction."

"What's more important?" the mystif asked him, turning from the painting it had been so fixated by. "Your satisfaction, or succeeding in what we came here to do?"

"You know my answer to that."

"Then trust me. I have to go on alone. Wait for me here if you like."

Lu 'chur' chem made a phlegm-hawking growl, like Culus' growl, only coarser. "I came here to kill the Autarch," he said.

"No. You came here to help me, and you've done that. It's my hands that have to dispatch him, not yours. That's the judgment."

"Suddenly it's the judgment, the judgment! I shit on the judgment! I want to see the Autarch dead. I want to look on his face."

"I'll bring you his eyes," Pie said. "That's the best I can do. I mean it, Lu 'chur' chem. We have to part here."

Lu 'chur' chem spat on the ground between them.

"You don't trust me, do you?" he said.

"If that's what you want to believe."

"Mystif shite!" he exploded. "If you come out of this alive, I'll kill you, I swear, I'll kill you!"

There was no further argument. He simply spat again and turned his back, stalking off down the gallery, leaving the mystif to return its gaze to the picture which had quickened its pulse and breath.

Though it was curious to see a rendering of Oxford Street and St. Bartholomew's Fair in this setting, so far in years and

Dominions from the scene that had inspired them, Pie might have suppressed the suspicion—growing in its belly while Lu 'chur' chem talked of revolution—that this was no coincidence, had the final image in the cycle not been so unlike those that had preceded it. The rest had been public spectacles, rendered countless times in satirical prints and paintings. This last was not. The rest had been well-known sites and streets, famous across the world. This last was not. It was an unremarkable thoroughfare in Clerkenwell, almost a backwater, which Pie doubted any artist of the Fifth had ever turned his pen or brush to depicting. But here it was, represented in meticulous detail: Gamut Street, to the brick, to the leaf. And taking pride of place in the center of the picture, number 28, the Maestro Sartori's house.

It had been lovingly re-created. Birds courted on its roof; on its step, dogs fought. And in between the fighters and wooers stood the house itself, blessed by a dappled sunlight denied the others in the row. The front door was closed, but the upper windows were flung wide, and the artist had painted somebody watching from one of them, his face too deeply shadowed to be recognized. The object of his scrutiny was not in doubt, however: the girl in the window across the street, sitting at her mirror with her dog on her lap, her fingers teasing from its bow the ribbon that would presently unlace her bodice. In the street between this beauty and her doting voyeur were a dozen details that could only have come from firsthand experience. On the pavement beneath the girl's window a small procession of charity children passed, wards of the parish, dressed all in white and carrying their wands. They marched raggedly behind their beadle, a brute of a man called Willis, whom Sartori had once beaten senseless on that very spot for cruelty to his charges. Around the far corner came Roxborough's carriage, drawn by his favorite bay, Bellamarre, named in honor of the Comte de St. Germain, who had swindled half the women of Venice under that alias a few years before. A dragoon was being ushered out of number 32 by the mistress of that house, who entertained officers of the Prince of Wales regiment—the Tenth, and no other—whenever her husband was away. The widow opposite watched enviously from her step.

All these and a dozen other little dramas were being played out in the picture, and there wasn't one Pie didn't remember seeing enacted countless times. But who was the unseen spectator who'd instructed the painters in their craft, so that carriage, girl, soldier, widow, dogs, birds, voyeurs, and all could be set down with such verisimilitude?

Having no solution to the puzzle, the mystif plucked its gaze from the picture and looked back along the immense length of the gallery. Lu 'chur' chem had disappeared, spitting as he went. The mystif was alone, the routes ahead and behind similarly deserted. It would miss Lu 'chur' chem's companionship and bitterly regretted that it had lacked the wit to persuade its comrade that it had to go on alone, without causing such offense. But the picture on the wall was proof of secrets here it had not yet fathomed, and when it did so it wanted no witnesses. They too easily became accusers, and Pie was weighed down with enough reproaches already. If the tyrannies of Yzordderrex were in some fashion linked with the house on Gamut Street—and if Pie, by extension, was an unwitting collaborator in those tyrannies—it was important to learn of this guilt unaccompanied.

As prepared as possible for such revelations, the mystif left its place in front of the painting, reminding itself as it went of the promise made to Lu 'chur' chem. If it survived this enterprise, it had to return with the eyes of the Autarch. Eyes which it now didn't doubt had once been laid on Gamut Street, studying it as obsessively as the watcher at the painted window studied his lady love, sitting across the street in thrall to her reflection.

—BOOK II—
THE
RECONCILIATION

I

LIKE THE THEATER DISTRICTS OF SO many great cities across the Imajica, whether in Reconciled Dominions or in the Fifth, the neighborhood in which the Ipse stood had been a place of some notoriety in earlier times, when actors of both sexes had supplemented their wages with the old five-acter—hiring, retiring, seduction, conjunction, and remittance—all played hourly, night and day. The center of these activities had moved away, however, to the other side of the city, where the burgeoning numbers of middle-class clients felt less exposed to the gaze of their peers out seeking more respectable entertainment. Lickerish Street and its environs had sprung up in a matter of months and quickly became the third richest Kesparate in the city, leaving the theater district to decline into legitimacy.

Perhaps because it was of so little interest to people, it had survived the traumas of the last few hours better than most Kesparates its size. It had seen some action. General Mattalaus' battalions had passed through its streets going south to the causeway, where rebels were attempting to build a makeshift bridge across the delta, and later a party of families from the Caramess had taken refuge in Koppocovi's Rialto. But no barricades had been erected, and none of the buildings burned. The Deliquium would meet the morning intact. Its survival, however, would not be accorded to general disinterest; rather to the presence at its perimeter of Pale Hill, a site which was neither a hill nor pale, but a circle of remembrance in the center of which lay a well, used from time immemorial as a repository for the corpses of executed men, suicides, paupers, and, on occasion, romantics who favored rotting in such company. Tomorrow's rumors would whisper that the ghosts of these forsaken souls had risen to defend their terrain, preventing the vandals and the barricade builders from destroying the Kesparate by haunting the steps of the Ipse and the Rialto and howling in the streets like dogs maddened from chasing the comet's tail.

With her clothes in rags and her throat uttering one seamless supplication, Quaisoir went through the heart of several battles quite unscathed. There were many such grief-stricken women on the streets of Yzordderrex tonight, all begging Hapexamendios to return children or husbands into their arms, and they were for the most part given passage through the lines, their sobs password enough.

The battles themselves didn't distress her; she'd organized and viewed mass executions in her time. But when the heads had rolled she'd always made a swift departure, leaving the aftermath for somebody else to shovel up. Now she had to tread barefoot in streets that were like abattoirs, and her legendary indifference to the spectacle of death was overtaken by a horror so profound she had several times changed her direction to avoid a street that stank too strongly of innards and burned blood. She knew she would have to confess this cowardice when she finally found the Man of Sorrows, but she was so laden with guilt that one more fault or less would scarcely matter.

Then, as she came to the corner of the street at the end of which lay Pluthero Quexos' playhouse, somebody called her name. She stopped and looked for her summoner. A man dressed in blue was rising from a doorstep, the fruit he'd been peeling in one hand, the peeling blade in the other. He seemed to be in no doubt as to her identity.

"You're his woman," he said.

Was this the Lord? she wondered. The man she'd seen on the rooftops at the harbor had been silhouetted against a bright sky; his features had been difficult to see. Could this be him?

He was calling someone from the interior of the house on the steps of which he'd been sitting, a sometime bordello to judge by its lewdly carved portico. The disciple, an Oethac, emerged with a bottle in one hand, the other ruffling the hair of a cretinous boy child, naked and glistening. She began to doubt her first judgment, but she didn't dare leave until she had her hopes confirmed or dashed.

"Are you the Man of Sorrows?" she said.

The fruit peeler shrugged. "Isn't everybody tonight?" he said, tossing the uneaten fruit away.

The cretin leapt down the steps and snatched it up, pushing the entire thing into his mouth so that his face bulged and the juice ran from his lips.

"You're the cause of this," the peeler said, jabbing his knife in Quaisoir's direction. He glanced around at the Oethac. "She was at the harbor. I saw her."

"Who is she?" the Oethac said.

"The Autarch's woman," came the reply. "Quaisoir." He took a step towards her. "You are, aren't you?"

She could no more deny this than she could take flight. If this man was indeed Jesu, she couldn't begin her pleas for forgiveness with a lie.

"Yes," she told him, "I'm Quaisoir. I was the Autarch's woman."

"She's fucking beautiful," the Oethac said.

"What she looks like doesn't matter," the fruit peeler told him. "It's what she's done that's important."

"Yes," Quaisoir said, daring to believe now that this was indeed the Son of David. "That's what's important. What I've done."

"The executions . . ."

"Yes."

"The purges . . ."

"Yes."

"I've lost a lot of friends, and you're the reason."

"Oh, Lord, forgive me," she said, and dropped to her knees.

"I saw you at the harbor this morning," Jesu said, approaching her as she knelt. "You were smiling."

"Forgive me."

"Looking around and smiling. And I thought, when I saw you—"

He was three paces away from her now.

"—your eyes glittering—"

His sticky hand took hold of her head.

"—I thought, those eyes—"

He raised the knife—

"—have to go."

—and brought it down again, quick and sharp, sharp and quick, pricking out his disciple's sight before she could start to scream.

The tears that suddenly filled Jude's eyes stung like no tears she'd ever shed before. She let out a sob, more of pain than of grief, pushing the heels of her hands against her eye sockets to stem the flow. But it wouldn't cease. The tears kept coming, hot and harsh, making her whole head throb. She felt Dowd's arm take hold of hers and was glad of it. Without his support, she was certain she would have fallen.

"What's wrong?" he said.

The answer—that she was sharing some agony with Quaisoir—was not one she could voice to Dowd. "It must be the smoke," she said. "I can barely see."

"We're almost at the Ipse," he replied. "But we have to keep moving for a little while longer. It's not safe in the open air."

That was true enough. Her eyes—which at present could only see pulsing red—had been laid on enough atrocities in the last hour to fuel a lifetime of nightmares. The Yzordderrex of her longings, the city whose spicy wind, blowing from the Retreat months before, had summoned her like the call of a lover to bed, was virtually in ruins. Perhaps that was why Quaisoir wept these burn-ing tears.

They dried after a time, but the pain lingered. Though she de-spised the man she was leaning upon, without his support she would have dropped to the ground and remained there. He coaxed her on, step by step. The Ipse was close now, he said: just a street or two away. She could rest there, while he soaked up the echoes of past glories. She barely attended to his monologue. It was her sister who filled her thoughts, her anticipation of their meeting now tinged with unease. She'd imagined Quaisoir would have come into these streets protected, and that at the sight of her Dowd would simply retreat, leaving them to their reunion. But what if Dowd was not overtaken by superstitious awe? What if, instead, he attacked one or both of them? Would Quaisoir have any de-fense against his mites? She began to wipe at her streaming eyes as she stumbled on, determined to be clear-sighted when the mo-ment came, and primed to escape Dowd's leash.

His monologue, when it ceased, did so abruptly. He halted, draw-ing Jude to a stop at his side. She raised her head. The street ahead was not well lit, but the glow of distant fires found its way between the buildings, and there, crawling into one such flickering shaft, she saw her sister. Jude let out a sob. Quaisoir's eyes had been stabbed out, and her torturers were coming in pursuit of her. One was a child, one an Oethac. The third, the most blood-spattered, was also the most nearly human, but his features were twisted out of true by the pleasure he was taking in Quaisoir's torment. The blinding knife was still in his hand, and now he raised it above his victim's naked back.

Before Dowd could move to stop her, Jude screamed, *"Stop!"*

The knife was arrested in mid-descent, and all three of Quaisoir's pursuers looked around at Jude. The child registered nothing; its face was an imbecilic blank. The knife wielder was equally silent, though his expression was one of disbelief. It was the Oethac that spoke, the words he uttered slurred but ripe with panic.

"You ... keep ... your distance," he said, his fearful glance going back and forth between the wounded woman and this echo of her, whole and strong.

The blinder found his voice now, and began to hush him, but the Oethac rattled on.

"Look at her!" he said. "What the fuck is this, eh? *Look at her.*"

"Just shut your trap," the blinder said. "She's not going to touch us."

"You don't know that," said the Oethac, picking up the child with one arm and slinging it over his shoulder. "It wasn't me," he went on, as he backed away. "I never laid a finger on her. I swear. On my scars, I swear."

Jude ignored his weaselings and took a step towards Quaisoir. As soon as she moved, the Oethac fled. The blinder, however, held his ground, taking courage from his blade.

"I'll do you the same way," he warned. "I don't care who the fuck you are, I'll do you!"

From behind her, Jude heard Dowd's voice, carrying an authority she'd never heard in it before.

"I'd leave her be if I were you," he said.

His utterance brought a response from Quaisoir. She raised her head and turned in Dowd's direction. Her eyes had not simply been stabbed out but virtually dug from their sockets. Seeing the holes, Jude was ashamed to have been so troubled by the little ache that she felt in sympathy; it was nothing beside Quaisoir's hurt. Yet the woman's voice was almost joyful.

"Lord?" she said. "Sweet Lord, is this punishment enough? Will you forgive me now?"

Neither the nature of the error Quaisoir was making here nor its profound irony was lost on Jude. Dowd was no savior. But he was happy enough to assume that role, it seemed. He replied to Quaisoir with a delicacy as feigned as the sonority he'd affected seconds before.

"Of course I'll forgive you," he said. "That's what I'm here to do."

Jude might have been tempted to disabuse Quaisoir of her illusions there and then, but that the blinder was usefully distracted by Dowd's performance.

"Tell me who you are, child," Dowd said.

"You know who the fuck she is," the blinder spat, "Quaisoir! It's fucking Quaisoir!"

Dowd glanced back at Jude, his expression one of comprehension rather than shock. Then he looked again at the blinder.

"So it is," he said.

"You know what she's done same as me," the man said. "She deserves worse than this."

"Worse, you think?" Dowd said, continuing to advance towards the man, who was nervously passing his knife from hand to hand, as though he sensed that Dowd's capacity for cruelty outstripped his own a hundredfold and was preparing to defend himself if need be.

"What worse would you do?" Dowd said.

"What she's done to others, over and over."

"She did these things personally, you think?"

"I wouldn't put it past her," he said. "Who knows what the fuck goes on up there? People disappear, and get washed up again in pieces. . . ." He tried a little smile, plainly nervous now. "You know she deserved it."

"And you?" Dowd asked. "What do you deserve?"

"I'm not saying I'm a hero," the blinder replied. "I'm just saying she had it coming."

"I see," said Dowd.

From Jude's vantage point, what happened next was more a matter of conjecture than observation. She saw Quaisoir's maimer take a step away from Dowd, repugnance on his face; then saw him lunge forward as if to stab Dowd through the heart. His attack put him in range of the mites, and before his blade could find Dowd's flesh they must have leapt at the blinder, because he dropped back with a shout of horror, his free hand going up to his face. Jude had seen what followed before. The man scrabbled at his eyes and nostrils and mouth, his legs giving out beneath him as the mites undid his system from the inside. He fell at Dowd's feet and rolled around in a fury of frustration, eventually putting his knife into his mouth and digging bloodily for the things that were unmaking him. The life went out of him as he was doing so, his hand dropping from his face, leaving the blade in his throat as though he'd choked upon it.

"It's over," Dowd said to Quaisoir, who had wrapped her arms around her shuddering body and was lying on the ground a few yards from her tormentor's corpse. "He won't hurt you again."

"Thank you, Lord."

"The things he accused you of, child?"

"Yes."

"Terrible things."

"Yes."

"Are you guilty of them?"

"I am," Quaisoir said. "I want to confess them before I die. Will you hear me?"

"I will," Dowd said, oozing magnanimity.

After being merely a witness to these events as they unraveled, Jude now stepped towards Quaisoir and her confessor, but Dowd heard her approach and turned to shake his head.

"I've sinned, my Lord Jesu," Quaisoir was saying. "I've sinned so many times. I beg you to forgive me."

It was the despair Jude heard in her sister's voice, rather than Dowd's rebuff, that kept her from making her presence known. Quaisoir was *in extremis,* and given that it was her clear desire to commune with some forgiving spirit, what right did Jude have to intervene? Dowd was not the Christ Quaisoir believed him to be, but did that matter? What would revealing the father confessor's true identity achieve now, besides adding to the sum of her sister's suffering?

Dowd had knelt beside Quaisoir and had taken her up into his arms, demonstrating a capacity for tenderness, or at least for its replication, that Jude would never have believed him capable of. For her part, Quaisoir was in bliss, despite her wounds. She clutched at Dowd's jacket and thanked him over and over for doing her this kindness. He hushed her softly, saying there was no need for her to make a catalogue of her crimes.

"You have them in your heart, and I see them there," he said. "I forgive them. Tell me instead about your husband. Where is he? Why hasn't he also come asking for forgiveness?"

"He didn't believe you were here," Quaisoir said. "I told him I'd seen you down at the harbor, but he has no faith."

"None?"

"Only in himself," she said bitterly.

Dowd began to rock backward and forward as he plied her with further questions, his focus so devoted to his victim he didn't notice Jude's approach. She envied Dowd his embrace, wishing it were her arms Quaisoir was lying in instead of his.

"Who *is* your husband?" Dowd was asking.

"You know who he is," Quaisoir replied. "He's the Autarch. He rules the Imajica."

"But he wasn't always Autarch, was he?"

"No."

"So what was he before?" Dowd wanted to know. "An ordinary man?"

"No," she said. "I don't think he was ever an ordinary man. I don't remember exactly."

He stopped rocking her. "I think you do," he said, his tone subtly shifting. "Tell me," he said. "Tell me: What was he before he ruled Yzordderrex? And what were you?"

"I was nothing," she said simply.

"Then how were you raised so high?"

"He loved me. From the very beginning, he loved me."

"You did no unholy service to be elevated?" Dowd said.

She hesitated, and he pressed her harder.

"What did you do?" he demanded. "What? What?" There was a distant echo of Oscar in that expletive: the servant speaking with his master's voice.

Intimidated by this fury, Quaisoir replied. "I visited the Bastion of the Banu many times," she confessed. "Even the Annex. I went there, too."

"And what's there?"

"Madwomen. Some who killed their spouses, or their children."

"Why did you seek such pitiful creatures out?"

"There are . . . *powers* . . . hidden among them."

At this, Jude attended more closely than ever.

"What kind of powers?" Dowd said, voicing the question she was silently asking.

"I did nothing unholy," Quaisoir protested. "I just wanted to be cleansed. The Pivot was in my dreams. Every night, its shadow on me, breaking my back. I only wanted to be cleansed of it."

"And were you?" Dowd asked her. Again she didn't answer at first, until he pressed her, almost harshly. *"Were* you?"

"I wasn't cleansed, I was changed," she said. "The women polluted me. I have a taint in my flesh and I wish it were out of me." She began to tear at her clothes, till her fingers found her belly and breasts. "I want it driven out!" she said. "It gave me new dreams, worse than before."

"Calm yourself," Dowd said.

"But I want it out! I want it out!" A kind of fit had suddenly taken her, and she flailed so violently in his arms she fell from them. "I can feel it in me now," she said, her nails raking her breasts.

Jude looked at Dowd, willing him to intervene, but he simply stood up, staring at the woman's distress, plainly taking pleasure in it. Quaisoir's self-assault was not theatrics. She was drawing blood from her skin, still yelling that she wanted the taint out of her. In her agony, a subtle change was coming over her flesh, as though she was sweating out the taint she'd spoken of. Her pores were oozing a sheen of iridescence, and the cells of her skin were subtly changing color. Jude knew the blue she saw spreading from her sister's neck, down over her body and up towards her contorted face. It was the blue of the stone eye, the blue of the Goddess.

"What is this?" Dowd demanded of his confessee.

"Out of me! Out of me!"

"Is this the taint?" He went down on his haunches beside her. *"Is it?"*

"Drive it out of me!" Quaisoir sobbed, and began assaulting her poor body afresh.

Jude could endure it no longer. Allowing her sister to die blissfully in the arms of a surrogate divinity was one thing. This self-mutilation was quite another. She broke her vow of silence.

"Stop her," she said.

Dowd looked up from his study, drawing his thumb across his throat to hush her. But it was too late. Despite her own commotion, Quaisoir had heard her sister speak. Her thrashings slowed, and her blind head turned in Jude's direction.

"Who's there?" she demanded.

There was naked fury on Dowd's face, but he hushed her softly. She would not be placated, however.

"Who's with you, Lord?" she asked him.

With his reply he made an error that unknitted the whole fiction. He lied to her.

"There's nobody," he said.

"I heard a woman's voice. Who's there?"

"I told you," Dowd insisted. "Nobody." He put his hand upon her face. "Now calm yourself. We're alone."

"No, we're not."

"Do you doubt me, child?" Dowd replied, his voice, after the harshness of his last interrogations, modulating with this question, so that he sounded almost wounded by her lack of faith. Quaisoir's reply was to silently take his hand from her face, seizing it tightly in her blue, blood-speckled fingers.

"That's better," he said.

Quaisoir ran her fingers over his palm. Then she said, "No scars."

"There'll always be scars," Dowd said, lavishing his best pontifical manner upon her. But he'd missed the point of her remark.

"There are no scars on your hand," she said.

He retrieved it from her grasp. "Believe in me," he said.

"No," she replied. "You're not the Man of Sorrows." The joy had gone from her voice. It was thick, almost threatening. "You can't save me," she said, suddenly flailing wildly to drive the pretender from her. "Where's my Savior? I want my Savior!"

"He isn't here," Jude told her. "He never was."

Quaisoir turned in Jude's direction. "Who are you?" she said. "I know your voice from somewhere."

"Keep your mouth shut," Dowd said, stabbing his finger in Jude's direction. "Or so help me you'll taste the mites—"

"Don't be afraid of him," Quaisoir said.

"She knows better than that," Dowd replied. "She's seen what I can do."

Eager for some excuse to speak, so that Quaisoir could hear more of the voice she knew but couldn't yet name, Jude spoke up in support of Dowd's conceit.

"What he says is right," she told Quaisoir. "He can hurt us both, badly. He's not the Man of Sorrows, sister."

Whether it was the repetition of words Quaisoir had herself used several times—Man of Sorrows—or the fact that Jude had called her sister, or both, the woman's sightless face slackened, the bafflement going out of it. She lifted herself from the ground.

"What's your name?" she murmured. "Tell me your name."

"She's nothing," Dowd said, echoing Quaisoir's own description of herself minutes earlier. "She's a dead woman." He made a move in Jude's direction. "You understand so little," he said. "And I've forgiven you a lot for that. But I can't indulge you any longer. You've spoiled a fine game. I don't want you spoiling any more."

He put his left hand, its forefinger extended, to his lips.

"I don't have many mites left," he said, "so one will have to do. A slow unraveling. But even a shadow like you can be undone."

"I'm a shadow now, am I?" Jude said to him. "I thought we were the same, you and I? Remember that speech?"

"That was in another life, lovey," Dowd said. "It's different here. You could do me harm here. So I'm afraid it's going to have to be *thank you and good night.*"

She started to back away from him, wondering as she did so how much distance she would have to put between them to be out of range of his wretched mites. He watched her retreat with pity on his face.

"No good, lovey," he said. "I know these streets like the back of my hand."

She ignored his condescension and took another backward step, her eye fixed on his mouth where the mites nested, but aware that Quaisoir had risen and was standing no more than a yard from her defender.

"Sister?" the woman said.

Dowd glanced around, distracted from Jude long enough for her to take to her heels. He let out a shout as she fled, and the blind woman lunged towards the sound, grabbing his arm and neck and dragging him towards her. The noise she made as she did so was like nothing Jude had heard from human lips, and she envied it: a cry to shatter bones like glass and shake color from the air. She was glad not to be closer, or it might have brought her to her knees.

She looked back once, in time to see Dowd spit the lethal mite at Quaisoir's empty sockets, and prayed her sister had better defenses against its harm than the man who'd emptied them. Whether or no, she could do little to help. Better to run while she had the chance, so that at least one of them survived the cataclysm.

She turned the first corner she came to, and kept turning corners thereafter, to put as many decisions between herself and her pursuer. No doubt Dowd's boast was true; he did indeed know these streets, where he claimed he'd once triumphed, like his own hand. It followed that the sooner she was out of them, and into terrain unfamiliar to them both, the more chance she had of losing him. Until then, she had to be swift and as nearly invisible as she could make herself. Like the shadow Dowd had dubbed her: darkness in a deeper dark, flitting and fleeting; seen and gone.

But her body didn't want to oblige. It was weary, beset with aches and shudders. Twin fires had been set in her chest, one in each lung.

Invisible hounds ripped her heels bloody. She didn't allow herself
to slow her pace, however, until she'd left the streets of playhouses
and brothels behind her and was delivered into a place that might
have stood as a set for a Pluthero Quexos tragedy: a circle a hundred yards wide, bounded by a high wall of sleek, black stone. The
fires that burned here didn't rage uncontrolled, as they did in so
many other parts of the city, but flickered from the tops of the walls
in their dozens; tiny white flames, like night-lights, illuminating
the inclined pavement that led down to an opening in the center
of the circle. She could only guess at its function. An entrance into
the city's secret underworld, perhaps, or a well? There were flowers everywhere, most of the petals shed and gone to rot, slicken-
ing the pavement beneath her feet as she approached the hole,
obliging her to tread with care. The suspicion grew that if this was
a well, its water was poisoned with the dead. Obituaries were
scrawled on the pavement—names, dates, messages, even crude
illustrations—their numbers increasing the closer to the edge she
came. Some had even been inscribed on the inner wall of the well,
by mourners brave or broken-hearted enough to dare the drop.

Though the hole exercised the same fascination as a cliff edge,
inviting her to peer into its depths, she refused its petitions and
halted a yard or two from the lip. There was a sickly smell out of
the place, though it wasn't strong. Either the well had not been used
of late, or else its occupants lay a very long way down.

Her curiosity satisfied, she looked around to choose the best
route out. There were no less than eight exits—nine, including the
well—and she went first to the avenue that lay opposite the one
she'd come in by. It was dark and smoky, and she might have taken
it had there not been signs that it was blocked by rubble some way
down its length. She went to the next, and it too was blocked, fires
flickering between fallen timbers. She was going to the third door
when she heard Dowd's voice. She turned. He was standing on the
far side of the well, with his head slightly cocked and a put-upon
expression on his face, like a parent who'd caught up with a truant
child.

"Didn't I tell you?" he said. "I know these streets."

"I heard you."

"It isn't so bad that you came here," he said, wandering towards
her. "It saves me a mite."

"Why do you want to hurt me?" she said.

"I might ask you the same question," he said. "You *do,* don't
you? You'd love to see me hurt. You'd be even happier if you could
do the hurting personally. Admit it!"

"I admit it."

"There. Don't I make a good confessor after all? And that's just the beginning. You've got some secrets in you I didn't even know you had." He raised his hand and described a circle as he spoke. "I begin to see the perfection of all this. Things coming round, coming round, back to the place where it all began. That is: to her. Or to you; it doesn't matter, really. You're the same."

"Twins?" Jude said. "Is that it?"

"Nothing so trite, lovey. Nothing so natural. I insulted you, calling you a shadow. You're more miraculous than that. You're—" He stopped. "Well, wait. This isn't strictly fair. Here's me telling you what *I* know and getting nothing from *you.*"

"I don't know anything," Jude said. "I wish I did."

Dowd stooped and picked up a blossom, one of the few underfoot that was still intact. "But whatever Quaisoir knows you also know," he said. "At least about how it all came apart."

"How what came apart?"

"The Reconciliation. You were there. Oh, yes, I know you think you're just an innocent bystander, but there's nobody in this, *nobody,* who's innocent. Not Estabrook, not Godolphin, not Gentle or his mystif. They've all got confessions as long as their arms."

"Even you?" she asked him.

"Ah, well, with me it's different." He sighed, sniffing at the flower. "I'm an actor chappie. I fake my raptures. I'd like to change the world, but I end up as entertainment. Whereas all you *lovers*"—he spoke the word contemptuously—"who couldn't give a fuck about the world as long as you're feeling passionate, you're the ones who make the cities burn and the nations tumble. You're the engines in the tragedy, and most of the time you don't even know it. So what's an actor chappie to do, if he wants to be taken seriously? I'll tell you. He has to learn to fake his feelings so well he'll be allowed off the stage and into the real world. It's taken me a lot of rehearsal to get where I am, believe me. I started small, you know; very small. Messenger. Spear-carrier. I once pimped for the Unbeheld, but it was just a one-night stand. Then I was back serving lovers—"

"Like Oscar."

"Like Oscar."

"You hated him, didn't you?"

"No, I was simply bored, with him and his whole family. He was so like his father, and his father's father, and so on, all the way back to crazy Joshua. I became impatient. I knew things would come around eventually, and I'd have my moment, but I got so tired of waiting, and once in a while I let it show."

"And you plotted."

"But of course. I wanted to hurry things along, towards the

moment of my . . . emancipation. It was all very calculated. But that's me, you see? I'm an artist with the soul of an accountant."

"Did you hire Pie to kill me?"

"Not knowingly," Dowd said. "I set some wheels in motion, but I never imagined they'd carry us all so far. I didn't even know the mystif was alive. But as things went on, I began to see how inevitable all this was. First Pie's appearance. Then your meeting Godolphin, and your falling for each other. It was all bound to happen. It was what you were born to do, after all. Do you miss him, by the way? Tell the truth."

"I've scarcely thought about him," she replied, surprised by the truth of this.

"Out of sight, out of mind, eh? Ah, I'm so glad I can't feel love. The misery of it. The sheer, unadulterated misery." He mused a moment, then said, "This is so much like the first time, you know. Lovers yearning, worlds trembling. Of course last time I was merely a spear-carrier. This time I intend to be the prince."

"What do you mean, I was born to fall for Godolphin? I don't even remember *being* born."

"I think it's time you did," Dowd said, tossing away the flower as he approached her. "Though these rites of passage are never very easy, lovey, so brace yourself. At least you've picked a good spot. We can dangle our feet over the edge while we talk about how you came into the world."

"Oh, no," she said. "I'm not going near that hole."

"You think I want to kill you?" he said. "I don't. I just want you to unburden yourself of a few memories. That's not asking too much, is it? Be fair. I've given you a glimpse of what's in my heart. Now show me yours." He took hold of her wrist. "I won't take no for an answer," he said, and drew her to the edge of the well.

She'd not ventured this close before, and its proximity was vertiginous. Though she cursed him for having the strength to drag her here, she was glad he had her in a tight hold.

"Do you want to sit?" he said. She shook her head. "As you like," he went on. "There's more chance of your falling, but it's your decision. You've become a very self-willed woman, lovey, I've noticed that. You were malleable enough at the beginning. That was the way you were bred to be, of course."

"I wasn't bred to be anything."

"How do you know?" he said. "Two minutes ago you were claiming you don't even remember the past. How do you know what you were meant to be? *Made* to be?" He glanced down the well. "The memory's in your head somewhere, lovey. You just have to be willing to coax it out. If Quaisoir sought some Goddess, maybe you did too, even if you don't remember it. And if you did, then maybe you're more than Joshua's Peachplum. Maybe you've got some place in the action I haven't accounted for."

"Where would I meet Goddesses, Dowd?" Jude replied. "I've lived in the Fifth, in London, in Notting Hill Gate. There are no Goddesses."

Even as she spoke she thought of Celestine, buried beneath the Tabula Rasa's tower. Was she a sister to the deities that haunted Yzordderrex? A transforming force, locked away by a sex that worshiped fixedness? At the memory of the prisoner, and her cell, Jude's mind grew suddenly light, as though she'd downed a whisky on an empty stomach. She had been touched by the miraculous, after all. So if once, why not many times? If now, why not in her forgotten past?

"I've got no way back," she said, protesting the difficulty of this as much for her own benefit as Dowd's.

"It's easy," he replied. "Just think of what it was like to be born."

"I don't even remember my childhood."

"You *had* no childhood, lovey. You had no adolescence. You were born just the way you are, overnight. Quaisoir was the first Judith, and you, my sweet, are only her replica. Perfect, maybe, but still a replica."

"I won't . . . I don't . . . believe you."

"Of course you must refuse the truth at first. It's perfectly understandable. But your body knows what's true and what isn't. You're shaking, inside and out. . . ."

"I'm tired," she said, knowing the explanation was pitifully weak.

"You're feeling more than weary," Dowd said. "Admit it."

As he pried, she remembered the results of his last revelations about her past: how she'd dropped to the kitchen floor, hamstrung by invisible knives. She dared not succumb to such a collapse now, with the well a foot from where she stood, and Dowd knew it.

"You have to face the memories," he was saying. "Just spit them out. Go on. You'll feel better for it, I promise you."

She could feel both her limbs and her resolve weakening as he spoke, but the prospect of facing whatever lay in the darkness at the back of her skull—and however much she distrusted Dowd, she didn't doubt there was something horrendous there—was almost as terrifying as the thought of the well taking her. Perhaps it would be better to die here and now, two sisters extinguished within the same hour, and never know whether Dowd's claims were true or not. But then suppose he'd been lying to her all along—the actor chappie's finest performance yet—and she was not a shadow, not a replica, not a thing bred to do service, but a natural child with natural parents: a creature unto herself, real, complete? Then she'd be giving herself to death out of fear of self-discovery, and Dowd would have claimed another victim. The only way to defeat him was to call his bluff; to do as he kept urging her to do and go into the darkness at the back of her head, ready to embrace whatever revelations it concealed. Whichever Judith she was, she was; whether real or replica, natural or bred. There was no escape from herself in the living world. Better to know the truth, once and for all.

The decision ignited a flame in her skull, and the first phantoms of the past appeared in her mind's eye.

"Oh, my Goddess," she murmured, throwing back her head. "What is this? What is this?"

She saw herself lying on bare boards in an empty room, a fire burning in the grate, warming her in her sleep and flattering her nakedness with its luster. Somebody had marked her body while she slept, daubing upon it a design she recognized—the glyph she'd first seen in her mind's eye when she'd made love with Oscar, then glimpsed again as she passed between Dominions—the spiraling sign of her flesh, here painted on flesh itself in half a dozen colors.

She moved in her sleep, and the whorls seemed to leave traces of themselves in the air where she'd been, their persistence exciting another motion, this other in the ring of sand that bounded her hard bed. It rose around her like the curtain of the Borealis, shimmering with the same colors in which her glyph had been painted, as though something of her essential anatomy was in the very air of the room. She was entranced by the beauty of the sight.

"What are you seeing?" she heard Dowd asking her.

"Me," she said, "lying on the floor . . . in a circle of sand. . . ."

"Are you sure it's you?" he said.

She was about to pour scorn on his question, when she realized its import. Perhaps this wasn't her, but her sister.

"Is there any way of knowing?" she said.

"You'll soon see," he told her.

So she did. The curtain of sand began to wave more violently, as if seized by a wind unleashed within the circle. Particles flew from it, intensifying as they were thrown against the dark air: motes of the purest color rising like new stars, then dropping again, burning in their descent, towards the place where she, the witness, lay. She was lying on the ground close to her sister, receiving the rain of color like a grateful earth, needing its sustenance if she was to grow and swell and become fruitful.

"What am I?" she said, following the fall of color to snatch a glimpse of the ground it was falling upon.

The beauty of what she'd seen so far had lulled her into vulnerability. When she saw her own unfinished body, the shock threw her out of the remembrance like a blow. Suddenly she was teetering on the wall's edge again, with Dowd's hand the only check upon her falling. Icewater sweat filled her pores.

"Don't let me go," she said.

"What are you seeing?" he asked her.

"Is this being born?" she sobbed. "Oh, Christ, is this being born?"

"Go back to the memory," he said. "You've begun it, so finish it!" He shook her. "Hear me? *Finish it!*"

She saw his face raging before her. She saw the well, yearning behind. And in between, in the firelit room awaiting her in her head, she saw a nightmare worse than both: her anatomy, barely made, lying in a circle of perverted enchantments, raw until the distillates of another woman's body put skin on her sinew and color in that skin, put the tint in her eyes and the gloss on her lips, gave her the same breasts, belly, and sex. This was not birth, it was duplication. She was a facsimile, a likeness stolen from a slumbering original.

"I can't bear it," she said.

"I did warn you, lovey," Dowd replied. "It's never easy, reliving the first moments."

"I'm not even *real,*" she said.

"Let's stay clear of the metaphysics," came the reply. "What you are, you are. You had to know sooner or later."

"I can't bear it. I can't bear it."

"But you *are* bearing it," Dowd said. "You just have to take it slowly. Step by step."

"No more. . . ."

"Yes," he insisted. "A lot more. That was the worst. It'll get easier from now on."

That was a lie. When memory took her again, almost without her inviting it, she was raising her arms above her head, letting the colors congeal around her outstretched fingers. Pretty enough, until she let one arm drop beside her and her new-made nerves felt a presence at her side, sharing the womb. She turned her head and screamed.

"What is it?" Dowd said. "Did the Goddess come?"

It was no Goddess. It was another unfinished thing, gaping at her with lidless eyes, putting out its colorless tongue, which was still so rough it could have licked her new skin off her. She retreated from it, and her fear aroused it, the pale anatomy shaken by silent laughter. It too had gathered motes of stolen color, she saw, but it had not bathed in them; rather, it had caught them in its hands, postponing the moment it attired itself until it had luxuriated in its flayed nakedness.

Dowd was interrogating her again. "Is it the Goddess?" he was asking. "What are you seeing? Speak it out, woman! *Speak it—*"

His demand was cut suddenly short. There was a beat of silence, then a cry of alarm so shrill her conjuring of the circle and the thing she'd shared it with vanished. She felt Dowd's grip on her wrist slip, and her body toppled. She flailed as she fell, and more by luck than design her motion threw her sideways, along the rim of the well, rather than pitching her within. Instantly, she began to slip down the incline. She clutched at the pavement. But the stone had been polished by years of passage, and her body slid towards the edge as if the depths were calling in a long-neglected debt. Her legs kicked empty air, her hips sliding over the well's lip while her fingers sought some purchase, however slight—a name etched a little deeper than the rest; a rose thorn, wedged between stones—that would give her some defense against gravity. As she did so she heard Dowd cry out a second time, and she looked up to see a miracle.

Quaisoir had survived the mite. The change that had come over her flesh when she rose in defiance of Dowd was here completed. Her skin was the color of the blue eye; her face, so lately maimed, was bright. But these were little changes, beside the dozen ribbons of her substance, several yards in length, that were unraveled around her, their source her back, their purpose to touch in succession the ground beneath her and raise her up into a strange flight. The power she'd found in the Bastion was blazing in her, and Dowd could only retreat before it, to the edge of the well. He kept his silence now, dropping to his knees, preparing to crawl away beneath the spiraling skirts of filament.

Jude felt slip what little hold her fingers had and let out a cry for help.

"Sister?" Quaisoir said.

"Here!" Jude yelled. "Quickly."

As Quaisoir moved towards the well, the tendrils' lightest touch enough to propel her forward, Dowd made his move, ducking beneath the tendrils. He'd mistimed his escape, however. One of the filaments caught his shoulder and, spiraling around his neck, pitched him over the edge of the well. As he went, Jude's right hand lost its purchase entirely, and she began to slide, a final desperate yell coming from her as she did so. But Quaisoir was as swift in saving as dispatching. Before the well's rim rose to eclipse the scene above, Jude felt the filaments seize her wrist and arm, their spirals instantly tightening around her. She seized them in return, her exhausted muscles quickened by the touch, and Quaisoir drew her up over the edge of the well, depositing her on the pavement. She rolled over onto her back and panted like a sprinter at the tape, while Quaisoir's filaments unknitted themselves and returned to serve their mistress.

It was the sound of Dowd's begging, echoing up from the well where he was suspended, that made her sit up. There was nothing in his cries she might not have predicted from a man who'd rehearsed servitude over so many generations. He promised Quaisoir eternal obedience and utter self-abnegation if only she'd save him from this terror. Wasn't mercy the jewel in any heavenly crown, he sobbed, and wasn't she an angel?

"No," Quaisoir said. "Nor am I the bride of Christ."

Undeterred, he began a new cycle of descriptions and negotiations: what she was; what he would do for her, in perpetuity. She would find no better servant, no humbler acolyte. What did she want, his manhood?; it was nothing; he would geld himself there and then. She only had to ask.

If Jude had any doubt as to the strength Quaisoir had gained, she had evidence of it now, as the tendrils drew their prisoner up from the well. He gushed like a holed bucket as he came.

"Thank you, a thousand times, thank you—"

In view now, he was in double jeopardy, Jude saw, his feet hanging over empty air and the tendrils around his throat tight enough to throttle him, had he not relieved their pressure by thrusting his fingers between noose and neck. Tears poured down his cheeks, in theatrical excess.

"Ladies," he said. "How do I begin to make amends?"

Quaisoir's response was another question. "Why was I misled by you?" she said. "You're just a man. What do you know about divinities?"

Dowd looked afraid to reply, not certain which would be more likely to prove fatal, denial or affirmation.

"Tell her the truth," Jude advised him.

"I served the Unbeheld once," he said. "He found me in the desert and sent me to the Fifth Dominion."

"Why?"

"He had business there."

"What business?"

Dowd began to squirm afresh. His tears had dried up. The drama had gone from his voice.

"He wanted a woman," he said, "to bear him a son in the Fifth."

"And you found one?"

"Yes, I did. Her name was Celestine."

"And what happened to her?"

"I don't know. I did what I was asked to do, and—"

"What happened to her?" Quaisoir said again, more forcefully.

"She died," Dowd replied, trailing that possibility to see if it was challenged. When it wasn't he took it up with fresh gusto. "Yes, that's what happened. She perished. In childbirth, so I believe. Hapexamendios impregnated her, you see, and her poor body couldn't bear the responsibility."

Dowd's style was by now too familiar to deceive Jude. She knew the music he put into his voice when he lied, and heard it clearly now. He was well aware that Celestine was alive. There had been no such music in his early revelations, however—his talk of procuring for Hapexamendios—which seemed to indicate that this was indeed a service he'd done the God.

"What about the child?" Quaisoir asked him. "Was it a son or a daughter?"

"I don't know," he said. "Truly, I don't."

Another lie, and one his captor sensed. She loosened the noose, and he dropped a few inches, letting out a sob of terror and clutching at the filaments in his panic.

"Don't drop me! Please God, don't drop me!"

"What about the child?"

"What do I know?" he said, tears beginning again, only this time the real thing. "I'm nothing. I'm a messenger. A spear-carrier."

"A pimp," she said.

"Yes, that too. I confess it. I'm a pimp! But it's nothing, it's nothing. Tell her, Judith! I'm just an actor chappie. A fucking worthless actor chappie!"

"Worthless, eh?"

"Worthless!"

"Then good night," Quaisoir said, and let him go.

The noose slipped through his fingers with such suddenness he had no time to take a faster hold, and he dropped like a dead man from a cut rope, not even beginning to shriek for several seconds, as though sheer disbelief had silenced him until the iris of smoky sky above him had closed almost to a dot. When his din finally rose it was high-pitched, but brief.

As it stopped, Jude laid her palms against the pavement and, without looking up at Quaisoir, murmured her thanks, in part for her preservation but at least as much for Dowd's dispatch.

"Who was he?" Quaisoir asked.

"I only know a little part of this," Jude replied.

"Little by little," Quaisoir said. "That's how we'll understand it all. Little ... by ... little."

Her voice was exhausted, and when Jude looked up she saw the miracle was leaving Quaisoir's cells. She had sunk to the ground, her unfurled flesh withdrawing into her body, the beatific blue fading from her skin. Jude picked herself up and hobbled from the edge of the hole.

Hearing her footsteps, Quaisoir said, "Where are you going?"

"Just away from the well," Jude said, laying her brow and her palms against the welcome chill of the wall. "Do you know who I am?" she asked Quaisoir, after a little time.

"Yes," came the soft reply. "You're the me I lost. You're the other Judith."

"That's right." She turned to see that Quaisoir was smiling, despite her pain.

"That's good," Quaisoir said. "If we survive this, maybe you'll begin again for both of us. Maybe you'll see the visions I turned my back on."

"What visions?"

Quaisoir sighed. "I was loved by a great Maestro once," she said. "He showed me angels. They used to come to our table in sunbeams. I swear. Angels in sunbeams. And I thought we'd live forever, and I'd learn all the secrets of the sea. But I let him lead me out of the sun. I let him persuade me the spirits didn't matter. Only our will mattered, and if we willed pain, then that was wisdom. I lost myself in such a little time, Judith. Such a little time." She shuddered. "I was blinded by my crimes before anyone ever took a knife to me."

Jude looked pityingly on her sister's maimed face. "We've got to find somebody to clean your wounds," she said.

"I doubt there's a doctor left alive in Yzordderrex," Quaisoir replied. "They're always the first to go in any revolution, aren't they? Doctors, tax collectors, poets. . . ."

"If we can't find anybody else, I'll do it," Jude said, leaving the security of the wall and venturing back down the incline to where Quaisoir sat.

"I thought I saw Jesus Christ yesterday," she said. "He was standing on a roof with his arms open wide. I thought he'd come for me, so that I could make my confession. That's why I came here: to find Jesu. I heard his messenger."

"That was me."

"You were . . . in my thoughts?"

"Yes."

"So I found you instead of Christos. That seems like a greater miracle." She reached out towards Jude, who took her hand. "Isn't it, sister?"

"I'm not sure yet," Jude said. "I was myself this morning. Now what am I? A copy, a forgery."

The word brought Klein's Bastard Boy to mind: Gentle the faker, making profit from other people's genius. Is that why he'd obsessed upon her? Had he seen in her some subtle clue to her true nature and followed her out of devotion to the sham she was?

"I was happy," she said, thinking back to the good times she'd shared with him. "Maybe I didn't always realize I was happy, but I was. I was myself."

"You still are."

"No," she said, as close to despair as she could ever remember being. "I'm a piece of somebody else."

"We're all pieces," Quaisoir said. "Whether we were born or made." Her fingers tightened around Jude's hand. "We're all hoping to be whole again. Will you take me back up to the palace?" she said. "We'll be safer there than here."

"Of course," Jude replied, helping her up.

"Do you know which direction to go?"

She said she did. Despite the smoke and the darkness, the walls of the palace loomed above them, massive but remote.

"We've got quite a climb ahead of us," Jude said. "It may take us till morning."

"The night is long in Yzordderrex," Quaisoir replied.

"It won't last forever," Jude said.

"It will for me."

"I'm sorry. That was thoughtless. I didn't mean—"

"Don't be sorry," Quaisoir said. "I like the dark. I can remember the sun better. Sun, and angels at the table. Will you take my arm, sister? I don't want to lose you again."

IN ANY OTHER PLACE BUT THIS, Gentle might have been frustrated by the sight of so many sealed doors, but as Lazarevich led him closer to the Pivot Tower the atmosphere grew so thick with dread he was glad whatever lay behind those doors was locked away. His guide spoke scarcely at all. When he did it was to suggest that Gentle make the rest of the journey alone.

"It's a little way now," he kept saying. "You don't need me any more."

"That's not the deal," Gentle would remind him, and Lazarevich would curse and whine, then head on some distance in silence, until a shriek down one of the passages, or a glimpse of blood spilled on the polished floor, made him halt and start his little speech afresh.

At no point in this journey were they challenged. If these titanic halls had ever buzzed with activity—and given that small armies could be lost in them, Gentle doubted that they ever had—they were all but deserted now. Those few servants and bureaucrats they did encounter were busy leaving, burdened with hastily gathered belongings as they hurried down the corridors. Survival was their foremost priority. They gave the bleeding soldier and his ill-dressed companion scarcely a look.

At last they came to a door, this one unsealed, which Lazarevich refused point-blank to enter.

"This is the Pivot Tower," he said, his voice barely audible.

"How do I know you're telling the truth?"

"Can't you feel it?"

Now it was remarked upon, Gentle did indeed feel a subtle sensation, barely strong enough to be called a tingle, in his fingertips, testicles, and sinuses.

"That's the tower, I swear," Lazarevich whispered.

Gentle believed him. "All right," he said. "You've done your duty; you'd better go."

The man grinned. "You mean it?"

"Yes."

"Oh, thank you. Whoever you are. Thank you."

Before he could skip away, Gentle took hold of his arm and drew him close. "Tell your children," he said, "not to be soldiers. Poets, maybe, or shoeshiners. But not soldiers. Got it?"

Lazarevich nodded violently, though Gentle doubted he'd comprehended a word. His only thought was of escape, and he took to his heels the moment Gentle let go of him and was out of sight in two or three seconds. Turning to the beaten brass doors, Gentle pushed them a few inches wider and slipped inside. The nerve endings in his scrotum and palms knew that something of significance was nearby—what had been subtle sensation was almost painful now—even though his eyes were denied sight of it by the murk of the room he'd entered. He stood by the door until he was able to grasp some sense of what lay ahead. This was not, it seemed, the Pivot Tower itself but an antechamber of some kind, as stale as a sickroom. Its walls were bare, its only furniture a table upon which a canary cage lay overturned, its door open, its occupant flown. Beyond the table, another doorway, which he took, led him into a corridor, staler still than the room he'd left. The source of agitation in his nerve endings was audible now: a steady tone that might have been soothing under other circumstances. Not knowing which direction it was coming from, he turned to his right and crept down the corridor. A flight of stairs curved out of sight to his left. He chose not to take them, his instinct rewarded by a glimmer of light up ahead. The Pivot's tone became less insistent as he advanced, suggesting this route was a cul-de-sac, but he headed on towards the light to be certain Pie was not being held prisoner in one of these antechambers.

As he came within half a dozen strides of the room somebody moved across the doorway, flitting through his field of vision too quickly to be seen. He flattened himself against the wall and edged towards the room. A wick, set in a bowl of oil on a table, shed the light he'd been drawn to. Beside it, several plates contained the remains of a meal. When he reached the door he waited there for the man—the night watch, he supposed—to come back into view. He had no wish to kill him unless it was strictly necessary. There'd be enough widows and orphans in Yzordderrex by tomorrow morning without his adding to the sum. He heard the man fart, not once but several times, with the abandon of someone who believed himself alone, then heard him open another door, his footsteps receding.

Gentle chanced a glance around the doorjamb. The room was empty. He quickly stepped inside, intending to take from the table the two knives that were lying there. On one of the plates was an already rifled assortment of candies. He couldn't resist.

He picked the most luscious and had it to his mouth when the man behind said, "Rosengarten?"

He looked around, and as his gaze settled on the face across the room his jaw clenched in shock, breaking on the candy between his teeth. Sight and sugar mingled, tongue and eye feeding such a sweetness to his brain he reeled.

The face before him was a living mirror: *his* eyes, *his* nose, *his* mouth, *his* hairline, *his* bearing, *his* bafflement, *his* fatigue. In everything but the cut of his coat and the muck beneath his fingernails, another Gentle. But not by that name, surely.

Swallowing the sweet liqueur from the candy, Gentle very slowly said, "Who . . . in God's name . . . are you?"

The shock was draining from the other's face, and amusement replacing it. He shook his head. ". . . damn kreauchee . . ."

"That's your name?" Gentle replied. "Damn Kreauchee?"

He'd heard stranger in his travels. But the question only served to amuse the other more.

"Not a bad idea," he replied. "There's enough in my system. The Autarch Damn Kreauchee. That's got a ring to it."

Gentle spat the candy from his mouth. "Autarch?" he said.

The amusement fled from the other's face. "You've made your point, wisp. Now fuck off." He closed his eyes. "Get a hold of yourself," he half whispered. "It's the fucking kreauchee. It's happened before, it'll happen again."

Now Gentle understood. "You think you're dreaming me, don't you?" he said.

The Autarch opened his eyes, angered to find the hallucination still hanging around. "I told you—" he said.

"What *is* this kreauchee? Some kind of alcohol? Dope? Do you think I'm a bad trip? Well, I'm not."

He started towards the other, who retreated in alarm.

"Go on," Gentle said, extending his hand. "Touch me. I'm real. I'm here. My name's John Zacharias, and I've come a long way to see you. I didn't think that was the reason, but now I'm here, I'm sure it was."

The Autarch raised his fists to his temples, as if to beat this drug dream from his brain.

"This isn't possible," he said. There was more than disbelief in his voice; there was an unease that was close to fear. "You can't be here. Not after all these years."

"Well, I am," said Gentle. "I'm as confused as you, believe me. But I'm here."

The Autarch studied him, turning his head this way and that, as though he still expected to find some angle from which to view the visitor that would reveal him as an apparition. But after a minute of such study he gave it up and simply stared at Gentle, his face a maze of furrows.

"Where did you come from?" he said slowly.

"I think you know," Gentle replied.

"The Fifth?"

"Yes."

"You came to bring me down, didn't you? Why didn't I see it? You started this revolution! You were out in the streets, sowing the seeds! No wonder I couldn't root the rebels out. I kept wondering: Who is it? Who's out there, plotting against me? Execution after execution, purge after purge, and I never got to the one at the heart of it. The one who was as clever as me. The nights I lay awake thinking: Who is it? Who? I made a list as long as my arm. But never you, Maestro. Never *Sartori.*"

Hearing the Autarch name himself was shocking enough, but this second naming bred utter rebellion in Gentle's system. His head filled with the same din that had beset him on the platform at Mai-ké, and his belly disgorged its contents in one bilious heave. He put his hand out to the table to steady himself and missed the edge, slipping to the floor where his vomit was already spattered. Floundering in his own mess, he tried to shake the noise from his head, but all he did was unknot the confusion of sounds and let the words they concealed slip through.

Sartori! He was Sartori! He didn't waste breath questioning the name. It was his, and he knew it. And what worlds there were in that naming: more confounding than anything the Dominions had unveiled, opening before him like windows blown wide and shattered, never to be closed again.

He heard the name spoken out of a hundred memories. A woman sighed it as she begged him back into her disheveled bed.

A priest beat out the syllables on his pulpit, prophesying damnation. A gambler blew it into his cupped hands to bless his dice. Condemned men made prayers of it; drunkards, mockery; carousers, songs.

Oh, but he'd been famous! At St. Bartholomew Fair there'd been troupes who'd filled their purses, telling his life as farce. A bordello in Bloomsbury had boasted a sometime nun driven to nymphomania by his touch, who would chant his conjurations (so she said) as she was fucked. He was a paradigm of all things fabulous and forbidden: a threat to reasoning men; to their wives, a secret vice. And to the children—the children, trailing past his house after the beadle—he was a rhyme:

Maestro Sartori
Wants a bit o' glory.
He loves the cats,
He loves the dogs,
He turns the ladies into frogs,
He made some hats
Of baby rats;
But that's another story.

This chant, repeated in his head in the piping voices of parish orphans, was worse in its way than the pulpit curses, or the sobs, or the prayers. It rolled on and on, in its fatuous way, gathering neither meaning nor music as it went. Like his life, without this name: motion without purpose.

"Had you forgotten?" the Autarch asked him.

"Oh, yes," Gentle replied, unbidden and bitter laughter coming to his lips with the reply. "I'd forgotten."

Even now, with the voices rebaptizing him with their clamor, he could scarcely believe it. Had this body of his survived two hundred years and more in the Fifth Dominion, while his mind went on deceiving itself: holding only a decade of life in its consciousness and hiding the rest away? Where had he lived all those years? Who had he been? If what he'd just heard was true, this act of remembering was just the first. There were two centuries of memories concealed in his brain somewhere, waiting to be discovered. No wonder Pie had kept him in ignorance. Now that he knew, madness was very close.

He got to his feet, holding on to the table for support. "Is Pie 'oh' pah here?" he said.

"The mystif? No. Why? Did it come with you from the Fifth?"

"Yes, it did."

A twitch of a smile returned to the Autarch's face. "Aren't they exquisite creatures?" he said. "I've had one or two myself. They're an acquired taste, but once you've got it you never really lose it again. But no, I haven't seen it."

"Judith, then?"

"Ah." He sighed. "Judith. I assume you mean Godolphin's lady? She went by a lot of names, didn't she? Mind you, we all did. What do they call you these days?"

"I told you. John Furie Zacharias. Or Gentle."

"I have a few friends who know me as Sartori. I'd like to number you among them. Or do you want the name back?"

"Gentle will do. We were talking about Judith. I saw her this morning, down by the harbor."

"Did you see Christ down there?"

"What are you talking about?"

"She came back here saying she'd seen the Man of Sorrows. She had the fear of the Lord in her. Crazy bitch." He sighed. "It was sad, really, to see her that way. I thought it was just too much kreauchee at first, but no. She'd finally lost her mind. It was running out of her ears."

"Who are we talking about?" Gentle said, thinking one or the other of them had mislaid the path of the conversation.

"I'm talking about Quaisoir, my wife. She came with me from the Fifth."

"I was talking about Judith."

"So was I."

"Are you saying—"

"There are two. You made one of them yourself, for God's sake, or have you forgotten that too?"

"Yes. Yes, I'd forgotten."

"She was beautiful, but she wasn't worth losing the Imajica for. That was your big mistake. You should have served your hand and not your rod. Then I'd never have been born, and God would be in His heaven, and you'd be Pope Sartori. Ha! Is that why you came back? To become pope? It's too late, brother. By tomorrow morning Yzordderrex will be a heap of smoking ash. This is my last night here. I'm going to the Fifth. I'm going to build a new empire there."

"Why?"

"Don't you remember the rhyme they used to sing? For glory's sake."

"Haven't you had enough of that?"

"You tell me. Whatever's in my heart was plucked from yours. Don't tell me you haven't dreamed of power. You were the greatest Maestro in Europe. There was nobody could touch you. That didn't all evaporate overnight."

He moved towards Gentle for the first time in this exchange, reaching out to lay his steady hand on Gentle's shoulder.

"I think you should see the Pivot, brother Gentle," he said. "That'll remind you of what power feels like. Are you steady on your feet?"

"Reasonably."

"Come on, then."

He led the way back into the passage, to the flight of stairs Gentle had declined to take. Now he did so, following Sartori around the curve of the staircase to a door without a handle.

"The only eyes laid on the Pivot since the tower was built are mine," he said. "Which has made it very sensitive to scrutiny."

"My eyes are yours," Gentle reminded him.

"It'll know the difference," Sartori replied. "It'll want to . . . probe you." The sexual subtext of this wasn't lost on him. "You'll just have to lie back and think of England," he said. "It's over quickly."

So saying he licked his thumb and laid it on the rectangle of slate-colored stone set in the middle of the door, inscribing a figure in spittle upon it. The door responded to the signal. Its locks began to grind into motion.

"Spit too, huh?" Gentle said. "I thought it was just breath."

"You use pneuma?" Sartori said. "Then I should be able to. But I haven't got the trick of it. You'll have to teach me, and I'll . . . remind you of a few sways in return."

"I don't understand the mechanics of it."

"Then we'll learn together," Sartori replied. "The principles are simple enough. Matter and mind, mind and matter. Each transforming the other. Maybe that's what *we're* going to do. Transform one another."

With that thought, Sartori put his palm on the door and pushed it open. Though it was fully six inches thick it moved without a sound, and with an extended hand Sartori invited Gentle to enter, speaking as he did so.

"It's said that Hapexamendios set the Pivot in the middle of the Imajica so that His fertility would flow from it into every Dominion." He lowered his voice, as if for an indiscretion. "In other words," he said. "This is the phallus of the Unbeheld."

Gentle had seen this tower from the outside, of course; it soared above every other pylon and dome in the palace. But he hadn't grasped its enormity until now. It was a square stone tower, seventy or eighty feet from side to side and so tall that the lights blazing in the walls to illuminate its sole occupant receded like cat's eyes in a highway till sheer distance dimmed then erased them. An extraordinary sight: but nothing beside the monolith around which the tower had been constructed. Gentle had been steeling himself for an assault when the door was opened: the tone he'd heard in his skull as he'd crept along the passage below rattling his teeth, the charge burning in his fingers. But there was nothing, not even a murmur, which was in its way more distressing. The Pivot knew he was here in its chamber but was keeping its counsel, silently assessing him as he assessed it.

There were several shocks. The first, and the least, how beautiful it was, its sides the color of thunderclouds, hewn so that seams of brightness flowed in them like hidden lightning. The second, that it was not set on the ground but hovered, in all its enormity, ten feet from the floor of the tower, casting a shadow so dense that the dark air was almost a plinth.

"Impressive, huh?" Sartori remarked, his cocky tone as inappropriate as laughter at an altar. "You can walk underneath it. Go on. It's quite safe."

Gentle was reluctant, but he was all too aware that his other was watching for his weaknesses, and any sign of fear now might be used against him later. Sartori had already seen him sickened and down on his knees; he didn't want the bastard to get another glimpse of frailty.

"Aren't you coming with me?" he said, glancing around at the Autarch.

"It's a very private moment," the other replied, and stood back to let Gentle venture into the shadow.

It was like stepping back into the wastes of the Jokalaylau. Cold cut him to the marrow. His breath was snatched from his lungs and appeared before him in a bitter cloud. Gasping, he turned his face to the power above him, his mind divided between the rational urge to study the phenomenon and the barely controllable desire to drop to his knees and beg it not to crush him. The heaven above him had five sides, he saw. One for each Dominion, perhaps. And like the hewn flanks, flickers of lightning appeared in it here and there. But it wasn't simply a trick of seam and shadow that gave the stone the look of a thundercloud. There was motion in it, the solid rock roiling above him. He threw a glance towards Sartori, who was standing at the door, casually putting a cigarette between his lips. The flame he struck to light it with was a world away, but Gentle didn't envy him its warmth. Icy as this shadow was, he wanted the stone sky to unfurl above him and deliver its judgment down; he wanted to see whatever power the Pivot possessed unleashed, if only to know that such powers and such judgments existed. He looked away from Sartori almost contemptuously, the thought shaping in his head that for all the other's talk of possessing this monolith, the years it had spent in this tower were moments in its incalculable span, and he and Sartori would have come and gone, their little mark eroded by those that followed, in the time it took the stone to blink its cloudy eye.

Perhaps it read that thought from his cortex and approved, because the light, when it came, was kind. There was sun in the stone as well as lightning, warmth as well as a killing fire. It brightened the mantle, then fell in shafts, first around him, then upon his upturned face. The moment had antecedents: events in the Fifth that had prophesied this, their parent's, coming. He'd stood on Highgate Hill once, when the city road was still a muddy track, and looked up to see the clouds drop glory down as they were doing now. He'd gone to the window of his room in Gamut Street and seen the same. He'd watched the smoke clear after a night of bombing—1941, the Blitz at its height—and seeing the sun burn through, had known in some place too tender to be touched that he'd forgotten something momentous, and that if he ever remembered—if a light like this ever burned the veil away—the world would unravel.

That conviction came again, but this time there was more than a vague unease to support it. The tone that had sounded in his skull had come again, attendant on the light, and in it, described by the subtlest variation in its monotony, he heard words.

The Pivot was addressing him.

Reconciler, it said.

He wanted to cover his ears and shut the word out. Drop to the ground like a prophet begging to be unburdened of some divine duty. But the word was inside as well as out. There was no escaping it.

The work's not finished yet, the Pivot said.

"What work?" he said.

You know what work.

He did, of course. But so much pain had come with that labor, and he was ill equipped to bear it again.

Why deny it? the Pivot said.

He stared up into the brightness. "I failed before, and so many people died. I can't do it again. Please. I can't."

What did you come here for? the Pivot asked him, its voice so tenuous he had to hold his breath to catch the shape of the words. The question took him back to Taylor's bedside, to that plea for comprehension.

"To understand . . ." he said.

To understand what?

"I can't put it into words . . . it sounds so pitiful. . . ."

Say it.

"To understand why I was born. Why anybody's born."

You know why you were born.

"No, I don't. I wish I did, but I don't."

You're the Reconciler of Dominions. You're the healer of the Imajica. Hide from that, and you hide from understanding. Maestro, there's a worse anguish than remembering, and another suffers it because you leave your work unfinished. Go back into the Fifth Dominion and complete what you began. Make the many One. This is the only salvation.

The stone sky began to roil again, and the clouds closed over the sun. With the darkness, the cold returned, but he didn't relinquish his place in the Pivot's shadow for several seconds, still hoping some crack would open and the God speak a last consoling word, a whisper perhaps, of how this onerous duty might be passed to another soul more readily equipped to accomplish it. But there was nothing. The vision had passed, and all he could do was wrap his arms around his shuddering frame and stumble out to where Sartori stood. The other's cigarette lay smoking at his feet, where it had dropped from his fingers. By the expression on his face it was apparent that even if he'd not comprehended every detail of the exchange that had just taken place, he had the gist.

"The Unbeheld speaks," he said, his voice as flat as the God's.

"I don't want this," Gentle said.

"I don't think this is any place to talk about denying Him," Sartori said, giving the Pivot a queasy glance.

"I didn't say I was denying Him," Gentle replied. "Just that I didn't want it."

"Still better discussed in private," Sartori whispered, turning to open the door.

He didn't lead Gentle back to the mean little room where they'd met, but to a chamber at the other end of the passageway, which boasted the only window he'd seen in the vicinity. It was narrow and dirty, but not as dirty as the sky on the other side. Dawn had begun to touch the clouds, but the smoke that still rose in curling columns from the fires below all but canceled its frail light.

"This isn't what I came for," Gentle said as he stared out at the murk. "I wanted answers."

"You've had 'em."

"I have to take what's mine, however foul it is?"

"Not yours, *ours*. The responsibility. The pain"—he paused—"and the glory, of course."

Gentle glanced at him. "It's mine," he said simply.

Sartori shrugged, as though this were of no consequence to him whatsoever. Gentle saw his own wiles working in that simple gesture. How many times had he shrugged in precisely that fashion—

raised his eyebrows, pursed his lips, looked away with feigned indifference? He let Sartori believe the bluff was working.

"I'm glad you understand," he said. "The burden's mine."

"You've failed before."

"But I came close," Gentle said, feigning access to a memory he
didn't yet have in the hope of coaxing an informative rebuttal.

"Close isn't good enough," Sartori said. "Close is lethal. A
tragedy. Look what it did to you. The great Maestro. You crawl back
here with half your wits missing."

"The Pivot trusts me."

That struck a tender place. Suddenly Sartori was shouting.

"Fuck the Pivot! Why should you be the Reconciler? Huh?
Why? One hundred and fifty years I've ruled the Imajica. I know
how to use power. You don't."

"Is that what you want?" Gentle said, trailing the bait of that
possibility. "You want to be the Reconciler in my place?"

"I'm better equipped than you," Sartori raged. "All you're good
for is sniffing after women."

"And what are you? Impotent?"

"I know what you're doing. I'd do the same. You're stirring me
up, so I'll spill my secrets. I don't care. There's nothing you can do
I can't do better. You wasted all those years, hiding away, but I *used*
them. I turned myself into an empire builder. What did you do?"
He didn't wait for an answer. He knew his subject too well. "You've
learned nothing. If you began the Reconciliation now, you'd make
the same mistakes."

"And what were they?"

"It comes down to one," Sartori said. "Judith. If you hadn't
wanted her—" He stopped, studying his other. "You don't even remember that, do you?"

"No," Gentle said. "Not yet."

"Let me tell you, brother," Sartori said, coming face to face with
Gentle. "It's a sad story."

"I don't weep easily."

"She was the most beautiful woman in England. Some people
said, in Europe. But she belonged to Joshua Godolphin, and he
guarded her like his soul."

"They were married?"

"No. She was his mistress, but he loved her more than any wife.
And of course he knew what you felt, you didn't disguise it, and
that made him afraid—oh, *God,* was he afraid—that sooner or
later you were going to seduce her and spirit her away. It'd be easy.
You were the Maestro Sartori; you could do anything. But he was
one of your patrons, so you bided your time, thinking maybe he'd
tire of her, and then you could have her without bad blood between

you. It didn't happen. The months went by, and his devotion was as intense as ever. You'd never waited this long for a woman before. You started to suffer like a lovesick adolescent. You couldn't sleep. Your heart palpitated at the sound of her voice. This wasn't good for the Reconciliation, of course, having the Maestro pining away, and Godolphin came to want a solution as badly as you did. So when you found one, he was ready to listen."

"What was it?"

"That you make another Judith, indistinguishable from the first. You had the feits to do it."

"Then he'd have one . . ."

"And so would you. Simple. No, not simple. Very difficult. Very dangerous. But those were heady days. Dominions hidden from human eyes since the beginning of time were just a few ceremonies away. Heaven was possible. Creating another Judith seemed like small potatoes. You put it to him, and he agreed—"

"Just like that?"

"You sweetened the pill. You promised him a Judith better than the first. A woman who wouldn't age, wouldn't tire of his company or the company of his sons, or the sons of his sons. This Judith would belong to the men of the Godolphin family in perpetuity. She'd be pliant, she'd be modest, she'd be perfect."

"And what did the original think of this?"

"She didn't know. You drugged her, you took her up to the Meditation room in the house in Gamut Street, you lit a blazing fire, stripped her naked, and began the ritual. You anointed her; you laid her in a circle of sand from the margin of the Second Dominion, the holiest ground in the Imajica. Then you said your prayers, and you waited." He paused, enjoying this telling. "It is, let me remind you, a long conjuration. Eleven hours at the minimum, watching the doppelgänger grow in the circle beside its source. You'd made sure there was nobody else in the house, of course, not even your precious mystif. This was a very secret ritual. So you were alone, and you soon got bored. And when you got bored, you got drunk. So there you were, sitting in the room with her, watching her perfection in the firelight, obsessing on her beauty. And eventually— half out of your mind with brandy—you made the biggest mistake of your life. You tore off your clothes, you stepped into the circle, and you did about everything a man can do to a woman, even though she was comatose, and you were hallucinating with fasting and drink. You didn't fuck her once, you did it over and over, as though you wanted to get up inside her. Over and over. Then you fell into a stupor at her side."

Gentle began to see the error looming. "I fell asleep in the circle?" he said.

"In the circle."

"And *you* were the consequence."

"I was. And let me tell you, it was quite a birth. People say they don't remember the moment they came into the world, but I do. I remember opening my eyes in the circle, with her beside me, and these rains of matter coming down on me, congealing around my spirit. Becoming bone. Becoming flesh." All expression had gone from his face. "I remember," he said, "at one point she realized she wasn't alone and she turned and saw me lying beside her. I was unfinished. An anatomy lesson, raw and wet. I've never forgotten the noise she made—"

"I didn't wake up through any of this?"

"You'd crawled away downstairs to douse your head, and you'd fallen asleep. I know because I found you, later on, sprawled on the dining room table."

"The conjuration still worked, even though I'd left the circle?"

"You're quite the technician, aren't you? Yes, it still worked. You were an easy subject. It took hours to decode Judith and make *her* doppelgänger. But you were incandescent. The sway read you in minutes and made me in a couple of hours."

"You knew who you were from the beginning?"

"Oh, yes. I was *you,* in your lust. I was *you,* full of drunken visions. I was *you,* wanting to fuck and fuck, and conquer and conquer. But I was also you when you'd done your worst, with your balls empty and your head empty, like death had got in, sitting there between her legs trying to remember what it was you were living for. I was that man too, and it was terrifying to have both those feelings in me at the same time."

He paused a moment.

"It still is, brother."

"I would have helped you, surely, if I'd known what I'd done."

"Or put me out of my misery," Sartori said. "Taken me into the garden and shot me like a rabid dog. I didn't know what you'd do. I went downstairs. You were snoring like a trooper. I watched you for a long while, wanting to wake you, wanting to share the terror I felt, but Godolphin arrived before I got up the courage. It was just before dawn. He'd come to take Judith home. I hid myself. I watched Godolphin wake you; I heard you talk together, I saw you climb the stairs like two expectant fathers and go into the Meditation Room. Then I heard your whoops of celebration, and I knew once and for all that I wasn't an intended child."

"What did you do?"

"I stole some money and some clothes. Then I made my escape. The fear passed after a time. I began to realize what I was, the knowledge I possessed. And I realized I had this ... appetite. Your appetite. I wanted glory."

"And this is what you did to get it?" Gentle said, turning back to the window. The devastation below was clearer by the minute, as the comet's light strengthened. "Brave work, brother."

"This was a great city once. And there'll be others, just as great. Greater, because this time there'll be two of us to build it. And two of us to rule."

"You've got me wrong," Gentle said. "I don't want an empire."

"But it's bound to come," Sartori said, fired up with this vision. "You're the Reconciler, brother. You're the healer of the Imajica. You know what that could mean for us both? If you reconcile the Dominions there'll have to be one great city—a new Yzordderrex—to rule it from end to end. I'll found it and administrate it, and you can be pope."

"I don't want to be pope."

"What *do* you want then?"

"Pie 'oh' pah for one. And some sense of what all this means."

"Being born to be the Reconciler's enough meaning for anyone. It's all the purpose you need. Don't run from it."

"And what were you born to do? You can't build cities forever." He glanced out at the desolation. "Is that why you've destroyed it?" he said. "So you can start again?"

"I didn't destroy it. There was a revolution."

"Which you fueled, with your massacres," Gentle said. "I was in a little village called Beatrix, a few weeks ago—"

"Ah, yes. Beatrix." Sartori drew a heavy breath. "It was you, of course. I knew somebody was watching me, but I didn't know who. The frustration made me cruel, I'm afraid."

"You call that cruel? I call it inhuman."

"It may take you a little time to understand, but every now and again such extremes are necessary."

"I knew some of those people."

"You won't ever have to dirty your hands with that kind of unpleasantness. I'll do whatever's necessary."

"So will I," said Gentle.

Sartori frowned. "Is that a threat?" he said.

"This began with me, and it'll end with me."

"But *which me,* Maestro? That one"—he pointed at Gentle—"or this? Don't you see, we weren't meant to be enemies. We can achieve so much more if we work together." He put his hand on Gentle's shoulder. "We were meant to meet this way. That's why the Pivot kept silent all these years. It was waiting for you to come, and us to be reunited." His face slackened. "Don't be my enemy," he said. "The thought of—"

A cry of alarm from outside the room cut him short. He turned from Gentle and started towards the door as a soldier appeared in the passageway beyond, his throat opened, his hand ineptly staunching the spurts. He stumbled and fell against the wall, sliding to the ground.

"The mob must be here," Sartori remarked, with a hint of satisfaction. "It's time to make your decision, brother. Do we go on from here together, or shall I rule the Fifth alone?"

A new din rose, loud enough to blot out any further exchange, and Sartori left off his counseling, stepping out into the passageway.

"Stay here," he told Gentle. "Think about it while you wait."

Gentle ignored the instruction. As soon as Sartori was around the corner, he followed. The commotion died away as he did so, leaving only the low whistle from the soldier's windpipe to accompany his pursuit. Gentle picked up his pace, suddenly fearing that an ambush awaited his other. No doubt Sartori deserved death. No doubt they both did. But there was a good deal he hadn't prized from his brother yet, especially concerning the failure of the Reconciliation. He had to be preserved from harm, at least until Gentle had every clue to the puzzle out of him. The time would come for them both to pay the penalty for their excesses. But it wasn't yet.

As he stepped over the dead soldier, he heard the mystif's voice. The single word it said was: "Gentle."

Hearing that tone—like no other he'd heard or dreamt—all concern for Sartori's preservation, or his own, was overwhelmed. His only thought was to get to the place where the mystif was; to lay his eyes on it and his arms around it. They'd been parted for far too long. Never again, he swore to himself as he ran. Whatever edicts or obligations were set before them, whatever malice sought to divide them, never again would he let the mystif go.

He turned the corner. Ahead lay the doorway that led out into the antechamber. Sartori was on the other side, partially eclipsed, but hearing Gentle's approach he turned, glancing back into the passageway. The smile of welcome he was wearing for Pie 'oh' pah decayed, and in two strides he was at the door to slam it in his maker's face. Realizing he was outpaced, Gentle yelled Pie's name, but the door was closed before the syllable was out, plunging Gentle into almost total darkness. The oath he'd made seconds before was broken; they were divided again, before they could even be reunited. In his rage Gentle threw himself against the door, but like everything else in this tower it was built to last a millennium. However hard he hit it, all he got was bruises. They hurt; but the memory of Sartori's leer when he'd talked about his taste for mystifs stung more. Even now, the mystif was probably in Sartori's arms. Embraced, kissed, possessed.

He threw himself against the door one final time, then gave up on such primitive assaults. Drawing a breath, he blew it into his fist and slammed the pneuma against the door the way he'd learned to do in the Jokalaylau. It had been a glacier beneath his hand on that first occasion, and the ice had cracked only after several attempts. This time, either because his will to be on the other side of the door was stronger than his desire to free the women in the ice, or simply because he was the Maestro Sartori now, a named man who knew at least a little about the power he wielded, the steel succumbed at the first blow, and a jagged crack opened in the door.

He heard Sartori shouting on the other side, but he didn't waste time trying to make sense of it. Instead he delivered a second pneuma against the fractured steel, and this time his hand passed all the way through the door as pieces flew from beneath his palm. He put his fist to his mouth a third time, smelling his own blood as he did so, but whatever harm this was doing him, it had not yet registered as pain. He caught a third breath and delivered it against the door with a yell that wouldn't have shamed a samurai. The hinges shrieked, and the door flew open. He was through it before it had struck the floor, only to find the antechamber beyond deserted, at least by the living. Three corpses, companions to the soldier who'd raised the alarm, lay sprawled on the floor, all opened with single slashes. He leapt over them to the door, his broken hand adding its drops to the pools he trod.

The corridor beyond was rank with smoke, as though something half rotted was burning in the bowels of the palace. But through the murk, fifty yards from him, he saw Sartori and Pie 'oh' pah. Whatever fiction Sartori had invented to dissuade the mystif from completing its mission, it had proved potent. They were racing from the tower without so much as a backward glance, like lovers just escaped from death's door.

Gentle drew breath, not to issue a pneuma this time but a call. He shouted Pie's name down the passageway, the smoke dividing as his summons went, as though the syllables from a Maestro's mouth had a literal presence. Pie stopped and looked back. Sartori took hold of the mystif's arm as if to hurry it on, but Pie's eyes had already found Gentle, and it refused to be ushered away. Instead it shrugged off Sartori's hold and took a step in Gentle's direction. The curtain of smoke divided by his cry had come together again and made a blur of the mystif's face, but Gentle read its confusion from its body. It seemed not to know whether to advance or retreat.

"It's me!" Gentle called. "It's me!"

He saw Sartori at the mystif's shoulder and caught fragments of the warnings he was whispering: something about the Pivot having hold of their heads.

"I'm not an illusion, Pie," Gentle said as he advanced. "This is me. Gentle. I'm real."

The mystif shook its head, looking back at Sartori, then again at Gentle, confounded by the sight.

"It's just a trick," Sartori said, no longer bothering to whisper. "Come away, Pie, before it really gets a hold. It can make us crazy."

Too late, perhaps, Gentle thought. He was close enough to see the look on the mystif's face now, and it was lunatic: eyes wide, teeth clenched, sweat making red rivulets of the blood spattered on its cheek and brow. The sometime assassin had long since lost its appetite for slaughter—that much had been apparent back in the Cradle, when it had hesitated to kill though their lives had depended upon it—but it had done so here, and the anguish it felt was written in every furrow of its face. No wonder Sartori had found it so easy to make the mystif forsake its mission. It was teetering on mental collapse. And now, confronted with two faces it knew, both speaking with the voice of its lover, it was losing what little equilibrium it had left.

Its hand went to its belt, from which hung one of the ribbon blades the execution squad had wielded. Gentle heard it sing as it came, its edge undulled by the slaughter it had already committed.

Behind the mystif, Sartori said, "Why not? It's only a shadow."

Pie's crazed look intensified, and it raised the fluttering blade above its head. Gentle halted. Another step and he was in range of the blade; nor did he doubt that Pie was ready to use it.

"Go on!" Sartori said. *"Kill it!* One shadow more or less. . . ."

Gentle glanced towards Sartori, and that tiny motion seemed enough to spur the mystif. It came at Gentle, the blade whining. He threw himself backwards to avoid the swipe, which would have opened his chest had it caught him, but the mystif was determined not to make the same error twice, and closed the gap between them with a stride. Gentle retreated, raising his arms in surrender, but the mystif was indifferent to such signs. It wanted this madness gone, and quickly.

"Pie?" Gentle gasped. "It's me! It's me! I left you at the Kesparate! Remember that?"

Pie swung again, not once but twice, the second slash catching Gentle's upper arm and chest, opening the coat, shirt, and flesh beneath. Gentle pivoted on his heel to avoid the following cut, putting his already bloodied hand to the wound. Taking another stumbling step of retreat, he felt the wall of the passageway hard against his spine. He had nowhere else to run.

"Don't I get a last supper then?" he said, not looking at the blade but at Pie's eyes, attempting to stare past the slaughter fugue to the sane mind that cowered behind it. "You promised we'd eat together, Pie. Don't you remember? A fish inside a fish inside—"

The mystif stopped. The blade fluttered at its shoulder.

"—a fish."

The blade fluttered on, but it didn't descend.

"Say you remember, Pie. *Please* say you remember."

Somewhere behind Pie, Sartori began a new round of exhortations, but to Gentle they were just a din. He continued to meet Pie's blank gaze, looking for some sign that his words had moved his executioner. The mystif drew a tiny, broken breath, and the knots that bound its brow and mouth slipped.

"Gentle?" it said.

He didn't reply. He just let his hand drop from his shoulder and stood open-armed against the wall.

"Kill it!" Sartori was still saying. "Kill it! It's just an illusion!"

Pie turned, the blade still raised.

"Don't!" Gentle said, but the mystif was already starting in the Autarch's direction. Gentle called after it again, pushing himself from the wall to stop it. "Pie! Listen to me—"

The mystif glanced around, and as it did so Sartori raised his hand to his eye and in one smooth motion snatched at it, extending his arm and opening his fist to let fly what it had plucked. Not the eye itself but some essence of his glance went from the palm like a ball trailing smoke. Gentle reached for the mystif to drag it out of the sway's path, but his hand fell inches short of Pie's back, and as he reached again the sway struck. The fluttering blade dropped from the mystif's hand as it was thrown backwards by the impact, its gaze fixed on Gentle as it fell into his arms. The momentum carried them both to the ground, but Gentle was quick to roll from under the mystif's weight and put his hand to his mouth to defend them with a pneuma. Sartori was already retreating into the smoke, however, on his face a look that would vex Gentle for many days and nights to come. There was more distress in it than triumph; more sorrow than rage.

"Who will reconcile us now?" he said, and then he was gone into the murk, as though he had mastery of the smoke and had pulled it around him to duck away behind its folds.

Gentle didn't give chase but went back to the mystif, lying where it had fallen. He knelt beside it.

"Who was he?" Pie said.

"Something I made," Gentle said, "when I was a Maestro."

"Another Sartori?" Pie said.

"Yes."

"Then go after him. Kill him. Those creatures are the most—"

"Later."

"Before he escapes."

"He can't escape, lover. There's nowhere he can go I won't find him."

Pie's hands were clutching at the place in mid-chest where Sartori's malice had struck.

"Let me see," Gentle said, drawing Pie's fingers away and tearing at the mystif's shirt. The wound was a stain on its flesh, black at the center and fading to a pustular yellow at its edges.

"Where's Huzzah?" Pie asked him, breath labored.

"She's dead," Gentle replied. "She was murdered by a Nullianac."

"So much death," Pie said. "It blinded me. I would have killed you and not even known I'd done it."

"We're not going to talk about death," Gentle said. "We're going to find some way of healing you."

"There's more urgent business than that," Pie said. "I came to kill the Autarch—"

"No, Pie. . . ."

"That was the judgment," Pie insisted. "But now I can't finish it. Will you do it for me?"

Gentle put his hand beneath the mystif's head and raised Pie up.

"I can't do that," he said.

"Why not? You could do it with a breath."

"No, Pie. I'd be killing myself."

"What?"

The mystif stared up at Gentle, baffled. But its puzzlement was short-lived. Before Gentle had time to explain, Pie let out a long, sorrowful sigh, in the shape of three soft words.

"Oh, my Lord."

"I found him in the Pivot Tower. I didn't believe it at first. . . ."

"The Autarch Sartori," Pie said, as if trying the words for their music. Then, its voice a dirge, it said, "It has a ring."

"You knew I was a Maestro all along, didn't you?"

"Of course."

"But you didn't tell me."

"I got as close as I dared. But I had sworn an oath never to remind you of who you were."

"Who made you swear that oath?"

"You did, Maestro. You were in pain, and you wanted to forget your suffering."

"How did I come to forget?"

"A simple feit."

"Your doing?"

Pie nodded. "I was your servant in that, as in everything. I swore an oath that when it was done, when the past was hidden away, I would never show it to you again. And oaths don't decay."

"But you kept hoping I'd ask the right questions—"

"Yes."

"—and invite the memory back in."

"Yes. And you came close."

"In Mai-ké. And in the mountains."

"But never close enough to free me from my responsibility. I had to keep my silence."

"Well, it's broken now, my friend. When you're healed—"

"No, Maestro," Pie said. "A wound like this can't be healed."

"It can and will," Gentle said, not willing to countenance the thought of failure.

He remembered Nikaetomaas' talk of the Dearthers' encampment on the margin of the Second and First Dominions, where she'd said Estabrook had been taken. Miracles of healing were possible there, she'd boasted.

"We're going to make quite a journey, my friend," he said, starting to lift the mystif up.

"Why break your back?" it said to him. "Let's say our farewells here."

"I'm not saying goodbye to you here or anywhere," Gentle said. "Now put your arms around me, lover. We've got a long way to go together yet."

3

1

The Comet's ascent into the heavens above Yzordderrex, and the light it shed upon the city's streets, didn't shame the atrocities there into hiding or cessation; quite the other way around. The city was ruled by Ruin now, and its court was everywhere: celebrating the enthronement, parading its emblems—the luckiest already dead—and rehearsing its rites in preparation for a long and inglorious reign. Children wore ash today, and carried their parents' heads like censers, still smoking from the fires where they'd been found. Dogs had the freedom of the city and devoured their masters without fear of punishment. The carrion birds Sartori had once tempted off the desert winds to feed on bad meat were gathered on the streets in garrulous hordes, to dine on the men and women who'd gossiped there the day before.

There were those survivors, of course, who clung to the dream of Order and banded together to do what they could under the new regime, digging through the rubble in the hope of finding survivors, dousing fires in buildings that were whole enough to save, giving succor to the grieving and quick dispatch for those too wounded to bear another breath. But they were easily outnumbered by the souls whose faith in sanity had been shattered and met the comet's eye with dissolution in their hearts. By midmorning, when Gentle and Pie reached the gate that led out of the city into the desert, many of those who'd begun the day determined to preserve something from this calamity had given up and were leaving while they still had their lives. The exodus that would empty Yzordderrex of much of its population within half a week had begun.

Beyond the vague instruction, gleaned from Nikaetomaas, that the encampment to which Estabrook had been taken lay in the desert at the limits of this Dominion, Gentle was traveling blind. He'd hoped to find somebody along the way to give him some better directions, but he encountered nobody who looked fit enough, mentally or physically, to lend him assistance. He'd bound the hand he'd wounded beating down the door of the Pivot Tower as best he could before leaving the palace. The stab wound he'd sustained when Huzzah had been snatched and the cut the mystif's ribbon blade had opened were slight enough to cause him little discomfort. His body, possessed of a Maestro's resilience, had survived three times a natural human span without significant deterioration, and it was quick to begin the process of mending itself now.

The same could not be said for Pie 'oh' pah's wounded frame. Sartori's sway was venomous, draining the mystif's strength and consciousness. By the time Gentle left the city, the mystif was barely able to move its legs, obliging Gentle to half-hoist it up beside him. He only hoped they found some means of transport before too long, or this journey would be over before it was begun.

There was little chance of hitching a ride with any of their fellow refugees. Most were on foot, and those who had transport— carts, cars, runty mules—were already laden with passengers. Several overburdened vehicles had given up the ghost within sight of the city gates, and those who'd paid for their ride were arguing on the roadside. But most of the travelers went on their way with an eerie hush, barely raising their eyes from the road a few feet in front of them, at least until they reached the spot where that road divided.

Here a bottleneck had been created, as people milled around, deciding on which of the three routes available to them they were going to take. Straight ahead, though a considerable distance from the crossroads, lay a mountain range as impressive as the Jokalay-lau. The road to the left led off into greener terrain, and, not surprisingly perhaps, this was the most favored way. The least favored, and for Gentle's purposes the most promising, was the road that lay to the right. It was dusty and badly laid, the terrain it wound through the least lush and therefore the most likely to deteriorate into desert. But he knew from his months in the Dominions that the terrain could change considerably within the space of a few miles, and that perhaps out of sight along this road lay verdant pastures, while the track behind him could just as easily lead into a wilderness. While he was standing in the mill of travelers debating with himself, he heard a high-pitched voice and, peering through the dust, caught sight of a small fellow—young, spectacled, barechested, and bald—making his way towards him, arms raised.

"Mr. Zacharias! Mr. Zacharias!"

He knew the face, but from precisely where he couldn't recall, nor could he put a name to it. But the man, perhaps used to being only half remembered, was quick to supply the information.

"Floccus Dado," he said. "You remember?"

Now he did. This was Nikaetomaas' comrade-in-arms.

Floccus snatched off his glasses and peered at Pie. "Your lady friend looks sick," he said.

"It's not a she. It's a mystif."

"Sorry. Sorry," Floccus said, slipping his spectacles back on and blinking violently. "My error. Sex was never my strong point. Is it very sick?"

"I'm afraid so."

"Is Nikae with you?" Floccus said, peering around. "Don't tell me she's gone on ahead. I told her I was going to wait for her here if we got separated."

"She won't be coming, Floccus," Gentle said.

"Why in the Hyo not?"

"I'm afraid she's dead."

Dado's nervous tics and blinks ceased on the instant. He stared at Gentle with a tiny smile on his face, as if he was used to being the butt of jokes and wanted to believe that this was one. "No," he said.

"I'm afraid so," Gentle replied. "She was killed in the palace."

Floccus took off his glasses again and ran his thumb and middle finger from the bridge of his nose along his lower lids. "That's grim," he said.

"She was a very brave woman."

"She was that."

"And she put up a very spirited defense. But we were outnumbered."

"How did *you* escape?" Floccus asked, the inquiry innocent of accusation.

"That's a very long story," Gentle said, "and I don't think I'm quite ready to tell it yet."

"Which way are you heading?" Dado said.

"Nikaetomaas told me you Dearthers have an encampment of some kind, at the margin of the First. Is that right?"

"Indeed we do."

"Then that's where I'm going. She said a man I knew—do you know Estabrook?—was healed there. I want to heal Pie."

"Then we'd best go together," Floccus said. "It's no use my waiting here any longer. Nikae's spirit will have passed by a long time ago."

"Do you have any kind of transport?"

"Indeed I do," he said, brightening. "A very fine car I found in the Caramess. It's parked over there." He pointed through the crush.

"If it's still there," Gentle remarked.

"It's guarded," Dado said, with a grin. "May I help you with the mystif?"

He put his arm beneath Pie, who had now lost consciousness completely; then they started to make their way through the crowd, Dado shouting to clear the route ahead. His demands were almost entirely ignored until he started shouting "Ruukassh! Ruukassh!" which had the desired effect of dividing the throng.

"What's Ruukassh?" Gentle asked him.

"Contagious," Dado replied. "Not far now."

A few paces on, and the vehicle came into view. Dado had good taste in loot. Not since that first glorious trip along the Patashoqua Highway had Gentle set eyes on a vehicle so sleek, so polished—or so wholly inappropriate for desert travel. It was powder-blue with silver trim, its tires white, its interior fur lined. Sitting on the hood, its leash tied to one of the wing mirrors, was its guard and antithesis: an animal related to the ragemy—via the hyena—and boasting the least pleasant attributes of both. It was as round and lardy as a pig, but its back and flanks were covered with a coat of mottled fur. Its head was short-snouted but heavily whiskered. Its ears pricked like a dog's at the sight of Dado, and it set up a round of barks and squeals so high they made Dado sound basso profundo by contrast.

"Good girl! Good girl!" he said.

The creature was up on its stubby legs, shaking its rear in delight at its master's return. Its belly was laden with teats, which shook to the rhythm of its welcome.

Dado opened the door, and there on the passenger seat was the reason the creature was so defensive of the vehicle: a litter of five yapping offspring, perfect miniatures of their mother. Dado suggested Gentle and Pie take the back seat, while Mama Sighshy, as he called her, sat with her children. The interior stank of the animals, but the previous owner had been fond of comfort, and there were cushions to support the mystif's head and neck. When Sighshy herself was invited back into the vehicle the stench increased tenfold, and she growled at Gentle in a less than friendly manner, but Dado placated her with baby talk, and she was soon curled up on the seat beside him, suckling her fat babes. With the travelers assembled, they headed off towards the mountains.

Exhaustion claimed Gentle after a mile or two, and he slept, his head on Pie's shoulder. The road steadily deteriorated over the next few hours, and the discomfort of the journey repeatedly brought him up to the surface of sleep, with scraps of dreams clinging to him. They were not dreams of Yzordderrex, nor were they memories of the adventures he and Pie had shared on their travels across the Imajica. It was the Fifth his mind was returning to in these fitful slumbers, shunning the horrors and the murders of the Reconciled Dominions for safer territory.

Except that it wasn't safe any longer, of course. The man he'd been in that Dominion—Klein's Bastard Boy, the lover and the faker—was a fabrication, and he could never return to that simple, sybaritic life again. He'd lived a lie, the scale of which even the most suspicious of his mistresses (Vanessa, whose abandoning of him had begun this whole endeavor) could never have imagined; and from that lie, three human spans of self-deceit had come. Thinking of Vanessa, he remembered the empty mews house in London, and the desolation he'd felt wandering it with nothing to show for his life but a string of broken romances, a few forged paintings, and the clothes he was wearing. It was laughable now, but that day he'd thought he could fall no further. Such naïveté! He'd learned lessons in despair since then numerous enough to fill a book, the bitterest reminder lying in wounded sleep beside him.

Though it was distressing to conceive of losing Pie, he refused himself the indulgence of denying the possibility. He'd turned a blind eye on the unpalatable too often in the past, with catastrophic results. Now the facts had to be faced. The mystif was becoming frailer by the hour, its skin icy, its breath so shallow that on occasion it was barely discernible. Even if all that Nikaetomaas had said

about the Erasure's healing powers proved correct, there would
be no miracle cure for such a profound malady. Gentle would have
to go back to the Fifth alone, trusting that Pie 'oh' pah would be
fit enough to follow after a time. The longer he delayed that return,
the less opportunity he'd have to muster assistance in the war
against Sartori.

That war would come, he had no doubt of it. The urge to conquer burned bright in his other, as it had perhaps once burned in
him, until desire and luxury and forgetfulness had dimmed it. But
where would he find such allies? Men and women who wouldn't
laugh (the way he'd have laughed, six months before) when he
started to talk about the Dominion-hopping he'd done and the
jeopardy the world was in from a man with his face? Certainly
he wouldn't find imaginations among his peer group supple
enough to embrace the vistas he was returning to describe. They
were fashionably disdainful of belief, having had the flesh-as-star-
stuff hopes of youth dashed by midnight sweats and their morning reflection. The most he'd heard any of them confess to was a
vague pantheism, and they'd deny even that when sober. Of them
all he'd only ever heard Clem espouse any belief in organized religion, and those dogmas were as antithetical to the message he was
bringing from the Dominions as the tenets of a nihilist. Even if
Clem could be persuaded from the Communion rail to join Gentle, they would be an army of two against a Maestro who had
honed his powers until they could command Dominions.

There was one other possibility, and that was Judith. She would
certainly not mock his wanderer's tales, but she'd been treated so
heinously from the start of this tragedy that he dared not expect
forgiveness from her, much less fellowship. Besides, who knew
where her true sympathies lay? Though she might resemble
Quaisoir to the last hair, she'd been made in the same bloodless
womb that had produced the Autarch. Was she not therefore his
spiritual sister: not born, but made? If she had to choose between
the butcher of Yzordderrex and those seeking to destroy him,
could she be trusted to side with the destroyers, when their victory
would mean she'd lose the only creature in the Imajica who shared
her condition? Though she and Gentle had meant much to each
other (who knew how many liaisons they'd enjoyed over the centuries; reigniting the desire which had brought them together in the
first place, then parting again, forgetting they'd even met?) he had
to treat her with the utmost caution from this point on. She'd been
innocent in the dramas of an earlier age, a toy in cruel and careless hands. But the woman she'd become over the decades was neither victim nor toy, and if (or perhaps *when*) she became aware of
her past she was perfectly capable of revenging herself upon the

man who'd made her, however much she'd claimed to love him
once.

Seeing that his passenger was now awake, Floccus gave Gentle
a progress report. They were making good time, he said. Within an
hour they'd be in the mountains, on the other side of which the
desert lay.

"How long do you estimate to the Erasure?" Gentle asked him.

"We'll be there before nightfall," Floccus promised. "How's the
mystif faring?"

"Not well, I'm afraid."

"There'll be no cause to mourn," Floccus said brightly, "I've
known people on death's door who were healed at the Erasure. It's
a place of miracles. But then everywhere is, if we just knew how to
look. That's what Father Athanasius taught me. You were in prison
with Athanasius, weren't you?"

"I was never exactly imprisoned. Not the way he was."

"But you met him?"

"Oh, yes. He was priest at our wedding."

"You and mystif, you mean? You're married?" He whistled.
"Now you, sir, are what I call a lucky man. I've heard a lot about
these mystifs, and I never heard of one getting married before.
They're usually lovers. Heartbreakers." He whistled again. "Well,
that's wonderful," he said. "We'll make sure she makes it, sir, don't
you worry. Oh, I'm sorry. She's not a she, is she? I've got to get that
right. It's just that when I look at her—I mean it—I see a she, you
know? I suppose that's the wonder of them."

"It's part of it."

"Can I ask you something?"

"Ask away."

"When you look at her, what do you see?"

"I've seen all kinds of things," Gentle replied. "I've seen women.
I've seen men. I've even seen myself."

"But at the moment," Floccus said. "What do you see right
now?"

Gentle looked at the mystif. "I see Pie," he said. "I see the face
I love."

Floccus made no reply to this, and after such gushing enthusiasm Gentle knew there had to be some significance in his silence.

"What are you thinking?" he asked.

"Do you really want to know?"

"I do. We're friends, aren't we? At least getting that way.
Tell me."

"I was thinking it's not good you care too much about the way
she looks. The Erasure's no place to be in love with things as they
are. People heal there, but they also change, you understand?" He

took both hands off the wheel to make cupped palms, like scales. "There's got to be a balance. Something given, something taken away."

"What kind of changes?" Gentle said.

"Different from one to another," Floccus said. "But you'll see for yourself, very soon. When we get close to the First Dominion, nothing's quite as it seems."

"Isn't that true of everything?" Gentle said. "The more I live, the less I seem to be certain about."

Floccus' hands were back on the wheel, his burst of sunny talk suddenly overcast. "I don't think Father Athanasius ever talked about that," he said. "Maybe he did. I don't remember everything he said."

The conversation ended there, leaving Gentle to wonder if in bringing the mystif back to the borders of the Dominion from which its people had been exiled, returning the great transformer to a land in which transformation was a commonplace, he was undoing the knot Athanasius had tied in the Cradle of Chzercemit.

2

Jude had never been much impressed with architectural rhetoric, and she found nothing in the courtyards or corridors of the Autarch's palace to dissuade her from that indifference. There were some sights that put her in mind of natural splendors: smoke drifting across the forsaken gardens like morning mist, or clinging to the cold stone of the towers like cloud to a mountain spire. But such punnish pleasures were few. It was mostly bombast: everything built on a scale intended to be awe-inspiring but to her eye merely monolithic.

She was glad when they finally reached Quaisoir's quarters, which for all their absurd ornamentation were at least humanized by their excesses. And they also heard there the first friendly voice in many hours, though its welcoming tones turned to horror when its owner, Quaisoir's many-tailed handmaiden, Concupiscentia, saw that her mistress had gained a twin and lost her eyes in the night she'd spent looking for salvation. Only after a good deal of lamentation could she be persuaded to tend to Quaisoir, which she did with trembling hands. The comet was by now making its steep ascent, and from Quaisoir's window Jude had a panoramic view of the desolation. She'd heard and seen enough in her short time here to realize that Yzordderrex had been ripe for the calamity that had overtaken it, and some in this city, perhaps many, had fanned the fire that had destroyed the Kesparates, calling it a just and cleansing flame. Even Peccable—who hadn't got an anarchist bone in his body—had intimated that Yzordder-rex's time had come. But Jude still mourned its passing. This was the city she'd begged Oscar to show her, whose air had smelled so temptingly spicy, and whose warmth, issuing from the Retreat that day, had seemed paradisiacal. Now she would return to the Fifth Dominion with its ash on her soles and its smuts in her nose, like a tourist back from Venice with pictures of bubbles in a lagoon.

"I'm so tired," Quaisoir said. "Will you mind if I sleep?"

"Of course not," Jude said.

"Is Seidux's blood still on the bed?" she asked Concupiscentia.

"It is, ma'am."

"Then I won't lie there, I think." She put out her arm. "Lead me to the little blue room. I'll sleep there. Judith, you should sleep too. Bathe and sleep. We've got so much to plan together."

"We do?"

"Oh, yes, sister," Quaisoir said. "But later . . ."

She let Concupiscentia lead her away, leaving Jude to wander through the chambers which Quaisoir had occupied all her years of power. There was indeed a little blood on the sheets, but the bed looked tempting nevertheless, the scent off it dizzyingly strong. She refused its lush blandishments, however, and moved in search of a bathroom, anticipating another chamber of baroque excess. In fact it proved to be the only room in the suite that came within shouting distance of restraint, and she happily lingered there, running a hot bath and soaking some of the ashes out of her body while contemplating her misty reflection in its black tiles.

When she emerged, her skin tingling, the clothes she'd sloughed off—which were filthy and stinking—revolted her. She left them on the floor and, instead, putting on the most subdued of the robes that lay scattered around the bedroom, took to the scented sheets. A man had been killed here only a few hours before, but that thought—which would once have driven her from the room, much less the bed—concerned her not at all. She didn't discount the possibility that this disinterest in the bed's sordid past was in part the influence of the scents off the pillow she laid her head upon. They conspired with fatigue, and with the heat of the bath from which she'd risen, to induce a languor she couldn't have resisted had her life depended upon it. The tension went from her sinews and joints; her belly gave up its jitters. Closing her eyes, she let her sister's bed lull her into dreaming.

Even during his most despondent meditations at the Pivot pit, Sartori had never felt the emptiness of his condition as acutely as he did now that he was parted from his other. Meeting Gentle in the tower and witnessing the Pivot's call to Reconciliation, he'd sensed new possibilities in the air: a marriage of self and self which would heal him into wholeness. But Gentle had poured contempt on that vision, preferring his mystif spouse over his brother. Perhaps he'd change his mind now that Pie 'oh' pah was dead, but Sartori doubted it. If *he* were Gentle—and he was—the mystif's death would be obsessed upon and magnified until such time as it could be revenged. The enmity between them was confirmed. There'd be no reunion.

He shared none of this with Rosengarten, who found him up in the gazebo, guzzling chocolate and musing on his anguish. Nor did he allow Rosengarten to recount the disasters of the night (the generals dead, the army murdered or mutinied) for very long without stopping him. They had plans to lay together, he told the piebald man, and it was little use fretting over what was lost.

"We're going to go to the Fifth, you and I," he informed Rosengarten. "We're going to build a new Yzordderrex."

It wasn't often he'd won a response from the man, but he got one now. Rosengarten smiled.

"The Fifth?" he said.

"I knew it many years ago, of course, but by all accounts it's naked now. The Maestros I knew are dead. Their wisdoms are dishonored. The place is defenseless. We'll take them with such sways they won't even know they've given up their Dominion until the New Yzordderrex is in their hearts and inviolate."

Rosengarten made a murmur of approval.

"Make any farewells you have to make," Sartori said. "And I'll make mine."

"We're going now?"

"Before the fires are out," the Autarch said.

It was a strange sleep Jude fell into, but she'd traveled in the country of the unconscious often enough to feel unintimidated there. This time she didn't move from the room in which she lay but luxuriated in its excesses, rising and falling like the veils around the bed, and on the same smoky breeze. Once in a while she heard some sound from the courtyards far below and allowed her eyes to flutter open for the sheer lazy pleasure of closing them again, and once she was woken by the sound of Concupiscentia's reedy voice as she sang in a distant room. Though the words were incomprehensible, Jude knew it was a lament, full of yearning for things that had passed and could never be again, and she slipped back into sleep with the thought that sad songs were the same in any language, whether Gaelic, Navaho, or Patashoquan. Like the

glyph of her body, this melody was essential, a sign that could pass
between Dominions.

The music and the scent she lay upon were potent narcotics, and
after a few melancholy verses of Concupiscentia's song she was no
longer sure whether she was asleep, and hearing the lament in her
dreams, or awake, but freed by Quaisoir's perfumes and wafted up
into the folds of silks above her bed like a dreamer. Whichever it
was, she scarcely cared. The sensations were pleasurable, and she'd
had too little pleasure of late.

Then came proof that this was indeed a dream. A doleful phantom appeared at the door and stood watching her through the
veils. She knew him even before he drew close to the bed. This was
not a face she'd thought of much in recent times, so it was somewhat strange that she'd conjured him, but conjure him she had, and
there was no denying the erotic charge she felt at his dreamed presence. It was Gentle, perfectly remembered, his expression troubled
the way it so often was, his hands stroking the veils as though they
were her legs and could be parted with caresses.

"I didn't think you'd be here," he said to her. His voice was raw,
and his expression as full of loss as Concupiscentia's song. "When
did you come back?"

"A little while ago."

"You smell so sweet."

"I bathed."

"Looking at you like this . . . it makes me wish I could take you
with me."

"Where are you going?"

"Back to the Fifth," he said. "I've come to say goodbye."

"From such a distance?" she said.

His face broke into an immoderate smile, and she remembered,
seeing it, how easy seduction had always been for him: how women
had slid their wedding rings off and their knickers down when he
shone this way. But why be churlish? This was an erotic whimsy,
not a trial. She dreamed that he saw the accusation in her eyes,
however, and was begging her forgiveness.

"I know I've done you harm," he said.

"That's in the past," she replied magnanimously.

"Looking at you now . . ."

"Don't be sentimental," she said. "I don't want sentiment. I want
you here."

Opening her legs, she let him see the niche she had for him. He
didn't hesitate any longer, but pulled the veil aside and climbed
onto the bed, wrenching the robe from her shoulders as he put his
mouth against hers. For some reason, she'd conjured him tasting
of chocolate. Another oddity, but not one that spoiled his kisses.

She tugged at his clothes, but they were a dream invention: the dark blue fabric of his shirt, its laces and buttons in fetishistic profusion, covered in tiny scales, as though a family of lizards had shed their skins to clothe him.

She was tender from the bath, and when he let his weight descend on her, and began to work his body against hers, the scales pricked her stomach and breasts in the most arousing way. She wrapped her legs around him, and he acceded to her capture, his kisses becoming fiercer by the moment.

"The things we've done," he murmured as she kissed his face. "The things we've done. . . ."

Her heart made her mind nimble; it leapt from memory to memory, back to the book she'd found in Estabrook's flat all those months before—one of Oscar's gifts from the Dominions—a manual of sexual possibilities that had shocked her at the time. Images of its couplings appeared in her head now: intimacies that were perhaps only possible in the profligacy of sleep, unknitting both male and female and weaving them together again in new and ecstatic combinations. She put her mouth to her dream lover's ear and whispered to him that she forbade him nothing; that she wanted them to share the most extreme sensations they were capable of inventing. He didn't grin this time, which pleased her, but raised himself up on his hands, which were plunged into the downy pillows to either side of her head, and looked down at her with some of the same sadness he'd had on his face when he'd first arrived.

"One last time?" he said.

"It doesn't have to be the last time," she said. "I can always dream you."

"And me, you," he said with the greatest fondness and courtesy.

She reached down between their bodies and slipped off his belt, then pulled his trousers open with some violence, unwilling to be delayed by his buttons. What filled her hand was as silken as the fabric hiding it was rough: still only half engorged, but all the more entertaining for that. She stroked him. He sighed as he bent his head towards her, licking her lips and teeth, letting his chocolate-sweetened spittle run off his tongue into her mouth. She raised her hips and moved the groove of her sex against the underside of his erection, wetting it. He started to murmur to her, terms of endearment, she presumed, though—like Concupiscentia's song—they were in no language she understood. They sounded as sweet as his spittle, however, and lulled her like a cradle song, as though to slip her into a dream within a dream. As her eyes closed she felt him raise his hips, lifting the thickness of his sex from between her labia, and with one thrust, hard enough to stab the breath from her, he entered, dropping down on top of her as he did so.

The endearments ceased; the kisses too. He put one hand on her brow, his fingers laced into her hair, and the other at her neck, his thumb rubbing her windpipe and coaxing sighs from it. She'd forbidden him nothing and would not rescind that invitation simply because his possession of her was so sudden. Instead, she raised her legs and crossed them behind his back, then started to whip him on with insults. Was this the most he could give her, the deepest he could go? He wasn't hard enough, wasn't hot enough. She wanted more. His thrusts speeded up, his thumb tightening against her throat, but not so much it kept her from drawing breath and expelling it again in a fresh round of provocations.

"I could fuck you forever," he said to her, his tone halfway between devotion and threat. "There's nothing I can't make you do. There's nothing I can't make you say. I could fuck you forever."

This was not talk she would have welcomed from a flesh-and-blood lover, but in a dream it was arousing. She let him continue in the same mode, opening her arms and legs beneath him, while he recited all that he would do to her, a litany of ambition that matched the rhythm of his hips. The room her dream had raised around them split here and there, and another seeped in through the cracks to occupy the same space: this one darker than Quaisoir's veil-draped chamber and lit by a fire that blazed off to her left. Her dream lover didn't fade, however; he remained with her and in her, more frenzied in his thrusts and promises than ever. She saw him above her as if lit by the same flames that warmed her nakedness, his face knotted and sweaty, his index of desires coming between clenched teeth. She would be his doll, his whore, his wife, his Goddess; he would fill every hole of her, forever and ever: own her, worship her, turn her inside out. Hearing this, she remembered the images in Estabrook's book again, and the memory made her cells swell as if each was a tiny bud ready to burst, their petals pleasure, their scent the shouts she was making, rising off her to draw fresh adoration from him. It came, cruel and exquisite by turns. One moment he wanted to be her prisoner, bound to her every whim, nourished on her shit and the milk he'd win from her breasts with suckling. The next she was less than the excrement he'd hungered for, and he was her only hope for life. He'd resurrect her with his fuck. He'd fill her with a fiery stream, till her eyes were washed from her head and she drowned in him. There was more, but her cries of pleasure were mounting with every moment, and she heard less and less. Saw less too, closing her eyes against the mingled rooms, fire-lit and veiled, letting her head fill with the geometries that always attended pleasure, forms like her glyph unraveled and reworked.

And then, just as she was reaching the first of the peaks—a

range of stratospheric heights ahead—she felt him shudder and his thrusts stop. She didn't believe he'd finished, not at first. This was a dream, and she'd conjured him to perform the way actualities never did: to go on when lovers of flesh and blood had spilled their promises and were panting their apologies beside her. He couldn't desert her now! She opened her eyes. The fire-lit chamber had gone, and the flames in Gentle's eyes had gone with it. He had already withdrawn, and all she felt between her legs was his fingers, dabbling in the dribble he'd supplied. He looked at her lazily.

"You almost tempt me to stay," he said. "But I've got work to do."

Work? What work did dreams have besides the dreamer's commandments?

"Don't leave," she demanded.

"I'm done," he said.

He was getting off the bed. She reached for him, but even in sleep the languor of the pillow was upon her, and he was away between the veils before her fingers came close to catching hold. She sank back in a slow swoon, watching his figure become remoter as the layers of gossamer between them multiplied.

"Stay beautiful," he told her. "Maybe I'll come back for you when I've built the New Yzordderrex."

This made little sense to her, but she didn't care. It was her own wretched invention, and worthless. She let it go, the figure seeming to halt at the door as if for one backward glance, then disappearing altogether. Her mind had no sooner let him slip than it conjured a compensation, however. The veils at the bottom of the bed parted and the many-tailed Concupiscentia appeared, her eyes bright with craving. She didn't wait for any word to pass between them but crawled up onto the bed, her gaze fixed on Judith's groin, her bluish tongue flicking as she approached. Jude raised her knees. The creature put her head down and began to lick out what the dream lover had left, her silky palms caressing Jude's thighs. The sensation soothed her, and she watched through the slits of her drugged eyes as Concupiscentia bathed her clean. Before she'd finished the dream grew dimmer, and the creature was still at its caressing work when another veil descended, this so dense she lost both sight and sensation in its folds.

4

I

Like galleons turned to the desert wind and in full sail before it, the tents of the Dearthers presented a pretty spectacle from a distance, but Gentle's admiration turned to awe as the car drew closer and their scale became apparent. They were the height of five-story houses and more, billowing towers of ocher and scarlet fabric, the colors all the more vivid given that the desert floor, which had been sand-colored at the outset, was now almost black, and the heavens they rose against were gray, being the wall between the Second Dominion and the unknown world haunted by Hapexamendios.

Floccus halted the car a quarter of a mile from the perimeter of the encampment. "I should go ahead," he said, "and explain who we are and what we're doing here."

"Make it quick," Gentle told him.

Floccus was away like a gazelle, over ground that was no longer sand but a flinty carpet of stone shards, like the clippings from some stupendous sculpture. Gentle looked at the mystif, lying in his arms as if in a charmed sleep, its brow innocent of frowns. He stroked its cold cheek.

How many friends and loved ones must he have seen pass away in the two centuries and more of his life on earth? Though he'd wiped those griefs from his conscious mind, could he doubt they'd made their mark, fueling his terror of sickness and hardening his heart over the years? Perhaps he'd always been a philanderer and plagiarist, a master of counterfeited emotion, but was that so surprising in a man who knew in his gut that the drama, however soul-searing, was cyclic? The faces changed and changed, but the story remained essentially the same. As Klein had been fond of pointing out, there was no such thing as originality. It had all been said before, suffered before. If a man knew that, was it any wonder love became mechanical and death just a scene to be shunned? There was no absolute knowledge to be gained from either. Just another ride on the merry-go-round, another blurred scene of faces smiling and faces grieved.

But his feelings for the mystif had been no sham, and with good reason. In Pie's self-denials ("I'm nothing and nobody," it had said at the beginning) he'd heard an echo of the anguish he himself felt; and in Pie's gaze, so heavy with the freight of years, seen a comrade soul who understood the nameless pain he carried. It had stripped him of his shams and chicanery and given him a taste of the Maestro he'd been and might be again. There was good to be done with such power, he now knew: breaches to be healed, rights to be restored, nations to be roused, and hopes reawakened. He needed his inspiration beside him if he was to be a great Reconciler.

"I love you, Pie 'oh' pah," he murmured.

"Gentle."

The voice was Floccus', calling him from outside the window.

"I've seen Athanasius. He says we're to come straight in."

"Good! Good!" Gentle threw open the door.

"Do you want help?"

"No. I'll carry Pie." He got out, then reached back into the car and picked up the mystif.

"Gentle, you do understand that this is a sacred place?" Floccus said as he led the way towards the tents.

"No singing, dancing, or farting, huh? Don't look so pained, Floccus. I understand."

As they approached, Gentle realized that what he'd taken to be an encampment of closely gathered tents was in fact a continuum, the various pavilions, with their swooping roofs, joined by smaller tents to form a single golden beast of wind and canvas.

Inside its body, the gusts kept everything in motion. Tremors moved through even the most tautly erected walls, and in the heights of the roof swaths of fabric whirled like the skirts of dervishes, giving off a constant sigh. There were people up among the folds, some walking on webs of rope as if they were solid board, others sitting in front of immense windows opened in the roof, their faces turned to the wall of the First World as though they anticipated a summons out of that place at any moment. If such a summons came, there'd be no hectic rush. The atmosphere was as measured and soothing as the motion of the dancing sails above.

"Where do we find the doctor?" Gentle asked Floccus.

"There is no doctor," he replied. "Follow me. We've been given a place to lay the mystif down."

"There must be some kind of medical attendants."

"There's fresh water and clothes. Maybe some laudanum and the like. But Pie's beyond that. The uredo won't be dislodged with medications. It's the proximity of the First Dominion that'll heal it."

"Then we should go outside right now," he said. "Get Pie closer to the Erasure."

"Any closer than this would take more resilience than either you or I possess, Gentle," Floccus said. "Now follow me, and be respectful of this place."

He led Gentle through the beast's tremulous body to a smaller tent, where a dozen plain low beds were set, some occupied, most not. Gentle laid the mystif down in one and proceeded to unbutton its shirt while Floccus went in search of cool water for its now-burning skin and some sustenance for Gentle and himself. While he waited, Gentle examined the spread of the uredo, which was too extensive to be fully examined without stripping Pie completely, which he was loath to do with so many strangers in the vicinity. The mystif had been covetous of its privacy—it had been many weeks before Gentle had glimpsed its beauty naked—and he wanted to respect that modesty, even in Pie's present condition. In fact, very few of those who passed by even glanced their way, and after a time he began to feel the fear lose its grip on him. There was very little more that he could do. They were at the edge of the known Dominions, where all maps stopped and the enigma of enigmas began. What use was fear in the face of such imponderables? He had to put it aside and proceed with dignity and containment, trusting to the powers that occupied the air here.

When Floccus returned with the means to wash Pie, Gentle asked if he might be left alone to do so.

"Of course," Floccus replied. "I've got friends here. I'd like to seek them out."

When he left, Gentle began to bathe the suppurating eruptions of the uredo, which oozed not blood but a silvery pus, the smell of which pricked his sinuses like ammonia. The body it fed upon seemed not only enfeebled but somehow unfocused, as though its contours and musculature were about to become a vapor, and the flesh disperse. Whether this was the uredo's doing or simply the condition of a mystif when life, and therefore its capacity to shape the sight of those gazing upon it, was fading, Gentle didn't know, but it made him think back over the way this body had appeared to him. As Judith, of course; as an assassin, armored in nakedness; and as the loving androgyne of their wedding night in the Cradle, that had momentarily taken his face and stared back at him like a prophecy of Sartori. Now, finally, it seemed to be a form of burnished mist, receding from his hand even as he touched it.

"Gentle? Is that you? I didn't know you could see in the dark."

Gentle looked up from Pie's body to find that in the time he'd been washing the mystif, half mesmerized by memory, the evening had fallen. There were lights burning at the bedsides of those nearby, but none near Pie 'oh' pah. When he returned his gaze to the body he'd been washing, it was barely discernible in the gloom.

"I didn't know I could either."

He stood up to greet the newcomer. It was Athanasius, a lamp in his hand. By its flame, which was as subject to the wind's whim as the canvas overhead, Gentle saw he'd been wounded in the fall of Yzordderrex. There were several cuts on his face and neck and a larger, livid injury on his belly. For a man who'd celebrated Sundays by making himself a new crown of thorns, these were probably welcome discomforts.

"I'm sorry I didn't come to welcome you earlier," he said. "But with such numbers of casualties coming in I spend a lot of time administering last rites."

Gentle didn't remark on this, but the fear crept back up his spine.

"We've had a lot of the Autarch's soldiers find their way here, and that makes me nervous. I'm afraid we'll let in someone on a suicide mission, and he'll blow the place apart. That's the way the bastard thinks. If he's destroyed, he'll want to bring everything down with him."

"I'm sure he's much more concerned with making his getaway," Gentle said.

"Where can he go? The word's already spread across the Imajica. There's armed uprising in Patashoqua. There's hand-to-hand combat on the Lenten Way. Every Dominion's shaking. Even the First."

"The First? How?"

"Haven't you seen? No, obviously you haven't. Come with me." Gentle glanced back towards Pie.

"The mystif's safe here," Athanasius said. "We won't be long."

He led Gentle through the body of the beast to a door that took them out into the deepening dusk. Though Floccus had counseled against what they were doing, hinting that the Erasure's proximity could do harm, there was no sign of any consequence. He was either protected by Athanasius or resistant to any malign influence on his own account. Either way, he was able to study the spectacle laid before him without ill effect.

There was no wall of fog, or even deeper twilight, to mark the division between the Second Dominion and the haunt of Hapexamendios. The desert simply faded away into nothingness, like a drawing erased by the power on the other side, first becoming unfocused, then losing its color and its detail. This subtle removal of solid reality, the world wiped away and replaced with nothing, was the most distressing sight Gentle had ever set eyes on. Nor was the similarity between what was happening here and the state of Pie's body lost on him.

"You said the Erasure was moving," Gentle whispered.

Athanasius scanned the emptiness, looking for some sign, but nothing caught his eye.

"It's not constant," he said. "But every now and then ripples appear in it."

"Is that rare?"

"There are accounts of this happening in earlier times, but this isn't an area that encourages accurate study. Observers get poetic here. Scientists turn to sonnets. Sometimes literally." He laughed. "That was a joke, by the way. Just in case you start worrying about your legs rhyming."

"How does looking at this make you feel?" Gentle asked him.

"Afraid," Athanasius said. "Because I'm not ready to be there."

"Nor am I," Gentle said. "But I'm afraid Pie is. I wish I'd never come, Athanasius. Maybe I should take Pie away now, while I still can."

"That's your decision," Athanasius replied. "But I don't believe the mystif will survive if you move it. A uredo's a terrible poison, Gentle. If there's any chance of Pie being healed, it's here, close to the First."

Gentle looked back towards the distressing absence of the Erasure.

"Is going to nothing being healed?" he said. "It seems more like death to me."

"They may be closer than we think, death and healing," Athanasius said.

"I don't want to hear that," Gentle said. "Are you staying out here?"

"For a while," Athanasius replied. "If you do decide to go, come and find me first, will you, so that we can say goodbye?"

"Of course."

He left Athanasius to his void-watching and went back inside, thinking as he did so that this would be a fine time to find a bar and order up a stiff drink. As he started back in the direction of Pie's bed, he was brought to a halt by a voice too abrasive for this hallowed place, and sufficiently slurred to suggest the speaker had found a bar himself and drunk it dry.

"Gentle, you old bugger!"

Estabrook stepped into view, grinning expansively, though several of his teeth were missing.

"I heard you were here and I didn't believe it." He seized Gentle's hand and shook it. "But here you are, large as life. Who'd have thought it, eh? The two of us, here."

Life in the encampment had wrought its changes on Charlie. He could scarcely have been further from the grief-wasted plotter Gentle had met on Kite Hill. Indeed, he could almost have passed for a clown, with his motley of pinstripe trousers, tattered braces, and unbuttoned tunic dyed half a dozen colors, all crowned with bald head and gap-toothed smile.

"It's so good to see you!" he kept saying, his pleasure unalloyed. "We must talk. This is the perfect time. They're all going outside to meditate on their ignorance, which is fine for a few minutes, but God! it gets drab. Come with me, come on! They've given me a little nook of my own, to keep me out of the way."

"Maybe later," Gentle said. "I've got a friend here who's sick."

"I heard somebody talking about that. A mystif? Is that the word?"

"That's the word."

"They're extraordinary, I heard. Very sexy. Why don't I come and see the patient with you?"

Gentle had no wish to keep Estabrook's company for longer than he needed to, but suspected that the man would beat a hasty retreat as soon as he set eyes on Pie and realized the creature he'd come to gawk at was the same he'd hired to assassinate his wife. They went back to Pie's bedside together. Floccus was there, with a lamp and an ample supply of food. Mouth crammed, he rose to be introduced, but Estabrook barely noticed him. His gaze was on Pie, whose head was turned away from the brightness of the lamp in the direction of the First Dominion.

"You lucky bugger," he said to Gentle. "She's beautiful."

Floccus glanced at Gentle to see if he intended to remark on Estabrook's error in sexing the patient, but Gentle made a tiny shake of his head. He was surprised that Pie's power to respond to the gaze of others was still intact, especially as his eyes saw an altogether more distressing sight: the substance of his beloved growing more insubstantial as the hours passed. Was this a sight and understanding reserved for Maestros? He knelt beside the bed and studied the fading features on the pillow. Pie's eyes were roving beneath the lids.

"Dreaming of me?" Gentle murmured.

"Is she getting better?" Estabrook inquired.

"I don't know," Gentle said. "This is supposed to be a healing place, but I'm not so sure."

"I really think we should talk," Estabrook said, with the strained nonchalance of a man who had something vital to impart, but was not able to do so in present company. "Why don't you pop along with me and have a quick drink? I'm sure Floccus will come and find you if anything untoward happens."

Floccus chewed on, nodding in accord with this, and Gentle agreed to go, hoping Estabrook had some insight into conditions here that would help him to decide whether to go or stay.

"I'll be five minutes," he promised Floccus, and let Estabrook lead him off through the lamp-lit passages to what he'd earlier called his nook.

It was off the beaten track somewhat, a little canvas room he'd made his own with what few possessions he'd brought from Earth. A shirt, its bloodstains now brown, hung above the bed like the tattered standard from some noteworthy battle. On the table beside the bed his wallet, his comb, a box of matches, and a roll of mints had been arranged, along several symmetrical columns of change, into an altar to the spirit of the pocket.

"It's not much," Estabrook said, "but it's home."

"Are you a prisoner here?" Gentle said as he sat in the plain chair at the bottom of the bed.

"Not at all," Estabrook said.

He brought a small bottle of liquor out from under the pillow. Gentle recognized it from the hours he and Huzzah had lingered in the café in the Oke T'Noon. It was the fermented sap of a swamp flower from the Third Dominion: kloupo. Estabrook took a swig from the bottle, reminding Gentle of how he'd supped brandy from a flask on Kite Hill. He'd refused the man's liquor that day, but not now.

"I could go anytime I wanted to," he went on. "But I think to myself, Where would you go, Charlie? And where *would* I go?"

"Back to the Fifth?"

"In God's name, why?"

"Don't you miss it, even a little?"

"A little, maybe. Once in a while I get maudlin, I suppose, and then I get drunk—drunker—and I have dreams."

"Of what?"

"Mostly childhood things, you know. Odd little details that wouldn't mean a damn thing to anyone else." He reclaimed the bottle and drank again. "But you can't have the past back, so what's the use of breaking your heart? When things are gone, they're gone."

Gentle made a noncommittal noise.

"You don't agree."

"Not necessarily."

"Name one thing that stays."

"I don't—"

"No, go on. Name *one* thing."

"Love."

"Ha! Well, that certainly brings us full circle, doesn't it? Love! You know, I'd have agreed with you half a year ago. I can't deny that. I couldn't conceive of ever being out of love with Judith. But I am. When I think back to the way I felt about her, it seems ludicrous. Now, of course, it's Oscar's turn to be obsessed by her. First you, then me, then Oscar. But he won't survive long."

"What makes you say that?"

"He's got his fingers in too many pies. It'll end in tears, you see if it doesn't. You know about the Tabula Rasa, I suppose?"

"No."

"Why should you?" Estabrook replied. "You were dragged into this, weren't you? I feel guilty about that, I really do. Not that my feeling guilty's going to do either of us much good, but I want you to know I never understood the ramifications of what I was doing. If I had, I swear I'd have left Judith alone."

"I don't think either of us would have been capable of that," Gentle remarked.

"Leaving her alone? No, I don't suppose we would. Our paths were already beaten for us, eh? I'm not saying I'm a total innocent, mind you. I'm not. I've done some pretty wretched things in my time, things I squirm to think about. But compared with the Tabula Rasa, or a mad bastard like Sartori, I'm not so bad. And when I look out every morning, into God's Nowhere—"

"Is that what they call it?"

"Oh, hell, no; they're much more reverential. That's my little nickname. But when I look out at it, I think, Well, it's going to take us all one of these days, whoever we are: mad bastards, lovers, drunkards, it's not going to pick and choose. We'll all go to nothing sooner or later. And you know, maybe it's my age, but that doesn't worry me any longer. We all have our time, and when it's over, it's over."

"There must be something on the other side, Charlie," Gentle said.

Estabrook shook his head. "That's all guff," he said. "I've seen a lot of people get up and walk into the Erasure, praying and carrying on. They take a few steps and they're gone. It's like they'd never lived."

"But people are healed here. You were."

"Oscar certainly made a mess of me, and I didn't die. But I don't know whether being here had much to do with that. Think about it. If God really was on the other side of that wall, and He was so damn eager to heal the sick, don't you think He'd reach out a little further and stop what's going on in Yzordderrex? Why would He put up with horrors like that, right under His nose? No, Gentle. I call it God's Nowhere, but that's only half-right. God isn't there. Maybe He was once. . . ."

He trailed away and filled the silence with another throatful of kloupo.

"Thank you for this," Gentle said.

"What is there to thank me for?"

"You've helped me to make up my mind about something."

"My pleasure," Estabrook said. "It's damn difficult to think straight, isn't it, with this bloody wind blowing all the time? Can you find your way back to that lovely lady of yours, or shall I go with you?"

"I'll find my way," Gentle replied.

2

He rapidly regretted declining Estabrook's offer, discovering after turning a few corners that one lamp-lit passageway looked much like the next, and that not only could he not retrace his steps to Pie's bedside, he couldn't be certain of finding his way back to Estabrook either.

One route he tried brought him into a kind of chapel, where several Dearthers were kneeling facing a window that gave onto God's Nowhere. The Erasure presented in what was now total darkness the same blank face it had by dusk, lighter than the night but shedding none upon it, its nullity more disturbing than the atrocities of Beatrix or the sealed rooms of the palace.

Turning his back on both window and worshipers, Gentle continued his search for Pie, and accident finally brought him back into what he thought was the room where the mystif lay. The bed was empty, however. Disoriented, he was about to go and quiz one of the other patients to confirm that he had the right room when he caught sight of Floccus' meal, or what was left of it, on the floor beside the bed: a few crusts, half a dozen well-picked bones. There could be no doubt that this was indeed Pie's bed. But where was the occupant? He turned to look at the others. They were all either asleep or comatose, but he was determined to have the truth of this, and was crossing to the nearest bed, when he heard Floccus running in pursuit, calling after him.

"There you are! I've been looking all over for you."

"Pie's bed is empty, Floccus."

"I know, I know. I went to empty my bladder—I was away two minutes, no more—and when I got back it had gone. The mystif, not my bladder. I thought maybe you'd come and taken it away."

"Why would I do that?"

"Don't get angry. There's no harm going to come to it here. Trust me."

After his discussion with Estabrook, Gentle was by no means certain this was true, but he wasn't going to waste time arguing with Floccus while Pie was wandering unattended.

"Where have you looked?" he asked.

"All around."

"Can't you be a little more precise?"

"I got lost," Floccus said, becoming exasperated. "All the tents look alike."

"Did you go outside?"

"No, why?" Floccus' agitation sank from sight. What surfaced instead was deep dismay. "You don't think it's gone to the Erasure?"

"We won't know till we look," Gentle said. "Which way did Athanasius take me? There was a door—"

"Wait! Wait!" Floccus said, snatching hold of Gentle's jacket. "You can't just step out there."

"Why not? I'm a Maestro, aren't I?"

"There are ceremonies—"

"I don't give a shit," Gentle said, and without waiting for further objections from Floccus, he headed off in what he hoped was the right direction.

Floccus followed, trotting beside Gentle, opening new arguments against what Gentle was planning with every fourth or fifth step. The Erasure was restless tonight, he said, there was talk of ruptures in it; to wander in its vicinity when it was so volatile was dangerous, possibly suicidal; and besides, it was a desecration. Gentle might be a Maestro, but it didn't give him the right to ignore the etiquette of what he was planning. He was a guest, invited in on the understanding that he obey the rules. And rules weren't written for the fun of it. There were good reasons to keep strangers from trespassing there. They were ignorant, and ignorance could bring disaster on everybody.

"What's the use of rules, if nobody really understands what's going on out there?" Gentle said.

"But we do! We understand this place. It's where God begins."

"So if the Erasure kills me, you know what to write in my obituary. 'Gentle ended where God begins.' "

"This isn't funny, Gentle."

"Agreed."

"It's life or death."

"Agreed."

"So why are you doing it?"

"Because wherever Pie is, that's where I belong. And I would have thought even someone as half-sighted and short-witted as you would have seen that!"

"You mean shortsighted and halfwitted."

"You said it."

Ahead lay the door he and Athanasius had stepped through. It was open and unguarded.

"I just want to say—" Floccus began.

"Leave it alone, Floccus."

"—it's been too short a friendship," the man replied, bringing Gentle to a halt, shamed by his outburst.

"Don't mourn me yet," he said softly.

Floccus made no reply, but backed away from the open door, leaving Gentle to step through it alone. The night outside was hushed, the wind having dropped to little more than a breeze. He scanned the terrain, left and right. There were worshipers in both directions, kneeling in the gloom, their heads bowed as they meditated on God's Nowhere. Not wishing to disturb them, he moved as quietly as he could over the uneven ground, but the smaller shards of rock ahead of him skipped and rolled as he approached, as though to announce him with their rattle and clatter. This was not the only response to his presence. The air he exhaled, which he'd turned to killing use so many times now, darkened as it left his lips, the cloud shot through with threads of bright scarlet. They didn't disperse, these breaths, but sank as though weighed down by their own lethality, wrapping around his torso and legs like funeral robes. He made no attempt to shrug them off, even though their folds soon concealed the ground and slowed his step. Nor did he have to puzzle much over their purpose. Now that he was unaccompanied by Athanasius, the air was determined to deny him the defense of walking here as an innocent, as a man in pursuit of an errant lover. Wrapped in black and attended by drums, his profounder nature was here revealed: he was a Maestro with a murderous power at his lips, and there would be no concealing that fact, either from the Erasure or from those who were meditating upon it.

Several of the worshipers had been stirred from their contemplations by the sound of the stones and now looked up to see they had an ominous figure in their midst. One, kneeling alone close to Gentle's path, rose in panic and fled, uttering a prayer of protection. Another fell prostrate, sobbing. Rather than intimidate them further with his gaze, Gentle turned his eyes on God's Nowhere, scouring the ground close to the margin of solid earth and void for some sign of Pie 'oh' pah. The sight of the Erasure no longer distressed him as it had when he'd first stepped out here with Athanasius. Clothed as he was, and thus announced, he came before the void as a man of power. For him to have attempted the rites of Reconciliation, he must have made his peace with this mystery. He had nothing to fear from it.

By the time he set eyes on Pie 'oh' pah he was three or four hundred yards from the door, and the assembly of meditators had thinned to a brave few who'd wandered from the main knot of the congregation in search of solitude. Some had already retreated,

seeing him approach, but a stoical few kept their praying places and
let this stranger pass by without so much as glancing up at him.
Now so folded in sable breath he feared Pie would not recognize
him, Gentle began to call the mystif's name. The call went unac-
knowledged. Though the mystif's head was no more than a dark
blur in the murk, Gentle knew what its hungry eyes were fixed
upon: the enigma that was coaxing its steady step the way a cliff
edge might coax a suicide. He picked up his pace, his momentum
moving steadily larger stones as he went. Though there was no sign
that the mystif was in any hurry, he feared that once it was in the
equivocal region between solid ground and nothingness, it would
be irretrievable.

"Pie!" he yelled as he went. "Can you hear me? Please, stop!"

The words went on clouding and clothing him, but they had no
effect upon Pie until Gentle turned his requests into an order.

"Pie 'oh' pah. This is your Maestro. Stop."

The mystif stumbled as Gentle spoke, as though his demand had
put an obstacle in its way. A small, almost bestial sound of pain escaped it. But it did as its sometime summoner had ordered and
stopped in its tracks like a dutiful servant, waiting until the Maestro reached its side.

Gentle was within ten paces, now, and saw how far advanced the
process of unknitting was. The mystif was barely more than a
shadow among shadows, its features impossible to read, its body
insubstantial. If Gentle needed any further proof that the Erasure
was not a place of healing, it was in the sight of the uredo, which
was more solid than the body it had fed upon, its livid stains intermittently brightening like embers caught by a gusting wind.

"Why did you leave your bed?" Gentle said, his pace slowed
once again as he approached the mystif. Its form seemed so tenuous he feared any violent motion might disperse it entirely.
"There's nothing beyond the Erasure you need, Pie. Your life's
here, with me."

The mystif took a little time to reply. When it did its voice was
as ethereal as its substance, a slender, exhausted plea emerging
from a spirit at the edge of total collapse.

"I don't have any life left, Maestro," it said.

"Let me be the judge of that. I swore to myself I wouldn't let
you go again, Pie. I want to look after you, make you well. Bringing you here was a mistake, I see that now. I'm sorry if it's brought
you pain, but I'll take you away—"

"It wasn't a mistake. You found your way here for your own
reasons."

"You're my reason, Pie. I didn't know who I was till you found
me, and I'll forget myself again if you go."

"No, you won't," it said, the dubious outline of its head turning in Gentle's direction. Though there was no gleam to mark the place where its eyes had been, Gentle knew it was looking at him. "You're the Maestro Sartori. The Reconciler of the Imajica." It faltered for a long moment. When its voice came again, it was frailer than ever. "And you are also my master, and my husband, and my dearest brother. . . . If you order me to stay, then I will stay. But if you love me, Gentle, then please . . . let . . . me . . . go."

The request could scarcely have been made more simply or more eloquently, and had Gentle known without question there was an Eden on the other side of the Erasure, ready to receive Pie's spirit, he would have let the mystif go there and then, agonizing as it would be. But he believed differently and was ready to say it, even in such proximity to the void.

"It's not heaven, Pie. Maybe God's there, maybe not. But until we know—"

"Why not just let me go now and see for myself? I'm not afraid. This is the Dominion where my people were made. I want to see it." In these words there was the first hint of passion Gentle had so far heard. "I'm dying, Maestro. I need to lie down and sleep."

"What if there's nothing there, Pie? What if it's only emptiness?"

"I'd prefer the absence to the pain."

The reply defeated Gentle utterly. "Then you'd better go," he said, wishing he could find some more tender way to relinquish his hold, but unable to conceal his desolation with platitudes. However much he wanted to save Pie from suffering, his sympathy could not outweigh the need he felt, nor quite annul the sense of ownership which, however unsavory, was a part of what he felt towards this creature.

"I wish we could have taken this last journey together, Maestro," Pie said. "But you've got work to do, I know. Great work."

"And how do I do it without you?" Gentle said, knowing this was a wretched gambit—and half ashamed of it—but unwilling to let the mystif pass from life without voicing every desire he knew to keep it from going.

"You're not alone," Pie said. "You've met Tick Raw and Scopique. They were both members of the last Synod, and they're ready to work the Reconciliation with you."

"They're Maestros?"

"They are now. They were novices the last time, but they're prepared now. They'll work in their Dominions while you work in the Fifth."

"They waited all this time?"

"They knew you'd come. Or, if not you, somebody in your place."

He'd treated them both so badly, he thought, Tick Raw especially.

"Who'll represent the Second?" he said. "And the First?"

"There was a Eurhetemec in Yzordderrex, waiting to work for the Second, but he's dead. He was old the last time, and he couldn't wait. I asked Scopique to find a replacement."

"And here?"

"I'd hoped that honor might fall to me, but now you'll need to find someone in my place. Don't look so lost, Maestro, please. You were a great Reconciler—"

"I failed. How great is that?"

"You won't fail again."

"I don't even know the ceremonies."

"You'll remember, after a time."

"How?"

"All that we did and said and felt is still waiting in Gamut Street. All our preparations, all our debates. Even me."

"Memory isn't enough, Pie."

"I know. . . ."

"I want you real. I want you . . . forever."

"Maybe, when the Imajica is whole again and the First Dominion opens, you'll find me."

There was some tiny hope in that, he thought, though whether it would be enough to keep him from despair when the mystif had disappeared he didn't know.

"May I go?" Pie said.

Gentle had never uttered a harder syllable than his next. "Yes," he said.

The mystif raised its hand, which was no more than a five-fingered wisp of smoke, and put it against Gentle's lips. He felt no physical contact, but his heart jumped in his chest.

"We're not lost," Pie said. "Trust in that."

Then the fingers dropped away, and the mystif started from Gentle's side towards the Erasure. There were perhaps a dozen yards to cover, and as the gap diminished Gentle's heart, already pounding after Pie's touch, beat faster, its drum tolling in his head. Even now, knowing he couldn't rescind the freedom he'd granted, it was all he could do not to pursue the mystif and delay it just another moment: to hear its voice, to stand beside it, to be the shadow of its shadow.

It didn't glance back, but stepped with cruel ease into the no-man's-land between solidity and nothingness. Gentle refused to look away but stared on with a steadfastness more defiant than heroic. The place was well named. As the mystif walked it was erased, like a sketch that had served its Creator's purpose and was no longer needed on the page. But unlike the sketch, which however fastidiously erased always left some trace to mark the artist's error, when Pie finally disappeared the vanishing was complete, leaving the spot flawless. If Gentle had not had the mystif in his memory—that unreliable book—it might never have existed.

5

I

When he returned inside, it was to meet the stares of fifty or more people gathered at the door, all of whom had obviously witnessed what had just happened, albeit at some distance. Nobody so much as coughed until he'd passed; then he heard the whispers rise like the sound of swarming insects. Did they have nothing better to do than gossip about his grief? he thought. The sooner he was away from here, the better. He'd say his farewells to Estabrook and Floccus and leave immediately.

He returned to Pie's bed, hoping the mystif might have left some keepsake for him, but the only sign of its presence was the indentation in the pillow on which its beautiful head had lain. He longed to lie there himself for a little time, but it was too public for such an indulgence. He would grieve when he was away from here.

As he prepared to leave, Floccus appeared, his wiry little body twitching like a boxer anticipating a blow.

"I'm sorry to interrupt," he said.

"I was coming to find you anyway," Gentle said. "Just to say thank you, and goodbye."

"Before you go," Floccus said, blinking maniacally, "I've a message for you." He'd sweated all the color from his face and stumbled over every other word.

"I'm sorry for my behavior," Gentle said, trying to soothe him. "You did all you could have done, and all you got for it was my foul temper."

"No need to apologize."

"Pie had to go, and I have to stay. That's the way of it."

"It's a pleasure to have you back," Floccus gushed. "Really, Maestro, really."

That *Maestro* gave Gentle a clue to this performance. "Floccus? Are you afraid of me?" he said. "You are, aren't you?"

"Afraid? Ah, well—ah, yes. In a manner of speaking. Yes. What happened out there, your getting so close to the Erasure and not being claimed, and the way you've changed"—the dark garb still clung about him, he realized, its slow dispersal draping shreds of smoke around his limbs—"it puts a different complexion on things. I hadn't understood; forgive me, it was stupid; I hadn't understood, you know, that I was in the company of, well, such a power. If I, you know, caused any offense—"

"You didn't."

"I can be frivolous."

"You were fine company, Floccus."

"Thank you, Maestro. Thank you. Thank you."

"Please stop thanking me."

"Yes. I will. Thank you."

"You said you had a message."

"I did? I did."

"Who from?"

"Athanasius. He'd like very much to see you."

Here was the third farewell he owed, Gentle thought. "Then take me to him, if you would," he said, and Floccus, his face flooded with relief that he'd survived this interview, turned and led him from the empty bed.

In the few minutes it took for them to thread their way through the body of the tent, the wind, which had dropped almost to nothing at twilight, began to rise with fresh ferocity. By the time Floccus ushered him into the chamber where Athanasius waited, it was beating at the walls wildly. The lamps on the floor flickered with each gust, and by their panicky light Gentle saw what a melancholy place Athanasius had chosen for their parting. The chamber was a mortuary, its floor littered with bodies wrapped in every kind of rag and shroud, some neatly parceled, most barely covered: further proof—as if it were needed—of how poor a place of healing this was. But that argument was academic now. This was neither the time nor the place to bruise the man's faith, not with the night wind thrashing at the walls and the dead everywhere underfoot.

"Do you want me to stay?" Floccus asked Athanasius, clearly desperate to be shunned.

"No, no. Go by all means," the other replied.

Floccus turned to Gentle and made a little bow. "It was an honor, sir," he said, then beat a hasty retreat.

When Gentle looked back towards Athanasius, the man had wandered to the far end of the mortuary and was staring down at one of the shrouded bodies. He had dressed for this somber place, the loose bright garb he'd been wearing earlier discarded in favor of robes so deep a blue they were practically black.

"So, Maestro," he said. "I was looking for a Judas in our midst and I missed you. That was careless, eh?"

His tone was conversational, which made a statement Gentle already found confusing doubly so.

"What do you mean?" he said.

"I mean you tricked your way into our tents, and now you expect to depart without paying a price for your desecration."

"There was no trick," Gentle said. "The mystif was sick, and I thought it could be healed here. If I failed to observe the formalities out there, you'll excuse me. I didn't have time to take a theology lesson."

"The mystif was never sick. Or if it was you sickened it yourself, so you could worm your way in here. Don't even bother to protest. I saw what you did out there. What's the mystif going to do, make some report on us to the Unbeheld?"

"What are you accusing me of exactly?"

"Do you even come from the Fifth, I find myself wondering, or is that also part of the plot?"

"There is no plot."

"Only I've heard that revolution and theology are bad bedfellows there, which of course seems strange to us. How can one ever be separated from the other? If you want to change even a little part of your condition, you must expect the consequences to reach the ears of divinities sooner or later, and then you must have your reasons ready."

Gentle listened to all of this, wondering if it might not be simplest to quit the room and leave Athanasius to ramble. Clearly none of this really made any sense. But he owed the man a little patience, perhaps, if only for the words of wisdom he'd bestowed at the wedding.

"You think I'm involved in some conspiracy," Gentle said. "Is that it?"

"I think you're a murderer, a liar, and an agent of the Autarch," Athanasius said.

"You call *me* a liar? Who's the one who seduced all these poor fuckers into thinking they could be healed here, you or me? Look at them!" He pointed along the rows. "You call this healing? I don't. And if they had the breath—"

He reached down and snatched the shroud off the corpse closest to him. The face beneath was that of a pretty woman. Her open eyes were glazed. So was her face: painted and glazed. Carved, painted, and glazed. He tugged the sheet farther back, hearing Athanasius' hard, humorless laugh as he did so. The woman had a painted child perched in the crook of her arm. There was a gilded halo around its head, and its tiny hand was raised in benediction.

"She may lie very still," Athanasius said. "But don't be deceived. She's not dead."

Gentle went to another of the bodies and drew back its covering. Beneath lay a second Madonna, this one more baroque than the first, its eyes turned up in a beatific swoon. He let the shroud drop from between his fingers.

"Feeling weak, Maestro?" Athanasius said. "You conceal your fear very well, but you don't deceive me."

Gentle looked around the room again. There were at least thirty bodies laid out here. "Are all of them Madonnas?" he said.

Reading Gentle's bewilderment as anxiety, Athanasius said, "Now I begin to see the fear. This ground is sacred to the Goddess."

"Why?"

"Because tradition says a great crime was committed against Her sex near this spot. A woman from the Fifth Dominion was raped hereabouts, and the spirit of the Holy Mother calls sacred any ground thus marked." He went down on his haunches and uncovered another of the statues, touching it reverentially. "She's with us here," he said. "In every statue. In every stone. In every gust of wind. She blesses us, because we dare to come so close to Her enemy's Dominion."

"What enemy?"

"Are you not allowed to utter his name without dropping to your knees?" Athanasius said. "Hapexamendios, Your Lord, the Unbeheld. You can confess it. Why not? You know my secret now, and I know yours. We're transparent to each other. I do have one question, however, before you leave."

"What's that?"

"How did you find out we worship the Goddess? Was it Floccus who told you or Nikaetomaas?"

"Nobody. I didn't know and I don't much care." He started to walk towards the man. "I'm not afraid of your Virgins, Athanasius."

He chose one nearby and unveiled her, from starry crown to cloud-treading toe. Her hands were clasped in prayer. Stooping, just as Athanasius had, Gentle put his hand over the statue's knitted fingers.

"For what it's worth," he said, "I think they're beautiful. I was an artist once myself."

"You're strong, Maestro, I'll say that for you. I expected you to be brought to your knees by Our Lady."

"First I'm supposed to kneel for Hapexamendios; now for the Virgin."

"One in fealty, one in fear."

"I'm sorry to disappoint you, but my legs are my own. I'll kneel when I choose to. *If* I choose to."

Athanasius looked puzzled. "I think you half believe that," he said.

"Damn right I do. I don't know what kind of conspiracy you think I'm guilty of, but I swear there's none."

"Maybe you're more His instrument than I thought," Athanasius said. "Maybe you're ignorant of His purpose."

"Oh, no," Gentle said. "I know what work I'm meant to do, and I see no reason to be ashamed of it. If I can reconcile the Fifth I will. I want the Imajica whole, and I'd have thought you would too. You can visit the Vatican. You'll find it's full of Madonnas."

As though inspired to fury by his words, the wind beat at the walls with fresh venom, a gust finding its way into the chamber, raising several of the lighter shrouds into the air and extinguishing one of the lamps.

"He won't save you," Athanasius said, clearly believing this wind had come to carry Gentle away. "Nor will your ignorance, if that's what's kept you from harm."

He looked back towards the bodies he'd been studying as Floccus departed.

"Lady, forgive us," he said, "for doing this in your sight."

The words were a signal, it seemed. Four of the figures moved as he spoke, sitting up and pulling the shrouds from their heads. No Madonnas these. They were men and women of the Dearth, carrying blades like crescent moons. Athanasius looked back at Gentle.

"Will you accept the blessing of Our Lady before you die?" he said.

Somebody had already begun a prayer behind him, Gentle heard, and he glanced around to see that there were another three assassins there, two of them armed in the same lunatic fashion, the third—a girl no more than Huzzah's age, bare-breasted, doe-faced—darting between the rows uncovering statues as she went. No two were alike. There were Virgins of stone, Virgins of wood, Virgins of plaster. There were Virgins so crudely carved they were barely recognizable, and others so finely hewn and finished they looked ready to draw breath. Though minutes before, Gentle had laid his hand on one of this number without harm, the spectacle faintly sickened him. Did Athanasius know something about the condition of Maestros that he, Gentle, didn't? Might he somehow be subjugated by this image, the way in an earlier life he'd been enthralled by the sight of a woman naked, or promising nakedness?

Whatever mystery was here, he wasn't about to let Athanasius murder him while he puzzled it out. He drew breath and put his hand to his mouth as Athanasius drew a weapon of his own and started towards him at speed. The breath proved faster than the blade. Gentle unleashed the pneuma, not at Athanasius directly, but at the ground in front of him. The stones it struck flew into pieces, and Athanasius fell back as the fusillade hit him. He dropped his knife and clamped his hands to his face, yelling as much in rage as in pain. If there was a command in his clamor the assassins missed or ignored it. They kept a respectful distance from Gentle as he walked towards their wounded leader, through an air still gray with motes of pulverized stone. Athanasius was lying on his side, propped on his elbow. Gentle went down on his haunches beside the man and carefully drew Athanasius' hands from his face. There was a deep cut beneath his left eye, and another above his right. Both were bleeding copiously, as were a score of littler cuts. None of them, however, would be calamitous for a man who wore wounds the way others wore jewelry. They would heal and add to his sum of scars.

"Call your assassins off, Athanasius," Gentle told him. "I didn't come here to hurt anybody, but if you press me to it I'll kill every last one of them. Do you understand me?" He put his arm beneath the man and hauled him to his feet. "Now call them off."

Athanasius shrugged himself free of Gentle's hold and scanned his cohorts through a drizzle of blood.

"Let him pass," he said. "There'll be another time."

The assassins between Gentle and the door parted, though none of them lowered or sheathed their weapons. Gentle stood up and left Athanasius' side, passing only to offer one final observation.

"I wouldn't want to kill the man who married me to Pie 'oh' pah," he said, "so before you come after me again, examine the evidence against me, whatever it is. And search your heart. I'm not your enemy. All I want to do is to heal Imajica. Isn't that what your Goddess wants too?"

If Athanasius had wanted to respond, he was too slow. Before he could open his mouth a cry rose from somewhere outside, and a moment later another, then another, then a dozen: all howls of pain and panic, twisted into eardrum-bruising screeches by the gusts that carried them. Gentle turned back to the door, but the wind had hold of the entire chamber, and even as he made to depart, one of the walls rose as if a titanic hand had seized hold of it and lifted it up into the air. The wind, bearing its freight of screams, rushed in, flinging the lamps over, their fuel spilled as they rolled before it. Caught by the very flames it had fed, the oil burst into bright yellow balls, by which light Gentle saw scenes of chaos on all sides. The assassins were being thrown over like the lamps, unable to withstand the power of the wind. One he saw impaled on her own blade. Another was carried into the oil and was instantly consumed by flame.

"What have you summoned?" Athanasius yelled.

"This isn't my doing," Gentle replied.

Athanasius screeched some further accusation, but it was snatched from his lips as the rampage escalated. Another of the chamber's walls was summarily snatched away, its tatters rising into the air like a curtain to unveil a scene of catastrophe. The storm was at work throughout the length of the tents, disemboweling the glorious and scarlet beast Gentle had entered with such awe. Wall after wall was shredded or wrenched from the ground, the ropes and pegs that had held them lethal as they flew. And visible beyond the turmoil, its cause: the once featureless wall of the Erasure, featureless no longer. It roiled the way the sky Gentle had seen beneath the Pivot had roiled, a maelstrom whose place of origin seemed to be a hole torn in the Erasure's fabric. The sight gave substance to Athanasius' charges. Threatened by assassins and Madonnas, had Gentle unwittingly summoned some entity out of the First Dominion to protect him? If so, he had to find it and subdue it before he had more innocent lives to add to the roster of those who'd perished because of him.

With his eyes fixed on the tear, he vacated the chamber and headed towards the Erasure. The route between was the storm's highway. It carried the detritus of its deeds back and forth, returning to places it had already destroyed in its first assault to pick up the survivors and pitch them into the air like sacks of bloody down, tearing them open up above. There was a red rain in the gusts, which spattered Gentle as he went, yet the same authority that was condemning men and women all around left him untouched. It could not so much as knock him off his feet. The reason? His breath, which Pie had once called the source of all magic. Its cloak clung to him as it had before, apparently protecting him from the tumult, and, though it didn't impede his steps, it lent him a mass beyond that of flesh and bone.

With half the distance covered, he glanced back to see if there was any sign of life among the Madonnas. The place was easy to find, even amid this carnage; the fire burned with a wind-fed fervor, and through air thickened by blood and shards Gentle saw that several of the statues had been raised from their stony beds and now formed a circle in which Athanasius and several of his followers were taking shelter. They'd offer little defense against this havoc, he thought, but several other survivors could be seen crawling towards the place, eyes fixed on the Holy Mothers.

Gentle turned his back on the sight and strode on towards the Erasure, catching sight of another soul here weighty enough to resist the assault: a man in robes the color of the shredded tents, sitting cross-legged on the ground no more than twenty yards from the fury's source. His head was hooded, his face turned towards the maelstrom. Was this monkish creature the force he'd summoned? Gentle wondered. If not, how was this fellow surviving so close to the engine of destruction?

He started to yell to the man as he approached, by no means certain that his voice would carry in the din of wind and screams. But the monk heard. He looked round at Gentle, the hood half eclipsing his face. There was nothing untoward about his placid features. His face was in need of a shave; his nose, which had been broken at some time, in need of resetting; his eyes in need of nothing. They had all they wanted, it seemed, seeing the Maestro approach. A broad grin broke over the monk's face, and he instantly rose to his feet, bowing his head.

"Maestro," he said. "You do me honor." His voice wasn't raised, but it carried through the commotion. "Have you seen the mystif yet?"

"The mystif's gone," Gentle said. He didn't need to yell, he realized. His voice, like his limbs, carried an unnatural weight here.

"Yes, I saw it go," the monk replied. "But it's come back, Maestro. It broke through the Erasure, and the storm came after it."

"Where? Where?" Gentle said, turning full circle. "I don't see it!" He looked accusingly at the man. "It would have found me if it was here," he said.

"Trust me, it's trying," the man replied. He pulled back his hood. His gingery curls were thinning, but there was the vestige of a chorister's charm there. "It's very close, Maestro."

Now it was he who stared into the storm: not to left and right, however, but up into the labyrinthine air. Gentle followed his gaze. There were swaths of tattered canvas on the wind high above them, rising and falling like vast wounded birds. There were pieces of furniture, shredded clothes, and fragments of flesh. And in among these clouds of dross, a darting form darker than either sky or storm, descending even as he set his eyes upon it. The monk drew closer to Gentle.

"That's the mystif," he said. "May I protect you, Maestro?"

"It's my friend," Gentle said. "I don't need protecting."

"I think you do," the other replied, and raised his arms above his head, palms out as if to deflect the approaching spirit.

It slowed at the sight of this gesture, and Gentle had time to see the form above him plainly. It was indeed the mystif, or its remains. Either by stealth or sheer force of will it had breached the Erasure. But its escape had brought it no comfort whatsoever. The uredo burned more venomously than ever, almost entirely consuming the shadow body it had fixed upon and poisoned; and from

the sufferer's mouth, a howl that could not have been more pained
had its guts been drawn out of its belly in front of its eyes.

It had come to a complete halt now and hovered above the two
men like a diver arrested in mid-descent, arms outstretched, head,
or its traces, thrown back.

"Pie?" Gentle said. "Have you done this?"

The howl went on. If there were words in its anguish, Gentle
couldn't make them out.

"I have to speak to it," Gentle said to his protector. "If you're
causing it pain, for God's sake stop."

"It came out of the margin howling like this," the man said.

"At least drop your defenses."

"It'll attack us."

"I'll take that risk," he replied.

The man let his shunning hands fall to his side. The form above
them twisted and turned but did not descend. Another force had
a claim upon it, Gentle realized. It was thrashing to resist a summons from the Erasure, which was calling it back into the place
from which it had escaped.

"Can you hear me, Pie?" Gentle asked it.

The howl went on, unabated.

"If you can speak, do it!"

"It's already speaking," the monk said.

"I only hear howls," Gentle said.

"Past the howls," came the reply, "there are words."

Drops of fluid fell from the mystif's wounds as its struggles to
resist the Erasure's power intensified. They stank of putrescence
and burned Gentle's upturned face, but their sting brought comprehension of the words encoded in Pie's screeches.

"Undone," the mystif was saying. "We're . . . undone. . . ."

"Why did you do this?" Gentle asked.

"It wasn't . . . me. The storm was sent to claim me back."

"Out of the First?"

"It's . . . His will," Pie said. "His . . . will. . . ."

Though the tortured form above him resembled the creature
he'd loved and wed scarcely at all, Gentle could still hear fragments of Pie 'oh' pah in these replies and, hearing them, wanted
to raise his own voice in anguish at the thought of Pie's pain. The
mystif had gone into the First to end its suffering; but here it was,
suffering still, and he was powerless to help it or heal it. All he
could do by way of comfort was tell it that he understood, which
he did. Its message was perfectly clear. In the trauma of their parting Pie had sensed some equivocation in him. But there was none,
and he said so.

"I know what I have to do," he told the sufferer. "Trust me, Pie.

I understand. I'm the Reconciler. I'm not going to run from that."

At this, the mystif writhed like a fish on a hook, no longer able to keep itself from being hauled in by the fisherman in the First. It started to scrabble at the air, as if it might gain another moment in this Dominion by catching hold of a mote. But the power that had sent such furies in pursuit of it had too strong a hold, and the spirit was drawn back towards the Erasure. Instinctively Gentle reached up towards it, hearing and ignoring a cry of alarm from the man at his side. The mystif reached for his hand, extending its shadowy substance to do so, and curling grotesquely long fingers around Gentle's. The contact sent such a convulsion through his system he would have been thrown to the ground but that his protector took hold of him. As it was his marrow seemed to burn in his bones, and he smelled the stench of rot off his skin, as though death were coming upon him inside and out. It was hard, in that agony, to hold on to the mystif, much less to the words it was trying to say. But he fought the urge to let go, struggling for the sense of the few syllables he was able to grasp. Three of them were his name.

"Sartori . . ."

"I'm here, Pie," Gentle said, thinking perhaps the thing was blinded now. "I'm still here."

But the mystif wasn't naming its Maestro.

"The other," it said. "The *other* . . ."

"What about him?"

"He knows," Pie murmured. "Find him, Gentle. He knows."

With this command, their fingers separated. The mystif reached to take hold of Gentle again, but with its frail hold lost it was prey to the Erasure and was instantly snatched towards the tear through which it had appeared. Gentle started after it, but his limbs had been more severely traumatized by the convulsion than he'd thought, and his legs simply folded up beneath him. He fell heavily, but raised his head in time to catch sight of the mystif disappearing into the void. Sprawled on the hard ground, he remembered his first pursuit of Pie, through the empty, icy streets of Manhattan. He'd fallen then, too, and looked up as he did now to see the riddle escaping him, unsolved. But it had turned that first time; turned and spoken to him across the river of Fifth Avenue, offering him the hope, however frail, of another meeting. Not so now. It went into the Erasure like smoke through a drafty door, its cry stopping dead.

"Not again," Gentle murmured.

The monk was crouching at his side. "Can you stand," he asked, "or shall I get help?"

Gentle put his hands beneath him and pushed himself up into

a kneeling position, making no reply to the question. With the mystif's disappearance, the malignant wind that had come after it, and brought such devastation, was dropping away, and as it did so the debris it had been keeping aloft descended in a grim hail. For a second time the monk raised his hands to ward off the descending force. Gentle was barely aware of what was happening. His eyes were on the Erasure, which was rapidly losing its roiling motion. By the time the rain of canvas, stones, and bodies had stopped, every last trace of detail had gone from the divide, and it was once again an absence over which the eye slid, finding no purchase.

Gentle got to his feet and, turning his eyes from the nullity, scanned the desolation that lay in every other direction but one. The circle of Madonnas he'd glimpsed through the storm was still intact, and sheltering in its midst were half a hundred survivors, some of them on their knees sobbing or praying, many kissing the feet of the statues that had shielded them, still others gazing towards the Erasure from which the destruction that claimed all but these fifty, plus the Maestro and the monk, had come.

"Do you see Athanasius?" Gentle asked the man at his side.

"No, but he's alive somewhere," came the reply. "He's like you, Maestro; he's got too much purpose in him to die."

"I don't think any purpose would have saved me if you hadn't been here," Gentle remarked. "You've got real power in your bones."

"A little, maybe," the monk replied, with a modest smile. "I had a fine teacher."

"So did I," Gentle said softly. "But I lost it." Seeing the Maestro's eyes filling, the monk made to withdraw, but Gentle said, "Don't worry about the tears. I've been running from them too long. Let me ask you something. I'll quite understand if you say no."

"What, Maestro?"

"When I leave here, I'm going back to the Fifth to prepare for a Reconciliation. Would you trust me enough to join the Synod; to represent the First?"

The monk's face broke into bliss, shedding years as he smiled. "It would be my honor, Maestro," he said.

"There's risk in it," Gentle warned.

"There always was. But I wouldn't be here if it weren't for you."

"How so?"

"You're my inspiration, Maestro," the man replied, inclining his head in deference. "Whatever you require of me, I'll perform as best I can."

"Stay here, then. Watch the Erasure and wait. I'll find you when the time comes." He spoke with more certainty than he felt, but then perhaps the illusion of competence was part of every Maestro's repertoire.

"I'll be waiting," the monk replied.

"What's your name?"

"When I joined the Dearthers they called me Chicka Jackeen."

"Jackeen?"

"It means worthless fellow," the man replied.

"Then we've got much in common," Gentle said. He took the man's hand and shook it. "Remember me, Jackeen."

"You've never left my mind," the man replied.

There was some subtext here Gentle couldn't grasp, but this was no time to delve. He had two demanding and dangerous journeys ahead of him: the first to Yzordderrex, the second from that city back to the Retreat. Thanking Jackeen for his good offices, Gentle left him at the Erasure and picked his way back through the devastation towards the circle of Madonnas. Some of the survivors were leaving its shelter to begin a search of the site, presumably in the hope—vain, he suspected—of finding others alive. It was a scene of grief and bewilderment he'd witnessed too many times on his journey through the Dominions. Much as he would have liked to believe it was mere happenstance that these scenes of devastation coincided with his presence, he couldn't afford to indulge such self-delusion. He was as surely wedded to the storm as he was to Pie. More so now, perhaps, with the mystif gone.

Jackeen's observation that Athanasius was too purposeful a soul to have perished was confirmed as Gentle drew closer to the circle. The man was standing at the center of a knot of Dearthers, leading a prayer of thanks to the Holy Mother for their survival. As Gentle reached the perimeter, Athanasius raised his head. One eye was closed beneath a scab of blood and dirt, but there was enough hatred in the other to burn in a dozen eyes. Meeting its gaze, Gentle advanced no further, but the priest dropped the volume of his prayer to a whisper anyway, preventing the trespasser from hearing the terms of his devotion. Gentle's ears were not so dulled by the din he didn't catch a few of the phrases, however. Though the woman represented in so many modes around the circle was clearly the Virgin Mary, she apparently went by other names here; or else had sisters. He heard her called Uma Umagammagi, Mother Imajica; and heard too the name Huzzah had first whispered to him in her cell beneath the *maison de santé*: Tishalullé. There was a third, though it took Gentle a little time to be certain he'd understood the naming aright, and that was Jokalaylau. Athanasius prayed that she'd keep a place for them at her side in the snows of paradise, which made Gentle wonder rather sourly if the man had ever trodden those wastes, that he could think them a heavenly place.

Though the names were strange, the inspiring spirit was not. Athanasius and his forlorn congregation were praying to the same loving Goddess at whose shrines in the Fifth countless candles were lit every day. Even Gentle at his most pagan had conceded the presence of that woman in his life and worshiped her the only way he'd known how: with the seduction and temporary possession of her sex. Had he known a mother or a loving sister he might have learned a better devotion than lust, but he hoped and believed the Holy Woman would forgive him his trespasses, even if Athanasius would not. The thought comforted him. He would need all the protection he could assemble in the battle that lay ahead, and it was no little solace to think that the Mother Imajica had her worshiping places in the Fifth, where that battle would be fought.

With the ad hoc service over, Athanasius let his congregation go about the business of searching the wreckage. For his part, he stayed in the middle of the circle, where a few survivors who'd made it that far, but perished, lay sprawled.

"Come here, Maestro," Athanasius said. "There's something you should see."

Gentle stepped into the circle, expecting Athanasius to show him the corpse of a child or some fragile beauty, broken. But the face at his feet was male, and far from innocent.

"You knew him, I think."

"Yes. His name was Estabrook."

Charlie's eyes were closed, his mouth too: sealed up in the moment of his passing. There was very little sign of physical damage. Perhaps his heart had simply given out in the excitement.

"Nikaetomaas said you brought him here because you thought he was me."

"We thought he was a Messiah," Athanasius said. "When we realized he wasn't we kept looking, expecting a miracle. Instead—"

"You got me. For what it's worth, you were right. I *did* bring all this destruction with me. I don't quite know why, and I don't expect you to forgive me for it, but I want you to understand that I take no pleasure in it. All I want to do is make good the damage I've done."

"And how will you do that, Maestro?" Athanasius said. His one good eye brimmed with tears as he surveyed the bodies. "How will you make this good? Can you resurrect them with what's between your legs? Is that the trick of it? Can you fuck them back into life?"

Gentle made a guttural sound of disgust.

"Well, that's what you Maestros think, isn't it? You don't want to suffer, you just want the glory. You lay your rod on the land, and the land bears fruit. That's what you think. But it doesn't work that way. It's your *blood* the land wants; it's your sacrifice. And as long as you deny that, others are going to die in your place. Believe me, I'd cut my throat now if I thought I could raise these people, but I've been played a wretched trick. I've the will to do it, but my blood's not worth a damn. Yours is. I don't know why. I wish it weren't. But it is."

"Would Uma Umagammagi like to see me bleed?" Gentle said. "Or Tishalullé? Or Jokalaylau? Is that what your loving mothers want from this child?"

"You don't belong to them. I don't know who you belong to, but you didn't come from their sweet bodies."

"I must have come from somewhere," Gentle said, voicing that thought for the first time in his life. "I've got a purpose in me, and I think God put it there."

"Don't look too far, Maestro. Your ignorance may be the only defense the rest of us have got against you. Give up your ambition now, before you find out what you're really capable of."

"I can't."

"Oh, but it's easy," Athanasius said. "Kill yourself, Maestro. Let the land have your blood. That's the greatest service you could do the Dominions now."

There was the bitterest echo, in these words, of a letter he'd read months ago, in another kind of wilderness.

Do this for the women of the world, Vanessa had written. *Slit your lying throat.*

Had he really traveled the Dominions simply to have the advice he'd been given by a woman whom he'd cheated in love returned to him? After all this striving for comprehension, was he finally as injurious and fraudulent a Maestro as he was a lover?

Athanasius read the accuracy of this last dart off his target's face and with a feral grin hammered it home.

"Do it soon, Maestro," he said. "There are enough orphans in the Dominions already, without you indulging your ambitions for another day."

Gentle let these cruelties go. "You married me to the love of my life, Athanasius," he said. "I won't ever forget that kindness."

"Poor Pie 'oh' pah," the other man replied, grinding the point home. "Another of your victims. What a *poison* there must be in you, Maestro."

Gentle turned and left the circle without responding, with Athanasius repeating his earlier advice to usher him on his way.

"Kill yourself soon, Maestro," he said. "For you, for Pie, for all of us. Kill yourself soon."

2

It took Gentle a quarter of an hour to make his way through the ravagement to open ground, hoping as he went that he'd find some vehicle—Floccus', perhaps—that he could commandeer for the return journey to Yzordderrex. If he found nothing, it would be a long trek on foot, but that would have to be the way of it. What little illumination the fires behind him proffered soon dwindled, and he was obliged to search by starlight, which would most probably have failed to show him the vehicle had his path not been redirected by the squeals of Floccus Dado's porcine pet Sighshy, who, along with her litter, was still inside. The car had been thrown over in the storm, and so he went to it simply to let the animals out, planning to go on to find another. But as he struggled with the handle a human face appeared at the steamed-up window. Floccus was inside and greeted Gentle's appearance with a clamor of relief almost as high-pitched as Sighshy's. Gentle clambered up onto the side of the car and after much swearing and sweating wrenched the door open with brute force.

"Oh, you're a sight to behold, Maestro," Floccus said. "I thought I was going to suffocate in there."

The stench was piercing, and it came with Floccus when he clambered out. His clothes were caked in the litter's excrement, and Mama's too.

"How the hell did you get in there?" Gentle asked him.

Floccus wiped a turd trail off his spectacles and blinked at his savior through them.

"When Athanasius told me to summon you, I thought, Something's wrong here, Dado. You'd better go while you can. I'd just got into the car when the storm started, and it was simply turned over, with all of us inside. The windows are unbreakable, and the locks were jammed. I couldn't get out."

"You were lucky to be in there."

"So I see," Floccus observed, surveying the distant vista of destruction. "What happened out here?"

"Something came out of the First, in pursuit of Pie 'oh' pah."

"The Unbeheld did this?"

"So it would seem."

"Unkind," Floccus said softly, which was surely the understatement of the night.

Floccus lifted Sighshy and her litter—two of which had perished when their mother fell on them—out of the vehicle; then he and Gentle set to the task of putting it back on four wheels. It took some doing, but Floccus made up in strength what he lacked in height, and between the two of them the job was done.

Gentle had made plain his intention to return to Yzordderrex but wasn't certain of Floccus' intentions until the engine was running. Then he said, "Are you coming with me?"

"I should stay," Floccus replied. There was a fretful pause. "But I've never been much good with death."

"You said the same thing about sex."

"It's true."

"That doesn't leave much, does it?"

"Would you prefer to go without me, Maestro?"

"Not at all. If you want to come, come. But let's get going. I want to be in Yzordderrex by dawn."

"Why, what happens at dawn?" Floccus said, a superstitious flutter in his voice.

"It's a new day."

"Should we be grateful for that?" the other man inquired, as though he sniffed some profound wisdom in the Maestro's reply but couldn't quite grasp it.

"Indeed we should, Floccus, indeed we should. For the day, and for the chance."

"What . . . er . . . what *chance* would that be exactly?"

"The chance to change the world."

"Ah," said Floccus. "Of course. To change the world. I'll make that my prayer from now on."

"We'll compose it together, Floccus. We've got to invent everything from now on: who we are, what we believe. There's been too many old roads taken. Too many old dramas repeated. We've got to find a new way by tomorrow."

"A new way."

"That's right. We'll make that our ambition, agreed? To be new men by the time the comet comes up."

Floccus' doubt was visible, even by starlight. "That doesn't give us very long," he observed.

True enough, Gentle thought. In the Fifth, midsummer could not be very far off, and though he didn't yet comprehend the reasons, he knew the Reconciliation could only be performed on that day. There was a fine irony. Having frittered away lifetimes in pursuit of sensation, the span he had left in which to make good the error of that waste could be measured in terms of hours.

"There'll be time," he said, hoping to answer Floccus' doubts, and subdue his own, but knowing in his heart of hearts that he was doing neither.

6

I

Jude was stirred from the torpor Quaisoir's narcotic bed had induced in her not by sound—she'd long since become accustomed to the anarchy that had raged unabated throughout the night—but by a sense of unease too vague to be identified and too insistent to be ignored. Something of consequence had happened in the Dominion, and though her wits were dulled by indulgence, she woke too agitated to return to the comfort of a scented pillow. Head throbbing, she heaved herself up out of the bed and went in search of her sister. Concupiscentia was at the door, with a sly smile on her face. Jude half remembered the creature slipping into one of her drugged dreams, but the details were hazy, and the foreboding she'd woken with was more important now than remembering the fantasies that had gone before. She found Quaisoir in a darkened room, sitting beside the window.

"Did something wake you, sister?" Quaisoir asked her.

"I don't quite know what, but yes. Do you know what it was?"

"Something in the desert," Quaisoir replied, turning her head towards the window, though she lacked the eyes to see what lay outside. "Something momentous."

"Is there any way of finding out what?"

Quaisoir took a deep breath. "No easy way."

"But there is one?"

"Yes, there's a place beneath the Pivot Tower . . ."

Concupiscentia had followed Judith into the room, but now, at the mention of this place, she made to withdraw. She was neither quiet nor fast enough, however. Quaisoir summoned her back.

"Don't be afraid," she told the creature. "We don't need you with us once we're inside. But fetch a lamp, will you? And something to eat and drink. We may be there awhile."

It was half a day and more since Jude and Quaisoir had taken refuge in the suite of chambers, and in that time any last occupants of the palace had made their escape, doubtless fearing the revolutionary zeal that would want the fortress cleansed of the Autarch's excesses down to the last bureaucrat. Those bureaucrats had fled, but the zealots hadn't appeared in their place. Though Jude had heard commotion in the courtyards as she'd dozed, it had never come close. Either the fury that had moved the tide was exhausted, and the insurgents were resting before they began their assault on the palace, or else their fervor had lost its singular purpose altogether, and the commotion she'd heard was factions battling with each other for the right to plunder, which conflicts had destroyed them all, left, right, and center. Whatever, the consequence was the same: a palace built to house many thousands of souls—servants, soldiers, pen pushers, cooks, stewards, messengers, torturers, and majordomos—was deserted, and they went through it, Jude led by Concupiscentia's lamp, Quaisoir led by Jude, like three tiny specks of life lost in a vast and dark machine. The only sounds were their footsteps, and those that said machine made as it ran down: hotwater pipes ticking as the furnaces that fed them guttered out; shutters beating themselves to splinters in empty rooms; guard dogs barking on gnawed leashes, fearful their masters would not come again. Nor would they. The furnaces would cool, the shutters break, and the dogs, trained to bring death, would have it come to them in their turn. The age of the Autarch Sartori was over, and no new age had yet begun.

As they walked Jude asked for an explanation of the place to which they were going, and by way of reply Quaisoir offered first a history of the Pivot. Of all the Autarch's devices to subdue and rule the Reconciled Dominions, she said—subverting the religions and governments of his enemies; setting nation against nation— none would have kept him in power for more than a decade had he not possessed the genius to steal and to set at the center of his empire the greatest symbol of power in the Imajica. The Pivot was Hapexamendios' marker, and the fact that the Unbeheld had allowed the architect of Yzordderrex to even touch, much less move, his pylon was for many proof that however much they might despise the Autarch, he was touched by divinity and could never be toppled. What powers it had conferred on its possessor even she didn't know.

"Sometimes," she said, "when he was high on kreauchee, he'd talk about the Pivot as though he was married to it, and he was the wife. Even when we made love he'd talk that way. He'd say it was in him the way he was in me. He'd always deny it afterward, of course, but it was in his mind always. It's in every man's mind."

Jude doubted this, and said so.

"But they so want to be *possessed*," Quaisoir replied. "They want some Holy Spirit inside them. You listen to their prayers."

"That's not something I hear very often."

"You will when the smoke clears," Quaisoir replied. "They'll be afraid, once they realize the Autarch's gone. They may have hated him, but they'll hate his absence more."

"If they're afraid they'll be dangerous," Jude said, realizing as she spoke how well these sentiments might have come from Clara Leash's mouth. "They won't be devout."

Concupiscentia halted, before Quaisoir could take up her account afresh, and began to murmur a little prayer of her own.

"Are we here?" Quaisoir asked.

The creature broke the rhythm of her entreaty to tell her mistress that they were. There was nothing remarkable about the door in front of them, or the staircases that wound out of sight to either side of it. All were monumental, and therefore commonplace. They'd passed through dozens of portals like this as they'd made their way through the place's cooling belly. But Concupiscentia was plainly in terror of it, or rather of what lay on the other side.

"Are we near the Pivot?" Jude said.

"The tower's directly above us," Quaisoir replied.

"That's not where we're going?"

"No. The Pivot would probably kill us both. But there's a chamber below the tower, where the messages the Pivot collects drain away. I've spied there often, though he never knew it."

Jude let go of Quaisoir's arm and went to the door, keeping to herself the irritation she felt at being denied the tower itself. She wanted to see this power, which had reputedly been shaped and planted by God Himself. Quaisoir had talked of it as lethal, and perhaps it was, but how was anyone to know until they'd tested themselves against it? Perhaps its reputation was the Autarch's invention, his way of keeping its gifts for himself. Under its aegis, he'd prospered, no doubt of that. What might others do, if they had its blessing conferred upon them? Turn night to day?

She turned the handle and pushed open the door. Sour and chilly air issued from the darkened space beyond. Jude summoned Concupiscentia to her side, took the lamp from the creature, and held it high. Ahead lay a small inclined corridor, its walls almost burnished.

"Do I wait here, lady?" Concupiscentia asked.

"Give me whatever you brought to eat," Quaisoir replied, "and stay outside the door. If you hear or see anybody, I want you to come and find us. I know you don't like to go in there, but you must be brave. Understand me, dearling?"

"I understand, lady," Concupiscentia replied, handing to her mistress the bundle and the bottle she'd carried with her.

Thus laden, Quaisoir took Jude's arm and they stepped into the passage. One part of the fortress's machine was still operational, it seemed, because as soon as they closed the door after them a circuit, broken as long as the door stood wide, was completed, and the air began to vibrate against their skin: vibrate and whisper.

"Here they are," Quaisoir said. "The intimations."

That was too civilized a word for this sound, Jude thought. The passageway was filled with a quiet commotion, like snatches from a thousand radio stations, all incomprehensible, coming and going as the dial was flipped, and flipped again. Jude raised the lamp to see how much farther they had to travel. The passageway ended ten yards ahead, but with every yard they covered the din increased—not in volume but in complexity—as new stations were added to the number the walls were already tuned into. None of it was music. There were multitudes of voices raised as a single sound, and there were solitary howls; there were sobs, and shouts, and words spoken like a recitation.

"What is this noise?" Jude asked.

"The Pivot hears every piece of magic in the Dominions. Every invocation, every confession, every dying oath. This is the Unbeheld's way of knowing what Gods are being worshiped besides Him. And what Goddesses, too."

"He spies on deathbeds?" Jude said, more than faintly disgusted by the thought.

"On every place where a mortal thing speaks to the divine, whether the divinity exists or not, whether the prayer's answered or not, He's there."

"Here, too?" Jude said.

"Not unless you start praying," Quaisoir said.

"I won't."

They were at the end of the passage, and the air was busier than ever; colder, too. The lamp's light illuminated a room shaped like a colander, maybe twenty feet across, its curved walls as polished as those of the passage. In the floor was a grille, like a gutter beneath a butcher's table, through which the detritus of prayers, ripped from the hearts of those in grief or washed up in tears of joy, ran off into the mountain upon which Yzordderrex was built. It was difficult for Jude to grasp the notion of prayer as a solid thing—a kind of matter to be gathered, analyzed, and sluiced away—but she knew her incomprehension was a consequence of living in a world out of love with transformation. There was nothing so solid that it couldn't be abstracted, nothing so ethereal that it couldn't find a place in the material world. Prayer might be substance after a time, and thought (which she'd believed skull-bound until the dream of the blue stone) fly like a bright-eyed bird, seeing the world remote from its sender; a flea might unravel flesh if wise to its code; and flesh in its turn move between worlds as a picture drawn in the mind of passage. All these mysteries were, she knew, part of a single system if she could only grasp it: one form becoming another, and another, and another, in a glorious tapestry of transformations, the sum of which was Being itself.

It was no accident that she embraced that possibility here. Though the sounds that filled the room were incomprehensible as yet, their purpose was known to her, and it raised the ambition of her thoughts. She let go of Quaisoir's arm and walked into the middle of the room, setting the lamp down beside the grille in the floor. They'd come here for a specific reason, and she knew she had to hold fast to that; otherwise her thoughts would be carried away on the swell of sound.

"How do we make sense of it?" she said to Quaisoir.

"It takes time," her sister replied. "Even for me. But I marked the compass points on the walls. Do you see?"

She did. Crude marks, scratched in the surface sheen.

"The Erasure is north-northwest of here. We can narrow the possibilities a little by turning in that direction." She extended her arms, like a haunting spirit. "Will you lead me to the middle?" she said.

Jude obliged, and they both turned in the direction of the Erasure. As far as Jude was concerned, doing so did little good. The din continued in all its complexity. But Quaisoir dropped her hands and listened intently, moving her head slightly from side to side as she did so. Several minutes passed, Jude keeping her silence for fear an inquiry would break her sister's concentration, and was rewarded for her diligence, finally, with some murmured words.

"They're praying to the Madonna," Quaisoir said.

"Who are?"

"Dearthers. Out at the Erasure. They're giving thanks for their deliverance and asking for the souls of the dead to be received into paradise."

She fell silent again for a time, and now, with some clue as to what she had to listen for, Jude attempted to sort through the intimations that filled her head. But although she was refining her focus, and could now snatch words and phrases out of the confusion, she couldn't hold that focus long enough to make any sense of what she heard. After a time Quaisoir's body relaxed, and she shrugged.

"There's just glimpses now," she said. "I think they're finding bodies. I hear little sobs of prayers and little oaths."

"Do you know what happened?"

"This was some time ago," Quaisoir said. "The Pivot's had these prayers for several hours. But it was something calamitous, that's certain," she said. "I think there are a lot of casualties."

"It's as if what happened in Yzordderrex is spreading," Jude said.

"Maybe it is," Quaisoir said. "Do you want to sit down and eat?"

"In here?"

"Why not? I find it very soothing." Reaching for Jude to help her, Quaisoir squatted down. "You get used to it after a time. Maybe a little addicted. Speaking of which . . . where's the food?" Jude put the bundle into Quaisoir's outstretched hands. "I hope the child packed kreauchee."

Her fingers were strong and, having scoured the surface of the bundle, dug deep, passing the contents over to Jude one by one. There was fruit, there were three loaves of black bread, there was some meat, and—the finding enough to bring a gleeful yelp from Quaisoir—a small parcel which she did not pass over to Jude but put to her nose.

"Bright thing," Quaisoir said. "She knows what I need."

"Is it some kind of drug?" Jude said, laying down the food. "I don't want you taking it. I need you here, not drifting off."

"Are you trying to forbid me my pleasure, after the way you dreamed on my pillows?" Quaisoir said. "Oh, yes, I heard your gasping and your groaning. Who were you imagining?"

"That's my business."

"And this is mine," Quaisoir replied, discarding the tissue in which Concupiscentia had fastidiously wrapped the kreauchee. It looked appetizing, like a cube of fudge. "When you've got no addiction of your own, sister, then you can moralize," Quaisoir said. "I won't listen, but you can moralize."

With that, she put the whole of the kreauchee into her mouth, chewing on it contentedly. Jude, meanwhile, sought more conventional sustenance, choosing among the various fruits one that resembled a diminutive pineapple and peeling it to discover it was just that, its juice tart but its meat tasty. That eaten, she went on to the bread and slivers of meat, her hunger so stimulated by the first few bites that she steadily devoured the lot, washing it down with bitter water from the bottle. The fall of prayers that had seemed so insistent when she'd first entered the chamber could not compete with the more immediate sensations of fruit, bread, meat, and water; the din became a background burble which she scarcely thought about until she'd finished her meal. By that time, the kreauchee was clearly working in Quaisoir's system. She was swaying back and forth as though in the arms of some invisible tide.

"Can you hear me?" Jude asked her.

She took awhile to reply. "Why don't you join me?" she said. "Kiss me, and we can share the kreauchee. Mouth to mouth. Mind to mind."

"I don't want to kiss you."

"Why not? Do you hate yourself too much to make love?" She smiled to herself, amused by the perverse logic of this. "Have you ever made love to a woman?"

"Not that I remember."

"I have. At the Bastion. It was better than being with a man."

She reached out towards Jude and found her hand with the accuracy of one sighted.

"You're cold," she said.

"No, you're hot," Jude replied, moving to break the contact.

"You know what air makes this place so cold, sister?" Quaisoir said. "It's the pit beneath the city, where the fake Redeemer went."

Jude looked down at the grille and shuddered. The dead were down there somewhere.

"You're cold like the dead are cold," Quaisoir went on. "Icy heart." All this she said in a singsong voice, to the rhythm of her rocking. "Poor sister. To be dead already."

"I don't want to hear any more of this," Jude said. She'd preserved her equanimity so far, but Quaisoir's fugue talk was beginning to irritate her. "If you don't stop," she said quietly, "I'm going to leave you here."

"Don't do that," Quaisoir replied. "I want you to stay and make love to me."

"I've told you—"

"Mouth to mouth. Mind to mind."

"You're talking in circles."

"That's the way the world was made," she said. "Joined together, round and round." She put her hand to her mouth, as if to cover it, then smiled, with almost fiendish glee. "There's no way in and there's no way out. That's what the Goddess says. When we make love, we go round and round—"

She searched for Jude a second time, with the same unerring ease, and a second time Jude withdrew her hand, realizing as she did so that this repetition was part of her sister's egocentric game. A sealed system of mirrored flesh, moving round and round. Was that truly how the world was made? If so, it sounded like a trap, and she wanted her mind out of it, there and then.

"I can't stay in here," she said to Quaisoir.

"You'll come back?" her sister replied.

"Yes, in a while."

The answer was more repetition. "You'll come back."

This time Jude didn't bother replying, but crossed to the passageway and climbed back up to the door. Concupiscentia was still waiting on the other side, asleep now, her form delineated by the first signs of dawn through the window on the sill of which she rested. The fact that day was breaking surprised Jude; she'd assumed that there were several hours yet before the comet reared its burning head. She was obviously more disoriented than she'd thought, the time she'd spent in the room with Quaisoir—

listening to the prayers, eating, and arguing—not minutes but hours. She went to the window and looked down at the dim court- yards. Birds stirred on a ledge somewhere below her and rose sud- denly, heading into the brightening sky, taking her eye with them, up towards the tower. Quaisoir had been unequivocal about the dangers of venturing there. But for all her talk of love between women, wasn't she still in thrall to the mythologies of the man who'd made her Queen of Yzordderrex, and therefore bound to believe that the places he kept her from would do her harm? There was no better time to challenge that mythology than now, Jude thought, with a new day beginning, and the power that had up- rooted the Pivot and raised such walls around it gone.

She went to the stairs and started to climb. After a few steps their curve took her into utter darkness, and she was obliged to ascend as blind as the sister she'd left below, her palm flat against the cold wall. But after maybe thirty stairs her outstretched arm encoun- tered a door, so heavy she first assumed it to be locked. It required all her strength to open, but her effort was well rewarded. On the other side was a passageway lighter than the staircase she'd climbed, though still gloomy enough to limit her sight to less than ten yards. Hugging the wall, she advanced with great caution, her route bringing her to the corner of a corridor, the door that had once sealed it off from the chamber at its end blown from its hinges and lying, fractured and twisted, on the tiled floor beyond. She paused here, in order to listen for any sign of the wrecker's pres- ence. There was none, so she moved on past the place, her gaze drawn to a flight of stairs that led up to her left. Forsaking the pas- sageway, she began a second ascent, this one also leading into darkness, until she rounded a corner and a sliver of light descended to meet her. Its source was the door at the summit of the stairs, which stood slightly ajar.

Again, she halted a moment. Though there was no overt indi- cation of power here—the atmosphere was almost tranquil—she knew that the force she'd come to confront was undoubtedly wait- ing in its silo at the top of the stairs, and more than likely sentient. She didn't discount the possibility that this hush was contrived to soothe her, and the light sent to coax. But if it wanted her up there, it must have a reason. And if it didn't—if it was as lifeless as the stone underfoot—she had nothing to lose.

"Let's see what you're made of," she said aloud, the challenge delivered at least as much to herself as the Unbeheld's Pivot. And so saying, she went to the door.

2

Though there were undoubtedly more direct routes to the Pivot Tower than the one he'd taken with Nikaetomaas, Gentle decided to go the way he half remembered rather than attempt a shortcut and find himself lost in the labyrinth. He parted company with Floccus Dado, Sighshy, and litter at the Gate of Saints and began his climb through the palace, checking on his position relative to the Pivot Tower from every window.

Dawn was in the offing. Birds rose singing from their nests beneath the colonnades and swooped over the courtyards, indifferent to the bitter smoke that passed for mist this morning. Another day was imminent, and his system was badly in need of sleep. He'd dozed a little on the journey from the Erasure, but the effect had been cosmetic. There was a fatigue in his marrow which would bring him to his knees very soon now, and the knowledge of that made him eager to complete the day's business as quickly as possible. He'd come back here for two reasons. First, to finish the task Pie's appearance and wounding had diverted him from: the pursuit and execution of Sartori. Second, whether he found his doppelgänger here or not, to make his way back to the Fifth, where Sartori had talked of founding his New Yzordderrex. It wouldn't be difficult to get home, he knew, now that he was alive to his capacities as a Maestro. Even without the mystif to point the way, he'd be able to dig from memory the means to pass between Dominions.

But first, Sartori. Though two days had passed since he'd let the Autarch slip, he nursed the hope that his other would still be haunting his palace. After all, removal from this self-made womb, where his smallest word had been law and his tiniest deed worshipful, would be painful. He'd linger awhile, surely. And if he was going to linger anywhere, it would be close to the object of power that had made him the undisputed master of the Reconciled Dominions: the Pivot.

He was just beginning to curse himself for losing his way when he came upon the spot where Pie had fallen. He recognized it instantly, as he did the distant door that led into the tower. He allowed himself a moment of meditation at the spot where he'd cradled Pie, but it wasn't their fond exchanges here that filled his head, it was the mystif's last words, uttered in anguish as the force behind the Erasure claimed it.

Sartori, Pie had said. *Find him . . . he knows. . . .*

Whatever knowledge Sartori possessed—and Gentle guessed it would concern plots laid against the Reconciliation—he, Gentle, was ready to do whatever was required in order to squeeze this information from his other before he delivered the coup de grace. There were no moral niceties here. If he had to break every bone in Sartori's body, it would be a little hurt set beside the crimes he'd committed as Autarch, and Gentle would perform such duties gladly.

Thought of torture, and the pleasure he'd take in it, had tempted him from his meditation entirely, and he gave up on his pursuit of equilibrium. Venom swilling in his belly, he headed down the corridor, through the door, and into the tower. Though the comet was climbing towards midmorning, very little of its light gained access to the tower, but those few beams that did creep in showed him empty passageways in all directions. He still advanced with caution; this was a maze of chambers, any one of which might conceal his enemy. Fatigue left him less light-footed than he'd have liked, but he reached the stairs that curled up towards the silo itself without his stumblings attracting any attention, and began to climb. The door at the top had been opened, he remembered, with the key of Sartori's thumb, and he'd have to repeat the feit himself in order to enter. That was no great challenge. They had the same thumbs, to the tiniest whorl.

As it was, he needed no feit. The door was open wide, and somebody was moving about inside. Gentle halted ten steps from the threshold and drew breath. He'd need to incapacitate his other quickly if he was to prevent retaliation: a pneuma to take off his right hand, another for his left. Breath readied, he climbed swiftly to the top of the stairs and stepped into the tower.

His enemy was standing beneath the Pivot, arms raised, reaching for the stone. He was all in shadow, but Gentle caught the motion of his head as he turned towards the door, and before the other could lower his arms in defense, Gentle had his fist to his mouth, the breath rising in his throat. As it filled his palm his enemy spoke, but the voice when it came was not his own, as he'd expected, but that of a woman. Realizing his error, he clamped his fist around the pneuma to quench it, but the power he'd unleashed wasn't about to be cheated of its quarry. It broke from between his fingers, its force fragmented but no less eager for that. The pieces flew off around the silo, some darting up the sides of the Pivot, others entering its shadow and extinguished there. The woman cried out in alarm and retreated from her attacker, backing against the opposite wall. There the light found her perfection. It was Judith; or at least it seemed to be. He'd seen this face in Yzordderrex once already and been mistaken.

"Gentle?" she said. "Is that you?"

It sounded like her, too. But then hadn't that been his promise to Roxborough, that he'd fashion a copy indistinguishable from the original?

"It's me," she said. "It's Jude."

Now he began to believe it was, for there was more proof in that last syllable than sight could ever supply. Nobody in her circle of admirers, besides Gentle, had ever called her Jude. Judy, sometimes; Juju, even; but never Jude. That was his diminution, and to his certain knowledge she'd never suffered another to use it.

He repeated it now, his hand dropping from his mouth as he spoke, and seeing the smile spread across his face she ventured back towards him, returning into the shadow of the Pivot as he came to meet her. The move saved her life. Seconds after she left the wall a slab of rock, blasted from the heights of the silo by the pneuma, fell on the spot where she'd stood. It initiated a hard, lethal rain, shards of stone falling on all sides. There was safety in the shelter of the Pivot, however, and there they met and kissed and embraced as though they'd been parted a lifetime, not weeks, which in a sense was true. The din of falling rock was muted in the shadow, though its thunder was only yards from where they stood. When she cupped his face in her hands and spoke, her whispers were quite audible; as were his.

"I've missed you," she said. There was a welcome warmth in her voice, after the days of anguish and accusation he'd heard. "I even dreamed about you. . . ."

"Tell me," he murmured, his lips close to hers.

"Later, maybe," she said, kissing him again. "I've so much to tell you."

"Likewise," Gentle said.

"We should find ourselves somewhere safer than this," she said.

"We're out of harm's way here," Gentle said.

"Yes, but for how long?"

The scale of the demolition was increasing, its violence out of all proportion to the force Gentle had unleashed, as though the Pivot had taken the pneuma's power and magnified it. Perhaps it knew—how could it not?—that the man it had been in thrall to had gone and was now about the business of shrugging off the prison Sartori had raised around it. Judging by the size of the slabs falling all around, the process would not take long. They were monumental, their impact sufficient to open cracks in the floor of the tower, the sight of which brought a cry of alarm from Jude.

"Oh, God, Quaisoir!" she said.

"What about her?"

"She's down there!" Jude said, staring at the gaping ground. "There's a chamber below this! She's in it!"

"She'll be out of there by now."

"No, she's high on kreauchee! We have to get down there!"

She left Gentle's side and crossed to the edge of their shelter, but before she could make a dash for the open door a new fall of rubble and dust obliterated the way ahead. It wasn't simply blocks of the tower that were falling now, Gentle saw. There were vast shards of the Pivot itself in this hail. What was it doing? Destroying itself, or shedding skins to uncover its core? Whichever, their place in the shadow was more precarious by the second. The cracks underfoot were already a foot wide and widening, the hovering monolith above them shuddering as if it was about to give up the effort of suspension and drop. They had no choice but to brave the rockfall.

He went to join Jude, searching his wits for a means to survival and picturing Chicka Jackeen at the Erasure, his hands high to ward off the detritus dropped by the storm. Could he do the same? Not giving himself pause to doubt, he lifted his hands above his head as he'd seen the monk do, palms up, and stepped out of the Pivot's shadow. One heavenward glance confirmed both the Pivot's shedding and the scale of his jeopardy. Though the dust was thick, he could see that the monolith was sloughing off scales of stone, the pieces large enough to smash them both to pulp. But his defense held. The slabs shattered two or three feet above his naked head, their smithereens dropping like a fleeting vault around him. IIe felt the impact nevertheless, as a succession of jolts through his wrists, arms, and shoulders, and knew he lacked the strength to preserve the feit for more than a few seconds. Jude had already grasped the method in her madness, however, and stepped from the shadow to join him beneath this flimsy shield. There were perhaps ten paces between where they stood and the safety of the door.

"Guide me," he told her, unwilling to take his eyes off the rain for fear his concentration slip and the feit lose its potency.

Jude slipped her arm around his waist and navigated for them both, telling him where to step to find clear ground and warning him when the path was so heavily strewn they were obliged to stumble over stone. It was a tortuous business, and Gentle's upturned hands were steadily beaten down until they were barely above his head, but the feit held to the door, and they slid through it together, with the Pivot and its prison throwing down such a hail of debris that neither was now visible.

Then Jude was off at speed, down the murky stairs. The walls were shaking, and laced with cracks as the demolition above took its toll below, but they negotiated both the trembling passageway and the second flight of stairs down to the lower level unharmed. Gentle was startled at the sight and sound of Concupiscentia, who was screeching in the passageway like a terrified ape, unwilling to go in search of her mistress. Jude had no such qualms. She'd already thrown open the door and was heading down an incline into a lamp-lit chamber beyond, calling Quaisoir's name to stir her from her stupor. Gentle followed, but was slowed by the cacophony that greeted him, a mingling of manic whispers and the din of capitulation from above. By the time he reached the room itself, Jude had bullied her sister to her feet. There were substantial cracks in the ceiling and a constant drizzle of dust, but Quaisoir seemed indifferent to the hazard.

"I said you'd come back," she said. "Didn't I? Didn't I say you'd come back? Do you want to kiss me? Please kiss me, sister."

"What's she talking about?" Gentle asked.

The sound of his voice brought a cry from the woman. She flung herself out of Jude's arms.

"What have you done?" she yelled. "Why did you bring *him* here?"

"He's come to help us," Jude replied.

Quaisoir spat in Gentle's direction. "Leave me alone!" she screeched. "Haven't you done enough? Now you want to take my sister from me! You bastard! I won't let you! We'll die before you touch her!" She reached for Jude, sobbing in panic. *"Sister! Sister!"*

"Don't be frightened," Jude said. "He's a friend." She looked at Gentle. "Reassure her," she begged him. "Tell her who you are, so we can get out of here."

"I'm afraid she already knows," Gentle replied.

Jude was mouthing the word *what?* when Quaisoir's panic boiled up again.

"Sartori!" she screeched, her denunciation echoing around the room. "He's Sartori, sister! Sartori!"

Gentle raised his hands in mock surrender, backing away from the woman. "I'm not going to touch you," he said. "Tell her, Jude. I don't want to hurt her!"

But Quaisoir was in the throes of another outburst. "Stay with me, sister," she said, grabbing hold of Jude. "He can't kill us both!"

"You can't stay in here," Jude said.

"I'm not going out!" Quaisoir said. "He's got soldiers out there! Rosengarten! That's who he's got! And his torturers!"

"It's safer out there than it is in here," Jude said, casting her eyes up at the roof. Several carbuncles had appeared in it, oozing debris. "We have to be quick!"

Still she refused, putting her hand up to Jude's face and stroking her cheek with her clammy palm: short, nervy strokes.

"We'll stay here together," she said. "Mouth to mouth. Mind to mind."

"We can't," Jude told her, speaking as calmly as circumstance allowed. "I don't want to be buried alive, and neither do you."

"If we die, we die," said Quaisoir. "I don't want him touching me again, do you hear?"

"I know. I understand."

"Not ever! Not ever!"

"He won't," Jude said, laying her own hand over Quaisoir's, which was still stroking her face. She laced her fingers through those of her sister and locked them. "He's gone," she said. "He won't be coming near either of us again."

Gentle had indeed retreated as far as the passageway, but even though Jude waved him away he refused to go any further. He'd had too many reunions cut short to risk letting her out of his sight.

"Are you certain he's gone?"

"I'm certain."

"He could still be waiting outside for us."

"No, sister. He was afraid for his life. He's fled."

Quaisoir grinned at this. "He was afraid?" she said.

"Terrified."

"Didn't I tell you? They're all the same. They talk like heroes, but there's piss in their veins." She began to laugh out loud, as careless now as she'd been in terror moments before. "We'll go back to my bedroom," she said when the outburst subsided, "and sleep for a while."

"Whatever you want to do," Jude said. "But let's do it soon."

Still chuckling to herself, Quaisoir allowed Jude to lift her up and escort her towards the door. They had covered maybe half that distance, Gentle standing aside to let them pass, when one of the carbuncles in the ceiling burst and threw down a rain of wreckage from the tower above. Gentle saw Jude struck and felled by a chunk of stone; then the chamber filled with an almost viscous dust that blotted out both sisters in an instant. With his only point of reference the lamp, the flame of which was just visible through the dirt, he headed into the fog to fetch her, as a thundering from above announced a further escalation of the tower's collapse. There was no time for protective feits or for keeping his silence. If he failed to find her in the next few seconds, they'd all be buried. He started to yell her name through the rising roar and, hearing her call back to him, followed her voice to where she was lying, half buried beneath a cairn of rubble.

"There's time," he said to her as he began to dig. "There's time. We can make it out."

With her arms unpinned she began to speed her own excavation, hauling herself up out of the debris and locking her arms around Gentle's neck. He started to stand, pulling her free of the remaining rocks, but as he did so another commotion began, louder

than anything that had preceded it. This was not the din of destruction but a shriek of white fury. The dust above their heads
parted, and Quaisoir appeared, floating inches from the fissured
ceiling. Jude had seen this transformation before—ribbons of flesh
unfurled from her sister's back and bearing her up—but Gentle
had not. He gaped at the apparition, distracted from thoughts of
escape.

"*She's mine!*" Quaisoir yelled, swooping towards them with the
same sightless but unerring accuracy she'd possessed in more intimate moments, her arms outstretched, her fingers ready to twist
the abductor's head from his neck.

But Jude was quick. She stepped in front of Gentle, calling
Quaisoir's name. The woman's swoop faltered, the hungry hands
inches from her sister's upturned face.

"I don't belong to you!" she yelled back at Quaisoir. "I don't belong to *anybody!* Hear me?"

Quaisoir threw back her head and loosed a howl of rage at this.
It was her undoing. The ceiling shuddered and abandoned its duty
at her din, collapsing beneath the weight of rubble heaped behind
it. There was, Jude thought, time for Quaisoir to escape the consequences of her cry. She'd seen the woman move like lightning at
Pale Hill, when she had the will to do so. But that will had gone.
Face to the killing dirt, she let the debris rain upon her, inviting it
with her unbroken cry, which didn't become alarm or plea, but remained a solid howl of fury until the rocks broke and buried her.
It wasn't quick. She went on calling down destruction as Gentle
took Jude's hand and hauled her away from the spot. He'd lost all
sense of direction in the chaos, and had it not been for the screeching of Concupiscentia in the passageway beyond they'd never have
made it to the door.

But make it they did, emerging with half their senses deadened
by dust. Quaisoir's death cry had ceased by now, but the roar behind them was louder than ever and drove them from the door as
the canker spread across the roof of the corridor. They outran it,
however, Concupiscentia giving up her keening when she knew her
mistress was lost and overtaking them, fleeing to some sanctuary
where she could raise a song of lamentation.

Jude and Gentle ran until they were out from under any stone,
roof, arch, or vault that might collapse upon them, into a courtyard
full of bees feasting on bushes that had chosen that day, of all days,
to blossom. Only then did they put their arms around each other
again, each sobbing for private griefs and gratitudes, while the
ground shook under them to the din of the demolition they'd escaped.

3

In fact the ground didn't stop reverberating until they were well outside the walls of the palace and wandering in the ruins of Yzordderrex. At Jude's suggestion they made their way back at all speed to Peccable's house, where, she explained to Gentle, there was a well-used route between this Dominion and the Fifth. He put up no resistance to this. Though he hadn't exhausted Sartori's hiding places by any means (could he ever, when the palace was so vast?) he *had* exhausted his limbs, his wits, and his will. If his other was still here in Yzordderrex, he posed very little threat. It was the Fifth that needed to be defended against him: the Fifth, which had forgotten magic and could so easily be his victim.

Though the streets of many Kesparates were little more than bloody valleys between rubble mountains, there were sufficient landmarks for Jude to trace her way back towards the district where Peccable's house had stood. There was no certainty, of course, that it would still be standing after a day and a night of cataclysm, but if they had to dig to reach the cellar, so be it.

They were silent for the first mile or so of the trek, but then they began to talk, begining—inevitably—with an explanation from Gentle as to why Quaisoir, hearing his voice, had taken him for her husband. He prefaced his account with the caveat that he wouldn't mire it in apology or justification but would tell it simply, like some grim fable. Then he went on to do precisely that. But the telling, for all its clarity, contained one significant distortion. When he described his encounter with the Autarch he drew in Jude's mind the portrait of a man to whom he bore only a rudimentary resemblance, a man so steeped in evil that his flesh had been corrupted by his crimes. She didn't question this description, but pictured an individual whose inhumanity seeped from every pore, a monster whose very presence would have induced nausea.

Once he'd unraveled the story of his doubling, she began to supply details of her own. Some were culled from dreams, some from clues she'd had from Quaisoir, yet others from Oscar Godolphin. His entrance into the account brought with it a fresh cycle of revelations. She started to tell Gentle about her romance with Oscar, which in turn led on to the subject of Dowd, living and dying; thence to Clara Leash and the Tabula Rasa.

"They're going to make it very dangerous for you back in London," she told him, having related what little she knew about the purges they'd undertaken in the name of Roxborough's edicts. "They won't have the slightest compunction about murdering you, once they know who you are."

"Let them try," Gentle said flatly. "Whatever they want to throw at me, I'm ready. I've got work to do, and they're not going to stop me."

"Where will you start?"

"In Clerkenwell. I had a house in Gamut Street. Pie says it's still standing. My life's there, ready for the remembering. We both need the past back, Jude."

"Where do I get mine from?" she wondered aloud.

"From me and from Godolphin."

"Thanks for the offer, but I'd like a less partial source. I've lost Clara, and now Quaisoir. I'll have to start looking." She thought of Celestine as she spoke, lying in darkness beneath the Tabula Rasa's tower.

"Have you got somebody in mind?" Gentle asked.

"Maybe," she said, as reluctant as ever to share that secret.

He caught the whiff of evasion. "I'm going to need help, Jude," he said. "I hope, whatever's been between us in the past—good and bad—we can find some way to work together that'll benefit us both."

A welcome sentiment, but not one she was willing to open her heart for. She simply said, "Let's hope so," and left it at that.

He didn't press the issue, but turned the conversation to lighter matters. "What was the dream you had?" he asked her. She looked confounded for a moment. "You said you had a dream about me, remember?"

"Oh, yes," she replied. "It was nothing, really. Past history."

When they reached Peccable's house it was still intact, though several others in the street had been reduced to blackened rubble by missiles or arsonists. The door stood open, and the interior had been comprehensively looted, down to the tulips and the vase on the dining room table. There was no sign of bloodshed, however, except those scabby stains Dowd had left when he'd first arrived, so she presumed that Hoi-Polloi and her father had escaped unharmed. The signs of frantic thieving did not extend to the cellar. Here, though the shelves had been cleared of the icons, talismans, and idols, the removal had been made calmly and systematically. There was not a rosary remaining, or any sign that the thieves had broken a single charm. The only relic of the cellar's life as a trove was set in the floor: the ring of stones that echoed that of the Retreat.

"This is where we arrived," Jude said.

Gentle stared down at the design in the floor. "What is it?" he said. "What does it mean?"

"I don't know. Does it matter? As long as it gets us back to the Fifth—"

"We've got to be careful from now on," Gentle replied. "Everything's connected. It's all one system. Until we understand our place in the pecking order, we're vulnerable."

One system; she'd speculated on that possibility in the room beneath the tower: the Imajica as a single, infinitely elaborate pattern of transformation. But just as there were times for such musings, so there were also times for action, and she had no patience with Gentle's anxieties now.

"If you know another way out of here," she said, "let's take it. But this is the only way I know. Godolphin used it for years and it never harmed him, till Dowd screwed it up."

Gentle had gone down on his haunches and was laying his fingers on the stones that bound the mosaic.

"Circles are so powerful," he said.

"Are we going to use it or not?"

He shrugged. "I don't have a better way," he said, still reluctant. "Do we just step inside?"

"That's all."

He rose. She laid her hand on his shoulder, and he reached up to clasp it.

"We have to hold tight," she said. "I only got a glimpse of the In Ovo, but I wouldn't want to get lost there."

"We won't get lost," he said, and stepped into the circle.

She was with him a heartbeat later, and already the Express was getting up steam. The solid cellar walls and empty shelves began to blur. The forms of their translated selves began to move in their flesh.

The sensation of passage awoke in Gentle memories of the outward journey, when Pie 'oh' pah had stood beside him where Jude was now. Remembering, he felt a stab of inconsolable loss. There were so many people he'd encountered in these Dominions whom he'd never set eyes on again. Some, like Efreet Splendid and his mother, Nikaetomaas, and Huzzah, because they were dead. Others, like Athanasius, because the crimes Sartori had committed were *his* crimes now, and whatever good he hoped to do in the future would never be enough to expunge them. The hurt of these losses was of course negligible beside the greater grief he'd sustained at the Erasure, but he'd not dared dwell too much upon that, for fear it incapacitated him. Now, however, he thought of it, and the tears started to flow, washing the last glimpse of Peccable's cellar away before the mosaic had removed the travelers from it.

Paradoxically, had he been leaving alone the despair might not have cut so deep. But as Pie had been fond of saying, there was only ever room for three players in any drama, and the woman in the flux beside him, her glyph burning through his tears, would from this moment on remind him that he had departed Yzordderrex with one of those three left behind.

7

I

One hundred and fifty-seven days after beginning his journey across the Reconciled Dominions, Gentle once again set foot on the soil of England. Though it wasn't yet the middle of June, spring had arrived prematurely, and the season on its heels was at its height. Flowers not due to blossom for another month were already blowsy and heavy-headed with seeds; bird and insect life abounded, as species that normally appeared months apart flourished simultaneously. This summer's dawns were announced not with choruses but with full-throated choirs; by midday the skies from coast to coast were cloudy with feeding millions, the wheels slowing through the afternoon, until by dusk the din had become a music (sated and survivors alike giving thanks for the day) so rich it lulled even the crazy into remedial sleep. If a Reconciliation could indeed be planned and achieved in the little time before midsummer, then it would be burgeoning country that the rest of the Imajica would greet: an England of bountiful harvests, spread beneath a melodious heaven.

It was full of music now, as Gentle wandered from the Retreat out across the dappled grass to the perimeter of the copse. The parkland was familiar to him, though its lovingly tended arbors were jungles now, and its lawns were veldt.

"This is Joshua's place, isn't it?" he said to Jude. "Which way's the house?"

She pointed across a wilderness of gilded grass. The roof of the mansion was barely visible above the surf of fronds and butterflies.

"The very first time I saw you was in that house," he told her, "I remember ... Joshua called you down the stairs. He had a pet name you despised. Peachblossom, was it? Something like that. As soon as I set eyes on you—"

"It wasn't me," Jude said, halting this romantic reverie. "It was Quaisoir."

"Whatever she was then, you are now."

"I doubt that. It was a long time ago, Gentle. The house is in ruins, and there's only one Godolphin left. History isn't going to repeat itself. I don't want it to. I don't want to be anybody's object."

He acknowledged the warning in these words with an almost formal statement of intent.

"Whatever I did that caused you or anybody else harm," he said, "I want to make good. Whether I did it because I was in love, or because I was a Maestro and I thought I was above common decency. . . . I'm here to heal the hurt. I want Reconciliation, Jude. Between us. Between the Dominions. Between the living and the dead if I can do it."

"That's a hell of an ambition."

"The way I see it, I've been given a second chance. Most people don't get that."

His plain sincerity mellowed her. "Do you want to wander to the house, for old time's sake?" she asked him.

"Not unless you do."

"No, thanks. I had my little fit of déjà vu when I convinced Charlie to bring me here."

Gentle had of course told her about his encounter with Estabrook in the Dearthers' tents and about the man's subsequent demise. She'd been unmoved.

"He was a difficult old bugger, you know," she now remarked. "I must have known in my gut he was a Godolphin, or I'd never have put up with his damn fool games."

"I think he was changed by the end," Gentle said. "Maybe you'd have liked him a little more."

"You've changed, too," she said, as they started to wander towards the gate. "People are going to be asking a lot of questions, Gentle. Like: Where have you been and what have you been doing?"

"Why does anybody even have to know I'm back?" he said. "I never meant that much to any of them, except Taylor, and he's gone."

"Clem, too."

"Maybe."

"It's your choice," she said. "But when you've got so many enemies, you may need some of your friends."

"I'd prefer to stay invisible," he told her. "That way nobody sees me, enemies *or* friends."

As the bounding wall came in sight the skies changed with almost eerie haste, the few fluffy clouds that minutes before had been drifting in the blue now congregating into a lowering bank that first shed a light drizzle and a minute later was bursting like a dam. The downpour had its advantages, however, sluicing from their clothes, hair, and skin all trace of Yzordderrexian dust. By the time they'd clambered through the mesh of timbers and convolvulus around the gate and trudged along the muddied road to the village—there to take shelter in the post office—they could have passed for two tourists (one with a somewhat bizarre taste in hiking clothes) who'd strayed too far from the beaten track and needed help to find their way home.

2

Though neither of them had any valid currency in their pockets, Jude was quick to persuade one of two lads who stopped in the post office to drive them back into London, promising a healthy fee at the other end if he did so. The storm worsened as they traveled, but Gentle rolled down the window in the back and stared at the passing panorama of an England he hadn't seen for half a year, content to let the rain soak him all over again.

Jude was meanwhile left to endure a monologue from their driver. He had a mutinous palate, which rendered every third word virtually unintelligible, but the gist of his chatter was plain enough. It was the opinion of every weather watcher he knew, he said, and these were folk who lived by the land and had ways of predicting floods and droughts no fancy-talking meteorologist ever had, that the country was in for a disastrous summer.

"We'll either be cooked or drowned," he said, prophesying months of monsoons and heatwaves.

She'd heard talk like this before, of course; the weather was an English obsession. But having come from the ruins of Yzordderrex, with the burning eye of the comet overhead and the air stinking of death, the youth's casually apocalyptic chatter disturbed her. It was as if he was willing some cataclysm to overtake his little world, not comprehending for a moment what that implied.

When he grew bored with predicting ruination, he started to ask her questions about where she and her friend had been coming from or going to when the storm had caught them. She saw no reason not to tell him they'd been at the estate, so she did so. Her reply earned her what studied disinterest had failed to achieve for three quarters of an hour: his silence. He gave her a baleful look in the mirror and then turned on the radio, proving, if nothing else, that the shadow of the Godolphin family was sufficient to hush even a doomsayer. They traveled to the outskirts of London without further exchange, the youth only breaking the silence when he needed directions.

"Do you want to be dropped at the studio?" she asked Gentle.

He was slow to answer, but when he did it was to reply that, yes, that's where he wanted to go. Jude furnished instructions to the driver and then turned her gaze back towards Gentle. He was still staring out the window, rain speckling his brow and cheeks like sweat, drops hanging off his nose, chin, and eyelashes. The smallest of smiles curled the corners of his mouth. Catching him unawares like this, she almost regretted her dismissal of his overtures at the estate. This face, for all that the mind behind it had done, was the face that had appeared to her while she slept in Quaisoir's bed: the dream lover whose imagined caresses had brought from her cries so loud her sister had heard them two rooms away. Certainly, they could never again be the lovers who'd courted in the great house two centuries before. But their shared history marked them in ways they had yet to discover, and perhaps when those discoveries were all made they'd find a way to put into flesh the deeds she dreamed in Quaisoir's bed.

The rainstorm had preceded them to the city, unleashed its torrent, and moved off, so that by the time they reached the outskirts there was sufficient blue sky overhead to promise a warm, if glistening, evening. The traffic was still clogged, however, and the last three miles of the journey took almost as long as the previous thirty. By the time they reached Gentle's studio their driver, used to the quiet roads around the estate, was out of sympathy with the whole endeavor and had several times broken his silence to curse the traffic and warn his passengers that he was going to require very considerable recompense for his troubles.

Jude got out of the car along with Gentle and on the studio step—out of the driver's earshot—asked him if he had enough money inside to pay the man. She would rather take a taxi from here, she said, than endure his company any longer. Gentle replied that if there was any cash in the studio, it certainly wouldn't be sufficient.

"It looks like I'm stuck with him then," Jude said. "Never mind. Do you want me to come up with you? Have you got a key?"

"There'll be somebody in downstairs," he replied. "They've got a spare."

"Then I suppose this is it." It was so bathetic, parting like this after all that had gone before. "I'll ring you when we've both slept."

"The phone's probably been cut off."

"Then ring me from a box, huh? I won't be at Oscar's, I'll be at home."

The conversation might have guttered out there, but for his reply.

"Don't stay away from him on my account," he said.

"What do you mean by that?"

"Just that you've got your love affairs," he said.

"And what? You've got yours?"

"Not exactly."

"What then?"

"I mean, not exactly love affairs." He shook his head. "Never mind. We'll talk about it some other time."

"No," Jude told him, taking his arm as he tried to turn from her. "We'll talk about it now."

Gentle sighed wearily. "Look, it doesn't matter," he said.

"If it doesn't matter, just tell me."

He hesitated for several seconds. Then he said, "I got married."

"Did you indeed?" she said, with feigned lightness. "And who's the lucky girl? Not the kid you were talking about?"

"Huzzah? Good God, no."

He paused for a tiny time, frowning deeply.

"Go on," she said. "Spit it out."

"I married Pie 'oh' pah."

Her first impulse was to laugh—the thought was absurd—but before the sound escaped her she caught the frown on his face and revulsion overtook laughter. This was no joke. He'd married the assassin, the sexless thing who was a function of its lover's every desire. And why was she so stunned? When Oscar had described the species to her, hadn't she herself remarked that it was Gentle's idea of paradise?

"That's some secret," she said.

"I would have told you about it sooner or later."

Now she allowed herself a little laughter, soft and sour. "Back there you almost had me believing there was something between us."

"That's because there was," he replied. "Because there always will be."

"Why should that matter to you now?"

"I have to hold on to a little of what I was. What I dreamed."

"And what did you dream?"

"That the three of us—" He stopped, sighing. Then: "That the three of us would find some way to be together." He wasn't looking at her but at the empty ground between them, where he'd clearly wanted his beloved Pie to stand. "The mystif would have learned to love you," he said.

"I don't want to hear this," she snapped.

"It would have been anything you desired. *Anything.*"

"Stop," she told him. "Just *stop.*"

He shrugged. "It's all right," he said. "Pie's dead. And we're going our different ways. It was just some stupid dream I had. I thought you'd want to know it, that's all."

"I don't want anything from you," she replied coldly. "You can keep your lunacies to yourself from now on!"

She'd long since let go of his arm, leaving him to retreat up the steps. But he didn't go. He simply stood watching her, squinting like a drunkard trying to hook one thought to another. It was she who retreated, shaking her head as she turned her back on him and crossed the puddled pavement to the car. Once in, the door slammed, she told the driver to get going, and the car sped from the curb.

On the step Gentle watched the corner where the car turned long after the vehicle had gone from sight, as though some words of peace might yet come to his lips and be carried from them to call her back. But he was out of persuasions. Though he'd returned to his place as a Reconciler, he knew he'd here opened a wound he lacked the gift to heal, at least until he'd slept and recovered his faculties.

3

Forty-five minutes after she'd left Gentle on his doorstep, Jude was throwing open the windows of her house to let in the late-afternoon sun and some fresh air. The journey from the studio had passed with her scarcely being aware of the fact, so stunned had she been by Gentle's revelation. Married! The thought was absurd, except that she couldn't find it in herself to be amused.

Though it was now many weeks since she'd occupied the house (all but the hardiest of her plants had died from loneliness, and she'd forgotten how the percolator and the locks on the windows worked), it was still a place she felt at home in, and by the time she'd downed a couple of cups of coffee, showered, and changed into some clean clothes, the Dominion from which she'd stepped only hours before was receding. In the presence of so many familiar sights and smells the strangeness of Yzordderrex wasn't its strength but its frailty. Without invitation, her mind had already drawn a line between the place she'd left and the one which she was now in, as solid as the division between a thing dreamt and a thing lived. No wonder Oscar had made a ritual of going up to his treasure room, she thought, and communing with his collection. It was a way of holding on to a perception that was under constant siege by the commonplace.

With several jolts of coffee buzzing around her bloodstream, the fatigue she'd felt on the journey back into the city had disappeared, so she decided to use the evening to visit Oscar's house. She'd called him several times since she'd got back, but the fact that nobody had answered was not, she knew, proof of his absence or demise. He'd seldom picked up the telephone in the house—that duty had fallen to Dowd—and more than once he'd stated his abhorrence of the machines. In paradise, he'd once said, the common blessed use telegrams and the saints have talking doves; all the telephones are down below.

She left the house at seven or so, caught a cab, and went to Regent's Park Road. She found the house securely locked, without so much as a window standing ajar, which on such a clement evening surely meant there was nobody home. Just to be sure, she went around to the rear of the house and peered in. At the sight of her, the three parrots Oscar kept in the back room rose from their perches in alarm. Nor did they settle, but squawked on in panic as she cupped her hands over her brow and peered in to see if their seed and water bowls were full. Though their perches were too far from the window for her to see, their level of agitation was enough to make her fear the worst. Oscar, she suspected, hadn't soothed their feathers in a long time. So where was he? Back at the estate, lying dead in the long grass? If so, it would be folly to go back there now and look for him, with darkness an hour away at most. Besides, when she thought back to her last glimpse of him, she was reasonably certain she'd seen him rising to his feet, framed against the door. He was robust, despite his excesses. She couldn't believe he was dead. In hiding, more like: concealing himself from the Tabula Rasa. With that thought in mind she returned to the front door and scribbled an anonymous note, telling him she was alive and well, and slipped it into the letter box. He'd know who'd penned it. Who else would write that the Express had brought her home, safe and sound?

A little after ten-thirty she was preparing for bed when she heard somebody calling her name from the street. She went to the balcony and looked out to see Clem standing on the pavement below, hollering for all he was worth. It was many months since they'd spoken, and her pleasure at the sight of him was tinged with guilt at her neglect. But from the relief in his voice at her appearance, and the fervor of his hug, she knew he hadn't come to squeeze apologies out of her. He needed to tell her something extraordinary, he said, but before he did (she'd think he was crazy, he warned), he needed a drink. Could she get him a brandy?

She could and did.

He fairly guzzled it, then said, "Where's Gentle?"

The question, and his demanding tone, caught her off guard, and she floundered. Gentle wanted to be invisible, and furious as she was with him, she felt obliged to respect that wish. But Clem needed to know badly.

"He's been away, hasn't he? Klein told me he tried calling, but the phone was cut off. Then he wrote Gentle a letter, and it was never answered—"

"Yes," Jude said. "I believe he's been away."

"But he just came back."

"Did he?" she replied, more puzzled by the moment. "Maybe you know better than I do."

"Not me," he said, pouring himself another brandy. "Taylor."

"Taylor? What are you talking about?"

Clem downed the liquor. "You're going to say I'm crazy, but hear me out, will you?"

"I'm listening."

"I haven't been sentimental about losing him. I haven't sat at home reading his love letters and listening to the songs we danced to. I've tried to get out and be useful for a change. But I have left his room the way it was. I couldn't bring myself to go through his clothes or even strip the bed. I kept putting it off. And the more I didn't do it, the more impossible it seemed to be. Then tonight, I came in just after eight, and I heard somebody talking."

Every particle of Clem's body but his lips was still as he spoke, transfixed by the memory.

"I thought I'd left the radio on, but no, no, I realized it was coming from upstairs, from his bedroom. It was *him*, Judy, talking clear as day, calling me up the way he used to. I was so afraid I almost fled. Stupid, isn't it? There I was, praying and praying for some sign he was in God's hands, and as soon as it came I practically shat myself. I tell you, I was half an hour on the stairs, hoping he'd stop calling me. And sometimes he did for a while, and I'd half convince myself I'd imagined it. Then he'd start again. Nothing melodramatic. Just him trying to persuade me not to be afraid and come up and say hello. So, eventually, that's what I did."

His eyes were filling with tears, but there was no grief in his voice.

"He liked that room in the evening. The sun fills it up. That's what it was like tonight: full of sun. And he was there, in the light. I couldn't see him but I knew he was next to me because he said so. He told me I looked well. Then he said, 'It's a glad day, Clem. Gentle came back, and he's got the answers.' "

"What answers?" Jude said.

"That's what I asked him. I said, 'What answers, Tay?' But you know Tay when he's happy. He gets delirious, like a child." Clem spoke with a smile, his gaze on sights remembered from better days. "He was so full of the fact that Gentle was back, I couldn't get much more from him."

Clem looked up at Jude.

"The light was going," he said. "And I think he wanted to go with it. He said that it was our duty to help Gentle. That was why he was showing himself to me this way. It wasn't easy, he said. But then neither was being a guardian angel. And I said, Why only one? One angel when there's two of us? And he said, Because we *are* one, Clem, you and I. We always were, and we always will be. Those were his exact words, I swear. Then he went away. And you know what I kept thinking?"

"What?"

"That I wished I hadn't waited on the stairs and wasted all that time I could have had with him." Clem set down his glass, pulled a tissue from his pocket, and blew his nose. "That's all," he said.

"I think that's plenty."

"I know what you're thinking," he said with a little laugh. "You're thinking, Poor Clem. He couldn't grieve so he's having hallucinations."

"No," she said, very softly. "I'm thinking, Gentle doesn't know how lucky he is, having angels like you two."

"Don't humor me."

"I'm not," she said. "I believe everything you've just told me happened."

"You do?"

"Yes."

Again, a laugh. "Why?"

"Because Gentle came home tonight, Clem, and I was the only one who knew it."

He left ten minutes later, apparently content to know that even if he was crazy there was another lunatic in his circle he could turn to when he wanted to share his insanities. Jude told him as much as she felt able at this juncture, which was very little, but she promised to contact Gentle on Clem's behalf and tell him about Taylor's visitation. Clem wasn't so grateful that he was blinded to her discretion.

"You know a lot more than you're telling me, don't you?" he said.

"Yes," she said. "But maybe in a little while I'll be able to tell you more."

"Is Gentle in danger?" Clem asked. "Can you tell me that at least?"

"We all are," she said. "You. Me. Gentle. Taylor."

"Taylor's dead," Clem said. "He's in the light. Nothing can hurt him."

"I hope you're right," she said grimly. "But please, Clem, if he finds you again—"

"He will."

"—then when he does, tell him nobody's safe. Just because Gentle's back in the—back home doesn't mean the troubles are over. In fact, they're just beginning."

"Tay says something sublime's going to happen. That's his word: sublime."

"And maybe it will. But there's a lot of room for error. And if anything goes wrong—" She halted, her head filled with memories of the In Ovo and the ruins of Yzordderrex.

"Well, whenever you feel you can tell me," Clem said, "we'll be ready to hear. Both of us." He glanced at his watch. "I should be out of here. I'm late."

"Party?"

"No, I'm working with a hospice for the homeless. We're out most nights, trying to get kids off the streets. The city's full of them." She took him to the door, but before he stepped out he said, "You remember our pagan party at Christmas?"

She grinned. "Of course. That was quite a shindig."

"Tay got stinking drunk after everybody had gone. He knew he wasn't going to be seeing most of them again. Then of course he got sick in the middle of the night, so we stayed up together talking about—oh, I don't know, everything under the sun. And he told me how much he'd always loved Gentle. How Gentle was the mystery man in his life. He'd been dreaming about him, he said: speaking in tongues."

"He told me the same thing," Jude said.

"Then, out of the blue, he said that next year I should have the Nativity back, and go to Midnight Mass the way we used to, and I told him I thought we'd decided none of that made much sense. And you know what he said to me? He said light was light, whatever name you call it, and it was better to think of it coming in a face you knew." Clem smiled. "I thought he was talking about Christ. But now . . . now I'm not so sure."

She hugged him hard, pressing her lips against his flushed cheek. Though she suspected that there was truth in what he said, she couldn't bring herself to voice the possibility. Not knowing that the same face Tay had imagined as that of the returning sun was also the face of the darkness that might soon eclipse them all.

I

Though the bed Gentle had collapsed into the night before had been stale, and the pillow beneath his head damp, he couldn't have slept more soundly had he been rocked in the arms of Mother Earth Herself. When he woke, fifteen hours later, it was to a fine

June morning, and the dreamless time behind him had put new strength into his sinews. There was no gas, electricity, or hot water, so he was obliged to shower and shave in cold water, which was respectively a bracing and a bloody experience. That done, he took some time to assess the state of the studio. It had not remained entirely untouched in his absence. At some juncture either an old girlfriend or a very particular thief had come in—he'd left two of the windows open, so gaining access had presented no difficulty—and the interloper had stolen both clothes and more private bric-a-brac. It was such a long time since he'd been here, however, that he couldn't remember precisely what was missing: some letters and postcards from the mantelpiece, a few photographs (though he'd not liked to be recorded this way, for what were now obvious reasons), and a few items of jewelry (a gold chain; two rings; a crucifix). The theft didn't much bother him. He'd never been a sentimentalist or a hoarder. Objects were like glossy magazines: fetching for a day, then readily discarded.

There were other, more disgusting, signs of his absence in the bathroom, where clothes he'd left to dry before his departure had grown green fur, and in the refrigerator, the shelves of which were scattered with what looked like pupating zarzi, stinking of putrefaction. Before he could really begin to clean up he had to have some power in the house, and to get it would require some politicking. He'd had the gas, telephone, and electricity cut off in the past, when, in the lean times between forgeries and sugar mamas, he'd run out of funds. But he had the patter to get them turned back on again well honed, and that had to be the priority of the hour.

He dressed in the freshest of his clothes and went downstairs to present himself to the venerable but dotty Mrs. Erskine, who occupied the ground-floor flat. It was she who'd let him in the day before, remarking with her characteristic candor that he looked as though he'd been kicked half to death, to which he'd replied that he felt the same way. She didn't question his absence, which was not surprising given that his occupation of the studio had always been sporadic, but she did ask him if he was going to be staying awhile this time. He said he thought so, and she replied that she was pleased at this, because during these summer days people always got crazy, and since Mr. Erskine's death she was sometimes frightened.

She made tea while he availed himself of her telephone, calling around the services he'd lost. It turned out to be a frustrating business. He'd lost the knack of charming the women he spoke to into some action on his behalf. Instead of an exchange of

flatteries he was served a chilly salad of officiousness and condescension. He had unpaid bills, he was told, and his supplies would
not be reconnected until payment was forthcoming. He ate some
toast Mrs. Erskine had made, drank several cups of tea, then went
down into the basement and left a note for the caretaker that he
was now back in residence and could he please have his hot water
turned on.

That done, he ascended to the studio again and bolted the door
behind him. One conversation for the day was enough, he'd decided. He drew the blinds at the windows and lit two candles. They
smoked as their dusty wicks first burned, but their light was kinder
than the glare of the day, and by it he started to go through the
snowdrift of mail that had gathered behind the door. There were
bills in abundance, of course, printed in increasingly irate colors,
plus the inevitable junk mail. There were very few personal letters,
but among them were two that gave him pause. Both were from
Vanessa, whose advice that he should slit his lying throat had found
such a distressing echo in Athanasius' exhortation at the Erasure.
Now she wrote that she missed him, and a day didn't go by without her thinking of him. The second missive was even more direct.
She wanted him back in her life. If he wanted to play around with
other women she would learn to accommodate that. Would he not
at least make contact with her? Life was too short to bear grudges,
on either side.

He was buoyed up somewhat by her appeals, and even more so
by a letter from Klein, scrawled in red ink on pink paper. Chester's
faintly camp tones rose from the page as Gentle scanned it.

Dear Bastard Boy, Klein had written. *Whose heart are you breaking, and where? Scores of forlorn women are presently weeping on
my lap, begging me to forgive you your trespasses and invite you
back into the bosom of the family. Among them, the delectable
Vanessa. For God's sake come home and save me from seducing her.
My groin is wet for you.*

So Vanessa had gone to Klein; desperation indeed. Though she'd
met Chester only once that Gentle could recall, she'd subsequently
professed to loathing him. Gentle kept all three letters, though he
had no intention of acting upon their appeals. There was only one
reunion he was eager for, and that was with the house in Clerkenwell. He couldn't face the idea of venturing out in daylight, however. The streets would be too bright and too busy. He'd wait until
dark, when he could move across the city as the invisible he aspired
to be. He set a match to the rest of the letters and watched them
burn. Then he went back to bed and slept through the afternoon
in preparation for the business of the night.

2

He waited until the first stars appeared in a sky of elegiac blue before he raised the blinds. The street outside was quiet, but given that he lacked the cash for a cab he knew he'd have to brush shoulders with a lot of people before he reached Clerkenwell. On a fine evening like this, the Edgware Road would be busy, and there'd be crowds on the Underground. His best hope of reaching his destination unscrutinized was to dress as blandly as possible, and he took some time hunting through his depleted wardrobe for those clothes that would render him most invisible. Once dressed, he walked down to Marble Arch and boarded the Underground. It was only five stations to Chancery Lane, which would put him on the borders of Clerkenwell, but after two he had to get off, gasping and sweating like a claustrophobic. Cursing this new weakness in himself, he sat in the station for half an hour while more trains passed through, unable to bring himself to board. What an irony! Here he was, a sometime wanderer in the wilds of the Imajica, incapable of traveling a couple of miles by tube without panicking. He waited until his shaking subsided and a less crowded train came along. Then he reboarded, sitting close to the door with his head in his hands until the journey was over.

By the time he emerged at Chancery Lane the sky had darkened, and he stood for several minutes on High Holborn, his head thrown back, soaking up the sky. Only when the tremors had left his legs did he head up Gray's Inn Road towards the environs of Gamut Street. Almost all the property on the main thoroughfares had long since been turned to commercial use, but there was a network of streets and squares behind the barricade of darkened office buildings which, protected perhaps by the patronage of notoriety, had been left untouched by the developers. Many of these streets were narrow and mazy, their lamps unlit, their signs missing, as though blind eyes had been turned to them over the generations. But he didn't need signs and lamps; his feet had trodden these ways countless times. Here was Shiverick Square, with its little park all overgrown, and Flaxen Street, and Almoth, and Sterne. And in their midst, cocooned by anonymity, his destination.

He saw the corner of Gamut Street twenty yards ahead and slowed his pace to take pleasure in the moment of reunion. There were innumerable memories awaiting him there, the mystif among them. But not all would be so sweet, or so welcome. He would have to ingest them carefully, like a diner with a delicate stomach coming to a lavish table. Moderation was the way. As soon as he felt a surfeit, he'd retreat and return to the studio to digest what he'd learned, let it strengthen him. Only then would he return for a second helping. The process would take time, he knew, and time was of the essence. But so was his sanity. What use would he be as a Reconciler if he choked on the past?

With his heart thumping hard, he came to the corner and, turning it, finally laid his eyes upon the sacred street. Perhaps, during his years of forgetfulness, he'd wandered through these backwaters all unknowing and seen the sight before him now. But he doubted it. More likely, his eyes were seeing Gamut Street for the first time in two centuries. It had changed scarcely at all, preserved from the city planners and their hammer-wielding hordes by the feits whose makers were still rumored here. The trees planted along the pavement were weighed down with unkempt foliage, but their sap's tang was sharp, the air protected from the fumes of Holborn and Gray's Inn Road by the warren of thoroughfares between. Was it just his fancy, or was the tree outside number 28 particularly lush, fed perhaps by a seepage of magics from the step of the Maestro's house?

He began towards them, tree and step, the memories already returning in force. He heard the children singing behind him, the song that had so tormented him when the Autarch had told him who he was. *Sartori,* he'd said, and this charmless ditty, sung by piping voices, had come in pursuit of the name. He'd loathed it then. Its melody was banal; its words were nonsense. But now he remembered how he'd first heard it, walking along this very pavement with the children in procession on the opposite shore, and how flattered he'd been that he was famous enough to have reached the lips of children who would never read or write or, most probably, reach the age of puberty. All of London knew who he was, and he liked his fame. He was talked about at court, Roxborough said, and should soon expect an invitation. People who'd not so much as touched his sleeve were claiming intimate association.

But there were still those, thank God, who kept an exquisite distance, and one such soul had lived, he remembered, in the house opposite: a nymph called Allegra who liked to sit at her dressing table near the window with her bodice half unlaced, knowing she had an admirer in the Maestro across the street. She'd had a little curly-haired dog, and sometimes in the evening he'd hear her piping voice summon the lucky hound onto her lap, where she'd let it snuggle. One afternoon, a few paces from where he stood now, he'd met the girl out walking with her mother and had made much of the dog, suffering its little tongue on his mouth for the smell of her sex in its fur. What had become of that child? Had she died a virgin or grown old and fat, wondering about the man who'd been her most ardent admirer?

He glanced up at the window where Allegra had sat. No light burned in it now. The house, like almost all these buildings, was dark. Sighing, he turned his gaze towards number 28 and, crossing the street, went to the door. It was locked, of course, but one of the lower windows had been broken at some point and never repaired. He reached through the smashed pane and unlocked it, then slid the window up and himself inside. Slowly, he reminded himself; go slowly. Keep the flow under control.

It was dark, but he'd come prepared for that eventuality, with candle and matches. The flame guttered at first, and the room rocked at its indecision, but by degrees it strengthened, and he felt a sensation he'd not expected swelling like the light: pride. In its time, this, his house, had been a place of great souls and great ambition, where all commonplace debate had been banned. If you wanted to talk politics or tittle-tattle you went to the coffee house; if you wanted commerce, to the Exchange. Here, only miracles. Here, only the rising of the spirit. And, yes, love, if it was pertinent (which it was, so often); and sometimes bloodletting. But never the prosaic, never the trivial. Here the man who brought the strangest tale was the most welcome. Here every excess was celebrated if it brought visions, and every vision analyzed for the hints it held to the nature of the Everlasting.

He lifted the candle and, holding it high, began to walk through the house. The rooms—there were many—were badly dilapidated, the boards creaking under his feet, weakened by rot and worm, the walls mapping continents of damp. But the present didn't insist upon him for long. By the time he reached the bottom of the stairs, memory was lighting candles everywhere, their luminescence spilling through the dining room door and from the rooms above. It was a generous light, clothing naked walls, putting lush carpets underfoot, and setting fine furniture on their pile. Though the debaters here might have aspired to pure spirit, they were not averse to comforting the flesh while still cursed with it. Who would have guessed, seeing the modest façade of the house from the street, that the interior would be so finely furnished and ornamented? And seeing these glories appear, he heard the voices of those who'd wallowed in that luxury. Laughter first; then vociferous argument from somebody at the top of the stairs. He couldn't see the debaters yet—perhaps his mind, which he'd instructed in caution, was holding the flood back—but he could put names to both of them, sight unseen. One was Horace Tyrwhitt, the other Isaac Abelove. And the laughter? That was Joshua Godolphin, of course. He had a laugh like the Devil's laugh, full and throaty.

"Come on, then," Gentle said aloud to the memories. "I'm ready to see your faces."

And as he spoke, they came: Tyrwhitt on the stairs, overdressed and overpowered, as ever, keeping his distance from Abelove in case the magpie his pursuer was nursing flew free.

"It's bad luck," Tyrwhitt was protesting. "Birds in the house are bad luck!"

"Luck's for fishermen and gamblers," Abelove replied.

"One of these days you'll turn a phrase worth remembering," Tyrwhitt replied. "Just get the thing out before I wring its neck." He turned towards Gentle. "Tell him, Sartori."

Gentle was shocked to see the memory's eyes fix so acutely upon him. "It does no harm," he found himself replying. "It's one of God's creatures."

At which point the bird rose flapping from Abelove's grasp, emptying its bowels as it did so on the man's wig and face, which brought a hoot of laughter from Tyrwhitt.

"Now don't wipe it off," he told Abelove as the magpie fluttered away. "It's good luck."

The sound of his laughter brought Joshua Godolphin, imperious as ever, out of the dining room. "What's the row?"

Abelove was already clattering after the bird, his calls merely alarming it more. It fluttered around the hallway in panic, cawing as it went.

"Open the damned door!" Godolphin said. "Let the bloody thing out!"

"And spoil the sport?" Tyrwhitt said.

"If everyone would but calm their voices," Abelove said, "it would settle."

"Why did you bring it in?" Joshua wanted to know.

"It was sitting on the step," Abelove replied. "I thought it was injured."

"It looks quite well to me," Godolphin said, and turned his face, ruddied with brandy, towards Gentle. "Maestro," he said, inclining his head a little. "I'm afraid we began dinner without you. Come in. Leave these bird brains to play."

Gentle was crossing to the dining room when there was a thud behind him, and he turned to see the bird dropping to the floor beneath one of the windows, where it had struck the glass. Abelove let out a little moan, and Tyrwhitt's laughter ceased.

"There now!" he said. "You killed the thing!"

"Not me!" Abelove said.

"You want to resurrect it?" Joshua murmured to Gentle, his tone conspiratorial.

"With a broken neck and wings?" Gentle mourned. "That wouldn't be very kind."

"But amusing," Godolphin replied with mischief in his puffy eyes.

"I think not," Gentle said, and saw his distaste wipe the humor off Joshua's face. He's a little afraid of me, Gentle thought; the power in me makes him nervous.

Joshua headed into the dining room, and Gentle was about to step through the door after him when a young man—eighteen at most, with a plain, long face and chorister's curls—came to his side.

"Maestro?" he said.

Unlike Joshua and the others, these features seemed more familiar to Gentle. Perhaps there was a certain modernity in the languid lidded gaze and the small, almost effeminate, mouth. He didn't look that intelligent, in truth, but his words, when they came, were well turned, despite the boy's nervousness. He barely dared look at Sartori, but with those lids downcast begged the Maestro's indulgence.

"I wondered, sir, if you had perhaps considered the matter of which we spoke?"

Gentle was about to ask, What matter?, when his tongue replied, his intellect seizing the memory as the words spilled out. "I know how eager you are, Lucius."

Lucius Cobbitt was the boy's name. At seventeen he already had the great works by heart, or at least their theses. Ambitious and apt at politics, he'd taken Tyrwhitt as a patron (for what services only his bed knew, but it was surely a hanging offense) and had secured himself a place in the house as a menial. But he wanted more than that, and scarcely an evening went by without his politely plying the Maestro with coy glances and pleas.

"I'm more than eager, sir," he said. "I've studied all the rituals. I've mapped the In Ovo, from what I've read in Flute's *Visions*. They're just beginnings, I know, but I've also copied all the known glyphs, and I have them by heart."

He had a little skill as an artist, too: something else they shared, besides ambition and dubious morals.

"I can help you, Maestro," he was saying. "You're going to need somebody beside you on the night."

"I commend you on your discipline, Lucius, but the Reconciliation's a dangerous business. I can't take the responsibility—"

"I'll take that, sir."

"Besides, I have my assistant."

The boy's face fell. "You do?" he said.

"Certainly. Pie 'oh' pah."

"You'd trust your life to a familiar?"

"Why shouldn't I?"

"Well, because . . . because it's not even human."

"That's why I trust it, Lucius," Gentle said. "I'm sorry to disappoint you—"

"Could I at least *watch,* sir? I'll keep my distance, I swear, I swear. Everybody else is going to be there."

This was true enough. As the night of the Reconciliation approached, the size of the audience swelled. His patrons, who'd at first taken their oaths of secrecy very seriously, now sensed triumph and had become indiscreet. In hushed and often embarrassed tones they'd admit to having invited a friend or a relation to witness the rites, and who was he, the performer, to forbid his paymasters their moment of reflected glory? Though he never gave them an easy time when they made these confessions, he didn't much mind. Admiration charged the blood. And when the Reconciliation had been achieved, the more tongues there were to say they'd seen it done, and sanctify the doer, the better.

"I beg you, sir," Lucius was saying. "I'll be in your debt forever."

Gentle nodded, ruffling the youth's ginger hair. "You may watch," he said.

Tears started to the boy's eyes, and he snatched up Gentle's hand, laying his lips to it. "I am the luckiest man in England," he said. "Thank you, sir, thank you."

Quieting the boy's profusions, Gentle left him at the door and stepped through into the dining room. As he did so he wondered if all these events and conversations had actually dovetailed in this fashion, or whether his memory was collecting fragments from different nights and days, knitting them together so that they appeared seamless. If the latter was the case—and he guessed it was—then there were probably clues in these scenes to mysteries yet to be unveiled, and he should try to remember their every detail. But it was difficult. He was both Gentle and Sartori here, both witness and actor. It was hard to live the moments when he was also observing them, and harder still to dig for the seam of their significance when their surface gleamed so fetchingly, and when he was the brightest jewel that shone there. How they had idolized him! He'd been like a divinity among them, his every belch and fart attended to like a sermon, his cosmological pronouncements—of which he was too fond—greeted with reverence and gratitude, even by the mightiest.

Three of those mighty awaited him in the dining room, gathered at one end of a table, set for four but laden with sufficient food to sate the street for a week. Joshua was one of the trio, of course. Roxborough and his long-time foil Oliver McGann were the others, the latter well in his cups, the former, as ever, keeping his counsel, his ascetic features, dominated by the long hook of his nose, always half masked by his hands. He despised his mouth, Gentle thought, because it betrayed his nature, which despite his incalculable wealth and his pretensions to metaphysics was peevish, penurious, and sullen.

"Religion's for the faithful," McGann was loudly opining. "They say their prayers, their prayers aren't answered, and their faith increases. Whereas magic—" He stopped, laying his inebriated gaze on the Maestro at the door. "Ah! The very man! The *very* man! Tell him, Sartori! Tell him what magic is."

Roxborough had made a pyramid of his fingers, the apex at the bridge of his nose. "Yes, Maestro," he said. "Do tell."

"My pleasure," Gentle replied, taking the glass of wine McGann poured for him and wetting his throat before he provided tonight's profundities. "Magic is the first and last religion of the world," he said. "It has the power to make us whole. To open our eyes to the Dominions and return us to ourselves."

"That sounds very fine," Roxborough said flatly. "But what does it mean?"

"It's obvious what it means," McGann protested.

"Not to me it isn't."

"It means we're born divided, Roxborough," the Maestro replied. "But we long for union."

"Oh, we do, do we?"

"I believe so."

"And why should we seek union with ourselves?" Roxborough said. "Tell me that. I would have thought we're the only company we're certain we have."

There was a riling smugness to the man's tone, but the Maestro had heard these niceties before and had his answers well honed.

"Everything that isn't us is also ourselves," he said. He came to the table and set down his glass, peering through the smoky candle flames at Roxborough's black eyes. "We're joined to everything that was, is, and will be," he said. "From one end of the Imajica to another. From the tiniest mote dancing over this flame to the Godhead Itself."

He took breath, leaving room for a retort from Roxborough. But none came.

"We'll not be subsumed at our deaths," he went on. "We'll be increased: to the size of Creation."

"*Yes...*" McGann said, the word coming long and loud from between teeth clenched in a tigerish smile.

"Magic's our means to that Revelation," the Maestro said, "while we're still in our flesh."

"And is it your opinion that we are *given* that Revelation?" Roxborough replied. "Or are we stealing it?"

"We were born to know as much as we *can* know."

"We were born to suffer in our flesh," Roxborough said.

"You may suffer; I don't."

The reply won a guffaw from McGann.

"The flesh isn't punishment," the Maestro said, "it's there for joy. But it also marks the place where we end and the rest of Creation begins. Or so we believe. It's an illusion, of course."

"Good," said Godolphin. "I like that."

"So are we about God's business or not?" Roxborough wanted to know.

"Are you having second thoughts?"

"Third and fourth, more like," McGann said.

Roxborough gave the man at his side a sour glance. "Did we swear an oath not to doubt?" he said. "I don't think so. Why should I be castigated because I ask a simple question?"

"I apologize," McGann said. "Tell the man, Maestro. We're doing God's work, aren't we?"

"Does God want us to be more than we are?" Gentle said. "Of course. Does God want us to love, which is the desire to be joined and made whole? Of course. Does It want us in Its glory, forever and ever? Yes, It does."

"You always say It," McGann observed. "Why's that?"

"Creation and its maker are one and the same. True or false?"

"True."

"And Creation's as full of women as it is of men. True or false?"

"Oh, true, true."

"Indeed, I give thanks for the fact night and day," Gentle said, glancing at Godolphin as he spoke. "Beside my bed and in it."

Joshua laughed his Devil's laugh.

"So the Godhead is both male and female. For convenience, an It."

"Bravely said!" Joshua announced. "I never tire of hearing you speak, Sartori. My thoughts get muddy, but after I've listened to you awhile they're like spring water, straight from the rock!"

"Not too clean, I hope," the Maestro said. "We don't want any Puritan souls spoiling the Reconciliation."

"You know me better than that," Joshua said, catching Gentle's eye.

Even as he did so, Gentle had proof of his suspicion that these encounters, though remembered in one continuous stream, had not occurred sequentially but were fragments his mind was knitting together as the rooms he was walking through evoked them. McGann and Roxborough faded from the table, as did most of the candlelight and the litter of carafes, glasses, and food it had illuminated. Now there was only Joshua and himself, and the house

was still above and below. Everyone asleep, but for these conspir-
ators.

"I want to be with you when you perform the working," Joshua
was saying. There was no hint of laughter now. He looked harassed
and nervous. "She's very precious to me, Sartori. If anything were
to happen to her I'd lose my mind."

"She'll be perfectly safe," the Maestro said, sitting down at the
table.

There was a map of the Imajica laid out in front of him, with the
names of the Maestros and their assistants in each Dominion
marked beside their places of conjuration. He scanned them and
found he knew one or two. Tick Raw was there, as the deputy to
Uter Musky; Scopique was there too, marked as an assistant to an
assistant to Heratae Hammeryock, the latter a distant relation, perhaps, of the Hammeryock whom Gentle and Pie had encountered
in Vanaeph. Names from two pasts, intersecting here on the map.

"Are you listening to me?" Joshua said.

"I told you she'd be perfectly safe," came the Maestro's reply.
"The workings are delicate, but they're not dangerous."

"Then let me be there," Godolphin said, wringing his hands.
"I'll be your assistant instead of that wretched mystif."

"I haven't even told Pie 'oh' pah what we're up to. This is our
business and only ours. You just bring Judith here tomorrow
evening, and I'll see to the rest."

"She's so vulnerable."

"She seems very self-possessed to me," the Maestro observed.
"Very heated."

Godolphin's fretful expression soured into ice. "Don't parade
it, Sartori," he said. "It's not enough that I've got Roxborough at
my ear all yesterday, telling me he doesn't trust you; I have to bear
you parading your arrogance."

"Roxborough understands nothing."

"He says you're obsessed with women, so he understands that,
at least. You watch some girl across the street, he says—"

"What if I do?"

"How can you give yourself to the Reconciliation if you're so
distracted?"

"Are you trying to talk me out of wanting Judith?"

"I thought magic was a religion to you."

"So's she."

"A discipline, a sacred mystery."

"Again, so's she." He laughed. "When I first saw her, it was like
my first glimpse of another world. I knew I'd risk my life to be inside her skin. When I'm with her, I feel like an adept again, creeping towards a miracle, step by step. Tentative, excited—"

"Enough!"

"Really? You don't want to know why I need to be inside her so badly?"

Godolphin eyed him ruefully. "Not really," he said. "But if you don't tell me, I'll only wonder."

"Because for a little time, I'll forget who I am. Everything petty and particular will go out of me. My ambition. My history. Everything. I'll be unmade. And that's when I'm closest to divinity."

"Somehow you always manage to bring everything back to that. Even your lust."

"It's all One."

"I don't like your talk of the One," Godolphin said. "You sound like Roxborough with his dictums! *Simplicity is strength* and all the rest."

"That's not what I mean and you know it. It's just that women are where everything begins, and I like—how shall I put it?—to touch the source as often as possible."

"You think you're perfect, don't you?" Godolphin said.

"Why so sour? A week ago you were doting on my every word."

"I don't like what we're doing," Godolphin replied. "I want Judith for myself."

"You'll have her. And so will I. That's the glory of this."

"There'll be no difference between them?"

"None. They'll be identical. To the pucker. To the lash."

"So why must I have the copy?"

"You know the answer to that. Because the original loves me, not you."

"I should never have let you set eyes on her."

"You couldn't have kept us apart. Don't look so forlorn. I'm going to make you a Judith that'll dote on you and your sons, and your son's sons, until the name Godolphin disappears off the face of the earth. Now where's the harm in that?"

As he asked the question all the candles but the one he held went out, and the past was extinguished with them. He was suddenly back in the empty house, a police siren whooping nearby. He stepped back into the hallway as the car sped down Gamut Street, its blue light pulsing through the windows. Seconds later, another came howling after. Though the din of the sirens faded and finally disappeared, the flashes did not. They brightened from blue to white, however, and lost their regularity. By their brilliance he saw the house once more restored to glory. It was no longer a place of debate and laughter however. There was sobbing above and below, and the animal smells of fear in every corner. Thunder rattled the roof, but there was no rain to soothe its choler.

I don't want to be here, he thought. The other memories had

entertained him. He'd liked his role in the proceedings. But this darkness was another matter entirely. It was full of death, and he wanted to run from it.

The lightning came again, horribly livid. By it, he saw Lucius Cobbitt standing halfway up the stairs, clutching the banister as though he'd fall if he didn't. He'd bitten his tongue or lip, or both, and blood dribbled from his mouth and chin, made stringy by the spit with which it was mingled. When Gentle climbed the stairs he smelt excrement. The boy had loosed his bowels in his breeches. Seeing Gentle, he raised his eyes.

"How did it fail, Maestro?" he sobbed. *"How?"*

Gentle shuddered as the question brought images flooding into his head, more horrendous than all the scenes he'd witnessed at the Erasure. The failure of the Reconciliation had been sudden, and calamitous, and had caught the Maestros representing the five Dominions at such a delicate time in the working that they'd been ill-equipped to prevent it. The spirits of all five had already risen from their circles across Imajica and, carrying the analogues of their worlds, had converged on the Ana, the zone of inviolability that appeared every two centuries in the heart of the In Ovo. There, for a tender time, miracles could be worked, as the Maestros, safe from the In Ovo's inhabitants but freed and empowered by their immaterial state, unburdened themselves of their similitudes and allowed the genius of the Ana to complete the fusing of the Dominions. It was a precarious time, but they'd been reaching its conclusion when the circle in which the Maestro Sartori's physical body sat, its stones protecting the outside world from the flux which let on to the In Ovo, broke. Of all the potential places for failure in the ceremonies, this was the unlikeliest: tantamount to transubstantiation failing for want of salt in the bread. But fail it did, and once the breach was opened, there was no way to seal it until the Maestros had returned to their bodies and mustered their feits. In that time the hungry tenants of the In Ovo had free access to the Fifth. Not only to the Fifth, but to the exulted flesh of the Maestros themselves, who vacated the Ana in confusion, leading the hounds of the In Ovo back to their flesh.

Sartori's life would certainly have been forfeited along with all the others had Pie 'oh' pah not intervened. When the circle broke, Pie was being forcibly removed from the Retreat on Godolphin's order, for voicing a prophetic murmur of alarm and disturbing the audience. The duty of removal had fallen to Abelove and Lucius Cobbitt, but neither had possessed the strength to hold the mystif. It had broken free, racing across the Retreat and plunging into the circle, where its master was visible to the assembly only as a blaze of light. The mystif had learned well at Sartori's feet. It had defenses against the flux of power that roared in the circle and had pulled the Maestro from under the noses of the approaching Oviates.

The rest of the assembly, however, caught between the mystif's yells of warning and Roxborough's attempts to maintain the status quo, were still standing around in confusion when the Oviates appeared.

The entities were swift. One moment the Retreat was a bridge to the transcendental; the next, it was an abattoir. Dazed by his sudden fall from grace, the Maestro had seen only snatches of the massacre, but they were burned on his eyes, and Gentle remembered them now in all their wretched detail: Abelove, scrabbling at the ground in terror as an Oviate the size of a felled bull, but resembling something barely born, opened its toothless maw and drew him between its jaws with tongues the length of whips; McGann, losing his arm to a sleek dark animal that rippled as it ran but hauling himself away, his blood a scarlet fountain, while the thing was distracted by fresher meat; and Flores—poor Flores, who'd come to Gamut Street the day before, carrying a letter of introduction from Casanova—caught by two beasts whose skulls were as flat as spades and whose translucent skin had given Sartori a terrible glimpse of their victim's agony as his head was taken down the throat of one while his legs were devoured by the other.

But it was the death of Roxborough's sister that Gentle remembered with profoundest horror, not least because the man had been at such pains to keep her from coming and had even abased himself to the Maestro, begging him to talk to the woman and persuade her to stay away. He'd had the talk, but he'd knowingly made his caution a seduction—almost literally, in fact—and she'd come to see the Reconciliation as much to meet the eyes of the man who'd wooed her with his warnings as for the ceremony itself. She'd paid the most terrible price. She'd been fought over like a bone among hungry wolves, shrieking a prayer for deliverance as a trio of Oviates drew out her entrails and dabbled in her open skull. By the time the Maestro, with Pie 'oh' pah's help, had raised sufficient feits to drive the entities back into the circle, she was dying in her own coils, thrashing like a fish half filleted by a hook.

Only later did the Maestro hear of the atrocities visited on the other circles. It was the same story there as in the Fifth: the Oviates appearing in the midst of innocents; carnage ensuing, which was only brought to a halt when one of the Maestro's assistants drove them back. With the exception of Sartori, the Maestros themselves had all perished.

"It would be better if I'd died like the others," he said to Lucius.

The boy tried to persuade him otherwise, but tears overwhelmed him. There was another voice, however, rising from the bottom of the stairs, raw with grief but strong.

"Sartori! Sartori!"

He turned. Joshua was there in the hallway, his fine powder-blue coat covered with blood. As were his hands. As was his face.

"What's going to happen?" he yelled. "This storm! It's going to tear the world apart!"

"No, Joshua."

"Don't lie to me! There's never been a storm like this! Ever!"

"Control yourself—"

"Jesus Christ our Lord, forgive us our trespasses."

"That's not going to help, Joshua."

Godolphin had a crucifix in his hand and put it to his lips.

"You Godless trash! Are you a demon? Is that it? Were you sent to have our souls?" Tears were pouring down his crazed face. "What Hell did you come out of?"

"The same as you. The human hell."

"I should have listened to Roxborough. He knew! He said over and over you had some plan, and I didn't believe him, wouldn't believe him, because Judith loved you, and how could anything so pure love anything unholy? But you hid yourself from her too, didn't you? Poor, sweet Judith! How did you make her love you? How did you do it?"

"Is that all you can think of?"

"Tell me! *How?*"

Barely coherent in his fury, Godolphin started up the stairs towards the seducer.

Gentle felt his hand go to his mouth. Godolphin halted. He knew this power.

"Haven't we shed enough blood tonight?" the Maestro said.

"*You,* not me," Godolphin replied. He jabbed a finger in Gentle's direction, the crucifix hanging from his fist. "You'll have no peace after this," he said. "Roxborough's already talking about a purge, and I'm going to give him every guinea he needs to break your back. You and all your works are damned!"

"Even Judith?"

"I never want to see that creature again."

"But she's yours, Joshua," the Maestro said flatly, descending the stairs as he spoke. "She's yours forever and ever. She won't age. She won't die. She belongs to the family Godolphin until the sun goes out."

"Then I'll kill her."

"And have her innocent soul on your blotted conscience?"

"She's got no soul!"

"I promised you Judith to the last, and that's what she is. A religion. A discipline. A sacred mystery. Remember?"

Godolphin buried his face in his hands.

"She's the one truly innocent soul left among us, Joshua. Preserve her. Love her as you've never loved any living thing, because she's our only victory." He took hold of Godolphin's hands and unmasked him. "Don't be ashamed of our ambition," he said. "And don't believe anyone who tells you it was the Devil's doing. We did what we did out of love."

"Which?" Godolphin said. "Making her, or the Reconciliation?"

"It's all One," he replied. "Believe that, at least."

Godolphin claimed his hands from the Maestro's grip. "I'll never believe anything again," he said and, turning his back, began his weary descent.

Standing on the stairs, watching the memory disappear, Gentle said a second farewell. He had never seen Godolphin again after that night. A few weeks later the man had retreated to his estate and sealed himself up there, living in silent self-mortification until despair had burst his tender heart.

"It was my fault," said the boy on the stairs behind him.

Gentle had forgotten Lucius was still there, watching and listening. He turned back to the child.

"No," he said. "You're not to blame."

Lucius had wiped the blood from his chin, but he couldn't control his trembling. His teeth chattered between his stumbling words. "I did everything you told me to do," he said. "I swear. I swear. But I must have missed some words from the rites or . . . I don't know . . . maybe mixed up the stones."

"What are you talking about?"

"The stones you gave me, to replace the flawed ones."

"I gave you no stones, Lucius."

"But Maestro, you did. Two stones, to go in the circle. You told me to bury the ones I took, at the step. Don't you remember?"

Listening to the boy, Gentle finally understood how the Reconciliation had come to grief. His other—born in the upper room of this very house—had used Lucius as his agent, sending him to replace a part of the circle with stones that resembled the originals (forging ran in the blood), knowing they would not preserve the circle's integrity when the ceremony reached its height.

But while the man who was remembering these scenes understood how all this had come about, to Maestro Sartori, still ignorant of the other self he'd created in the womb of the doubling circle, this remained an unfathomable mystery.

"I gave you no such instruction," he said to Lucius.

"I understand," the youth replied. "You have to lay the blame at my feet. That's why Maestros need adepts. I begged you for the responsibility, and I'm glad to have had it even if I failed." He reached into his pocket as he spoke. "Forgive me, Maestro," he said and, drawing out a knife, had it at his heart in the space of a thunderclap. As the tip drew blood the Maestro caught hold of the youth's hand and, wrenching the blade from his fingers, threw it down the stairs.

"Who gave you permission to do that?" he said to Lucius. "I thought you wanted to be an adept?"

"I did," the boy said.

"And now you're out of love with it. You see humiliation and you want no more of the business."

"No!" Lucius protested. "I still want wisdom. But I failed tonight."

"We *all* failed tonight!" the Maestro said. He took hold of the trembling boy and spoke to him softly. "I don't know how this tragedy came about," he said. "But I sniff more than your shite in the air. Some plot was here, laid against our high ambition, and perhaps if I hadn't been blinded by my own glory I'd have seen it. The fault isn't yours, Lucius. And stopping your own life won't bring Abelove, or Esther, or any of the others back. Listen to me."

"I'm listening."

"Do you still want to be my adept?"

"Of course."

"Will you obey my instructions now, to the letter?"

"Anything. Just tell me what you need from me."

"Take my books, all that you can carry, and go as far from here as you're able to go. To the other end of the Imajica, if you can learn the trick of it. Somewhere Roxborough and his hounds won't ever find you. There's a hard winter coming for men like us. It'll kill all but the cleverest. But you can be clever, can't you?"

"Yes."

"I knew it." The Maestro smiled. "You must teach yourself in secret, Lucius, and you must learn to live outside time. That way, the years won't wither you, and when Roxborough's dead you'll be able to try again."

"Where will you be, Maestro?"

"Forgotten, if I'm lucky. But never forgiven, I think. That would be too much to hope for. Don't look so dejected, Lucius. I have to know there's some hope, and I'm charging you to carry it for me."

"It's my honor, Maestro."

As he replied, Gentle was once again grazed by the déjà vu he'd first felt when he'd encountered Lucius outside the dining room door. But the touch was light, and passed before he could make sense of it.

"Remember, Lucius, that everything you learn is already part of you, even to the Godhead Itself. Study nothing except in the knowledge that you already knew it. Worship nothing except in adoration of your true self. And fear nothing"—there the Maestro stopped and shuddered, as though he had a presentiment—"fear nothing except in the certainty that you are your enemy's begetter and its only hope of healing. For everything that does evil is in pain. Will you remember those things?"

The boy looked uncertain. "As best I can," he said.

"That will have to suffice," the Maestro said. "Now . . . get out of here before the purgers come."

He let go of the boy's shoulders, and Cobbitt retreated down the stairs, backwards, like a commoner from the king, only turning and heading away when he was at the bottom.

The storm was overhead now, and with the boy gone, taking his sewer stench with him, the smell of electricity was strong. The candle Gentle held flickered, and for an instant he thought it was going to be extinguished, signaling the end of these recollections, at least for tonight. But there was more to come.

"That was kind," he heard Pie 'oh' pah say, and turned to see the mystif standing at the top of the stairs. It had discarded its soiled clothes with its customary fastidiousness, but the plain shirt and trousers it wore were all the finery it needed to appear in perfection. There was no face in the Imajica more beautiful than this, Gentle thought, nor form more graceful, and the scenes of terror and recrimination the storm had brought were of little consequence while he bathed in the sight of it. But the Maestro he had been had not yet made the error of losing this miracle and, seeing the mystif, was more concerned that his deceits had been discovered.

"Were you here when Godolphin came?" he asked.

"Yes."

"Then you know about Judith?"

"I can guess."

"I kept it from you because I knew you wouldn't approve."

"It's not my place to approve or otherwise. I'm not your wife, that you should fear my censure."

"Still, I do. And I thought, well, when the Reconciliation was done this would seem like a little indulgence, and you'd say I deserved it because of what I'd achieved. Now it seems like a crime, and I wish it could be undone."

"Do you? Truly?" the mystif said.

The Maestro looked up. "No, I don't," he said, his tone that of a man surprised by a revelation. He started to climb the stairs. "I suppose I must believe what I told Godolphin, about her being our . . ."

"Victory," Pie prompted, stepping aside to let the summoner step into the Meditation Room. It was, as ever, bare. "Shall I leave you alone?" Pie asked.

"No," the Maestro said hurriedly. Then, more quietly: "Please. No."

He went to the window from which he had stood those many evenings watching the nymph Allegra at her toilet. The branches of the tree he'd spied her through thrashed themselves to splinter and pulp against the panes.

"Can you make me forget, Pie 'oh' pah? There are such feits, aren't there?"

"Of course. But is that what you want?"

"No, what I really want is death, but I'm too afraid of that at the moment. So . . . it will have to be forgetfulness."

"The true Maestro folds pain into his experience."

"Then I'm not a true Maestro," he returned. "I don't have the courage for that. Make me forget, mystif. Divide me from what I've done and what I am forever. Make a feit that'll be a river between me and this moment, so that I'm never tempted to cross it."

"How will you live?"

The Maestro puzzled over this for a few moments. "In increments," he finally replied. "Each part ignorant of the part before. Well. You can do this for me?"

"Certainly."

"It's what I did for the woman I made for Godolphin. Every ten years she'll start to undo her life and disappear. Then she'll invent another one and live it, never knowing what she left behind."

Listening to himself plot the life he'd lived, Gentle heard a perverse satisfaction in his voice. He had condemned himself to two hundred years of waste, but he'd known what he was doing. He'd made the same arrangements precisely for the second Judith and had contemplated every consequence on her behalf. It wasn't just cowardice that made him shun these memories. It was a kind of revenge upon himself for failing, to banish his future to the same limbo he'd made for his creature.

"I'll have pleasure, Pie," he said. "I'll wander the world and enjoy the moments. I just won't have the sum of them."

"And what about me?"

"After this, you're free to go," he said.

"And do what? Be what?"

"Whore or assassin, I don't care," the Maestro said.

The remark had been thrown off casually—surely not intended as an order to the mystif. But was it a slave's duty to distinguish between a command made for the humor of it and one to be followed absolutely? No, it was a slave's duty to obey, especially if the dictate came, as did this, from a beloved mouth. Here, with a throw-away remark, the master had circumscribed his servant's life for two centuries, driving it to deeds it had doubtless abhorred.

Gentle saw the tears shining in the mystif's eyes and felt its suffering like a hammer pounding at his heart. He hated himself then, for his arrogance and his carelessness, for not seeing the harm he was doing a creature that only wanted to love him and be near him. And he longed more than ever to be reunited with Pie, so that he could beg forgiveness for this cruelty.

"Make me forget," he said again. "I want an end to this."

The mystif was speaking, Gentle saw, though whatever incantations its lips shaped were spoken in a voice he couldn't hear. The breath that bore them made the flame he'd set on the floor flicker, however, and as the mystif instructed its master in forgetfulness the memories went out with the flame.

Gentle rummaged for the box of matches and struck one, using its light to find the smoking wick, then reigniting it. But the night of storm had passed back into history, and Pie 'oh' pah, beautiful, obedient, loving Pie 'oh' pah, had gone with it. He sat down in front of the candle and waited, wondering if there was some coda to come. But the house was dead from cellar to eaves.

"So," he said to himself. "What now, Maestro?"

He had his answer from his stomach, which made a little thunder of its own.

"You want food?" he asked it, and it gurgled its reply. "Me too," he said.

He got up and started down the stairs, preparing himself for a return to modernity. As he reached the bottom, however, he heard something scraping across the bare boards. He raised the candle, and his voice.

"Who's there?"

Neither the light nor his demand brought an answer. But the sound went on, and others joined it, none of them pleasant: a low, agonized moan; a wet, dragging sound; a whistling inhalation. What melodrama was his memory preparing to stage for him, he wondered, that had need of these hoary devices? They might have inspired fear in him once upon a time, but not now. He'd seen too many horrors face to face to be chilled by imitations.

"What's this about?" he asked the shadows, and was somewhat surprised to have his question answered.

"We've waited for you a long time," a wheezing voice told him.

"Sometimes we thought you'd never come home," another said. There was a fluting femininity in its tone.

Gentle took a step in the direction of the woman, and the rim of the candle's reach touched what looked to be the hem of a scarlet skirt, which was hastily twitched out of sight. Where it had lain, the bare boards shone with fresh blood. He didn't advance any further, but listened for another pronouncement from the shadows. It came soon enough. Not the woman this time, but the wheezer.

"The fault was yours," he said. "But the pain's been ours. All these years, waiting for you."

Though corrupted by anguish, the voice was familiar. He'd heard its lilt in this very house.

"Is that Abelove?" he said.

"Do you remember the maggot-pie?" the man said, confirming his identity. "The number of times I've thought: That was my error, bringing the bird into the house. Tyrwhitt would have no part of it, and he survived, didn't he? He died in his dotage. And Roxborough, and Godolphin, and you. All of you lived and died intact. But me, I just suffered here, flying against the glass but never hard enough to cease." He moaned, and though his rebuke was as absurd as it had been when first uttered, this time Gentle shuddered. "I'm not alone, of course," Abelove said. "Esther's here. And Flores. And Byam-Shaw. And Bloxham's brother-in-law; do you remember him? So there'll be plenty of company for you."

"I'm not staying," Gentle said.

"Oh, but you are," said Esther. "It's the least you can do."

"Blow out the candle," Abelove said. "Save yourself the distress of seeing us. We'll put out your eyes, and you can live with us blind."

"I'll do no such thing," Gentle said, raising the light so that it cast its net wider.

They appeared at its farthest edge, their viscera catching the gleam. What he'd taken to be Esther's skirt was a train of tissue, half flayed from her hip and thigh. She clutched it still, pulling it up around her, seeking to conceal her groin from him. Her decorum was absurd, but then perhaps his reputation as a womanizer had so swelled over the passage of the years that she believed he might be aroused by her, even in this appalling state. There was worse, however. Byam-Shaw was barely recognizable as a human being, and Bloxham's brother-in-law looked to have been chewed by tigers. But whatever their condition they were ready for revenge, no doubt of that. At Abelove's command they began to close upon him.

"You've already been hurt enough," Gentle said. "I don't want to hurt you again. I advise you to let me pass."

"Let you pass to do what?" Abelove replied, his terrible wounding clearer with every step he took. His scalp had gone, and one of his eyes lolled on his cheek. When he lifted his arm to point his next accusation at Gentle, it was with the littlest finger, which was the only one remaining on that hand. "You want to try again, don't you? Don't deny it! You've got the old ambition in your head!"

"You died for the Reconciliation," Gentle said. "Don't you want to see it achieved?"

"It's an abomination!" Abelove replied. "It was never meant to be! We died proving that. You render our sacrifice worthless if you try, then fail again."

"I won't fail," Gentle said.

"No, you won't," Esther replied, dropping her skirt to uncoil a garrote of her gut. "Because you won't get the chance."

He looked from one wretched face to the next and realized that he didn't have a hope of dissuading them from their intentions. They hadn't waited out the years to be diverted by argument. They'd waited for revenge. He had no choice but to stop them with a pneuma, regrettable as it was to add to their sum of suffering. He passed the candle from his right hand to his left, but as he did so somebody reached around him from behind and pinned his arms to his torso. The candle went from his fingers and rolled across the floor in the direction of his accusers. Before it could drown in its own wax, Abelove picked it up in his fingered hand.

"Good work, Flores," Abelove said.

The man clutching Gentle grunted his acknowledgment, shaking his prey to prove he had it securely caught. His arms were flayed, but they held Gentle like steel bands.

Abelove made something like a smile, though on a face with flaps for cheeks and blisters for lips it was a misbegotten thing.

"You don't struggle," he said, approaching Gentle with the candle held high. "Why's that? Are you already resigned to joining us, or do you think we'll be moved by your martyrdom and let you go?" He was very close to Gentle now. "It is pretty," he said. He cocked his eye a little, sighing. "How your face was loved!" he went on. "And this chest. How women fought to lay their heads upon it!" He slid his stump of a hand into Gentle's shirt and tore it open. "Very pale! And hairless! It's not Italian flesh, is it?"

"Does it matter?" said Esther. "As long as it bleeds, what do you care?"

"He never deigned to tell us anything about himself. We had to take him on trust because he had power in his fingers and his wits. He's like a little God, Tyrwhitt used to say. But even little Gods have fathers and mothers." Abelove leaned closer, allowing the candle flame within singeing distance of Gentle's lashes. "Who are you *really?*" Abelove said. "You're not an Italian. Are you Dutch? You could be Dutch. Or a Swiss. Chilly and precise. Huh? Is that you?" He paused. Then: "Or are you the Devil's child?"

"Abelove," Esther protested.

"I want to know!" Abelove yelped. "I want to hear him admit he's Lucifer's son." He peered at Gentle more closely. "Go on," he said. "Confess it."

"I'm not," Gentle said.

"There was no Maestro in Christendom could match you for feits. That kind of power has to come from somebody. *Who,* Sartori?"

Gentle would have gladly told, if he'd had an answer. But he had none. "Whoever I am," he said, "and whatever hurt I've done—"

" 'Whatever,' he says!" Esther spat. "Listen to him! *Whatever! Whatever!*"

She pushed Abelove aside and tossed a loop of her gut over Gentle's head. Abelove protested, but he'd prevaricated long enough. He was howled down from all sides, Esther's howls the loudest. Tightening the noose around Gentle's neck, she tugged on it, preparing to topple him. He felt rather than saw the devourers awaiting him when he fell. Something was gnawing at his leg, something else punching his testicles. It hurt like hell, and he started to struggle and kick. There were too many holds upon him, however—gut, arms, and teeth—and he earned himself not an inch of latitude with his thrashings. Past the red blur of Esther's fury, he caught sight of Abelove, crossing himself with his one-fingered hand, then raising the candle to his mouth.

"Don't!" Gentle yelled. Even a little light was better than none. Hearing him shout, Abelove looked up and shrugged. Then he blew out the flame. Gentle felt the wet flesh around him rise like a tide to claw him down. The fist gave up beating at his testicles and seized them instead. He screamed with pain, his clamor rising an octave as someone began to chew on his hamstrings.

"Down!" he heard Esther screech. "Down!"

Her noose had cut off all but the last squeak of breath. Choked, crushed, and devoured, he toppled, his head thrown back as he did so. They'd take his eyes, he knew, as soon as they could, and that would be the end of him. Even if he was saved by some miracle, it would be worthless if they'd taken his eyes. Unmanned, he could go on living; but not blind. His knees struck the boards, and fingers clawed for access to his face. Knowing he had mere seconds of sight left to him, he opened his eyes as wide as he could and stared up into the darkness overhead, hoping to find some last lovely thing to spend them on: a beam of dusty moonlight; a spider's web, trembling at the din he raised. But the darkness was too deep. His eyes would be thumbed out before he could use them again.

And then, a motion in that darkness. Something unfurling, like smoke from a conch, taking figmental shape overhead. His pain's invention, no doubt, but it sweetened his terror a little to see a face, like that of a beatific child, pour his gaze upon him.

"Open yourself to me," he heard it say. "Give up the struggle and let me be in you."

More cliché, he thought. A dream of intercession to set against the nightmare that was about to geld and blind him. But one was real—his pain was testament to that—so why not the other?

"Let me into your head and heart," the infant's lips said.

"I don't know how," he yelled, his cry taken up in parody by Abelove and the rest.

"How? How? How?" they chanted.

The child had its reply. "Give up the fight," he said.

That wasn't so hard, Gentle thought. He'd lost it anyway. What was there left to lose? With his eyes fixed on the child, Gentle let every muscle in his body relax. His hands gave up their fists; his heels, their kicks. His head tipped back, mouth open.

"Open your heart and head," he heard the infant say.

"Yes," he replied.

Even as he uttered his invitation, a moth's-wing doubt fluttered in his ear. At the beginning hadn't this smacked of melodrama? And didn't it still? A soul snatched from Purgatory by cherubim; opened, at the last, to simple salvation. But his heart was wide, and the saving child swooped upon it before doubt could seal it again. He tasted another mind in his throat and felt its chill in his veins. The invader was as good as its word. He felt his tormentors melt from around him, their holds and howls fading like mists.

He fell to the floor. It was dry beneath his cheek, though seconds before Esther's skirts had been seeping on it. Nor was there any trace of the creatures' stench in the air. He rolled over and cautiously reached to touch his hamstrings. They were intact. And his testicles, which he'd presumed nearly pulped, didn't even ache. He laughed with relief to find himself whole and, while he laughed, scrabbled for the candle he'd dropped. Delusion! It had all been delusion! Some final rite of passage conducted by his mind so that he might supersede his guilt and face his future as a Reconciler unburdened. Well, the phantoms had done their duty. Now he was free.

His fingers had found the candle. He picked it up, fumbled for the matches, struck one, and put the flame to the wick. The stage he'd filled with ghouls and cherubim was empty from boards to gallery. He got to his feet. Though the hurts he'd felt had been imagined, the fight he'd put up against them had been real enough, and his body—which was far from healed after the brutalities of Yzordderrex—was the worse for his resistance.

As he hobbled towards the door, he heard the cherub speak again. "Alone at last," it said.

He turned on his heel. The voice had come from behind him, but the staircase was empty. So was the landing and the passageways that led off the hall. The voice came again, however.

"Amazing, isn't it?" the putto said. "To hear and not to see. It's enough to drive a man mad."

Again Gentle wheeled, the candle flame fluttering at his speed.

"I'm still here," the cherub said. "We'll be together for quite a time, just you and I, so we'd better get to like each other. What do you enjoy chatting about? Politics? Food? I'm good for anything but religion."

This time, as he turned, Gentle caught a glimpse of his tormentor. It had put off the cherubic illusion. What he saw resembled a small ape, its face either anemic or powdered, its eyes black beads, its mouth enormous. Rather than waste his energies pursuing something so nimble (it had hung from the ceiling minutes before), Gentle stood still and waited. The tormentor was a chatterbox. It would speak again and eventually show itself entirely. He didn't have to wait long.

"Those demons of yours must have been appalling," it said. "The way you kicked and cursed."

"You didn't see them?"

"No. Nor do I want to."

"But you've got your fingers in my head, haven't you?"

"Yes. But I don't delve. It's not my business."

"What *is* your business?"

"How do you live in this brain? It's so small and sweaty."

"Your business?"

"To keep you company."

"I'm leaving soon."

"I don't think so. Of course, that's just my opinion. . . ."

"Who are you?"

"Call me Little Ease."

"That's a name?"

"My father was a jailer. Little Ease was his favorite cell. I used to say, Thank God he didn't circumcise for a living, or I'd be—"

"Don't."

"Just trying to keep the conversation light. You seem very agitated. There's no need. You're not going to come to any harm, unless you defy my Maestro."

"Sartori."

"The very man. He knew you'd come here, you see. He said you'd pine and you'd preen, and how very right he was. But then I'm sure he'd have done the same thing. There's nothing in your head that isn't in his. Except for me, that is. I must thank you for being so prompt, by the way. He said I'd have to be patient, but here you are, after less than two days. You must have wanted these memories badly."

The creature went on in similar vein, burbling at the back of Gentle's head, but he was barely aware of it. He was concentrating on what to do now. This creature, whatever it was, had tricked its way into him—*Open your head and heart,* it had said, and he'd done just that, fool that he was: opened himself up to its possession—and now he had to find some way to be rid of it.

"There's more where those came from, you know," it was saying.

He'd temporarily lost track of its monologue and didn't know what it was prattling about.

"More of what?" he said.

"More memories," it replied. "You wanted the past, but you've only had a tiny part of a tiny part. The best's still to come."

"I don't want it," he said.

"Why not? It's *you,* Maestro, in all your many skins. You should have what's yours. Or are you afraid you'll drown in what you've been?"

He didn't answer. It knew damn well how much damage the past could do if it came over him too suddenly; he'd laid plans for that very eventuality as he'd come to the house.

Little Ease must have heard his pulse quicken, because it said, "I can see why it'd frighten you. There's so much to be guilty for, isn't there? Always, so much."

He had to be out and away, he thought. Staying here, where the past was all too present, invited disaster.

"Where are you going?" Little Ease said as Gentle started towards the door.

"I'd like to get some sleep," he said. An innocent enough request.

"You can sleep here," his possessor replied.

"There's no bed."

"Then lie down on the floor. I'll sing a lullaby."

"And there's nothing to eat or drink."

"You don't need sustenance right now," came the reply.

"I'm hungry."

"So fast for a while."

Why was it so eager to keep him here? he wondered. Did it simply want to wear him down with sleeplessness and thirst before he even stepped outside? Or did its sphere of influence cease at the threshold? That hope leapt in him, but he tried not to let it show. He sensed that the creature, though it had spoken of entering his head and heart, did not have access to every thought in his cranium.

If it did, it'd have no need of threats in order to keep him here. It would simply direct his limbs to be leaden and drop him to the ground. His intentions were still his own, even if the entity had his memories at its behest, and it followed therefore that he might get to the door, if he was quick, and be beyond its grasp before it opened the floodgates. In order to placate it until he was ready to make his move, he turned his back on the door.

"Then I suppose I stay," he said.

"At least we've got each other for company," Little Ease said. "Though let me make it clear, I draw the line at any carnal relations, however desperate you get. Please don't take it personally. It's just that I know your reputation, and I want to state here and now I have no interest in sex."

"Will you never have children?"

"Oh, yes, but that's different. I lay them in the heads of my enemies."

"Is that a warning?" he asked.

"Not at all," it replied. "I'm sure you could accommodate a family of us. It's all One, after all. Isn't that right?" It left off its voice for a moment and imitated him perfectly. *"We'll not be subsumed at our deaths, Roxborough, we'll be increased to the size of Creation.* Think of me as a little sign of that increase, and we'll get along fine."

"Until you murder me."

"Why would I do that?"

"Because Sartori wants me dead."

"You do him an injustice," Little Ease said. "I've no brief as an assassin. All he wants me to do is keep you from your work until after midsummer. He doesn't want you playing the Reconciler and letting his enemies into the Fifth. Who can blame him? He intends to build a New Yzordderrex here, to rule over the Fifth from pole to pole. Did you know that?"

"He did mention it."

"And when that's done, I'm sure he'll embrace you as a brother."

"But until then—"

"—I have his permission to do whatever I must to keep you from being a Reconciler. And if that means driving you insane with memories—"

"—then you will."

"Must, Maestro, *must.* I'm a dutiful creature."

Keep talking, Gentle thought, as it waxed poetic describing its powers of subservience. He wouldn't make for the door, he'd decided. It was probably double- or treble-locked. Better that he went for the window by which he'd entered. He'd fling himself through if need be. If he broke a few bones in the process, it'd be a small price to pay for escape.

He glanced around casually, as if deciding where he was going to lay his head, never once allowing his eyes to stray to the front door. The room with the open window lay ten paces at most from where he stood. Once inside, there'd be another ten to reach the window. Little Ease, meanwhile, was lost in loops of its own humility. Now was as good a time as any.

He took a pace towards the bottom of the stairs as a feint, then changed direction and darted for the door. He'd made three paces before it even realized what he was up to.

"Don't be so stupid!" it snapped.

He'd been conservative in his calculation, he realized. He'd be through the door in eight paces, not ten, and across the room in another six.

"I'm warning you," it shrieked, then, realizing its appeals would gain it nothing, acted.

Within a pace of the door, Gentle felt something open in his head. The crack through which he allowed the past to trickle suddenly gaped. In a pace the rivulet was a stream; in two, white waters; in three, a flood. He saw the window across the room, and the street outside, but his will to reach it was washed away in the deluge of the past.

He'd lived nineteen lives between his years as Sartori and his time as John Furie Zacharias, his unconscious programmed by Pie to ease him out of one life and into another in a fog of self-ignorance that only lifted when the deed was done, and he awoke in a strange city, with a name filched from a telephone book or a conversation. He'd left pain behind him, of course, wherever he'd gone. Though he'd always been careful to detach himself from his circle, and cover his tracks when he departed, his sudden disappearances had undoubtedly caused great grief to everyone who'd held him in their affections. The only one who'd escaped unscathed had been himself. Until now. Now all these lives were upon him at once, and the hurts he'd scrupulously avoided caught up with him. His head filled with fragments of his past, pieces of the nineteen unfinished stories that he'd left behind, all lived with the same infantile greed for sensation that had marked his existence as John Furie Zacharias. In every one of these lives he'd had the comfort of adoration. He'd been loved and lionized: for his charm, for his profile, for his mystery. But that fact didn't sweeten the flood of memories. Nor did it save him from the panic he felt as the little self he knew and understood was overwhelmed by the sheer profusion of details that arose from the other histories.

For two centuries he'd never had to ask the questions that vexed every other soul at some midnight or other: "Who am I? What was I made for, and what will I be when I die?"

Now he had too many answers, and that was more distressing than too few. He had a small tribe of selves, put on and off like masks. He had trivial purposes aplenty. But there had never been enough years held in his memory at one time to make him plumb the depths of regret or remorse, and he was the poorer for that. Nor, of course, had there been the imminence of death or the hard wisdom of mourning. Forgetfulness had always been on hand to smooth his frowns away, and it had left his spirit unproved.

Just as he'd feared, the assault of sights and scenes was too much to bear, and though he fought to hold on to some sense of the man he'd been when he'd entered the house, it was rapidly subsumed. Halfway between the door and the window his desire to escape, which had been rooted in the need to protect himself, went out of him. The determination fell from his face, as though it were just another mask. Nothing replaced it. He stood in the middle of the room like a stoic sentinel, with no flicker of his inner turmoil rising to disturb the placid symmetry of his face.

The night hours crawled on, marked by a bell in a distant steeple, but if he heard it he showed no sign. It wasn't until the first light of day crept over Gamut Street, slipping through the window he'd been so desperate to reach, that the world outside his confounded head drew any response from him. He wept. Not for himself, but rather for the delicacy of this amber light falling in soft pools on the hard floor. Seeing it, he conceived the vague notion of stepping out into the street and looking for the source of this miracle, but there was somebody in his head, its voice stronger than the muck of confusion that swilled there, who wanted him to answer a question before it would allow him out to play. It was a simple enough inquiry.

"Who are you?" it wanted to know.

The answer was difficult. He had a lot of names in his head, and pieces of lives to go with them, but which one of them was his? He'd have to sort through many fragments to get a sense of himself, and that was too wretched a task on a day like this, when there were sunbeams at the window, inviting him out to spy their father in Heaven.

"Who are you?" the voice asked him again, and he was obliged to tell the simple truth.

"I don't know."

The questioner seemed content with this. "You may as well go, then," it said. "But I'd like you to come back once in a while, just to see me. Will you do that?"

He said that of course he would, and the voice replied that he was free to go. His legs were stiff, and when he tried to walk he fell instead, and had to crawl to where the sun was brightening the boards. He played there for a time and then, feeling stronger, climbed out of the window into the street.

Had he possessed a cogent memory of the previous night's pursuits he'd have realized, as he jumped down onto the pavement, that his guess concerning Sartori's agent had been correct, and its jurisdiction did indeed halt at the limits of the house. But he comprehended not at all the fact of his escape. He'd entered number 28 the previous night as a man of purpose, the Reconciler of the Imajica come to confront the past and be strengthened by self-knowledge. He left it undone by that same knowledge and stood in the street like a bedlamite, staring up at the sun in ignorance of the fact that its arc marked the year's progression to midsummer, and thus to the hour when the man of purpose he'd been had to act—or fail forever.

9

I

Although Jude had not slept well after Clem's visit (dreams of light bulbs, talking in a code of flickers she couldn't crack), she woke early and had laid her plans for the day by eight. She'd drive up to Highgate, she decided, and try and find some way into the prison beneath the tower, where the only woman left in the Fifth who might help empower her languished. She knew more about Celestine now than she had when she'd first visited the tower on New Year's Eve. Dowd had procured her for the Unbeheld, or so he claimed, plucking her from the streets of London and taking her to the borders of the First. That she'd survived such traumas at all was extraordinary. That she might be sane at the end of them, after divine violation and centuries of imprisonment, was almost certainly too much to hope for. But mad or not, Celestine was a much needed source of insight, and Jude was determined to dare whatever she had to in order to hear the woman speak.

The tower was so perfectly anonymous she drove past it before realizing that she'd done so. Doubling back, she parked in a side street and approached on foot. There were no vehicles in the forecourt and no sign of life at any of the windows, but she marched to the front door and rang the bell, hoping there might be a caretaker she could persuade to let her in. She'd use Oscar's name as a reference, she decided. Though she knew this was playing with fire, there was no time for niceties. Whether Gentle's ambitions as

a Reconciler were realized or not, the days ahead would be charged
with possibilities. Things sealed were cracking; things silent were
drawing breath to speak.

The door remained closed, though she rang and rapped several
times. Frustrated, she headed around the back of the building, the
route more choked by barbs and stings than ever. The tower's
shadow chilled the ground where Clara had dropped and died, and
the earth, which was badly drained, smelled of stagnancy. Until she
walked here the thought of finding any fragments of the blue eye
had not occurred to her, but perhaps it had been part of her unconscious agenda from the start. Finding no hope of access on this
side of the building, she turned her attention to seeking the pieces.
Though her recollections of what had happened here were strong,
she couldn't pinpoint with any accuracy the place where Dowd's
mites had devoured the stone, and she wandered around for fully
an hour, searching through the long grass for some sign. Her patience was finally rewarded, however. Much farther from the tower
than she'd ever have guessed, she found what the devourers had
left. It was little more than a pebble, which anybody but herself
would have passed over. But to her eyes its blue was unmistakable,
and when she knelt to pick it up she was almost reverential. It
looked like an egg, she thought, lying there in a nest of grass, waiting for the warmth of a body to kindle the life in it.

As she stood up she heard the sound of car doors slamming
on the other side of the building. Keeping the stone in her hand
she slipped back down the side of the tower. There were voices
in the forecourt: men and women exchanging words of welcome.
At the corner, she had a glimpse of them. Here they were, the Tabula Rasa. In her imagination she'd elevated them to the dubious
status of Grand Inquisitors, austere and merciless judges whose
cruelty would be gouged into their faces. There was perhaps one
among this quartet—the eldest of the three men—who would not
have looked absurd in robes, but the others had an insipidity about
their features and a sloth in their bearing that would have made
them bathetic in any garb but the most bland. None looked particularly happy with his lot. To judge by their leaden eyes, sleep had
failed to befriend them lately. Nor could their expensive clothes
(everything charcoal and black) conceal the lethargy in their limbs.

She waited at the corner until they'd disappeared through the
front door, hoping the last had left it ajar. But it was once again
locked, and this time she declined to knock. While she might have
brazened or flattered her way past a caretaker, none of the quartet she'd seen would have spared her an inch. As she stepped away
from the door another car turned off the road and glided into the
forecourt. Its driver was a male, and the youngest of the arrivees.

It was too late to dodge for cover, so she raised her hand in a cheery way and picked up her pace to a smart trot.

As she came abreast of the vehicle it halted. She kept on walking. Once past it, she heard the car door open and a fruity, overeducated voice said, "You there! What are you doing?"

She kept up her trot, resisting the temptation to run even though she heard his feet on the gravel, then another haughty holler as he came in pursuit. She ignored him until she was at the property line and he was within grasping distance of her. Then she turned, with a pretty smile, and said, "Did you call?"

"This is a private ground," he replied.

"I'm sorry, I must have the wrong address. You're not a gynecologist, are you?" Where this invention sprang from she didn't know, but it colored his cheeks in two pulses. "I need to see a doctor as soon as possible."

He shook his head, covered in confusion. "This isn't the hospital," he spluttered. "It's halfway down the hill."

Lord bless the English male, she thought, who could be reduced to near idiocy at the very mention of matters vaginal.

"Are you sure you're not a doctor?" she said, enjoying his discomfiture. "Even a student? I don't mind."

He actually took a step back from her at this, as though she was going to pounce on him and demand an examination on the spot.

"No, I'm—I'm sorry."

"So am I," she said, extending her hand. He was too baffled to refuse, and shook it. "I'm Sister Concupiscentia," she said.

"Bloxham," he replied.

"You should be a gynecologist," she said appreciatively. "You've got lovely warm hands." And with that she left him to his blushes.

2

There was a message from Chester Klein on the answering machine when she got back, inviting her to a cocktail party at his house that evening, in celebration of what he called the Bastard Boy's return to the land of the living. She was at first startled that Gentle had decided to make contact with his friends after all his talk of invisibility, then flattered that he'd taken her advice. Perhaps she'd been over-hasty in her rejection of him. Even in the short time she'd spent in Yzorderrex, the city had made her think and behave in ways she'd never have countenanced in the Fifth. How much more so for Gentle, whose catalogue of adventures in the Dominions would have filled a dozen diaries. Now he was back in the Fifth, perhaps he was resisting some of those bizarrer influences, like a man returned to civilization from some lost tribe, sluicing off the war paint and learning to wear shoes again. She called Klein back and accepted the invitation.

"My dear child, you are a sight for sore eyes," he said when she appeared on his doorstep that evening. "So stylishly unnourished! Malnutrition à la mode. Perfection."

She hadn't seen him in a long time, but she didn't remember his ever being so fulsome in his flattery before. He kissed her on both cheeks and led her through the house into the back garden. There was still warmth in the descending sun, and his other guests—two of whom she knew, two of whom were strangers—were sipping cocktails on the lawn. Though small and high-walled, the garden was almost tropically lush. Inevitably, given Klein's nature, it was entirely given over to flowering species, no bush or plant welcomed if it didn't bloom with immoderate abandon. He introduced her to the company one by one, starting with Vanessa, whose face—though much changed since they'd last met—was one of the two she knew. She had put on a good deal of weight and even more makeup, as though to cover one excess with another. Her eyes, Jude saw when she said hello, were those of a woman who was only holding back a scream for decorum's sake.

"Is Gentle with you?" was Vanessa's first question.

"No, he's not," Klein said. "Now have another drink and go and dally in the rosebushes."

The woman took no offense at his condescension but made straight for the champagne bottle, while Klein introduced Jude to the two strangers in the party. One, a balding young man in sunglasses, he introduced as Duncan Skeet.

"A painter," he said. "Or, more precisely, an impressionist. Isn't that right, Duncan? You do impressions, don't you? Modigliani, Corot, Gauguin. . . ."

The joke was lost on its butt, though not on Jude. "Isn't that illegal?" she said.

"Only if you don't talk about it," Klein replied, which remark brought a guffaw from the fellow in conversation with the faker, a heavily mustached and accented individual called Luis.

"Who's not a painter of any persuasion. You're not anything at all, are you, Luis?"

"How about a Lotos-eater?" Luis said. The scent Jude had taken to be that of the blossoms in the borders was in fact Luis' aftershave.

"I'll drink to that," Klein said, moving Jude on to the last of the company. Though Jude knew the woman's face she couldn't place it, until Klein named her—Simone—and she remembered the conversation she'd had at Clem and Taylor's, which had ended with this woman heading off in search of seduction. Klein left them to talk while he went inside to break open another bottle of champagne.

"We met at Christmas," Simone said. "I don't know if you remember?"

"Instantly," Jude said.

"I've had my hair chopped since then, and I swear half my friends don't recognize me."

"It suits you."

"Klein says I should have kept it and had it made into jewelry. Apparently hair brooches were the height of fashion at the turn of the century."

"Only as memento mori," Jude said. Simone looked blank. "The hair was usually from someone who'd died."

The woman's fizz-addled features still took a little time to register what she was being told, but when she grasped the point she let out a groan of disgust.

"I suppose that's his idea of a joke," she said. "He has no sense of fucking decency, that man." Klein was appearing from the back door, bearing champagne. "Yes, you!" Simone said. "Don't you take death seriously?"

"Have I missed something?" Klein said.

"You are a tasteless old fart sometimes!" Simone went on, striding toward him and throwing the glass down at his feet.

"What did I do?" Klein said.

Luis went to his assistance, cooing at Simone to calm her. Jude had no desire to get further embroiled. She retreated down one of the paths, her hand slipping into the deep pocket of her skirt, where the egg of the blue eye was lying. She closed her palm around it and stooped to sniff at one of the perfect roses. It had no scent, not even of life. She thumbed its petals. They were dry. She stood up again, casting her eyes over the spectacle of blossoms. Fake, every last one.

Simone's caterwauling had ceased behind her, and now so did Luis' chatter. Jude looked around, and there at the back door, stepping out of the house into the warm evening light, was Gentle.

"Save me," she heard Klein imploring. "Before I'm flayed alive."

Gentle smiled his sun-shamer and opened his arms to Klein.

"No more arguments," he said, hugging the man.

"Tell Simone," Klein replied.

"Simone. Are you bullying Chester?"

"He was being a bastard."

"No, I'm the bastard. Give me a kiss, and tell me you forgive him."

"I forgive him."

"Peace on earth, goodwill to Chester."

There was laughter from all parties, and Gentle passed through the company with kisses, hugs, and handshakes, reserving the longest, and perhaps the cruelest, embrace for Vanessa.

"You're missing somebody," Klein said, and steered Gentle's glance towards Jude.

He didn't lavish his smile upon her. She was wise to his devices, and he knew it. Instead he offered her an almost apologetic look and raised the glass Klein had already put in his hand in her direction. He'd always been a slick transformer (perhaps it was the Maestro in him, surfacing as a trivial skill), and in the twenty-four hours or so since she'd left him on his doorstep he'd made himself new. The ragged locks were trimmed, the grimy face washed and shaved. Dressed in white, he looked like a cricketer returned from the crease, glowing with vigor and victory. She stared at him, searching for some sign of the haunted man he'd been the evening before, but he'd put his anxieties entirely out of sight, for which she could only admire him. More than admire. Tonight he was the lover she'd imagined as she'd lain in Quaisoir's bed, and she couldn't help but be stirred by the sight of him. Once before a dream had led her into his arms, and the consequence, of course, had been pain and tears. It was a form of masochism to invite a repeat of that experience, and a distraction from weightier matters.

And yet; and yet. Was it perhaps *inevitable* that they found their way back into one another's arms sooner or later? And if it was, maybe this game of glances was a greater distraction still, and they would serve their ambitions better to dispense with the dalliance and accept that they were indivisible. This time, instead of being dogged by a past neither of them had comprehended, they knew their histories and could build on solid ground. That is, if he had the will to do so.

Klein was beckoning her, but she stayed in her bower of fake blossoms, seeing how eager he was to watch the drama he'd engineered unfold. He, Luis, and Duncan were merely spectators. The scene they'd come to watch was the Judgment of Paris, with Vanessa, Simone, and herself cast as the Goddesses, and Gentle as the hero obliged to choose between them. It was grotesque, and she was determined to keep herself from the tableau, instead wandering up to the far end of the garden while the banter continued on the lawn. Close to the wall she came upon a strange sight. A clearing had been made in the artificial jungle, and a small rosebush—real, but far less sumptuous than the fakery surrounding it—had been planted there. As she was puzzling over this, Luis appeared at her side with a glass of champagne.

"One of his cats," Luis said. "Gloriana. She was killed by a car

in March. He was devastated. Couldn't sleep. Wouldn't even talk
to anybody. I thought he was going to kill himself."

"He's a strange one," Jude said, casting a glance back at Klein,
who had his arm around Gentle's shoulder and was laughing up-
roariously. "He pretends everything's a game—"

"That's because he feels everything too much," Luis replied.

"I doubt that," she said.

"I've been in business with him twenty-one, twenty-two years.
We have fights. We make up. We have fights again. He's a good
man, believe me. But so afraid of feeling, he must make it all a joke.
You're not English, huh?"

"No, I'm English."

"Then you understand this," he said. "You also have the little
graves, hidden away." He laughed.

"Thousands," she said, watching Gentle step back into the house.
"Would you excuse me a moment?" she said, and headed back
down the garden with Luis in pursuit.

Klein made a move to intercept her, but she simply handed him
her empty glass and went inside. Gentle was in the kitchen, rooting through the refrigerator, peeling the lids off bowls and peering into them.

"So much for invisibility," Jude said.

"Would you have preferred it if I hadn't come?"

"Meaning that if I'd asked you'd have stayed away?"

He grinned as he found something that suited his palate. "Meaning," he said, "that the rest of them don't have a prayer. I came because I knew you'd be here."

He plunged his first and middle fingers into the ramekin he'd
brought out and laid a dollop of chocolate mousse on his tongue.

"Want some?" he said.

She hadn't, until she saw the abandon with which he was devouring the stuff. His appetite was contagious. She scooped a fin-
gerful herself. It was sweet and creamy.

"Good?" he said.

"Sinful," she replied. "What made you change your mind?"

"About what?"

"About hiding yourself away."

"Life's too short," he said, taking his laden fingers to his mouth
again. "Besides, I just said: I knew you'd be here."

"You're a mind reader now?"

"I'm flourishing," he said, his grin more chocolate than teeth.
The sophisticate she'd seen step out into the garden minutes before was here a guzzling boy.

"You've got chocolate all around your mouth," she said.

"Do you want to kiss it off?" he replied.

"Yes," she said, seeing no purpose misrepresenting her feeling. Secrets had done them too much harm in the past.

"Then why are we still here?" he said.

"Klein'll never forgive us if we leave. The party's in your honor."

"They can talk about us when we've gone," he said, setting down the ramekin and wiping his mouth with the back of his hand. "In fact, they'd probably prefer that. I say we go now, before we're spotted. We're wasting time making conversation—"

"—when we could be making love."

"I thought *I* was the mind reader," he said.

As they opened the front door they heard Klein calling them from the back, and Jude felt a pang of guilt, until she remembered the proprietorial look she'd caught on Klein's face when Gentle had first appeared and he'd known that he had the cast gathered for a fine farce. Guilt turned to irritation, and she slammed the front door hard to make sure he heard.

3

As soon as they got back to the flat Jude threw open the windows to let the breeze, which was still balmy though the night had long since fallen, come and go. News from the streets outside came with it, of course, but nothing momentous: the inevitable sirens; chatter from the pavement; jazz from the club down the block. With the windows wide, she sat down on the bed beside Gentle. It was time for them to speak without any other agenda but the truth.

"I didn't think we'd end up this way," she said. "Here. Together."

"Are you glad we have?"

"Yes, I'm glad," she said, after a pause. "It feels right."

"Good," he replied. "It feels perfectly natural to me too."

He slid around the back of her and, threading his hands through her hair, began to work his fingers against her scalp. She sighed.

"You like that?" he asked.

"I like that."

"Do you want to tell me how you feel?"

"About what?"

"About me. About us."

"I told you, it feels right."

"That's all?"

"No."

"What else?"

She closed her eyes, the persuasive fingers almost easing the words out of her. "I'm glad you're here because I think we can learn from one another. Maybe even love each other again. How does that sound?"

"Fine by me," he said softly.

"And what about you? What's in your head?"

"That I'd forgotten how strange this Dominion is. That I need your help to make me strong. That I'm afraid I may act strangely sometimes, make mistakes, and I want you to love me enough to forgive me if I do. Will you?"

"You know I will," she said.

"I want you to share my visions, Judith. I want you to see what's shining in me and not be afraid of it."

"I'm not afraid."

"That's good to hear," he said. "That's so very good." He leaned towards her, putting his mouth close to her ear. "We make the rules from now on," he whispered. "And the world follows. Yes? There's no law but us. What we want. What we feel. We'll let that consume us, and the fire'll spread. You'll see."

He kissed the ear into which he'd poured these seductions, then her cheek, and finally her mouth. She started to kiss him back, fervently, putting her hands around his head as he had hers, kneading the flesh from which his hair sprang and feeling its motion against his skull. He had his hands on the neck of her blouse, but he didn't bother to unbutton it. Instead he tore it open, not in a frenzy but rhythmically, rent after rent, like a ritual of uncovering. As soon as her breasts were bare his mouth was on them. Her skin was hot, but his tongue was hotter, painting her with spiral tracks of spittle, then closing his mouth around her nipples until they were harder than the tongue that teased them. His hands were reducing her skirt to tatters in the same efficient way he'd torn open her blouse. She let herself drop back onto the bed, with the rags of blouse and skirt beneath her. He looked down at her, laying his palm at her crotch, which was still protected from his touch by the thin fabric of her underwear.

"How many men have had this?" he asked her, the question murmured without inflection. His head was silhouetted against the pale billows at the window, and she could not read his expression. "How many?" he said, moving the ball of his hand in a circular motion. From any other source but this the question would have offended or even enraged her. But she liked his curiosity.

"A few."

He ran his fingers down into the space between her legs and worked his middle fingers under the fabric to touch her other hole. "And this?" he said, pushing at the place.

She was less comfortable with this inquiry, verbal or digital, but he insisted. "Tell me," he said. "Who's been in here?"

"Just one," she said.

"Godolphin?" he replied.

"Yes."

He removed his finger and rose from the bed. "A family enthusiasm," he remarked.

"Where are you going?"

"Just closing the curtains," he said. "The dark's better for what we're going to do." He drew the drapes without closing the window. "Are you wearing any jewelry?" he asked her.

"Just my earrings."

"Take them off," he said.

"Can't we have a little light?"

"It's too bright as it is," he replied, though she could barely see him. He was watching her as she undressed, that much she knew. He saw her slide her earrings from the holes in her lobes and then take off her underwear. By the time she was completely naked so was he.

"I don't want a little part of you," he said, approaching the bottom of the bed. "I want all of you, every last piece. And I want you to want all of me."

"I do," she said.

"I hope you mean that."

"How can I prove it?"

His gray form seemed to darken as she spoke, receding into the shadows of the room. He'd said he'd be invisible, and now he was. Though she felt his hand graze her ankle, and looked down the bed to find him, he was beyond the grasp of her eye. But pleasure flowed from his touch nevertheless.

"I want this," he said as he caressed her foot. "And this." Now her shin and thigh. "And this"—her sex—"as much as the rest, but no more. And this, and these." Belly, breasts. His touch was on them all, so he had to be very close to her now, but still invisible. "And this sweet throat, and this wonderful head." Now the hands slid away again, down her arms. "And these," he said, "to the ends of your fingers."

The touch was back at her foot again, but everywhere his hands had been—which was to say her entire body—trembled with anticipation at the touch coming again. She raised her head from the pillow a second time in the hope of glimpsing her lover.

"Lie back," he told her.

"I want to see you."

"I'm here," he said, his eyes stealing a gleam from somewhere as he spoke: two bright dots in a space that, had she not known it was bounded, could have been limitless. After his words, there was only his breath. She couldn't help but let the rhythm of her own inhalations and exhalations fall in with his, a lulling regularity which steadily slowed.

After a time, he raised her foot to his mouth and licked the sole from heel to toe in one motion. Then his breath again, cooling the fluid he'd bathed her with, and slowing still further as it came and went, until her system seemed to teeter on termination at the end of each breath, only to be coaxed back into life again as she inhaled. This was the substance of every moment, she realized: the body— never certain if the next lungful would be its last—hovering for a tiny time between cessation and continuance. And in that space out of time, between a breath expelled and another drawn, the miraculous was easy, because neither flesh nor reason had laid their edicts there. She felt his mouth open wide enough to encompass her toes and then, impossible as it was, slide her foot into his throat.

He's going to swallow me, she thought, and the notion conjured once again the book she'd found in Estabrook's study, with its sequence of lovers enclosed in a circle of consumption: a devouring so prodigious it had ended with mutual eclipse. She felt no unease at the prospect. This wasn't the business of the visible world, where fear got fat because there was so much to win and lose. This was a place for lovers, where there was only ever gain.

She felt him draw her other leg up to his head and immerse it in the same heat; then felt him take hold of her hips and use them as purchase to impale himself upon her, inch by inch. Perhaps he'd become vast: his maw monstrous, his throat a tunnel; or perhaps she was pliant as silk, and he was drawing her into him like a magician threading fake flowers into a wand. She reached up towards him in the darkness, to feel the miracle, but her fingers couldn't interpret what buzzed beneath them. Was this *her* flesh or *his?* Ankle or cheek? There was no way of knowing. Nor, in truth, any need to know. All she wanted now was to do as the lovers in the book had done and match his devouring with her own.

She reached for the edge of the bed and turned herself half over, bringing him down beside her. Now, though her eyes were besotted by darkness, she saw the outline of his body, folded into the shadows of her own. There was nothing changed about his anatomy. Though he was consuming her, his body was in no way distorted. He lay beside her like a sleeper. She reached out to touch him a second time, not expecting to make sense of his body now but finding she could. This was his thigh; this his shin; this his ankle and foot. As she ran her palm across his flesh a delicate wave of change came with it, and his substance seemed to soften beneath her touch. The scent of his sweat was appetizing. It quickened the juices in her throat and belly. She drew her head towards his feet and touched her lips to the substance of him. Then she was feeding; spreading her hunger around him like a mouth and closing her mind on his glistening skin. He shuddered as she took him in, and she felt the thrill of his pleasure as her own. He had already consumed her to the hips, but she quickly matched his appetite, taking his legs down into her, swallowing both his prick and the belly it lay hard against. She loved the excess of this, and its absurdity, their bodies defying physics and physique, or else making fresh proofs of both as the configuration closed upon itself. Was anything ever so easy and yet so impossible, besides love? And what was this, if not that paradox laid on a sheet? He had slowed his swallows to allow her to catch up, and now, in tandem, they closed the loop of their consumption, until their bodies were figments, and they were mouth to mouth.

Something from outside—a shout in the street, a sour saxophone chord—threw her back into the plausible world again, and she saw the root from which their invention had flowered. It was a commonplace conjunction: her legs crossed around his hips, his erection high inside her. She couldn't see his face, but she knew he wasn't here in this fugitive place with her. He was still dreaming their devouring. She panicked, wanted to regain the vision but not knowing how. She tightened her grip on his body and, in so doing, inspired his hips to motion. He began to move in her, breathing oh so slowly against her face. She forgot her panic and let her rhythm once again slow until it matched his. The solid world dissolved as she did so, and she returned to the place from which she'd been called to find that the loop was tightening by the moment, his mind enveloping her head as she enveloped his, like layers of an impossible onion, each one smaller than the layer it concealed: an enigma that could only exist where substance collapsed into the very mind which begged its being.

This bliss could not be sustained indefinitely, however. Before long it began once more to lose its purity, tainted by further sounds from the outside world, and this time she sensed that he was also relinquishing his hold on the delirium. Perhaps, as they learned to be lovers again, they'd find a way to sustain the state for longer: spend nights and days, perhaps, lost in the precious space between a breath expelled and another drawn. But for now she would have to be content with the ecstasy they'd had. Reluctantly, she let the tropic night in which they'd devoured each other be subsumed into a simpler darkness, and, without quite knowing where consciousness began and ended, she fell asleep.

When she awoke she was alone in the bed. That disappointment apart, she felt both lively and light. What they'd shared was a commodity more marketable than a cure for the common cold: a high without a hangover. She sat up, reaching for a sheet to drape around her, but before she could stand she heard his voice in the predawn gloom. He was standing by the window, with a fold of curtain clipped between middle and forefinger, his eye to the chink he'd opened.

"It's time for me to get working," he said softly.

"It's still early," she said.

"The sun's almost up," he replied. "I can't waste time."

He let the curtain drop and crossed to the bed. She sat up and put her arms around his torso. She wanted to spend time with him, luxuriating in the calm she felt, but his instinct was healthier. They both had work to do.

"I'd rather stay here than return to the studio," he said. "Would you mind?"

"Not at all," she replied. "In fact, I'd like you to stay."

"I'll be coming and going at odd hours."

"As long as you find your way back into bed once in a while," she said.

"I'll be with you," he said, running his hand down from her neck to rub her belly. "From now on, I'll be with you night and day."

10

I

Though Jude's memory of the night before was vivid, she had no recollection of either herself or Gentle taking the telephone off the hook, and it wasn't until nine-thirty the following morning, when she decided to call Clem, that she realized that one of them had done so. She replaced the receiver, only to have the telephone ring seconds later. At the other end of the line was a voice she'd almost given up expecting to hear again: Oscar. At first she thought he was breathless, but after a few stumbling sentences she realized his pantings were barely suppressed sobs.

"Where have you been, my darling? I've rung and rung since I got your note. I thought you were dead."

"The phone was off the hook, that's all. Where are you?"

"At the house. Will you come? Please. I need you here!" He spoke with escalating panic, as though she were punctuating his appeals with refusals. "We don't have much time."

"Of course I'll come," she told him.

"Now," he insisted. "You've got to come now."

She told him she'd be on his doorstep within the hour, and he replied that she'd find him waiting. Putting off her call to Clem and putting on a little makeup, she headed out. Though it wasn't yet midmorning the sun was blazing hot, and as she drove she

remembered the monologue that she and Gentle had been treated
to on their ride back from the estate. Monsoons and heat waves
all through the summer, the doomsayer had predicted; and how
he'd relished his prophecies! She'd thought his enthusiasm
grotesque at the time, a petty mind indulging in apocalyptic fantasies. But now, after the extraordinary night she'd had with Gentle, she found herself wondering how these bright streets might be
made to experience the miracles of the previous midnight: sluiced
of vehicles by an almighty rain, then softened in the blaze of sun,
so that solid matter flowed like warm treacle and a city divided into
public places and private, into wealthy ghettoes and gutters, became a continuum. Was this what Gentle had meant when he'd
talked about her sharing his vision? If so, she was ready for more.

Regent's Park Road was quieter than usual. There were no kids
playing on the pavement and, though she'd had a hellish time carv-
ing her way through the traffic just two streets away, no vehicles
parked within half a mile of the house. It stood shunned, but for
her. She didn't need to knock. Before she'd even set her heel on
the step the door was opening, and there was Oscar, looking harried, beckoning her in. He answered the door dry-eyed, but as
soon as it was closed and locked and bolted, he put his arms around
her and the tears began, great sobs that racked his bulk. Over and
over he told her how much he loved her, missed her, and needed
her, now more than ever. She embraced him and calmed him as
best she could. After a time he controlled himself and ushered her
through to the kitchen. The lights were burning throughout the
house, but after the blaze of the day their contribution looked
jaundiced and didn't flatter him. His face was pale, where it wasn't
discolored with bruises; his hands were puffed and raw. There were
other wounds, she guessed, beneath his unpressed clothes. Watching him brew Earl Grey for them, she saw a look of discomfort
cross his face when he moved too fast. Their talk, of course, rapidly
turned to their parting at the Retreat.

"I was certain Dowd would slit your throat as soon as you got
to Yzordderrex."

"He didn't lay a finger on me," she said. Then added, "That's not
quite true. He did later. But when we arrived he was too badly
hurt." She paused. "So are you."

"I was in a pretty wretched state," he said. "I wanted to follow
you, but I could barely stand. I came back here, got a gun, licked
my wounds awhile, then crossed over. But by that time you'd gone."

"So you *did* follow?"

"Of course. Did you think I'd leave you in Yzordderrex?"

He set a large cup of tea in front of her, and honey to sweeten
it with. She didn't usually indulge, but she hadn't breakfasted, so

she put enough spoonfuls of honey into the tea to turn it into an aromatic syrup.

"By the time I reached Peccable's house," Oscar went on, "it was empty. There were riots going on outside. I didn't know where to start looking for you. It was a nightmare."

"You know the Autarch was deposed?"

"No, I didn't, but I'm not surprised. Every New Year, Peccable would say, He'll go this year, he'll go this year. What happened to Dowd, by the way?"

"He's dead," she said, with a little smile of satisfaction.

"Are you sure? His type is difficult to kill, my dear, let me tell you. I speak from bitter experience."

"You were saying—"

"Yes. What *was* I saying?"

"That you followed us and found Peccable's house empty."

"And half the city in flames." He sighed. "It was tragic, seeing it like that. All that mindless destruction. The revenge of the proles. Oh, I know, I should be celebrating a victory for democracy, but what's going to be left? My lovely Yzordderrex: rubble. I looked at it and I said, This is the end of an era, Oscar. After this, everything'll be different. Darker." He looked up from the tea into which he'd been staring. "Did Peccable survive, do you know?"

"He was going to leave with Hoi-Polloi. I assume he did. He emptied the cellar."

"No, that was me. And I'm glad I did it."

He cast a glance towards the windowsill. Nestling among the domestic bric-a-brac were a series of diminutive figurines. Talismans, she guessed: part of the horde from Peccable's cellar. Some were looking into the room, others out. They were all little paradigms of aggression, with positively rabid expressions on their garishly painted faces.

"But you're my best protection," he said. "Just having you here, I feel we've got some chance of surviving this mess." He put his hand over hers. "When I got your note and knew you'd survived, I began to hope a little. Then of course I couldn't get hold of you, and I began to imagine the worst."

She looked up from his hand and saw on his plagued face a family resemblance she'd never glimpsed before. There was an echo of Charlie in him, the Charlie of the Hampstead hospice, sitting at his window talking about bodies being dug up in the rain.

"Why didn't you just come to the flat?" she said.

"I couldn't leave here."

"Are you that badly hurt?"

"It's not what's in here that held me back," he said, putting his hand to his chest. "It's what's out there."

"You still think the Tabula Rasa's going to come after you?"

"God, no. They're the least of our worries. I half thought of warning one or two of them: anonymously, you know. Not Shales or McGann, or that idiot Bloxham. They can fry in Hell. But Lionel was always friendly, even when he was sober. And the ladies. I don't like the idea of their deaths on my conscience."

"So who are you hiding from?"

"The fact is, I don't know," he admitted. "I see images in the bowl, and I can't quite make them out."

She'd forgotten the Boston Bowl, with its blur of prophetic stones. Now Oscar was apparently hanging on its every rattle.

"Something's crossed over from the Dominions, my dear," he said. "I'm certain of that. I saw it coming after you. Trying to smother you. . . ."

He looked as though tears were going to overtake him again, but she reassured him, lightly patting his hand as though he were some addled old man.

"Nothing's going to harm me," she said. "I've survived too much in the last few days."

"You've never seen a power like this," he warned her. "And neither's the Fifth."

"If it came from the Dominions, then it's the Autarch's doing."

"You sound very certain."

"That's because I know who he is."

"You've been listening to Peccable," he said. "He's full of theories, darling, but they're not worth a damn."

His not-so-faint condescension irritated her, and she drew her hand out from under his. "My source is a lot more reliable than Peccable," she said.

"Oh?" He realized he'd caused offense and indulged her. "Who's that?"

"Quaisoir."

"Quaisoir? How the hell did you get to her?" His surprise seemed to be as genuine as his humoring had been feigned.

"Don't you have any idea?" she asked him. "Didn't Dowd ever talk to you about the old days?"

Now his expression became guarded, almost suspicious.

"Dowd served generations of Godolphins," she said. "Surely you knew that? Right back to crazy Joshua. In fact, he was Joshua's right-hand man, if man's the word."

"I was aware of that," Oscar said softly.

"Then you knew about me too?"

He said nothing.

"Did you, Oscar?"

"I didn't debate you with Dowd, if that's what you mean."

"But you knew why you and Charlie kept me in the family?"

Now it was he who was offended; he grimaced at her vocabulary.

"That's what it was, Oscar. You and Charlie, trading me; knowing I was bound to stay with the Godolphins. Maybe I'd wander off for a while and have a few romances, but sooner or later I'd be back in the family."

"We both loved you," he said, his voice as blank as the look he now gave her. "Believe me, neither of us understood the politics of it. We didn't care."

"Oh really?" she said, her doubt plain.

"All I know is: I love you. It's the one certainty left in my life."

She was tempted to sour this saccharine with chapter and verse of his family's conspiracies against her, but what was the use? He was a fractured man, locked away in his house for fear of what the sun might invite over his threshold. Circumstance had already undone him. Any further work on her part would be malice, and though she didn't doubt that there was much in him to despise—his talk of the revenge of the proles had been particularly unattractive—she'd shared too many intimacies with him, and been too comforted by them, to be cruel. Besides, she had something to impart that would be a harder blow than any accusation.

"I'm not staying, Oscar," she said. "I haven't come back here to lock myself away."

"But it's not safe out there," he replied. "I've seen what's coming. It's in the bowl. You want to see for yourself?" He stood up. "You'll change your mind."

He led her up the stairs to the treasure room, talking as he went.

"The bowl's got a life of its own since this power came into the Fifth. It doesn't need anybody watching, it just goes on repeating the same images. It's panicking. It knows what's coming, and it's panicking."

She could hear it before they even reached the door: a din like the drumming of hailstones on sun-baked earth.

"I don't think it's wise to watch for too long," he warned. "It gets hypnotic."

So saying, he opened the door. The bowl was sitting in the middle of the floor, surrounded by a ring of votive candles, their fat flames jumping as the air was agitated by the spectacle they lit. The prophetic stones were moving like a swarm of enraged bees in and above the bowl, which Oscar had been obliged to set in a small mound of earth to keep it from being thrown over by their violence. The air smelled of what he'd called their panic: a bitter odor mingled with the metallic tang that came before lightning. Though the motion of the stones was reasonably contained, she hung back from the bowl lest a rogue find its way out of the dance and strike her. At the speed they were moving, the smallest of them could have taken out an eye. But even from a distance, with the shelves and their treasures to distract her, the motion of the stones was all consuming. The rest of the room, Oscar included, faded into insignificance as the frenzy drew her in.

"It may take a little time," Oscar was saying. "But the images are there."

"I see," she said.

The Retreat had already appeared in the blur, its dome half hidden behind the screen of the copse. Its appearance was brief. The Tabula Rasa's tower took its place a moment after, only to be superseded by a third building, quite different from the pair that had gone before, except that it too was half concealed by foliage, in this case a single tree planted in the pavement.

"What's that house?" she asked Oscar.

"I don't know, but it comes up over and over again. It's somewhere in London, I'm certain of that."

"How can you be sure?"

The building was unremarkable: three stories, flat-fronted, and, as far as she could judge, in a dilapidated state. It could have stood in any inner city in England or for that matter in Europe.

"London's where the circle's going to close," Oscar replied. "It's where everything began, and it's where everything'll end."

The remark brought echoes: of Dowd at the wall on Pale Hill, talking about history coming around, and of Gentle and herself, mere hours before, devouring each other into perfection.

"There it is again," Oscar said.

The image of the house had briefly flickered out but now reappeared, brightly lit. There was somebody near the step, she saw, with his arms hanging by his sides and his head back as he stared up at the sky. The resolution of the image was not good enough for her to make out his features. Perhaps he was just some anonymous sun worshiper, but she doubted it. Every detail of this parade had its significance. Now the image decayed again, and the noonday scene, with its gleaming foliage and its pristine sky, gave way to a roiling juggernaut of smoke, all black and gray.

"Here it comes," she heard Oscar say.

There were forms in the smoke, rising, withering, and falling as ash, but their nature defied her interpretation. Scarcely aware of what she was doing, she took a step towards the bowl.

"Don't, darling," Oscar said.

"What are we seeing?" she asked, ignoring his caution.

"The power," he said. "That's what's coming into the Fifth. Or already here."

"But that's not Sartori."

"Sartori?" he said.

"The Autarch."

Defying his own warning, he came to her side and again said, "Sartori? The Maestro?"

She didn't look around at him. The juggernaut demanded her utter devotion. Much as she hated to admit it to herself, Oscar had been right, talking of immeasurable powers. This was no human agency at work. It was a force of stupendous scale, advancing over a landscape she'd first thought covered by a stubble of gray grass but which she now realized was a city, those frail stalks buildings, toppling as the power burned out their foundations and over-turned them.

No wonder Oscar was trembling behind locked doors; this was a terrible sight, and one for which she was unprepared. However atrocious Sartori's deeds, he was just a tyrant in a long and squalid history of tyrants, men whose fear of their own frailty made them monstrous. But this was a horror of another order entirely, beyond curing by politics or poisonings: a vast, unforgiving power, capa-ble of sweeping all the Maestros and despots that had carved their names on the face of the world away without pausing to think about it. Had Sartori unleashed this immensity? she wondered. Was he so insane that he thought he could survive such devasta-tion and build his New Yzordderrex on the rubble it left behind? Or was his lunacy profounder still? Was this juggernaut the true city of which he'd dreamed: a metropolis of storm and smoke that would stand to the World's End because that was its true name?

Now the sight was consumed by total darkness, and she let go of the breath she'd been holding.

"It isn't over," Oscar said, his voice close to her ear.

The darkness began to shred in several places, and through the gashes she saw a single figure, lying on a gray floor. It was herself: a crude representation, but recognizable.

"I warned you," Oscar said.

The darkness this image had appeared through didn't entirely evaporate, but lingered like a fog, and out of it a second figure came and sank down beside her. She knew before the action had un-raveled that Oscar had made an error, thinking this was a prophecy of harm. The shadow between her legs was no killer. It was Gen-tle, and this scene was here, in the bowl's report, because the Rec-onciler stood as a sign of hope to set against the despair that had come before. She heard Oscar moan as the shadow lover reached for her, putting his hand between her legs, then raising her foot to his mouth to begin his devouring.

"It's killing you," Oscar said.

Watched remotely, this was a rational interpretation. But it wasn't death, of course, it was love. And it wasn't prophecy, it was history: the very act they'd performed the night before. Oscar was viewing it like a child, seeing its parents make love and thinking violence was being done in the marital bed. She was glad of his error, in a way, saving her as it did from the problem of explaining this coupling.

She and the Reconciler were quickly intertwined, the veils of darkness attending on the act and deepening their mingled shadows, so that the lovers became a single knot, which shrank and shrank and finally disappeared altogether, leaving the stones to rattle on as an abstraction.

It was a strangely intimate conclusion to the sequence. From temple, tower, and house to the storm had been a grim progression, but from the storm to this vision of love was altogether more optimistic: a sign, perhaps, that union could bring an end to the darkness that had gone before.

"That's all there is," Oscar said. "It just begins again from here. Round and round."

She turned from the bowl as the din of stones, which had quieted as the love scene was sketched, became loud again.

"You see the danger you're in?" he said.

"I think I'm just an afterthought," she said, hoping to steer him away from an analysis of what had been depicted.

"Not to me you're not," he replied, putting his arms around her. For all his wounds, he was not a man to be resisted easily. "I want to protect you," he said. "That's my duty. I see that now. I know you've been mistreated, but I can make reparations for that. I can keep you here, safe and sound."

"So you think we can hole up here and Armageddon will just pass over?"

"Have you got a better idea?"

"Yes. We resist it, at all costs."

"There's no victory to be had against the likes of that," he said.

She could hear the stones' thunder behind her and knew they were picturing the storm again.

"At least we've got some defenses here," he went on. "I've got spirit guards at every door and every window. You saw those in the kitchen? They're the tiniest."

"All male, are they?"

"What's that got to do with it?"

"They're not going to protect you, Oscar."

"They're all we've got."

"Maybe they're all *you've* got—"

She slipped from his arms and headed for the door. He followed her out onto the landing, demanding to know what she meant by this, and finally, inflamed by his cowardice, she turned back to him.

"There's been a power under your nose for years."

"What power? Where?"

"Sealed up beneath Roxborough's tower."

"What the hell are you talking about?"

"You don't know who she is?"

"No," he said, angered now. "This is nonsense."

"I've seen her, Oscar."

"How? Nobody but the Tabula Rasa gets into the tower."

"I could show her to you. Take you to the very place."

She dropped her volume, studying Oscar's anxious, ruddy features as she spoke. "I think maybe she's some kind of Goddess. I've tried to get her out twice and failed. I need help. I need *your* help."

"It's impossible," he replied. "The tower's a fortress, now more than ever. I tell you, this house is the only safe place left in the city. It would be suicide for me to step out of here."

"Then that's that," she said, not about to debate with such timidity. She started down the stairs, ignoring his calls for her to wait.

"You can't leave me," he said, as though amazed. "I love you. Do you hear me? I love you."

"There's more important things than love," she returned, thinking as she spoke that this was easy to say with Gentle awaiting her at home. But it was also true. She'd seen this city overturned and pitched into dust. Preventing that was indeed more important than love, especially Oscar's spineless variety.

"Don't forget to lock up after me," she said as she reached the bottom of the stairs. "You never know what's going to come knocking on the door."

2

On the way home she stopped to buy groceries, which had never been her favorite chore but was today elevated into the realms of the surreal by the sense of foreboding she brought with her. Here she was going about the business of purchasing domestic necessities, while the image of the killing cloud turned in her head. But life had to go on, even if oblivion waited in the wings. She needed milk, bread, and toilet paper; she needed deodorant and waste bags to line the bin in the kitchen. It was only in fiction that the daily round of living was ignored so that grand events could take center stage. Her body would hunger, tire, sweat, and digest until the final pall descended. There was peculiar comfort in this thought, and though the darkness gathering at the threshold of her world should have distracted her from trivialities, its presence had precisely the reverse effect. She was more pernickety than usual about the cheese she bought and sniffed at half a dozen deodorants before she found a scent that pleased her.

The shopping done, she headed home through streets buzzing with the business of a sunlit day, contemplating the problem of Celestine as she went. With Oscar plainly unwilling to aid her, she would have to look for help elsewhere, and with her circle of trusted souls so shrunk, that only left Clem and Gentle. The Reconciler had his own agenda, of course, but after the promises of the night before—the commitments to be with each other, sharing the fears and the visions—he'd surely understand her need to liberate Celestine, if only to put an end to the mystery. She would tell him all she knew about Roxborough's prisoner, she decided, as soon as possible.

He wasn't home when she got back, which was no surprise. He'd warned her that he'd be keeping odd hours as he laid the groundwork for the Reconciliation. She prepared some lunch, then decided she hadn't got an appetite and went to work one up by tidying the bedroom, which was still chaos after the night's traffic. As she straightened the sheets she discovered they had a tiny occupant: the blue stone (or, as she preferred to think of it, the egg), which had been in one of the pockets of her ravaged clothes. The sight of it diverted her from her bed making, and she sat on the edge of the mattress, passing the egg from hand to hand, wondering if perhaps it could deliver her, even briefly, into the cell where Celestine was locked. It had of course been much reduced by Dowd's mites, but even when she'd first discovered it in Estabrook's safe it had been a fragment of a greater form and possessed some jurisdiction. Did it still?

"Show me the Goddess," she said, clutching the egg tight. "Show me the Goddess."

Spoken plainly that way, the notion of her mind's removal from the physical world, and its flight, seemed absurd. That wasn't the way the world worked, except perhaps at enchanted midnights. Now it was the middle of the afternoon, and the noise of day rose through the open window. She was loath to go and close it, however. She couldn't exile the world every time she wanted to alter her consciousness. The street and the people in it—the dirt and the din and the summer sky—all had to be made part of the mechanism for transcendence, or else she'd come to grief the way her sister had, bound up and blind long before her eyes went from her head.

As was her wont, she began to talk to herself, coaxing the miracle. "It's happened before," she said. "It can happen again. Be patient, woman."

But the longer she sat, the stronger the sense of her own ludicrousness became. The image of her idiot devotion appeared in her mind's eye. There she was, sitting on the bed, staring at a piece of dead stone: a study in fatuity.

"Fool," she said to herself.

Suddenly weary of the whole fiasco, she got up from the bed. In that rising she realized her error. Her mind's eye showed her the motion as if it was detached from her, hovering near the window. She felt a sudden pang of panic and for the second time in the space of thirty seconds called herself fool, not for wasting time with the egg but for failing to realize that the image she'd taken as evidence of her own failure, that of herself sitting waiting for something to happen, was in fact proof that it had. Her sight had drifted from her so subtly she'd not even known it had gone.

"The cell," she said, instructing her subtle eye. "Show me the Goddess's cell."

Though it was close to the window, and could have flown from there, her eye instead rose at a sickening speed, till she was looking down at herself from the ceiling. She saw her body rock below her, as the flight giddied her. Then her sight descended. The top of her head loomed like a planet beneath her, and she was plunged into her skull, down, down into the darkness of her body. She felt her own panic on all sides: the frantic labor of her heart, her lungs drawing shallow breaths. There was none of the brightness she'd found in Celestine's body, no hint of that luminous blue the Goddess had shared with the stone. There was only the dark and its turmoil. She wanted to make the egg understand its mistake and draw her mind's eye up out of this pit, but if her lips were making such pleas, which she doubted, they were ignored, and her fall went on, and on, as though her sight had become a fly speck in a well and would fall for hours without reaching its bowels.

And then, below her, a tiny point of light, which grew as she approached, to show itself not a point but a strip of rippling luminescence, like the purest glyph imaginable. What was this doing inside her? Was it some relic of the working that had created her, a fragment of Sartori's feit, like Gentle's signature hidden in the brushwork of his forged canvases? She was upon it now, or rather *in* it, its brightness a blaze that made her mind's eye squint.

And out of the blaze, images. Such images! She knew neither their origins nor their purpose, but they were exquisite enough to make her forgive the misdirection that had led her here rather than to Celestine. She seemed to be in a paradisiacal city, half overgrown with glorious flora, the profusion of which was fed by waters that rose like arches and colonnades on every side. Flocks of stars flew overhead and made perfect circles at her zenith; mists hung at her ankles, laying their veils beneath her feet to ease her step. She passed through this city like a hallowed daughter and came to rest in a large airy room, where water cascaded in place of doors, and the merest stab of sun brought rainbows. There she sat and with these borrowed eyes saw her own face and breasts, so vast they might have been sculpted for a temple, raised above her. Did milk seep from her nipples, and did she sing a lullaby? She thought so; but her attention strayed too quickly from breasts and face to be sure, her gaze turned towards the far end of the chamber. Somebody had entered: a man, so wounded and ill-mended she didn't recognize him at first. It was only when he was almost upon her that she realized the company she kept. It was Gentle, unshaven and badly fed, but greeting her with tears of joy in his eyes. If words were exchanged she didn't hear them, but he fell to his knees in front of her, and her gaze went between his upturned face and the monumental effigy behind her. It was not, after all, a thing of painted stone, but was in this vision made of living flesh, moving, weeping, even glancing down at the worshiper she was.

All this was strange enough, but there was stranger still to come, as she looked back towards Gentle and saw him pluck from a hand too tiny to be hers the very stone that had given her this dream. He took it with gratitude, his tears finally abating. Then he rose, and as he made his way back towards the liquid door, the day beyond it blazed, and the scene was washed away in light.

She sensed that the enigma, whatever it signified, was passing away, but she had no power to hold it. The glyph in her core appeared before her, and she rose from it like a diver from some treasure the deep would not relinquish, up through the dark and out into the place she'd left.

Nothing had changed in the room, but a sudden squall was on the world outside, its torrent heavy enough to drop a sheet of water between the raised window and the sill. She stood up, clutching the stone. The journey had left her light-headed, however, and she knew if she tried to go to the kitchen and put some food in her belly her legs would fold up beneath her, so she lay down and let the pillow have her head awhile.

3

She didn't think she slept, but it was as difficult to distinguish between sleep and wakefulness as it had been in Quaisoir's bed. The visions she'd seen in the darkness of her own belly were as insistent as some prophetic dream and stayed with her, the music of the rain a perfect accompaniment to the memory. It was only when the clouds moved on, taking their deluge south, and the sun appeared between the sodden curtains, that sleep overcame her.

When she woke, it was to the sound of Gentle's key in the lock. It was night, or close to it, and he switched on the light in the adjacent room. She sat up and was about to call to him when she thought better of it and, instead, watched through the partially open door. She saw his face for only an instant, but the glimpse was enough to make her want him to come in to her with kisses. He didn't. Instead, he paced back and forth next door, massaging his hands as though they ached, working first at the fingers, then at the palms.

Finally, she couldn't be patient any longer and got up, sleepily murmuring his name. He didn't hear her at first, and she had to speak again before he realized it was being called. Only then did he turn and put on a smile for her.

"Still awake?" he said fondly. "You shouldn't have stayed up."

"Are you all right?"

"Yes. Yes, of course." He put his hands to his face. "This is a hard business, you know. I didn't expect it to be so difficult."

"Do you want to tell me about it?"

"Some other time," he said, approaching the door. She took his hands in hers. "What's this?" he said.

She was still holding the egg, but not for long. He had it from her palm with the ease of a pickpocket. She wanted to snatch it back, but she fought the instinct and let him study his prize.

"Pretty," he said. Then, less lightly: "Where did it come from?"

Why did she hesitate to answer? Because he looked so weary, and she didn't want to burden him with new mysteries when he had a surfeit of his own? It was that in part; but there was another part that was altogether less clear to her. Something to do with the fact that in her vision she'd seen him far more broken that he was at present, wounded and wretched, and somehow that condition had to remain her secret, at least for a time.

He put the egg to his nose and sniffed it. "I smell you," he said.

"No. . . ."

"Yes, I do. Where have you been keeping it?" He put his empty hand between her legs. "In here?"

The thought was not so preposterous. Indeed she might slip it into that pocket, when she had it back, and enjoy its weight.

"No?" he said. "Well, I'm sure it wishes you would. I think half the world would like to creep up there if it could." He pressed his hand against her. "But it's mine, isn't it?"

"Yes."

"Nobody goes in there but me."

"No."

She answered mechanically, her thoughts as much on reclaiming the egg as on his proprietorial talk.

"Have you got anything we can get high on?" he said.

"I had some dope. . . ."

"Where is it?"

"I think I smoked the last of it. I'm not sure. Do you want me to look?"

"Yes, please."

She reached up for the egg, but before her fingers could take hold of it he put it to his lips.

"I want to keep it," he said. "Sniff it for a while. You don't mind, do you?"

"I'd like it back."

"You'll have it back," he said, with a faint air of condescension, as though her possessiveness was childish. "But I need a keepsake, something to remind me of you."

"I'll give you some of my underwear," she said.

"It's not quite the same."

He laid the egg against his tongue and turned it, coating it in his spittle. She watched him, and he watched her back. He knew damn well she wanted her toy, but she wasn't going to stoop to begging him for it.

"You mentioned dope," he said.

She went back into the bedroom, put on the lamp beside the bed, and searched through the top drawer of her dresser where she'd last stashed her marijuana.

"Where did you go today?" he asked her.

"I went to Oscar's house."

"Oscar?"

"Godolphin."

"And how's Oscar? Alive and kicking?"

"I can't find the dope. I must have smoked it all."

"You were telling me about Oscar."

"He's locked himself up in his house."

"Where does he live? Maybe I should call on him. Reassure him."

"He won't see you. He won't see anybody. He thinks the world's coming to an end."

"And what do you think?"

She shrugged. She was quietly raging at him, but she wasn't exactly sure why. He'd taken the egg for a while, but that wasn't a capital crime. If the stone afforded him a little protection, why should she be covetous of it? She was being petty, and she wished she could be other, but without the heat of sex shimmering between them he seemed crass. It was not a flaw she expected to find in him. Lord knows she'd accused him of countless deficiencies in her time, but a lack of finesse had never been one of them. If anything, he'd been too much the polished operator, discreet and suave.

"You were telling me about the end of the world," he said.

"Was I?"

"Did Oscar frighten you?"

"No. But I saw something that did."

She told him, briefly, about the bowl and its prophecies. He listened without comment, then said, "The Fifth's teetering. We both know that. But it won't touch us."

She'd heard the same sentiments from Oscar, or near enough. Both these men, wanting to offer her a haven from the storm. She should have been flattered. Gentle looked at his watch.

"I've got to go out again," he said. "You'll be safe here, won't you?"

"I'll be fine."

"You should sleep. Make yourself strong. There's going to be some dark times before it gets light again, and we're going to find some of that darkness in each other. It's perfectly natural. We're not angels, after all." He chuckled. "At least, you may be, but I'm not."

So saying, he pocketed the egg.

"Go back to bed," he said. "I'll be back in the morning. And don't worry, nothing's going to come near you but me. I swear. I'm with you, Judith, all the time. And that's not love talking."

With that, he smiled at her and headed off, leaving her to wonder what indeed had been talking, if it wasn't love.

I

"And who the fuck are you?" the filthy, bearded face demanded of the stranger who'd had the misfortune to stumble into its bleary sight.

The man he was questioning, whom he had by the neck, shook his head. Blood had run from a crown of cuts and scrapes along his brow, where he'd earlier beaten his skull against a stone wall to try and silence the din of voices that echoed between his temples. It hadn't worked. There were still too many names and faces in there to be sorted out. The only way he could answer his interrogator was with that shaking of his head. Who was he? He didn't know.

"Well, get the fuck out of here," the man said.

There was a bottle of cheap wine in his hand, and its stench, mingled with a deeper rot, on his breath. He pushed his victim against the concrete wall of this underpass and closed upon him.

"You can't sleep where you fuckin' want. If you want to lie down, you fuckin' ask me first. I say who sleeps here. Isn't that right?"

He swung his bloodshot eyes in the direction of the tribe who'd clambered from their beds of trash and newspapers to watch their leader have his sport. There'd be blood, for certain. There always was when Tolland got riled, and for some reason he was more riled by this trespasser than by others who'd laid down their homeless heads without his permission.

"Isn't that right?" he said again. "Irish? Tell him! *Isn't that right?*"

The man he'd addressed muttered something incoherent. The woman beside him, with a head of hair bleached to near extinction but black at the roots, came within striking distance of Tolland—something only a very few dared to do.

"That's right, Tolly," she said. "That's right." She looked at the victim without pity. "D'you think he's a Jew-boy? He's got a Jew-boy's nose."

Tolland took down a throatful of wine. "Are you a fuckin' yid?" he said.

Someone in the crowd said they should strip him and see. The woman, who went by a number of names but whom Tolland called Carol when he fucked her, made to do just that, but he aimed a blow at her and she retreated.

"You get your fuckin' hands off him," Tolland said. "He'll tell us, won't you, matey? You'll tell us. Are you a fuckin' yid or not?"

He took hold of the man by the lapel of his jacket.

"I'm waitin'," he said.

The victim dug for a word, and found: ". . . Gentle . . ."

"Gentile?" Tolland said. "Yeah? You a Gentile? Well, I don't give a fuck *what* you are! I don't want you here."

The other nodded and tried to detach Tolland's fingers, but his captor hadn't finished. He slammed the man against the wall, so hard the breath went out of him.

"Irish? Take the fuckin' bottle."

The Irishman claimed the bottle from Tolland's hands and stepped back to let him do his worst.

"Don't kill him," the woman said.

"What the fuck do you care?" Tolland spat and delivered two, three, four punches to the Gentile's solar plexus, followed by a knee jab to his groin. Pinned against the wall by his neck, the man could do little to defend himself, but even that little he failed to do, accepting the punishment even though tears of pain ran from his eyes. He stared through them with a look of bewilderment on his face, small exclamations of pain coming with every blow.

"He's a head case, Tolly," the Irishman said. "Look at him! He's a friggin' head case."

Tolland didn't glance the Irishman's way, or slow his beating, but delivered a new fusillade of punches. The Gentile's body now hung limply from the pinion of his hand, the face above it blanker by the blow.

"You hear me, Tolly?" the Irishman said. "He's a nutter. He's not feeling it."

"You keep the fuck out of this."

"Why don't you leave him alone?"

"He's on my fuckin' patch," Tolland said.

He dragged the Gentile away from the wall and swung him around. The small crowd backed off to give their leader room to play. With Irish silenced, there were no objections raised from any quarter. Tolland was left to beat the Gentile to the ground. Then he followed through with a barrage of kicks. His victim put his hands around his head and curled up to protect himself as best he could, whimpering. But Tolland wasn't about to let the man's face go unbroken. He reached down and dragged the hands away, raising his boot to bring it down. Before he could do so, however, Tolland's bottle hit the floor, spattering wine as it smashed. He turned on Irish.

"What the fuck d'you that for?"

"You shouldn't beat up head cases," the man replied, by his tone already regretting the breakage.

"You goin' to stop me?"

"All I'm sayin'—"

"Are you goin' to try and fuckin' stop me?"

"He's not right in the head, Tolly."

"So I'll kick some sense into him," Tolland replied.

He dropped his victim's arms, turning all his crazed attention on the dissenter.

"Or do _you_ want to do it?" he said.

Irish shook his head.

"Go on," said Tolland. "You do it for me." He stepped over the Gentile in the Irishman's direction. "Go on . . ." he said again. "Go on. . . ."

Irish began to retreat, Tolland bearing down on him. The Gentile had meanwhile turned himself over and was starting to crawl away, blood running from his nose and from the wounds reopened on his brow. Nobody moved to help him. When Tolland was roused, as now, his fury knew no bounds. Anyone who stepped in his way—whether man, woman, or child—was forfeit. He broke bones and heads without a second thought; had ground a broken bottle into a man's eye once, not twenty yards from this spot, for the crime of looking at him too long. There wasn't a cardboard city north or south of the river where he wasn't known, and prayers said in the hope that he'd not come visiting.

Before he could grab hold of Irish the man threw up his hands in defeat.

"All right, Tolly, all right," he said. "It was my mistake. I swear, I'm sorry."

"You broke my fuckin' bottle."

"I'll fetch you another. I will. I'll do it now."

Irish had known Tolland longer than anyone else in this circle and was familiar with the rules of placation: copious apology, witnessed by as many of Tolland's tribe as possible. It wasn't foolproof, but today it worked.

"Will I be fetchin' you a bottle now?" Irish said.

"Get me two, you fuckin' scab."

"That's what I am, Tolly. I'm a scab."

"And one for Carol," Tolland said.

"I'll do that."

Tolland leveled a grimy finger at Irish. "And don't you ever try crossin' me again, or I'll have your fuckin' balls."

With this promise made, Tolland turned back to his victim. Seeing that the Gentile had already crawled some distance from him, he let out an incoherent roar of fury, and those of the crowd who were standing within a yard or two of the path between him and his target retreated. Tolland didn't hurry, but watched as the wounded Gentile laboriously got to his feet and began to make a staggering escape through the chaos of boxes and strewn bedding.

Up ahead, a youth of sixteen or so was kneeling on the ground, covering the concrete slabs underfoot with designs in colored chalk, blowing the pastel dust off his handiwork as he went. Engrossed in his art he'd ignored the beating that had claimed the attention of the others, but now he heard Tolland's voice echoing through the underpass, calling his name.

"Monday, you fuckhead! Get hold of him!"

The youth looked up. His hair was cropped to a dark fuzz, his skin pockmarked, his ears sticking out like handles. His gaze was clear, however, despite the track marks that disfigured his arms, and it took him only a second to realize his dilemma. If he brought down the bleeding man, he'd condemn him. If he didn't, he'd condemn himself. To gain a little time he feigned bafflement, cupping his hand behind his ear as if he'd missed Tolland's instruction.

"Stop him!" came the brute's command.

Monday started to get to his feet, murmuring, "Get the fuck out of here," to the escapee as he did so.

But the idiot had stumbled to a halt, his eyes fixed on the picture Monday had been making. It was filched from a newspaper photo of a starlet, wide-eyed, posing with a koala in her arms. Monday had rendered the woman with loving accuracy, but the koala had become a patchwork beast, with a single burning eye in its brooding head.

"Didn't you hear me?" Monday said.

The man ignored him.

"It's your funeral," he said, rising now as Tolland approached, pushing the man from the edge of his picture. "Go on," he said, "or he'll bust it up! Get away!" He pushed hard, but the man remained fixated. "You're gettin' blood on it, dickhead!"

Tolland yelled for Irish, and the man hurried to his side, eager to make good.

"What, Tolly?"

"Collar that fuckin' kid."

Irish was obedient and headed straight for Monday, taking hold of the boy. Tolland, meanwhile, had caught up with the Gentile, who hadn't moved from his place on the edge of the colored paving.

"Don't let him bleed on it!" Monday begged.

Tolland threw the youth a glance, then stepped onto the picture, scraping his boots over the carefully worked face. Monday raised a moan of protest as he watched the bright chalk colors reduced to a gray-brown dust.

"Don't, man, don't," he pleaded.

But his complaints only riled the vandal further. Seeing Monday's tobacco tin of chalks within reach of his boot, Tolland went to scatter them, but Monday, dragging himself out of Irish's grip, flung himself down to preserve them. Tolland's kick landed in the boy's flank, and he was sent sprawling, rolled in chalk dust. Tolland's heel booted the tin and its contents, then he came after its protector a second time. Monday curled up, anticipating the blow. But it never landed. The Gentile's voice came between Tolland and his intention.

"Don't do that," he said.

Nobody had custody of him, and he could have made another attempt to escape while Tolland went after Monday, but he was still at the edge of the picture, his gaze no longer on it but on its spoiler.

"What the fuck did you say?" Tolland's mouth opened like a toothed wound in his matted beard.

"I said: *Don't . . . do . . . that.*"

Whatever pleasure Tolland had derived from this hunt was over now, and there wasn't one among the spectators who didn't know it. The sport that would have ended with an ear bitten off or a few broken ribs had become something else entirely, and several of the crowd, having no stomach for what they knew was coming, retired from their places at the ringside. Even the hardiest of them backed away a few paces, their drugged, drunken, or simply addled minds dimly aware that something far worse than bloodletting was imminent.

Tolland turned on the Gentile, reaching into his jacket as he did so. A knife emerged, its nine-inch blade marked with nicks and scratches. At the sight of it, even Irish retreated. He'd seen Tolland's blade at work only once before, but it was enough.

There were no jabs or taunts now, just Tolland's drink-rotted bulk lurking towards his victim to bring the man down. The Gentile stepped back as the knife came, his eyes going to the designs underfoot. They were like the pictures that filled his head to overflowing; brightnesses that had been smeared into gray dust. But somewhere in the midst of that dust he remembered another place like this: a makeshift town, full of filth and rage, where somebody or something had come for his life as this man was coming, except that this other executioner had carried a fire in his head, to burn the flesh away, and all that he, the Gentile, had owned by way of defense was empty hands.

He raised them now. They were as marked as the knife the executioner was carrying, their backs bloodied from his attempt to stem the flow from his nose. He uncurled them, as he'd done many times before, drawing breath as he chose his right over his left and, without understanding why, put it to his mouth.

The pneuma flew before Tolland had time to raise his blade, hitting him on the shoulder with such force he was thrown to the ground. Shock took his voice away for several seconds, then his hand went to his gushing shoulder and he loosed a noise more shriek than roar. The few witnesses who'd remained to watch the killing were rooted to the spot, their eyes not on their fallen lord but on his deposer. Later, when they told this story, they'd all describe what they'd seen in different ways. Some would talk of a knife produced from hiding, used, and concealed again so fast the eye could barely catch it. Others of a bullet, spat from between the Gentile's teeth. But nobody doubted that something remarkable had taken place in these seconds. A wonder worker had appeared among them and laid the tyrant Tolland low without even touching him.

The wounded man wasn't bested so easily, however. Though his blade had gone from his fingers (and been surreptitiously swiped by Monday) he still had his tribe to defend him. He summoned them now, with wild screeches of rage.

"See what he did? What are you fuckin' waitin' for? *Take him!* Take the fucker! No one does that to me! Irish? Irish? Where the fuck are you? Somebody help me!"

It was the woman who came to his aid, but he pushed her aside. "Where the fuck's Irish?"

"I'm here."

"Take hold of the bastard," Tolland said.

Irish didn't move.

"D'you hear me? He used some fuckin' Jew-boy trick on me! You saw him. Some yid trick, it was."

"I saw him," said Irish.

"He'll do it again! He'll do it to you!"

"I don't think he's goin' to do anything to anybody."

"Then break his fuckin' head."

"You can do it if you like," Irish said. "I'm not touching him."

Despite his wounding and his bulk, Tolland was up on his feet in seconds, and going at his sometime lieutenant like a bull, but the Gentile's hand was on his shoulder before his fingers could get to the man's throat. He stopped in his tracks, and the spectators had sight of the day's second wonder: fear on Tolland's face. There'd be no ambiguity in their reports of this. When word went out across the city—as it did within the hour, passed from one asylum Tolland had spoiled with blood to another—the account, though embroidered in the telling, was at root the same. Drool had run from Tolland's mouth, it said, and his face had got sweaty. Some said piss ran from the bottom of his trousers and filled his boots.

"Let Irish alone," the Gentile told him. "In fact . . . *let us all alone.*"

Tolland made no reply. He simply looked at the hand laid on him and seemed to shrink. It wasn't his wounding that made him so quiescent, or even fear of the Gentile attacking a second time. He'd sustained injuries far worse than the wound on his shoulder and simply been inflamed to fresh cruelties. It was the touch he shrank from: the Gentile's hand laid lightly on his shoulder. He turned and backed away from his wounder, glancing from side to side as he did so, in the hope that there would be somebody to support him. But everyone, including Irish and Carol, gave him a wide berth.

"You can't do this," he said when he'd put five yards between himself and the Gentile. "I've got friends all over! I'll see you dead, fucker. I will. I'll see you dead!"

The Gentile simply turned his back on this and stooped to claim from the ground the scattered shards of Monday's chalks. This casual gesture was in its way more eloquent than any counter-threat or show of power, announcing as it did his complete indifference to the other man's presence. Tolland stared at the Gentile's bent back for several seconds, as if calculating the risk of mounting another attack. Then, calculations made, he turned and fled.

"He's gone," said Monday, who was crouching beside the Gentile and watching over his shoulder.

"Do you have any more of these?" the stranger said, rocking the colors in the cradle of his palm.

"No. But I can get some. Do you draw?"

The Gentile stood up. "Sometimes," he said.

"Do you copy stuff, like me?"

"I don't remember."

"I can teach you, if you want."

"No," the Gentile replied. "I'll copy from my head." He looked down at the crayons in his hand. "I can empty it that way."

"Could you be doin' with paint as well?" Irish asked, as the Gentile's gaze went to the gray concrete all around them.

"You could get paint?"

"Me and Carol here, we can get anything. Whatever you want, Gentile, we'll get it for you."

"Then . . . I want all the colors you can find."

"Is that all? You don't want something to drink?"

But the Gentile didn't reply. He was wandering towards the pillar against which Tolland had first pinned him and was applying a color to it. The chalk in his fingers was yellow, and with it he began to draw the circle of the sun.

2

When Jude woke it was almost noon: eleven hours or more since Gentle had come home, relieved her of the egg that had brought her a glimpse of Nirvana, then headed out again into the night. She felt sluggish and pained by the light. Even when she turned the hot water in her shower to a trickle and let it run near cold, it failed to fully waken her. She toweled herself half dry and padded through to the kitchen naked. The window was open there, and the breeze brought goose bumps. At least this was some sign of life, she thought, negligible though it was.

She put on some coffee and the television, flipping the channels from one banality to another, then letting it burble along with the percolator while she dressed. The telephone rang while she was looking for her second shoe. There was a din of traffic at the other end of the line, but no voice, and after a couple of seconds the line went dead. She put down the receiver and stayed by the phone, wondering if this was Gentle trying to get through. Thirty seconds later the phone rang again. This time there was a speaker: a man, whose voice was barely more than a ragged whisper.

"For Christ's sake ..."

"Who is this?"

"Oh, Judith ... God, God ... Judith? ... It's Oscar. ..."

"Where are you?" she said. He was very clearly not locked up in his house.

"They're dead, Judith."

"Who are?"

"Now it's me. Now it wants me."

"I'm not getting this, Oscar. Who's dead?"

"Help me ... you've got to help me. ... Nowhere's safe."

"Come to the flat then."

"No ... you come here. ..."

"Where's here?"

"I'm at St. Martin-in-the-Fields. Do you know it?"

"What the hell are you doing there?"

"I'll be waiting inside. But hurry. It's going to find me. It's going to find me."

The traffic around the square was locked, as was often the case at noon, the breeze that had brought gooseflesh an hour before too meek to disperse the fog of countless exhausts and the fumes of as many frustrated drivers. Nor was the air inside the church any less stale, though it was pure ozone beside the smell of fear that came off the man sitting close to the altar, his thick hands knitted so tightly the bone of his knuckles showed through the fat.

"I thought you said you weren't going to leave the house," she reminded him.

"Something came for me," Oscar said, his eyes wide. "In the middle of the night. It tried to get in, but it couldn't. Then this morning—in broad daylight—I heard the parrots kicking up a din, and the back door was blown off its hinges."

"Did you see what it was?"

"Do you think I'd be here if I had? No; I was ready, after the first time. As soon as I heard the birds I ran for the front door. Then this terrible din, and all the lights went out. ..."

He divided his hands and took light hold of her arm.

"What am I going to do?" he said. "It'll find me, sooner or later. It's killed all the rest of them—"

"Who?"

"Haven't you seen the headlines? They're all dead. Lionel, McGann, Bloxham. Even the ladies. Shales was in his bed. Cut up in pieces in his own bed. I ask you, what kind of creature does that?"

"A quiet one."

"How can you joke?"

"I joke, you sweat. We deal with it the best way we know how."

She sighed. "You're a better man than this, Oscar. You shouldn't be hiding away. There's work to do."

"Don't tell me about your damn Goddess, Judith. It's a lost cause. The tower'll be rubble by now."

"If there's any help for us," she said, "it's there. I know it. Come with me, won't you? I've seen you brave. What's happened to you?"

"I don't know," he said. "I wish I did. All these years I've been crossing over to Yzordderrex, not giving a damn where I put my nose, not caring whether I was at risk or not, as long as there were new sights to see. It was another world. Maybe another me, too."

"And here?"

He made a baffled face. "This is England," he said. "Safe, rainy, boring England, where the cricket's bad and the beer's warm. This isn't supposed to be a dangerous place."

"But it is, Oscar, whether we like it or not. There's a darkness here worse than anything in Yzordderrex. And it's got your scent. There's no escaping that. It's coming after you. And me, for all I know."

"But why?"

"Maybe it thinks you can do it some harm."

"What can I do? I don't know a damn thing."

"But we could learn," she said. "That way, if we're going to die, at least it won't be in ignorance."

12

DESPITE OSCAR'S PREDICTION, the Tabula Rasa's tower was still standing, any trace of distinction it might have once owned eroded by the sun, which blazed with noonday fervor at well past three. Its ferocity had taken its toll on the trees that shielded the tower from the road, leaving their leaves to hang like dishrags from their branches. If there were any birds taking cover in the foliage, they were too exhausted to sing.

"When were you last here?" Oscar asked Jude as they drove into the empty forecourt.

She told him about her encounter with Bloxham, squeezing the account for its humorous effect in the hope of distracting Oscar from his anxiety.

"I never much liked Bloxham," Oscar replied. "He was so damn full of himself. Mind you, so were we all...." His voice trailed away, and with all the enthusiasm of a man approaching the execution block, he got out of the car and led her to the front door.

"There's no alarms ringing," he said. "If there's anybody inside, they got in with a key."

He'd pulled a cluster of his own keys out of his pocket and selected one.

"Are you sure this is wise?" he asked her.

"Yes, I am."

Resigned to this insanity, he unlocked the door and, after a moment's hesitation, headed inside. The foyer was cold and gloomy, but the chill only served to make Jude brisk.

"How do we get down into the cellar?" she said.

"You want to go straight down there?" he replied. "Shouldn't we check upstairs first? Somebody could be here."

"Somebody *is* here, Oscar. She's in the cellar. You can check upstairs if you want to, but I'm going down. The less time we waste the sooner we're out of here."

It was a persuasive argument, and he conceded to it with a little nod. He dutifully fished through the bunch of keys a second time and, having chosen one, went over to the farthest and smallest of the three closed doors ahead. Having taken his time selecting the right key, he now took even longer to get it into the lock and coax it into turning.

"How often have you been down there?" she asked him while he worked.

"Only twice," he replied. "It's a pretty grim place."

"I know," she reminded him.

"On the other hand, my father seemed to make quite a habit of exploring down there. There's rules and regulations, you know, about nobody looking through the library on their own, in case they're tempted by something they read. I'm sure he flouted all that. Ah!" The key turned. "That's one of them!" He selected a second key and started on the other lock.

"Did your father talk to you about the cellar?" she asked him.

"Once or twice. He knew more about the Dominions than he should have done. I think he even knew a few feits. I can't be sure. He was a cagey bugger. But at the end, when he was delirious, he'd mutter these names. *Patashoqua,* I remember. He repeated that over and over."

"Do you think he ever crossed into the Dominions?"

"I doubt it."

"So you worked out how to do that on your own?"

"I found a few books down here and smuggled them out. It wasn't difficult to get the circle working. Magic doesn't decay. It's about the only thing"—he paused, grunted, forced the key—"that doesn't." It began to turn, but not all the way. "I think Papa would have liked Patashoqua," he went on. "But it was only a name to him, poor sod."

"It'll be different after the Reconciliation," Jude said. "I know it's too late for him—"

"On the contrary," Oscar said, grimacing as he bullied the key. "From what I hear, the dead are just as locked up as the rest of us. There's spirits everywhere, according to Peccable, ranting and raving."

"Even in here?"

"Especially in here," he said.

With that, the lock gave up its resistance, and the key turned.

"There," he said. "Just like magic."

"Wonderful." She patted his back. "You're a genius."

He grinned at her. The dour, defeated man she'd found sweating in the pews an hour ago had lightened considerably now there was something to distract him from his death sentence. He withdrew the key from the lock and turned the handle. The door was stout and heavy, but it opened without much resistance. He preceded her into the darkness.

"If I remember right," he said, "there's a light here. No?" He patted the wall to the side of the door. "Ah! Wait!"

A switch flipped, and a row of bare bulbs, strung from a cable, illuminated the room. It was large, wood-paneled, and austere.

"This is the one part of Roxborough's house still intact, besides the cellar." There was a plain oak table in the middle of the room, with several chairs around it. "This is where they met, apparently: the first Tabula Rasa. And they kept meeting here, over the years, until the house was demolished."

"Which was when?"

"In the late twenties."

"So a hundred and fifty years of Godolphin bums sat on one of those seats?"

"That's right."

"Including Joshua."

"Presumably."

"I wonder how many of them I knew?"

"Don't you remember?"

"I wish I did. I'm still waiting for the memories to come back. In fact, I'm begining to wonder if they ever will."

"Maybe you're repressing them for a reason?"

"Why? Because they're so appalling I can't face them? Because I acted like a whore; let myself be passed around the table with the port, left to right? No, I don't think that's it at all. I can't remember because I wasn't really living. I was sleepwalking, and nobody wanted to wake me."

She looked up at him, almost defying him to defend his family's ownership of her. He said nothing, of course. Instead, he moved to the vast grate, ducking beneath the mantelpiece, selecting a third key as he went. She heard him slot it in the lock and turn it, heard the motion of cogs and counterweights its turning initiated, and, finally, heard the groan of the concealed door as it opened. He glanced back at her.

"Are you coming?" he said. "Be careful. The steps are steep."

The flight was not only steep but long. What little light spilled from the room above dwindled after half a dozen steps, and she descended twice that number in darkness before Oscar found a switch below, and lights ran off along the labyrinth. A sense of triumph ran through her. She'd put her desire to find a way into this underworld aside many times since the dream of the blue eye had brought her to Celestine's cell, but it had never died. Now, finally, she was going to walk where her dream sight had gone, through this mine of books with its seams to the ceiling, to the place where the Goddess lay.

"This is the single largest collection of sacred texts since the library at Alexandria," Oscar said, his museum-guide tone a defense, she suspected, against the sense of moment he shared with her. "There are books here even the Vatican doesn't know exist." He lowered his voice, as though there might be other browsers here that he'd disturb if he spoke too loudly. "The night he died, Papa told me he found a book here written by the Fourth King."

"The what?"

"There were three kings at Bethlehem, remember? According to the Gospels. But the Gospels lied. There were four. They were looking for the Reconciler."

"Christ was a Reconciler?"

"So Papa said."

"And you believe that?"

"Papa had no reason to lie."

"But the book, Oscar; the book could have lied."

"So could the Bible. Papa said this Magi wrote his story because he knew he'd been cut out of the Gospels. It was this fellow named the Imajica. Wrote the word down in this book. There it was on the page for the first time in history. Papa said he wept."

Jude surveyed the labyrinth that spread from the foot of the stairs with fresh respect. "Have you tried to find the book since?"

"I didn't need to. When Papa died I went in search of the real thing. I traveled back and forth as though Christos had succeeded and the Fifth was reconciled. And there they were, the Unbeheld's many mansions."

And there, too, the most enigmatic player in this inter-Dominional drama: Hapexamendios. If Christos was a Reconciler, did that make the Unbeheld Christos' Father? Was the force in hiding behind the fogs of the First Dominion the Lord of Lords, and, if so, why had He crushed every Goddess across the Imajica, as legend said He had? One question begged another, all from a few claims made by a man who'd knelt at the Nativity. No wonder Roxborough had buried these books alive.

"Do you know where your mystery woman's lurking?" Oscar said.

"Not really."

"Then we've got a hell of a search on our hands."

"I remember there was a couple making love down here, near her cell. One of them was Bloxham."

"Dirty little bugger. So we should be looking for some stains on the floor, is that it? I suggest we split up, or we'll be here all summer."

They parted at the stairs and made their separate ways. Jude soon discovered how strangely sound carried in the tunnels. Sometimes she could hear Godolphin's footsteps so clearly she thought he must be following her. Then she'd turn a corner (or else he would) and the noise would not simply fade but vanish altogether, leaving only the pad of her own soles on the cold stone to keep her company. They were buried too deeply for even the remotest murmur from the street above to penetrate, nor was there any suspicion of sound from the earth around them: no hum of cables; no sluicing of drains.

She was several times tempted to pluck one of the tomes from its shelf, thinking perhaps serendipity would put her in reach of the diary of the Fourth King. But she resisted, knowing that even if she had time to browse here, which she didn't, the volumes were written in the great languages of theology and philosophy: Latin, Greek, Hebrew, and Sanskrit, all incomprehensible to her. As ever on this journey, she'd have to beat a track to the truth by instinct and wit alone. Nothing had been given to her to illuminate the way except the blue eye, and that was in Gentle's possession now. She'd reclaim it as soon as she saw him again, give him something else as a talisman: the hair of her sex, if that's what he wanted. But not her egg; not her cool blue egg.

Maybe it was these thoughts that ushered her to the place where the lovers had stood; maybe it was that same serendipity she'd hoped might lead her hand to the King's book. If so, this was a finer leading. Here was the wall where Bloxham and his mistress had coupled; she knew it without a trace of doubt. Here were the shelves the woman had clung to while her ridiculous beau had labored to fulfill her. Between the books they bore, the mortar was tinged with the faintest trace of blue. She didn't call Oscar but went to the shelves and took down several armfuls of books, then put her fingers to the stains. The wall was bitterly cold, but the mortar crumbled beneath her touch, as though her sweat was sufficient agent to unbind its elements. She was shocked at what she'd caused, and gratified, retreating from the wall as the message of dissolution spread with extraordinary rapidity. The mortar began to run from between the bricks like the finest of sand, its trickle becoming a torrent in seconds.

"I'm here," she told the prisoner behind the wall. "God knows, I've taken my time. But I'm here."

Oscar didn't catch Jude's words, not even the remotest echo. His attention had been claimed two or three minutes before by a sound from overhead, and he'd climbed the stairs in pursuit of its source. He'd disgraced his manhood enough in the last few days, hiding himself away like a frightened widow, and the thought that he might reclaim some of the respect he'd lost in Jude's eyes by confronting the trespasser above gave purpose to the chase. He'd armed himself with a piece of timber he'd found at the bottom of the stairs and was almost *hoping* as he went that his ears weren't playing tricks on him, and that there was indeed something tangible up above. He was sick of being in fear of rumors, and of pictures half glimpsed in flying stones. If there was something to see, he wanted to see it and either be damned in the seeing or cured of fear.

At the top of the stairs he hesitated. The light spilling through the door from Roxborough's room was moving, very slightly. He took his bludgeon in both hands and stepped through the door. The room swung with the lights, the solid table and its solid chairs giddied by the motion. He surveyed the room from corner to corner. Finding every shadow empty, he moved towards the door that led out into the foyer, as delicately as his bulk allowed. The rocking of the lights settled as he went, and they were still by the time he reached the door. As he stepped outside a perfume caught his nostrils, as sweet as the sudden, sharp pain in his side was sour. He tried to turn but his attacker dug a second time. The timber went from his hand, and a shout came from his lips....

"Oscar?"

She didn't want to leave the wall of Celestine's cell when it was undoing itself with such gusto—the bricks were dropping onto each other as the mortar between them decayed, and the shelves were creaking, ready to fall—but Oscar's shout demanded her attention. She headed back through the maze, the sound of the wall's capitulation echoing through the passageways, confounding her. But she found her way back to the stairs after a time, yelling for Oscar as she went. There was no reply from the library itself, so she decided to climb back up into the meeting room. That too was silent and empty, as was the foyer when she got to it, the only sign that Oscar had passed through a block of wood lying close to the door. What the hell was he up to? She went out to see if he'd returned to the car for some reason, but there was no sign of him in the sun, which narrowed the options to one: the tower above.

Irritated, but a little anxious now, she looked towards the open door that led back into the cellar, torn between returning to welcome Celestine and following Oscar up the tower. A man of his bulk was perfectly capable of defending himself, she reasoned, but she couldn't help but feel some residue of responsibility, given that she'd cajoled him into coming here in the first place.

One of the doors looked to be a lift, but when she approached she heard the hum of its motor in action, so rather than wait she went to the stairs and began to climb. Though the flight was in darkness, she didn't let that slow her but mounted the stairs three and four at a time until she reached the door that led out onto the top floor. As she groped for the handle she heard a voice from the suite beyond. The words were indecipherable, but the voice sounded cultivated, almost clipped. Had one of the Tabula Rasa survived after all? Bloxham, perhaps, the Casanova of the cellar?

She pushed the door open. It was brighter on the other side, though not by that much. All the rooms along the corridor were murky pits, their drapes drawn. But the voice led her on through the gloom towards a pair of doors, one of which was ajar. A light was burning on the other side. She approached with caution, the carpet underfoot lush enough to silence her tread. Even when the speaker broke off from his monologue for a few moments she continued to advance, reaching the suite without a sound. There was little purpose in delay, she thought, once she was at the threshold. Without a word, she pushed open the door.

There was a table in the room, and on it lay Oscar, in a double pool: one of light, the other of blood. She didn't scream, or even sicken, even though he was laid open like a patient in mid-surgery. Her thoughts flew past the horror to the man and his agonies. He was alive. She could see his heart beating like a fish in a red pool, gasping its last.

The surgeon's knife had been cast onto the table beside him, and its owner, who was presently concealed by shadow, said, "There you are. Come in, why don't you? Come in." He put his hands, which were clean, on the table. "It's only me, lovey."

"Dowd...."

"Ah! To be remembered. It seems such a little thing, doesn't it? But it's not. Really, it's not."

The old theatricality was still in his manner, but the mellifluous quality had gone from his voice. He sounded, and indeed looked, like a parody of himself, his face a mask carved by a hack.

"Do join us, lovey," he said. "We're in this together, after all."

Startled as she was to see him (though hadn't Oscar warned her that his type was difficult to kill?) she didn't feel intimidated by him. She'd seen his tricks and deceits and performances; she'd seen him hanging over an abyss, begging for life. He was ridiculous.

"I wouldn't touch Godolphin, by the way," he said.

She ignored the advice and went to the table.

"His life's hanging by a thread," Dowd went on. "If he's moved, I swear his innards will just drop out. My advice is let him lie. Enjoy the moment."

"*Enjoy?*" she said, the revulsion she felt surfacing, though she knew it was exactly what the bastard wanted to hear.

"Not so loud, sweetie," Dowd said, as if pained by her volume. "You'll wake the baby." He chuckled. "He *is* a baby, really, compared to us. Such a little life. . . ."

"Why did you do this?"

"Where do I begin? With the petty reasons? No. With the big one. I did it to be free." He leaned in towards her, his face a chiaroscuro jigsaw beneath the lamp. "When he breathes his last, lovey—which'll be very soon now—that's the end of the Godolphins. When he's gone, we're in thrall to nobody."

"You were free in Yzordderrex."

"No. On a long leash, maybe, but never free. I felt his desires, I felt his discomforts. A little part of me knew I should be at home with him, making his tea and drying between his toes. In my heart, I was still his slave." He looked at the body again. "It seems almost miraculous, how he manages to linger."

He reached for the knife.

"Leave him!" she snapped, and he retreated with surprising alacrity.

She leaned towards Oscar, afraid to touch him for fear of shocking his traumatized system further and stopping it. There were tics in his face, and his white lips were full of tiny tremors.

"Oscar?" she murmured. "Can you hear me?"

"Oh, look at you, lovey," Dowd cooed. "Getting all doe-eyed over him. Remember how he *used* you. How he *oppressed* you."

She leaned closer to Oscar and said his name again.

"He never loved either of us," Dowd went on. "We were his goods and chattels. Part of his . . ."

Oscar's eyes flickered open.

". . . inheritance," Dowd said, but the word was barely audible. As the eyes opened, Dowd retreated a second step, covering himself in shadow.

Oscar's white lips shaped the syllables of Judith's name, but there was no sound to accompany the motion.

"Oh, God," she murmured, "can you hear me? I want you to know this wasn't all for nothing. I found her. Do you understand? I found her."

Oscar made a tiny nod, then, with agonizing delicacy, ran his tongue over his lips and drew enough breath to say, "It wasn't true. . . ."

She caught the words, but not their sense. "What wasn't true?" she said.

He licked again, his face knotting up with the effort of speech. This time there was only one word: "Inheritance . . ."

"Not an inheritance?" she said. "I know that."

He made the very tiniest smile, his gaze going over her face from brow to cheek, from cheek to lips, then back to her eyes, meeting them unabashed.

"I . . . loved . . . you," he said.

"I know that too," she whispered.

Then his gaze lost its clarity. His heart stopped beating in its bloody pool; the knots on his face slipped with its cessation. He was gone. The last of the Godolphins, dead on the Tabula Rasa's table.

She stood upright, staring at the cadaver, though it distressed her to do so. If she was ever tempted to toy with darkness, let this sight be a scourge to that temptation. There was nothing poetic or noble in this scene, only waste.

"So there it is," Dowd said. "Funny. I don't feel any different. It may take time, of course. I suppose freedom has to be learned, like anything else." She could hear desperation beneath this babble, barely concealed. He was in pain. "You should know something," he said.

"I don't want to hear."

"No, listen, lovey, I want you to know. . . . He did exactly this to me, on this very table. He gutted me in front of the Society. Maybe it's a petty thing, wanting revenge, but then I'm just an actor chappie. What do I know?"

"You killed them all for that?"

"Who?"

"The Society."

"No, not yet. But I'll get to them. For us both."

"You're too late. They're already dead."

This hushed him for fully fifteen seconds. When he began again, it was more chatter, as empty as the silence he wanted to fill.

"It was that damn purge, you know; they made themselves too many enemies. There's going to be a lot of minor Maestros crawling out of the woodwork in the next few days. It's quite an anniversary, isn't it? I'm going to get stinking drunk. What about you? How will you celebrate, alone or with friends? This woman you found, for instance. Is she the partying type?"

Jude silently cursed her indiscretion.

"Who is she?" Dowd went on. "Don't tell me Clara had a sister." He laughed. "I'm sorry, I shouldn't laugh, but she was crazy as a coot; you must see that now. She didn't understand you. Nobody understands you but me, lovey, and I understand you—"

"—because we're the same."

"Exactly. We don't belong to anybody any more. We're our own inventions. We'll do what we want, when we want, and we won't give a fuck for the consequences."

"Is that freedom?" she said flatly, finally taking her eyes off Oscar and looking up at Dowd's misshapen form.

"Don't try and tell me you don't want it," Dowd said. "I'm not asking you to love me for this, I'm not that stupid, but at least admit it was *just*."

"Why didn't you murder him in his bed years ago?"

"I wasn't strong enough. Oh, I realize I may not radiate health and efficiency just at the moment, but I've changed a lot since we last met. I've been down among the dead. It was very . . . educational. And while I was down there, it began to rain. Such a *hard* rain, lovey, let me tell you. I never saw its like before. You want to see what fell on me?"

He pulled up his sleeve and put his arm into the pool of light. Here was the reason for his lumpen appearance. His arm, and presumably his entire body, was a patchwork, with the flesh half sealed over fragments of stone which he'd slid into his wounds. She instantly recognized the iridescence that ran in the fragments, lending their glamour to his wretched meat. The rain that had fallen on his head was the sloughings of the Pivot.

"You know what it is, don't you?"

She hated the ease with which he read her face, but there was no use denying what she knew.

"Yes, I do," she said. "I was in the tower when it started to collapse."

"What a Godsend, eh? It makes me slow, of course, carrying this kind of weight, but after today I won't be fetching and carrying, so what do I care if it takes me half an hour to cross the room? I've got power in me, lovey, and I don't mind sharing—"

He stopped and withdrew his arm from the light.

"What was that?"

She'd heard nothing, but she did now: a distant rumbling from below.

"Whatever were you up to down there? Not destroying the library, I hope. I wanted that satisfaction for myself. Oh, dear. Well, there'll be plenty of other chances to play the barbarian. It's in the air, don't you think?"

Jude's thoughts went to Celestine. Dowd was perfectly capable of doing her harm. She had to go back down and warn the Goddess, perhaps find some means of defense. In the meantime, she'd play along.

"Where will you go after this?" she asked Dowd, lightening her tone as best she could.

"Back to Regent's Park Road, I thought. We can sleep in our master's bed. Oh, what am I saying? Please don't think I want your body. I know the rest of the world thinks heaven's in your lap, but I've been celibate for two hundred years and I've completely lost the urge. We can live as brother and sister, can't we? That doesn't sound so bad, now, does it?"

"No," she said, fighting the urge to spit her disgust in his face. "No, it doesn't."

"Well, look, why don't you wait for me downstairs? I've got a bit of business left to do here. Rituals have to be observed."

"Whatever you say," she replied.

She left him to his farewells, whatever they were, and headed back to the stairs. The rumbling that had caught his attention had ceased, but she hurried down the concrete flight with high hopes. The cell was open, she knew it. In a matter of moments she'd set her eyes on the Goddess and, perhaps as importantly, Celestine would set her eyes on Jude. In one sense, what Dowd had expressed above was true. With Oscar dead, she was indeed free from the curse of her creation. It was time to know herself and be known.

As she walked through the remaining room of Roxborough's house and started down the stairs into the cellar, she sensed the change that had come over the maze below. She didn't have to search for the cell; the energy in the air moved like an invisible tide, carrying her towards its source. And there it was, in front of her: the cell wall a heap of splinters and rubble, the gap its collapse had made rising to the ceiling. The dissolution she'd initiated was still going on. Even as she approached, further bricks fell away, their mortar turned to dust. She braved the fall, clambering up over the wreckage to peer into the cell. It was dark inside, but her eyes soon found the mummified form of the prisoner, lying in the dirt.

There was no movement in the body whatsoever. She went to it and fell to her knees to tear at the fine threads that Roxborough

or his agents had bound Celestine with. They were too tough for
her fingers, so she went at them with her teeth. The threads were
bitter, but her teeth were sharp, and once one succumbed to her
bites others quickly followed. A tremor passed through the body,
as if the captive sensed liberation. As with the bricks, the message
of unmaking was contagious, and she'd only snapped half a dozen
of the threads when they began to stretch and break of their own
volition, aided by the motion of the body they'd bound. Her cheek
was stung by the flight of one, and she was obliged to retreat as the
unfettering spread, the threads describing sinuous motions as they
broke, their severed ends bright.

The tremors in Celestine's body were now convulsions, growing as the ambition of the threads increased. They weren't simply
flying wildly, Jude realized; they were reaching out in all directions,
up towards the ceiling of the cell and to its walls. Stung by them
once, the only way she could avoid further contact was by backing
away to the hole through which she'd come and then out, stumbling over the rubble.

As she emerged she heard Dowd's voice, somewhere in the
labyrinth behind her. "What have you been doing, lovey?"

She wasn't quite sure, was the truth. Though she'd been the ini-
tiator of this unbinding, she wasn't its mistress. The cords had an
urgency of their own, and whether it was Celestine who moved
them, or Roxborough who'd plaited into them the instruction to
destroy anyone who came seeking his prisoner's release, they were
not about to be placated or contained. Some were snatching at the
edge of the hole, dragging away more of the bricks. Others, demonstrating an elasticity she hadn't expected, were nosing over the rubble, turning over stones and books as they advanced.

"Oh, my Lord," she heard Dowd say, and turned to see him
standing in the passageway half a dozen yards behind her, with his
surgeon's knife in one hand and a bloody handkerchief in the
other.

This was the first sight she had of him head to foot, and the burden of Pivot shards he carried was apparent. He looked utterly
maladroit, his shoulders mismatched and his left leg turned inward,
as though a shattered bone had been badly set.

"What's in there?" he said, hobbling towards her. "Is this your
friend?"

"I suggest you keep your distance," she said.

He ignored her. "Did Roxborough wall something up? Look at
those things! Is it an Oviate?"

"No."

"What then? Godolphin never told me about this."

"He didn't know."

"But you did?" he said, glancing back at her as he advanced to study the cords, which were emerging all the time. "I'm impressed. We've both kept our little secrets, haven't we?"

One of the cords reared suddenly from the rubble, and he jumped back, the handkerchief dropping from his hand. It unfolded as it fell, and the piece of Oscar's flesh Dowd had wrapped in it landed in the dirt. It was vestigial, but she knew it well enough. He'd cut off the curiosity and carried it away as a keepsake.

She let out a moan of disgust. Dowd started to stoop to pick it up, but her rage—which she'd concealed for Celestine's sake—erupted.

"You scumbag!" she said, and went at him with both hands raised above her head, locked into a single fist.

He was heavy with shards and couldn't rise fast enough to avoid her blow. She struck the back of his neck, a clout that probably hurt her more than him, but unbalanced a body already too asymmetrical for its own good. He stumbled, prey to gravity, and sprawled in the rubble. He knew his indignity, and it enraged him.

"Stupid cow!" he said. "Stupid, sentimental cow! Pick it up! Go on, pick it up! Have it if you want to."

"I don't want it."

"No, I *insist.* It's a gift, brother to sister."

"I'm not your sister! I never was and I never will be!"

Mites were appearing from his mouth as he lay on the rubble, some of them grown fat as cockroaches on the power he carried in his skin. Whether they were for her benefit or to protect him against the presence in the wall she didn't know, but seeing them she took a step away from him.

"I'm going to forgive you this," he said, all magnanimity. "You're overwrought, I know." He raised his arm. "Help me up," he said. "Tell me you're sorry, and it's forgotten."

"I loathe everything you are," she said.

Despite the mites, it was self-preservation that made her speak, not courage. This was a place of power. The truth would serve her better here than a lie, however politic.

He withdrew his arm and started to haul himself up. As he did so she took two steps forward and, picking up the bloodied handkerchief, claimed with it the last of Oscar. As she stood up again, almost guilty at what she'd done, she caught sight of a motion in the wall. A pale form had appeared against the darkness of the cell, as ripe and rounded a form as the wall that framed it was ragged. Celestine was floating, or rather was borne up as Quaisoir had been borne up, on ribbons of flesh, the filaments that had once smothered her clinging to her limbs like the remnants of a coat and draped around her head as a living hood. The face beneath was delicately boned, but severe, and what beauty it might have possessed was spoiled by the dementia that burned in it. Dowd was still in the process of rising and turned to follow Jude's astonished gaze. When he set eyes on the apparition his body failed him, and he fell back onto the rubble, belly down. From his mite-spawning mouth came one terrified word.

"*Celestine?*"

The woman had approached the limits of her cell and now raised her hands to touch the bricks that had sealed her in for so long. Though she merely brushed them, they seemed to flee her fingers, tumbling down to join the rest. There was ample room for her to emerge, but she hung back and spoke from the shadows, her pupils flicking back and forth maniacally, her lips curling back from her teeth as though in rehearsal for some ghastly revelation. She matched Dowd's single utterance with a word of her own: "Dowd."

"Yes . . ." he murmured, "it's me."

So he'd been honest in some part of his biography at least, Jude thought. She knew him, just as he'd claimed to know her.

"Who did this to you?" he said.

"Why ask me," Celestine said, "when you were part of the plot?" In her voice was the same mingling of lunacy and composure her body exhibited, her mellifluous tones accompanied by a fluttering that was almost a second voice, speaking in tandem with the first.

"I didn't know, I swear," Dowd said. He craned his heavy head to appeal to Jude. "Tell her," he said.

Celestine's oscillating gaze rose to Jude. "You?" she said. "Did you conspire against me?"

"No," Jude said. "I'm the one who freed you."

"I freed myself."

"But I began it," Jude said.

"Come closer. Let me see you better."

Jude hesitated to approach, with Dowd's face still a nest of mites. But Celestine made her demand again, and Jude obeyed. The woman raised her head as she approached, turning it this way and that, perhaps to coax her torpid muscles back into life.

"Are you Roxborough's woman?" she said.

"No."

"That's close enough," she told Jude. "Who's then? Which one of them do you belong to?"

"I don't belong to any of them," Jude said. "They're all dead."

"Even Roxborough?"

"He's been gone two hundred years."

At last the eyes stopped flickering, and their stillness, now it came, was more distressing than their motion. She had a gaze that could slice steel.

"Two hundred years," she said. It wasn't a question, it was an accusation. And it wasn't Jude she was accusing, it was Dowd. "Why didn't you come for me?"

"I thought you were dead and gone," he told her.

"Dead? No. That would have been a kindness. I bore His child. I raised it for a time. You knew this."

"How could I? It was none of my business."

"You *made* me your business," she said. "The day you took me from my life and gave me to God. I didn't ask for that, and I didn't want it—"

"I was just a servant."

"Dog, more like. Who's got your leash now? This woman?"

"I serve nobody."

"Good. Then you can serve me."

"Don't trust him," Jude said.

"Who would you prefer I trust?" Celestine replied, not deigning to look at Jude. "You? I don't think so. You've got blood on your hands, and you smell of coitus."

These last words were tinged with such disgust Jude couldn't stem her retort. "You wouldn't be awake if I hadn't found you."

"Consider your freedom to go from this place my thanks," Celestine replied. "You wouldn't wish to know my company for very long."

Jude didn't find that difficult to believe. After all the months she'd waited for this meeting, there were no revelations to be had here: only Celestine's insanity and the ice of her rage.

Dowd, meanwhile, was getting to his feet. As he did so, one of the woman's ribbons unfurled itself from the shadows and reached towards him. Despite his earlier protests, he made no attempt to avoid it. A suspicious air of humility had come over him. Not only did he put up no resistance, he actually proffered his hands to Celestine for binding, placing them pulse to pulse. She didn't scorn his offer. The ribbon of her flesh wrapped itself around his wrists, then tightened, tugging at him to haul him up the incline of brick.

"Be careful," Jude warned her. "He's stronger than he looks."

"It's all stolen." Celestine replied, "His tricks, his decorums, his power. None of it belongs to him. He's an actor. Aren't you?"

As if in acquiescence, Dowd bowed his head. But as he did so he dug his heels into the rubble and refused to be drawn any further. Jude started to voice a second warning; but before it was out of her mouth, his fingers closed around the flesh and pulled hard. Caught unawares, Celestine was dragged against the raw edge of the hole, and before the rest of her filaments could come to her aid Dowd had raised his wrists above his head and casually snapped the flesh that bound them. Celestine let out a howl of pain and retreated into the sanctuary of her cell, trailing the severed ribbon.

Dowd gave her no respite, however, but went in instant pursuit, yelling to her as he shambled up over the heaped rubble, "I'm not your slave! I'm not your dog! And you're no fucking Goddess! You're a whore!"

Then he was gone into the darkness of the cell, roaring. Jude ventured a few steps closer to the hole, but the combatants had retreated into its recesses, and she saw nothing of their struggle. She heard it, however: the hiss of breaths expelled in pain; the sound of bodies pitched against the stone. The walls shook, and books all along the passageway were thrown from their shelves, the tide of power snatching loose sheets and pamphlets up into the air like birds in a hurricane, leaving the heavier tomes to thrash on the ground, broken-backed.

And then, suddenly, it was over. The commotion in the cell ceased utterly, and there were several seconds of motionless hush, broken by a moan and the sight of a hand reaching out of the murk to clutch at the broken wall. A moment later Dowd stumbled into view, his other hand clamped to his face. Though the shards he carried were powerful, the flesh they were seated in was weak, and Celestine had exploited that frailty with the efficiency of a warrior. Half his face was missing, stripped to the bone, and his body was more unknitted than the corpse he'd left on the table above; his abdomen gaping, his limbs battered.

He fell as he emerged. Rather than attempting to get to his feet—which she doubted he was capable of doing—he crawled over the rubble like a blind man, his hands feeling out the wreckage ahead. Sobs came from him now and then, and whimpers, but the effort of escape was quickly consuming what little strength he had, and before he reached clear ground his noises gave out. So, a little time after, did he. His arms folded beneath him, and he collapsed, face to the floor, surrounded by twitching books.

Jude watched his body for a count of ten, then moved back towards the cell. As she came within two yards of his body, she saw a motion and froze in her tracks. There was life in him still, though it wasn't his. The mites were exiting his open mouth, like fleas hastening from a cooling host. They came from his nostrils, too, and from his ears. Without his will to direct them they were probably harmless, but she wasn't going to test that notion. She stepped as wide of them as she could, taking an indirect route up over the rubble to the threshold of Celestine's asylum.

The shadows were much thickened by the dust that danced in the air, an aftermath of the forces that had been unleashed inside. But Celestine was visible, lying crookedly against the far wall. He'd

done her harm, no doubt of that. Her pale skin was seared and rup-
tured at thigh, flank, and shoulder. Roxborough's purgative zeal
still had some jurisdiction in his tower, Jude thought. She'd seen
three apostates laid low in the space of an hour: one above and two
below.

Of them all, his prisoner Celestine seemed to have suffered
least. Wounded though she was, she still had the will to turn her
fierce eyes in Jude's direction and say, "Have you come to crow?"

"I tried to warn you," Jude said. "I don't want us to be enemies,
Celestine. I want to help you."

"On whose command?"

"On my own. Why'd you assume everybody's a slave or a whore
or somebody's damn dog?"

"Because that's the way the world is," she said.

"It's changed, Celestine."

"What? Are the humans gone then?"

"It's not human to be a slave."

"What would you know?" the woman said. "I don't sniff much
humanity in you. You're some kind of pretender, aren't you? Made
by a Maestro."

It would have pained Jude to hear such dismissal from any
source, but from this woman, who'd been for so long a beacon of
hope and healing, it was the bitterest condemnation. She'd fought
so hard to be more than a fake, forged in a manmade womb. But
with a few words Celestine had reduced her to a mirage.

"You're not even natural," she said.

"Nor are you," Jude snapped back.

"But I was once," Celestine said. "And I cling to that."

"Cling all you like, it won't change the facts. No natural woman
could have survived in here for two centuries."

"I had my revenge to nourish me."

"On Roxborough?"

"On them all, all except one."

"Who?"

"The Maestro . . . Sartori."

"You knew him?"

"Too little," Celestine said.

There was a weight of sorrow here Jude didn't comprehend, but
she had the means to ameliorate it on her tongue, and for all
Celestine's cruelties Jude wasn't about to withhold the news.

"Sartori isn't dead," she said.

Celestine had turned her face to the wall, but now looked back
at Jude. "Not dead?"

"I'll find him for you if you want," Jude said.

"You'd do that?"

"Yes."

"Are you his mistress?"

"Not exactly."

"Where is he? Is he near?"

"I don't know where he is. Somewhere in the city."

"Yes. Fetch him. Please, fetch him." She hauled herself up the wall. "He doesn't know my name, but I know him."

"So who shall I tell him you are?"

"Ask him . . . ask him if he remembers Nisi Nirvana."

"Who?"

"Just tell him."

"Nisi Nirvana?"

"That's right."

Jude stood up and returned to the hole in the wall, but as she was about to step out Celestine recalled her.

"What's your name?" she asked.

"Judith."

"Well, Judith, not only do you stink of coitus, but you have in your hand some piece of flesh which you haven't given up clutching. Whatever it is, let it go."

Appalled, Jude looked down at her hand. The curiosity was still in her possession, half hanging from her fist. She pitched it away, into the dust.

"Do you wonder I took you for a whore?" Celestine remarked.

"Then we've both made mistakes," Jude replied, looking back at her. "I thought you were my salvation."

"Yours was the greater error," Celestine replied.

Jude didn't grace this last piece of spite with a reply but headed out of the cell. The mites that had exited Dowd's body were still crawling around aimlessly, looking for a new bolthole, but the flesh they'd vacated had upped and gone. She wasn't altogether surprised. Dowd was an actor to his core. He would postpone his farewell scene as long as possible, in the hope that he'd be at center stage when the final curtain fell. A hopeless ambition, given the fame of his fellow players, and one Jude wasn't foolish enough to share. The more she learned about the drama unfolding around her, with its roots in the tale of Christos the Reconciler, the more resigned she was to having little or no role in it. Like the Fourth Magi, expunged from the Nativity, she wasn't wanted in the Gospel about to be written; and having seen the pitiful place a king's testament had come to, she was not about to waste time writing her own.

13

I

Clem's duties were done for the night. He'd been out since seven the previous evening, about the same business that took him out every night: the shepherding of those among the city's homeless too frail or too young to survive long on its streets with only concrete and cardboard for a bed. Midsummer Night was only two days away, and the hours of darkness were short and relatively balmy, but there were other stalkers besides the cold that preyed on the weak—all human—and the work of denying them their quarry took him through the empty hours after midnight and left him, as now, exhausted, but too full of feeling to lay down his head and sleep. He'd seen more human misery in the three months he'd been working with the homeless than in the four decades preceding that. People living in the extremes of deprivation within spitting distance of the city's most conspicuous symbols of justice, faith, and democracy: without money, without hope, and many (these the saddest) without much left of their sanity. When he returned home after these nightly treks, the hole left in him by Taylor's passing not filled but at least forgotten for a while, it was with expressions of such despair in his head that his own, met in the mirror, seemed almost blithe.

Tonight, however, he lingered in the dark city longer than usual. Once the sun was up he knew he'd have little or no chance of sleeping, but sleep was of little consequence to him at the moment. It was two days since he'd had the visitation that had sent him to Judy's doorstep with tales of angels, and since then there'd been no further hint of Taylor's presence. But there were other hints, not in the house but out here in the streets, that powers were abroad which his dear Taylor was just one sweet part of.

He'd had evidence of this only a short time ago. Just after midnight a man called Tolland, apparently much feared among the fragile communities that gathered to sleep under the bridges and in the stations of Westminster, had gone on a rampage in Soho. He'd wounded two alcoholics in a back street, their sole offense to be in his path when his temper flowed. Clem had witnessed none of this, but had arrived after Tolland's arrest to see if he could coax from the gutter some of those whose beds and belongings had been demolished. None would go with him, however, and in the course of his vain persuasions one of the number, a woman he'd never seen without tears on her face until now, had smiled at him and said he should stay out in the open with them tonight rather than hiding in his bed, because the Lord was coming, and it would be the people on the streets who saw Him first. Had it not been for Taylor's fleeting reappearance in his life, Clem would have dismissed the woman's blissful talk, but there were too many imponderables in the air for him to ignore the vaguest signpost to the miraculous. He'd asked the woman what Lord this was that was coming, and she'd replied, quite sensibly, that it didn't matter. Why should she care what Lord it was, she said, as long as He came?

Now it was an hour before dawn, and he was trudging across Waterloo Bridge because he'd heard the psychopathic Tolland had usually kept to the South Bank and something odd must have happened to drive him across the river. A faint clue, to be sure, but enough to keep Clem walking, though hearth and pillow lay in the opposite direction.

The concrete bunkers of the South Bank complex had been a favorite *bête grise* of Taylor's, their ugliness railed against whenever the subject of contemporary architecture came up in conversation. The darkness presently concealed their drab, stained façades, but it also turned the maze of underpasses and walkways around them into terrain no bourgeois would tread for fear of his life or his wallet. Recent experience had taught Clem to ignore such anxieties. Warrens such as this usually contained individuals more aggressed against than aggressive, souls whose shouts were defenses against imagined enemies and whose tirades, however terrifying they might seem emerging from shadow, usually dwindled into tears.

In fact, he'd not heard a whisper from the murk as he descended from the bridge. The cardboard city was visible where its suburbs spilled out into the meager lamplight, but the bulk of it lay under cover of the walkways, out of sight and utterly quiet. He began to suspect that the lunatic Tolland was not the only tenant who'd left his plot to travel north and, stooping to peer into the boxes on the outskirts, had that suspicion confirmed. He headed into shadow, fishing his pencil torch from his pocket to light the way. There was the usual detritus on the ground: spoiled scraps of food, broken bottles, vomit stains. But the boxes, and the beds of newspaper and filthy blankets they contained, were empty. More curious than ever, he wandered on through the rubbish, hoping to find a soul here too weak or too crazy to leave, who could explain this migration. But he passed through the city without finding a single occupant, emerging into what the planners of this concrete hell had designed as a children's playground. All that remained of their good intentions were the grimy bones of a slide and a jungle gym.

The paving beyond them, however, was covered in fresh color, and advancing to the spot Clem found himself in the middle of a kitsch exhibition: crude chalk copies of movie-star portraits and glamour girls everywhere underfoot.

He ran the beam over the ground, following the trail of images. It led him to a wall, which was also decorated, but by a very different hand. Here was no mere copyist's work. This image was on such a grand scale Clem had to play his torch beam back and forth across it to grasp its splendor. A group of philanthropic muralists had apparently taken it upon themselves to enliven this underworld, and the result was a dream landscape, its sky green, with streaks of brilliant yellow, the plain beneath orange and red. Set on the sands, a walled city, with fantastical spires.

The torch beam caught a glint off the paint, and Clem approached the wall to discover that the muralists had only recently left off their labors. Patches of the paint were still tacky. Seen at close quarters, the rendering was extremely casual, almost slapdash. Barely more than half a dozen marks had been used to indicate the city and its towers, and only a single snaking stroke to show the highway running from the gates. Moving his beam off the picture to illuminate the way ahead, Clem realized why the muralists had been so haphazard. They had been at work on every available wall, creating a parade of brightly colored images, many of which were far stranger than the landscape with the green sky. To Clem's left was a man with two cupped hands for a head, lightning jumping between the palms; to his right a family of freaks, with fur on their faces. Farther on was an alpine scene, fantasticated by the addition of several naked women, hovering above the snows; beyond it a skull-strewn veldt, with a distant train belching smoke against a dazzling sky; and beyond that again, an island set in the middle of a sea disturbed by a single wave, in the foam of which a face could be discovered. All were painted with the same passionate haste as the first, which fact lent them the urgency of sketches and added to their power. Perhaps it was his exhaustion, or simply the bizarre setting for this exhibition, but Clem found himself oddly moved by the images. There was nothing ingratiating or sentimental about them. They were glimpses into the minds of strangers, and he was exhilarated to find such wonders there.

With his gaze following the journey of pictures, he'd lost all sense of his own direction, but when he turned out his torch to look for the lamplight he saw a small fire burning up ahead, and in lieu of any other beacon he made his way towards it. The fire makers had occupied a small garden laid amid the concrete. It had perhaps once boasted a rose bed or flowering shrubs; benches, perhaps, dedicated to some dead city father. But now there was only a pitiful lawn, which barely greened the dirt it peered from. Gathered upon it were the tenants of the cardboard city, or some part of their number. Most were asleep, bundled up in their coats and blankets. But five or six were awake, standing around the fire and passing a cigarette between them as they talked.

A dreadlocked black squatted on the low wall beside the garden's gate and, spotting Clem, rose to guard the entrance. Clem didn't retreat. There was no threat visible in the man's posture, nor anything but calm in the garden beyond. The sleepers did so quietly, their dreams seemingly kind. And the debaters around the fire spoke in whispers. When they laughed, which they did now and then, it wasn't the hard, desperate noise he'd heard among these clans, but light.

"Who are you, man?" the black asked him.

"My name's Clem. I got lost."

"You don't look like you been sleepin' rough, man."

"I haven't."

"So why you here?"

"Like I said: I got lost."

The man shrugged. "Waterloo Station's over in that direction," he said, pointing roughly back the way Clem had come. "But you got a long wait for the first train." He caught Clem's glance into the garden. "Sorry, man, you can't come in. If you got a bed, go to it."

Clem didn't move, however. Something about one of the men at the fire, standing with his back to the gate, rooted him to the spot.

"Who is that, who's talking now?" he asked the guard.

The man glanced around. "That's the Gentile," he said.

"The Gentile?" he said. "Surely you mean *Gentle*."

He hadn't raised his voice in order to name the man, but the syllables must have carried on the tranquil air, because as they went from Clem's lips the speaker stopped talking and slowly turned towards the gate. With the fire burning at his back his features were hard to make out, but Clem knew he'd made no error. The man turned back to his fellow debaters and said something to them Clem didn't catch. Then he left their fire and walked down to the gate.

"Gentle?" his visitor said. "It's Clem."

The black stood aside, opening the gate to let the man he'd called the Gentile step out of the garden. There he stood and studied the stranger.

"Do I know you?" he said. There was no enmity in his voice, but there was no warmth either. "I do, don't I?"

"Yes, you do, my friend," Clem replied. "Yes, you do."

They walked together along the river, leaving the sleepers and the fire behind them. The many changes in Gentle soon became apparent. He was of course far from certain of who he was, but there were other changes which were, Clem sensed, profounder still. There was a plainness about his speech, and about the expression on his face, which was by turns disturbing and calming. Something of the Gentle he and Taylor had known had gone, perhaps forever. But something was on its way to being gained in its place, and Clem wanted to be there when it was: to be the angel guarding that tender self.

"Did you paint the pictures?" he asked.

"With my friend Monday," Gentle said. "We made them together."

"I never saw you paint anything like that before."

"They're places I've been," Gentle told him, "and people I've known. They start coming back to me when I've got the colors. But it's slow. There's so much filling my head"—he put his fingers to his brow, which bore a series of ill-healed lacerations—"confusing me. You call me Gentle, but I've got other names."

"John Zacharias?"

"That's one. Then there's a man in me called Joseph Bellamy, and another called Michael Morrison, and one called Almoth, and one called Fitzgerald, and one called Sartori. They all seem to be me, Clem. But that's not possible, is it? I asked Monday, and Carol, and Irish, and they said people have two names, sometimes three, but never ten."

"Maybe you've lived other lives, Gentle, and you're remembering them."

"If that's true, I don't want to remember. It hurts too much. I can't think straight. I want to be one man with one life. I want to know where I begin and where I end, instead of going on and on."

"Why's that so terrible?" Clem said, genuinely unable to see the horror in such expansion.

"Because I'm afraid there'll be no end to it," Gentle replied. He spoke steadily, like a metaphysician who'd reached a precipice and was calmly describing the abyss below for the benefit of those who couldn't—or wouldn't—be with him there. "I'm afraid I'm joined to everything else," he said. "And then I'm going to be lost. I want to be this man, or that man, but not every man. If I'm everyone I'm no one, and nothing."

He stopped his even stride and turned to Clem, putting his hands on Clem's shoulders.

"Who am I?" he said. "Just tell me. If you love me, tell me. Who am I?"

"You're my friend."

It wasn't an eloquent reply, but it was the only one Clem had. Gentle studied his companion's face for a minute or more, as if calculating the potency of this axiom against his dread. And slowly, as he scanned Clem's features, a smile plucked at the corners of his mouth, and tears began to glisten in his eyes.

"You see me, don't you?" he said softly.

"Of course I see you."

"I don't mean with your sight, I mean with your mind. I exist in your head."

"Clear as crystal," Clem said.

That was truer now than it had ever been. Gentle nodded, and his smile spread.

"Somebody else tried to teach me this," he said. "But I didn't understand." He paused, musing. Then he said, "It doesn't matter what I'm called. Names are nothing. I am what I am *in you.*" His arms slipped around Clem, into an embrace. "I'm your friend."

He hugged Clem hard, then stood away, the tears clearing.

"Who was it who taught me that?" he wondered.

"Judith, maybe?"

He shook his head. "I see her face over and over," he said. "But it wasn't her. It was somebody who went away."

"Was it Taylor?" Clem said. "Do you remember Taylor?"

"He knew me, too?"

"He loved you."

"Where is he now?"

"That's a whole other story."

"Is it?" Gentle replied. "Or is it all one?"

They walked on along the river, exchanging questions and answers as they went. At Gentle's request Clem recounted Taylor's story, from life to deathbed, from deathbed to light, and Gentle in his turn offered what clues he had to the nature of the journey he'd returned from. Though he could remember very few of the details, he knew that unlike Taylor's it had not taken him into brightness. He'd lost many friends along the way—their names mingled with those of the lives he'd lived—and seen the deaths of many others. But he'd also witnessed the wonders he'd painted on the walls. Sunless skies that shimmered green and gold; a palace of mirrors, like Versailles; vast, mysterious deserts and ice cathedrals full of bells. Listening to these traveler's tales, the vistas of hitherto unknown worlds spreading in all directions, Clem felt his earlier ease with the notion of an unbounded self, going into some limitless adventure, falter. The very divisions he'd happily tried to persuade Gentle from at the outset of this report looked tempting now. But they were a trap, and he knew it. Their comfort would smother and hobble him eventually. He had to unburden himself of his old, stale ways of thinking if he was to travel alongside this man into places where dead souls were light and being was a function of thought.

"Why did you come back?" he asked Gentle after a time.

"I wish I knew," Gentle replied.

"We should find Judith. I think maybe she knows more about this than either of us."

"I don't want to leave these people, Clem. They took me in."

"I understand that," Clem said. "But Gentle, they can't help you now. They don't understand what's going on."

"Nor do we," Gentle reminded him. "But they listened when I told my story. They watched me paint, and they asked me questions, and when I told them the visions I'd had they didn't mock me." He stopped and pointed over the river towards the Houses of Parliament. "The lawgivers'll be coming there soon," he said. "Would you trust what I just told you to them? If we said to them that the dead come back in sunlight and there are worlds where the sky's green and gold, what would they say?"

"They'd say we were crazy."

"Yes. And throw us into the gutter with Monday and Carol and Irish and all the rest."

"They're not in the gutter because they had visions, Gentle," Clem said. "They're there because they've been abused, or they've abused themselves."

"Which means they can't cover their despair the way the rest can. They've got no distractions from their pain. So they get drunk and crazy, and the next day they're even more lost than they were the day before. But I'd still rather trust them than all the bishops and the ministers. Maybe they're naked, but isn't that a holy state?"

"It's also a vulnerable one," Clem pointed out. "You can't drag them into this war."

"Who said there's going to be a war?"

"Judith," Clem replied. "But even if she hadn't, it's in the air."

"Does she know who the enemy's going to be?"

"No. But it'll be a hard battle, and if you care for these people you won't put them in the front line. They'll be there when the war's over."

Gentle pondered this for a time. Finally, he said, "So they'll be the peacemakers."

"Why not? They can spread the good news."

Gentle nodded. "I like that," he said. "And so will they."

"So shall we go and find Judith?"

"I think that'd be wise. But first, I have to say goodbye."

The day came with them as they retraced their steps along the bank, and by the time they reached the underpass the shadows

were no longer black but gray-blue. Some of the beams had found
their way through the concrete bridges and barricades and were
edging towards the threshold of the garden.

"Where did you go?" Irish said, meeting his Gentile at the gate.
"We thought you'd slipped away."

"I want you to meet a friend of mine," Gentle said. "This is
Clem. Clem, this is Irish; this is Carol and Benedict. Where's
Monday?"

"Asleep," said Benedict, the sometime guard.

"What's Clem short for?" Carol asked.

"Clement."

"I've seen you before," she said. "Didn't you used to bring round
soup? You did, didn't you? I never forget faces."

Gentle led the way through the gate and into the garden. The
fire was almost out, but there were enough embers to thaw chilled
fingers. He squatted down beside the fire and poked at it with a
stick to stir some flame, beckoning Clem to warm himself. But as
Clem bent to do so he stopped.

"What is it?" Gentle said.

Clem's eyes went from the fire to the bundled forms still slumbering all around: twenty or more, still lost in dreams, though the
light was creeping over them.

"Listen," he said.

One of the sleepers was laughing, so softly it was barely audible.

"Who is that?" Gentle said. The sound was contagious and
brought a smile to his face.

"It's Taylor," Clem said.

"There's no one here called Taylor," Benedict said.

"Well, he's here," Clem replied.

Gentle stood up and scanned the sleepers. In the far corner of
the garden Monday was lying flat on his back, with a blanket barely
covering his paint-spattered clothes. A beam of morning light had
found its straight, bright way between the concrete pillars and was
settled on his chest, catching his chin and his pale lips. As if its gilding tickled, he laughed in his sleep.

"That's the boy who made the paintings with me," Gentle said.

"Monday," Clem remembered.

"That's right."

Clem picked his way through the dormitory to the youth's side.
Gentle followed, but before he reached the sleeper the laughter
faded. Monday's smile lingered, however, the sun catching the
blond hairs on his upper lip. His eyes didn't open, but when he
spoke it was as if he saw.

"Look at you, Gentle," he said. "The traveler returned. No, I'm
impressed, really I am."

It wasn't quite Taylor's voice—the larynx shaping it was twenty years too young—but the cadences were his; so was the sly warmth.

"Clem told you I was hanging around, I presume."

"Of course," Clem said.

"Strange times, eh? I used to say I'd been born into the wrong age. But it looks as though I died into the right one. So much to gain. So much to lose."

"Where do I begin?" Gentle said.

"You're the Maestro, Gentle, not me."

"Maestro, am I?"

"He's still remembering, Tay," Clem explained.

"Well, he should be quick about it," Taylor said. "You've had your holiday, Gentle. Now you've got some healing to do. There's a hell of a void waiting to take us all if you fuck up. And if it comes"—the smile went from Monday's face—"if it comes there won't be any more spirits in the light, because there won't *be* any light. Where's your familiar, by the way?"

"Who?"

"The mystif."

Gentle's breath quickened.

"You lost it once, and I went looking for it. I found it too, mourning its children. Don't you remember?"

"Who was this?" Clem asked.

"You never met it," Taylor said. "If you had, you'd remember."

"I don't think Gentle does," Clem said, looking at the Maestro's troubled face.

"Oh, the mystif's in there somewhere," Taylor said. "Once seen, never forgotten. Go on, Gentle. Name it for me. It's on the tip of your tongue."

Gentle's expression became pained.

"It's the love of your life, Gentle," Taylor said, coaxing Gentle on. "Name it. I dare you. Name it."

Gentle frowned and mouthed silence. But finally his throat gave up its hostage. "Pie . . ." he murmured.

Taylor smiled through Monday's face. "Yes . . . ?"

"Pie 'oh' pah."

"What did I tell you? Once seen, never forgotten."

Gentle said the name again and again, breathing it as though the syllables were an incantation. Then he turned to Clem.

"That lesson I never learned," he said. "It came from Pie."

"Where's the mystif now?" Taylor asked. "Do you have any idea?"

Gentle went down on his haunches beside Tay's sleeping host. "Gone," he said, closing his hands around the sunlight.

"Don't do that," Taylor said softly. "You only catch the dark that

way." Gentle opened his hand again and let the light lie on his palm.
"You say the mystif's gone?" Tay went on. "Where, for God's sake?
How can you lose it twice?"

"It went into the First Dominion," Gentle replied. "It died and
went where I couldn't follow."

"I'm sorry to hear that."

"But I'll see it again, when I've done my work," Gentle said.

"Finally, we get to it," Tay said.

"I'm the Reconciler," Gentle said. "I've come to open the Dominions . . ."

"So you have, Maestro," Tay said.

". . . on Midsummer Night."

"You're cutting it fine," Clem said. "That's tomorrow."

"It can be done," Gentle said, standing up again. "I know who I
am now. He can't hurt me any more."

"Who can't?" Clem asked.

"My enemy," Gentle replied, turning his face into the sunlight.
"Myself."

2

After only a few days in this city that enemy, the sometime Autarch
Sartori, had begun yearning for the languid dawns and elegaic
dusks of the Dominion he'd left. The day came altogether too
quickly here and was snuffed out with the same alacrity. That
would have to change. Among his plans for the New Yzordderrex
would be a palace made of mirrors, and of glass made possessive
by feits, that would hold the glory of these inkling dawns and pro-
tract them, so that they met the glow of dusk coming in other directions. Then he might be happy here.

There would be, he knew, little in the way of resistance to his
taking of the Fifth, to judge by the ease with which the members
of the Tabula Rasa had succumbed to him. All but one of them was
now dead, cornered in their burrows like rabid vermin. Not one
had detained him more than minutes; they had given up their lives
quickly, with few sobs and still fewer prayers. He wasn't surprised.
Their ancestors had been strong-willed men, but even the most
pungent blood thinned over generations, and the children of their
children of their children (and so on) were faithless cowards.

The only surprise he'd had in this Dominion, and it was a sweet
one, was the woman whose bed he was returning to: the peerless
and eternal Judith. His first taste of her had been in Quaisoir's
chambers when, mistaking her for the woman he'd married, he'd
made love to her on the bed of veils. Only later, as he'd prepared
to quit Yzordderrex, had Rosengarten informed him of Quaisoir's

maiming and gone on to report the presence of a doppelgänger in the corridors of the palace. That report had been Rosengarten's last as a loyal commander. When, a few minutes later, he'd been ordered to join his Autarch on the journey to the Fifth, he'd unconditionally refused. The Second was his home, he said, and Yzordderrex his pride, and if he was to die then he wanted it to be in sight of the comet. Tempted as he was to punish the man for this dereliction of duty, Sartori had no desire to enter his new world with blood on his hands. He'd let the man go and departed for the Fifth, believing the woman he'd made love to on Quaisoir's bed was somewhere in the city behind him. But no sooner had he taken up the mask of his brother's life than he'd met her again, in Klein's garden of scentless flowers.

He never ignored omens, good or bad. Judith's reappearance in his life was a sign that they belonged together, and it seemed that she, all unknowing, felt the same. Here was the woman for the love of whom this whole sorry catalogue of death and desolation had been started, and in her company he felt himself renewed, as though the sight of her reminded his cells of the self he'd been before his fall. He was being offered a second chance: an opportunity to start again with the creature he'd loved and make an empire that would erase all memory of his previous failure. He'd had proof of their compatibility when they'd made love. A more perfect welding of erotic impulses he could scarcely have imagined. After it, he'd gone out into the city about the business of murder with more vigor than ever.

It would take time, of course, to persuade her that this was a marriage decreed by fate. She believed him to be his other and would be vengeful when he disabused her of this fiction. But he would bring her around in time. He had to. He had intimations, even in this blithe city, of intolerable things: whispers of oblivion that made the foulest Oviate he'd ever dredged up look alluring. She could save him from that, lick off his sweats and rock him to sleep. He had no fear that she'd reject him. He had a claim on her that would make her put aside all moral niceties: his child, planted in her two nights before.

It was his first. Though he and Quaisoir had attempted to found a dynasty many times, she'd repeatedly miscarried, then later corrupted her body with so much kreauchee it refused to produce another egg. But this Judith was a wonder. Not only had she made surpassing love with him, there was fruit from that coupling. And when the time came to tell her (once the irksome Oscar Godolphin was dead, and the line for whom she'd been made stopped), then she would see the perfection of their union and feel it, kicking in her womb.

3

Jude hadn't slept, waiting for Gentle to return from another night of wanderings. The summons she carried from Celestine was too heavy to sleep with; she wanted it said and done, so she could put her thoughts of the woman away. Nor did she want to be unconscious when he returned. The idea of his coming in and watching her sleep, which would have been comforting two nights before, unsettled her now. He was the egg licker, and its thief. When she had her possession back and he was gone off to Highgate, she'd rest, but not before.

The day was creeping up when he finally returned, but there was insufficient light for her to read much on his face until he was within a few yards of her, by which time he was wreathed in smiles. He chastised her fondly for waiting up. There was no need, he said; he was quite safe. The pleasantries stopped here, however. He saw her unease and wanted to know what was wrong.

"I went to Roxborough's tower," she told him.

"Not on your own, I hope. Those people can't be trusted."

"I took Oscar."

"And how's Oscar?"

She was in no mood to prettify. "He's dead," she said.

He looked genuinely saddened at this. "How did that happen?" he asked.

"It doesn't matter."

"It does to me," he insisted. "Please. I want to know."

"Dowd was there. He killed Godolphin."

"Did he hurt you?"

"No. He tried. But no."

"You shouldn't have gone up there without me. What on earth possessed you?"

She told him, as plainly as she knew: "Roxborough had a prisoner," she said. "A woman he buried under the tower."

"He kept that little kink to himself," came the reply. She thought there was something almost admiring in his tone, but she fought the temptation to accuse him. "So you went to dig up her bones, did you?"

"I went to release her."

Now she had every scrap of his attention. "I don't follow," he said.

"She's not dead."

"So she's not human." He made a curt little smile. "What was Roxborough doing up there? Raising wantons?"

"I don't know what wantons are."

"They're ethereal whores."

"That doesn't describe Celestine." She trailed the bait of the name, but he failed to bite. "She's human. Or at least she was."

"And what is she now?"

Jude shrugged. "Something . . . else. I don't quite know what. She's powerful, though. She almost killed Dowd."

"Why?"

"I think you're better off hearing that from her."

"Why should I want to?" he said lightly.

"She asked to see you. She says she knows you."

"Really? Did she say from where?"

"No. But she told me to mention Nisi Nirvana."

He chuckled at this.

"Does it mean something to you?" Jude said.

"Yes, of course. It's a story for children. Don't you know it?"

"No."

Even as she spoke, she realized why, but it was he who voiced the reason.

"Of course you don't," he said. "You were never a child, were you?"

She studied his face, wishing she could be certain he meant to be cruel, but still not sure that the indelicacy she'd sensed in him, and now sensed again, wasn't a newfound naïveté.

"So will you go to her?"

"Why should I? I don't know her."

"But *she* knows you."

"What is this?" he said. "Are you trying to palm me off on another woman?"

He took a step towards her, and though she tried to conceal her reluctance to be touched, she failed.

"Judith," he said. "I swear I don't know this Celestine. It's you I think about when I'm not here—"

"I don't want to discuss that now."

"What do you suspect me of?" he said. "I've done nothing. I swear." He laid both his hands on his chest. "You're hurting me, Judith. I don't know if that's what you want to do, but you are. You're hurting me."

"That's a new experience for you, is it?"

"Is that what this is about? A sentimental education? If it is, I beg you, don't torment me now. We've got too many enemies to be fighting with each other."

"I'm not fighting. I don't want to fight."

"Good," he said, opening his arms. "So come here."

She didn't move.

"*Judith.*"

"I want you to go and see Celestine. I promised her I'd find you, and you'll make a liar of me if you don't go."

"All right, I'll go," he said. "But I'm going to come back, love, you can depend on that. Whoever she is, whatever she looks like, it's you I want." He paused. "Now more than ever," he said.

She knew he wanted her to ask him why, and for fully ten seconds she kept her silence rather than satisfy him. But the look on his face was so brimming she couldn't keep her curiosity from putting the question on her tongue.

"Why now?" she said.

"I wasn't going to tell you yet . . ."

"Tell me what?"

"We're going to have a child, Judith."

She stared at him, waiting for some further explanation: that he'd found an orphan on the street or was bringing a babe from the Dominions. But that wasn't what he meant at all, and her pounding heart knew it. He meant a child born from the act they'd performed: a consequence.

"It'll be my first," he said. "Yours too, yes?"

She wanted to call him liar. How could *he* know when *she* didn't? But he was quite certain of his facts.

"He'll be a prophet," he said. "You'll see."

She already had, she realized. She'd entered its tiny life when the egg had plunged her consciousness down into her own body. She'd seen with its stirring spirit: a jungle city, and living waters; Gentle, wounded, and coming to take the egg from tiny fingers. Had that perhaps been the first of its prophecies?

"We made a kind of love no other beings in this Dominion could make," Gentle was saying. "The child came from that."

"You knew what you were doing?"

"I had my hopes."

"And didn't I get a choice in the matter? I'm just a womb, am I?"

"That's not how it was."

"A walking womb!"

"You're making it grotesque."

"It *is* grotesque."

"What are you saying? How can anything that comes from us be less than perfection?" He spoke with almost religious zeal. "I'm changing, sweet. I'm discovering what it is to love, and cherish, and plan for the future. See how you're changing me?"

"From what? From the great lover to the great father? Another day, another Gentle?"

He looked as though he had an answer on his tongue but bit it back. "We know what we mean to each other," he said. "There should be proof of that. Judith, please—" His arms were still open, but she refused to go into them. "When I came here I said I'd make mistakes, and I asked you to forgive me if I did. I'm asking you again now."

She bowed her head and shook it. "Go away," she said.

"I'll see this woman if you want me to. But before I go, I want you to swear something to me. I want you to swear you won't try and harm what's in you."

"Go to hell."

"It's not for me. It's not even for the child. It's for you. If you were to do any harm to yourself because of something I did, my life wouldn't be worth living."

"I'm not going to slit my wrists, if that's what you think."

"It's not that."

"What then?"

"If you try to abort the child, it won't go passively. It's got *our* purpose in it; it's got *our* strength. It'll fight for its life, and it may take yours in the process. Do you understand what I'm saying?" She shuddered. "Speak to me."

"I've got nothing to say to you that you want to hear. Go talk to Celestine."

"Why don't you come with me?"

"Just . . . go . . . away."

She looked up. The sun had found the wall behind him and was celebrating there. But he remained in shadow. For all his grand purpose, he was still made to be fugitive: a liar and a fraud.

"I want to come back," he said.

She didn't answer.

"If you're not here, I'll know what you want from me."

Without a further word he went to the door and let himself out. Only as she heard the front door slam did she shake herself from her stupor and realize he'd taken the egg with him as he went. But then like all mirror lovers he was fond of symmetry, and it probably pleased him to have that piece of her in his pocket, knowing she had a piece of him in a deeper place still.

14

1

Even though Gentle had known the tribe of the South Bank only a few hours, parting from them wasn't easy. He'd felt more secure in their company for that short time than he'd felt with many men and women he'd known for years. They, for their part, were used

to loss—it was the theme of almost every life story he'd heard—
so there were no histrionics or accusations, just a heavy silence.
Only Monday, whose victimization had first stirred the stranger
from his passivity, made any attempt to have Gentle linger.

"We've only got a few more walls to paint," he said, "and we'll
have covered them all. A few days. A week at the most."

"I wish I had that long," Gentle told him. "But I can't postpone
the work I came back to do."

Monday had of course been asleep while Gentle talked with Tay
(and had woken much confounded by the respect he got), but the
others, especially Benedict, had new words to add to the vocabulary of miracles.

"So what does a Reconciler do?" he asked Gentle. "If you're
goin' off to the Dominions, man, we want to be comin' with you."

"I'm not leaving Earth. But if and when I do, you'll be the first
to know about it."

"What if we never see you again?" Irish said.

"Then I'll have failed."

"And you're dead and gone?"

"That's right."

"He won't fuck up," Carol said. "Will you, love?"

"But what do we do with what we know?" Irish said, clearly
troubled by this burden of mysteries. "With you gone, it won't
make sense to us."

"Yes, it will," Gentle said. "Because you'll be telling other people, and that way the stories will stay alive until the door to the Dominions is open."

"So we should tell people?"

"Anyone who'll listen."

There were murmurs of assent from the assembly. Here at least
was a purpose, a connection with the tale they'd heard and its teller.

"If you need us for anything," Benedict purred, "you know
where to find us."

"Indeed I do," Gentle said, and went with Clem to the gate.

"And what if anybody comes looking for you?" Carol called
after them.

"Tell 'em I was a mad bastard and you kicked me over the
bridge."

This earned a few grins.

"That's what we'll say, Maestro," Irish said. "But I'm tellin' you,
if you don't come back for us one of these days, we're goin' to come
lookin' for you."

The farewells over, Clem and Gentle headed up onto Waterloo
Bridge in search of a cab to take them across the city to Jude's

place. It wasn't yet six, and though the flow of northbound traffic was beginning to thicken as the first commuters appeared, there were no taxis to be had, so they started across the bridge on foot in the hope of finding a cab on the Strand.

"Of all the company to have found you in," Clem remarked as they went, "that has to be the strangest."

"You came looking for me there," Gentle pointed out, "so you must have had some inkling."

"I suppose I must."

"And believe me, I've kept stranger company. A lot stranger."

"I believe it. I'd like you to tell me about the whole journey one day soon. Will you do that?"

"I'll do my best. But it'll be difficult without a map. I kept telling Pie I'd draw one, so that if I ever passed through the Dominions again and got lost . . ."

"You'd be found."

"Exactly."

"And did you make a map?"

"No. There was never time, somehow. There always seemed to be something new to distract me."

"Tell me as much as— Whoa! I see a cab!"

Clem stepped out into the street and waved the vehicle down. They both got in and Clem supplied the driver with directions. As he was doing so, the man peered into his mirror.

"Is that someone you know?"

They looked back along the bridge to see Monday pelting towards them. Seconds later the paint-smeared face was at the taxi window, and Monday was begging to join them.

"You've got to let me come with you, boss. It's not fair if you don't. I gave you my colors, didn't I? Where would you be without my colors?"

"I can't risk your getting hurt," Gentle said.

"If I get hurt it's my hurt and it's my fault."

"Are we going, or what?" the driver wanted to know.

"Let me come, boss. Please."

Gentle shrugged, then nodded. The grin, which had gone from Monday's face during his appeal, returned in glory, and he clambered into the cab, rattling his tobacco tin of chalks like a ju-ju as he did so.

"I brought the colors," he said, "just in case we need 'em. You never know when we might have to draw a quick Dominion or something, right?"

Though the journey to Judith's flat was relatively short, there were signs everywhere—mostly small, but so numerous their sum became significant—that the days of venomous heat and un-cleansing storm were taking their toll on the city and its occu-pants. There were vociferous altercations at every other corner, and some in the middle of the street; there were scowls and furrows on every passing face.

"Tay said there was a void coming," Clem remarked as they waited at an intersection for two furious motorists to be stopped from making nooses of each other's neckties. "Is this all part of it?"

"It's bloody madness is what it is," the cabbie chimed in. "There's been more murders in the last five days than in all of last year. I read that somewhere. And it's not just murders, neither, it's peo-ple toppin' themselves. A mate of mine, a cabbie like, was up the Arsenal on Tuesday and this woman just throws herself in front of his cab. Straight under the front wheels. Bloody tragic."

The fighters had finally been refereed and were being escorted to opposite pavements.

"I don't know what the world's coming to," the cabbie said. "It's bloody madness."

His piece said, he turned on the radio as the traffic began mov-ing again, and began whistling an out-of-tune accompaniment to the ballad that emerged.

"Is this something we can help stop?" Clem asked Gentle. "Or is it just going to get worse?"

"I hope the Reconciliation will put an end to it. But I can't be certain. This Dominion's been sealed up for so long, it's poisoned itself with its own shit."

"So we just have to pull down the soddin' walls," Monday said, with the glee of a born demolisher. He rattled his tin of colors again. "You mark 'em," he said, "and I'll knock 'em down. Easy."

2

The child, Jude had been told, had more purpose in it than most, and she believed it. But what did that mean, besides the risk of its fury if she tried to unhouse it? Would it grow faster than others? Would she be big with it by dusk, and her water ready to break be-fore morning? She lay in the bedroom now, the day's heat already weighing on her limbs, and hoped the stories she'd heard from ra-diant mothers were true, that her body would pour palliatives into her bloodstream to ease the traumas of nurturing and expelling another life.

When the doorbell rang her first instinct was to ignore it, but her visitors, whoever they were, kept on ringing and eventually began to shout up at the window. One called for Judy; the other, more oddly, for Jude. She sat up, and for a moment it was as though her anatomy had shifted. Her heart thumped in her head, and her thoughts had to be dragged up out of her belly to form the intention to leave the room and go down to the door. The voices were still summoning her from below, but they petered out as she headed down the stairs, and she was ready to find the doorstep empty when she got there. Not so. There was an adolescent there, besmirched with color, who upon sight of her turned and hollered to her other visitors, who were across the street, peering up at her flat.

"She's here!" he yelled. "Boss? She's here!"

They started back across the road towards the step, and as they came her heart, still beating in her head, took up a suicidal tempo. She reached out for some support as the man at Clem's side met her eyes and smiled. This wasn't Gentle. At least it wasn't the egg-thief Gentle who'd left a couple of hours before, his face flawless. This one hadn't shaved for several days and had a brow of scabs.

She backed away from the step, her hand failing to find the door though she wanted to slam it. "Keep away from me," she said.

He stopped a yard or two from the threshold, seeing the panic on her face. The youth had turned to him, and the imposter signaled that he should retreat, which he did, leaving the line of vision between them clear.

"I know I look like shit," the scabby face said. "But it's me, Jude."

She took two steps back from the blaze in which he stood (How the light liked him! Not like the other, who'd been in shadow every time she'd set eyes on him), her sinews fluttering from toes to fingertips, their motion escalating as though a fit was about to seize her. She reached for the banister and took hold of it to keep herself from falling over.

"It can't be," she said.

This time the man made no reply. It was his accomplice in this deceit—Clem, of all people—who said, "Judy. We have to talk to you. Can I come in?"

"Just you," she said. "Not them. Just you."

"Just me."

He came to the door, approaching her slowly, palms out. "What's happened here?" he said.

"That's not Gentle," she told him. "Gentle's been with me for the last two days. And nights. That's . . . I don't know who."

The imposter heard what she was telling Clem. She could see his face over the other man's shoulder, so shocked the words might have been blows. The more she tried to explain to Clem what had happened, the more she lost faith with what she was saying. This Gentle, waiting outside, was the man she'd left on the studio step, standing bewildered in the sun as he was now. And if this was he, then the lover who'd come to her, the egg licker and fertilizer, was some other: some terrible other.

She saw Gentle make the man's name with his lips: "Sartori."

Hearing the name and knowing it was true—knowing that the butcher of Yzordderrex had found a place in her bed, heart, and womb—the convulsions threatened to overtake her completely. But she clung to the solid, sweaty world as best she could, determined that these men, his enemies, should know what he'd done.

"Come in," she said to Gentle. "Come in and close the door."

He brought the boy with him, but she didn't have the will to waste on objecting. He also brought a question: "Did he harm you?"

"No," she said. She almost wished he had, wished he'd given her a glimpse of his atrocious self. "You told me he was changed, Gentle," she said. "You said he was a monster; he was corrupted, you said. But he was exactly like you."

She let her rage simmer in her as she spoke, working its alchemy on the abhorrence she felt and turning it into purer, wiser stuff. Gentle had misled her with his descriptions of his other, creating in her mind's eye a man so tainted by his deeds he was barely human. There'd been no malice in his deception; only the desire to be utterly divided from the man who shared his face. But now he knew his error and was plainly ashamed. He hung back, watching her while the tremors in her body slowed. There was steel in her sinew and it held her up, lent her the strength to finish the account. There was no sense in keeping the last part of Sartori's deceit from either Gentle or Clem. It would be apparent soon enough. She laid her hand on her belly.

"I'm pregnant," she said. "His child. Sartori's child."

In a more rational world she might have been able to interpret the expression on Gentle's face as he received the news, but its complexity defied her. There was anger in the maze, certainly, and bafflement too. But was there also a little jealousy? He hadn't wanted her company when they'd returned from the Dominions; his mission as Reconciler had scourged his libido. But now that she'd been touched by his other, *pleasured* by him (did he see that guilt somewhere on her face, as ineptly buried as his jealousy?) he was feeling pangs of possessiveness. As ever with their story, there was no sentiment untainted by paradox.

It was Clem, dear comforting Clem, who opened his arms now and said, "Any chance of a hug?"

"Oh, God, yes," she said. "Every chance."

He crossed to her and wrapped his embrace around her. They rocked together.

"I should have known, Clem," she said, too quietly for Gentle or the boy to hear.

"Hindsight's easy," he said, kissing her hair. "I'm just glad you're alive."

"He never threatened me. He never laid a finger on me that I didn't . . ."

"Ask for?"

"I didn't need to ask," she said. "He knew."

The sound of the front door reopening made her raise her head from Clem's shoulder. Gentle was stepping out into the sun again, with the youth following. Once outside, he looked up, cupping his hand over his brow to study the sky at his zenith. Seeing him do so, Jude realized who the sky watcher she'd glimpsed in the Boston Bowl had been. It was a small solving, but she wasn't about to spurn the satisfaction it provided.

"Sartori is Gentle's brother, is that right?" Clem said. "I'm afraid I'm still hazy on the family relations."

"They're not brothers, they're twins," she replied. "Sartori is his perfect double."

"How perfect?" Clem asked, looking at her with a small, almost mischievous smile on his face.

"Oh . . . very perfect."

"So it wasn't so bad, his being here?"

She shook her head. "It wasn't bad at all," she replied. Then, after a moment: "He told me he loved me, Clem."

"Oh, Lord."

"And I believed him."

"How many dozens of men have told you that?"

"Yes, but he was different. . . ."

"Famous last words."

She looked at the sun watcher for a few seconds, puzzled by the calm that had come over her. Was the mere memory of his commitment to her enough to assuage every dread?

"What are you thinking?" Clem asked her.

"That he feels something Gentle never did," she replied. "Maybe never could. Before you say it, I know the whole thing's repulsive. He's a destroyer. He's wiped out whole countries. How can I be feeling anything for him?"

"You want the clichés?"

"Tell me."

"You feel what you feel. Some people go for sailors, some people go for men in rubber suits and feather boas. We do what we do. Never explain, never apologize. There. That's all you're getting."

Her hands went to his face. She cupped it, then kissed it. "You are sublime," she said. "We're going to survive, aren't we?"

"Survive and prosper," he said. "But I think we'd better find your beau, for everybody's—"

He stopped as her grip on him tightened. All trace of joy had gone from her face.

"What's wrong?"

"Celestine. I sent him up to Highgate. To Roxborough's tower."

"I'm sorry, I'm not following this."

"It's bad news," she said, leaving his embrace and hurrying to the front door.

Gentle relinquished his zenith watching at her summons and returned to the step as she repeated what she'd just told Clem.

"What's up in Highgate?" he said.

"A woman who wanted to see you. Does the name Nisi Nirvana mean anything to you?"

Gentle puzzled over this for a moment. "It's something from a story," he said.

"No, Gentle. She's real. She's alive. At least she was."

3

It hadn't been sentiment alone that had moved the Autarch Sartori to have the streets of London depicted in such loving detail on the walls of his palace. Though he'd spent only a little time in this city—no more than weeks, between his birth and his departure for the Reconciled Dominions—Mother London and Father Thames had educated him right royally. Of course the metropolis visible from the summit of Highgate Hill, where he stood now, was vaster and grimmer than the city he'd wandered then, but there were enough signs remaining to stir some poignant and pungent memories. He'd learned sex in these streets, from the professionals around Drury Lane. He'd learned murder at the riverside, watching the bodies washed up in the mud on a Sunday morning after the slaughters of Saturday night. He'd learned law at Lincoln's Inn Field and seen justice done at Tyburn. All fine lessons, that had helped to make him the man he was. The only lesson he couldn't remember learning, whether in these streets or any other, was how to be an architect. He must have had a tutor in that, he presumed, at some time. After all, wasn't he the man whose vision had built a palace that would stand in legend, even though its towers were now rubble? Where, in the furnace of his genes or in his history, was the kindling spark of that genius? Perhaps he'd only discover the answer in the raising of his New Yzordderrex. If he was patient and watchful, the face of his mentor would sooner or later appear in its walls.

There would have to be a great demolishing, however, before

the foundations were laid, and banalities like the Tabula Rasa's tower, which he now came in sight of, would be the first to be condemned. He crossed the forecourt to the front door, whistling as he went and wondering if the woman Judith had been so insistent he meet—this Celestine—could hear his trill. The door stood open, but he doubted any thief, however opportunist, had dared enter. The air around the threshold fairly pricked with power, putting him in mind of his beloved Pivot Tower.

Still whistling, he crossed the foyer to a second door and stepped through it into a room he knew. He'd walked these ancient boards twice in his life: the first time the day before the Reconciliation, when he'd presented himself to Roxborough here, passing himself off as the Maestro Sartori for the perverse pleasure of shaking the hands of the Reconciler's patrons before the sabotage he'd planned took them to Hell; the second time, the night after the Reconciliation, with storms tearing up the skies from Hadrian's Wall to Land's End. On this occasion he'd come with Chant, his new familiar, intending to kill Lucius Cobbitt, the boy he'd made his unwitting agent in the sabotage. Having searched for him in Gamut Street and found him gone, he'd braved the storm—there were forests uprooted and lifted in the air, and a man struck by lightning burning on Highgate Hill—only to discover that Roxborough's house was empty. He'd never found Cobbitt. Driven from the safety of Gamut Street by his sometime Maestro, the youth had probably fallen prey to the storm, as so many others had that night.

Now the room stood silent, and so did he. The lords who'd built this house, and their children, who'd raised the tower above, were dead. It was a welcome hush; in it, there'd be time for dalliance. He wandered over to the mantelpiece and headed down the stairs, descending into a library he'd never known existed until this moment. He might have been tempted to linger, perusing the laden shelves, but the pricking power he'd felt at the front door was stronger than ever and drew him on, more intrigued with every yard.

He heard the woman's voice before he set eyes on her, emanating from a place where the restless dust was so thick it was like walking in a delta fog. Barely visible through it, a scene of sheer vandalism: books, scrolls, and manuscripts reduced to shreds or buried in the wreckage of the shelves they'd been laid upon. And beyond the rubble, a hole in the brick; and from the hole, a call.

"Is that Sartori?"

"Yes," he said.

"Come closer. Let me see you."

He presented himself at the bottom of the heap of rubble.

"I thought she'd failed to find you," Celestine said. "Or else you'd refused to come."

"How could I refuse a summons like this?" he said softly.

"Do you think this is some kind of liaison?" she replied. "Some secret tryst?"

Her voice was raw with the dust, and bitter. He liked the sound of it. Women who had anger in them were always so much more interesting than their contented sisters.

"Come in, Maestro," she said to him. "Let me put you to rights."

He clambered up over the stones and peered into the darkness. The cell was a wretched hole, as sordid as anything beneath his palace, but the woman who'd occupied it was no anchorite. Her flesh hadn't been chastened by incarceration, but looked lush, for all the marks upon it. The tendrils that clung to her body extolled her fluency, moving over her thighs and breasts and belly like unctuous snakes. Some clung to her head and paid court at her honey lips; others lay between her legs in bliss. He felt her tender gaze on him and luxuriated in it.

"Handsome," she said.

He took her compliment as an invitation to approach, but as he did so she made a murmur of distress, and he stopped in his tracks.

"What's this shadow in you?" she said.

"Nothing to be afraid of," he told her.

Some of the filaments parted, and longer tendrils, these not courtiers but part of her substance, uncurled from behind her, clinging to the rough wall and hauling her up.

"I've heard that before," she said. "When a man tells you there's nothing to be afraid of, he's lying. Even you, Sartori."

"I won't come any closer if it bothers you," he said.

It wasn't respect for the woman's unease that moved him to compliance, but the sight of the ribbons that had lifted her. Quaisoir had sprouted such appendages, he recalled, after her intimacies with the women of the Bastion of the Banu. They were evidence of some facility in the other sex he had no real comprehension of: a remnant of crafts all but banished from the Reconciled Dominions by Hapexamendios. Perhaps they'd seen a new, poisonous flowering in the Fifth in the time since he'd left. Until he knew the scope of their authority, he'd be circumspect.

"I'd like to ask a question, if I may?" he said.

"Yes?"

"How do you know who I am?"

"First, tell me where you've been all these years."

Oh, the temptation he felt to tell her the truth, then, and parade his achievements in the hope of impressing her. But he'd come here in the guise of his other, and, as with Judith, he'd have to choose the moment of his unmasking carefully.

"I've been wandering," he said. It wasn't so untrue.

"Where?"

"In the Second Dominion, and occasionally the Third."

"Were you ever in Yzordderrex?"

"Sometimes."

"And in the desert outside the city?"

"There too. Why do you ask?"

"I was there once. Before you were born."

"I'm older than I look," he told her. "I know it doesn't show—"

"I know how long you've lived, Sartori," she replied. "To the very day."

Her certainty nourished the discomfort bred by the sight of the tendrils. Could she read his thoughts, this woman? If so—if she knew what he was and all he'd done—why wasn't she in awe of him?

There was no profit in pretending that he didn't care that she seemed to know so much. Plainly but politely, he asked her how, preparing as he spoke a profusion of excuses if she was simply one of the Maestro's casual conquests and accused him of forgetting her. But the accusation, when it came, was of another kind entirely.

"You've done great harm in your life, haven't you?" she said to him.

"No more than most," he protested mildly. "I've been tempted to a few excesses, certainly. But then hasn't everybody?"

"A few excesses?" she said. "I think you've done more than that. There's evil in you, Sartori. I smell it in your sweat, the way I smelled coitus in the woman."

Her mention of Judith—who else could this venereal woman be?—reminded him of the prophecy he'd made to her two nights before. They would find darkness in each other, he'd said; and that was a perfectly human condition. The argument had proved potent then. Why not now?

"It's just the humanity in me you can sense," he said to Celestine.

She was clearly unpersuaded. "Oh, no," she replied. *"I'm* the humanity in you."

He was about to laugh this absurdity off, but her stare hushed him.

"What part of me are you?" he murmured.

"Don't you know yet?" she said. "Child, I'm your mother."

Gentle led the way as they stepped into the cool of the tower's foyer. There was no sound from anywhere in the building, above or below.

"Where's Celestine?" he asked Jude. She led him to the door into the Tabula Rasa's meeting room, where he told them all, "This is something for me to do, brother to brother."

"I'm not afraid," Monday piped up.

"No, but I am," Gentle said with a smile. "And I wouldn't want you to see me piss my pants. Stay up here. I'll be out double quick."

"Make sure you are," Clem said. "Or we're coming down to get you."

With that promise as comfort, Gentle slipped through the door into what remained of Roxborough's house. Though he'd felt nothing in the way of memories as he'd entered the tower, he felt them now. They weren't as material as those that visited him in Gamut Street, where the very boards seemed to have recorded the souls that had trodden them. These were vague recollections of the times he'd drunk and debated around the great oak table. He didn't allow nostalgia to delay him, however, but passed through the room like a man vexed by admirers, arms raised against their blandishments, and headed down into the cellar. He'd had this labyrinth and its contents (all spined and skin-bound, whether human or not) described to him by Jude, but the sight still amazed him. All this wisdom, buried in darkness. Was it any wonder the Imajical life of the Fifth had been so anemic in the last two centuries, when all the liquors that might have fortified it had been hidden here?

But he hadn't come to browse, glorious as that prospect was. He'd come for Celestine, who'd trailed, of all things, the name Nisi Nirvana to bring him here. He didn't know why. Though he vaguely remembered the name, and knew there was some story to go with it, he could neither remember the tale nor recall whose knee he'd first heard it at. Perhaps she knew the answer.

There was a wonderful agitation here. Even the dust would not lie down and die, but moved in giddy constellations, which he divided as he strode. He made no false turns, but the route from the steps to the place where Celestine lay was still a long one, and before he'd reached it he heard a cry. It wasn't a woman's cry, he thought, but the echoes disfigured it, and he couldn't be certain. He picked up his speed, turning corner after corner, knowing as he went that his other had preceded him every step of the way. There were no further cries after the first, but as his destination came in view—it looked like a cave, raggedly dug from the wall; an oracle's home—he heard a different sound: that of bricks, grinding their gritty faces together. There were small but constant falls of dried mortar from the ceiling, and a subtle trembling in the ground. He started up over the litter of fallen rock, which was strewn like a battlefield with gutted books, to the inviting crack. As he did so he caught a glimpse of a violent motion inside, which had him to the threshold in a stumbling rush.

"Brother?" he said, even before he'd found Sartori in the gloom. "What are you doing?"

Now he saw his other, closing on the woman in the corner of the cave. She was almost naked, but far from defenseless. Ribbons, like the rags of a bridal train but made of her flesh, were springing from her shoulders and back, their power clearly more substantial than their delicacy implied. Some were clinging to the wall above her head, but the bulk were extended towards Sartori and wrapped around his head like a smothering hood. He clawed at them, working his fingers between them to get a better grip. Fluid ran from the gouged flesh, and cobs of matter came away in his fists. It could only be a matter of time before he released himself, and when he did he'd do her no little harm.

Gentle didn't call to his brother a second time. What was the use? The man was deafened. Instead, he crossed the cave at a stumbling rush and took hold of Sartori from behind, dragging his brother's arms from their maiming work and pinning them to his sides. As he did so he saw Celestine's gaze go between the two figures in front of her, and either the shock of what she was witnessing or her exhaustion took its toll on her strength. The wounded ribbons loosened and fell in wreaths around Sartori's neck, uncovering the other face and confirming Celestine in her distress. She withdrew the ribbons entirely, gathering them into her lap.

With his sight returned, Sartori wrenched his head around to identify his captor. Seeing Gentle, he instantly gave up his struggle to free himself and stood in the Reconciler's arms, quite pacified.

"Why do I always find you doing harm, brother?" Gentle asked him.

"Brother?" said Sartori. "Since when was it brother?"

"That's what we are."

"You tried to kill me in Yzordderrex, or have you forgotten? Has something changed?"

"Yes," said Gentle. "*I* have."

"Oh?"

"I'm ready to accept our . . . kinship."

"A fine word."

"In fact, I accept my responsibility for everything I was, am, or will be. I've got your Oviate to thank for that."

"That's good to hear," Sartori said. "Especially in this company."

He looked back at Celestine. She was still standing, though it was plainly the filaments hugging the wall that held her up, not her legs. Her eyes were flickering closed, and there were tremors running through her body. Gentle knew she needed aid, but he could do nothing while he was burdened with Sartori, so he turned and pitched his brother towards the cave door. Sartori went from him like a doll, only raising his arms to break his fall at the very last.

"Help her if you want," he said, staring back at Gentle with slackened features. "It's no skin off my nose."

Then he lifted himself up. For an instant Gentle thought he intended some reprisal, and drew breath to defend himself.

But the other simply said, "I'm on my belly, brother. Would you harm me here?"

As if to prove how low he'd fallen and was willing to stay, he began to slink over the earth, like a snake driven from a hearth.

"You're welcome to her," he said, and disappeared into the brighter murk beyond the door.

Celestine's eyes had closed by the time Gentle looked back, her body hanging limply from the tenacious ribbons. He went towards her, but as he approached her lids flickered open.

"No . . ." she said. "I don't want . . . you . . . near . . . me."

Could he blame her? One man with his face had already attempted murder, or violation, or both. Why should she trust another? Nor was this any time to be pleading his innocence; she needed help, not apology. The question was, from whom? Jude had made it clear on the way up that she'd been sent from this woman's side the same way he was being sent. Perhaps Clem could nurse the woman.

"I'll send somebody to help you," he said, and headed out into the passageway.

Sartori had disappeared. lifted himself off his belly and taken to his heels. Once again Gentle went in his footsteps, back towards the stairs. He'd covered half that distance when Jude, Clem, and Monday appeared. Their frowns evaporated when they saw Gentle.

"We thought he'd murdered you," Jude said.

"He didn't touch me. But he's hurt Celestine, and she won't let me near her. Clem, will you see if you can help? But be careful. She may look sick, but she's strong."

"Where is she?"

"Jude'll take you. I'm going after Sartori."

"He's gone up the tower," Monday said.

"He didn't even look at us," Jude said. She sounded almost offended. "He just stumbled out and up the stairs. What the hell did you do to him?"

"Nothing."

"I never saw an expression like that on his face before. Or yours, come to that."

"Like what?"

"Tragic," said Clem.

"Maybe we're going to win a quicker victory than I thought," Gentle said, starting past them to the stairs.

"Wait," Jude said. "We can't tend to Celestine here. We need to take her somewhere safer."

"Agreed."

"The studio, maybe?"

"No," Gentle said. "There's a house I know in Clerkenwell where we'll be safe. He drove me out of it once. But it's mine, and we're going back to it. All of us."

15

I

The sun that met Gentle in the foyer put him in mind of Taylor, whose wisdom, spoken through a sleeping boy, had begun this day. That dawn already seemed an age ago, the hours since then had been so filled with journeys and revelations. It would be this way until the Reconciliation, he knew. The London he'd wandered in his first years, brimming with possibilities—a city Pie had once said hid more angels than God's skirts—was once again a place of presences, and he rejoiced in the fact. It gave heat to his heels as he mounted the stairs, two and three at a time. Strange as it was, he was actually eager to see Sartori's face again: to speak with his other and know his mind.

Jude had prepared him for what he'd find on the top floor: bland corridors leading to the Tabula Rasa's table, and the body sprawled there. The scent of Godolphin's undoing was there to meet him as he stepped into the passageway: a sickening reminder, though he scarcely needed one, that revelation had a grimmer face and that those last halcyon days, when he'd been the most lauded metaphysician in Europe, had ended in atrocity. It would not happen again, he swore to himself. Last time the ceremonies had been brought to grief by the brother waiting for him at the end of this corridor, and if he had to commit fratricide to remove the danger of a recurrence, then so be it. Sartori was the spirit of his own imperfections made flesh. To kill him would be a cleansing, and welcome, perhaps, to them both.

As he advanced along the corridor the sickly smell of Godolphin's putrefaction grew stronger. He held his breath against it and came to the door in utter silence. It nevertheless swung open as he approached, his own voice inviting him in.

"There's no harm in here, brother; not from me. And I don't need you on your belly to prove your good intentions."

Gentle stepped inside. All the drapes were drawn against the sun, but even the sturdiest fabric usually let some trace of light through its weave. Not so here. The room was sealed by something more than curtains and brick, and Sartori was sitting in this darkness, his form visible only because the door was ajar.

"Will you sit?" he said. "I know this isn't a very wholesome slab"—the body of Oscar Godolphin had gone, the mess of his blood and rot remaining in pools and smears—"but I like the formality. We should negotiate like civilized beings, yes?"

Gentle acceded to this, walking to the other end of the table and sitting down, content to demonstrate good faith unless or until Sartori showed signs of treachery. Then he'd be swift and calamitous.

"Where did the body go?" he asked.

"It's here. I'll bury it after we've talked. This is no place for a man to rot. Or maybe it's the perfect place, I don't know. We can vote on it later."

"Suddenly you're a democrat."

"You said you were changing. So am I."

"Any particular reason?"

"We'll get to that later. First—"

He glanced towards the door, and it swung closed, plunging them both into utter darkness.

"You don't mind, do you?" Sartori said. "This isn't a conversation we should have looking at ourselves. The mirror's bad enough."

"You didn't mind in Yzordderrex."

"I was incarnate there. Here I feel . . . immaterial. I was really impressed by what you did in Yzordderrex, by the way. One word from you, and it just crumbled away."

"Your handiwork, not mine."

"Oh, don't be obtuse. You know what history'll say. It won't give a fuck about the politics. It'll say the Reconciler arrived, and the walls came tumbling down. And you're not going to argue with that. It feeds the legend; it makes you look messianic. That's what you really want, isn't it? The question is: if you're the Reconciler, *what am I?*"

"We don't have to be enemies."

"Didn't I say the very same thing in Yzordderrex? And didn't you try and murder me?"

"I had good reason."

"Name one."

"You destroyed the first Reconciliation."

"It wasn't the first. There've been three other attempts to my certain knowledge."

"It was my first. My Great Work. And you destroyed it."

"Who did you hear that from?"

"From Lucius Cobbitt," Gentle replied.

There was a silence then, and in it Gentle thought he heard the darkness move, a sound like silk on silk. But his head was never quite silent these days, and before he could clear a path through the whispers Sartori had recovered his equilibrium.

"So Lucius is alive," he said.

"Just in memory. In Gamut Street."

"That fuckhead Little Ease let you have quite an education, didn't he? I'll have his guts." He sighed. "I miss Rosengarten, you know. He was so very loyal. And Racidio and Mattalaus. I had some good people in Yzordderrex. People I could trust; people who loved me. It's the face, I think; it inspires devotion. You must have noticed that. Is it the divine in you, or is it just the way we smile? I resist the notion that one's a symptom of the other. Hunchbacks can be saints and beauties perfect monsters. Haven't you found that?"

"Certainly."

"You see how much we agree? We sit here in the dark, and we talk like friends. I truly think if we never again stepped out into the light we could learn to love each other, after a time."

"That can't happen."

"Why not?"

"Because I've work to do, and I won't let you delay me."

"You did terrible harm last time, Maestro. Remember that. Put it in your mind's eye. Remember how it looked, seeing the In Ovo spilling out. . . ."

By the sound of Sartori's voice, Gentle guessed that the man had risen to his feet. But again it was difficult to be certain, when the darkness was so profound. He stood up himself, his chair tipping over behind him.

"The In Ovo's a filthy place," Sartori was saying. "And believe me, I don't want it dirtying up this Dominion. But I'm afraid that may be inevitable."

Now Gentle was certain there was some duplicity here. Sartori's voice no longer had a single source but was being subtly disseminated throughout the room, as though he was seeping into the darkness.

"If you leave this room, brother—if you leave me alone—there'll be such horror unleashed on the Fifth."

"I won't make any errors this time."

"Who's talking about error?" Sartori said. "I'm talking about what I'll do for righteousness' sake, if you desert me."

"So come with me."

"What for? To be your disciple? Listen to what you're saying! I've got as much right to be called Messiah as you. Why should I be a piddling acolyte? Do me the courtesy of understanding that, at least."

"So do I have to kill you?"

"You can try."

"I'm ready to do it, brother, if you force me."

"So am I. So am I."

There was no purpose in further debate, Gentle thought. If he was going to kill the man, as it seemed he must, he wanted to do it swiftly and cleanly. But he needed light for the deed. He moved towards the door, intending to open it, but as he did so something touched his face. He put his hand up to snatch it away, but it had already gone, flitting towards the ceiling. What defense was this? He'd sensed no living thing when he'd entered the room, other than Sartori. The darkness had been inert. Either it had now taken on some illusory life as an extension of Sartori's will, or else his other had used the darkness as a cover for some summoning. But what? There'd been no evocations spoken, no hint of a feit. If he'd managed to call up some defender, it was flimsy and witless. He heard it flapping against the ceiling like a blinded bird.

"I thought we were alone," he said.

"Our last conversation needs witnesses, or how would the world know I gave you a chance to save it?"

"Biographers, now?"

"Not exactly. . . ."

"What then?" Gentle said, his outstretched hand reaching the wall and sliding along it towards the door. "Why don't you show me?" he said, his palm closing around the handle. "Or are you too ashamed?"

With this, he pulled not one but both doors open. The phenomenon that followed was more startling than dire. The meager light in the passageway outside was drawn into the room in a rush, as though it were milk, sucked from day's teat to feed what waited inside. It flew past him, dividing as it went, going to a dozen places around the room, high and low. Then the handles were snatched from Gentle's grip, and the doors slammed.

He turned back to face the room and as he did so heard the table being thrown over. Some of the light had been drawn to what lay beneath. There was Godolphin, gutted, his entrails splayed around him, his kidneys laid on his eyes, his heart at his groin. And skittering around his body, some of the entities this arrangement had called forth, carrying fragments of the light stolen through the door. None of them made much sense to Gentle's eye. They had no limbs recognizable as such, nor any trace of features, nor, in most cases, heads upon which features might have sat. They were scraps of nonsense, some strung together like the cloggings of a drain, and mindlessly busy, others lying like bloated fruit, splitting and splitting and showing themselves seedless.

Gentle looked towards Sartori. He hadn't taken any light for himself, but a loop of wormy life hung over his head and cast its baleful brightness down.

"What have you done?" Gentle asked him.

"There are workings a Reconciler would never stoop to know. This is one. These beasts are Oviates. Peripeteria. You can't raise the weightier beasts with a corpse that's cold. But these things know how to be compliant, and that's all either you or I have ever really asked for from our abettors, isn't it? Or our loved ones, come to that."

"Well, you've shown me them now," Gentle said. "You can send them home."

"Oh, no, brother. I want you to know what they can do. They're the least of the least, but they've got some maddening tricks."

Sartori glanced up, and the loop of wretchedness above him went from its cherished place, moving towards Gentle, then to the ground, its target not the living but the dead. It was around Godolphin's neck in moments, while in the air above it an alliance of its fellows formed, congealing into a peristaltic cloud. The loop tightened like a noose and rose, hauling Godolphin up. The kidneys fell from his eyes; they were open beneath. The heart dropped from his groin; there was a wound where his manhood had been. Then the remaining innards spilled from his carcass, preserved in a jelly of cold blood. The peripeteria overhead offered themselves as a gallows for the ascending noose and, having it in their midst, rose again, so that the dead man's feet were pulled clear off the ground.

"This is obscene, Sartori," Gentle said. "Stop it."

"It's not very pretty, is it? But think, brother, *think* what an army of them could do. You couldn't even heal this single little horror, never mind this a thousandfold." He paused, then said, with genuine inquiry in his voice, "Or could you? Could you raise poor Oscar? From the dead, I mean. Could you do that?"

He left his place at the other end of the room and moved towards Gentle, the look on his face, lit by the gallows, one of exhilaration at this possibility. "If you could do that," he said, "I swear I'd be your perfect disciple. I would."

He was past the hanged man now and coming within a yard or two of Gentle. "I swear," he said again.

"Let him down."

"Why?"

"Because it's pointless and pathetic."

"Maybe that's what I am," Sartori said. "Maybe that's what I've been from the beginning, and I never had the wit to realize it."

This was a new tack, Gentle thought. Five minutes before the man had been demanding due respect as an aspirant Messiah; now he was wallowing in self-abnegation.

"I've had so many dreams, brother. Oh, the cities I've imagined! The empires! But I could never quite remove the niggling doubt, you know? The worm at the back of the skull that keeps saying, It'll come to nothing, it'll come to nothing. And you know what? The worm was right. All I ever attempted was doomed from the beginning, because of what we are to each other."

Tragic, Clem had said, describing the look on Sartori's face as he'd fled the cellar. And perhaps in his way he was. But what had he learned, that had brought him so low? It had to be goaded out of him, now or never.

"I saw your empire," Gentle replied. "It didn't fall apart because there was some judgment on it. You built it out of shit. That's why it collapsed."

"But don't you see? That *was* the judgment. I was the architect, and I was also the judge who found it unworthy. I was set against myself from the beginning, and I never realized it."

"But you realize it now?"

"It couldn't be plainer."

"Why? Do you see yourself in this filth? Is that it?"

"No, brother," Sartori said. "It's when I look at you—"

"At me?"

Sartori stared at him, tears beginning to fill his eyes. "She thought I was you," he murmured.

"Judith?"

"*Celestine.* She didn't know there were two of us. How could she? So when she saw me she was pleased. At first, anyway."

There was a weight of pain in his speech Gentle hadn't anticipated, and it was no pretense. Sartori was suffering like a damned man.

"Then she smelled me," he went on. "She said I stank of evil, and I disgusted her."

"Why should you care?" Gentle said. "You wanted to kill her anyway."

"No," he protested. "That wasn't what I wanted at all. I wouldn't have laid a finger on her if she hadn't attacked me."

"You're suddenly very loving."

"Of course."

"I don't see why."

"Didn't you say we were brothers?"

"Yes."

"Then she's my mother too. Don't I have some right to be loved by her?"

"Mother?"

"Yes. Mother. She's your mother, Gentle. She was raped by the Unbeheld, and you're the consequence."

Gentle was too shocked to reply. His mind was gathering puzzles from far and wide—all of them solved by this revelation—and the solving filled him to brimming.

Sartori wiped his face with the heels of his hands. "I was born to be the Devil, brother," he said. "Hell to your Heaven. Do you see? Every plan I ever laid, every ambition I ever had, is a mockery, because the part of me that's you wants love and glory and great works, and the part of me that's our Father knows it's shite and brings it down. I'm my own destroyer, brother. All I can do is live with destruction, until the end of the world."

2

In the foyer six stories below, Celestine's rescuers had, after much coaxing, persuaded the woman out of the labyrinth and into the light. Weak though she'd been when Clem had entered her cell, she'd resisted his consolations for a good while, telling him that she wanted no part of them. She preferred to remain underground, she said, and perish there.

His experience on the streets had given him a way with such recalcitrance. He didn't argue with her, nor did he leave. He bided his time at the threshold, telling her she was probably right; there was nothing to be gained from seeing the sun.

After a while she balked at this, telling him that wasn't her opinion at all and if he had any decency about him he'd give her some comfort in her distress. Did he want her to die like an animal, she said, locked away in the dark? He then allowed that the fault was his, and if she wanted to be taken up into the outside world, he'd do what he could.

With his tactic successful, he sent Monday off to bring Jude's car to the front of the tower and began the business of getting Celestine out. There was a delicate moment at the door of the cell when the woman, setting eyes on Jude, almost recanted her desire to leave, saying she wanted no truck with this tainted creature. Jude kept her silence, and Clem, tact personified, sent her up to fetch blankets from the car while he escorted Celestine to the stairs. It was a slow business, and several times she asked him to stop, holding on to him fiercely and telling him that she wasn't trembling because she was afraid, but because her body was unused to such freedom, and that if anybody, particularly the tainted woman, was to remark on these tremors, he was to hush them.

Thus, clinging to Clem one moment, then demanding he not lean on her the next, slowing at times, then rising up with preternatural strength in her sinews the instant after, Roxborough's captive quit her prison after two centuries of incarceration, and went up to meet the day.

But the tower's sum of surprises, whether above or below, was not yet exhausted. As Clem escorted her across the foyer, he stopped, his eyes on the door ahead, or rather on the sunlight that poured through it. It was laden with motes: pollen and seeds from the trees and plants outside; dust from the road beyond. Though there was scarcely a breeze outside, they were in lively motion.

"We've got a visitor," he remarked.

"Here?" Jude said.

"Up ahead."

She looked at the light. Though she could see nothing that resembled a human form in it, the particles were not moving arbitrarily. There was some organizing principle among them, and Clem, it seemed, knew its name.

"Taylor," he said, his voice thick with feeling. "Taylor's here."

He glanced across at Monday, who without being told stepped in to take Celestine's weight. The woman had been hovering on unconsciousness again, but now she raised her head and watched, as did they all, while Clem started to walk towards the light-filled door.

"It's you, isn't it?" he said softly.

In reply, the motion in the light became more agitated.

"I thought so," Clem said, coming to a halt a couple of yards from the edge of the pool.

"What does he want?" Jude said. "Can you tell?"

Clem glanced back at her, his expression both awed and afraid.

"He wants me to let him in," he replied. "He wants to be here." He tapped his chest. "Inside me."

Jude smiled. The day had brought little in the way of good news, but here was some: the possibility of a union she'd never have believed possible. Still Clem hesitated, keeping his distance from the light.

"I don't know if I can do it," he said.

"He's not going to hurt you," Jude said.

"I know," Clem said, glancing back at the light. Its gilded dust was more hectic than ever. "It's not the hurt . . ."

"What then?"

He shook his head.

"I did it, man," Monday said. "Just close your eyes and think of England."

This earned a little laugh from Clem, who was still staring at the light when Jude voiced the final persuasion.

"You loved him," she said.

The laugh caught in Clem's throat, and in the utter hush that followed he murmured, "I still do."

"Then be with him."

He looked back at her one last time and smiled. Then he stepped into the light.

To Jude's eyes there was nothing so remarkable about the sight. It was just a door, and a man stepping through it into sunlight. But there was significance in it now she'd never understood before, and as she stood witness a warning of Oscar's returned to her head, spoken as they'd prepared to leave for Yzordderrex. She'd come back changed, he'd said, seeing the world she'd left with clearer eyes. Here was proof of that. Perhaps sunlight had always been numinous, and doorways signs of a greater passage than that of one room to another. But she'd not seen it, until now.

Clem stood in the beams for perhaps thirty seconds, his hands palm up in front of him. Then he turned back towards her, and she saw that Taylor had come with him. If she'd been asked to name the places where she saw his presence, she couldn't have done so. There was no change in his physiognomy, no particular in which they could be seen, unless it was in signs so subtle—the angle of his head, the fixedness of his mouth—that she couldn't distinguish them. But he was there, no doubt of it. And so was an urgency that had not been in Clem a minute before.

"Take Celestine out of here," he said to Jude and Monday. "There's something terrible going on upstairs."

He left the doorway, heading for the stairs.

"Do you want help?" Jude said.

"No. Stay with her. She needs you."

At this, Celestine uttered her first words since leaving the cell. "I don't need her," she said.

Clem reeled around on one heel, coming back to the woman and putting his nose an inch from hers.

"You know, I'm finding you hard to like, madam!" he snapped.

Jude laughed out loud, hearing Tay's irascible tones so clearly. She'd forgotten how his and Clem's natures had dovetailed, before sickness had taken the piss and vinegar out of Tay.

"We're here because of you, remember that," Tay said. "And you'd still be down there picking the fluff from your navel if Judy hadn't brought us."

Celestine narrowed her eyes. "Put me back, then," she said.

"Just for that"—Jude held her breath; he wouldn't, surely?— "I'm going to give you a big kiss and ask you very politely to stop being a cantankerous old bag." He kissed her on the nose. "Now let's get going," he said to Monday, and before Celestine could summon a reply he headed to the stairs and was up them and out of sight.

3

Exhausted by his outpouring of pain, Sartori turned from Gentle and began to wander back to the chair where he'd been sitting at the start of their interview. He idled as he went, kicking over those servile scraps that came to dote on him and pausing to look up at Godolphin's gutted body, then setting it in motion with a touch, so that its bulk eclipsed and uncovered him by turns, as he went to his little throne. There were peripeteria gathered around in a sycophantic horde, but Gentle didn't wait for him to order them against him. Sartori was no less dangerous for the despair he'd just expressed; all it did was free him from any last hope of peace between them. It freed Gentle too. This had to end in Sartori's dispatch, or the Devil he'd decided to be would undo the Great Work all over again. Gentle drew breath. As soon as his brother turned he'd let the pneuma fly and be done.

"What makes you think you can kill me, brother?" Sartori said, still not turning. "God's in the First Dominion, and Mother's nearly dead downstairs. You're alone. All you have is your breath."

Godolphin's body continued to swing between them, but the man kept his back turned.

"And if you unknit me, what do you do to yourself in the process? Have you thought about that? Kill me, and maybe you kill yourself."

Gentle knew Sartori was capable of planting such doubts all night. It was the complement to his own lost skill with seduction: dropping these possibilities into promising earth. He wouldn't be delayed by them. His pneuma readied, he started after the man, pausing only for the swing of Godolphin's corpse, then stopping on the other side of it. Sartori still refused to show his face, and Gentle had no option but to waste a little of the killing breath with words.

"Look at me, brother," he said.

He read the intention to do so in Sartori's body, a motion beginning in his heels and torso and head. But before his face came in sight Gentle heard a sound behind him and glanced back to see the third actor here—the dead Godolphin—dropping from his gallows. He had time to glimpse the Oviates in the carcass; then it was upon him. It should have been easy to stand aside, but the beasts had done more than nest in the corpse. They were busy in

Godolphin's rotted muscle, engineering the resurrection Sartori had begged Gentle to perform. The corpse's arms snatched hold of him, and its bulk, all the vaster for the weight of parasites, bore him to his knees. The breath went out of him as harmless air, and before he could take another his arms were caught and twisted to breaking point behind his back.

"Never turn your back on a dead man," Sartori said, finally showing his face.

There was no triumph on it, though he'd incapacitated his enemy in one swift maneuver. He turned his sorrowful eyes up to the host of peripeteria that had been Godolphin's gallows and, with the thumb of his left hand, described a tiny circle. They took their cue instantly, the motion appearing in their cloud.

"I'm more superstitious than you, brother," Sartori said, reaching behind him and throwing over his chair. It didn't lie where it fell, but rolled on around the room as though the motion overhead had some correspondence below. "I'm not going to lay a hand on you," he went on. "In case there *is* some consequence for a man who takes his other's life." He raised his palms. "Look, I'm blameless," he said, stepping back towards the draped windows. "You're going to die because the world is coming apart."

While he spoke the motion around Gentle increased, as the peripeteria took their summoner's cue. They were insubstantial as individuals, but en masse they had considerable authority. As their circling speeded up, it generated a current strong enough to lift the chair Sartori had overthrown into the air. The light fixtures were sheared off the walls, taking cobs of plaster with them; the handles were ripped from the doors; and the rest of the chairs snatched up to join the tarantella, smashed to firewood as they collided with each other. Even the table, enormous as it was, began to move. At the eye of this storm Gentle struggled to free himself from Godolphin's cold embrace. He might have done so, given time, but the circle and its freight of shards closed on him too quickly. Unable to protect himself, all he could do was bow his head against the hail of wood, plaster, and glass, the breath pummeled from him by the assault. Only once did he lift his eyes to look for Sartori through the storm. His brother stood flat against the wall, his head thrown back as he watched the execution. If there was any feeling on his face, it was that of a man offended by what he saw, a lamb obliged to watch helplessly as his companion was pulped.

It seemed he didn't hear the voice raised in the corridor outside, but Gentle did. It was Clem, calling the Maestro's name and beating on the door. Gentle didn't have the strength left to reply. His body sagged in Godolphin's arms as the fusillade increased, striking his skull and rib cage and thighs. Clem, God love him, didn't need an answering call. He slammed himself against the door repeatedly, and the lock suddenly burst, throwing both doors open at once.

There was more light outside than in, of course, and just as before it was drawn into the darkened room at a rush, sweeping past the astonished Clem. The peripeteria were as desperate as ever to have a sliver of illumination for themselves, and their swirling ranks fell into confusion at the appearance of the light. Gentle felt the hold on him loosen as those Oviates who'd quickened Godolphin's corpse left off their labors and went to join the mêlée. With the energies in the room diverted, the circling wreckage began to lose momentum, but not before a piece of the splintered table struck one of the open doors, sheering it off at the hinges. Clem saw the collision coming and retreated before he too was struck, his shout of alarm stirring Sartori.

Gentle looked towards his brother. He'd left off his sham of innocence and was studying the stranger in the hallway with gleaming eyes. He didn't leave his place at the wall, however. A rain of wreckage was falling now, littering the room from end to end, and he clearly had no desire to step into it. Instead he reached up to snatch a uredo from his eye, intending to strike Clem down before he could intervene again.

Godolphin's bulk was doubling Gentle over, but he strained to raise himself from beneath it, yelling a warning to Clem, who was back at the threshold now, as he did so. Clem heard the shout and saw Sartori snatch at his eye. Though he had no knowledge of what the gesture meant, he was quick to defend himself, ducking behind the surviving door as the killing blow flew his way. In the same instant, Gentle heaved himself to his feet, throwing off Godolphin's body. He glanced in Clem's direction to be certain his friend had survived and, seeing that he had, started towards Sartori. He had breath in his body now, and might easily have dispatched a pneuma at his enemy. But his hands wanted more than air in them. They wanted flesh; they wanted bone.

Careless of the trash that was both underfoot and falling from the air, he ran at his brother, who sensed his approach and turned his way. Gentle had time to see the face before him smile a feral welcome; then he was upon him. His momentum carried them both back against the drapes. The window behind Sartori shattered, and the rail above him broke, bringing the curtain down.

This time the light that filled the room was a blaze, and it fell directly on Gentle's face. He was momentarily blinded, but his body still knew its business. He pushed his brother to the sill and hauled him up over it. Sartori reached for a handhold and snatched at the fallen drape, but its folds were of little use. The cloth tore as he tipped backwards, carried over the sill by his brother's arms. Even then he fought to keep himself from falling, but Gentle gave him no quarter. Sartori flailed for a moment, scrabbling at the air. Then he was gone from Gentle's hands, his scream going with him, down and down and down.

Gentle didn't see the fall and was glad of it. Only when the cry stopped did he retreat from the window and cover his face, while the circle of the sun blazed blue and green and red behind his lids. When he finally opened his eyes, it was to devastation. The only whole thing in the room was Clem, and even he was the worse for wear. He'd picked himself up and was watching the Oviates, who'd fought so vehemently for a piece of light, withering for excess of it. Their matter was drab slough, their skitters and flights reduced to a wretched crawling retreat from the window.

"I've seen prettier turds," Clem remarked.

Then he started around the room, pulling all the rest of the drapes down, the dust he raised making the sun solid as it came and leaving no shadow for the peripeteria to retreat to.

"Taylor's here," he said, when the job was done.

"In the sun?"

"Better than that," Clem replied. "In my head. We think you need guardian angels, Maestro."

"So do I," said Gentle. "Thank you. Both."

He turned back to the window and looked down at the wasteland into which Sartori had fallen. He didn't expect to see a body there; nor did he. Sartori hadn't survived all those years as Autarch without finding a hundred feits to protect his flesh.

They met Monday, who had heard the window breaking above, coming up the stairs as they descended.

"I thought you was a goner, boss," he said.

"Almost," came the reply.

"What do we do about Godolphin?" Clem said as the trio headed down together.

"We don't need to do anything," Gentle said. "There's an open window—"

"I don't think he's going to be flying anywhere."

"No, but the birds can get to him," Gentle said lightly. "Better to fatten birds than worms."

"There's a morbid sense in that, I suppose," Clem said.

"And how's Celestine?" Gentle asked the boy.

"She's in the car, all wrapped up and not saying very much. I don't think she likes the sun."

"After two hundred years in the dark, I'm not surprised. We'll make her comfortable once we get to Gamut Street. She's a great lady, gentlemen. She's also my mother."

"So that's where you get your bloody-mindedness from," Tay remarked.

"How safe is this house we're going to?" Monday asked.

"If you mean how do we stop Sartori getting in, I don't think we can."

They'd reached the foyer, which was as sun-filled as ever.

"So what do you think the bastard's going to do?" Clem wondered.

"He won't come back here, I'm sure of that," Gentle said. "I think he'll wander the city for a while. But sooner or later he'll be driven back to where he belongs."

"Which is where?"

Gentle opened his arms. "Here," he said.

16

I

There was surely no more haunted thoroughfare in London that blistering afternoon than Gamut Street. Neither those locations in the city famous for their phantoms, nor those anonymous spots— known only to psychics and children—where revenants gathered, boasted more souls eager to debate events in the place of their decease as that backwater in Clerkenwell. While few human eyes, even those ready for the marvelous (and the car that turned into Gamut Street at a little past four o'clock contained several such eyes), could see the phantoms as solid entities, their presence was clear enough, marked by the cold, still places in the shimmering haze rising off the road and by the stray dogs that gathered in such numbers at the corners, drawn by the high whistle some of the dead were wont to make. Thus Gamut Street cooked in a heat of its own, its stew potent with spirits.

Gentle had warned them all that there was no comfort to be had at the house. It was without furniture, water, or electricity. But the past was there, he said, and it would be a comfort to them all, after their time in the enemy's tower.

"I remember this house," Jude said as she emerged from the car.

"We should both be careful," Gentle warned, as he climbed the steps. "Sartori left one of his Oviates inside, and it nearly drove me crazy. I want to get rid of it before we all go in."

"I'm coming with you," Jude said, following him to the door.

"I don't think that's wise," he said. "Let me deal with Little Ease first."

"That's Sartori's beast?"

"Yes."

"Then I'd like to see it. Don't worry, it's not going to hurt me. I've got a little of its Maestro right here, remember?" She laid her hand upon her belly. "I'm safe."

Gentle made no objection but stood aside to let Monday force the door, which he did with the efficiency of a practiced thief. Before the boy had even retreated down the steps again, Jude was over the threshold, braving the stale, cold air.

"Wait up," Gentle said, following her into the hallway.

"What does this creature look like?" she wanted to know.

"Like an ape. Or a baby. I don't know. It talks a lot, I'm certain of that much."

"Little Ease . . ."

"That's right."

"Perfect name for a place like this."

She'd reached the bottom of the stairs and was staring up towards the Meditation Room.

"Be careful," Gentle said.

"I heard you the first time."

"I don't think you quite understand how powerful—"

"I was born up there, wasn't I?" she said, her tone as chilly as the air. He didn't reply; not until she swung around and asked him again. "Wasn't I?"

"Yes."

Nodding, she returned to her study of the stairs. "You said the past was waiting here," she said.

"Yes."

"My past, too?"

"I don't know. Probably."

"I don't feel anything. It's like a bloody graveyard. A few vague recollections, that's all."

"They'll come."

"You're very certain."

"We have to be whole, Jude."

"What do you mean by that?"

"We have to be . . . reconciled . . . with everything we ever were before we can go on."

"Suppose I don't want to be reconciled? Suppose I want to invent myself all over again, starting now?"

"You can't do it," he said simply. "We have to be whole before we can get home."

"If that's home," she said, nodding in the direction of the Meditation Room, "you can keep it."

"I don't mean the cradle."

"What then?"

"The place before the cradle. Heaven."

"Fuck Heaven. I haven't got Earth sorted out yet."

"You don't need to."

"Let me be the judge of that. I haven't even had a life I could call my own, and you're ready to slot me into the grand design. Well, I don't think I want to go. I want to be my own design."

"You can be. As part of—"

"Part of nothing. I want to be me. A law unto myself."

"That isn't you talking. It's Sartori."

"What if it is?"

"You know what he's done," Gentle replied. "The atrocities. What are you doing taking lessons from him?"

"When I should be taking them from you, you mean? Since when were you so damn perfect?" He made no reply, and she took his silence as further sign of his new high-mindedness. "Oh, so you're not going to stoop to mudslinging, is that it?"

"We'll debate it later," he said.

"Debate it?" she mocked. "What are you going to give us, Maestro, an ethics lesson? I want to know what makes you so damn rare."

"I'm Celestine's son," he said quietly.

She stared at him, agog. "You're what?"

"Celestine's son. She was taken from the Fifth—"

"I know where she was taken. Dowd did it. I thought he'd told me the whole story."

"Not this part?"

"Not this part."

"There were kinder ways to tell you. I'm sorry I didn't find one."

"No," she said. "Where better?"

Her gaze went back up the stairs. When she spoke again, which was not for a little time, it was in a whisper.

"You're lucky," she said. "Home and Heaven are the same place."

"Maybe that's true for us all," he murmured.

"I doubt it."

A long silence followed, punctuated only by Monday's forlorn attempts to whistle on the step outside.

At last, Jude said, "I can see now why you're so desperate to get all this right. You're . . . how does it go? . . . you're about your Father's business."

"I hadn't thought of it quite like that. . . ."

"But you are."

"I suppose I am. I just hope I'm equal to it, that's all. One minute I feel it's all possible. The next . . ."

He studied her, while outside Monday attempted the tune afresh.

"Tell me what you're thinking," he said.

"I'm thinking I wish I'd kept your love letters," she replied.

There was another aching pause; then she turned from him and wandered off towards the back of the house. He lingered at the bottom of the stairs, thinking he should probably go with her, in case Sartori's agent was hiding there, but he was afraid to bruise her further with his scrutiny. He glanced back towards the open door and the sunlight on the step. Safety wasn't far from her, if she needed it.

"How's it going?" he called to Monday.

"Hot," came the reply. "Clem's gone to fetch some food and beer. Lots of beer. We should have a party, boss. We fuckin' deserve it, don't we?"

"We do. How's Celestine?"

"She's asleep. Is it okay to come in yet?"

"Just a little while longer," Gentle replied. "But keep up the whistling, will you? There's a tune in there somewhere."

Monday laughed, and the sound, which was utterly commonplace of course, yet as unlikely as whale song, pleased him. If Little Ease was still in the house, Gentle thought, his malice could do no great harm on a day as miraculous as this. Comforted, he set off up the stairs, wondering as he went if perhaps the daylight had shooed all the memories into hiding. But before he was halfway up the flight, he had proof that they hadn't. The phantom form of Lucius Cobbitt, conjured in his mind's eye, appeared beside him, snotty, tearful, and desperate for wisdom. Moments later, the sound of his own voice, offering the advice he'd given the boy that last, terrible night.

"Study nothing except in the knowledge that you already knew it. Worship nothing . . ."

But before he'd completed the second dictum, the phrase was taken up by a mellifluous voice from above.

". . . except in adoration of your true self. And fear nothing . . ."

The figment of Lucius Cobbitt faded as Gentle continued to climb, but the voice became louder.

". . . except in the certainty that you are your enemy's begetter and its only hope of healing."

And with the voice came the realization that the wisdom he'd bestowed on Lucius had not been his at all. It had originated with the mystif. The door to the Meditation Room was open, and Pie was perched on the sill, smiling out of the past.

"When did you invent that?" the Maestro asked.

"I didn't invent it, I learned it," the mystif replied. "From my mother. And she learned it from her mother, or her father, who knows? Now you can pass it on."

"And what am I?" he asked the mystif. "Your son or your daughter?"

Pie looked almost abashed. "You're my Maestro."

"Is that all? We're still masters and servants here? Don't say that."

"What should I say?"

"What you feel."

"Oh." The mystif smiled. "If I told you what I feel we'd be here all day."

The gleam of mischief in its eye was so endearing, and the memory so real, it was all Gentle could do to prevent himself crossing the room and embracing the space where his friend had sat. But there was work to be done—his Father's business, as Jude had called it—and it was more pressing than indulging his memories. When Little Ease had been ousted from the house, then he'd return here and search for a profounder lesson: that of the workings of the Reconciliation. He needed that education quickly, and the echoes here were surely rife with exchanges on the subject.

"I'll be back," he said to the creature on the sill.

"I'll be waiting," it replied.

He glanced back towards it, and the sun, catching the window behind, momentarily ate into its silhouette, showing him not a whole figure but a fragment. His gut turned, as the image called another back to mind, with appalling force: the Erasure, in roiling chaos, and in the air above his head, the howling rags of his beloved, returned into the Second with some words of warning.

"*Undone,*" it had said, as it fought the claim of the Erasure. "*We are . . . undone.*"

Had he made some placating reply, snatched from his lips by the storm? He didn't remember. But he heard again the mystif telling him to find Sartori, instructing him that his other knew something that he, Gentle, didn't. And then it had gone, been snatched away into the First Dominion and silenced there.

His heart racing, Gentle shook this horror from his head and looked back towards the sill. It was empty now. But Pie's exhortation to find Sartori was still in his head. Why had that been so important? he wondered. Even if the mystif had somehow discovered the truth of Gentle's origins in the First Dominion and had failed to communicate the fact, it must have known that Sartori was as much in ignorance of the secret as his brother. So what was the knowledge the mystif had believed Sartori possessed, that it had defied the limits of God's Kingdom to spur him into pursuit?

A shout from below had him give up the enigma. Jude was calling out to him. He headed down the stairs at speed, following her voice through the house and into the kitchen, which was large and chilly. Jude was standing close to the window, which had gone to ruin many years ago, giving access to the convolvulus from the garden behind, which having entered had rotted in a darkness its own abundance had thickened. The sun could only get pencil beams through this snare of foliage and wood, but they were sufficient to illuminate both the woman and the captive whose head she had pinned beneath her foot. It was Little Ease, his oversized mouth drawn down like a tragic mask, his eyes turned up towards Jude.

"Is this it?" she said.

"This is it."

Little Ease set up a round of thin mewling as Gentle approached, which it turned into words. "I didn't do a thing! You ask her, ask her please, ask her did I do a thing? No, I didn't. Just keeping out of harm's way, I was."

"Sartori's not very happy with you," Gentle said.

"Well, I didn't have a hope," it protested. "Not against the likes of you. Not against a Reconciler."

"So you know that much."

"I do now. 'We have to be whole,' " it quoted, catching Gentle's tone perfectly. " 'We have to be reconciled with everything we ever were—' "

"You were listening."

"I can't help it," the creature said. "I was born inquisitive. I didn't understand it, though," it hastened to add. "I'm not spying, I swear."

"Liar," Jude said. Then to Gentle, "How do we kill it?"

"We don't have to," he said. "Are you afraid, Little Ease?"

"What do you think?"

"Would you swear allegiance to me if you were allowed to live?"

"Where do I sign? Show me the place!"

"You'd let *this* live?" Jude said.

"Yes."

"What for?" she demanded, grinding her heel upon it. "Look at it."

"Don't," Little Ease begged.

"Swear," said Gentle, going down on his haunches beside it.

"I swear! I swear!"

Gentle looked up at Jude. "Lift your foot," he said.

"You trust it?"

"I don't want death here," he said. "Even this. Let it go, Jude." She didn't move. "I said, *let it go.*"

Reluctance in every sinew, she raised her foot half an inch and Little Ease scrabbled free, instantly taking hold of Gentle's hand.

"I'm yours, Liberatore," it said, touching its clammy brow to Gentle's palm. "My head's in your hands. By Hyo, by Heretea, by Hapexamendios, I commit my heart to you."

"Accepted," Gentle said, and stood up.

"What should I do now, Liberatore?"

"There's a room at the top of the stairs. Wait for me there."

"For ever and ever."

"A few minutes will do."

It backed off to the door, bowing woozily, then took to its heels.

"How can you trust a thing like that?" Jude said.

"I don't. Not yet."

"But you're willing to try."

"You're damned if you can't forgive, Jude."

"You could forgive Sartori, could you?" she said.

"He's me, he's my brother, and he's my child," Gentle replied. "How could I not?"

2

With the house made safe, the rest of the company moved in. Monday, ever the scavenger, went off to scour the neighboring houses and streets in search of whatever he could find to offer some modicum of comfort. He returned three times with bounty, the third time taking Clem off with him. They returned half an hour later with two mattresses and armfuls of bed linen, all too clean to have been found abandoned.

"I missed my vocation," Clem said, with Tay's mischief in his features. "Burglary's much more fun than banking."

At this juncture Monday requested permission to borrow Jude's car and drive back to the South Bank, there to collect the belongings he'd left behind in his haste to follow Gentle. She told him yes, but urged him to return as fast as possible. Though it was still bright on the street outside, they would need as many strong arms and wills as they could muster to defend the house when night fell. Clem had settled Celestine in what had been the dining room, laying the larger of the two mattresses on the floor and sitting with her until she slept. When he emerged Tay's feisty presence was mellowed, and the man who came to join Jude on the step was serene.

"Is she asleep?" Jude asked him.

"I don't know if it's sleep or a coma. Where's Gentle?"

"Upstairs, plotting."

"You've argued."

"That's nothing new. Everything else changes, but that remains the same."

He opened one of the bottles of beer sitting on the step and drank with gusto. "You know, I catch myself every now and then wondering if this is all some hallucination. You've probably got a better grasp of it than I have—you've seen the Dominions; you know it's all real—but when I went off with Monday to get the mattresses, there were people just a few streets away, walking around in the sun as though it was just another day, and I thought, There's a woman back there who's been buried alive for two hundred years, and her son whose Father's a God I never heard of—"

"So he told you that."

"Oh, yes. And thinking about it, I wanted to just go home, lock the door, and pretend it wasn't happening."

"What stopped you?"

"Monday, mostly. He just takes everything in stride. And knowing Tay's inside me. Though that feels so natural it's like he was always there."

"Maybe he was," she said. "Is there any more beer?"

"Yep."

He handed over a bottle, and she struck it on the step the way he had. The top flew; the beer foamed.

"So what made you want to run?" she said, when she'd slaked her thirst.

"I don't know," Clem replied. "Fear of what's coming, I suppose. But that's stupid, isn't it? We're here at the beginning of something sublime, just the way Tay promised. Light coming into the world, from a place we never even dreamed existed. It's the Birth of the Unconquered Son, isn't it?"

"Oh, the sons are going to be fine," Jude said. "They usually are."

"But you're not so sure about the daughters?"

"No, I'm not," she said. "Hapexamendios killed the Goddesses throughout the Imajica, Clem, or at least tried to. Now I find He's Gentle's Father. That doesn't make me feel too comfortable about doing His work."

"I can understand that."

"Part of me thinks . . ." She let her voice trail into the silence, the thought unfinished.

"What?" he asked. "Tell me."

"Part of me thinks we're fools to trust either of them, Hapexamendios *or* His Reconciler. If He was such a loving God, why did He do so much harm? And don't tell me He moves in mysterious ways, because that's so much horse shit and we both know it."

"Have you talked to Gentle about this?"

"I've tried, but he's got one thing on his mind—"

"Two," Clem said. "The Reconciliation's one. Pie 'oh' pah's the other."

"Oh, yes, the glorious Pie 'oh' pah."

"Did you know he married it?"

"Yes, he told me."

"It must have been quite a creature."

"I'm a little biased, I'm afraid," she said dryly. "It tried to kill me."

"Gentle said that wasn't Pie's nature."

"No?"

"He told me he ordered it to live its life as an assassin or a whore. It's all his fault, he said. He blames himself for everything."

"Does he blame himself or does he just take responsibility?" she said. "There's a difference."

"I don't know," Clem said, unwilling to be drawn on such niceties. "He's certainly lost without Pie."

She kept her counsel here, wanting to say that she too was lost, that she too pined, but not trusting even Clem with this admission.

"He told me Pie's spirit is still alive, like Tay's," Clem was saying. "And when this is all over—"

"He says a lot of things," Jude cut in, weary of hearing Gentle's wisdoms repeated.

"And you don't believe him?"

"What do I know?" she said, flinty now. "I don't belong in this Gospel. I'm not his lover, and I won't be his disciple."

A sound behind them, and they turned to find Gentle standing in the hallway, the brightness bouncing up from the step like footlights. There was sweat on his face, and his shirt was stuck to his chest. Clem rose with guilty speed, his heel catching his bottle. It rolled down two steps, spilling frothy beer as it went, before Jude caught it.

"It's hot up there," Gentle said.

"And it's not getting any cooler," Clem observed.

"Can I have a word?"

Jude knew he wanted to speak out of her earshot, but Clem was either too guileless to realize this, which she doubted, or unwilling to play his game. He stayed on the step, obliging Gentle to come to the door.

"When Monday gets back," he said, "I'd like you to go to the estate and bring back the stones in the Retreat. I'm going to perform the Reconciliation upstairs, where I've got my memories to help me."

"Why are you sending Clem?" Jude said, not rising or even

turning. "I know the way; he doesn't. I know what the stones look like; he doesn't."

"I think you'd be better off here," Gentle replied.

Now she turned. "What for?" she said. "I'm no use to anyone. Unless you simply want to keep an eye on me."

"Not at all."

"Then let me go," she said. "I'll take Monday to help me. Clem and Tay can stay here. They're your angels, aren't they?"

"If that's the way you'd prefer it," he said, "I don't mind."

"I'll come back, don't worry," she said derisively, raising her beer bottle. "If it's only to toast the miracle."

3

A little while after this conversation, with the blue tide of dusk rising in the street and lifting the day to the rooftops, Gentle left off his debates with Pie and went to sit with Celestine. Her room was more meditative than the one he'd left, where the memories of Pie had become so easy to conjure it was sometimes hard to believe the mystif wasn't there in the flesh. Clem had lit candles beside the mattress upon which Celestine was sleeping, and their light showed Gentle a woman so deeply asleep that no dreams troubled her. Though she was far from emaciated, her features were stark, as though her flesh was halfway to becoming bone. He studied her for a time, wondering if his own face would one day possess such severity; then he returned to the wall at the bottom of the bed and sat on his haunches there, listening to the slow cadence of her breath.

His mind was reeling with all that he'd learned, or recollected, in the room above. Like so much of the magic he'd become acquainted with, the working of the Reconciliation was not a great ceremonial. Whereas most of the dominant religions of the Fifth wallowed in ritual in order to blind their flocks to the paucity of their understanding—the liturgies and requiems, charts and sacraments all created to amplify those tiny grains of comprehension the holy men actually possessed—such theatrics were redundant when the ministers had truth in their grasp, and with the help of memory he might yet become one such minister.

The principle of the Reconciliation was not very difficult to grasp, he'd discovered. Every two hundred years, it seemed, the In Ovo produced a kind of blossom: a five-petaled lotus which floated for a brief time in those lethal waters, immune to either their poison or their inhabitants. This sanctuary was called by a variety of names but most simply, and most often, the Ana. In it, the Maestros would gather, carrying there analogues of the Dominions

they each represented. Once the pieces were assembled, the
process had its own momentum. The analogues would fuse and,
empowered by the Ana, burgeon, driving the In Ovo back and
opening the way between the Reconciled Dominions and the Fifth.

"The flow of things is towards success," the mystif had said,
speaking from a better time. "It's the natural instinct of every broken thing to make itself whole. And the Imajica is broken until it's
Reconciled."

"Then why have there been so many failures?" Gentle had
asked.

"There haven't been that many," Pie had replied. "And they
were always destroyed by outside forces. Christos was brought
down by politics. Pineo was destroyed by the Vatican. Always people from the outside, destroying the Maestro's best intentions. We
don't have such enemies."

Ironic words, with hindsight. Gentle could not afford such complacency again, not with Sartori still alive and the chilling image
of Pie's last frantic appearance at the Erasure still in his head.

It was no use dwelling on it. He put the sight away as best he
could, settling his gaze on Celestine instead. It was difficult to
think of her as his mother. Maybe, among the innumerable memories he'd garnered in this house, there was some faint recollection
of being a babe in these arms, of putting his toothless mouth to
these breasts and being nourished there. But if it was there, it escaped him. Perhaps there were simply too many years, and lives,
and women, between now and that cradling. He could find it in him
to be grateful for the life she'd given him, but it was hard to feel
much more than that.

After a time the vigil began to depress him. She was too like a
corpse, lying there, and he too much a dutiful but loveless mourner.
He got up to go, but before he quit the room he halted at her bedside and stooped to touch her cheek. He'd not laid his flesh to hers
in twenty-three or -four decades, and perhaps, after this, he
wouldn't do so again. She wasn't chilly, as he'd expected her to be,
but warm, and he kept his hand upon her longer than he'd intended.

Somewhere in the depths of her slumber she felt his touch and
seemed to rise into a dream of him. Her austerity softened, and her
pale lips said, "Child?"

He wasn't sure whether to answer, but in the moment of hesitation she spoke again, the same question. This time he replied.

"Yes, Mama?" he said.

"Will you remember what I told you?"

What now? he wondered. "I'm . . . not certain," he told her.
"I'll try."

"Shall I tell you again? I want you to remember, child."

"Yes, Mama," he said. "That would be good. Tell me again."

She smiled an infinitesimal smile and began to repeat a story she'd apparently told many times.

"There was a woman once, called Nisi Nirvana. . . ."

She'd no sooner started, however, than the dream she was having lost its claim on her, and she began to slip back into a deeper place, her voice losing power as she went.

"Don't stop, Mama," Gentle prompted. "I want to hear. There was a woman . . ."

"Yes . . ."

". . . called Nisi Nirvana."

"Yes. And she went to a city full of iniquities, where no ghost was holy and no flesh was whole. And something there did a great hurt to her. . . ."

Her voice was getting stronger again, but the smile, even that tiniest hint, had gone.

"What hurt was this, Mama?"

"You needn't know the hurt, child. You'll learn about it one day, and on that day you'll wish you could forget it. Just understand that it's a hurt only men can do to women."

"And who did this hurt to her?" Gentle asked.

"I told you, child, a man."

"But *what* man?"

"His name doesn't matter. What matters is that she escaped him, and came back into her own city, and knew she must make a good thing from this bad that had been done to her. And do you know what that good thing was?"

"No, Mama."

"It was a little baby. A perfect little baby. And she loved it so much it grew big after a time, and she knew it would be leaving her, so she said, 'I have a story to tell you before you go.' And do you know what the story was? I want you to remember, child."

"Tell me."

"There was a woman called Nisi Nirvana. And she went into a city of iniquities—"

"That's the same story, Mama."

"—where no ghost was holy—"

"You haven't finished the first story. You've just begun again."

"—and no flesh was whole. And something there—"

"Stop, Mama," Gentle said. "Stop."

"—did a great hurt to her. . . ."

Distressed by this loop, Gentle took his hand from his mother's cheek. She didn't halt her recitation, however; at least not at first. The story went on exactly as it had before: the escape from the city;

the good thing made from the bad; the baby, the perfect little baby. But with the hand no longer on her cheek Celestine was sinking back into unthinking slumber, her voice steadily growing more indistinct. Gentle got up and backed away to the door, as the whispered wheel came full circle again.

"So she said: I have a story to tell you before you go."

Gentle reached behind him and opened the door, his eyes fixed on his mother as the words slurred.

"And do you know what the story was?" she said. "I want . . . you . . . to . . . remember . . . child."

He went on watching her as he slipped out into the hallway. The last sounds he heard would have been nonsense to any ear other than this, but he'd heard this story often enough now to know that she was beginning again as she'd dropped into dreamlessness.

"There was a woman once . . ."

On that, he closed the door. For some inexplicable reason, he was shaking, and had to stand at the threshold for several seconds before he could control the tremor. When he turned, he found Clem at the bottom of the stairs, sorting through a selection of candles.

"Is she still asleep?" he asked as Gentle approached.

"Yes. Has she talked to you at all, Clem?"

"Very little. Why?"

"I've just been listening to her tell a story in her sleep. Something about a woman called Nisi Nirvana. Do you know what that means?"

"Nisi Nirvana. Unless Heaven. Is that somebody's name?"

"Apparently. And it must mean a lot to her, for some reason. That's the name she sent Jude with to fetch me."

"And what's the story?"

"Damn strange," Gentle said.

"Maybe you liked it better when you were a kid."

"Maybe."

"If I hear her talking again, do you want me to call you down?"

"I don't think so," Gentle said. "I've got it by heart already."

He started up the stairs.

"You're going to need some candles up there," Clem said. "And matches to light 'em with."

"So I am," Gentle said, turning back.

Clem handed over half a dozen candles, thick, stubby, and white. Gentle handed one of them back.

"Five's the magic number," he said.

"I left some food at the top of the stairs," Clem said as Gentle started to climb again. "It's not exactly haute cuisine, but it's sustenance. And if you don't claim it now it'll be gone as soon as the boy gets back."

Gentle called his thanks back down the flight, picked up the bread, strawberries, and bottle of beer waiting at the top, then returned to the Meditation Room, closing the door behind him. Perhaps because he was still preoccupied with what he'd heard from his mother's lips, the memories of Pie were not waiting at the threshold. The room was empty, a cell of the present. It wasn't until Gentle had set the candles on the mantelpiece, and was lighting one of them, that he heard the mystif speaking softly behind him.

"Now I've distressed you," it said.

Gentle turned into the room and found the mystif at the window, where it so often loitered, with a look of deep concern on its face.

"I shouldn't have asked," Pie went on. "It's just idle curiosity. I heard Abelove asking the boy Lucius a day or two ago, and it made me wonder."

"What did Lucius say?"

"He said he remembered being suckled. That was the first thing he could recall: the teat at his mouth."

Only now did Gentle grasp the subject under debate here. Once again his memory had found some fragment of conversation between himself and the mystif pertinent to his present concerns. They'd talked of childhood memories in this very room, and the Maestro had been plunged into the same distress which he felt now; and for the same reason.

"But to remember a story," Pie was saying. "Particularly one you didn't like—"

"It wasn't that I didn't like it," the Maestro said. "At least, it didn't frighten me, the way a ghost story might have done. It was worse than that. . . ."

"We don't have to talk about this," Pie said, and for a moment Gentle thought the conversation was going to fizzle out there. He wasn't altogether certain he'd have minded if it had. But it seemed to have been one of the unwritten rules of this house that no inquiry was ever fled from, however discomfiting.

"No, I want to explain if I can," the Maestro said. "Though what a child fears is sometimes hard to fathom."

"Unless we can listen with a child's heart," Pie said.

"That's harder still."

"We can try, can't we? Tell me the story."

"Well, it always began the same way. My mother would say, *I want you to remember, child,* and I'd know right away what was going to follow. *There was a woman called Nisi Nirvana, and she went into a city full of iniquities. . . .*"

Now Gentle heard the story again, this time from his own lips, told to the mystif. The woman; the city; the crime; the child; and then, with a sickening inevitability, the story beginning again with the woman and the city and the crime.

"Rape isn't a very pretty subject for a nursery tale," Pie observed.

"She never used that word."

"But that's what the crime is, isn't it?"

"Yes," he said softly, though he was uncomfortable with the admission. This was his mother's secret, his mother's pain. But yes, of course, Nisi Nirvana was Celestine, and the city of terrors was the First Dominion. She'd told her child her own story, encoded in a grim little fable. But more bizarrely than that, she'd folded the listener into the tale, and even the telling of the tale itself, creating a circle impossible to break because all of its constituent elements were trapped inside. Was it that sense of entrapment that had so distressed him as a child? Pie had another theory, however, and was voicing it from across the years.

"No wonder you were so afraid," the mystif said, "not knowing what the crime was, but knowing it was terrible. I'm sure she meant no harm by it. But your imagination must have run riot."

Gentle didn't reply; or, rather, couldn't. For the first time in these conversations with Pie he knew more than history did, and the discontinuity fractured the glass in which he'd been seeing the past. He felt a bitter sense of loss, adding to the distress he'd carried into this room. It was as though the tale of Nisi Nirvana marked the divide between the self who'd occupied these rooms two hundred years before, ignorant of his divinity, and the man he was now, who knew that the story of Nisi Nirvana was his mother's story, and the crime she'd told him about was the act that had brought him into being. There could be no more dallying in the past after this. He'd learned what he needed to know about the Reconciliation, and he couldn't justify further loitering. It was time to leave the comfort of memory, and Pie with it.

He picked up the bottle of beer and struck off the cap. It probably wasn't wise to be drinking alcohol at this juncture, but he wanted to toast the past before it faded from view entirely. There must have been a time, he thought, when he and Pie had raised a glass to the millennium. Could he conjure such a moment now and join his intention with the past one last time? He raised the bottle to his lips and, as he drank, heard Pie laughing across the room. He looked in the mystif's direction, and there, fading already, he caught a glimpse of his lover, not with a glass in hand but a carafe, toasting the future. He lifted the beer bottle to touch the carafe, but the mystif was fading too fast. Before past and present could share the toast, the vision was gone. It was time to begin.

Downstairs, Monday was back, talking excitedly. Setting the bottle down on the mantelpiece, Gentle went out onto the landing to find out what all the furor was about. The boy was at the door, in the middle of describing the state of the city to Clem and Jude. He'd never seen a stranger Saturday night, he said. The streets were practically empty. The only thing that was moving was the traffic lights.

"At least we'll have an easy trip," Jude said.

"Are we going somewhere?"

She told him, and he was well pleased.

"I like it out in the country," he said. "We can do what the fuck we like."

"Let's just make it back alive," she said. "He's relying on us."

"No problem," Monday said cheerily. Then, to Clem: "Look after the boss-man, huh? If things get weird, we can always call on Irish and the rest."

"Did you tell them where we are?" Clem said.

"They're not going to fetch up lookin' for a bed, don't worry," Monday said. "But the way I reckon it, the more friends we got, the better." He turned to Jude. "I'm ready when you are," he said, and headed back outside.

"This shouldn't take more than two or three hours," Jude told Clem. "Look after yourself. And him."

She glanced up the stairs as she spoke, but the candles at the bottom threw too frail a light to reach the top, and she failed to see Gentle there. It was only when she'd gone from the step, and the car was roaring away down the street, that he made his presence known.

"Monday's come back," Clem said.

"I heard."

"Did he disturb you? I'm sorry."

"No, no. I was finished anyway."

"The night's so hot," Clem said, gazing up at the sky.

"Why don't you sleep for a while? I can stand guard."

"Where's that bloody pet of yours?"

"He's called Little Ease, Clem, and he's on the top floor, keeping watch."

"I don't trust him, Gentle."

"He'll do us no harm. Go and lie down."

"Have you finished with Pie?"

"I think I've learned what I can. Now I've got to check on the rest of the Synod."

"How'll you do that?"

"I'll leave my body upstairs and go traveling."

"That sounds dangerous."

"I've done it before. But my flesh and blood'll be vulnerable while I'm out of it."

"As soon as you're ready to go, wake me. I'll watch over you like a hawk."

"Have an hour's nap first."

Clem picked up one of the candles and went to look for a place to lie down, leaving Gentle to take over his post at the front door. He sat on the step with his head laid against the door frame and enjoyed what little breeze the night could supply. There were no lamps working in the street. It was the light of the moon, and the stars in array around it, that picked out the details in the house opposite and caught the pale undersides of the leaves when the wind lifted them. Lulled, he fell into a doze and missed the shooting stars.

4

"Oh, how beautiful," the girl said. She couldn't have been more than sixteen, and when she laughed, which her beau had made her do a lot tonight, she sounded even younger. But she wasn't laughing now. She was standing in the darkness staring up at the meteor shower, while Sartori looked on admiringly.

He'd found her three hours earlier, wandering through the Midsummer Fair on Hampstead Heath, and had easily charmed himself into her company. The fair was doing poor business, with so few people out and about, so when the rides closed down, which they did at the first sign of dusk, he talked her into coming into the City with him. They'd buy some wine, he said, and wander; find a place to sit and talk and watch the stars. It was a long time since he'd indulged himself in a seduction—Judith had been another kind of challenge entirely—but the tricks of the trade came back readily enough, and the satisfaction of watching her resistance crumble, plus the wine he imbibed, did much to assuage the pain of recent defeats.

The girl—her name was Monica—was both lovely and compliant. She met his gaze only coyly at first, but that was all part of the game, and it contented him to play it for a while, as a diversion from the coming tragedy. Coy as she was, she didn't reject him when he suggested they take a stroll around the fields of demolished buildings at the back of Shiverick Square, though she made some remark about wanting him to treat her carefully. So he did. They walked together in the darkness until they found a spot where the undergrowth thinned and made a kind of grove. The sky was clear overhead, and she had a fine, swooning sight of the meteor shower.

"It always makes me feel a little bit afraid," she told him in a charmless Cockney. "Looking at the stars, I mean."

"Why's that?"

"Well . . . we're so small, aren't we?"

He'd asked her earlier to tell him about her life, and she'd volunteered scraps of biography, first about a boy called Trevor, who'd said he loved her but had gone off with her best friend; then about her mother's collection of china frogs, and how much she'd like to live in Spain, because everybody was so much happier there. But now, without prompting, she told him she didn't care about Spain or Trevor or the china frogs. She was happy, she said; and the sight of the stars, which usually scared her, tonight made her want to fly, to which he said that they could indeed fly, together, if she just said the word.

At this she looked away from the sky, with a resigned sigh.

"I know what you want," she said. "You're all the same. Flying. Is that your fancy word for it then?"

He said she'd misunderstood him completely. He hadn't brought her here to fumble and fuss with her. That was beneath them both.

"What then?" she said.

He answered her with his hand, too swiftly to be contradicted. The second primal act, after the one she'd thought he'd brought her here to perform. Her struggles were almost as resigned as her sigh, and she was dead on the ground in less than a minute. Overhead, the stars continued to fall in an abundance he remembered from this time two hundred years before. An unseasonal rain of heavenly bodies, to presage the business of tomorrow night.

He dismembered and disemboweled her with the greatest care and laid the pieces around the grove in time-honored fashion. There was no need to hurry. This working was better completed in the bleak moments before dawn, and they were still some hours away. When they came, and the working was performed, he had high hopes for it. Godolphin's body had been cold when he'd used it, and its owner scarcely an innocent. The creatures he'd tempted from the In Ovo with such unappetizing bait had therefore been primitive. Monica, on the other hand, was warm and had not lived long enough to be much soiled. Her death would open a deeper crack in the In Ovo than Godolphin's, and through it he hoped to draw a particular species of Oviate uniquely suited for the work tomorrow would bring: a sleek, bitter-throated kind, that would help him prove, by tomorrow night, what a child born to destruction could do.

17

AFTER ALL THAT MONDAY HAD SAID about the state of the city, Jude had expected to find it completely deserted, but this proved not to be the case. In the time between his returning from the South Bank and their setting out for the estate, the streets of London, which were as devoid of romancing tourists and partiers as Monday had claimed, had become the territory of a third and altogether stranger tribe: that of men and women who had simply got up out of their beds and gone wandering. Almost all of them were alone, as though whatever unease had driven them out into the night was too painful to share with their loved ones. Some were dressed for a day at the office: suits and ties, skirts and sensible shoes. Others were wearing the minimum for decency: many barefoot, many more bare-chested. All wandered with the same languid gait, their eyes turned up to scan the sky.

As far as Jude could see, the heavens had nothing untoward to show them. She caught sight of a few shooting stars, but that wasn't so unusual on a clear summer night. She could only assume that these people had in their heads the idea that revelation would come from on high and, having woken with the irrational suspicion that such revelation was imminent, had gone out to look for it.

The scene was not so different when they reached the suburbs: ordinary men and women in their nightclothes, standing at street corners or on their front lawns, watching the sky. The phenomenon petered out the farther from the center of London—from Clerkenwell, perhaps—they traveled, only to reappear when they reached the outskirts of the village of Yoke, where, just a few days before, she and Gentle had stood soaked in the post office. Passing down the lanes they'd trudged in the rain reminded her of the naïve ambition she'd returned into the Fifth bearing: the possibility of some reunion between Gentle and herself. Now she was retracing her route with all such hopes dashed, carrying a child that belonged to his enemy. Her two-hundred-year courtship with Gentle was finally, and irredeemably, over.

The undergrowth around the estate had swelled monstrously, and it took more than the switch Estabrook had wielded to clear a way to the gates. Despite the fact that it was flourishing, the greenery smelled rank, as if it was decaying as quickly as it was growing, and its buds would not be blossoms but rot. Thrashing to left and right with his knife, Monday led the way to the gates and through the corrugated iron into the parkland beyond. Though it was an hour for moths and owls, the park was swarming with all manner of daylight life. Birds circled the air as though misdirected by a change in the poles and blind to their nests. Gnats, bees, dragonflies, and all the mazing species of a summer's day flitted in desperate confusion through the moonlit grass. Like the sky gazers in the streets they'd passed through, Nature sensed imminence and could not rest.

Jude's own sense of direction served her well, however. Though the copses scattered ahead of them looked much the same in the blue-gray light, she fixed upon the Retreat, and they trudged towards it, slowed by the muddy ground and the thickness of the grass. Monday whistled as he went, with that same blissful indifference to melody that Clem had remarked upon a few hours before.

"Do you know what's going to happen tomorrow?" Jude asked him, almost envious of his strange serenity.

"Yeah, sort of," he said. "There's these heavens, see? And the boss is going to let us go there. It's going to be amazin'."

"Aren't you afraid?" she said.

"What of?"

"Everything's going to change."

"Good," he said. "I'm fucked off with the way things are."

Then he picked up the thread of his whistle again and headed on through the grass for another hundred yards, until a sound more insistent than his din silenced him.

"Listen to that."

The activity in the air and the grass had steadily increased as they approached the copse, but with the wind blowing in the opposite direction the din of such an assembly as was gathered there had not been audible until now.

"Birds and bees," Monday remarked. "And a fuck of a lot of 'em."

As they continued their advance, the scale of the parliament ahead steadily became more apparent. Though the moonlight did not pierce the foliage very deeply, it was clear that every branch of every tree around the Retreat, to the tiniest twiglet, was occupied with birds. The smell of their massing pricked their nostrils; its din, their ears.

"We're going to get our heads right royally shat on," Monday said. "Either that or we'll get stung to death."

The insects were by now a living veil between them and the copse, so thick that they gave up attempting to flail it aside after a few strides and bore the deaths on their brows and cheeks, and the countless flutterings in their hair, in order to pick up speed and dash for their destination. There were birds in the grass now, commoners among the parliament, denied a seat on the branches. They rose in a squawking cloud before the runners, and their alarm caused consternation in the trees. A thunderous ascent began, the mass of life so vast that the violence of its motion beat the tender leaves down. By the time Jude and Monday reached the corner of the copse, they were running through a double rain: one green and falling, the other rising and feathered.

Picking up her pace, Jude overtook Monday and headed around the Retreat—the walls of which were black with insects—to the door. At the threshold, she halted. There was a small fire burning inside, built close to the edge of the mosaic.

"Some bugger got here first," Monday remarked.

"I don't see anyone."

He pointed to a bundle lying on the floor beyond the fire. His eyes, more accustomed than hers to seeing life in rags, had found the fire maker. She stepped into the Retreat, knowing before he raised his head who this creature was. How could she not? Three times before—once here, once in Yzordderrex, and once, most recently, in the Tabula Rasa's tower—this man had made an unexpected arrival, as though to prove what he'd claimed not so long ago: that their lives would be perpetually interwoven, because they were the same.

"Dowd?"

He didn't move.

"Knife," she said to Monday.

He passed it over and, armed, she advanced across the Retreat towards the bundle. Dowd's hands were crossed on his chest, as though he expected to expire where he lay. His eyes were closed, but they were the only part of his face that was. Almost every other inch had been laid open by Celestine's assault, and despite his legendary powers of recuperation he'd been unable to make good the damage done. He was unmasked to the bone. Yet he breathed, albeit weakly, and moaned to himself now and then, as though dreaming of punishment or revenge. She was half tempted to kill him in his sleep and have this bitter business brought to an end on the spot. But she was curious to know why he was here. Had he attempted to return to Yzordderrex, and failed, or was he expecting someone to come back this way and meet him here? Either could be significant in these volatile times, and though in her present venomous state she felt perfectly capable of dispatching him, he'd always been an agent in the dealings of greater souls and might still have some fragment of use as a messenger. She went down on her haunches beside him and spoke his name above the din of birds coming back to roost on the roof. He opened his eyes only slowly, adding their glisten to the wetness of his features.

"Look at you," he said. "You're radiant, lovey." It was a line from a boulevard comedy, and despite his wretched condition he spoke it with élan. "I, of course, look like ordure. Will you come closer to me? I don't have the energy for volume."

She hesitated to comply. Though he was on the verge of extinction, he had boundless capacity for malice in him and, with the Pivot's sloughings still fixed in his flesh, the power to do harm.

"I can hear you perfectly well where I am," she said.

"I'm good for a hundred words at this volume," he bargained. "Twice that at a whisper."

"What have we got left to say to each other?"

"Ah," he said. "So much. You think you've heard everybody's stories, don't you? Mine. Sartori's. Godolphin's. Even the Reconciler's, by now. But you're missing one."

"Oh, am I?" she said, not much caring. "Whose is that?"

"Come closer."

"I'll hear it from here or not at all."

He looked at her beadily. "You're a bitch, you really are."

"And you're wasting words. If you've got something to say, say it. Whose story am I missing?"

He bided his time before replying, to squeeze what little drama he could out of this. Finally, he said, "The Father's."

"What father?"

"Is there more than one? Hapexamendios. The Aboriginal. The Unbeheld. He of the First Dominion."

"You don't know that story," she said.

He reached up with sudden speed, and his hand was clamped around her arm before she could move out of range. Monday saw the attack and came running, but she halted him before he plowed into Dowd and sent him back to sit by the fire.

"It's all right," she told him. "He's not going to hurt me. Are you?" She studied Dowd. "Well, are you?" she said again. "You can't afford to lose me. I'm the last audience you'll have, and you know it. If you don't tell this story to me, you're not going to tell it to anybody. Not this side of Hell."

The man quietly conceded her point. "True," he said.

"So tell. Unburden yourself."

He drew a laborious breath; then he began.

"I saw Him once, you know," he said. "The Father of the Imajica. He came to me in the desert."

"He appeared in person, did He?" she said, her skepticism plain.

"Not exactly. I heard Him speaking out of the First. But I saw hints, you know, in the Erasure."

"And what did He look like?"

"Like a man, from what I could see."

"Or what you imagined."

"Maybe I did," Dowd said. "But I didn't imagine what He told me—"

"That He'd raise you up. Make you His procurer. You've told me all this before, Dowd."

"Not all of it," he said. "When I'd seen Him, I came back to the Fifth, using feits He'd whispered to me to cross the In Ovo, and I searched the length and breadth of London for a woman to be blessed among women."

"And you found Celestine?"

"Yes. I found Celestine—at Tyburn, as a matter of fact—watching a hanging. I don't know why I chose her. Perhaps because she laughed so hard when the man kissed the noose, and I thought, She's no sentimentalist, this woman; she won't weep and wail if she's taken into another Dominion. She wasn't beautiful, even then, but she had a clarity, you know? Some actresses have it. The great ones, anyway. A face that could carry extremes of emotion and not look bathetic. Maybe I was a little infatuated with her. . . ." He shivered. "I was capable of that when I was younger. So . . . I made myself known to her, and told her I wanted to show her a living dream, the like of which she'd never forget. She resisted at first, but I could have talked the face off the moon in those days, and she let me drug her with sways and take her away. It was a hell of a journey. Four months, across the Dominions. But I got her there eventually, back to the Erasure. . . ."

"And what happened?"

"It opened."

"And?"

"I saw the City of God."

Here at least was something she wanted to know about. "What was it like?" she said.

"It was just a glimpse—"

Having denied him her proximity for so long, she leaned towards him and repeated her question inches from his ravaged face. "What was it like?"

"Vast and gleaming and exquisite."

"Gold?"

"All colors. But it was just a glimpse. Then the walls seemed to burst, and something reached for Celestine and took her."

"Did you see what it was?"

"I've tried to remember, over and over. Sometimes I think it was like a net; sometimes like a cloud. I don't know. Whatever it was, it took her."

"You tried to help her, of course," Jude said.

"No, I shat my pants and crawled away. What could I do? She belonged to God. And in the long run, wasn't she the lucky one?"

"Abducted and raped?"

"Abducted, raped, and made a little divine. Whereas I, who'd done all the work, what was I?"

"A pimp."

"Yes. A pimp. Anyway, she's had her revenge," he said sourly. "Look at me! She's had more than enough."

That was true. The life both Oscar and Quaisoir had failed to extinguish in Dowd, Celestine had virtually put out.

"So that's the Father's tale?" Jude said. "I've heard most of it before."

"That's the tale. But what's the moral?"

"You tell me."

He shook his head slightly. "I don't know whether you're mocking or not."

"I'm listening, aren't I? Be grateful for small mercies. You could be lying here without an audience."

"Well, that's part of it, isn't it? I'm not. You could have come here when I was dead. You could maybe not have come here at all. But our lives have collided one last time. That's fate's way of telling me to unburden myself."

"Of what?"

"I'll tell you." Again, a labored breath. "All these years I've wondered: Why did God pluck a scabby little actor chappie up out of the dirt and send him across three Dominions to fetch Him a woman?"

"He wanted a Reconciler."

"And He couldn't find a wife in His own city?" Dowd said. "Isn't that a little odd? Besides, why does He care whether the Imajica's Reconciled or not?"

Now that was a good question, she thought. Here was a God who'd sealed Himself away in His own city, and showed no desire to lower the wall between His Dominion and the rest, yet went to immense lengths to breed a child who would bring all such walls tumbling down.

"It's certainly strange," she said.

"I'd say so."

"Have you got any answers to any of this?"

"Not really. But I think He must have some purpose, don't you, or why go to all this trouble?"

"A plot . . ."

"Gods don't plot. They create. They protect. They proscribe."

"So which is He doing?"

"That's the nub of it. Maybe you can find out. Maybe the other Reconcilers already did."

"The others?"

"The sons He sent before Sartori. Maybe they realized what He was up to, and they defied Him."

There was a thought.

"Maybe Christos didn't die saving mortal man from his sins—"

"But from his Father?"

"Yes."

She thought of the scenes she'd glimpsed in the Boston Bowl— the terrible spectacle of the city, and most likely the Dominion, overwhelmed by a great darkness—and her body, that had been driven to fits and convulsions by the torments visited upon her, grew suddenly still. There was no panic, no frenzy: just a deep, cold dread.

"What do I do?"

"I don't know, lovey. You're free to do whatever you like, re-member?"

A few hours before, sitting on the step with Clem, her lack of a place in the Gospel of Reconciliation had depressed her spirits. But now it seemed that fact offered her some frail thread of hope. As Dowd had been so eager to claim at the tower, she belonged to no one. The Godolphins were dead, and so was Quaisoir. Gentle had gone to walk in the footsteps of Christos, and Sartori was either out building his New Yzordderrex or digging a hole to die in. She was on her own, and in a world in which everyone else was blinded by obsession and obligation, that was a significant condition. Per-haps only she could see this story remotely now and make a judg-ment unswayed by fealty.

"This is some choice," she said.

"Perhaps you'd better forget I even spoke, lovely," Dowd said. His voice was becoming frailer by the phrase, but he preserved as best he could his jaunty tone. "It's just gossip from an actor chappie."

"If I try and stop the Reconciliation—"

"You'll be flying in the face of the Father, the Son, and proba-bly the Holy Ghost as well."

"And if I don't?"

"You take the responsibility for whatever happens."

"Why?"

"Because"—the power in his voice was now so diminished the sound of the fire he'd built was louder—"because I think only *you* can stop it."

As he spoke, his hand lost its grip on her arm. "Well . . ." he said, "that's done. . . ." His eyes began to flicker closed.

"One last thing, lovey?" he said.

"Yes?"

"It's maybe asking too much . . ."

"What is?"

"I wonder . . . could you . . . forgive me? I know it's absurd . . . but I don't want to die with you despising me."

She thought of the cruel scene he'd played with Quaisoir, when her sister had asked for some kindness. While she hesitated, he began whispering again.

"We were . . . just a little . . . the same, you know?"

At this, she put out her hand to touch him and offer what comfort she could, but before her fingers reached him his breath stopped and his eyes flickered closed.

Jude let out a tiny moan. Against all reason, she felt a pang of loss at Dowd's passing.

"Is something wrong?" Monday said.

She stood up. "That rather depends on your point of view," she said, borrowing an air of comedic fatalism from the man at her feet. It was a tone worth rehearsing. She might need it quite a bit in the next few hours. "Can you spare a cigarette?" she asked Monday.

Monday fished out his pack and lobbed it over. She took one and threw the pack back as she returned to the fire, stooping to pluck up a burning twig to light the tobacco.

"What happened to fella, m'lad?"

"He's dead."

"So what do we do now?"

What indeed? If ever a road divided, it was here. Should she prevent the Reconciliation—it wouldn't be difficult; the stones were at her feet—and let history call her a destroyer for doing so? Or should she let it proceed and risk an end to all histories, and futures, too?

"How long till it's light?" she asked Monday.

The watch he was wearing had been part of the booty he'd brought back to Gamut Street on his first trip. He consulted it with a flourish. "Two and a half hours," he said.

There was so little time to act, and littler still to decide on a course. Returning to Clerkenwell with Monday was a cul-de-sac; that at least was certain. Gentle was the Unbeheld's agent in this, and he wasn't going to be diverted from his Father's business now, especially on the word of a man like Dowd, who'd spent his life a stranger to truth. He'd argue that this confession had been Dowd's revenge on the living: a last desperate attempt to spoil a glory he knew he couldn't share. And maybe that was true; maybe she'd been duped.

"Are we going to collect these stones or what?" Monday said.

"I think we have to," she said, still musing.

"What are they for?"

"They're ... like stepping stones," she said, her voice losing momentum as a thought distracted her.

Indeed they were stepping stones. They were a way back to Yzordderrex, which suddenly seemed like an open road, along which she might yet find some guidance, in these last hours, to help her make a choice.

She threw her cigarette down into the embers. "You're going to have to take the stones back to Gamut Street on your own, Monday."

"Where are you going?"

"To Yzordderrex."

"Why?"

"It's too complicated to explain. You just have to swear to me that you'll do exactly as I tell you."

"I'm ready," he said.

"All right. So listen up. When I'm gone I want you to take the stones back to Gamut Street and carry a message along with them. It has to go to Gentle personally, you understand? Don't trust anybody else with it. Even Clem."

"I understand," Monday said, beaming with pleasure at this unlooked-for honor. "What have I got to tell him?"

"Where I've gone, for one thing."

"Yzordderrex."

"That's right."

"Then tell him"—she pondered for a moment—"tell him the Reconciliation isn't safe, and he mustn't start the working until I contact him again."

"It isn't safe, and he mustn't start the working—"

"—until I contact him again."

"I've got that. Is there any more?"

"That's it," she said. "Now, all I've got to do is find the circle."

She started to scan the mosaic, looking for the subtle differences in tone that marked the stones. From past experience, she knew that once they'd been lifted from their niches the Yzordderrexian Express would be under way, so she told Monday to wait outside until she'd gone. He looked worried now, but she told him she'd come to no harm.

"It's not that," he said. "I want to know what the message means. If you're telling the boss it's not safe, does that mean he won't open the Dominions?"

"I don't know."

"But I want to see Patashoqua and L'Himby and Yzordderrex," he said, listing the places like charms.

"I know that," she said. "And believe me, I want the Dominions opened just as much as you do."

She studied his face in the dying firelight, looking for some clue as to whether he was being placated, but for all his youth he was a master of concealment. She'd have to trust that he'd put his duties as a messenger above his desire to see the Imajica and relay the spirit of her warning, if not its precise text.

"You've *got* to make Gentle understand the danger he's in," she said, hoping this tack would make him conscientious.

"I will," he said, now faintly irritated by her insistence.

She let the subject lie and returned to the business of finding the stones. He didn't offer his assistance, but retreated to the door, from which he said, "How will you get back?"

She'd found four of the stones already, and the birds on the roof had set up a fresh cacophony, suggesting that they felt some tremor of change below.

"I'll deal with that problem when I get to it," she replied.

The birds suddenly rose up and, unnerved, Monday stepped out of the Retreat altogether. Jude glanced up at him as she dug out another stone. The fire between them had already been fanned into flame, and now its ashes were stirred up, rising in a smutty cloud to hide the door from view. She scanned the mosaic, checking to see if she'd missed a stone, but the itches and aches she remembered from her first crossing were already creeping through her body, proof that the passing place was about its work.

Oscar had told her, on this very spot, that the discomforts of passage diminished with repetition, and his words proved correct. She had time, as the walls blurred around her, to glimpse the door through the swirling ash and realize, all too late, that she should have looked out at the world one last time before leaving it. Then the Retreat disappeared, and the In Ovo's delirium was oppressing her, its prisoners rising in their legions to claim her. Traveling alone, she went more quickly than she had with Oscar (at least that was her impression), and she was out the other side before the Oviates had time to sniff the heels of her glyph.

The walls of the merchant Peccable's cellar were brighter than she remembered them. The reason: a lamp which burned on the floor a yard from the circle and beyond it a figure, its face a blur, which came at her with a bludgeon and laid her unconscious on the floor before she'd uttered a word of explanation.

18

I

The mantle of night was falling on the Fifth Dominion, and Gentle found Tick Raw near the summit of the Mount of Lipper Bayak, watching the last dusky colors of day drop from the sky. He was eating while he did so, a bowl each of sausage and pickle between his feet and a large pot of mustard between these, into which meat and vegetable alike were plunged. Though Gentle had come here as a projection—his body left sitting cross-legged in the Meditation Room in Gamut Street—he didn't need nose or palate to appreciate the piquancy of Raw's meal; imagination sufficed.

He looked up when Gentle approached, unperturbed by the phantom watching him eat.

"You're early, aren't you?" he remarked, glancing at his pocket watch, which hung from his coat on a piece of string. "We've got hours yet."

"I know. I just came—"

"—to check up on me," Tick Raw said, the sting of pickle in his voice. "Well, I'm here. Are you ready in the Fifth?"

"We're getting there," Gentle said, somewhat queasily.

Though he'd traveled this way countless times as the Maestro Sartori—his mind, empowered by feits, carrying his image and his voice across the Dominions—and had reacquainted himself with the technique easily enough, the sensation was damn strange.

"What do I look like?" he asked Tick Raw, remembering as he spoke how he'd attempted to describe the mystif on these very slopes.

"Insubstantial," Tick Raw replied, squinting up at him, then returning to his meal. "Which is fine by me, because there's not enough sausage for two."

"I'm still getting used to what I'm capable of."

"Well, don't take too long about it," Tick Raw said. "We've got work to do."

"And I should have realized that you were part of that work when I was first here, but I didn't, and for that I apologize."

"Accepted," Tick Raw said.

"You must have thought I was crazy."

"You certainly—how shall I put this?—you certainly *confounded* me. It took me days to work out why you were so damn obstreperous. Pie talked to me, you know, tried to make me understand. But I'd been waiting for somebody to come from the Fifth for so long I was only listening with half an ear."

"I think Pie probably hoped my meeting with you would make me remember who the hell I was."

"How long did it take?"

"Months."

"Was it the mystif who hid you from yourself in the first place?"

"Yes, of course."

"Well, it did too good a job. That'll teach it. Where's your flesh and blood, by the way?"

"Back in the Fifth."

"Take my advice, don't leave it too long. I find the bowels mutiny, and you come back to find you're sitting in shite. Of course, that could be a personal weakness."

He selected another sausage and chewed on it as he asked Gentle why the hell he'd let the mystif make him forget.

"I was a coward," Gentle replied. "I couldn't face my failure."

"It's hard," Tick Raw said. "I've lived all these years wondering if I could have saved my Maestro, Uter Musky, if I'd been quicker witted. I still miss him."

"I'm responsible for what happened to him, and I've no excuses."

"We've all got our frailties, Maestro: my bowels; your cowardice. None of us is perfect. But I presume your being here means we're finally going to have another try?"

"That's my intention, yes."

Again, Tick Raw looked at his watch, doing a mute calculation as he chewed. "Twenty of your Fifth Dominion hours from now, or thereabouts."

"That's right."

"Well, you'll find me ready," he said, consuming a sizable pickle in one bite.

"Do you have anyone to help you?"

His mouth full, all Tick could manage was: "on't 'eed un." He chewed on, then swallowed. "Nobody even knows I'm here," he explained. "I'm still wanted by the law, even though I hear Yzordderrex is in ruins."

"It's true."

"I also hear the Pivot's quite transformed," Tick Raw said. "Is that right?"

"Into what?"

"Nobody can get near enough to find out," he replied. "But if you're planning to check on the whole Synod—"

"I am."

"Then maybe you'll see for yourself while you're in the city.

There was a Eurhetemec representing the Second, if I
remember—"

"He's dead."

"So who's there now?"

"I'm hoping Scopique's found someone."

"He's in the Third, isn't he? At the Pivot pit?"

"That's right."

"And who's at the Erasure?"

"A man called Chicka Jackeen."

"I've never heard of him," Tick Raw said. "Which is odd. I get
to hear about most Maestros. Are you sure he's a Maestro?"

"Certainly."

Tick Raw shrugged. "I'll meet him in the Ana then. And don't
worry about me, Sartori. I'll be here."

"I'm glad we've made our peace."

"I fight over food and women but never metaphysics," Tick Raw
said. "Besides, we've joined in a great mission. This time tomorrow
you'll be able to walk home from here!"

Their exchange ended on that optimistic note, and Gentle left Tick
to his night watch, heading with a thought towards the Kwem,
where he hoped to find Scopique keeping his place beside the site
of the Pivot. He would have been there in the time it took to think
himself over the border between Dominions, but he allowed his
journey to be diverted by memory. His thoughts turned to Beatrix
as he left the Mount of Lipper Bayak, and it was there rather than
the Kwem his spirit flew to, arriving on the outskirts of the village.

It was night here too, of course. Doeki lowed softly on the dark
slopes around him, their neck bells tinkling. Beatrix itself was
silent, however, the lamps that had flickered in the groves around
the houses gone, and the children who'd tended them gone too: all
extinguished. Distressed by this melancholy sight, Gentle almost
fled the village there and then, but that he glimpsed a single light
in the distance and, advancing a little way, saw a figure he recognized crossing the street, his lamp held high. It was Coaxial Tasko,
the hermit of the hill who'd granted Pie and Gentle the means to
dare the Jokalaylau. Tasko paused, halfway across the street, and
raised his lamp, peering out into the darkness.

"Is somebody there?" he asked.

Gentle wanted to speak—to make his peace, as he had with Tick
Raw, and to talk about the promise of tomorrow—but the expression on Tasko's face forbade him. The hermit wouldn't thank him
for apologies, Gentle thought, or for talk of a bright new day. Not
when there were so many who'd never see it. If Tasko had some
inkling of his visitor, he also judged a meeting pointless. He simply

shuddered, lowered his lamp, and moved on about his business.

Gentle didn't linger another minute, but turned his face up towards the mountains and thought himself away, not just from Beatrix but from the Dominion. The village vanished, and the dusty daylight of the Kwem appeared around him. Of the four sites where he hoped to find his fellow Maestros—the Mount, the Kwem, the Eurhetemec Kesparate, and the Erasure—this was the only one he hadn't visited in his travels with Pie, and he'd been prepared to have some difficulty locating the spot. But Scopique's presence was a beacon in this wasteland. Though the wind raised blinding clouds of dust, he found the man within a few moments of his arrival, squatting in the shelter of a primitive blind, constructed from a few blankets hung on poles which were stuck in the gray earth.

Uncomfortable though it was, Scopique had suffered worse privations in his life as a seditionist—not least his incarceration in the *maison de santé*—and when he rose to meet Gentle it was with the brio of a fit and contented man. He was dressed immaculately in a three-piece suit and bow tie, and his face, despite the peculiarity of his features (the nose that was barely two holes in his head, the popping eyes), was much less pinched than it had been, his cheeks made florid by the gritty wind. Like Tick Raw, he was expecting his visitor.

"Come in! Come in!" he said. "Not that you're feeling the wind much, eh?"

Though this was true (the wind blew through Gentle in the most curious way, eddying around his navel), he joined Scopique in the lee of his blankets, and there they sat down to talk. As ever, Scopique had a good deal to say and poured his tales and observations out in a seamless monologue. He was ready, he said, to represent this Dominion in the sacred space of the Ana, though he wondered how the equilibrium of the working would be affected by the absence of the Pivot. It had been set at the center of the Five Dominions, he reminded Gentle, to be a conduit, and perhaps an interpreter, of power through the Imajica. Now it was gone, and the Third was undoubtedly the weaker for its removal.

"Look," he said, standing up and leading his phantom visitor out to the tip of the pit. "I'm left conjuring beside a hole in the ground!"

"And you think that'll affect the working?"

"Who knows? We're all amateurs pretending to be experts. All I can do is cleanse the place of its previous occupant and hope for the best."

He directed Gentle's attention away from the pit, to the smoking shell of a sizable building, which was only occasionally visible through the dust.

"What was that?" Gentle asked.

"The bastard's palace."

"And who destroyed it?"

"I did, of course," Scopique said. "I didn't want his handiwork looming over our working. This is going to be a delicate operation as it is, without his filthy influence fucking it up. It looked like a bordello!" He turned his back on it. "We should have had months to prepare for this, not hours."

"I realize that—"

"And then there's the problem of the Second. You know Pie charged me with finding a replacement? I'd have liked to discuss all of this with you, of course, but when we last met you were in a fugue state, and Pie forbade me to acquaint you with who you were, though—may I be honest?"

"Could I stop you?"

"No. I was sorely tempted to slap you out of it." Scopique looked at Gentle fiercely, as though he might have done so now, if Gentle had been material enough. "You caused the mystif so much grief, you know," he said. "And like a damned fool it loved you anyway."

"I had my reasons," Gentle said softly. "But you were talking about this replacement—"

"Ah, yes. Athanasius."

"Athanasius?"

"He's now our man in Yzordderrex, representing the Second. Don't look so appalled. He knows the ceremony, and he's completely committed to it."

"There's not a sane bone in his body, Scopique. He thought I was Hapexamendios' agent."

"Well, of course, that's nonsense—"

"He tried to kill me with Madonnas. He's crazy!"

"We've all had our moments, Sartori."

"Don't call me that."

"Athanasius is one of the most holy men I've ever met."

"How can he believe in the Holy Mother one moment and claim he's Jesus the next?"

"He can believe in his own mother, can't he?"

"Are you seriously saying—"

"—that Athanasius is literally the resurrected Christos? No. If we have to have a Messiah among us, I vote for you." He sighed. "Look, I realize you have difficulties with Athanasius, but I ask you, who else was I to find? There aren't that many Maestros left, Sartori."

"I told you—"

"Yes, yes, you don't like the name. Well, forgive me, but for as long as I live you'll be the Maestro Sartori, and if you want to find somebody else to sit here instead of me, who'll call you something prettier, find him."

"Were you always this bloody-minded?" Gentle replied.

"No," said Scopique. "It's taken years of practice."

Gentle shook his head in despair. "Athanasius. It's a nightmare."

"Don't be so sure he hasn't got the spirit of Jesu in him, by the way," Scopique said. "Stranger things have been known."

"Any more of this," Gentle said, "and I'll be as crazy as he is. Athanasius! This is a disaster!"

Furious, he left Scopique at the blind and moved off through the dust, trailing imprecations as he went, the optimism with which he'd set out on his journey severely bruised. Rather than appear in front of Athanasius with his thoughts so chaotic, he found a spot on the Lenten Way to ponder. The situation was far from encouraging. Tick Raw was holding his position on the Mount as an outlaw, still in danger of arrest. Scopique was in doubt as to the efficacy of his place now that the Pivot had been removed. And now, of all people to join the Synod, Athanasius, a man without the wit to come out of the rain.

"Oh, God, Pie," Gentle murmured to himself. "I need you now."

The wind blew mournfully along the highway as he loitered, gusting towards the place of passage between the Third and Second Dominions, as if to usher him with it, on towards Yzordderrex. But he resisted its coaxing, taking time to examine the options available to him. There were, he decided, three. One, to abandon the Reconciliation right away, before the frailties he saw in the system were compounded and brought on another tragedy. Two, to find a Maestro who could replace Athanasius. Three, to trust Scopique's judgment and go into Yzordderrex to make his peace with the man. The first of these options was not to be seriously countenanced. This was his Father's business, and he had a sacred duty to perform it. The second, the finding of a replacement for Athanasius, was impractical in the time remaining. Which left the third. It was unpalatable, but it seemed to be unavoidable. He'd have to accept Athanasius into the Synod.

The decision made, he succumbed to the message of the gusts and at a thought went with them, along the straight road, through the gap between the Dominions, and across the delta into the city-god's entrails.

2

"Hoi-Polloi?"

Peccable's daughter had put down her bludgeon and was kneeling beside Jude with tears pouring from her crossed eyes.

"I'm sorry, I'm so sorry," she kept saying. "I didn't know. I didn't know."

Jude sat up. A team of bell ringers was tuning up between her temples, but she was otherwise unharmed. "What are you doing here?" she asked Hoi-Polloi. "I thought you'd gone with your father."

"I did," she explained, fighting the tears. "But I lost him at the causeway. There were so many people trying to find a way over. One minute he was beside me, and the next he'd vanished. I stayed there for hours, looking for him; then I thought he'd be bound to come back here, to the house, so I came back too—"

"But he wasn't here."

"No."

She started to sob again, and Jude put her arms around her, murmuring condolences.

"I'm sure he's still alive," Hoi-Polloi said. "He's just being sensible and staying under cover. It's not safe out there." She cast a nervous glance up towards the cellar roof. "If he doesn't come back after a few days, maybe you can take me to the Fifth, and he can follow."

"It's no safer there than it is here, believe me."

"What's happening to the world?" Hoi-Polloi wanted to know.

"It's changing," Jude said. "And we have to be ready for the changes, however strange they are."

"I just want things the way they were: Poppa, and the business, and everything in its place—"

"Tulips on the dining room table."

"Yes."

"It's not going to be that way for quite a while," Jude said. "In fact, I'm not sure it'll ever be that way again." She got to her feet.

"Where are you going?" Hoi-Polloi said. "You can't leave."

"I'm afraid I've got to. I came here to work. If you want to come with me, you're welcome, but you'll have to be responsible for yourself."

Hoi-Polloi sniffed hard. "I understand," she said.

"Will you come?"

"I don't want to be alone," she replied. "I'll come."

Jude had been prepared for the scenes of devastation awaiting them beyond the door of Peccable's house, but not for the sense of rapture that accompanied them. Though there were sounds of lamentation rising from somewhere nearby, and that grief was doubtless being echoed in innumerable houses across the city, there was another message on the balmy noonday air.

"What are you smiling at?" Hoi-Polloi asked her.

She hadn't been aware she was doing so, until the girl pointed it out.

"I suppose because it feels like a new day," she said, aware as she spoke that it was also very possibly the last. Perhaps this brightness in the city's air was its acknowledgement of that: the final remission of a sickened soul before decline and collapse.

She voiced none of this to Hoi-Polloi, of course. The girl was already terrified enough. She walked a step behind Jude as they climbed the street, her fretful murmurs punctuated by hiccups. Her distress would have been profounder still if she'd been able to sense the confusion in Jude, who had no clue, now that she was here, as to where to find the instruction she'd come in search of. The city was no longer a labyrinth of enchantments, if indeed it had ever been that. It was a virtual wasteland, its countless fires now guttering out but leaving a pall overhead. The comet's light pierced these grimy skirts in several places, however, and where its beams fell won color from the air, like fragments of stained glass shimmering in solution above the griefs below.

Having no better place to head for, Jude directed them towards the nearest of these spots, which was no more than half a mile away. Long before they'd reached the place, a faint drizzle was carried their way by the breeze, and the sound of running water announced the phenomenon's source. The street had cracked open, and either a burst water main or a spring was bubbling up from the tarmac. The sight had brought a number of spectators from the ruins, though very few were venturing close to the water, their fear not of the uncertain ground but of something far stranger. The water issuing from the crack was not running away down the hill but *up* it, leaping the steps that occasionally broke the slope with a salmon's zeal. The only witnesses unafraid of this mystery were the children, several of whom had wrested themselves from their parents' grip and were playing in the law-defying stream, some running in it, others sitting in the water to let it play over their legs. In the little shrieks they uttered, Jude was sure she heard a note of sexual pleasure.

"What is this?" Hoi-Polloi said, her tone more offended than astonished, as though the sight had been laid on as a personal affront to her.

"Why don't we follow it and find out?" Jude replied.

"Those children are going to drown," Hoi-Polloi observed, somewhat primly.

"In two inches of water? Don't be ridiculous."

With this, Jude set off, leaving Hoi-Polloi to follow if she so wished. She apparently did, because she once again fell into step behind Jude, her hiccups now abated, and they climbed in silence until, two hundred yards or more from where they'd first encountered the stream, a second appeared, this from another direction entirely and large enough to carry a light freight from the lower slopes. The bulk of the cargo was debris—items of clothing, a few drowned graveolents, some slices of burned bread—but among this trash were objects clearly set upon the stream to be carried wherever it was going: boat missives of carefully folded paper; small wreaths of woven grass, set with tiny flowers; a doll laid on a little flood in a shroud of ribbons.

Jude plucked one of the paper boats out of the water and unfolded it. The writing inside was smeared but legible.

Tishalullé, the letter read. *My name is Cimarra Sakeo. I send this prayer for my mother and for my father, and for my brother, Boem, who is dead. I have seen you in dreams, Tishalullé, and know you are good. You are in my heart. Please be also in the hearts of my mother and father, and give them your comfort.*

Jude passed the letter over to Hoi-Polloi, her gaze following the course of the married streams.

"Who's Tishalullé?" she asked.

Hoi-Polloi didn't reply. Jude glanced around at her, to find that the girl was staring up the hill.

"Tishalullé?" Jude said again.

"She's a Goddess," Hoi-Polloi replied, her voice lowered although there was nobody within earshot. She dropped the letter onto the ground as she spoke, but Jude stooped to pick it up.

"We should be careful of people's prayers," she said, refolding the boat and letting it return to its voyage.

"She'll never get it," Hoi-Polloi said. "She doesn't exist."

"Yet you refuse to say her name out loud."

"We're not supposed to name any of the Goddesses. Poppa taught us that. It's forbidden."

"There are others, then?"

"Oh, yes. There's the sisters of the Delta. And Poppa said there's even one called Jokalaylau, who lived in the mountains."

"Where does Tishalullé come from?"

"The Cradle of Chzercemit, I think. I'm not sure."

"The Cradle of what?"

"It's a lake in the Third Dominion."

This time, Jude knew she was smiling. "Rivers, snows, and lakes," she said, going down on her haunches beside the stream and putting her fingers into it. "They've come in the waters, Hoi-Polloi."

"Who have?"

The stream was cool and played against Jude's fingers, leaping up against her palm. "Don't be obtuse," she said. "The Goddesses. They're here."

"That's impossible. Even if they still existed—and Poppa told me they don't—why would they come here?"

Jude lifted a cupped handful of water to her lips and supped. It tasted sweet. "Perhaps somebody called them," she said. She looked at Hoi-Polloi, whose face was still registering her distaste at what Jude had just done.

"Somebody up there?" the girl said.

"Well, it takes a lot of effort to climb a hill," Jude said. "Especially for water. It's not heading up there because it likes the view. Somebody's pulling it. And if we go with it, sooner or later—"

"I don't think we should do that," Hoi-Polloi replied.

"It's not just the water that's being called," Jude said. "We are, too. Can't you feel it?"

"No," the girl said bluntly. "I could turn around now and go back home."

"Is that what you want to do?"

Hoi-Polloi looked at the river running a yard from her foot. As luck would have it, the water was carrying some of its less lovely cargo past them: a flotilla of chicken heads and the partially incinerated carcass of a small dog.

"You drank that," Hoi-Polloi said.

"It tasted fine," Jude said, but looked away as the dog went by.

The sight had confirmed Hoi-Polloi in her unease. "I think I *will* go home," she said. "I'm not ready to meet Goddesses, even if they are up there. I've sinned too much."

"That's absurd," said Jude. "This isn't about sin and forgiveness. That kind of nonsense is for the men. This is . . ." she faltered, uncertain of the vocabulary, then said, "This is *wiser* than that."

"How do you know?" Hoi-Polloi replied. "Nobody really understands these things. Even Poppa. He used to tell me he knew how the comet was made, but he didn't. It's the same with you and these Goddesses."

"Why are you so afraid?"

"If I wasn't I'd be dead. And don't condescend to me. I know you think I'm ridiculous, but if you were a bit politer you'd hide it."

"I don't think you're ridiculous."

"Yes, you do."

"No, I just think you loved your Poppa a little too much. There's no crime in that. Believe me, I've made the same mistake myself, over and over again. You trust a man, and the next thing . . ." She sighed, shaking her head. "Never mind. Maybe you're right. Maybe you should go home. Who knows, perhaps he'll be waiting for you. What do I know?"

They turned their backs on each other without further word, and

Jude headed on up the hill, wishing as she went that she'd found a more tactful way of stating her case.

She'd climbed fifty yards when she heard the soft pad of Hoi-Polloi's step behind her, then the girl's voice, its rebuking tone gone, saying, "Poppa's not going to come home, is he?"

Jude turned back, meeting Hoi-Polloi's cross-eyed gaze as best she could. "No," she said, "I don't think he is."

Hoi-Polloi looked at the cracked ground beneath her feet. "I think I've always known that," she said, "but I just haven't been able to admit it." Now she looked up again and, contrary to Jude's expectation, was dry-eyed. Indeed, she almost looked happy, as though she was lighter for this admission. "We're both alone now, aren't we?" she said.

"Yes, we are."

"So maybe we should go on together. For both our sakes."

"Thank you for thinking of me," Jude said.

"We women should stick together," Hoi-Polloi replied, and came to join Jude as she resumed the climb.

3

To Gentle's eye Yzordderrex looked like a fever dream of itself. A dark *borealis* hung above the palace, but the streets and squares were everywhere visited by wonders. Rivers sprang from the fractured pavements and danced up the mountainside, spitting their climb in gravity's face. A nimbus of color painted the air over each of the springing places, bright as a flock of parrots. It was a spectacle he knew Pie would have reveled in, and he made a mental note of every strangeness along the way, so that he could paint the scene in words when he was back at the mystif's side.

But it wasn't all wonders. These prisms and waters rose amid scenes of utter devastation, where keening widows sat, barely distinguishable from the blackened rubble of their houses. Only the Eurhetemec Kesparate, at the gates of which he presently stood, seemed to be untouched by the fire raisers. There was no sign of any inhabitant, however, and Gentle wandered for several minutes, silently honing a fresh set of insults for Scopique, when he caught sight of the man he'd come to find. Athanasius was standing in front of one of the trees that lined the boulevards of the Kesparate, staring up at it admiringly. Though the foliage was still in place, the arrangement of branches it grew upon was visible, and Gentle didn't have to be an aspirant Christos to see how readily a body might be nailed to them. He called Athanasius' name several times as he approached, but the man seemed lost in reverie and didn't look around, even when Gentle was at his shoulder. He did, however, reply.

"You came not a moment too soon," he said.

"Auto-crucifixion," Gentle replied. "Now that would be a miracle."

Athanasius turned to him. His face was sallow and his forehead bloody. He looked at the scabs on Gentle's brow and shook his head.

"Two of a kind," he said. Then he raised his hands. The palms bore unmistakable marks. "Have you got these, too?"

"No. And these"—Gentle pointed to his forehead—"aren't what you think. Why do you do this to yourself?"

"I didn't do it," Athanasius replied. "I woke up with these wounds. Believe me, I don't welcome them."

Gentle's face registered his skepticism, and Athanasius responded with vim.

"I've never wanted any of this," he said. "Not the stigmata. Not the dreams."

"So why were you looking at the tree?"

"I'm hungry," came the reply, "and I was wondering if I had the strength to climb."

The gaze directed Gentle's attention back to the tree. Amid the foliage on the higher branches were clusters of comet-ripened fruit, like zebra tangerines.

"I can't help you, I'm afraid," Gentle said. "I don't have enough substance to catch hold of them. Can't you shake them down?"

"I tried. Never mind. We've got more important business than my belly."

"Finding you bandages, for one," Gentle said, his suspicions chastened out of him by this misunderstanding, at least for the moment. "I don't want you bleeding to death before we begin the Reconciliation."

"You mean these?" he said, looking at his hands. "No, it stops and starts whenever it wants. I'm used to it."

"Well, then, we should at least find you something to eat. Have you tried any of the houses?"

"I'm not a thief."

"I don't think anybody's coming back, Athanasius. Let's find you some sustenance before you pass out."

They went to the nearest house, and after a little encouragement from Gentle, who was surprised to find such moral nicety in his companion, Athanasius kicked open the door. The house had either been looted or vacated in haste, but the kitchen had been left untouched and was well stocked. There Athanasius daintily prepared himself a sandwich with his wounded hands, bloodying the bread as he did so.

"I've such a hunger on me," he said. "I suppose you've been fasting, have you?"

"No. Was I supposed to?"

"Each to their own," Athanasius replied. "Everybody walks to Heaven by a different road. I knew a man who couldn't pray unless he had his loins in a zarzi nest."

Gentle winced. "That's not religion, it's masochism."

"And masochism isn't a religion?" the other replied. "You surprise me."

Gentle was startled to find that Athanasius had a capacity for wit, and found himself warming to the man as they chatted. Perhaps they could profit from each other's company after all, though any truce would be cosmetic if the subject of the Erasure and all that had happened there wasn't broached.

"I owe you an explanation," he said.

"Oh?"

"For what happened at the tents. You lost a lot of your people, and it was because of me."

"I don't see how you could have handled it much differently," Athanasius said. "Neither of us knew the forces we were dealing with."

"I'm not sure I do now."

Athanasius made a grim face. "Pie 'oh' pah went to a good deal of trouble to come back and haunt you," he said.

"It wasn't a haunting."

"Whatever it was, it took will to do it. The mystif must have known what the consequences would be, for itself and for my people."

"It hated to cause harm."

"So what was so important that it caused so much?"

"It wanted to make certain I understood my purpose."

"That's not reason enough," Athanasius said.

"It's the only one I've got," Gentle replied, skirting the other part of Pie's message, the part about Sartori. Athanasius had no answers to such puzzles, so why vex him with them?

"I believe there's something going on we don't understand," Athanasius said. "Have you seen the waters?"

"Yes."

"Don't they perturb you? They do me. There are other powers at work here besides us, Gentle. Maybe we should be seeking them out, taking their advice."

"What do you mean by *powers?* Other Maestros?"

"No. I mean the Holy Mother. I think she may be here in Yzord-derrex."

"But you're not certain."

"Something's moving the waters."

"If She was here, wouldn't you know it? You were one of her high priests."

"I was never that. We worshiped at the Erasure because there was a crime committed there. A woman was taken from that spot into the First."

Floccus Dado had told Gentle this story as they'd driven across the desert, but with so much else to vex and excite him, he'd forgotten the tale: his mother's of course.

"Her name was Celestine, wasn't it?"

"How do you know?"

"Because I've met her. She's still alive, back in the Fifth."

The other man narrowed his eyes, as though to sharpen his gaze and prick this if it was a lie. But after a few moments a tiny smile appeared.

"So you've had dealings with holy women," he said. "There's hope for you yet."

"You can meet her yourself, when all this is over."

"I'd like that."

"But for now, we have to hold to our course. There can be no deviations. Do you understand? We can go looking for the Holy Mother when the Reconciliation's done, but not before."

"I feel so damn naked," Athanasius said.

"We all do. It's inevitable. But there's something more inevitable still."

"What's that?"

"The wholeness of things," Gentle said. "Things mended. Things healed. That's more certain than sin, or death, or darkness."

"Well said," Athanasius replied. "Who taught you that?"

"You should know. You married me to it."

"Ah." He smiled. "Then may I remind you why a man marries? So that he can be made whole: by a woman."

"Not this man," Gentle said.

"Wasn't the mystif a woman to you?"

"Sometimes. . . ."

"And when it wasn't?"

"It was neither man nor woman. It was bliss."

Athanasius looked intensely discomfited by this. "That sounds profane to me," he remarked.

Gentle had never thought of the bond between himself and the mystif in such terms before, nor did he welcome the burden of such doubts now. Pie had been his teacher, his friend, and his lover, a selfless champion of the Reconciliation from the very beginning. He could not believe that his Father would ever have sanctioned such a liaison if it were anything but holy.

"I think we should let the subject lie," he told Athanasius, "or we'll be at each other's throats again, and I for one don't want that."

"Neither do I," Athanasius replied. "We'll not discuss it any further. Tell me, where do you go from here?"

"To the Erasure."

"And who represents the Synod there?"

"Chicka Jackeen."

"Ah! So you chose him, did you?"

"You know him?"

"Not well. I know he came to the Erasure long before I did. In fact, I don't think anyone quite knew how long he'd been there. He's a strange fellow."

"If that were a disqualification, we'd both be out of a job," Gentle remarked.

"True enough."

With that, Gentle offered Athanasius his good wishes, and they parted—civilly if not fondly—Gentle turning his thoughts from Yzordderrex to the desert beyond. Instantly, the domestic interior flickered and was replaced seconds later by the vast wall of the Erasure, rising from a fog in which he dearly hoped the last member of his Synod was awaiting him.

4

The streams kept converging as the women climbed, until they were walking beside a flow that would soon be too wide to leap and too furious to ford. There were no embankments to contain these waters, only the gullies and gutters of the street, but the same intentionality that drew them up the hill also limited their lateral spread. That way the river didn't dissipate its energies, but climbed like an animal whose skin was growing at a prodigious rate to accommodate the power it gained every time it assimilated another of its kind. By now its destination would not be in doubt. There was only one structure on the city's highest peak—the Autarch's palace—and unless an abyss opened up in the street and swallowed the waters before they reached the gates it would be there that the trail would deliver them.

Jude had mixed memories of the palace. Some, like the Pivot Tower and the chamber of sluiced prayers beneath it, were terrifying. Others were sweetly erotic, like the hours she'd spent dozing in Quaisoir's bed while Concupiscentia sang and the lover

she'd thought too perfect to be real had covered her with kisses.
He was gone, of course, but she would be returning into the
labyrinth he'd built, now turned to some new purpose, not only
with the scent of him upon her (you smell of coitus, Celestine had
said) but with the fruit of that coupling in her womb. Her hope of
sharing wisdom with Celestine had undoubtedly been blighted by
that fact. Even after Tay's disparagement and Clem's conciliation,
the woman had contrived to treat Jude as a pariah. And if *she*,
merely brushed by divinity, had sniffed Sartori on Jude's skin, then
surely Tishalullé would sniff the same and know the child was
there too. If challenged, Jude had decided to tell the truth. She had
reasons for doing all that she'd done, and she would not make false
apologies, but come to the altars of these Goddesses with humility and self-respect in equal measure.

The gates were now in view, the river gushing towards them, its
flood a whitewater roar. Either its assault or some previous violence had thrown both gates off their hinges, and the water surged
through the gap ecstatically.

"How do we get through?" Hoi-Polloi yelled above the din.

"It's not that deep," Jude said. "We'll be able to wade it if we go
together. Here. Take my hand."

Without giving the girl time to argue or retreat, she took firm
hold of Hoi-Polloi's wrist and stepped into the river. As she'd said,
it wasn't very deep. Its spumy surface only climbed to the middle
of their thighs. But there was considerable force in it, and they were
obliged to proceed with extreme care. Jude couldn't see the ground
she was leading them over, the water was too wild, but she could
feel through her soles how the river was digging up the paving,
eroding in a matter of minutes what the tread of soldiers, slaves,
and penitents had not much impressed in two centuries. Nor was
this erosion the only threat to their equilibrium. The river's freight
of alms, petitions, and trash was very heavy now, gathered as it was
from five or six places in the lower Kesparates. Slabs of wood
knocked at their hamstrings and shins; swaths of cloth wrapped
around their knees. But Jude remained surefooted and advanced
with a steady tread until they were through the gates, glancing back
over her shoulder now and then to reassure Hoi-Polloi with a look
or a smile that, though there was discomfort here, there was no
great hazard.

The river didn't slow once it was inside the palace walls. Instead
it seemed to find fresh impetus, its spume thrown ever higher as it
climbed through the courtyards. The comet's beams were falling
here in greater abundance than on the Kesparates below, and their
light, striking the water, threw silver filigrees up against the joy-
less stone. Distracted by the beauty of this, Jude momentarily lost

her footing as they cleared the gates and, despite a cry of warning, fell back into the river, taking Hoi-Polloi with her. Though they were in no danger of drowning, the water had sufficient momentum to carry them along, and Hoi-Polloi, being much the lighter of the two, was swept past Jude at some speed. Their attempts to stand up again were defeated by the eddies and countercurrents its enthusiasm was generating, and it was only by chance that Hoi-Polloi—thrown against a dam of detritus that was choking part of the flow—was able to use its accrued bulk to bring herself to a halt and haul herself to her knees. The water broke against her with considerable vehemence as she did so, its will to carry her off undiminished, but she defied it, and by the time Jude was carried to the place, Hoi-Polloi was getting to her feet.

"Give me your hand!" she yelled, returning the invitation Jude had first offered when they'd stepped into the flood.

Jude reached to do so, half turning in the water to stretch for Hoi-Polloi's fingers. But the river had other ideas. As their hands came within inches of clasping, the waters conspired to spin her and snatch her away, their hold on her so tight the breath was momentarily squeezed out of her. She couldn't even yell a word of reassurance but was hauled off by the flood, up through a monolithic archway and out of sight.

Violent as the waters were, pitching her around as it raced through the cloisters and colonnades, she wasn't in fear of them; quite the opposite. The exhilaration was contagious. She was part of their purpose now, even if they didn't know it, and happy to be delivered to their summoner, who was surely also their source. Whether that summoner—be she Tishalullé or Jokalaylau or any other Goddess who might be resident here today—judged her to be a petitioner or simply another piece of trash, only the end of this ride would tell.

5

If Yzordderrex had become a place of glorious particulars—every color singing, every bubble in its waters crystalline—the Erasure had given itself over to ambiguity. There was no breath of wind to stir the heavy mist that hung over the fallen tents and over the dead, shrouded but unburied, who lay in their folds; nor did the comet have fire enough to pierce a higher fog, the fabric of which left its light dusky and drab. Off to the left of where Gentle's projection stood, the ring of Madonnas that Athanasius and his disciples had sheltered in was visible through the murk. But the man he'd come here to find wasn't in residence there, nor was there any sign of him to the right, though here the fog was so thick it blotted out everything that lay beyond an eight- or ten-yard range. He nevertheless headed into it, loath to try calling Chicka Jackeen's name, even if his voice had possessed sufficient strength. There was a conspiracy of suppression upon the landscape, and he was unwilling to challenge it. Instead he advanced in silence, his body barely displacing the mist, his feet making little or no impression on the ground. He felt more like a phantom here than in any of the other meeting places. It was a landscape for such souls: hushed but haunted.

He didn't have to walk blindly for long. The mist began to thin out after a time, and through its shreds he caught sight of Chicka Jackeen. He'd dug a chair and small table from the wreckage and was sitting with his back to the great wall of the First Dominion, playing a solitary game of cards and talking furiously to himself as he did so. We're all crazies, Gentle thought, catching him like this. Tick Raw half mad on mustard; Scopique become an amateur arsonist; Athanasius marking sacramental sandwiches with his pierced hands; and finally Chicka Jackeen, chattering away to himself like a neurotic monkey. Crazies to a man. And of all of them he, Gentle, was probably the craziest: the lover of a creature that defied the definitions of gender, the maker of a man who had destroyed nations. The only sanity in his life—burning like a clear white light—was that which came from God: the simple purpose of a Reconciler.

"Jackeen?"

The man looked up from his cards, somewhat guiltily. "Oh. Maestro. You're here."

"Don't say you weren't expecting me?"

"Not so soon. Is it time for us to go to the Ana?"

"Not yet. I came to be sure you were ready."

"I am, Maestro. Truly."

"Were you winning?"

"I was playing myself."

"That doesn't mean you can't win."

"No? No. As you say. Then yes, I was winning." He rose from the table, taking off the spectacles he'd been wearing to study his cards.

"Has anything come out of the Erasure while you've been waiting?"

"No, not come out. In fact, yours is the first voice I've heard since Athanasius left."

"He's part of the Synod now," Gentle said. "Scopique induced him to join us, to represent the Second."

"What happened to the Eurhetemec? Not murdered?"

"He died of old age."

"Will Athanasius be equal to the task?" Jackeen asked; then, thinking his question overstepped the bounds of protocol, he said, "I'm sorry. I've no right to question your judgment in this."

"You've every right," Gentle said. "We've got to have complete faith in each other."

"If you trust Athanasius, then so do I," Jackeen said simply.

"So we're ready."

"There *is* one thing I'd like to report, if I may."

"What's that?"

"I said nothing's come *out* of the Erasure, and that's true—"

"But something went in?"

"Yes. Last night, I was sleeping under the table here"—he pointed to his bed of blankets and stone—"and I woke chilled to the marrow. I wasn't sure whether I was dreaming at first, so I was slow to get up. But when I did I saw these figures coming out of the fog. Dozens of them."

"Who were they?"

"Nullianacs," Jackeen said. "Are you familiar with them?"

"Certainly."

"I counted fifty at least, just within sight of me."

"Did they threaten you?"

"I don't think they even saw me. They had their eyes on their destination—"

"The First?"

"That's right. But before they crossed over, they shed their clothes, and made some fires, and burned every last thing they wore or brought with them."

"All of them did this?"

"Every one that I saw. It was extraordinary."

"Can you show me the fires?"

"Easily," Jackeen said, and led Gentle away from the table, talking as he went. "I'd never seen a Nullianac before, but of course I've heard the stories."

"They're brutes," Gentle said. "I killed one in Vanaeph, a few months ago, and then I met one of its brothers in Yzordderrex, and it murdered a child I knew."

"They like innocence, I've heard. It's meat and drink to them. And they're all related to each other, though nobody's ever seen the female of the species. In fact, some say there isn't one."

"You seem to know a lot about them."

"Well, I read a good deal," Jackeen said, glancing at Gentle. "But you know what they say: Study nothing except in the knowledge—"

"—that you already knew it."

"That's right."

Gentle looked at the man with fresh interest, hearing the old saw from his lips. Was it so commonplace a dictum that every student had it by heart, or did Chicka Jackeen know the significance of what he was saying? Gentle stopped walking, and Jackeen stopped beside him, offering a smile that verged on the mischievous. Now it was Gentle who did the studying, his text the other man's face: and, reading, saw the dictum proved.

"My God," he said. "Lucius?"

"Yes, Maestro. It's me."

"Lucius! Lucius!"

The years had taken their toll, of course, though not insufferably. While the face in front of him was no longer that of the eager acolyte he had sent from Gamut Street, it was not marked by more than a tenth of the two centuries in between.

"This is extraordinary," Gentle said.

"I thought maybe you knew who I was, and you were playing a game with me."

"How could I know?"

"Am I really so different?" the other said, clearly a little deflated. "It took me twenty-three years to master the feit of holding, but I thought I'd caught the last of my youth before it went entirely. A little vanity. Forgive me."

"When did you come here?"

"It seems like a lifetime, so it probably is. I wandered back and forth through the Dominions first, studying with one evocator after another, but I was never content with any of them. I had you to judge them by, you see. So I was always dissatisfied."

"I was a lousy teacher," Gentle said.

"Not at all. You taught me the fundamentals, and I've lived by them and prospered. Maybe not in the world's eyes, but in mine."

"The only lesson I gave you was on the stairs. Remember, that last night?"

"Of course I remember. The laws of study, workings, and fear. Wonderful."

"But they weren't mine, Lucius. The mystif taught them to me. I just passed them along."

"Isn't that what most teachers do?"

"I think the great ones refine wisdom, they don't simply repeat it. I refined nothing. I thought every word I uttered was perfect, because it was falling from my lips."

"So my idol has feet of clay?"

"I'm afraid so."

"You think I didn't know that? I saw what happened at the Retreat. I saw you fail, and it's because of that I've waited here."

"I don't follow."

"I knew you wouldn't accept failure. You'd wait, and you'd plan, and someday, even if it took a thousand years, you'd come back to try again."

"One of these days I'll tell you how it really happened, and you won't be so impressed."

"However it went, you're here," Lucius said. "And I have my dream at last."

"Which is what?"

"To work with you. To join you in the Ana, Maestro to Maestro." He grinned. "God is in His Heaven today," he said. "If I'm ever happier than this, it'll kill me. Ah! There, Maestro!" He stopped and pointed to the ground a few yards from them. "That's one of the Nullianacs' fires."

The place was blasted, but there were some remains of the Nullianacs' robes among the ashes. Gentle approached.

"I don't have the wherewithal to sort through them, Lucius. Will you do it for me?"

Lucius obliged, stooping to turn over the cinders and pluck out what remained of the clothes. There were fragments of suits, robes, and coats in a variety of styles, one finely embroidered, after the fashion of Patashoqua, another barely more than sackcloth, a third with medals attached, as if its owner had been a soldier.

"They must have come from all over the Imajica," Gentle said.

"Summoned," Lucius replied.

"That seems like a reasonable assumption."

"But why?"

Gentle mused a moment. "I think the Unbeheld has taken them into His furnace, Lucius. He's burned them away."

"So He's wiping the Dominions clean?"

"Yes, He is. And the Nullianacs knew it. They threw off their clothes like penitents, because they knew that they were going to their judgment."

"You see," Lucius said, "you *are* wise."

"When I'm gone, will you burn even these last pieces?"

"Of course."

"It's His will that we cleanse this place."

"I'll start right away."

"And I'll go back to the Fifth and finish my preparations."

"Is the Retreat still standing?"

"Yes. But that's not where I'll be. I've returned to Gamut Street."

"That was a fine house."

"It's still fine in its way. I saw you there on the stairs only a few nights ago."

"A spirit there and flesh here? What could be more perfect?"

"Being flesh and spirit in the whole of Creation," Gentle said.

"Yes. That would be finer still."

"And it'll happen. It's all One, Lucius."

"I hadn't forgotten that lesson."

"Good."

"But if I may ask—"

"Yes?"

"Would you call me Chicka Jackeen from now on? I've lost the bloom of youth, so I may as well lose the name."

"Maestro Jackeen it is."

"Thank you."

"I'll see you in a few hours," Gentle said, and with that put his thoughts to his return.

This time there were no diversions or loiterings, for sentiment's sake or any other. He went at the speed of his intention back through Yzordderrex and along the Lenten Way, over the Cradle and the benighted heights of the Jokalaylau, passing across the Mount of Lipper Bayak and Patashoqua (within whose gates he had yet to step), finally returning into the Fifth, to the room he'd left in Gamut Street.

Day was at the window and Clem was at the door, patiently awaiting the return of his Maestro. As soon as he saw a flicker of animation in Gentle's face he began to speak, his message too urgent to be delayed a second longer than it had to be.

"Monday's back," he said.

Gentle stretched and yawned. His nape and lumbar regions ached, and his bladder was ready to burst, but at least he hadn't returned to discover his bowels had given out, as Tick Raw had predicted.

"Good," he said. He got to his feet and hobbled to the mantelpiece, clinging to it as he kicked some life back into his deadened legs. "Did he get all the stones?"

"Yes, he did. But I'm afraid Jude didn't come back with him."

"Where the hell is she?"

"He won't tell me. He's got a message from her, he says, but he won't trust it to anyone but you. Do you want to speak to him? He's downstairs, eating breakfast."

"Yes, send him up, will you? And if you can, find me something to eat. Anything but sausages."

Clem headed off down the stairs, leaving Gentle to cross to the window and throw it open. The last morning that the Fifth would see Unreconciled had dawned, and the temperature was already high enough to wilt the leaves on the tree outside. Hearing Monday's feet clattering up the stairs, Gentle turned to greet the messenger, who appeared with a half-eaten hamburger in one hand and a half-smoked cigarette in the other.

"You've got something to tell me?" he said.

"Yes, boss. From Jude."

"Where did she go?"

"Yzordderrex. That's part of what I'm supposed to tell you. She's gone to Yzordderrex."

"Did you see her go?"

"Not exactly. She made me stand outside while she went, so that's what I did."

"And the rest of the message?"

"She told me"—he made a great show of concentration now—"to tell you where she'd gone, and I've done that; then she said to tell you that the Reconciliation isn't safe, and that you weren't to do nothing until she contacted you again."

"*Isn't safe?* Those were her words?"

"That's what she said. No kiddin'."

"Do you know what she was talking about?"

"Search me, boss." His eyes had gone from Gentle to the darkest corner of the room. "I didn't know you had a monkey," he said. "Did you bring it back with you?"

Gentle looked to the corner. Little Ease was there, staring up at the Maestro fretfully, having presumably crept down into the Meditation Room sometime during the night.

"Does it eat hamburgers?" Monday said, going down on his haunches.

"You can try," Gentle said distractedly. "Monday, is that all Jude said: It isn't safe?"

"That's it, boss. I swear."

"She just arrived at the Retreat and told you she wasn't coming back?"

"Oh, no, she took her time," Monday said, pulling a face as the creature he'd taken to be an ape skulked from its corner and started towards the proffered hamburger.

He made to stand up, but it bared its teeth in a grin of such ferocity he thought better of doing so and simply extended his arm as far as he could to keep the beast from his face. Little Ease slowed as it came within sniffing distance and, instead of snatching the meal, claimed it from Monday's hand with the greatest delicacy, pinkies raised.

"Will you finish the story?" Gentle said.

"Oh, yeah. Well, there was this fella in the Retreat when we got there, and she had a long jaw with him."

"This was somebody she knew?"

"Oh, yeah."

"Who?"

"I forget his name," Monday said, but seeing Gentle's brow frown protested, "That wasn't part of the message, boss. If it had been I'd have remembered."

"Remember anyway," Gentle said, beginning to suspect conspiracy. "Who was he?"

Monday stood up and drew nervously on his cigarette. "I don't recall. There were all these birds, you know, and bees an' stuff. I wasn't really listening. It was something short, like Cody or Coward or—"

"Dowd."

"Yeah! That's it. It was Dowd. And he was really fucked up, let me tell you."

"But alive."

"Oh, yeah, for a while. Like I said, they talked together."

"And it was after this that she said she was going to Yzordderrex?"

"That's right. She told me to bring the stones back to you, and the message with 'em."

"Both of which you've done. Thank you."

"You're the boss, boss," Monday said. "Is that all? If you want me I'm on the step. It's going to be a scorcher."

He thundered off downstairs.

"Shall I leave the door open, Liberatore?" Little Ease said, as it nibbled on the hamburger.

"What are you doing here?"

"I got lonely up there," the creature said.

"You promised obedience," Gentle reminded it.

"You don't trust her, do you?" Little Ease replied. "You think she's gone off to join Sartori."

He hadn't until now. But the notion, now that it was floated, didn't seem so improbable. Jude had confessed what she felt for Sartori, in this very house, and clearly believed that he loved her in return. Perhaps she'd simply slipped away from the Retreat while Monday's back was turned and had gone to find the father of her child. If that was the case, it was paradoxical behavior, to seek out the arms of a man whose enemy she'd just helped towards victory. But this was not a day to waste analyzing such conundrums. She'd done what she'd done, and there was an end to it.

Gentle hoisted himself up onto the sill, from which perch he'd often planned his itinerary, and attempted to push all thoughts of her defection out of his head. This was a bad room in which to try and forget her, however. It was, after all, the womb in which she'd been made. The boards most likely still concealed motes of the sand that had marked her circle and stains, deep in their grain, of the liquors he'd anointed her nakedness with. Try as he might to keep the thoughts from coming, one led inevitably to another. Imagining her naked, he pictured his hands upon her, slick with oils. Then his kisses. Then his body. And before a minute had passed he was sitting on the sill with an erection nuzzling against his underwear.

Of all the mornings to be plagued with such distraction! The beguilements of the flesh had no place in the work ahead of him. They'd brought the last Reconciliation to tragedy, and he would not allow them to lead him from his sanctified path by a single step. He looked down at his groin, disgusted with himself.

"Cut it off," Little Ease advised.

If he could have done the deed without making an invalid of himself, he'd have done so there and then, and gladly. He had nothing but contempt for what rose between his legs. It was a hot-headed idiot, and he wanted rid of it.

"I can control it," he replied.

"Famous last words," the creature said.

A blackbird had come into the tree and was singing blithely there. He looked its way and beyond, up through the branches into the burnished blue sky. His thoughts abstracted as he studied it, and by the time he heard Clem coming up the stairs with food and drink the spasm of carnality had passed, and he greeted his angels with a cooling brow.

"So now we wait," he told Clem.

"What for?"

"For Jude to come back."

"And if she doesn't?"

"She will," Gentle replied. "This is where she was born. It's her home, even if she wishes it weren't. She'll have to make her way back here eventually. And if she's conspired against us, Clem—if she's working with the enemy—then I swear I'll draw a circle right *here*"—he pointed to the boards—"and I'll unmake her so well it'll be as though she never drew breath."

19

I

The law-defying waters were compassionate. Though they carried Jude through the palace at considerable speed, roaming through corridors their passage had already stripped of tapestries and furnishings, they treated their cargo with care. She wasn't thrown

against the walls or the pillars, but was borne up on a ship of surf
that neither faltered nor foundered but hurried, remotely helmed,
to its destination. That place could scarcely be in doubt. The mystery at the heart of the Autarch's maze had always been the Pivot
Tower, and though she'd witnessed the beginning of the tower's undoing, it was still, surely, her place of debarkation. Prayers and petitions had gone there for an age, attracted by the Pivot's authority.
Whatever force had replaced it, calling these waters, it had set its
throne on the rubble of the fallen lord.

And now she had proof of that, as the waters carried her out of
the naked corridors and into the still severer environs of the tower,
slowing to deliver her into a pool so thick with detritus it was almost solid. Out of this wreckage rose a staircase, and she hauled
herself from the debris and lay on the lower steps, giddy but exhilarated. The waters continued to surge around the staircase like
an eager spring tide, and their clear desire to be up the flight was
contagious. She got to her feet, after a little time, and proceeded
to climb.

Although there were no lights burning at the top, there was
plenty of illumination spilling down the stairs to meet her, and like
the light at the springing places it was prismatic, suggesting there
were more waters ahead that had come into the palace via other
routes. Before she was even halfway up the flight, two women appeared and stared down at her. Both were dressed in simple off-
white shifts, the fatter of the pair, a woman of gargantuan
proportions, unbuttoned to bare her breasts to the baby she was
nursing. She looked almost as infantile as her charge, her hair
wispy, her face, like her breasts, heavy and sugar-almond pink. The
woman beside her was older and slimmer, her skin substantially
darker than that of her companion, her gray hair braided and
combed out to her shoulders like a cowl. She wore gloves, and
glasses, and regarded Jude with almost professorial detachment.

"Another soul saved from the flood," she said.

Jude had stopped climbing. Though neither woman had made
any sign that she was forbidden entry, she wanted to come into this
miraculous place as a guest, not a trespasser.

"Am I welcome?"

"Of course," said the mother. "Have you come to meet the
Goddesses?"

"Yes."

"Are you from the Bastion, then?"

Before Jude could reply, her companion supplied the answer.
"Of course not! Look at her!"

"But the waters brought her."

"The waters'll bring any woman who dares. They brought us, didn't they?"

"Are there many others?" Jude asked.

"Hundreds," came the reply. "Maybe thousands by now."

Jude wasn't surprised. If someone like herself, a stranger in the Dominions, had come to suspect that the Goddesses were still extant, how much more hopeful must the women who lived here have been, living with the legends of Tishalullé and Jokalaylau.

When Jude reached the top of the stairs, the bespectacled woman introduced herself.

"I'm Lotti Yap."

"I'm Judith."

"We're pleased to see you, Judith," the other woman said. "I'm Paramarola. And this fellow"—she looked down at the baby—"is Billo."

"Yours?" Jude asked.

"Now where would I have found a man to give me the likes of this?" Paramarola said.

"We've been in the Annex for nine years," Lotti Yap explained. "Guests of the Autarch."

"May his thorn rot and his berries wither," Paramarola added.

"And where have you come from?" Lotti asked.

"The Fifth," Jude said.

She was not fully attending to the women now, however. Her interest had been claimed by a window that lay across the puddle-strewn corridor behind them: or, rather, by the vista visible through it. She went to the sill, both awed and astonished, and gazed out at an extraordinary spectacle. The flood had cleared a circle half a mile wide or more in the center of the palace, sweeping walls and pillars and roofs away and drowning the rubble. All that was left, rising from the waters, were islands of rock where the taller towers had stood, and here and there a corner of one of the palace's vast amphitheaters, preserved as if to mock the overweening pretensions of its architect. Even these fragments would not stand for much longer, she suspected. The waters circled this immense basin without violence, but their sheer weight would soon bring these last remnants of Sartori's masterwork down.

At the center of this small sea was an island larger than the rest, its lower shores made up of the half-demolished chambers that had clustered around the Pivot Tower, its rocks the rubble of that tower's upper half, mingled with vast pieces of its tenant, and its height the remains of the tower itself, a ragged but glittering pyramid of rubble in which a white fire seemed to be burning. Looking at the transformation these waters had wrought, eroding in a matter of days, perhaps hours, what the Autarch had taken decades to devise and build, Jude wondered that she'd reached this place intact. The power she'd first encountered on the lower slopes as an innocent, if willful, brook was here revealed as an awesome force for change.

"Were you here when this happened?" she asked Lotti Yap.

"We saw only the end of it," she replied. "But it was quite a sight, let me tell you. Seeing the towers fall—"

"We were afraid for our lives," Paramarola said.

"Speak for yourself," Lotti replied. "The waters didn't set us free just to drown us. We were prisoners in the Annex, you see. Then the floor cracked open, and the waters just bubbled up and washed the walls away."

"We knew the Goddesses would come, didn't we?" Paramarola said. "We always had faith in that."

"So you never believed they were dead?"

"Of course not. Buried alive, maybe. Sleeping. Even lunatic. But never dead."

"What she says is right," Lotti observed. "We knew this day would come."

"Unfortunately, it may be a short victory," Jude said.

"Why do you say that?" Lotti replied. "The Autarch's gone."

"Yes, but his Father hasn't."

"His Father?" said Paramarola. "I thought he was a bastard."

"Who's his father then?" said Lotti.

"Hapexamendios."

Paramarola laughed at this, but Lotti Yap nudged in her well-padded ribs.

"It's not a joke, Rola."

"It has to be," the other protested.

"Do you see the woman laughing?" Then, to Jude: "Do you have any evidence for this?"

"No, I don't."

"Then where'd you get such an idea?"

Jude had guessed it would be difficult to persuade people of Sartori's origins, but she'd optimistically supposed that when the moment came she'd be possessed by a sudden lucidity. Instead she felt a rage of frustration. If she was obliged to unravel the whole sorry history of her involvement with the Autarch Sartori to every soul who stood between her and the Goddesses, the worst would be upon them all before she was halfway there. Then, inspiration.

"The Pivot's the proof," she said.

"How so?" said Lotti, who was now studying this woman the flood had brought to their feet with fresh intensity.

"He could never have moved the Pivot without his Father's collaboration."

"But thc Pivot doesn't belong to the Unbeheld," Paramorola said. "It never did."

Jude looked confounded.

"What Rola says is true," Lotti told her. "He may have used it to control a few weak men. But the Pivot was never His."

"Whose then?"

"Uma Umagammagi was in it."

"And who's that?"

"The sister of Tishalullé and Jokalaylau. Half-sister of the daughters of the Delta."

"There was a *Goddess* in the Pivot?"

"Yes."

"And the Autarch didn't know it?"

"That's right. She hid Herself there to escape Hapexamendios when He passed through the Imajica. Jokalaylau went into the snow and was lost there. Tishalullé—"

"—in the Cradle of Chzercemit," Jude said.

"Yes indeed," said Lotti, plainly impressed.

"And Uma Umagammagi hid Herself in solid rock," Paramarola went on, telling the tale as though to a child, "thinking He'd pass over the place not seeing Her. But He chose the Pivot as the center of the Imajica and laid His power upon it, sealing Her in."

This was surely the ultimate irony, Jude thought. The architect of Yzordderrex had built his fortress, indeed his entire empire, around an imprisoned Goddess. Nor was the parallel with Celestine lost on her. It seemed Roxborough had been unwittingly working in a grim tradition when he'd scaled Celestine up beneath his house.

"Where are the Goddesses now?" Jude asked Lotti.

"On the island. We'll all be allowed into their presence in time, and we'll be blessed by them. But it'll take days."

"I don't have days," Jude said. "How do I get to the island?"

"You'll be called when your time comes."

"That has to be now," Jude said, "or it'll be never." She looked left and right along the passageway. "Thank you for the education," she said. "Maybe I'll see you again."

Choosing right over left she made to leave, but Lotti took hold of her sleeve.

"You don't understand, Judith," she said. "The Goddesses have come to make us safe. Nothing can harm us here. Not even the Unbeheld."

"I hope that's true," Jude said. "To the bottom of my heart, I hope that's true. But I have to warn them, in case it isn't."

"Then we'd better come with you," Lotti said. "You'll never find your way otherwise."

"Wait," Paramarola said. "Should we be doing this? She may be dangerous."

"Aren't we all?" Lotti replied. "That's why they locked us away in the first place, remember?"

2

If the atmosphere of the streets outside the palace had suggested some post-apocalyptic carnival—the waters dancing, the children laughing, the air pavonine—then that sense was a hundred times stronger in the passageways around the rim of the flood-scoured basin. There were children here too, their laughter more musical than ever. None was over five or so, but there were both boys and girls in the throng. They turned the corridors into playgrounds, their din echoing off walls that had not heard such joy since they'd been raised. There was also water, of course. Every inch of ground was blessed by a puddle, a rivulet, or a stream, every arch had a liquid curtain cascading from its keystone, every chamber was refreshed by burbling springs and roof-grazing fountains. And in every tinkling trickle there was the same sentience that Jude had felt in the tide that had brought her up here: water as life, filled to the last drop with the purpose of the Goddesses. Overhead, the comet was at its height and sent its straight white beams through any chink it could find, turning the humblest puddle into an oracular pool and plaiting its light into the gush of every spout.

The women in these glittering corridors came in all shapes and sizes. Many, Lotti explained, were like themselves, former prisoners of the Bastion or its dreaded Annex; others had simply found their way up the hill following their instincts and the streams, leaving their husbands, dead or alive, below.

"Are there no men here at all?"

"Only the little ones," said Lotti.

"They're all little ones," Paramarola observed.

"There was a captain at the Annex who was a brute," Lotti said, "and when the waters came he must have been emptying his bladder, because his body floated by our cell with his trousers unbuttoned."

"And you know, he was still holding on to his manhood," Paramarola said. "He had the choice between that and swimming—"

"—and instead of letting go, he drowned," Lotti said.

This entertained Paramarola no end, and she laughed so hard the baby's mouth was dislodged from her teat. Milk spurted in the child's face, which brought a further round of merriment. Jude didn't ask how Paramarola came to be so nourishing when she was neither the mother of the child nor, presumably, pregnant. It was just one of the many enigmas this journey showed her: like the pool that clung to one of the walls, filled to brimming with luminous fish; or the waters that imitated fire, from which some of the women had made crowns; or the immensely long eel she saw carried past, its gaping head on a child's shoulder, its body looped between half a dozen women, back and forth across their shoulders ten times or more. If she'd requested an explanation for any one of these sights she'd have been obliged to inquire about them all, and they'd never have got more than a few yards down the corridor.

The journey brought them, at last, to a place where the waters had carved out a shallow pool at the edge of the main basin, served by several rivulets that climbed through rubble to fill it to brimming, its overflow running into the basin itself. In it and around it were perhaps thirty women and children, some playing, some talking, but most, their clothes shed, waiting silently in the pool, gazing out across the turbulent waters of the basin to Uma Umagammagi's island. Even as Jude and her guides approached the place, a wave broke against the lip of the pool and two women, standing there hand in hand, went with it as it withdrew and were carried away towards the island. There was an eroticism about the scene which in other circumstances Jude would certainly have denied she felt. But here, such priggishness seemed redundant, even ludicrous. She allowed her imagination to wonder what it would be like to sink into the midst of this nakedness, where the only scrap of masculinity was between the legs of a suckling infant; to brush breast to breast, and let her fingers be kissed and her neck be caressed, and kiss and caress in her turn.

"The water in the basin's very deep," Lotti said at her side. "It goes all the way down into the mountain."

What had happened to the dead, Jude wondered, whose company Dowd had found so educative? Had the waters sluiced them away, along with the invocations and entreaties that had dropped into that same darkness from beneath the Pivot Tower? Or had they been dissolved into a single soup, the sex of dead men forgiven, the pain of dead women healed, and—all mingled with the prayers—become part of this indefatigable flood? She hoped so. If the powers here were to have authority against the Unbeheld, they would have to reclaim every forsaken strength they could. The walls between Kesparates had already been dragged down, and the plashing streams were making a continuum of city and palace. But the past had to be reclaimed as well, and whatever miracles it had boasted—surely there'd been some, even here—preserved. This was more than an abstract desire on Jude's part. She was, after all, one of those miracles, made in the image of the woman who'd ruled here with as much ferocity as her husband.

"Is this the only way of getting to the island?" she asked Lotti.

"There aren't ferries, if that's what you mean."

"I'd better start swimming, then," Jude said.

Her clothes were an encumbrance, but she wasn't yet so easy with herself that she could strip off on the rocks and go into the waters naked, so with a brief thanks to Lotti and Paramarola she started to climb down the tumble of blocks that surrounded the pool.

"I hope you're wrong, Judith," Lotti called after her.

"So do I," Jude replied. "Believe me, so do I."

Both this exchange and her ungainly descent drew the puzzled gaze of several of the bathers, but none made any objection to her appearing in their midst. The closer she got to the waters of the basin, the more anxious she became about the crossing, however. It was several years since she'd swum any distance, and she doubted she'd have the strength to resist the currents and eddies if they chose to keep her from her destination. But they wouldn't drown her, surely. They'd borne her all the way up here, after all, sweeping her through the palace unharmed. The only difference between this journey and that (though it was a profound one, to be sure) was the depth of the water.

Another wave was approaching the lip of the pool, and there was a woman and child floating forward to take it. Before they could do so, she took a running jump off the boulder she was perched on, clearing the heads of the bathers below by a hair's breadth and plunging into the tide. It wasn't so much a dive as a plummet, and it took her deep. She flailed wildly to right herself, opening her eyes but unable to decide which way was up. The waters knew. They lifted her out of their depths like a cork and threw her up into the spume. She was already twenty yards or more from the rocks and being carried away at speed. She had time to glimpse Lotti searching for her in the surf, then the eddies turned her around, and around again, until she no longer knew the direction in which the pool lay. Instead, she fixed her eyes on the island and began to swim as best she could towards it. The waters seemed content to supplement her efforts with energies of their own, though they were describing a spiral around the island, and as they carried her closer to its shore they also swept her in a counterclockwise motion around it.

The comet's light fell on the waves all around her, and its glitter kept the depths from sight, which she was glad of. Buoyed up though she was, she didn't want to be reminded of the pit beneath her. She put all her will into the business of swimming, not even allowing herself to enjoy the roiling of the waters against her body.

Such luxury, like the questions she'd wanted to ask as she'd walked with Lotti and Paramarola, was for another day.

The shore was within fifty yards of her now, but her strokes became increasingly irrelevant the closer to the island she came. As the spiral tightened, the tide became more authoritative, and she finally gave up any attempt at self-propulsion and surrendered herself utterly to the hold of the waters. They carried her around the island twice before she felt her feet scraping the steeply inclined rocks beneath the surge, presenting her with a fine, if giddying, view of Uma Umagammagi's temple. Not surprisingly, the waters had been more inspired here than in any other spot she'd seen. They'd worked at the blocks of which the tower was built, monumental though they were, eroding the mortar between them, then eating at them top and bottom, replacing their severity with a mathematics of undulation. Slabs of stone the height of the masons who'd first carved them were no longer locked together but balanced like acrobats, one corner laid against another, while radiant water ran through the cavities and carried on its work of turning the once-impregnable tower into a wedded column of water, stone, and light. The eroded motes had run off in the rivulets and been deposited on the shore as a fine, soft sand, in which Jude lay when she emerged from the basin, given a giggling welcome by a quartet of children playing nearby.

She allowed herself only a minute to catch her breath; then she got to her feet and started up the beach towards the temple. Its doorway was as elaborately eroded as the blocks, a veil of bright water concealing the interior from those waiting nearby. There were perhaps a dozen women at the threshold. One, a girl barely past pubescence, was walking on her hands; somebody else seemed to be singing, but the music was so close to the sound of running water that Jude couldn't decide whether a voice was flowing or some stream was aspiring to melody. As at the pool, nobody objected to her sudden appearance, nor remarked on the fact that she was weighed down by waterlogged clothes while they were in various states of undress. A benign languor was on them all, and had it not been for Jude's willpower she might have let it claim her, too. She didn't hesitate, however, but stepped through the water door without so much as a murmur to those waiting at the threshold.

Inside, there was no solid sight to greet her. Instead, the air was filled with forms of light, folding and unfolding as though invisible hands were performing a lucid origami. They weren't working towards petty resemblance, but transforming their radiant stuff over and over, each new shape on its way to becoming another before it was fixed. She looked down at her arms. They were still visible, but not as flesh and blood. They'd learned the trick of the light

already and were blossoming into a multiplicity of forms in order
to join the play. She reached out to touch one of her fellow visitors with her burgeoning fingers and, brushing her, caught a
glimpse of the woman from whom this origami had emerged. She
appeared the way a body might if a damp sheet billowed against
it, momentarily clinging to the shape of her hip, her cheek, her
breast, then billowing again and snatching the glimpse away. But
there'd been a smile there, she was certain of that.

Reassured that she was neither alone nor unwelcome here, she
began to advance into the temple. The promise of eroticism she'd
first felt as she gazed into the pool was now realized. She felt the
forms of her own body spreading like milk dropped into the fluid
air and grazing the bodies of those she was passing between. Musings, most no more than half formed, mingled with the sensation.
Perhaps she would dissolve here and flow out through the walls to
join the waters around the islands; or perhaps she was already in
that sea, and the flesh and blood she thought she'd owned was just
a figment of those waters, conjured to comfort the lonely land. Or
perhaps ... or perhaps ... or perhaps. These speculations were not
divorced from the brushing of form against form but were part of
the pleasure, her nerves bearing these fruits, which in turn made
her more tender to the touches of her companions.

They were falling away as she advanced, she realized. Her
progress was taking her up into the heights of the temple. If there
had been solid ground beneath her feet, she'd lost all sense of it as
she crossed the threshold and rose without effort, her stuff possessed of the same law-defying genius as had been the waters
below. There was another motion ahead and above her, more sinuous than the forms she'd met at the door, and she rose towards it
as if summoned, praying that when the moment came she'd have
the words and lips to shape the thoughts in her head. The motion
was getting clearer and if she'd had any doubt below as to whether
these sights were imagined or seen, she now had such dichotomies
swept away.

She was both seeing with her imagination and imagining she saw
the glyph that hung in the air in front of her: a Möbius strip of light-
haunted water, a steady rhythm passing through its seamless loop
and throwing off waves of brilliant color, which shed bright rains
around her. Here was the raiser of springs; here was the summoner
of rivers; here was the sublime presence whose strength had
brought the palace to rubble and made a home for oceans and children where there'd only been terror before. Here was Uma
Umagammagi.

Though she studied the Goddess's glyph, Jude could see no hint
of anything that breathed, sweated, or corrupted in it. But there

was such an emanation of tenderness from the form that, faceless
as the Goddess was, it seemed to Jude she could feel Her smile, Her
kiss, Her loving gaze. And love it was. Though this power knew her
not at all, Jude felt embraced and comforted as only love could embrace and comfort. There'd never been a time in her life, until now,
when some part of her had not been afraid. It was the condition
of being alive that even bliss was attended by the imminence of its
decease. But here such terrors seemed absurd. This face loved her
unconditionally and would do so forever.

"Sweet Judith," she heard the Goddess say, the voice so charged,
so resonant, that these few syllables were an aria. "Sweet Judith,
what's so urgent that you risk your life to come here?"

As Uma Umagammagi spoke, Jude saw her own face appear-
ing in the ripples, brightening, then teased out into a thread of light
that was run into the Goddess's glyph. She's reading me, Jude
thought. She's trying to understand why I'm here, and when She
does She'll take the responsibility away. I'll be able to stay in this
glorious place with Her, always.

"So," said the Goddess after a time. "This is a grim business. It
falls to you to choose between stopping this Reconciliation or letting it go on and risking some harm from Hapexamendios."

"Yes," Jude replied, grateful that she'd been relieved of the need
to explain herself. "I don't know what the Unbeheld is planning.
Maybe nothing . . ."

". . . and maybe the end of the Imajica."

"Could He do that?"

"Very possibly," said Uma Umagammagi. "He's done harm to
Our temples and Our sisters many, many times, both in His own
person and through His agents. He's a soul in error, and lethal."

"But would He destroy a whole Dominion?"

"I can no more predict Him than you can," Umagammagi said.
"But I'll mourn if the chance to complete the circle is missed."

"The circle?" said Jude. "What circle?"

"The circle of the Imajica," the Goddess replied. "Please understand, sister, the Dominions were never meant to be divided this
way. That was the work of the first human spirits, when they came
into their terrestrial life. Nor was there any harm in it, at the beginning. It was their way of learning to live in a condition that intimidated them. When they looked up, they saw stars. When they
looked down, they saw Earth. They couldn't make their mark on
what was above, but what was below could be divided and owned
and fought over. From that division, all others sprang. They lost
themselves to territories and nations, all shaped by the other sex,
of course; all named by them. They even buried themselves in the
Earth to have it more utterly, preferring worms to the company of

light. They were blinded to the Imajica, and the circle was broken, and Hapexamendios, who was made by the will of these men, grew strong enough to forsake His makers and so passed from the Fifth Dominion into the First—"

"—murdering Goddesses as He went."

"He did harm, yes, but He could have done greater harm still if He'd known the shape of the Imajica. He could have discovered what mystery it circled and gone there instead."

"What mystery's that?"

"You're going back into a dangerous place, sweet Judith, and the less you know the safer you'll be. When the time comes, we will unravel these mysteries together, as sisters. Until then take comfort that the error of the Son is also the error of the Father, and in time all errors must undo themselves and pass away."

"So if they'll solve themselves," Jude said, "why do I have to go back to the Fifth?"

Before Uma Umagammagi could resume speaking, another voice intruded. Particles rose between Jude and the Goddess as this other woman spoke, pricking Jude's flesh where they touched, reminding her of a state that knew ice and fire.

"Why do you trust this woman?" the stranger said.

"Because she came to us openhearted, Jokalaylau," the Goddess replied.

"How openhearted is a woman who treads dry-eyed in the place where her sister died?" Jokalaylau said. "How openhearted is a woman who comes into Our presence without shame, when she has the Autarch Sartori's child in her womb?"

"We have no place for shame here," Umagammagi said.

"*You* may have no place," Jokalaylau said, rising into view now. "I have plenty."

Like her sister, Jokalaylau was here in Her essential form: a more complex shape than that of Uma Umagammagi, and less pleasing to the eye, because the motions that ran in it were more hectic, Her form not so much rippling as boiling, shedding its pricking darts as it did so.

"Shame is wholly appropriate for a woman who has lain with one of Our enemies," she said.

Despite the intimidation Jude felt from the Goddess, she spoke out in her own defense.

"It's not as simple as that," she said, her courage fueled by the frustration she felt, having this intruder spoil the congress between herself and Uma Umagammagi. "I didn't know he was the Autarch."

"Who did you imagine he was? Or didn't you care?"

The exchange might have escalated, but that Uma Umagammagi spoke again, her tone as serene as ever.

"Sweet Judith," she said, "let me speak with my sister. She's suffered at the hands of the Unbeheld more than either Tishalullé or
myself, and She'll not readily forgive any flesh touched by Him or
His children. Please understand Her pain, as I hope to make Her
understand yours."

She spoke with such delicacy that Jude now felt the shame
Jokalaylau had accused her of lacking: not for the child, but for her
rage.

"I'm sorry," she said. "That was . . . inappropriate."

"If you'll wait on the shore," said Uma Umagammagi, "we'll
speak together again in a little while."

From the moment that the Goddess had talked of Jude's returning to the Fifth, she'd known this parting would come. But she
hadn't prepared herself to leave the Goddess's embrace so soon,
and now that she felt gravity claiming her again, it was an agony.
There was no help for it, however. If Uma Umagammagi knew
what she suffered—and how could She not?—She did nothing to
ameliorate the hurt, but folded Her glyph back into the matrix,
leaving Jude to fall like a petal from a blossom tree, lightly enough,
but with a sense of separation worse than any bruising. The forms
of the women she'd passed through were still unfolding and folding below, as exquisite as ever, and the water music at the door was
as soothing, but they could not salve the loss. The melody that had
sounded so joyous when she'd entered was now elegaic, like a
hymn for harvest home, thankful for the gifts bestowed but
touched by fears for a colder season to come.

It was waiting on the other side of the curtain, that season.
Though the children still laughed on the shore, and the basin was
still a glorious spectacle of light and motion, she had gone from the
presence of a loving spirit and couldn't help but mourn. Her tears
astonished the women at the threshold, and several rose to con-
sole her, but she shook her head as they approached, and they quietly parted to let her go her way alone, down to the water. There
she sat, not daring to glance back at the temple where her fate was
being decided, but gazing out over the basin.

What now? she wondered. If she was called back into the presence of the Goddesses to be told she wasn't fit to make any decision concerning the Reconciliation, she'd be quite happy with the
judgment. She'd leave the problem in surer hands than hers and
return to the corridors around the basin, where she might after a
time reinvent herself and come back into this temple as a novice,
ready to learn the way to fold light. If, on the other hand, she was
simply shunned, as Jokalaylau clearly wanted, if she was driven

from this miraculous place back into the wilderness outside, what would she do? Without anyone to guide her, what knowledge did she possess to help choose between the ways ahead? None. Her tears dried after a time, but what came in their place was worse: a sense of desolation that could only be Hell itself, or some neighboring province, divided from the main by infernal jailers, made to punish women who had loved immoderately and who had lost perfection, for want of a little shame.

20

I

In his last letter to his son, written the night before he boarded a ship bound for France—his mission to spread the gospel of the Tabula Rasa across Europe—Roxborough, the scourge of Maestros, had set down the substance of a nightmare from which he'd just woken.

> *I dreamed that I drove in my coach through the damnable streets of Clerkenwell, he wrote, I need not name my destination. You know it, and you know too what infamies were planned there. As is the way in dreams, I was bereft of self-government, for though I called out many times to the driver, begging him, for my soul's sake, not to take me back to that house, my words had no power to persuade him. As the coach turned the corner, however, and the Maestro Sartori's house came in sight, Bellamare reared up affrighted and would go no further. She was ever my favorite bay, and I felt such a flood of gratitude towards her for refusing to carry me to that unholy step that I climbed from the coach to speak my thanks into her ear.*
>
> *And lo! as my foot touched the ground the cobbles spoke up like living things, their voices stony but raised in a hideous lamentation, and at the sound of their anguish the very bricks of the houses in that street, and the roofs and railings and chimneys, all made similar cry, their voices joined in sorrowful testament to Heaven. I never heard a din its like, but I could not stop my ears against it, for was their pain not in some part of my making? And I heard them say:*
>
> *Lord, we are but unbaptized things and have no hopes to come into your Kingdom, but we beseech you to bring some storm down upon us and grind us into dust with your*

*righteous thunder, that we may be scoured and destroyed
and not suffer complicity with the deeds performed in our
sight.*

*My son, I marveled at their clamor, and wept too, and was
ashamed, hearing them make this appeal to the Almighty,
knowing that I was a thousand times more accountable than
they. O! how I wished my feet might carry me away to some
less odious place! I swear at that moment I would have
judged the heart of a fiery furnace an agreeable place, and
lain my head there with hosannahs, rather than be where
these deeds had been done. But I could not retreat. On the
contrary, my mutinous limbs carried me to the very doorstep
of that house. There was foamy blood upon the threshold, as
though the martyrs had that night marked the place so that
the Angel of Destruction might find it, and cause the earth to
gape 'neath it, and commit it to the Abyss. And from within
was a sound of idle chatter as the men I had known debated
their profane philosophies.*

*I went down on my knees in the blood, calling to those
within to come out and join me in begging forgiveness of the
Almighty, but they scorned me with much laughter, and
called me coward and fool, and told me to go on my way.
This I presently did, with much haste, and did escape the
street with the cobbles telling me I should go about my cru
sade without fear of God's retribution, for I had turned my
back on the sin of that house.*

*That was my dream. I am setting it down straightway, and
will have this letter sent post haste, that you may be warned
what harm there is in that place and not be tempted to enter
Clerkenwell or even stray south of Islington while I am gone
from you. For my dream instructs me that the street will be
forfeit, in due course, for the crimes it has entertained, and I
would not wish one hair of your sweet head harmed for the
deeds I in my delirium committed against the edicts of Our
Lord. Though the Almighty did offer His only begotten Son
to suffer and die for our sins, I know that He would not ask
that same sacrifice of me, knowing that I am His humblest
servant, and pray only to be made His instrument until I quit
this vale and go to Judgment.*

*May the Lord God keep you in His care until I embrace
you again.*

The ship Roxborough boarded a few hours after finishing this
letter went down a mile out of Dover harbor, in a squall that
troubled no other vessel in the vicinity but overturned the purger's

ship and sank it in less than a minute. All hands were lost.

The day after the letter arrived, the recipient, still tearful with the news, went to seek solace at the stables of his father's bay, Bellamare. The horse had been jittery since her master's departure and, though she knew Roxborough's son well, kicked out at his approach, striking him in the abdomen. The blow was not instantly fatal, but with stomach and spleen split wide, the youth was dead in six days. Thus he preceded his father, whose body was not washed up for another week, to the family grave.

2

Pie 'oh' pah had recounted this sorry story to Gentle as they'd traveled from L'Himby to the Cradle of Chzercemit in search of Scopique. It was one of many tales the mystif had told on that journey, offering them not as biographical details, though of course many of them were precisely that, but as entertainment, comedic, absurd, or melancholy, that usually opened with: "I heard about this fellow once . . ."

Sometimes the stories were told within a few minutes, but Pie had lingered over this one, repeating word for word the text of Roxborough's letter, though to this day Gentle didn't know how the mystif had come by it. He understood why it had committed the prophecy to memory, however, and why it had taken such trouble to repeat it for Gentle. It had half believed there was some significance in Roxborough's dream, and just as it had educated Gentle on other matters pertaining to his concealed self, so it had told this tale to warn the Maestro of dangers the future might bring.

That future was now. As the hours since Monday's return crept on, and Jude still didn't return, Gentle was reduced to picking his recollections of Roxborough's letter apart, looking for some clue in the purger's words as to what threat might be coming to the doorstep. He even wondered if the man who'd written the letter was numbered among the revenants who by midmorning could be glimpsed in the heat haze. Had Roxborough come back to watch the demise of the street he'd called damnable? If he had—if he listened at the step the way he had in his dream—he was most likely as frustrated as the occupants, wishing they'd get on with the work he hoped would invite calamity.

But however many doubts Gentle harbored concerning Jude, he could not believe she would conspire against the Great Work. If she said it was unsafe she had good reason for so saying, and, though every sinew in Gentle's body raged at inactivity, he refused to go downstairs and bring the stones up into the Meditation Room, for fear their very presence might tempt him into warming the circle. Instead he waited, and waited, and waited, while the heat outside rose and the air in the Meditation Room grew sour with his frustration. As Scopique had said, a working like this required months of preparation, not hours, and now even those hours were being steadily whittled away. How late could he afford to postpone the ceremony before he gave up on Jude and began? Until six? Until nightfall? It was an imponderable.

There were signs of unease outside the house as well as in. Scarcely a minute went by without a new siren being added to the chorus of whoops and wails from every compass point. Several times through the morning, bells began chiming from steeples in the vicinity, their peals neither summons nor celebration but alarm. There were even cries occasionally: shouts and screams from distant streets carried to the open windows on air now hot enough to make the dead sweat.

And then, just after one in the afternoon, Clem came up the stairs, his eyes wide. It was Taylor who spoke, and there was excitement in his voice.

"Somebody's come into the house, Gentle."

"Who?"

"A spirit of some kind, from the Dominions. She's downstairs."

"Is it Jude?"

"No. This is a real power. Can't you smell her? I know you've given up women, but your nose still works, doesn't it?"

He led Gentle out onto the landing. The house lay quiet below. Gentle sensed nothing.

"Where is she?"

Clem looked puzzled. "She was here a moment ago, I swear."

Gentle went to the top of the stairs, but Clem held him back.

"Angels first," he said, but Gentle was already beginning his descent, relieved that the torpor of the last few hours was over and eager to meet this visitor. Perhaps she carried a message from Jude.

The front door stood open. There was a pool of beer glinting on the step, but no sign of Monday.

"Where's the boy?" Gentle asked.

"He's outside, sky watching. He says he saw a flying saucer."

Gentle threw his companion a quizzical look. Clem didn't reply but laid his hand on Gentle's shoulder, his eyes going to the door of the dining room. From inside came the barely audible sound of sobbing.

"Mama," Gentle said, and gave up any caution, hurrying down the rest of the flight with Clem in pursuit.

By the time he reached Celestine's room, the sound of her sobs had already disappeared. Gentle drew a defensive breath, took hold of the handle, and put his shoulder to the door. It wasn't locked but swung open smoothly, delivering him inside. The room was ill-lit, the drooping, mildewed curtains still heavy enough to keep the sun to a few dusty beams. They fell on the empty mattress in the middle of the floor. Its sometime occupant, whom Gentle had not expected to see standing again, was at the other end of the room, her tears subsided to whimpers. She had brought one of the sheets from her bed with her and, seeing her son enter, drew it up to her breastbone. Then she turned her attention back towards the wall she was standing close to and studied it. A pipe had burst somewhere behind the brick, Gentle supposed. He could hear water running freely.

"It's all right, Mama," he said. "Nothing's going to hurt you."

Celestine didn't reply. She'd raised her left hand in front of her face and was looking at the palm, as if into a mirror.

"It's still here," Clem said.

"Where?" Gentle asked him.

He nodded in the direction of Celestine, and Gentle instantly left his side, opening his arms as he went to offer the haunted air a fresh target.

"Come on," he said. "Wherever you are. Come on."

Halfway between the door and his mother he felt a cool drizzle strike his face, so fine it was invisible. Its touch was not unpleasant. In fact it was refreshing, and he let out an appreciative gasp.

"It's raining in here," he said.

"It's the Goddess," Celestine replied.

She looked up from studying her hand, which Gentle now saw was running with water, as though a spring had appeared in her palm.

"What Goddess?" Gentle asked her.

"Uma Umagammagi," his mother replied.

"Why were you crying, Mama?"

"I thought I was dying. I thought She'd come to take me."

"But She hasn't."

"I'm still here, child."

"Then what does She want?"

Celestine extended her arm to Gentle. "She wants us to make peace," she said. "Join me in the waters, child."

Gentle took hold of his mother's hand, and she drew him towards her, turning her face up to the rain as she did so. The last traces of her tears were being washed away, and a look of ecstasy appeared where there had been grief. Gentle felt it too. His eyes wanted to flicker closed; his body wanted to swoon. But he resisted the rain's blandishments, tempting as they were. If it carried some message for him, he needed to know it quickly and end these delays before they cost the Reconciliation dearly.

"Tell me," he said, as he came to his mother's side, "whether you're here to stay; tell me. . . ."

But the rain made no reply, at least none that he could grasp. Perhaps his mother heard more than he did, however, because there were smiles on her glistening face, and her grip on Gentle's hand became more possessive. She let the sheet she'd held to her bosom drop, so that the rains could stroke her breasts and belly, and Gentle's gaze took full account of her nakedness. The wounds she'd sustained in her struggles with Dowd and Sartori still marked her body, but they only served to prove her perfection, and although he knew the felony here, he couldn't stem his feelings.

She put her free hand up to her face and with thumb and forefingers emptied the shallow pools of her sockets, then once again opened her eyes. They found Gentle too quickly for him to conceal himself, and he felt a shock as their looks met, not just because she read his desire, but because he found the same in her face.

He wrested his hand from hers and backed away, his tongue fumbling with denials. She was far less abashed than he. Her eyes remained fixed on him, and she called him back into the rain with words of invitation so soft they were barely more than sighs. When he continued to retreat, she turned to more specific exhortations.

"The Goddess wants to know you," she said. "She needs to understand your purpose."

"My . . . Father's . . . business," Gentle replied, the words as much defense as explanation, shielding him from this seduction with the weight of his purpose.

But the Goddess, if that was what this rain really was, wouldn't be shaken off so easily. He saw a look of distress cross his mother's face as the vapors deserted her to move in pursuit of him. They passed through a spear of sun as they came, and threw out rainbows.

"Don't be afraid of Her," Gentle heard Clem say behind him. "You've got nothing to hide."

Perhaps this was true, but he kept on retreating nevertheless, as much from his mother as from the vapor, until he felt the comfort of his angels at his back.

"Guard me," he told them, his voice tremulous.

Clem wrapped his arms around Gentle's shoulders. "It's a woman, Maestro," he murmured. "Since when were you afraid of women?"

"Since always," Gentle replied. "Hold on, for Christ's sake."

Then the rain broke against their faces, and Clem let out a sigh of pleasure as its languor enclosed them. Gentle seized hard hold of his protector's arms, his fingers digging deep, but if the rain had the sinew to detach him from Clem's embrace it didn't attempt to do so. It lingered around their heads for no more than thirty seconds, then simply passed away through the open door.

As soon as it had gone, Gentle turned to Clem. "Nothing to hide, eh?" he said. "I don't think She believed you."

"Are you hurt?"

"No. She just got inside my head. Why does every damn thing want to get inside my head?"

"It must be the view," Tay remarked, grinning with his lover's lips.

"She only wanted to know if your purpose was pure, child," Celestine said.

"Pure?" Gentle said, staring at his mother venomously. "What right has She got to judge me?"

"What you call your Father's business is the business of every soul in the Imajica."

She had not yet claimed her modesty from the floor, and as she approached him he averted his eyes.

"Cover yourself, Mother," he said. "For God's sake, cover yourself."

Then he turned and headed out into the hallway, calling after the intruder as he went.

"Wherever you are," he yelled, "I want you out of this house! Clem, look downstairs. I'll go up."

He pelted up the flight, his fury mounting at the thought of this spirit invading the Meditation Room. The door stood open. Little Ease was cowering in the corner when he entered.

"Where is She?" Gentle demanded. "Is She here?"

"Is *who* here?"

Gentle didn't reply but went from wall to wall like a prisoner, beating his palms against them. There was no sound of running water from the brick, however, nor any drizzle, however fine, in the air. Content that the room was free of the visitor's taint, he returned to the door.

"If it starts raining in here," he said to Little Ease, "yell blue murder."

"Any color you like, Liberatore."

Gentle slammed the door and headed along the landing, searching all the rooms in the same manner. Finding them empty he climbed the last flight and went through the rooms above. Their air was bone-dry. But as he started back down the stairs he heard laughter from the street. It was Monday, though the sound he was making was lighter than Gentle had ever heard from his lips before. Suspicious of this music, he picked up the speed of his descent, meeting Clem at the bottom of the stairs and telling him the rooms were empty below, then racing across the hallway to the front door.

Monday had been busy with his chalks since Gentle had last crossed the threshold. The pavement at the bottom of the steps was covered with his designs: not copies of glamour girls this time but elaborate abstractions that spilled over the curb and onto the sun-softened tarmac. The artist had left off his work, however, and was now standing in the middle of the street. Gentle recognized the language of his body instantly. Head thrown back, eyes closed, he was bathing in the air.

"Monday!"

But the boy didn't hear. He continued to luxuriate in this unction, the water running over his close-cropped skull like rippling fingers, and he might have gone on bathing until he drowned in it had Gentle's approach not driven the Goddess off. The rain went from the air in a heartbeat, and Monday's eyes opened. He squinted against the sky, his laughter faltering.

"Where'd the rain go?" he said.

"There was no rain."

"What do you call this, boss?" Monday said, proffering arms from which the last of the waters still ran.

"Take it from me, it wasn't rain."

"Whatever it was, it was fine by me," Monday said. He hauled his sodden T-shirt up over his head and used it as a mop to wipe his face. "Are you all right, boss?"

Gentle was scanning the street, looking for some sign of the Goddess.

"I will be," he said. "You go back to work, huh? You haven't decorated the door yet."

"What do you want on it?"

"You're the artist," Gentle said, distracted from the conversation by the state of the street.

He hadn't realized until now how full of presences it had become, the revenants not simply occupying the pavement but hovering in the wilted foliage like hanged men or keeping their vigils on the eaves. They were benign enough, he thought. They had good reason to wish him well in this endeavor. Half a year ago, on the night he and Pie had left on their travels, the mystif had given Gentle a grim lesson in the pain that the spirits of this and every other Dominion suffered.

"No spirit is happy," Pie had said. "They haunt the doors, waiting to leave, but there's nowhere for them to go."

But hadn't there been some hope mooted then, that at the end of the journey ahead lay a solution to the anguish of the dead? Pie had known that solution even then, and must have longed to call Gentle Reconciler, to tell him that the wit lay somewhere in his head to open the doors at which the dead stood waiting and let them into Heaven.

"Be patient," he murmured, knowing the revenants heard. "It'll be soon, I swear. It'll be soon."

The sun was drying the Goddess's rain from his face, and, happy to stay out in the heat until he was dry, he wandered away from the house, while Monday resumed his whistling on the step. What a place this had become, Gentle thought: angels in the house behind him, lascivious rains in the street, ghosts in the trees. And he, the Maestro, wandering among them, ready to do the deed that would change their worlds forever. There would never be such a day again.

His optimistic mood darkened, however, as he approached the end of the street, for other than the sound of his footsteps, and the shrill noise of Monday's whistle, the world was absolutely quiet. The alarms that had raised such a din earlier in the day were now hushed. No bell rang, no voice cried out. It was as if all life beyond this thoroughfare had taken a vow of silence. He picked up his pace. Either his agitation was contagious or else the revenants that lingered at the end of the street were more jittery than those closer to the house. They milled around, their numbers, and perhaps their unease, sufficient to disturb the baked dust in the gutter. They made no attempt to impede his progress but parted like a cold curtain, allowing him to step over the invisible boundary of Gamut Street. He looked in both directions. The dogs that had gathered here for a time had gone; the birds had fled every eave and telephone wire. He held his breath and listened through the whine in his head for some evidence of life: an engine, a siren, a shout. But there was nothing. His unease now profound, he glanced back into Gamut Street. Loath though he was to leave it, he supposed it would be safe while the revenants remained at the perimeter. Though they were too insubstantial to protect the street from attackers, it was doubtful that anyone would dare enter while they milled and churned at the corner. Taking that small comfort, he headed towards Gray's Inn Road, his walk becoming a run as he went. The heat was less welcome now. It made his legs heavy and his lungs burn. But he didn't slacken his pace until he reached the intersection.

Gray's Inn Road and High Holborn were two of the city's major conduits. Had he stood at this corner on the coldest December midnight, there would have been some traffic upon one or the other. But there was nothing now; nor was there a murmur from any street, square, alleyway, or circus within earshot. The sphere of

influence that had left Gamut Street untrammeled for two centuries had apparently spread, and if the citizens of London were
still in residence they were keeping clear of this harrowed terrain.

And yet, despite the silence, the air was not unfreighted. There
was something else upon it, which kept Gentle from turning on his
heel and wandering back to Gamut Street: a smell so subtle that
the tang of cooking asphalt almost overwhelmed it, but so unmistakable he could not ignore even the traces that came his way. He
lingered at the corner, waiting for another gust of wind. It came
after a time, confirming his suspicions. There was only one source
for this sickly perfume, and only one man in this city—no, in this
Dominion—who had access to that source. The In Ovo had been
opened again, and this time the beasts that had been called forth
were not the nonsense stuff he'd encountered at the tower. These
were of another magnitude entirely. He'd seen and smelled their
like only once, two hundred years before, and they'd done incalculable mischief. Given that the breeze was so languid, their scent
could not be coming all the way from Highgate. Sartori and his legion were considerably closer than that: perhaps ten streets away,
perhaps two, perhaps about to turn the corner of Gray's Inn Road
and come in sight.

There was no time left for prevarication. Whatever danger Jude
had discovered, or believed she'd discovered, it was notional. This
scent, on the other hand, and the entities that oozed it, were not.
He could not afford to delay his final preparations any longer. He
forsook his watching place and started back toward the house as
though these hordes were already on his heels. The revenants scattered as he rounded the corner and raced down the street. Monday was working on the door, but he dropped his colors as he
heard the Maestro's summons.

"It's time, boy!" Gentle yelled, mounting the steps in a single
bound. "Start bringing the stones upstairs."

"We're starting?"

"We're starting."

Monday grinned, whooped, and ducked into the house, leaving
Gentle to pause and admire what now adorned the door. It was
just a sketch as yet, but the boy's draftsmanship was sufficient for
his purpose. He'd drawn an enormous eye, with beams of light emanating from it in all directions. Gentle stepped into the house,
pleased at the thought that this burning gaze would greet anyone,
friend or foe, who came to the threshold. Then he closed the door
and bolted it. When I next step out, he thought, the work of my Father will be done.

21

WHATEVER DEBATES AND QUARRELS went on in Uma Umagam-magi's temple while Jude waited on the shore, they brought the procession of postulants to a halt. The tide carried no more women or children to the shore, and after a time the waters became sub-dued and finally becalmed, as if their inspiring forces were so pre-occupied that all other matters had become inconsequential. Without a watch Jude could only guess at how long a time passed while she waited, but occasional glances up at the comet showed her that it was to be measured in hours rather than minutes. Did the Goddesses fully comprehend how urgent a business this was, she wondered, or had the ages they'd spent in captivity and exile so slowed their sensibilities that their debate might last days and they not realize how much time had passed?

She blamed herself for not making the urgency of this more plain to them. The day would be creeping on in the Fifth, and even if Gentle had been persuaded to postpone his preparations for a time, he would not do so indefinitely. Nor could she blame him. All he had was a message—brought by a less than reliable courier—that things were not safe. That wouldn't be enough to make him put the Reconciliation in jeopardy. He hadn't seen the horrors she'd seen in the Boston Bowl, so he had no real comprehension of what was at stake here. He was, in her own words, about his Fa-ther's business, and the possibility that such business might mark the end of the Imajica was surely very far from his mind.

She was twice distracted from these melancholy thoughts: the first time when a young girl came down to the shore to offer her something to eat and drink, which she gratefully accepted; the sec-ond when nature called and she was obliged to scout around the island for a sheltered place to squat and empty her bladder. To be shy about passing water in this place was of course absurd and she knew it, but she was still a woman of the Fifth, however many mir-acles she'd seen. Maybe she'd learn to become blithe about such functions eventually, but it would take time.

As she returned from the place she'd found among the rocks, lighter by a bladderful, the song at the temple door, which had dropped away to a murmur and disappeared a long time before, began again. Instead of going back to her place of vigil, she headed around the temple to the door, her stride lent spring by the sight of the waters in the basin, which were stirring from their inertia and once again breaking against the shore. It seemed the God-desses had made their decision. She wanted to hear the news as soon as possible, of course, but she couldn't help but feel a little like an accused woman returning into a courtroom.

There was an air of expectancy among those at the door. Some of the women were smiling; others looked grim. If they had any knowledge of the judgment, they were interpreting it in radically different ways.

"Should I go in?" Jude asked the woman who'd brought her food.

The other nodded vigorously, though Jude suspected she simply wanted to expedite a process which had delayed them all. Jude stepped back through the water curtain and into the temple. It had changed. Though the sense that her inner and outer sights were here united was as strong as ever, what they perceived was far less reassuring than it had been. There was no sign of the origami light, nor of the bodies these forms had been derived from. She was, it seemed, the sole representative of the fleshly here, and scrutinized by an incandescence far less tender than Uma Umagammagi's gaze had been. She squinted against it, but her lids and lashes could do little to mellow a light that burned in her head rather than her corneas. Its blaze intimidated her, and she wanted to retreat before it, but the thought that Uma Umagammagi's consolation lay somewhere in its midst kept her from doing so.

"Goddess?" she ventured.

"We're here together," came the reply. "Jokalaylau, Tishalullé, and Myself."

As the roll was called, Jude began to distinguish shapes within the brilliance. They were not the inexhaustible glyphs she'd last seen in this place. What she saw suggested not abstractions but sinuous human forms, hovering in the air above her. This was a strange turnabout, she thought. Why, when she'd previously been able to share the essential natures of Jokalaylau and Uma Umagammagi, was she now being presented with lowlier faces? It didn't augur well for the exchange ahead. Had They clothed Themselves in trivial matter because They'd decided she wasn't worthy to lay eyes on the truth of Them? She concentrated hard to grasp the details of Their appearance, but either her sight wasn't sophisticated enough or They were resisting her. Whichever, she could hold only impressions in her head: that They were naked, that Their eyes were incandescent, that Their bodies ran with water.

"Do you see Us?" Jude heard a voice she didn't recognize— Tishalullé's, she presumed—ask.

"Yes, of course," she said. "But not . . . not completely."

"Didn't I tell You?" Uma Umagammagi said.

"Tell me what?" Jude wanted to know, then realized the remark wasn't directed at her but at the other Goddesses.

"It's extraordinary," said Tishalullé.

The pliancy of Her voice was seductive, and as Jude attended to it Her nebulous form became more particular, the syllables bringing sight along with them. Her face was Oriental in cast, and without a trace of color in cheek or lip or lash. Yet what should have been bland was instead exquisitely subtle, its symmetry and its curves delineated by the light that flickered in Her eyes. Below its calm, Her body was another matter entirely. Her entire length was covered by what Jude at first took to be tattoos of some kind, following the sweep of Her anatomy. But the more she studied the Goddess—and she did so without embarrassment—the more she saw movement in these marks. They weren't *on* Her but *in* Her, thousands of tiny flaps opening and closing rhythmically. There were several shoals of them, she saw, each swept by independent waves of motion. One rose up from Her groin, where the inspiration of them all had its place; others swept down Her limbs, out to Her fingertips and toes, the motion of each shoal converging every ten or fifteen seconds, at which point a second substance seemed to spring from these slits, forming the Goddess afresh in front of Jude's astonished eyes.

"I think you should know that I've met your Gentle," Tishalullé said. "I embraced him in the Cradle."

"He's not mine any longer," Jude replied.

"Do you care, Judith?"

"Of course she doesn't care," came Jokalaylau's response. "She's got his brother to keep her bed warm. The Autarch. The butcher of Yzordderrex."

Jude turned her gaze towards the Goddess of the High Snows. The particulars of Her form were more elusive than Tishalullé's had been, but Jude was determined to know what She looked like, and fixed her gaze on the spiral of cold flame that burned in Her core, watching until it spat bright arcs out against the limits of Jokalaylau's body. The light of this collision was brief, but by it Jude got her glimpse. An imperious Negress, Her blazing eyes heavy-lidden, hovered there, Her hands crossed at the wrist, then turned back on themselves to knit their fingers. She was not, after all, such a terrifying sight. But sensing that Her face had been found, the Goddess responded with a sudden transformation. Her lush features were mummified in a heartbeat, the eyes sinking away, the lips withering and retracting. Worms devoured the tongue that poked between Her teeth.

Jude let out a cry of revulsion, and the eyes reignited in Jokalaylau's sockets, the wormy mouth gaping as hard laughter rose from Her throat and echoed around the temple.

"She's not so remarkable, sister," Jokalaylau said. "Look at her shake."

"Let her alone," Uma Umagammagi replied. "Why must You always be testing people?"

"We've endured because We've faced the worse and survived," Jokalaylau replied. "This one would have died in the snow."

"I doubt that," Umagammagi said. "Sweet Judith—"

Still shaking, Jude took a moment to respond. "I'm not afraid of death," she said to Jokalaylau. "Or cheap tricks."

Again, Umagammagi spoke. "Judith," she said. "Look at Me."

"I just want Her to understand—"

"Sweet Judith . . ."

"—I'm not going to be bullied."

". . . look at Me."

Now Jude did so, and this time there was no need to pierce the ambiguities. The Goddess appeared to Jude without challenge or labor, and the sight was a paradox. Uma Umagammagi was an ancient, Her body so withered it was almost sexless, Her hairless skull subtly elongated, Her tiny eyes so wreathed in creases they were barely more than gleams. But the beauty of Her glyph was here in this flesh: its ripples, its flickers, its ceaseless, effortless motion.

"Do you see now?" Uma Umagammagi said.

"Yes, I see."

"We haven't forgotten the flesh We had," She said to Jude. "We've known the frailties of your condition. We remember its pains and discomforts. We know what it is to be wounded: in the heart, in the head, in the womb."

"I see that," Jude said.

"Nor would We have trusted you with knowledge of Our frailty, unless We believed that you might one day be among Us."

"Among You?"

"Some divinities arise from the collective will of peoples; some are made in the heat of stars; some are abstractions. But some— dare we say the finest, the most loving?—are the higher minds of living souls. We are such divinities, sister, and Our memories of the lives We lived and the deaths We died are still sharp. We understand you, sweet Judith, and We don't accuse you."

"Not even Jokalaylau?" Jude said.

The Goddess of the High Snows made Herself apparent to Her length and breadth, showing Jude Her entire form in a single glance. There was a paleness moving beneath Her skin, and Her eyes, that had been so luminous, were dark. But they were fixed on Jude. She felt the stare like a stab.

"I want you to see," She said, "what the Father of the father of the child in you did to My devotees."

Jude recognized the paleness now. It was a blizzard, driven through the Goddess's form by pain, and pricking every part of Her. Its drifts were mountainous, but at Jokalaylau's behest they moved and uncovered the site of an atrocity. The bodies of women lay frozen where they'd fallen, their eyes carved out, their breasts taken off. Some lay close to smaller bodies: violated children, dismembered babes.

"This is a little part of a little part of what He did," Jokalaylau said.

Appalling as the sight was, Jude didn't flinch this time, but stared on at the horror until Jokalaylau drew a cold shroud back over it.

"What are You asking me to do?" Jude said. "Are You telling me I should add another body to the heap? Another child?" She laid her hand on her belly. "*This* child?"

She hadn't realized until now how covetous she felt of the soul she was nurturing.

"It belongs to the butcher," Jokalaylau said.

"No," Jude quietly replied. "It belongs to me."

"You'll be responsible for its works?"

"Of course," she said, strangely exhilarated by this promise. "Bad can be made from good, Goddess; whole things from broken."

She wondered as she spoke if They knew where these sentiments originated; whether They understood that she was turning the Reconciler's philosophies to her own maternal ends. If They did, They seemed not to think less of her for it.

"Then Our spirits go with you, sister," Tishalullé said.

"Are You sending me away again?" Jude asked.

"You came here looking for an answer, and We can provide it."

"We understand the urgency of this," Uma Umagammagi said. "And We haven't held you here without cause. I've been across the Dominions while you waited, looking for some clue to this puzzle. There are Maestros waiting in every Dominion to undertake the Reconciliation—"

"Then Gentle didn't begin?"

"No. He's waiting for your word."

"And what should I tell him?"

"I've searched their hearts, looking for some plot—"

"Did You find any?"

"No. They're not pure, of course. Who is? But all of them want the Imajica whole. All of them believe the working they're ready to perform can succeed."

"Do You believe it too?"

"Yes, We do," said Tishalullé. "Of course they don't realize they're completing the circle. If they did, perhaps they'd think again."

"Why?"

"Because the circle belongs to Our sex, not to theirs," Jokalaylau put in.

"Not true," Umagammagi said. "It belongs to any mind that cares to conceive it."

"Men are incapable of conceiving, sister," Jokalaylau replied. "Or hadn't You heard?"

Umagammagi smiled. "Even that may change, if We can coax them from their terrors."

Her words begged many questions, and She knew it. Her eyes fixed on Jude, and She said, "We'll have time for these works when you come back. But now I know you need to be fleet."

"Tell Gentle to be a Reconciler," Tishalullé said. "But share nothing that We've said with him."

"Do I have to be the one to tell him?" Jude said to Umagammagi. "If You've been there once, can't You go again and give him the news? I want to stay here."

"We understand. But he's in no mood to trust Us, believe me. The message must come from you, in the flesh."

"I see," Jude said.

There was no room for persuasion, it seemed. She had the plain answer she'd come here hoping to find. Now she had to return to the Fifth with it, unpalatable as that journey would be.

"May I ask one question before I go?" she said.

"Ask it," said Umagammagi.

"Why did You show Yourselves to me this way?"

It was Tishalullé who replied. "So that you'll know Us when We come to sit at your table or walk beside you in the street," She said.

"Will you come to the Fifth?"

"Perhaps, in time. We'll have work there, when the Reconciliation's achieved."

Jude imagined the transformations she'd seen outside wrought in London: Mother Thames climbing her banks, depositing the filth she'd been choked by in Whitehall and the Mall, then sweeping through the city, making its squares into swimming pools and its cathedrals into playgrounds. The thought made her light.

"I'll be waiting for you," she said and, thanking them, made her departure.

When she got outside the waters were waiting for her, the surf lush as pillows. She didn't delay, but went straight down the beach and threw herself into its comfort. This time there was no need to swim; the tide knew its business. It picked her up and carried her across the basin like a foamy chariot, delivering her back to the rocks from which she'd first taken her plunge. Lotti Yap and Paramarola had gone, but finding her way out of the palace would be easier now than when she'd first arrived. The waters had been at work on many of the corridors and chambers that ran around the basin, and on the courtyards beyond, opening up vistas of glittering pools and fountains that stretched to the rubble of the palace gates. The air was clearer than it had been, and she could see the Kesparates spread below. She could even see the harbor, and the sea at its walls, its own tide longing, no doubt, to share this enchantment.

She made her way back to the staircase, to find that the waters that had carried her here had receded from the bottom, leaving heaps of flotsam and jetsam behind. Picking through it, like a beachcomber granted her paradise, was Lotti Yap, and sitting on the lower steps, chatting to Paramarola, Hoi-Polloi Peccable.

After they'd greeted each other, Hoi-Polloi explained how she'd prevaricated before committing herself to the river that had separated her from Jude. Once she jumped in, however, it had carried her safely through the palace and delivered her to this spot. Minutes later it had been called to other duties and disappeared.

"We'd pretty much given up on you," said Lotti Yap. She was busy plucking the petitions and prayers from among the trash, unfolding them, scanning them, then pocketing them. "Did you get to see the Goddesses?"

"Yes, I did."

"Are They beautiful?" Paramarola asked.

"In a way."

"Tell us every detail."

"I haven't time. I have to get back to the Fifth."

"You got your answer, then," Lotti said.

"I did. And we've got nothing to fear."

"Didn't I tell you?" she replied. "Everything's well with the world."

As Jude started to pick her way through the debris, Hoi-Polloi said, "Can two of us go?"

"I thought you were going to wait with us," Paramarola said.

"I'll come back and see the Goddesses," Hoi-Polloi replied. "I'd like to see the Fifth before everything changes. It *is* going to change, isn't it?"

"Yes, it is," Jude said.

"Do you want something to read on your travels?" Lotti asked them, proffering a fistful of petitions. "It's amazing, what people write."

"All those should go to the island," Jude said. "Take them with you. Leave them at the temple door."

"But the Goddesses can't answer every prayer," Lotti said. "Lost lovers, crippled children—"

"Don't be so sure," Jude told her. "It's going to be a new day."

Then, with Hoi-Polloi at her side, she made the hour's second round of farewells and headed away in the general direction of the gate.

"Do you really believe what you said to Lotti?" Hoi-Polloi asked her when they'd left the staircase far behind. "Is tomorrow going to be so different from today?"

"One way or another," Jude said.

The reply was more ambiguous than she'd intended, but then perhaps her tongue was wiser than it knew. Though she was going from this holy place with the word of powers far more discerning than she, their reassurance could not quite erase the memory of the bowl in Oscar's treasure room and the prophecy of dust it had shown her.

She silently admonished herself for her lack of faith. Where did this seam of arrogance come from, that she could doubt the wisdom of Uma Umagammagi Herself? From now on, she would put such ambivalence away. Maybe tomorrow, or some blissful day after, she'd meet the Goddesses on the streets of the Fifth and tell Them that even after Their comforts she'd still nursed some ridiculous nub of doubt. But for today she'd bow to Their wisdoms and return to the Reconciler as a bearer of good news.

22

I

Gentle wasn't the only occupant of the house in Gamut Street who'd smelled the In Ovo on the late-afternoon breeze; so had one who'd once been a prisoner in that Hell between Dominions: Little Ease. When Gentle returned to the Meditation Room, having set Monday the task of bringing the stones up the stairs and sent Clem around the house securing it, he found his sometime tormentor up at the window. There were tears on its cheeks, and its teeth were chattering uncontrollably.

"He's coming, isn't he?" it said. "Did you see him, Liberatore?"

"Yes, he is, and no, I didn't," Gentle said. "Don't look so terrified, Easy. I'm not going to let him lay a finger on you."

The creature put on its wretched grin, but with its teeth in such motion the effect was grotesque.

"You sound like my mother," it said. "Every night she used to tell me: nothing's going to hurt you, nothing's going to hurt you."

"I remind you of your mother?"

"Give or take a tit," Little Ease replied. "She was no beauty, it has to be said. But all my fathers loved her."

There was a din from downstairs, and the creature jumped.

"It's all right," Gentle said. "It's just Clem closing the shutters."

"I want to be of some use. What can I do?"

"You can do what you're doing. Watch the street. If you see anything out there—"

"I know. Scream blue murder."

With the windows shuttered below, the house was thrown into a sudden dusk, in which Clem, Monday, and Gentle labored without word or pause. By the time all the stones had been fetched upstairs the day outside had also dwindled into twilight, and Gentle found Little Ease leaning out of the window, stripping fistfuls of leaves from the tree outside and flinging them back into the room. When he asked it what it was up to it explained that, with evening fallen, the street was invisible through the foliage, so it was clearing it away.

"When I begin the Reconciliation maybe you should keep watch from the floor above," Gentle suggested.

"Whatever you suggest, Liberatore," Little Ease said. It slid down from the sill and stared up at him. "But before I go, if you don't mind, I have a little request," it said.

"Yes?"

"It's delicate."

"Don't be afraid. Ask it."

"I know you're about to start the working, and I think this may be the last time I have the honor of your company. When the Reconciliation's achieved you'll be a great man. I don't mean to say you're not one already," it added hurriedly. "You are, of course. But after tonight everyone will know you're the Reconciler, and you did what Christos Himself couldn't do. You'll be made Pope, and you'll write your memoirs"—Gentle laughed—"and I'll never see you again. And that's as it should be. That's right and proper. But before you become hopelessly famous and feted, I wondered: would you . . . bless me?"

"Bless you?"

Little Ease raised its long-fingered hands to ward off the rejection it thought was coming. "I understand! I understand!" it said. "You've already been kind to me beyond measure—"

"It's not that," said Gentle, going down on his haunches in front of the creature the way he had when its head had been beneath Jude's heel. "I'd do it if I could. But Ease, I don't know how. I'm not a Messiah. I've never had a ministry. I've never preached a gospel or raised the dead."

"You've got your disciples," Little Ease said.

"No. I've had some friends who've endured me, and some mistresses who've humored me. But I've never had the power to inspire. I frittered it away on seductions. I don't have the right to bless anybody."

"I'm sorry," the creature said. "I won't mention it again."

Then it did again what it had done when Gentle had set it free: took his hand and laid its brow upon his palm.

"I'm ready to die for you, Liberatore."

"I'm hoping that won't be necessary."

Little Ease looked up. "Between us?" it said. "So am I."

Its oath made, it returned to gathering up the leaves it had deposited on the floor, putting plugs of them up its nose to stop the stench. But Gentle told it to let the rest lie. The scent of the sap was sweeter than the smell that would permeate the house if, or rather when, Sartori arrived. At the mention of the enemy, Little Ease hoisted itself back up onto the sill.

"Any sign?" Gentle asked it.

"Not that I see."

"But what do you *feel?*"

"Ah," it said, looking up through the canopy of leaves. "It's such a beautiful night, Liberatore. But he's going to try and spoil it."

"I think you're right. Stay here a while longer, will you? I want to go around the house with Clem. If you see anything—"

"They'll hear me in L'Himby," Ease promised.

The beast was as good as its word. Gentle hadn't reached the bottom of the stairs when it set up a din so loud it brought dust from the rafters. Yelling for Monday and Clem to make sure all the doors were bolted, Gentle started up the stairs again, reaching the summit in time to see the door of the Meditation Room flung open and Little Ease backing through it at speed, shrieking. Whatever warning the creature was trying to offer, it was incomprehensible. Gentle didn't try and interpret it, but raced towards the room, drawing his breath in readiness to drive Sartori's invaders out. The window was empty when he entered, but the circle was not. Within the ring of stones two forms were unknotting themselves. He'd never seen the phenomenon of passage from this perspective before, and he stood as much aghast as awed. There were too many raw surfaces in this process for comfortable viewing. But he studied the forms with mounting excitement, certain long before they were reconstituted that one of the travelers was Jude. The other, when she appeared, was a cross-eyed girl of seventeen or so, who fell to her knees sobbing with terror and relief the moment her muscles were her own again. Even Jude, who'd made this journey four times now, was shaking violently and would have fallen when she stepped from the circle had Gentle not caught her up.

"The In Ovo . . ." she gasped, "almost had us. . . ."

Her leg had been gouged from knee to ankle.

". . . felt teeth in me. . . ."

"You're all right," Gentle said. "You've still got two legs. Clem! Clem!"

He was already at the door, with Monday in pursuit.

"Have we got something to bind this up?"

"Of course! I'll go—"

"No," said Jude. "Take me down. This is no floor to bleed on."

Monday was left to comfort Hoi-Polloi, while Clem and Gentle carried Jude to the door.

"I've never seen the In Ovo like that before," she said. "Crazy. . . ."

"Sartori's been in," Gentle said, "finding himself an army."

"He certainly stirred them up."

"We were about to give up on you," Clem said.

Jude raised her head. Her skin was waxen with shock, and her smile too tentative to be joyful. But it was there, at least.

"Never give up on the messenger," she said. "Especially if she's got good news."

It was three hours and four minutes to midnight, and there wasn't time for a lengthy exchange, but Gentle wanted some explanation—however brief—of what had taken Jude to Yzordderrex. So she was made comfortable in the front room, which Monday's scavengings had furnished with pillows, foodstuffs, and even magazines, and there, while Clem bound her leg and foot, she did her best to encapsulate all that had happened to her since she'd left the Retreat.

It didn't make easy telling, and there were a couple of occasions when she attempted to describe scenes in Yzordderrex and simply gave up, saying that she knew no words to describe what she'd witnessed and felt. Gentle listened without once interrupting her, though his expression grew grimmer when she told of how Uma Umagammagi had passed through the Dominions, seeking out the Synod to be certain their motives were pure.

When she was finished he said, "I was in Yzordderrex, too. It's changed quite a bit."

"For the better," Jude said.

"I don't like ruin, however picturesque it is," Gentle replied.

Jude eyed him strangely at this, but she said nothing.

"Are we safe here?" Hoi-Polloi said, addressing nobody in particular. "It's so dark."

" 'Course we're safe," Monday said, putting his arm around the girl's shoulders. "We got the whole fuckin' place sealed up. He's not going to get in, is he, boss?"

"Who?" Jude asked.

"Sartori," said Monday.

"Is he somewhere in the vicinity?"

Gentle's silence was reply enough.

"And you think a few locks are going to keep him out?"

"Won't they?" said Hoi-Polloi.

"Not if he wants to get in," Jude said.

"He won't," Gentle replied. "When the Reconciliation begins, there's going to be a flow of power through this house . . . my Father's power."

The thought was as distasteful to Jude as Gentle assumed it would be to Sartori, but her response was subtler than revulsion.

"He's your brother," she reminded him. "Don't be so sure he won't want a taste of what's in here. And if he does, he'll come and get it."

He stared hard at her.

"Are we talking about power, here, or you?"

Jude took a moment before replying. Then she said, "Both."

Gentle shrugged. "If that happens, you'll make your decision," he said. "You've made them before, and you've been wrong. Maybe it's time to have a little faith, Jude." He stood up. "Share what the rest of us already know," he said.

"And what's that?"

"That in a few hours we'll be standing in a legendary place."

Monday softly said, "Yeah," and Gentle smiled.

"Take care down here, all of you," he said, and headed to the door.

Jude reached for Clem, and with his help hauled herself to her feet. By the time she reached the door Gentle was already on the stairs.

She didn't say his name. He simply stopped for a moment and, without turning, said, "I don't want to hear."

Then he continued his ascent, and she knew by the slope of his shoulders and the weight of his tread that for all his prophetic talk there was a little worm of doubt in him just as there was in her, and he was afraid that if he turned and saw her, it would fatten on their look and choke him.

The scent of sap was waiting for him on the threshold, and as he'd hoped it masked the sourer smell from the darkened streets outside. Otherwise his room, in which he'd lounged and laughed and debated the conundrums of the cosmos, offered no solace. It suddenly seemed to him a stagnant place, too well feited and swayed for its own good: the last place on earth to perform his work. But then hadn't he berated Jude, just moments ago, for not having sufficient faith? There was no great power in geography. It was all rooted in the Maestro's faith in the miraculous, and in the will that sprang from that faith.

In preparation for the work ahead, he undressed. Once naked, he crossed to the mantelpiece, intending to fetch the candles off it and set them around the circle. But the sight of their flames in flickering array made him think instead of worship, and he dropped to his knees in front of the empty grate to pray. The Lord's Prayer came most readily to his lips, and he recited it aloud. Its sentiments had never been apter, of course. But after tonight it would be a museum piece, a relic of a time before the Lord's Kingdom had come and His will been done, on Earth and in Heaven.

A touch on the back of his neck brought this recitation to a halt. He opened his eyes, raised his head, turned. The room was empty, but his nape still tingled where the touch had come. This wasn't memory, he knew. It was something more delicate than that, a reminder of the other prize that lay at the end of this night's work. Not glory, not the gratitude of the Dominions: Pie 'oh' pah. He looked up at the stained wall above the mantelpiece and seemed for a moment to see the mystif's face there, changing with each flicker of the candlelight. Athanasius had called the love he felt for the mystif profane. He hadn't believed it then, and he didn't now. The purpose that was in him as Reconciler and the desire he felt for reunion were part of the same plan.

The prayer was gone from his tongue. No matter, he thought; I'm its executor now. He got up, took one of the candles from the mantelpiece, and, smiling, stepped over the perimeters of the circle, not as a simple traveler but as a Maestro, ready to use its engine to miraculous end.

2

Lying on the cushions in the lounge below, Jude felt the flow of energies start. They ached in her chest and belly, like mild dyspepsia. She rubbed her stomach, in the hope of soothing the discomfort, but it did little good, so she got to her feet and hobbled out, leaving Monday to entertain Hoi-Polloi with his chatter and his handiwork. He'd taken to drawing on the walls with the smoke from one of the candles, enhancing the marks with his chalks. Hoi-Polloi was much impressed, and her laughter, the first Jude had ever heard from the girl, followed her out into the hallway, where she found Clem standing guard beside the locked front door.

They stared at each other in the candlelight for several seconds before she said, "Do you feel it too?"

"Yep. It's not very pleasant, is it?"

"I thought it was only me," she said.

"Why only you?"

"I don't know, some kind of punishment. . . ."

"You still think he's got some secret agenda, don't you?"

"No," Jude said, glancing up the stairs. "I think he's doing what he believes is best. In fact I know it. Uma Umagammagi got inside his head—"

"God, he hated that."

"She gave him a good report, whether he hated it or not."

"So?"

"So there's still a conspiracy somewhere."

"Sartori?"

"No. It's something to do with their Father and this damn Reconciliation." She winced as the discomfort in her belly became more severe. "I'm not afraid of Sartori. It's what's going on in this house"—she gritted her teeth as another wave of pain passed through her system—"that I can't quite trust."

She looked back at Clem and knew that, as ever, he'd listen as a loving friend, but she could expect no support from him. He and Tay were the angels of the Reconciliation, and if she pressed them to decide between her welfare and that of the working, she'd be the loser.

The sound of Hoi-Polloi's laughter came again, not as feathery as before, but with an undertow of mischief Jude knew was sexual. She turned her back on the sound and on Clem, and her gaze came to rest on the door of the one room in this house she'd never entered. It stood a little ajar, and she could see that candles were burning inside. Of all the company to seek out when she was in need of comfort, Celestine's was the least promising, but all other avenues were closed to her. She crossed to the door and pushed it open. The mattress was empty, and the candle beside it was burning low. The room was too large to be illuminated by such a fitful flame, and she had to study the darkness until she found its occupant. Celestine was standing against the far wall.

"I'm surprised you came back," she said.

Jude had heard many exquisite speakers since she'd last heard Celestine, but there was still something extraordinary in the way the woman mingled voices: one running beneath the other, as though the part of her touched by divinity had never entirely married with a baser self.

"Why surprised?"

"Because I thought you'd stay with the Goddesses."

"I was tempted," Jude replied.

"But finally you had to come back. For him."

"I was a messenger, that's all. I've got no claims on Gentle now."

"I didn't mean Gentle."

"I see."

"I meant—"

"I know who you meant."

"Can't you bear to have his name spoken?"

Celestine had been staring at the candle flame, but now she looked up at Jude.

"What will you do when he's dead?" she asked. "He *will* die, you realize that? He has to. Gentle'll want to be magnanimous, the way victors are supposed to be; he'll want to forgive all his brother's trespasses. But there'll be too many demands for his head."

Until now Jude hadn't contemplated the possibility of Sartori's demise. Even in the tower, knowing Gentle had gone in pursuit of his brother intending to stop his malice, she'd never believed he'd die. But what Celestine said was undoubtedly true. There were countless claims upon his head, both secular and divine. Even if Gentle was forgiving, Jokalaylau wouldn't be; nor would the Unbeheld.

"You're very alike, you know, you and he," Celestine said. "Both copies of a finer original."

"You never knew Quaisoir," Jude replied. "You don't know whether she was finer or not."

"Copies are always coarser. It's their nature. But at least your instinct's good. You and he belong together. That's what you're pining for, isn't it? Why don't you admit it?"

"Why should I pour out my heart to you?"

"Isn't that what you came in here to do? You won't get any sympathy out there."

"Listening by the door now?"

"I've heard everything that's gone on in this house since I was brought here. And what I haven't heard, I've felt. And what I haven't felt, I've predicted."

"Like what?"

"Well, for one thing that child Monday will end up coupling with the little virgin you brought back from Yzordderrex."

"That scarcely takes an oracle."

"And the Oviate isn't long for this world."

"The Oviate?"

"It calls itself Little Ease. The beast you had under your heel. It asked the Maestro to bless it a little while ago. It'll murder itself before daybreak."

"Why would it do that?"

"It knows when Sartori perishes it'll be forfeit too, however much allegiance it's sworn to the winning side. It's sensible. It wants to choose its moment."

"Am I supposed to find some lesson in that?"

"I don't think you're capable of suicide," Celestine said.

"You're right. I've got too much to live for."

"Motherhood?"

"And the future. There's going to be a change in this city. I've seen it in Yzordderrex already. The waters will rise—"

"—and the great sisterhood will dispense love from on high."

"Why not? Clem told me what happened when the Goddess came. You were in ecstasies, so don't try and deny it."

"Maybe I was. But do you imagine that's going to make you and me sisters? What have we got in common, besides our sex?"

The question was meant to sting, but its plainness made Jude see the questioner with fresh eyes. Why was Celestine so eager to deny any other link between them but womanhood? Because another such link existed, and it was at the very heart of their enmity. Nor, now that Celestine's contempt had freed Jude from reverence, was it difficult to see where their stories intersected. From the beginning, Celestine had marked Jude out as a woman who stank of coitus. Why? Because she too stank of coitus. And this business with the child, which came up again and again: that had the same root. Celestine had also borne a baby for this dynasty of Gods and demigods. She too had been used and had never quite come to terms with the fact. When she raged against Jude, the tainted woman who would not concede her error in being sexual, in being fecund, she was raging against some fault in herself.

And the nature of that fault? It wasn't difficult to guess, or to put words to. Celestine had asked a plain question. Now it was Jude's turn.

"Was it really rape?" she said.

Celestine glanced up, her look venomous. The denial that followed, however, was measured. "I'm afraid I don't know what you mean," she said.

"Well, now," Jude replied, "how else can I put it?" She paused. "Did Sartori's Father take you against your will?"

The other woman now put on a show of comprehension, followed by one of shock.

"Of course He did," she said. "How could you ask such a thing?"

"But you knew where you were going, didn't you? I realize Dowd drugged you at the start, but you weren't in a coma all the way across the Dominions. You knew something extraordinary was waiting at the end of the trip."

"I don't—"

"Remember? Yes, you do. You remember every mile of it. And I don't think Dowd kept his mouth shut all those weeks. He was pimping for God, and he was proud of it. Wasn't he?"

Celestine offered no riposte. She simply stared at Jude, daring her to go on, which Jude was happy to do.

"So he told you what lay ahead, didn't he? He said that you were going to the Holy City and you were going to see the Unbeheld Himself. Not just see Him but be loved by Him. And you were *flattered.*"

"It wasn't like that."

"How was it then? Did He have His angels hold you down while He did the deed? No, I don't think so. You lay there and you let Him do what the hell He wanted, because it was going to make you into the bride of God and the mother of Christ—"

"Stop!"

"If I'm wrong, tell me how it was. Tell me you screamed and fought and tried to tear out His eyes."

Celestine continued to stare, but said nothing.

"That's why you despise me, isn't it?" Jude went on. "That's why I'm the woman who stinks of coitus. Because I lay down with a piece of the same God that you did, and you don't like to be reminded of the fact."

"Don't judge me, woman!" Celestine suddenly shouted.

"Then don't you judge me! *Woman.* I did what I wanted with the man I wanted, and I'm carrying the consequences. You did the same. I'm not ashamed of it. You are. That's why we're not sisters, Celestine."

She'd said her piece, and she wasn't much interested in a further round of insults and denials, so she turned her back and had her hand on the door when Celestine spoke. There were no denials. She spoke softly, half lost to memory.

"It was a city of iniquities," she said. "But how was I to know that? I thought I was blessed among women, to have been chosen. To be God's—"

"Bride?" Jude said, turning back from the door.

"That's a kind word," Celestine said. "Yes. Bride." She drew a deep breath. "I never even saw my husband."

"What did you see?"

"Nobody. The city was full, I know it was full, I saw shadows at the window, I saw them close up the doors when I passed, but nobody showed their faces."

"Were you afraid?"

"No. It was too beautiful. The stones were full of light, and the houses were so high you could barely see the sky. It was like nothing I'd ever seen. And I walked, and I walked, and I kept thinking, He'll send an angel for me soon, and I'll be carried to His palace. But there were no angels. There was just the city, going on and on in every direction, and I got tired after a time. I sat down, just to rest for a few minutes, and I fell asleep."

"You fell asleep?"

"Yes. Imagine! I was in the City of God, and I fell asleep. And I dreamed I was back at Tyburn, where Dowd had found me. I was watching a man being hanged, and I dug through the crowd until I was standing under the gallows." She raised her head. "I remember looking up at him, kicking at the end of his rope. His breeches were unbuttoned, and his rod was poking out."

The look on her face was all disgust, but she drove herself on to finish the story.

"And I lay down under him. I lay down in the dirt in front of all these people, with him kicking, and his rod getting redder and redder. And as he died he spilled his seed. I wanted to get up before it touched me, but my legs were open, and it was too late. Down it came. Not much. Just a few spurts. But I felt every drop inside me like a little fire, and I wanted to cry out. But I didn't, because that was when I heard the voice."

"What voice?"

"It was in the ground underneath me. Whispering."

"What did it say?"

"The same thing, over and over again: *Nisi Nirvana. Nisi Nirvana. Nisi . . . Nirvana.*"

In the process of repeating the words, tears began to flow copiously. She made no attempt to stem them, but the repetition faltered.

"Was it Hapexamendios talking to you?" Jude asked.

Celestine shook her head. "Why should He speak to me? He had what He needed. I'd lain down and dreamed while He dropped His seed. He was already gone, back to His angels."

"So who was it?"

"I don't know. I've thought about it over and over. I even made it into a story, to tell the child, so that when I'd gone he'd have the mystery for himself. But I don't think I ever really wanted to know. I was afraid my heart would burst if I ever knew the answer. I was afraid the heart of the world would burst."

She looked up at Jude.

"So now you know my shame," she said.

"I know your story," said Jude. "But I don't see any reason for shame."

Her own tears, which she'd been holding back since Celestine had begun to share this horror with her, fell now, flowing a little for the pain she felt and a little for the doubt that still churned in her, but mostly for the smile that came onto Celestine's face when she heard Jude's reply, and for the sight of the other woman opening her arms and crossing the room, to embrace her like a loved one who'd been lost and found again before some final fire.

23

I

If coming to the moment of Reconciliation had been for Gentle a series of rememberings, leading him back to himself, then the greatest of those rememberings, and the one he was least prepared for, was the Reconciliation itself.

Though he'd performed the working before, the circumstances had been radically different. For one, there'd been all the hoopla of a grand event. He'd gone into the circle like a prizefighter, with an air of congratulation hanging around his head before he'd even worked up a sweat, his patrons and admirers a cheering throng at the sidelines. This time he was alone. For another, he'd had his eyes on what the world would shower on him when the work was done: what women would fall to him, what wealth and glory would come. This time, the prize in sight was a different thing entirely, and wouldn't be counted in stained sheets and coinage. He was the instrument of a higher and wiser power.

That fact took the fear away. When he opened his mind to the process, he felt a calm come upon him, subduing the unease he'd felt climbing the stairs. He'd told Jude and Clem that forces would run through the house the likes of which its bricks had never known, and it was true. He felt them fuel his weakening mind, ushering his thoughts out of his head to gather the Dominion to the circle.

That gleaning began with the place he was sitting in. His mind spread to all compass points, and up and down, to have the sum of the room. It was an easy space to grasp. Generations of prison poets had made the analogies for him, and he borrowed them freely. The walls were his body's limits, the door his mouth, the windows his eyes: commonplace similitudes, taxing his power of comparison not a jot. He dissolved the boards, the plaster, the glass, and all the thousand tiny details in the same lyric of confinement and, having made them part of him, broke their bounds to stray farther afield.

As his imagination headed down the stairs and up onto the roof, he felt the beginnings of momentum. His intellect, dogged by literalism, was already lagging behind a sensibility more mercurial, which was delivering back to him similitudes for the whole house before his logical faculties had even reached the hallway.

Once again, his body was the measure of all things: the cellar, his bowels; the roof, his scalp; the stairs, his spine. Their proofs delivered, his thoughts flew out of the house, rising up over the slates and spreading through the streets. He gave passing consideration to Sartori as he went, knowing his other was out here in the night somewhere, skulking. But his mind was quicksilver, and too exhilarated by its speed and capacity to go searching in the shadows for an enemy already defeated.

With speed came ease. The streets were no more difficult to claim than the house he'd already devoured. His body had its conduits and its intersections, had its places of excrement and its fine, dandified façades; had its rivers, moving from a springing place, and its parliament, and its holy seat.

The whole city, he began to see, could be analogized to his flesh, bone, and blood. And why should that be so surprising? When an architect turned his mind to the building of a city, where would he look for inspiration? To the flesh where he'd lived since birth. It was the first model for any creator. It was a school and an eating house and an abattoir and a church; it could be a prison and a brothel and Bedlam. There wasn't an edifice in any street in London that hadn't begun somewhere in the private city of an architect's anatomy, and all Gentle had to do was open his mind to that fact and the districts were his, running back to swell the assembly in his head.

He flew north, through Highbury and Finsbury Park, to Palmer's Green and Cockfosters. He went east with the river, past Greenwich, where the clock that marked the coming of midnight stood, and on towards Tilbury. West took him through Marylebone and Hammersmith, south through Lambeth and Streatham, where he'd first met Pie 'oh' pah, long ago.

But the names soon became irrelevant. Like the ground seen from a rising plane, the particulars of a street or a district became part of another pattern, even more appetizing to his ambitious spirit. He saw the Wash glittering to the east, and the Channel to the south, becalmed on this humid night. Here was a fine new challenge. Was his body, which had proved the equal of a city, also the measure of this vaster geography? Why not? Water flowed by the same laws everywhere, whether the conduit was a groove in his brow or a rift between the continents. And were his hands not like two countries, laid side by side in his lap, their peninsulas almost touching, their landscapes scarred and grooved?

There was nothing outside his substance that was not mirrored within: no sea, no city, no street, no roof, no room. He was in the Fifth, and the Fifth in him, gathering to be carried into the Ana as a proof and a map and a poem, written in praise of all things being One.

In the other Dominions the same pursuit of similitude was under way.

From his circle on the Mount of Lipper Bayak, Tick Raw had already drawn into his net of dissolution both the city of Patashoqua and the highway that ran from its gates towards the mountains. In the Third, Scopique—his fears that the absence of the Pivot would invalidate his working allayed—was spreading his grasp across the Kwem towards the dust bowls around Mai-ké. In L'Himby, where he was soon to arrive, there were celebrants gathering at the temples, their hopes raised by prophetics who'd appeared from hiding the night before to spread the word that the Reconciliation was imminent.

No less inspired, Athanasius was presently traveling back along the Lenten Way to the borders of the Third and skimming the ocean to the islands, while a self more tender trod the changed streets of Yzordderrex. He found challenges there unknown to Scopique, Tick Raw, or even Gentle. There were slippery wonders loose on the streets that defied easy analogy. But in inviting Athanasius to join the Synod, Scopique had chosen better than he knew. The man's obsession with Christos, the bleeding God, gave him a grasp of what the Goddesses had wrought that a man less preoccupied by death and resurrection would never have owned. In Yzordderrex's ravaged streets he saw a reflection of his own physical ravagement. And in the music of the iconoclastic waters an echo of the blood that ran from his wounds, transformed—by love of the Holy Mother he had worshiped—into a sublime and healing liquor.

Only Chicka Jackeen, at the borders of the First Dominion, had to work with abstractions, for there was nothing of a physical nature he could win similitudes from. All he had was the blank wall of the Erasure to set his mind on. Of the Dominion that lay beyond—which it fell to him to encapsulate and carry into the Ana—he had no knowledge.

He hadn't spent so many years studying the mystery without finding some means to tussle with it, however. Although his body offered no analogy for the enigma that lay on the other side of the

divide, there was a place in him just as sealed from sight, and just
as open to the inquiries made by dreaming explorers like himself.
He let mind—the unbeheld process that empowered every mean-
ingful action, that made the very devotion that kept him in his
circle—be his similitude. The blank wall of the Erasure was the
white bone of his skull, scoured of every scrap of meat and hair.
The force inside, incapable of impartial self-study, was both the
God of the First and the thoughts of Chicka Jackeen, bonded by
mutual scrutiny.

After tonight, both would be free of the curse of invisibility. The
Erasure would drop and the Godhead come back into view to
walk the Imajica. When that happened, when the same Godhead
who'd taken the Nullianacs into His furnace and burned their malice away, was no longer divided from His Dominions, there would
be a revelation such as had never been known before. The dead,
trapped in their condition and unable to find the door, would have
a light to lead the way. And the living, no longer afraid to show their
minds, would step from their houses like divinities, carrying their
private heavens upon their heads for all to see.

About his own work, Gentle had little grasp of what his fellow
Maestros were achieving, but the absence of alarm from the other
Dominions reassured him that all was well. All the pains and hu-
miliations he'd endured to reach this place had been repaid in the
little hours since he'd stepped into the circle. An ecstasy he'd only
known for the duration of a heartbeat suffused him, confounding
the conviction he'd had that such feelings only came in glimpses
because to know them for longer would burst the heart. It wasn't
so. The ecstasy went on and on, and he was surviving it: more than
surviving, burgeoning, his authority over the working stronger with
every city and sea he retrieved into the circle where he sat.

The Fifth was almost there with him now, sharing the space,
teaching him with its coming where the true power of a Reconciler
lay. It wasn't a skill with feits and sways, nor was it pneumas, nor
resurrections, nor the driving out of demons. It was the strength to
call the myriad wonders of an entire Dominion by the names of
his body and not be broken by the simile; to allow that he was in
the world to its smallest degree, and the world in him, and not be
driven to insanity by the intricacies he contained or else so enam-
ored of the panoramas he was spread through that he lost all memory of the man he'd been.

There was such pleasure in this process that laughter began to
shake him as he sat in the circle. His good humor wasn't a distraction from his purpose but instead made it easier still, his

laugh-lightened thoughts running from the circle out to regions both bright and benighted and coming back with their prizes like runners sent with poems to a promised land, and returning with it on their backs, flowering as it came.

2

In the room above, Little Ease heard the laughter and capered in sympathy with the Liberatore's joy. What else could such a sound mean, but that the deed was close to being done? Even if it didn't see the consequences of this triumph, it thought, its last night in the living world had been immeasurably sweetened by all it had been a party to. And should there be an afterlife for such creatures as itself (although of this it was by no means certain), then its account of this night would be a fine tale to tell when it went into the company of its ancestors.

Anxious not to disturb the Reconciler, it gave up its dance of celebration and was about to return to the window and its duties as night watchman when it heard a sound its paddings had concealed. Its gaze went from the sill to the ceiling. The wind had got up in the last little while and was skittering across the roof, rattling the slates as it went, or so Ease thought, until it realized the tree outside was as still as the Kwem at equinox.

Little Ease didn't come from a tribe of heroes; quite the reverse. The legends of its people concerned famous apologists, humblers, deserters, and cowards. Its instinct, hearing this sound from above, was to be away downstairs as fast as its bandy legs knew how. But it fought what came naturally, for the Reconciler's sake, and cautiously approached the window in the hope of gaining a glimpse of what was happening above.

It climbed up onto the sill and, belly up, slid itself out a little way, peering up at the eaves. A mist dirtied the starlight, and the roof was dark. It leaned a little farther out, the sill hard beneath its bony back. From the window below, the sound of the Reconciler's laughter floated up, its music reassuring. Little Ease had time to smile, hearing it. Then something as dark as the roof and as dirty as the fog that covered the stars reached down and stopped its mouth. The attack came so suddenly Little Ease lost its grip on the window frame and toppled backwards, but its smotherer had too tight a hold on it to let it drop, and hauled it up onto the roof. Seeing the assembly there, Ease knew its errors instantly. One, it had stopped its nostrils and so failed to smell this congregation. Two, it had believed too much in a theology which taught that evil came from below. Not so, not so. While it had watched the street for Sartori and his legion, it had neglected the route along the roofs, which was just as secure for creatures as nimble as these.

There were not more than six of them, but then there didn't need to be. The gek-a-gek were feared among the feared; Oviates that only the most overweening of Maestros would have called into the Dominions. As massive as tigers, and as sleek, they had hands the size of a man's head and heads as flat as a man's hand. Their flanks were translucent in some lights, but here they had made a pact with darkness, and they lay—all but the smotherer—at the apex of the roof, their silhouettes concealing the Maestro until he rose and murmured that the captive be brought to his feet.

"Now, Little Ease," he said, the words too soft to be heard in the rooms below, but loud enough to make the creature evacuate its bowels in terror, "I want you to spill more than your shite for me."

3

It gave Sartori no satisfaction to watch Little Ease's life go out. The sense of exhilaration he'd felt at dawn when, having summoned the gek-a-gek, he'd contemplated the confrontation that lay a few hours off, had been all but sweated out of him by the heat of the intervening day. The gek-a-gek were powerful beasts and might well have survived the journey from Shiverick Square to Gamut Street, but no Oviate was fond of the light from any heaven, and rather than risk their debilitation, he'd stayed beneath the trees with his pride, counting off the hours. Only once had he ventured from their company and had found the streets deserted. The sight should have heartened him. With the area deserted he and the creatures would be unwitnessed when they moved on the enemy. But sitting in the silent bower with his dozing legion, undistracted by even the sound of a fly, his mind had been preyed upon by fears he'd always put away until now, fears fueled by the sight of these empty streets.

Was it possible that his revisionist purposes were about to be overwhelmed by some still greater revision? He realized his dreams of a New Yzordderrex were valueless. He'd said as much to his brother in the tower. But even if he wasn't to be an empire builder here, he still had something to live for. She was in the house in Gamut Street, yearning for him, he hoped, as he yearned for her. He wanted continuance, even if it was as Hell to Gentle's Heaven. But the desertion of this city made him wonder if even that was a pipe dream.

As the afternoon had crept on, he'd begun to look forward to reaching Gamut Street, simply for the signs of life it would provide. But he'd arrived to find precious little comfort here. The phantoms that lingered at the perimeters only reminded him of how uncharitable death really was, and the sounds that issued from the house itself (a girl's giggling from one of the lower rooms, and later full-throated laughter, his brother's, from the Meditation Room) only seemed to him signs of an idiot optimism.

He wished he could scour these thoughts from his head, but there was no escape from them except, possibly, in the arms of his Judith. She was in the house, that he knew. But with the currents unleashed inside so strong, he dared not enter. What he wanted, and what he finally got from Little Ease, was intelligence as to her state and whereabouts. He'd assumed, wrongly as it turned out, that Judith was with the Reconciler. She'd taken herself off to Yzord-derrex, Little Ease said, and come back with fabulous tales. But the Reconciler had not been much impressed by them. There'd been a fracas, and he'd begun his working alone.

Why had she gone in the first place? he inquired, but the creature claimed it didn't know and could not be persuaded to supply an answer even though its limbs were half twisted off and its brain pan opened to the gek-a-gek's tongue. It had died protesting its ignorance, and Sartori had left the pride to toy with the carcass, taking himself off along the roof to turn over what he'd learned.

Oh, for a wad of kreauchee, to subdue his impatience, or else make him brave enough to beat on the door and tell her to come out and make love among the phantoms. But he was too tender to face the currents. There'd come a time, very soon, when the Reconciler, his gathering completed, would retire to the Ana. At that juncture the circle, its power no longer needed as a conduit to carry the analogues back into its reservoir, would turn off those currents and turn its attention to conveying the Reconciler through the In Ovo. There, in that window between the Reconciler's removal to the Ana and the completion of the working, he would act. He'd enter the house and let the gek-a-gek take Gentle (and any who rose to protect him) while he claimed Judith.

Thinking of her, and of the kreauchee he yearned for, he brought the blue egg out of his pocket and put it to his lips. He'd kissed its cool a thousand times in the last few hours; licked it; sucked it. But he wanted it deeper inside him, locked up in his belly as she would be when they'd mated again. He put it in his mouth, threw back his head, and swallowed. It went down easily, and granted him a few minutes of calm while he waited for the hour of his deliverance.

Had Clem's head not had two tenants he might well have forsaken his place at the front door during the hours in which the Reconciler worked above. The currents which that process had unleashed had made his belly ache at the outset, but after a time their effect mellowed, suffusing his system with a serenity so persuasive he'd wanted to find a place to lie down and dream. But Tay had policed such dereliction of duty severely, and whenever Clem's attention strayed he felt his lover's presence—which was so subtly wed and interwoven with his thoughts it only became apparent when there was a conflict of interests—rousing him to fresh vigilance. So he kept his post, though by now it was surely an academic exercise.

The candle he had set beside the door was drowning in its own wax, and he had just stooped to wick the lip and let the excess flow off when he heard something hitting the step outside, the sound like that of a fish being slapped on a slab. He gave up his candle work and put his ear to the door. There was no further sound. Had a fruit fallen from the tree outside the house, he wondered, or was there some stranger rain tonight? He went from the door, through to the room where Monday had been entertaining Hoi-Polloi. They'd left it for some more private place, taking two of the cushions with them. The thought that there were lovers in the house tonight pleased him, and he silently wished them well as he crossed to the window. It was darker outside than he'd expected, and though he had a view of the step he couldn't distinguish between objects lying upon it and the designs that Monday had drawn there.

Perplexed rather than anxious, he went back to the front door and listened again. There were no further sounds, and he was tempted to let the matter alone. But he half hoped some visionary rain had indeed begun to fall, and he was too curious to ignore the mystery. He moved the candle from the door, the wax snuffing the flame as he did so. No matter. There were other candles burning at the bottom of the stairs, and he had sufficient light to find the bolts and slide them back.

In Celestine's room, Jude woke and raised her head from the mattress where she'd laid it an hour before. The conversation between the women had continued for some while after their peacemaking, but Jude's exhaustion had finally caught up with her, and Celestine had suggested she rest for a while, which, reassured by Celestine's presence, she'd gladly done. Now she stirred to find that Celestine had also succumbed, her head on the mattress, her body on the floor. She was snoring softly, undisturbed by whatever had woken Jude.

The door was slightly ajar, and a perfume was coming through it, stirring a faint nausea in Jude's system. She sat up and rubbed at the crick in her neck, then got to her feet. She'd slipped off her shoes before she lay down, but rather than search for them in the darkened room she went out into the hallway barefoot. The smell was much stronger now. It was coming from the street outside, its route plain. The front door was open, and the angels who'd been guarding it were gone.

Calling Clem's name, she crossed the hallway, her step slowing as she approached the open door. The candles at the stairs were bright enough to shed some light upon the step. There was something glistening there. She picked up her speed again, asking for the Goddesses to be with her and with Clem. Don't let this be him, she murmured, seeing that it was tissue glistening, and blood in a pool around it; please don't let this be him.

It wasn't. Now that she was almost at the threshold she saw the remnants of a face there and knew it: Sartori's agent, Little Ease. Its eyes had been scooped out, and its mouth, which had spewed pleas and flattery in such abundance, was tongueless. But there was no doubting its identity. Only a creature of the In Ovo could still twitch as this did, refusing to give up the semblance of life even if the fact of it had gone.

She looked beyond the trophy into the murk of the street, calling Clem's name again. There was no answer at first. Then she heard him, his shout half smothered.

"Go back inside! For—God's—sake, go back!"

"Clem?" She stepped out of the house, bringing new cries of alarm from the darkness.

"Don't! Don't!"

"I'm not going back without you," she said, avoiding the Oviate's head as she advanced.

She heard something let out a soft sound as she did so, like a creature growling with its maw full of bees.

"Who's there?" she said.

There was no reply at first, but she knew it would come if she waited, and whose voice it would be when it did. She did not anticipate the nature of the reply, however, or its falling note.

"It wasn't supposed to happen this way," Sartori said.

"If you've hurt Clem—"

"I've no wish to hurt anybody."

She knew that was a lie. But she also knew he'd do Clem no harm as long as he needed a hostage.

"Let Clem go," she said.

"Will you come to me if I do?"

She left a decent pause before replying, so as not to seem too eager. "Yes," she said. "I'll come."

"No, Judy!" Clem said. *"Don't.* He's not alone."

She could see that now, as her eyes became more accustomed to the darkness. Sleek, ugly beasts prowled back and forth. One was up on its back legs, sharpening its claws on the tree. Another was in the gutter, close enough for her to see its innards through its translucent skin. Their ugliness didn't distress her. Around the fringes of any drama such detritus was bound to accrue: scraps of discarded characters, soiled costumes, cracked masks. They were irrelevancies, and her lover had taken them for company because he felt a kinship with them. She pitied them. But him, who'd been most high, she pitied more.

"I want to see Clem here on the step before I make a move," she said.

There was a pause, then Sartori said, "I'm going to trust you."

His words were followed by further sounds from the Oviates that paced in the murk, and Jude saw two of them slope out of the shadows, with Clem between them, his arms in their throats. They came close enough to the pavement for her to see the foam of appetite that rose from their lips; then they literally spat their prisoner free. Clem fell face down on the road, his hands and arms covered in their muck. She wanted to go to his aid there and then, but though the captors had retreated, the tree gouger had turned and lowered its shovel head, its eyes, black as a shark's, flickering back and forth in their bulbous sockets, hungry to have the frail meat on the road. If she moved she feared it would pounce, so she kept her place on the step while Clem hauled himself to his feet. His arms were blistered by the Oviate's spittle, but he was otherwise intact.

"I'm all right, Judy," he murmured. "Go back inside."

She stayed put, however, waiting until he was up and staggering across the pavement before she started down the steps.

"Go back!" he told her again.

She put her arms around him and whispered. "Clem. I don't want you to argue with this. Go into the house and lock the door. I'm not coming with you."

He started to speak, but she hushed him.

"No argument, I said. I want to see him, Clem. I want to . . . be with him. Now, *please,* if you love me, go inside and close the door."

She felt reluctance in his every sinew, but he knew too much about the business of love, especially love that defied orthodoxy, to attempt to reason with her.

"Just remember what he's done," he said, as he let her go.

"That's all part of it, Clem," she said, and slipped past him.

It was easy to leave the light behind. The ache which the currents had woken in her marrow diminished with every yard she put between herself and the house, and the thought of the embrace ahead quickened her step. This was what she wanted, and what he wanted, too. Though the first causes of this passion were gone—

one to dust, one to divinity—she and the man in the darkness were its embodiments and could not be denied each other.

She glanced back towards the house once only, to see that Clem was lingering on the step. She didn't waste time trying to persuade him to go inside, but simply turned back to the shadows.

"Where are you?" she said.

"Here," her lover replied, and stepped from the folds of his legion.

A single strand of luminescent matter came with him, fine enough to have been woven by Oviate spiders, but clotted here and there with beads like pearls, which swelled and dropped from the filaments, running down his arms and face and mottling the ground where he walked. The light flattered him, but she was too hungry for the truth of his face to be deceived, and piercing the glamour with her stare found him much reduced. The shining dandy she'd first met in Klein's plastic garden had gone. Now his eyes were heavy with despair, his mouth drawn down at the corners, his hair awry. Perhaps he'd always looked like this, and he'd simply used some piffling sway to mask the fact, but she doubted it. He was changed on the outside because something had changed within.

Though she stood before him defenseless, he made no move to touch her, but hung back like a penitent in need of invitation before he approached the altar. She liked this new fastidiousness.

"I didn't hurt the angels," he said softly.

"You shouldn't even have touched them."

"It wasn't supposed to happen like this," he said again. "The gek-a-gek were clumsy. They dropped some meat from the roof."

"I saw."

"I was going to wait until the power subsided and come for you in style." He paused, then asked, "Would you have let me take you?"

"Yes."

"I wasn't certain. I was a little afraid you'd reject me, and then I'd become cruel. You're my sanity now. I can't go on without you."

"You went on all those years in Yzordderrex."

"I had you there," he said, "only by a different name."

"And you were still cruel."

"Imagine how much crueler I would have been," he said, as if amazed at the possibility, "if I hadn't had your face to mellow me."

"Is that all I am to you? A face?"

"You know better than that," he said, his voice dropping to a whisper.

"Tell me," she said, inviting his affections.

He glanced back over his shoulder, towards the legion. If he spoke to them she didn't hear it. They simply retreated, cowed by his glance. When they were gone, he put his hands to her face, his little fingers just beneath the line of her jaw, his thumbs laid lightly at the corners of her mouth. Despite the heat that was still rising from the cooked asphalt, his skin was chilly.

"One way or another," he said, "we don't have very long, so I'll keep this simple. There's no future for us now. Maybe there was yesterday, but tonight . . ."

"I thought you were going to build a New Yzordderrex."

"I was. I have the perfect model for it, here." His thumbs went from the corners of her mouth to the middle of her lips and stroked them. "A city made in your image, built in place of these miserable streets."

"But now?"

"We don't have the time, love. My brother's about his work up there, and when he's finished"—he sighed, his voice dropping lower still—"when he's finished—"

"What?" she said. There was something he wanted to share, but he was forbidding himself.

"I hear you went back to Yzordderrex," he said.

She wanted to press him to complete his earlier explanation, but she knew better than to push too hard, so she answered him, knowing his earlier doubts could surface again if she was patient. Yes, she said, she had indeed been to Yzordderrex, and she'd found the palace much changed. This sparked his interest.

"Who's taken it over? Not Rosengarten? No. The Dearthers. That damn priest Athanasius—"

"None of those."

"Who then?"

"Goddesses."

The web of luminescence fluttered around his head, shaken by his distress.

"They were always there," she told him. "Or at least one was, a Goddess called Uma Umagammagi. Have you ever heard of Her?"

"Legends—"

"She was in the Pivot."

"That's impossible," he said. "The Pivot belongs to the Unbeheld. The whole of the Imajica belongs to the Unbeheld."

She'd never heard of a breath of subservience in him before, but she heard it now.

"Does He own us, too?" she asked him.

"We may escape that," he said. "But it'll be hard, love. He's the Father of us all. He expects to be obeyed, even to the very end." Again an aching pause, but this time a request on its heels. "Will you embrace me?" he asked her.

She answered with her arms. His hands slid from her face and through her hair to clasp behind her.

"I used to think it was a godlike thing to build cities," he murmured. "And if I built one fine enough it would stand forever, and so would I. But everything passes away sooner or later, doesn't it?"

She heard in his words a despair that was the inverse of Gentle's visionary zeal, as though in the time she'd known them they'd exchanged their lives. Gentle the faithless lover had become a dealer in heavens, while Sartori, the sometime maker of hells, was here holding out love as his last salvation.

"What is God's work," she asked him quietly, "if it's not the building of cities?"

"I don't know," he said.

"Well . . . maybe it's none of our business," she said, pretending a lover's indifference to matters of moment. "We'll forget about the Unbeheld. We've got each other. We've got the child. We can be together for as long as we like."

There was enough truth in these sentiments, enough hope in her that this vision might come true, that using it for manipulative purpose sickened her. But having turned her back on the house and all it contained, she could hear in her lover's whispers echoes of the same doubts that had made her an outcast, and if she had to use the feelings between them as a way to finally solve the enigma, so be it. Her queasiness at her deceit wasn't soothed by its effectiveness. When Sartori let out a tiny sob, as he did now, she wanted to confess her motives. But she fought the desire and let him suffer, hoping that he'd finally purge himself of all he knew, even though she suspected he'd never dared even *shape* these thoughts before, much less speak them.

"There'll be no child," he said, "no being together."

"Why not?" she said, still striving to keep her tone optimistic. "We can leave now, if you want. We can go anywhere and hide away."

"There are no hiding places left," he said.

"We'll find one."

"No. There are none."

He drew away from her. She was glad of his tears. They were a veil between his gaze and her duplicity.

"I told the Reconciler I was my own destroyer," he said. "I said I saw my works, and I conspired against them. But then I asked myself, Whose eyes am I seeing with? And you know what the answer is? My Father's eyes, Judith. My Father's eyes. . . ."

Of all the voices to return into Jude's head as he spoke, it was Clara Leash's she heard. Man the destroyer, willfully undoing the world. And what more perfect manhood was there than the God of the First Dominion?

"If I see my works with these eyes and want to destroy them," Sartori murmured, "what does He see? What does He want?"

"Reconciliation," she said.

"Yes. But why? It's not a beginning, Judith. It's the end. When the Imajica's whole, He'll turn it into a wasteland."

She drew away from him. "How do you know?"

"I think I've always known."

"And you said nothing? All your talk about the future—"

"I didn't dare admit it to myself. I didn't want to believe I was anything but my own man. You understand that. I've seen you fight to see with your own eyes. I did the same. I couldn't admit He had any part of me, until now."

"Why now?"

"Because I see you with *my* eyes. I love you with *my* heart. I love you, Judith, and that means I'm free of Him. I can admit . . . what . . . I . . . *know*."

He dissolved in grief, but his hands kept hold of her as he shook.

"There's nowhere to hide, love," he said. "We've got a few minutes together, you and I: a few sweet moments. Then it's over."

She heard everything he said, but her thoughts were as much with what was going on in the house behind her. Despite all she'd heard from Uma Umagammagi, despite the zeal of the Maestro, despite all the calamities that would come with her interference, the Reconciliation had to be halted.

"We can still stop Him," she said to Sartori.

"It's too late," he replied. "Let Him have His victory. We can defy Him a better way. A purer way."

"How?"

"We can die together."

"That's not defying Him. It's defeat."

"I don't want to live with His presence in me. I want to lie down with you and die. It won't hurt, love."

He opened his jacket. There were two blades at his belt. They glittered by the light of the floating threads, but his eyes glittered more dangerously still. His tears had dried. He looked almost happy.

"It's the only way," he said.

"I can't."

"If you love me you will."

She drew her arm from his grasp. "I want to live," she said, backing away from him.

"Don't desert me," he replied. There was warning in his voice as well as appeal. "Don't leave me to my Father. *Please.* If you love me don't leave me to my Father. Judith!"

He drew the knives out of his belt and came after her, offering the handle of one as he came, like a merchant selling suicide. She swiped at the proffered blade, and it went from his grasp. As it flew she turned, hoping to the Goddess that Clem had left the door open. He had; and lit every candle he could find, to judge by the spill of light onto the step. She picked up her pace, hearing Sartori's voice behind her as she went. He only spoke her name, but the threat in it was unmistakable. She didn't reply—her flight from him was answer enough—but when she reached the pavement she glanced back at him. He was picking up the dropped knife, and rising.

Again he said, "*Judith—*"

But this time it was a warning of a different order. Off to her left a motion drew her glance. One of the gek-a-gek, the sharpener, was coming at her, its flat head now wide as a manhole and toothed to its gut.

Sartori yelled an order, but the thing was rogue and came on at her unchecked. She raced for the step, and as she did so heard a whoop from the door. Monday was there, naked but for his grimy underwear: in his hand, a homemade bludgeon, which he swung around his head like a man possessed. She ducked beneath its sweep as she made the step. Clem was behind him, ready to haul her in, but she turned to call Monday to retreat, in time to see the gek-a-gek mounting the step in pursuit. Her defender didn't retreat, but brought the weapon down in a whistling arc, striking the gek-a-gek's gaping head. The bludgeon shattered, but the blow sheared off one of the beast's bulbous eyes. Though wounded, its mass was still sufficient to carry it forward, and one of its freshly honed claws found Monday's back as he turned to dodge it. The boy shrieked and might have fallen beneath the Oviate's attack if Clem hadn't grabbed his arms and all but thrown him into the house.

The half-blinded beast was a yard from Jude's feet, its head thrown back as it raged in pain. But it wasn't the maw she was watching. It was Sartori. He was once again walking towards the house, a knife in each hand, and a gek-a-gek at each heel. His eyes were fixed on her. They shone with sorrow.

"*In!*" Clem yelled, and she relinquished both sight and step to pitch herself back over the threshold.

The one-eyed Oviate came after her as she did so, but Clem was fast. The heavy door swung closed, and Hoi-Polloi was there to fling the bolts across, leaving the wounded beast and its still more wounded master out in the darkness.

On the floor above, Gentle heard nothing of this. He had finally passed, via the circle's good offices, through the In Ovo and into what Pie had called the Mansion of the Nexus, the Ana, where he

and the other Maestros would undertake the penultimate phase
of the working. The conventional life of the senses was redundant
in this place, and for Gentle being here was like a dream in which
he was knowing but unknown, potent but unfixed. He didn't mourn
the body he'd left in Gamut Street. If he never inhabited it again
it would be no loss, he thought. He had a far finer condition here,
like a figure in some exquisite equation that could neither be removed nor reduced but was all it had to be—no more, no less—to
change the sum of things.

He knew the others were with him, and though he had no sight
to see them with, his mind's eye had never owned so vast a palette
as it did now, nor had his invention ever been finer. There was no
need for cribbing and forgery here. He had earned with his
metempsychosis access to a visionary grasp he'd never dreamt of
possessing, and his imagination brimmed with correlatives for the
company he kept.

He invented Tick Raw dressed in the motley he'd first seen the
man wear in Vanaeph, but fashioned now from the wonders of the
Fourth. A suit of mountains, dusted in Jokalaylaurian snow; a shirt
of Patashoqua, belted by its walls; a shimmering halo of green and
gold, casting its light down on a face as busy as the highway.
Scopique was a less gaudy sight, the gray dust of the Kwem billowing around him like a shredded coat, its particles etching the
glories of the Third in its folds. The Cradle was there. So were the
temples at L'Himby; so was the Lenten Way. There was even a
glimpse of the railroad track, the smoke of its locomotive rising to
add its murk to the storm.

Then Athanasius, dressed in a clout of dirty cloth and carrying
in his bleeding hands a perfect representation of Yzordderrex,
from the causeway to the desert, from the harbor to Ipse. The
ocean ran from his wounded flank, and the crown of thorns he wore
was blossoming, throwing petals of rainbow light down upon all he
bore. Finally, there was Chicka Jackeen, here in lightning, the way
he'd looked two hundred midsummers before. He'd been weeping,
then, and waxen with fright. But now the storm was his possession,
not his scourge, and the arcs of fire that leapt between his fingers
were a geometry, austere and beautiful, that solved the mystery of
the First, and in unveiling it made perfection the new enigma.

Inventing them this way, Gentle wondered if they in turn were
inventing him, or whether his painter's hunger to *see* was an irrel-
evancy to them, and what they imagined, knowing he was with
them, was a body subtler than any sight. It would be better that way,
he supposed, and with time he'd learn to rise out of his literalisms,
just as he'd shrug off the self that wore his name. He had no at-
tachment to this Gentle left, nor to the tale that hung behind. It

was tragedy, that self; any self. It was a marriage made with loss, and had he not wanted one last glimpse of Pie 'oh' pah, he might have prayed that his reward for Reconciliation would be this state in perpetuity.

He knew that wasn't plausible, of course. The Ana's sanctuary existed for only a brief time, and while it did so it had more ecumenical business than nurturing a single soul. The Maestros had served their purpose in bringing the Dominions into this sacred space, and would soon be redundant. They would return to their circles, leaving Dominion to meld with Dominion, and in so doing drive the In Ovo back like a malignant sea. What would happen then was a matter of conjecture. He doubted there'd be an instant of revelation—all the nations of the Fifth waking to their unfettered state in the same moment. It would most likely be slow, the work of years. Rumors at first, that bridges wreathed in fogs could be found by those eager enough to look. Then the rumors becoming certainties, and the bridges becoming causeways, and the fogs great clouds, until, in a generation or two, children were born who knew without being taught that the species had five Dominions to explore and would one day discover its own Godhood in its wanderings. But the time it took to reach that blessed day was unimportant. The moment the first bridge, however small, was forged, the Imajica was whole; and at that moment every soul in the Dominion, from cradle to deathbed, would be healed in some tiny part and take their next breath lighter for the fact.

Jude waited in the hall long enough to be sure that Monday wasn't dead; then she headed towards the stairs. The currents which had induced such discomforts were no longer circling in the system of the house: sure sign that some new phase of the working— possibly its last—was under way above. Clem joined her at the bottom of the stairs, armed with another two of Monday's homemade bludgeons.

"How many of these creatures are there out there?" he demanded.

"Maybe half a dozen."

"You'll have to watch the back door then," he said, thrusting one of the weapons at Jude.

"You use it," she said, pressing past him. "Keep them out for as long as you can."

"Where are you going?"

"To stop Gentle."

"Stop him? In God's name, why?"

"Because Dowd was right. If he completes the Reconciliation we're dead."

He cast the bludgeons aside and took hold of her. "No, Judy," he said. "You know I can't let you do that."

It wasn't just Clem speaking, but Tay as well: two voices and a single utterance. It was more distressing than anything she'd heard or seen outside, to have this command issue from a face she loved. But she kept her calm.

"Let go of me," she said, reaching for the banister to haul herself up the stairs.

"He's twisted your mind, Judy," the angels said. "You don't know what you're doing."

"I know damn well," she said, and fought to wrest herself free.

But Clem's arms, despite their blistering, were unyielding. She looked for some help from Monday, but he and Hoi-Polloi had their backs to the door, against which the gek-a-gek were beating their massive limbs. Stout as the timbers were, they'd splinter soon. She had to get to Gentle before the beasts got in, or it was all over.

And then, above the din of assault, came a voice she'd only heard raised once before.

"Let her go."

Celestine had emerged from her bedroom, draped in a sheet. The candlelight shook all around her, but she was steady, her gaze mesmeric. The angels looked around at her, Clem's hands still holding Jude fast.

"She wants to—"

"I know what she wants to do," Celestine said. "If you're our guardians, guard us now. *Let her go.*"

Jude felt doubt loosen the hold on her. She didn't give the angels time to change their mind, but dragged herself free and started up the stairs again. Halfway up, she heard a shout and glanced down to see both Hoi-Polloi and Monday thrown forward as the door's middle panel broke and a prodigious limb reached through to snatch at the air.

"Go on!" Celestine yelled up to her, and Jude returned to her ascent as the woman stepped onto the bottom stair to guard the way.

Though there was far less light above than below, the details of the physical world became more insistent as she climbed. The flight beneath her bare feet was suddenly a wonderland of grains and knotholes, its geography entrancing. Nor was it simply her sight that filled to brimming. The banister beneath her hand was more alluring than silk; the scent of sap and the taste of dust begged to be sniffed and savored. Defying these distractions, she fixed her attention on the door ahead, holding her breath and removing her hand from the banister to minimize the sources of sensation. Even so, she was assailed. The creaks of the stairs were rich enough to be orchestrated. The shadows around the door had nuances to parade and called for her devotion. But she had a rod at her back: the commotion from below. It was getting louder all the time, and now—cutting through the shouts and roars—came the sound of Sartori's voice.

"Where are you going, love?" he asked her. "You can't leave me. I won't let you. Look! Love? *Look!* I've brought the knives."

She didn't turn to see, but closed her eyes and stopped her ears with her hands, stumbling up the rest of the stairs blind and deaf. Only when her toes were no longer stubbed, and she knew she was at the top, did she dare the sight again. The seductions began again, instantly. Every nick in every nail of the door said, *Stop and study me.* The dust rising around her was a constellation she could have lost herself in forever. She pitched herself through it, with her gaze glued to the door handle, and clasped it so hard the discomfort canceled the beguilings long enough for her to turn it and throw the door open. Behind her Sartori was calling again, but this time his voice was slurred, as though he was distracted by profusion.

In front of her was his mirror image, naked at the center of the stones. He sat in the universal posture of the meditator: legs crossed, eyes closed, hands laid palms out in his lap to catch whatever blessings were bestowed. Though there was much in the room to call her attention—mantelpiece, window, boards, and rafters—their sum of enticements, vast as it was, could not compete with the glory of human nakedness, and *this* nakedness, that she'd loved and lain beside, more than any other. Neither the blandishments of the walls—their stained plaster like a map of some unknown country—nor the persuasions of the crushed leaves at the sill could distract her now. Her senses were fixed on the Reconciler, and she crossed the room to him in a few short strides, calling his name as she went.

He didn't move. Wherever his mind wandered, it was too far from this place—or rather, this place was too small a part of his arena—for him to be claimed by any voices here, however desperate. She halted at the edge of the circle. Though there was nothing to suggest that what lay inside was in flux, she'd seen the harm done to both Dowd and his voider when the bounds had been injudiciously breached. From down below she heard Celestine raise a cry of warning. There was no time for equivocation. What the circle would do it would do, and she'd have to take the consequences.

Steeling herself, she stepped over the perimeter. Instantly, the myriad discomforts that attended passage afflicted her—itches, pangs, and spasms—and for a moment she thought the circle intended to dispatch her across the In Ovo. But the work it was about had overruled such functions, and the pains simply mounted and mounted, driving her to her knees in front of Gentle. Tears spilled from her knitted lids, and the ripest curses from her lips. The circle hadn't killed her, but another minute of its persecutions and it might. She had to be quick.

She forced open her streaming eyes and set her gaze on Gentle. Shouts hadn't roused him, nor had curses, so she didn't waste her breath with more. Instead she seized his shoulders and began to shake him. His muscles were lax, and he lolled in her grasp, but either her touch or the fact of her trespass in this charmed circle won a response. He gasped as though he'd been drawn up from some airless deep.

Now she began to talk.

"Gentle? Gentle! Open your eyes! Gentle. I said, *Open your fucking eyes!*"

She was causing him pain, she knew. The tempo and volume of his gasps increased, and his face, which had been beatifically placid, was knotted with frowns and grimaces. She liked the sight. He'd been so smug in his messianic mode. Now there had to be an end to that complacency, and if it hurt a little it was his own damn fault for being too much his Father's child.

"Can you hear me?" she yelled at him. "You've got to stop the working. Gentle! You've got to stop it!"

His eyes started to flicker open.

"Good! Good!" she said, talking at his face like a schoolmarm trying to coax a delinquent pupil.

"You can do it! You can open your eyes. Go on! *Do it!* If you won't, I'll do it for you, I'm warning you!"

She was as good as her word, lifting her right hand to his left eye and thumbing back the lid. His eyeball was rolled back into its socket. Wherever he was, it was still a long way off, and she wasn't sure her body had the strength to resist its harrowment while she coaxed him home.

Then, from the landing behind her, Sartori's voice.

"It's too late, love," he said. "Can't you feel it? It's too late."

She didn't need to look back at him. She could picture him well enough, with the knives in his hands and elegy on his face. Nor did she reply. She needed every last ounce of will and wit to stir the man in front of her.

And then inspiration! Her hand went from his face to his groin, from his eyelid to his testicles. Surely there was enough of the old Gentle left in the Reconciler to value his manhood. The flesh of his scrotum was loose in the warmth of the room. His balls were heavy in her hand, heavy and vulnerable. She held them hard.

"Open your eyes," she said, "or so help me I'm going to hurt you."

He remained impassive. She tightened her grip.

"Wake up," she said.

Still nothing. She squeezed harder, then twisted.

"Wake up!"

His breath quickened. She twisted again, and his eyes suddenly opened, his gasps becoming a yell which didn't stop until there was no breath left in his lungs to loose it on. As he inhaled his arms rose to take hold of Jude at the neck. She lost her grip on his balls, but it didn't matter. He was awake and raging. He started to rise and, as he did so, pitched her out of the circle. She landed clumsily, but began harassing him before she'd even raised her head.

"You've got to stop the working!"

"Crazy . . . woman . . ." he growled.

"I mean it! You've got to stop the working! It's all a plot!" She hauled herself up. "Dowd was right, Gentle! It's got to be stopped."

"You're not going to spoil it now," he said. "You're too late."

"Find a way!" she said. "There's got to be a way!"

"If you come near me again I'll kill you," he warned. He scanned the circle, to be certain it was still intact. It was. "Where's Clem?" he yelled. *"Clem?"*

Only now did he look beyond Judith to the door, and beyond the door to the shadowy figure on the landing. His frown deepened into a scowl of revulsion, and she knew any hope of persuading him was lost. He saw conspiracy here.

"There, love," said Sartori. "Didn't I tell you it was too late?"

The two gek-a-gek fawned at his feet. The knives gleamed in his fists. This time he didn't offer the handle of either one. He'd come to take her life if she refused to take her own.

"Dearest one," he said, "it's over."

He took a step and crossed the threshold.

"We can do it here," he said, looking down at her, "where we were made. What better place?"

She didn't need to look back at Gentle to know he was hearing this. Was there some sliver of hope in that fact? Some persuasion that might drop from Sartori's lips and move Gentle where hers had failed?

"I'm going to have to do it for us both, love," he said. "You're too weak. You can't see clearly."

"I don't . . . want . . . to die," she said.

"You don't have any choice," he said. "It's either by the Father or the Son. That's all. Father or Son."

Behind her, she heard Gentle murmur two syllables.

"Oh, Pie."

Then Sartori took a second step, out of the shadow into the candlelight. When he did, the obsessive scrutiny of the room fixed him in every wretched morsel. His eyes were wet with despair, his lips so dry they were dusty. His skull gleamed through his pallid skin,

and his teeth, in their array, made a fatal smile. He was Death, in
every detail. And if *she* recognized that fact—she who loved him—
then so, surely, did Gentle.

He took a third step toward her and raised the knives above his
head. She didn't look away, but turned her face up towards him,
daring him to spoil with his blades what he'd caressed with his fingers only minutes before.

"I would have died for you," he murmured. The blades were at
the top of their gleaming arc, ready to fall. "Why wouldn't you die
for me?"

He didn't wait for an answer, even if she'd had one to give, but
let the knives descend. As they came for her eyes she looked away,
but before they caught her cheek and neck the Reconciler howled
behind her, and the whole room shook. She was thrown from her
knees, Sartori's blades missing her by inches. The candles on the
mantelpiece guttered and went out, but there were other lights to
take their place. The stones of the circle were flickering like tiny
bonfires flattened by a high wind, flecks of their brightness racing
from them to strike the walls. At the circle's edge stood Gentle. In
his hand, the reason for this turmoil. He'd picked up one of the
stones, arming himself and breaking the circle in the same moment.
He clearly knew the gravity of his deed. There was grief on his face,
so profound it seemed to have incapacitated him. Having raised
the stone he was now motionless, as if his will to undo the working had already lost momentum.

She got to her feet, though the room was shaking more violently
than ever. The boards felt solid enough beneath her, but they'd
darkened to near invisibility. She could see only the nails that kept
them in place; the rest, despite the light from the stones, was pitch
black, and as she started towards the circle she seemed to be treading a void.

There was a noise accompanying every tremor now: a mingling
of tortured wood and cracking plaster, all underscored by a guttural boiling, the source of which she didn't comprehend until she
reached the edge of the circle. The darkness beneath them was
indeed a void—the In Ovo, opened by Gentle's breaking of the
circle—and in it, already woken by Sartori's dabblings, the prisoners that connived and suppurated there, rising at the scent of
escape.

At the door, the gek-a-gek set up a clamor of anticipation, sensing the release of their fellows. But for all their power they'd have
few of the spoils in the coming massacre. There were forms appearing below that made them look kittenish: entities of such
elaboration neither Jude's eyes nor wits could encompass them.
The sight terrified her, but if this was the only way to halt the

Reconciliation, then so be it. History would repeat itself, and the Maestro be twice damned.

He'd seen the Oviates' ascent as clearly as she and was frozen by the sight. Determined to prevent him from reestablishing the status quo at all costs, she reached to snatch the stone from his hand, so as to pitch it through the window. But before her fingers could grasp it he looked up at her. The anguish went from his face, and rage replaced it.

"Throw the stone away!" she yelled.

His eyes weren't on her, however. They were on a sight at her shoulder. Sartori! She threw herself aside as the knives came down and, clutching the mantelpiece, turned back to see the brothers face to face, one armed with blades, the other with the stone.

Sartori's glance had gone to Jude as she leapt, and before he could return it to his enemy Gentle brought the stone down with a two-handed blow, striking sparks from one of the blades as he dashed it from his brother's fingers. While the advantage was his, Gentle went after the second blade, but Sartori had it out of range before the stone could connect, so Gentle swung at the empty hand, the cracking of his brother's bones audible through the din of Oviates and boards and cracking walls.

Sartori made a pitiful yell and raised his fractured hand in front of his brother, as if to win remorse for the hurt. But as Gentle's eyes went to Sartori's broken hand, the other, whole and sharp, came at his flank. He glimpsed the blade and half turned to avoid it, but it found his arm, opening it to the bone from wrist to elbow. He dropped the stone, a rain of blood coming after, and as his palm went up to stem the flow Sartori entered the circle, slashing back and forth as he came.

Defenseless, Gentle retreated before the blade and, arching back to avoid the cuts, lost his footing and went down beneath his attacker. One stab would have finished him there and then. But Sartori wanted intimacy. He straddled his brother's body and squatted down upon it, slashing at Gentle's arms as he attempted to ward off the coup de grace.

Jude scoured the unsolid boards for the fallen knife, her gaze distracted by the malignant forms that were everywhere turning their faces to freedom. The blade, if she could find it, would be of no use against them, but it might still dispatch Sartori. He'd planned to take his own life with one of these knives. She could still turn it to such work, if she could only find it.

But before she could do so, she heard a sob from the circle and, glancing back, saw Gentle sprawled beneath his brother's weight, horrendously wounded, his chest sliced open, his jaw, cheeks, and temples slashed, his hands and arms crisscrossed with cuts. The sob wasn't his, but Sartori's. He'd raised the knife and was uttering this last cry before he plunged the blade into his brother's heart.

His grief was premature. As the knife came down, Gentle found the strength to thrash one final time, and instead of finding his heart the blade entered his upper chest below his clavicle. Slickened, the handle slipped through Sartori's fingers. But he had no need to reclaim it. Gentle's rally was over as suddenly as it had begun. His body uncurled, its spasms ceased, and he lay still.

Sartori rose from his seat on his brother's belly and looked down at the body for a time, then turned to survey the spectacle of the void. Though the Oviates were close to the surface now, he didn't hurry to act or retreat, but surveyed the whole panorama at the center of which he stood, his eyes finally coming to rest on Jude.

"Oh, love," he said softly. "Look what you've done. You've given me to my Heavenly Father."

Then he stooped and reached out of the circle to take hold of the stone that Gentle had removed and, with the finesse of a painter laying down a final stroke, put it back in place.

The status quo wasn't instantly restored. The forms below continued to rise, seething with frustration as they sensed that their route into the Fifth had been sealed. The fire in the stone began to go out, but before their last gutterings Sartori murmured an order to the gek-a-gek and they sloped from their places at the door, their flat heads skimming the ground. Jude thought at first they were coming for her, but it was Gentle they'd been ordered to collect. They divided around the circle and reached over its perimeter, taking hold of the body almost tenderly and lifting it out of their Maestro's way.

"Down the stairs," he told them, and they retreated to the door with their burden, leaving the circle in Sartori's sole possession.

A terrible calm had descended. The last glimpses of the In Ovo had disappeared; the light in the stones was all but gone. In the gathering darkness she saw Sartori find his place at the center of the circle and sit.

"Don't do this," she murmured to him.

He raised his head and made a little grunt, as though he was surprised she was still in the room.

"It's already done," he said. "All I have to do is hold the circle till midnight."

She heard a moan from below, as Clem saw what the Oviates had brought to the top of the stairs. Then came the *thump, thump, thump* as the body was thrown down the flight. There could only be seconds before they came back for her, seconds to coax him from the circle. She knew only one way, and if it failed there could be no further appeal.

"I love you," she said.

It was too dark to see him, but she felt his eyes.

"I know," he said, without feeling. "But my Heavenly Father will love me more. It's in His hands now."

She heard the Oviates moving behind her, their breaths chilly on her neck.

"I don't ever want to see you again," Sartori said.

"Please call them off," she begged him, remembering the way Clem had been apprehended by these beasts, his arms half swallowed.

"Leave of your volition, and they won't touch you," he said. "I am about my Father's business."

"He doesn't love you. . . ."

"Leave."

"He's incapable. . . ."

"*Leave.*"

She got to her feet. There was nothing left to say or do. As she turned her back on the circle the Oviates pressed their cold flanks against her legs and kept her trapped between them until she reached the threshold, to be certain she made no last attempt on their summoner's life. Then she was allowed to go unescorted onto the landing. Clem was halfway up the stairs, bludgeon in hand, but she instructed him to stay where he was, fearful that the gek-a-gek would claw him to shreds if he climbed another step.

The door to the Meditation Room slammed behind her, and she glanced back to confirm what she'd already guessed: that the Oviates had followed her out and were now standing guard at the threshold. Still nervous that they'd land some last blow, she crossed to the top of the flight as though she were walking on eggs and only picked up her speed once she was on the stairs.

There was light below, but the scene it illuminated was as grim as anything above. Gentle was lying at the bottom of the stairs, his head laid on Celestine's lap. The sheet she'd worn had fallen from her shoulders, and her breasts were bare, bloodied where she'd held her son's face to her skin.

"Is he dead?" Jude murmured to Clem.

He shook his head. "He's holding on."

She didn't have to ask what for. The front door was open, hanging half demolished from its hinges, and through it she could hear the first stroke of midnight from a distant steeple.

"The circle's complete," she said.

"What circle?" Clem asked her.

She didn't reply. What did it matter now? But Celestine had looked up from her meditation on Gentle's face, and the same question was in her eyes as on Clem's lips, so Jude answered them as plainly as she could.

"The Imajica's a circle," she said.

"How do you know?" Clem asked.

"The Goddesses told me."

She was almost at the bottom of the stairs, and now that she was closer to mother and son she could see that Gentle was literally holding on to life, clutching at Celestine's arm and staring up into her face. Only when Jude sank down onto the bottom stair did Gentle's eyes go to her.

"I . . . never knew," he said.

"I know," she replied, thinking he was speaking of Hapexamendios' plot. "I didn't want to believe it either."

Gentle shook his head. "I mean the circle," he said. "I never knew it was a circle. . . ."

"It was the Goddesses' secret," Jude said.

Now Celestine spoke, her voice as soft as the flames that lit her lips. "Doesn't Hapexamendios know?"

Jude shook her head.

"So whatever fire he sends," Celestine murmured, "will burn its way around the circle."

Jude studied her face, knowing there was some profit in this knowledge but too exhausted to make sense of it. Celestine looked down at Gentle's face.

"Child?" she said.

"Yes, Mama."

"Go to Him," she said. "Take your spirit into the First and find your Father."

The effort of breathing seemed almost too much for Gentle, never mind a journey. But what his body was incapable of, maybe his spirit could achieve. He lifted his fingers towards his mother's face. She caught hold of them.

"What are you going to do?" Gentle said.

"Call His fire," Celestine said.

Jude looked towards Clem to see if this exchange made any more sense to him than it did to her, but he looked completely perplexed. What was the use of inviting death when it was going to come anyway, and all too quickly?

"Delay Him," Celestine was telling Gentle. "Go to Him as a loving son, and hold His attention for as long as you can. Flatter Him. Tell Him how much you want to see His face. Can you do that for me?"

"Of course, Mama."

"Good."

Content that her child would do as he was charged, Celestine

laid Gentle's hand back upon his chest and slid her knees out from
beneath his head, lowering it tenderly to the boards. She had one
last instruction for him.

"When you go into the First, go through the Dominions. He
mustn't know that there's another way, do you understand?"

"Yes, Mama."

"And when you get there, child, listen for the voice. It's in the
ground. You'll hear it, if you listen carefully. It says—"

"Nisi Nirvana."

"That's right."

"I remember," Gentle said. "Nisi Nirvana."

As if the name were a blessing and would protect him as he went
on his way, he closed his eyes and took his leave.

Celestine didn't indulge in sentiment but rose, pulling the sheet
up around her as she crossed to the bottom of the stairs. "Now I
have to speak to Sartori."

"That's going to be difficult," Jude said. "The door's locked and
guarded."

"He's my son," Celestine replied, looking up the flight. "He'll
open it for me."

And so saying, she ascended.

24

I

Gentle's spirit went from the house, thinking not of the Father that
awaited him in the First Dominion but of the mother he was leaving behind. In the hours since his return from the Tabula Rasa's
tower they'd shared all too brief a time together. He'd knelt beside her bed for a few minutes while she told the story of Nisi Nirvana. He'd held on to her in the Goddesses' rain, ashamed of the
desire he felt but unable to deny it. And finally, moments ago, he'd
lain in her arms while the blood seeped out of him. Child; lover;
cadaver. There was the arc of a little life there, and they'd have to
be content with it.

He didn't entirely comprehend her purpose in sending him from
her, but he was too confounded to do anything but obey. She had
her reasons, and he had to trust them, now that the work he'd labored to achieve had soured. That too he didn't entirely comprehend. It had happened too fast. One moment he'd been so remote
from his body he was almost ready to forget it entirely; the next
he was back in the Meditation Room, with Jude's grip earning his

screams, and his brother mounting the stairs behind her, his knives gleaming. He'd known then, seeing death in his brother's face, why the mystif had torn itself to shreds in order to make him seek Sartori out. Their Father was there in that face, in that despairing certainty, and had been all along, no doubt. But he'd never seen it. All he'd ever seen was his own beauty, twisted out of true, and told himself how fine it was to be Heaven to his other's Hell. What a mockery that was! He'd been his Father's dupe—His agent, His fool—and he might never have realized it if Jude hadn't dragged him raw from the Ana and showed him in terrible particulars the destroyer in the mirror.

But the recognition had come so late, and he was so ill equipped to undo the damage he'd done. He could only hope that his mother understood better than he where the little hope left to them lay. In pursuit of it, he'd be *her* agent now and go into the First to do whatever he could at her behest.

He went the long way round, as she'd instructed, his path taking him back over the territories he'd traveled when he'd sought out the Synod, and though he longed to swoop out of the air and pass the time of a new day with the others, he knew he couldn't linger.

He glimpsed them as he went, however, and saw that they'd survived the last hectic minutes in the Ana and were back in their Dominions, beaming with their triumph. On the Mount of Lipper Bayak, Tick Raw was howling to the heavens like a lunatic, waking every sleeper in Vanaeph and stirring the guards in the watchtowers of Patashoqua. In the Kwem, Scopique was clambering up the slope of the Pivot pit where he'd sat to do his part, tears of joy in his eyes as he turned them skyward. In Yzordderrex, Athanasius was on his knees in the street outside the Eurhetemec Kesparate, bathing his hands in a spring that was leaping up at his wounded face like a dog that wanted to lick him well. And on the borders of the First, where Gentle's spirit slowed, Chicka Jackeen was watching the Erasure, waiting for the blank wall to dissolve and give him a glimpse of Hapexamendios' Dominion.

His gaze left the sight, however, when he felt Gentle's presence. "Maestro?" he said.

More than any of the others, Gentle wanted to share something of what was afoot with Jackeen, but he dared not. Any exchange this close to the Erasure might be monitored by the God behind it, and he knew he'd not be able to converse with this man, who'd shown him such devotion, without offering some word of warning, so he didn't tempt himself. Instead he commanded his spirit on, hearing Jackeen call his name again as he went. But before the appeal could come a third time he passed through the Erasure and into the Dominion beyond. In the blind moments before the First appeared, his mother's voice echoed in his head.

"She went into a city of iniquities," he heard her saying, *"where no ghost was holy, and no flesh was whole."*

Then the Erasure was behind him, and he was hovering on the perimeters of the City of God.

No wonder his brother had been an architect, he thought. Here was enough inspiration for a nation of prodigies, a labor of ages, raised by a power for whom an age was the measure of a breath. Its majesty spread in every direction but the one behind, the streets wider than the Patashoquan Highway and so straight they only disappeared at their vanishing point, the buildings so monumental the sky was barely visible between their eaves. But whatever suns or satellites hung in the heavens of this Dominion, the city had no need of their illumination. Cords of light ran through the paving stones, and through the bricks and slabs of the great houses, their ubiquity ensuring that all but the most vapid shadows were banished from the streets and plazas.

He moved slowly at first, expecting soon to encounter one of the city's inhabitants, but after passing over half a dozen intersections and finding no soul on the streets, he began to pick up his speed, slowing only when he glimpsed some sign of life behind the façades. He wasn't nimble enough to catch a face, nor was he so presumptuous as to enter uninvited, but he several times saw curtains moving, as though some shy but curious citizen was retiring from the sill before he could return the scrutiny. Nor was this the only sign of such presences. Carpets left hanging over balustrades still shook, as if their beaters had just retired from their patios; vines dropped their leaves down as fruit gatherers fled for the safety of their rooms.

It seemed that however fast he traveled—and he was moving faster than any vehicle—he couldn't overtake the rumor that drove the populace into hiding. They left nothing behind: no pet, no child, no scrap of litter, no stroke of graffiti. Each was a model citizen and kept his or her life out of sight behind the drapes and the closed doors.

Such emptiness in a metropolis so clearly built to teem might have seemed melancholy had it not been for the structures themselves, which were built of materials so diverse in texture and color, and were lent such vitality by the light that ran in them, that, even though they were deserted, the streets and plazas had a life of their own. The builders had banished gray and brown from their palette and in its place had found slate, stone, paving, and tiles of every conceivable hue and nuance, mingling their colors with an audacity no architect of the Fifth would have dared. Street after street presented a spectacle of glorious color: façades of lilac and amber, colonnades of brilliant purples, squares laid out in ocher and blue. And everywhere, amid the riot, scarlet of eye-pricking intensity; and a white as perfect; and here and there, used more sparingly still, flicks and snippets of black: a tile, a brick, a seam in a slab.

But even such beauty could pall, and after a thousand such streets had slipped by—all as heroically built, all as lushly colored—the sheer excess of it became sickening, and Gentle was glad of the lightning that he saw erupt from one of the nearby streets, its brilliance sufficient to bleach the color from the façades for a flickering time. In search of its source, he redirected himself and came into a square, at the center of which stood a solitary figure, a Nullianac, its head thrown back as it unleashed its silent bolts into the barely glimpsed sky. Its power was many orders of magnitude greater than anything Gentle had witnessed from its like before. It, and presumably its brothers, had a piece of the God's power between the palms of its face, and its capacity for destruction was now stupendous.

Sensing the approach of the wanderer, the creature left off its rehearsals and floated up from the square as it searched for this interloper. Gentle didn't know what harm it could do to him in his present condition. If the Nullianacs were now Hapexamendios' elite, who knew what authority they'd been lent? But there was no profit in retreat. If he didn't seek some direction, he might wander here forever and never find his Father.

The Nullianac was naked, but there was neither sensuality nor vulnerability in that state. Its flesh was almost as bright as its fire, its form without visible means of procreation or evacuation: without hair, without nipples, without navel. It turned and turned and turned again, looking for the entity whose nearness it sensed, but perhaps the new scale of its destructive powers had made it insensitive, because it failed to find Gentle until his spirit hovered a few yards away.

"Are you looking for me?" he said.

It found him now. Arcs of energy played back and forth between the palms of its head, and out of their cracklings the creature's unmelodious voice emerged.

"Maestro," it said.

"You know who I am?"

"Of course," it said. "Of course."

Its head wove like that of a mesmerized snake as it drew closer to Gentle.

"Why are you here?" it said.

"To see my Father."

"Ah."

"I came here to honor Him."

"So do we all."

"I'm sure. Can you take me to Him?"

"He's everywhere," the Nullianac said. "This is His city, and He's in its every mote."

"So if I speak to the ground I speak to Him, do I?"

The Nullianac mused on this for a few moments. "Not the ground," it said. "Don't speak to the ground."

"Then what? The walls? The sky? *You?* Is my Father in you?"

The arcs in the Nullianac's head grew more excitable. "No," it said. "I wouldn't presume—"

"Then will you take me to where I *can* do Him devotion? There isn't much time."

It was this remark more than any other which gained the Nullianac's compliance. It nodded its death-laden head.

"I'll take you," it said, and rose a little higher, turning from Gentle as it did so. "But as you say, we must be swift. His business cannot wait long."

2

Though Jude had been loath to let Celestine climb the stairs above, knowing as she did what lay at the top, she also knew that her presence would only spoil what little chance the woman had of gaining access to the Meditation Room, so she reluctantly stayed below, listening hard—as did they all—for some clue to what was transpiring in the shadows of the landing.

The first sound they heard was the warning growls of the gek-a-gek, followed by Sartori's voice, telling trespassers that their lives would be forfeit if they attempted to enter. Celestine answered him, but in a voice so low the sense of what she said was lost before it reached the bottom of the flight, and as the minutes passed—were they minutes? perhaps only dreadful seconds, waiting for another eruption of violence—Jude could resist the temptation no longer and, snuffing out the candles closest to her, started a slow ascent.

She expected the angels to make some move to stop her, but they were too preoccupied with tending to Gentle's body, and she climbed unhindered by all but her caution. Celestine was still outside the door, she saw, but the Oviates were no longer blocking her way. At the instruction of the man inside they'd shrunk away and were waiting, bellies to the ground, for a cue to do mischief. Jude was now almost halfway up the flight, and she was able to catch fragments of the exchange that was under way between mother and son. It was Sartori's voice she heard first; a wasted whisper.

"It's over, Mama. . . ."

"I know, child," Celestine said. There was conciliation in her tone, not rebuke.

"He's going to kill everything. . . ."

"Yes. I know that too."

"I had to hold the circle for Him . . . it's what He wanted."

"And you had to do what He wanted. I understand that, child. Believe me, I do. I served Him too, remember? It's no great crime."

At these words of forgiveness, the door of the Meditation Room clicked open and slowly swung wide. Jude was too far down the staircase to see more than the rafters, lit either by a candle or the halo of Oviate tissue that had attended on Sartori when he was out in the street. With the door open, his voice was much clearer.

"Will you come in?" he asked Celestine.

"Do you want me to?"

"Yes, Mama. Please. I'd like us to be together when the end comes."

A familiar sentiment, Jude thought. Apparently he didn't much care what breast he laid his sobbing head on, as long as he wasn't left to die alone. Celestine put up no further show of ambivalence but accepted her child's invitation and stepped inside. The door didn't close, nor did the gek-a-gek creep back into place to block it. Celestine was quickly gone from sight, however. Jude was sorely tempted to continue her ascent and watch what unfolded inside, but she was afraid that any further advance would be sensed by the Oviates, so she gingerly sat down on the stairs, halfway between the Maestro at the top and the body at the bottom. There she waited, listening to the silence of the house; of the street; of the world.

In her mind, she shaped a prayer.

Goddess, she thought, *this is Your sister, Judith. There's a fire coming, Goddess. It's almost upon me, and I'm afraid.*

From above, she heard Sartori speak, his voice now so low she could catch none of his words even with the door open. But she heard the tears that they became, and the sound broke her concentration. The thread of her prayer was lost. No matter. She'd said enough to summarize her feelings.

The fire's almost upon me, Goddess. I am afraid.

What was there left to say?

3

The speed at which Gentle and the Nullianac traveled didn't diminish the scale of the city they were passing through: quite the opposite. As the minutes passed, and the streets continued to

flicker by, thousand upon thousand, their buildings all raised from
the same ripely colored stone, all built to obscure the sky, all laid
to the horizon, the magnitude of this labor began to seem not epic
but insane. However alluring its colors were, however satisfying its
geometries and exquisite its details, the city was the work of a collective madness: a compulsive vision that had refused to be placated until it had covered every inch of the Dominion with
monuments to its own relentlessness. Nor was there any sign of any
life on any street, leading Gentle to a suspicion that he finally
voiced, not as a statement but as a question.

"Who lives here?" he said.

"Hapexamendios."

"And who else?"

"It's His city," the Nullianac said.

"Are there no citizens?"

"It's His city."

The answer was plain enough: the place was deserted. The shaking of vines and drapes he'd seen when he'd first arrived had either been caused by his approach or, more likely, been a game of
illusion the empty buildings had devised to while away the centuries.

But at last, after traveling through innumerable streets that
were indistinguishable from each other, there were finally subtle
signs of change in the structures ahead. Their luscious colors were
steadily deepening, the stone so drenched it must soon surely ooze
and run. And there was a new elaboration in the façades, and a perfection in their proportions, that made Gentle think that he and
the Nullianac were approaching the First Cause, the district of
which the streets they'd passed through had been imitations, di-
luted by repetition.

Confirming his suspicion that the journey was nearing its end,
Gentle's guide spoke.

"He knew you'd come," it said. "He sent some of my brothers
to the perimeter to look for you."

"Are there many of you?"

"Many," the Nullianac said. "Minus one." It looked in Gentle's
direction. "But you know this, of course. You killed him."

"He would have killed *me* if I hadn't."

"And wouldn't that have been a proud boast for our tribe," it
said, "to have killed the Son of God?"

It made a laugh from its lightning, though there was more humor
in a death rattle.

"Aren't you afraid?" Gentle asked it.

"Why should I be afraid?"

"Talking this way when my Father may hear you?"

"He needs my service," came the reply. "And I do not need to live." It paused, then said, "Though I would miss burning the Dominions."

Now it was Gentle's turn to ask why.

"Because it's what I was born to do. I've lived too long, waiting for this."

"How long?"

"Many thousands of years, Maestro. Many, many thousands."

It silenced Gentle, to think that he was traveling beside an entity whose span was so much vaster than his own, and anticipated this imminent destruction as its life's reward. How far off was that prize? he wondered. His sense of time was impoverished without the tick of breath and heartbeat to aid it, and he had no clue as to whether he'd vacated his body in Gamut Street two minutes before, or five, or ten. It was in truth academic. With the Dominions reconciled, Hapexamendios could choose His moment, and Gentle's only comfort was the continued presence of his guide, who would be, he suspected, gone from his side at the first call to arms.

As the street ahead grew denser, the Nullianac's speed and height dropped, until they were hovering inches above the ground, the buildings around them grotesquely elaborate now, every fraction of their brick and stonework etched and carved and filigreed. There was no beauty in these intricacies, only obsession. Their surfeit was more morbid than lively, like the ceaseless, witless motion of maggots. And the same decadence had overcome the colors, the delicacy and profusion of which he'd so admired in the suburbs. Their nuances were gone. Every color now competed with scarlet, the mingled show not brightening the air but bruising it. Nor was there light here in the same abundance as there'd been at the outskirts of the city. Though seams of brightness still flickered in the stone, the elaboration that surrounded them devoured their glow and left these depths dismal.

"I can go no farther than this, Reconciler," the Nullianac said. "From here, you go alone."

"Shall I tell my Father who found me?" Gentle said, hoping that the offer might coax a few more tidbits from the creature before he came into Hapexamendios' presence.

"I have no name," the Nullianac replied. "I am my brother and my brother is me."

"I see. That's a pity."

"But you offered me a kindness, Reconciler. Let me offer you one."

"Yes?"

"Name me a place to destroy in your name, and I'll make it my business to do so: a city, a country, whatever."

"Why would I want that?" Gentle said.

"Because you're your Father's son," came the reply. "And what your Father wants, so will you."

Despite all his caution, Gentle couldn't help but give the destroyer a sour look.

"No?" it said.

"No."

"Then we're both without gifts to give," it said and, turning its back, rose and went from Gentle without another word.

He didn't call after it for directions. There was only one way to go now, and that was on, into the heart of the metropolis, choked though it was by gaud and elaboration. He had the power to go at the speed of thought, of course, but he wished to do nothing that might alarm the Unbeheld, so took his spirit into the garish gloom like a pedestrian, wandering between edifices so fraught with ornament they could not be far from collapse.

As the splendors of the suburbs had given way to decadence, so decadence had, in its turn, given way to pathology, a state that drove his sensibilities beyond distaste or antipathy to the borders of panic. That mere excess might squeeze such anguish out of him was revelation in itself. When had he become so rarefied? He, the crass copyist. He, the sybarite who'd never said *enough,* much less *too much.* What had he become? A phantom aesthete driven to terror by the sight of his Father's city.

Of the Architect Himself, there was no sign, and rather than advance into complete darkness Gentle stopped and simply said, "Father?"

Though his voice had very little authority here, it was loud in such utter silence, and must surely have gone to every threshold within the radius of a dozen streets. But if Hapexamendios was in residence behind any of these doors, He made no reply.

Gentle tried again. "Father. I want to see you."

As he spoke he peered down the shadowy street ahead, looking for some sign, however vestigial, of the Unbeheld's whereabouts. There was no murmur, no motion. But his study was rewarded by the slow comprehension that his Father, for all His apparent absence, was in fact here in front of him; and to his left, and to his right, and above his head, and beneath his feet. What were those gleaming folds at the windows, if they weren't skin? What were those arches, if they weren't bone? What was this scarlet pavement, and this light-shot stone, if it wasn't flesh? There was pith and marrow here. There was tooth and lash and nail. The Nullianac hadn't been speaking of spirit when it had said that Hapexamendios was everywhere in this metropolis. This was the City of God; and God was the city.

Twice in his life he'd had presentiments of this revelation. The
first time when he'd entered Yzordderrex, which had been com-
monly called a city-god itself and had been, he now understood,
his brother's unwitting attempt to re-create his Father's masterwork. The second when he'd undertaken the business of similitudes
and had realized, as the net of his ambition encompassed London,
that there was no part of it, from sewer to dome, that was not
somehow analogous to his anatomy.

Here was that theory proved. The knowledge didn't strengthen
him but, instead, fueled the dread he felt, thinking of his Father's
immensity. He'd crossed a continent and more to get here, and
there'd been no part of it that was not made as these streets were
made, his Father's substance replicated in unimaginable quantities
to become the raw materials for the masons and carpenters and
hod carriers of His will. And yet, for all its magnitude, what was
His city? A trap of corporeality, and its architect its prisoner.

"Oh, Father," he said, and perhaps because the formality had
gone from his voice, and there was sorrow in it, he was finally
granted a reply.

"You've done well for me," the voice said.

Gentle remembered its monotony well. Here was the same
barely discernible modulation he'd first heard as he'd stood in the
shadow of the Pivot.

"You've succeeded where all the others failed," Hapexamendios
said. *"They went astray or let themselves be crucified. But you, Reconciler, you held to your course."*

"For your sake, Father."

"And that service has earned you a place here," the God said. *"In
my city. In my heart."*

"Thank you," Gentle replied, fearful that this gift was going to
mark the end of the exchange.

If so, he'd have failed as his mother's agent. Tell Him you want
to see His face, she'd said. Distract Him. Flatter Him. Ah, yes,
flattery!

"I want to learn from You now, Father," he said. "I want to be
able to carry Your wisdom back into the Fifth with me."

"You've done all you need to do, Reconciler," Hapexamendios
said. *"You won't need to go back into the Fifth, for your sake or
mine. You'll stay with me and watch my work."*

"What work is that?"

"You know what work," came the God's reply. *"I heard you
speak with the Nullianac. Why are you pretending ignorance?"*

The inflexions in His voice were too subtle to be interpreted.
Was there genuine inquiry in the question, or a fury at His son's
deceit?

"I didn't wish to presume, Father," Gentle said, cursing himself for this gaffe. "I thought You'd want to tell me Yourself."

"Why would I tell you what you already know?" the God said, unwilling to be persuaded from this argument until He had a convincing answer. *"You already have every knowledge you need—"*

"Not every one," Gentle said, seeing now how he might divert the flow.

"What do you lack?" Hapexamendios said. *"I'll tell you everything."*

"Your face, Father."

"My face? What about my face?"

"That's what I lack. The sight of Your face."

"You've seen my city," the Unbeheld replied. *"That's my face."*

"There's no other? Really, Father? None?"

"Aren't you content with that?" Hapexamendios said. *"Isn't it perfect enough? Doesn't it shine?"*

"Too much, Father. It's too glorious."

"How can a thing be too glorious?"

"Part of me's human, Father, and that part's weak. I look at this city, and I'm agog. It's a masterwork—"

"Yes, it is."

"Genius."

"Yes, it is."

"But Father, grant me a simpler sight. Show a glimpse of the face that made my face, so that I can know the part of me that's You."

He heard something very like a sigh in the air around him.

"It may seem ridiculous to you," Gentle said, "but I've followed this course because I wanted to see one face. One loving face." There was enough truth in this to lend his words real passion. There was indeed a face he'd hoped to find at the end of his journey. "Is it too much to ask?" he said.

There was a flutter of movement in the dingy arena ahead, and Gentle stared into the murk, in the expectation of some colossal door opening. But instead Hapexamendios said, *"Turn your back, Reconciler."*

"You want me to leave?"

"No. Only avert your eyes."

Here was a paradox: to be told to look away when sight was requested. But there was something other than an unveiling afoot. For the first time since entering the Dominion, he heard sounds other than a voice: a delicate rustling, a muted patter, creaks and whirrings stealing on his ear. And all around him, tiny motions in the solid street, as the monoliths softened and inclined towards the mystery he'd turned his back upon. A step gaped and oozed marrow. A wall opened where stone met stone, and a scarlet deeper than any he'd seen, a scarlet turned almost black, ran in rills as the slabs yielded up their geometry, lending themselves to the Unbeheld's purpose. Teeth came down from an unknitted balcony above, and loops of gut unraveled from the sills, dragging down curtains of tissue as they came.

As the deconstruction escalated, he dared the look he'd been forbidden, glancing back to see the entire street in gross or petty motion: forms fracturing, forms congealing, forms drooping and rising. There was nothing recognizable in the turmoil, and Gentle was about to turn away when one of the pliant walls tumbled in the flux and for a heartbeat, no more, he glimpsed a figure behind it. The moment was long enough to know the face he saw and have it in his mind's eye when he looked away. There was no face its equal in the Imajica. For all the sorrow on it, for all its wounds, it was exquisite.

Pie was alive and waiting there, in his Father's midst, a prisoner of the prisoner. It was all Gentle could do not to turn there and then and pitch his spirit into the tumult, demanding that his Father give the mystif up. This was his teacher, he'd say, his renewer, his perfect friend. But he fought the desire, knowing such an attempt would end in calamity, and instead turned away again, doting on the glimpse he'd had while the street behind him continued to convulse. Though the mystif's body had been marked by the hurts it had suffered, it was more whole than Gentle had dared hope. Perhaps it had drawn strength from the land on which Hapexamendios's city was built, the Dominion its people had worked their feits upon, before God had come to raise this metropolis.

But how should he persuade his Father to give the mystif up? With pleas? With further flattery? As he chewed on the problem, the ructions around him began to subside, and he heard Hapexamendios speak behind him.

"Reconciler?"

"Yes, Father?"

"You wanted to see my face."

"Yes, Father?"

"Turn and look."

He did so. The street in front of him had not lost all semblance of a thoroughfare. The buildings still stood, their doors and windows visible. But their architect had claimed from their substance sufficient pieces of the body he'd once owned to re-create it for Gentle's edification. The Father was human, of course, and had perhaps been no larger than His son in His first incarnation. But He'd remade Himself three times Gentle's height and more, a teetering giant that was as much borne up by the street He'd racked for matter as of it.

For all His scale, however, His form was ineptly made, as if He'd forgotten what it was like to be whole. His head was enormous, the shards of a thousand skulls claimed from the buildings to construct it, but so mismatched that the mind it was meant to shield was visible between the pieces, pulsing and flickering. One of His arms was vast, yet ended in a hand scarcely larger than Gentle's, while the other was wizened, but finished with fingers that had three dozen joints. His torso was another mass of misalliances, His innards cavorting in a cage of half a thousand ribs, His huge heart beating against a breastbone too weak to contain it and already fractured. And below, at His groin, the strangest deformation: a sex He'd failed to conjure into a single organ, but which hung in rags, raw and useless.

"Now," the God said. *"Do you see?"*

The impassivity had gone from His voice, its monotony replaced by an assembly of voices, as many larynxes, none of them whole, labored to produce each word.

"Do you see," He said again, *"the resemblance?"*

Gentle stared at the abomination before him and, for all its patchworks and disunions, knew that he did. It wasn't in the limbs, this likeness, or in the torso, or in the sex. But it was there. When the vast head was raised, he saw his face in the ruin that clung to his Father's skull. A reflection of a reflection of a reflection, perhaps, and all in cracked mirrors. But oh! it was there. The sight distressed him beyond measure, not because he saw the kinship but because their roles seemed suddenly reversed. Despite its size, it was a child he saw, its head fetal, its limbs untutored. It was eons old, but unable to slough off the fact of flesh, while he, for all his naïvetés, had made his peace with that disposal.

"Have you seen enough, Reconciler?" Hapexamendios said.

"Not quite."

"What then?"

Gentle knew he had to speak now, before the likeness was undone again and the walls were resealed.

"I want what's in You, Father."

"In me?"

"Your prisoner, Father. I want Your prisoner."

"I have no prisoner."

"I'm your son," Gentle said. "The flesh of your flesh. Why do you lie to me?"

The unwieldy head shuddered. The heart beat hard against the broken bone.

"Is there something you don't want me to know?" Gentle said, starting towards the wretched body. "You told me I could know everything."

The hands, great and small, twitched and jittered.

"Everything, You said, because I've done You perfect service. But there's something You don't want me to know."

"There's nothing."

"Then let me see the mystif. Let me see Pie 'oh' pah."

At this the God's body shook, and so did the walls around it. There were eruptions of light from beneath the flawed mosaic of His skull: little raging thoughts that cremated the air between the folds of His brain. The sight was a reminder to Gentle that, however frail this figure looked, it was the tiniest part of Hapexamendios's true scale. He was a city the size of a world, and if the power that had raised that city, and sustained the bright blood in its stone, was ever allowed to turn to destruction, it would beggar the Nullianacs.

Gentle's advance, which had so far been steady, was now halted. Though he was a spirit here and had thought no barrier could be raised against him, there was one before him now, thickening the air. Despite it, and the dread he felt when reminded of his Father's powers, he didn't retreat. He knew that if he did so the exchange would be over and Hapexamendios would be about His final business, His prisoner unreleased.

"Where's the pure, obedient son I had?" the God said.

"Still here," Gentle replied. "Still wanting to serve You, if You'll deal with me honorably."

A series of more livid bursts erupted in the distended skull. This time, however, they broke from its dome and rose into the dark air above the God's head. There were images in these energies, fragments of Hapexamendios's thoughts, shaped from fire. One of them was Pie.

"You've no business with the mystif," Hapexamendios said. *"It belongs to me."*

"No, Father."

"To me."

"I married it, Father."

The lightning was quieted momentarily, and the God's pulpy eyes narrowed.

"It made me remember my purpose," Gentle said. "It made me remember to be a Reconciler. I wouldn't be here—I wouldn't have served you—if it weren't for Pie 'oh' pah."

"Maybe it loved you once," the many throats replied. *"But now I want you to forget it. Put it out of your head forever."*

"Why?"

In reply came the parent's eternal answer to a child who asks too many questions. *"Because I tell you to,"* the God said.

But Gentle wouldn't be hushed so readily. He pressed on. "What does it know, Father?"

"Nothing."

"Does it know where Nisi Nirvana comes from? Is that what it knows?"

The fire in the Unbeheld's skull seethed at this. *"Who told you that?"* He raged.

There was no purpose served by lying, Gentle thought. "My mother," he said.

Every motion in the God's bloated body ceased, even to its cage-battering heart. Only the lightning went on, and the next word came not from the mingled throats but from the fire itself. Three syllables, spoken in a lethal voice.

"Cel. Est. Ine."

"Yes, Father."

"She's dead," the lightning said.

"No, Father. I was in her arms a few minutes ago." He lifted his hand, translucent though it was. "She held these fingers. She kissed them. And she told me—"

"I don't want to hear!"

"—to remind You—"

"Where is she?"

"—of Nisi Nirvana."

"Where is she? Where? Where?"

He had been motionless, but now rose up in His fury, lifting His wretched limbs above His head as if to bathe them in His own lightning.

"Where is she?" he yelled, throats and fire making the demand together. *"I want to see her! I want to see her!"*

4

On the stairs below the Meditation Room, Jude stood up. The gek-a-gek had begun a guttural complaint that was, in its way, more distressing than any sound she'd ever heard from them. They were afraid. She saw them sloping away from their places beside the door like dogs in fear of a beating, their spines depressed, their heads flattened.

She glanced at the company below: the angels still kneeling beside their wounded Maestro; Monday and Hoi-Polloi leaving off their vigil at the step and coming back into the candlelight, as though its little ring could preserve them from whatever power was agitating the air.

"Oh, Mama," she heard Sartori whisper.

"Yes, child?"

"He's looking for us, Mama."

"I know."

"You can feel it?"

"Yes, child, I can."

"Will you hold me, Mama? Will you hold me?"

"Where? Where?" the God was howling, and in the arcs above His skull shreds of His mind's sight appeared.

Here was a river, serpentine; and a city, drabber than His metropolis but all the finer for that; and a certain street; and a certain house. Gentle saw the eye Monday had scrawled on the front door, its pupil beaten out by the Oviate's attack. He saw his own body, with Clem beside it; and the stairs; and Jude on the stairs, climbing.

And then the room at the top, and the circle in the room, with his brother sitting inside it, and his mother, kneeling at the perimeter.

"Cel. Est. Ine," the God said. *"Cel. Est. Ine!"*

It wasn't Sartori's voice that uttered these syllables, but it *was* his lips that moved to shape them. Jude was at the top of the stairs now, and she could see his face clearly. It was still wet with tears, but there was no expression upon it whatsoever. She'd never seen features so devoid of feeling. He was a vessel, filling up with another soul.

"Child?" Celestine said.

"Get away from him," Jude murmured.

Celestine started to rise. "You sound sick, child," she said.

The voice came again, this time a furious denial. *"I Am Not. A. Child."*

"You wanted me to comfort you," Celestine said. "Let me do that."

Sartori's eyes looked up, but it wasn't his sight alone that fixed on her.

"Keep. Away," he said.

"I want to hold you," Celestine said, and instead of retreating she stepped over the boundary of the circle.

On the landing the gek-a-gek were in terror now, their sly retreat become a dance of panic. They beat their heads against the wall as if to hammer out their brains rather than hear the voice issuing from Sartori; this desperate, monstrous voice that said over and over, *"Keep. Away. Keep. Away."*

But Celestine wouldn't be denied. She knelt down again, in front of Sartori. When she spoke, however, it wasn't to the child, it

was to the Father, to the God who'd taken her into this city of iniquities.

"Let me touch You, love," she said. "Let me touch You, the way
You touched me."

"No!" Hapexamendios howled, but His child's limbs refused to
rise and ward off the embrace.

The denial came again and again, but Celestine ignored it, her
arms encircling them both, flesh and occupying spirit in one embrace.

This time, when the God unleashed His rejection, it was no
longer a word but a sound, as pitiful as it was terrifying.

In the First, Gentle saw the lightning above his Father's head
congeal into a single blinding flame and go from Him, like a meteor.

In the Second, Chicka Jackeen saw the blaze brighten the Erasure and fell to his knees on the flinty ground. A signal fire was
coming, he thought, to announce the moment of victory.

In Yzordderrex, the Goddesses knew better. As the fire broke
from the Erasure and entered the Second Dominion, the waters
around the temple grew quiescent, so as not to draw death down
upon them. Every child was hushed, every pool and rivulet stilled.
But the fire's malice wasn't meant for them, and the meteor passed
over the city, leaving it unharmed, outblazing the comet as it went.

With the fire out of sight, Gentle turned back to his Father.

"What have You done?" he demanded.

The God's attention lingered in the Fifth for a little time, but as
Gentle's demand came again He withdrew His mind from His target, and His eyes regained their animation.

"I've sent a fire for the whore," He said. It was no longer the lightning that spoke, but His many throats.

"Why?"

"Because she tainted you . . . she made you want love."

"Is that so bad?"

"You can't build cities with love," the God said. *"You can't make
great works. It's weakness."*

"And what about Nisi Nirvana?" Gentle said. "Is that a weakness, too?"

He dropped to his knees and laid his phantom palms on the
ground. They had no power here, or else he'd have started digging.
Nor could his spirit pierce the ground. The same barrier that sealed
him from his Father's belly kept him from looking into His Dominion's underworld. But he could ask the questions.

"Who spoke the words, Father?" he asked. "Who said: *Nisi
Nirvana?"*

"Forget you ever heard those words," Hapexamendios replied. *"The whore is dead. It's over."*

In his frustration Gentle made fists of his hands and beat on the solid ground.

"There's nothing there but Me," the many throats went on. *"My flesh is everywhere. My flesh is the world, and the world is My flesh."*

On the Mount of Lipper Bayak, Tick Raw had given up his triumphal jig and was sitting at the edge of his circle, waiting for the curious to emerge from their houses and come up to question him, when the fire appeared in the Fourth. Like Chicka Jackeen, he assumed it was some star of annunciation, sent to mark the victory, and he rose again to hail it. He wasn't alone. There were several people below who'd spotted the blaze over the Jokalaylau and were applauding the spectacle as it approached. When it passed overhead it brought a brief noon to Vanaeph, before going on its way. It lit Patashoqua just as brightly, then flew out of the Dominion through a fog that had just appeared beyond the city, marking the first passing place between the Dominion of green-gold skies and that of blue.

Two similar fogs had formed in Clerkenwell, one to the southeast of Gamut Street and the other to the northwest, both marking doorways in the newly reconciled Dominion. It was the latter that became blinding now, as the fire sped through it from the Fourth. The sight was not unwitnessed. Several revenants were in the vicinity, and though they had no clue as to what this signified, they sensed some calamity and retreated before the radiance, returning to the house to raise the alarm. But they were too sluggish. Before they were halfway back to Gamut Street the fog divided, and the Unbeheld's fire appeared in the benighted streets of Clerkenwell.

Monday saw it first, as he forsook the little comfort of the candlelight and returned to the step. The remnants of Sartori's hordes were raising a cacophony in the darkness outside, but even as he crossed the threshold to ward them off, the darkness became light.

From her place on the top stair Jude saw Celestine lay her lips against her son's and then, with astonishing strength, lift his dead weight up and pitch him out of the circle. Either the impact or the coming fire stirred him, and he began to rise, turning back towards his mother as he did so. He was too late to reclaim his place. The fire had come.

The window burst like a glittering cloud and the blaze filled the room. Jude was flung off her feet, but clutched the banister long enough to see Sartori cover his face against the holocaust, as the woman in the circle opened her arms to accept it. Celestine was instantly consumed, but the fire seemed unappeased and would have spread to burn the house to its foundations had its momentum not been so great. It sped on through the room, demolishing the wall as it went. On, on, towards the second fog that Clerkenwell boasted tonight.

"What the fuck was that?" Monday said in the hallway below.

"God," Jude replied. "Coming and going."

In the First, Hapexamendios raised His misbegotten head. Even though He didn't need the assembly of sight that gleamed in His skull to see what was happening in His Dominion—He had eyes everywhere—some memory of the body that had once been His sole residence made Him turn now, as best He could, and look behind Him.

"What is this?" He said.

Gentle couldn't see the fire yet, but he could feel whispers of its approach.

"What is this?" Hapexamendios said again.

Without waiting for a reply, He began feverishly to unknit his semblance, something Gentle had both feared and hoped He'd do. Feared, because the body from which the fire had been issued would doubtless be its destination, and if it was too quickly undone, the fire would have no target. And hoped, because only in that undoing would he have a chance to locate Pie. The barrier around his Father's form softened as the God was distracted by the intricacies of this dismantling, and though Gentle had yet to get a second glimpse of Pie he turned his thought to entering the body; but for all His perplexity Hapexamendios was not about to be breached so readily. As Gentle approached, a will too powerful to be denied seized hold of him.

"What is this?" the God demanded a third time.

Hoping he might yet gain a few precious seconds' reprieve, Gentle answered with the truth.

"The Imajica's a circle," he said.

"A circle?"

"This is Your fire, Father. This is Your fire, coming around again."

Hapexamendios didn't respond with words. He understood instantly the significance of what He'd been told and let His hold on Gentle slip again, in order to turn all His will to the business of unknitting Himself.

The ungainly body began to unravel, and in its midst Gentle once again glimpsed Pie. This time, the mystif saw him. Its frail limbs thrashed to clear a way through the turmoil between them, but before Gentle could finally wrest himself from his Father's custody the ground beneath Pie 'oh' pah grew unsolid. The mystif reached up to take hold of some support in the body above, but it was decaying too fast. The ground gaped like a grave, and, with one last despairing look in Gentle's direction, the mystif sank from sight.

Gentle raised his head in a howl, but the sound he made was drowned out by that of his Father, who—as if in imitation of His child—had also thrown back His head. But His was a din of fury rather than sorrow, as He wrenched and thrashed in His attempts to speed His unmasking.

Behind Him, now, the fire. As it came Gentle thought he saw his mother's face in the blaze, shaped from ashes, her eyes and mouth wide as she returned to meet the God who'd raped, rejected, and finally murdered her. A glimpse, no more, and then the fire was upon its maker, its judgment absolute.

Gentle's spirit was gone from the conflagration at a thought, but His Father—the world His flesh, the flesh His world—could not escape it. His fetal head broke, and the fire consumed the shards as they flew, its blaze cremating His heart and innards and spreading through His mismatched limbs, burning them away to every last fingertip and toe.

The consequence for His city was both instantly felt and calamitous. Every street from one end of the Dominion to the other shook as the message of collapse went from the place where its First Cause had fallen. Gentle had nothing to fear from this dissolution, but the sight of it appalled him nevertheless. This was his Father, and it gave him neither pleasure nor satisfaction to see the body whose child he was now reel and bleed. The imperious towers began to topple, their ornament dropping in rococo rains, their arches forsaking the illusion of stone and falling as flesh. The streets heaved and turned to meat; the houses threw down their bony roofs. Despite the collapse around him, Gentle remained close to the place where his Father had been consumed, in the hope that he might yet find Pie 'oh' pah in the maelstrom. But it seemed Hapexamendios' last voluntary act had been to deny the lovers their reunion. He'd opened the ground and buried the mystif in the pit of His decay, sealing it with His will to prevent Gentle from ever finding Pie again.

There was nothing left for the Reconciler to do but leave the city to its decease, which in due course he did, not taking the route across the Dominions but going back the way the fire had come. As he flew, the sheer enormity of what was under way became apparent. If every living body that had passed a span on Earth had been left to putrefy here in the First, the sum of their flesh would

not begin to approach that of this city. Nor would this carrion rot
into the ground and its decomposition feed a new generation of
life. It *was* the ground; it *was* the life. With its passing, there would
only be putrescence here: decay laid on decay laid on decay. A Dominion of filth, polluted until the end of time.

Ahead, now, the fog that divided the city's outskirts from the
Fifth. Gentle passed through it, returning gratefully to the modest
streets of Clerkenwell. They were drab, of course, after the brilliance of the metropolis he'd left. But he knew the air had the
sweetness of summer leaves upon it, even if he couldn't smell that
sweetness, and the welcome sound of an engine from Holborn or
Gray's Inn Road could be heard, as some fleet fellow, knowing the
worst was past, got about his business. It was unlikely to be legal
work at such an hour. But Gentle wished the driver well, even in
his crime. The Dominion had been saved for thieves as well as
saints.

He didn't linger at the passing place but went as fast as his weary
thoughts would drive him, back to number 28 and the wounded
body that was still clinging to continuance at the bottom of the stairs.

At the top, Jude hadn't waited for the smoke to clear before venturing into the Meditation Room. Despite a warning shout from
Clem she'd gone up into the murk to find Sartori, hoping that he'd
survived. His creatures hadn't. Their corpses were twitching close
to the threshold, not struck by the blast, she thought, but laid low
by their summoner's decline. She found that summoner easily
enough. He was lying close to where Celestine had pitched him,
his body arrested in the act of turning towards the circle.

It had been his undoing. The fire that had carried his mother
to oblivion had seared every part of him. The ashes of his clothes
had been fused with his blistered back, his hair singed from his
scalp, his face cooked beyond tenderness. But like his brother,
lying in ribbons below, he refused to give up life. His fingers
clutched the boards; his lips still worked, baring teeth as bright as
a death's-head smile. There was even power in his sinews. When
his blood-filled eyes saw Jude he managed to push himself up,
until his body rolled over onto its charred spine, and he used his
agonies to fuel the hand that clutched at her, dragging her down
beside him.

"My mother . . ."

"She's gone."

There was bafflement on his face. "Why?" he said, shudders
convulsing him as he spoke. "She seemed . . . to want it. Why?"

"So that she'd be there when the fire took Hapexamendios,"
Jude replied.

He shook his head, not comprehending the significance of this.
"How . . . could that . . . be?" he murmured.

"The Imajica's a circle," she said. He studied her face, attempting to puzzle this out. "The fire went back to the one who sent it."

Now the sense of what she was telling him dawned. Even in his agony, here was a greater pain.

"He's gone?" he said.

She wanted to say, I hope so, but she kept that sentiment to herself and simply nodded.

"And my mother too?" Sartori went on. The trembling quieted; so did his voice, which was already frail. "I'm alone," he said.

The anguish in these last few words was bottomless, and she longed to have some way of comforting him. She was afraid to touch him for fear of causing him still greater discomfort, but perhaps there was more hurt in her not doing so. With the greatest delicacy she laid her hand over his.

"You're not alone," she said. "I'm here."

He didn't acknowledge her solace, perhaps didn't even hear it. His thoughts were elsewhere.

"I should never have touched him," he said softly. "A man shouldn't lay hands on his own brother."

As he squeezed out these words there was a moan from the bottom of the stairs, followed by a yelp of pure joy from Clem, and then Monday's ecstatic whoops.

"Boss oh boss oh boss!"

"Do you hear that?" Jude said to Sartori.

"Yes. . . ."

"I don't think you killed him after all."

A strange tic appeared around his mouth, which after a moment she realized was the shreds of a smile. She took it to be pleasure at Gentle's survival, but its source was more bitter.

"That won't save me now," he said.

His hand, which was laid on his stomach, began to knead the muscles there, its clutches so violent that his body began to spasm. Blood bubbled up between his lips, and he moved his hand to his mouth, as if to conceal it. There, he seemed to spit his blood into his palm. Then he removed his hand and offered its grisly contents to her.

"Take it," he said, uncurling his fist.

She felt something drop into her hand. She didn't glance at his gift, however, but kept her eyes fixed on his face as he looked away from her, back towards the circle. She realized, even before his gaze had found its resting place, that he was looking away from her for the final time, and she started to call him back. She said his name; she called him love; she said she'd never wanted to desert him, and never would again, if he'd only stay. But her words were wasted. As his eyes found the circle, the life went from them, his last sight not of her but of the place where he'd been made.

In her palm, bloody from his belly and throat, lay the blue egg.

After a time, she got up and went out onto the landing. The place at the bottom of the stairs where Gentle's body had lain was empty. Clem was standing in the candlelight with both tears and a broad smile on his face. He looked up at Jude as she started down the stairs.

"Sartori?" he said.

"He's dead."

"What about Celestine?"

"Gone," she said.

"But it's over, isn't it?" Hoi-Polloi said. "We're going to live."

"Are we?"

"Yes, we are," said Clem. "Gentle saw Hapexamendios destroyed."

"Where *is* Gentle?"

"He went outside," Clem said. "He's got enough life in him—"

"For another life?"

"For another twenty, the lucky bugger," came Tay's reply.

Reaching the bottom of the stairs, she put her arms around Gentle's protectors, then went out onto the step. Gentle was standing in the middle of the street, wrapped in one of Celestine's sheets. Monday was at his side, and he was leaning on the boy as he stared up at the tree that grew outside number 28. Hapexamendios' fire had charred much of its foliage, leaving the branches naked and blackened. But there was a breeze stirring the leaves that had survived, and after such a long motionless time even these shreds of wind were welcome: final, simple proof that the Imajica had survived its perils and was once again drawing breath.

She hesitated to join him, thinking perhaps he'd prefer to have these moments of meditation uninterrupted. But his gaze came her way after half a minute or so, and though there was only starlight and the last guttering flames in the fretwork above to see him by, the smile was as luminous as ever, and as inviting. She left the step but, as she approached, saw that his smile was slender and the wounds he'd sustained deeper than cuts.

"I failed," he said.

"The Imajica's whole," she replied. "That isn't failure."

He looked away from her, down the street. The darkness was full of agitation.

"The ghosts are still here," he said. "I swore to them I'd find a way out, and I failed. That was why I went with Pie in the first place, to find Taylor a way out—"

"Maybe there isn't one," came a third voice.

Clem had appeared on the doorstep, but it was Tay who spoke.

"I promised you an answer," Gentle said.

"And you found one. The Imajica's a circle, and there's no way out of it. We just go round and round. Well, that's not so bad, Gentle. We have what we have."

Gentle lifted his hand from Monday's shoulder and turned away from the tree, and from Jude, and from the angels on the step. As he hobbled out into the middle of the street, his head bowed, he murmured a reply to Tay too quiet for any but an angel's ear.

"It's not enough," he said.

25

I

For the living occupants of Gamut Street, the days that followed the events of that midsummer were as strange in their way as anything that had gone before. The world that returned to life around them seemed to be totally ignorant of the fact that its existence had hung in the balance, and if it now sensed the least change in its condition it concealed its suspicion very well. The monsoons and heat waves that had preceded the Reconciliation were replaced the next morning with the drizzles and tepid sunshine of an English summer, its moderation the model for public behavior in subsequent weeks. The eruptions of irrationality which had turned every junction and street corner into a little battleground summarily ceased; the night walkers Monday and Jude had seen watching for revelation no longer strayed out to peer quizzically at the stars.

In any city other than London, perhaps the mysteries now present in its streets would have been discovered and celebrated. If such fogs as lingered in Clerkenwell had appeared instead in Rome, the Vatican would have been pronouncing on them within a week. Had they appeared in Mexico City, the poor would have been through them in a shorter time still, desperate for a better life in the world beyond. But England: oh! England. It had never had much of a taste for the mystical, and with all but the weakest of its evocators and feit workers murdered by the Tabula Rasa, there was nobody to begin the labor of freeing minds locked up in dogmas and utilities.

The fogs were not entirely ignored, however. The animal life of the city knew something was afoot and came to Clerkenwell to

sniff it out. The runaway dogs who'd gathered in the vicinity of
Gamut Street when the revenants had come, only to be frightened
off by Sartori's horde, now returned, their noses twitching after
some piquant scent or other. Cats came too, yowling in the trees
at dusk, curious but casual. There were also visitations by bees, and
birds, who twice in the three days following midsummer gathered
in the same stupefying numbers as Monday and Jude had witnessed at the Retreat. In all these cases the packs, swarms, and
flocks disappeared after a time, having discovered the source of the
perfumes and poles that had directed them to the district and gone
into the Fourth to have a life under different skies.

But if no two-legged traffic passed into the Fourth, there was certainly some in the opposite direction. A little over a week after the
Reconciliation, Tick Raw arrived on the doorstep of number 28
and, having introduced himself to Clem and Monday, asked to see
the Maestro. He came into a house that was a good deal more comfortable than his quarters in Vanaeph, furnished as it was from a
score of recent burglaries by Monday and Clem. But the atmosphere of domesticity was cosmetic. Though the bodies of the gek-
a-gek had been removed and buried, along with their summoner,
beneath the long grass in Shiverick Square; though the front door
had been mended and the bloodstains mopped up; though the
Meditation Room had been scoured and the stones of the circle
individually wrapped in linen and locked away, the house was
charged with all that had happened here: the deaths, the love
scenes, the reunions and revelations.

"You're living in the middle of a history lesson," Tick Raw said
when he sat himself down beside the bed in which Gentle lay.

The Reconciler was healing, but even with his extraordinary
powers of recuperation it would be a lengthy business. He slept
twenty hours or more out of every twenty-four and barely ventured from his mattress when he was awake.

"You look as though you've seen some wars, my friend," Tick
Raw said.

"More than I'd like," Gentle replied wearily.

"I sniff something Oviate."

"Gek-a-gek," Gentle said. "Don't worry, they're gone."

"Did they break through during the ceremony?"

"No. It's more complicated than that. Ask Clem. He'll tell you
the whole story."

"No offense to your friends," Tick Raw said, fetching a jar of
pickled sausage from his pocket, "but I'd prefer to hear it from you."

"I've thought about it too much as it is," Gentle said. "I don't
want to be reminded."

"But we won the day," Tick Raw said. "Doesn't that merit a little celebration?"

"Celebrate with Clem, Tick. I need to sleep."

"As you like, as you like," Tick Raw said, retreating to the door. "Oh. I wonder? Do you mind if I stay here for a few days? There's a number of parties in Vanaeph who want the grand tour of the Fifth, and I've volunteered to show them the sights. But as I don't yet know them myself—"

"Be my guest," Gentle said. "And forgive me if I don't brim with bonhomie."

"No apology required," Tick Raw said. "I'll leave you to sleep."

That evening, Tick did as Gentle had suggested and plied both Clem and Monday with questions until he had the full story.

"So when do I meet the mesmeric Judith?" he asked when the tale was told.

"I don't know if you ever will," Clem said. "She didn't come back to the house after we buried Sartori."

"Where is she?"

"Wherever she is," Monday said dolefully, "Hoi-Polloi's with her. Just my fuckin' luck."

"Well, now, listen," Tick Raw said. "I've always had a way with the ladies. I'll make you a deal. If you show me this city, inside out, I'll show you a few ladies the same way."

Monday's palm went from his pocket, where it'd been stroking the consequence of Hoi-Polloi's absence, and seized hold of Tick Raw's hand before it was even extended.

"You're a gentleman an' a squalor," Monday said. "You got yourself a tour, mate."

"What about Gentle?" Tick Raw said to Clem. "Is he languishing for want of female company?"

"No, he's just tired. He'll get well."

"Will he?" said Tick Raw. "I'm not so sure. He's got the look of a man who'd be happier dead than alive."

"Don't say that."

"Very well. I didn't say it. But he has, Clement. And we all know it."

The vigor and noise Tick Raw brought into the house only served to emphasize the truth of that observation. As the days passed and turned to weeks, there was little or no improvement in Gentle's mood. He was, as Tick Raw had said, languishing, and Clem began to feel the way he had during Tay's final decline. A loved one was slipping away, and he could do nothing to prevent it. There weren't even those moments of levity that there'd been with Tay, when good times had been remembered and the pain superseded.

Gentle wanted no false comforts, no laughter, no sympathy. He simply wanted to lie in his bed and steadily become as bland as the sheets he lay upon. Sometimes, in his sleep, the angels would hear him speaking in tongues, the way Tay had heard him talk before. But it was nonsense that he muttered: reports from a mind that was rambling without map or destination.

Tick Raw stayed in the house a month, leaving with Monday at dawn and returning late, having had another day seeing the sights and acquiring the appetites of this new Dominion. His sense of wonder was boundless, his capacity for pleasure prodigal. He found he had a taste for eel pie and Elgar, for Speaker's Corner at Sunday noon and the Ripper's haunts at midnight; for dog races, for jazz, for waistcoats made in Saville Row and women hired behind King's Cross Station. As for Monday, it was clear from the face he wore whenever he returned that the hurt of Hoi-Polloi's desertion was being kissed away. When Tick Raw finally announced that it was time to return to the Fourth, the boy was crestfallen.

"Don't worry," Tick told him. "I'll be back. And I won't be alone."

Before he departed, he presented himself at Gentle's bedside with a proposal.

"Come to the Fourth with me," he said. "It's time you saw Patashoqua."

Gentle shook his head.

"But you haven't seen the Merrow Ti' Ti'," Tick protested.

"I know what you're trying to do, Tick," Gentle said. "And I thank you for it, really I do, but I don't want to see the Fourth again."

"Well, what *do* you want to see?"

The answer was simple: "Nothing."

"Oh, now stop this, Gentle," Tick Raw said. "It's getting damn boring. You're behaving as though we lost everything. We didn't."

"I did."

"She'll come back. You'll see."

"Who will?"

"Judith."

Gentle almost laughed at this. "It's not Judith I've lost," he said.

Tick Raw realized his error then, and came as near to dumbfounded as he ever got. All he could manage was: "Ah. . . ."

For the first time since Tick Raw had appeared at his bedside the month before, Gentle actually looked at his guest. "Tick," he said. "I'm going to tell you something I've told nobody else."

"What's that?"

"When I was in my Father's city . . ." He paused, as though the will to tell was going from him already, then began again. "When I was in my Father's city I saw Pie 'oh' pah."

"Alive?"

"For a time."

"Oh, Jesu. How did it die?"

"The ground opened up beneath it."

"That's terrible; terrible."

"Do you see now why it doesn't feel like a victory?"

"Yes, I see. But Gentle—"

"No more persuasions, Tick."

"—there are such changes in the air. Maybe there are the miracles in the First, the way there are in Yzordderrex. It's not out of the question."

Gentle studied his tormentor, eyes narrowed.

"The Eurhetemecs were in the First long before Hapexamendios, remember," Tick went on. "And they worked wonders there. Maybe those times have returned. The land doesn't forget. Men forget; Maestros forget. But the land? Never."

He stood up.

"Come with me to a passing place," he said. "Let's look for ourselves. Where's the harm? I'll carry you on my back if your legs don't work."

"That won't be necessary," Gentle said, and throwing off the sheets got out of bed.

Though the month of August had yet to begin, the early months of summer had been marked by such excesses that the season had burned itself out prematurely, and when Gentle, accompanied by Tick and Clem, stepped out into Gamut Street, he met the first chills of autumn on the step. Clem had found the fog that let onto the First Dominion within forty-eight hours of the Reconciliation, but had not entered it. After all that he'd heard about the state of the Unbeheld's city, he'd had no wish to see its horrors. He led the Maestros to the place readily enough, however. It was little more than half a mile from the house, hidden in a cloister behind an empty office building: a bank of gray fog, no more than twice the height of a man, which rolled upon itself in the shadowed corner of the empty yard.

"Let me go first," Clem said to Gentle. "We're still your guardians."

"You've done more than enough," Gentle said. "Stay here. This won't take long."

Clem didn't contradict the instruction but stepped aside to let the Maestros enter the fog. Gentle had passed between Dominions many times now and was used to the brief disorientation that always accompanied such passage. But nothing, not even the abattoir nightmares that had haunted him after the Reconciliation, could have prepared him for what was waiting on the other side. Tick Raw, ever a man of instant responses, vomited as the stench of putrescence came to meet them through the fog, and though he stumbled after Gentle, determined not to leave his friend to face the First alone, he covered his eyes after a single glance.

The Dominion was decayed from horizon to horizon. Everywhere rot, and more rot: suppurating lakes of it, and festering hills. Overhead, in skies Gentle had barely seen as he passed through his Father's city, clouds the color of old bruises half hid two yellowish moons, their light falling on a filth so atrocious the hungriest kite in the Kwem would have starved rather than feed here.

"This was the City of God, Tick," Gentle said. "This was my Father. This was the Unbeheld."

In a sudden fury he tore at Tick's hands, which were clamped to the man's face.

"Look, damn you, *look!* I want to hear you tell me about the wonders, Tick! Go on! Tell me! *Tell me!*"

Tick didn't go back to the house when he and Gentle emerged from the passing place, but with some murmured words of apology headed off into the dusk, saying he needed to be on his home turf for a while and that he'd come back when he'd regained his composure. Sure enough, three days later he reappeared at number 28, still a little queasy, still a little shamefaced, to find that Gentle had not returned to his bed but was up and about. The Reconciler's mood was brisk rather than blithe. His bed, he explained to Tick, was not the refuge it had previously been. As soon as he closed his eyes he saw the slaughterhouse of the First in every atrocious detail and could now only sleep when he'd driven himself to such exhaustion that there was no time between his head striking the pillow and oblivion for his mind to dwell on what he'd witnessed.

Luckily, Tick had brought distractions, in the form of a party of eight tourists (he preferred *excursionists*) from Vanaeph who were relying upon him to introduce them to the rites and rarities of the Fifth Dominion. Before the tour began, however, they were eager to pay their respects to the great Reconciler, and did so with a succession of painfully overworked speeches, which they read aloud before presenting Gentle with the gifts they'd brought: smoked meats, perfumes, a small picture of Patashoqua rendered in zarzi wings, a pamphlet of erotic poems by Pluthero Quexos' sister.

The group was the first of many Tick brought in the next few weeks, freely admitting to Gentle that he was turning a handsome profit from his new role. "Have a Holy Day in the City of Sartori" was his pitch, and the more satisfied customers who returned to Vanaeph with tales of eel pies and Jack the Ripper, the more who signed on to take the excursion. He knew the boom time couldn't last, of course. In a short while the professional tour operators in Patashoqua would start trading, and he'd be unable to compete with their slick packages, except in one particular regard. Only he could guarantee an audience, however brief, with the Maestro Sartori himself.

The time was coming, Gentle realized, when the Fifth would have to face the fact that it was Reconciled, whether it liked it or not. The first few sightseers from Vanaeph and Patashoqua might be ignored; but when their families came, and their families' families—creatures in shapes, size, and assemblies that demanded attention—the people of this Dominion would be able to overlook them no longer. It would not be long before Gamut Street became a sacred highway, with travelers passing down it in not one but both directions. When it did, living in the house would become untenable. He, Clem, and Monday would have to vacate number 28 and leave it to become a shrine.

When that day arrived—and it would be soon—he would be forced to make a momentous decision. Should he seek out some sanctuary here in Britain or leave the island for a country where none of his lives had ever taken him? Of one thing he was certain: he would not return to the Fourth, or any Dominion beyond it. Though it was true that he'd never seen Patashoqua, there had only ever been one soul he'd wanted to see it with, and that soul was gone.

2

Times were no less strange or demanding for Jude. She'd decided to leave the company in Gamut Street on the spur of the moment, expecting that she'd return there in due course. But the longer she stayed away, the harder it became to return. She hadn't realized, until Sartori was gone, how much she'd mourn. Whatever the source of the feelings she had for him, she felt no regrets. All she felt was loss. Night after night she'd wake up in the little flat she and Hoi-Polloi had rented together (the old place was too full of memories), shaken to tears by the same terrible dream. She was climbing those damn stairs in Gamut Street, trying to reach Sartori as he lay burning at the top, but for all her toil never managing to advance a single step. And always the same words on her lips when Hoi-Polloi woke her.

"Stay with me. Stay with me."

Though he'd gone forever, and she would have to make her peace with that eventually, he'd left a living keepsake, and as the autumn months came it began to make its presence felt in no uncertain fashion, its kicking keeping her awake when the nightmares didn't. She didn't like the way she looked in the mirror, her stomach a glossy dome, her breasts swelling and tender, but Hoi-Polloi was there to lend comfort and companionship whenever it was needed. She was all Jude could have asked for during those months: loyal, practical, and eager to learn. Though the customs of the Fifth were a mystery to her at first, she soon became familiar with its eccentricities and even fond of them. This was not, however, a situation that could continue indefinitely. If they stayed in the Fifth, and Jude had the child there, what could she promise it? A rearing and an education in a Dominion that might come to appreciate the miracles in its midst some distant day, but would in the meantime ignore or reject whatever extraordinary qualities the child was blessed with.

By the middle of October she'd made up her mind. She'd leave the Fifth, with or without Hoi-Polloi, and find some country in the Imajica where the child, whether it was a prophetic, a melancholic, or simply priapic, would be allowed to flourish. In order to take that journey, of course, she would have to return to Gamut Street or its environs, and though that was not a particularly attractive prospect, it was better to do so soon, she reasoned, before many more sleepless nights took their toll and she felt too weak. She shared her plans with Hoi-Polloi, who declared herself happy to go wherever Jude wished to lead. They made swift preparations and four days later left the flat for the last time, with a small collection of valuables to pawn when they got to the Fourth.

The evening was cold, and the moon, when it rose, had a misty halo. By its light the thoroughfares around Gamut Street were iridescent with the first etchings of frost. At Jude's request they went first to Shiverick Square, so that she could pay her last respects to Sartori. Both his grave and those of the Oviates had been well disguised by Monday and Clem, and it took her quite a while to find the place where he was buried. But find it she did and spent twenty minutes there while Hoi-Polloi waited at the railings. Though there were revenants in the nearby streets, she knew he would never join their ranks. He'd not been born, but made, the stuff of his life stolen. The only existence he had after his decease was in her memory and in the child. She didn't weep for that fact, or even for his absence. She'd done all she could, weeping and begging him to stay. But she did tell the earth that she'd loved what it was heaped upon and charged it to give Sartori comfort in his dreamless sleep.

Then she quit the graveside, and together she and Hoi-Polloi went looking for the passing place into the Fourth. It would be day there, bright day, and she'd call herself by another name.

Number 28 was noisy that night, the cause a celebration in honor of Irish, who'd that afternoon been released from prison, having served a three-month sentence for petty theft, and had arrived on the doorstep—with Carol, Benedict, and several cases of stolen whisky—to toast his release. The house was by now a trove of treasures—all gifts to the Maestro from Tick Raw's excursionists—and there was no end to the drunken fooling these artifacts, many of them total enigmas, inspired. Gentle was feeling as facetious as Irish, if not more so. After so many weeks of abstinence the substantial amounts of whisky he'd imbibed had his head spinning, and he resisted Clem's attempts to engage him in serious conversation, despite the latter's insistence that the matter was urgent. Only after some persuading did he follow Clem to a quieter place in the house, where his angels told him that Judith was in the vicinity. He was somewhat sobered by the news.

"Is she coming here?" he asked.

"I don't think so," Clem said, his tongue passing back and forth over his lips as though her taste was upon them. "But she's close."

Gentle didn't need further prompting. With Monday in tow he went out into the street. There were no living creatures in sight. Only the revenants, listless as ever, their joylessness made all the more apparent by the sound of merrymaking that emanated from the house.

"I don't see her," Gentle said to Clem, who had followed them out as far as the step. "Are you sure she's here?"

It was Tay who replied. "You think I wouldn't know when Judy was near? Of course I'm certain."

"Which direction?" Monday wanted to know.

Now Clem again, cautioning: "Perhaps she doesn't want to see us."

"Well, *I* want to see *her*," Gentle replied. "At least a drink, for old time's sake. Which direction, Tay?"

The angels pointed, and Gentle headed off down the street, with Monday, bottle in hand, close on his heels.

The fog that let onto the Fourth looked inviting: a slow wave of pale mist that turned and turned on itself, but never broke. Before she and Hoi-Polloi stepped into it, Jude took a few moments to look up. The Plow was overhead. She wouldn't be seeing it again. Then she said, "That's enough goodbyes," and together they took a step into the mist.

As they did so Jude heard the sound of running feet in the

alleyway behind them and Gentle, calling her name. She'd been aware that their presence might be detected and had schooled them both in how best to respond. Neither woman turned. They simply picked up their pace and headed on through the mist. It thickened as they went, but after a dozen steps daylight began to filter through from the other side, and the fog's clammy cold gave way to balm. Again, Gentle called after her, but there was a commotion up ahead, and it all but drowned out his call.

Back in the Fifth, Gentle came to a halt at the edge of the fog. He'd sworn to himself that he'd never leave the Dominion again, but the drink swilling in his system had weakened his resolve. His feet itched to go after her into the fog.

"Well, boss," Monday said. "Are we going or aren't we?"

"Do you care either way?"

"Yes, as it happens."

"You'd still like to get your hands on Hoi-Polloi, huh?"

"I dream about her, boss. Cross-eyed girls, every night."

"Ah, well," Gentle said. "If we're chasing dreams, then I think that's good reason to go."

"Yeah?"

"In fact it's the only reason."

He grabbed hold of Monday's bottle and took a healthy swig from it.

"Let's do it," he said, and together they plunged into the fog, running over ground that softened and brightened as they went, paving stones becoming sand, night becoming day.

They caught sight of the women briefly, gray silhouettes against the peacock sky ahead, then lost them again as they gave chase. The gleam of day grew, however, and so did the sound of voices, which rose to the din of an excited crowd as they emerged from the passing place. There were buyers, sellers, and thieves on every side, and, disappearing into the throng, the women. They followed with renewed fervor, but the tide of people conspired to keep them from their quarry, and after half an hour of fruitless pursuit, which finally brought them back to the fog and the commercial hubbub which surrounded it, they had to admit that they'd been outmaneuvered.

Gentle was tetchy now, his head no longer buzzing but aching. "They're away," he said. "Let's give up on it."

"Shit."

"People come, people go. You can't afford to get attached to anyone."

"It's too late," Monday said dolefully. "I am."

Gentle squinted at the fog, his lips pursed. It was a cold October on the other side.

"I tell you what," he said after a little time. "We'll wander over to Vanaeph and see if we can find Tick Raw. Maybe he can help us."

Monday beamed. "You're a hero, boss. Lead the way."

Gentle went on tiptoe, attempting to orient himself.

"Trouble is, I haven't a bloody clue where Vanaeph *is,*" he said.

He collared the nearest passerby and asked him how to get to the Mount. The fellow pointed over the heads of the crowd, leaving the boss and his boy to burrow their way to the edge of the market, where they had a view not of Vanaeph but of the walled city that stood between them and the Mount of Lipper Bayak. The grin reappeared on Monday's face, broader than ever, and on his lips the name he'd so often breathed like an enchantment.

"Patashoqua?"

"Yes."

"We painted it on the wall together, d'you remember?"

"I remember."

"What's it like inside?"

Gentle was peering at the bottle in his hand, wondering if the peculiar exhilaration he felt was going to pass with the headache that accompanied it.

"Boss?"

"What?"

"I said, what's it like inside?"

"I don't know. I've never been."

"Well, shouldn't we?"

Gentle thrust the bottle at Monday and sighed, a lazy, easy sigh that ended in a smile. "Yes, my friend," he said. "I think maybe we should."

3

Thus began the last pilgrimage of the Maestro Sartori—called John Furie Zacharias, or Gentle, the Reconciler of Dominions—across the Imajica.

He hadn't intended it to be a pilgrimage at all, but having promised Monday that they would find the woman of his dreams, he couldn't bring himself to desert the boy and return to the Fifth. They began their search, of course, in Patashoqua, which was more prosperous than ever these days, with its proximity to the newly reconciled Dominion creating businesses every day. After almost a year of wondering what the city would be like, Gentle was inevitably somewhat disappointed once he got inside its walls, but Monday's enthusiasm was a sight in itself, and a poignant reminder of his own astonishment when he and Pie had first entered the Fourth.

Unable to trace the women in the city, they went on to Vanaeph, hoping to find Tick. He was off traveling, they were told, but one sharp-sighted individual claimed to have seen two women who fitted the description of Jude and Hoi-Polloi hitching a ride at the edge of the highway. An hour later, Gentle and Monday were doing the same thing, and the pursuit that was to take them across the Dominions began in earnest.

For the Maestro the journey was very different from those that had preceded it. The first time he'd made this trek he'd traveled in ignorance of himself, failing to comprehend the significance of the people he'd met and the places he'd seen. The second time he'd been a phantom, flying at the speed of thought between members of the Synod, his business too urgent to allow him to appreciate the myriad wonders he was passing through. But now, finally, he had both the time and the comprehension to make sense of his pilgrimage, and, having begun the journey reluctantly, he soon had as much taste for it as his companion.

Word of the changes in Yzordderrex had spread even to the tiniest villages, and the demise of the Autarch's Empire was everywhere cause for jubilation. Rumors of the Imajica's healing had also spread, and when Monday told people where he and his quiet companion came from (which he was wont to do at the vaguest cue) they were plied with drinks and grilled for news of the paradisiacal Fifth. Many of their questioners, knowing that the door into that mystery finally stood open, were planning to visit the Fifth and wanted to know what gifts they should take with them into a Dominion that was already so full of marvels. When this question was put, Gentle, who usually let Monday do the talking during these interviews, invariably spoke up.

"Take your family histories," he'd say. "Take your poems. Take your jokes. Take your lullabies. Make them understand in the Fifth what glories there are here."

People tended to look at him askance when he answered in this fashion, and told him that their jokes and their family histories didn't seem particularly glorious. Gentle would simply say, "They're you. And you're the best gift the Fifth could be given."

"You know, we could have made a fortune if we'd brought a few maps of England with us," Monday remarked one day.

"Do we care about fortunes?" Gentle said.

"You might not, boss," Monday replied. "Personally, I'm much in favor."

He was right, Gentle thought. They could have sold a thousand maps already, and they were only just entering the Third: maps which would have been copied, and the copies copied, each transcriber inevitably adding their own felicities to the design. The thought of such proliferation led Gentle back to his own hand, which had seldom worked for any purpose other than profit, and which for all its labor had never produced anything of lasting value. But unlike the paintings he'd forged, maps weren't cursed by the notion of a definitive original. They grew in the copying, as their inaccuracies were corrected, their empty spaces filled, their legends redevised. And even when all the corrections had been made, to the finest detail, they could still never be cursed with the word *finished,* because their subject continued to change. Rivers widened and meandered, or dried up altogether; islands rose and sank again; even mountains moved. By their very nature, maps were always works in progress, and Gentle—his resolve strengthened by thinking of them that way—decided after many months of delay to turn his hand to making one.

Occasionally along the road they'd meet an individual who, in ignorance of his audience, would boast some association with the Fifth's most celebrated son, the Maestro Sartori, and would proceed to tell Gentle and Monday about the great man. The accounts varied, especially when it came to talk of his companion. Some said he'd had a beautiful woman at his side; some his brother, called Pie; others still (these the least numerous) told of a mystif. At first it was all Monday could do not to blurt the truth, but Gentle had insisted from the outset that he wanted to travel incognito, and having been sworn to secrecy the boy was as good as his word. He kept his silence while wild tales of the Maestro's doings were told: marriages celebrated on the ceiling; copses springing up overnight where he'd slept; women made pregnant drinking from his cup. The fact that he'd become a figment of the popular imagination amused Gentle at first, but after a time it began to weigh on him. He felt like a ghost among these living versions of himself, invisible among the listeners who gathered to hear tales of his exploits, the details of which were embroidered and embellished with every telling.

There was some comfort in the fact that he was not the only character around whom such parables occurred. There were other fables alive in the air between the ears and tongues of the populace, which the pilgrims were usually told when they asked after Jude and Hoi-Polloi: tales of miraculous women. A whole new nomadic tribe had appeared in the Dominions since the fall of Yzorderrex. Women of power were abroad, rising to the occasion of their liberation, and rites they'd only practiced at the hearth and cot were now performed in the open air for all to see. But unlike the stories of the Maestro Sartori, most of which were pure invention, Gentle and Monday saw ample evidence that the stories concerning these women were rooted in truth. In the province around Mai-ké, for instance, which had been a dust bowl during Gentle's first pilgrimage, they found fields green with the first crop in six seasons, courtesy of a woman who'd sniffed out the course of an underground river and coaxed it to the surface with sways and supplications. In the temples of L'Himby a sibyl had carved from a solid slab—using only her finger and her spittle—a representation of the city as she prophesied it would be in a year's time, her prophecy so mesmeric that her audience had gone out of the temple that very hour and had torn down the trash that had disfigured their city. In the Kwem—where Gentle took Monday in the hope of finding Scopique—they found instead that the once shallow pit where the Pivot had stood was now a lake, its waters crystalline but its bottom hidden by the congregation of life that was forming in it: birds, mostly, which rose in sudden excited flocks, fully feathered and ready for the sky.

Here they had a chance to meet the miracle worker, for the woman who'd made these waters (literally, her acolytes said; it was the pissing of a single night) had taken up residence in the blackened husk of the Kwem Palace. In the hope of gleaning some clue to Jude and Hoi-Polloi's whereabouts, Gentle ventured into the shadows to find the lake maker, and though she refused to show herself she answered his inquiry. No, she hadn't seen a pair of travelers such as he described, but yes, she could tell him where they'd gone. There were only two directions for wandering women these days, she explained: out of Yzordderrex and into it.

He thanked her for this information and asked her if there was anything he could do for her in return. She told him that there was nothing she wanted from him personally, but she'd be very glad of the company of his boy for an hour or two. Somewhat chagrined, Gentle went out and asked Monday if he was willing to chance the woman's embrace for a while. He said he was and left the Maestro to find himself a seat by the bird-breeding lake while he ventured into its maker's boudoir. It was the first time in Gentle's life that any woman in search of sexual attentions had passed him over for another. If ever he'd needed proof that his day was done, it was here.

When, after two hours, Monday reappeared (with a flushed face and ringing ears), it was to find Gentle sitting at the lakeside, long ago tired of working on his map, surrounded by several small cairns of pebbles.

"What are these?" the boy said.

"I've been counting my romances," Gentle replied. "Each one of them is a hundred women."

There were seven cairns.

"Is that them all?" Monday said.

"It's all that I remember."

Monday squatted down beside the stones. "I bet you'd like to love them all over again," he said.

Gentle thought about this for a little time and finally said, "No. I don't think so. I've done my best work. It's time to leave it to the younger men."

He tossed the stone he had in hand out into the middle of the teeming lake.

"Before you ask," he said. "That was Jude."

There were no diversions after that, nor any need to pursue rumors of women hither and thither. They knew where Jude and Hoi-Polloi had gone. Having left the lake, they were on the Lenten Way within a matter of hours. Unlike so much else, the Way hadn't changed. It was as busy and as wide as ever: an arrow, driving its straight way into the hot heart of Yzordderrex.

26

I

In the Fifth, winter came: not suddenly but certainly. Hallowe'en was the last time people chanced the night air without coats, hats, and gloves, and it saw the first substantial visitation of Londoners to Gamut Street—revelers who'd taken the spirit of All Hallow's Eve to heart and come to see if there was any truth in the bizarre rumors they'd heard about the neighborhood. Some retreated after a very short time, but the braver among them stayed to explore, a few lingering outside number 28, where they puzzled over the designs on the door and peered up at the carbonized tree that shaded the house from the stars.

After that evening the cold's nip became a bite, and the bite a gnaw, until by late November the temperatures were low enough to keep even the most ardent tomcat at the fire. But the flow of visitors—in both directions—didn't cease. Night after night ordinary citizens appeared in Gamut Street to brush shoulders with the excursionists who were coming in the opposite direction. Some of the former became such regular visitors that Clem began to recognize them and was able to watch their investigations grow less tentative as they realized that the sensations they felt were not the first signs of lunacy. There were wonders to be found here, and one by one these men and women must have discovered the source,

because they invariably disappeared. Others, perhaps too afraid to
venture into the passing places alone, came with trusted friends,
showing them the street as though it were a secret vice, talking in
whispers, then laughing out loud when they found their loved ones
could see the apparitions too.

Word was spreading. But that fact was the only pleasure those
bitter days and nights provided. Though Tick Raw spent more and
more time in the house and was lively company, Clem missed Gentle badly. He hadn't been altogether surprised at his abrupt departure (he'd known, even if Gentle hadn't, that sooner or later the
Maestro would leave the Dominion), but now his truest company
was the man with whom he shared his skull, and as the first anniversary of Tay's death approached the mood of both grew
steadily darker. The presence of so many living souls on the street
only served to make the revenants who'd occupied it through the
summer months feel further disenfranchised, and their distress
was contagious. Though Tay had been happy to stay with Clem
through the preparations for the Great Work, their time as angels
was over, and Tay felt the same need as those ghosts who roamed
outside the house: to be gone.

As December came, Clem began to wonder how many more
weeks he could keep his post, when it seemed every hour the despair of the ghost in him grew. After much debate with himself he
decided that Christmas would mark the last day of his service in
Gamut Street. After that he'd leave number 28 to be tramped
around by Tick's excursionists and go back to the house where a
year before he and Tay had celebrated the Return of the Unvan-
quished Sun.

2

Jude and Hoi-Polloi had taken their time crossing the Dominions,
but with so many roads to choose between, and so many inci-
dental joys along the way, going quickly seemed almost criminal.
They had no reason to hurry. There was nothing behind them to
drive them on, and nothing in front summoning them. At least,
so Jude pretended. Time and time again, when the issue of their
ultimate destination cropped up in conversation, she avoided
talking about the place she knew in her heart of hearts they
would eventually reach. But if the name of that city wasn't on *her*
lips, it was on the lips of almost every other woman they met, and
when Hoi-Polloi mentioned that it was her birthplace questions
from fellow travelers would invariably flow thick and fast. Was
it true that the harbor was now filled at every tide with fish that
had swum up from the depths of the ocean, ancient creatures that

knew the secret of the origins of women and swam up the rivered streets at night to worship the Goddesses on the hill? Was it true that the women there could have children without any need of men whatsoever, and that some could even *dream* babies into being? And were there fountains in that city that made the old young, and trees on which every fruit was new to the world? And so on, and so forth.

Though Jude was willing, if pressed, to supply descriptions of what she'd seen in Yzordderrex, her accounts of how the palace had been refashioned by water, and of streams that defied gravity, were not particularly remarkable in the face of what rumor was claiming about Yzordderrex. After a few conversations in which she was urged to describe marvels she had no knowledge of—as though the questioners were willing her to invent prodigies rather than disappoint them—she told Hoi-Polloi she'd not be drawn into any further debates on the subject. But her imagination refused to ignore the tales it heard, however preposterous, and with every mile they traveled along the Lenten Way, the *idea* of the city awaiting them at the end of their journey grew more intimidating. She fretted that perhaps the blessings bestowed on her there would be valueless after all the time she'd spent away from the place. Or that the Goddesses knew that she'd told Sartori—in all truth—that she loved him, and that Jokalaylau's condemnation of her would carry the day if she ever went back into their temple.

Once they were on the Lenten Way, however, such fears became academic. They were not going to turn back now, especially as both of them were becoming steadily more exhausted. The city called them out of the fogs that lay between Dominions, and they would go into it together and face whatever judgments, prodigies, and deep-sea fish were waiting there.

Oh, but it was changed. A warmer season was on the Second than when Jude had last been here, and with so much water running in the streets the air was tropical. But more breathtaking than the humidity was the growth it had engendered. Seeds and spores had been carried up from the seams and caverns beneath the city in vast numbers, and under the influence of the Goddesses' feits had matured with preternatural speed. Ancient forms of vegetation, most long believed extinct, had greened the rubble, turning the Kesparates into luxuriant jungle. In the space of half a year Yzordderrex had come to resemble a lost city, sacred to women and children, its desolation salved by flora. The smell of ripeness was everywhere, its source the fruits that glistened on vine and bough and bush, the abundance of which had in turn attracted animals that would never have dared Yzordderrex under its previous regime. And running through this cornucopia, feeding the seeds it had raised from the underworld, the eternal waters, still flowing up the hillsides in their riotous way but no longer carrying their fleets of prayers. Either the requests of those who lived here had been answered, or else their baptisms had made them their own healers and restorers.

Jude and Hoi-Polloi didn't go up to the palace the day they arrived. Nor the day after, nor the day after that. Instead, they searched for the Peccable house and there made themselves comfortable, though the tulips on the dining room table had been replaced by a throng of blossoms that had erupted through the floor, and the roof had become an aviary. After so long a journey, in which they'd not known from night to night where they were going to lay their heads, these were minor inconveniences, and they were grateful to be at rest, lulled to sleep by cooings and chatterings in beds that were more like bowers. When they woke, there was plenty to eat: fruit that could be picked off the trees, water that ran clear and cold in the street outside, and, in some of the larger streams, fish, which formed the staple diet of the clans that lived in the vicinity.

There were men as well as women among these extended families, some of whom must have been members of the mobs and armies that had run so brutally riot on the night the Autarch fell. But either gratitude at having survived the revolution or the calming influence of the growth and plenitude around them had persuaded them to better purpose. Hands that had maimed and murdered were now employed rebuilding a few of the houses, raising their walls not in defiance of the jungle, or the waters that fed it, but in league with both. This time, the architects were women, who'd come down from their baptisms inspired to use the wreckage of the old city to create a new one, and everywhere Jude saw echoes of the serene and elegant aesthetic that marked the Goddesses' handiwork.

There was no great sense of urgency attending these constructions, nor, she thought, any sign of a grand design being adhered to. The age of empire was over, and all dogmas, edicts, and conformities had gone with it. People solved the problems of putting a roof over their heads in their own way, knowing that the trees were both shady and bountiful in the meantime; the houses that resulted were as different as the faces of the women who supervised their construction. The Sartori she'd met in Gamut Street would have approved, Jude thought. Hadn't he touched her cheek during their penultimate encounter and told her he'd dreamed of a city built in her image? If that image was *woman* then here was that city, rising from the ruins.

So by day they had the murmuring canopy, the bubbling rivers, the heat, the laughter. And by night, slumbers beneath a feathered roof and dreams that were kind and uninterrupted. Such was the case, at least, for a week. But on the eighth night, Jude was woken by Hoi-Polloi, who called her to the window.

"Look."

She looked. The stars were bright above the city and ran silver in the river below. But there were other forms in the water, she realized: more solid but no less silver. The talk they'd heard on the road was true. Climbing the river were creatures that no fishing boat, however deep it trawled, would ever have found in its nets. Some had a trace of dolphin in them, or squid, or manta ray, but their common trait was a hint of humanity, buried as deep in their past (or future) as their homes were in ocean. There were limbs on some of them, and these few seemed to leap the slope rather than swim it. Others were as sinuous as eels but had heads that carried a mammalian cast, their eyes luminous, their mouths fine enough to make words.

The sight of their ascent was exhilarating, and Jude stayed at the window until the entire shoal had disappeared up the street. She had no doubt of their destination, nor indeed of her own, after this.

"We're as rested as we're ever going to be," she said to Hoi-Polloi.

"So it's time to go up the hill?"

"Yes. I think it is."

They left the Peccable house at dawn in order to make much of the ascent before the comet climbed too high and the humidity sapped their strength. It had never been an easy journey, but even in the cool early morning it became a backbreaking trudge, especially for Jude, who felt as though she were carrying a lead weight in her womb rather than a living soul. She had to call a halt to the climb several times and sit in the shade to catch her breath, but on the fourth such occasion she rose to find her gasps becoming steadily shallower and a pain in her belly so acute she could barely hold on to consciousness. Her agitation—and Hoi-Polloi's yelps—drew helping hands, and she was being lowered onto a knoll of flowering grasses when her waters broke.

A little less than an hour later, not more than half a mile from where the gate of the twin saints Creaze and Evendown had stood, in a grove busy with tiny turquoise birds, she gave birth to the Autarch Sartori's first and only child.

3

Though Jude and Hoi-Polloi's pursuers had left the lake maker in the Kwem with clear directions, they still reached Yzordderrex six weeks later than the women. This was in part because Monday's sexual appetite was significantly depleted after his liaison in the Kwem Palace, and he set a far less hectic pace than he had hitherto, but more particularly because Gentle's enthusiasm for cartography grew by leaps and bounds. Barely an hour would go by without his remembering some province he'd passed through, or some signpost he'd seen, and whenever he did so the journey was interrupted while he brought out his handmade album of charts and religiously set down the details, rattling off the names of uplands, lowlands, forests, plains, highways, and cities like a litany while he worked. He wouldn't be hurried, even if the chance of a ride was missed, or a good drenching gained in the process. This was, he told Monday, the true great work of his life, and he only regretted that he'd come to it so late.

These interruptions notwithstanding, the city got closer day by day, mile by mile, until one morning, when they raised their heads from their pillows beneath a hawthorn bush, the mists cleared to show them a vast green mountain in the distance.

"What is that place?" Monday wondered.

Astonished, Gentle said, "Yzordderrex."

"Where's the palace? Where's the streets? All I can see is trees and rainbows."

Gentle was as confounded as the boy. "It used to be gray and black and bloody," he said.

"Well, it's fucking green now."

It got greener the closer they came, the scent of its vegetation so sweetening the air that Monday soon lost his scowl of disappointment and remarked that perhaps this wouldn't be so bad after all. If Yzordderrex had turned into a wild wood, then maybe all the women had become savages, dressed in berry juice and smiles. He could suffer that awhile.

What they found on the lower slopes, of course, were scenes more extraordinary than Monday's most heated imaginings. So much of what the inhabitants of the New Yzordderrex took for granted—the anarchic waters, the primeval trees—left both man and boy agog. They gave up voicing their awe after a time and simply climbed through the lavish thicket, steadily sloughing off the weight of baggage they'd accrued on their journey and leaving it scattered in the grass.

Gentle had intended to go to the Eurhetemec Kesparate in the hope of locating Athanasius, but with the city so transformed it was a slow and difficult trek, so it was more luck than wit that brought them, after an hour or more, to the gate. The streets beyond it were as overgrown as those they'd come through, the terraces resembling some orchard that had been left to riot, its fallen fruit the rubble that lay between the trees.

At Monday's suggestion, they split up to search for the Maestro, Gentle telling the boy that if he saw Jesus somewhere in the trees then he'd discovered Athanasius. But they both came back to the gate having failed to find him, obliging Gentle to ask some children who'd come to play swinging games on the gate if any of them had seen the man who'd lived here. One of the number, a girl of six or so with her hair so plaited with vines she looked as though she was sprouting them, had an answer.

"He went away," she said.

"Do you know where?"

"Nope," she said again, speaking on behalf of her little tribe.

"Does anybody know?"

"Nope."

Which exchange brought the subject of Athanasius to a swift halt.

"Where now?" Monday asked, as the children returned to their games.

"We follow the water," Gentle replied.

They began to ascend again, while the comet, which had long since passed its zenith, made the contrary motion. They were both weary now, and the temptation to lie down in some tranquil spot grew with every stride they took. But Gentle insisted they go on, reminding Monday that Hoi-Polloi's bosom would be a far more comfortable place to lay his head than any hummock, and her kisses more invigorating than a dip in any pool. His talk was persuasive, and the boy found an energy Gentle envied, bounding on to clear the way for the Maestro, until they reached the mounds of dark rubble that marked the walls of the palace. Rising from them, the columns from which had once hung an enormous pair of gates were turned to playthings by the waters, which climbed the right pillar in rivulets and threw themselves across the gap in a drizzling arch that squarely struck the top of the left. It was a most beguiling spectacle, and one that claimed Gentle's attention completely, leaving Monday to head between the columns alone.

After a short time his shout came back to fetch Gentle, and it was blissful.

"Boss? Boss! Come here!"

Gentle followed where Monday's cries led, through the warm

rain beneath the arch and into the palace itself. He found Monday wading across a courtyard, fragrant with the lilies that trembled on its flood, towards a figure standing beneath the colonnade on the other side. It was Hoi-Polloi. Her hair was plastered to her scalp, as though she'd just swum the pool, and the bosom upon which Monday was so eager to lay his head was bare.

"So you're here at last," she said, looking past Monday towards Gentle.

Her eager beau lost his footing halfway across, and lilies flew as he hauled himself to his feet.

"You knew we were coming?" he said to the girl.

"Of course," she replied. "Not you. But the Maestro. We knew the Maestro was coming."

"But it's *me* you're glad to see, right?" Monday spluttered. "I mean, you *are* glad?"

She opened her arms to him. "What do you think?" she said.

He whooped his whoop and splashed on towards her, peeling off his soaked shirt as he went. Gentle followed in his wake. By the time he reached the other side Monday was stripped down to his underwear.

"How did you know we were coming here?" Gentle asked the girl.

"There are prophetics everywhere," she said. "Come on. I'll take you up."

"Can't he go on his own?" Monday protested.

"We'll have plenty of time later," Hoi-Polloi said, taking his hand. "But first I have to take him up to the chambers."

The trees within the ring of the demolished walls dwarfed those outside, inspired to unprecedented growth by the almost palpable sanctity of this place. There were women and children in their branches and among their gargantuan roots, but Gentle saw no men here and supposed that if Hoi-Polloi hadn't been escorting them they'd have been asked to leave. How such a request would have been enforced he could only guess, but he didn't doubt that the presences which charged the air and earth here had their ways. He knew what those presences were: the promised Goddesses, whose existence he'd first heard mooted in Beatrix, while sitting in Mother Splendid's kitchen.

The journey was circuitous. There were several places where the rivers ran too hard and deep to be forded, and Hoi-Polloi had to lead them to bridges or stepping stones, then double back along the opposite bank to pick up the track again. But the farther they went, the more sentient the air became, and though Gentle had countless questions to ask he kept them to himself rather than display his naïveté.

There were tidbits from Hoi-Polloi once in a while, so casually dropped they were enigmas in themselves. "... the fires are so comical ..." she said at one point, as they passed a pile of twisted metalwork that had been one of the Autarch's war machines. And at another place, where a deep blue pool housed fish the size of men, said: "... apparently they have their own city ... but it's so deep in the ocean I don't suppose I'll ever see it. The children will, though. That's what's wonderful. ..."

Finally, she brought them to a door that was curtained with running water and, turning to Gentle, said, "They're waiting for you."

Monday went to step through the curtain at Gentle's side, but Hoi-Polloi restrained him with a kiss on his neck.

"This is just for the Maestro," she said. "Come along. We'll go swimming."

"Boss?"

"Go ahead," Gentle told him. "No harm's going to come to me here."

"I'll see you later then," Monday said, content to have Hoi-Polloi tug him away.

Before they'd disappeared into the thicket, Gentle turned to the door, dividing the cool curtain with his fingers and stepping into the chamber beyond. After the riot of life outside, both its scale and its austerity came as a shock. It was the first structure he'd seen in the city that preserved something of his brother's lunatic ambition. Its vastness was uninvaded by all but a few shoots and tendrils, and the only waters that ran here were at the door behind him and those falling from an arch at the other end. The Goddesses had not left the chamber entirely unmarked, however. The walls of what had been built as a windowless hall were now pierced on all sides, so that for all its immensity the place was a honeycomb, penetrated by the soft light of evening. There was only one item of furniture: a chair, close to the distant arch, and seated upon it, with a baby on her lap, was Judith.

As Gentle entered, she looked up from the child's face and smiled at him. "I was beginning to think you'd lost your way," she said.

Her voice was light: almost literally, he thought. When she spoke, the beams that came through the walls flickered.

"I didn't know you were waiting," he said.

"It's been no great hardship," she said. "Won't you come closer?" As he crossed the chamber towards her, she said, "I didn't expect you to follow us at first, but then I thought, He will, he will, because he'll want to see the child."

"To be honest ... I didn't think about the child."

"Well, she thought about you," Jude said, without rebuke.

The baby in her lap could not be more than a few weeks old but, like the trees and flowers here, was burgeoning. She sat on Jude's lap rather than lay, one small strong hand clutching her mother's long hair. Though Jude's breasts were bare and comfortable, the child had no interest in nourishment or sleep. Her gray eyes were fixed on Gentle, studying him with an intense and quizzical stare.

"How's Clem?" Jude asked when Gentle stood before her.

"He was fine when I last saw him. But I left rather suddenly, as you know. I feel rather guilty about that. But once I'd started . . ."

"I know. There was no turning back. It was the same for me."

Gentle went down on his haunches in front of Jude and offered his hand, palm up, to the child. She grasped it instantly.

"What's her name?" he said.

"I hope you won't mind . . ."

"What?"

"I called her Huzzah."

Gentle smiled up at Jude. "You did?" Then back to the baby, called by her scrutiny: "Huzzah?" he said, leaning his face towards hers. "Huzzah. I'm Gentle."

"She knows who you are," Jude said, without a trace of doubt. "She knew about this room before it even existed. And she knew you'd come here, sooner or later."

Gentle didn't inquire as to how the child had shared her knowledge. It was just one more mystery to add to the catalogue in this extraordinary place.

"And the Goddesses?" he said.

"What about them?"

"They don't mind that she's Sartori's child?"

"Not at all," Jude said, her voice daintier at the mention of Sartori. "The whole city . . . the whole city's here to prove how good can come from bad."

"She's better than good, Jude," Gentle said.

She smiled, and so did the child. "Yes, she is."

Huzzah was reaching for Gentle's face, ready to topple from Jude's lap in pursuit of her object.

"I think she sees her father," Jude said, lifting the child back into the crook of her arm and standing up.

Gentle also stood, watching Jude carry Huzzah to a litter of playthings on the ground. The child pointed and gurgled.

"Do you miss him?" he said.

"I did in the Fifth," Jude replied, her back still turned while she picked up Huzzah's chosen toy. "But I don't here. Not since Huzzah. I never felt quite real till she appeared. I was a figment of the other Judith." She stood up again, turning to Gentle. "You know I still can't really remember all those missing years? I get snatches of them once in a while, but nothing solid. I suppose I was living in a dream. But she's woken me, Gentle." Jude kissed the baby's cheek. "She's made me real. I was only a copy until her. We both were. He knew it and I knew it. But we made something new." She sighed. "I don't miss him," she said. "But I wish he could have seen her. Just once. Just so he could have known what it was to be real too."

She started to cross back to the chair, but the child reached out for Gentle again, letting out a little cry to emphasize her wishes.

"My, my," Jude said. "You *are* popular."

She sat down again and put the toy she'd picked up in front of Huzzah. It was a small blue stone.

"Here, darling," she cooed. "Look. What's this? What's this?"

Gurgling with pleasure, the child claimed the plaything from her mother's finger with a dexterity far beyond her tender age. The gurgles became chuckles, as she laid it to her lips, as if to kiss it.

"She likes to laugh," Gentle said.

"She does, thank God. Oh, now listen to me. Still thanking God."

"Old habits . . ."

"That one'll die," Jude said firmly.

The child was putting the toy to her mouth.

"No, sweetie, don't do that," Jude said. Then, to Gentle: "Do you think the Erasure'll decay eventually? I have a friend here called Lotti; she says it will. It'll decay, and then we'll have to live with the stench from the First every time the wind comes that way."

"Maybe a wall could be built."

"By whom? Nobody wants to go near the place."

"Not even the Goddesses?"

"They've got their work here. And in the Fifth. They want to free the waters there too."

"That should be quite a sight."

"Yes, it should. Maybe I'll go back for that."

Huzzah's laughter had subsided during this exchange, and she was once again studying Gentle, reaching up towards him from her mother's lap. This time her tiny hand was not open but clutching the blue stone.

"I think she wants you to have it," Jude said.

He smiled at the child and said, "Thank you. But you should keep it."

Her gaze became more intent at this, and he was certain she understood every word he was saying. Her hand still proffered its gift, determined he should take it.

"Go on," Jude said.

As much at the behest of the eyes as at Jude's words, Gentle

reached down and gingerly took the stone from Huzzah's hand.
There was some considerable strength in her. The stone was heavy:
heavy and cool.

"Now our peace is really made," Jude said.

"I didn't know we'd been at war," Gentle replied.

"That's the worst kind, isn't it?" Jude said. "But it's over now.
It's over forever."

There was a subtle modulation in the plush of the water-
curtained arch behind her, and she glanced around. Her expression had been grave, but when she looked back at Gentle she had
a smile on her face.

"I have to go," she said as she stood.

The child was chuckling and clutching the air.

"Will I see you again?" Gentle said.

Jude shook her head slowly, looking at him almost indulgently.

"What for?" she murmured. "We've said all we have to say.
We've forgiven each other. It's finished."

"Will I be allowed to stay in the city?"

"Of course," she said with a little laugh. "But why would you
want to?"

"Because I've come to the end of the pilgrimage."

"Have you?" she said, turning from him to pad towards the
arch. "I thought you had one Dominion left."

"I've seen it. I know what's there."

There was a pause. Then Jude said, "Did Celestine ever tell you
her story? She did, didn't she?"

"The one about Nisi Nirvana?"

"Yes. She told it to me, too, the night before the Reconciliation.
Did you understand it?"

"Not really."

"Ah."

"Why?"

"It's just that I didn't either, and I thought maybe . . ." She
shrugged. "I don't know what I thought."

She was at the archway now, and the child was peering over her
shoulder at somebody who'd appeared behind the veil of water.
The visitor was not, Gentle thought, quite human.

"Hoi-Polloi mentioned our other guests, did she?" Jude said, seeing his astonishment. "They came up out of the ocean, to woo us."
She smiled. "Beautiful, some of them. There's going to be such
children. . . ."

The smile faltered, just a little.

"Don't be sad, Gentle," she said. "We had our time."

Then she turned from him and took the child through the curtain. He heard Huzzah laugh to see the face that awaited them on

the other side, and saw its owner put his silvery arms around mother and child. Then the light in his eyes brightened, running in the curtain, and when it dimmed the family had gone.

Gentle waited in the empty chamber for several minutes, knowing Jude wasn't going to come back, not even certain that he wanted her to but unable to depart until he had fixed in his memory all that had passed between them. Only then did he return to the door and step out into the evening air. There was a different kind of enchantment in the wild wood now. Soft blue mists drooped from the canopy and crept up from the pools. The mellifluous songs of dusk birds had replaced those of noon, and the busy drone of pollinators had given way to breath-wing moths.

He looked for Monday but failed to find him, and although there was nobody to prevent his loitering in this idyll, he felt ill at ease. This was not his place now. By day it was too full of life, and by night, he guessed, too full of love. It was a new experience for him to feel so utterly immaterial. Even on the road, hanging back from the fires while nonsense tales were told, he'd always known that if he'd simply opened his mouth and identified himself he would have been feted, encircled, adored. Not so here. Here he was nothing: nothing and nobody. There were new growths, new mysteries, new marriages.

Perhaps his feet understood that better than his head, because before he'd properly confessed his redundancy to himself they were already carrying him away, out under the water-clad arches and down the slope of the city. He didn't head towards the delta but towards the desert, and though he'd not seen the purpose in this journey when Jude had hinted at it, he didn't now deny his feet their passage.

When he'd last emerged from the gate that led out into the desert he'd been carrying Pie, and there'd been a throng of refugees around them. Now he was alone, and though he had no other weight to carry besides his own, he knew the trek ahead of him would exhaust what little sum of will was left to him. He wasn't much concerned at this. If he perished on the way, it scarcely mattered. Whatever Jude had said, his pilgrimage was at an end.

As he reached the crossroads where he'd encountered Floccus Dado, he heard a shout behind him and turned to see a bare-chested Monday galloping towards him through the dwindling light, mounted on a mule, or a striped variation thereof.

"What were you doing, going without me?" he demanded when he reached Gentle's side.

"I looked for you, but you weren't around. I thought you'd gone off to start a family with Hoi-Polloi."

"Nah!" said Monday. "She's got funny ideas, that girl. She said she wanted to introduce me to some fish. I said I wasn't too keen on fish, 'cause the bones get stuck in your throat. Well, that's right, innit? People choke on fish, regular. Anyhow, she looks at me like I just farted and says maybe I should go with you after all. An' I said, I didn't even know you was leaving. So she finds me this ugly little fuck"—he slapped the hybrid's flank—"an' points me in this direction." He glanced back at the city. "I think we're well out of there," he said, dropping his voice. "There was too much water, if you ask me. D'you see it at the gate? A great fuckin' fountain."

"No, I didn't. That must be recent."

"See? The whole place is going to drown. Let's get the fuck out of here. Hop on."

"What's the beast called?"

"Tolland," Monday said with a grin. "Which way are we headed?"

Gentle pointed towards the horizon.

"I don't see nothin'."

"Then that must be the right direction."

4

Ever the pragmatist, Monday hadn't left the city without supplies. He'd made a sack of his shirt and filled it to bursting with succulent fruits, and it was these that sustained them as they traveled. They didn't halt when night came, but kept up their steady pace, taking turns to walk beside the beast so as not to exhaust it and giving it at least as much of the fruit as they ate themselves, plus the piths, cores, and skins of their own portions.

Monday slept much of the time that he rode, but Gentle, despite his fatigue, remained wide awake, too vexed by the problem of how he was going to set this wasteland down in his book of maps to indulge himself in slumber. The stone Huzzah had given him was constantly in his hand, coaxing so much sweat from his pores that several times a little pool gathered in the cup of his palm. Discovering this, he would put the stone away, only to find a few minutes later that he'd taken it out of his pocket without even realizing that he'd done so, and his fingers were once again making play with it.

Now and then he'd cast a backward glance towards Yzordderrex, and it made quite a sight, the benighted flanks of the city glittering in countless places, as though the waters in its streets had become perfect mirrors for the stars. Nor was Yzordderrex the only source of such splendor. The land between the gates of the city and the track that they were following also gleamed here and there, catching its own fragments of the sky's display.

But all such enchantments were gone by the first sign of dawn. The city had long since disappeared into the distance behind them, and the thunderheads in front were lowering. Gentle recognized the baleful color of this sky from the glimpse he and Tick Raw had snatched of the First. Though the Erasure still sealed Hapexamendios' pestilence from the Second, its taint was too persuasive to be obliterated, and the bruisy heavens loomed vaster as they traveled, lying along the entire horizon and climbing to their zenith.

There was some good news, however: they weren't alone. As the wretched remains of the Dearthers' tents appeared on the horizon, so too did a congregation of God spotters, thirty or so, watching the Erasure. One of them saw Gentle and Monday approaching, and word of their arrival passed through the small crowd until it reached one who instantly pelted in the travelers' direction.

"Maestro! Maestro!" he yelled as he came.

It was Chicka Jackeen, of course, and he was in a fair ecstasy to see Gentle, though after the initial flood of greetings the talk became grim.

"What did we do wrong, Maestro?" he wanted to know. "This isn't the way it was meant to be, is it?"

Gentle did his weary best to explain, astonishing and appalling Chicka Jackeen by turns.

"So Hapexamendios is dead?"

"Yes, he is. And everything in the First is His body. And it's rotting to high heaven."

"What happens when the Erasure decays?"

"Who knows? I'm afraid there's enough rot to stink out the Dominion."

"So what's your plan?" Chicka Jackeen wanted to know.

"I don't have one."

The other looked confounded at this. "But you came all the way here," he said. "You must have had some notion or other."

"I'm sorry to disappoint you," Gentle replied, "but the truth is, this was the only place left for me to go." He stared at the Erasure. "Hapexamendios was my Father, Lucius. Perhaps in my heart of hearts I believe I should be in the First with Him."

"If you don't mind me saying so, boss—" Monday broke in.

"Yes?"

"That's a bloody stupid idea."

"If you're going to go in, so am I," Chicka Jackeen said. "I want to see for myself. A dead God's something to tell your children about, eh?"

"Children?"

"Well," said Jackeen, "it's either that or write my memoirs, and I haven't got the patience for that."

"You?" Gentle said. "You waited two hundred years for me, and you say you haven't got patience?"

"Not any more," came the reply. "I want a life, Maestro."

"I don't blame you."

"But not before I've seen the First."

They'd reached the Erasure by now, and while Chicka Jackeen went among his colleagues to tell them what he and the Reconciler were going to do, Monday once again piped up with his opinion on the venture.

"Don't do it, boss," he said. "You've got nothing to prove. I know you were pissed off that they didn't throw a party in Yzorderrex, but fuck 'em, I say—or, rather, don't. Let 'em have their fish."

Gentle laid his hands on Monday's shoulders. "Don't worry," he said. "This isn't a suicide mission."

"So what's the big hurry? You're dead beat, boss. Have a sleep. Eat something. Get strong. There's all of tomorrow not touched yet."

"I'm fine," Gentle said. "I've got my talisman."

"What's that?"

Gentle opened his palm and showed Monday the blue stone.

"A fuckin' egg?"

"An egg, eh?" Gentle said, tossing the stone in his hand. "Maybe it is."

He threw it up into the air a second time, and it rose, far higher than his muscle had propelled it, way up above their heads. At the summit of its ascent it seemed to hover for a beat and then returned into his hand at leisure, defying the claim of gravity. As it descended it brought the faintest drizzle down with it, cooling their upturned faces.

Monday cooed with pleasure. "Rain out of nowhere," he said. "I remember that."

Gentle left him bathing the grime from his face and went to join Chicka Jackeen, who had finished explaining his intentions to his colleagues. They all hung back, watching the Maestros with uneasy stares.

"They think we're going to die," Chicka Jackeen explained.

"They may very well be right," Gentle said quietly. "Are you certain you want to come with me?"

"I was never more certain of anything."

With that they started towards the ambiguous ground that lay between the solidity of the Second and the Erasure's vacancy. As they went, one of Jackeen's friends began to call after him, in distress at his departure. The cry was taken up by several others, their shouts too mingled to be interpreted. Jackeen halted for a moment and glanced back towards the company he was leaving. Gentle made no attempt to urge him on. He ignored the shouts and picked up his speed, the Erasure thickening around him and the smell of the devastation that lay on the other side growing stronger with every step he took. He was prepared for it, however. Instead of holding his breath, he drew the stench of his Father's rot deep into his lungs, defying its pungency.

There was another shout from behind him, but this time it wasn't one of Jackeen's friends, it was the Maestro himself, his voice colored more by wonder than alarm. Its tone piqued Gentle's curiosity, and he glanced back over his shoulder to seek Jackeen out, but the nullity had come between them. Unwilling to be delayed, Gentle forged on, a purpose in his stride he didn't comprehend. His enfeebled legs had found strength from somewhere; his heart was urgent in his chest.

Ahead, the blinding murk was stirring, the first vague forms of the First's terrain emerging. And from behind, Jackeen again.

"Maestro? Maestro! Where are you?"

Without slowing his stride, Gentle returned the call. "Here!"

"Wait for me!" Jackeen gasped. "Wait!" He emerged from the void to lay his hand on Gentle's shoulder.

"What is it?" Gentle said, looking around at Jackeen, who as if in bliss had dropped the toll of years and was once again a young man, sweaty with awe at the way of feits.

"The waters," he said.

"What about them?"

"They've followed you, Maestro. They've followed you!"

And as he spoke, they came. Oh, how they came! They ran to Gentle's feet in glittering rills that broke against his ankles and his shins and leapt like silver snakes towards his hands—or, rather, towards the stone he held in his hands. And seeing their elation and their zeal, he heard Huzzah's laughter and felt again her tiny fingers brushing his arm as she passed the blue egg on to him. He didn't doubt for a moment that she'd known what would come of the gift. So, most likely, had Jude. He'd become their agent at the last, just as he'd become his mother's, and the thought of that sweet service brought an echo of the child's laughter to his lips.

From above, the egg was calling down a drizzle to swell the waters swirling underfoot, and in the space of seconds the patter became a roar, and a deluge descended, violent enough to sluice the murk of the Erasure out of the air. After a few moments, light began to break around the Maestros, the first light this terrain had seen since Hapexamendios had drawn the void over his Dominion. By it, Gentle saw that Jackeen's exhilaration was rapidly turning to panic.

"We're going to drown!" he yelled, fighting to stay on his feet as the water deepened.

Gentle didn't retreat. He knew where his duty lay. As the surf broke against their backs, the tide threatening to drag them under, he raised Huzzah's gift to his lips and kissed it, just as she had done. Then he mustered all his strength and threw the stone out, over the landscape that was being uncovered before them. The egg went from his hand with a momentum that was not his sinews' work but its own ambition, and instantly the waters went in pursuit of it, dividing around the Maestros and taking their tides off into the wasteland of the First.

It would take the waters weeks, perhaps even months, to cover the Dominion from end to end, and most of that work would go unwitnessed. But in the next few hours, standing at their vantage point where the City of God had once begun, the Maestros were granted a glimpse of their labor. The clouds above the First, which had been as inert as the landscape beneath, now began to churn and roil and shed their anguish in stupendous storms, which in turn swelled the rivers that were driving their cleansing way across the rot.

Hapexamendios' remains were not despised. With the purpose of the Goddesses fueling their every drop, the waters turned the slaughterhouse over and over and over, scouring the matter of its poisons and sweeping it up into mounds, which the exhilarated air festooned with vapors.

The first ground that appeared from this tumult was close to the feet of the Maestros and rapidly became a ragged peninsula that stretched fully a mile into the Dominion. The waters broke against it constantly, bringing with every wave another freight of Hapexamendios' clay to increase its flanks. Gentle was patient for a time and stayed at the border. But he could not resist the invitation forever, and finally, ignoring Jackeen's words of caution, he set off down the spine of land to better see the spectacle visible from the far end. The waters were still draining from the new earth, and here and there lightning still ran on the slopes, but the ground was solid enough, and there were seedlings everywhere, carried, he presumed, from Yzordderrex. If so, there would be abundant life here in a little while.

By the time he'd reached the end of the peninsula the clouds overhead were begining to clear somewhat, lighter for their furies. Farther off, of course, the process he'd been privileged to witness was just beginning, as the storms spread in all directions from their point of origin. By their blazes he glimpsed the snaking rivers, going about their work with undiminished ambition. Here on the promontory, however, there was a more benign light. The First Dominion had a sun, it seemed, and though it wasn't yet warm, Gentle didn't wait for balmier weather to begin his last labors, but took his album and his pen from his jacket and sat down on the marshy headland to work. He still had the map of the desert between the gates of Yzordderrex and the Erasure to set down, and though these pages would doubtless be the barest in the album, they had to be drawn all the more carefully for that fact: he wanted their very spareness to have a beauty of its own.

After perhaps an hour of concentrated work he heard Jackeen behind him. First a footfall, then a question:

"Speaking in tongues, Maestro?"

Gentle hadn't even been aware of the inventory he was rattling off until his attention was drawn to it: a seamless list of names that must have been incomprehensible to anyone other than himself, the stopping places of his pilgrimage, as familiar to his tongue as his many names.

"Are you sketching the new world?" Jackeen asked him, hesitating to come too close to the artist while he worked.

"No, no," said Gentle, "I'm finishing a map." He paused, then corrected himself. "No, not finishing. Starting."

"May I look?"

"If you like."

Jackeen went down on his haunches behind Gentle and peered over his shoulder. The pages that depicted the desert were as complete as Gentle could make them. He was now attempting to delineate the peninsula he was sitting on, and something of the scene in front of him. It would be little more than a line or two, but it was a beginning.

"I wonder, would you fetch Monday for me?"

"Is there something you need?"

"Yes, I want him to take these maps back into the Fifth with him and give them to Clem."

"Who's Clem?"

"An angel."

"Ah."

"Would you bring him here?"

"Now?"

"If you would," Gentle said. "I'm almost done."

Ever dutiful, Jackeen stood up and started back towards the Second, leaving Gentle to work on. There was very little left to do. He finished making his crude rendering of the promontory; then he added a line of dots along it to mark his path and at the headland placed a small cross at the spot where he was sitting. That done, he went back through the album, to be certain that the pages were in proper order. It occurred to him as he did so that he'd fashioned a self-portrait. Like its maker, the map was flawed but, he hoped, redeemable: a rudimentary thing that might see finer versions in the fullness of time; be made and remade and made again, perhaps forever.

He was about to set the album down beside the pen when he heard a hint of coherence in the surf that was beating against the slope below. Unable to quite make sense of the sound, he ventured to the edge. The ground was too newly made to be solid and threatened to crumble away beneath his weight, but he peered over as far as he could, and what he saw and what he heard were enough to make him retreat from the edge, kneel down in the dirt, and with trembling hands start scribbling a message to accompany the maps.

It was necessarily brief. He could hear the words clearly now, rising from the surge of waves. They distracted him with promises.

"Nisi Nirvana," they said, "Nisi Nirvana. . . ."

By the time he'd finished his note, laid down the album and the pen beside it, and returned to the edge of the promontory, the sun of this Dominion was emerging from the storm clouds overhead to shed its light on the waves below. The beams placated them for a time, soothing their frenzy and piercing them, so that Gentle had a glimpse of the ground they were moving over. It was not, it seemed, an earth at all, but another sky, and in it was a sphere so majestic that to his eyes all the bodies in the heavens of the Imajica—all stars, all moons, all noonday suns—could not in their sum have touched its glory. Here was the door that his Father's city had been built to seal, the door through which his mother's name in fable had been whispered. It had been closed for millenniums, but now it stood open, and through it a music of voices was rising, going on its way to every wandering spirit in Imajica and calling them home to rapture.

In its midst was a voice Gentle knew, and before he'd even glimpsed its source his mind had shaped the face that called him, and his body felt the arms that would wrap him around and bear him up. Then they were there—those arms, that face—rising from the door to claim him, and he needed to imagine them no longer.

"Are you finished?" he was asked.

"Yes," he replied. "I'm finished."

"Good," said Pie 'oh' pah, smiling. "Then we can begin."

The congregation Chicka Jackeen had left at the perimeter of the First had steadily begun to venture along the peninsula as their courage and curiosity grew. Monday was of course among them, and Jackeen was just about to call the boy and summon him to the Reconciler's side when Monday let out a cry of his own, pointing back along the promontory. Jackeen turned and fixed his eyes— as did they all—on the two figures standing on the headland, embracing. Later there would be much discussion between these witnesses as to what they'd actually seen. All agreed that one of the pair was the Maestro Sartori. As to the other, opinions differed widely. Some said they saw a woman, others a man, still others a cloud with a piece of sun burning in it. But whatever these ambiguities, what followed was not in doubt. Having embraced, the two figures advanced to the limit of the promontory, where they stepped out into the air and were gone.

Two weeks later, on the penultimate day of a cheerless December, Clem was sitting in front of the fire in the dining room of number 28, a spot from which he'd seldom risen since Christmas, when he heard a hectic beating on the front door. He was not wearing a watch—what did time matter now?—but he assumed it was long after midnight. Anyone calling at such an hour was likely to be either desperate or dangerous, but in his present bleak mood he scarcely cared what harm might await him in the street outside. There was nothing left for him here: in this house, in this life. Gentle had gone, Judy had gone, and so, most recently, had Tay. It was five days since he'd heard his lover whisper his name.

"Clem . . . I have to go."

"Go?" he'd replied. "Where to?"

"Somebody opened the door," came Tay's reply. "The dead are being called home. I have to go."

They wept together for a while, tears pouring from Clem's eyes while the sound of Tay's anguish racked him from within. But there was no help for it. The call had come, and though Tay was grief-stricken at the thought of parting from Clem, his existence between conditions had become unbearable, and beneath the sorrow of parting was the joyful knowledge of imminent release. Their strange union was over. It was time for the living and the dead to part.

Clem hadn't known what loss really was until Tay left. The pain of losing his lover's physical body had been acute enough, but losing the spirit that had so miraculously returned to him was immeasurably worse. It was not possible, he thought, to be emptier than this and still be a living being. Several times during those dark days he'd wondered if he should simply kill himself and hope he would be able to follow his lover through whatever door now stood open. That he didn't was more a consequence of the responsibility he felt than from lack of courage. He was the only witness to the miracles of Gamut Street left in this Dominion. If he departed, who would there be to tell the tale?

But such imperatives seemed frail things at an hour like this, and as he rose from the fire and crossed to the front door, he allowed himself the thought that if these midnight callers came with death in their hands perhaps he would not refuse it. Without asking who was on the other side, he slid back the bolts and opened the door. To his surprise he discovered Monday standing in the driving sleet. Beside him stood a shivering stranger, his thinning curls flattened to his skull.

"This is Chicka Jackeen," Monday said as he hauled his sodden guest over the threshold. "Jackie, this is Clem, eighth wonder of the world. Well, am I too wet to get a hug?"

Clem opened his arms to Monday, who embraced him with fervor.

"I thought you and Gentle had gone forever," Clem said.

"Well, one of us has," came the reply.

"I guessed as much," Clem said. "Tay went after him. And the revenants too."

"When was this?"

"Christmas Day."

Jackeen's teeth were chattering, and Clem ushered him through to the fire, which he had been fueling with sticks of furniture. He threw on a couple of chair legs and invited Jackeen to sit by the blaze to thaw out. The man thanked him and did so. Monday, however, was made of sterner stuff. Availing himself of the whisky that sat beside the hearth, he put several mouthfuls into his system, then set about clearing the room, explaining as he dragged the table into the corner that they needed some working space. With the floor cleared, he opened his jacket and pulled Gentle's gazetteer from beneath his arm, dropping it in front of Clem.

"What's this?"

"It's a map of the Imajica," Monday said.

"Gentle's work?"

"Yep."

Monday went down on his haunches and flipped the album open, taking out the loose leaves and handing the cover back up to Clem.

"He wrote a message in it," Monday said.

While Clem read the few words Gentle had scribbled on the cover, Monday began to arrange the sheets side by side on the floor, carefully aligning them so that the maps became an unbroken flow. As he worked, he talked, his enthusiasm as unalloyed as ever.

"You know what he wants us to do, don't you? He wants us to draw this map on every fuckin' wall we can find! On the pavements! On our foreheads! Anywhere and everywhere."

"That's quite a task," said Clem.

"I'm here to help you," Chicka Jackeen said. "In whatever capacity I can."

He got up from the fire and came to stand beside Clem, where he could admire the pattern that was emerging on the floor in front of them.

"That's not the only thing you've come to do, is it?" Monday said. "Be honest."

"Well, no," said Jackeen. "I'd also like to find myself a wife. But that will have to wait."

"Damn right!" said Monday. *This* is our business now."

He stood up and stepped out of the circle which the pages of Gentle's album had formed. Here was the Imajica, or rather the tiny part of it which the Reconciler had seen: Patashoqua and Vanaeph; Beatrix and the mountains of the Jokalaylau; Mai-ké, the Cradle, L'Himby, and the Kwem; the Lenten Way, the delta, and Yzordderrex. And then the crossroads outside the city, and the desert beyond, with a single track leading to the borders of the Second Dominion. On the other side of that border, the pages were practically empty. The wanderer had sketched the peninsula he'd sat on, but beyond it he'd simply written: *This is a new world.*

"And this," said Jackeen, stooping to indicate the cross at the end of the promontory, "is where the Maestro's pilgrimage ended."

"Is that where he's buried?" Clem said.

"Oh, no," Jackeen said. "He's gone to places that'll make this life seem like a dream. He's left the circle, you see."

"No, I don't," said Clem. "If he's left the circle, then where's he gone? Where have they *all* gone?"

"Into it," Jackeen said.

Clem began to smile.

"May I?" said Jackeen, rising and claiming from Clem's fingers the sheet which carried Gentle's last message.

My friends, he'd written, *Pie is here. I am found. Will you show these pages to the world, so that every wanderer may find their way home?*

"I think our duty is plain, gentlemen," Jackeen said. He stooped again to lay the final page in the middle of the circle, marking the place of spirits to which the Reconciler had gone. "And when we've done that duty, we have here the map that will show us where we must go. We'll follow him. There's nothing more certain. We'll all of us follow him, by and by."